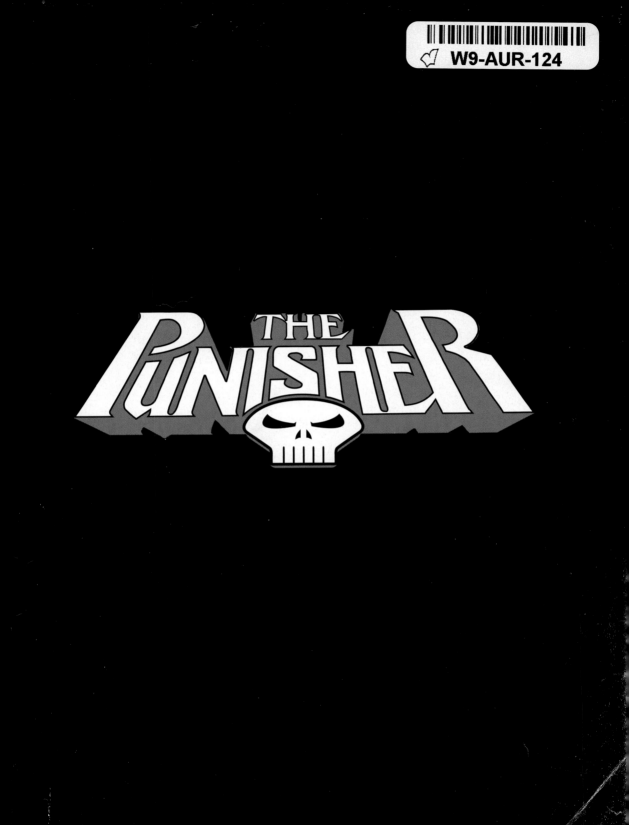

PUNISHER MAX: THE COMPLETE COLLECTION VOL. 1. Contains material originally published in magazine form as BORN #1-4 and PUNISHER (2004) #1-12. First printing 2016. ISBN# 978-1-302-90015-1. Published by MARVEL WORLDWIDE, INC., a subsidiary of MARVEL ENTERTAINMENT, LLC. OFFICE OF PUBLICATION: 135 West 50th Street, New York, NY 10020. Copyright © 2016 MARVEL No similarity between any of the names, characters, persons, and/or institutions in this magazine with those of any living or dead person or institution is intended, and any such similarity which may exist is purely coincidental. **Printed in the U.S.A.** ALAN FINE, President, Marvel Entertainment; DAN BUCKLEY, President, TV, Publishing and Brand Management; JOE QUESADA, Chief Creative Officer; TOM BREVOORT, SVP of Publishing; DAVID BOGART, SVP of Operations & Procurement, Publishing; C.B. CEBULSKI, VP of International Development & Brand Management; DAVID GABRIEL, SVP Print, Sales & Marketing; JIM O'KEEFE, VP of Operations & Logistics; DAN CARR, Executive Director of Publishing Technology; SUSAN CRESPI, Editorial Operations Manager; ALEX MORALES, Publishing Operations Manager; STAN LEE, Chairman Emeritus. For information regarding advertising in Marvel Comics or on Marvel.com, please contact Jonathan Rheingold, VP of Custom Solutions & Ad Sales, at jrheingold@marvel.com. For Marvel subscription inquiries, please call 800-217-9158. **Manufactured between 11/27/2015 and 1/4/2016 by R.R. DONNELLEY, INC., SALEM, VA, USA.**

10 9 8 7 6 5 4 3 2 1

The essential American soul is hard, isolate, stoic, and a killer.
It has never yet melted.

-- D.H. Lawrence

Writer: Garth Ennis

BORN
Born #1-6
Pencils: Darick Robertson
Inks: Tom Palmer
Colors: Paul Mounts
Letters: Virtual Calligraphy's Rus Wooton
Cover Art: Wieslaw Walkuski
Assistant Editor: Nick Lowe
Editor: Joe Quesada
Associate Managing Editor: Kelly Lamy
Managing Editor: Nanci Dakesian

IN THE BEGINNING
Punisher #1-6
Pencils: Lewis LaRosa
Inks: Tom Palmer
Colors: Dean White
Letters: Virtual Calligraphy's Randy Gentile, Dave Sharpe & Cory Petit
Cover Art: Tim Bradstreet
Assistant Editor: John Miesegaes
Editor: Axel Alonso

KITCHEN IRISH
Punisher #7-12
Artist: Leandro Fernandez
Colors: Dean White
Letters: Virtual Calligraphy's Randy Gentile
Cover Art: Tim Bradstreet
Assistant Editor: John Miesegaes
Editor: Axel Alonso

Collection Editor: Jennifer Grünwald • Assistant Editor: Sarah Brunstad
Associate Managing Editor: Alex Starbuck • Editor, Special Projects: Mark D. Beazley
Senior Editor, Special Projects: Jeff Youngquist • SVP Print, Sales & Marketing: David Gabriel

Editor in Chief: Axel Alonso • Chief Creative Officer: Joe Quesada
Publisher: Dan Buckley • Executive Producer: Alan Fine

INTRODUCTION

The first time I thought about the Punisher with any degree of seriousness was in September of 1988, during a panel discussion at UKCAC (the long-deceased United Kingdom Comic Art Convention). This was a few months before I began writing comics professionally, and was in fact the only convention I attended without being involved in the industry. The panel was entitled *Violence in Comics*, and I watched as half a dozen creative types debated the pros and cons of that very subject. All but one of them were British; the one in question being the writer/editor of Marvel Comics' *The Punisher*.

His take on the subject was a simple one. The Punisher was a violent character in a violent story, he said, but the violence neither made the world better nor relieved the character's torment. Frank Castle, the Punisher, was not a happy man and never would be. In short, he was careful to make clear when writing the book that violence solved nothing, at least in the long term.

What happened next was quite interesting. A couple of the other members of the panel stated quite plainly — with that breathtaking blend of condescension and arrogance that Brits always think plays well with Americans — that *The Punisher* was not even worthy of consideration in this particular discussion. They were talking on a different level. There was no need to waste time on *The Punisher*. So could they return to more serious matters, please? And, partly because these two weren't exactly producing *War & Peace* themselves — darlings of the British indie scene though they were — and partly because of their bloody awful manners, I found myself thinking... hmmm. That's why I decided to take a proper look at the Punisher.

I was aware of him, of course. As ignorant of most U.S. comics characters as I was, the Punisher was a hard one for me to miss: the white skull on the black suit, the permanently grim visage, the firepower. What I found when I looked more closely was interesting, although I have to admit it didn't exactly grab me. Nice art and some serviceable stories, maybe, but nothing really that memorable. And, with depressingly increasing frequency, these hard-boiled crime tales were ruined by the addition of costumed super heroes (truth to tell, the Punisher looked a bit like a super hero himself, with his white jackboots and giant skull motif). Not bad but not for me, I thought, and moved on.

All the same, there was potential.

*   *   *   *   *

Fast forward ten years. I'd enjoyed a degree of success in the American comics market, mostly writing characters I'd created myself, and now Joe Quesada and Jimmy Palmiotti were asking me to revive the Punisher for their Marvel Knights line. I started by taking another look at the character, and despite a degree of stagnation (and outright nonsense) I saw signs of hope. Writer Chuck Dixon in particular had done good work. The costume was more or less gone, replaced with less-conspicuous civilian clothing. The skull was still there, but as a target rather than a symbol — its purpose being to draw a nervous shooter's aim away from Frank Castle's unarmored head. Thinking about it, I began to see the Punisher as resembling the British comics characters of my youth, and that turned out to be my way in.

This is perhaps not as surprising as it might seem. The characters in question, grim-faced gunfighters like *2000AD*'s Judge Dredd and *Battle-Action*'s Dredger, were born of the 1970s — that uncertain era when TV and movies reflected society's growing unease with itself. Government, law and order, a nation's standing in the world, nothing could be comfortably relied upon anymore; and fiction such as *Dirty Harry* and *Death Wish* responded with protagonists who might provide a scrap of bleak and tattered hope in all the chaos. The action was vicious, the humor sardonic, the heroes themselves a brutal bunch, the justice they offered final and unyielding. The Punisher was of that time too.

Which to my mind was actually quite a healthy development, at least in creative terms. Most comic book characters are influenced only by other comic books; each super hero or super-team being essentially the same as the last, with only the costumes colored in differently. Suddenly throwing television, film and prose fiction into the mix helped stir things up and gave the stories an edge they badly needed. In the UK market this defined an entire decade, and resulted in what I believe are some of the greatest comics ever produced. Yet while there may have been other American characters so influenced, the Punisher is the only one to have stood the test of time. In fact, to this day, I like to think of Frank Castle as an essentially British character — born by a very happy accident on the wrong side of the Atlantic.

I wrote about fifty issues of *The Punisher* for Marvel Knights. Some of it's not bad. It went on too long, certainly longer than I meant it to, and it has an oddly goofy quality that reflected how I felt about the book at the time. I certainly saw the Punisher himself as serious enough, but I populated the world he moved through with freaks and

BORN #1

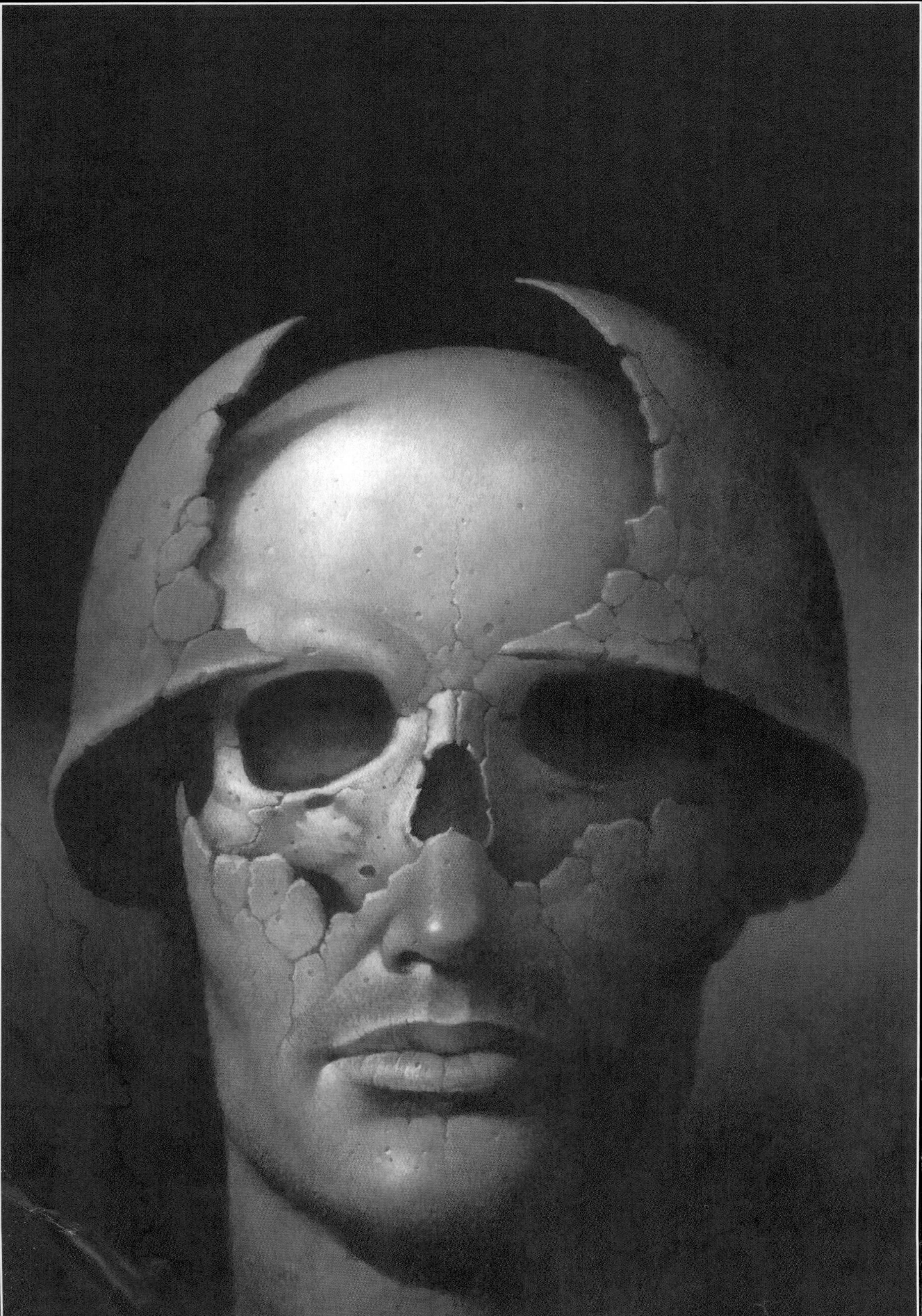

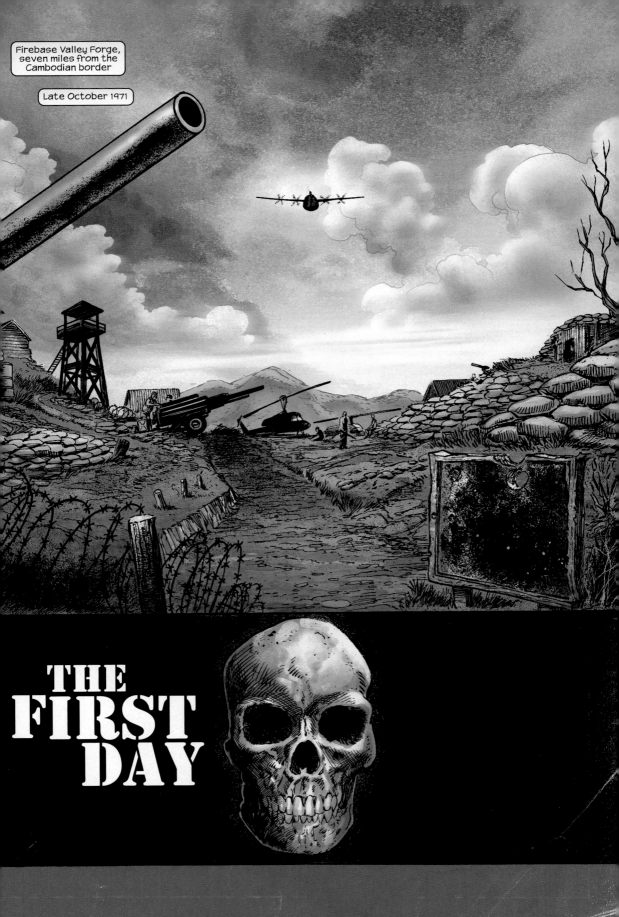

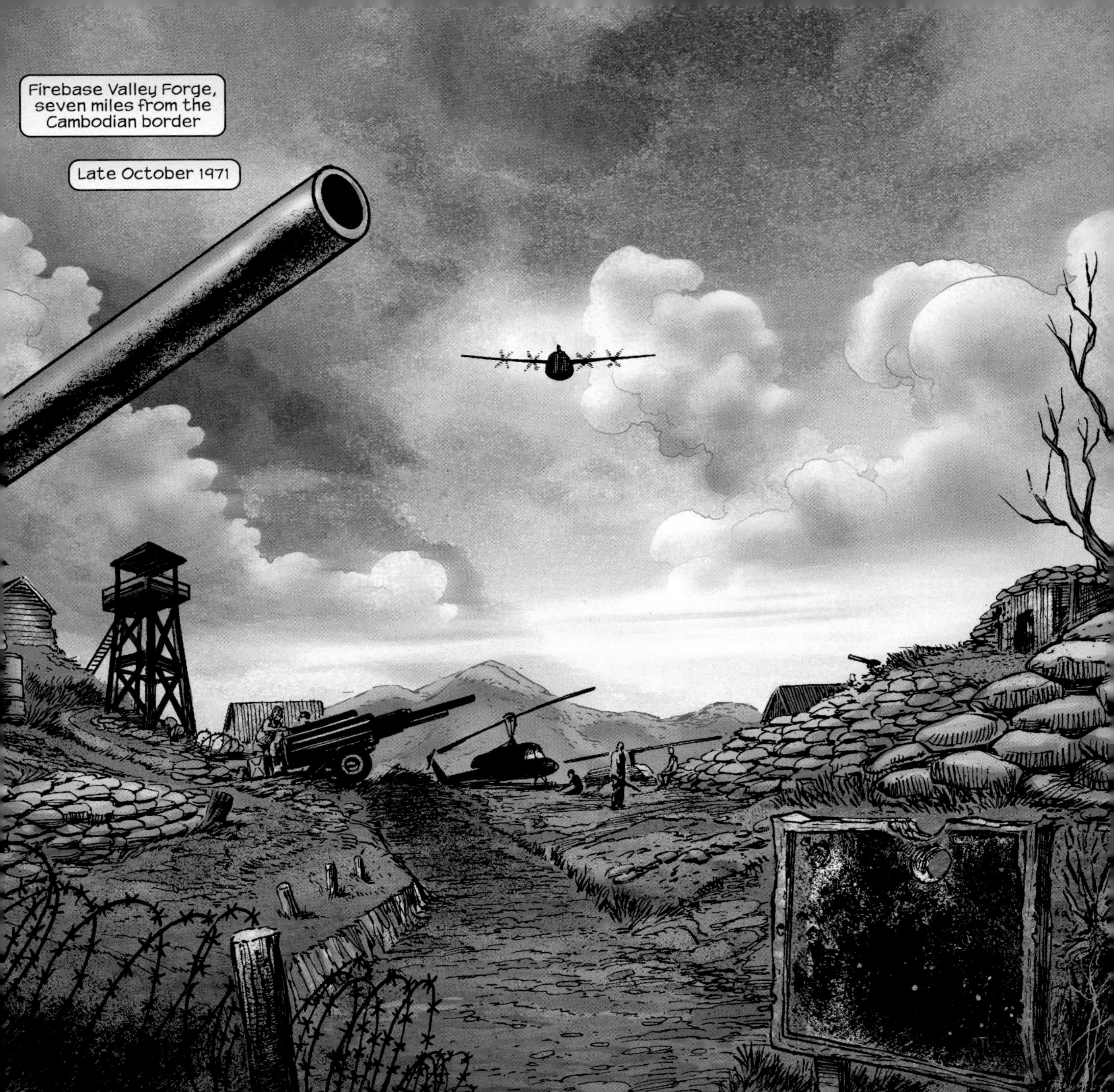
Firebase Valley Forge, seven miles from the Cambodian border
Late October 1971

THE FIRST DAY

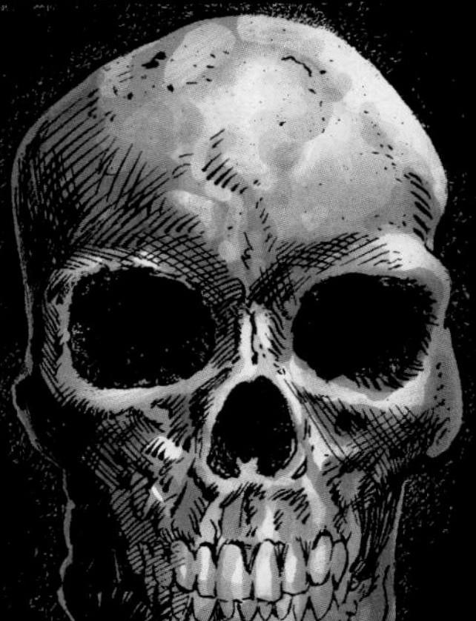

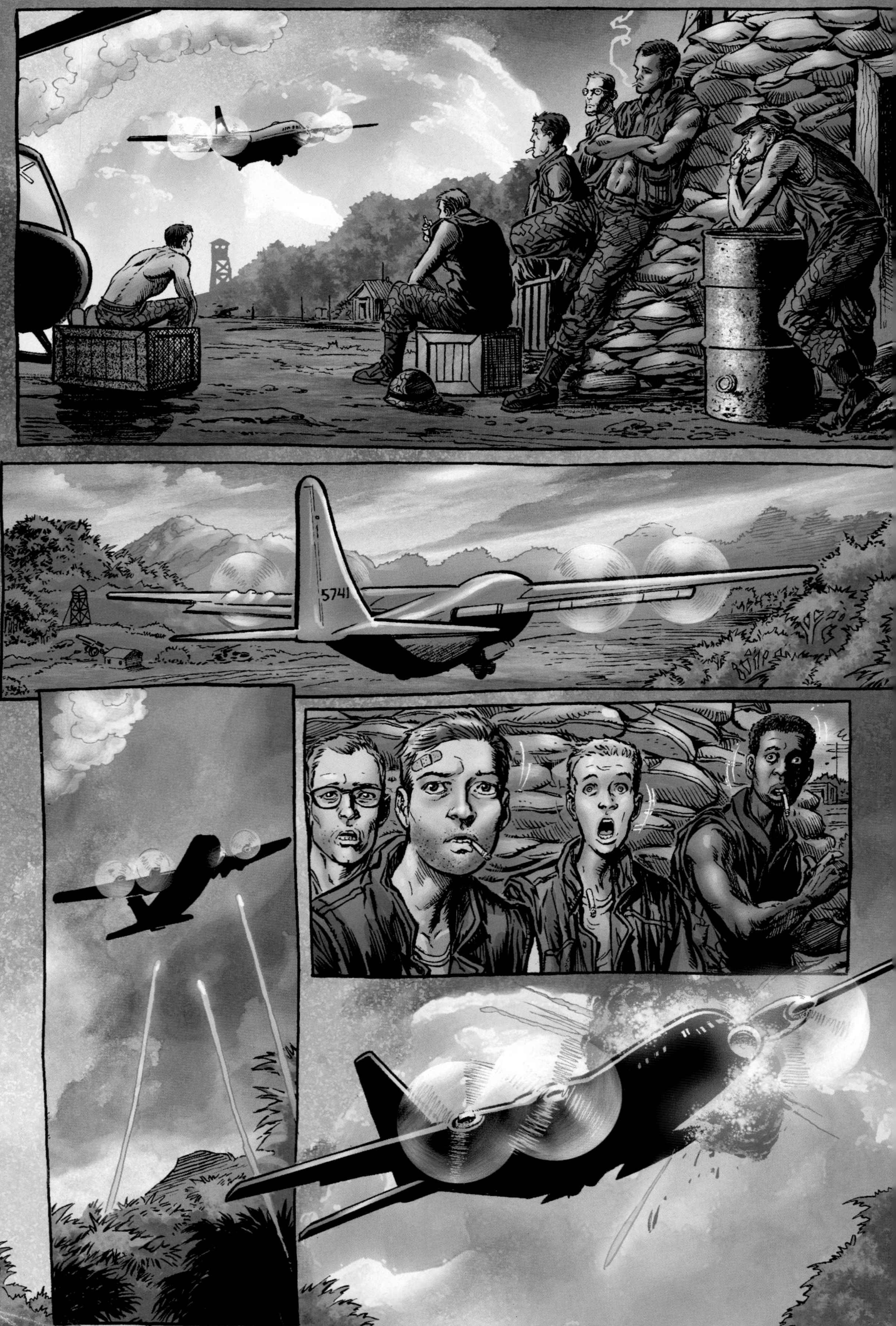
5741

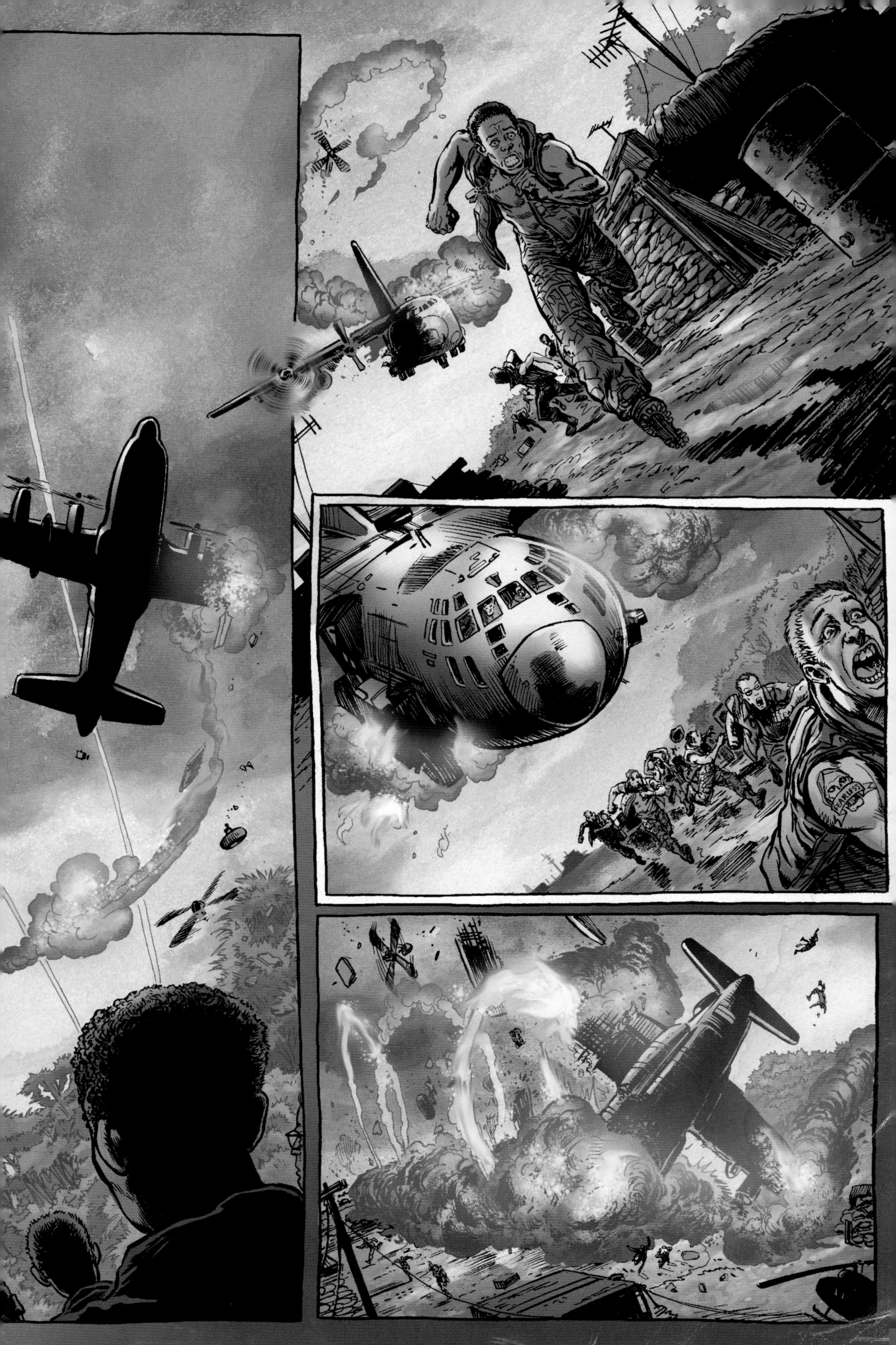
FEARLESS

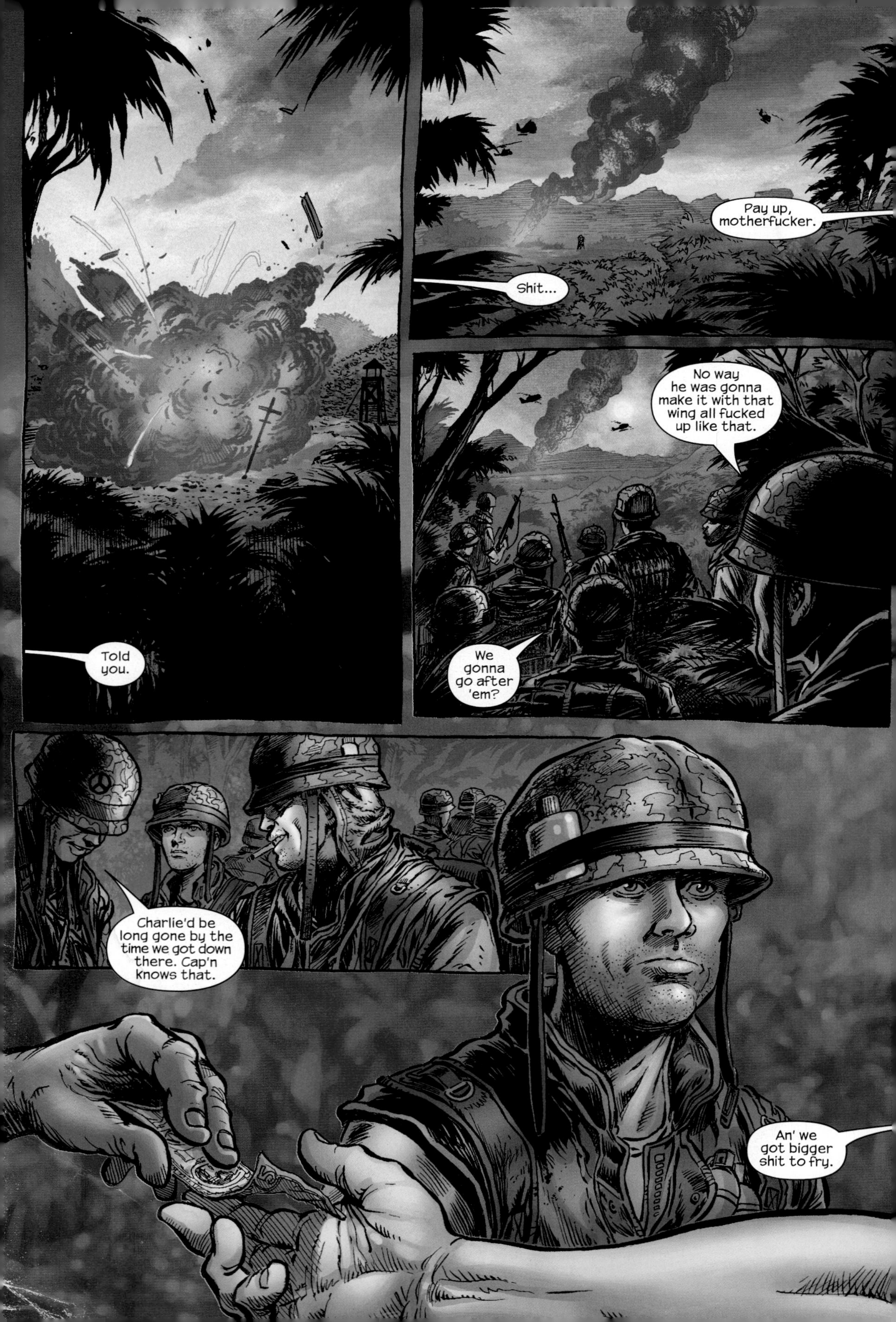
Told you.
Shit...
Pay up, motherfucker.
No way he was gonna make it with that wing all fucked up like that.
We gonna go after 'em?
Charlie'd be long gone by the time we got down there. Cap'n knows that.
An' we got bigger shit to fry.

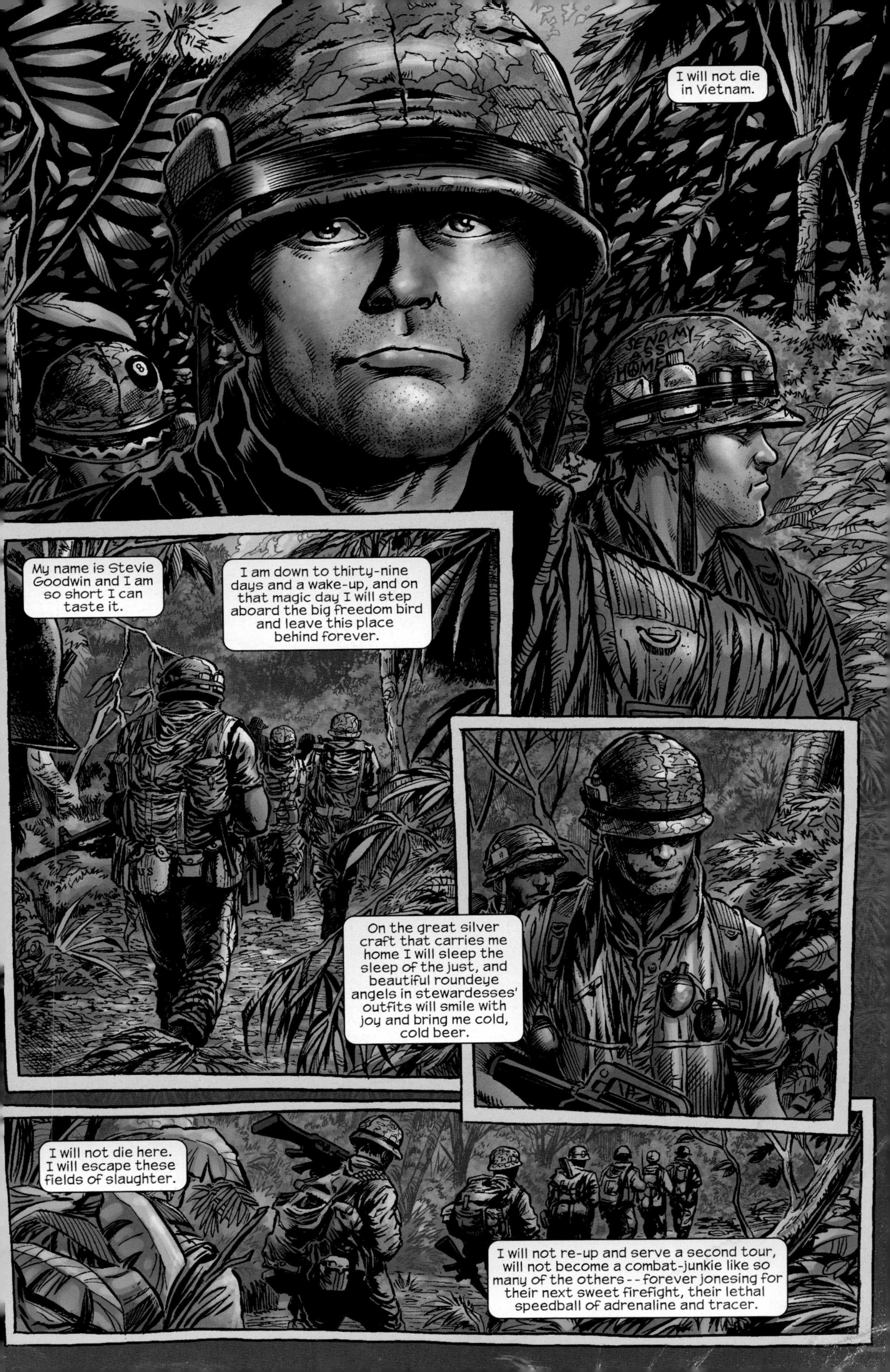

I will not die in Vietnam.
SEND MY ASS HOME
My name is Stevie Goodwin and I am so short I can taste it.
I am down to thirty-nine days and a wake-up, and on that magic day I will step aboard the big freedom bird and leave this place behind forever.
On the great silver craft that carries me home I will sleep the sleep of the just, and beautiful roundeye angels in stewardesses' outfits will smile with joy and bring me cold, cold beer.
I will not die here. I will escape these fields of slaughter.
I will not re-up and serve a second tour, will not become a combat-junkie like so many of the others--forever jonesing for their next sweet firefight, their lethal speedball of adrenaline and tracer.

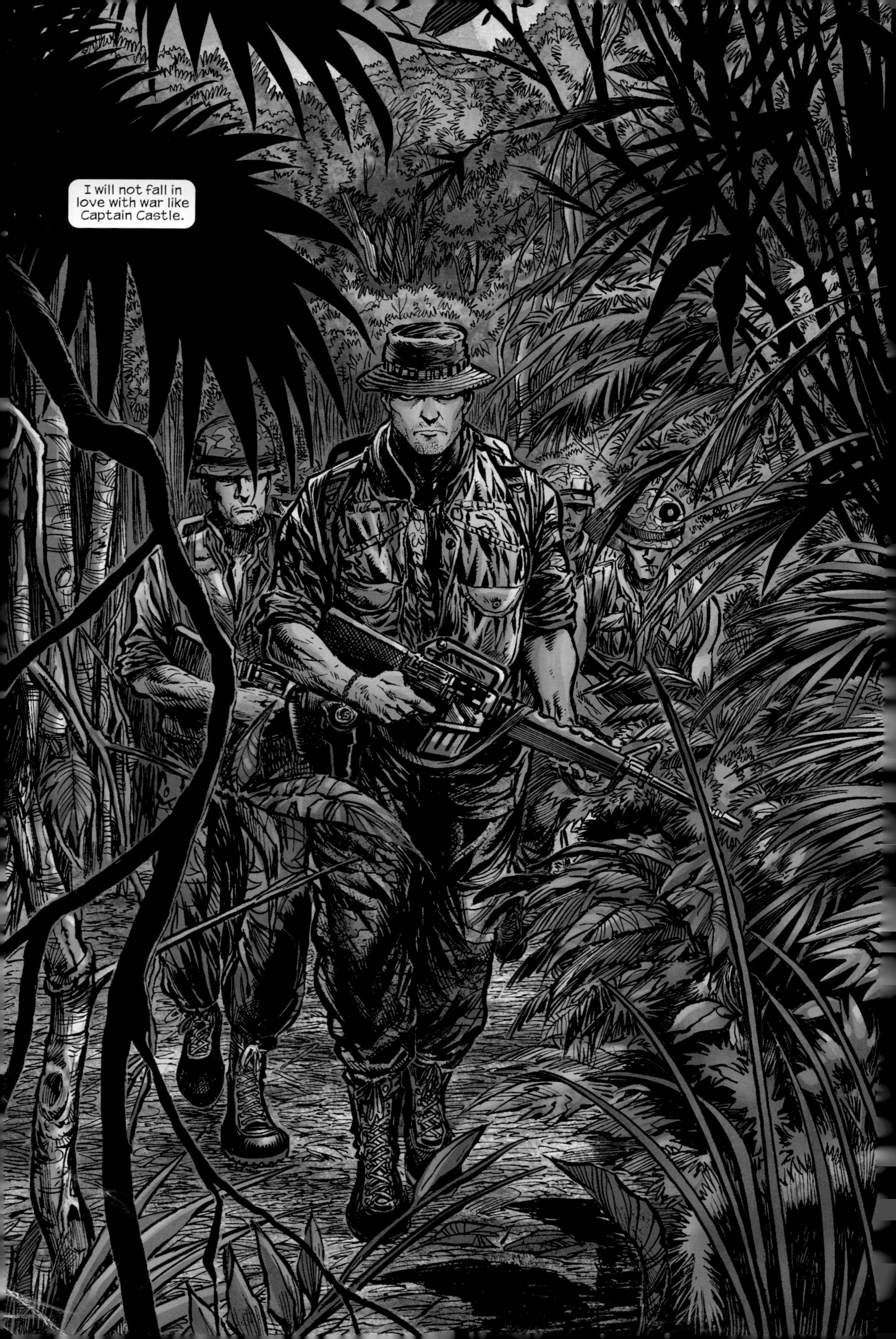
I will not fall in love with war like Captain Castle.

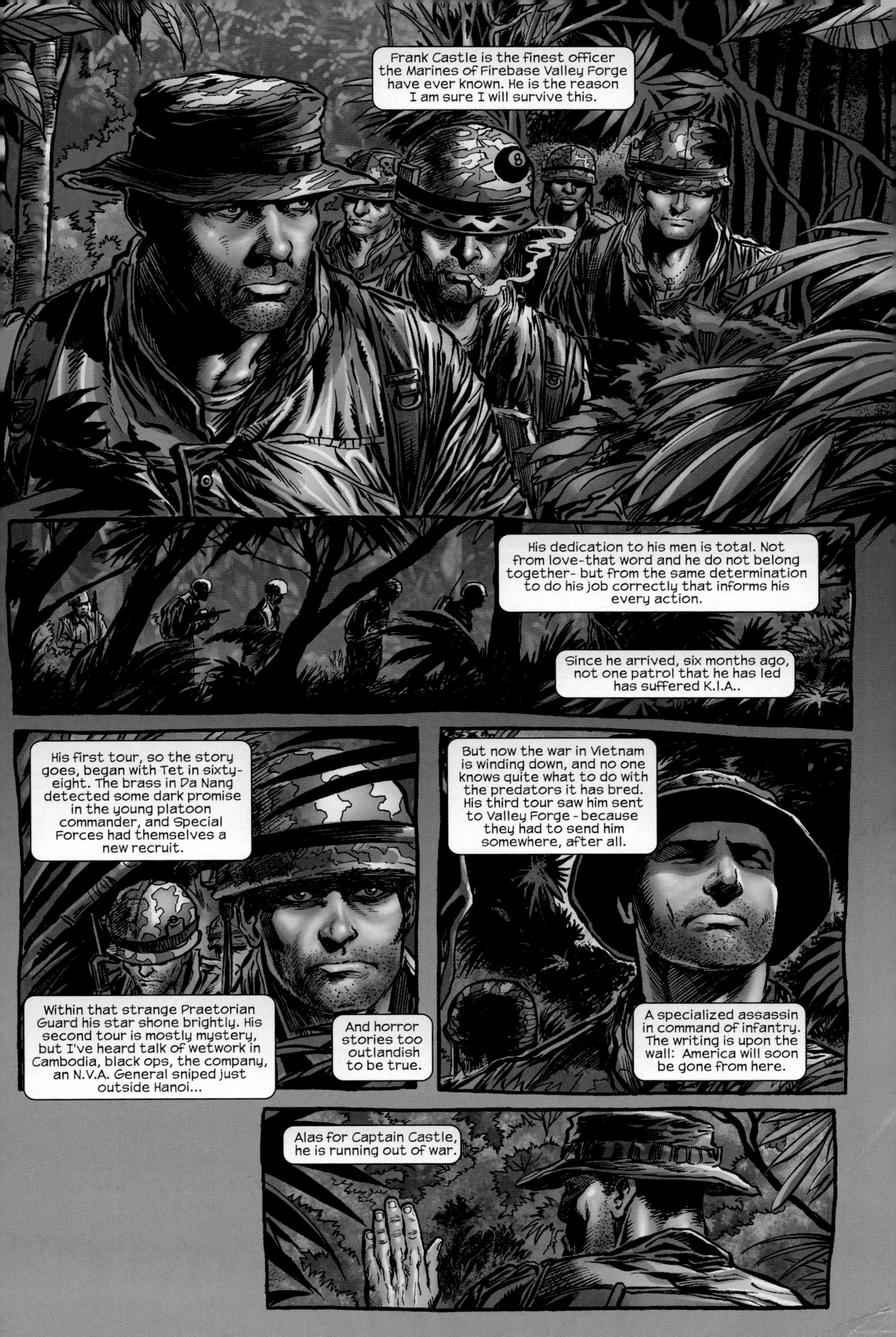
Frank Castle is the finest officer the Marines of Firebase Valley Forge have ever known. He is the reason I am sure I will survive this.
His dedication to his men is total. Not from love-that word and he do not belong together- but from the same determination to do his job correctly that informs his every action.
Since he arrived, six months ago, not one patrol that he has led has suffered K.I.A..
His first tour, so the story goes, began with Tet in sixty-eight. The brass in Da Nang detected some dark promise in the young platoon commander, and Special Forces had themselves a new recruit.
Within that strange Praetorian Guard his star shone brightly. His second tour is mostly mystery, but I've heard talk of wetwork in Cambodia, black ops, the company, an N.V.A. General sniped just outside Hanoi...
And horror stories too outlandish to be true.
But now the war in Vietnam is winding down, and no one knows quite what to do with the predators it has bred. His third tour saw him sent to Valley Forge - because they had to send him somewhere, after all.
A specialized assassin in command of infantry. The writing is upon the wall: America will soon be gone from here.
Alas for Captain Castle, he is running out of war.

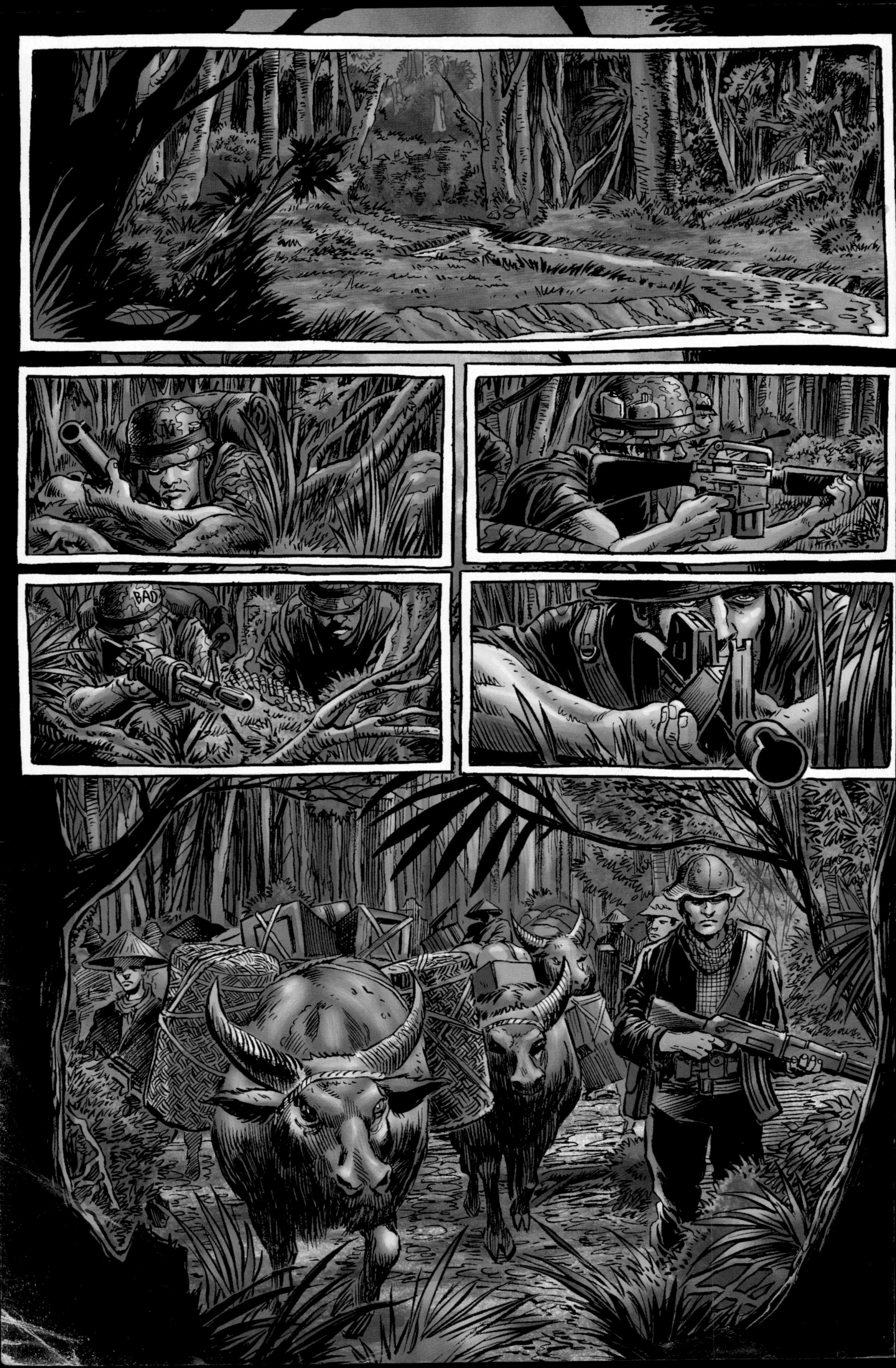
BAD

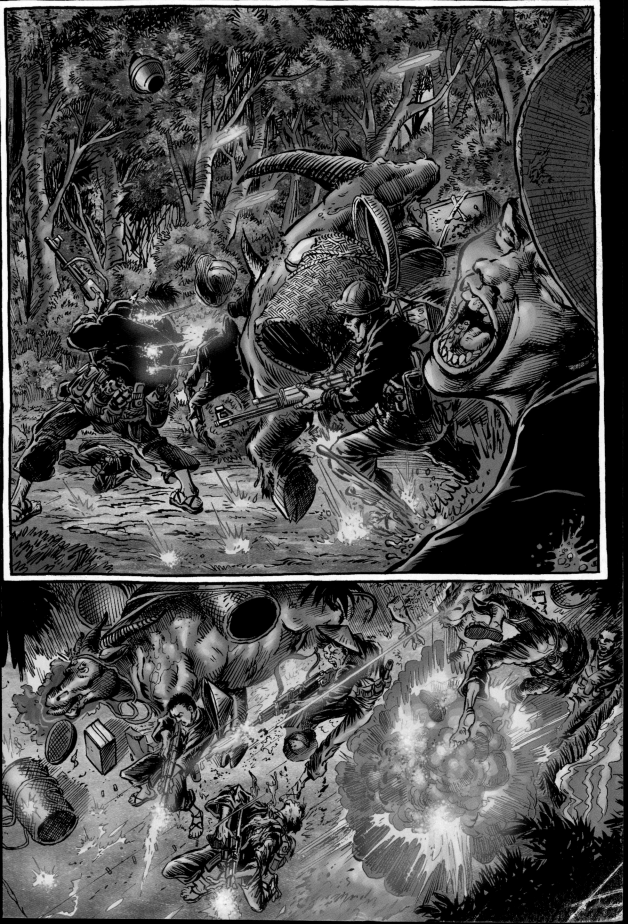

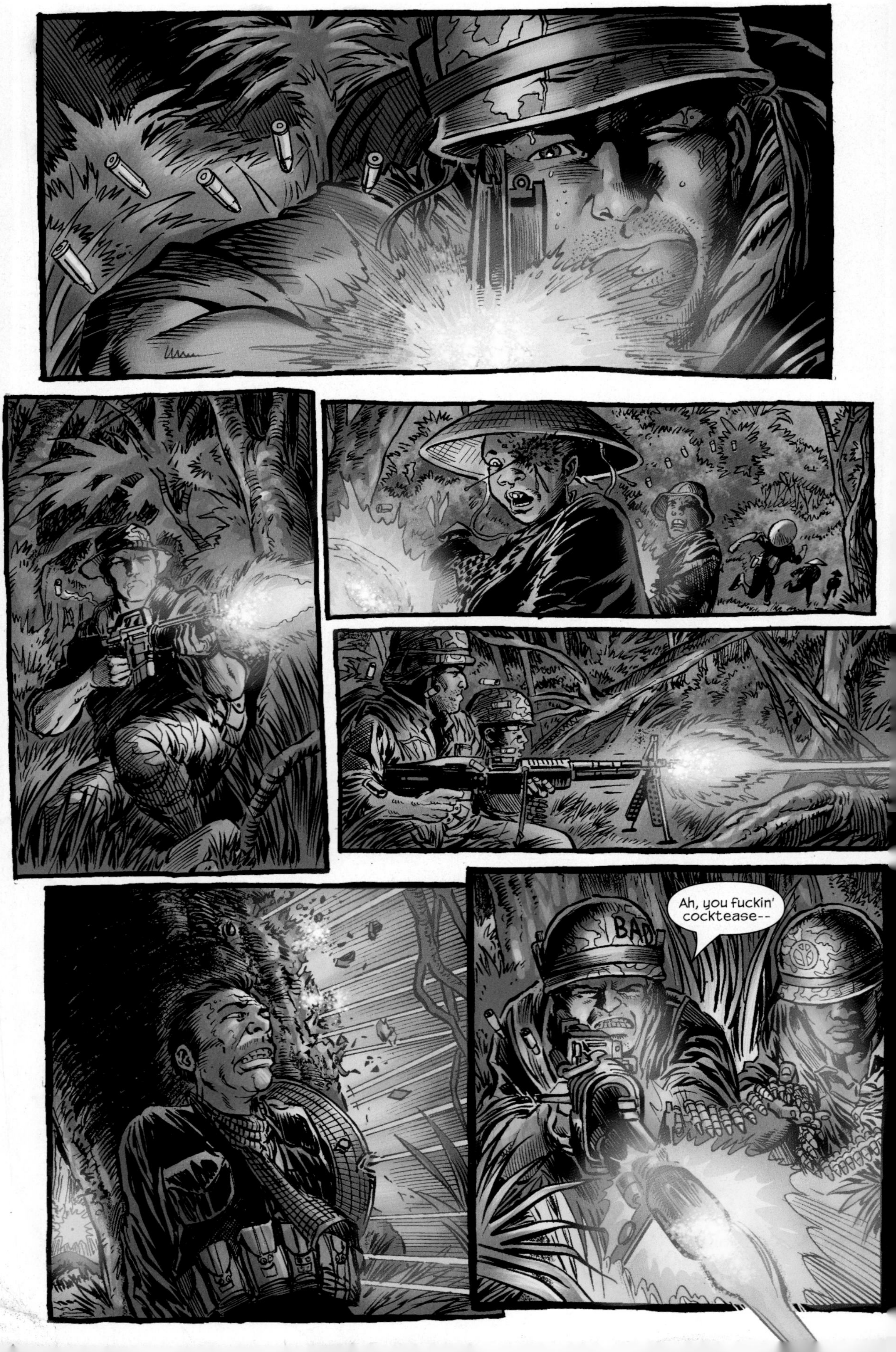
Ah, you fuckin' cocktease--
BAD

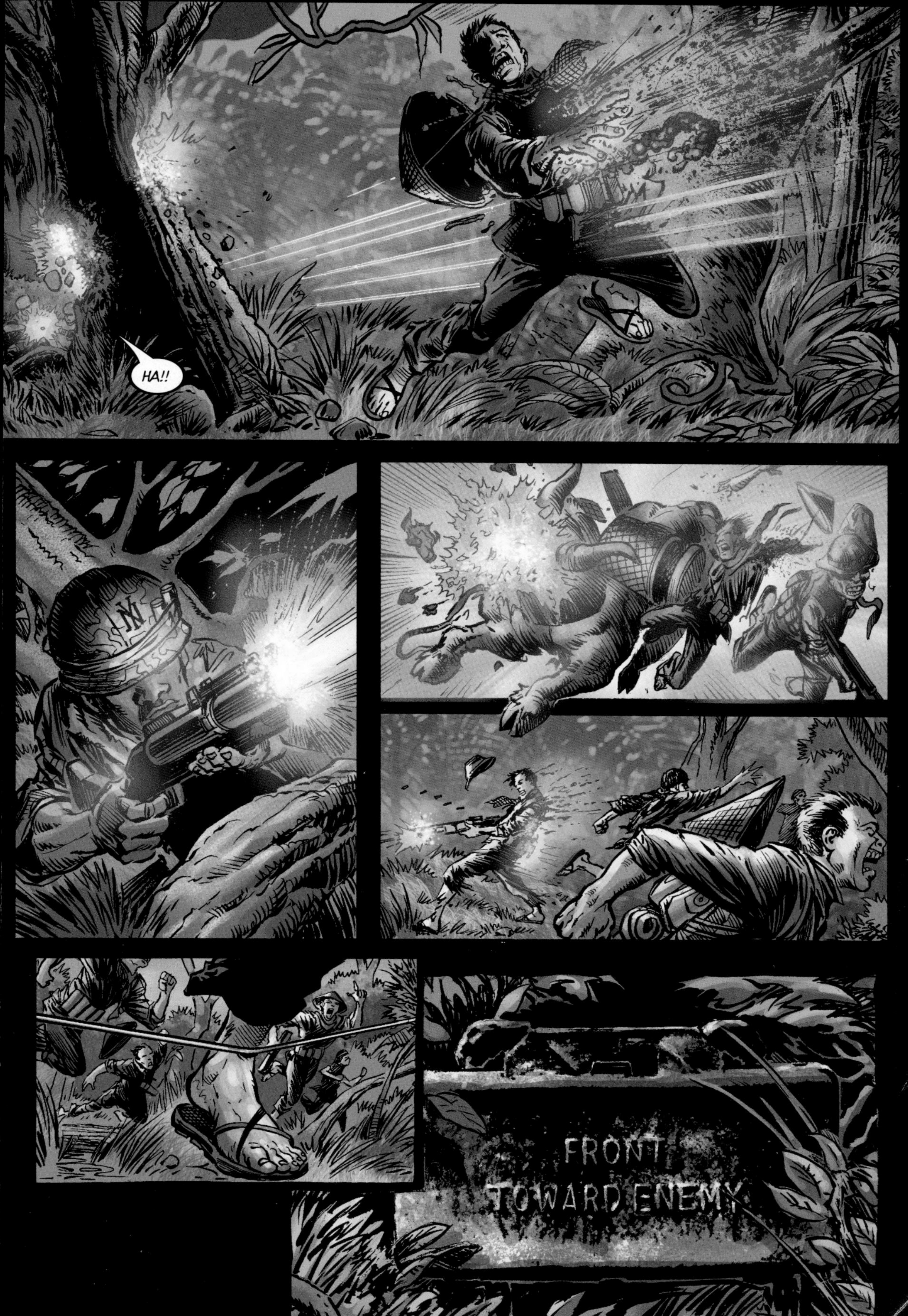
HA!!
FRONT
TOWARD ENEMY

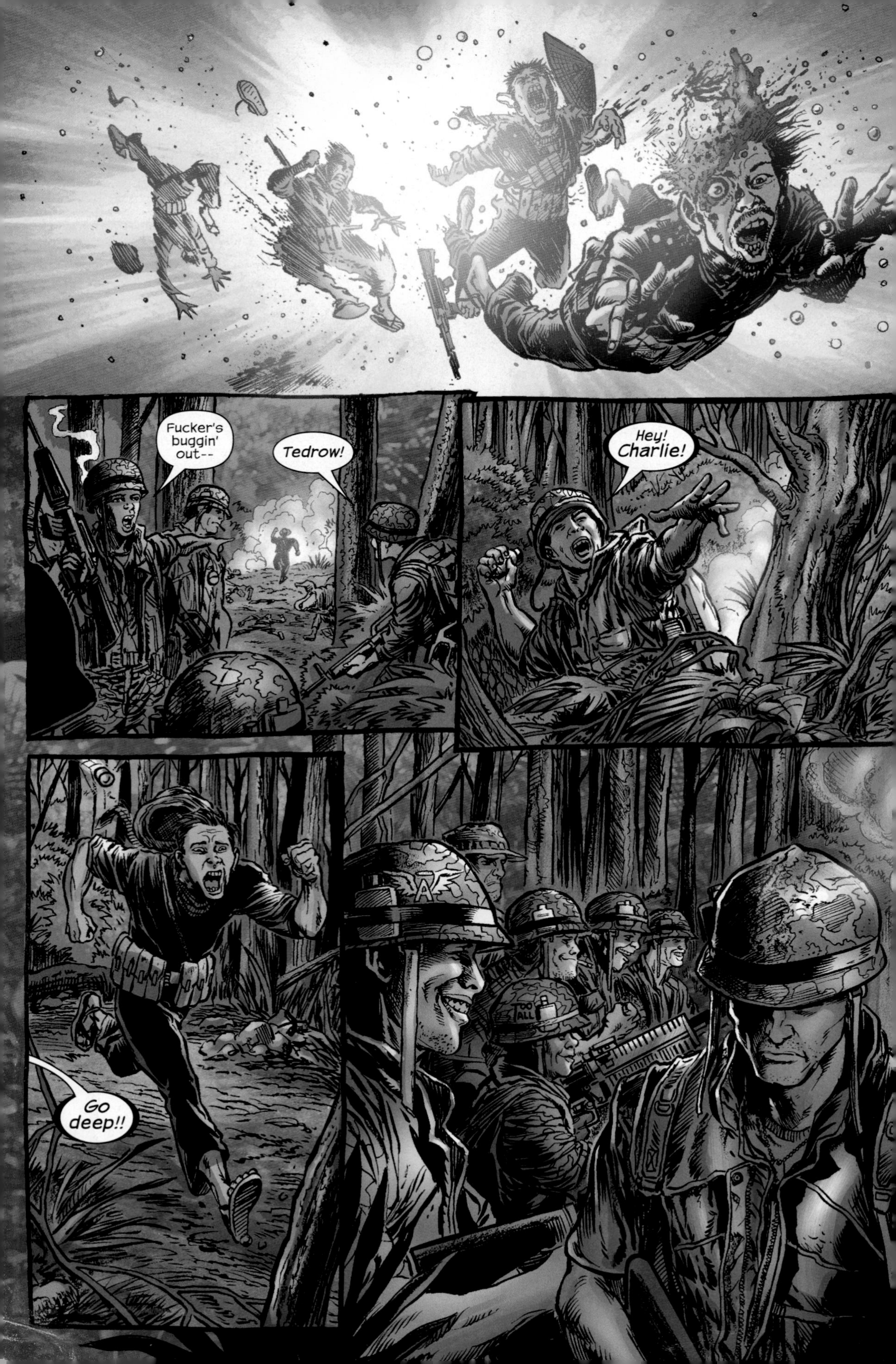
Fucker's buggin' out--
Tedrow!
Hey! Charlie!
Go deep!!

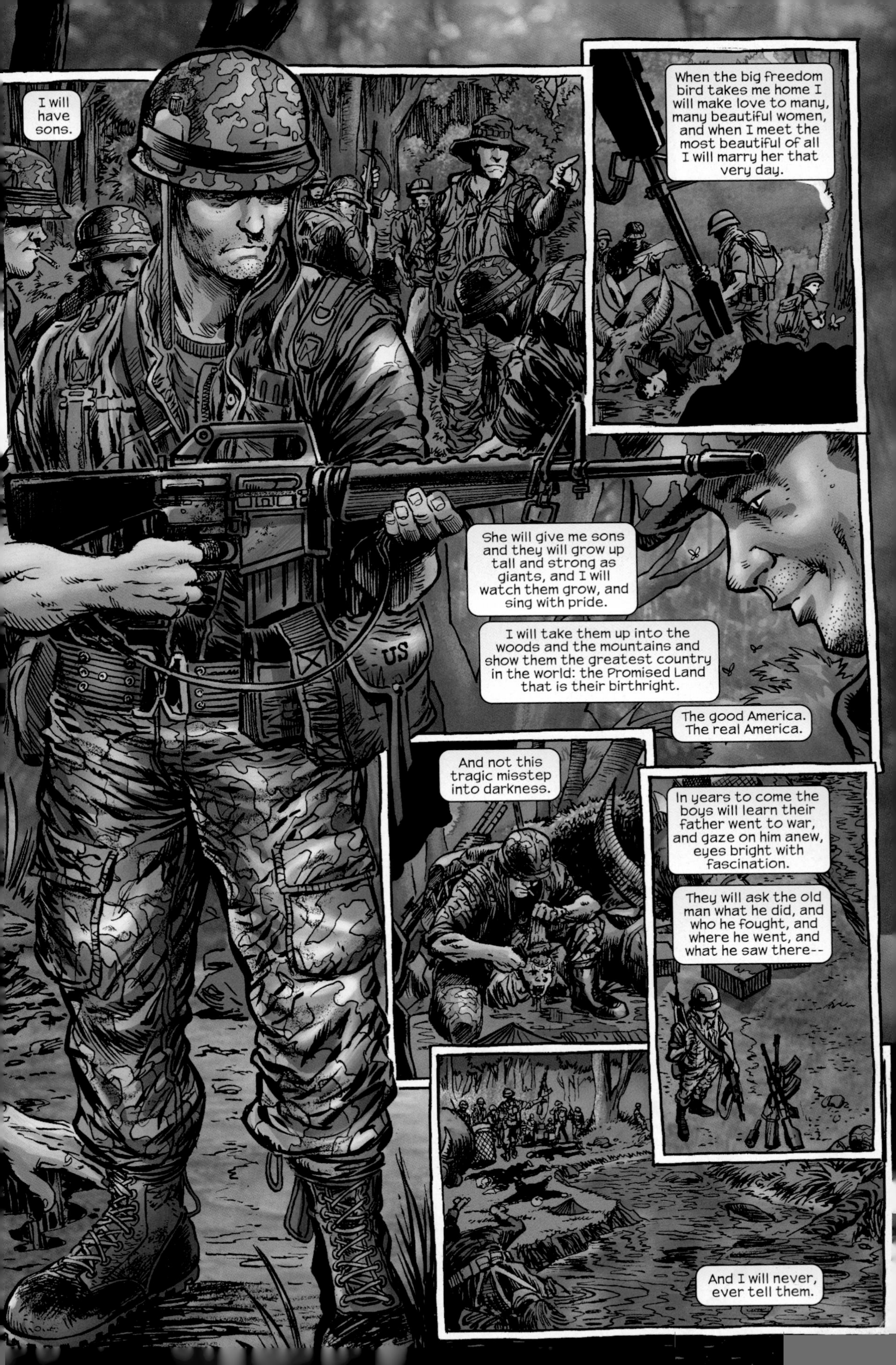
I will have sons.
When the big freedom bird takes me home I will make love to many, many beautiful women, and when I meet the most beautiful of all I will marry her that very day.
She will give me sons and they will grow up tall and strong as giants, and I will watch them grow, and sing with pride.
I will take them up into the woods and the mountains and show them the greatest country in the world: the Promised Land that is their birthright.
The good America. The real America.
And not this tragic misstep into darkness.
In years to come the boys will learn their father went to war, and gaze on him anew, eyes bright with fascination.
They will ask the old man what he did, and who he fought, and where he went, and what he saw there--
And I will never, ever tell them.
US

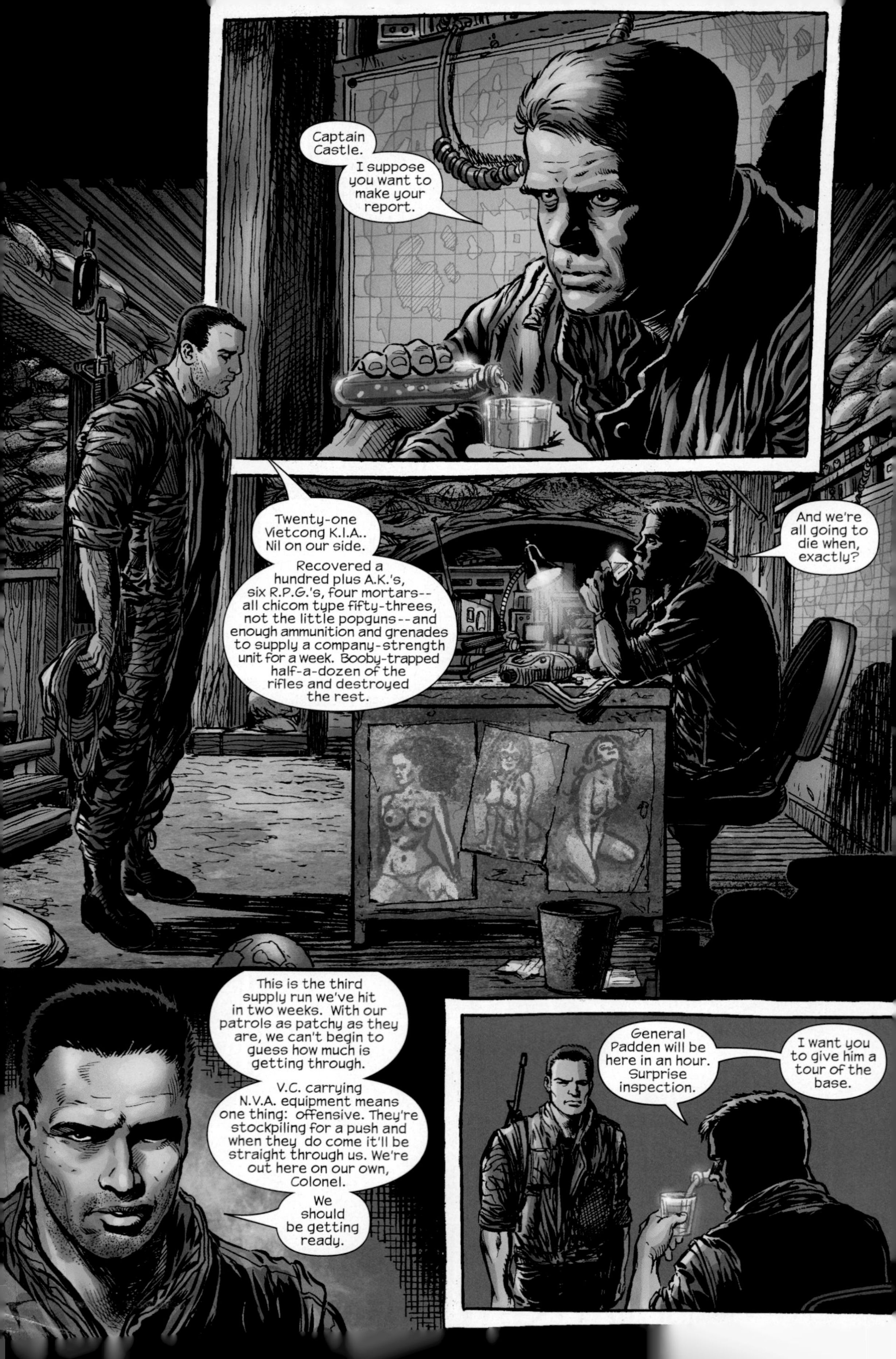
Captain Castle.
I suppose you want to make your report.
Twenty-one Vietcong K.I.A.. Nil on our side.
Recovered a hundred plus A.K.'s, six R.P.G.'s, four mortars--all chicom type fifty-threes, not the little popguns--and enough ammunition and grenades to supply a company-strength unit for a week. Booby-trapped half-a-dozen of the rifles and destroyed the rest.
And we're all going to die when, exactly?
This is the third supply run we've hit in two weeks. With our patrols as patchy as they are, we can't begin to guess how much is getting through.
V.C. carrying N.V.A. equipment means one thing: offensive. They're stockpiling for a push and when they do come it'll be straight through us. We're out here on our own, Colonel.
We should be getting ready.
General Padden will be here in an hour. Surprise inspection.
I want you to give him a tour of the base.

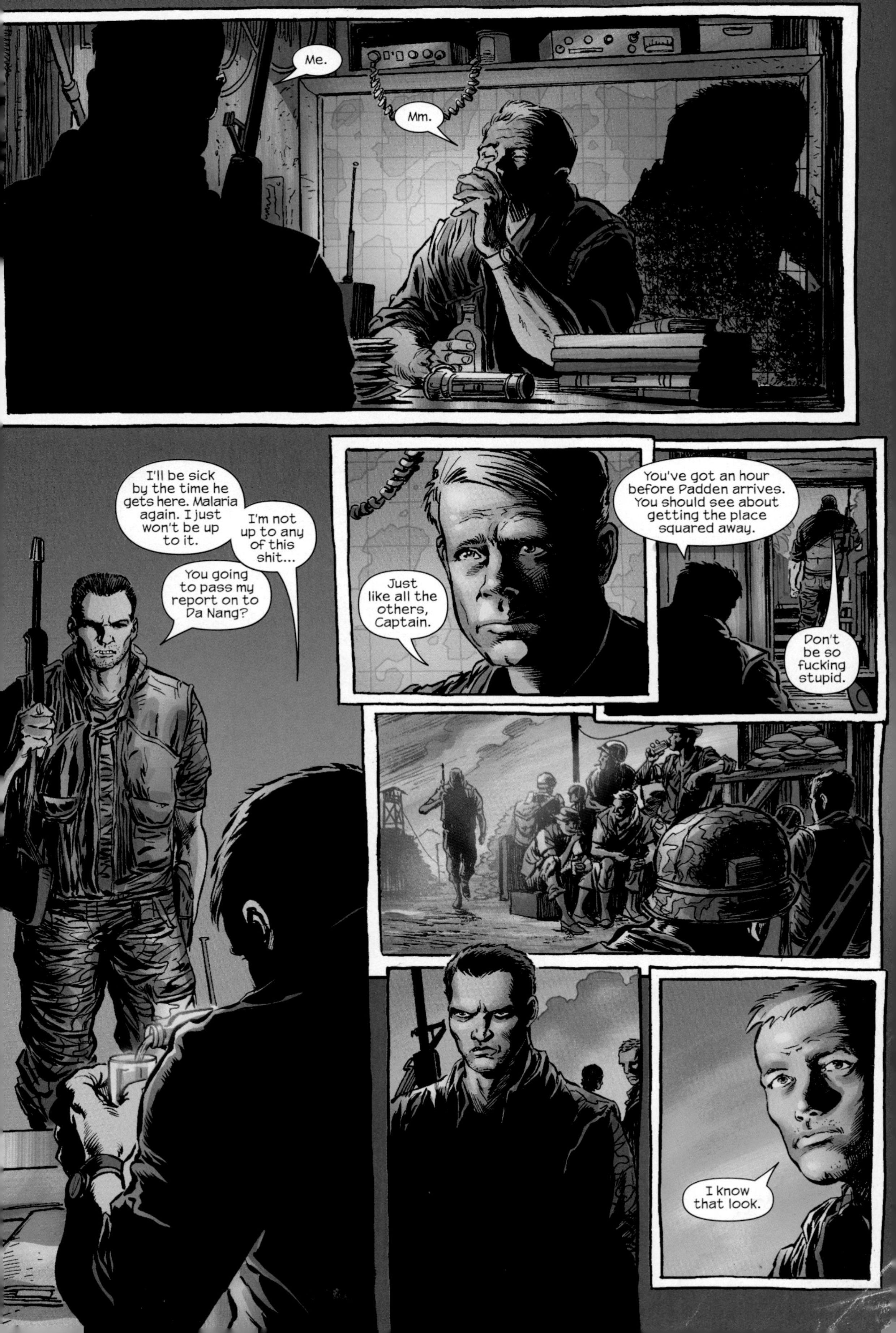
Me.
Mm.
I'll be sick by the time he gets here. Malaria again. I just won't be up to it.
I'm not up to any of this shit...
You going to pass my report on to Da Nang?
Just like all the others, Captain.
You've got an hour before Padden arrives. You should see about getting the place squared away.
Don't be so fucking stupid.
I know that look.

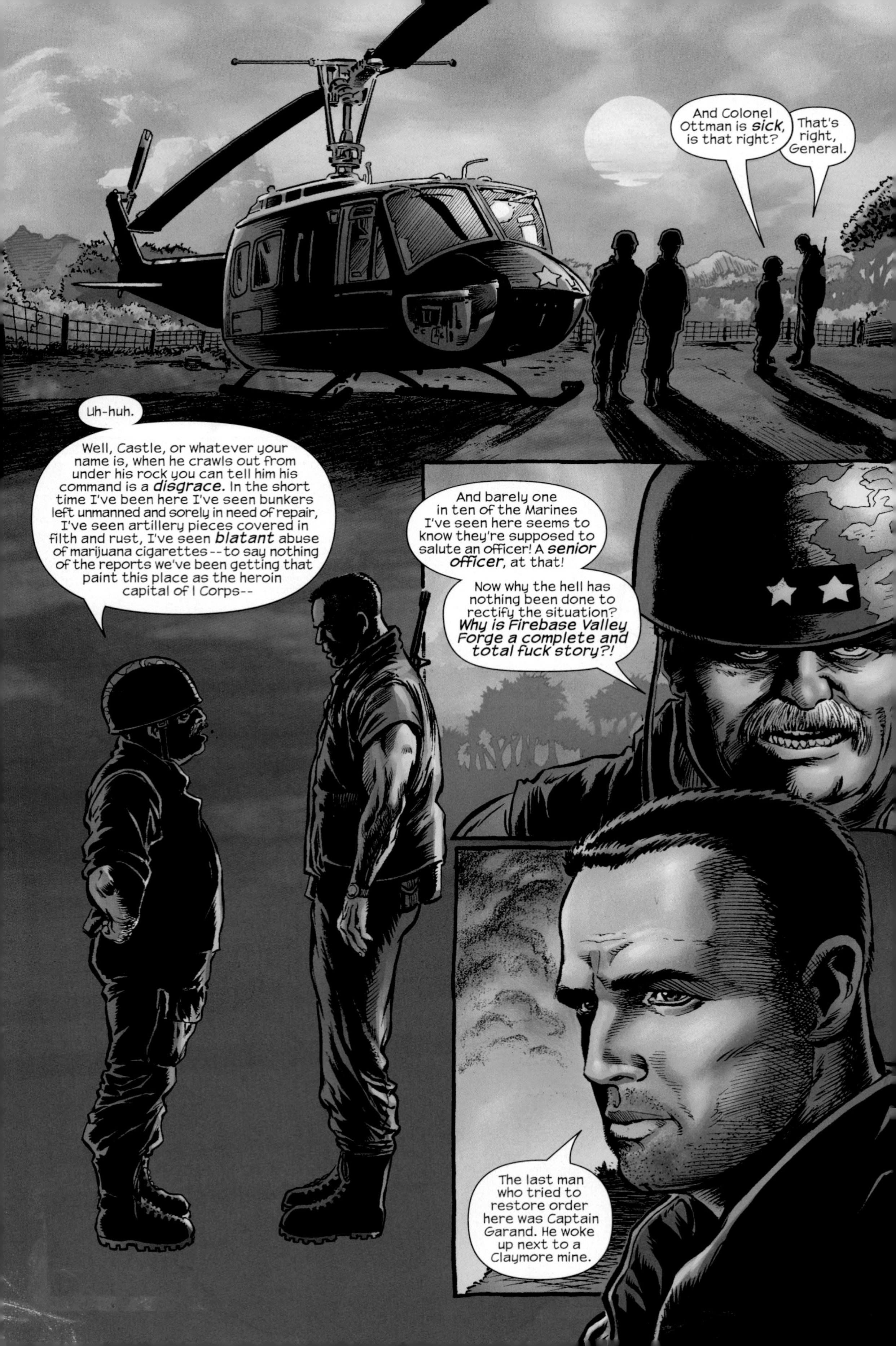
And Colonel Ottman is sick, is that right?
That's right, General.
Uh-huh.
Well, Castle, or whatever your name is, when he crawls out from under his rock you can tell him his command is a disgrace. In the short time I've been here I've seen bunkers left unmanned and sorely in need of repair, I've seen artillery pieces covered in filth and rust, I've seen blatant abuse of marijuana cigarettes --to say nothing of the reports we've been getting that paint this place as the heroin capital of I Corps--
And barely one in ten of the Marines I've seen here seems to know they're supposed to salute an officer! A senior officer, at that!
Now why the hell has nothing been done to rectify the situation? Why is Firebase Valley Forge a complete and total fuck story?!
The last man who tried to restore order here was Captain Garand. He woke up next to a Claymore mine.

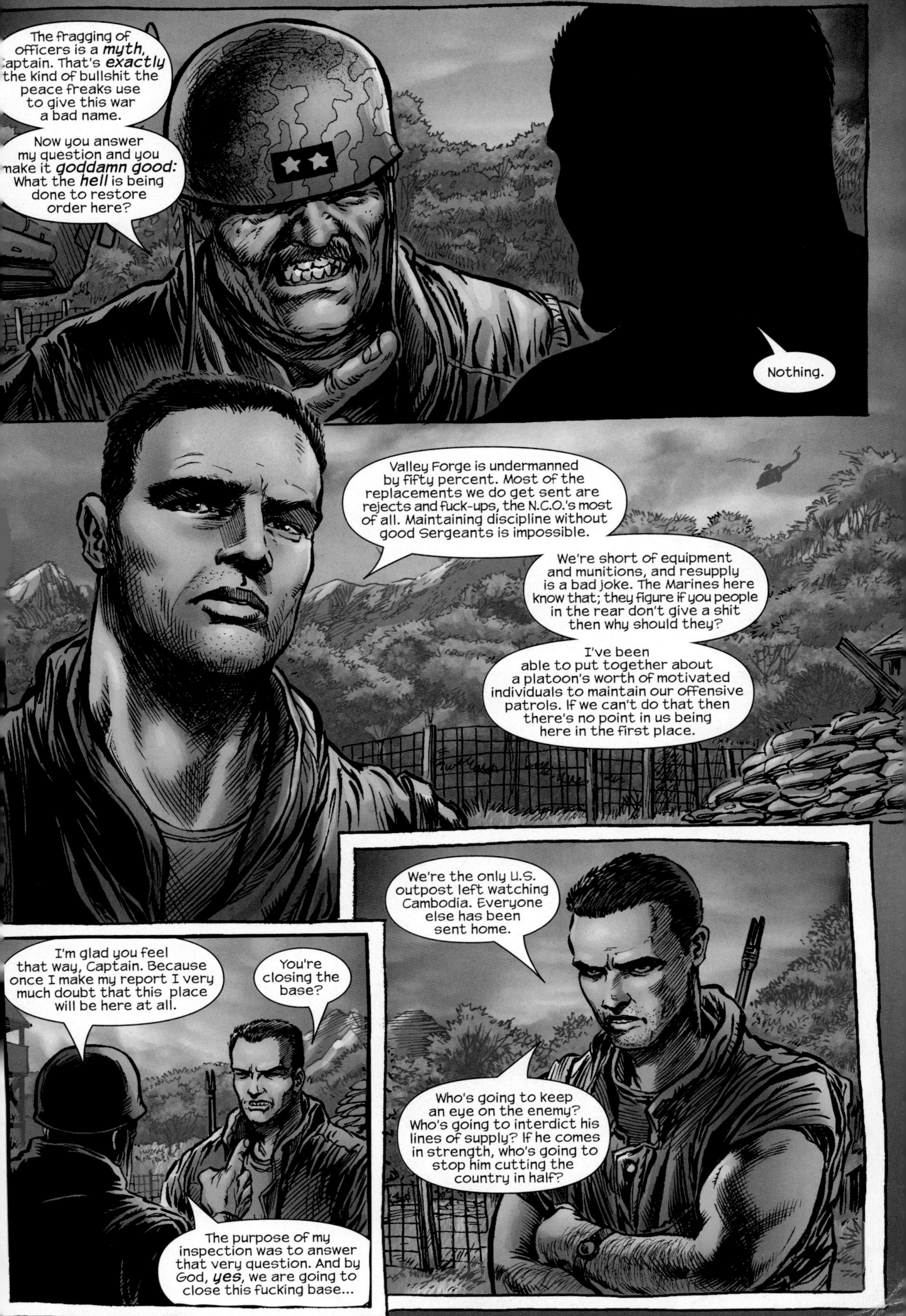
The fragging of officers is a *myth*, Captain. That's *exactly* the kind of bullshit the peace freaks use to give this war a bad name.
Now you answer my question and you make it *goddamn good:* What the *hell* is being done to restore order here?
Nothing.
Valley Forge is undermanned by fifty percent. Most of the replacements we do get sent are rejects and fuck-ups, the N.C.O.'s most of all. Maintaining discipline without good Sergeants is impossible.
We're short of equipment and munitions, and resupply is a bad joke. The Marines here know that; they figure if you people in the rear don't give a shit then why should they?
I've been able to put together about a platoon's worth of motivated individuals to maintain our offensive patrols. If we can't do that then there's no point in us being here in the first place.
We're the only U.S. outpost left watching Cambodia. Everyone else has been sent home.
Who's going to keep an eye on the enemy? Who's going to interdict his lines of supply? If he comes in strength, who's going to stop him cutting the country in half?
I'm glad you feel that way, Captain. Because once I make my report I very much doubt that this place will be here at all.
You're closing the base?
The purpose of my inspection was to answer that very question. And by God, *yes*, we are going to close this fucking base...

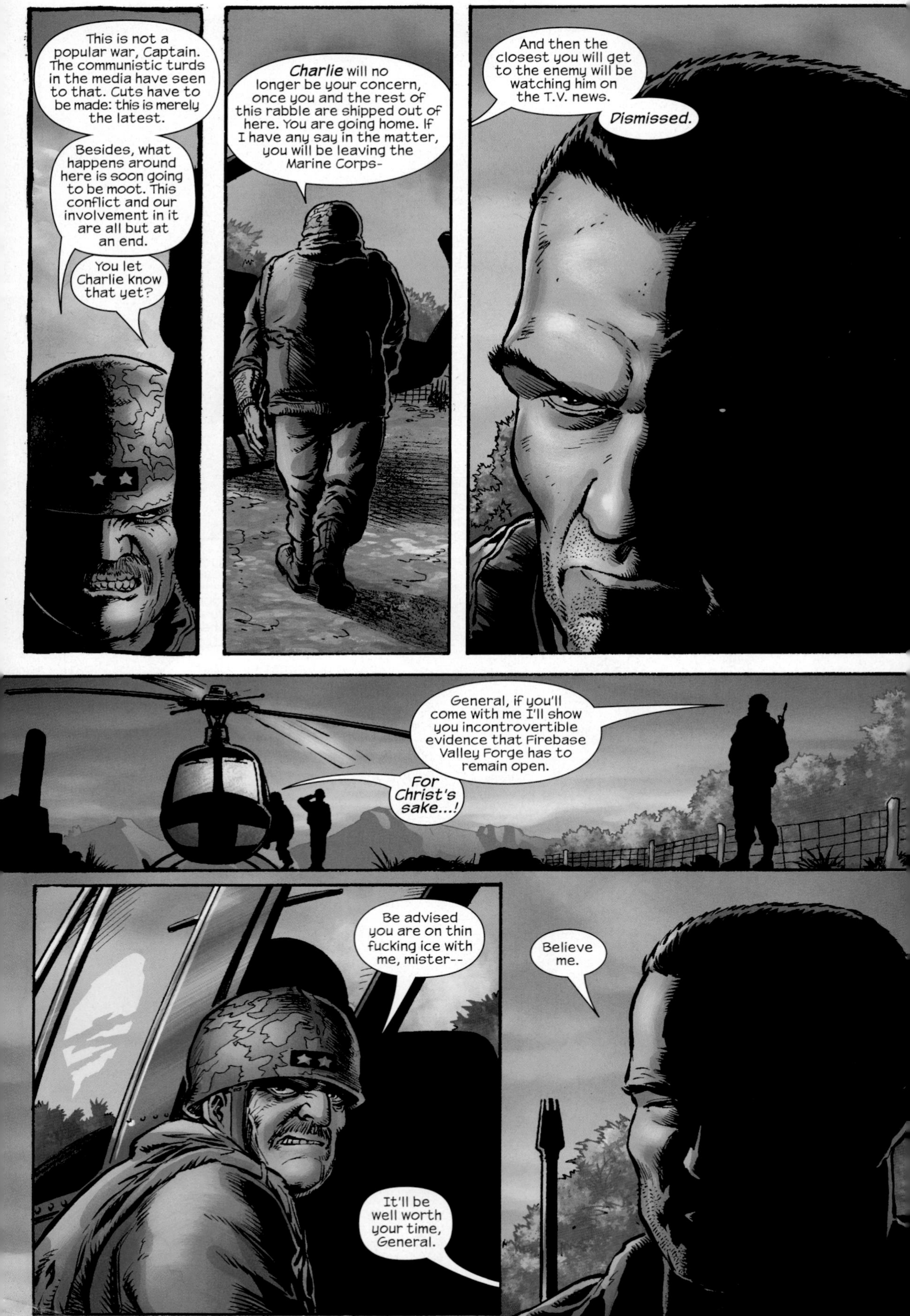
This is not a popular war, Captain. The communistic turds in the media have seen to that. Cuts have to be made: this is merely the latest.
Besides, what happens around here is soon going to be moot. This conflict and our involvement in it are all but at an end.
You let Charlie know that yet?
Charlie will no longer be your concern, once you and the rest of this rabble are shipped out of here. You are going home. If I have any say in the matter, you will be leaving the Marine Corps-
And then the closest you will get to the enemy will be watching him on the T.V. news.
Dismissed.
General, if you'll come with me I'll show you incontrovertible evidence that Firebase Valley Forge has to remain open.
For Christ's sake...!
Be advised you are on thin fucking ice with me, mister--
Believe me.
It'll be well worth your time, General.

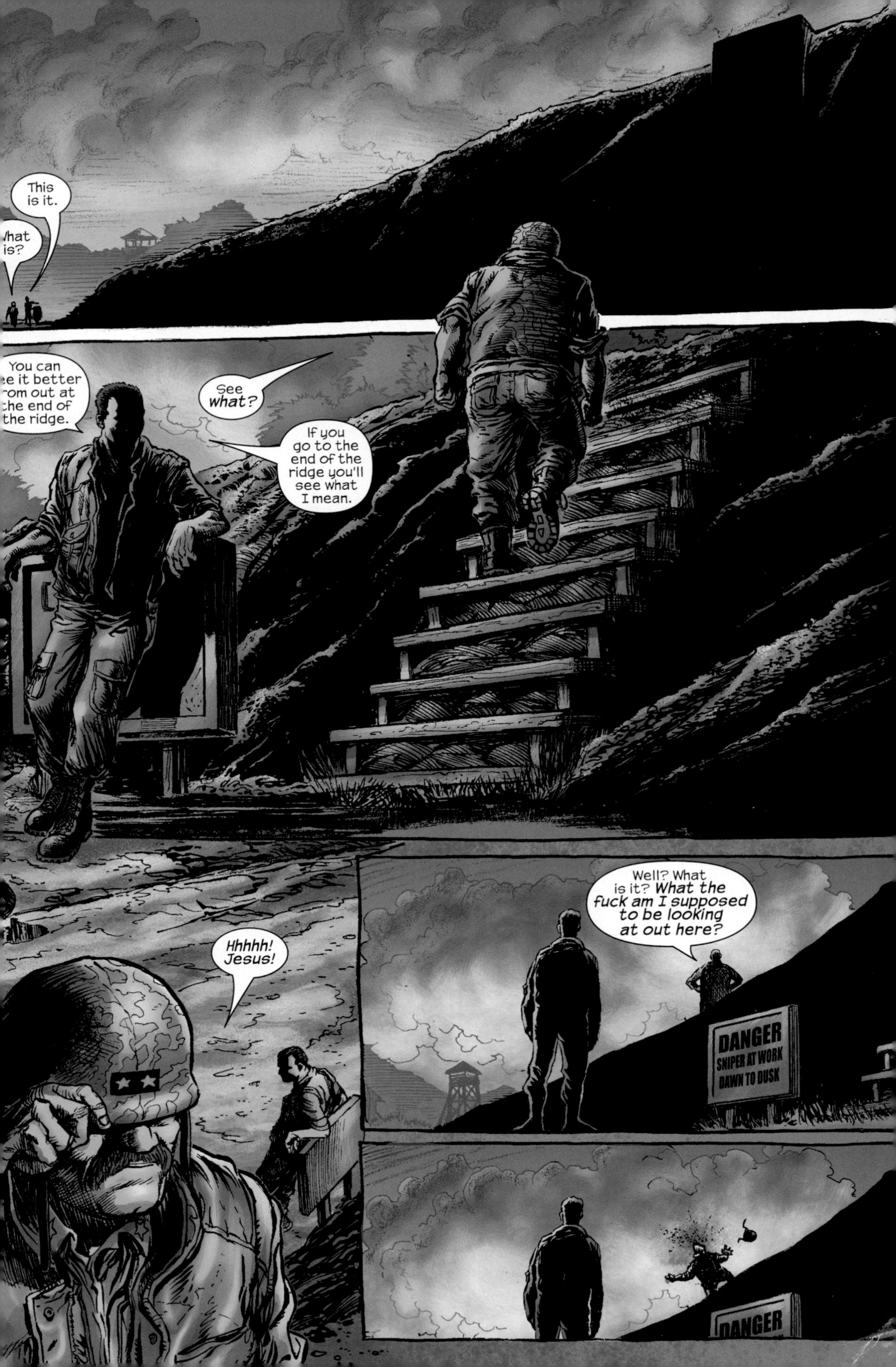
This is it.
What is?
You can see it better from out at the end of the ridge.
See what?
If you go to the end of the ridge you'll see what I mean.
Hhhhh! Jesus!
Well? What is it? What the fuck am I supposed to be looking at out here?
DANGER
SNIPER AT WORK
DAWN TO DUSK
DANGER

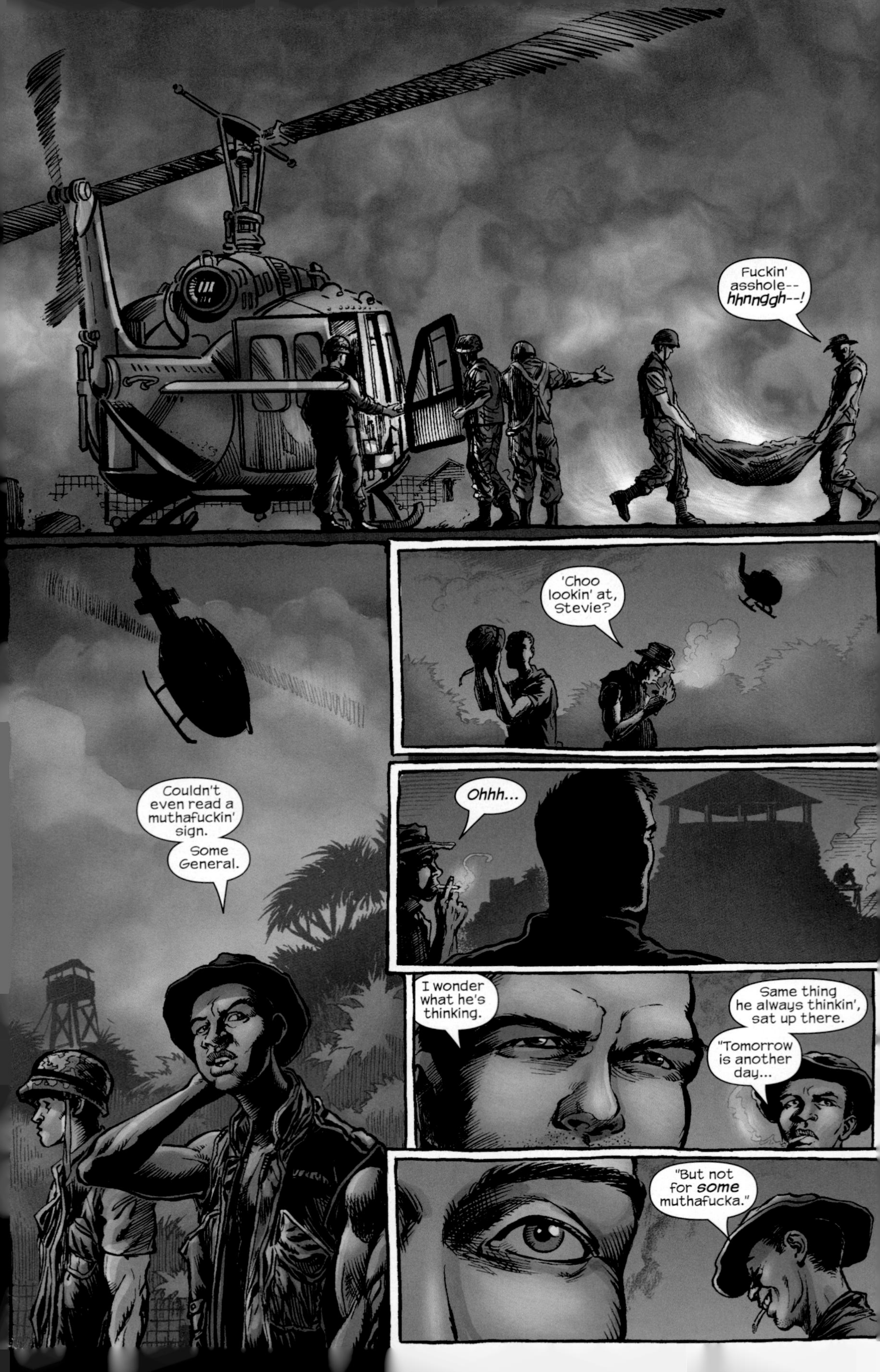
Fuckin' asshole-- hhnngh--!
'Choo lookin' at, Stevie?
Couldn't even read a muthafuckin' sign.
Some General.
Ohhh...
I wonder what he's thinking.
Same thing he always thinkin', sat up there.
"Tomorrow is another day...
"But not for *some* muthafucka."

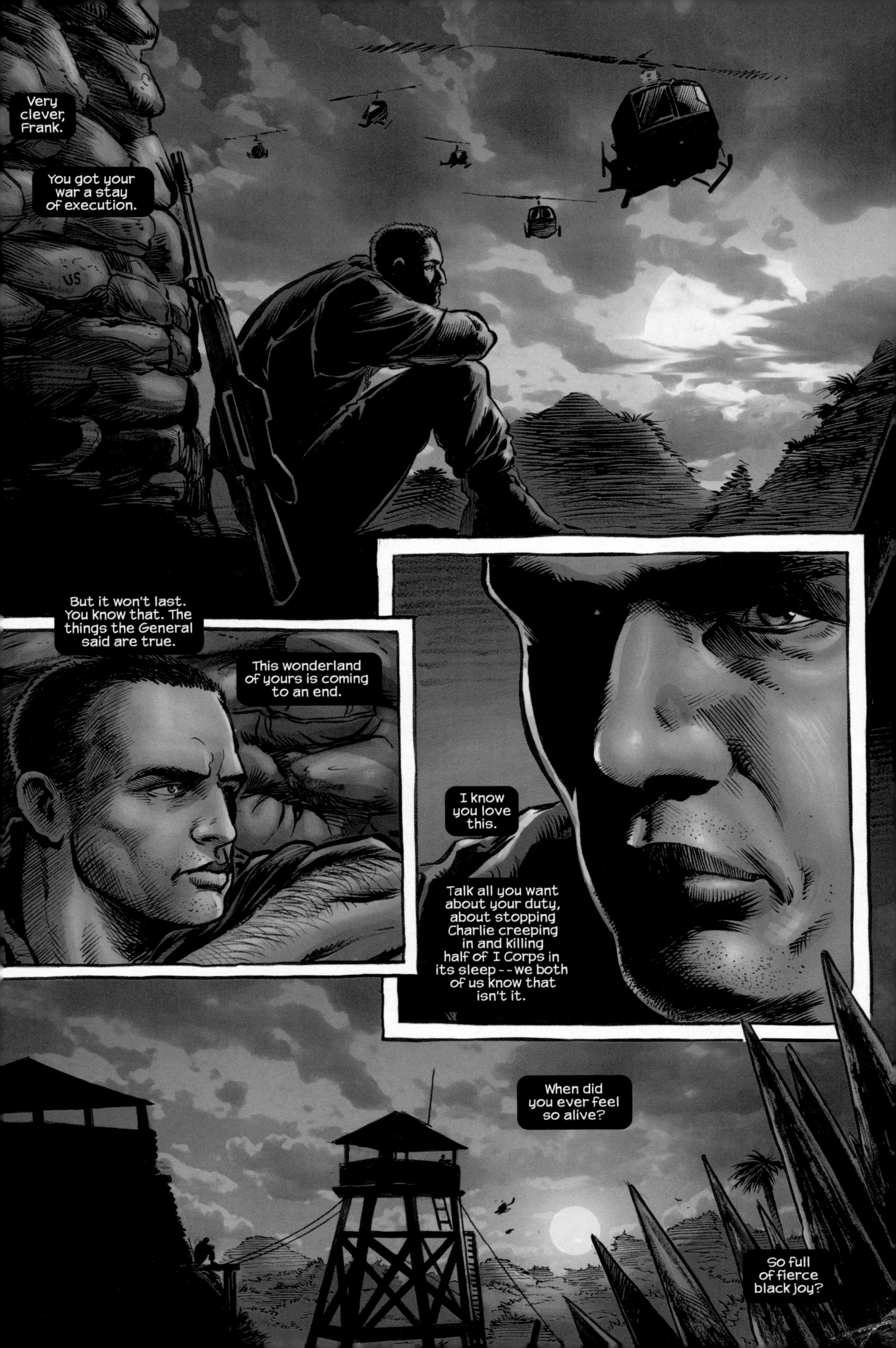
Very clever, Frank.
You got your war a stay of execution.
But it won't last. You know that. The things the General said are true.
This wonderland of yours is coming to an end.
I know you love this.
Talk all you want about your duty, about stopping Charlie creeping in and killing half of I Corps in its sleep--we both of us know that isn't it.
When did you ever feel so alive?
So full of fierce black joy?

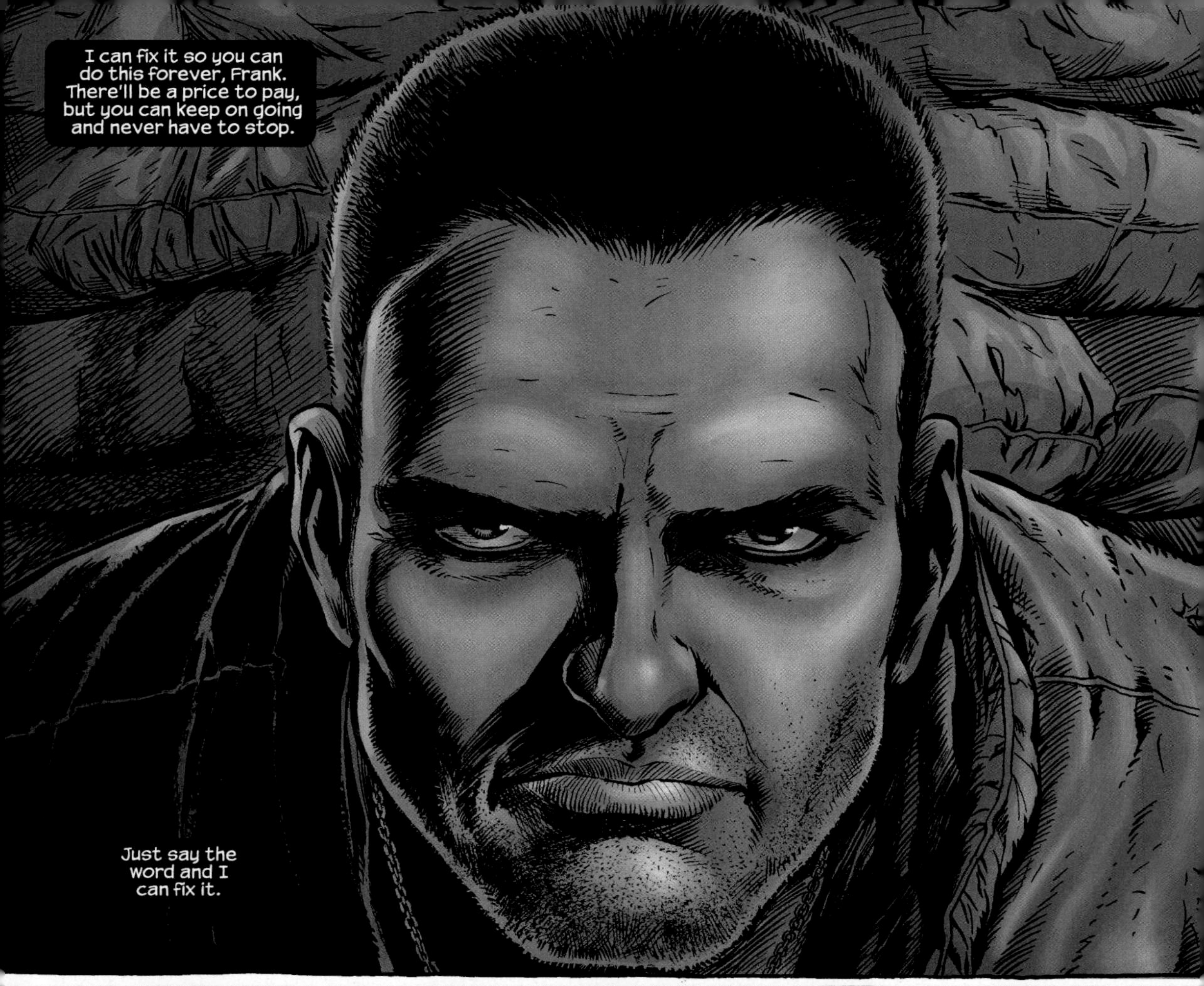
I can fix it so you can do this forever, Frank. There'll be a price to pay, but you can keep on going and never have to stop.
Just say the word and I can fix it.
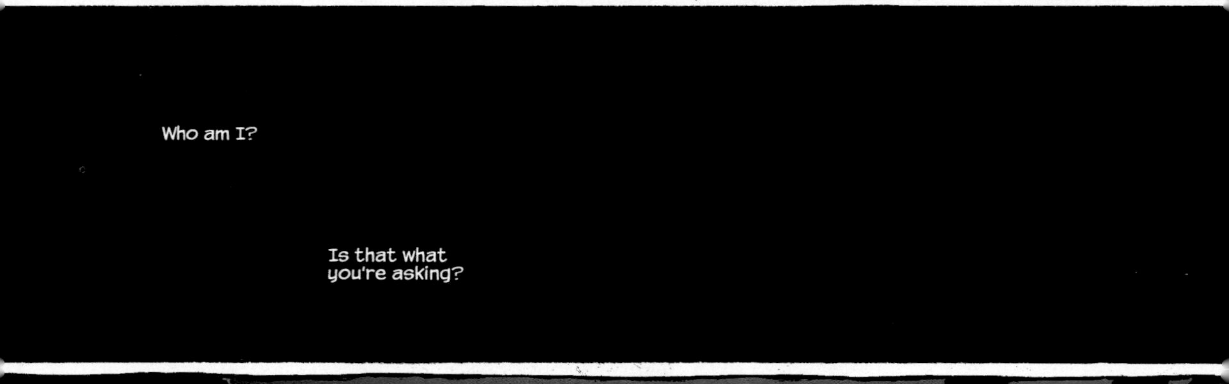
Who am I?
Is that what you're asking?
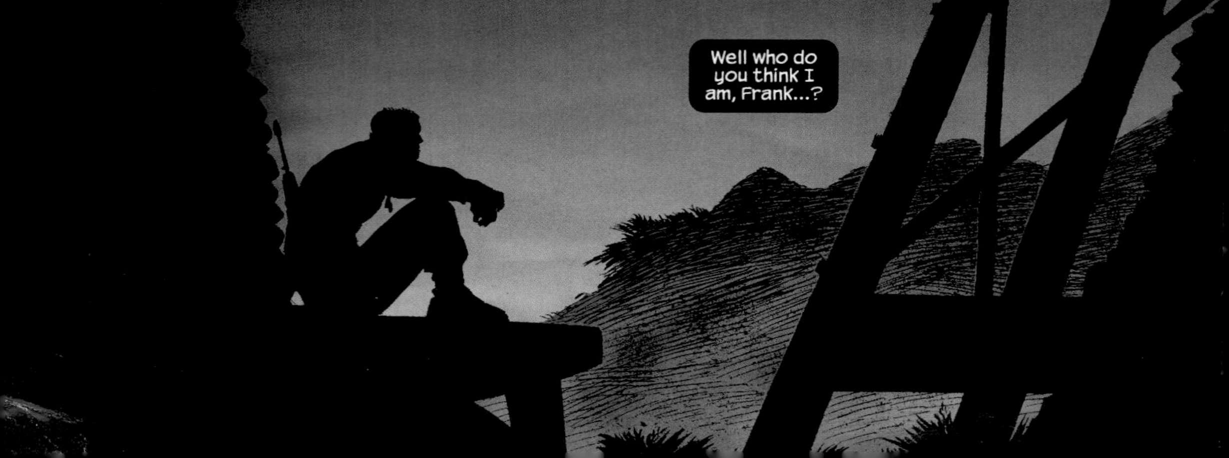
Well who do you think I am, Frank...?

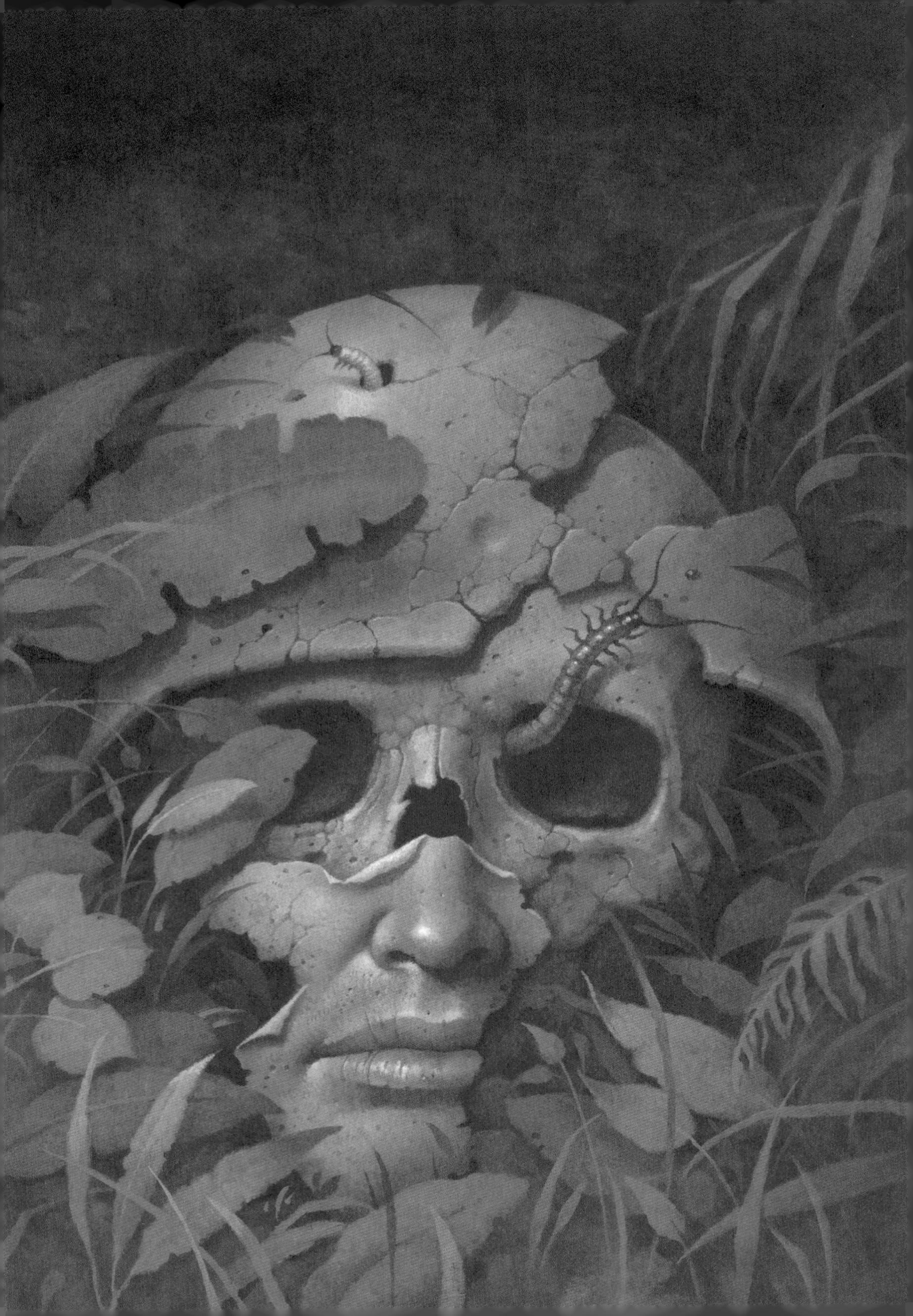

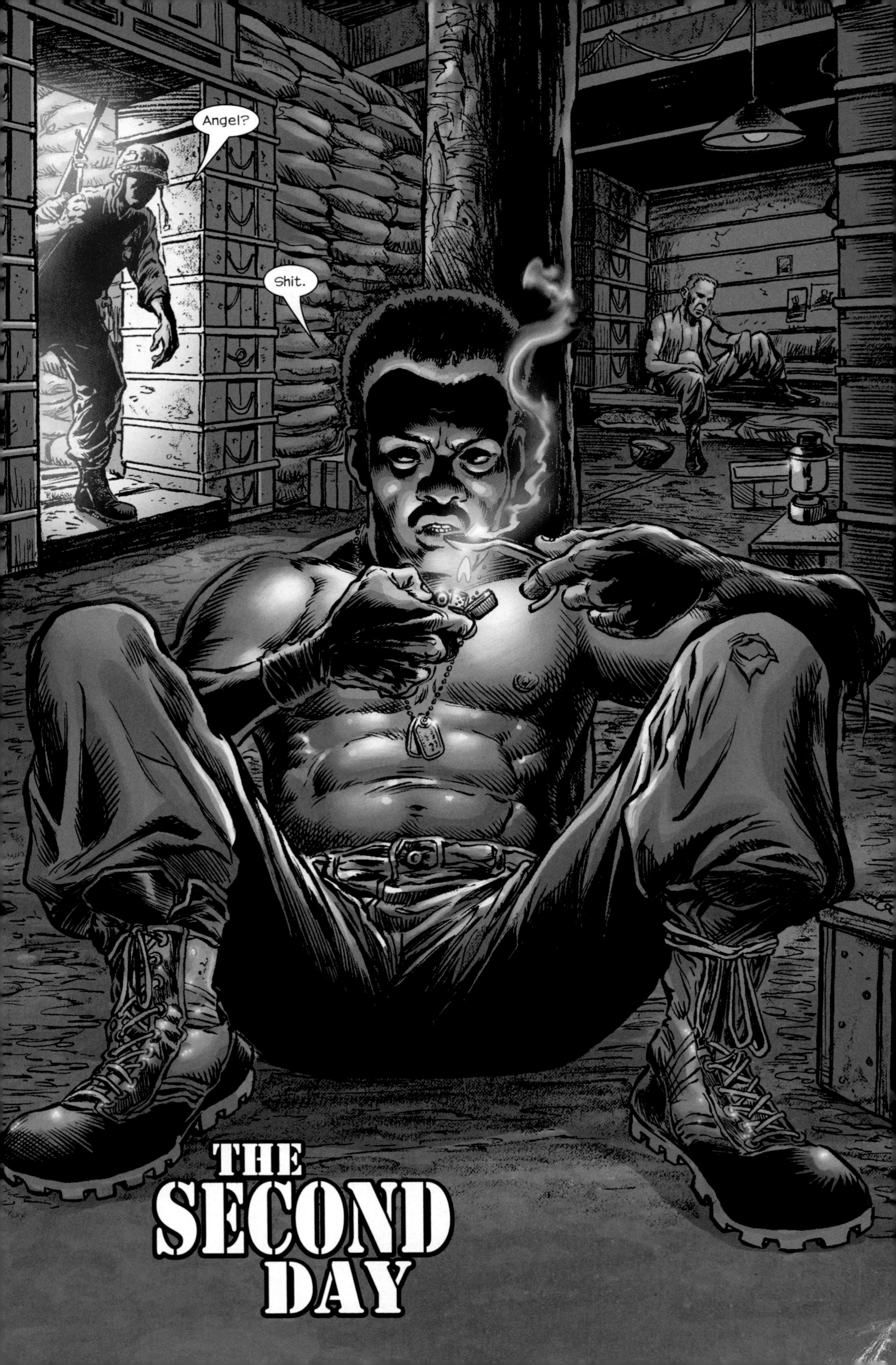
Angel?
Shit.
THE SECOND DAY

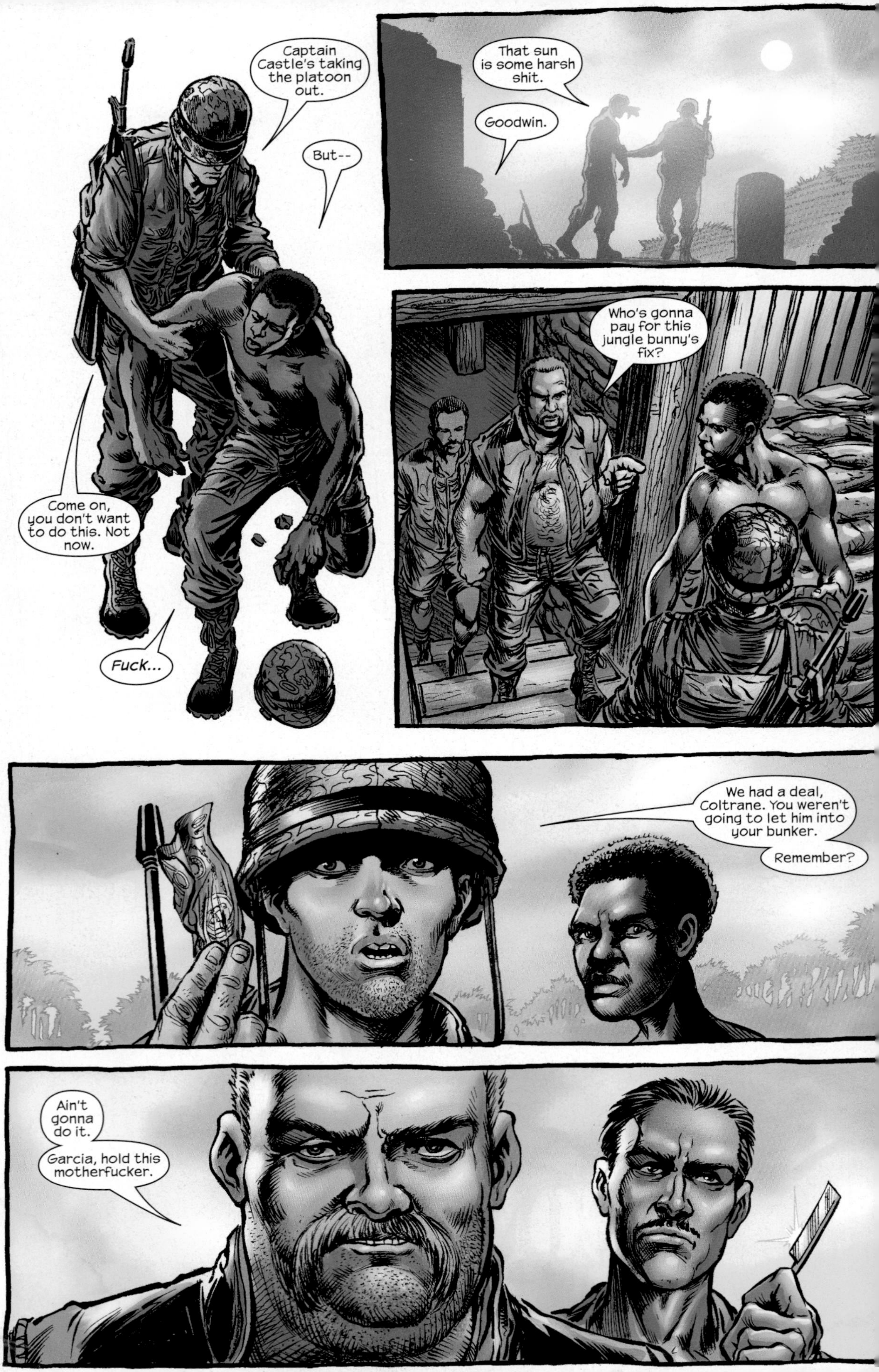
Captain Castle's taking the platoon out.
But--
Come on, you don't want to do this. Not now.
Fuck...
That sun is some harsh shit.
Goodwin.
Who's gonna pay for this jungle bunny's fix?
We had a deal, Coltrane. You weren't going to let him into your bunker.
Remember?
Ain't gonna do it.
Garcia, hold this motherfucker.

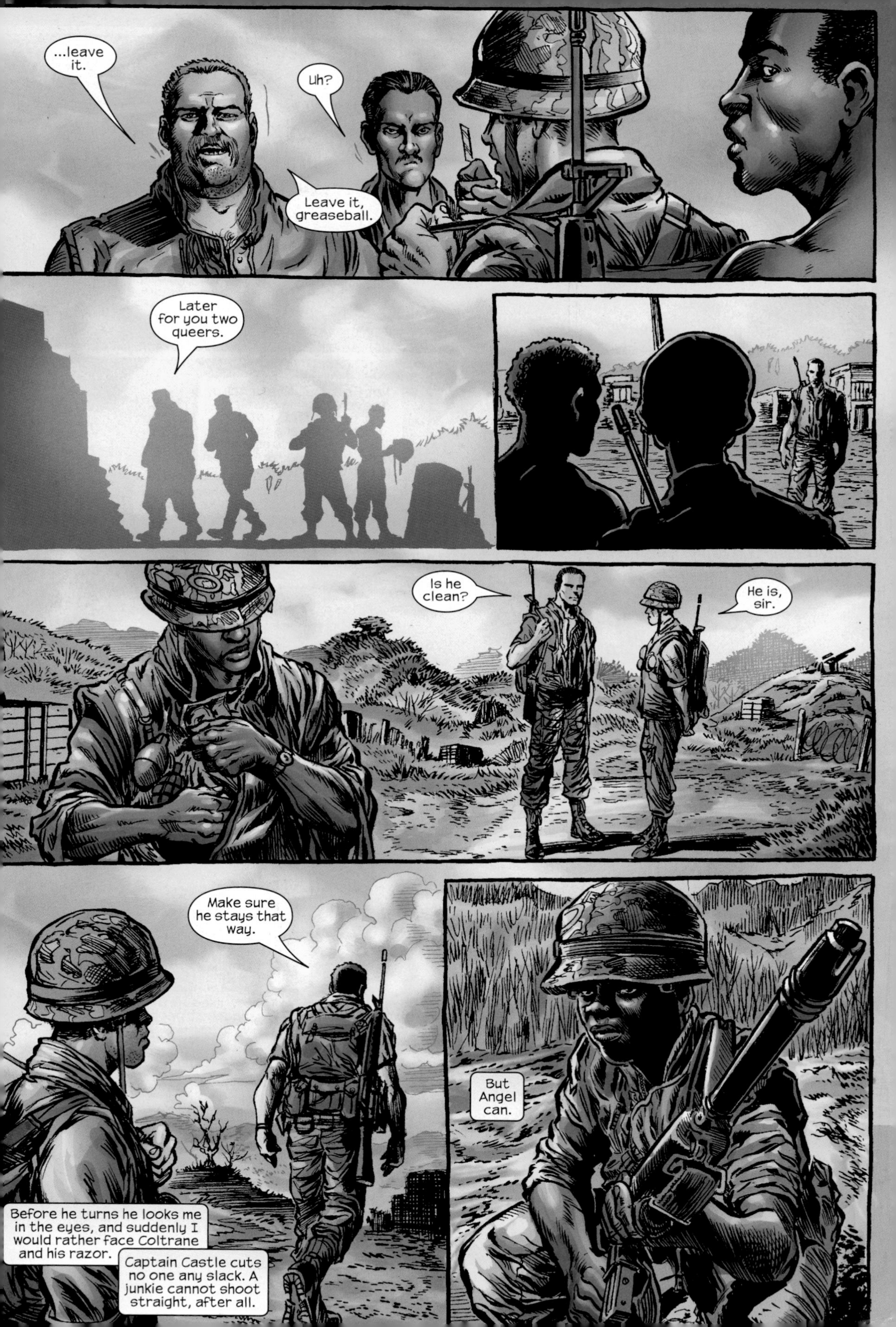
...leave it.
Uh?
Leave it, greaseball.
Later for you two queers.
Is he clean?
He is, sir.
Make sure he stays that way.
Before he turns he looks me in the eyes, and suddenly I would rather face Coltrane and his razor.
Captain Castle cuts no one any slack. A junkie cannot shoot straight, after all.
But Angel can.

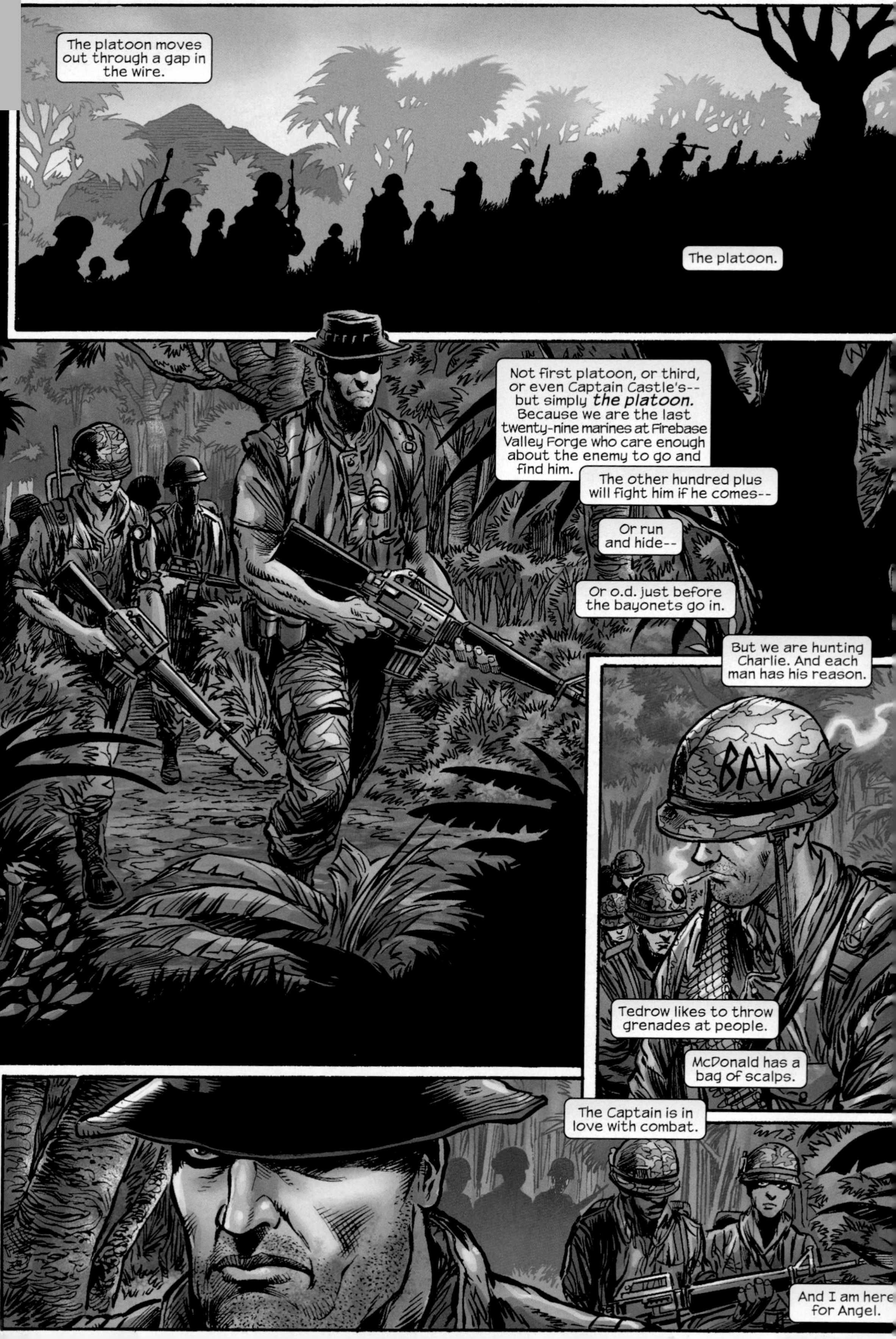
The platoon moves out through a gap in the wire.
The platoon.
Not first platoon, or third, or even Captain Castle's-- but simply *the platoon.* Because we are the last twenty-nine marines at Firebase Valley Forge who care enough about the enemy to go and find him.
The other hundred plus will fight him if he comes--
Or run and hide--
Or o.d. just before the bayonets go in.
But we are hunting Charlie. And each man has his reason.
BAD
Tedrow likes to throw grenades at people.
McDonald has a bag of scalps.
The Captain is in love with combat.
And I am here for Angel.

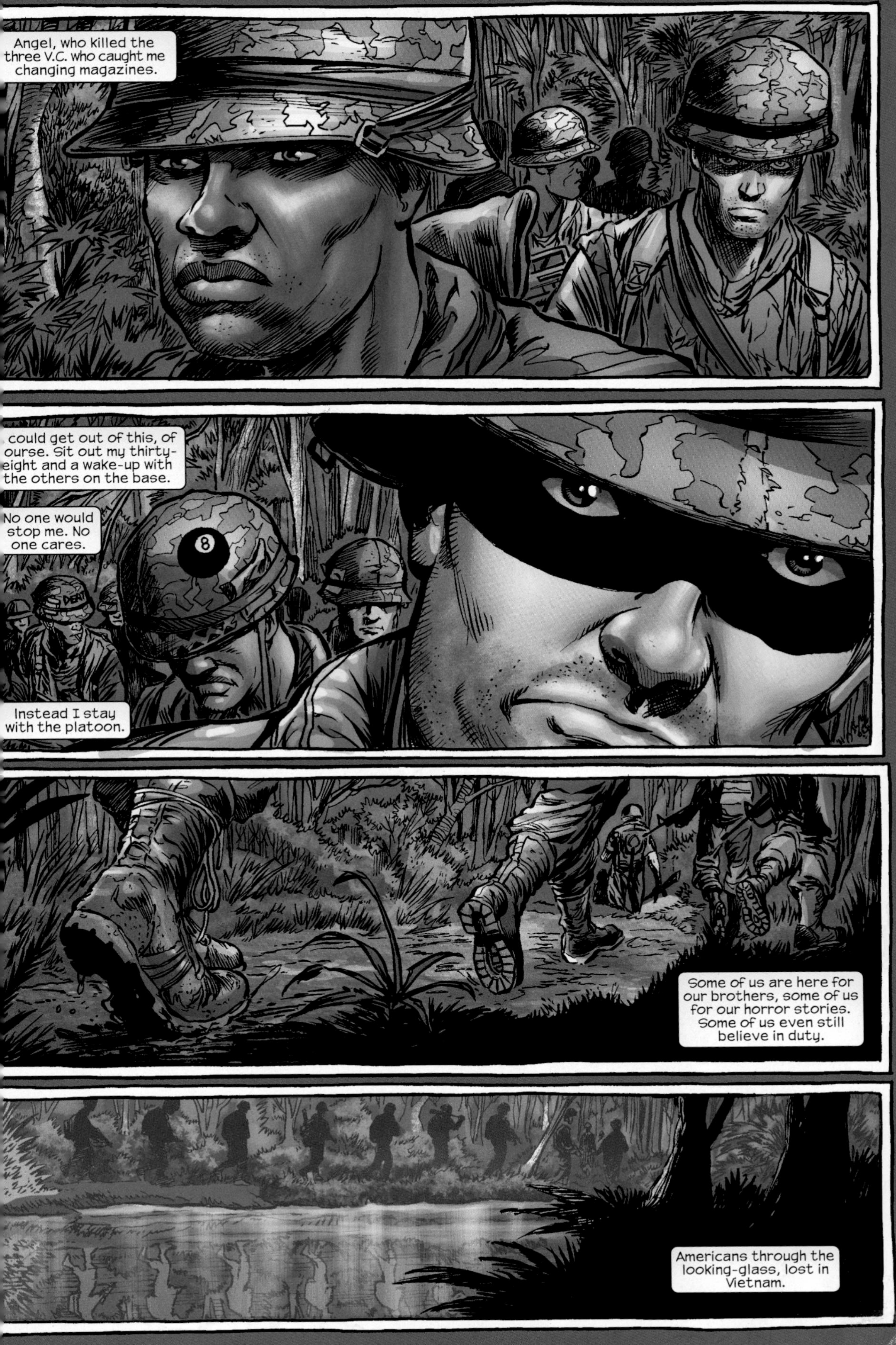
Angel, who killed the three V.C. who caught me changing magazines.
could get out of this, of ourse. Sit out my thirty-eight and a wake-up with the others on the base.
No one would stop me. No one cares.
Instead I stay with the platoon.
Some of us are here for our brothers, some of us for our horror stories. Some of us even still believe in duty.
Americans through the looking-glass, lost in Vietnam.

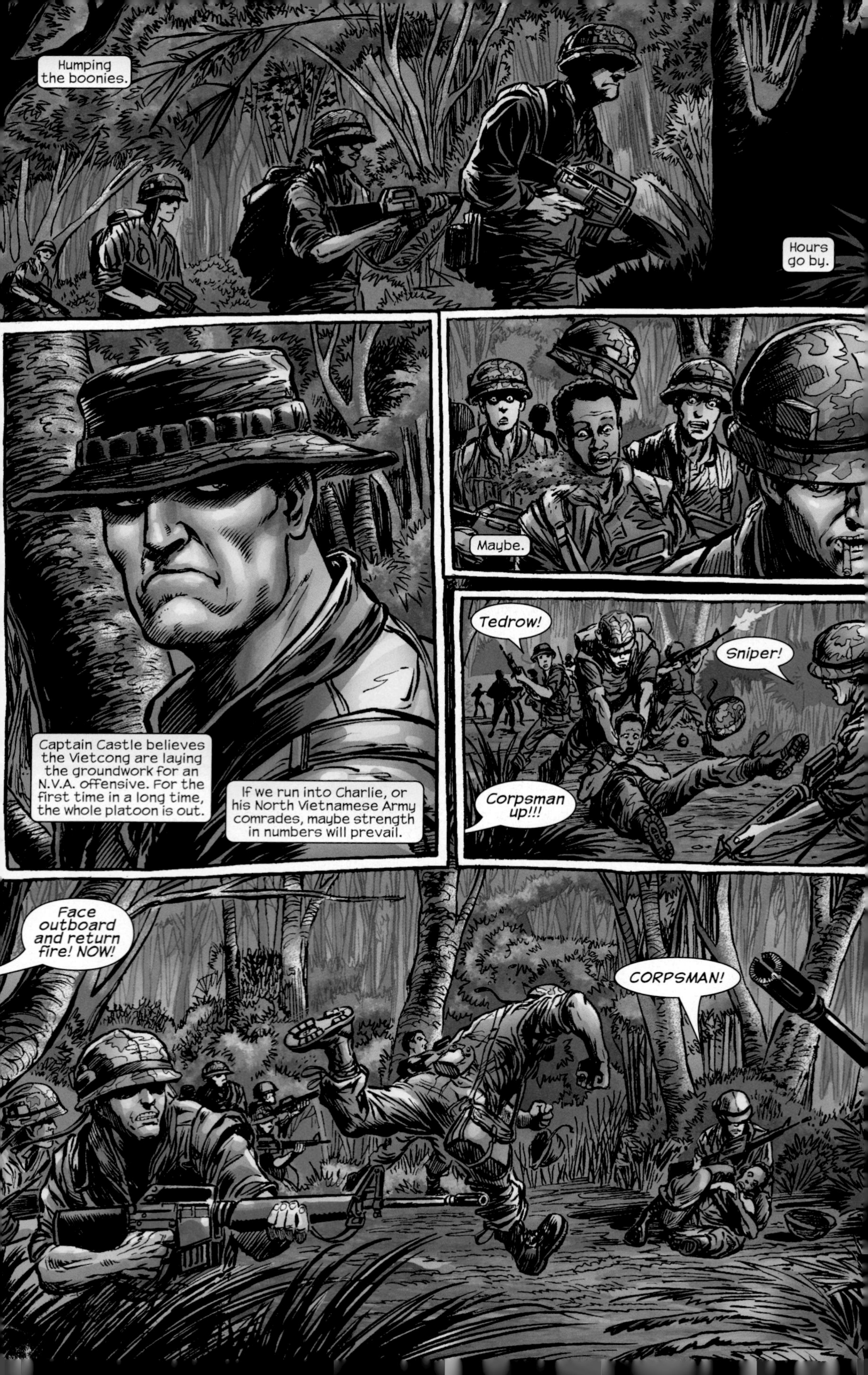
Humping the boonies.
Hours go by.
Captain Castle believes the Vietcong are laying the groundwork for an N.V.A. offensive. For the first time in a long time, the whole platoon is out.
If we run into Charlie, or his North Vietnamese Army comrades, maybe strength in numbers will prevail.
Maybe.
Tedrow!
Sniper!
Corpsman up!!!
Face outboard and return fire! NOW!
CORPSMAN!

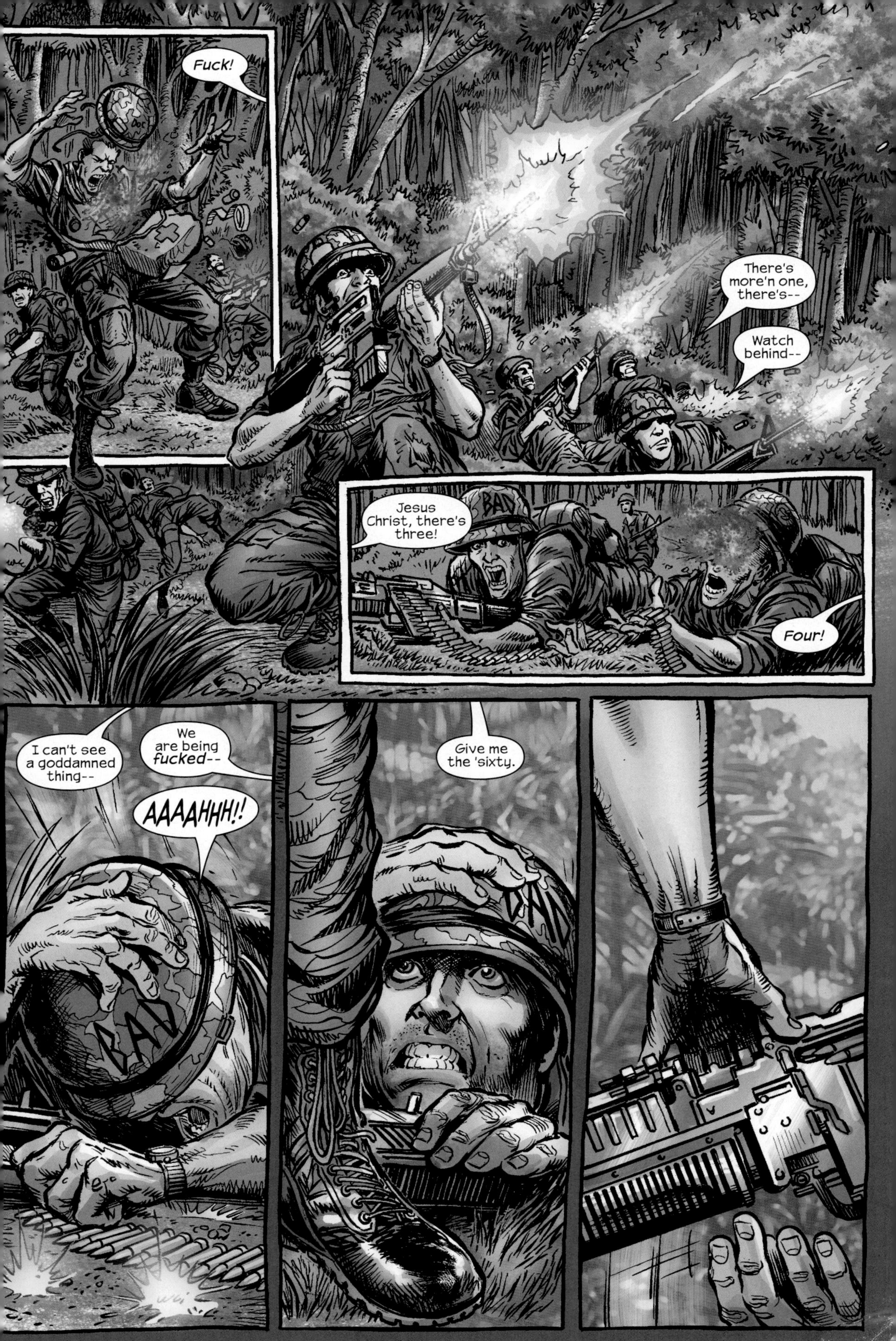
Fuck!
There's more'n one, there's--
Watch behind--
Jesus Christ, there's three!
Four!
I can't see a goddamned thing--
We are being *fucked*--
AAAAHHH!!
Give me the 'sixty.

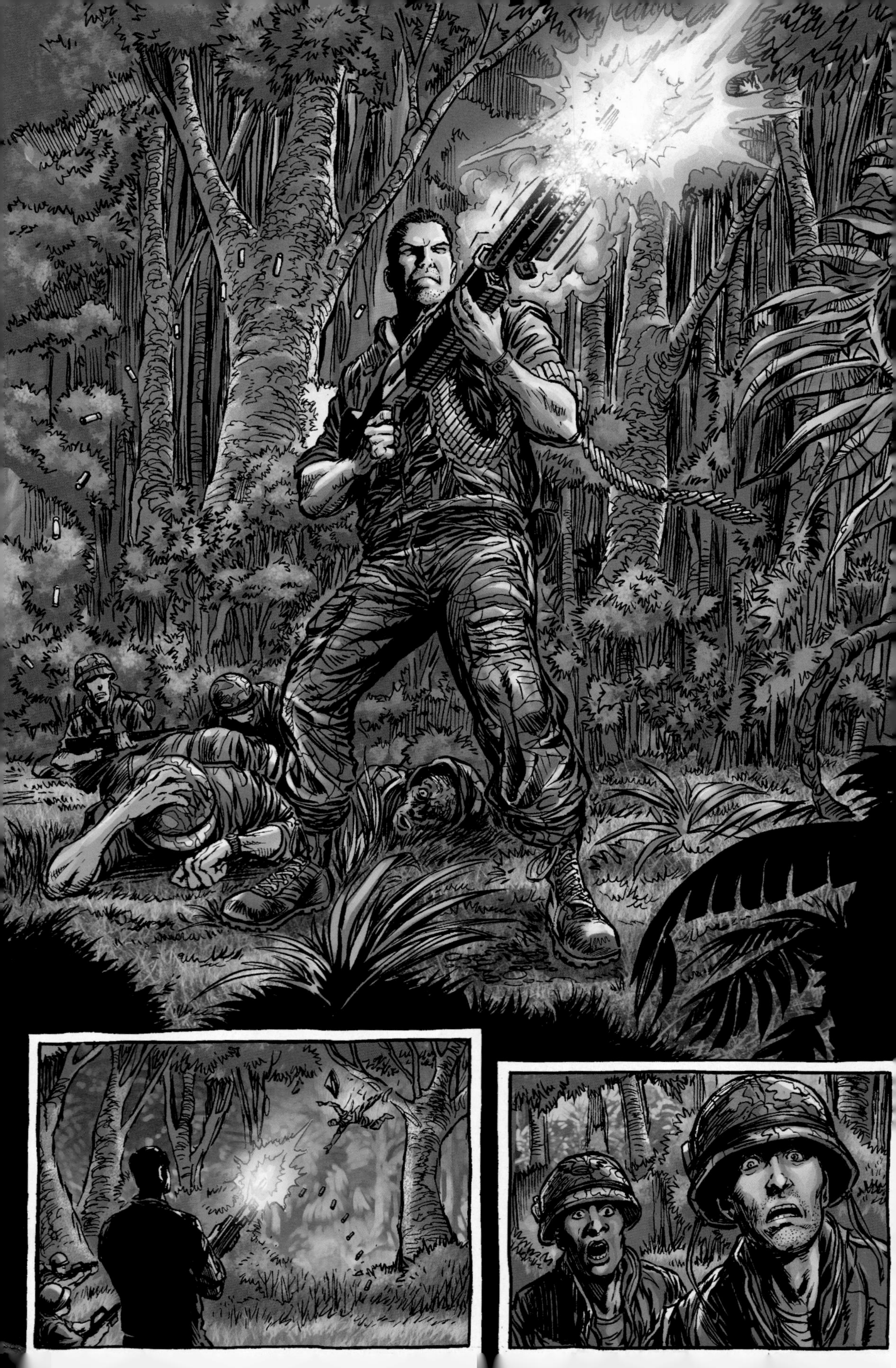

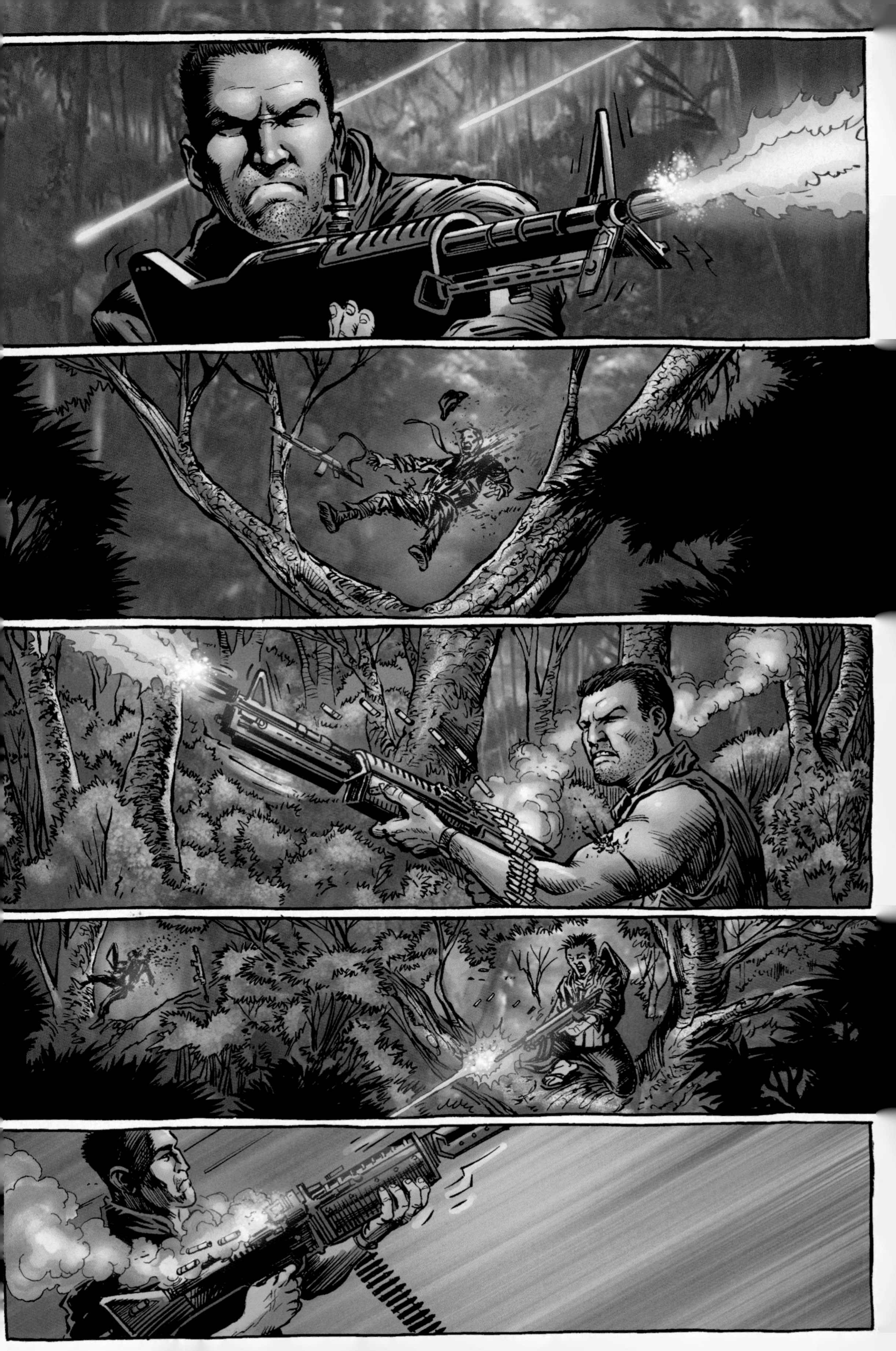

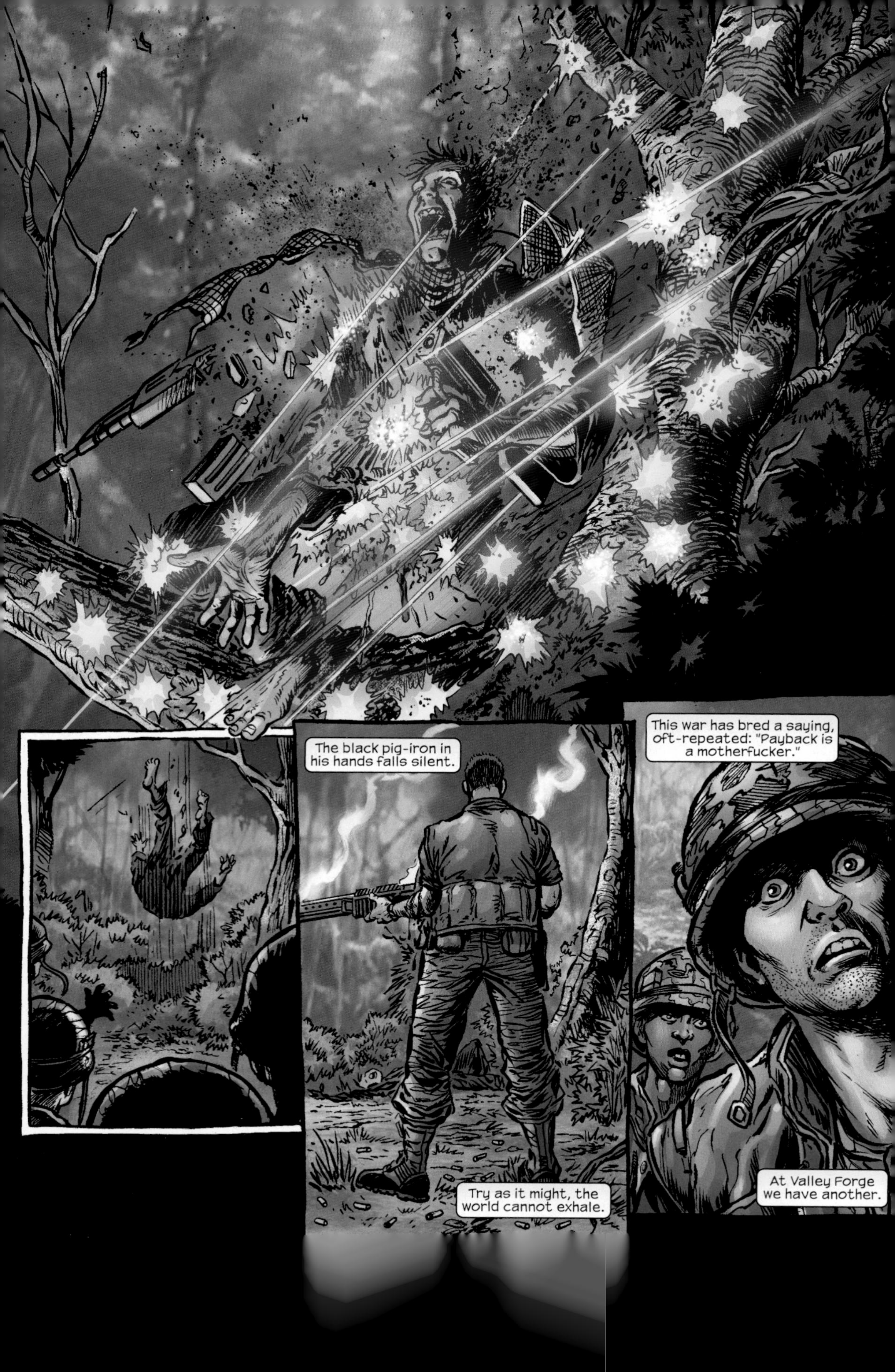
The black pig-iron in his hands falls silent.
Try as it might, the world cannot exhale.
This war has bred a saying, oft-repeated: "Payback is a motherfucker."
At Valley Forge we have another.

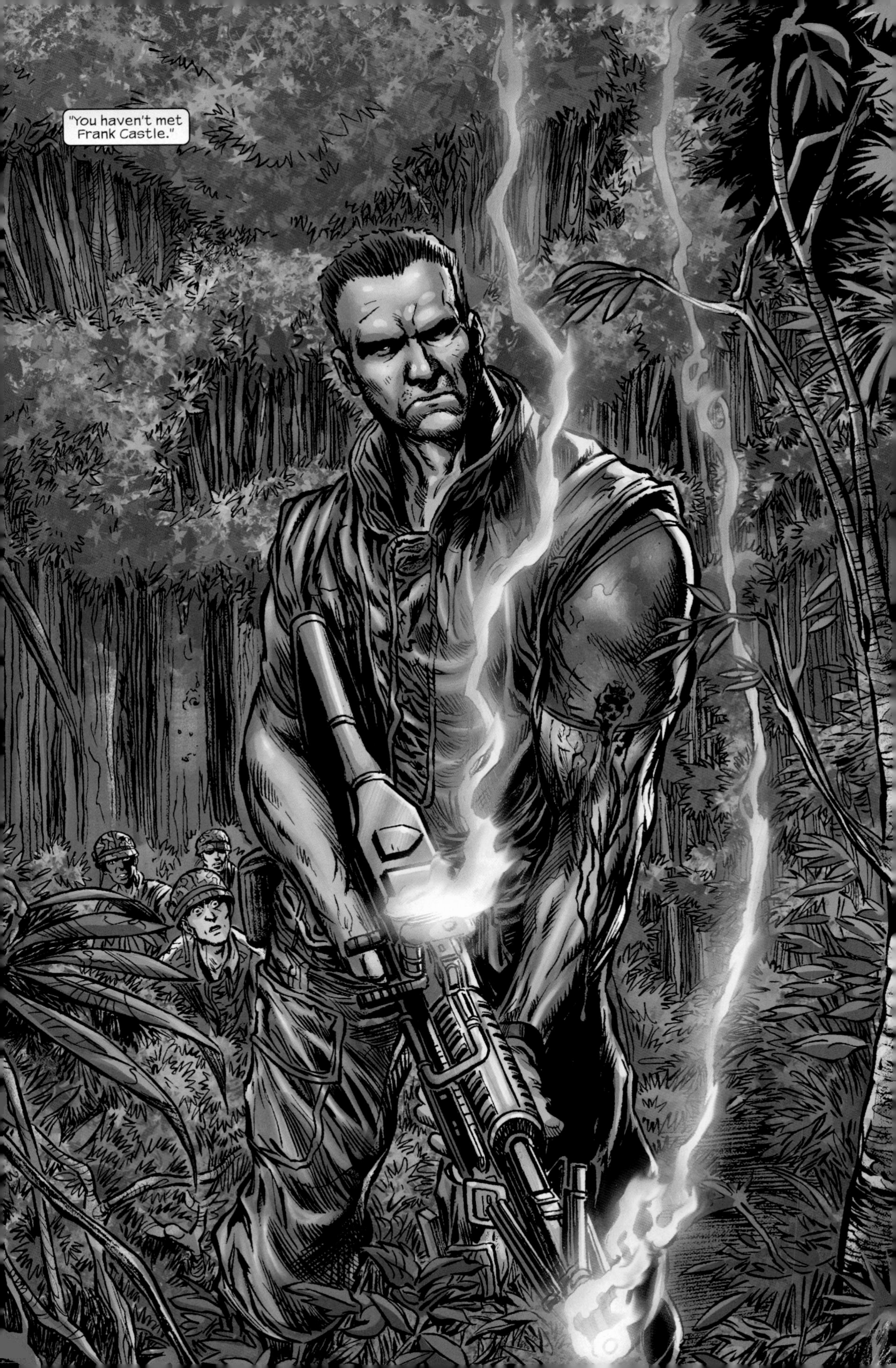
"You haven't met Frank Castle."

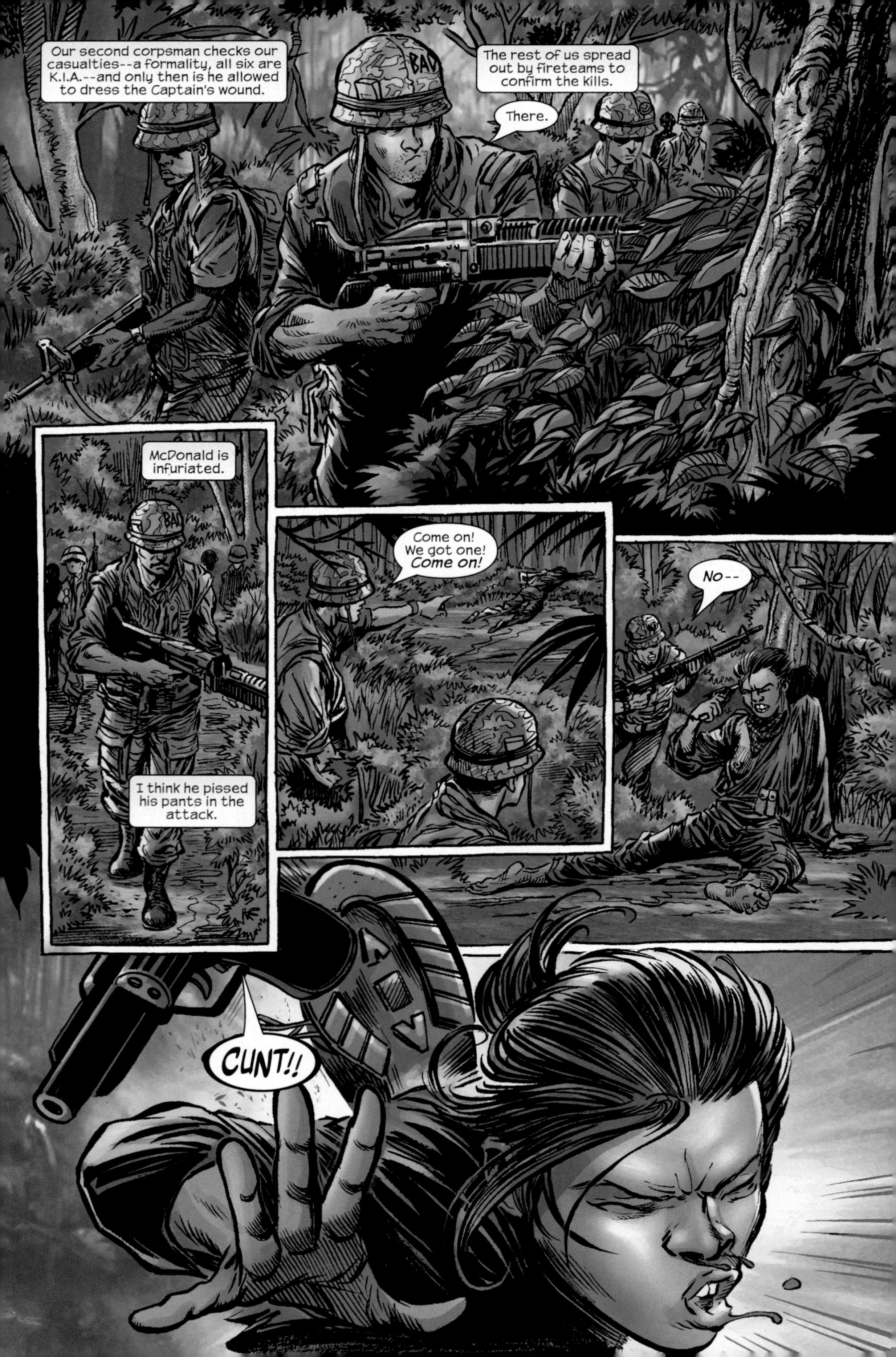
Our second corpsman checks our casualties--a formality, all six are K.I.A.--and only then is he allowed to dress the Captain's wound.
The rest of us spread out by fireteams to confirm the kills.
There.
McDonald is infuriated.
I think he pissed his pants in the attack.
Come on! We got one! *Come on!*
No--
CUNT!!

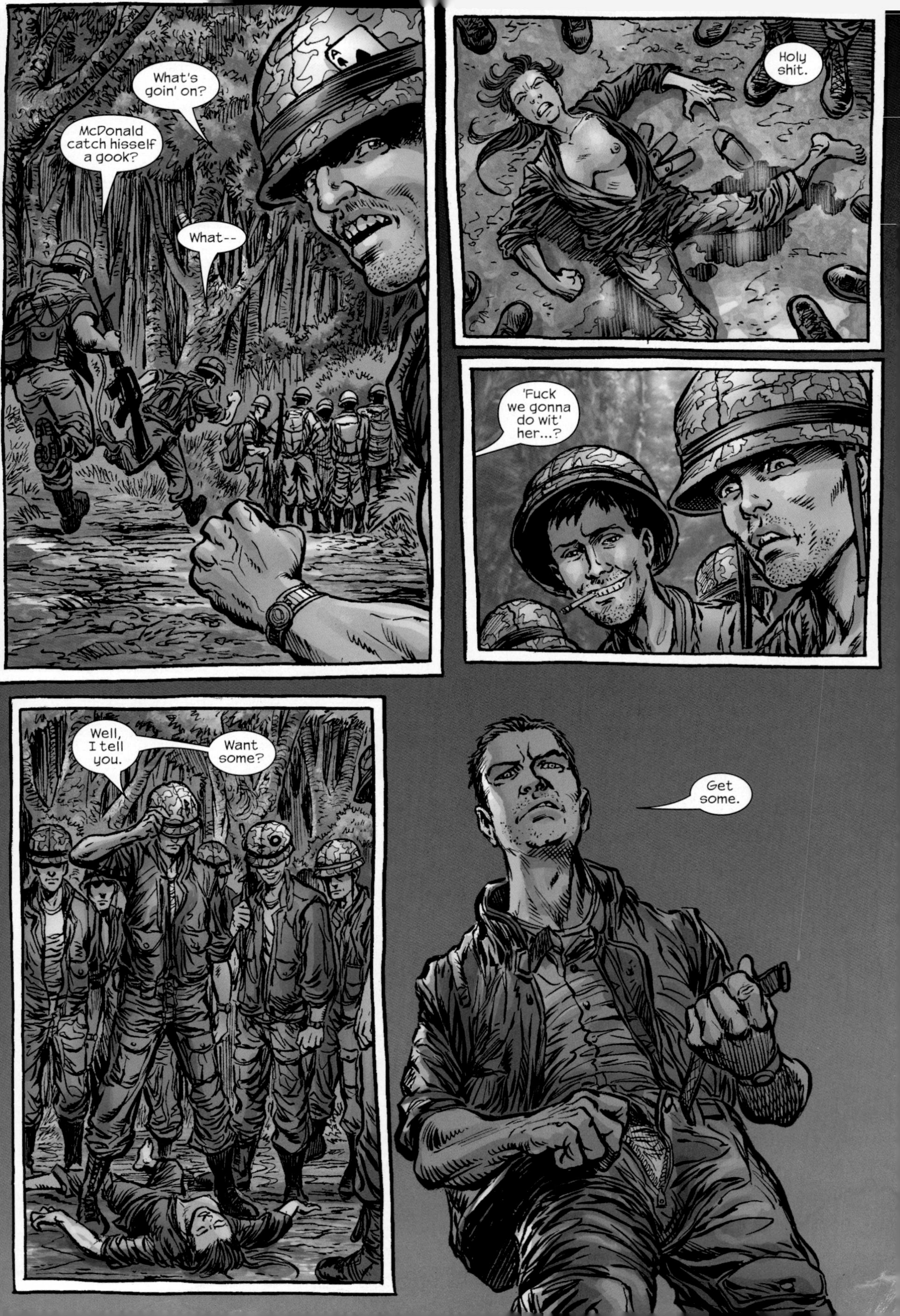
What's goin' on?
McDonald catch hisself a gook?
What--
Holy shit.
'Fuck we gonna do wit' her...?
Well, I tell you.
Want some?
Get some.

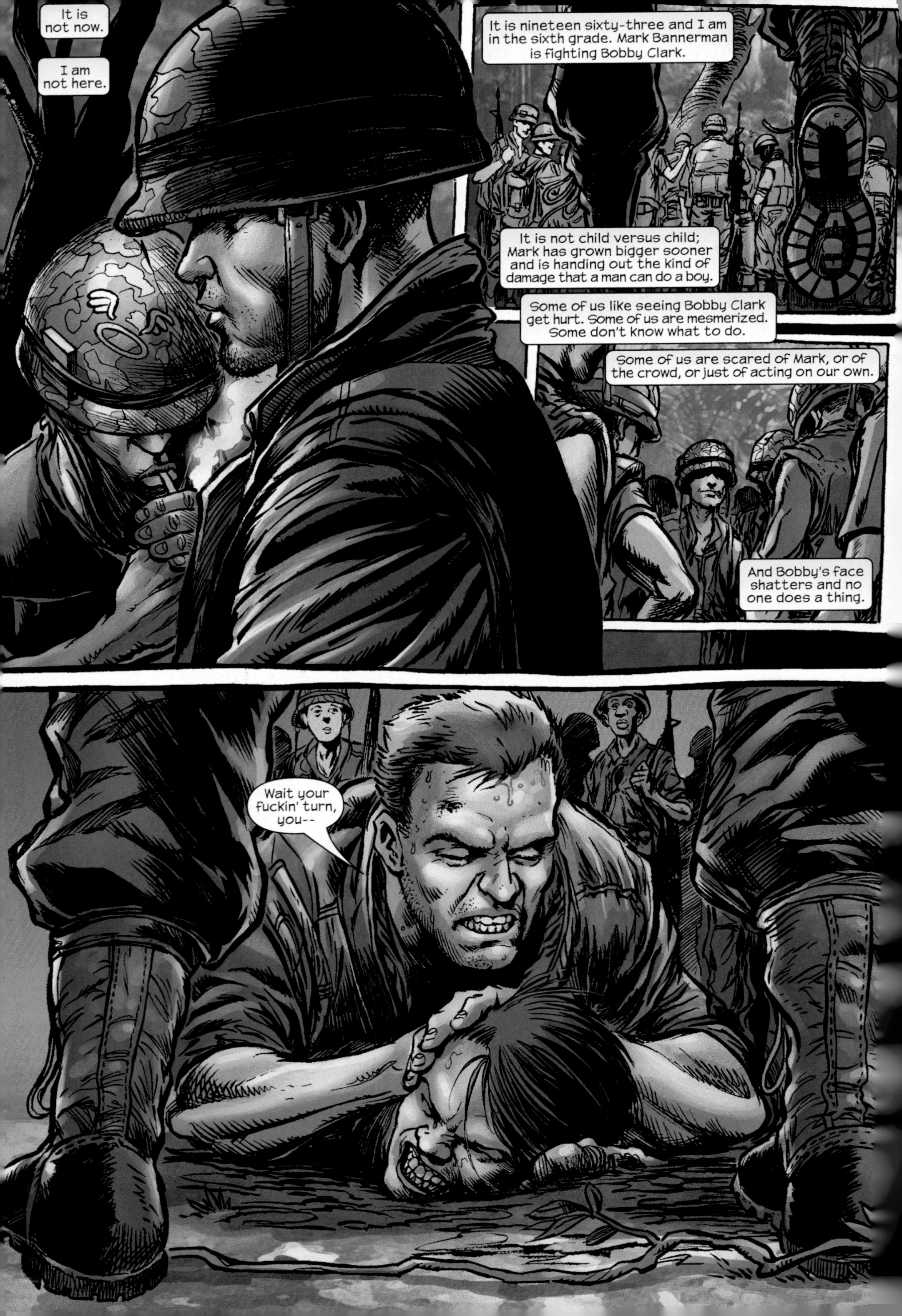
It is not now.
I am not here.
It is nineteen sixty-three and I am in the sixth grade. Mark Bannerman is fighting Bobby Clark.
It is not child versus child; Mark has grown bigger sooner and is handing out the kind of damage that a man can do a boy.
Some of us like seeing Bobby Clark get hurt. Some of us are mesmerized. Some don't know what to do.
Some of us are scared of Mark, or of the crowd, or just of acting on our own.
And Bobby's face shatters and no one does a thing.
Wait your fuckin' turn, you--

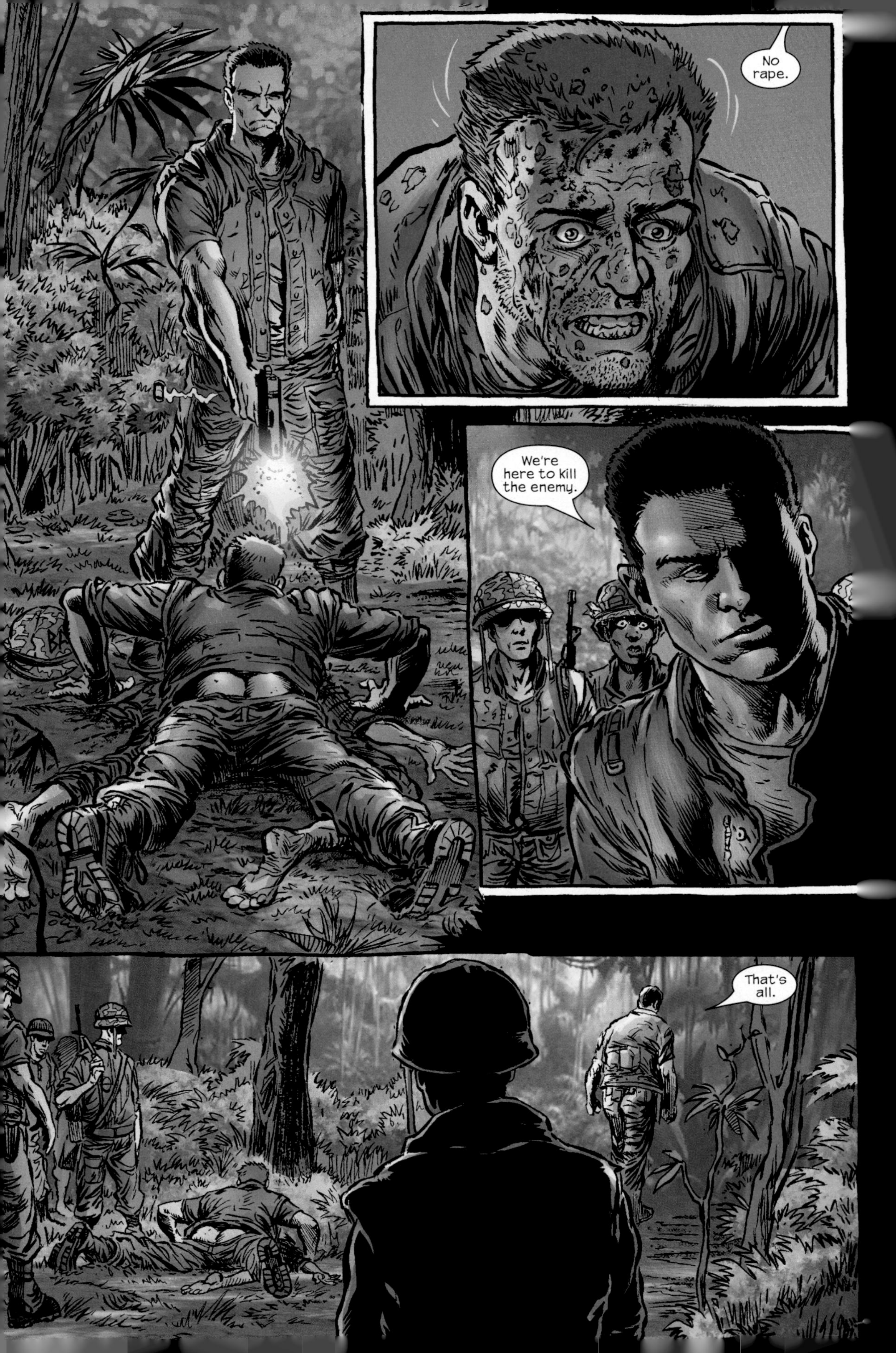
No rape.
We're here to kill the enemy.
That's all.

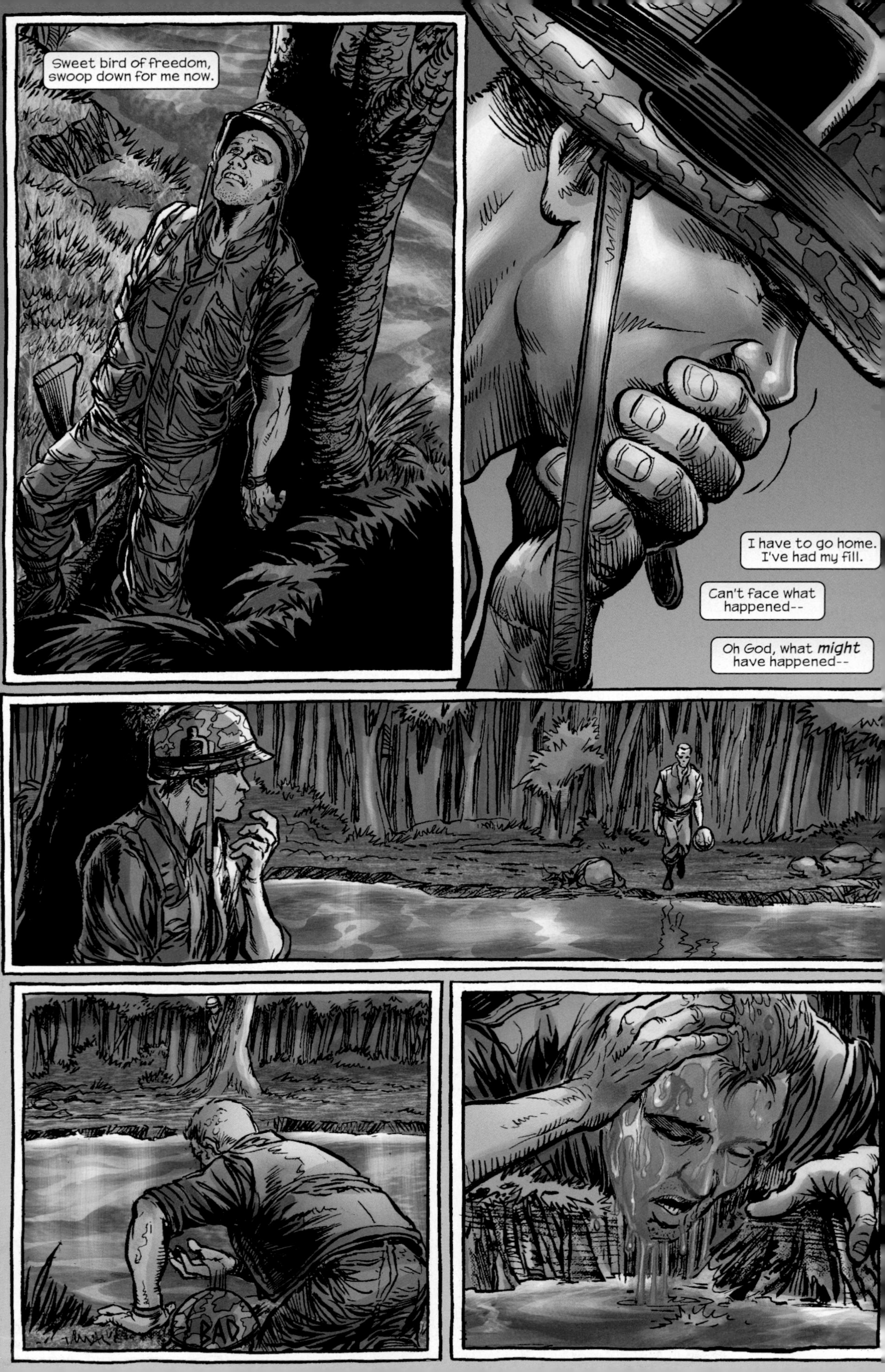
Sweet bird of freedom, swoop down for me now.
I have to go home. I've had my fill.
Can't face what happened--
Oh God, what *might* have happened--
BAD

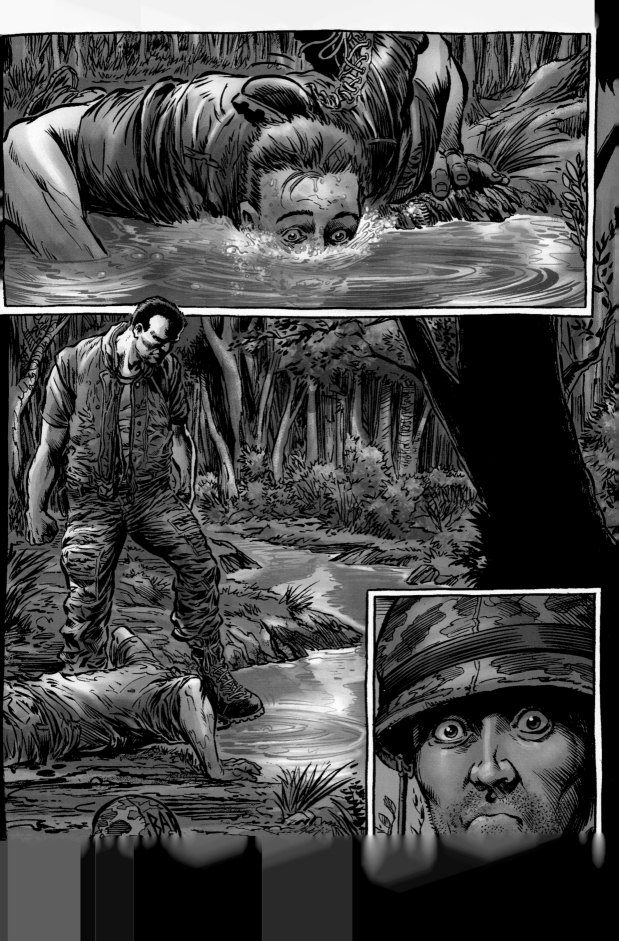

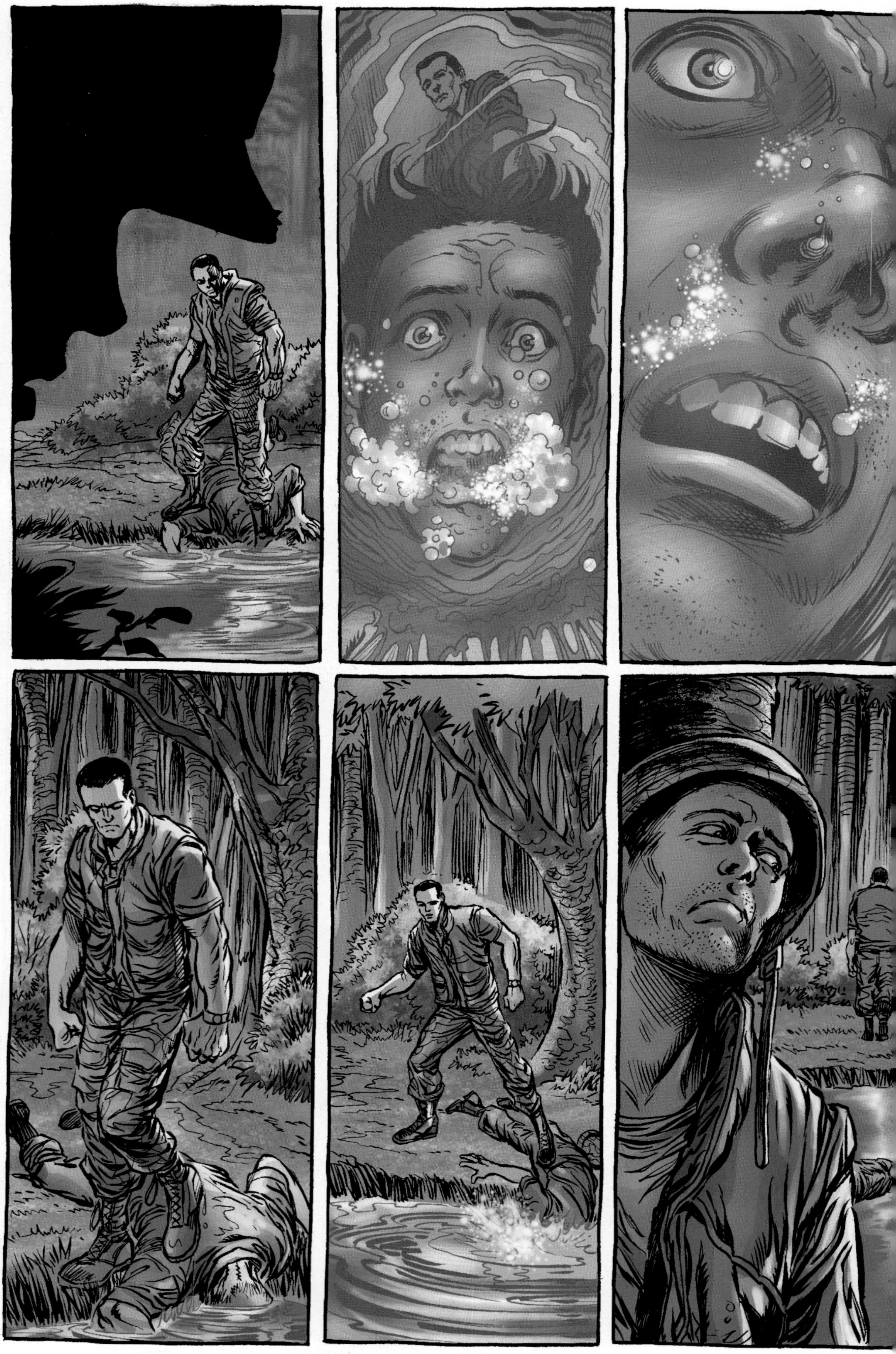

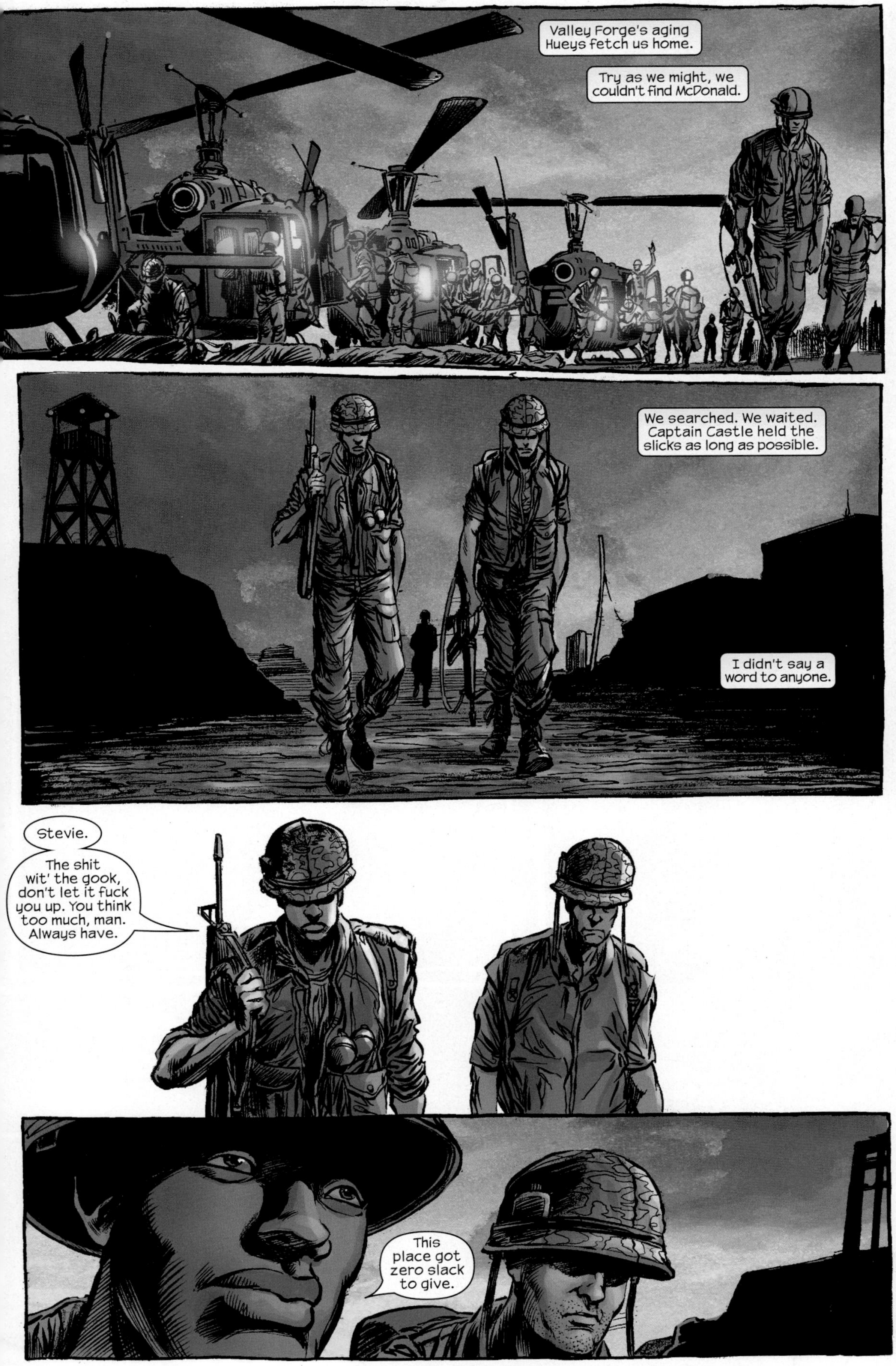
Valley Forge's aging Hueys fetch us home.
Try as we might, we couldn't find McDonald.
We searched. We waited. Captain Castle held the slicks as long as possible.
I didn't say a word to anyone.
Stevie.
The shit wit' the gook, don't let it fuck you up. You think too much, man. Always have.
This place got zero slack to give.

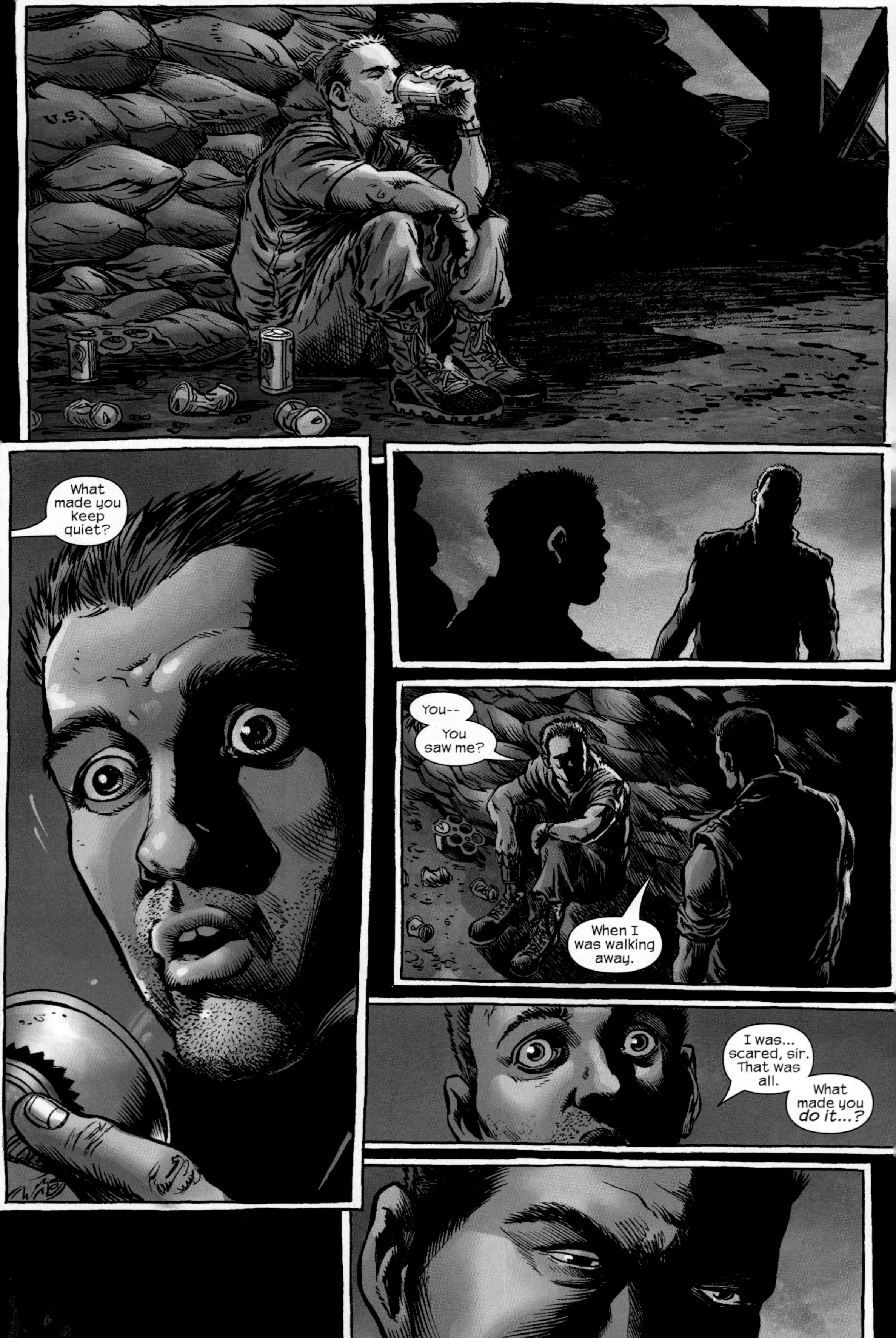
What made you keep quiet?
You--
You saw me?
When I was walking away.
I was... scared, sir. That was all.
What made you *do it*...?

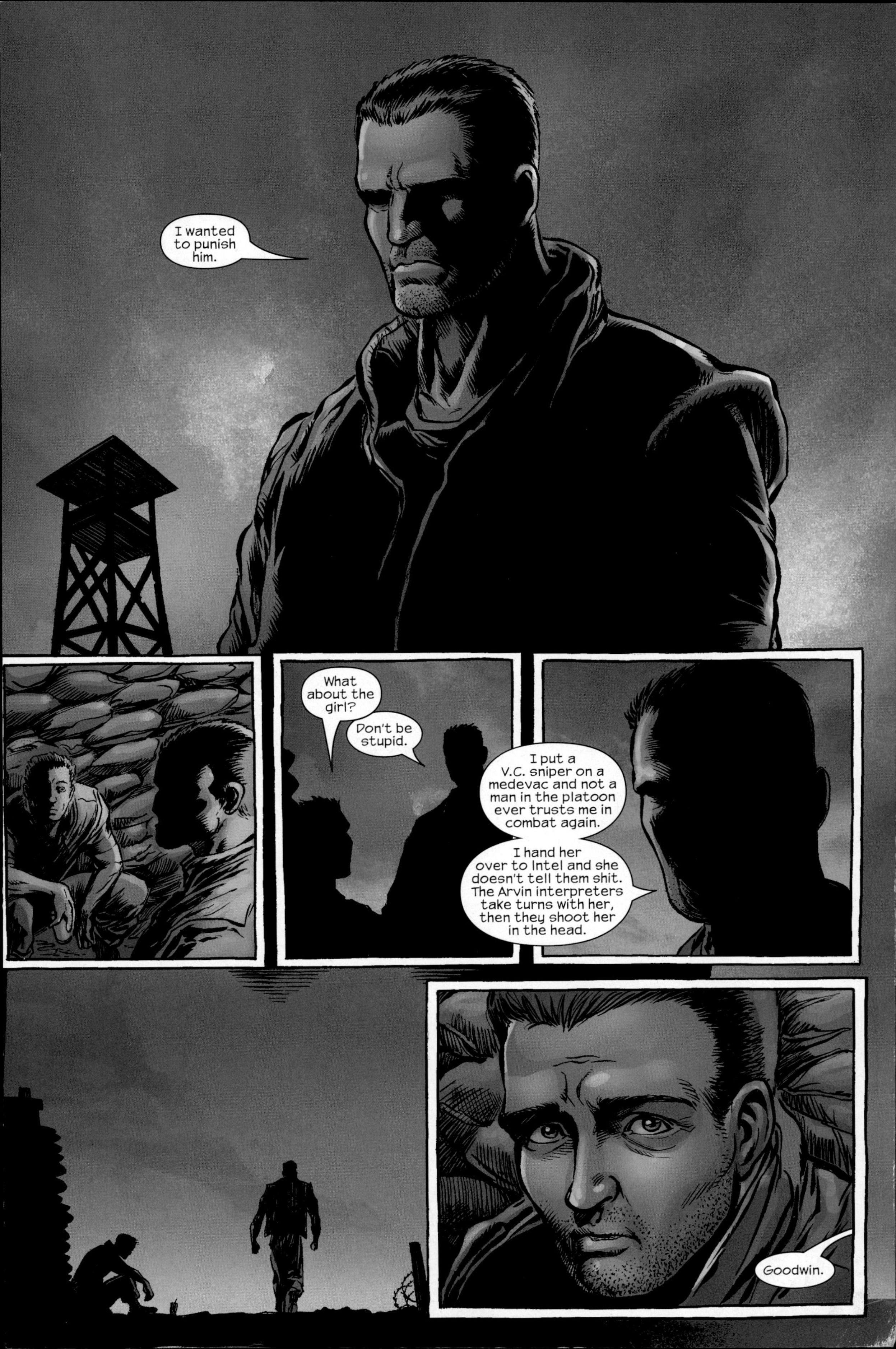
I wanted to punish him.
What about the girl?
Don't be stupid.
I put a V.C. sniper on a medevac and not a man in the platoon ever trusts me in combat again.
I hand her over to Intel and she doesn't tell them shit. The Arvin interpreters take turns with her, then they shoot her in the head.
Goodwin.

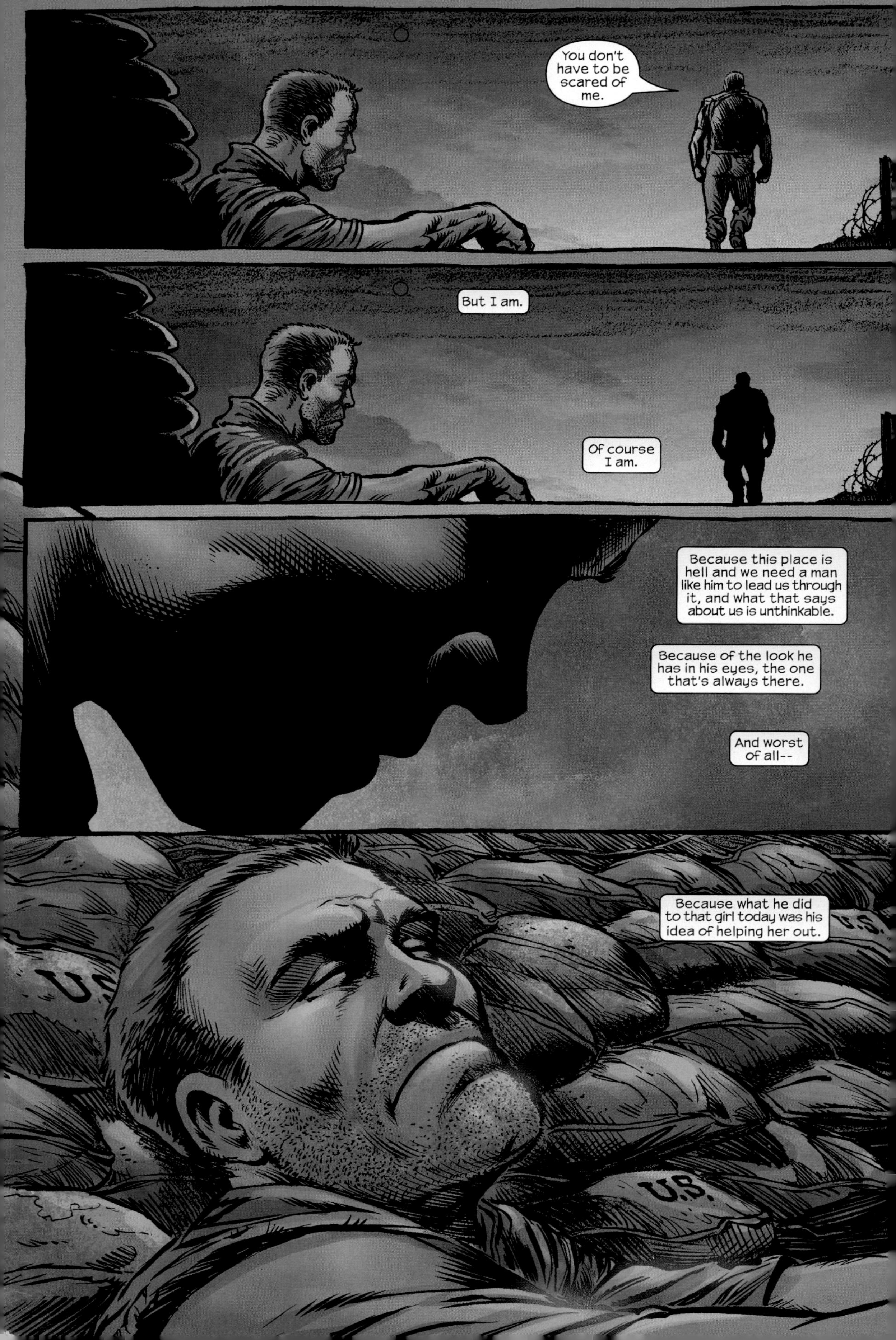
You don't have to be scared of me.
But I am.
Of course I am.
Because this place is hell and we need a man like him to lead us through it, and what that says about us is unthinkable.
Because of the look he has in his eyes, the one that's always there.
And worst of all--
Because what he did to that girl today was his idea of helping her out.
U.S.
U.S.
U.S.

BORN #3

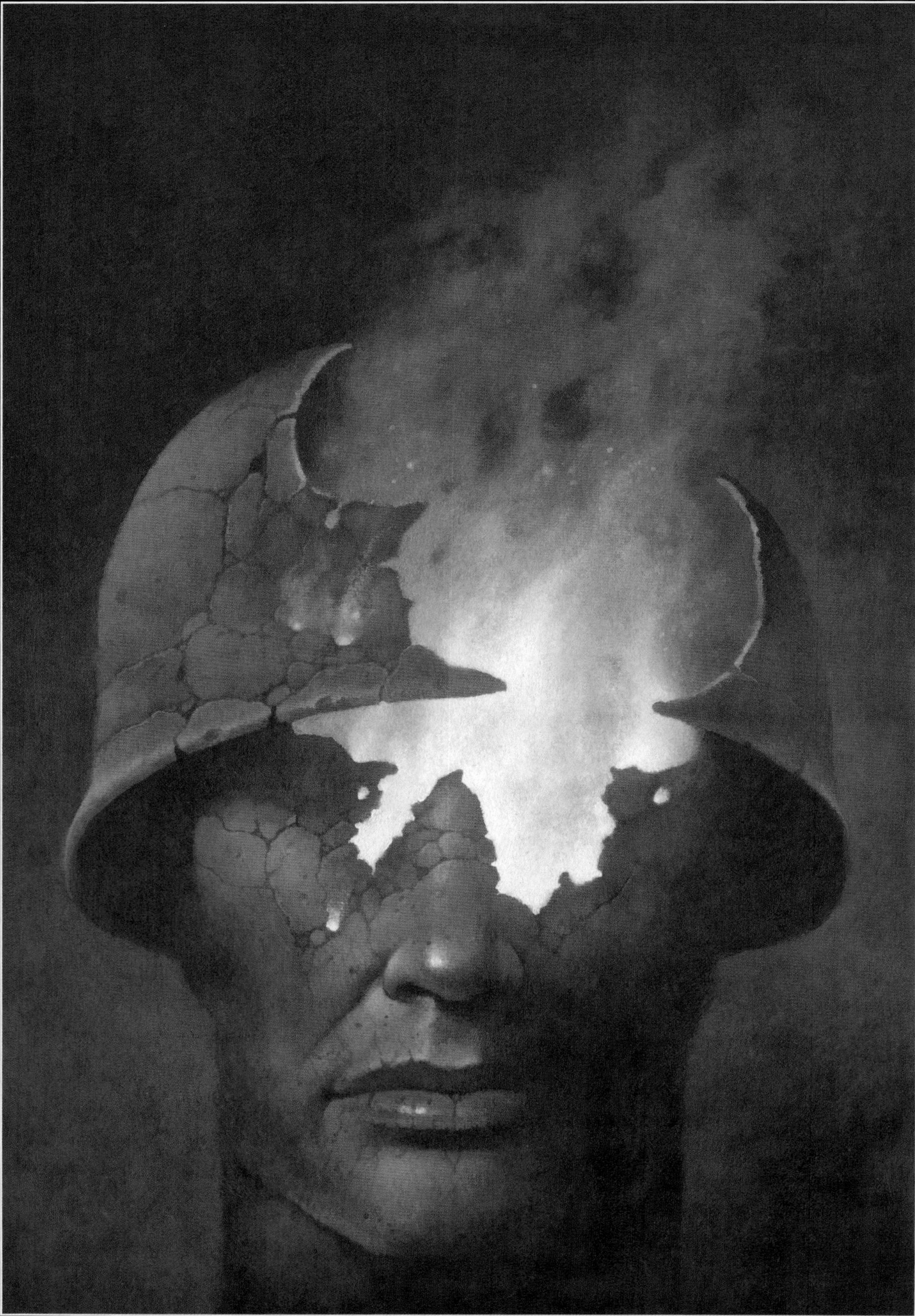

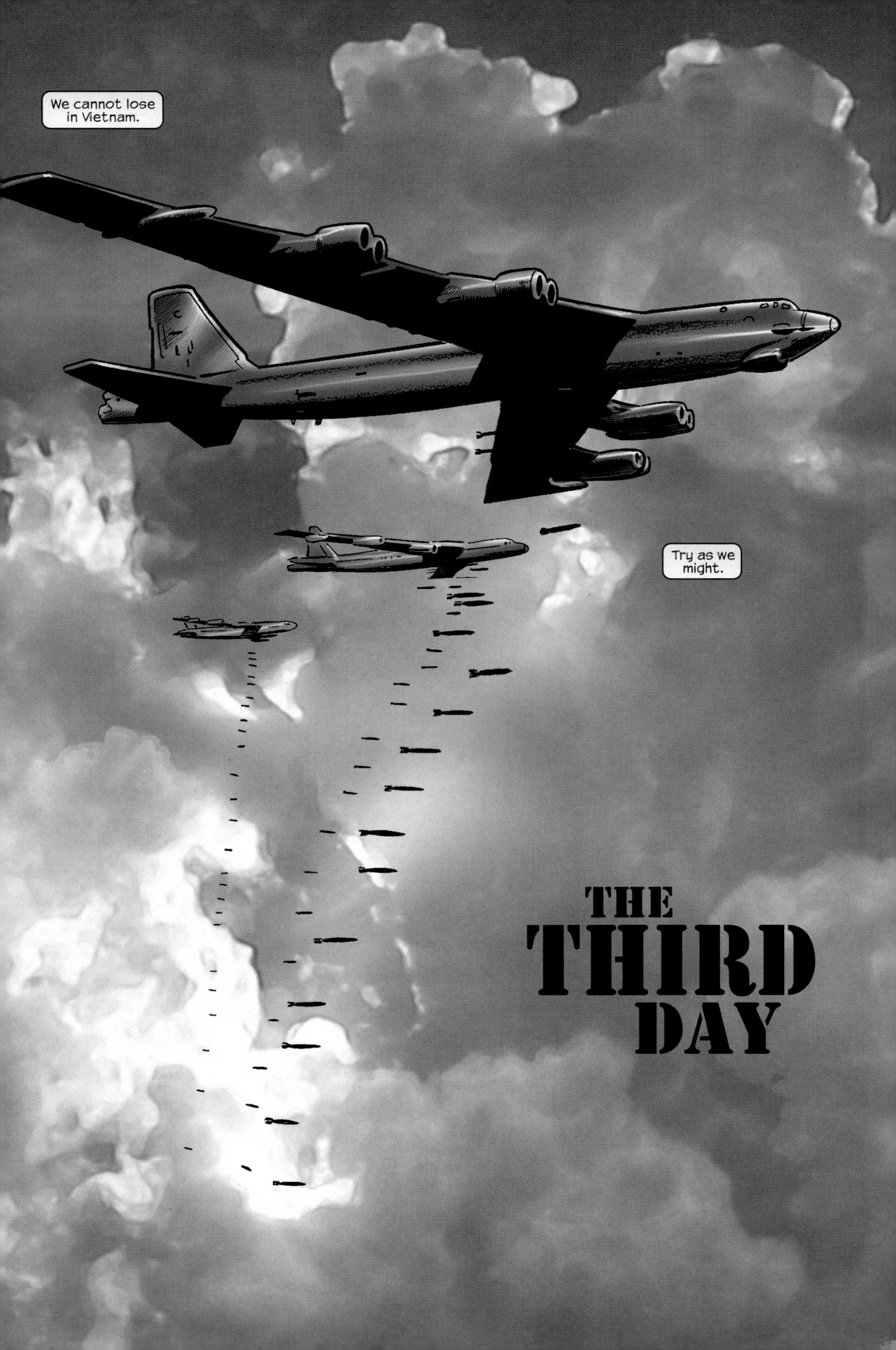
We cannot lose in Vietnam.
Try as we might.
THE THIRD DAY

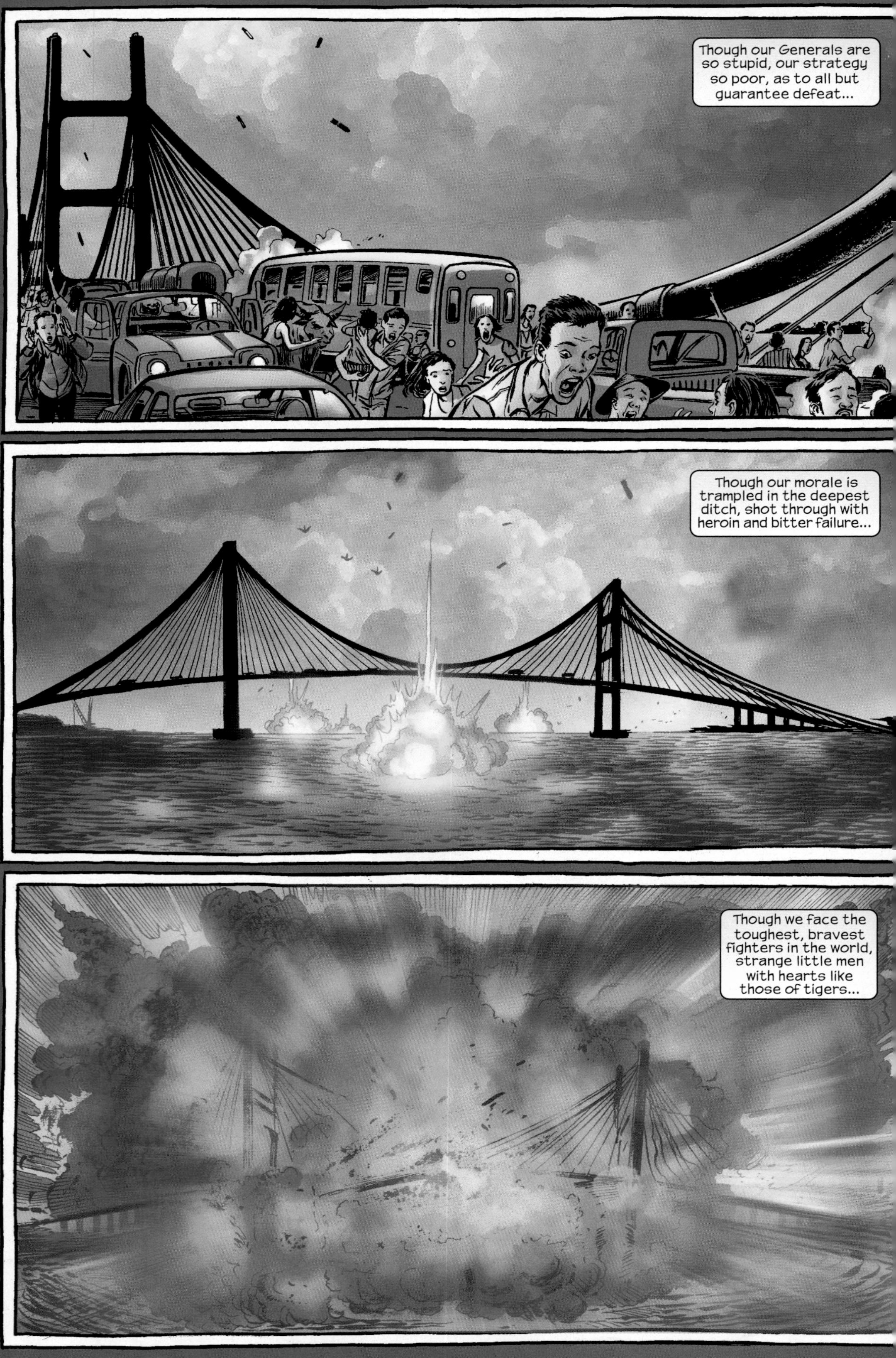
Though our Generals are so stupid, our strategy so poor, as to all but guarantee defeat...
Though our morale is trampled in the deepest ditch, shot through with heroin and bitter failure...
Though we face the toughest, bravest fighters in the world, strange little men with hearts like those of tigers...

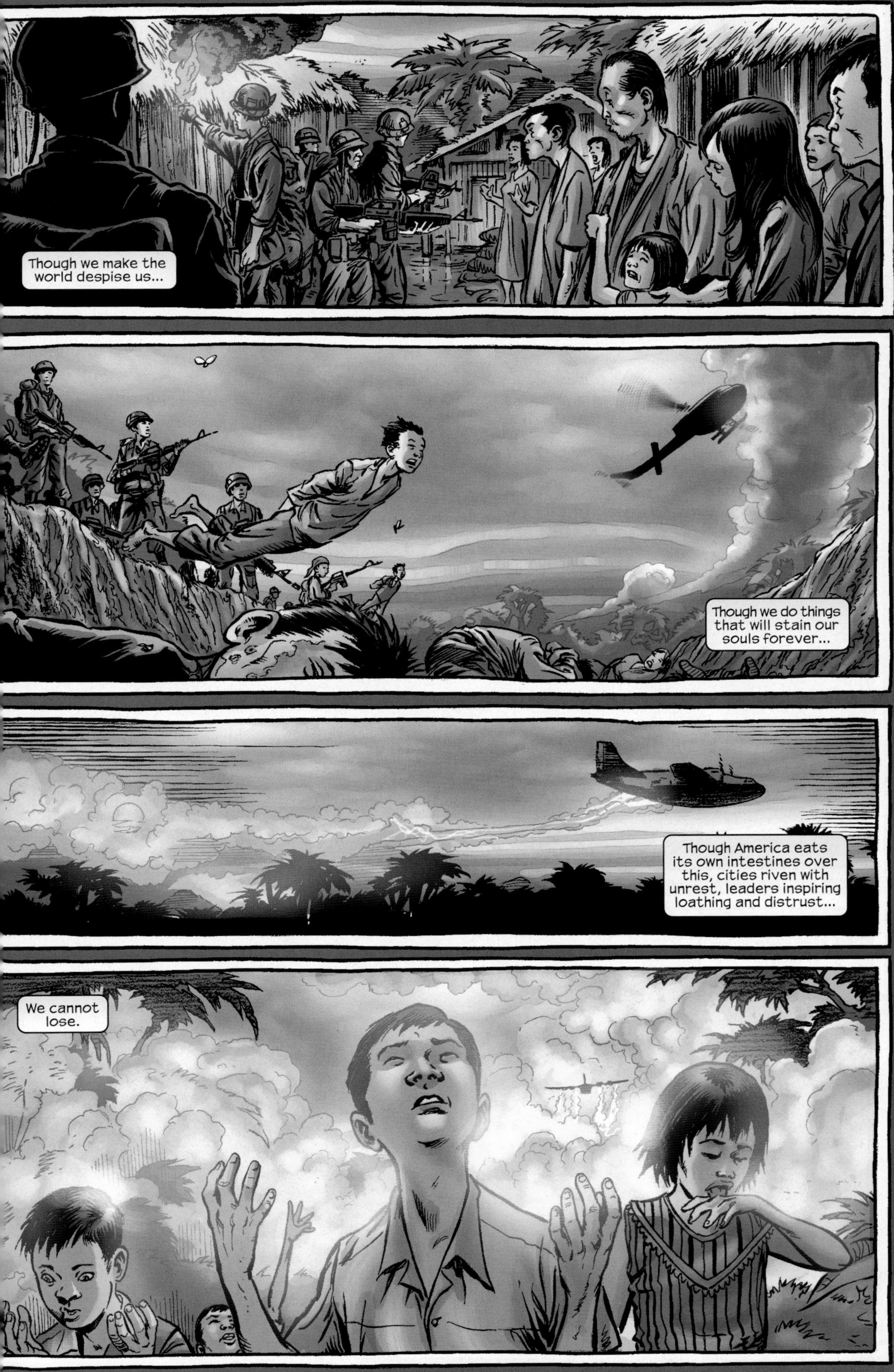
Though we make the world despise us...
Though we do things that will stain our souls forever...
Though America eats its own intestines over this, cities riven with unrest, leaders inspiring loathing and distrust...
We cannot lose.

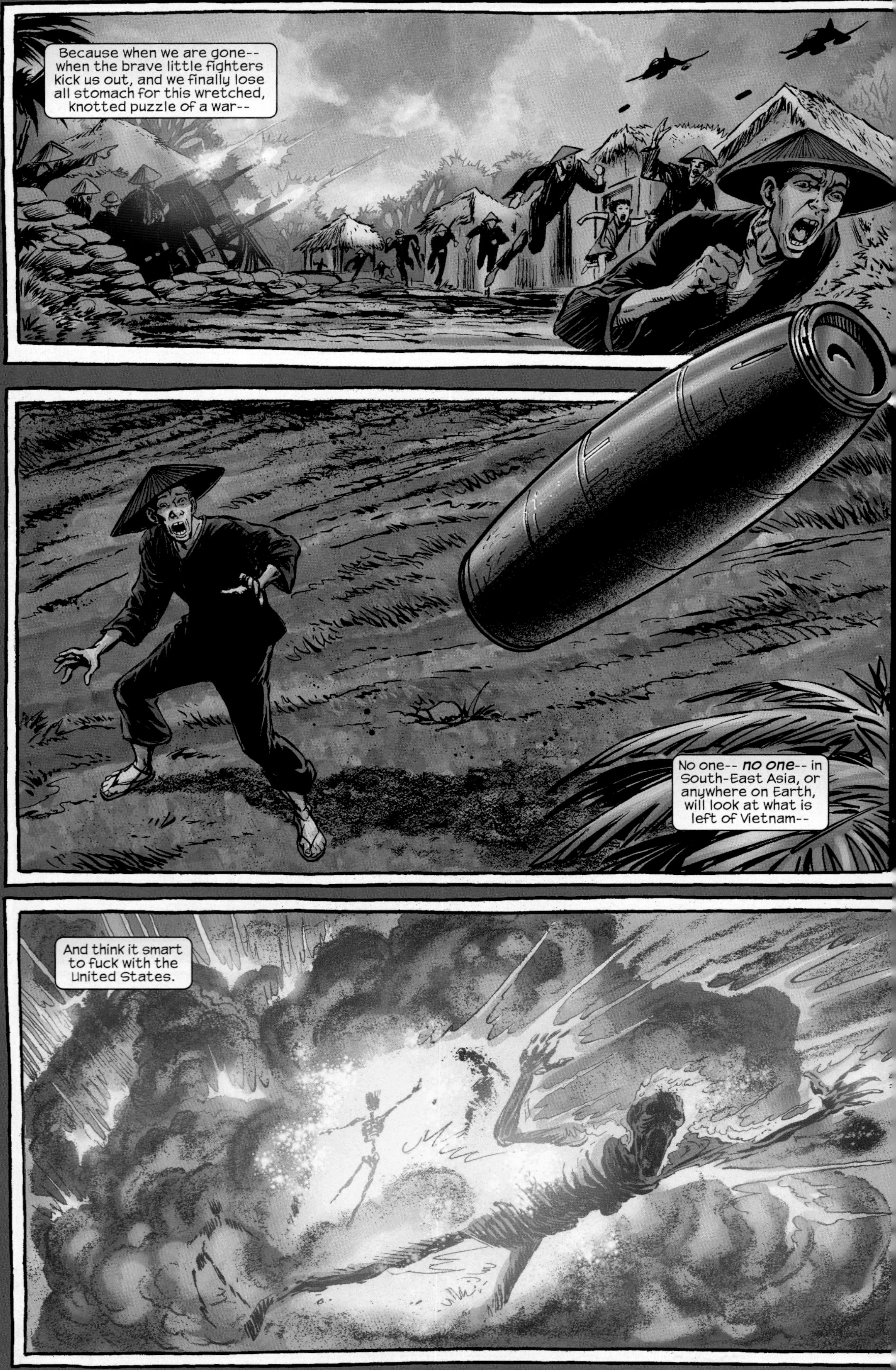
Because when we are gone--
when the brave little fighters
kick us out, and we finally lose
all stomach for this wretched,
knotted puzzle of a war--
No one-- *no one*-- in
South-East Asia, or
anywhere on Earth,
will look at what is
left of Vietnam--
And think it smart
to fuck with the
United States.

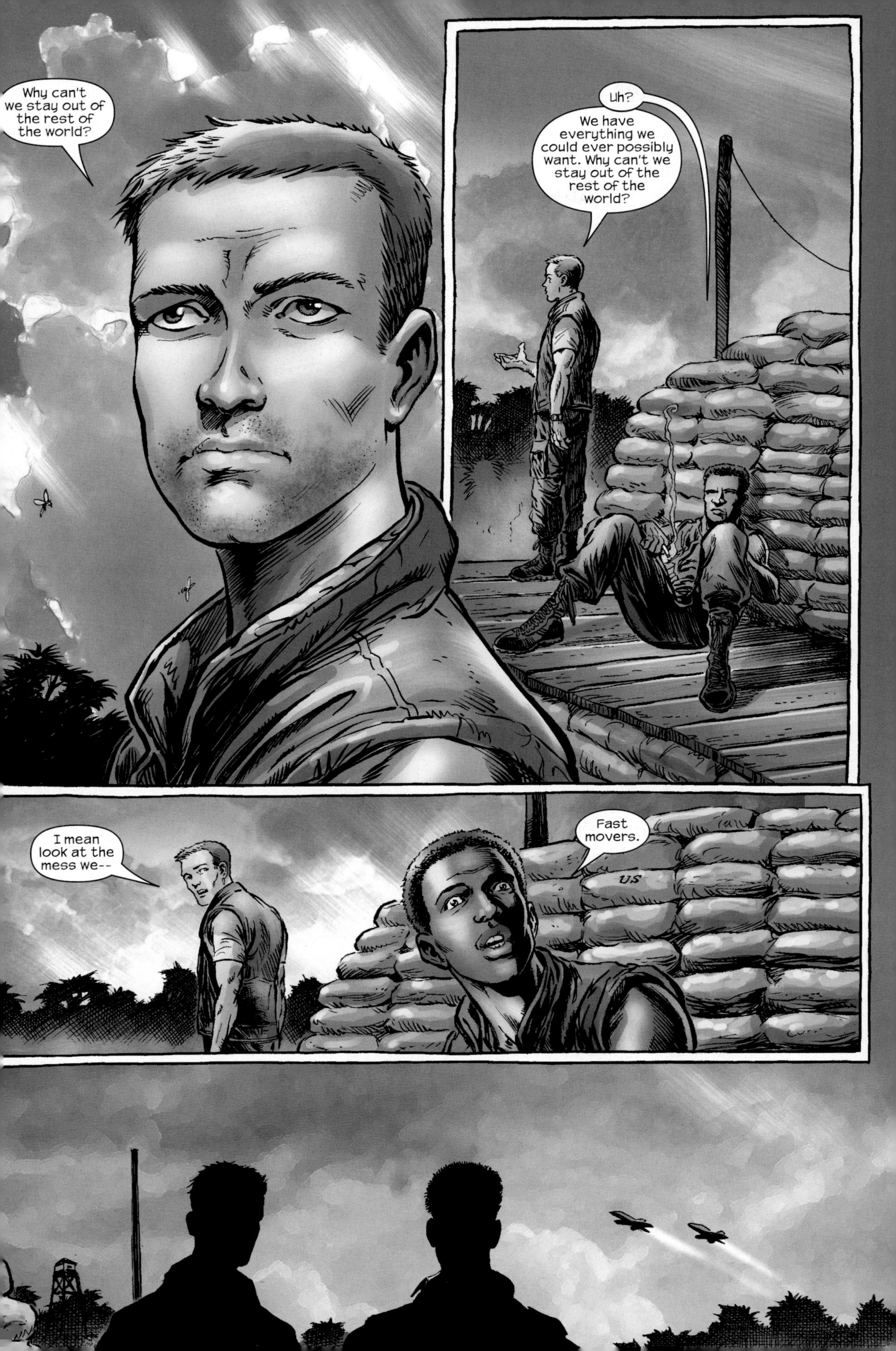
Why can't we stay out of the rest of the world?
Uh?
We have everything we could ever possibly want. Why can't we stay out of the rest of the world?
I mean look at the mess we--
Fast movers.
US

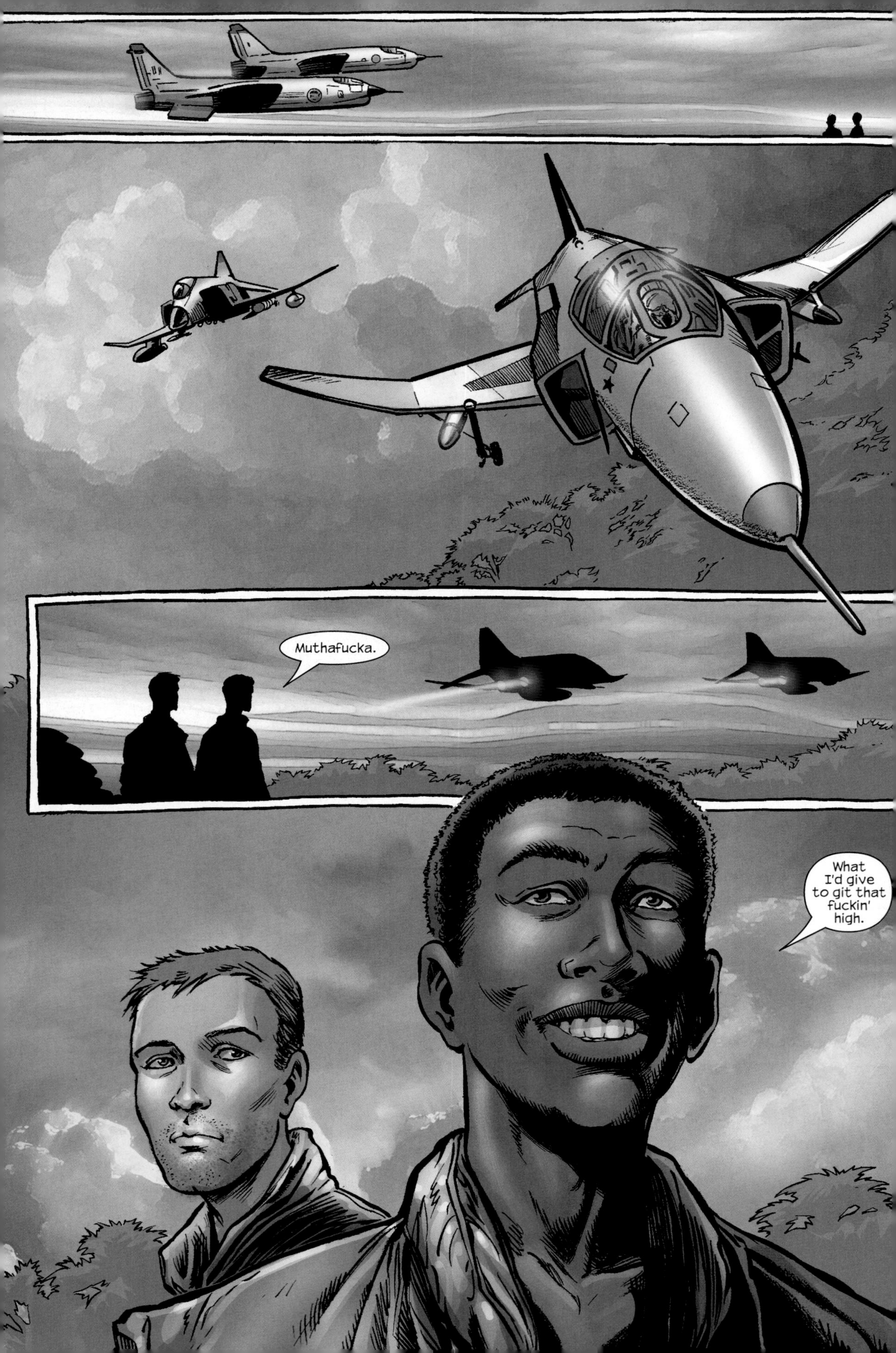
Muthafucka.
What I'd give to git that fuckin' high.

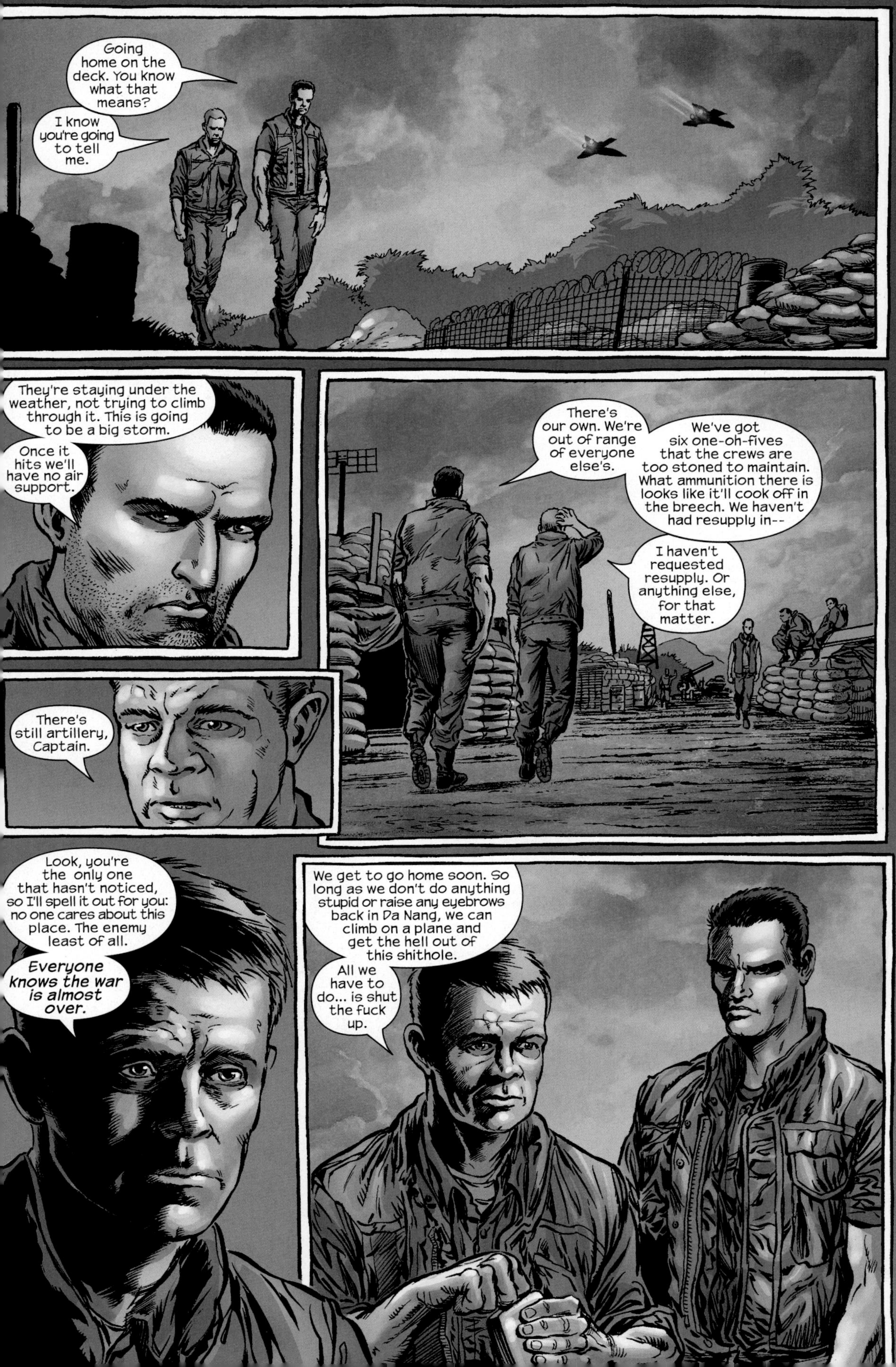

Going home on the deck. You know what that means?
I know you're going to tell me.
They're staying under the weather, not trying to climb through it. This is going to be a big storm.
Once it hits we'll have no air support.
There's still artillery, Captain.
There's our own. We're out of range of everyone else's.
We've got six one-oh-fives that the crews are too stoned to maintain. What ammunition there is looks like it'll cook off in the breech. We haven't had resupply in--
I haven't requested resupply. Or anything else, for that matter.
Look, you're the only one that hasn't noticed, so I'll spell it out for you: no one cares about this place. The enemy least of all.
Everyone knows the war is almost over.
We get to go home soon. So long as we don't do anything stupid or raise any eyebrows back in Da Nang, we can climb on a plane and get the hell out of this shithole.
All we have to do... is shut the fuck up.

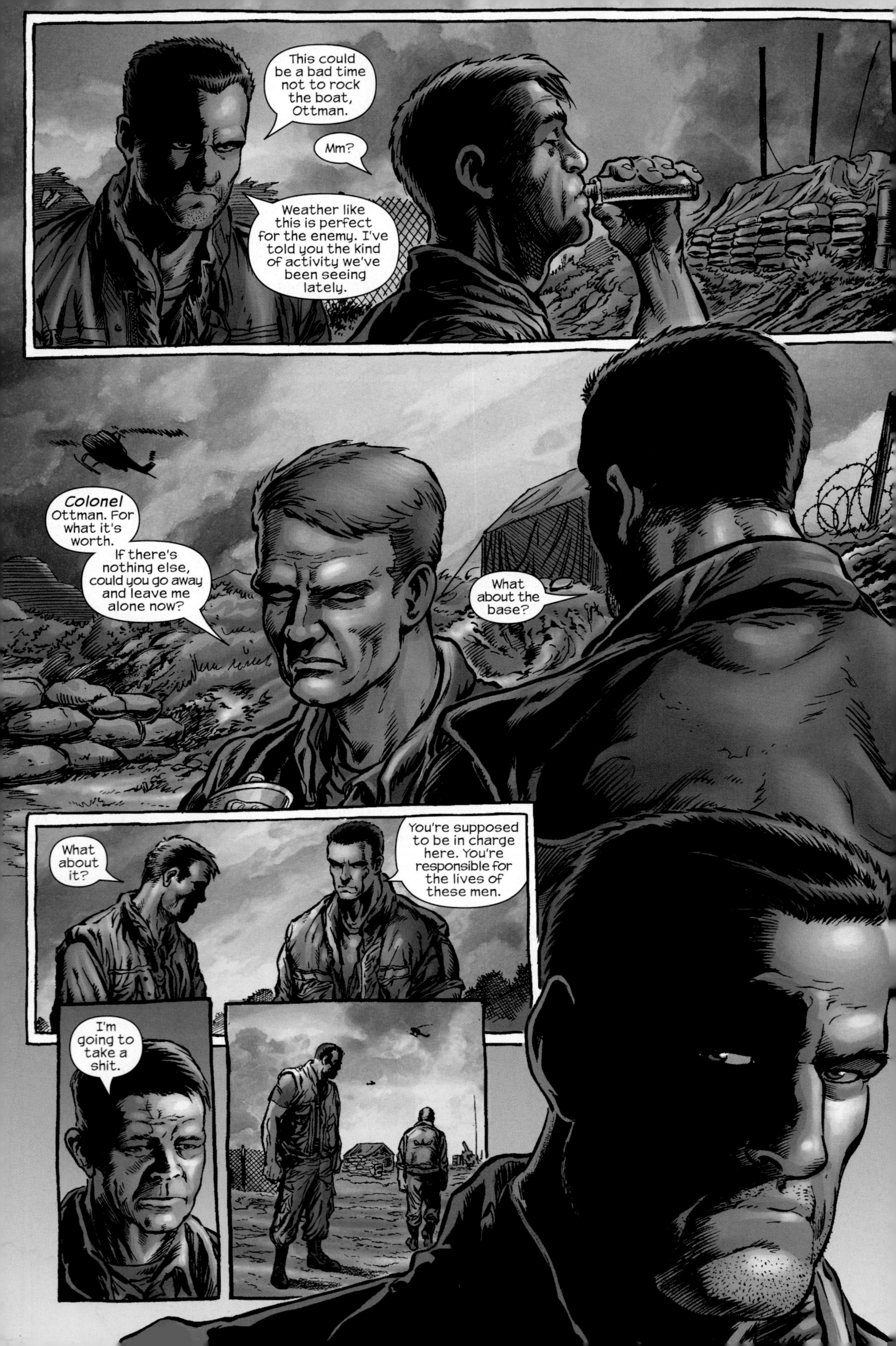
This could be a bad time not to rock the boat, Ottman.
Mm?
Weather like this is perfect for the enemy. I've told you the kind of activity we've been seeing lately.
Colonel Ottman. For what it's worth.
If there's nothing else, could you go away and leave me alone now?
What about the base?
What about it?
You're supposed to be in charge here. You're responsible for the lives of these men.
I'm going to take a shit.

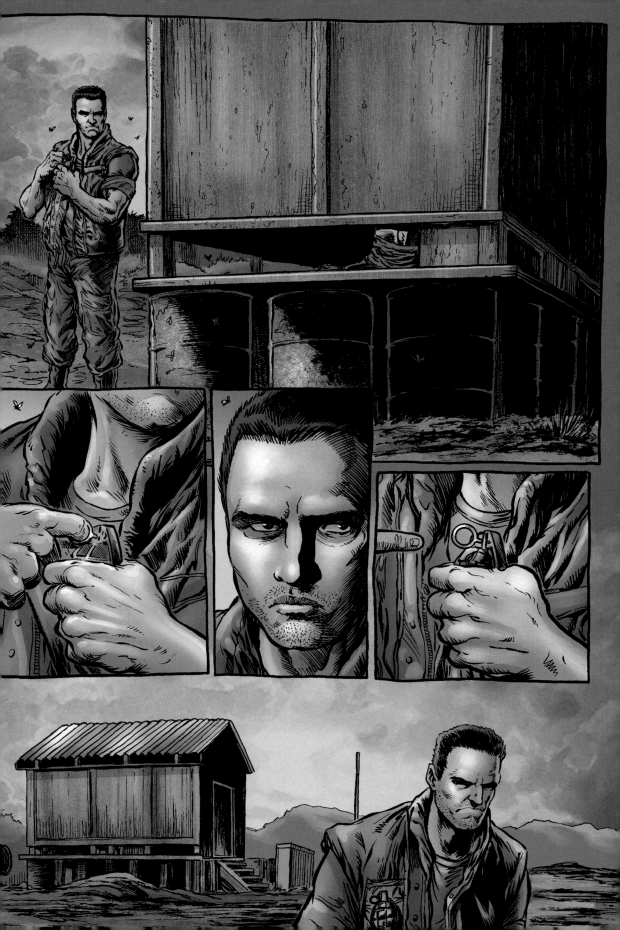

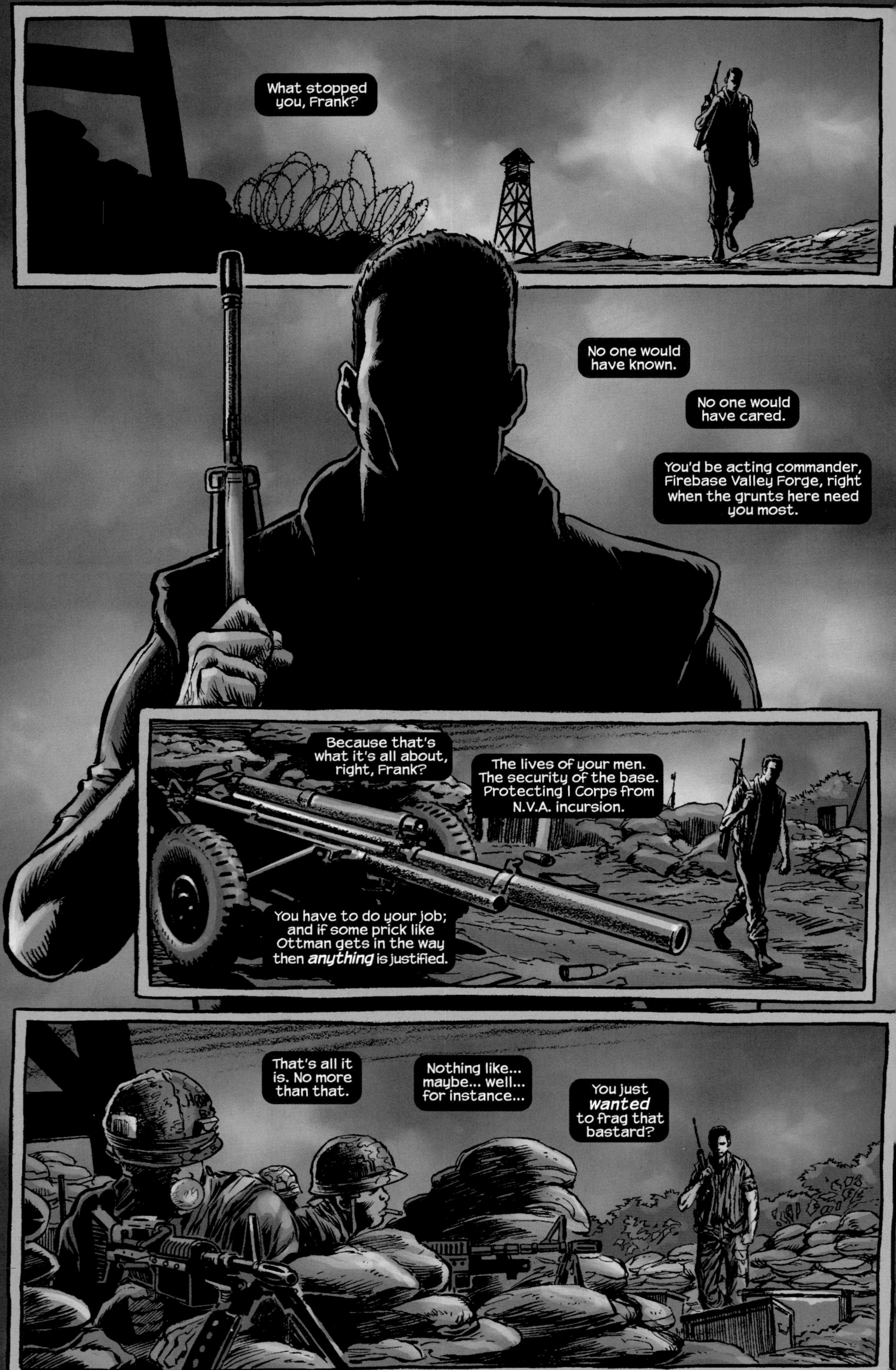

What stopped you, Frank?
No one would have known.
No one would have cared.
You'd be acting commander, Firebase Valley Forge, right when the grunts here need you most.
Because that's what it's all about, right, Frank?
The lives of your men. The security of the base. Protecting I Corps from N.V.A. incursion.
You have to do your job; and if some prick like Ottman gets in the way then *anything* is justified.
That's all it is. No more than that.
Nothing like... maybe... well... for instance...
You just *wanted* to frag that bastard?

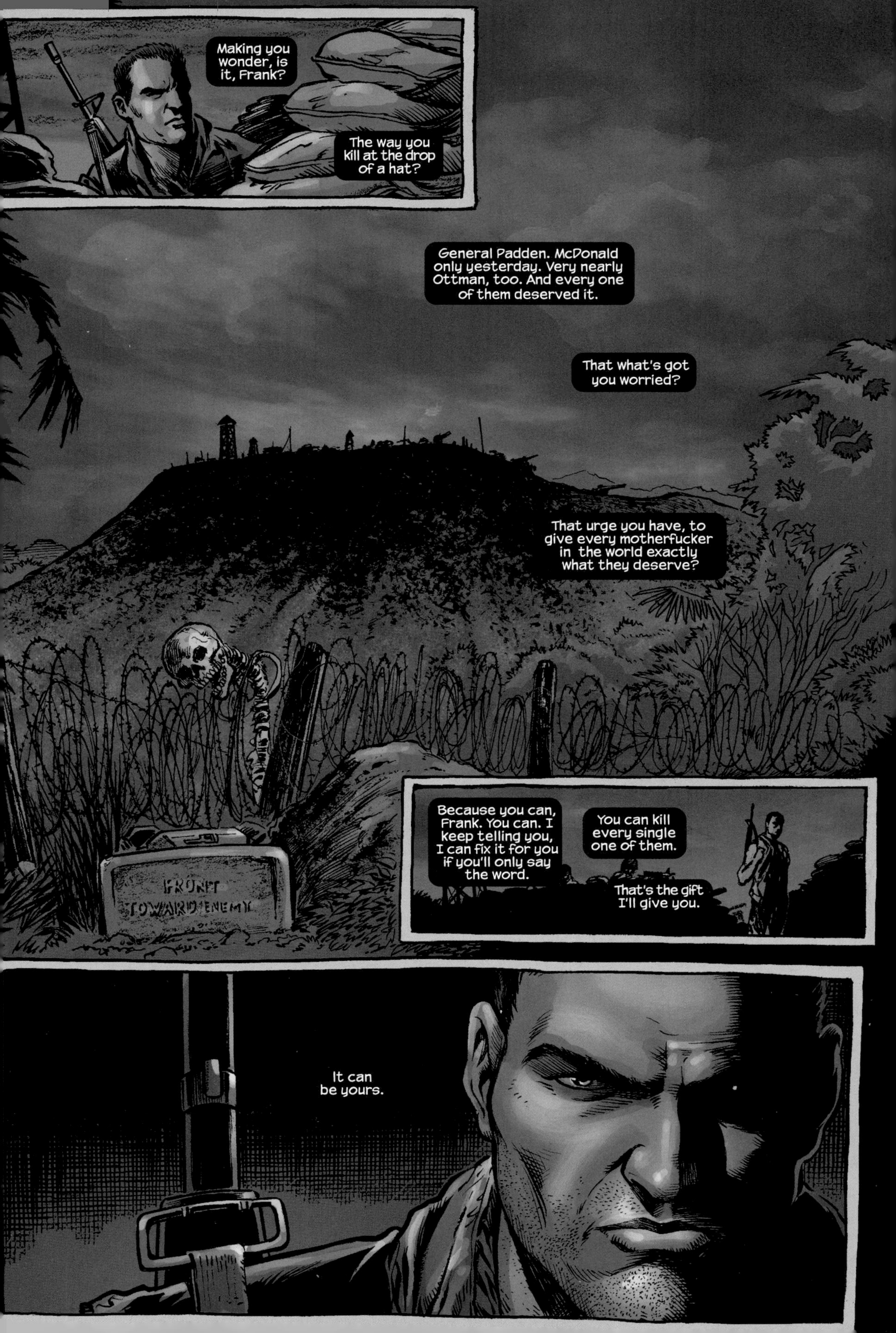
Making you wonder, is it, Frank?
The way you kill at the drop of a hat?
General Padden. McDonald only yesterday. Very nearly Ottman, too. And every one of them deserved it.
That what's got you worried?
That urge you have, to give every motherfucker in the world exactly what they deserve?
FRONT TOWARD ENEMY
Because you can, Frank. You can. I keep telling you, I can fix it for you if you'll only say the word.
You can kill every single one of them.
That's the gift I'll give you.
It can be yours.

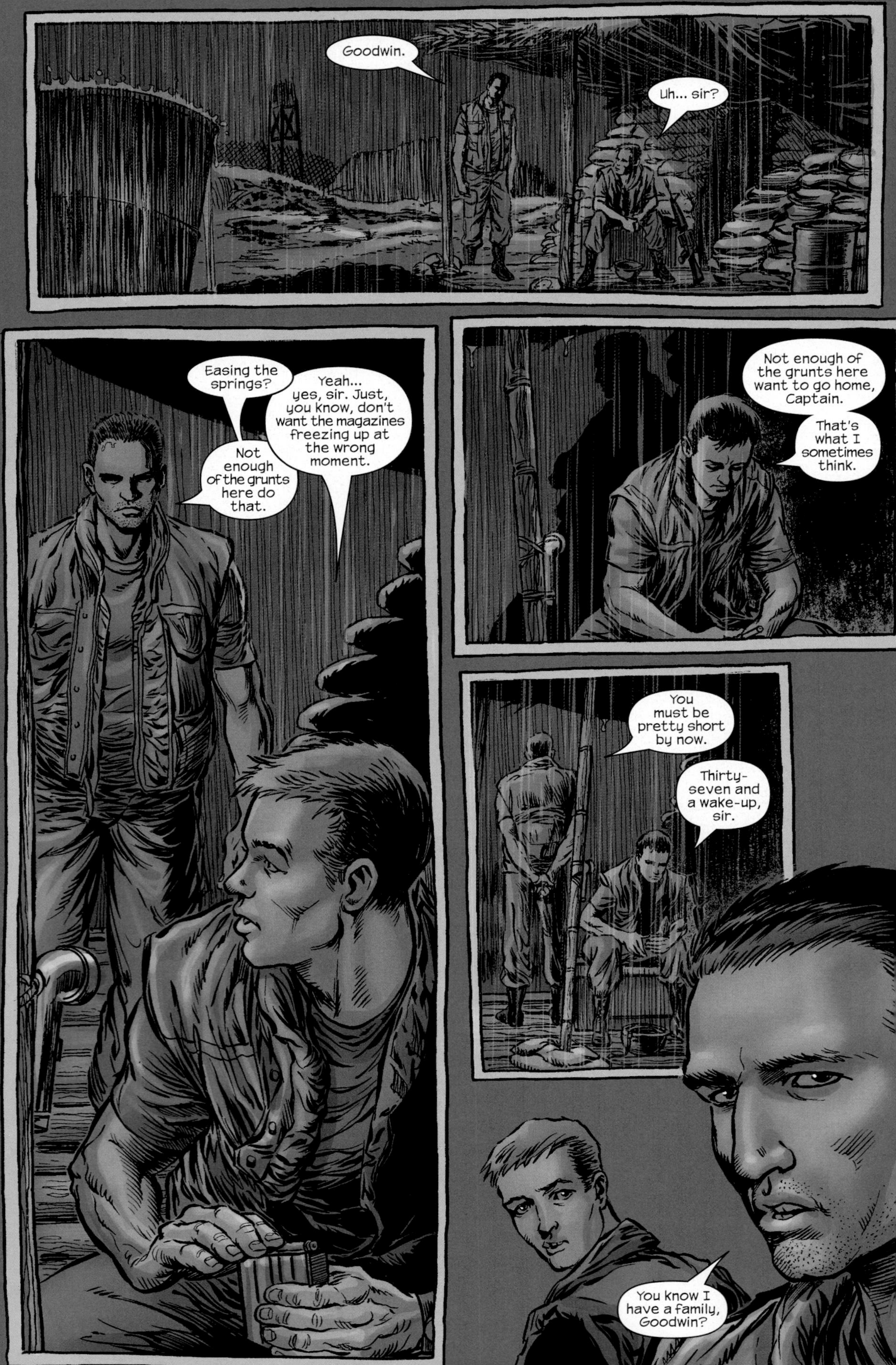
Goodwin.
Uh... sir?
Easing the springs?
Yeah... yes, sir. Just, you know, don't want the magazines freezing up at the wrong moment.
Not enough of the grunts here do that.
Not enough of the grunts here want to go home, Captain.
That's what I sometimes think.
You must be pretty short by now.
Thirty-seven and a wake-up, sir.
You know I have a family, Goodwin?

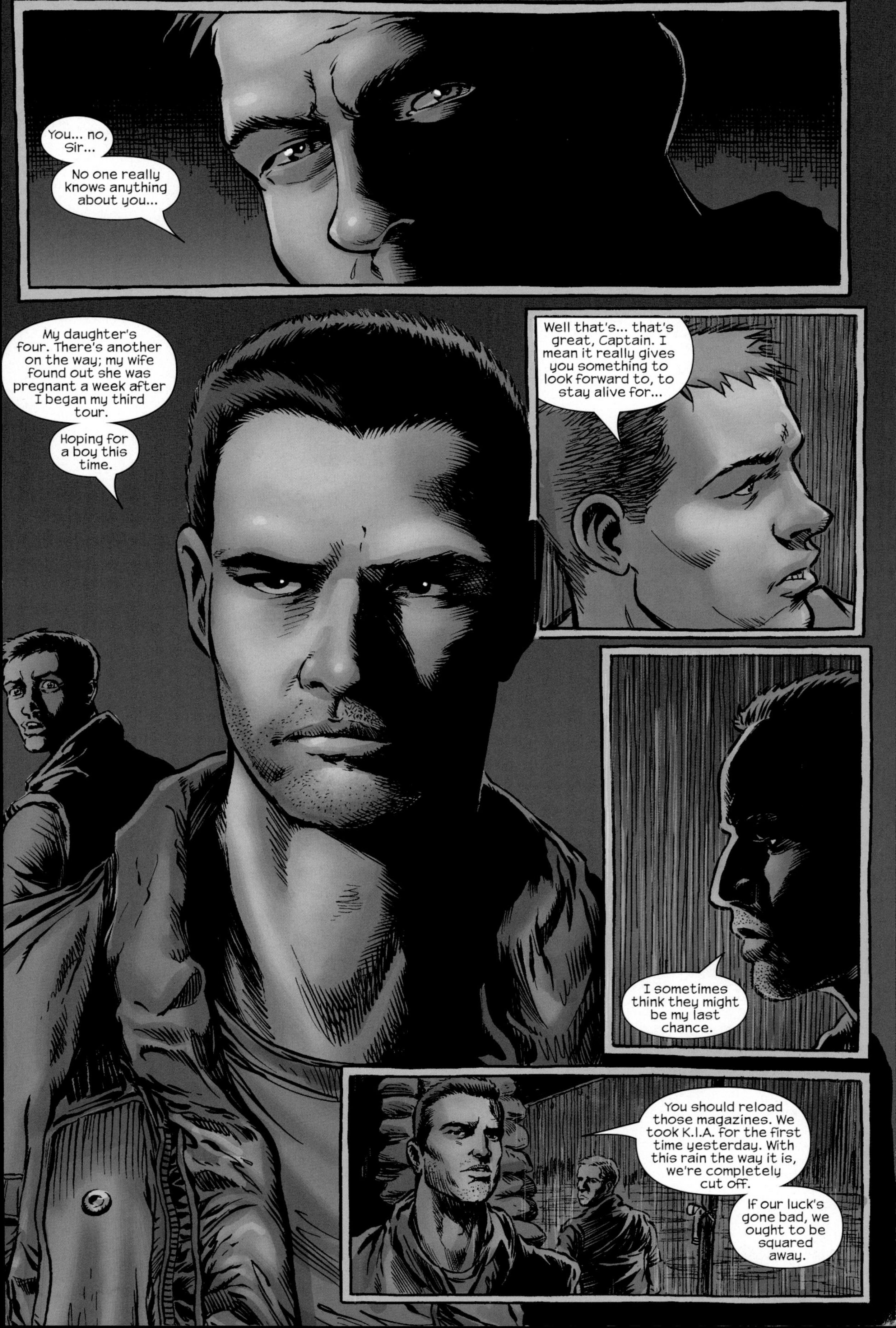
You... no, Sir...
No one really knows anything about you...
My daughter's four. There's another on the way; my wife found out she was pregnant a week after I began my third tour.
Hoping for a boy this time.
Well that's... that's great, Captain. I mean it really gives you something to look forward to, to stay alive for...
I sometimes think they might be my last chance.
You should reload those magazines. We took K.I.A. for the first time yesterday. With this rain the way it is, we're completely cut off.
If our luck's gone bad, we ought to be squared away.

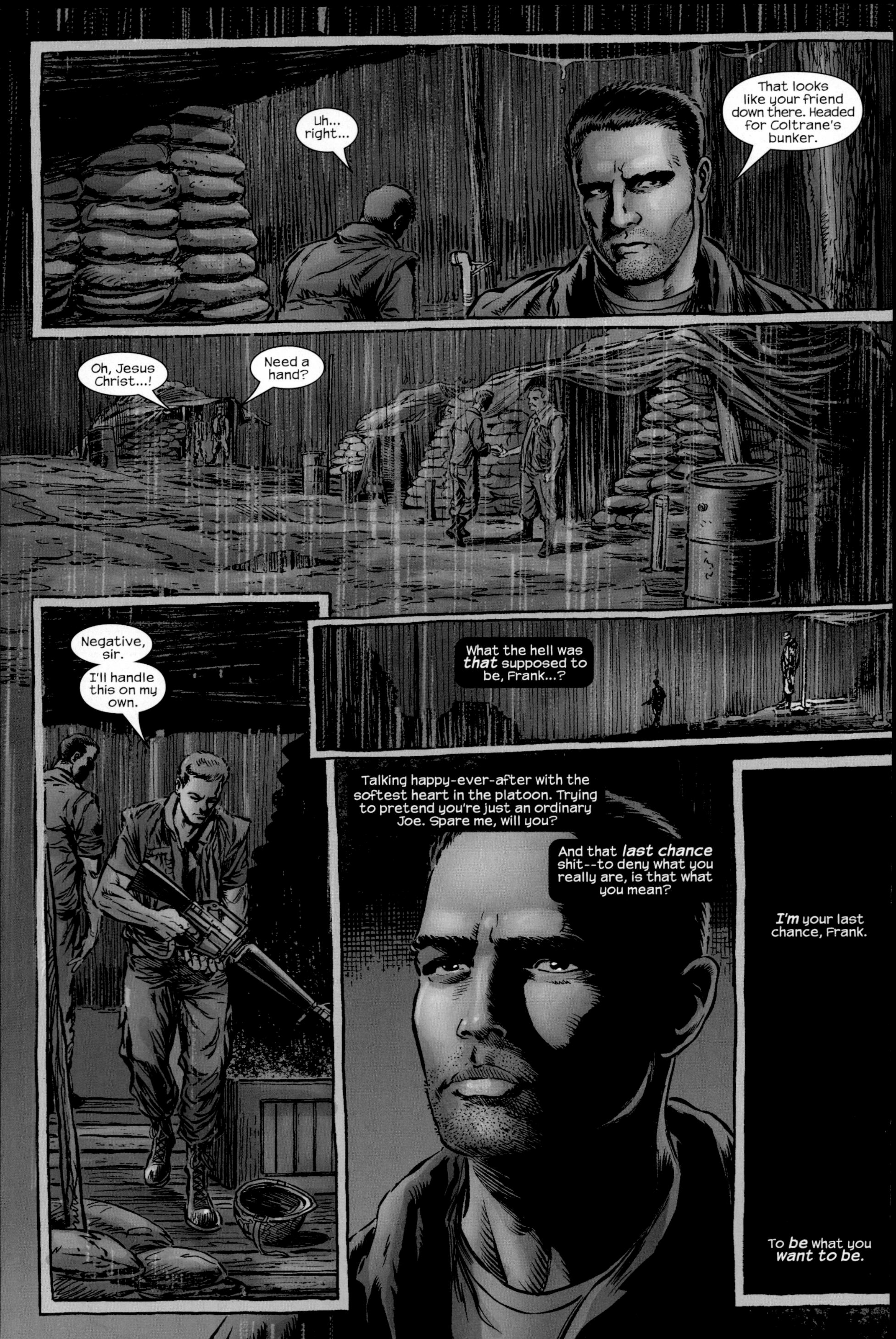

Uh... right...
That looks like your friend down there. Headed for Coltrane's bunker.
Oh, Jesus Christ...!
Need a hand?
Negative, sir.
I'll handle this on my own.
What the hell was *that* supposed to be, Frank...?
Talking happy-ever-after with the softest heart in the platoon. Trying to pretend you're just an ordinary Joe. Spare me, will you?
And that *last chance* shit--to deny what you really are, is that what you mean?
I'm your last chance, Frank.
To *be* what you *want to be.*

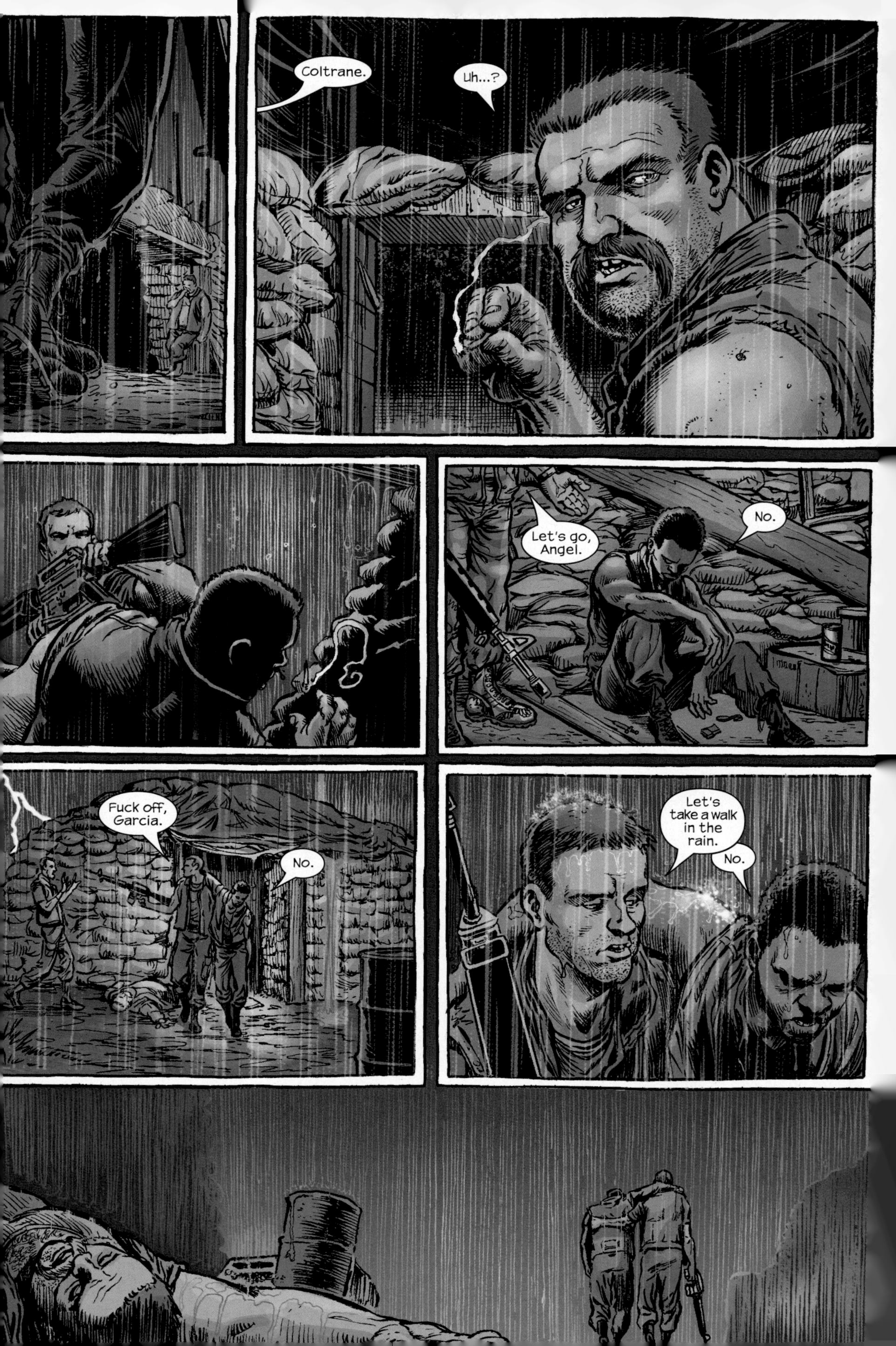
Coltrane.
Uh...?
Let's go, Angel.
No.
Fuck off, Garcia.
No.
Let's take a walk in the rain.
No.

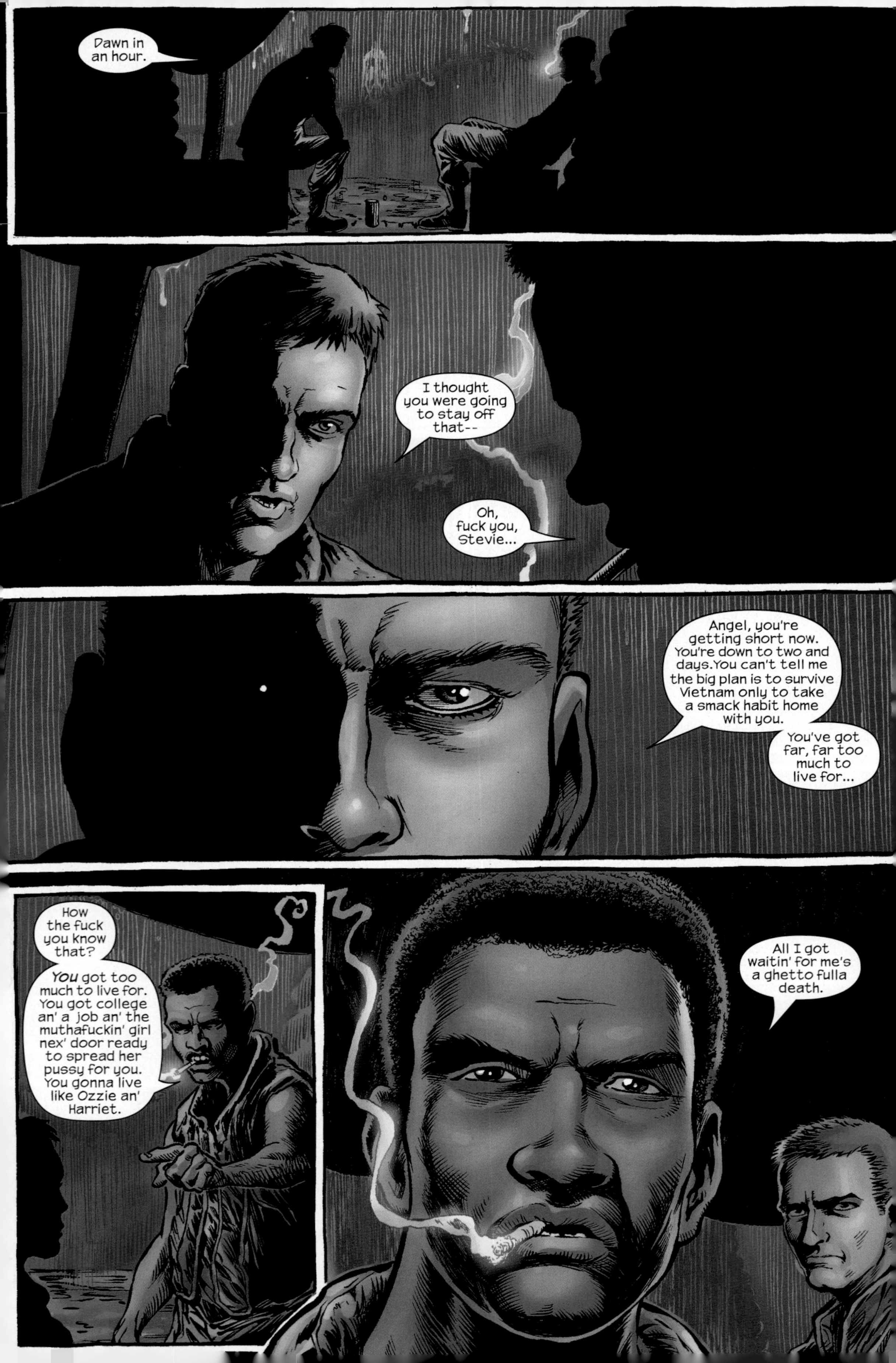
Dawn in an hour.
I thought you were going to stay off that--
Oh, fuck you, Stevie...
Angel, you're getting short now. You're down to two and days.You can't tell me the big plan is to survive Vietnam only to take a smack habit home with you.
You've got far, far too much to live for...
How the fuck you know that?
You got too much to live for. You got college an' a job an' the muthafuckin' girl nex' door ready to spread her pussy for you. You gonna live like Ozzie an' Harriet.
All I got waitin' for me's a ghetto fulla death.

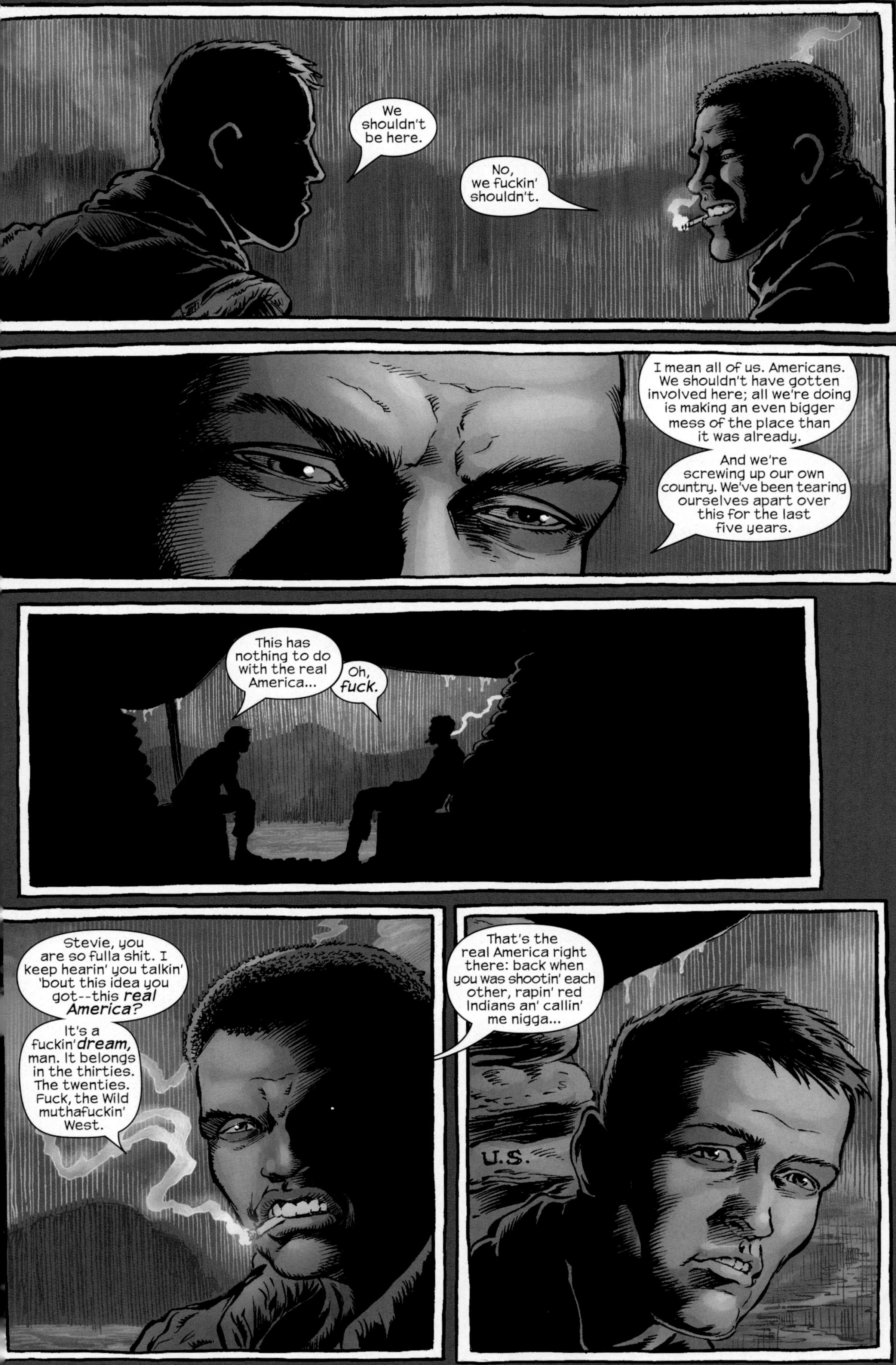
We shouldn't be here.
No, we fuckin' shouldn't.
I mean all of us. Americans. We shouldn't have gotten involved here; all we're doing is making an even bigger mess of the place than it was already.
And we're screwing up our own country. We've been tearing ourselves apart over this for the last five years.
This has nothing to do with the real America...
Oh, *fuck.*
Stevie, you are so fulla shit. I keep hearin' you talkin' 'bout this idea you got--this *real America?*
It's a fuckin' *dream,* man. It belongs in the thirties. The twenties. Fuck, the Wild muthafuckin' West.
That's the real America right there: back when you was shootin' each other, rapin' red Indians an' callin' me nigga...
U.S.

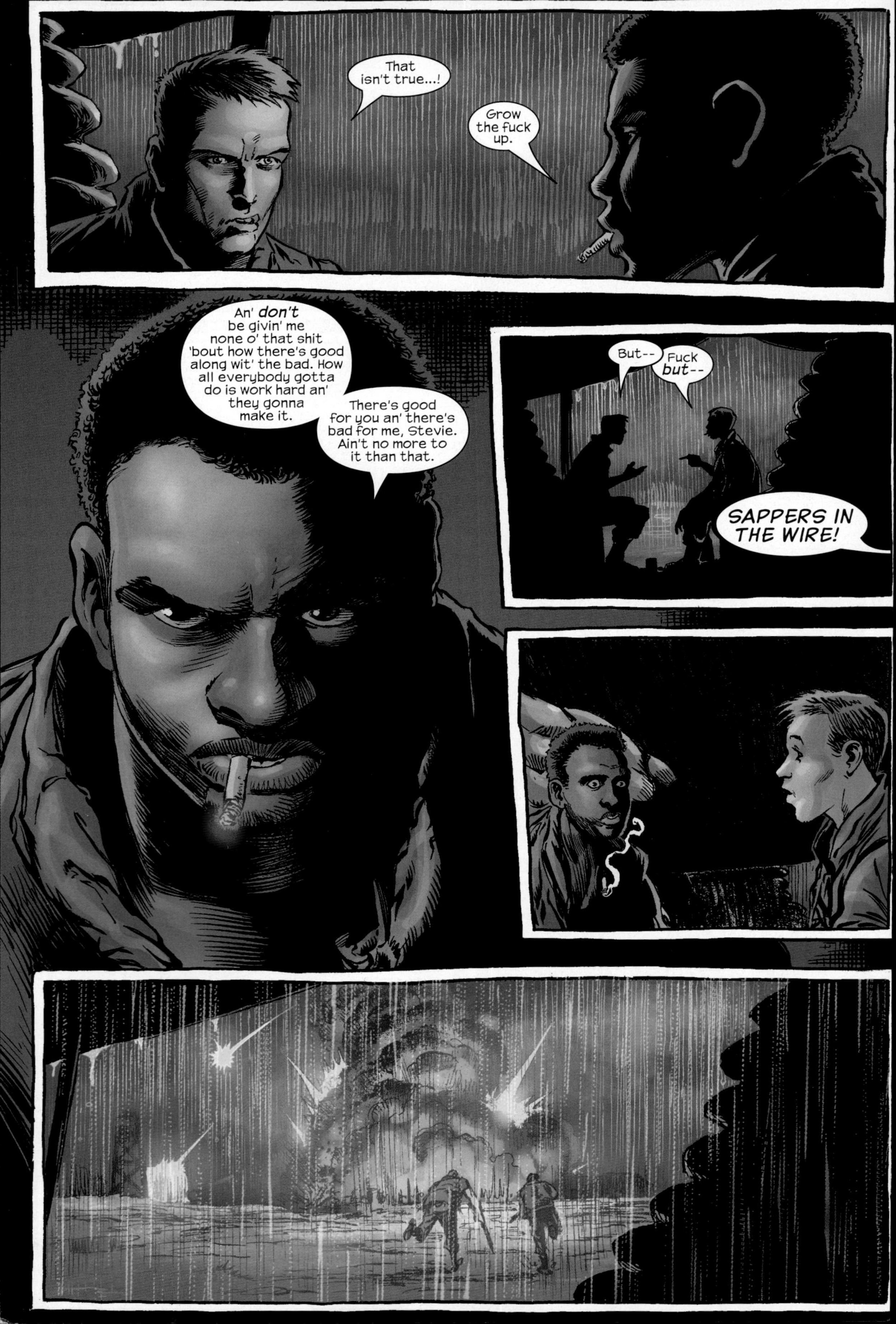
That isn't true...!
Grow the fuck up.
An' *don't* be givin' me none o' that shit 'bout how there's good along wit' the bad. How all everybody gotta do is work hard an' they gonna make it.
There's good for you an' there's bad for me, Stevie. Ain't no more to it than that.
But--
Fuck *but*--
SAPPERS IN THE WIRE!

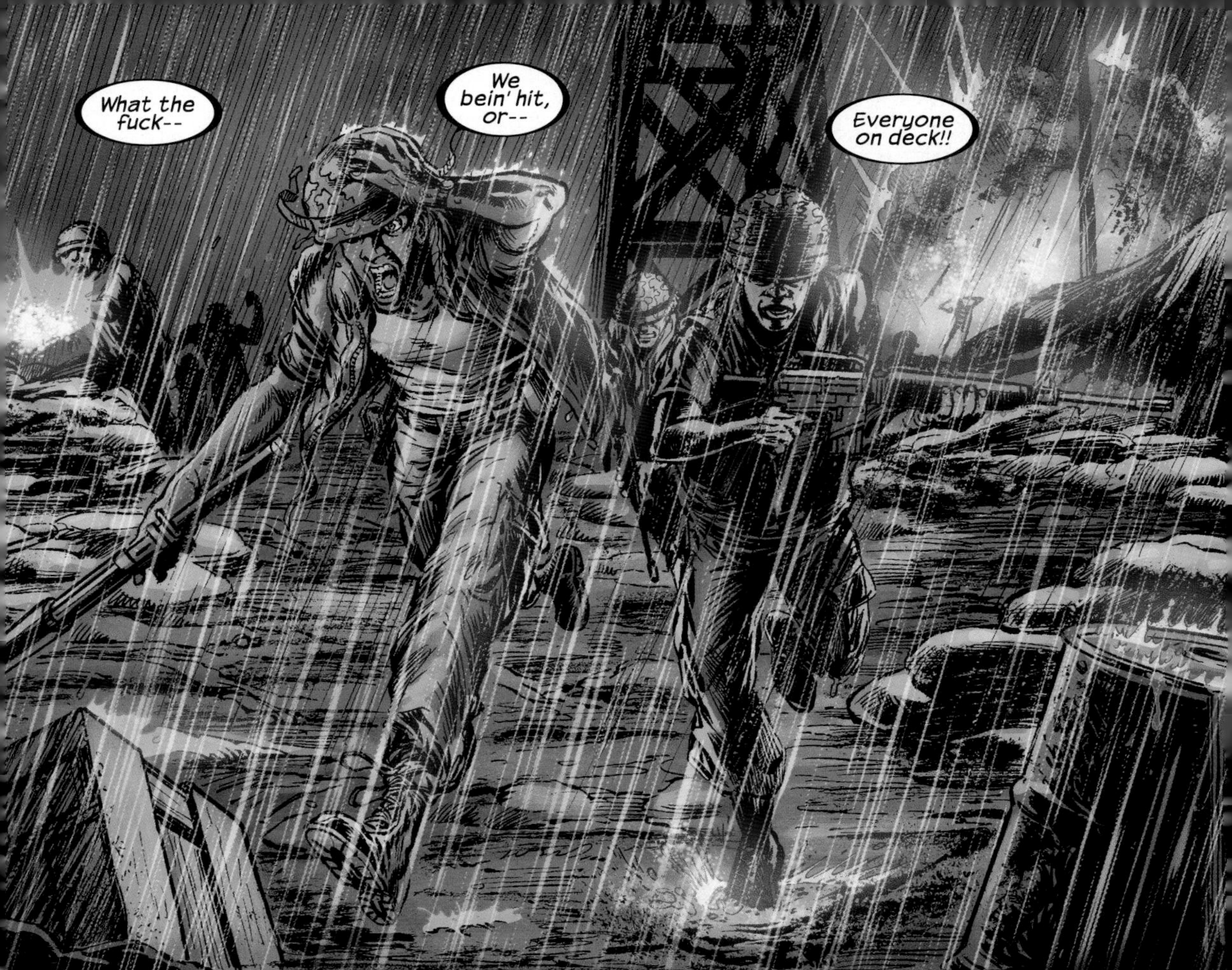
What the fuck--
We bein' hit, or--
Everyone on deck!!

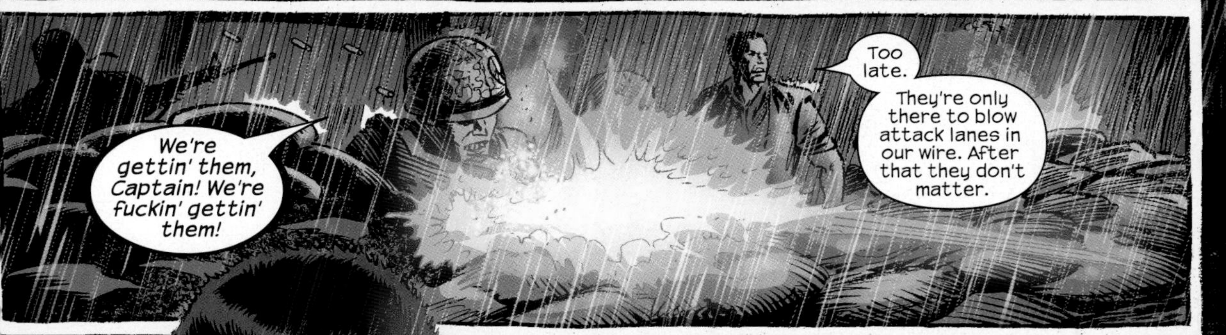
We're gettin' them, Captain! We're fuckin' gettin' them!
Too late.
They're only there to blow attack lanes in our wire. After that they don't matter.

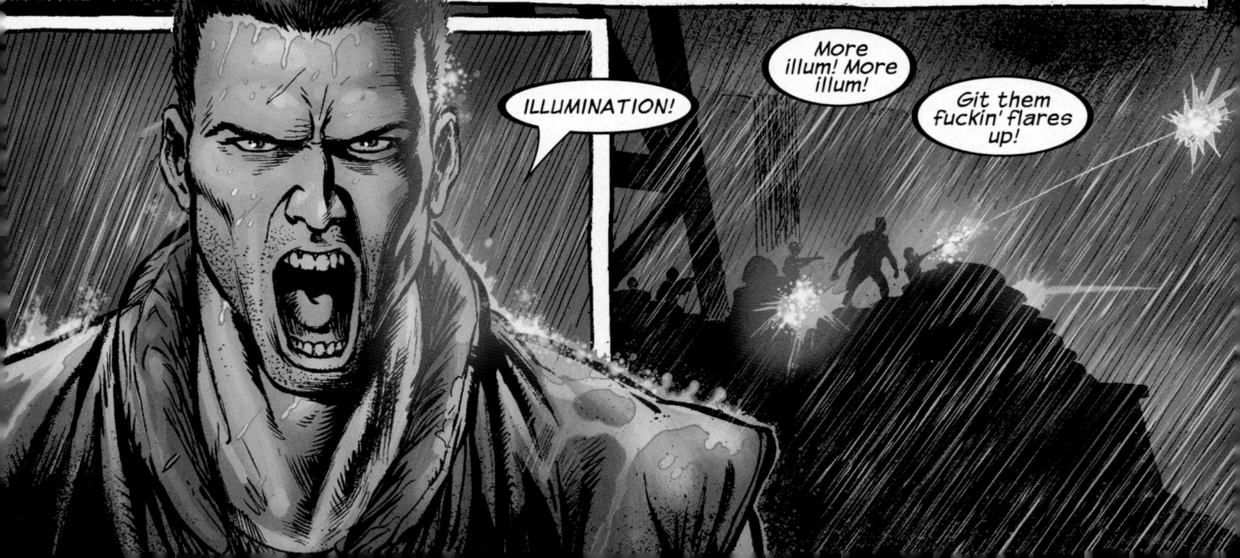
ILLUMINATION!
More illum! More illum!
Git them fuckin' flares up!

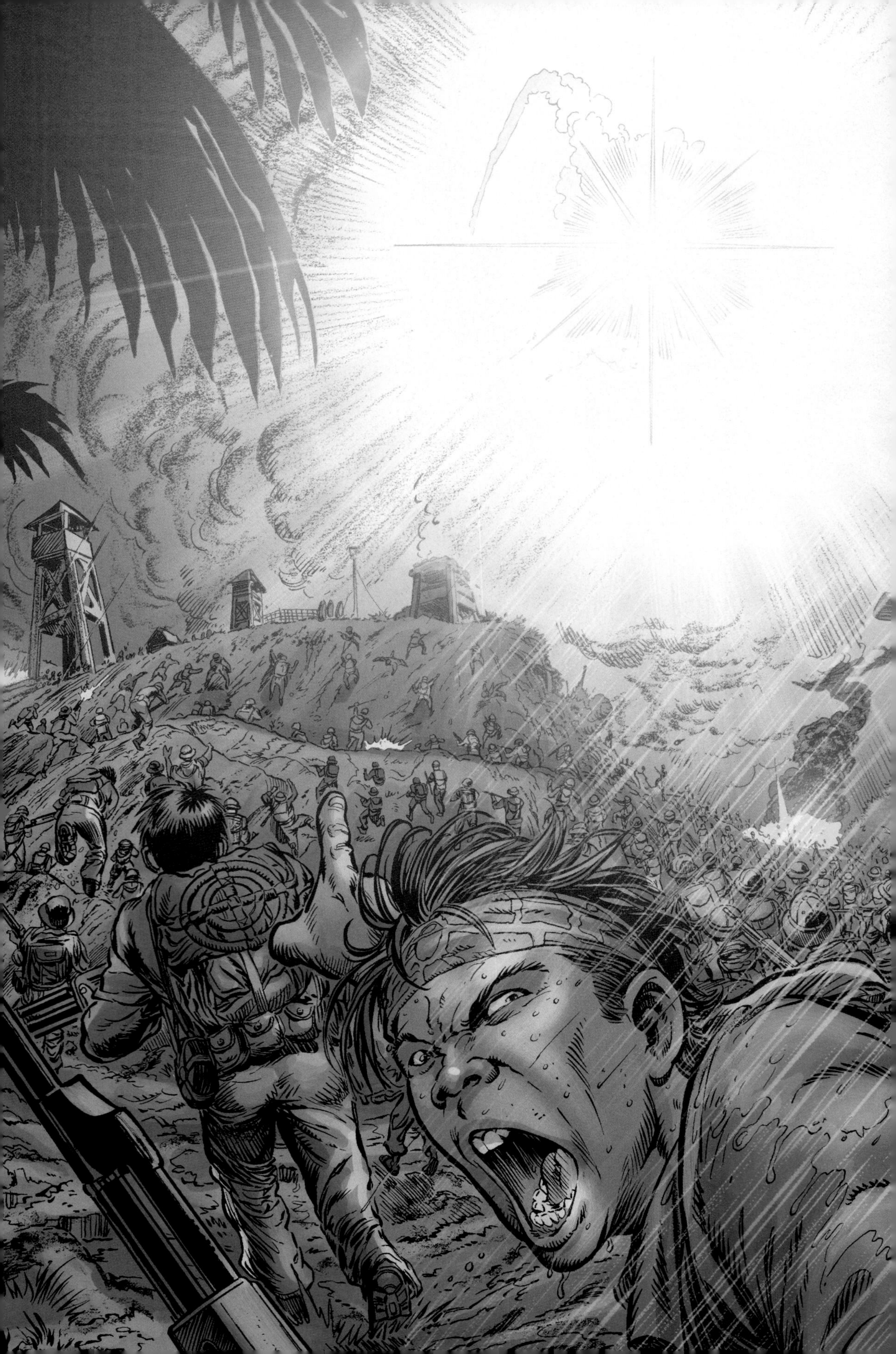

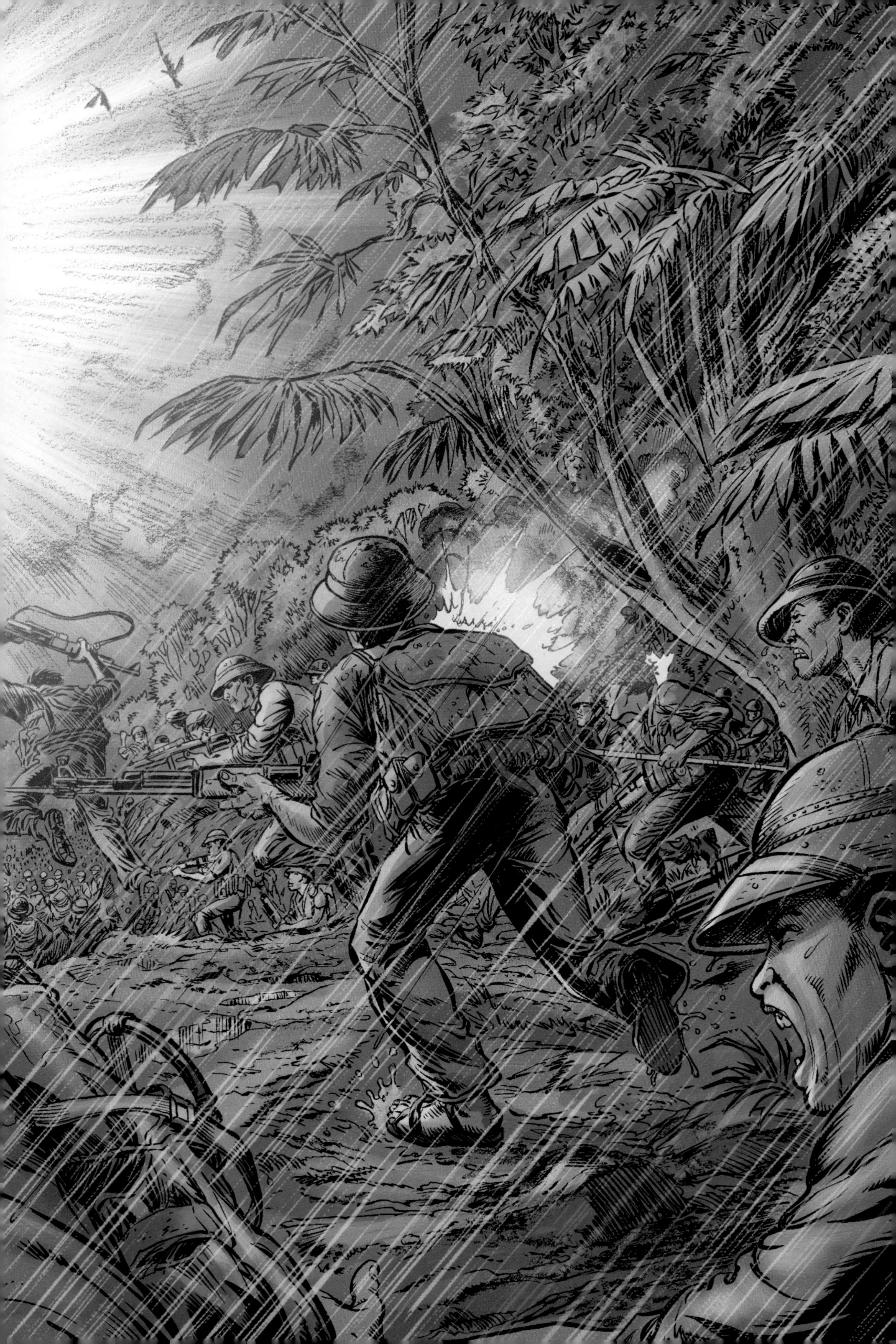

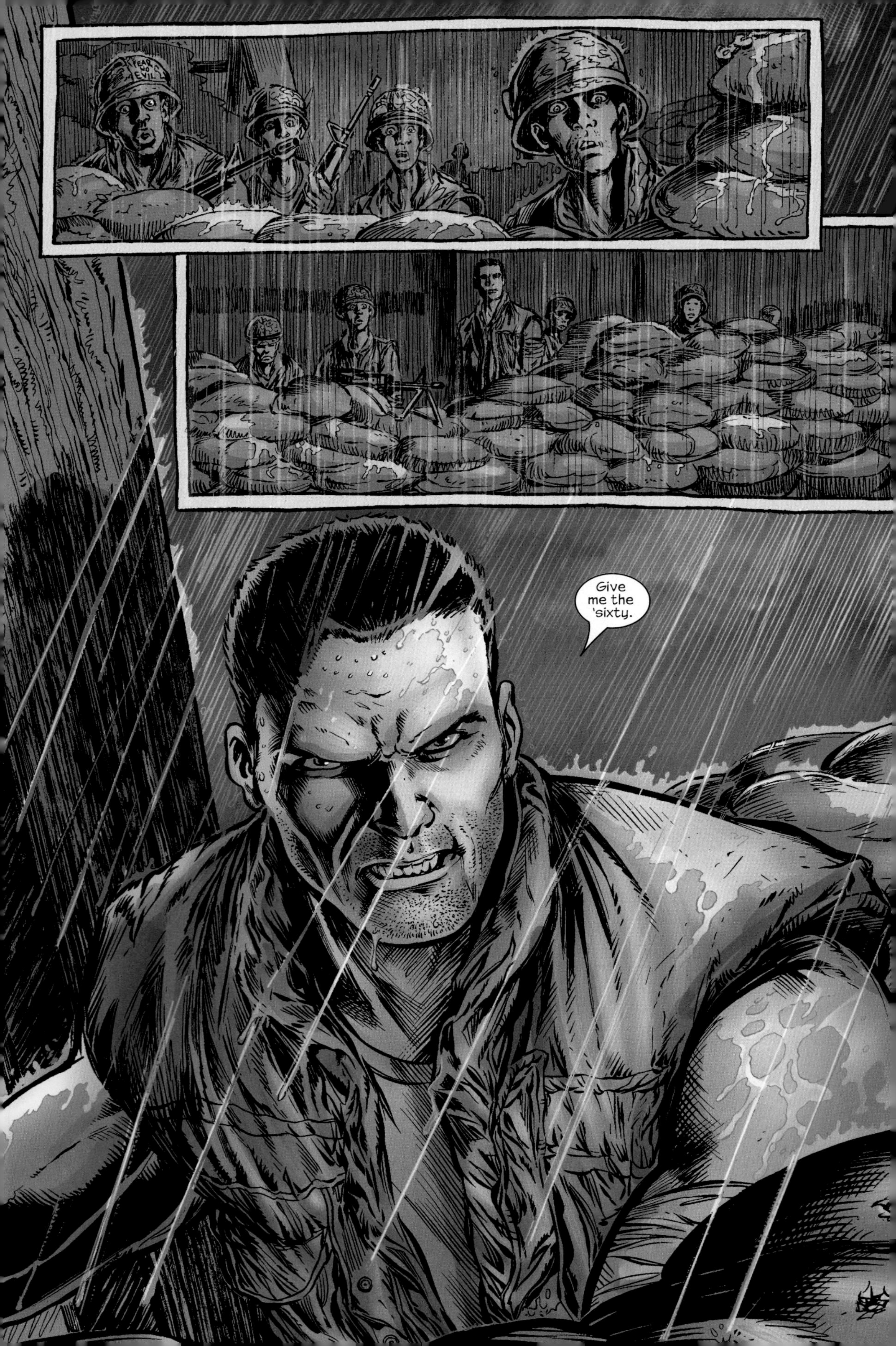
Give me the 'sixty.

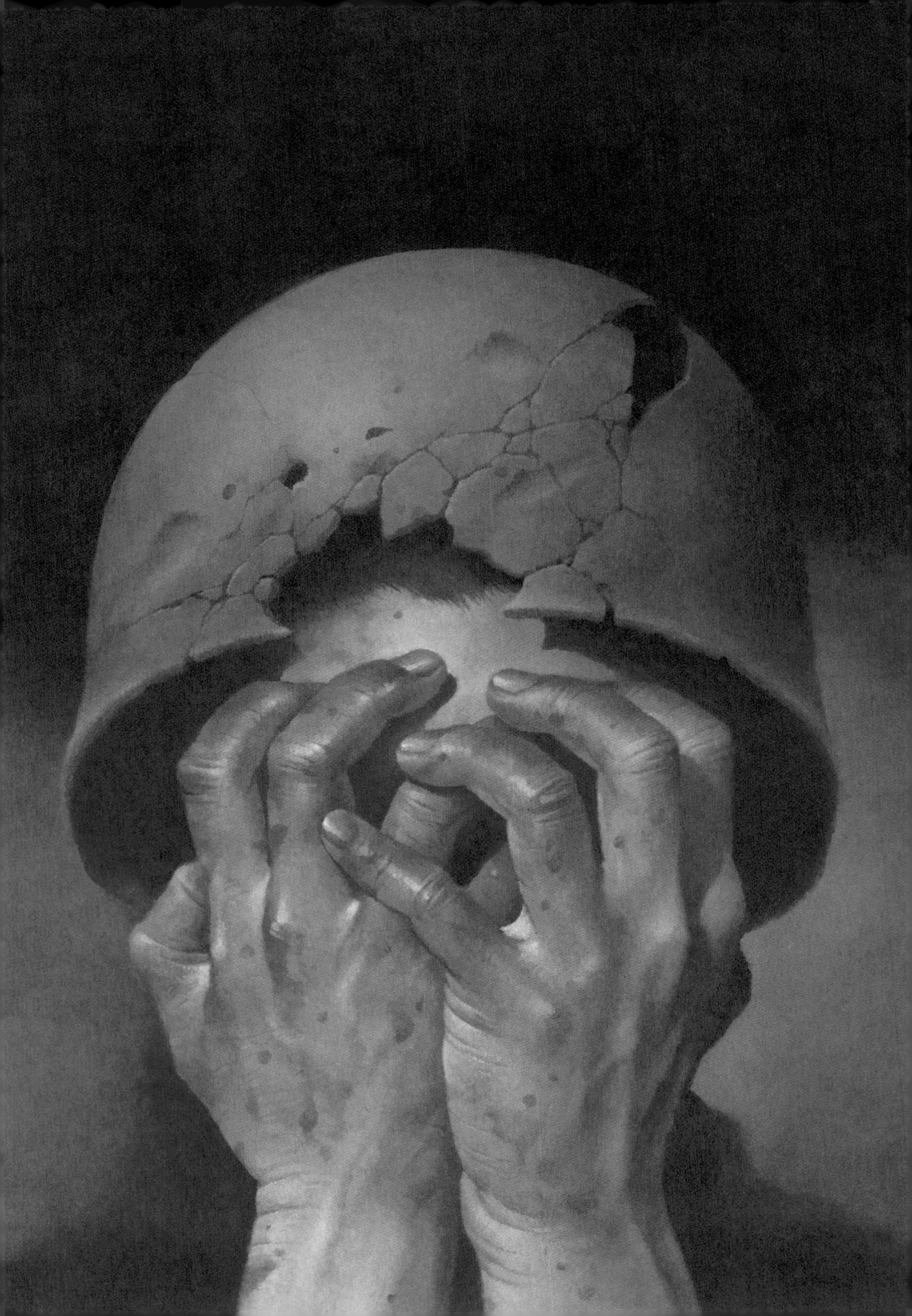

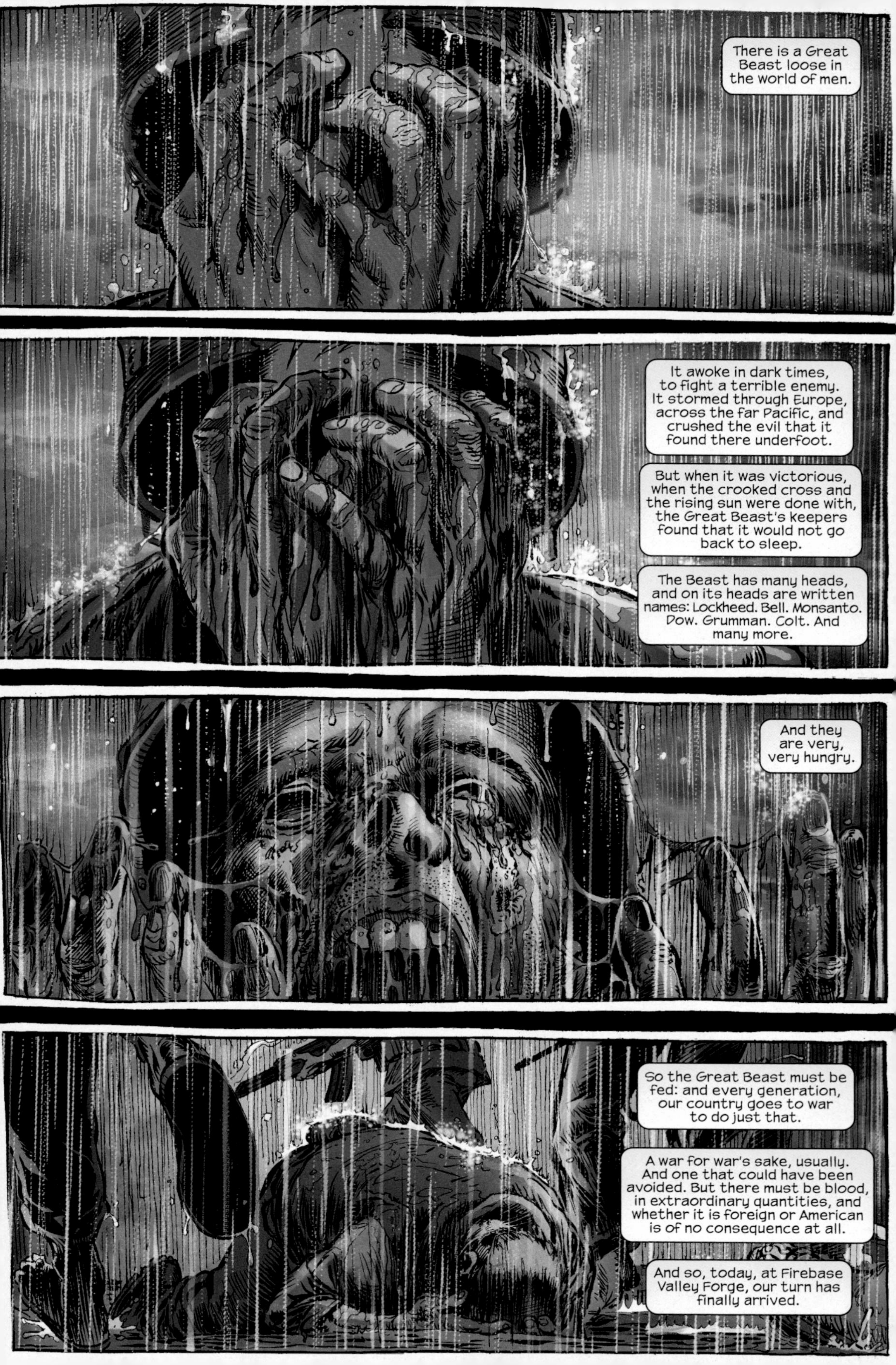
There is a Great Beast loose in the world of men.
It awoke in dark times, to fight a terrible enemy. It stormed through Europe, across the far Pacific, and crushed the evil that it found there underfoot.
But when it was victorious, when the crooked cross and the rising sun were done with, the Great Beast's keepers found that it would not go back to sleep.
The Beast has many heads, and on its heads are written names: Lockheed. Bell. Monsanto. Dow. Grumman. Colt. And many more.
And they are very, very hungry.
So the Great Beast must be fed: and every generation, our country goes to war to do just that.
A war for war's sake, usually. And one that could have been avoided. But there must be blood, in extraordinary quantities, and whether it is foreign or American is of no consequence at all.
And so, today, at Firebase Valley Forge, our turn has finally arrived.

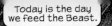

Today is the day
we feed the Beast.

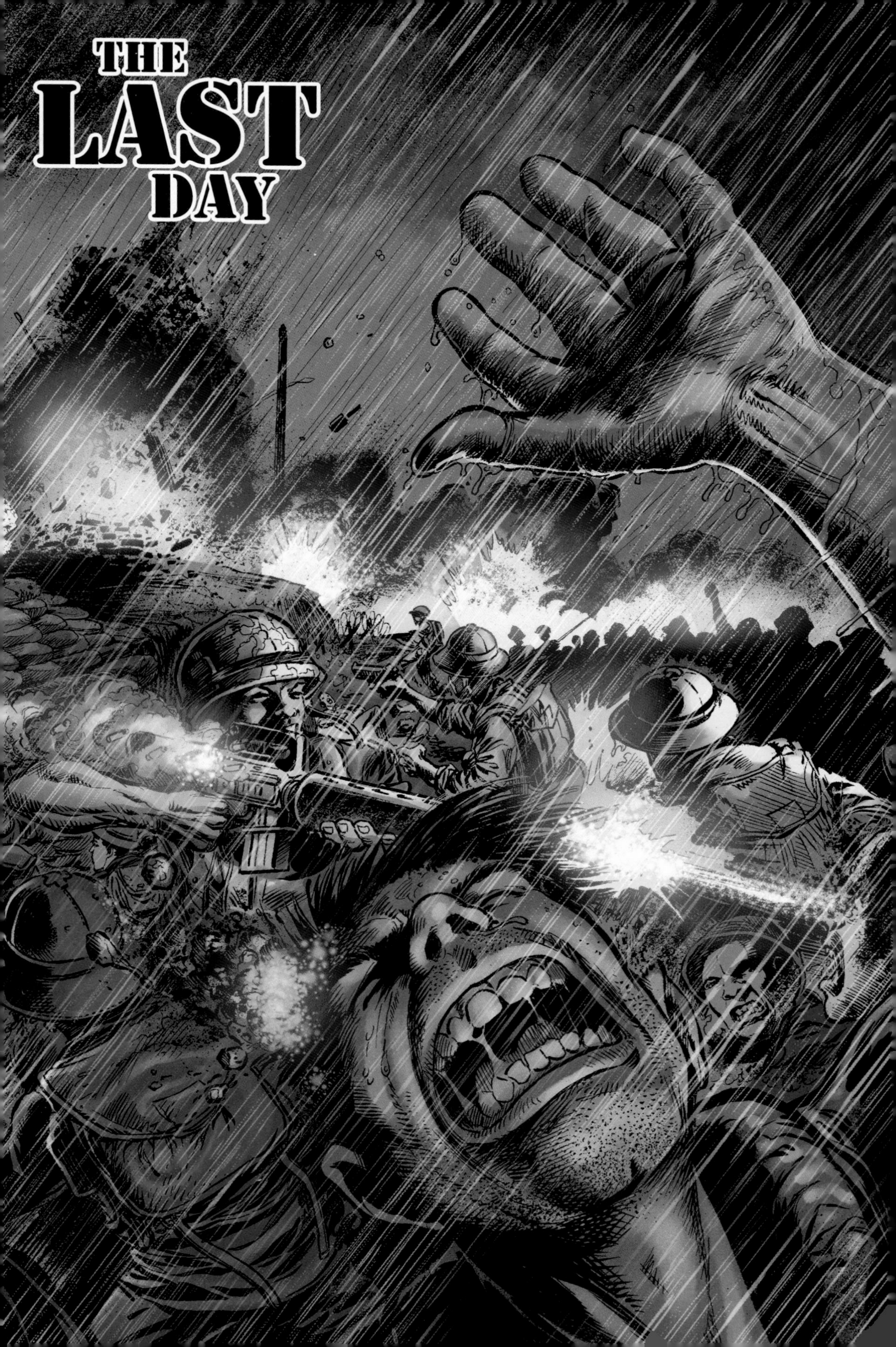
THE
LAST
DAY

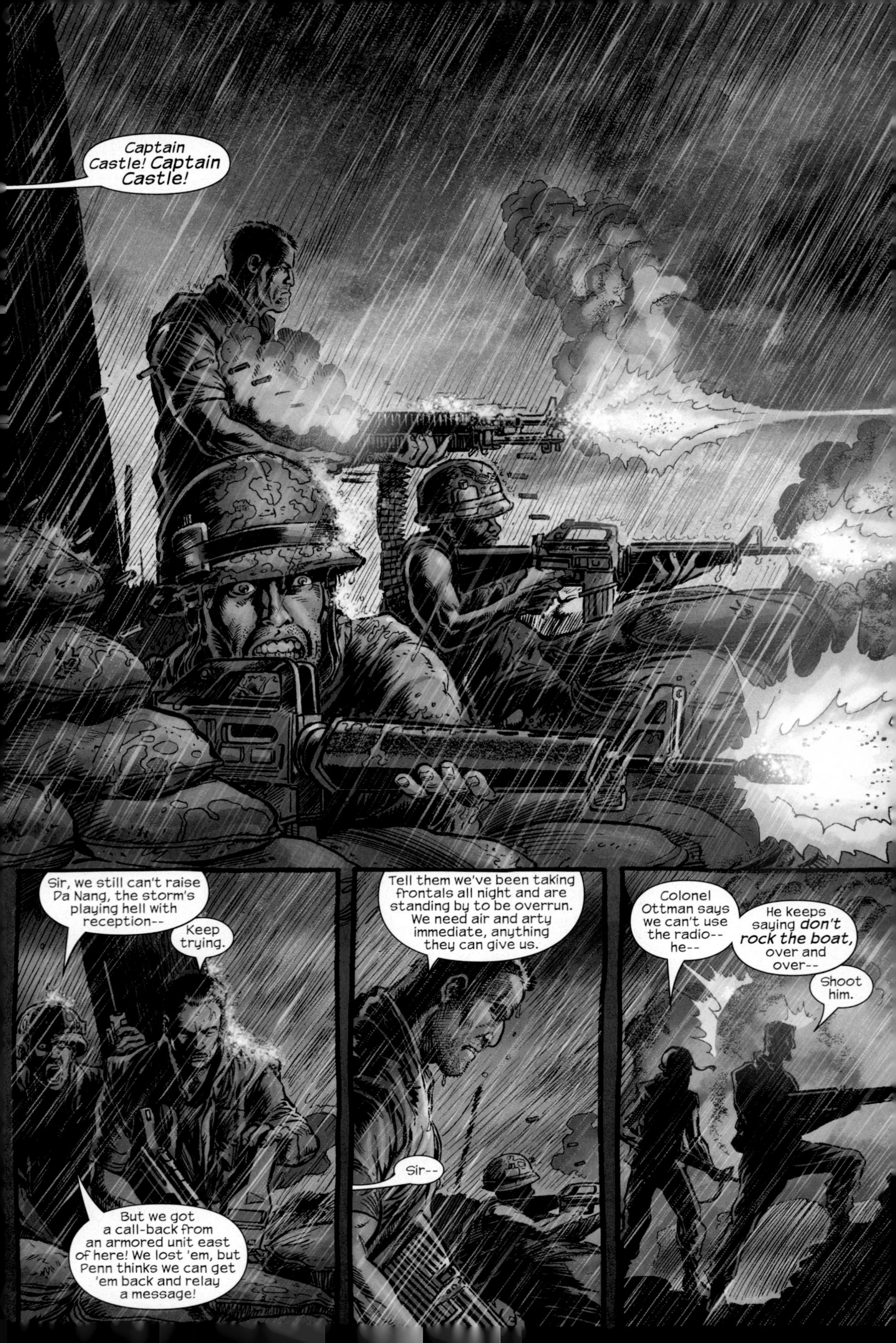

Captain Castle! Captain Castle!
Sir, we still can't raise Da Nang, the storm's playing hell with reception--
Keep trying.
But we got a call-back from an armored unit east of here! We lost 'em, but Penn thinks we can get 'em back and relay a message!
Tell them we've been taking frontals all night and are standing by to be overrun. We need air and arty immediate, anything they can give us.
Sir--
Colonel Ottman says we can't use the radio-- he--
He keeps saying *don't rock the boat,* over and over--
Shoot him.

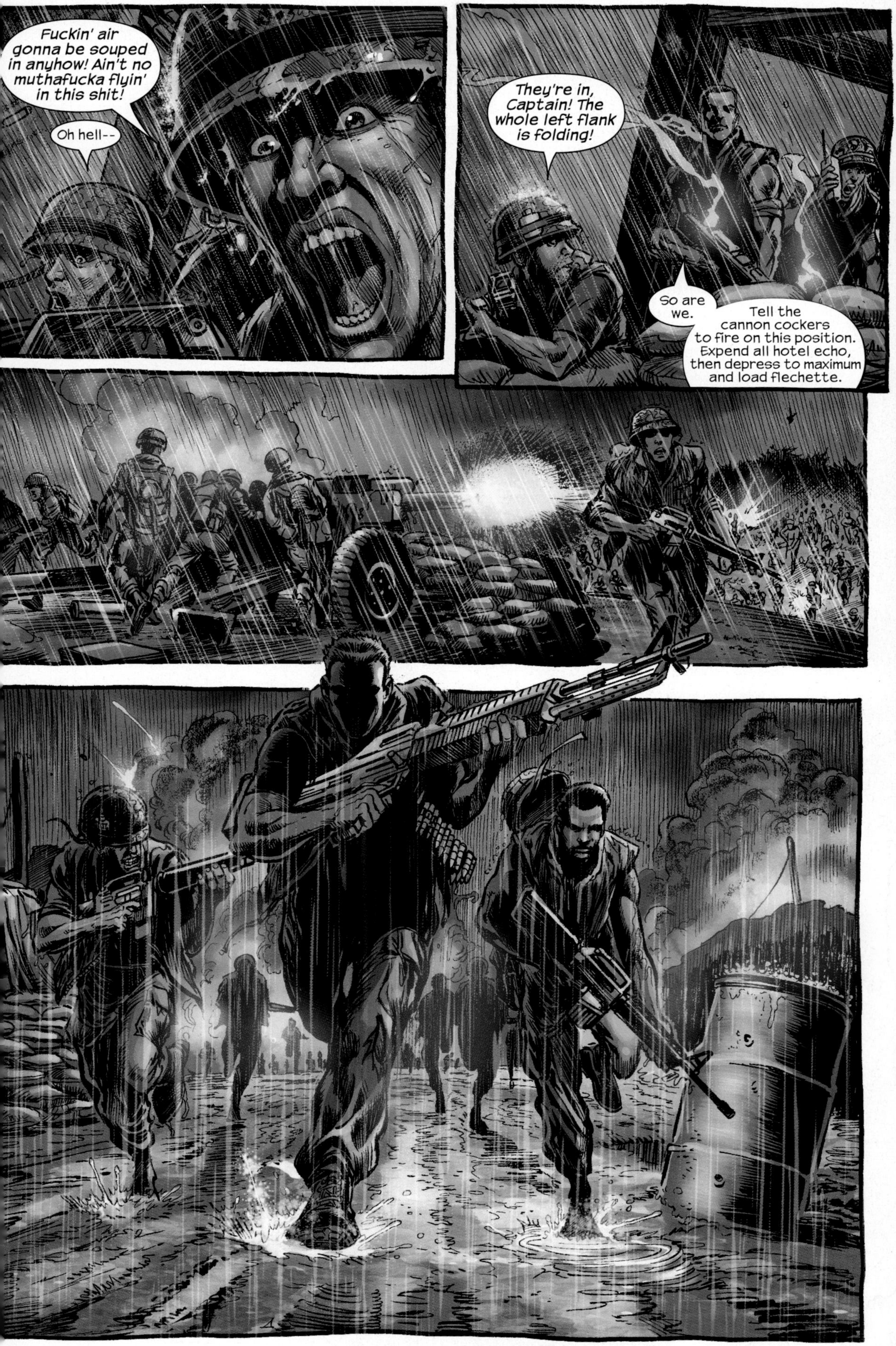
Fuckin' air gonna be souped in anyhow! Ain't no muthafucka flyin' in this shit!
Oh hell--
They're in, Captain! The whole left flank is folding!
So are we.
Tell the cannon cockers to fire on this position. Expend all hotel echo, then depress to maximum and load flechette.

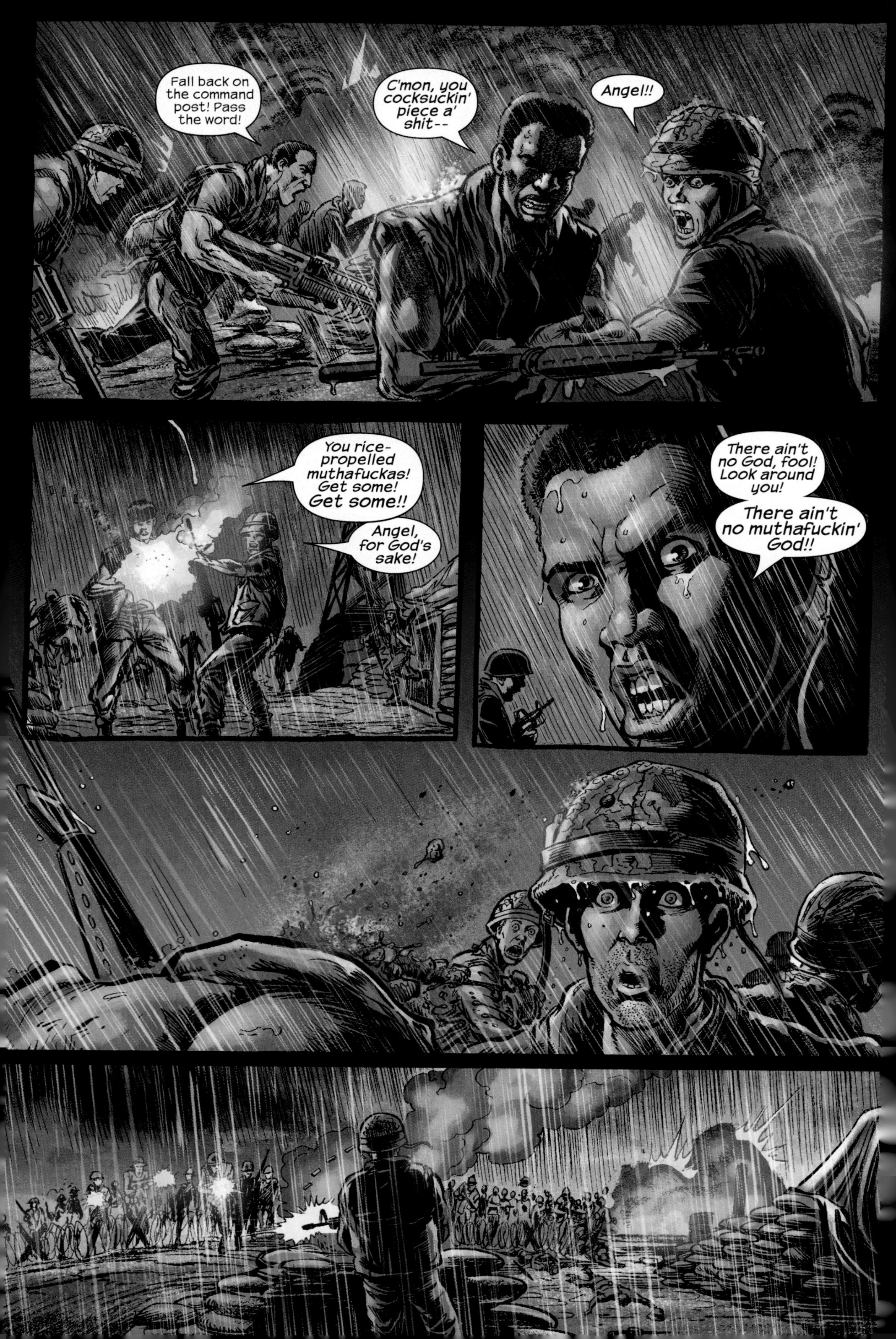

Fall back on the command post! Pass the word!
C'mon, you cocksuckin' piece a' shit--
Angel!!
You rice-propelled muthafuckas! Get some! Get some!!
Angel, for God's sake!
There ain't no God, fool! Look around you!
There ain't no muthafuckin' God!!

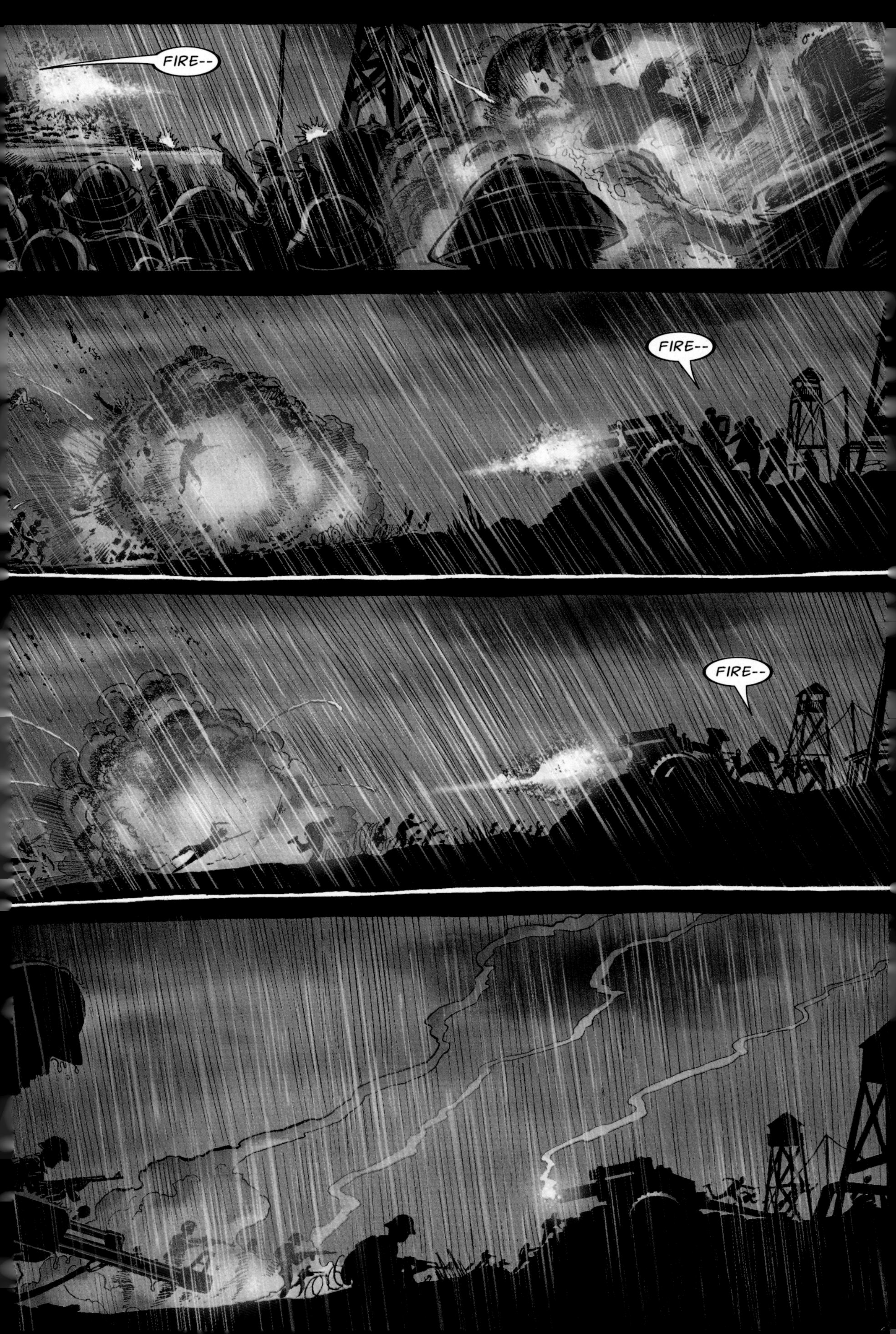
FIRE--
FIRE--
FIRE--

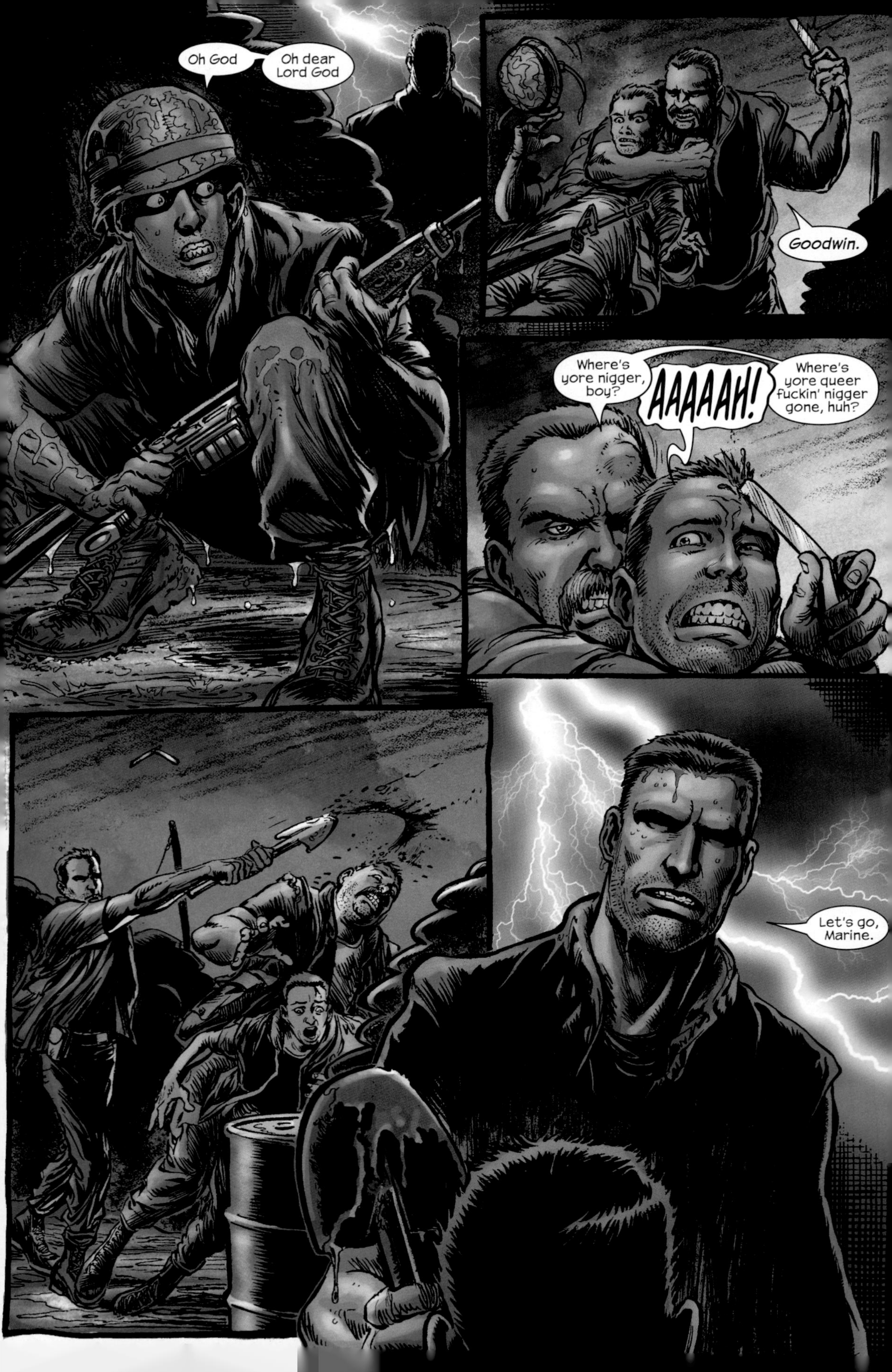
Oh God
Oh dear Lord God
Goodwin.
Where's yore nigger, boy?
AAAAAH!
Where's yore queer fuckin' nigger gone, huh?
Let's go, Marine.

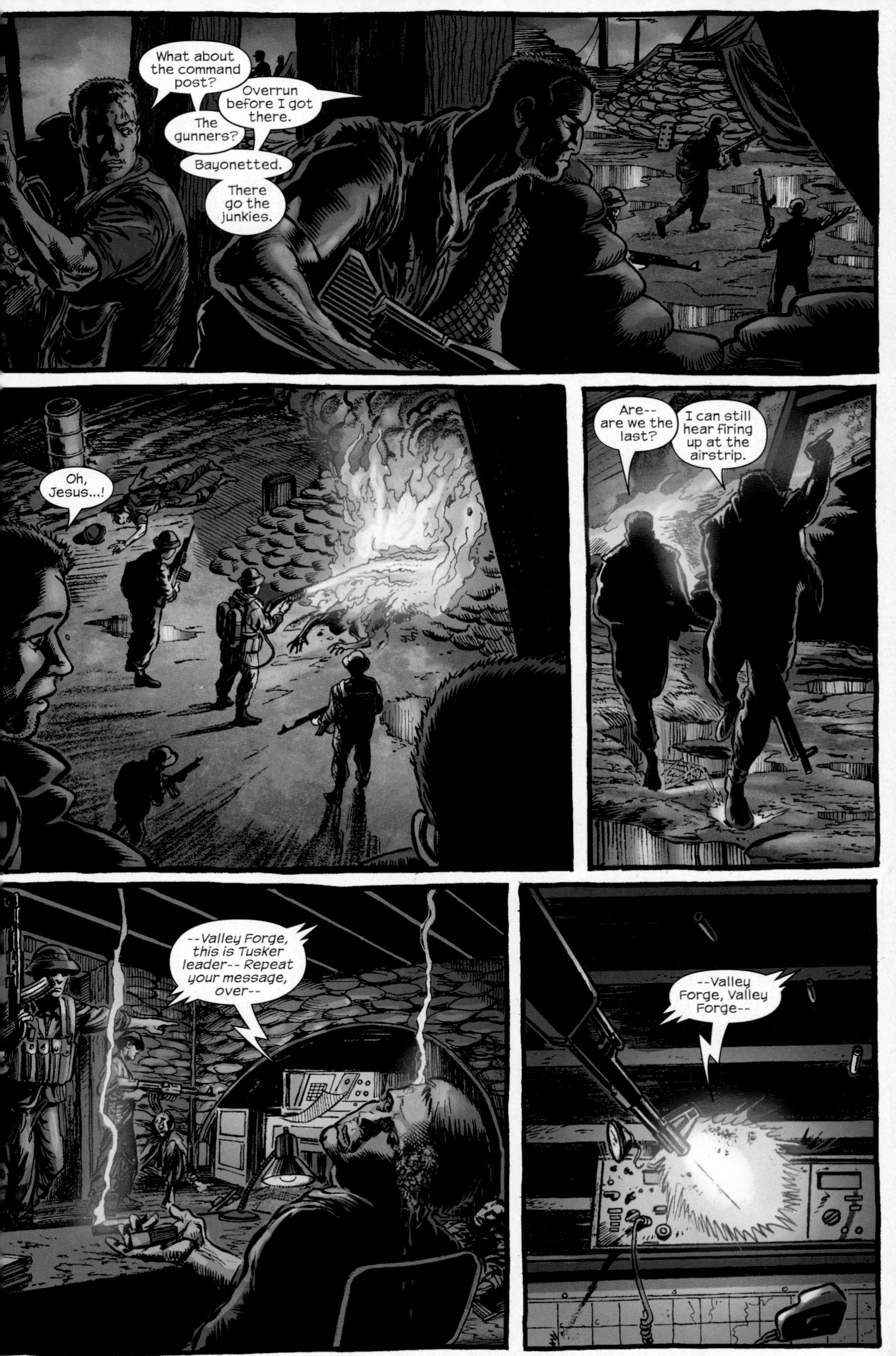
What about the command post?
Overrun before I got there.
The gunners?
Bayonetted.
There go the junkies.
Oh, Jesus...!
Are-- are we the last?
I can still hear firing up at the airstrip.
--Valley Forge, this is Tusker leader-- Repeat your message, over--
--Valley Forge, Valley Forge--

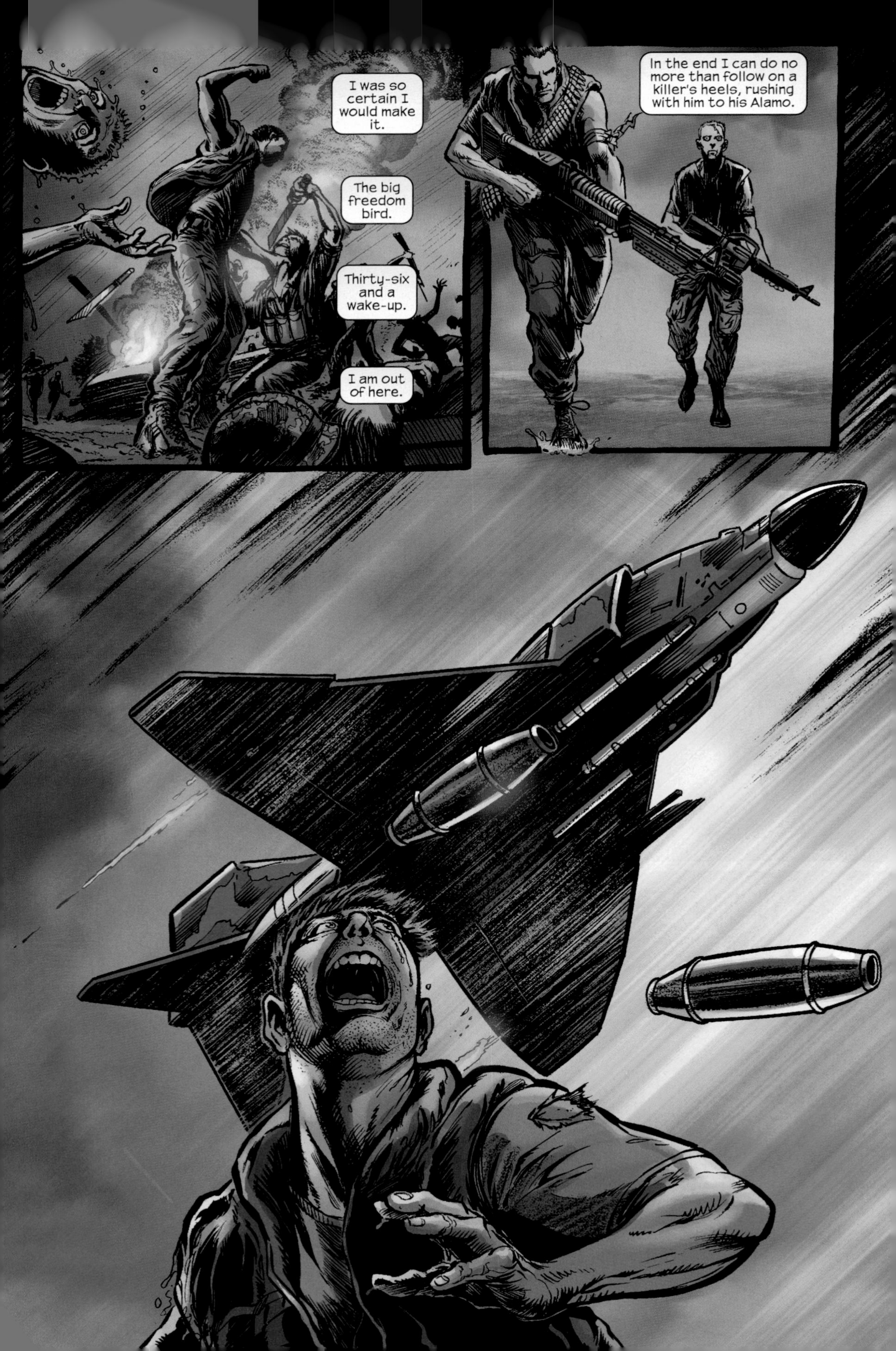
I was so certain I would make it.
The big freedom bird.
Thirty-six and a wake-up.
I am out of here.
In the end I can do no more than follow on a killer's heels, rushing with him to his Alamo.

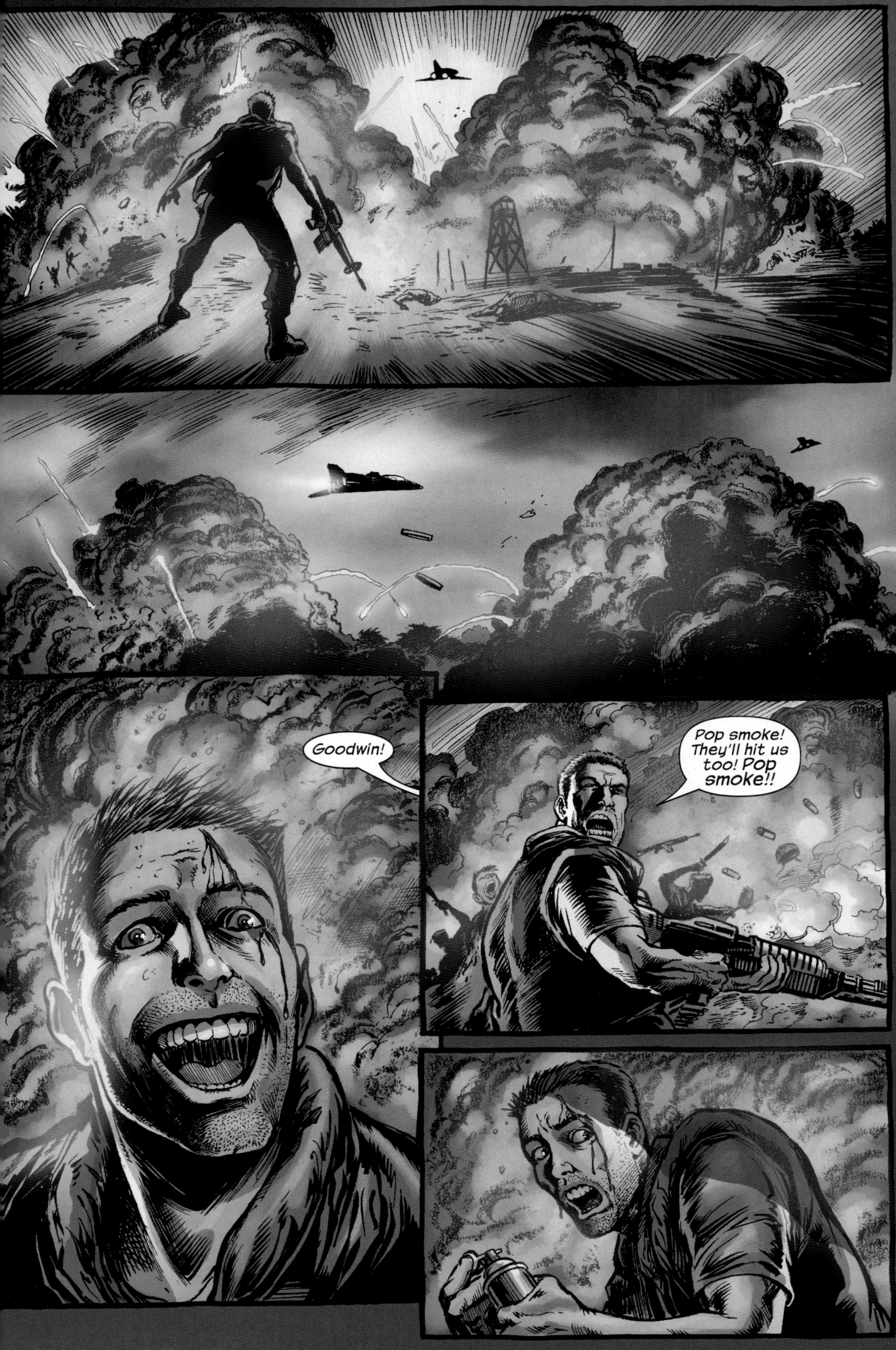
Goodwin!
Pop smoke! They'll hit us too! Pop smoke!!

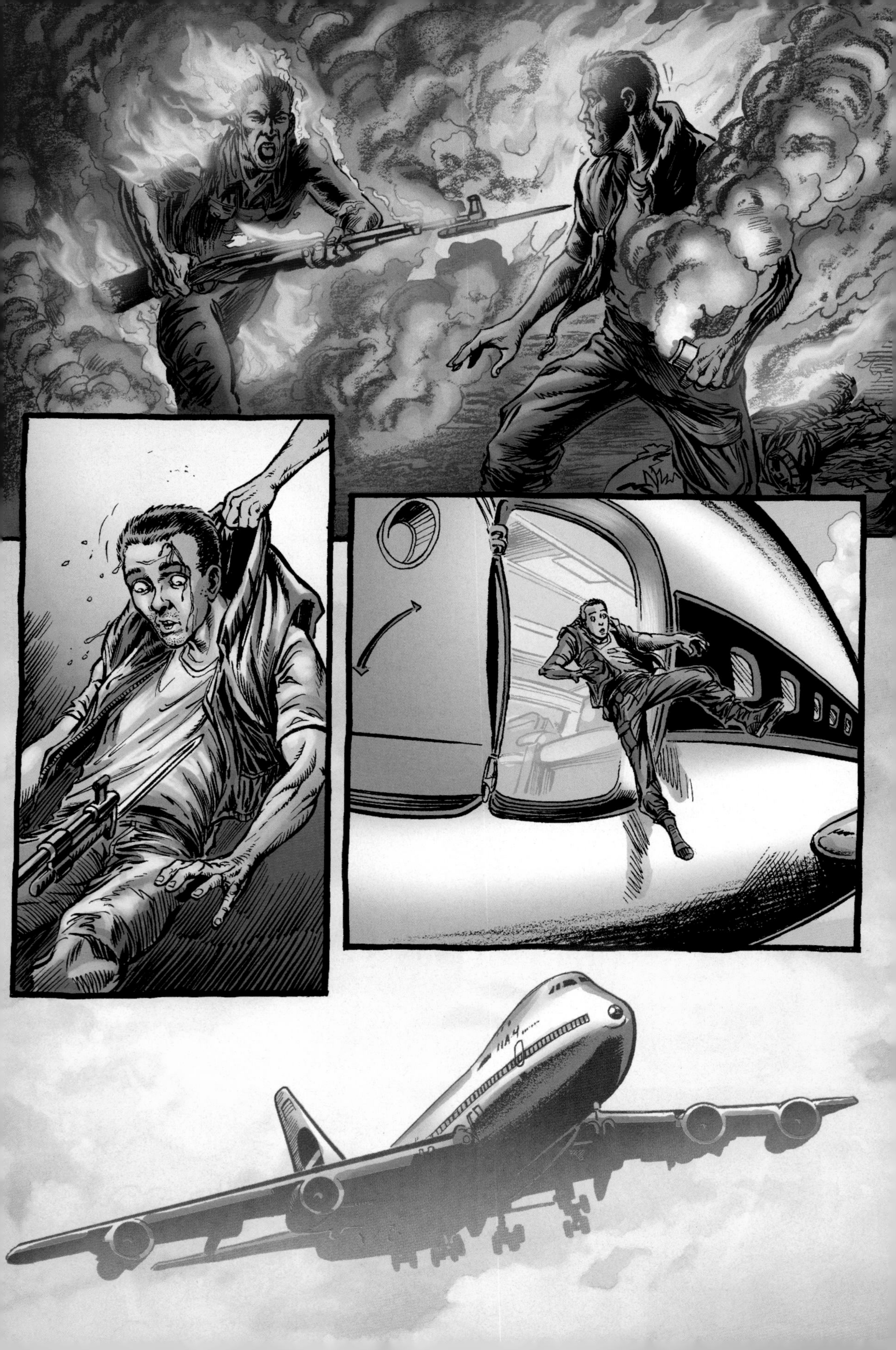

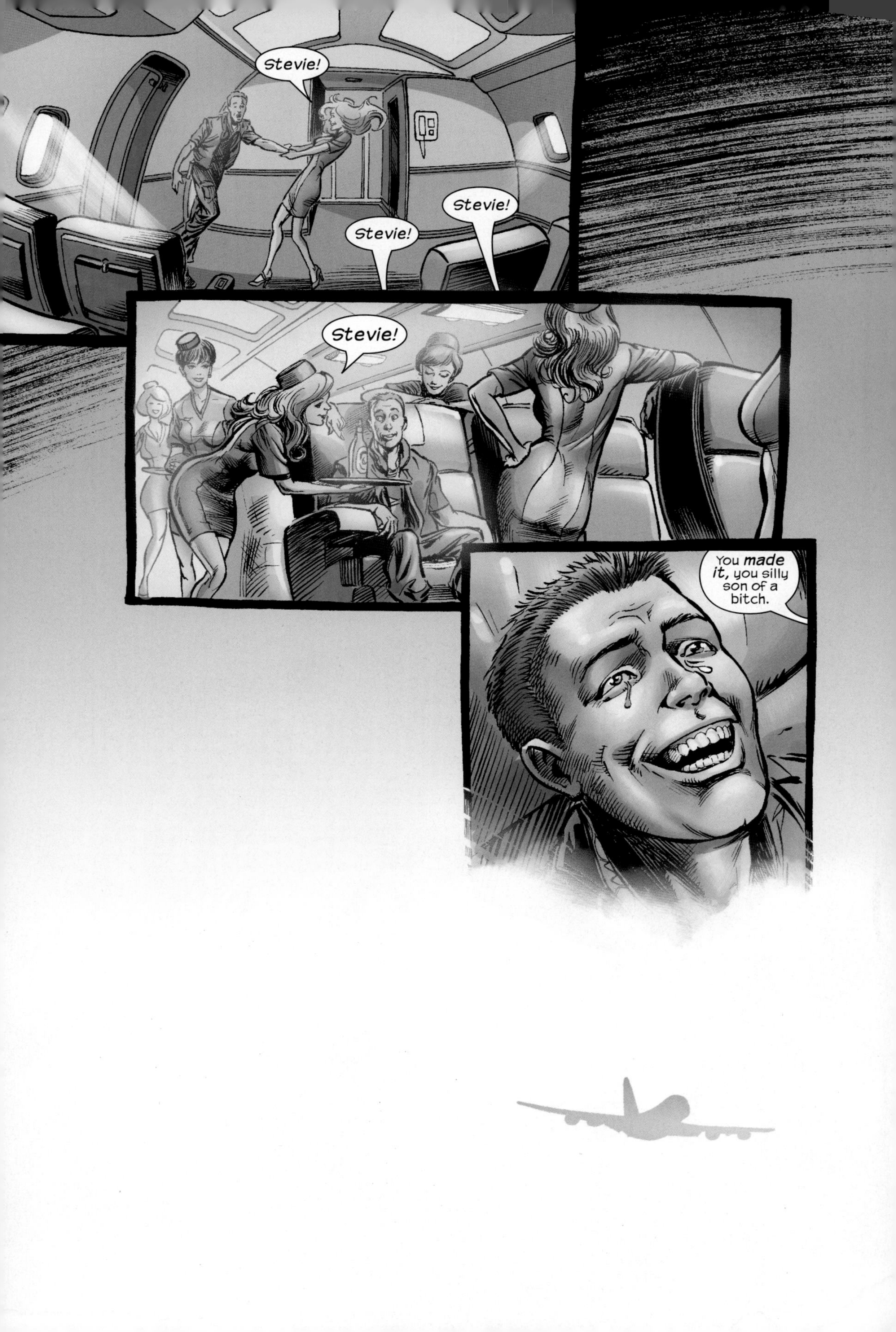
Stevie!
Stevie!
Stevie!
Stevie!
You made it, you silly son of a bitch.

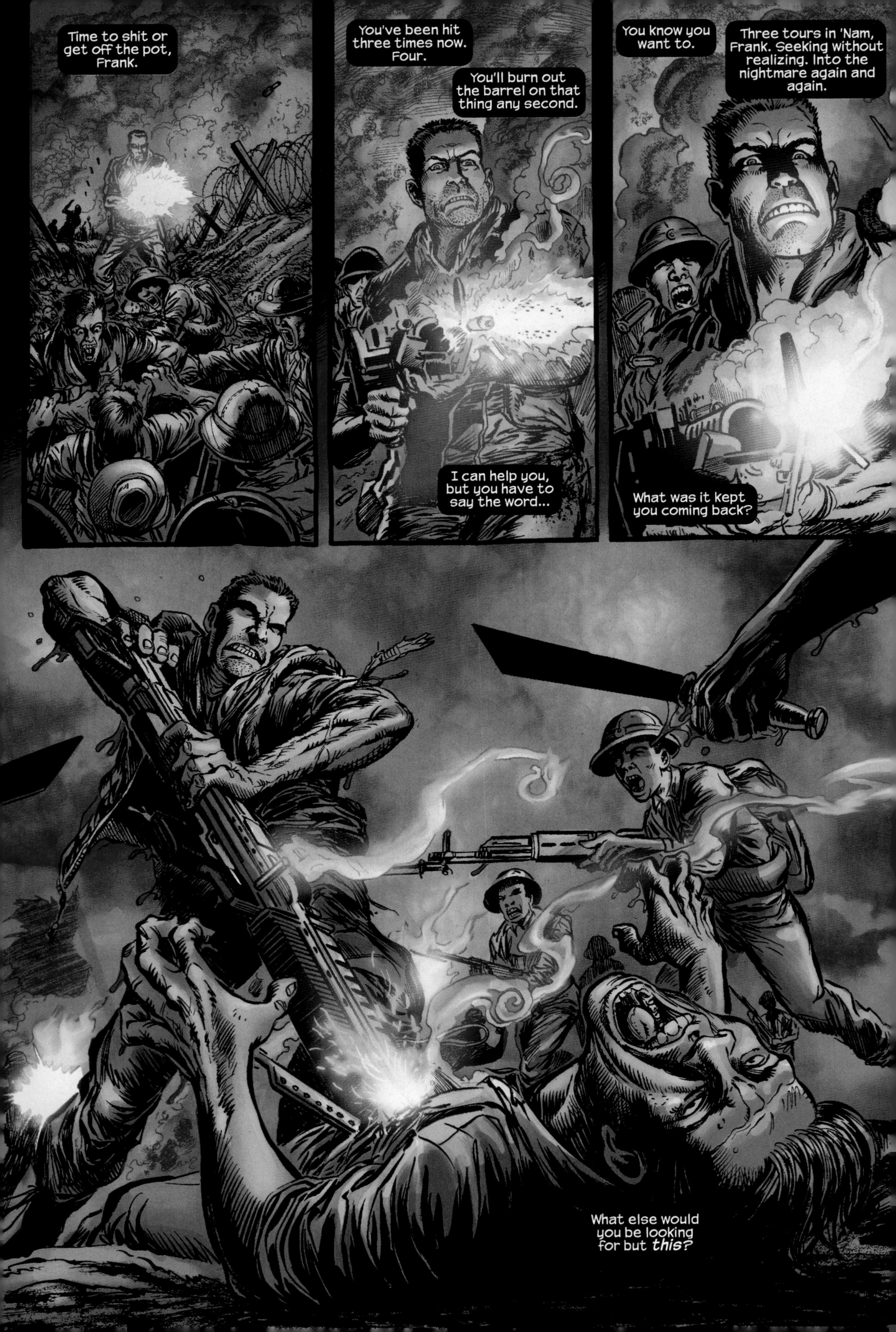
Time to shit or get off the pot, Frank.
You've been hit three times now. Four.
You'll burn out the barrel on that thing any second.
I can help you, but you have to say the word...
You know you want to.
Three tours in 'Nam, Frank. Seeking without realizing. Into the nightmare again and again.
What was it kept you coming back?
What else would you be looking for but *this?*

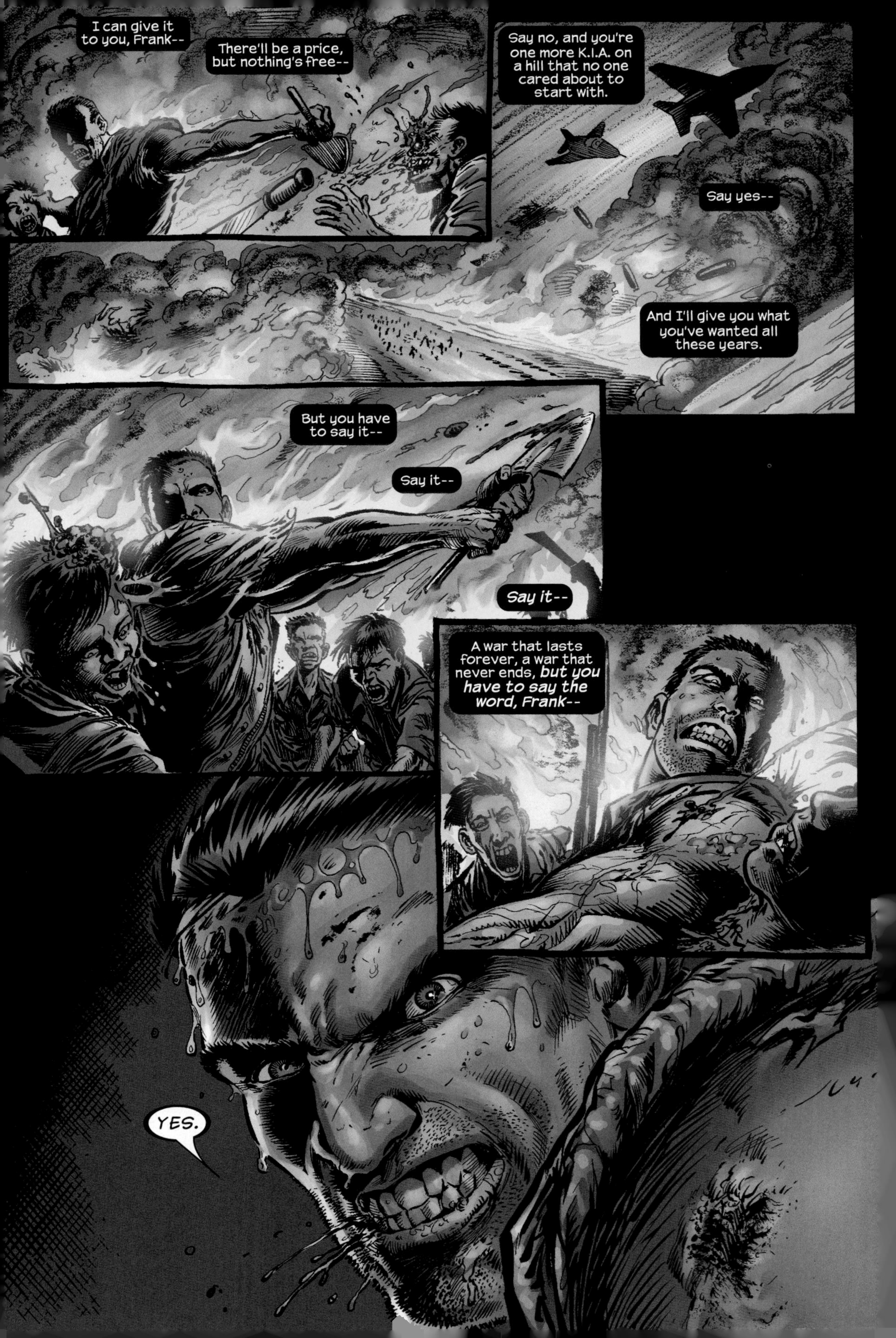
I can give it to you, Frank--
There'll be a price, but nothing's free--
Say no, and you're one more K.I.A. on a hill that no one cared about to start with.
Say yes--
And I'll give you what you've wanted all these years.
But you have to say it--
Say it--
Say it--
A war that lasts forever, a war that never ends, ***but you have to say the word, Frank--***
YES.

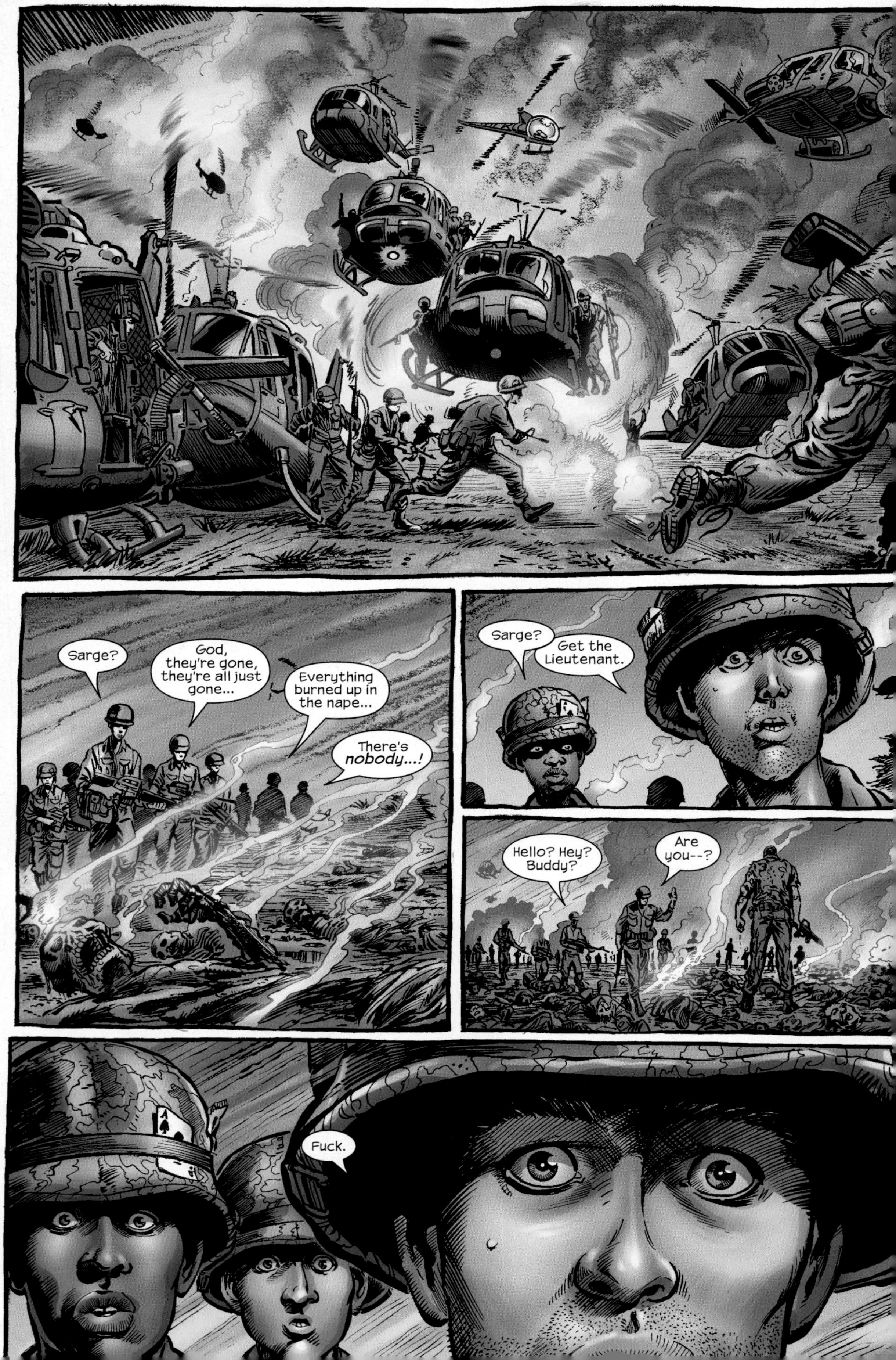
Sarge?
God, they're gone, they're all just gone...
Everything burned up in the nape...
There's *nobody...!*
Sarge?
Get the Lieutenant.
Hello? Hey? Buddy?
Are you--?
Fuck.

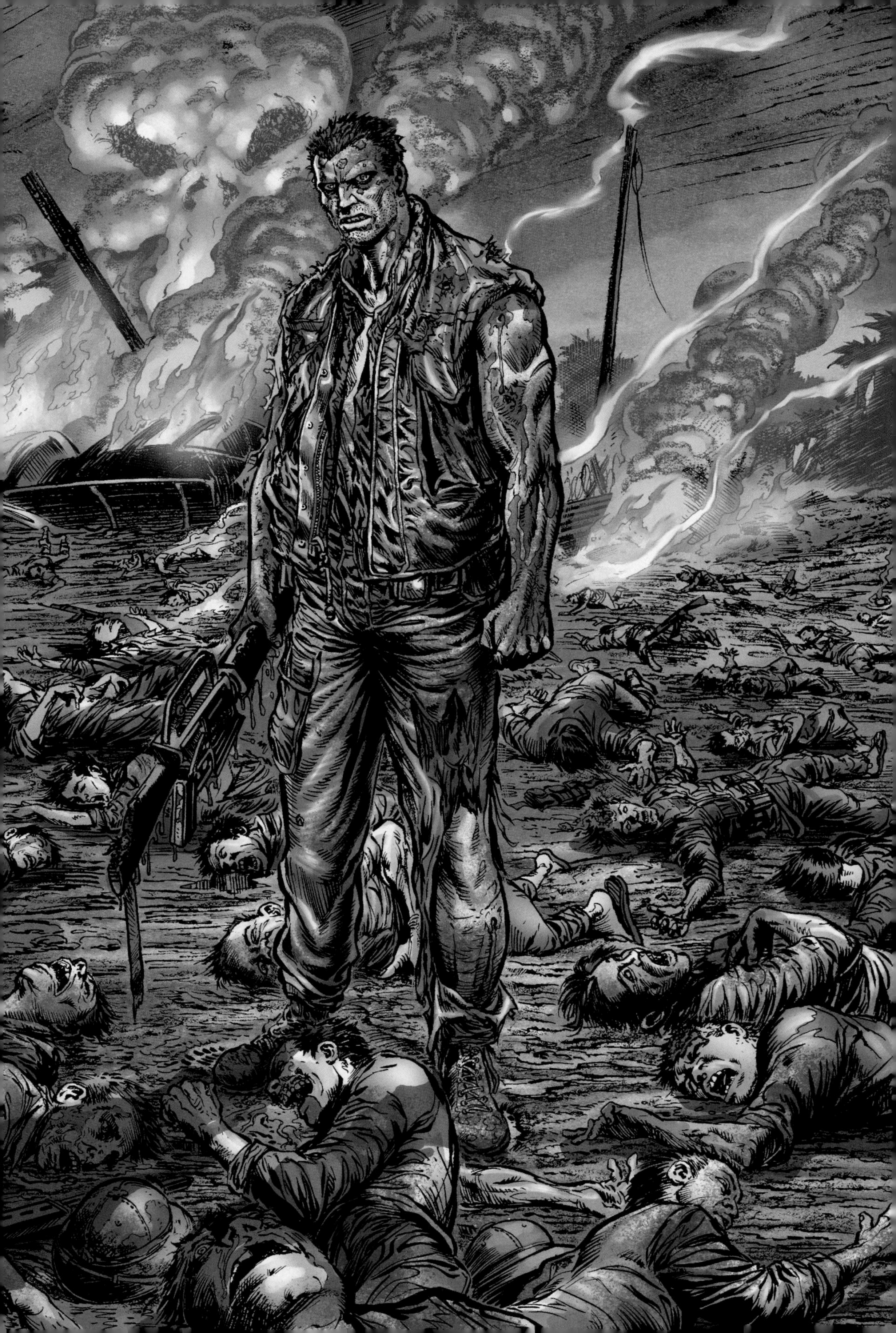

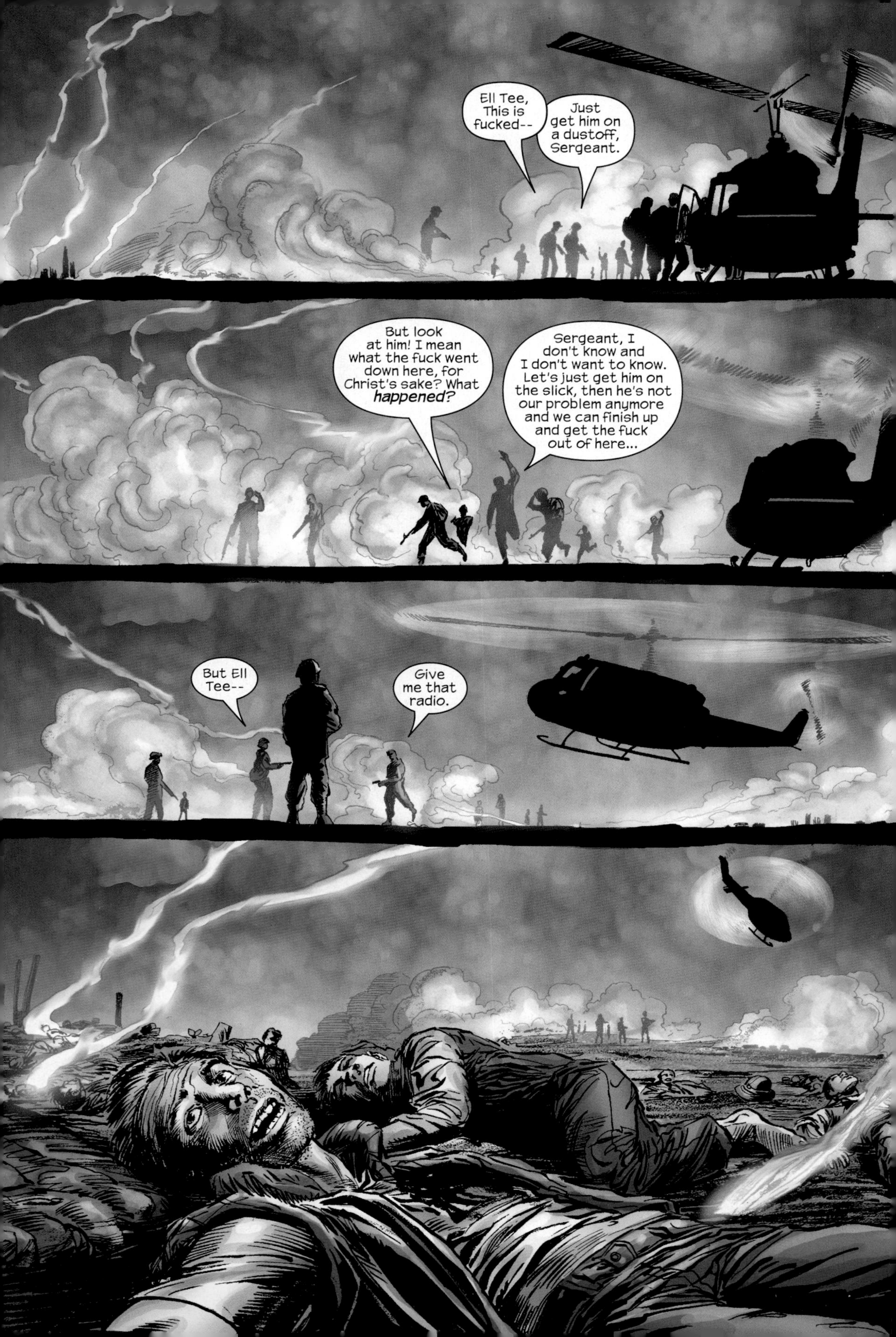
Ell Tee, This is fucked--
Just get him on a dustoff, Sergeant.
But look at him! I mean what the fuck went down here, for Christ's sake? What *happened*?
Sergeant, I don't know and I don't want to know. Let's just get him on the slick, then he's not our problem anymore and we can finish up and get the fuck out of here...
But Ell Tee--
Give me that radio.

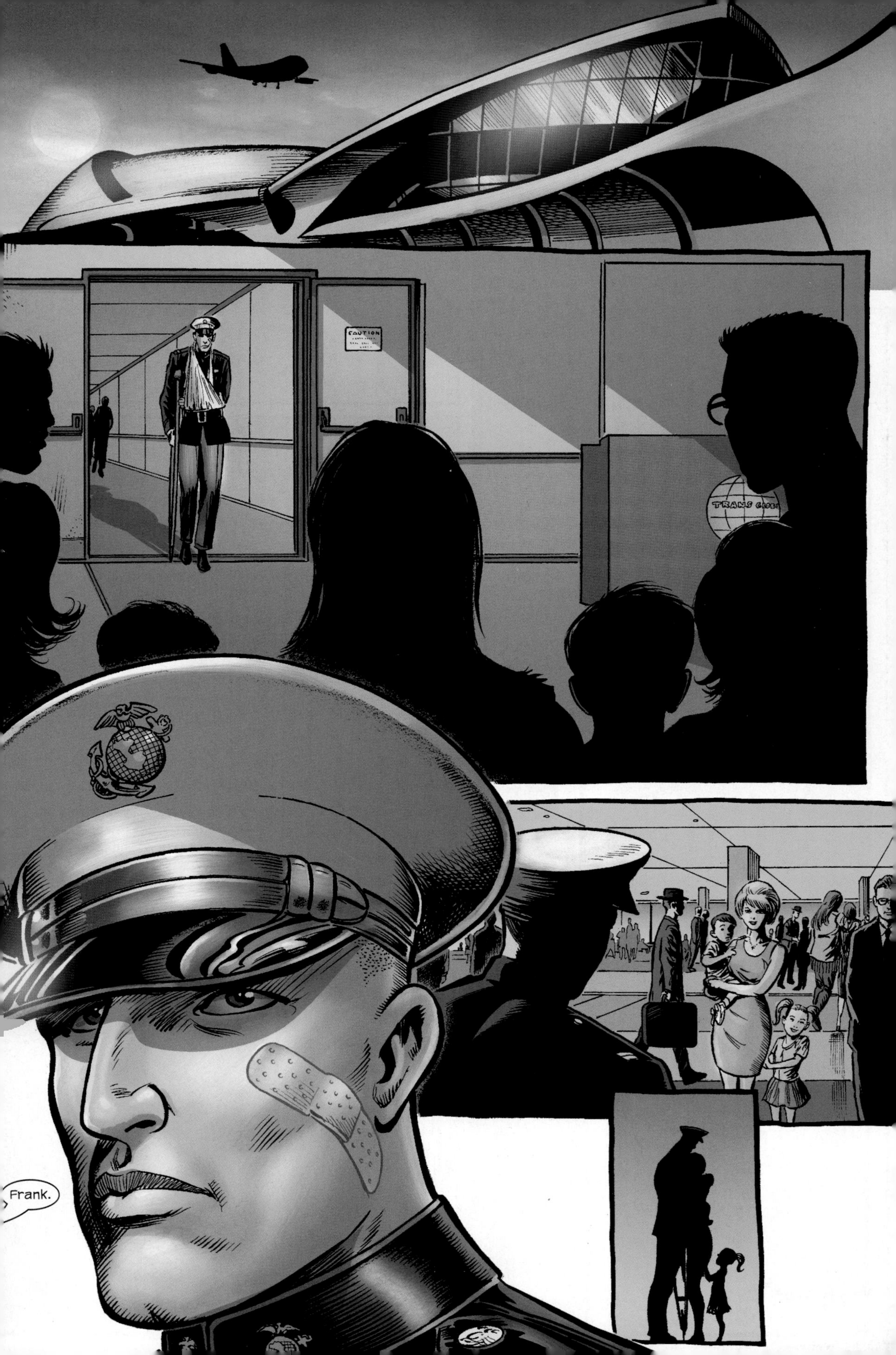
CAUTION
TRANS
Frank.

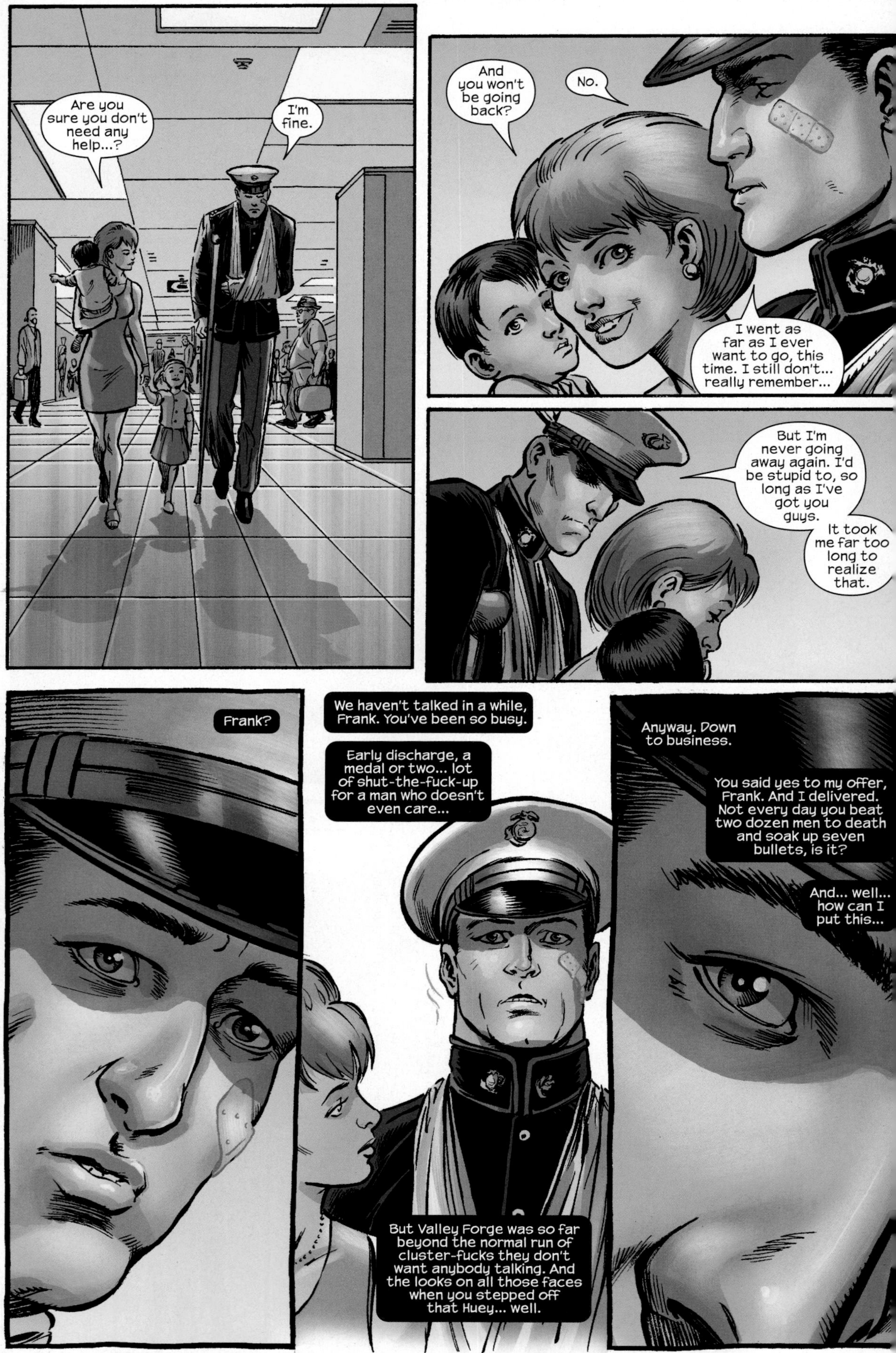
Are you sure you don't need any help...?
I'm fine.
And you won't be going back?
No.
I went as far as I ever want to go, this time. I still don't... really remember...
But I'm never going away again. I'd be stupid to, so long as I've got you guys.
It took me far too long to realize that.
Frank?
We haven't talked in a while, Frank. You've been so busy.
Early discharge, a medal or two... lot of shut-the-fuck-up for a man who doesn't even care...
But Valley Forge was so far beyond the normal run of cluster-fucks they don't want anybody talking. And the looks on all those faces when you stepped off that Huey... well.
Anyway. Down to business.
You said yes to my offer, Frank. And I delivered. Not every day you beat two dozen men to death and soak up seven bullets, is it?
And... well... how can I put this...

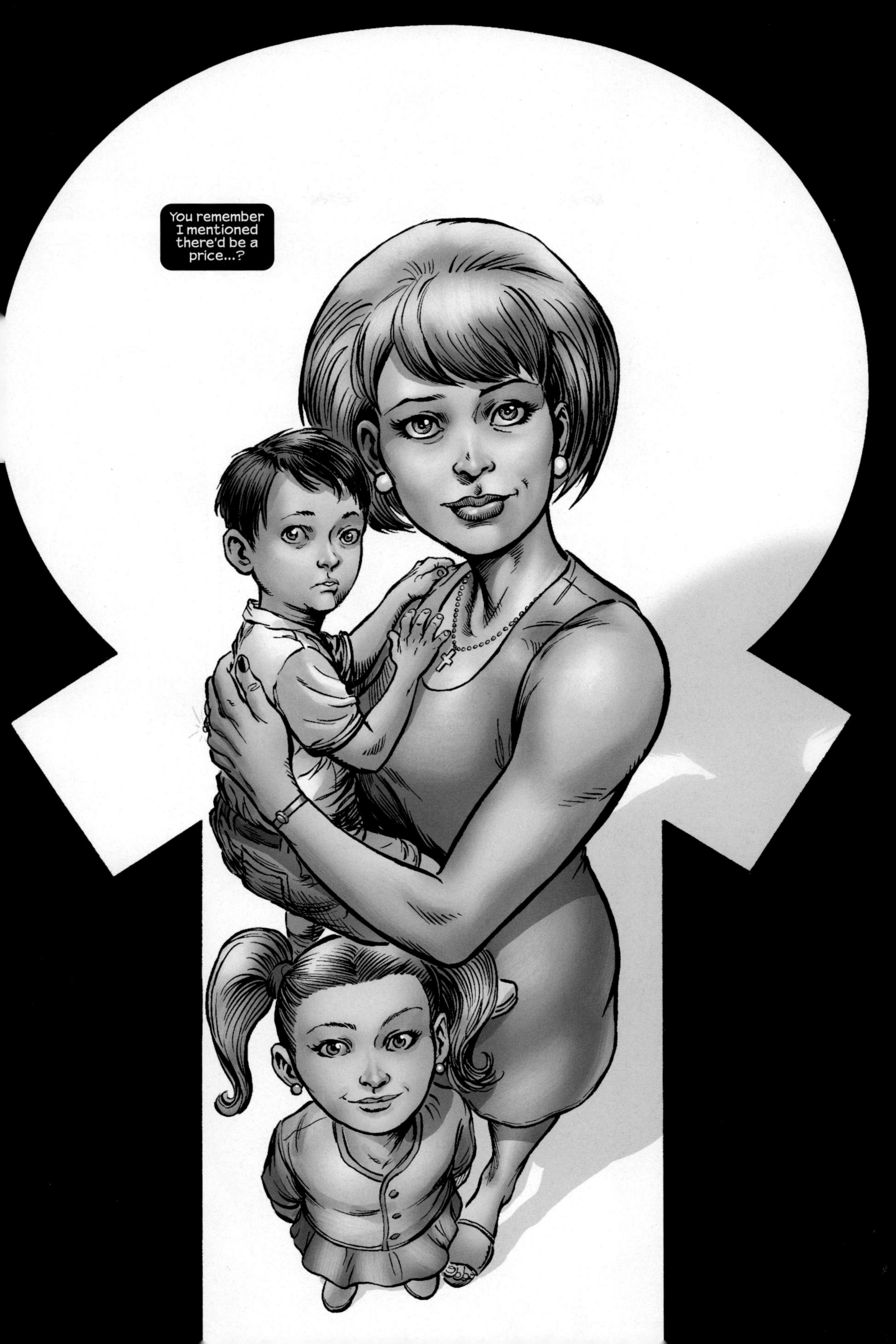
You remember I mentioned there'd be a price...?

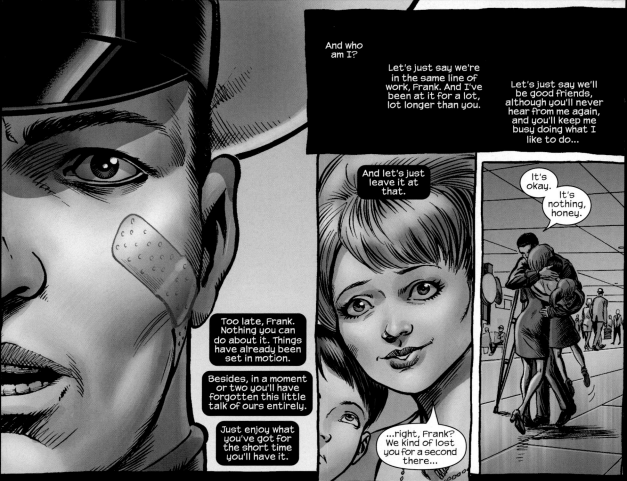

And who am I?

Let's just say we're in the same line of work, Frank. And I've been at it for a lot, lot longer than you.

Let's just say we'll be good friends, although you'll never hear from me again, and you'll keep me busy doing what I like to do...

And let's just leave it at that.

It's okay. It's nothing, honey.

Too late, Frank. Nothing you can do about it. Things have already been set in motion.

Besides, in a moment or two you'll have forgotten this little talk of ours entirely.

Just enjoy what you've got for the short time you'll have it.

...right, Frank? We kind of lost you for a second there...

Hold on tight.

The End

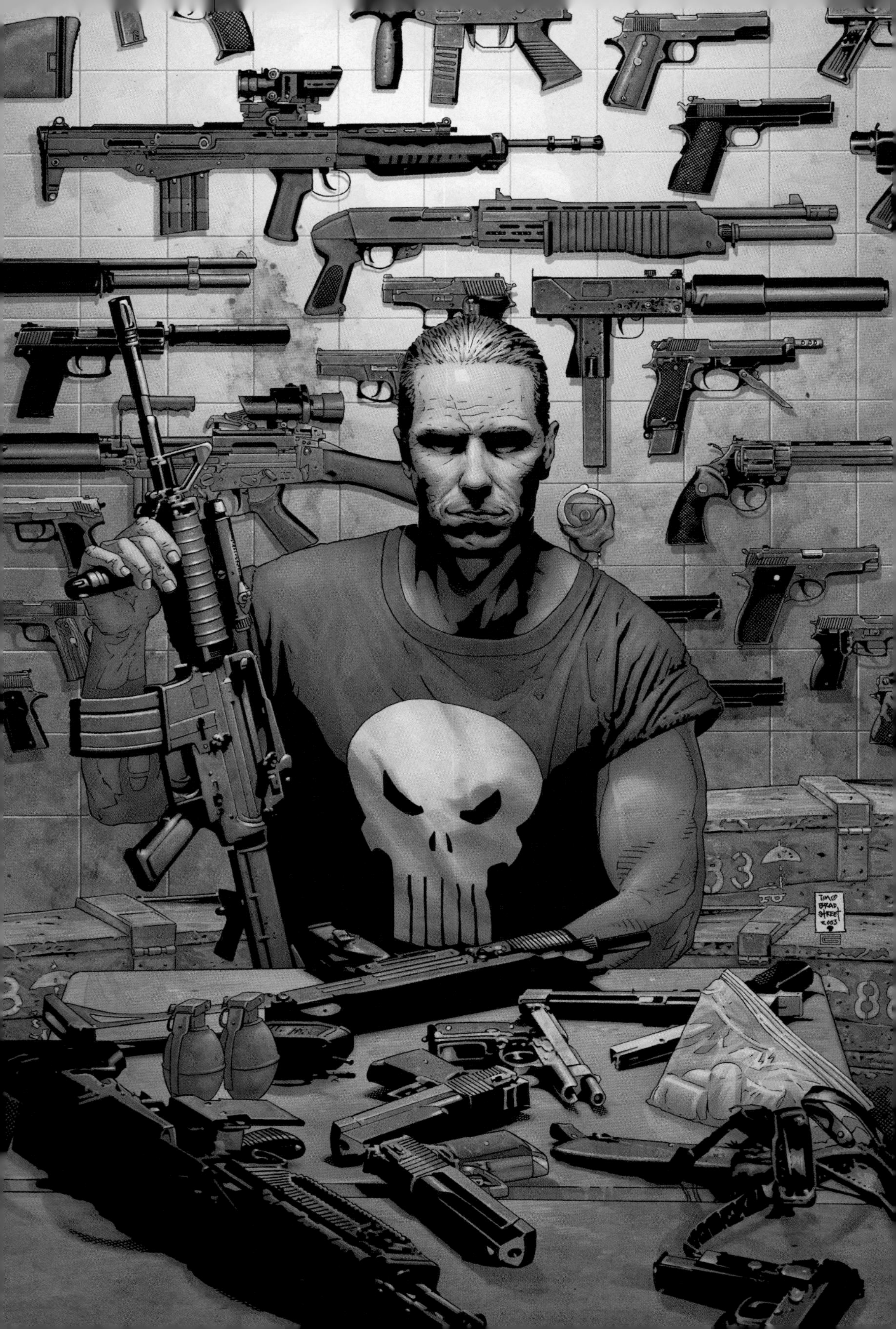

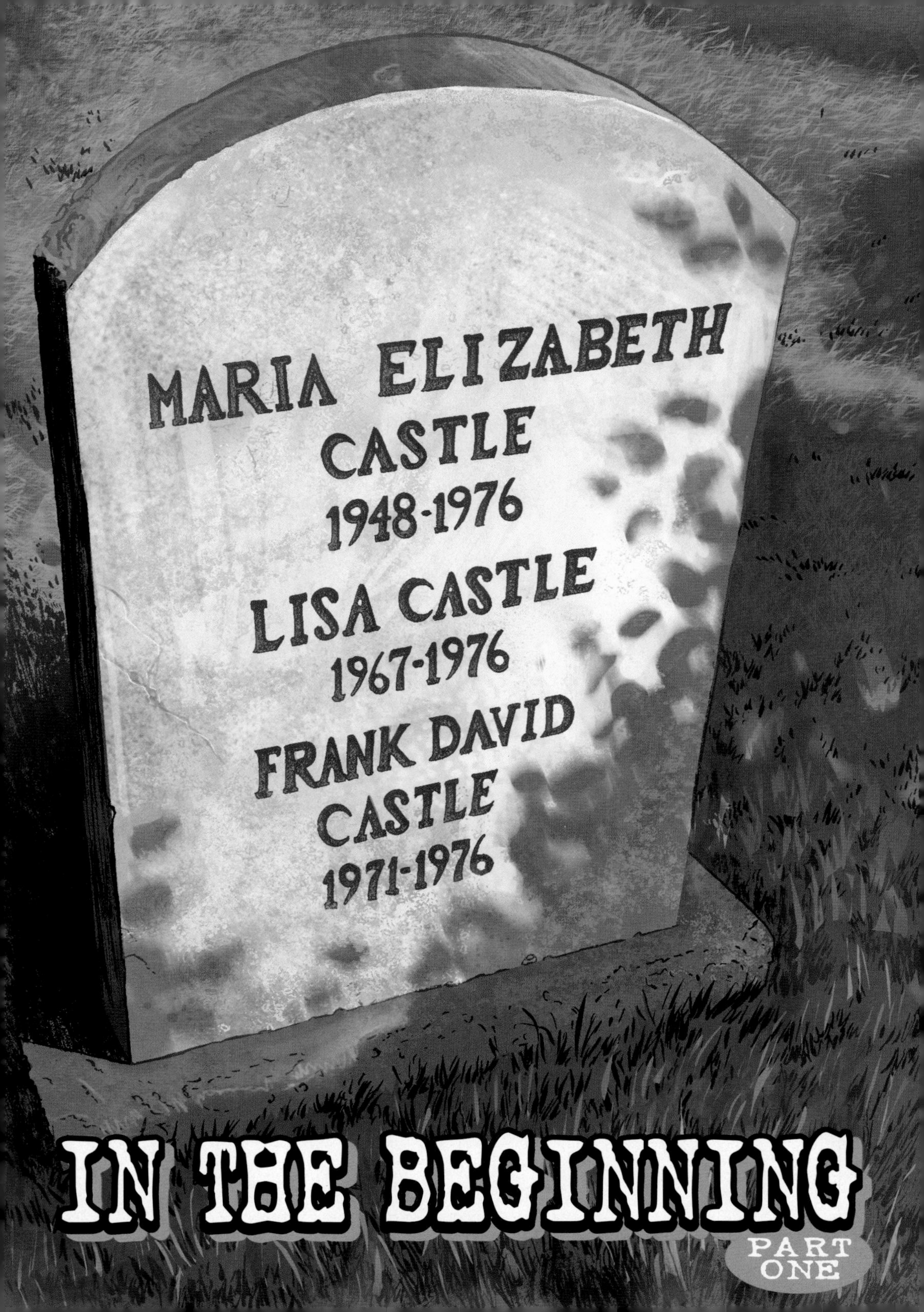
MARIA ELIZABETH
CASTLE
1948-1976
LISA CASTLE
1967-1976
FRANK DAVID
CASTLE
1971-1976
IN THE BEGINNING
PART ONE

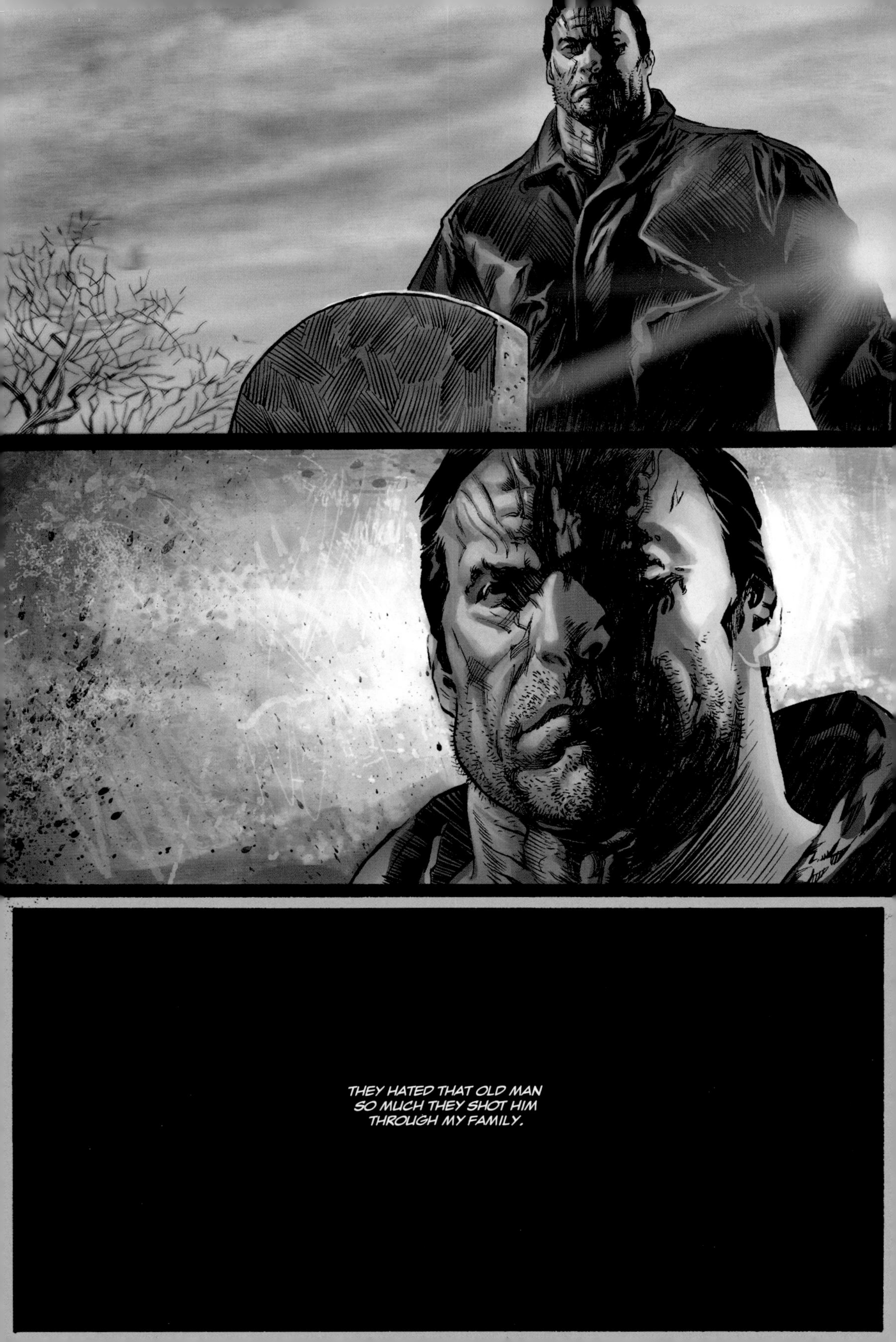
THEY HATED THAT OLD MAN SO MUCH THEY SHOT HIM THROUGH MY FAMILY.

THE WORLD WENT CRAZY ON A SUMMER'S DAY IN CENTRAL PARK, IN THE TIME BEFORE UZIS AND BERETTAS, BEFORE NINE MILLIMETER POPGUNS RULED THE STREETS.

IT WAS A THOMPSON, LIKE THE ONES OUR FATHERS CARRIED, AND I RECOGNIZED ITS RATTLE EVEN AS ITS BIG, MAN-STOPPING FORTY-FIVES PUNCHED BLOOD AND BREATH FROM MY LUNGS.

I HIT THE GROUND BESIDE MY DAUGHTER. SHE'D BEEN GUTSHOT, BADLY, AND WHEN SHE SAW THE THINGS THAT BOILED AND WRIGGLED FROM HER BELLY THE EXPRESSION ON HER FACE WAS NOT A LITTLE GIRL'S.

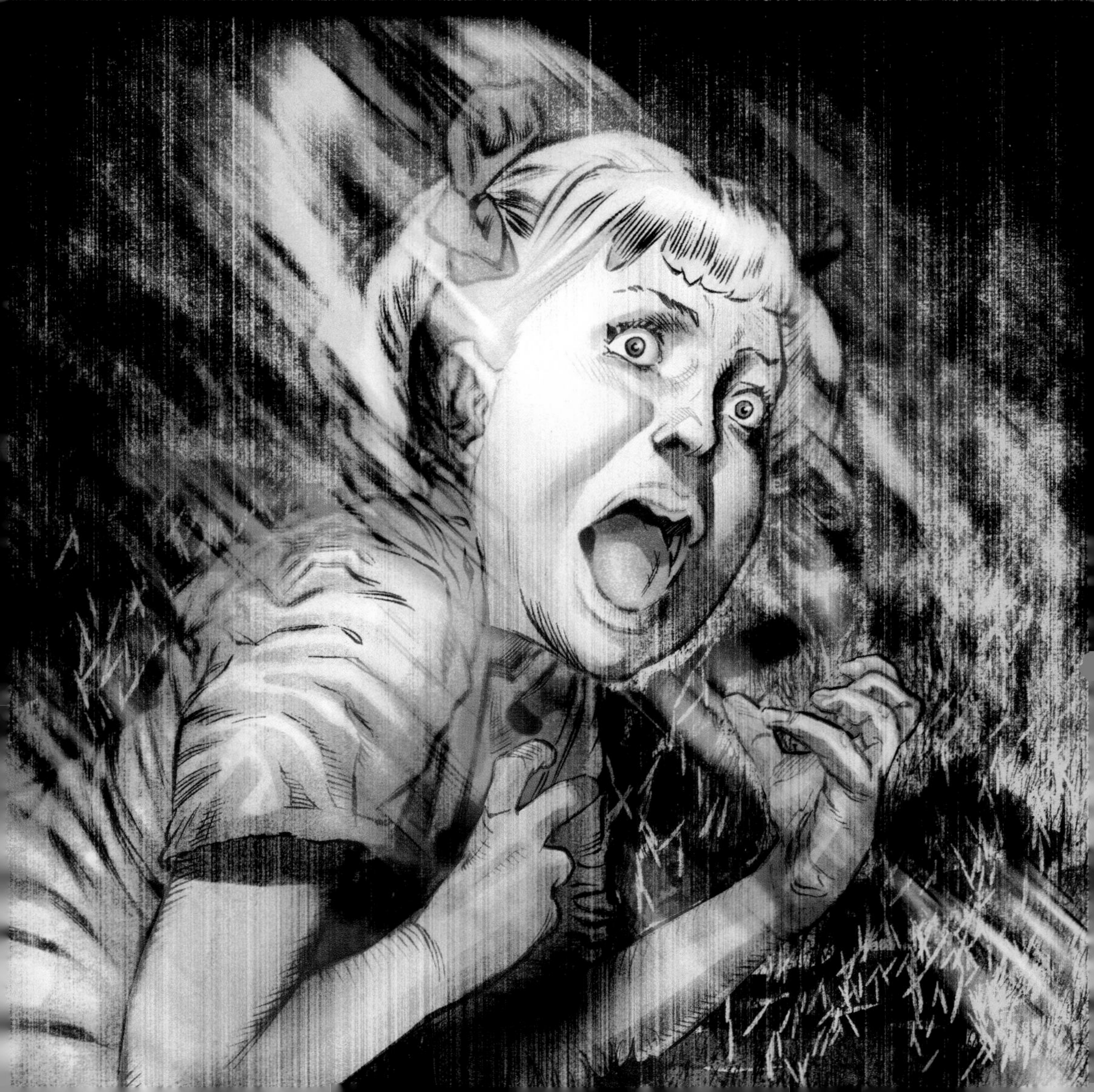

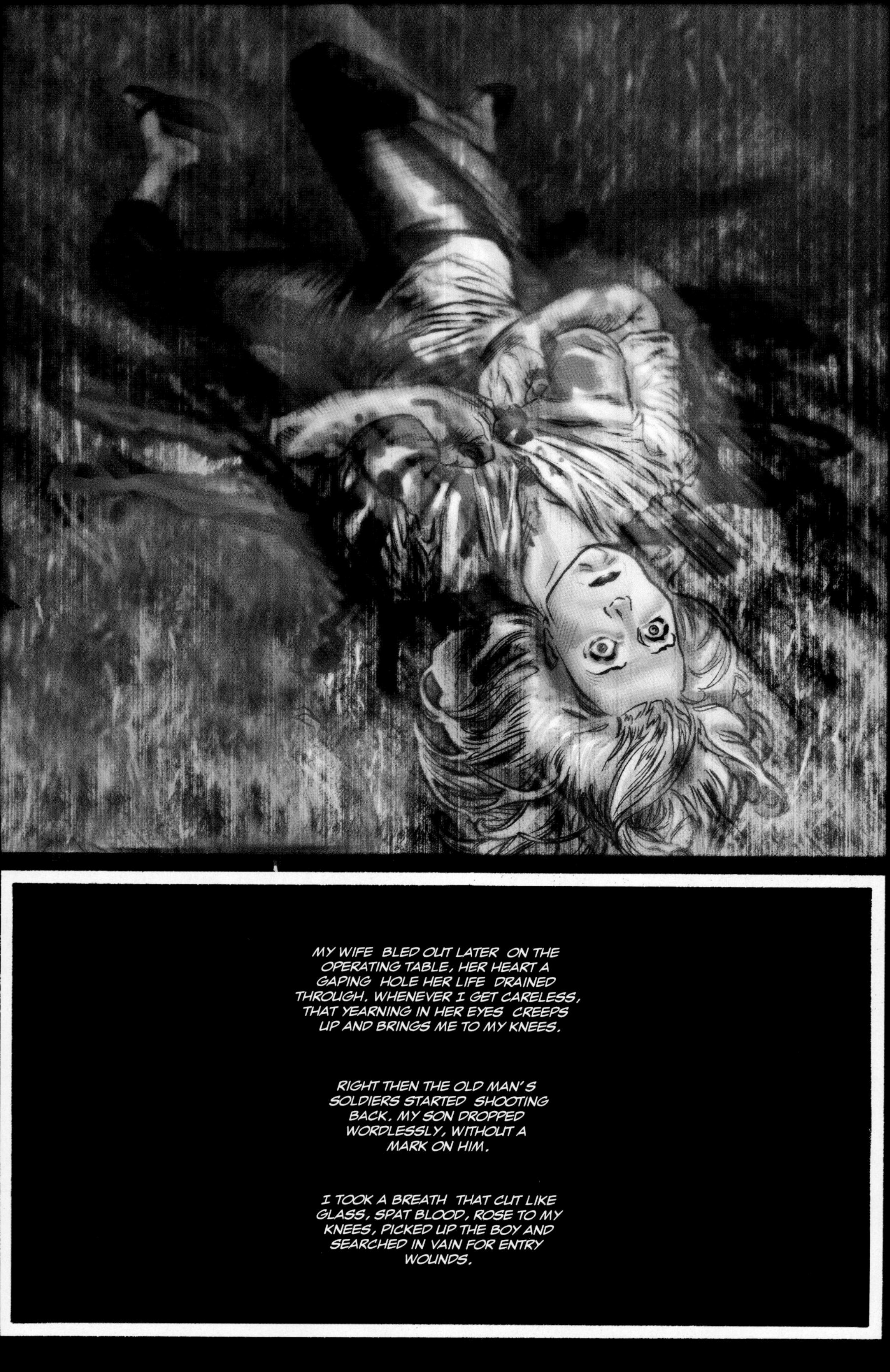
MY WIFE BLED OUT LATER ON THE OPERATING TABLE, HER HEART A GAPING HOLE HER LIFE DRAINED THROUGH. WHENEVER I GET CARELESS, THAT YEARNING IN HER EYES CREEPS UP AND BRINGS ME TO MY KNEES.
RIGHT THEN THE OLD MAN'S SOLDIERS STARTED SHOOTING BACK. MY SON DROPPED WORDLESSLY, WITHOUT A MARK ON HIM.
I TOOK A BREATH THAT CUT LIKE GLASS, SPAT BLOOD, ROSE TO MY KNEES, PICKED UP THE BOY AND SEARCHED IN VAIN FOR ENTRY WOUNDS.

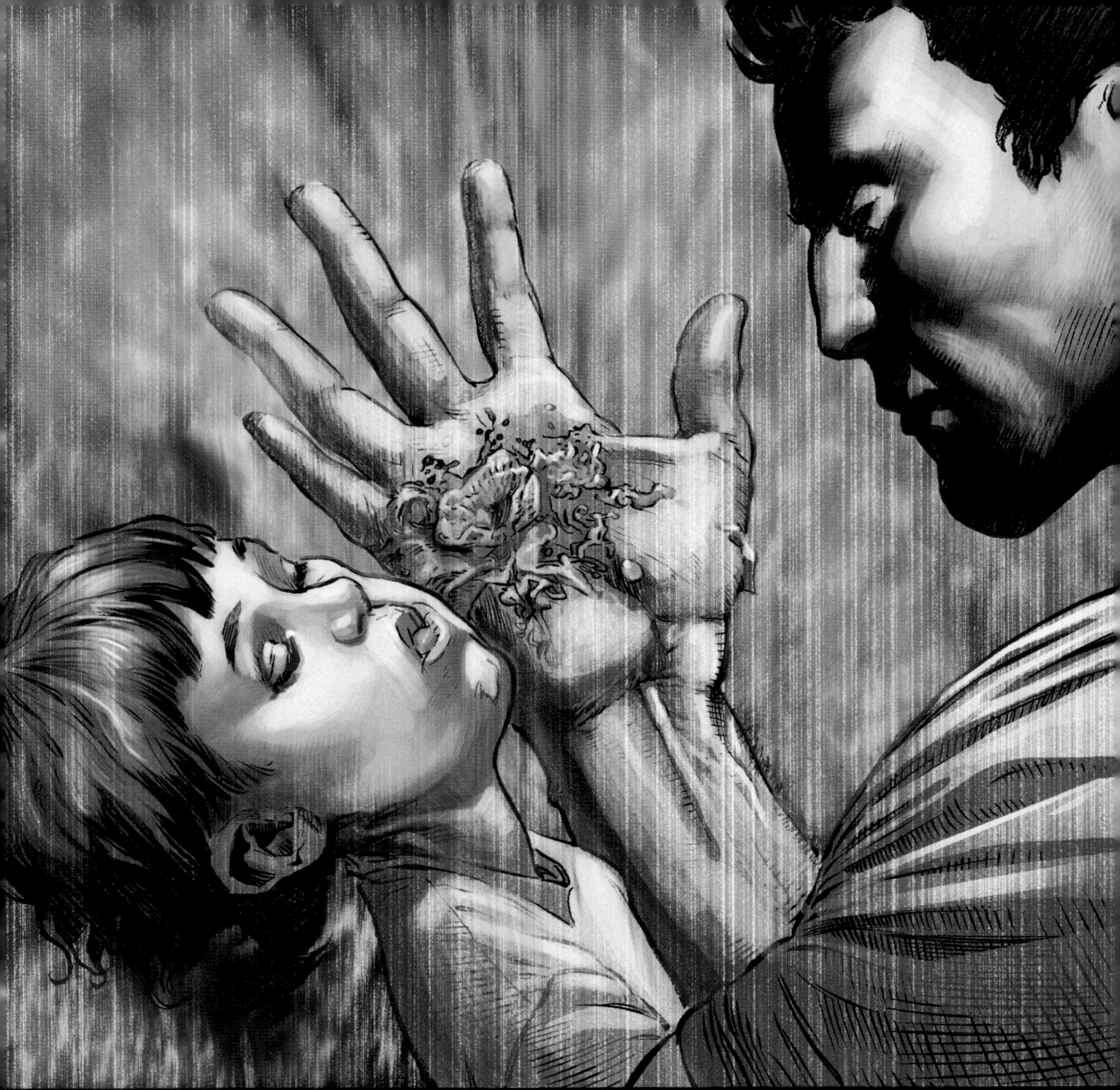

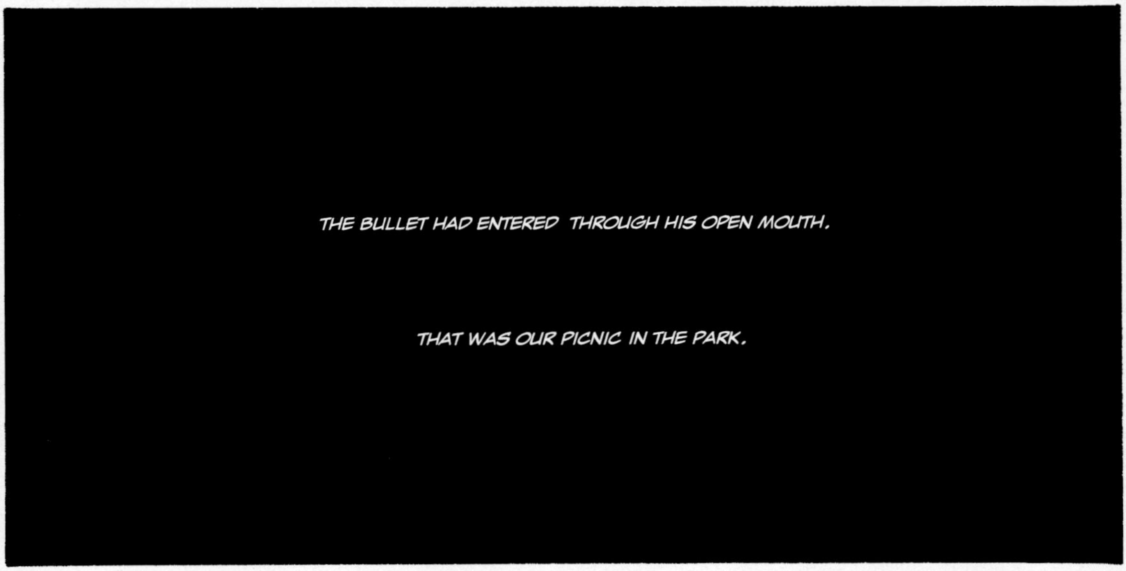
THE BULLET HAD ENTERED THROUGH HIS OPEN MOUTH.
THAT WAS OUR PICNIC IN THE PARK.

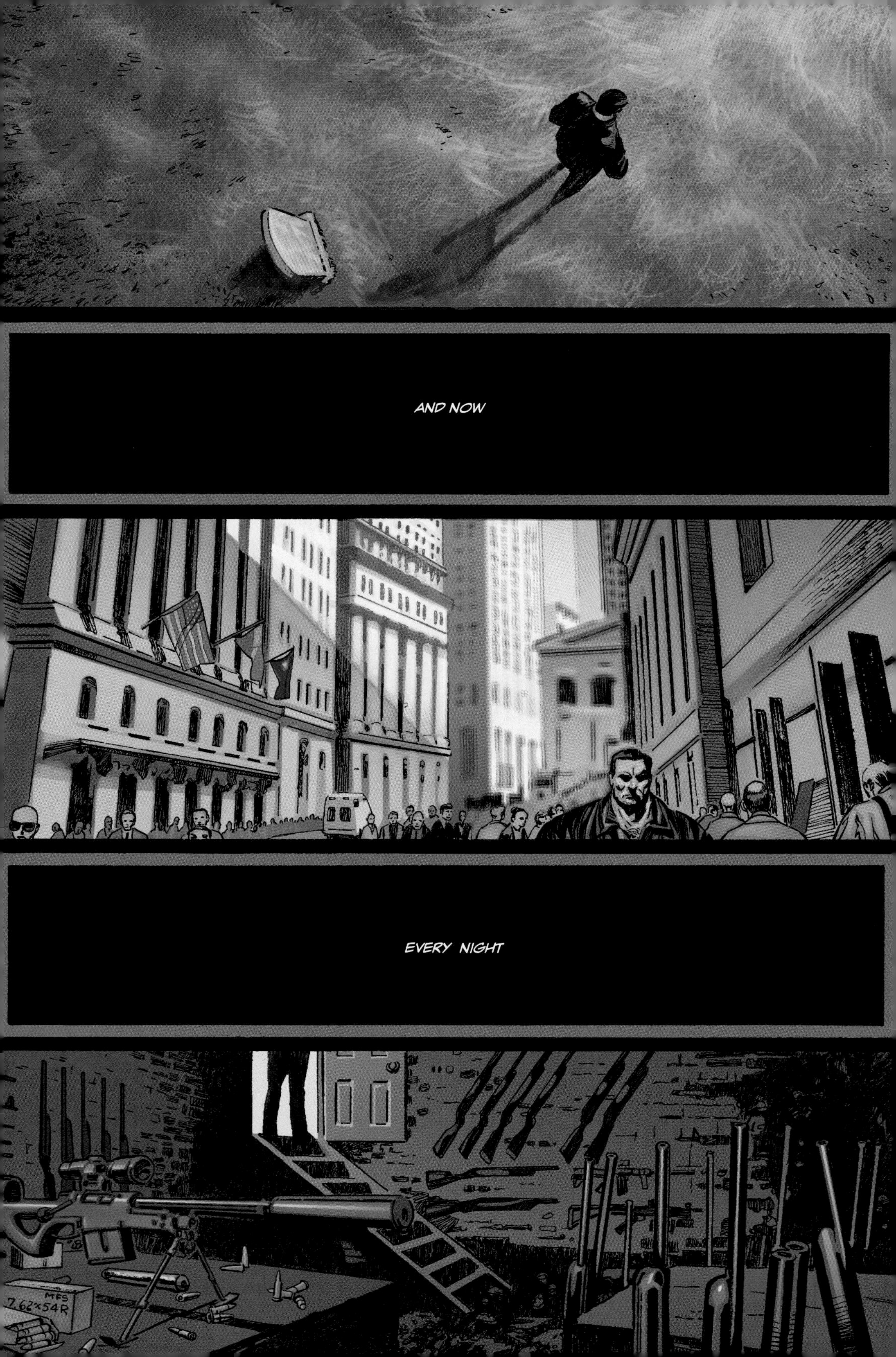
AND NOW
EVERY NIGHT
MFS
7.62x54R

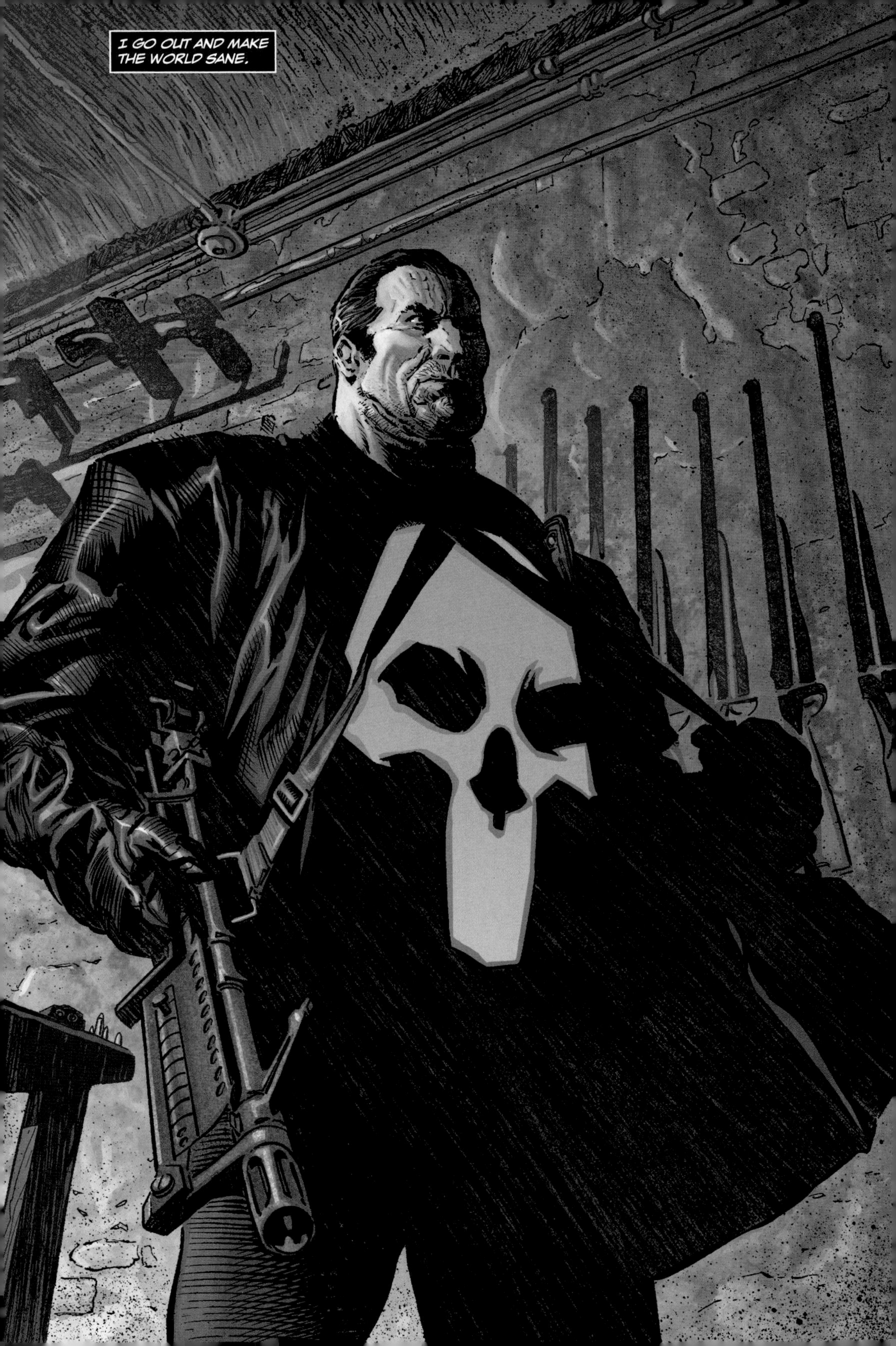
I GO OUT AND MAKE
THE WORLD SANE.

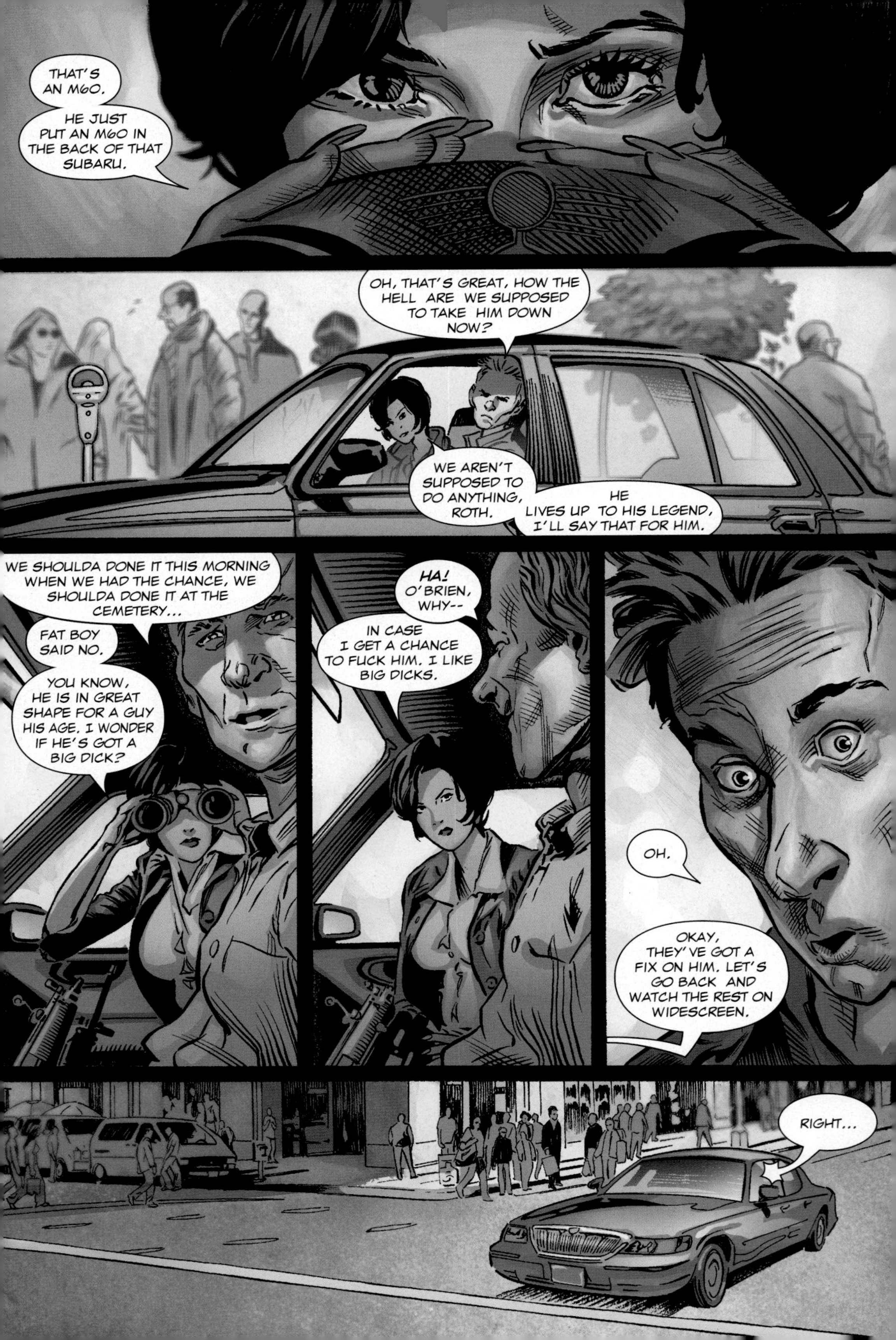
THAT'S AN M60.
HE JUST PUT AN M60 IN THE BACK OF THAT SUBARU.
OH, THAT'S GREAT, HOW THE HELL ARE WE SUPPOSED TO TAKE HIM DOWN NOW?
WE AREN'T SUPPOSED TO DO ANYTHING, ROTH.
HE LIVES UP TO HIS LEGEND, I'LL SAY THAT FOR HIM.
WE SHOULDA DONE IT THIS MORNING WHEN WE HAD THE CHANCE, WE SHOULDA DONE IT AT THE CEMETERY...
FAT BOY SAID NO.
YOU KNOW, HE IS IN GREAT SHAPE FOR A GUY HIS AGE. I WONDER IF HE'S GOT A BIG DICK?
HA! O'BRIEN, WHY--
IN CASE I GET A CHANCE TO FUCK HIM. I LIKE BIG DICKS.
OH.
OKAY, THEY'VE GOT A FIX ON HIM. LET'S GO BACK AND WATCH THE REST ON WIDESCREEN.
RIGHT...

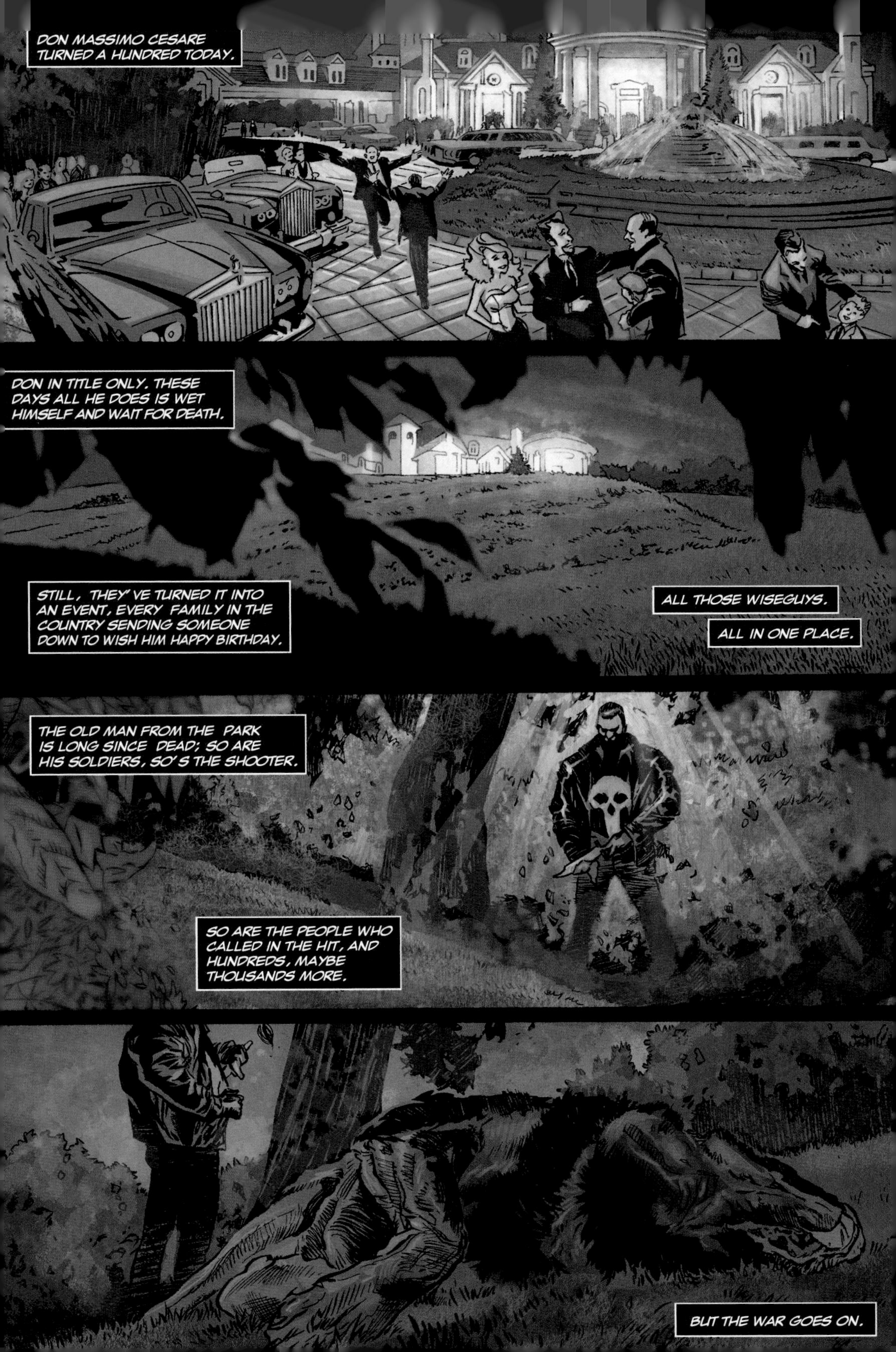
DON MASSIMO CESARE TURNED A HUNDRED TODAY.
DON IN TITLE ONLY. THESE DAYS ALL HE DOES IS WET HIMSELF AND WAIT FOR DEATH.
STILL, THEY'VE TURNED IT INTO AN EVENT, EVERY FAMILY IN THE COUNTRY SENDING SOMEONE DOWN TO WISH HIM HAPPY BIRTHDAY.
ALL THOSE WISEGUYS.
ALL IN ONE PLACE.
THE OLD MAN FROM THE PARK IS LONG SINCE DEAD; SO ARE HIS SOLDIERS, SO'S THE SHOOTER.
SO ARE THE PEOPLE WHO CALLED IN THE HIT, AND HUNDREDS, MAYBE THOUSANDS MORE.
BUT THE WAR GOES ON.

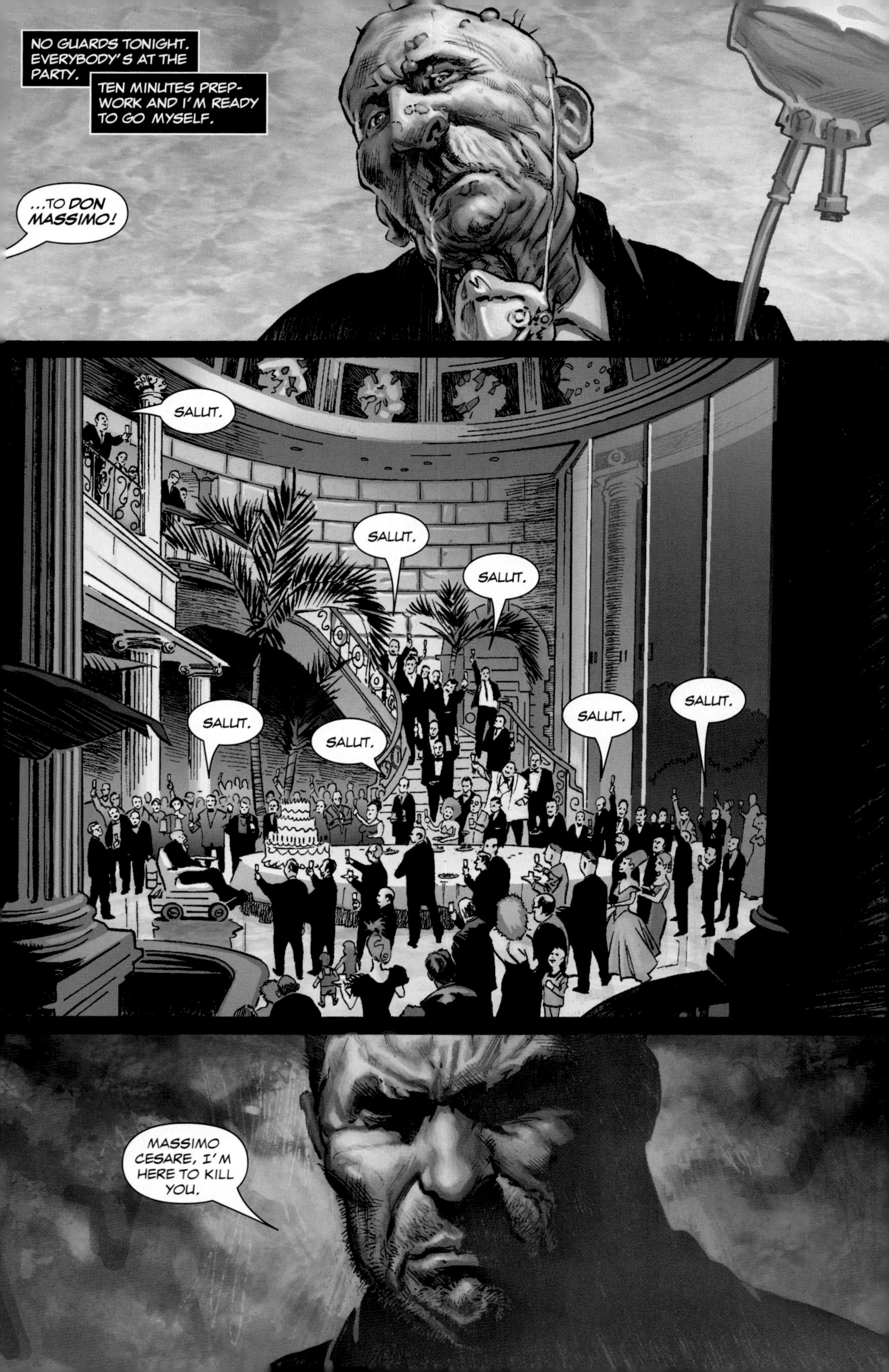

NO GUARDS TONIGHT. EVERYBODY'S AT THE PARTY.
TEN MINUTES PREP-WORK AND I'M READY TO GO MYSELF.
...TO DON MASSIMO!
SALUT.
SALUT.
SALUT.
SALUT.
SALUT.
SALUT.
SALUT.
MASSIMO CESARE, I'M HERE TO KILL YOU.

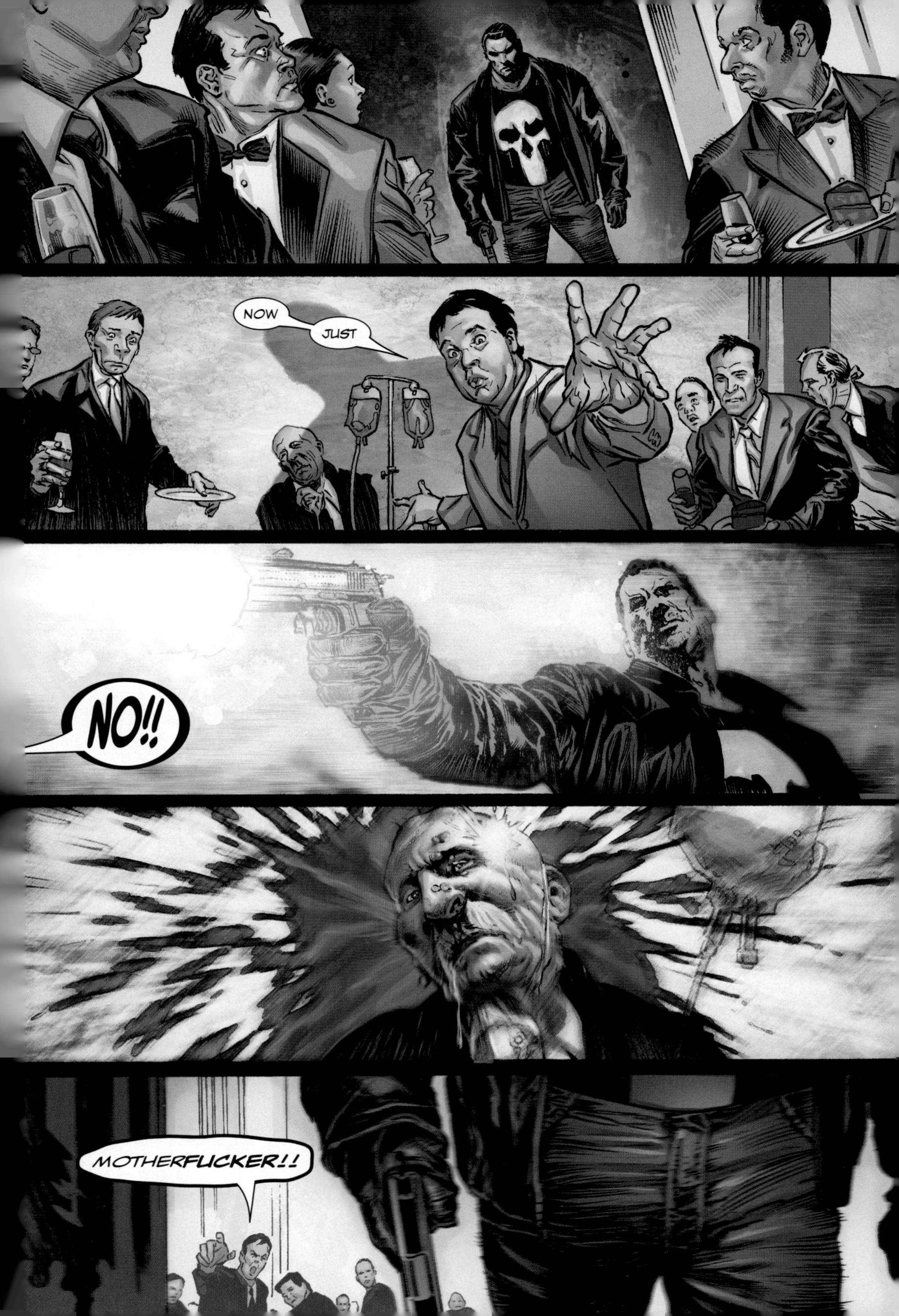
NOW
JUST
NO!!
MOTHERFUCKER!!

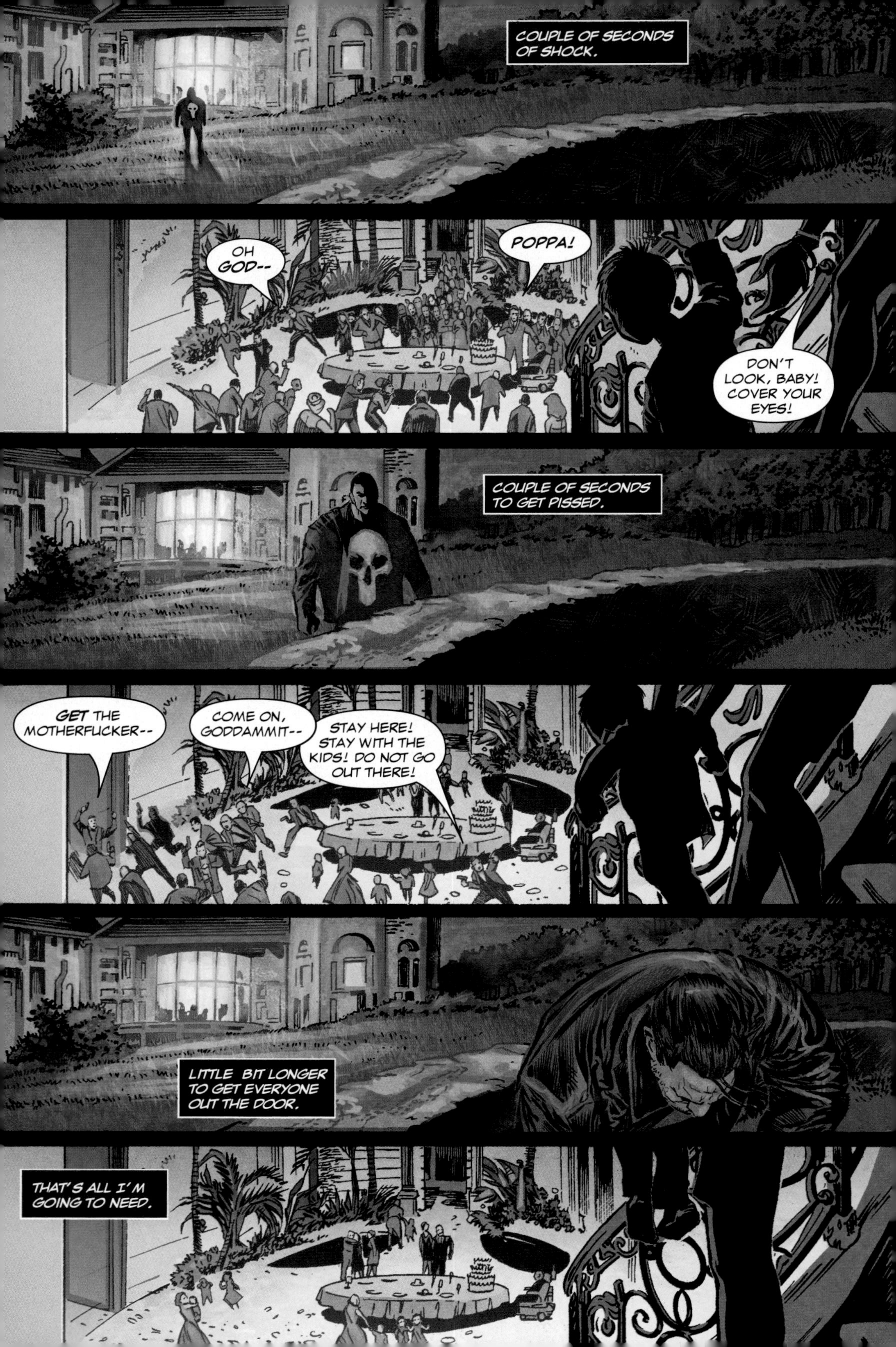
COUPLE OF SECONDS OF SHOCK.
OH GOD--
POPPA!
DON'T LOOK, BABY! COVER YOUR EYES!
COUPLE OF SECONDS TO GET PISSED.
GET THE MOTHERFUCKER--
COME ON, GODDAMMIT--
STAY HERE! STAY WITH THE KIDS! DO NOT GO OUT THERE!
LITTLE BIT LONGER TO GET EVERYONE OUT THE DOOR.
THAT'S ALL I'M GOING TO NEED.

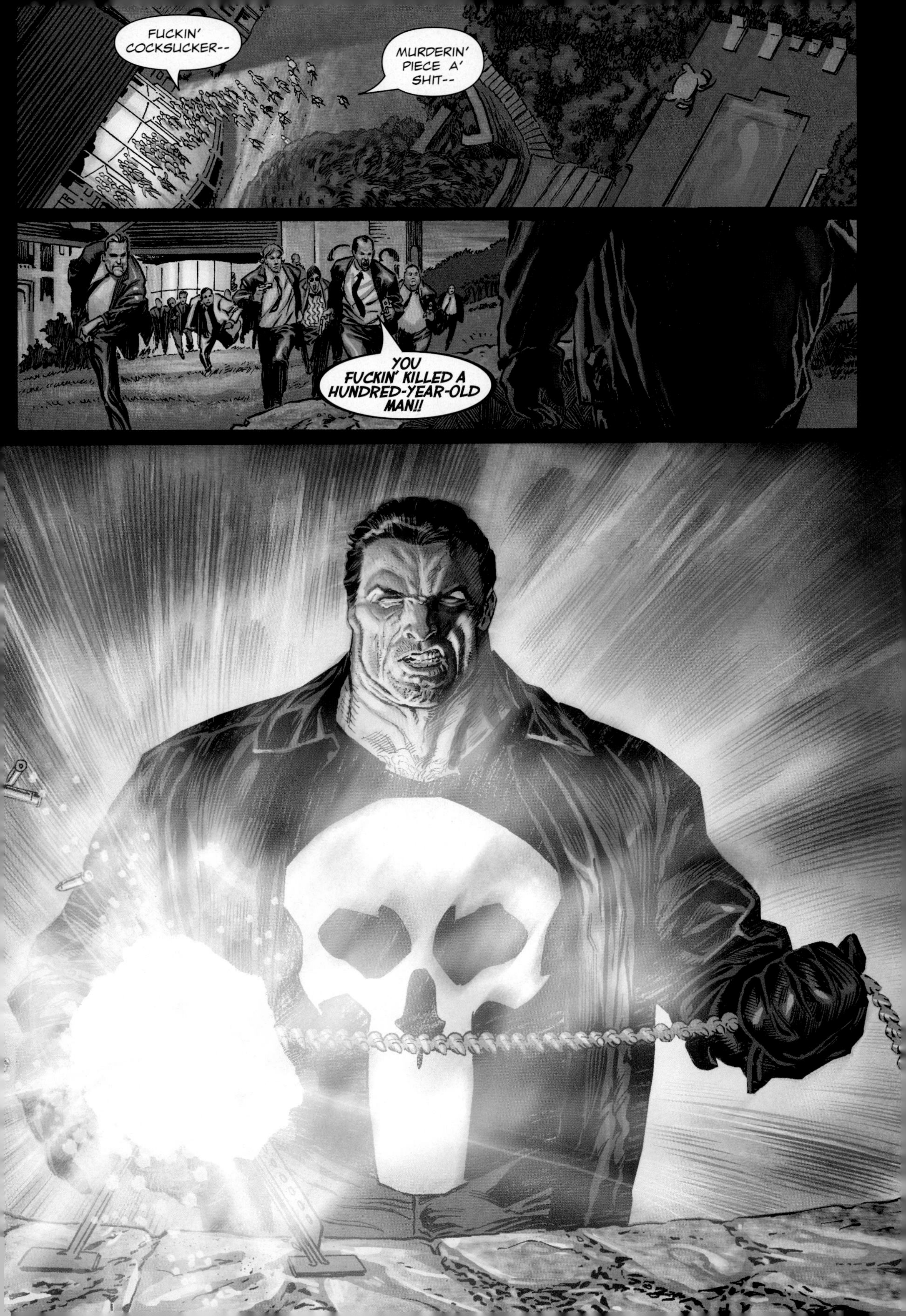

FUCKIN' COCKSUCKER--
MURDERIN' PIECE A' SHIT--
YOU FUCKIN' KILLED A HUNDRED-YEAR-OLD MAN!!

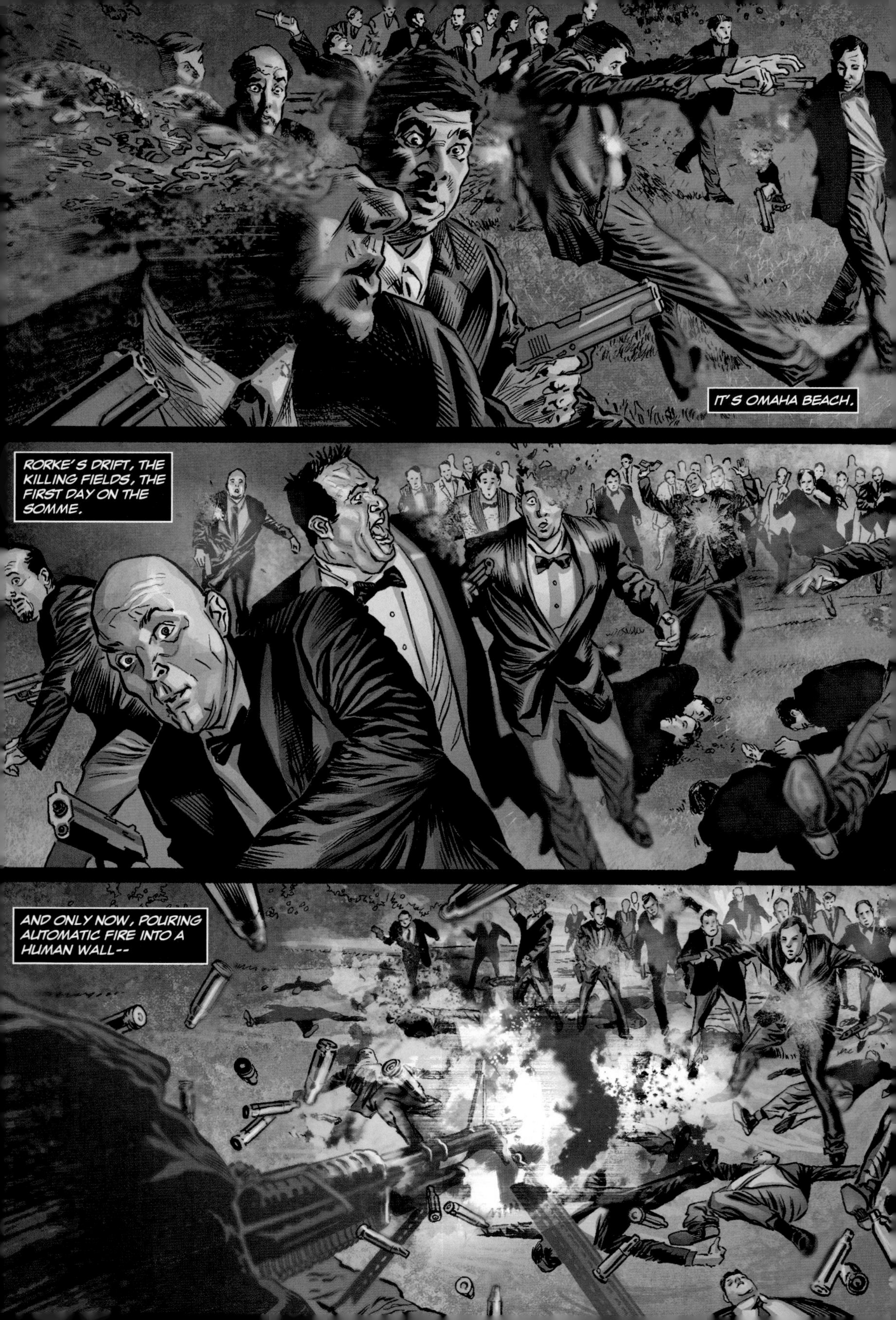
IT'S OMAHA BEACH.
RORKE'S DRIFT, THE KILLING FIELDS, THE FIRST DAY ON THE SOMME.
AND ONLY NOW, POURING AUTOMATIC FIRE INTO A HUMAN WALL--

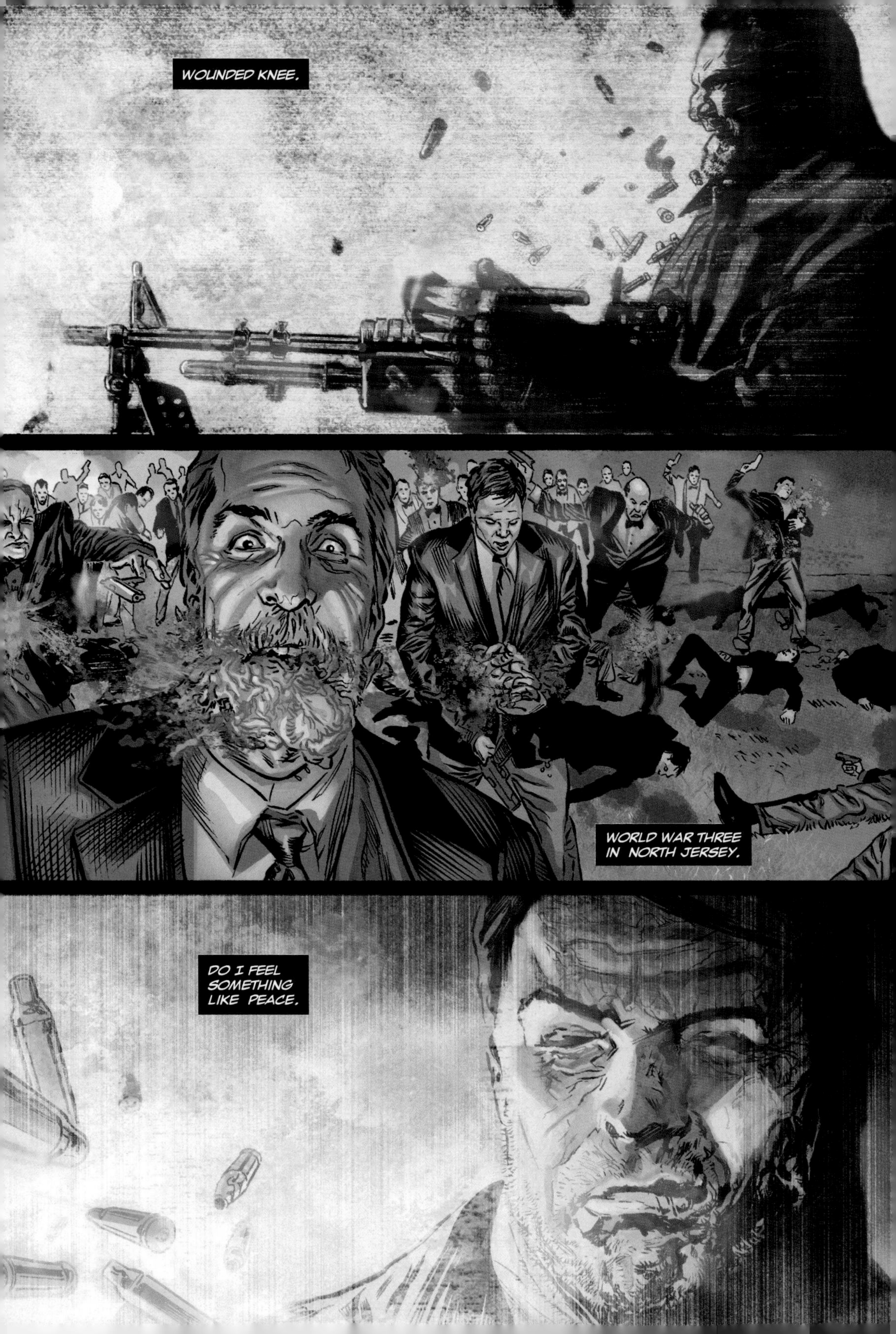
WOUNDED KNEE.
WORLD WAR THREE IN NORTH JERSEY.
DO I FEEL SOMETHING LIKE PEACE.

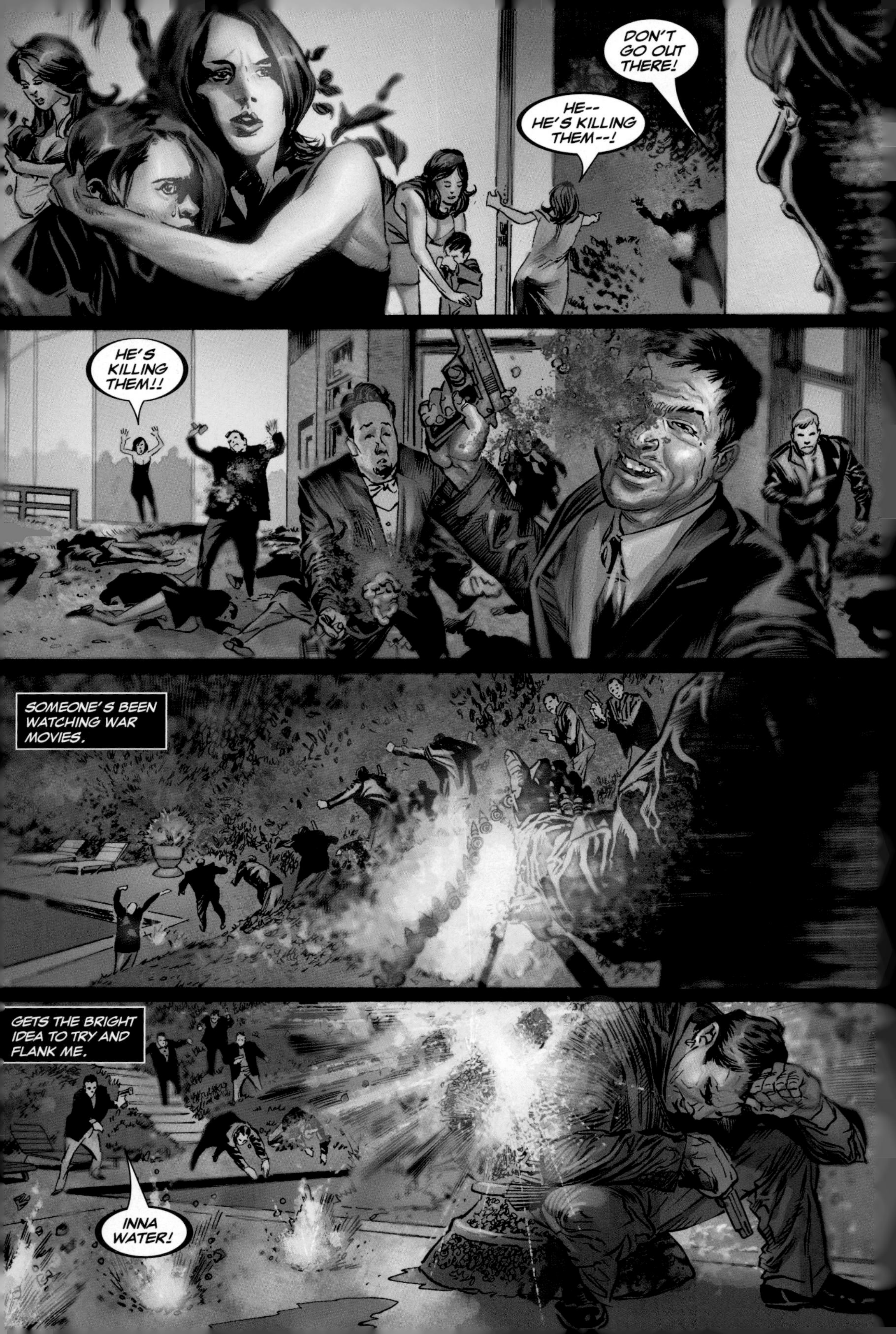
DON'T GO OUT THERE!
HE-- HE'S KILLING THEM--!
HE'S KILLING THEM!!
SOMEONE'S BEEN WATCHING WAR MOVIES.
GETS THE BRIGHT IDEA TO TRY AND FLANK ME.
INNA WATER!

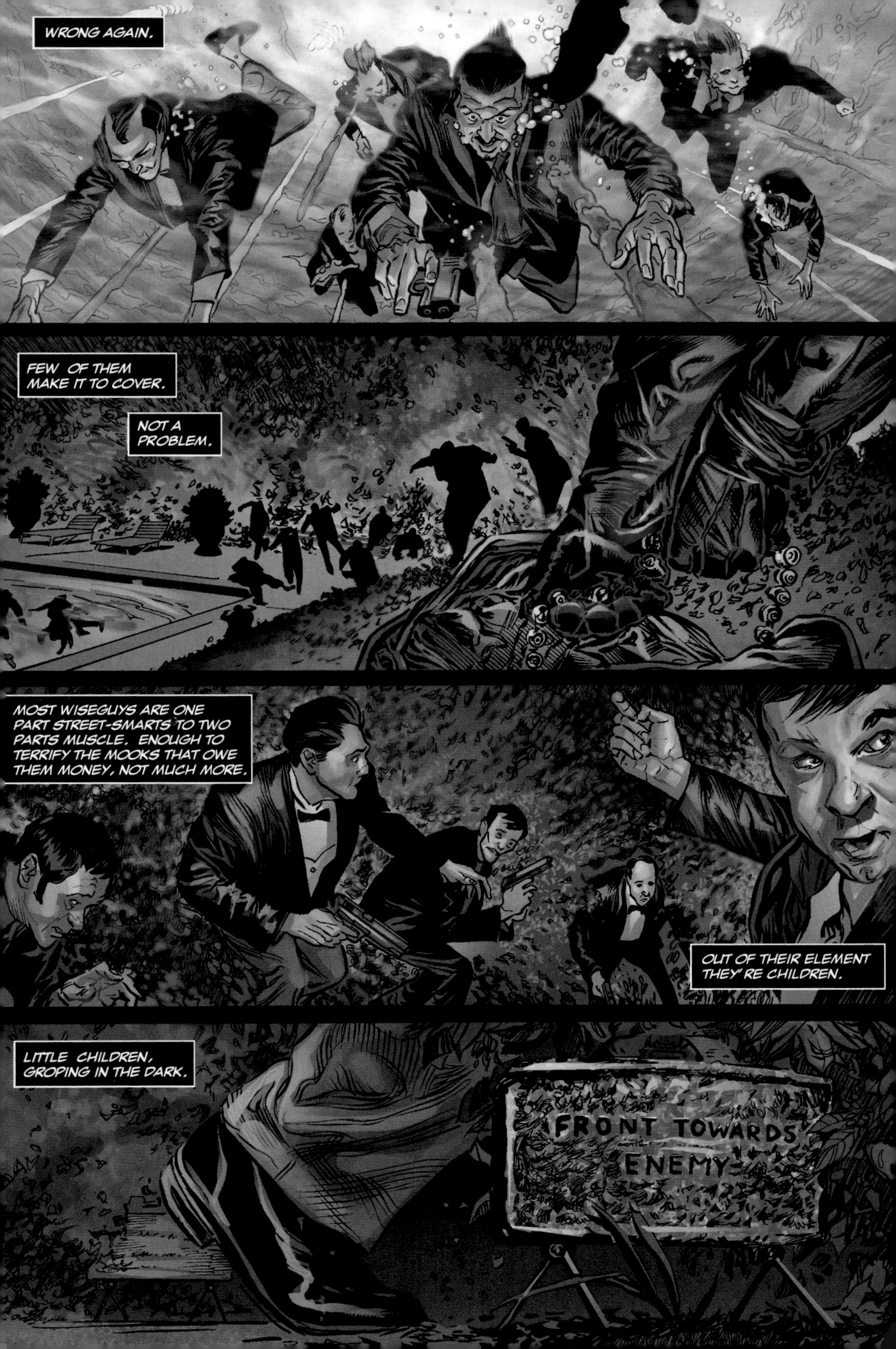
WRONG AGAIN.
FEW OF THEM MAKE IT TO COVER.
NOT A PROBLEM.
MOST WISEGUYS ARE ONE PART STREET-SMARTS TO TWO PARTS MUSCLE. ENOUGH TO TERRIFY THE MOOKS THAT OWE THEM MONEY, NOT MUCH MORE.
OUT OF THEIR ELEMENT THEY'RE CHILDREN.
LITTLE CHILDREN, GROPING IN THE DARK.
FRONT TOWARDS ENEMY

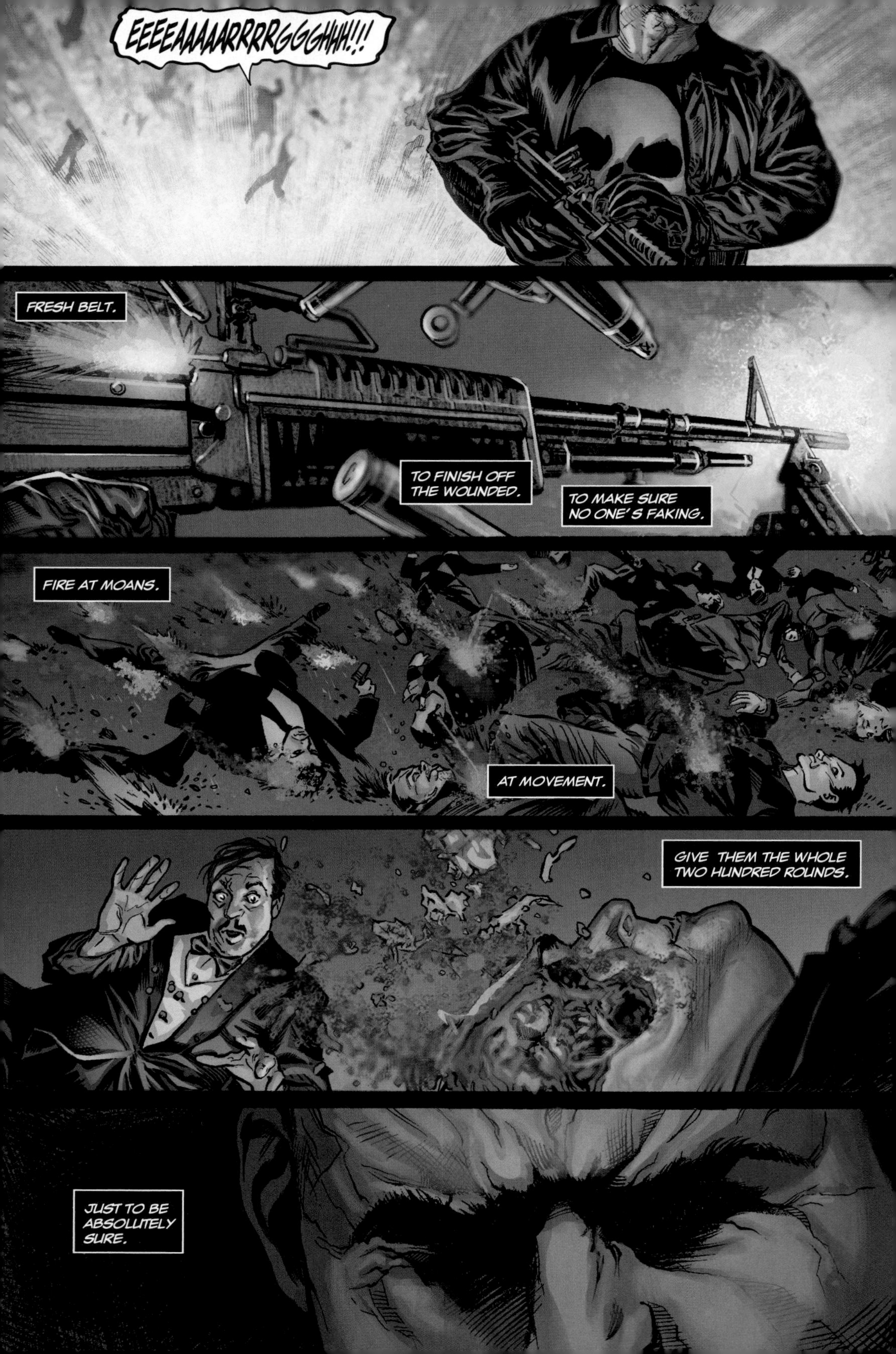
EEEEAAAAARRRRGGGHHH!!!
FRESH BELT.
TO FINISH OFF THE WOUNDED.
TO MAKE SURE NO ONE'S FAKING.
FIRE AT MOANS.
AT MOVEMENT.
GIVE THEM THE WHOLE TWO HUNDRED ROUNDS.
JUST TO BE ABSOLUTELY SURE.

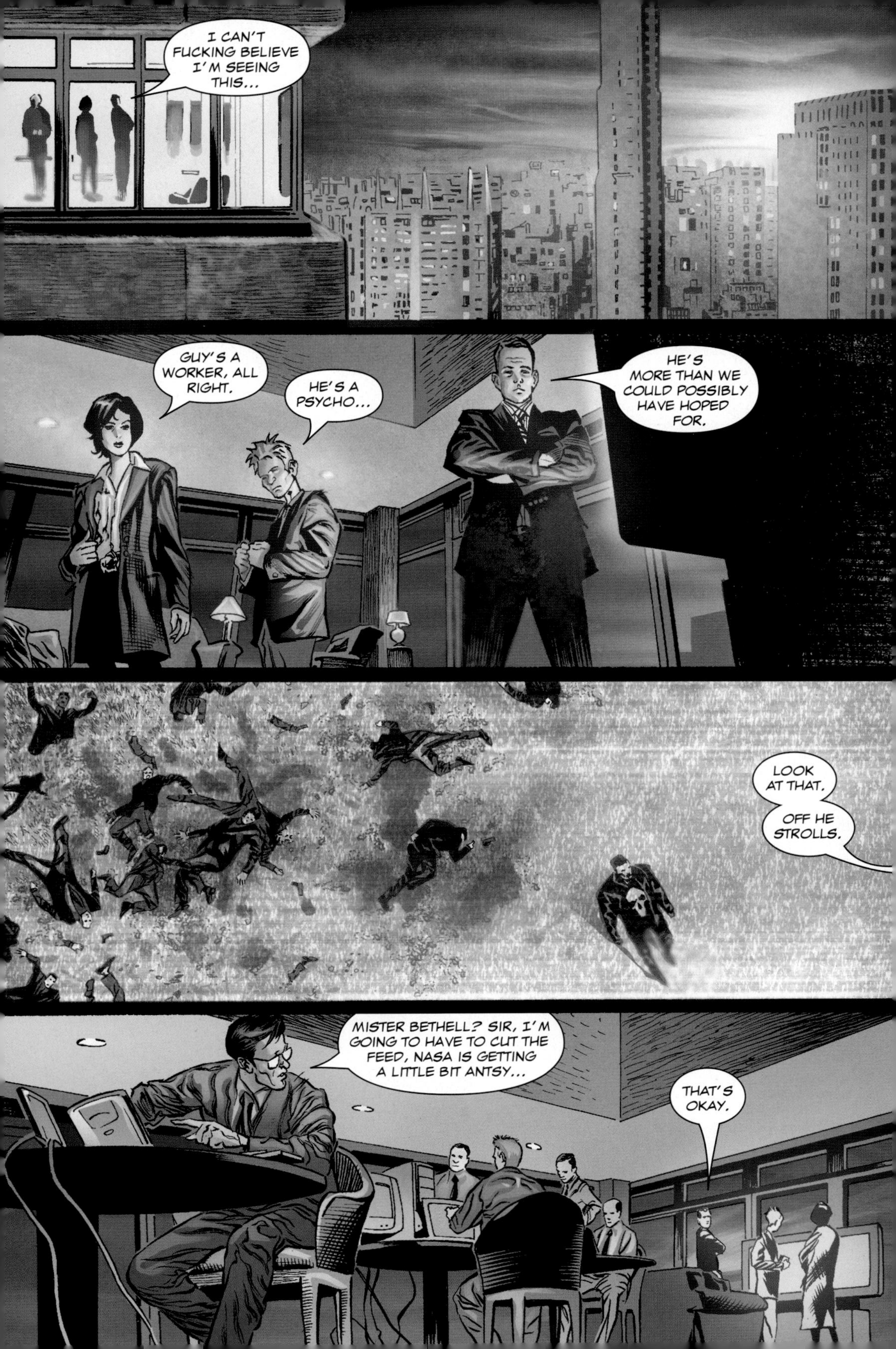
I CAN'T FUCKING BELIEVE I'M SEEING THIS...
GUY'S A WORKER, ALL RIGHT.
HE'S A PSYCHO...
HE'S MORE THAN WE COULD POSSIBLY HAVE HOPED FOR.
LOOK AT THAT.
OFF HE STROLLS.
MISTER BETHELL? SIR, I'M GOING TO HAVE TO CUT THE FEED, NASA IS GETTING A LITTLE BIT ANTSY...
THAT'S OKAY.

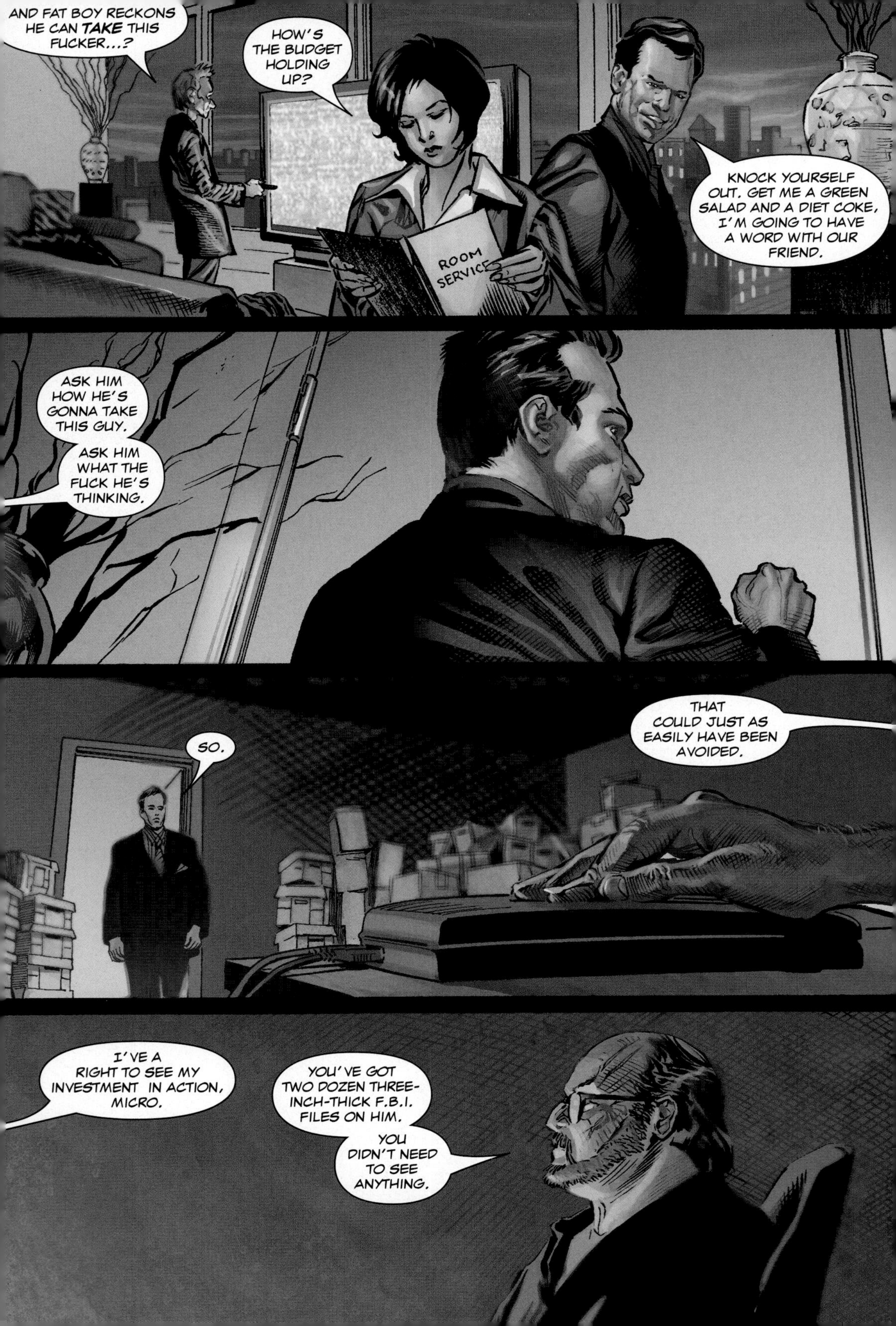
AND FAT BOY RECKONS HE CAN TAKE THIS FUCKER...?
HOW'S THE BUDGET HOLDING UP?
ROOM SERVICE
KNOCK YOURSELF OUT. GET ME A GREEN SALAD AND A DIET COKE, I'M GOING TO HAVE A WORD WITH OUR FRIEND.
ASK HIM HOW HE'S GONNA TAKE THIS GUY.
ASK HIM WHAT THE FUCK HE'S THINKING.
SO.
THAT COULD JUST AS EASILY HAVE BEEN AVOIDED.
I'VE A RIGHT TO SEE MY INVESTMENT IN ACTION, MICRO.
YOU'VE GOT TWO DOZEN THREE-INCH-THICK F.B.I. FILES ON HIM.
YOU DIDN'T NEED TO SEE ANYTHING.

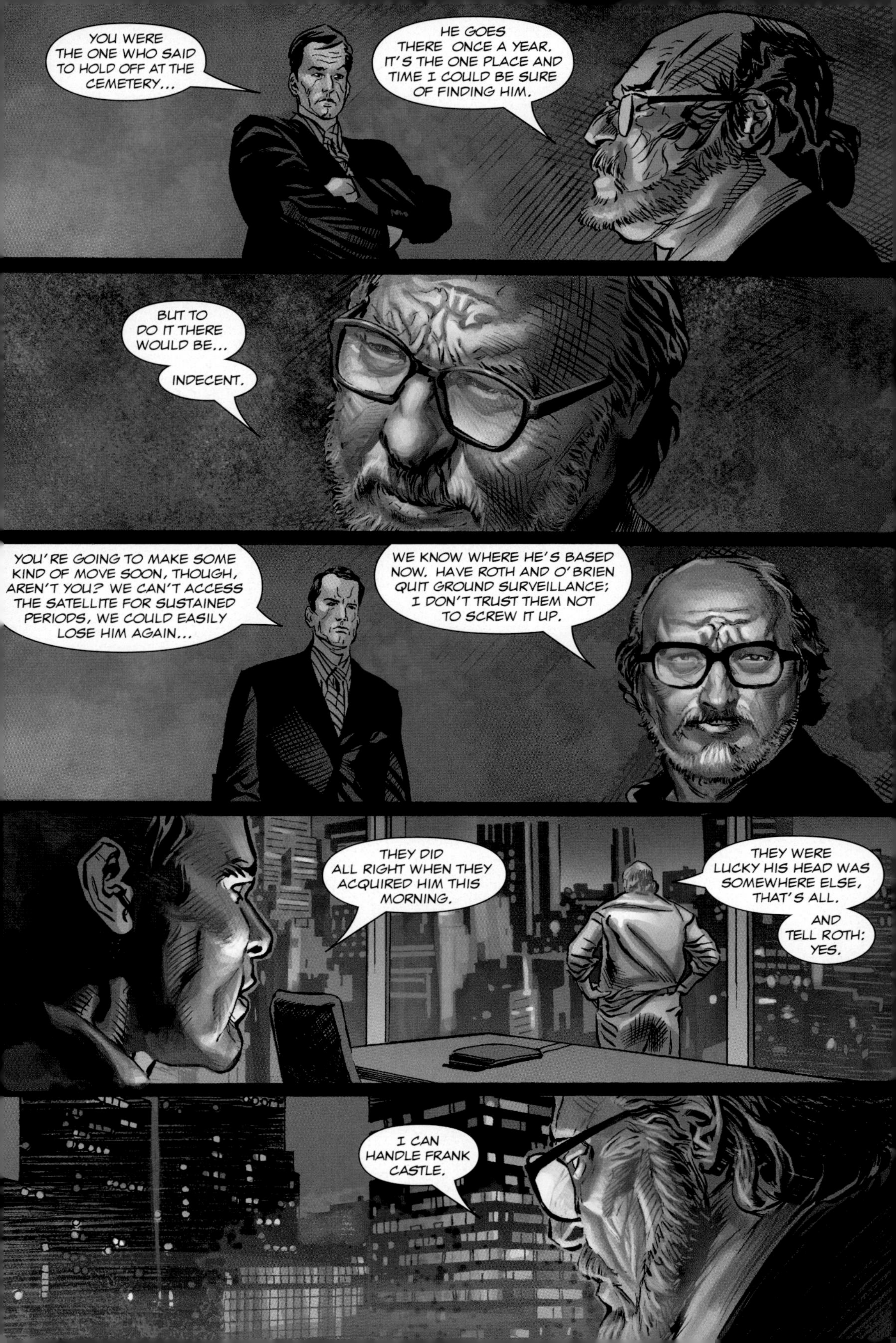
YOU WERE THE ONE WHO SAID TO HOLD OFF AT THE CEMETERY...
HE GOES THERE ONCE A YEAR. IT'S THE ONE PLACE AND TIME I COULD BE SURE OF FINDING HIM.
BUT TO DO IT THERE WOULD BE...
INDECENT.
YOU'RE GOING TO MAKE SOME KIND OF MOVE SOON, THOUGH, AREN'T YOU? WE CAN'T ACCESS THE SATELLITE FOR SUSTAINED PERIODS, WE COULD EASILY LOSE HIM AGAIN...
WE KNOW WHERE HE'S BASED NOW. HAVE ROTH AND O'BRIEN QUIT GROUND SURVEILLANCE; I DON'T TRUST THEM NOT TO SCREW IT UP.
THEY DID ALL RIGHT WHEN THEY ACQUIRED HIM THIS MORNING.
THEY WERE LUCKY HIS HEAD WAS SOMEWHERE ELSE, THAT'S ALL.
AND TELL ROTH: YES.
I CAN HANDLE FRANK CASTLE.

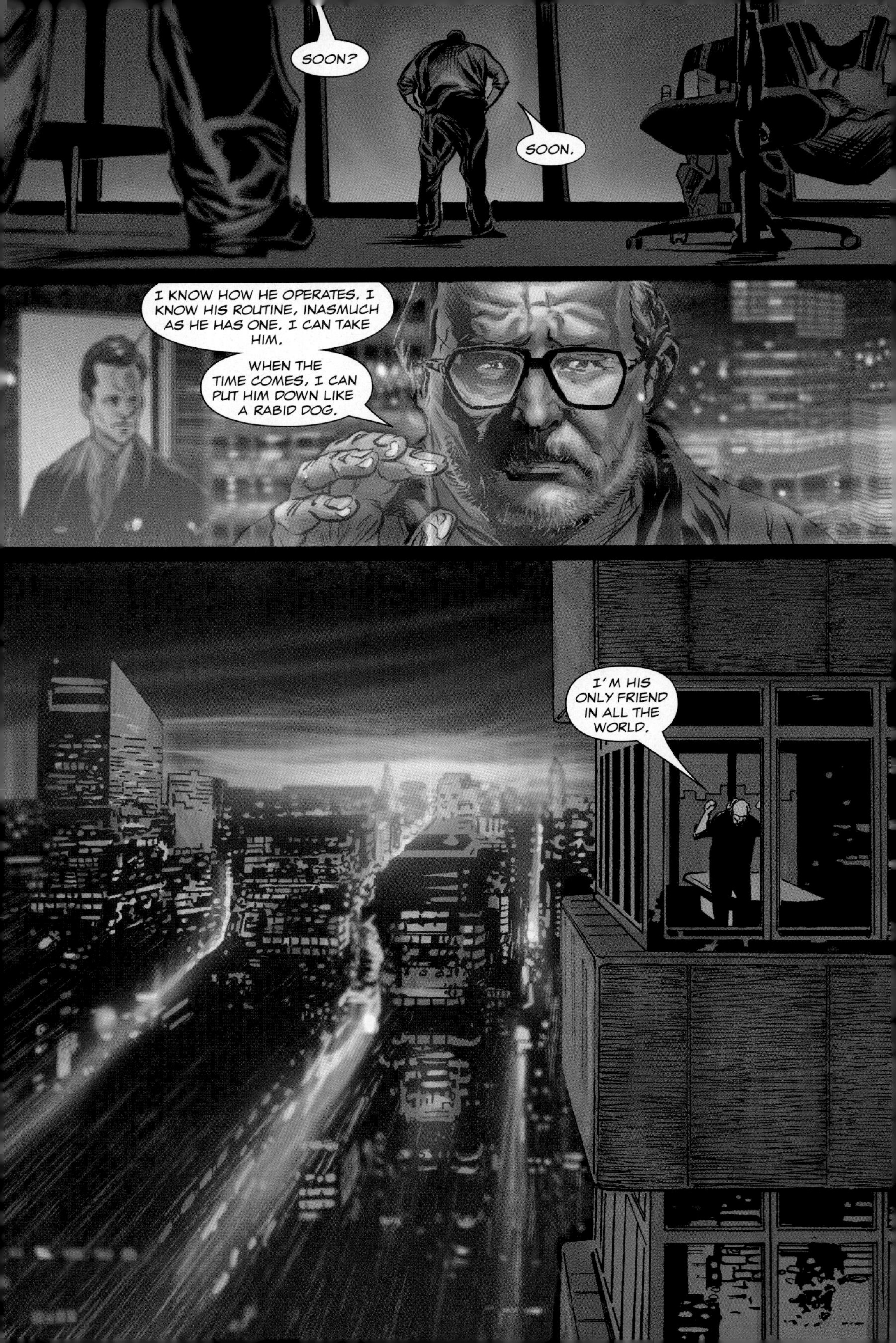
SOON?
SOON.
I KNOW HOW HE OPERATES. I KNOW HIS ROUTINE, INASMUCH AS HE HAS ONE. I CAN TAKE HIM.
WHEN THE TIME COMES, I CAN PUT HIM DOWN LIKE A RABID DOG.
I'M HIS ONLY FRIEND IN ALL THE WORLD.

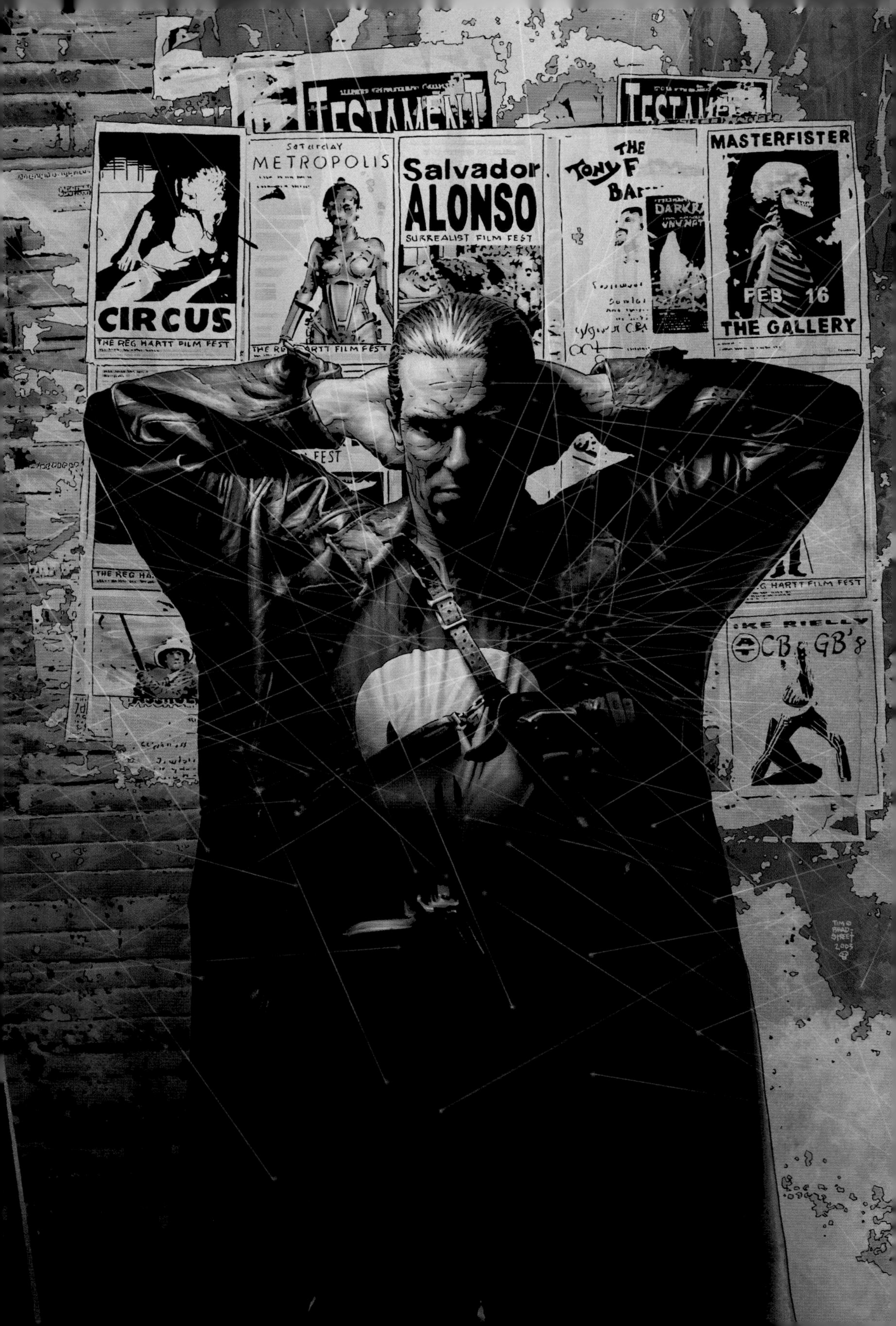
Saturday
METROPOLIS
THE REG HARTT FILM FEST
Salvador
ALONSO
SURREALIST FILM FEST
CIRCUS
THE REG HARTT FILM FEST
MASTERFISTER
FEB 16
THE GALLERY
TIM
BRADSTREET
2003

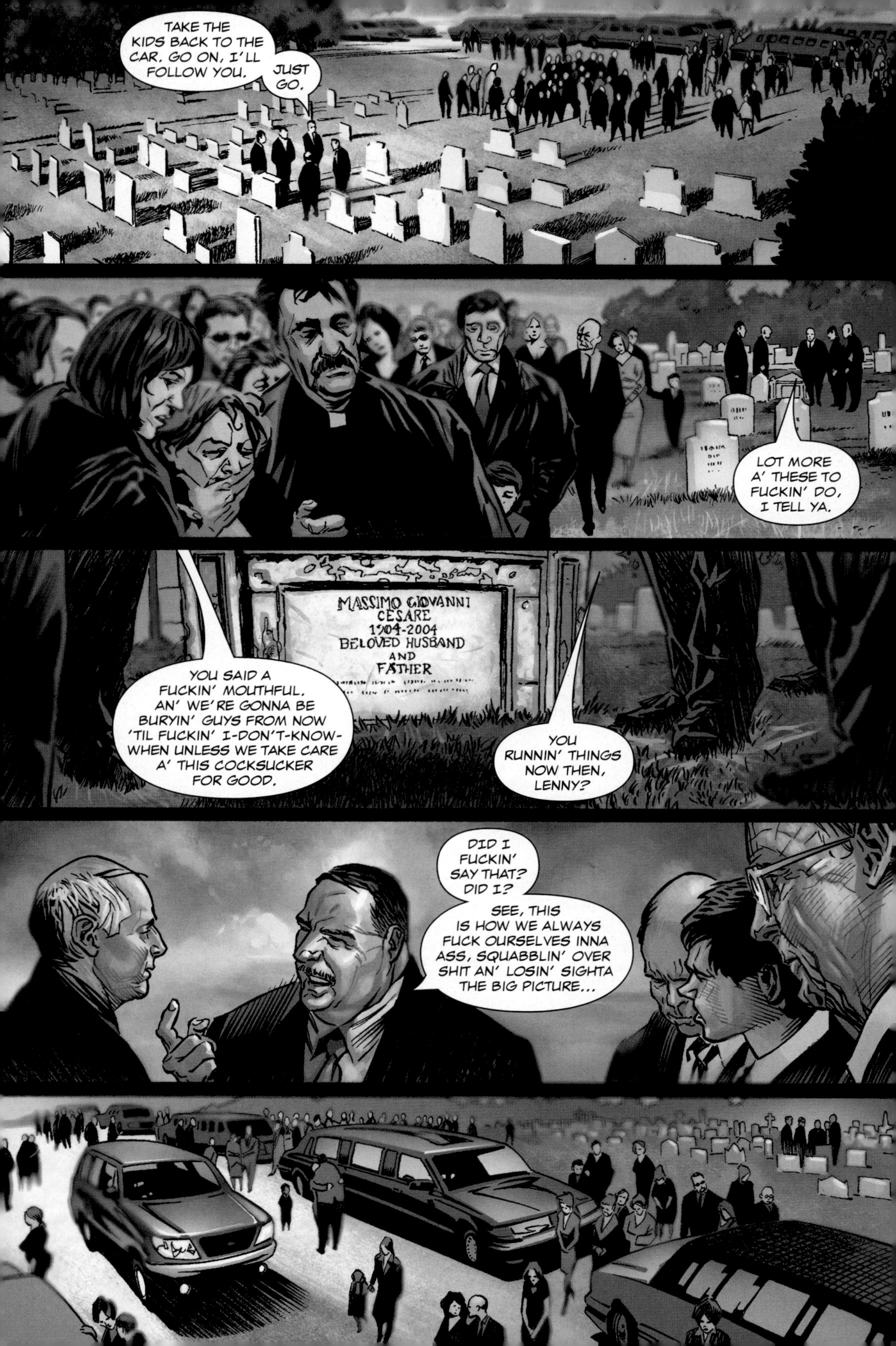

TAKE THE KIDS BACK TO THE CAR. GO ON, I'LL FOLLOW YOU.
JUST GO.
LOT MORE A' THESE TO FUCKIN' DO, I TELL YA.
MASSIMO GIOVANNI CESARE 1904-2004 BELOVED HUSBAND AND FATHER
YOU SAID A FUCKIN' MOUTHFUL. AN' WE'RE GONNA BE BURYIN' GUYS FROM NOW 'TIL FUCKIN' I-DON'T-KNOW-WHEN UNLESS WE TAKE CARE A' THIS COCKSUCKER FOR GOOD.
YOU RUNNIN' THINGS NOW THEN, LENNY?
DID I FUCKIN' SAY THAT? DID I?
SEE, THIS IS HOW WE ALWAYS FUCK OURSELVES INNA ASS, SQUABBLIN' OVER SHIT AN' LOSIN' SIGHTA THE BIG PICTURE...

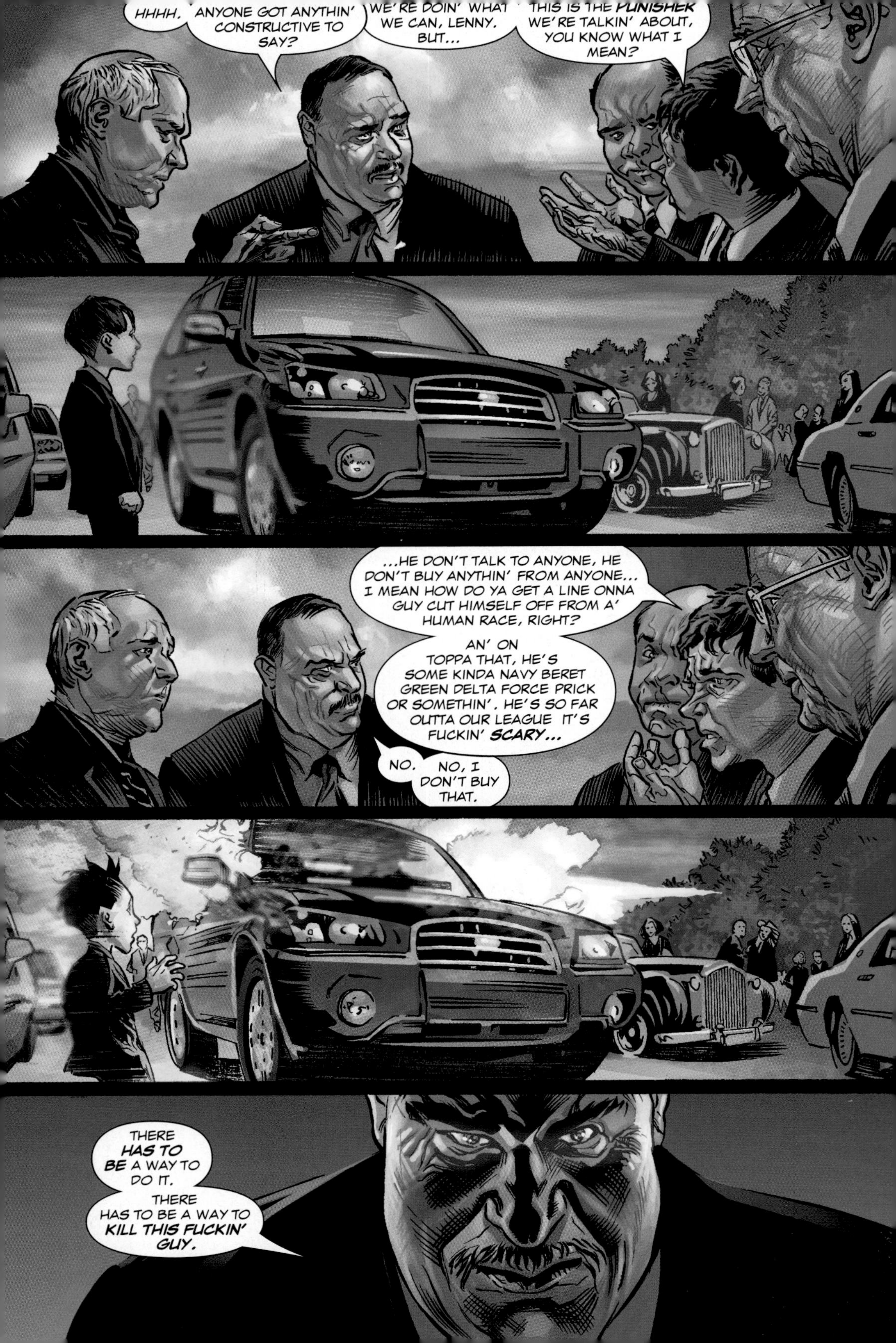
HHHH.
ANYONE GOT ANYTHIN' CONSTRUCTIVE TO SAY?
WE'RE DOIN' WHAT WE CAN, LENNY. BUT...
THIS IS THE PUNISHER WE'RE TALKIN' ABOUT, YOU KNOW WHAT I MEAN?
...HE DON'T TALK TO ANYONE, HE DON'T BUY ANYTHIN' FROM ANYONE... I MEAN HOW DO YA GET A LINE ONNA GUY CUT HIMSELF OFF FROM A' HUMAN RACE, RIGHT?
AN' ON TOPPA THAT, HE'S SOME KINDA NAVY BERET GREEN DELTA FORCE PRICK OR SOMETHIN'. HE'S SO FAR OUTTA OUR LEAGUE IT'S FUCKIN' SCARY...
NO.
NO, I DON'T BUY THAT.
THERE HAS TO BE A WAY TO DO IT.
THERE HAS TO BE A WAY TO KILL THIS FUCKIN' GUY.

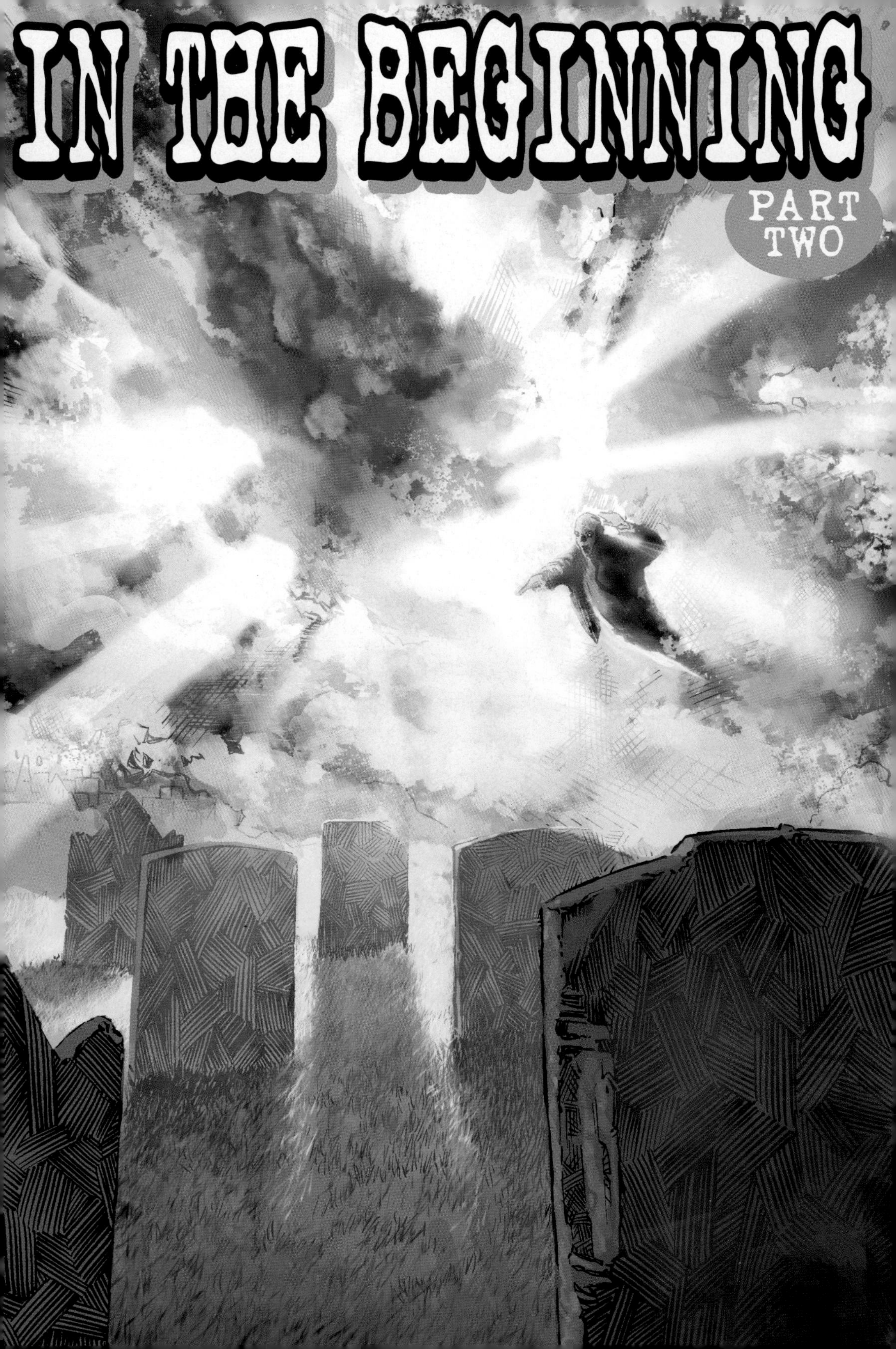
IN THE BEGINNING
PART TWO

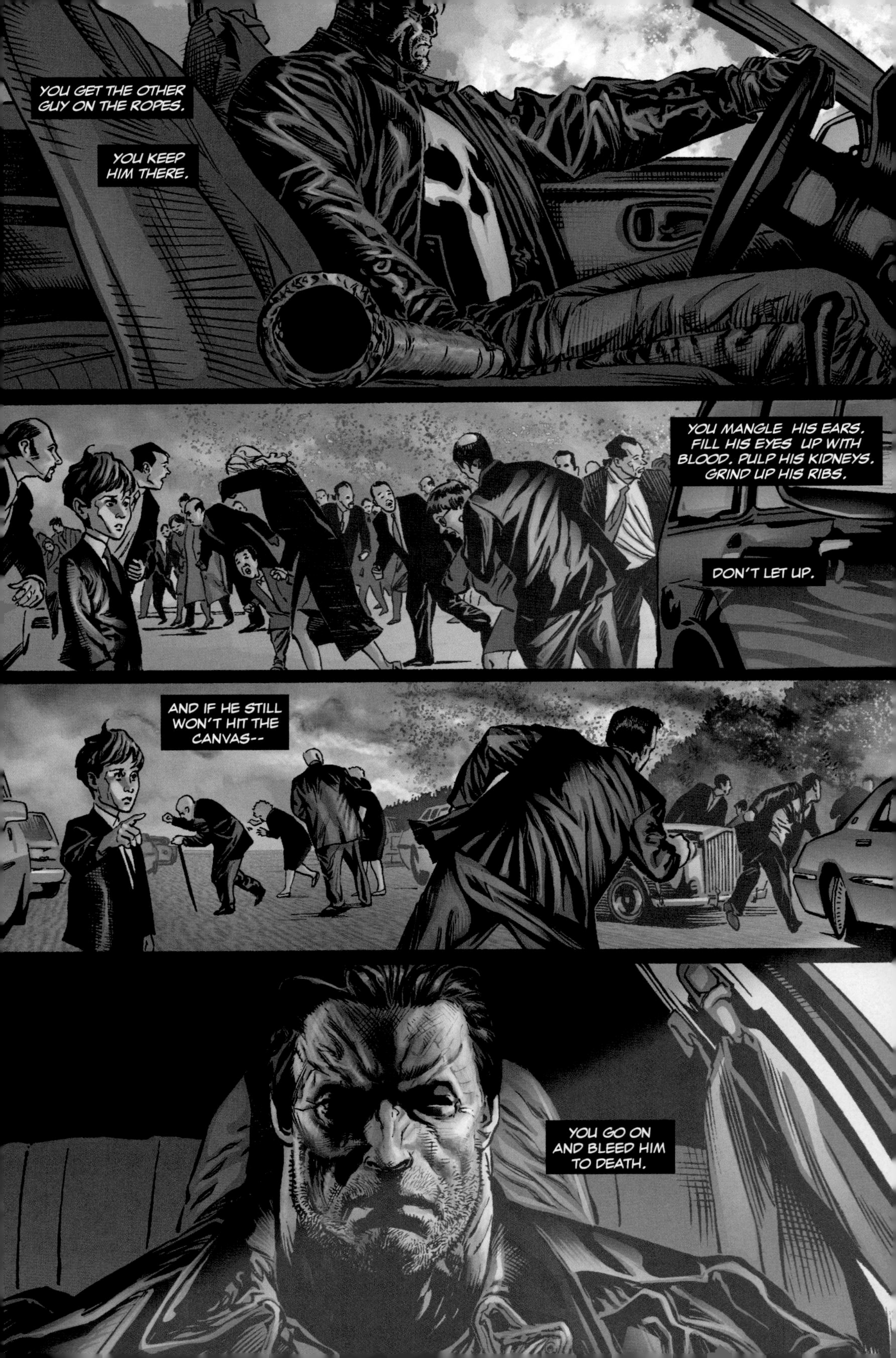
YOU GET THE OTHER GUY ON THE ROPES.
YOU KEEP HIM THERE.
YOU MANGLE HIS EARS. FILL HIS EYES UP WITH BLOOD. PULP HIS KIDNEYS. GRIND UP HIS RIBS.
DON'T LET UP.
AND IF HE STILL WON'T HIT THE CANVAS--
YOU GO ON AND BLEED HIM TO DEATH.

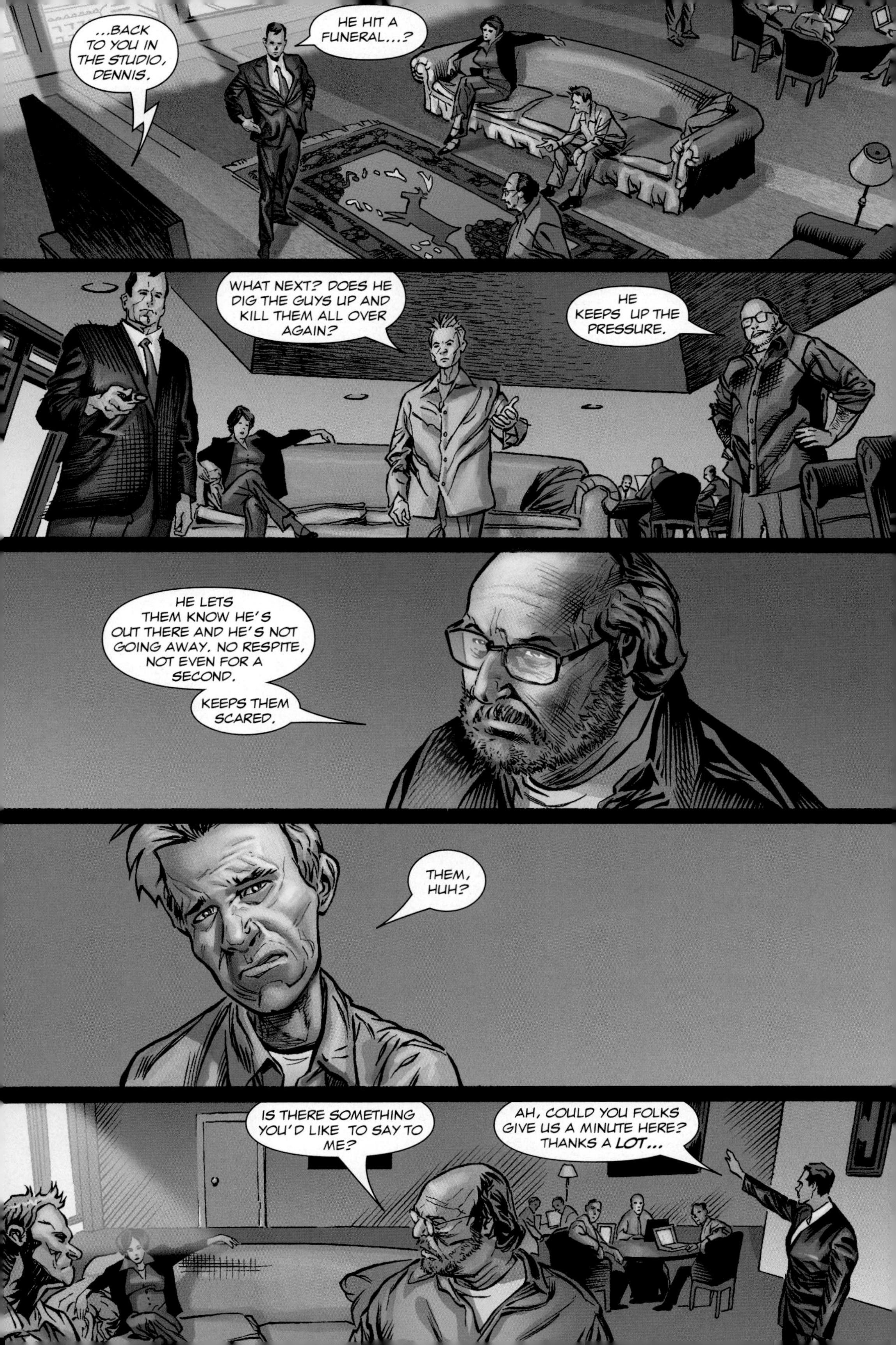
...BACK TO YOU IN THE STUDIO, DENNIS.
HE HIT A FUNERAL...?
WHAT NEXT? DOES HE DIG THE GUYS UP AND KILL THEM ALL OVER AGAIN?
HE KEEPS UP THE PRESSURE.
HE LETS THEM KNOW HE'S OUT THERE AND HE'S NOT GOING AWAY. NO RESPITE, NOT EVEN FOR A SECOND.
KEEPS THEM SCARED.
THEM, HUH?
IS THERE SOMETHING YOU'D LIKE TO SAY TO ME?
AH, COULD YOU FOLKS GIVE US A MINUTE HERE? THANKS A LOT...

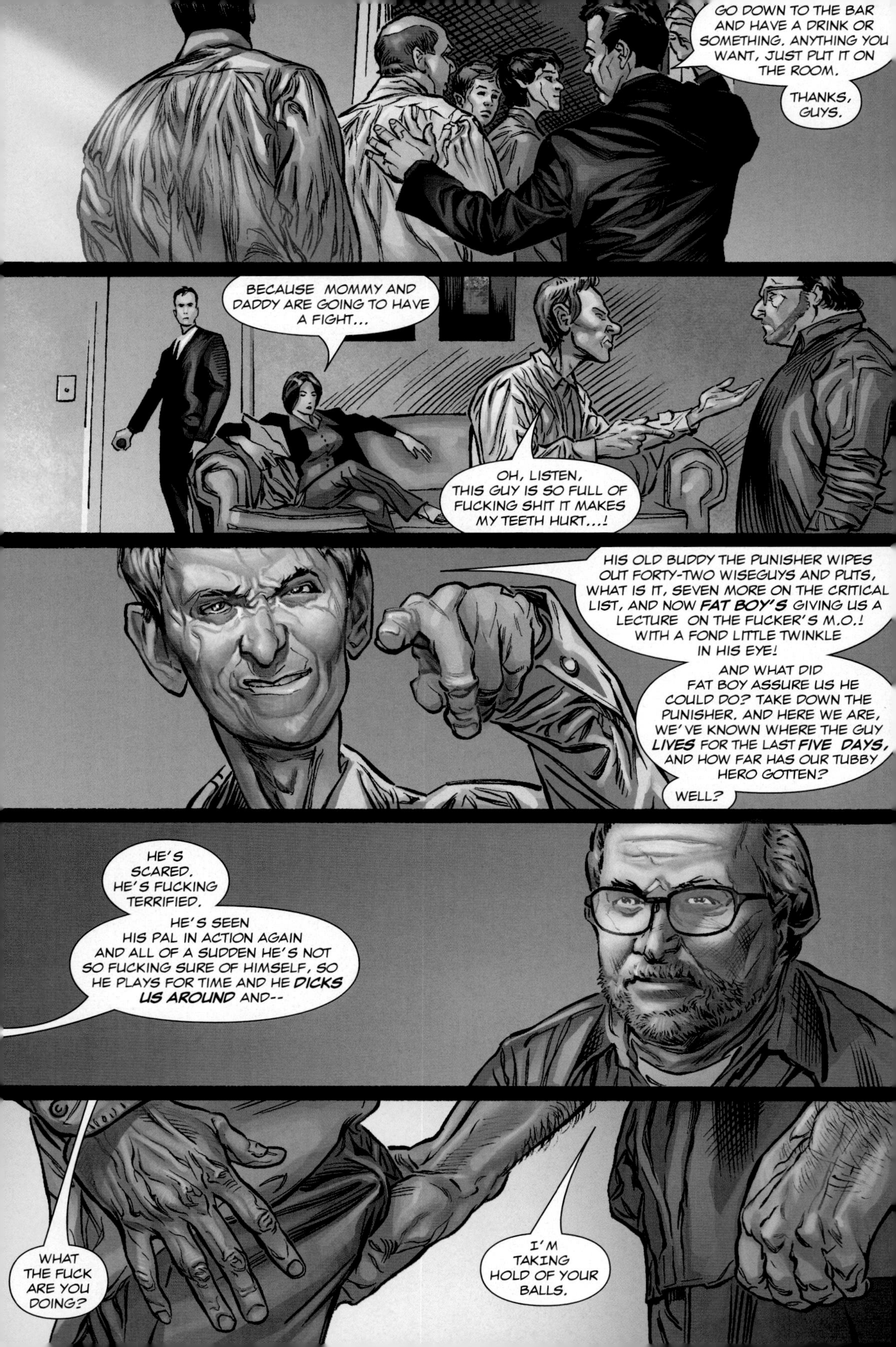
GO DOWN TO THE BAR AND HAVE A DRINK OR SOMETHING. ANYTHING YOU WANT, JUST PUT IT ON THE ROOM.
THANKS, GUYS.
BECAUSE MOMMY AND DADDY ARE GOING TO HAVE A FIGHT...
OH, LISTEN, THIS GUY IS SO FULL OF FUCKING SHIT IT MAKES MY TEETH HURT...!
HIS OLD BUDDY THE PUNISHER WIPES OUT FORTY-TWO WISEGUYS AND PUTS, WHAT IS IT, SEVEN MORE ON THE CRITICAL LIST, AND NOW FAT BOY'S GIVING US A LECTURE ON THE FUCKER'S M.O.! WITH A FOND LITTLE TWINKLE IN HIS EYE!
AND WHAT DID FAT BOY ASSURE US HE COULD DO? TAKE DOWN THE PUNISHER. AND HERE WE ARE, WE'VE KNOWN WHERE THE GUY LIVES FOR THE LAST FIVE DAYS, AND HOW FAR HAS OUR TUBBY HERO GOTTEN?
WELL?
HE'S SCARED. HE'S FUCKING TERRIFIED.
HE'S SEEN HIS PAL IN ACTION AGAIN AND ALL OF A SUDDEN HE'S NOT SO FUCKING SURE OF HIMSELF, SO HE PLAYS FOR TIME AND HE DICKS US AROUND AND--
WHAT THE FUCK ARE YOU DOING?
I'M TAKING HOLD OF YOUR BALLS.

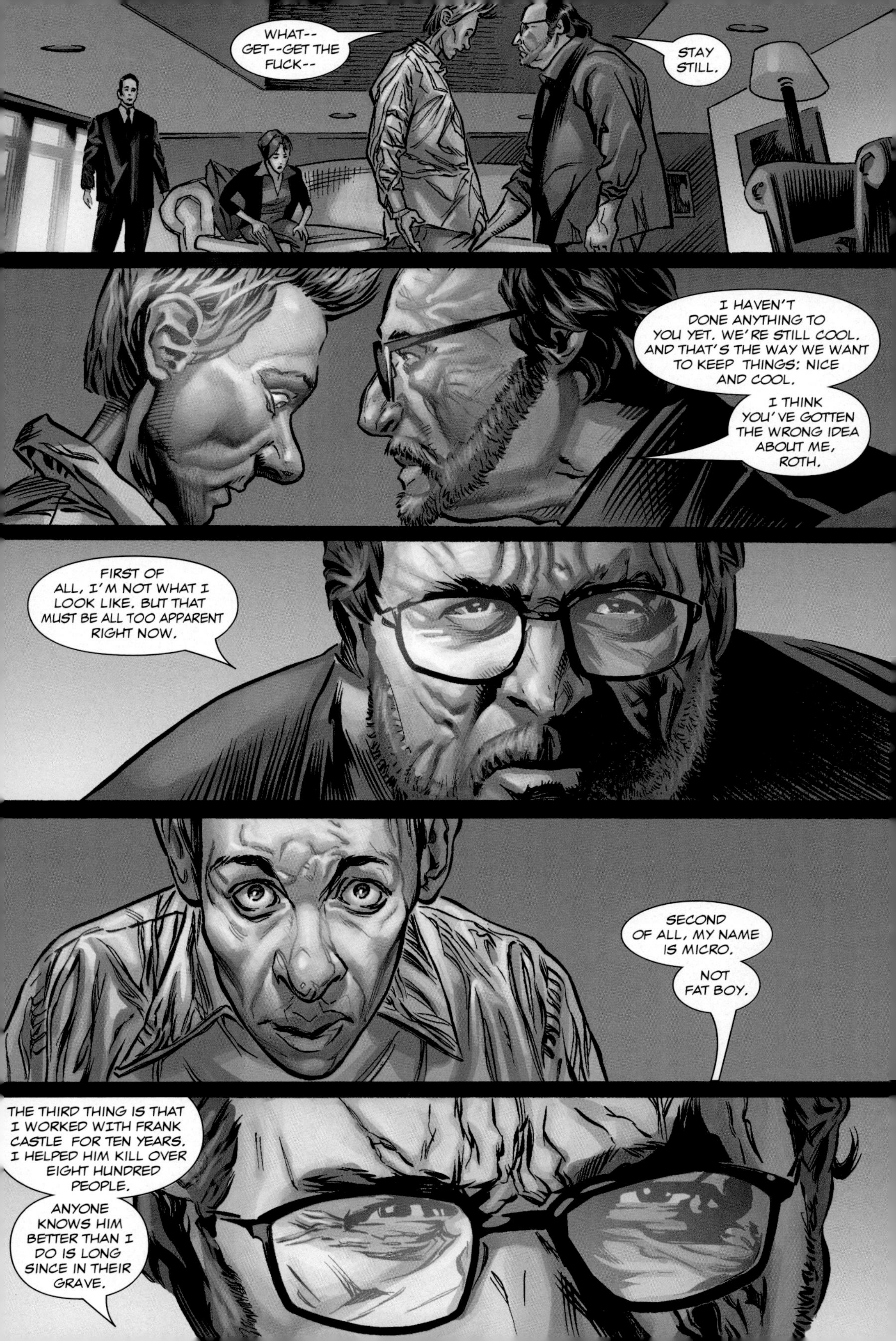
WHAT--
GET--GET THE FUCK--
STAY STILL.
I HAVEN'T DONE ANYTHING TO YOU YET. WE'RE STILL COOL. AND THAT'S THE WAY WE WANT TO KEEP THINGS: NICE AND COOL.
I THINK YOU'VE GOTTEN THE WRONG IDEA ABOUT ME, ROTH.
FIRST OF ALL, I'M NOT WHAT I LOOK LIKE. BUT THAT MUST BE ALL TOO APPARENT RIGHT NOW.
SECOND OF ALL, MY NAME IS MICRO.
NOT FAT BOY.
THE THIRD THING IS THAT I WORKED WITH FRANK CASTLE FOR TEN YEARS. I HELPED HIM KILL OVER EIGHT HUNDRED PEOPLE.
ANYONE KNOWS HIM BETTER THAN I DO IS LONG SINCE IN THEIR GRAVE.

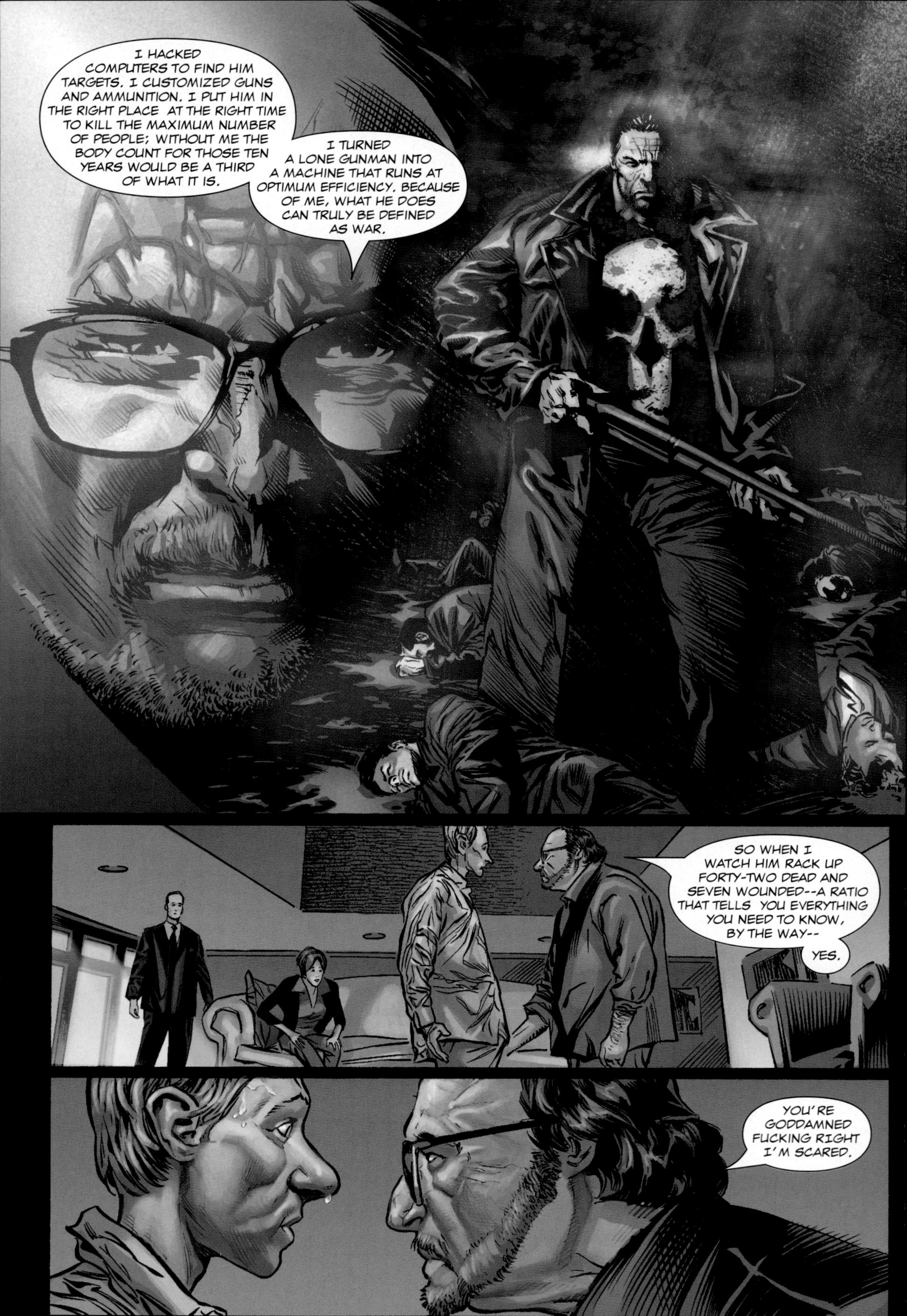
I HACKED COMPUTERS TO FIND HIM TARGETS. I CUSTOMIZED GUNS AND AMMUNITION. I PUT HIM IN THE RIGHT PLACE AT THE RIGHT TIME TO KILL THE MAXIMUM NUMBER OF PEOPLE; WITHOUT ME THE BODY COUNT FOR THOSE TEN YEARS WOULD BE A THIRD OF WHAT IT IS.
I TURNED A LONE GUNMAN INTO A MACHINE THAT RUNS AT OPTIMUM EFFICIENCY. BECAUSE OF ME, WHAT HE DOES CAN TRULY BE DEFINED AS WAR.
SO WHEN I WATCH HIM RACK UP FORTY-TWO DEAD AND SEVEN WOUNDED--A RATIO THAT TELLS YOU EVERYTHING YOU NEED TO KNOW, BY THE WAY--
YES.
YOU'RE GODDAMNED FUCKING RIGHT I'M SCARED.

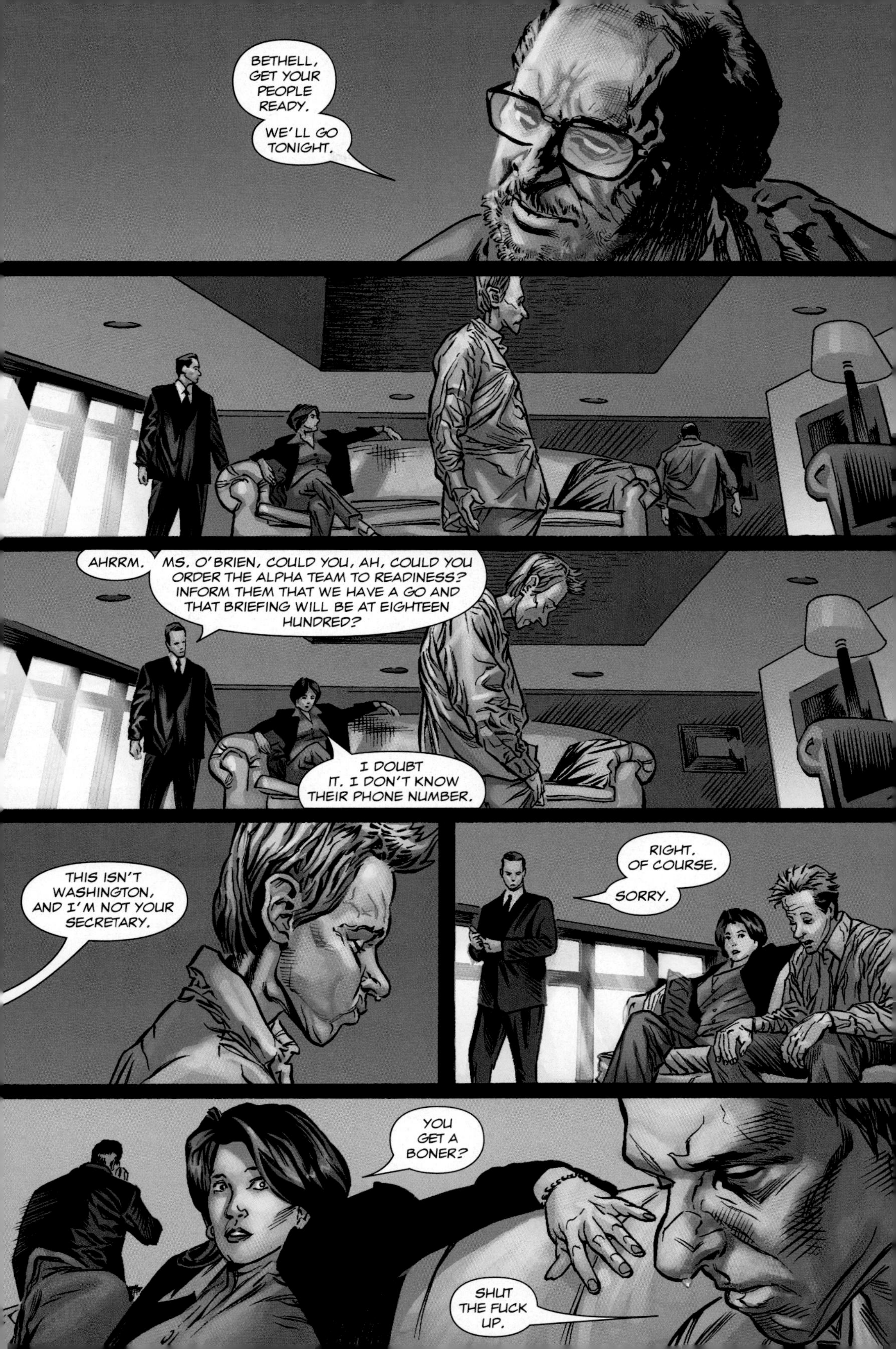
BETHELL, GET YOUR PEOPLE READY.
WE'LL GO TONIGHT.
AHRRM.
MS. O'BRIEN, COULD YOU, AH, COULD YOU ORDER THE ALPHA TEAM TO READINESS? INFORM THEM THAT WE HAVE A GO AND THAT BRIEFING WILL BE AT EIGHTEEN HUNDRED?
I DOUBT IT. I DON'T KNOW THEIR PHONE NUMBER.
THIS ISN'T WASHINGTON, AND I'M NOT YOUR SECRETARY.
RIGHT. OF COURSE.
SORRY.
YOU GET A BONER?
SHUT THE FUCK UP.

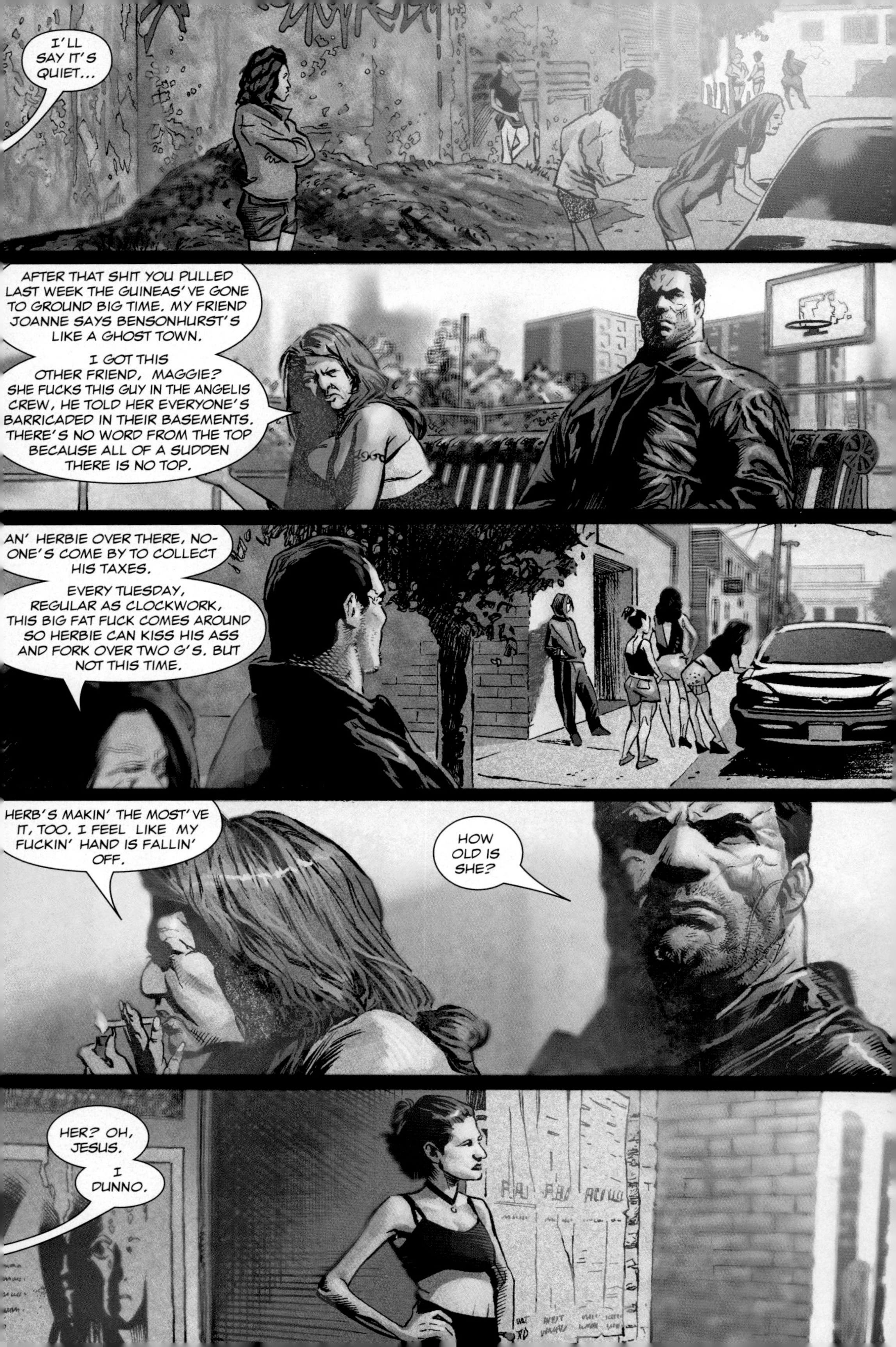

I'LL SAY IT'S QUIET...
AFTER THAT SHIT YOU PULLED LAST WEEK THE GUINEAS'VE GONE TO GROUND BIG TIME. MY FRIEND JOANNE SAYS BENSONHURST'S LIKE A GHOST TOWN.
I GOT THIS OTHER FRIEND, MAGGIE? SHE FUCKS THIS GUY IN THE ANGELIS CREW, HE TOLD HER EVERYONE'S BARRICADED IN THEIR BASEMENTS. THERE'S NO WORD FROM THE TOP BECAUSE ALL OF A SUDDEN THERE IS NO TOP.
AN' HERBIE OVER THERE, NO-ONE'S COME BY TO COLLECT HIS TAXES.
EVERY TUESDAY, REGULAR AS CLOCKWORK, THIS BIG FAT FUCK COMES AROUND SO HERBIE CAN KISS HIS ASS AND FORK OVER TWO G'S. BUT NOT THIS TIME.
HERB'S MAKIN' THE MOST'VE IT, TOO. I FEEL LIKE MY FUCKIN' HAND IS FALLIN' OFF.
HOW OLD IS SHE?
HER? OH, JESUS. I DUNNO.

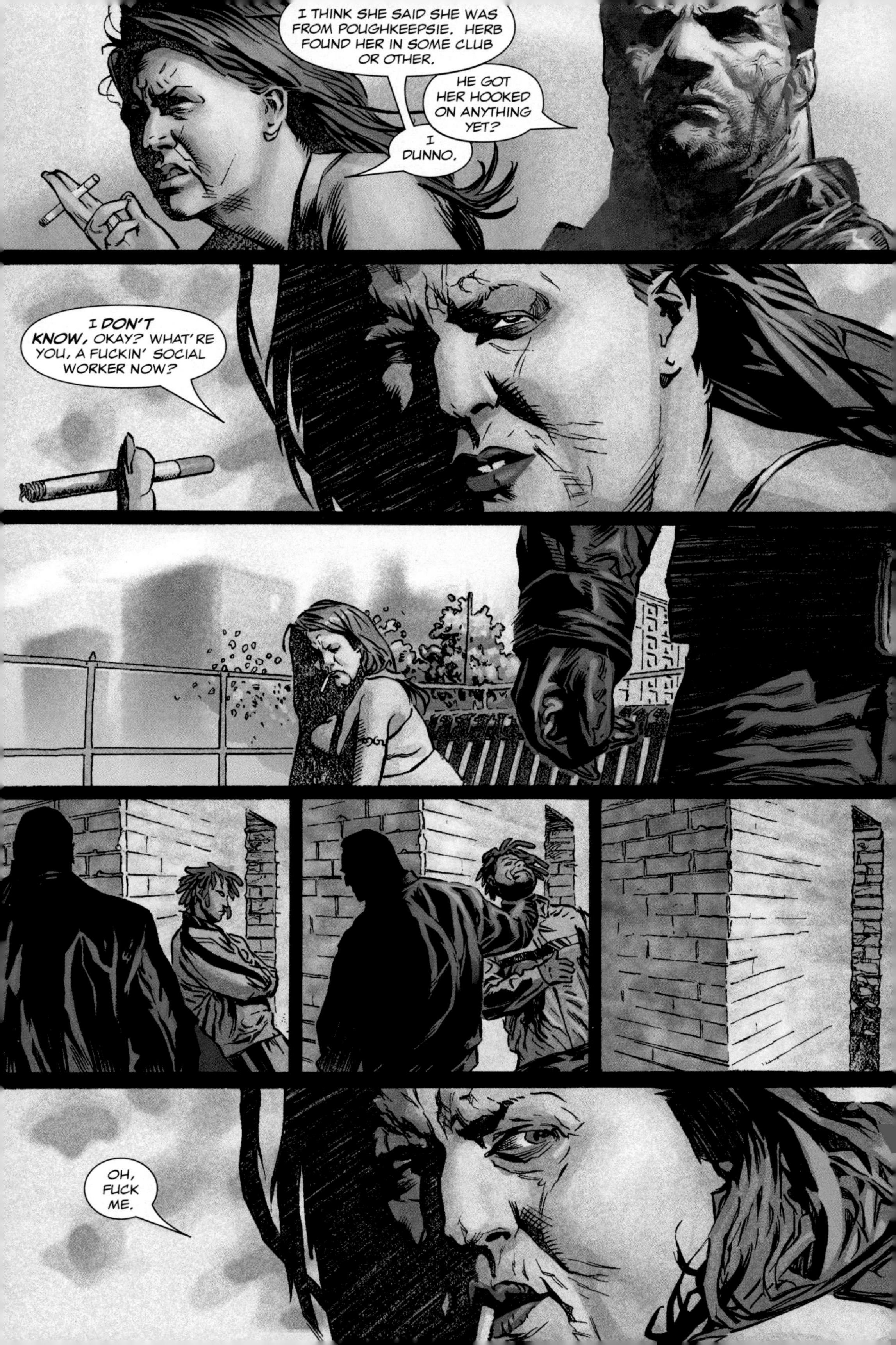
I THINK SHE SAID SHE WAS FROM POUGHKEEPSIE. HERB FOUND HER IN SOME CLUB OR OTHER.
HE GOT HER HOOKED ON ANYTHING YET?
I DUNNO.
I DON'T KNOW, OKAY? WHAT'RE YOU, A FUCKIN' SOCIAL WORKER NOW?
OH, FUCK ME.

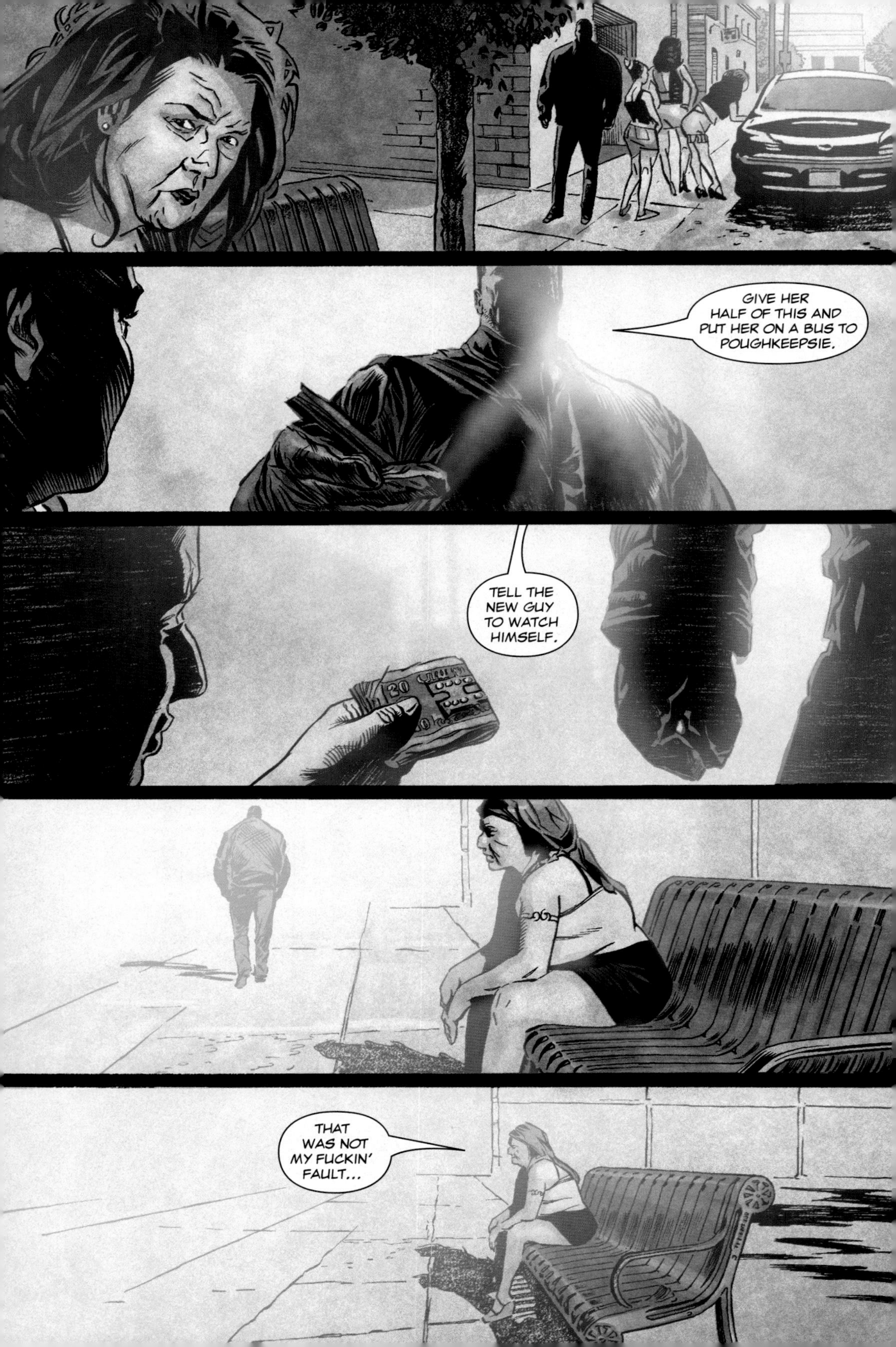
GIVE HER HALF OF THIS AND PUT HER ON A BUS TO POUGHKEEPSIE.
TELL THE NEW GUY TO WATCH HIMSELF.
THAT WAS NOT MY FUCKIN' FAULT...

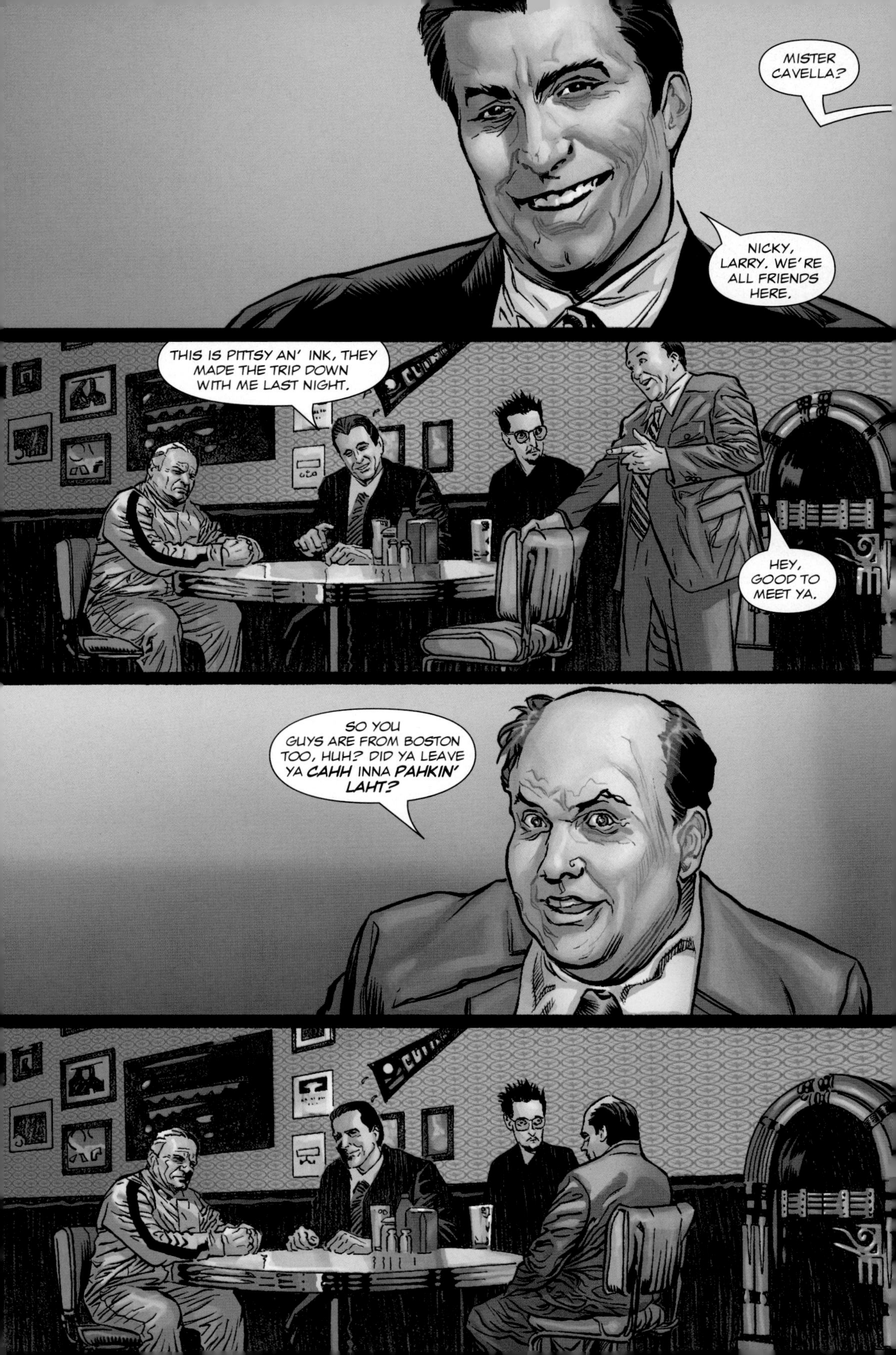
MISTER CAVELLA?
NICKY, LARRY. WE'RE ALL FRIENDS HERE.
THIS IS PITTSY AN' INK, THEY MADE THE TRIP DOWN WITH ME LAST NIGHT.
HEY, GOOD TO MEET YA.
SO YOU GUYS ARE FROM BOSTON TOO, HUH? DID YA LEAVE YA **CAHH** INNA **PAHKIN' LAHT?**

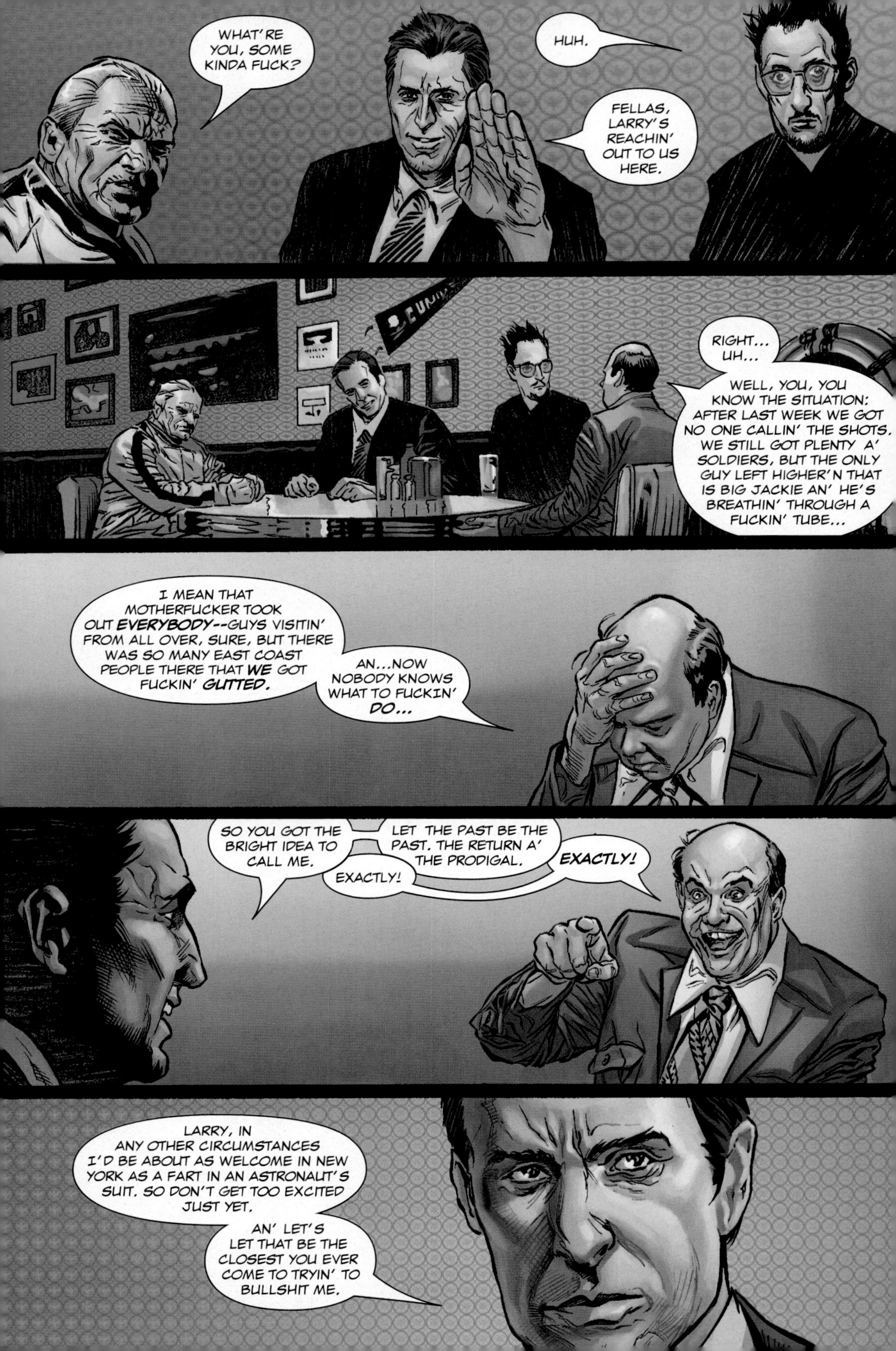
WHAT'RE YOU, SOME KINDA FUCK?
HUH.
FELLAS, LARRY'S REACHIN' OUT TO US HERE.
RIGHT... UH...
WELL, YOU, YOU KNOW THE SITUATION: AFTER LAST WEEK WE GOT NO ONE CALLIN' THE SHOTS. WE STILL GOT PLENTY A' SOLDIERS, BUT THE ONLY GUY LEFT HIGHER'N THAT IS BIG JACKIE AN' HE'S BREATHIN' THROUGH A FUCKIN' TUBE...
I MEAN THAT MOTHERFUCKER TOOK OUT **EVERYBODY**--GUYS VISITIN' FROM ALL OVER, SURE, BUT THERE WAS SO MANY EAST COAST PEOPLE THERE THAT **WE** GOT FUCKIN' **GUTTED.**
AN...NOW NOBODY KNOWS WHAT TO FUCKIN' **DO...**
SO YOU GOT THE BRIGHT IDEA TO CALL ME.
EXACTLY!
LET THE PAST BE THE PAST. THE RETURN A' THE PRODIGAL.
EXACTLY!
LARRY, IN ANY OTHER CIRCUMSTANCES I'D BE ABOUT AS WELCOME IN NEW YORK AS A FART IN AN ASTRONAUT'S SUIT. SO DON'T GET TOO EXCITED JUST YET.
AN' LET'S LET THAT BE THE CLOSEST YOU EVER COME TO TRYIN' TO BULLSHIT ME.

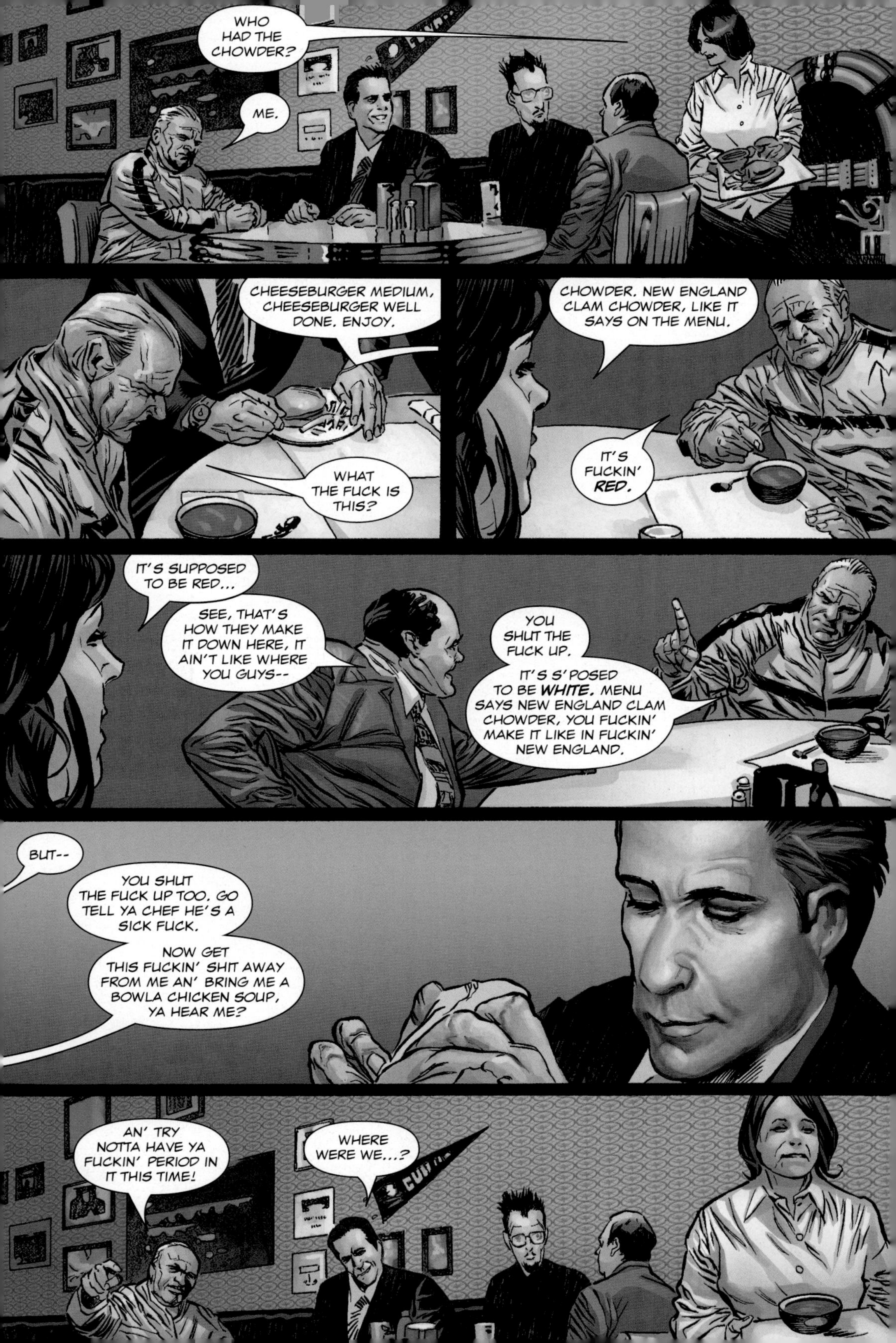
WHO HAD THE CHOWDER?
ME.
CHEESEBURGER MEDIUM, CHEESEBURGER WELL DONE. ENJOY.
WHAT THE FUCK IS THIS?
CHOWDER. NEW ENGLAND CLAM CHOWDER, LIKE IT SAYS ON THE MENU.
IT'S FUCKIN' **RED.**
IT'S SUPPOSED TO BE RED...
SEE, THAT'S HOW THEY MAKE IT DOWN HERE, IT AIN'T LIKE WHERE YOU GUYS--
YOU SHUT THE FUCK UP.
IT'S S'POSED TO BE **WHITE.** MENU SAYS NEW ENGLAND CLAM CHOWDER, YOU FUCKIN' MAKE IT LIKE IN FUCKIN' NEW ENGLAND.
BUT--
YOU SHUT THE FUCK UP TOO. GO TELL YA CHEF HE'S A SICK FUCK.
NOW GET THIS FUCKIN' SHIT AWAY FROM ME AN' BRING ME A BOWLA CHICKEN SOUP, YA HEAR ME?
AN' TRY NOTTA HAVE YA FUCKIN' PERIOD IN IT THIS TIME!
WHERE WERE WE...?

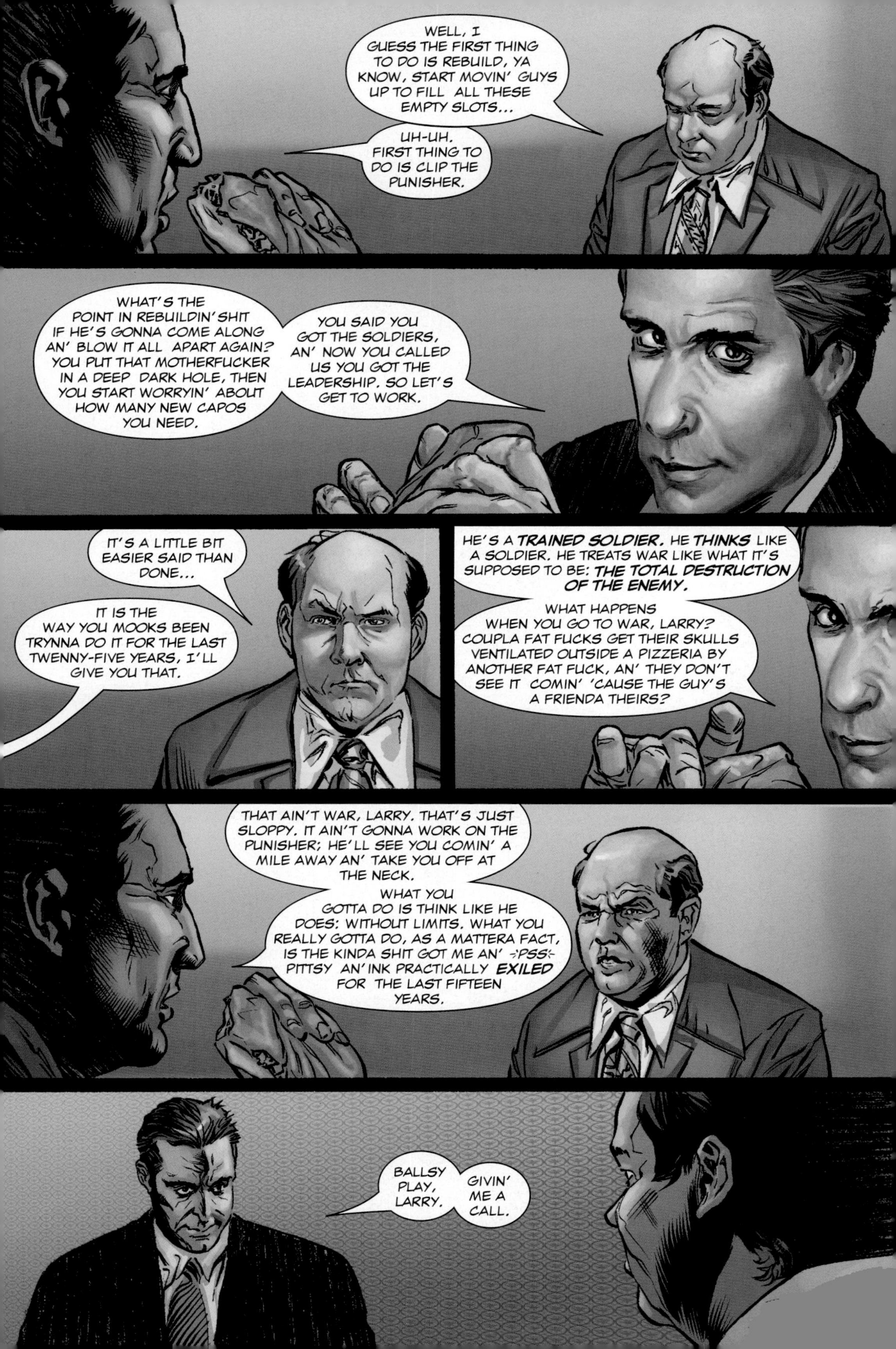
WELL, I GUESS THE FIRST THING TO DO IS REBUILD, YA KNOW, START MOVIN' GUYS UP TO FILL ALL THESE EMPTY SLOTS...
UH-UH. FIRST THING TO DO IS CLIP THE PUNISHER.
WHAT'S THE POINT IN REBUILDIN' SHIT IF HE'S GONNA COME ALONG AN' BLOW IT ALL APART AGAIN? YOU PUT THAT MOTHERFUCKER IN A DEEP DARK HOLE, THEN YOU START WORRYIN' ABOUT HOW MANY NEW CAPOS YOU NEED.
YOU SAID YOU GOT THE SOLDIERS, AN' NOW YOU CALLED US YOU GOT THE LEADERSHIP. SO LET'S GET TO WORK.
IT'S A LITTLE BIT EASIER SAID THAN DONE...
IT IS THE WAY YOU MOOKS BEEN TRYNNA DO IT FOR THE LAST TWENNY-FIVE YEARS, I'LL GIVE YOU THAT.
HE'S A **TRAINED SOLDIER.** HE **THINKS** LIKE A SOLDIER. HE TREATS WAR LIKE WHAT IT'S SUPPOSED TO BE: **THE TOTAL DESTRUCTION OF THE ENEMY.**
WHAT HAPPENS WHEN YOU GO TO WAR, LARRY? COUPLA FAT FUCKS GET THEIR SKULLS VENTILATED OUTSIDE A PIZZERIA BY ANOTHER FAT FUCK, AN' THEY DON'T SEE IT COMIN' 'CAUSE THE GUY'S A FRIENDA THEIRS?
THAT AIN'T WAR, LARRY. THAT'S JUST SLOPPY. IT AIN'T GONNA WORK ON THE PUNISHER; HE'LL SEE YOU COMIN' A MILE AWAY AN' TAKE YOU OFF AT THE NECK.
WHAT YOU GOTTA DO IS THINK LIKE HE DOES: WITHOUT LIMITS. WHAT YOU REALLY GOTTA DO, AS A MATTERA FACT, IS THE KINDA SHIT GOT ME AN' ⸗PSS⸗ PITTSY AN' INK PRACTICALLY **EXILED** FOR THE LAST FIFTEEN YEARS.
BALLSY PLAY, LARRY.
GIVIN' ME A CALL.

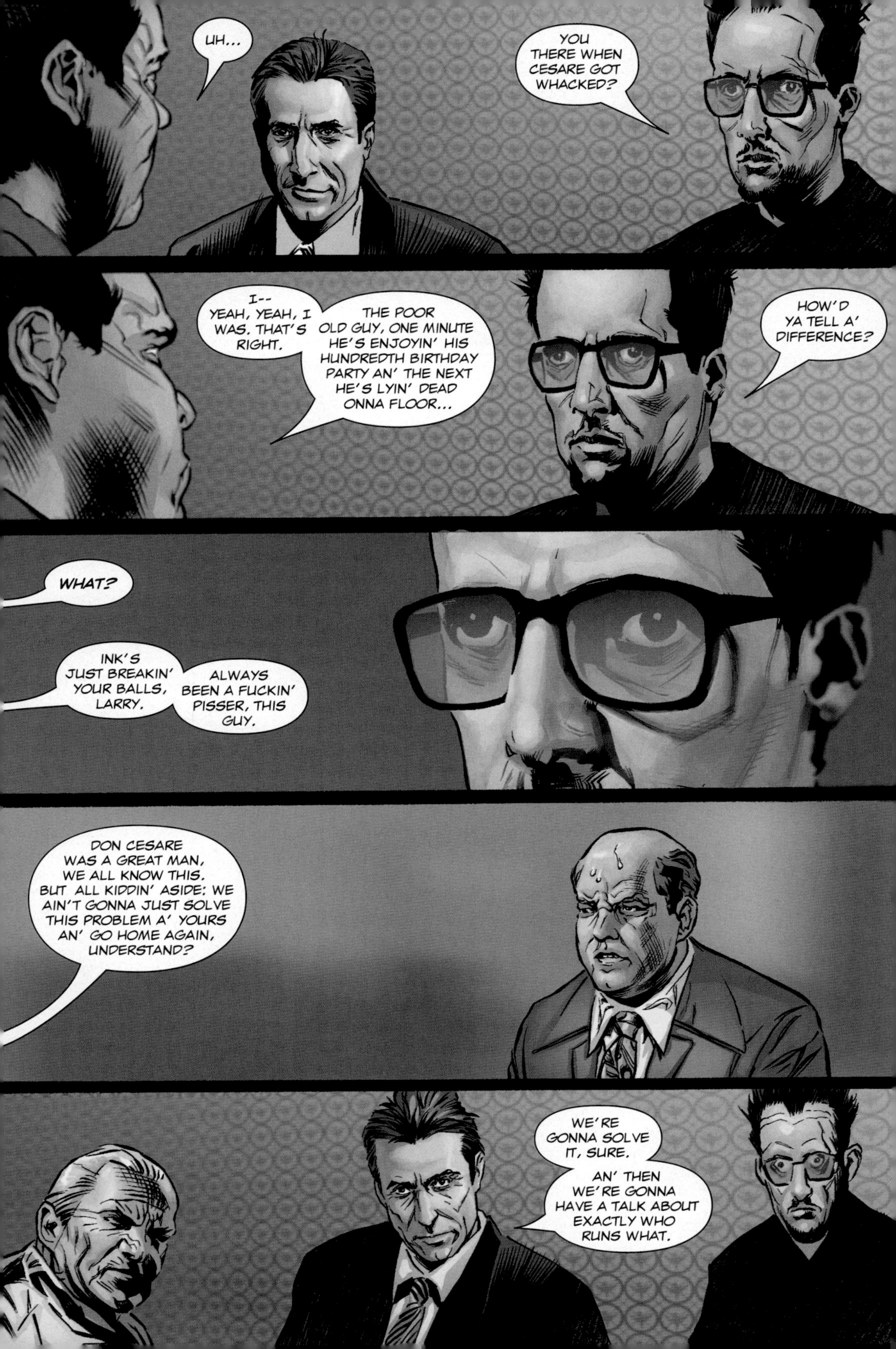
UH...
YOU THERE WHEN CESARE GOT WHACKED?
I-- YEAH, YEAH, I WAS. THAT'S RIGHT.
THE POOR OLD GUY, ONE MINUTE HE'S ENJOYIN' HIS HUNDREDTH BIRTHDAY PARTY AN' THE NEXT HE'S LYIN' DEAD ONNA FLOOR...
HOW'D YA TELL A' DIFFERENCE?
WHAT?
INK'S JUST BREAKIN' YOUR BALLS, LARRY.
ALWAYS BEEN A FUCKIN' PISSER, THIS GUY.
DON CESARE WAS A GREAT MAN, WE ALL KNOW THIS. BUT ALL KIDDIN' ASIDE: WE AIN'T GONNA JUST SOLVE THIS PROBLEM A' YOURS AN' GO HOME AGAIN, UNDERSTAND?
WE'RE GONNA SOLVE IT, SURE.
AN' THEN WE'RE GONNA HAVE A TALK ABOUT EXACTLY WHO RUNS WHAT.

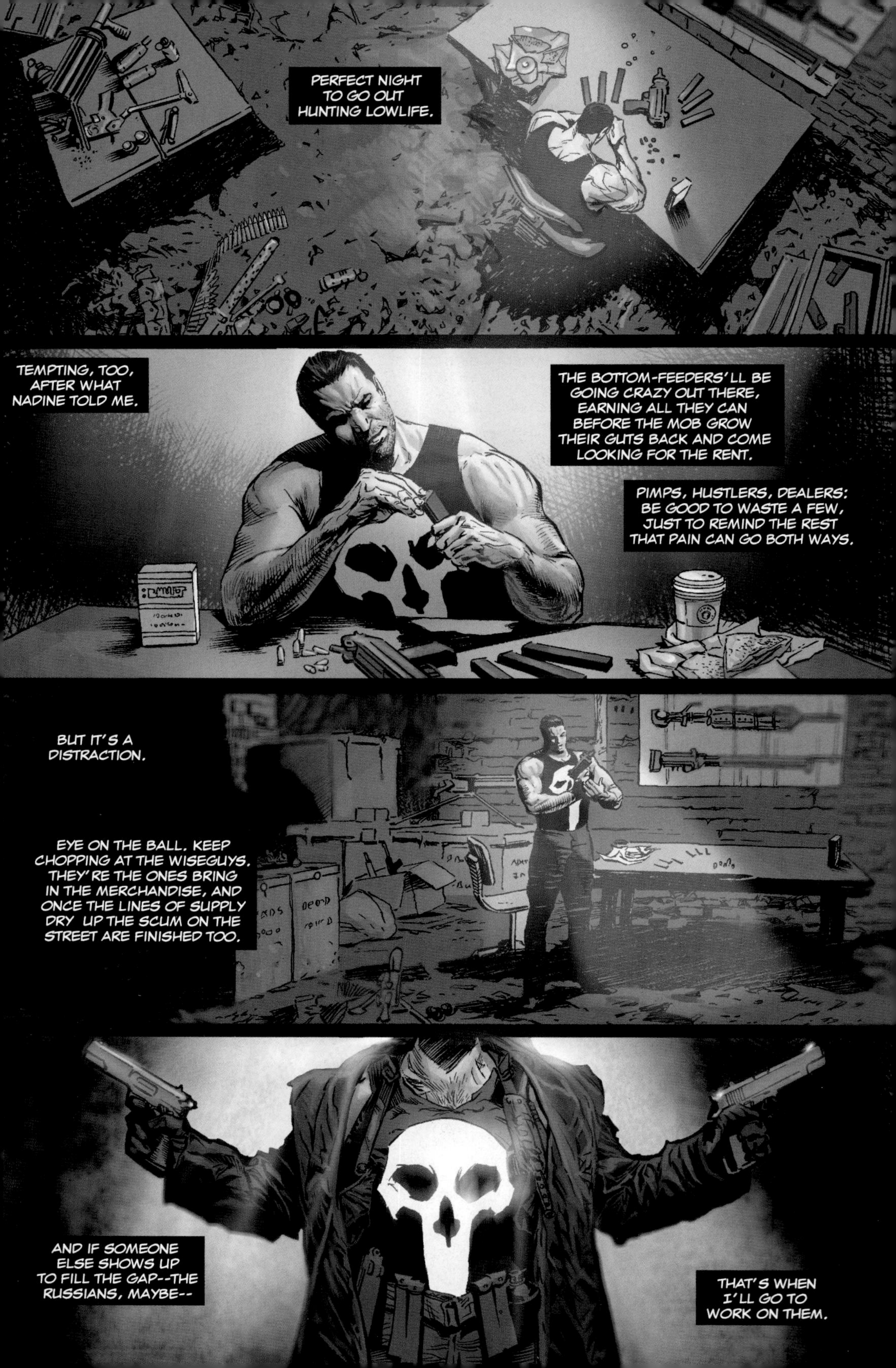
PERFECT NIGHT TO GO OUT HUNTING LOWLIFE.
TEMPTING, TOO, AFTER WHAT NADINE TOLD ME.
THE BOTTOM-FEEDERS'LL BE GOING CRAZY OUT THERE, EARNING ALL THEY CAN BEFORE THE MOB GROW THEIR GUTS BACK AND COME LOOKING FOR THE RENT.
PIMPS, HUSTLERS, DEALERS: BE GOOD TO WASTE A FEW, JUST TO REMIND THE REST THAT PAIN CAN GO BOTH WAYS.
BUT IT'S A DISTRACTION.
EYE ON THE BALL. KEEP CHOPPING AT THE WISEGUYS. THEY'RE THE ONES BRING IN THE MERCHANDISE, AND ONCE THE LINES OF SUPPLY DRY UP THE SCUM ON THE STREET ARE FINISHED TOO.
AND IF SOMEONE ELSE SHOWS UP TO FILL THE GAP--THE RUSSIANS, MAYBE--
THAT'S WHEN I'LL GO TO WORK ON THEM.

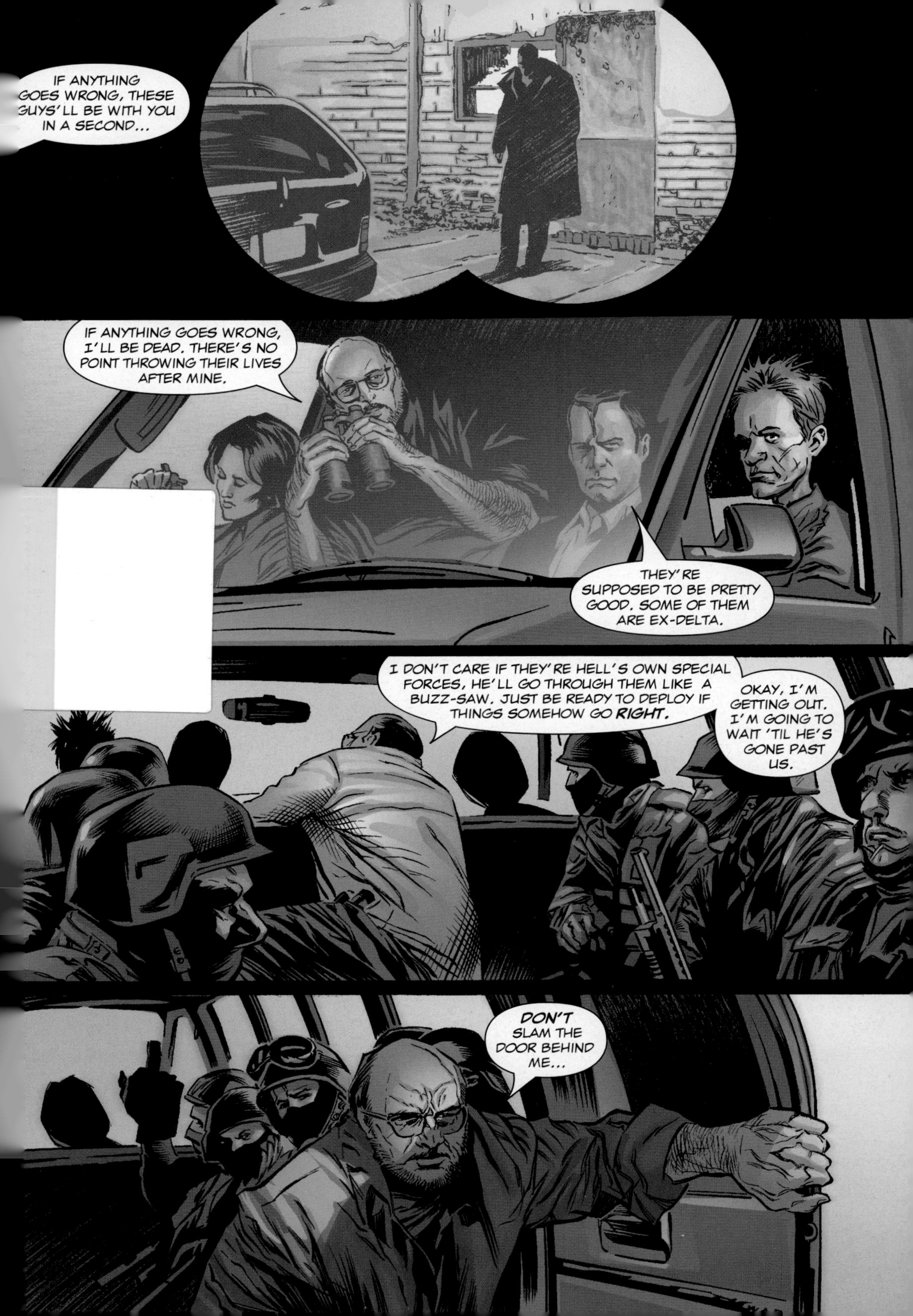
IF ANYTHING GOES WRONG, THESE GUYS'LL BE WITH YOU IN A SECOND...
IF ANYTHING GOES WRONG, I'LL BE DEAD. THERE'S NO POINT THROWING THEIR LIVES AFTER MINE.
THEY'RE SUPPOSED TO BE PRETTY GOOD. SOME OF THEM ARE EX-DELTA.
I DON'T CARE IF THEY'RE HELL'S OWN SPECIAL FORCES, HE'LL GO THROUGH THEM LIKE A BUZZ-SAW. JUST BE READY TO DEPLOY IF THINGS SOMEHOW GO **RIGHT.**
OKAY, I'M GETTING OUT. I'M GOING TO WAIT 'TIL HE'S GONE PAST US.
DON'T SLAM THE DOOR BEHIND ME...

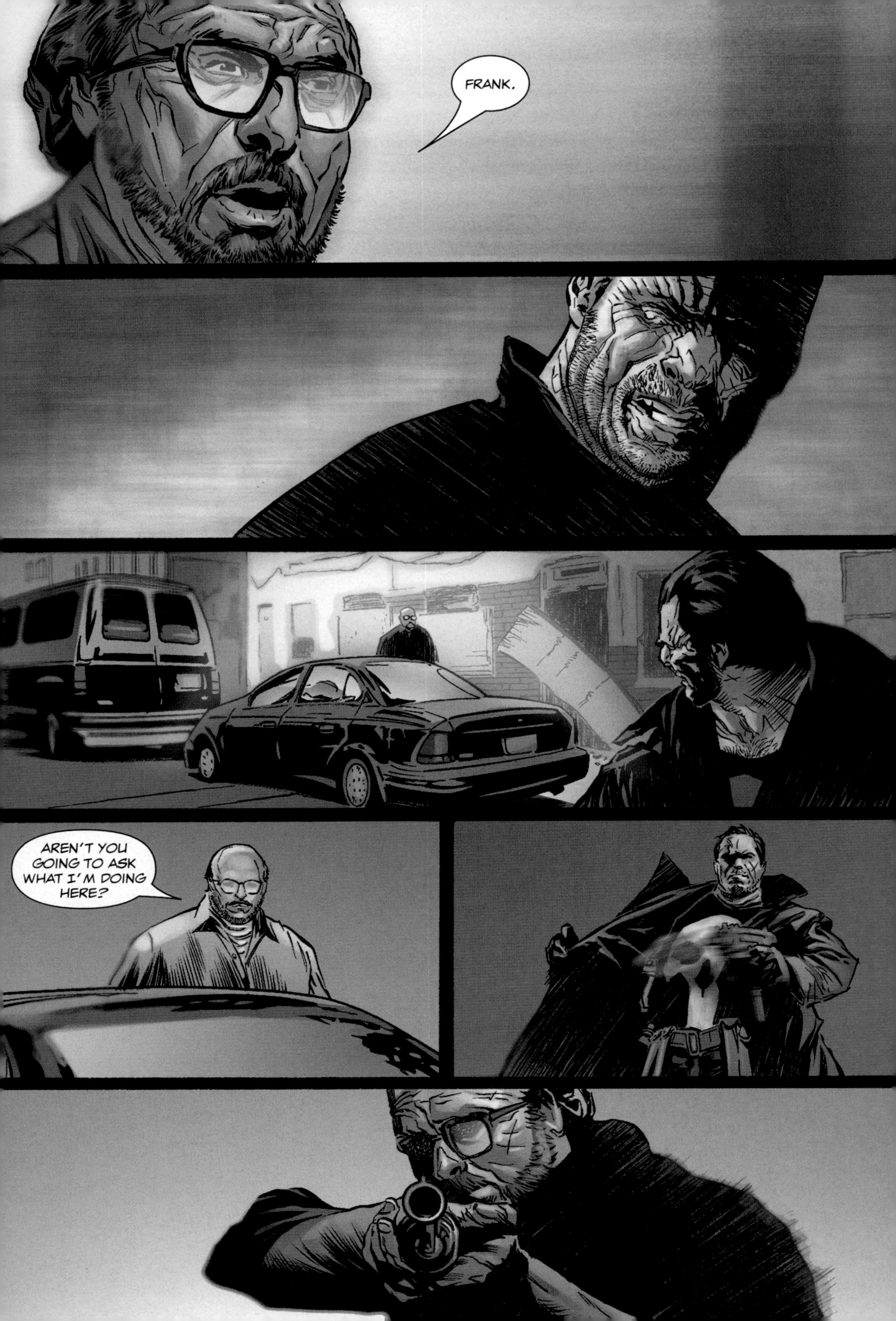
FRANK.
AREN'T YOU GOING TO ASK WHAT I'M DOING HERE?

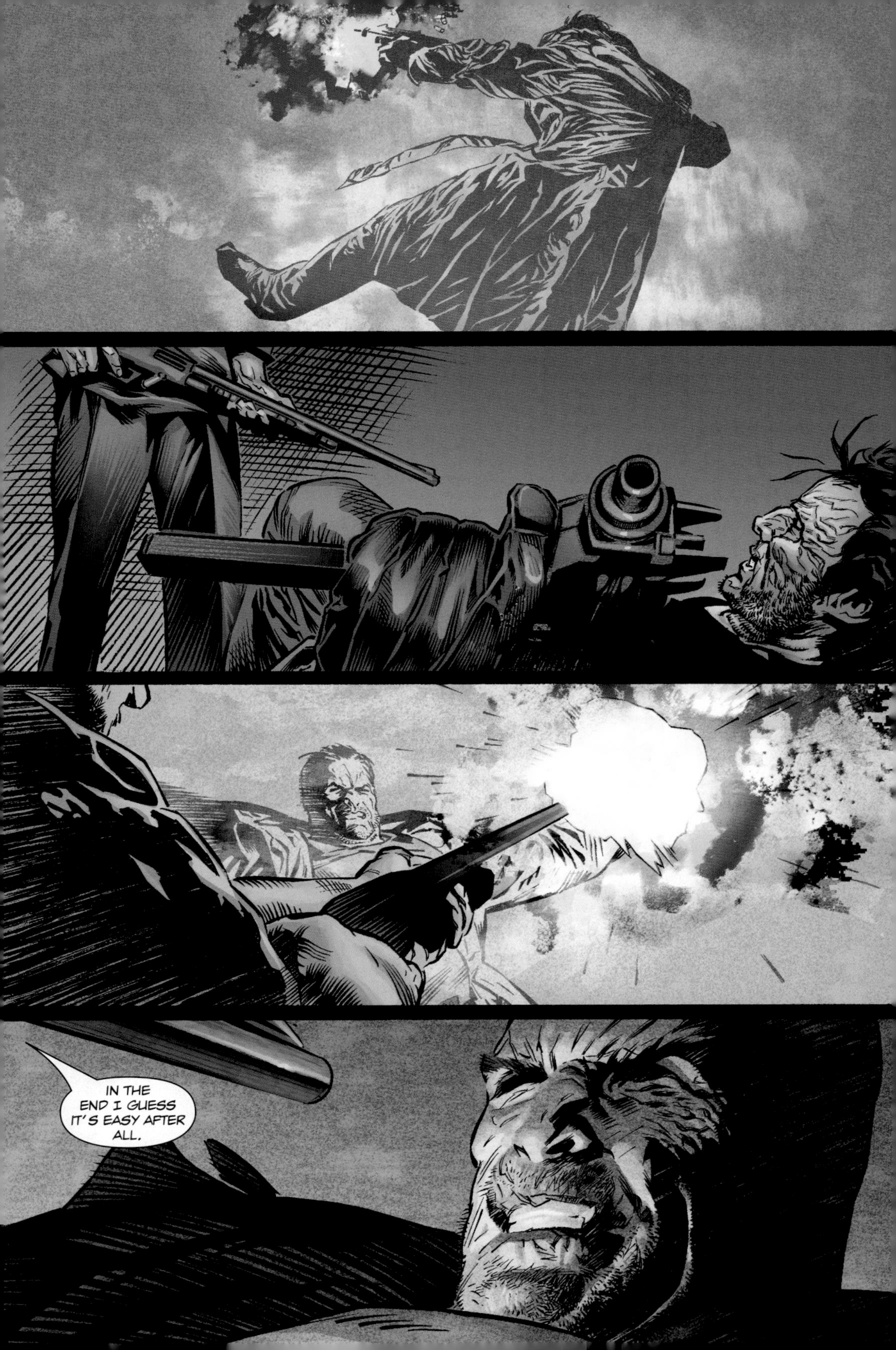
IN THE END I GUESS IT'S EASY AFTER ALL.

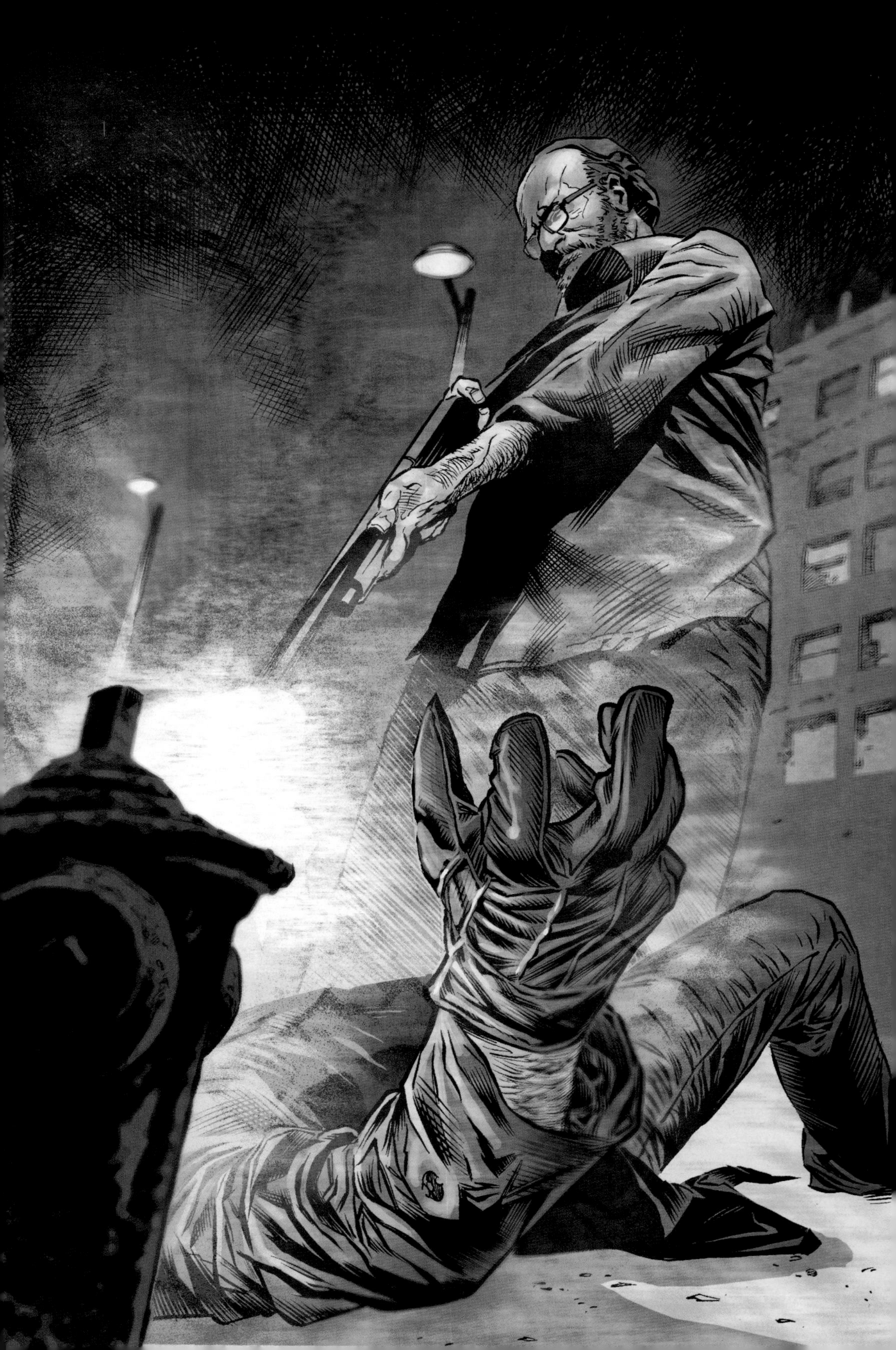

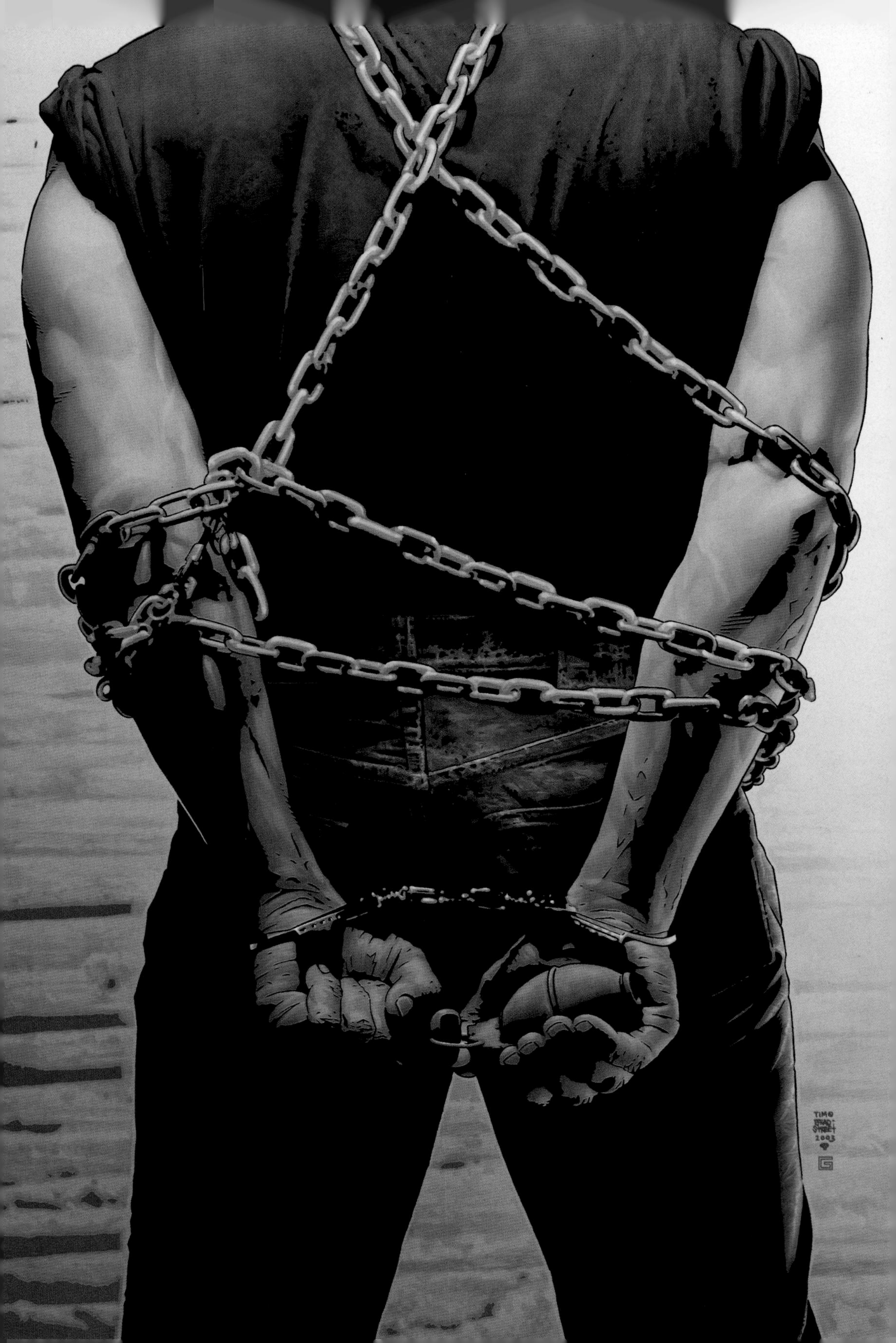
TIMO
2003

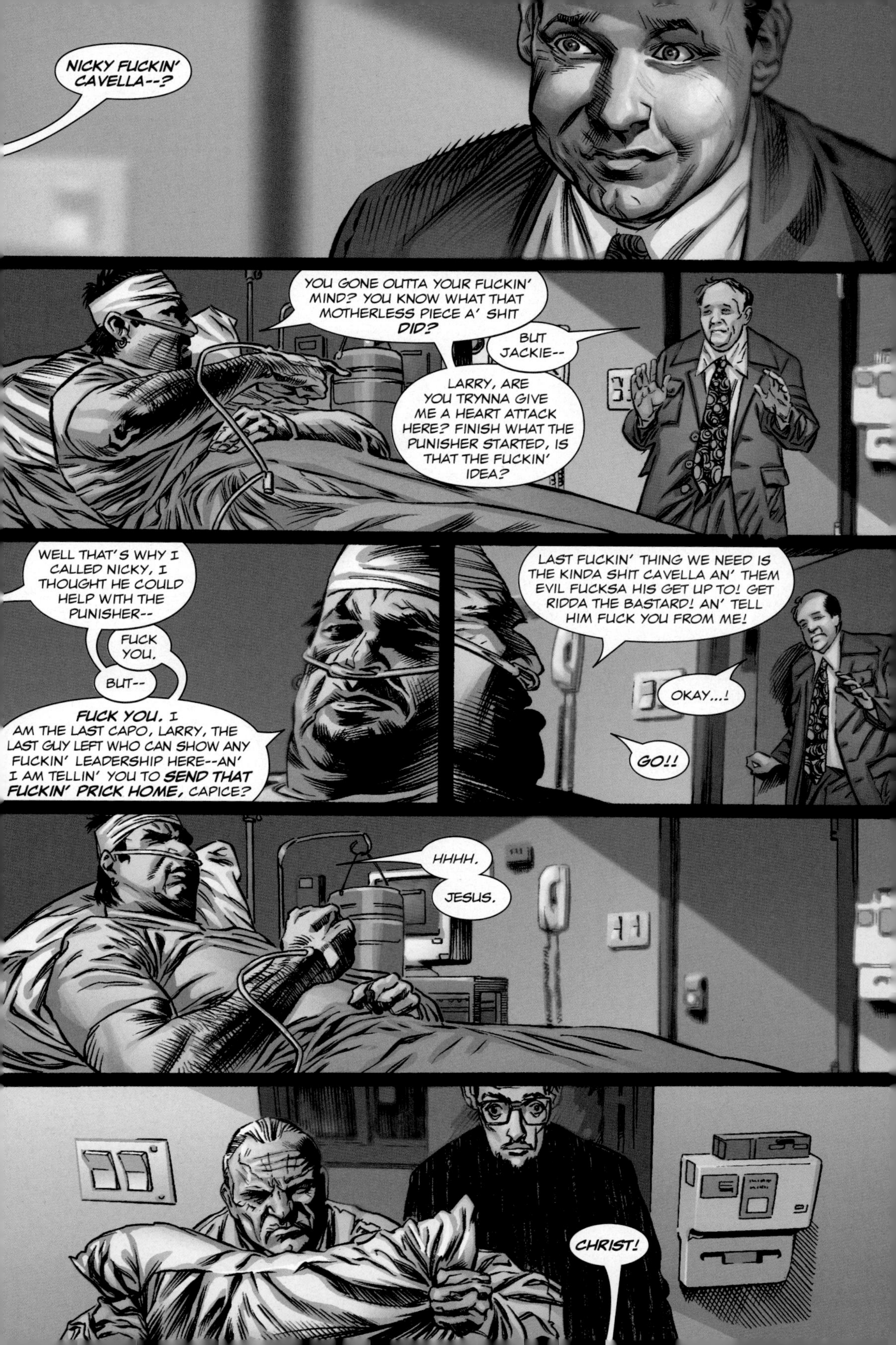
NICKY FUCKIN' CAVELLA--?
YOU GONE OUTTA YOUR FUCKIN' MIND? YOU KNOW WHAT THAT MOTHERLESS PIECE A' SHIT DID?
BUT JACKIE--
LARRY, ARE YOU TRYNNA GIVE ME A HEART ATTACK HERE? FINISH WHAT THE PUNISHER STARTED, IS THAT THE FUCKIN' IDEA?
WELL THAT'S WHY I CALLED NICKY, I THOUGHT HE COULD HELP WITH THE PUNISHER--
FUCK YOU.
BUT--
FUCK YOU. I AM THE LAST CAPO, LARRY, THE LAST GUY LEFT WHO CAN SHOW ANY FUCKIN' LEADERSHIP HERE--AN' I AM TELLIN' YOU TO SEND THAT FUCKIN' PRICK HOME, CAPICE?
LAST FUCKIN' THING WE NEED IS THE KINDA SHIT CAVELLA AN' THEM EVIL FUCKSA HIS GET UP TO! GET RIDDA THE BASTARD! AN' TELL HIM FUCK YOU FROM ME!
OKAY...!
GO!!
HHHH.
JESUS.
CHRIST!

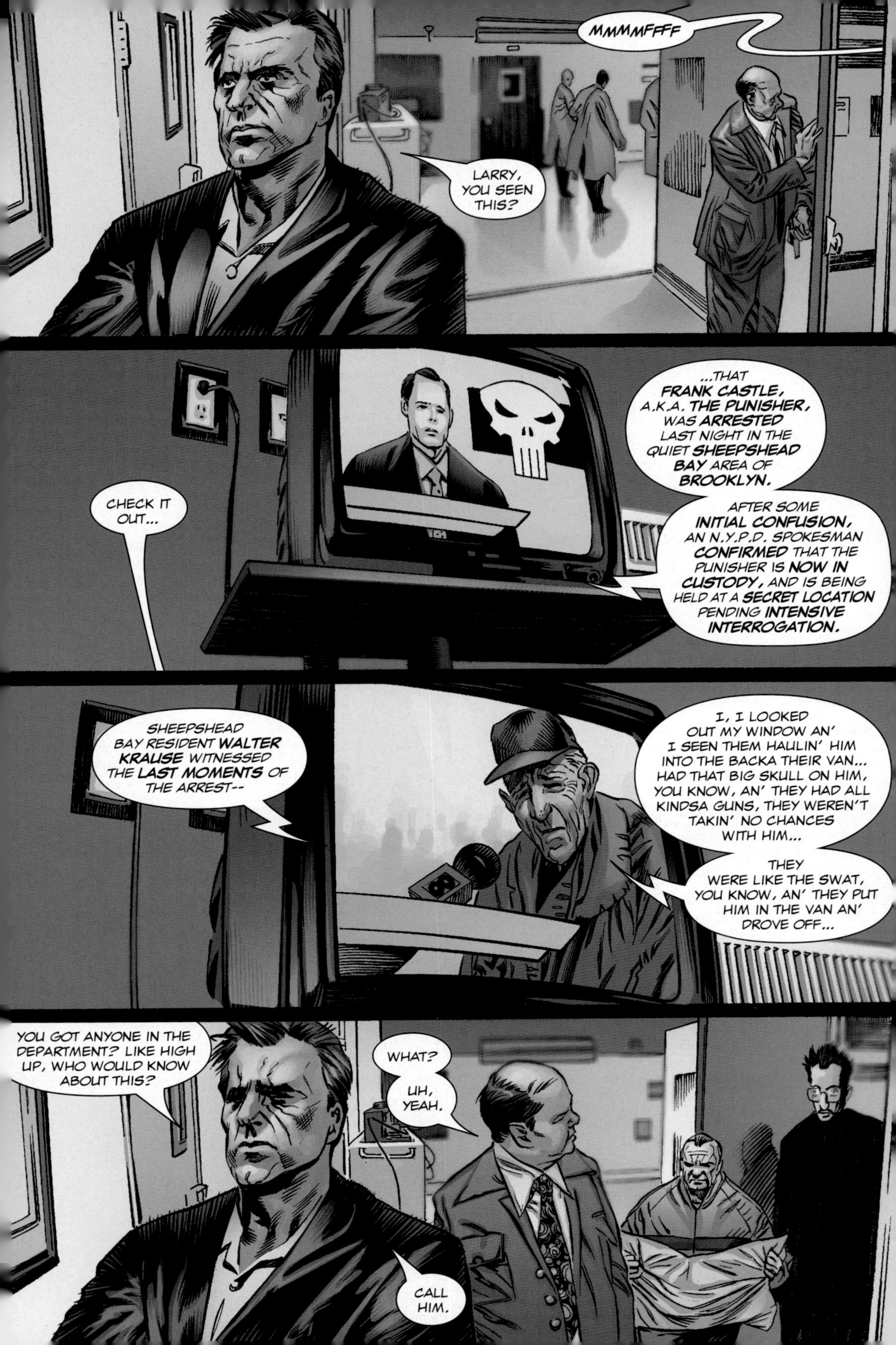
MMMMFFFF
LARRY, YOU SEEN THIS?
...THAT FRANK CASTLE, A.K.A. THE PUNISHER, WAS ARRESTED LAST NIGHT IN THE QUIET SHEEPSHEAD BAY AREA OF BROOKLYN.
CHECK IT OUT...
AFTER SOME INITIAL CONFUSION, AN N.Y.P.D. SPOKESMAN CONFIRMED THAT THE PUNISHER IS NOW IN CUSTODY, AND IS BEING HELD AT A SECRET LOCATION PENDING INTENSIVE INTERROGATION.
SHEEPSHEAD BAY RESIDENT WALTER KRAUSE WITNESSED THE LAST MOMENTS OF THE ARREST--
I, I LOOKED OUT MY WINDOW AN' I SEEN THEM HAULIN' HIM INTO THE BACKA THEIR VAN... HAD THAT BIG SKULL ON HIM, YOU KNOW, AN' THEY HAD ALL KINDSA GUNS, THEY WEREN'T TAKIN' NO CHANCES WITH HIM...
THEY WERE LIKE THE SWAT, YOU KNOW, AN' THEY PUT HIM IN THE VAN AN' DROVE OFF...
YOU GOT ANYONE IN THE DEPARTMENT? LIKE HIGH UP, WHO WOULD KNOW ABOUT THIS?
WHAT?
UH, YEAH.
CALL HIM.

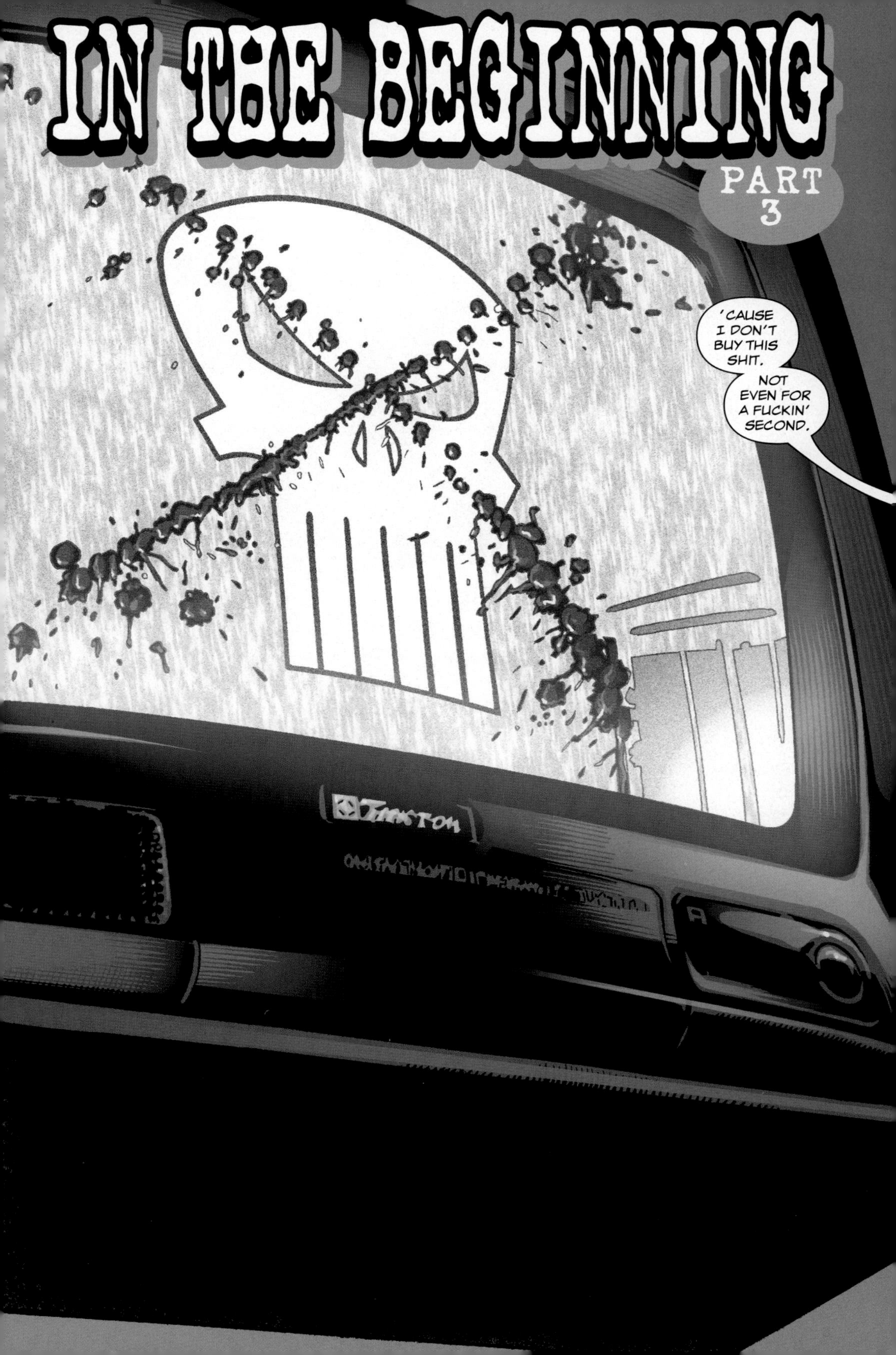
IN THE BEGINNING
PART 3
'CAUSE I DON'T BUY THIS SHIT.
NOT EVEN FOR A FUCKIN' SECOND.

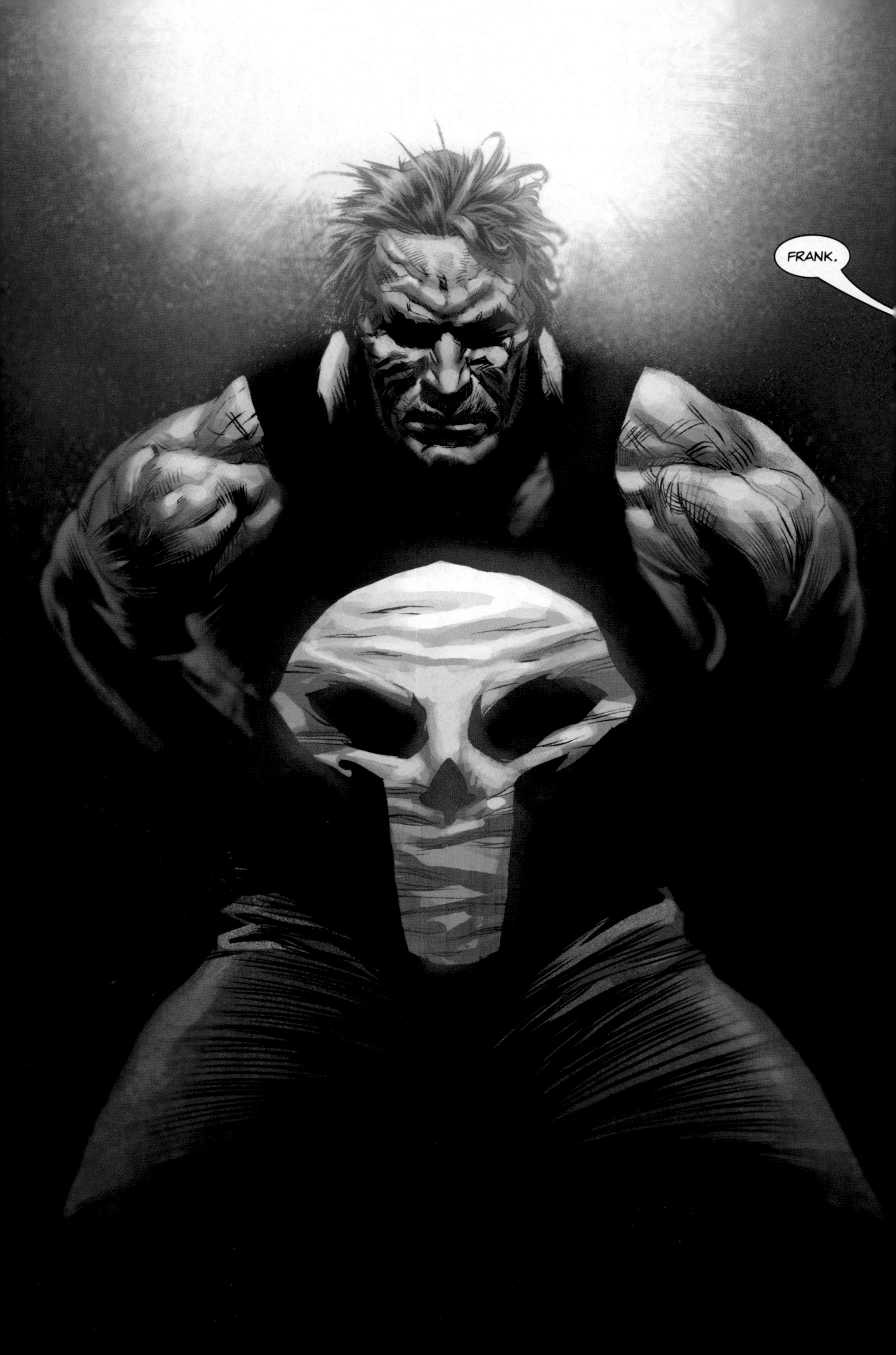
FRANK.

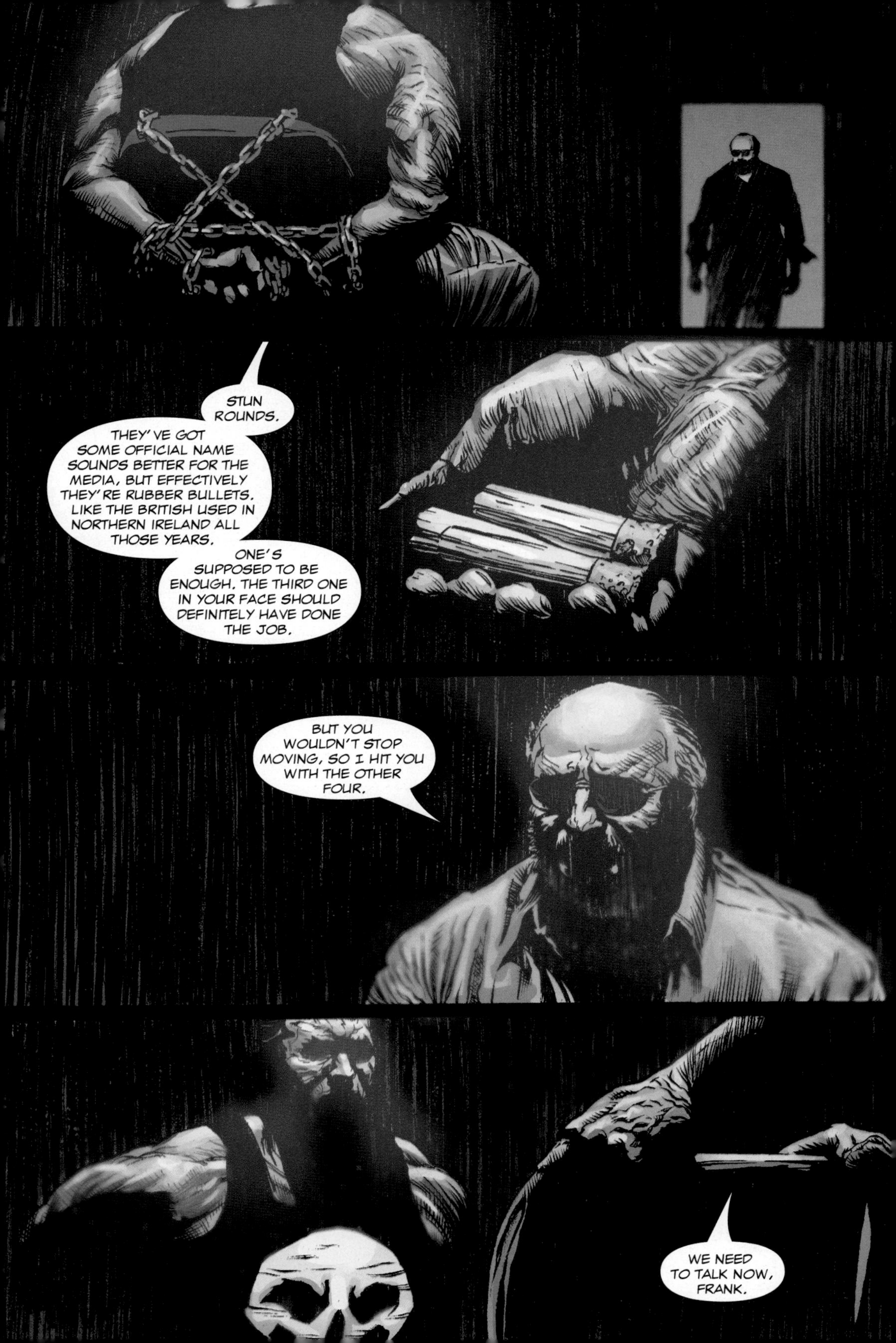
STUN ROUNDS.
THEY'VE GOT SOME OFFICIAL NAME SOUNDS BETTER FOR THE MEDIA, BUT EFFECTIVELY THEY'RE RUBBER BULLETS. LIKE THE BRITISH USED IN NORTHERN IRELAND ALL THOSE YEARS.
ONE'S SUPPOSED TO BE ENOUGH. THE THIRD ONE IN YOUR FACE SHOULD DEFINITELY HAVE DONE THE JOB.
BUT YOU WOULDN'T STOP MOVING, SO I HIT YOU WITH THE OTHER FOUR.
WE NEED TO TALK NOW, FRANK.

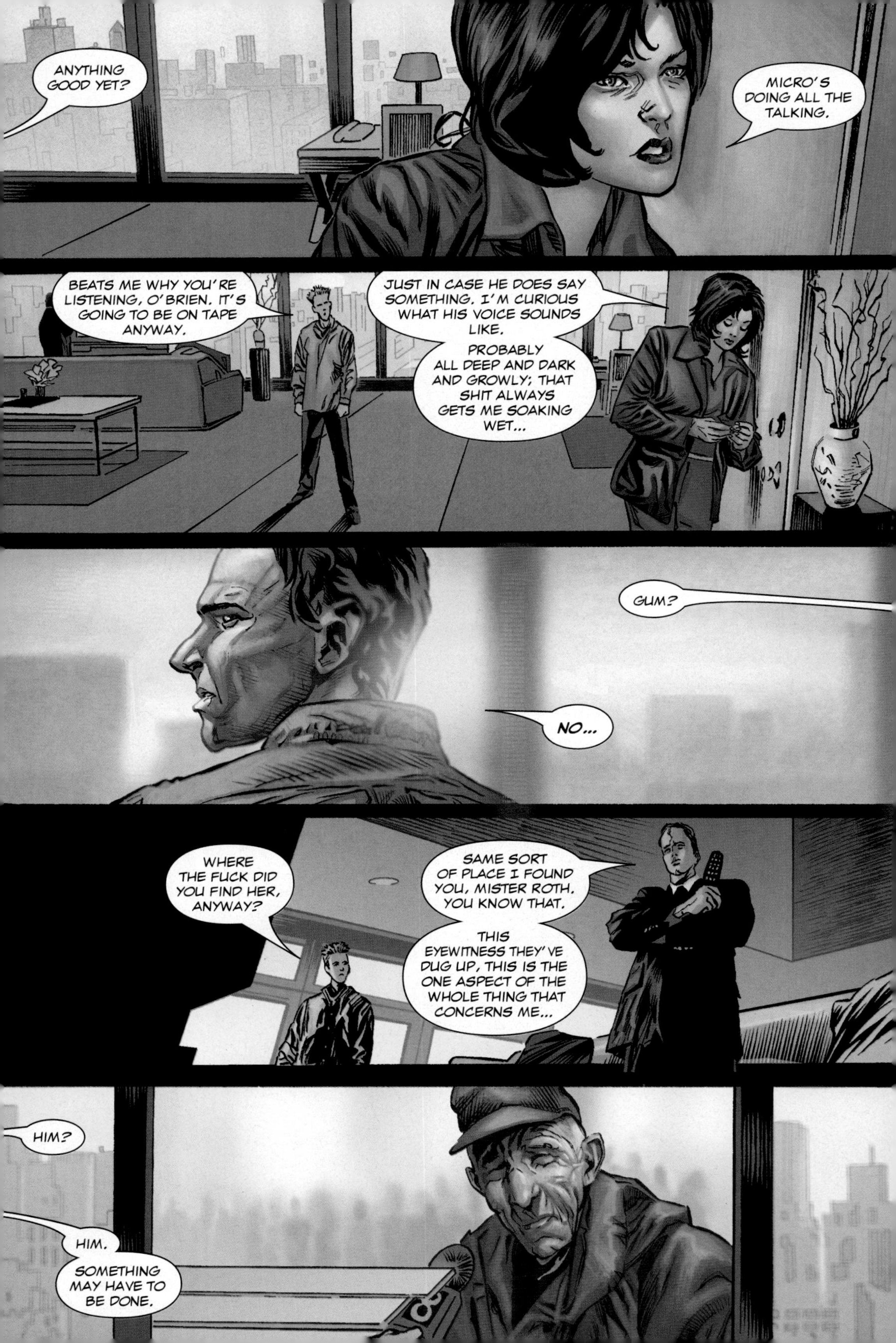
ANYTHING GOOD YET?
MICRO'S DOING ALL THE TALKING.
BEATS ME WHY YOU'RE LISTENING, O'BRIEN. IT'S GOING TO BE ON TAPE ANYWAY.
JUST IN CASE HE DOES SAY SOMETHING. I'M CURIOUS WHAT HIS VOICE SOUNDS LIKE.
PROBABLY ALL DEEP AND DARK AND GROWLY; THAT SHIT ALWAYS GETS ME SOAKING WET...
GUM?
NO...
WHERE THE FUCK DID YOU FIND HER, ANYWAY?
SAME SORT OF PLACE I FOUND YOU, MISTER ROTH. YOU KNOW THAT.
THIS EYEWITNESS THEY'VE DUG UP, THIS IS THE ONE ASPECT OF THE WHOLE THING THAT CONCERNS ME...
HIM?
HIM.
SOMETHING MAY HAVE TO BE DONE.

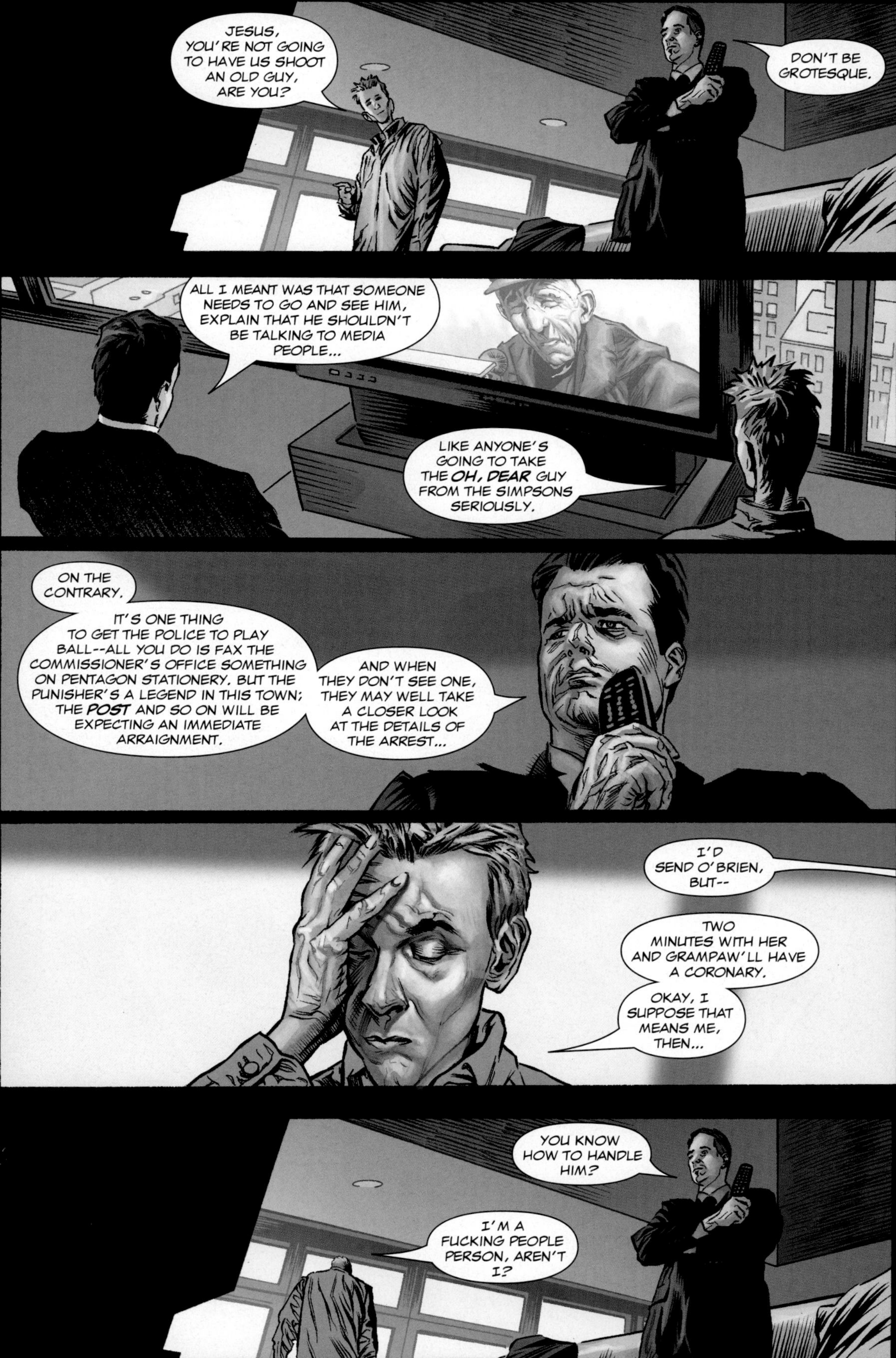
JESUS, YOU'RE NOT GOING TO HAVE US SHOOT AN OLD GUY, ARE YOU?
DON'T BE GROTESQUE.
ALL I MEANT WAS THAT SOMEONE NEEDS TO GO AND SEE HIM, EXPLAIN THAT HE SHOULDN'T BE TALKING TO MEDIA PEOPLE...
LIKE ANYONE'S GOING TO TAKE THE OH, DEAR GUY FROM THE SIMPSONS SERIOUSLY.
ON THE CONTRARY.
IT'S ONE THING TO GET THE POLICE TO PLAY BALL--ALL YOU DO IS FAX THE COMMISSIONER'S OFFICE SOMETHING ON PENTAGON STATIONERY. BUT THE PUNISHER'S A LEGEND IN THIS TOWN; THE POST AND SO ON WILL BE EXPECTING AN IMMEDIATE ARRAIGNMENT.
AND WHEN THEY DON'T SEE ONE, THEY MAY WELL TAKE A CLOSER LOOK AT THE DETAILS OF THE ARREST...
I'D SEND O'BRIEN, BUT--
TWO MINUTES WITH HER AND GRAMPAW'LL HAVE A CORONARY.
OKAY, I SUPPOSE THAT MEANS ME, THEN...
YOU KNOW HOW TO HANDLE HIM?
I'M A FUCKING PEOPLE PERSON, AREN'T I?

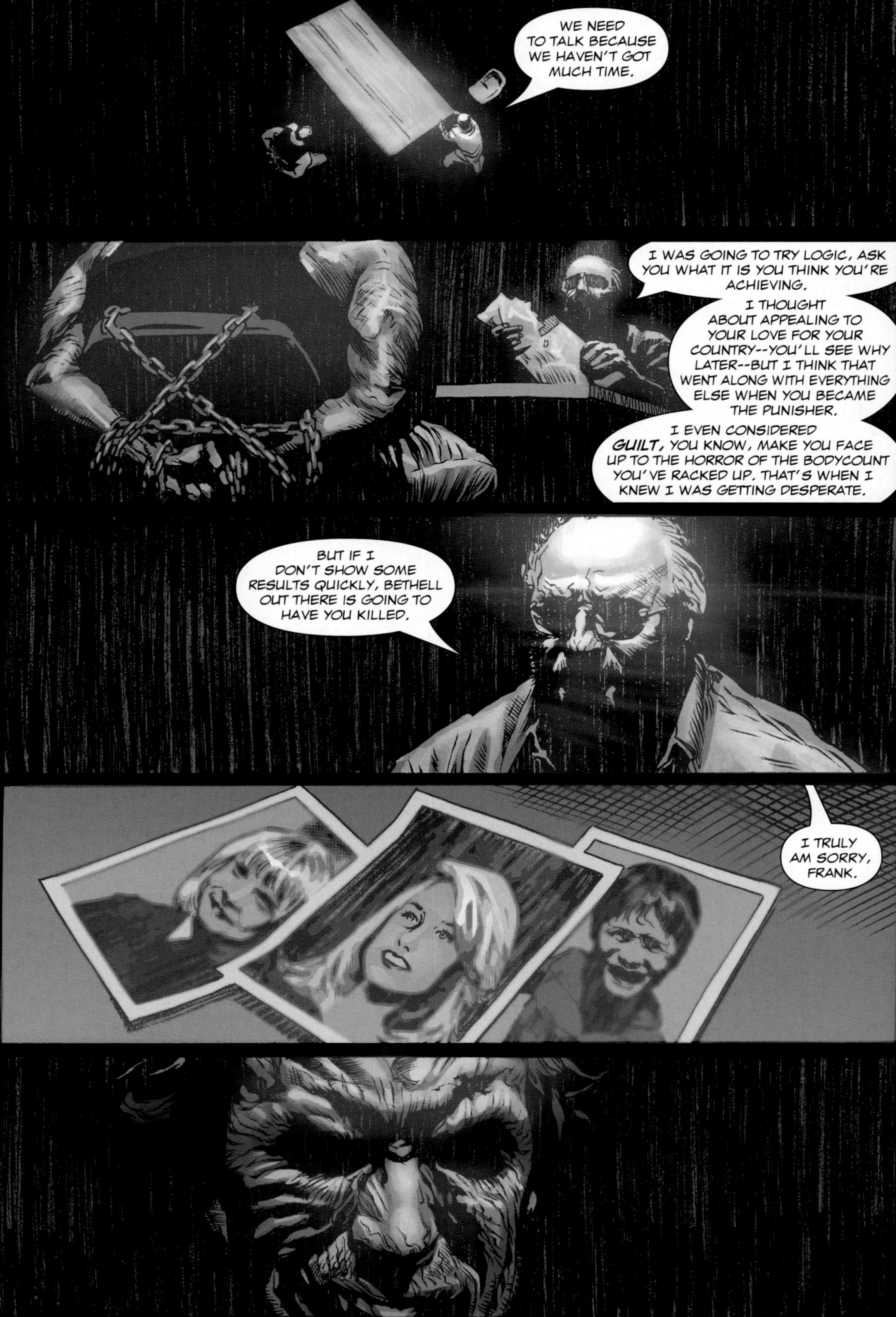
WE NEED TO TALK BECAUSE WE HAVEN'T GOT MUCH TIME.
I WAS GOING TO TRY LOGIC, ASK YOU WHAT IT IS YOU THINK YOU'RE ACHIEVING.
I THOUGHT ABOUT APPEALING TO YOUR LOVE FOR YOUR COUNTRY--YOU'LL SEE WHY LATER--BUT I THINK THAT WENT ALONG WITH EVERYTHING ELSE WHEN YOU BECAME THE PUNISHER.
I EVEN CONSIDERED **GUILT,** YOU KNOW, MAKE YOU FACE UP TO THE HORROR OF THE BODYCOUNT YOU'VE RACKED UP. THAT'S WHEN I KNEW I WAS GETTING DESPERATE.
BUT IF I DON'T SHOW SOME RESULTS QUICKLY, BETHELL OUT THERE IS GOING TO HAVE YOU KILLED.
I TRULY AM SORRY, FRANK.

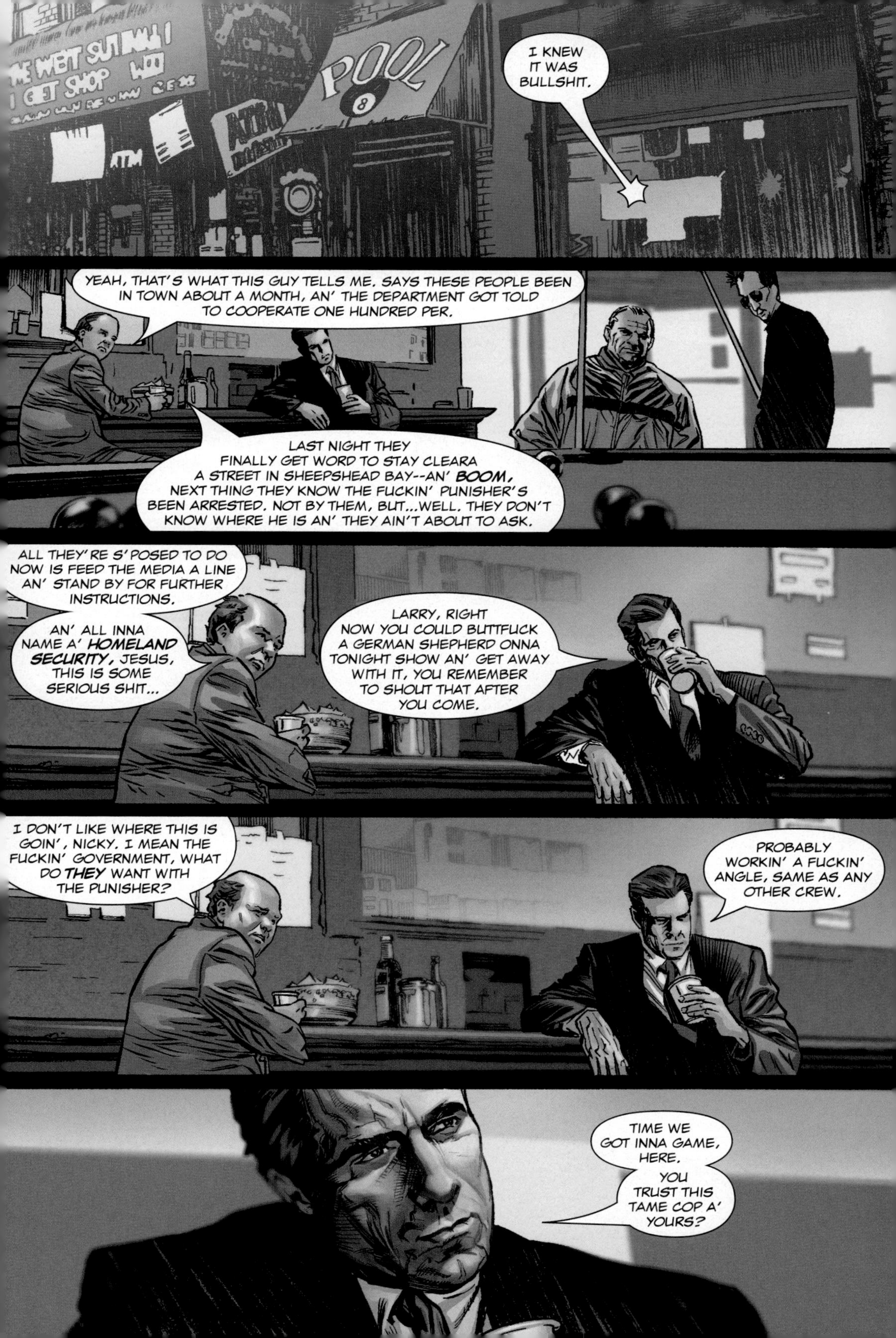

I KNEW IT WAS BULLSHIT.
YEAH, THAT'S WHAT THIS GUY TELLS ME. SAYS THESE PEOPLE BEEN IN TOWN ABOUT A MONTH, AN' THE DEPARTMENT GOT TOLD TO COOPERATE ONE HUNDRED PER.
LAST NIGHT THEY FINALLY GET WORD TO STAY CLEARA A STREET IN SHEEPSHEAD BAY--AN' BOOM, NEXT THING THEY KNOW THE FUCKIN' PUNISHER'S BEEN ARRESTED. NOT BY THEM, BUT...WELL. THEY DON'T KNOW WHERE HE IS AN' THEY AIN'T ABOUT TO ASK.
ALL THEY'RE S'POSED TO DO NOW IS FEED THE MEDIA A LINE AN' STAND BY FOR FURTHER INSTRUCTIONS.
AN' ALL INNA NAME A' HOMELAND SECURITY, JESUS, THIS IS SOME SERIOUS SHIT...
LARRY, RIGHT NOW YOU COULD BUTTFUCK A GERMAN SHEPHERD ONNA TONIGHT SHOW AN' GET AWAY WITH IT, YOU REMEMBER TO SHOUT THAT AFTER YOU COME.
I DON'T LIKE WHERE THIS IS GOIN', NICKY. I MEAN THE FUCKIN' GOVERNMENT, WHAT DO THEY WANT WITH THE PUNISHER?
PROBABLY WORKIN' A FUCKIN' ANGLE, SAME AS ANY OTHER CREW.
TIME WE GOT INNA GAME, HERE.
YOU TRUST THIS TAME COP A' YOURS?

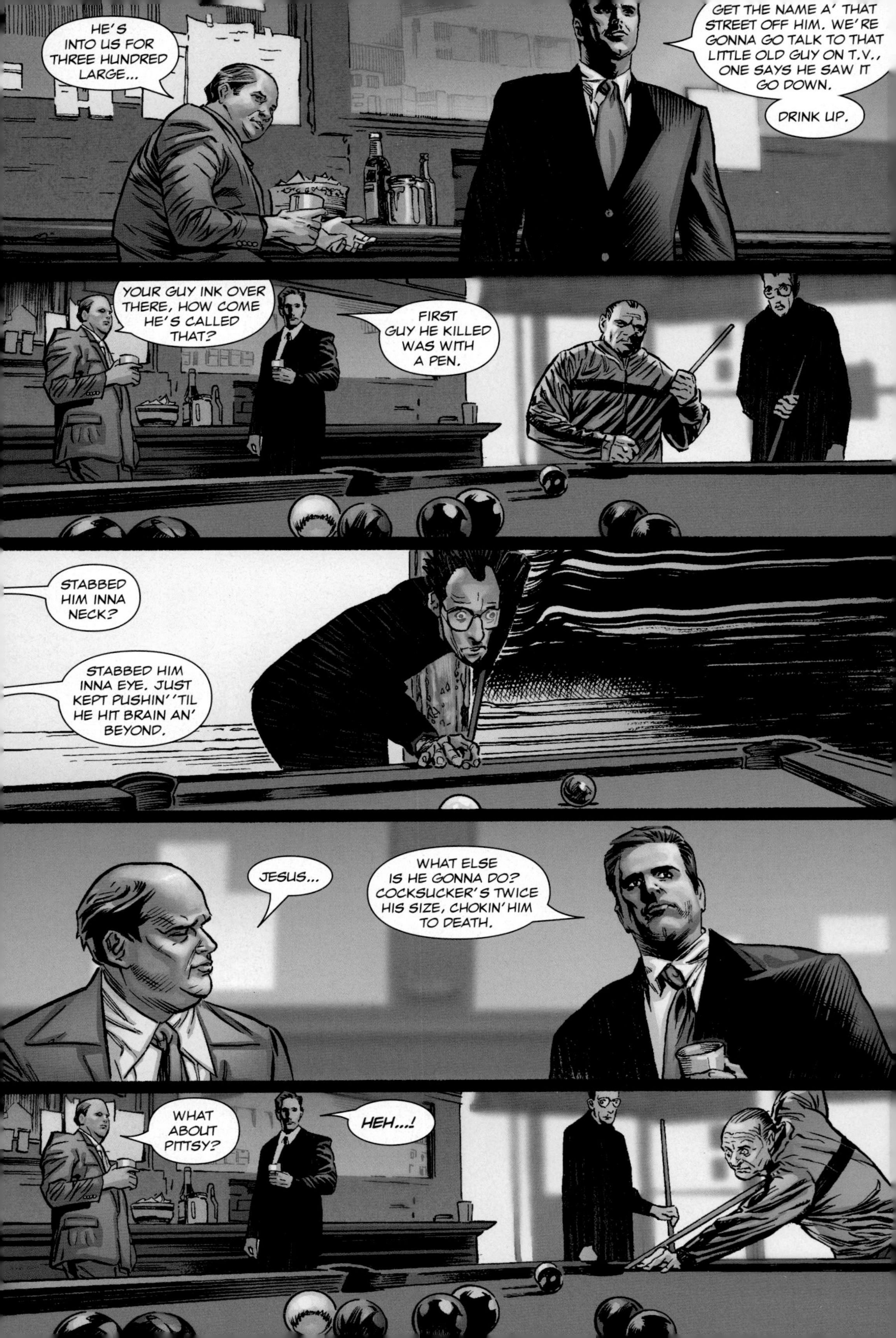
HE'S INTO US FOR THREE HUNDRED LARGE...
GET THE NAME A' THAT STREET OFF HIM. WE'RE GONNA GO TALK TO THAT LITTLE OLD GUY ON T.V., ONE SAYS HE SAW IT GO DOWN.
DRINK UP.
YOUR GUY INK OVER THERE, HOW COME HE'S CALLED THAT?
FIRST GUY HE KILLED WAS WITH A PEN.
STABBED HIM INNA NECK?
STABBED HIM INNA EYE. JUST KEPT PUSHIN' 'TIL HE HIT BRAIN AN' BEYOND.
JESUS...
WHAT ELSE IS HE GONNA DO? COCKSUCKER'S TWICE HIS SIZE, CHOKIN' HIM TO DEATH.
WHAT ABOUT PITTSY?
HEH...!

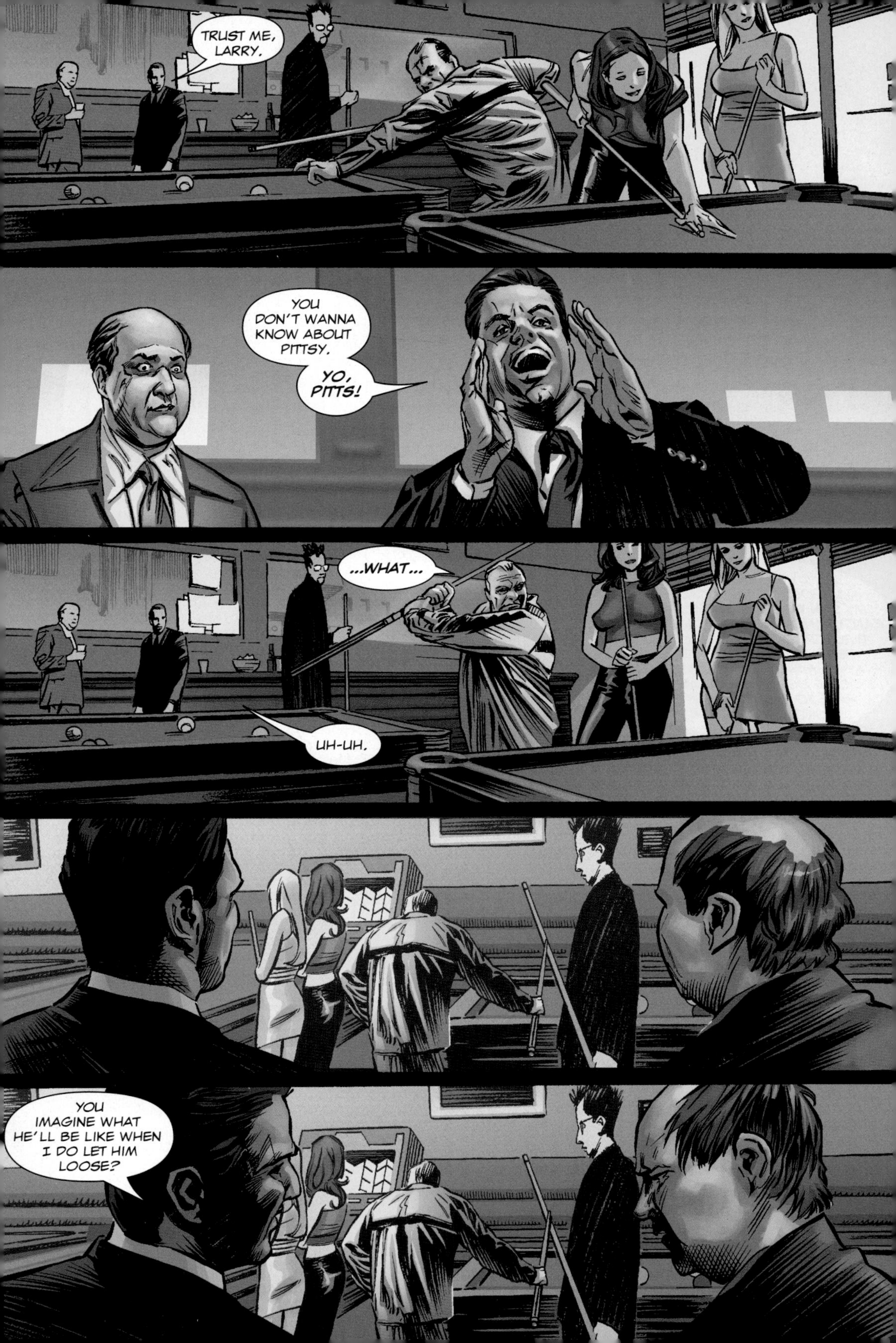
TRUST ME, LARRY.
YOU DON'T WANNA KNOW ABOUT PITTSY.
YO, PITTS!
...WHAT...
UH-UH.
YOU IMAGINE WHAT HE'LL BE LIKE WHEN I DO LET HIM LOOSE?

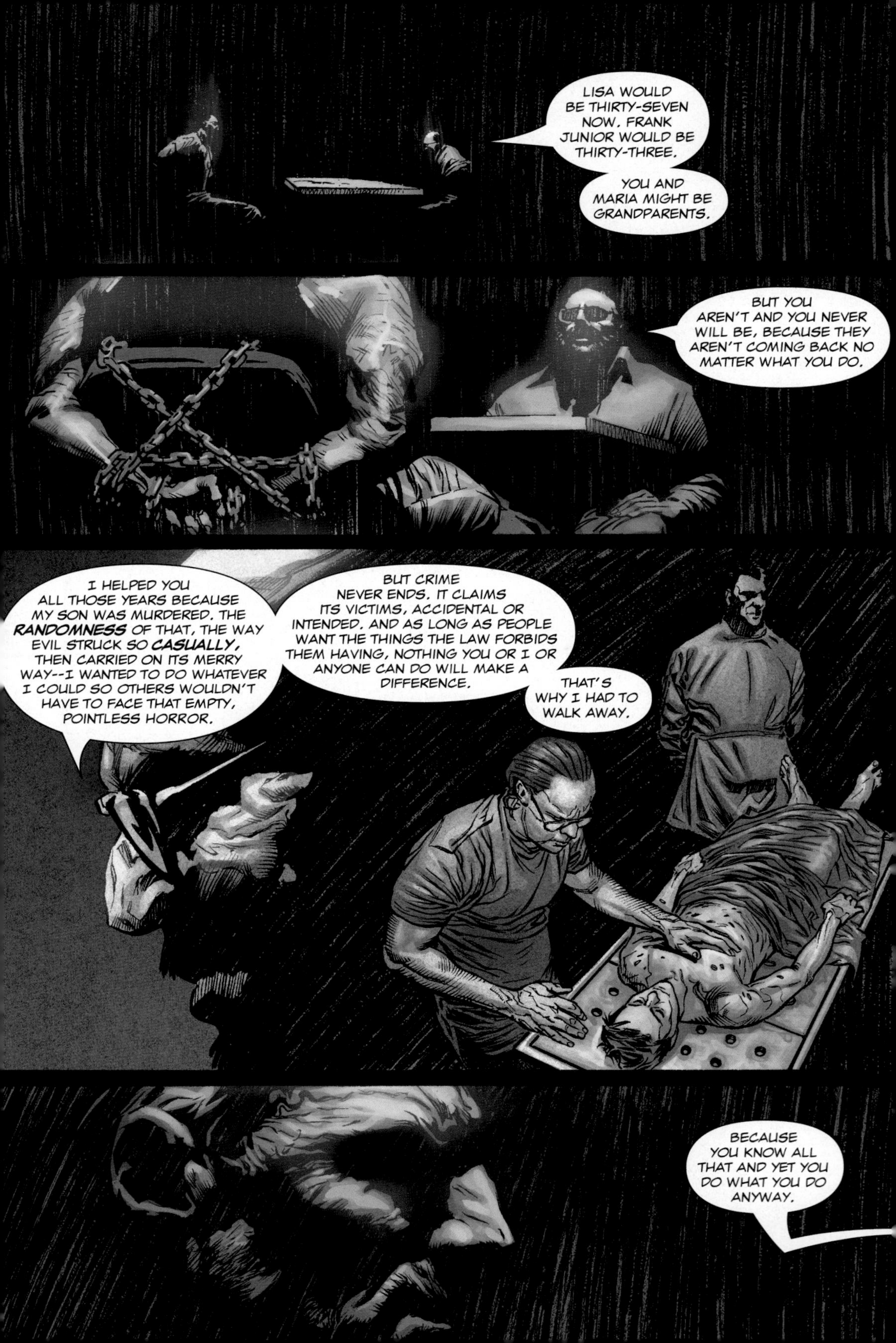

LISA WOULD BE THIRTY-SEVEN NOW. FRANK JUNIOR WOULD BE THIRTY-THREE.
YOU AND MARIA MIGHT BE GRANDPARENTS.
BUT YOU AREN'T AND YOU NEVER WILL BE, BECAUSE THEY AREN'T COMING BACK NO MATTER WHAT YOU DO.
I HELPED YOU ALL THOSE YEARS BECAUSE MY SON WAS MURDERED. THE RANDOMNESS OF THAT, THE WAY EVIL STRUCK SO CASUALLY, THEN CARRIED ON ITS MERRY WAY--I WANTED TO DO WHATEVER I COULD SO OTHERS WOULDN'T HAVE TO FACE THAT EMPTY, POINTLESS HORROR.
BUT CRIME NEVER ENDS. IT CLAIMS ITS VICTIMS, ACCIDENTAL OR INTENDED. AND AS LONG AS PEOPLE WANT THE THINGS THE LAW FORBIDS THEM HAVING, NOTHING YOU OR I OR ANYONE CAN DO WILL MAKE A DIFFERENCE.
THAT'S WHY I HAD TO WALK AWAY.
BECAUSE YOU KNOW ALL THAT AND YET YOU DO WHAT YOU DO ANYWAY.

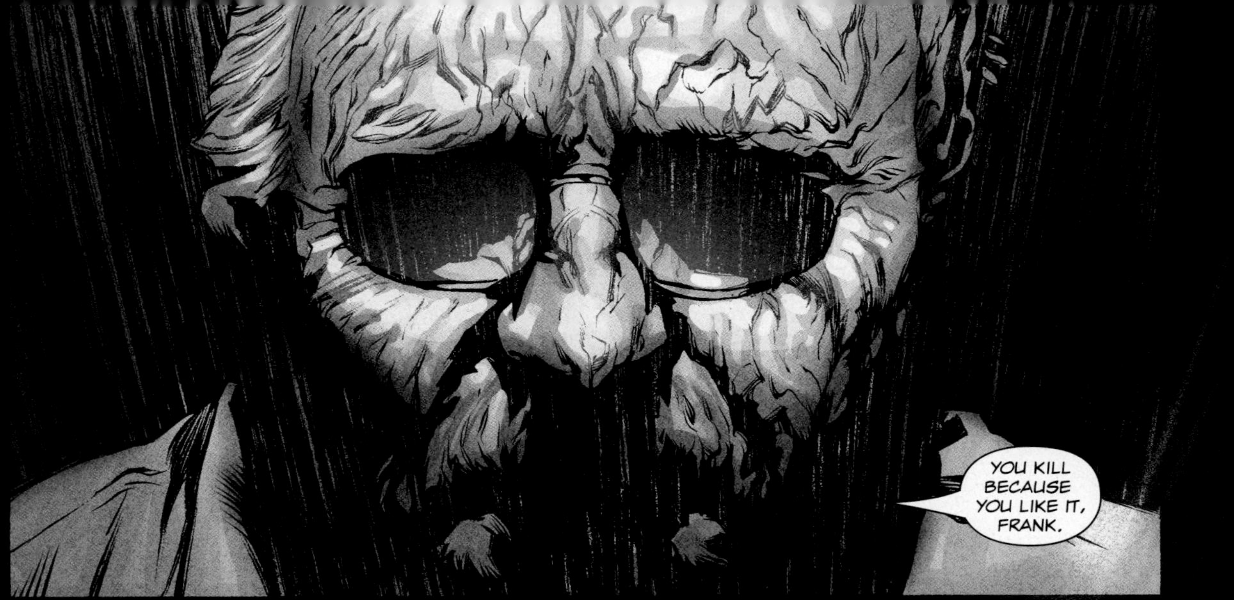
YOU KILL BECAUSE YOU LIKE IT, FRANK.

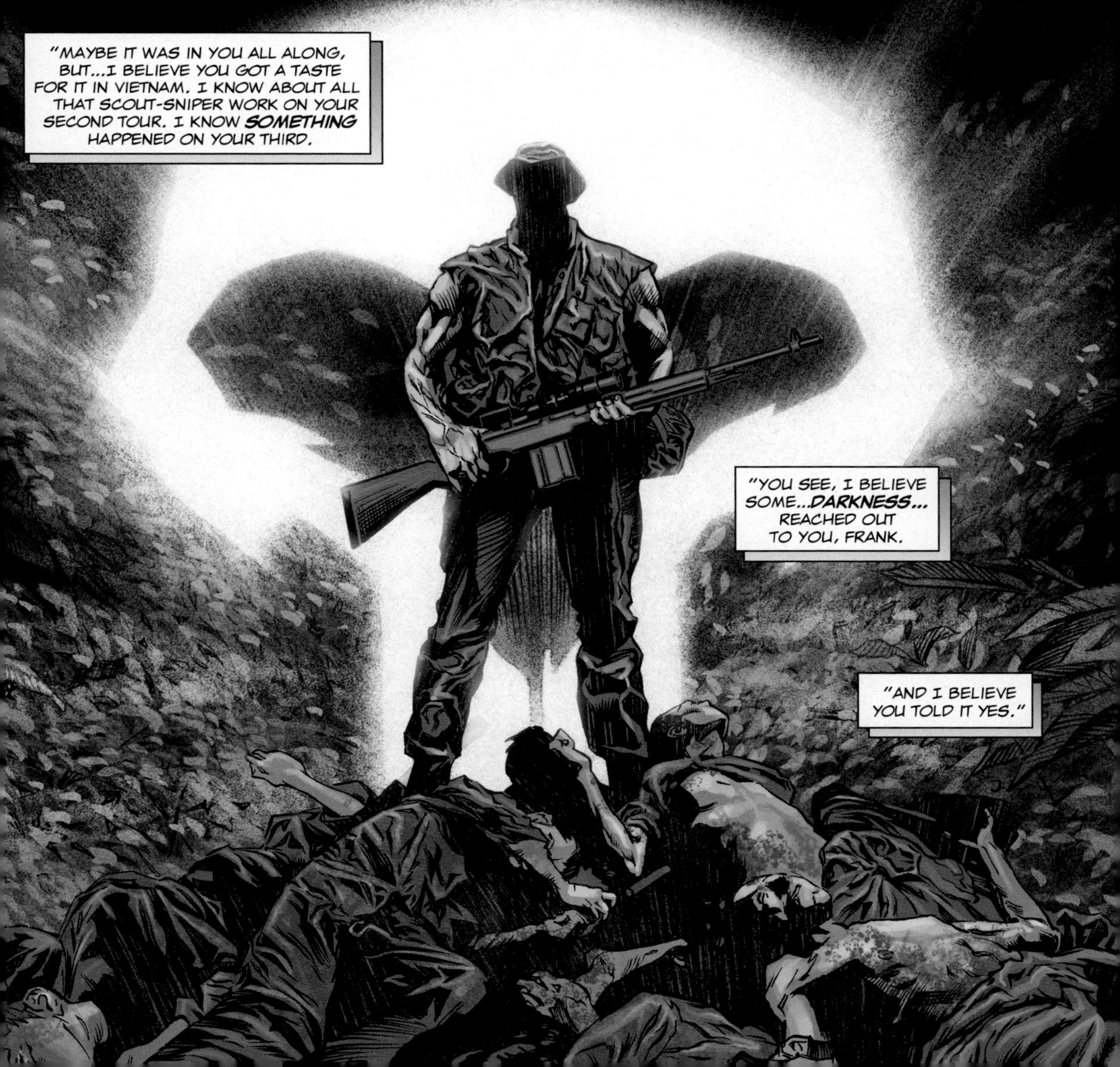
"MAYBE IT WAS IN YOU ALL ALONG, BUT...I BELIEVE YOU GOT A TASTE FOR IT IN VIETNAM. I KNOW ABOUT ALL THAT SCOUT-SNIPER WORK ON YOUR SECOND TOUR. I KNOW SOMETHING HAPPENED ON YOUR THIRD.
"YOU SEE, I BELIEVE SOME...DARKNESS... REACHED OUT TO YOU, FRANK.
"AND I BELIEVE YOU TOLD IT YES."

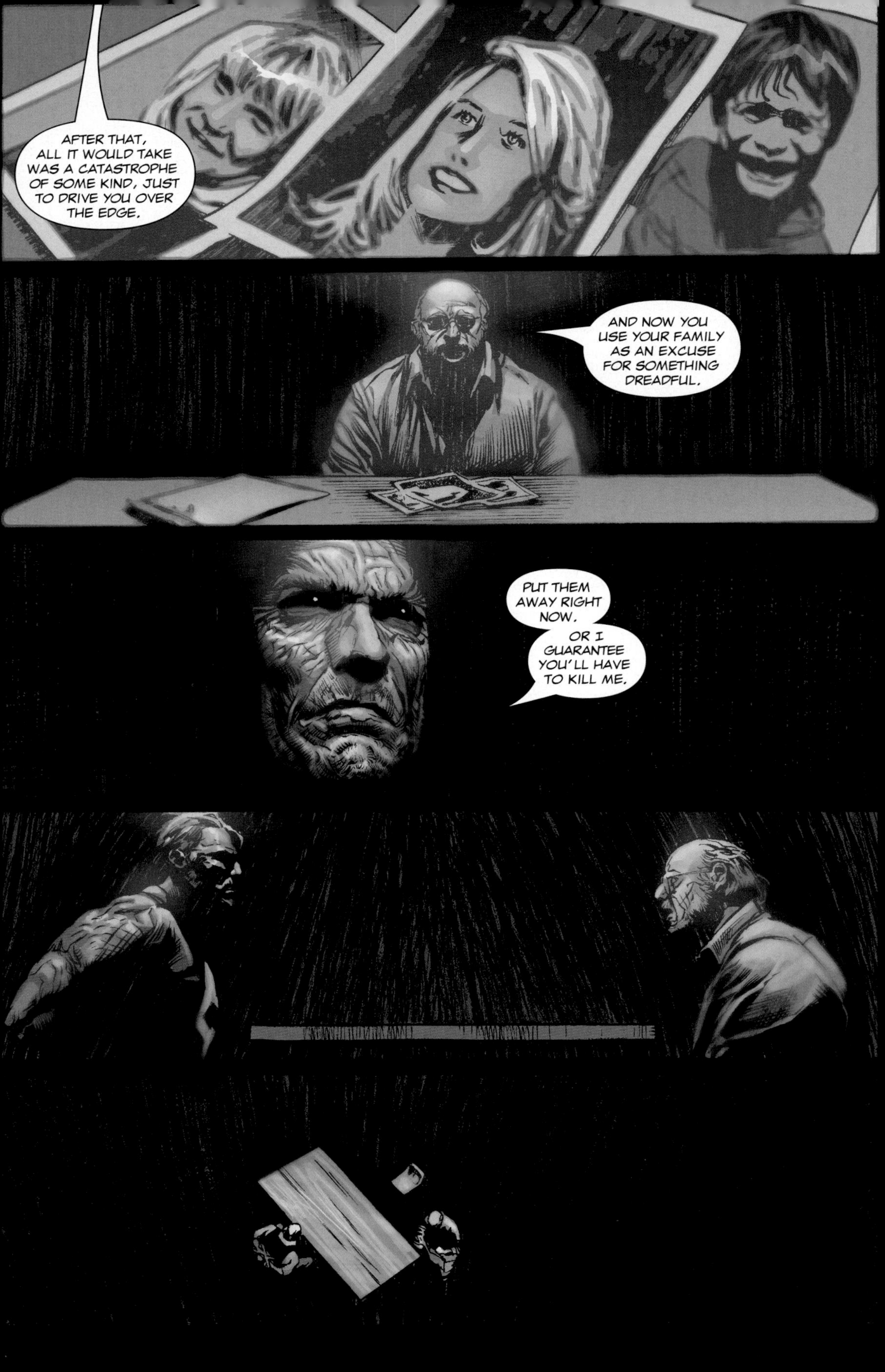
AFTER THAT, ALL IT WOULD TAKE WAS A CATASTROPHE OF SOME KIND, JUST TO DRIVE YOU OVER THE EDGE.
AND NOW YOU USE YOUR FAMILY AS AN EXCUSE FOR SOMETHING DREADFUL.
PUT THEM AWAY RIGHT NOW.
OR I GUARANTEE YOU'LL HAVE TO KILL ME.

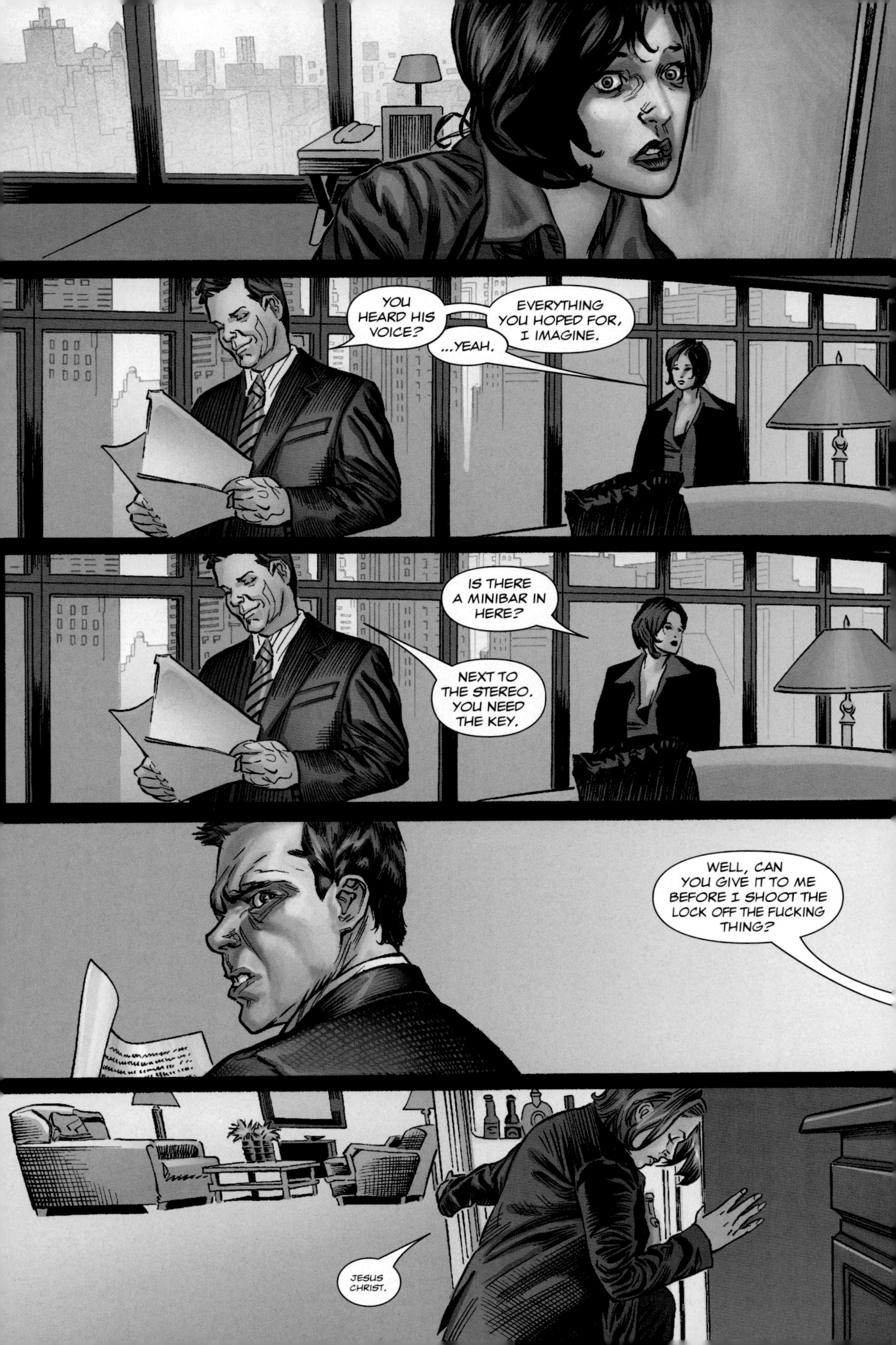
YOU HEARD HIS VOICE?
EVERYTHING YOU HOPED FOR, I IMAGINE.
...YEAH.
IS THERE A MINIBAR IN HERE?
NEXT TO THE STEREO. YOU NEED THE KEY.
WELL, CAN YOU GIVE IT TO ME BEFORE I SHOOT THE LOCK OFF THE FUCKING THING?
JESUS CHRIST.

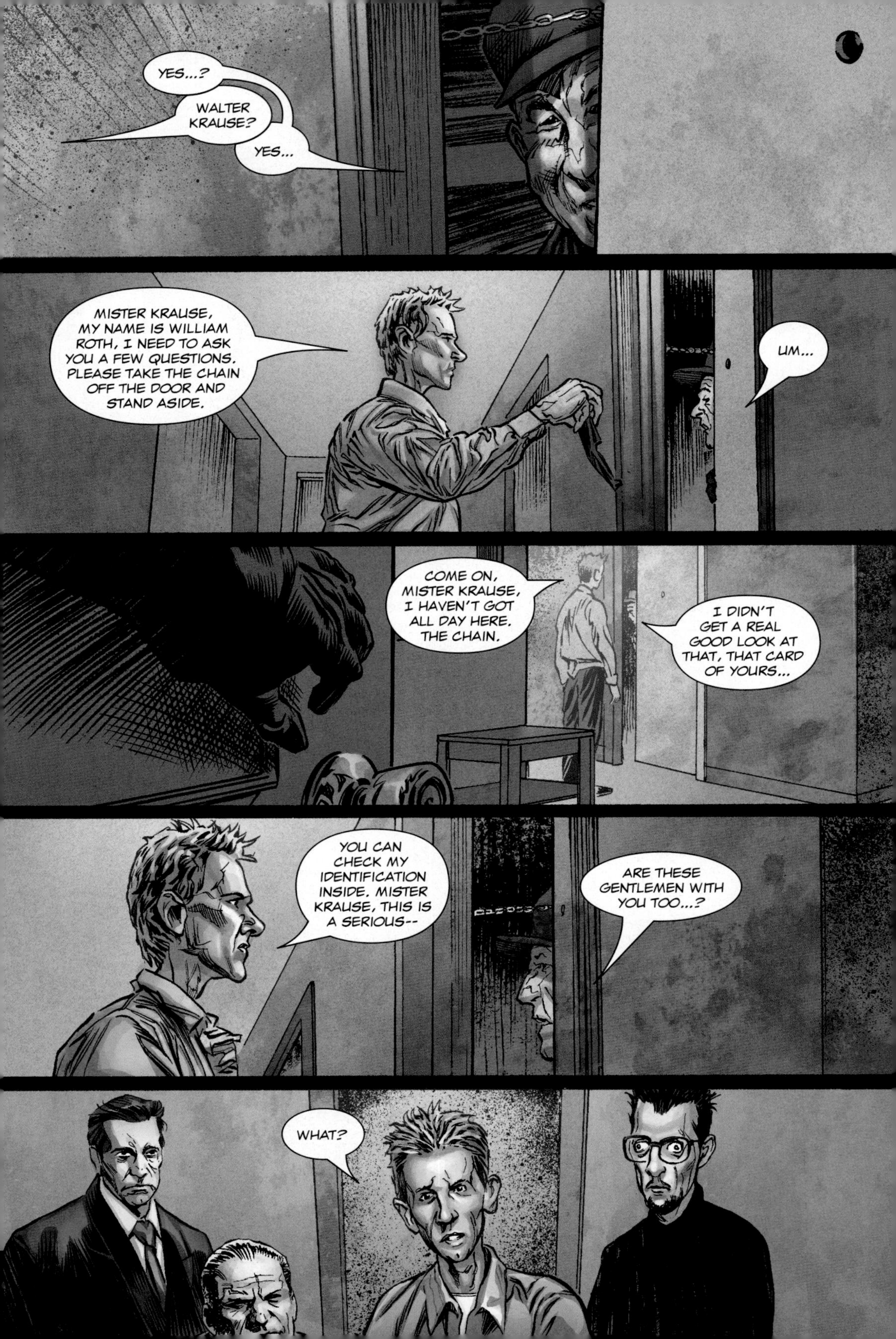
YES...?
WALTER KRAUSE?
YES...
MISTER KRAUSE, MY NAME IS WILLIAM ROTH, I NEED TO ASK YOU A FEW QUESTIONS. PLEASE TAKE THE CHAIN OFF THE DOOR AND STAND ASIDE.
UM...
COME ON, MISTER KRAUSE, I HAVEN'T GOT ALL DAY HERE. THE CHAIN.
I DIDN'T GET A REAL GOOD LOOK AT THAT, THAT CARD OF YOURS...
YOU CAN CHECK MY IDENTIFICATION INSIDE. MISTER KRAUSE, THIS IS A SERIOUS--
ARE THESE GENTLEMEN WITH YOU TOO...?
WHAT?

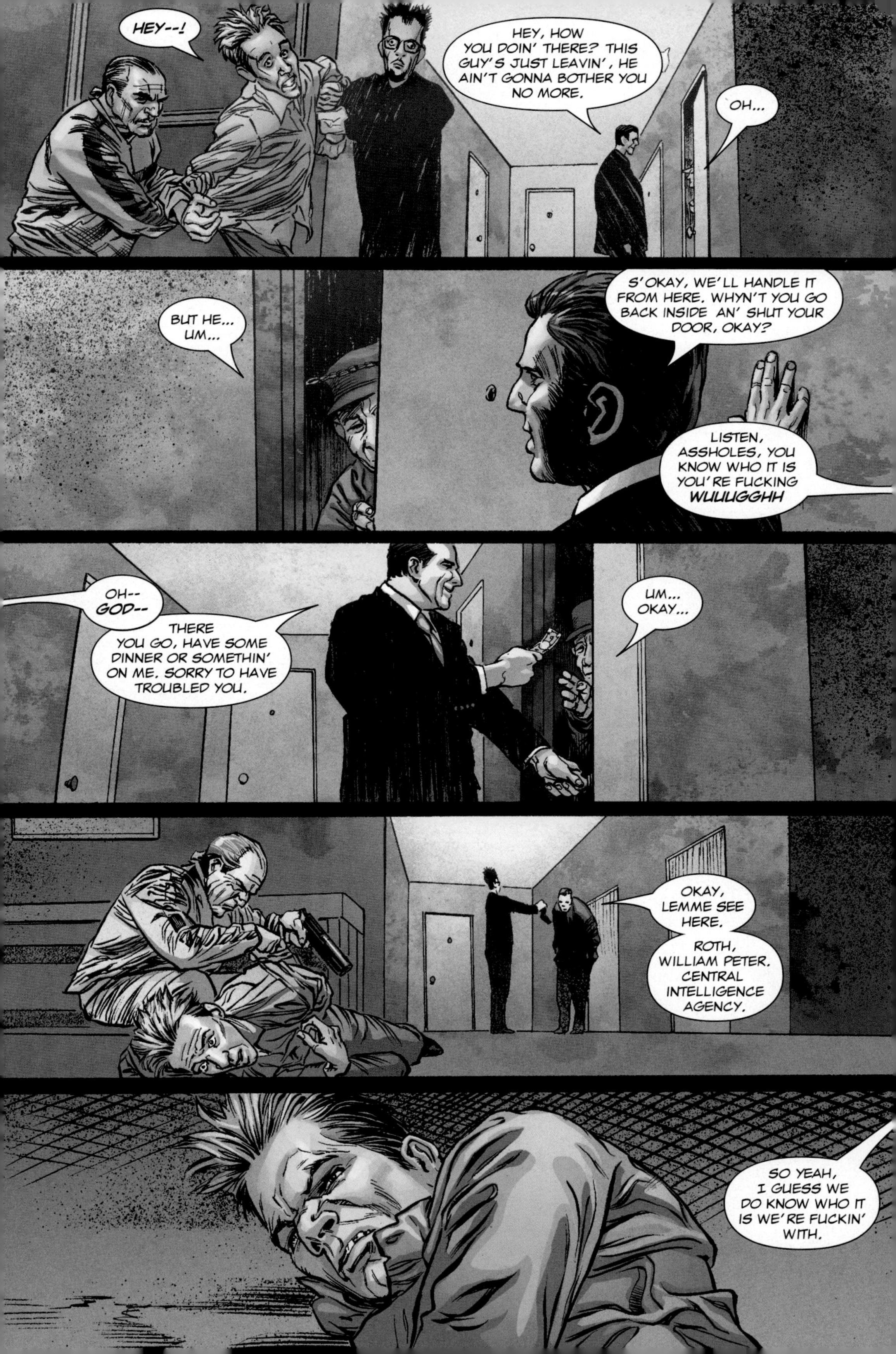
HEY--!
HEY, HOW YOU DOIN' THERE? THIS GUY'S JUST LEAVIN', HE AIN'T GONNA BOTHER YOU NO MORE.
OH...
BUT HE... UM...
S'OKAY, WE'LL HANDLE IT FROM HERE. WHYN'T YOU GO BACK INSIDE AN' SHUT YOUR DOOR, OKAY?
LISTEN, ASSHOLES, YOU KNOW WHO IT IS YOU'RE FUCKING *WUUUGGHH*
OH-- *GOD--*
THERE YOU GO, HAVE SOME DINNER OR SOMETHIN' ON ME. SORRY TO HAVE TROUBLED YOU.
UM... OKAY...
OKAY, LEMME SEE HERE.
ROTH, WILLIAM PETER. CENTRAL INTELLIGENCE AGENCY.
SO YEAH, I GUESS WE DO KNOW WHO IT IS WE'RE FUCKIN' WITH.

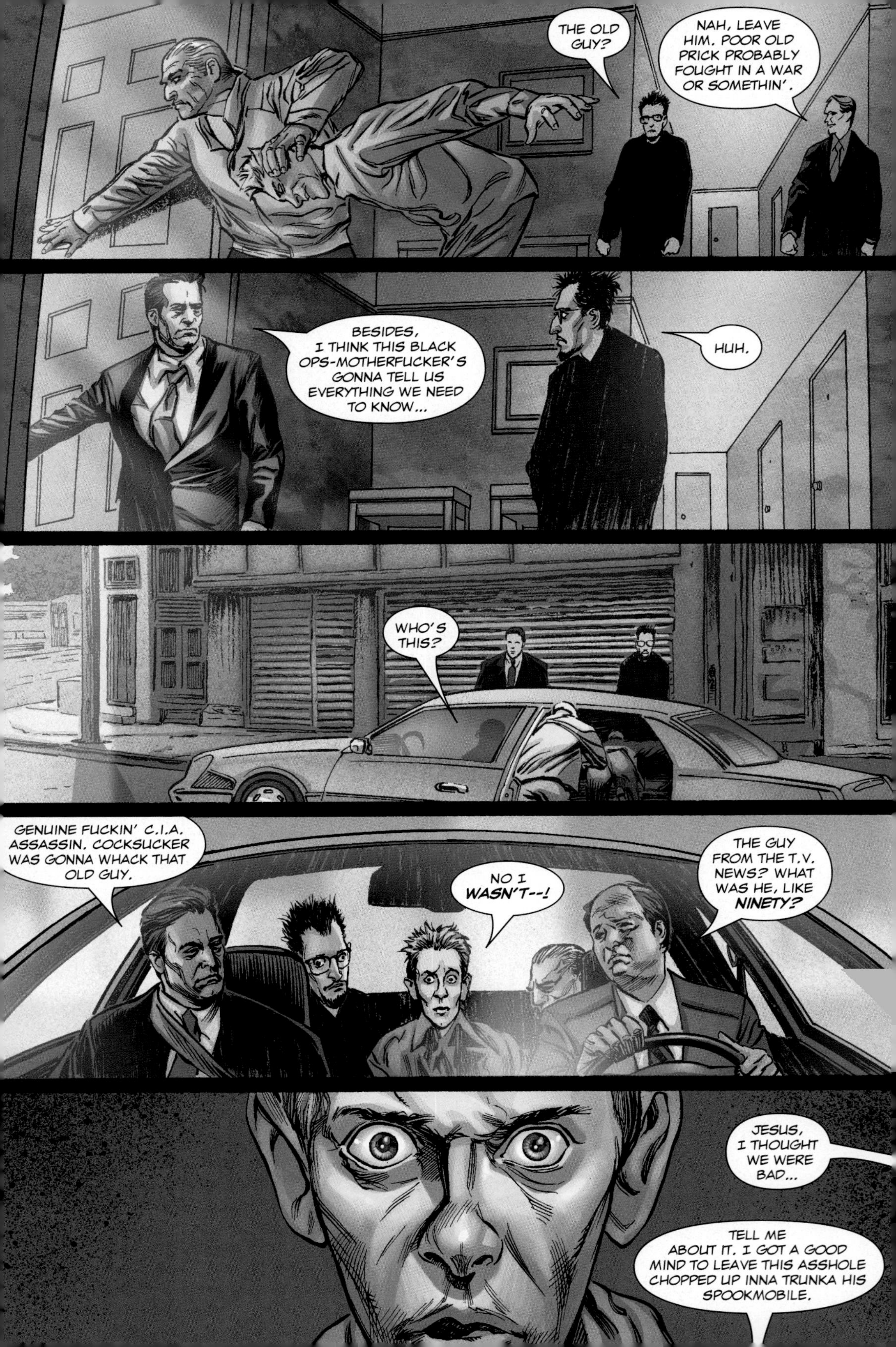
THE OLD GUY?
NAH, LEAVE HIM. POOR OLD PRICK PROBABLY FOUGHT IN A WAR OR SOMETHIN'.
BESIDES, I THINK THIS BLACK OPS-MOTHERFUCKER'S GONNA TELL US EVERYTHING WE NEED TO KNOW...
HUH.
WHO'S THIS?
GENUINE FUCKIN' C.I.A. ASSASSIN. COCKSUCKER WAS GONNA WHACK THAT OLD GUY.
NO I **WASN'T--!**
THE GUY FROM THE T.V. NEWS? WHAT WAS HE, LIKE **NINETY?**
JESUS, I THOUGHT WE WERE BAD...
TELL ME ABOUT IT. I GOT A GOOD MIND TO LEAVE THIS ASSHOLE CHOPPED UP INNA TRUNKA HIS SPOOKMOBILE.

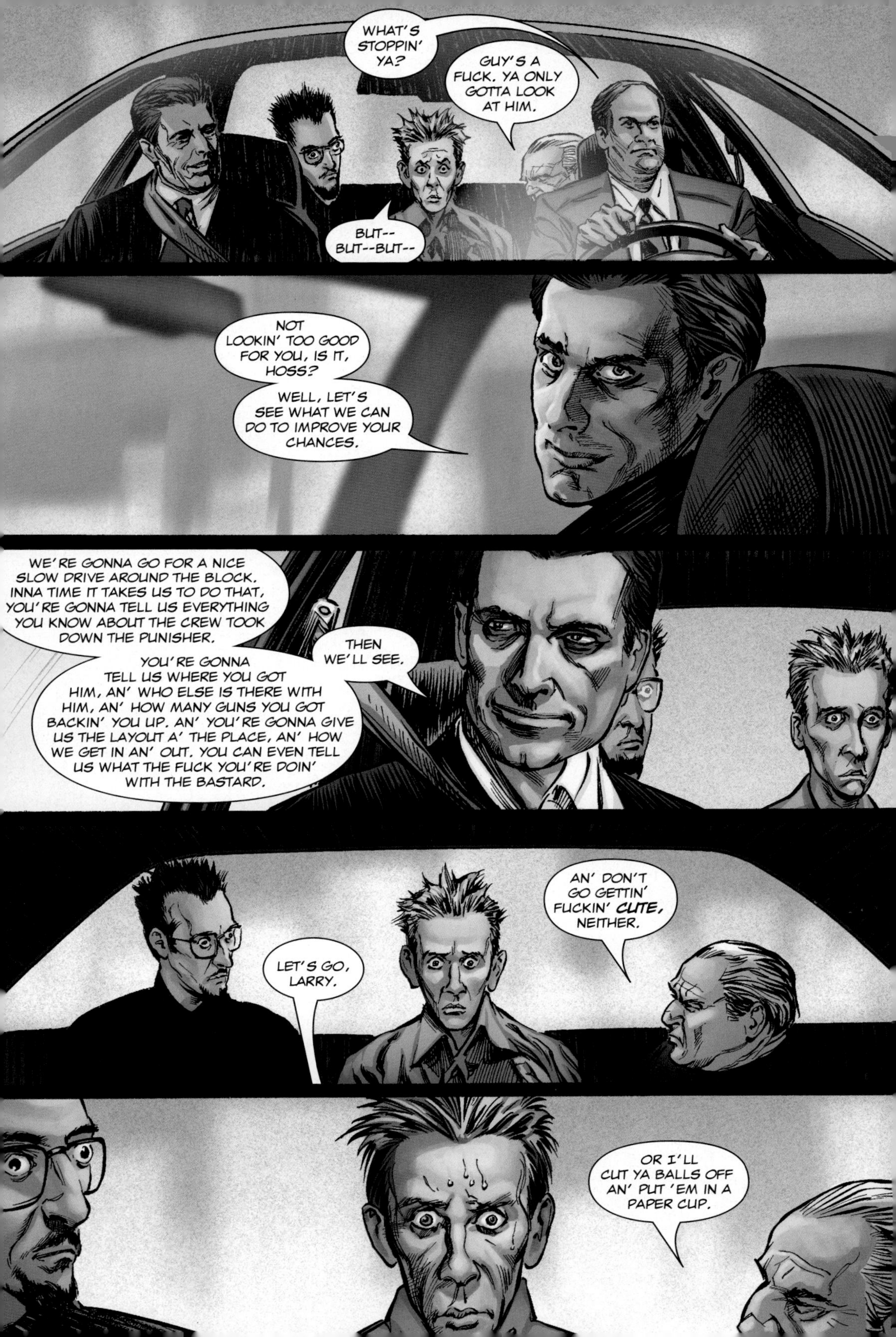
WHAT'S STOPPIN' YA?
GUY'S A FUCK. YA ONLY GOTTA LOOK AT HIM.
BUT-- BUT--BUT--
NOT LOOKIN' TOO GOOD FOR YOU, IS IT, HOSS?
WELL, LET'S SEE WHAT WE CAN DO TO IMPROVE YOUR CHANCES.
WE'RE GONNA GO FOR A NICE SLOW DRIVE AROUND THE BLOCK. INNA TIME IT TAKES US TO DO THAT, YOU'RE GONNA TELL US EVERYTHING YOU KNOW ABOUT THE CREW TOOK DOWN THE PUNISHER.
YOU'RE GONNA TELL US WHERE YOU GOT HIM, AN' WHO ELSE IS THERE WITH HIM, AN' HOW MANY GUNS YOU GOT BACKIN' YOU UP. AN' YOU'RE GONNA GIVE US THE LAYOUT A' THE PLACE, AN' HOW WE GET IN AN' OUT. YOU CAN EVEN TELL US WHAT THE FUCK YOU'RE DOIN' WITH THE BASTARD.
THEN WE'LL SEE.
LET'S GO, LARRY.
AN' DON'T GO GETTIN' FUCKIN' CUTE, NEITHER.
OR I'LL CUT YA BALLS OFF AN' PUT 'EM IN A PAPER CUP.

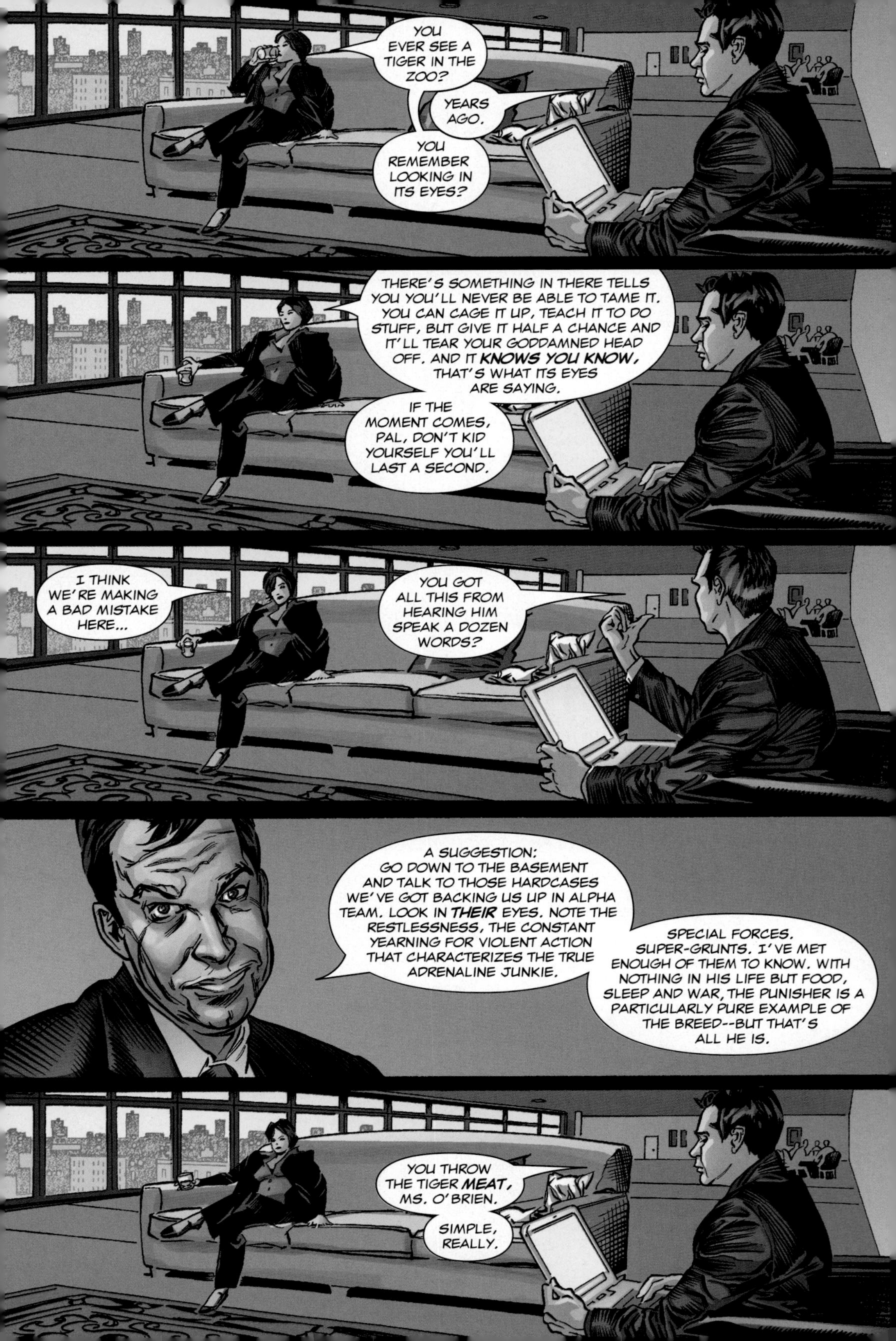

YOU EVER SEE A TIGER IN THE ZOO?
YEARS AGO.
YOU REMEMBER LOOKING IN ITS EYES?
THERE'S SOMETHING IN THERE TELLS YOU YOU'LL NEVER BE ABLE TO TAME IT. YOU CAN CAGE IT UP, TEACH IT TO DO STUFF, BUT GIVE IT HALF A CHANCE AND IT'LL TEAR YOUR GODDAMNED HEAD OFF. AND IT **KNOWS YOU KNOW,** THAT'S WHAT ITS EYES ARE SAYING.
IF THE MOMENT COMES, PAL, DON'T KID YOURSELF YOU'LL LAST A SECOND.
I THINK WE'RE MAKING A BAD MISTAKE HERE...
YOU GOT ALL THIS FROM HEARING HIM SPEAK A DOZEN WORDS?
A SUGGESTION: GO DOWN TO THE BASEMENT AND TALK TO THOSE HARDCASES WE'VE GOT BACKING US UP IN ALPHA TEAM. LOOK IN ***THEIR*** EYES. NOTE THE RESTLESSNESS, THE CONSTANT YEARNING FOR VIOLENT ACTION THAT CHARACTERIZES THE TRUE ADRENALINE JUNKIE.
SPECIAL FORCES. SUPER-GRUNTS. I'VE MET ENOUGH OF THEM TO KNOW. WITH NOTHING IN HIS LIFE BUT FOOD, SLEEP AND WAR, THE PUNISHER IS A PARTICULARLY PURE EXAMPLE OF THE BREED--BUT THAT'S ALL HE IS.
YOU THROW THE TIGER ***MEAT,*** MS. O'BRIEN.
SIMPLE, REALLY.

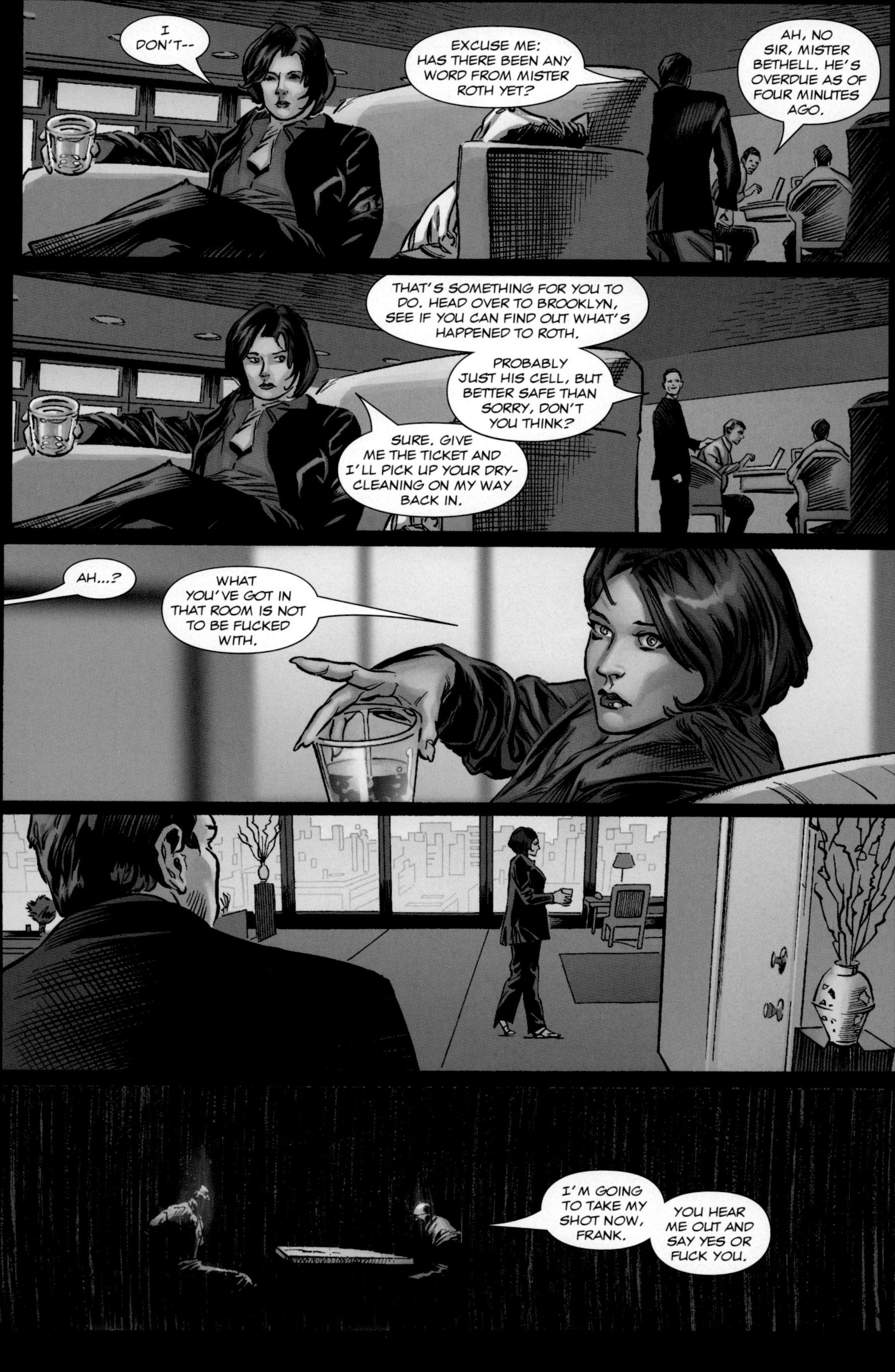

I DON'T--
EXCUSE ME: HAS THERE BEEN ANY WORD FROM MISTER ROTH YET?
AH, NO SIR, MISTER BETHELL. HE'S OVERDUE AS OF FOUR MINUTES AGO.
THAT'S SOMETHING FOR YOU TO DO. HEAD OVER TO BROOKLYN, SEE IF YOU CAN FIND OUT WHAT'S HAPPENED TO ROTH.
PROBABLY JUST HIS CELL, BUT BETTER SAFE THAN SORRY, DON'T YOU THINK?
SURE. GIVE ME THE TICKET AND I'LL PICK UP YOUR DRY-CLEANING ON MY WAY BACK IN.
AH...?
WHAT YOU'VE GOT IN THAT ROOM IS NOT TO BE FUCKED WITH.
I'M GOING TO TAKE MY SHOT NOW, FRANK.
YOU HEAR ME OUT AND SAY YES OR FUCK YOU.

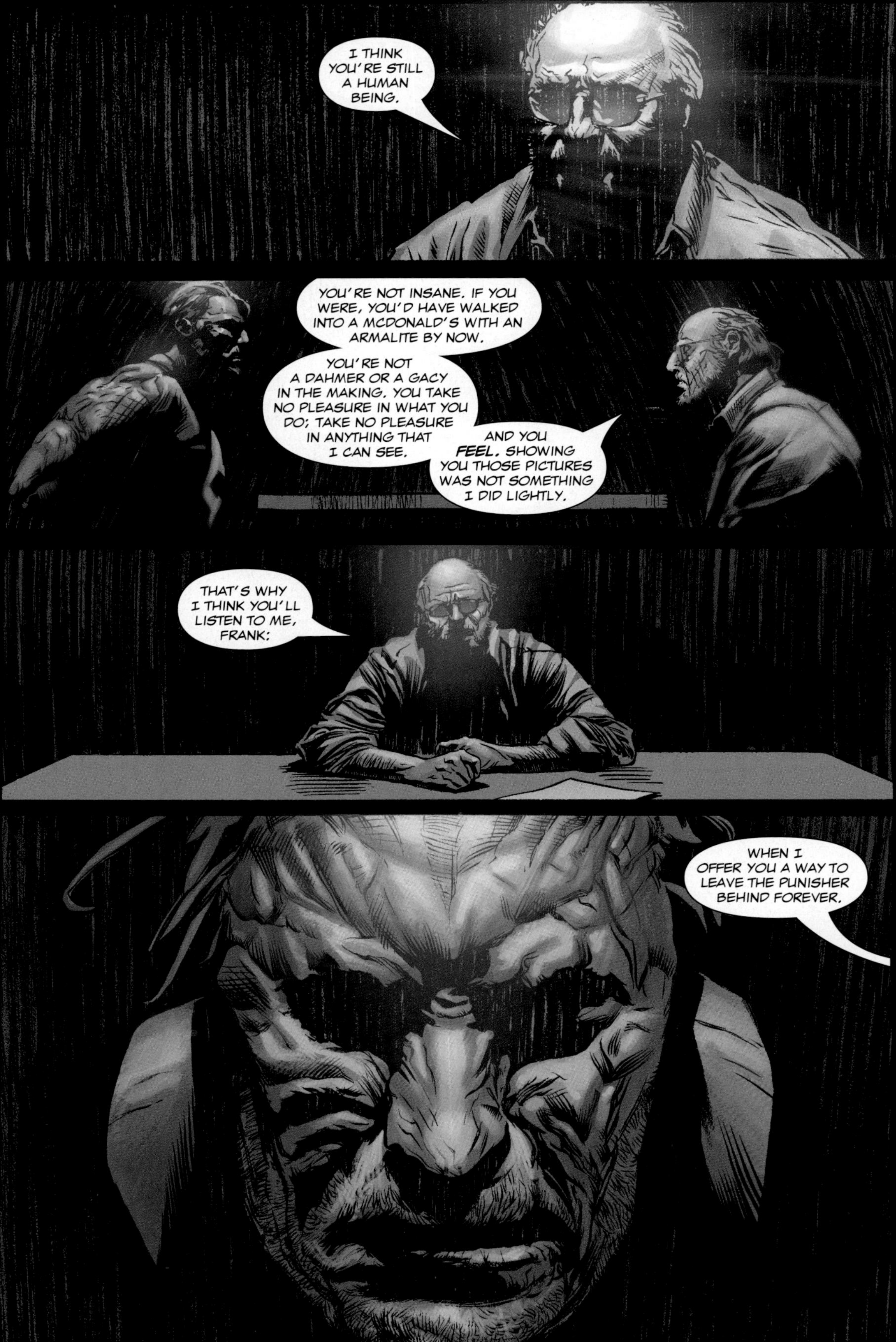
I THINK YOU'RE STILL A HUMAN BEING.
YOU'RE NOT INSANE. IF YOU WERE, YOU'D HAVE WALKED INTO A MCDONALD'S WITH AN ARMALITE BY NOW.
YOU'RE NOT A DAHMER OR A GACY IN THE MAKING. YOU TAKE NO PLEASURE IN WHAT YOU DO; TAKE NO PLEASURE IN ANYTHING THAT I CAN SEE.
AND YOU **FEEL.** SHOWING YOU THOSE PICTURES WAS NOT SOMETHING I DID LIGHTLY.
THAT'S WHY I THINK YOU'LL LISTEN TO ME, FRANK:
WHEN I OFFER YOU A WAY TO LEAVE THE PUNISHER BEHIND FOREVER.

PUNISHER #4

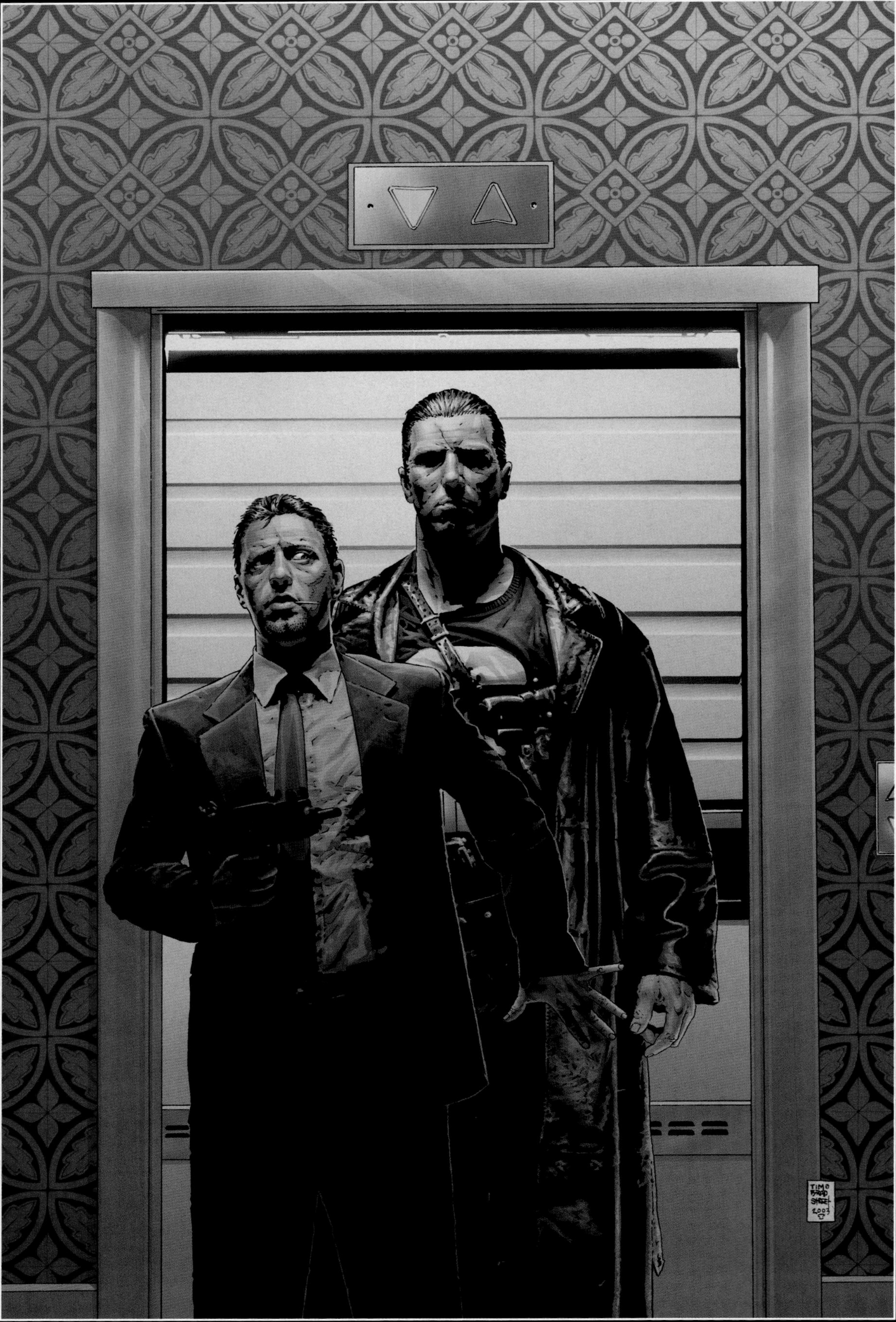

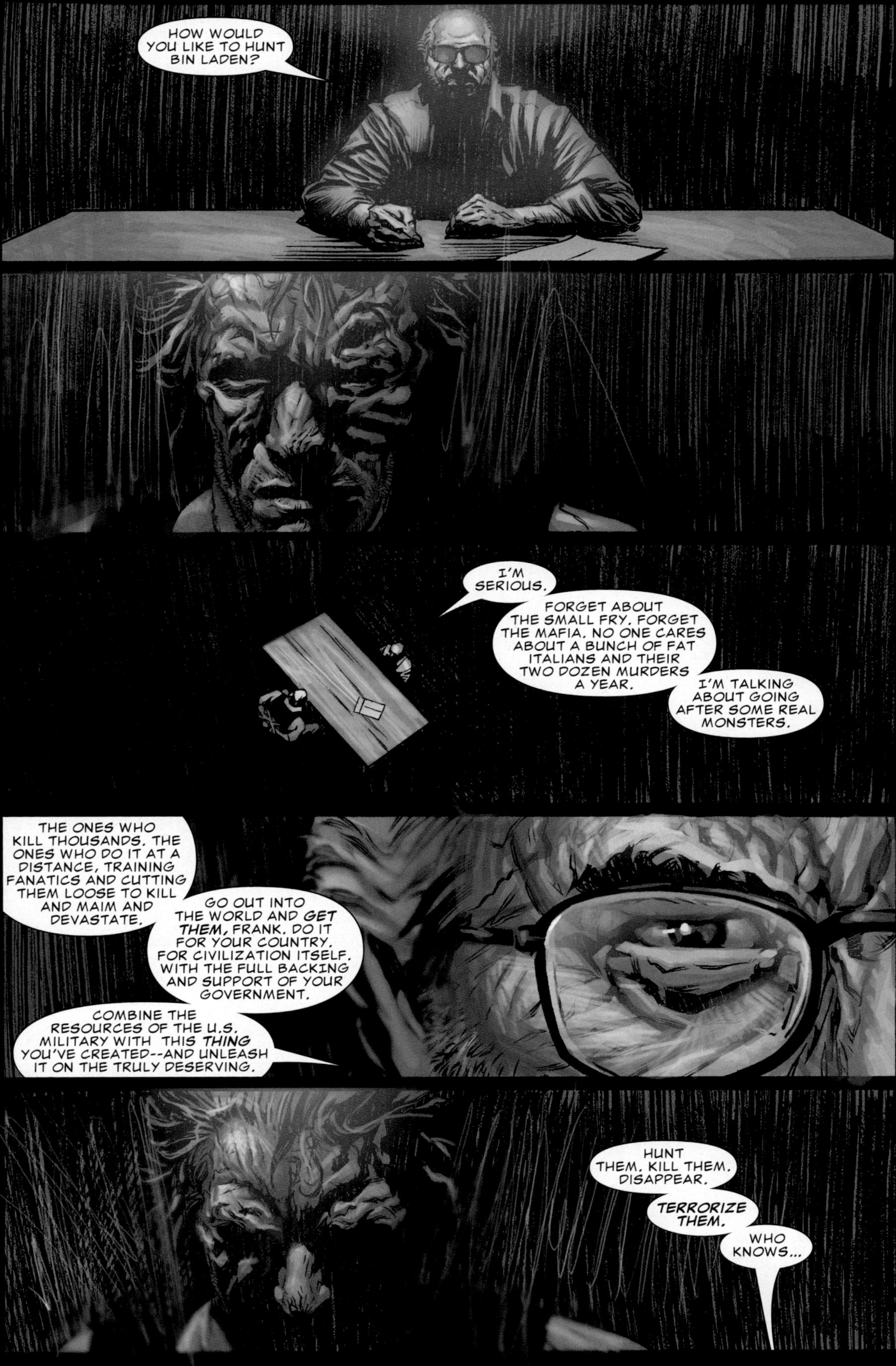
HOW WOULD YOU LIKE TO HUNT BIN LADEN?
I'M SERIOUS.
FORGET ABOUT THE SMALL FRY. FORGET THE MAFIA. NO ONE CARES ABOUT A BUNCH OF FAT ITALIANS AND THEIR TWO DOZEN MURDERS A YEAR.
I'M TALKING ABOUT GOING AFTER SOME REAL MONSTERS.
THE ONES WHO KILL THOUSANDS. THE ONES WHO DO IT AT A DISTANCE, TRAINING FANATICS AND CUTTING THEM LOOSE TO KILL AND MAIM AND DEVASTATE.
GO OUT INTO THE WORLD AND GET THEM, FRANK. DO IT FOR YOUR COUNTRY. FOR CIVILIZATION ITSELF. WITH THE FULL BACKING AND SUPPORT OF YOUR GOVERNMENT.
COMBINE THE RESOURCES OF THE U.S. MILITARY WITH THIS THING YOU'VE CREATED--AND UNLEASH IT ON THE TRULY DESERVING.
HUNT THEM. KILL THEM. DISAPPEAR.
TERRORIZE THEM.
WHO KNOWS...

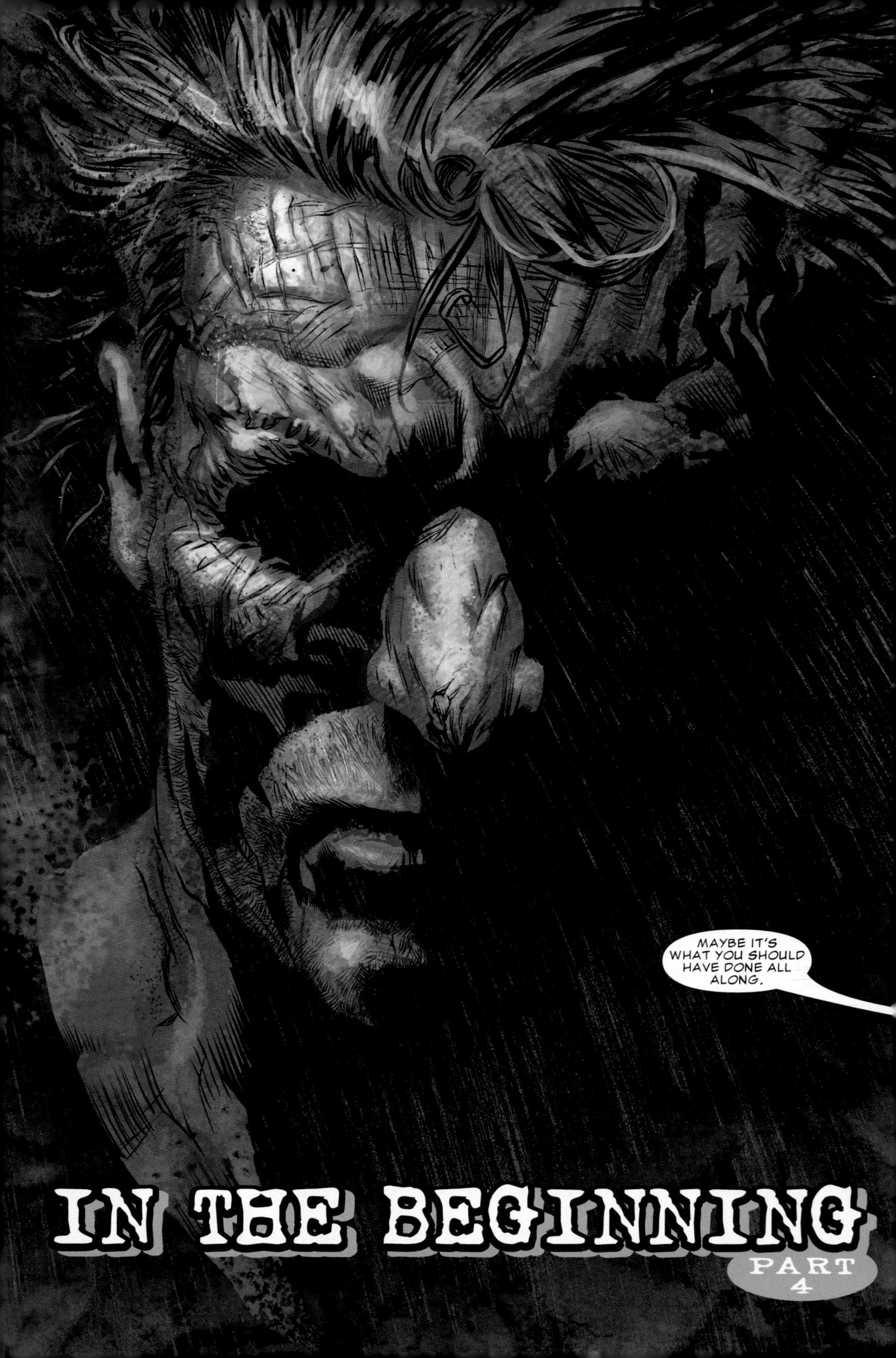
MAYBE IT'S WHAT YOU SHOULD HAVE DONE ALL ALONG.
IN THE BEGINNING
PART 4

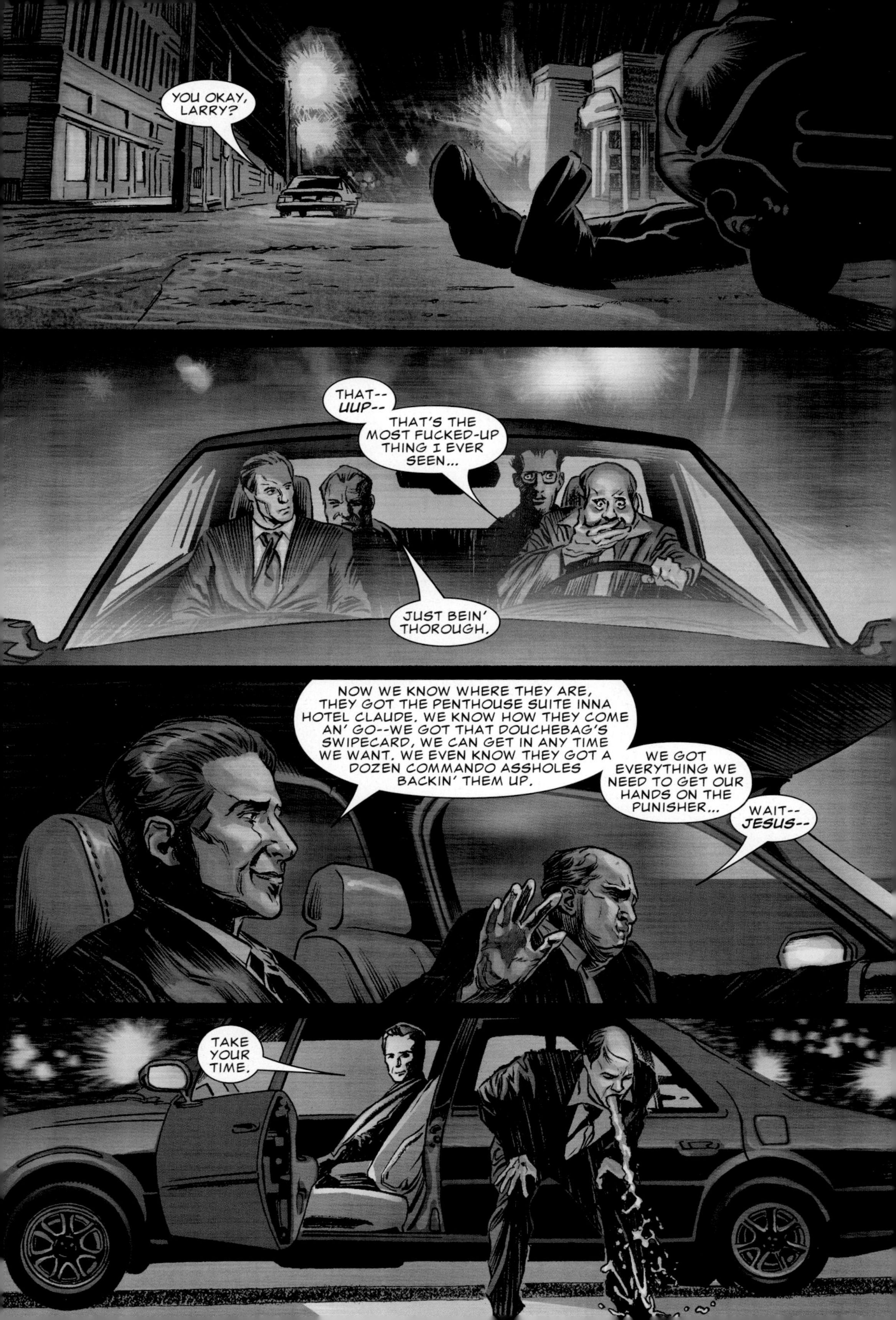
YOU OKAY, LARRY?
THAT-- UUP--
THAT'S THE MOST FUCKED-UP THING I EVER SEEN...
JUST BEIN' THOROUGH.
NOW WE KNOW WHERE THEY ARE, THEY GOT THE PENTHOUSE SUITE INNA HOTEL CLAUDE. WE KNOW HOW THEY COME AN' GO--WE GOT THAT DOUCHEBAG'S SWIPECARD, WE CAN GET IN ANY TIME WE WANT. WE EVEN KNOW THEY GOT A DOZEN COMMANDO ASSHOLES BACKIN' THEM UP.
WE GOT EVERYTHING WE NEED TO GET OUR HANDS ON THE PUNISHER...
WAIT-- JESUS--
TAKE YOUR TIME.

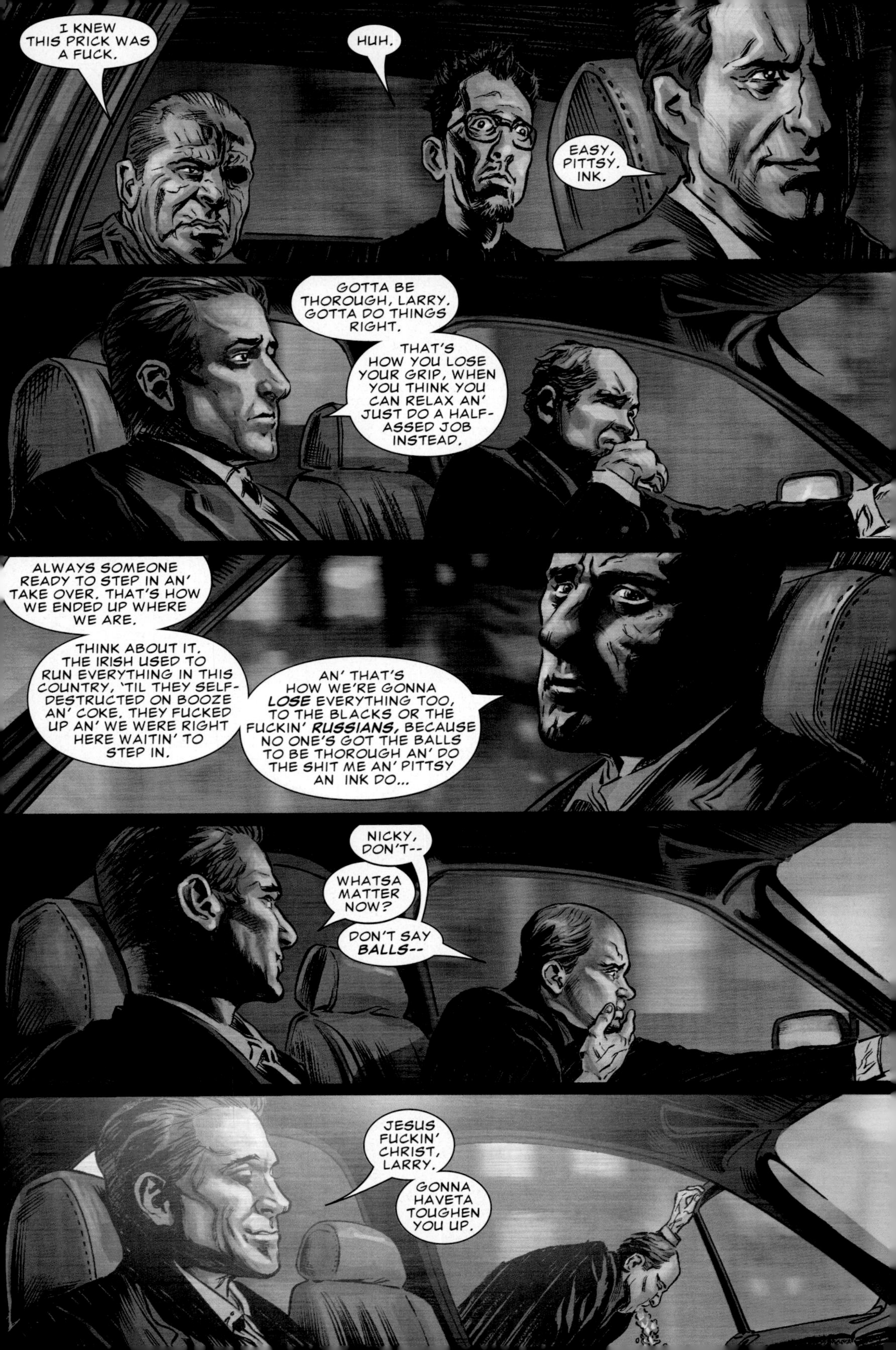
I KNEW THIS PRICK WAS A FUCK.
HUH.
EASY, PITTSY. INK.
GOTTA BE THOROUGH, LARRY. GOTTA DO THINGS RIGHT.
THAT'S HOW YOU LOSE YOUR GRIP, WHEN YOU THINK YOU CAN RELAX AN' JUST DO A HALF-ASSED JOB INSTEAD.
ALWAYS SOMEONE READY TO STEP IN AN' TAKE OVER. THAT'S HOW WE ENDED UP WHERE WE ARE.
THINK ABOUT IT. THE IRISH USED TO RUN EVERYTHING IN THIS COUNTRY, 'TIL THEY SELF-DESTRUCTED ON BOOZE AN' COKE. THEY FUCKED UP AN' WE WERE RIGHT HERE WAITIN' TO STEP IN.
AN' THAT'S HOW WE'RE GONNA *LOSE* EVERYTHING TOO, TO THE BLACKS OR THE FUCKIN' ***RUSSIANS,*** BECAUSE NO ONE'S GOT THE BALLS TO BE THOROUGH AN' DO THE SHIT ME AN' PITTSY AN INK DO...
NICKY, DON'T--
WHATSA MATTER NOW?
DON'T SAY ***BALLS--***
JESUS FUCKIN' CHRIST, LARRY.
GONNA HAVETA TOUGHEN YOU UP.

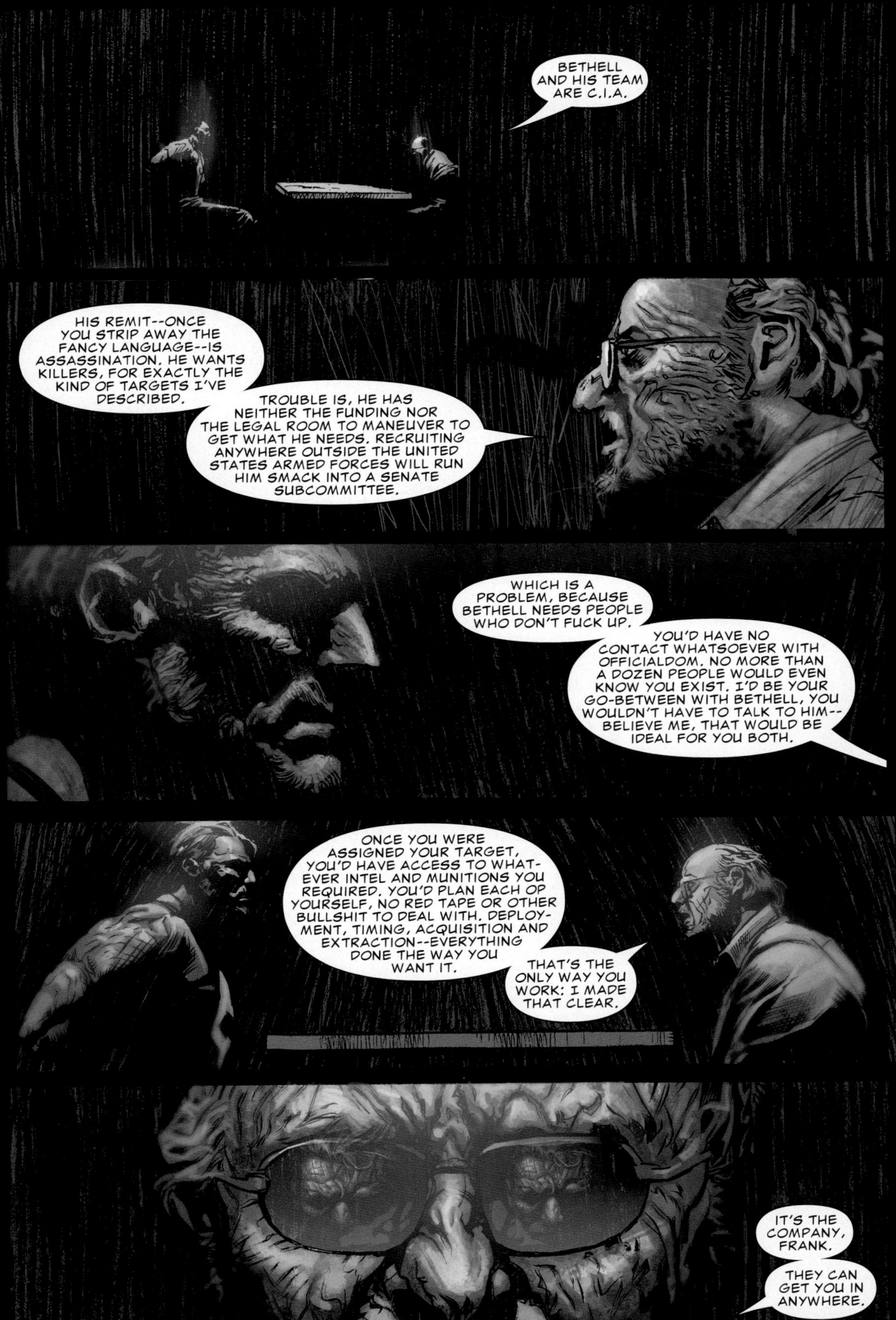
BETHELL AND HIS TEAM ARE C.I.A.
HIS REMIT--ONCE YOU STRIP AWAY THE FANCY LANGUAGE--IS ASSASSINATION. HE WANTS KILLERS, FOR EXACTLY THE KIND OF TARGETS I'VE DESCRIBED.
TROUBLE IS, HE HAS NEITHER THE FUNDING NOR THE LEGAL ROOM TO MANEUVER TO GET WHAT HE NEEDS. RECRUITING ANYWHERE OUTSIDE THE UNITED STATES ARMED FORCES WILL RUN HIM SMACK INTO A SENATE SUBCOMMITTEE.
WHICH IS A PROBLEM, BECAUSE BETHELL NEEDS PEOPLE WHO DON'T FUCK UP.
YOU'D HAVE NO CONTACT WHATSOEVER WITH OFFICIALDOM. NO MORE THAN A DOZEN PEOPLE WOULD EVEN KNOW YOU EXIST. I'D BE YOUR GO-BETWEEN WITH BETHELL, YOU WOULDN'T HAVE TO TALK TO HIM--BELIEVE ME, THAT WOULD BE IDEAL FOR YOU BOTH.
ONCE YOU WERE ASSIGNED YOUR TARGET, YOU'D HAVE ACCESS TO WHATEVER INTEL AND MUNITIONS YOU REQUIRED. YOU'D PLAN EACH OP YOURSELF, NO RED TAPE OR OTHER BULLSHIT TO DEAL WITH. DEPLOYMENT, TIMING, ACQUISITION AND EXTRACTION--EVERYTHING DONE THE WAY YOU WANT IT.
THAT'S THE ONLY WAY YOU WORK; I MADE THAT CLEAR.
IT'S THE COMPANY, FRANK.
THEY CAN GET YOU IN ANYWHERE.

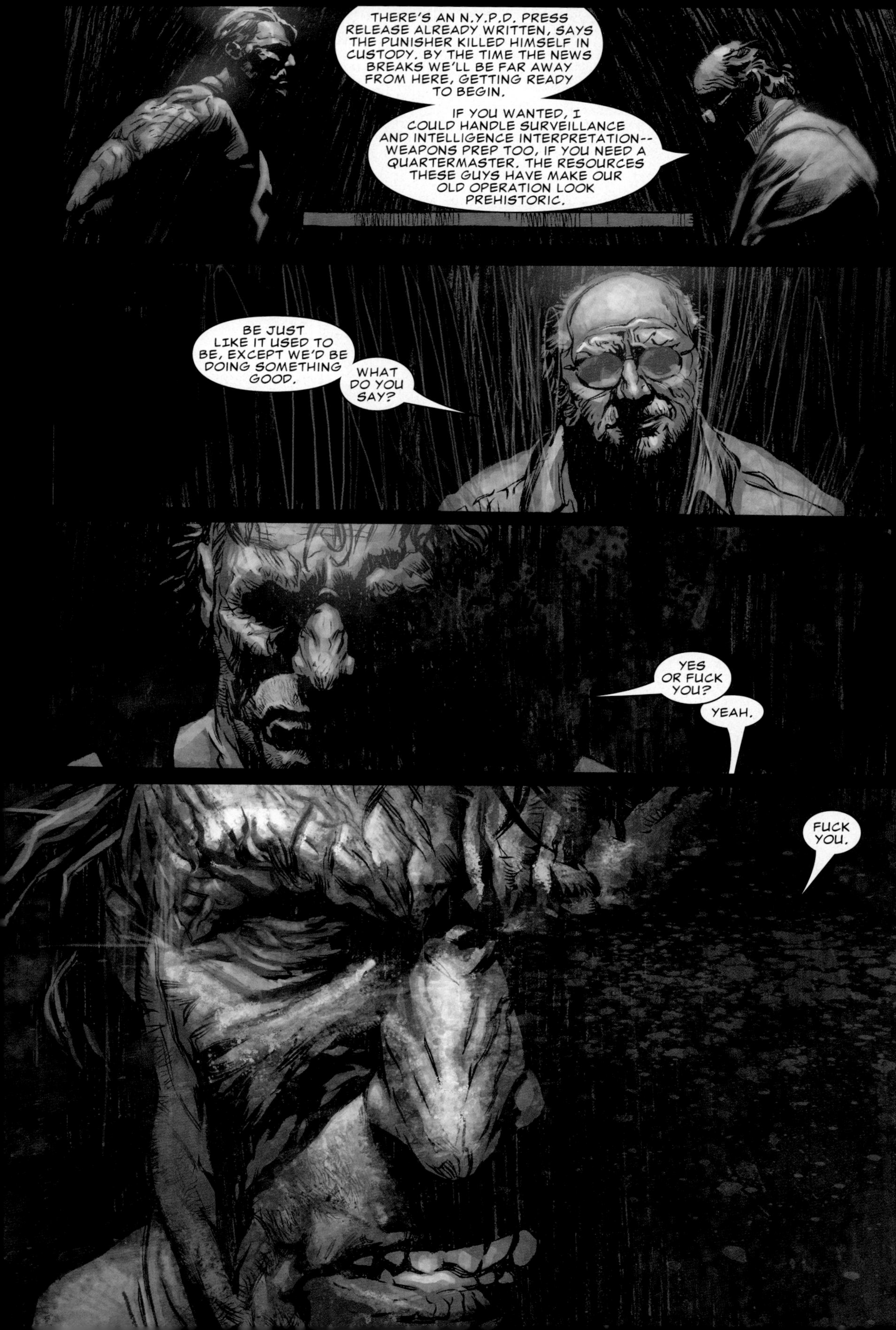
THERE'S AN N.Y.P.D. PRESS RELEASE ALREADY WRITTEN, SAYS THE PUNISHER KILLED HIMSELF IN CUSTODY. BY THE TIME THE NEWS BREAKS WE'LL BE FAR AWAY FROM HERE, GETTING READY TO BEGIN.
IF YOU WANTED, I COULD HANDLE SURVEILLANCE AND INTELLIGENCE INTERPRETATION-- WEAPONS PREP TOO, IF YOU NEED A QUARTERMASTER. THE RESOURCES THESE GUYS HAVE MAKE OUR OLD OPERATION LOOK PREHISTORIC.
BE JUST LIKE IT USED TO BE, EXCEPT WE'D BE DOING SOMETHING GOOD.
WHAT DO YOU SAY?
YES OR FUCK YOU?
YEAH.
FUCK YOU.

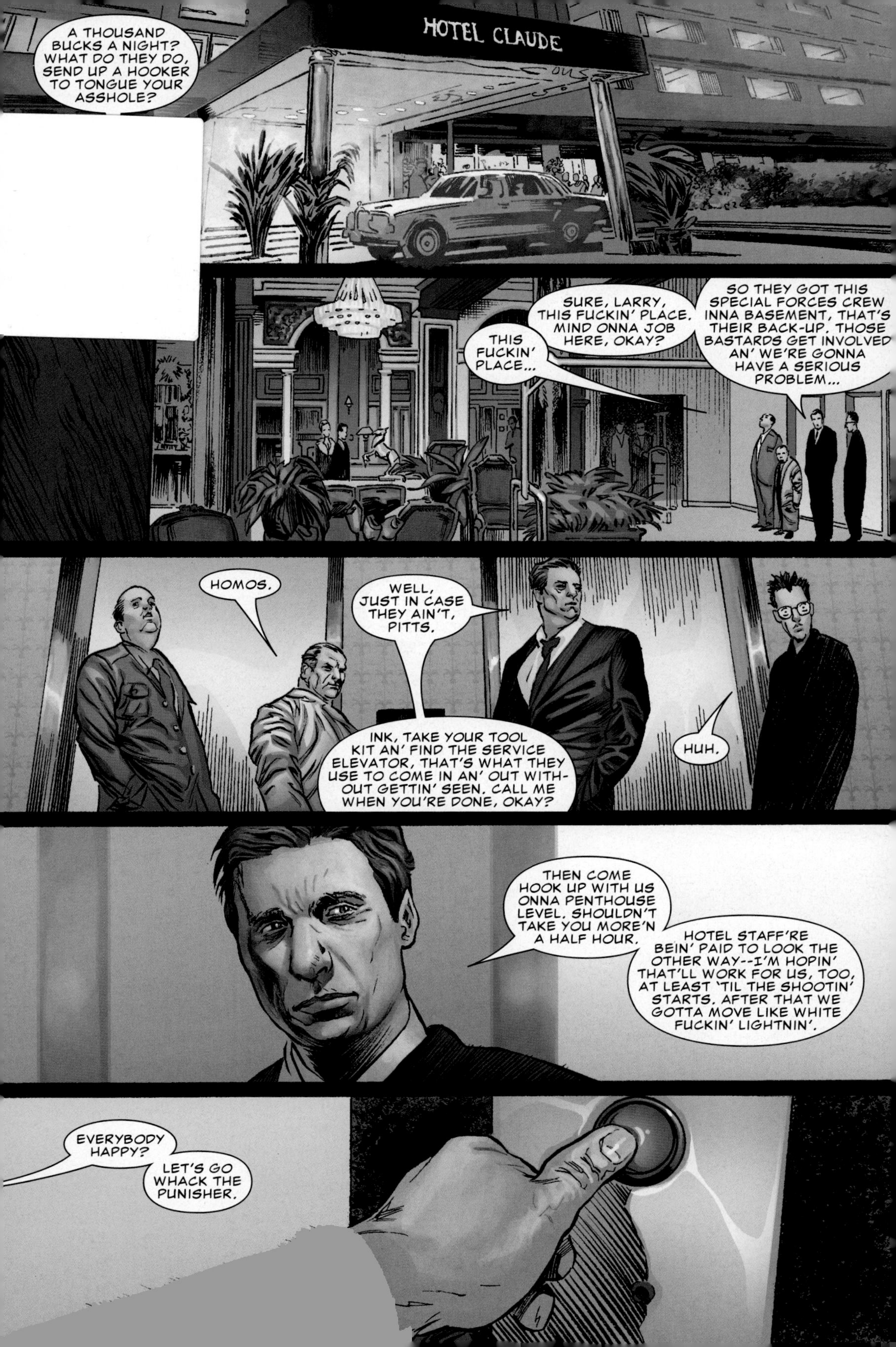
HOTEL CLAUDE
A THOUSAND BUCKS A NIGHT? WHAT DO THEY DO, SEND UP A HOOKER TO TONGUE YOUR ASSHOLE?
SO THEY GOT THIS SPECIAL FORCES CREW INNA BASEMENT, THAT'S THEIR BACK-UP. THOSE BASTARDS GET INVOLVED AN' WE'RE GONNA HAVE A SERIOUS PROBLEM...
SURE, LARRY, THIS FUCKIN' PLACE. MIND ONNA JOB HERE, OKAY?
THIS FUCKIN' PLACE...
HOMOS.
WELL, JUST IN CASE THEY AIN'T, PITTS.
INK, TAKE YOUR TOOL KIT AN' FIND THE SERVICE ELEVATOR, THAT'S WHAT THEY USE TO COME IN AN' OUT WITH-OUT GETTIN' SEEN. CALL ME WHEN YOU'RE DONE, OKAY?
HUH.
THEN COME HOOK UP WITH US ONNA PENTHOUSE LEVEL. SHOULDN'T TAKE YOU MORE'N A HALF HOUR.
HOTEL STAFF'RE BEIN' PAID TO LOOK THE OTHER WAY--I'M HOPIN' THAT'LL WORK FOR US, TOO, AT LEAST 'TIL THE SHOOTIN' STARTS. AFTER THAT WE GOTTA MOVE LIKE WHITE FUCKIN' LIGHTNIN'.
EVERYBODY HAPPY?
LET'S GO WHACK THE PUNISHER.

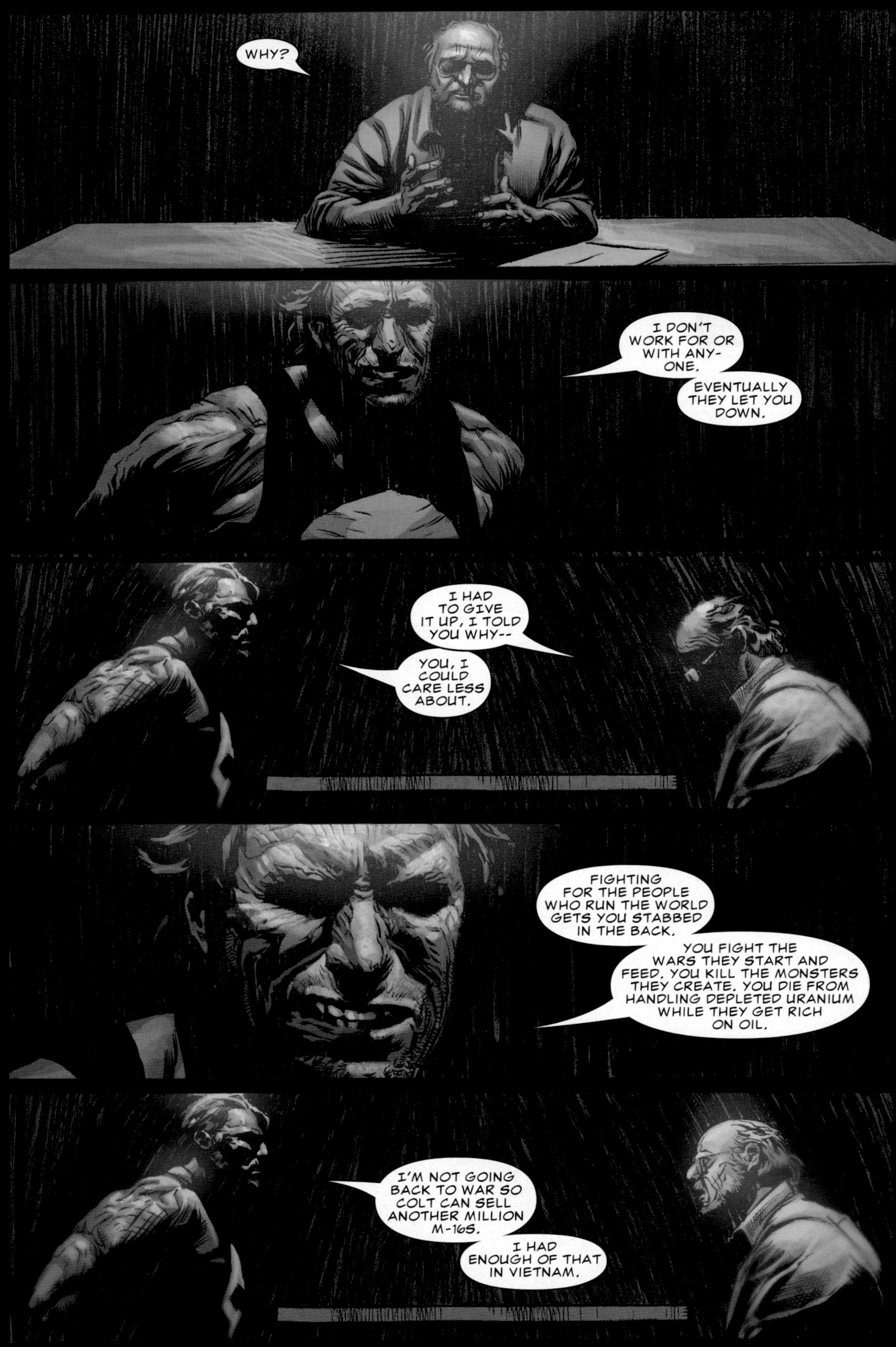
WHY?
I DON'T WORK FOR OR WITH ANY-ONE.
EVENTUALLY THEY LET YOU DOWN.
I HAD TO GIVE IT UP, I TOLD YOU WHY--
YOU, I COULD CARE LESS ABOUT.
FIGHTING FOR THE PEOPLE WHO RUN THE WORLD GETS YOU STABBED IN THE BACK.
YOU FIGHT THE WARS THEY START AND FEED. YOU KILL THE MONSTERS THEY CREATE. YOU DIE FROM HANDLING DEPLETED URANIUM WHILE THEY GET RICH ON OIL.
I'M NOT GOING BACK TO WAR SO COLT CAN SELL ANOTHER MILLION M-16S.
I HAD ENOUGH OF THAT IN VIETNAM.

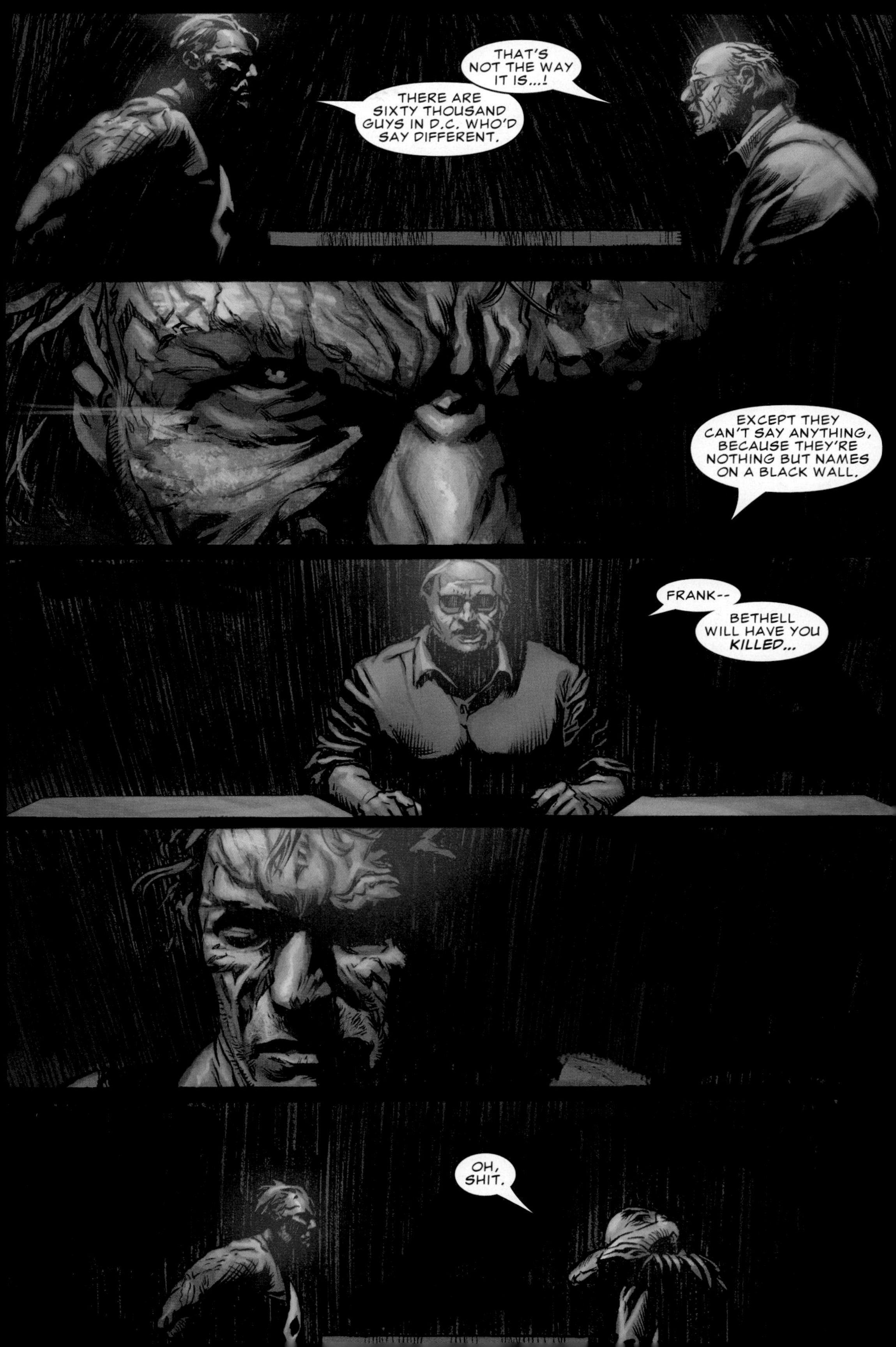
THAT'S NOT THE WAY IT IS...!
THERE ARE SIXTY THOUSAND GUYS IN D.C. WHO'D SAY DIFFERENT.
EXCEPT THEY CAN'T SAY ANYTHING, BECAUSE THEY'RE NOTHING BUT NAMES ON A BLACK WALL.
FRANK--
BETHELL WILL HAVE YOU KILLED...
OH, SHIT.

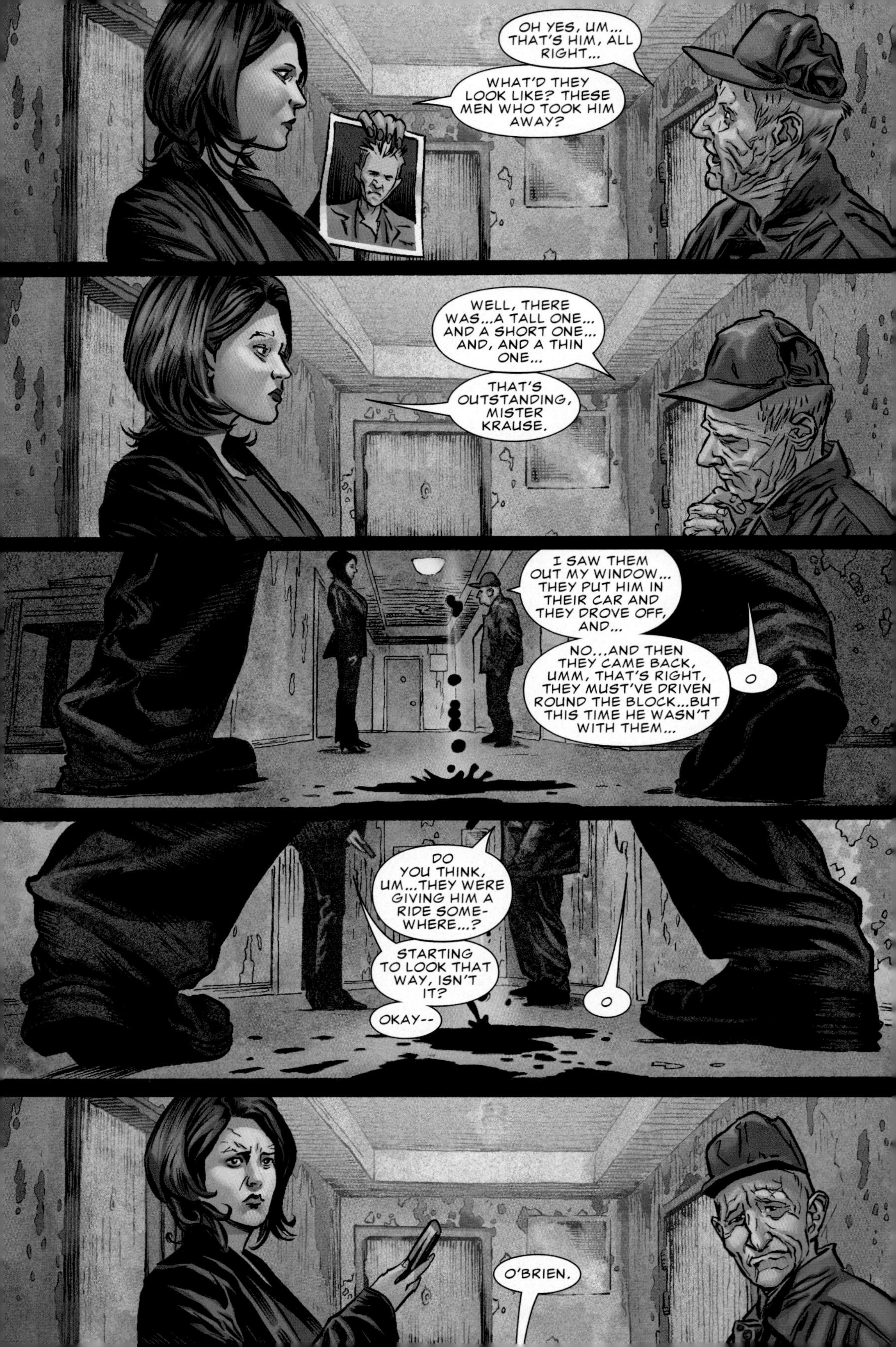
OH YES, UM... THAT'S HIM, ALL RIGHT...
WHAT'D THEY LOOK LIKE? THESE MEN WHO TOOK HIM AWAY?
WELL, THERE WAS...A TALL ONE... AND A SHORT ONE... AND, AND A THIN ONE...
THAT'S OUTSTANDING, MISTER KRAUSE.
I SAW THEM OUT MY WINDOW... THEY PUT HIM IN THEIR CAR AND THEY DROVE OFF, AND...
NO...AND THEN THEY CAME BACK, UMM, THAT'S RIGHT, THEY MUST'VE DRIVEN ROUND THE BLOCK...BUT THIS TIME HE WASN'T WITH THEM...
O
DO YOU THINK, UM...THEY WERE GIVING HIM A RIDE SOME-WHERE...?
STARTING TO LOOK THAT WAY, ISN'T IT?
OKAY--
O
O'BRIEN.

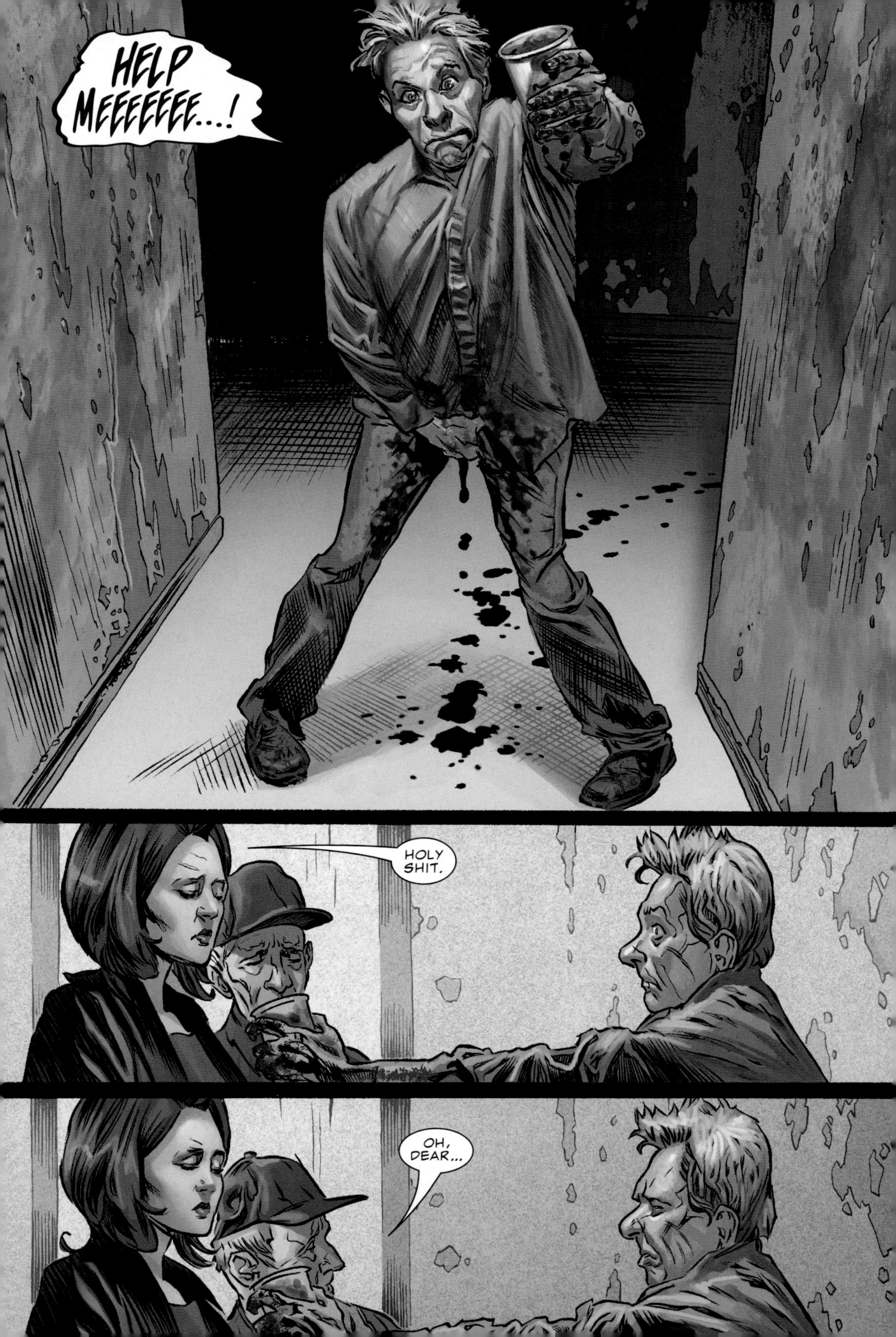
HELP MEEEEEEE...!
HOLY SHIT.
OH, DEAR...

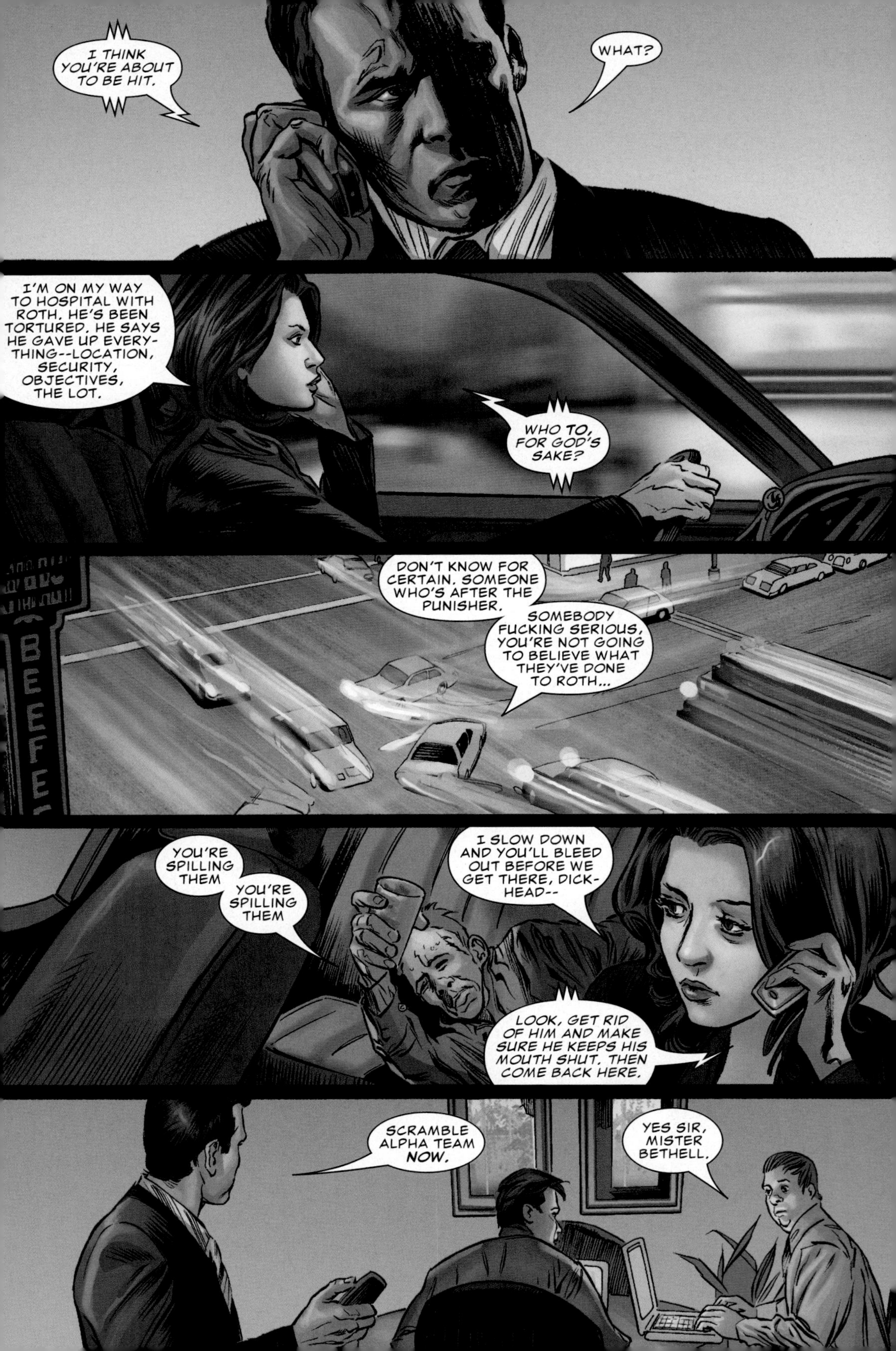
I THINK YOU'RE ABOUT TO BE HIT.
WHAT?
I'M ON MY WAY TO HOSPITAL WITH ROTH. HE'S BEEN TORTURED. HE SAYS HE GAVE UP EVERY-THING--LOCATION, SECURITY, OBJECTIVES, THE LOT.
WHO TO, FOR GOD'S SAKE?
DON'T KNOW FOR CERTAIN. SOMEONE WHO'S AFTER THE PUNISHER.
SOMEBODY FUCKING SERIOUS. YOU'RE NOT GOING TO BELIEVE WHAT THEY'VE DONE TO ROTH...
YOU'RE SPILLING THEM
YOU'RE SPILLING THEM
I SLOW DOWN AND YOU'LL BLEED OUT BEFORE WE GET THERE, DICK-HEAD--
LOOK, GET RID OF HIM AND MAKE SURE HE KEEPS HIS MOUTH SHUT. THEN COME BACK HERE.
SCRAMBLE ALPHA TEAM NOW.
YES SIR, MISTER BETHELL.

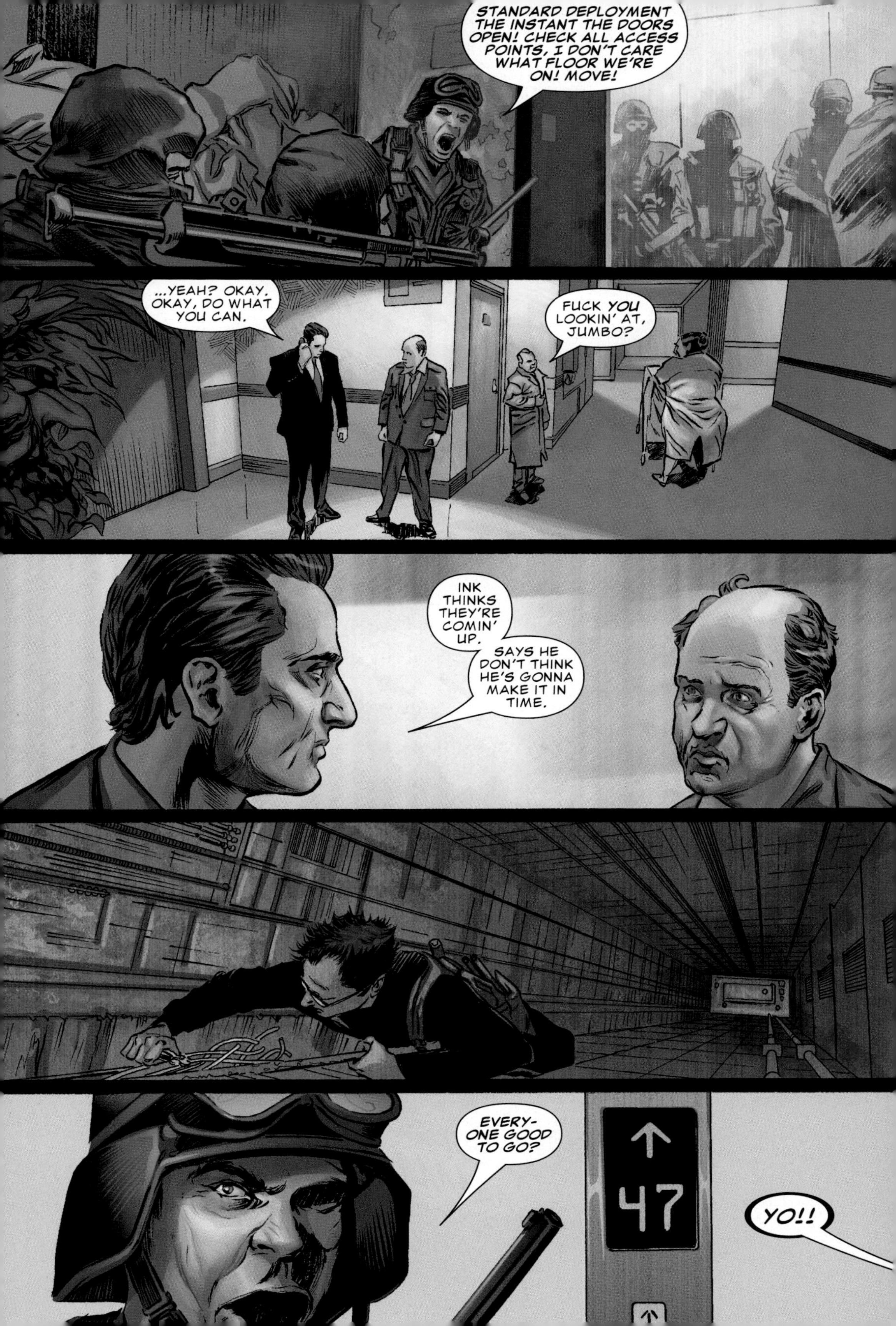
STANDARD DEPLOYMENT THE INSTANT THE DOORS OPEN! CHECK ALL ACCESS POINTS, I DON'T CARE WHAT FLOOR WE'RE ON! MOVE!
...YEAH? OKAY. OKAY, DO WHAT YOU CAN.
FUCK YOU LOOKIN' AT, JUMBO?
INK THINKS THEY'RE COMIN' UP.
SAYS HE DON'T THINK HE'S GONNA MAKE IT IN TIME.
EVERY-ONE GOOD TO GO?
47
YO!!

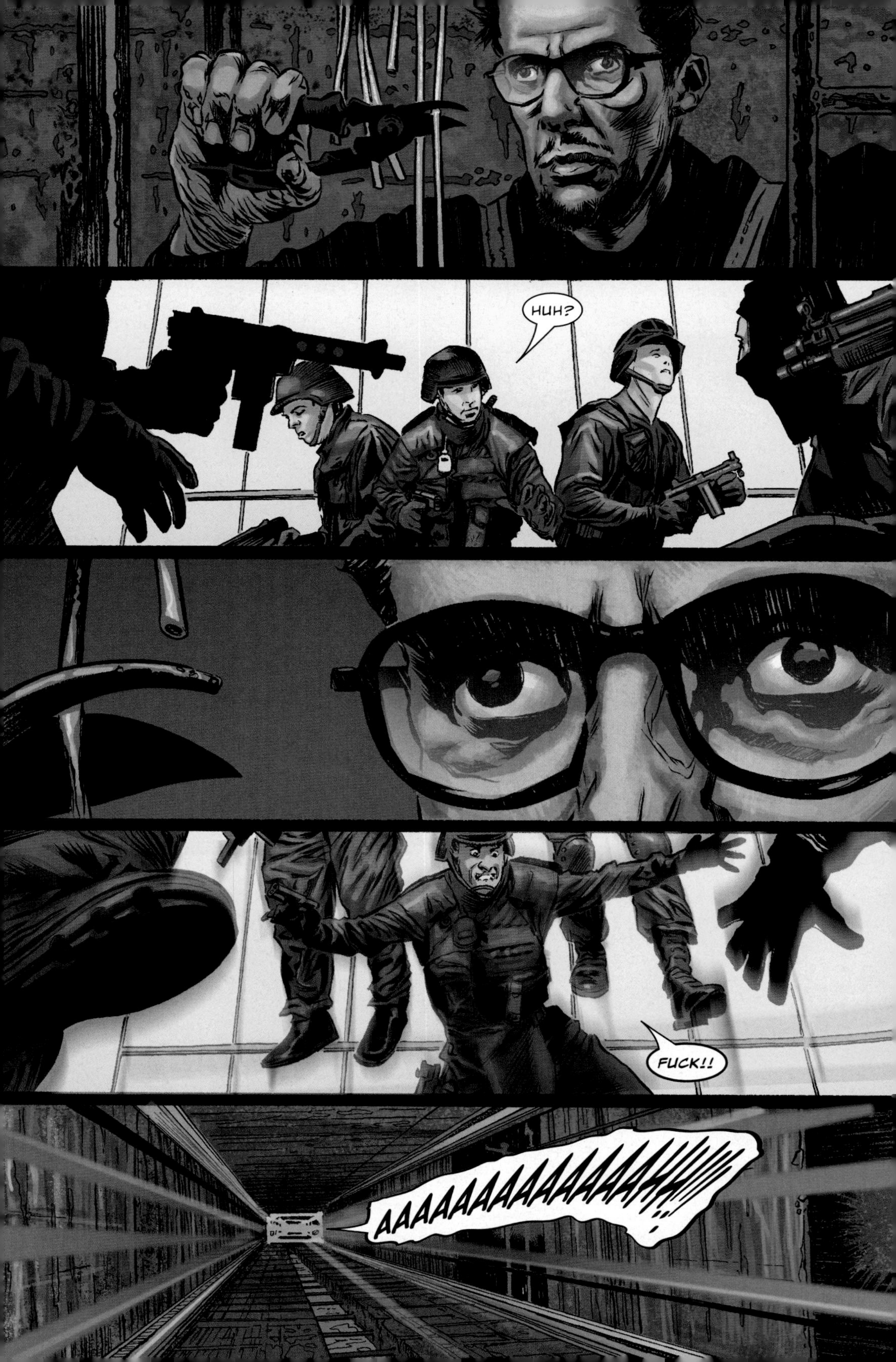
HUH?
FUCK!!
AAAAAAAAAAAAAAAAH!!!

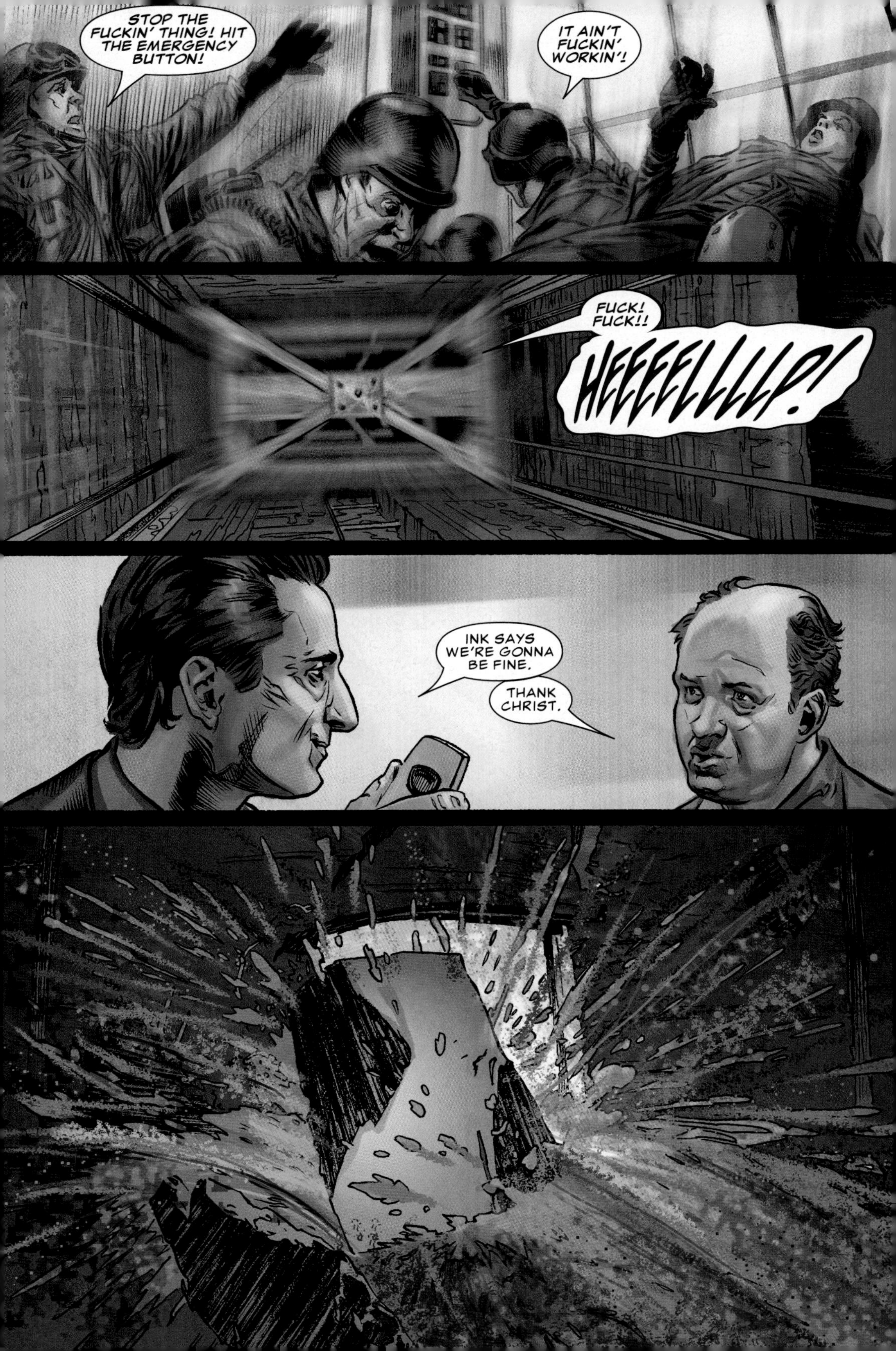
STOP THE FUCKIN' THING! HIT THE EMERGENCY BUTTON!
IT AIN'T FUCKIN' WORKIN'!
FUCK! FUCK!!
HEEEELLLLP!
INK SAYS WE'RE GONNA BE FINE.
THANK CHRIST.

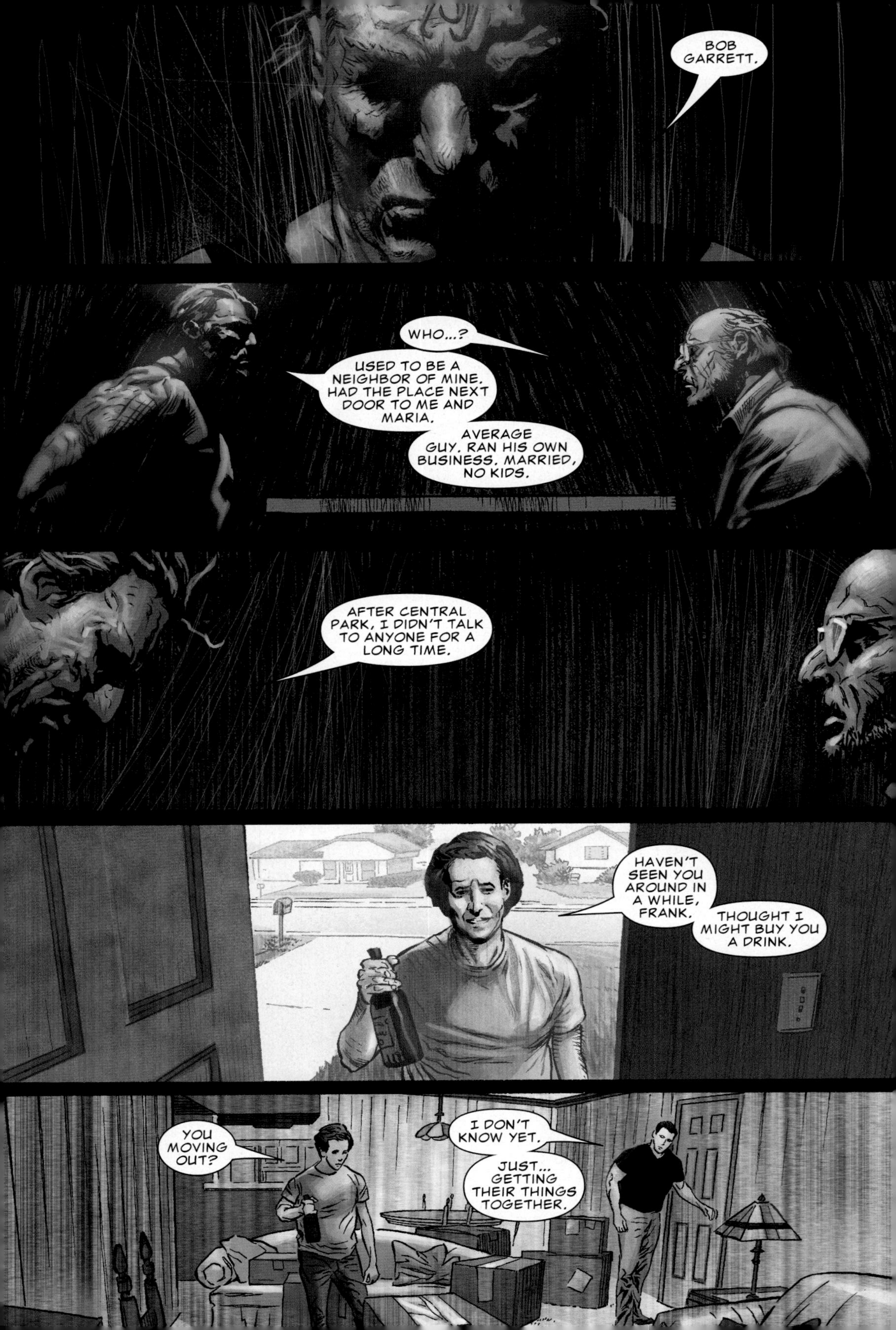
BOB GARRETT.
WHO...?
USED TO BE A NEIGHBOR OF MINE. HAD THE PLACE NEXT DOOR TO ME AND MARIA.
AVERAGE GUY. RAN HIS OWN BUSINESS. MARRIED, NO KIDS.
AFTER CENTRAL PARK, I DIDN'T TALK TO ANYONE FOR A LONG TIME.
HAVEN'T SEEN YOU AROUND IN A WHILE, FRANK.
THOUGHT I MIGHT BUY YOU A DRINK.
YOU MOVING OUT?
I DON'T KNOW YET.
JUST... GETTING THEIR THINGS TOGETHER.

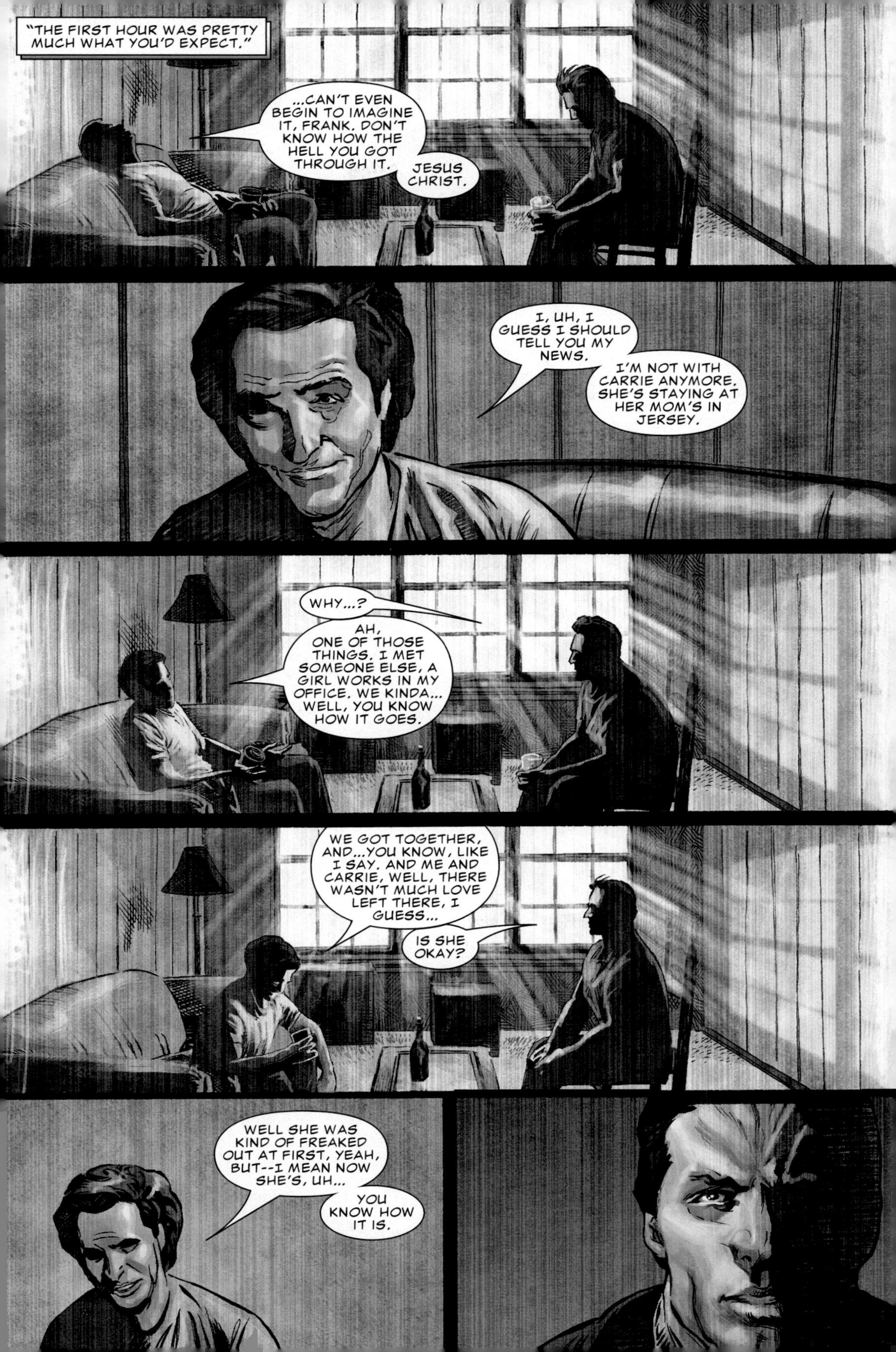
"THE FIRST HOUR WAS PRETTY MUCH WHAT YOU'D EXPECT."
...CAN'T EVEN BEGIN TO IMAGINE IT, FRANK. DON'T KNOW HOW THE HELL YOU GOT THROUGH IT.
JESUS CHRIST.
I, UH, I GUESS I SHOULD TELL YOU MY NEWS.
I'M NOT WITH CARRIE ANYMORE. SHE'S STAYING AT HER MOM'S IN JERSEY.
WHY...?
AH, ONE OF THOSE THINGS. I MET SOMEONE ELSE, A GIRL WORKS IN MY OFFICE. WE KINDA... WELL, YOU KNOW HOW IT GOES.
WE GOT TOGETHER, AND...YOU KNOW, LIKE I SAY. AND ME AND CARRIE, WELL, THERE WASN'T MUCH LOVE LEFT THERE, I GUESS...
IS SHE OKAY?
WELL SHE WAS KIND OF FREAKED OUT AT FIRST, YEAH, BUT--I MEAN NOW SHE'S, UH...
YOU KNOW HOW IT IS.

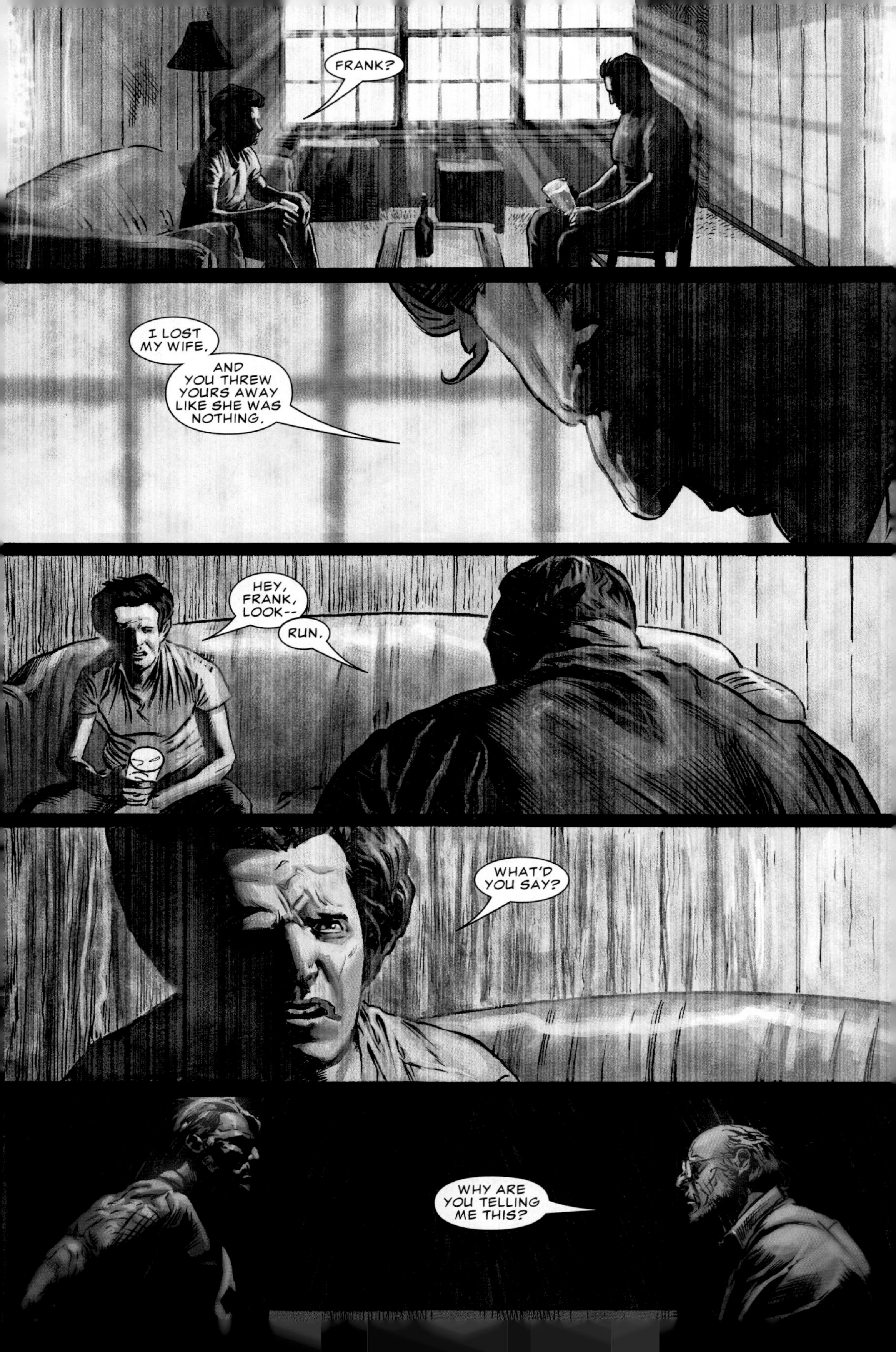
FRANK?
I LOST MY WIFE.
AND YOU THREW YOURS AWAY LIKE SHE WAS NOTHING.
HEY, FRANK, LOOK--
RUN.
WHAT'D YOU SAY?
WHY ARE YOU TELLING ME THIS?

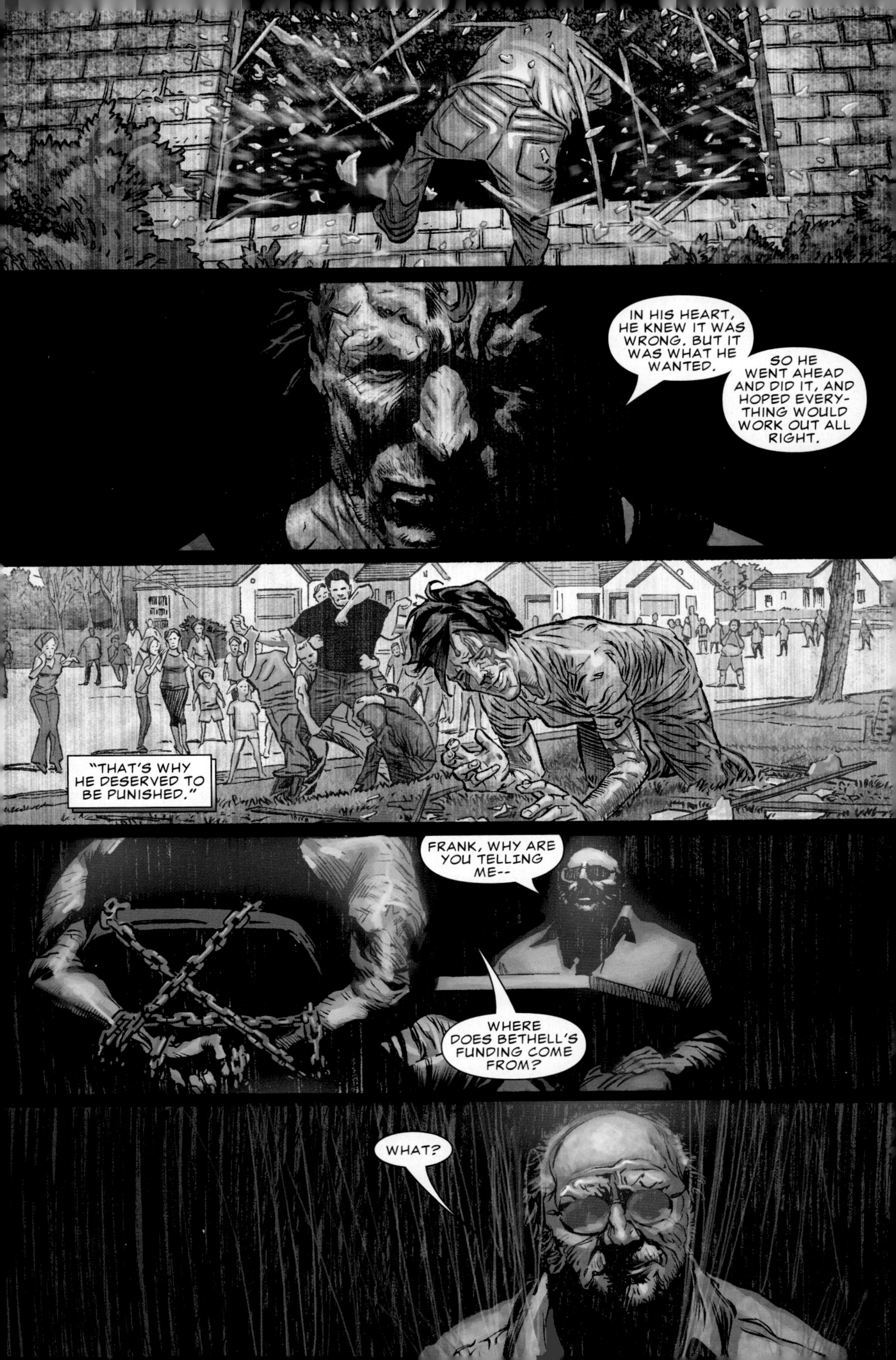

IN HIS HEART, HE KNEW IT WAS WRONG. BUT IT WAS WHAT HE WANTED.
SO HE WENT AHEAD AND DID IT, AND HOPED EVERY-THING WOULD WORK OUT ALL RIGHT.
"THAT'S WHY HE DESERVED TO BE PUNISHED."
FRANK, WHY ARE YOU TELLING ME--
WHERE DOES BETHELL'S FUNDING COME FROM?
WHAT?

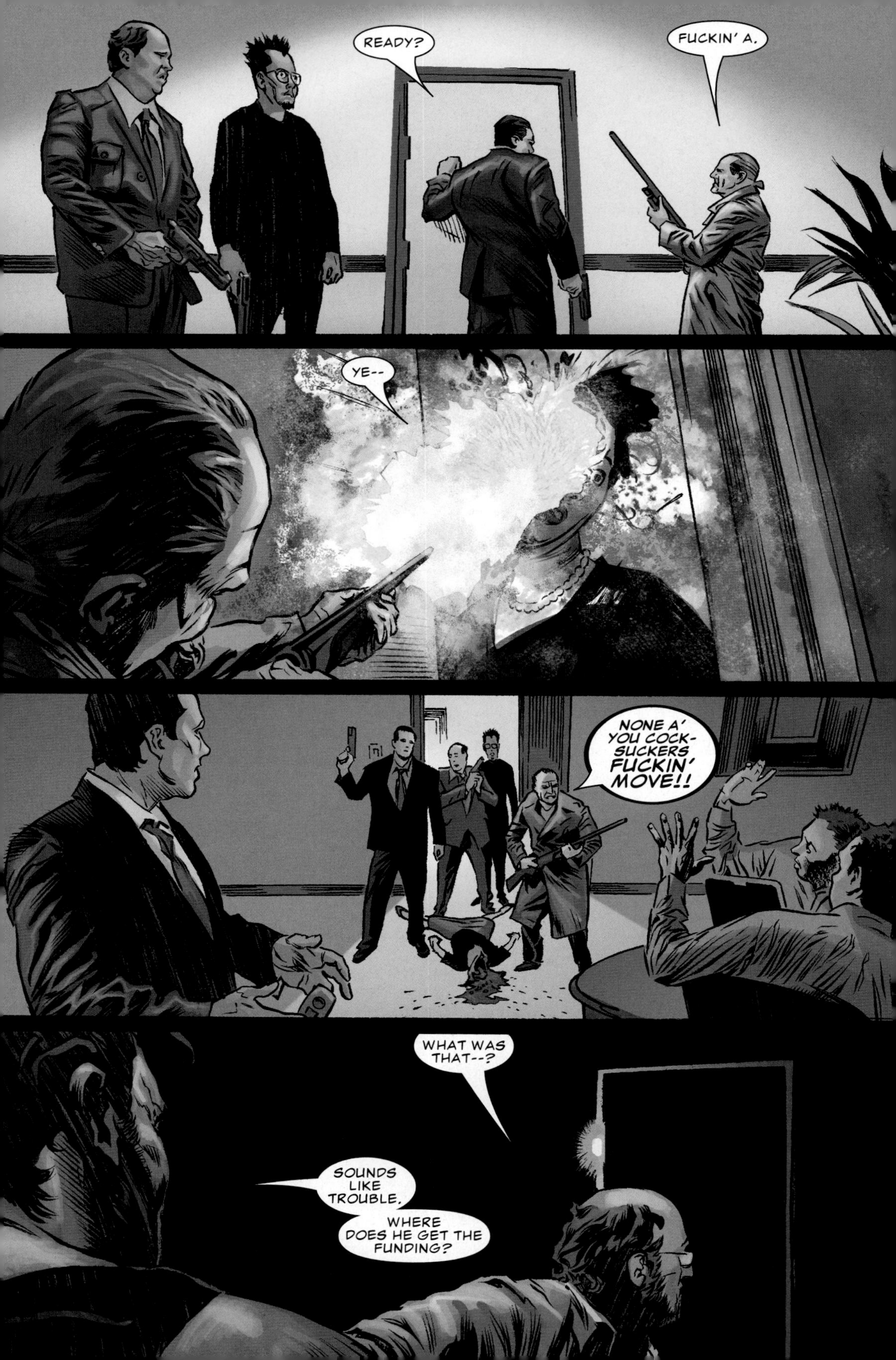
READY?
FUCKIN' A.
YE--
NONE A' YOU COCK-SUCKERS FUCKIN' MOVE!!
WHAT WAS THAT--?
SOUNDS LIKE TROUBLE.
WHERE DOES HE GET THE FUNDING?

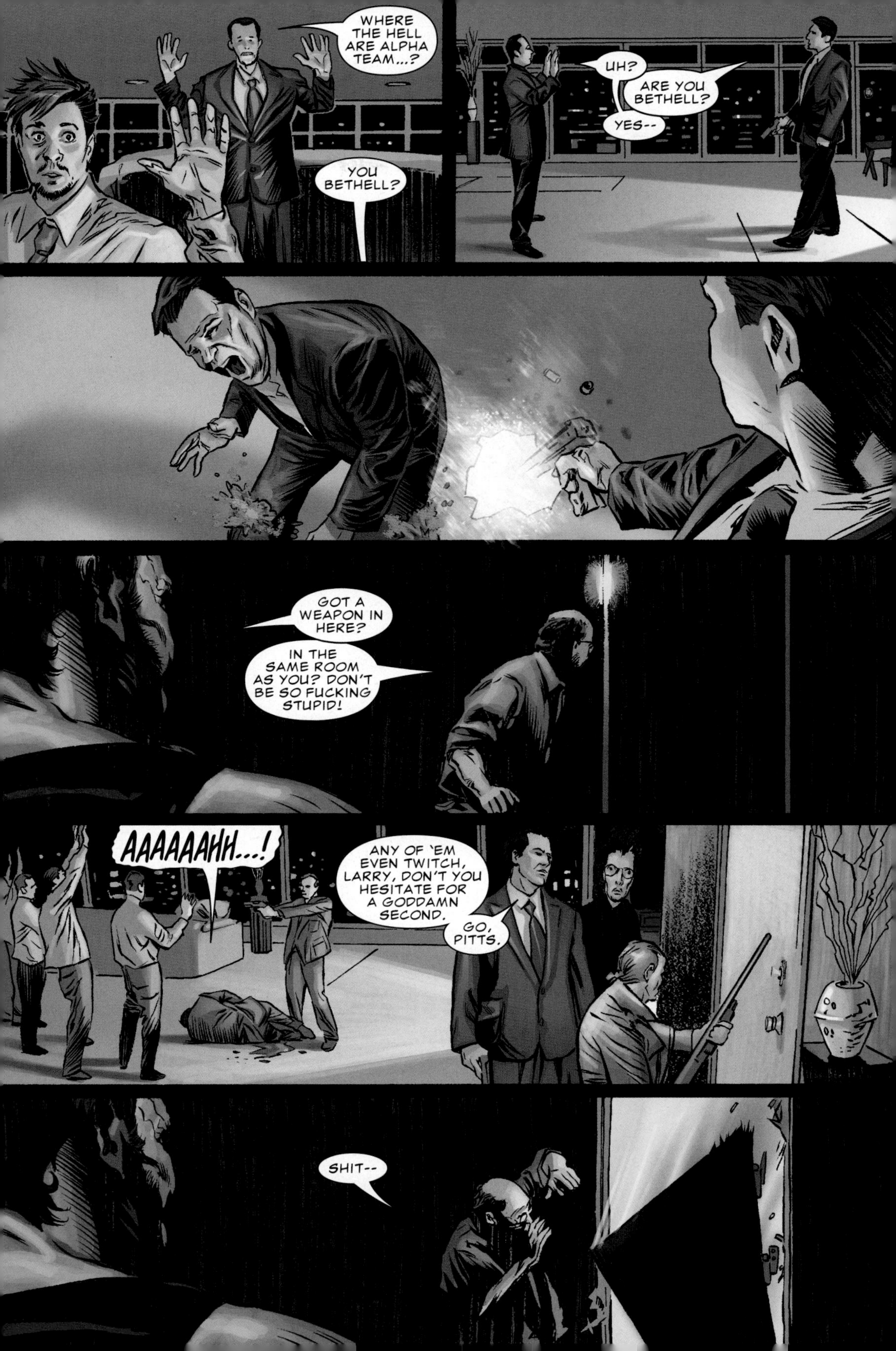
WHERE THE HELL ARE ALPHA TEAM...?
YOU BETHELL?
UH?
ARE YOU BETHELL?
YES--
GOT A WEAPON IN HERE?
IN THE SAME ROOM AS YOU? DON'T BE SO FUCKING STUPID!
AAAAAAHH...!
ANY OF 'EM EVEN TWITCH, LARRY, DON'T YOU HESITATE FOR A GODDAMN SECOND.
GO, PITTS.
SHIT--

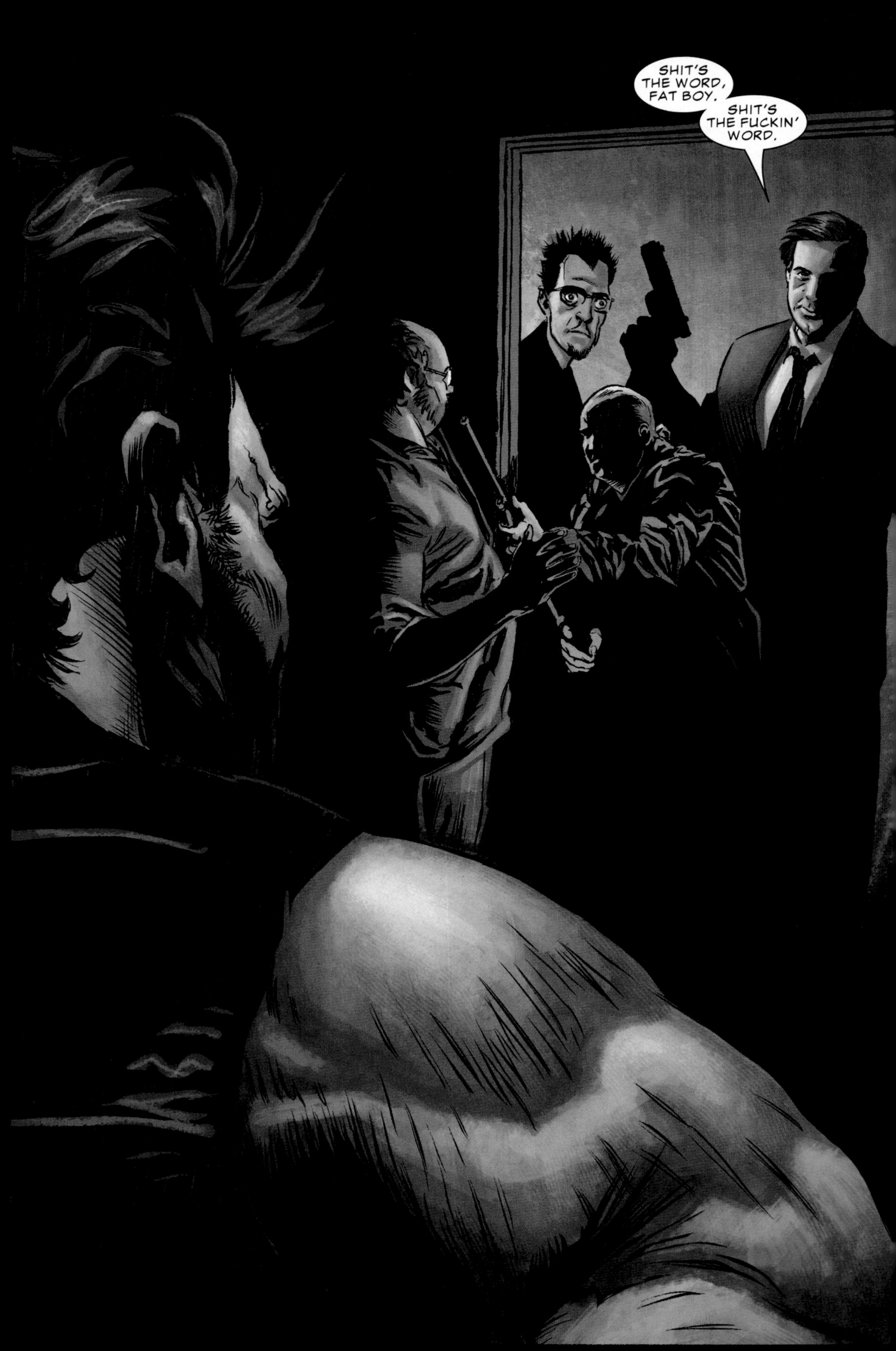
SHIT'S THE WORD, FAT BOY.
SHIT'S THE FUCKIN' WORD.

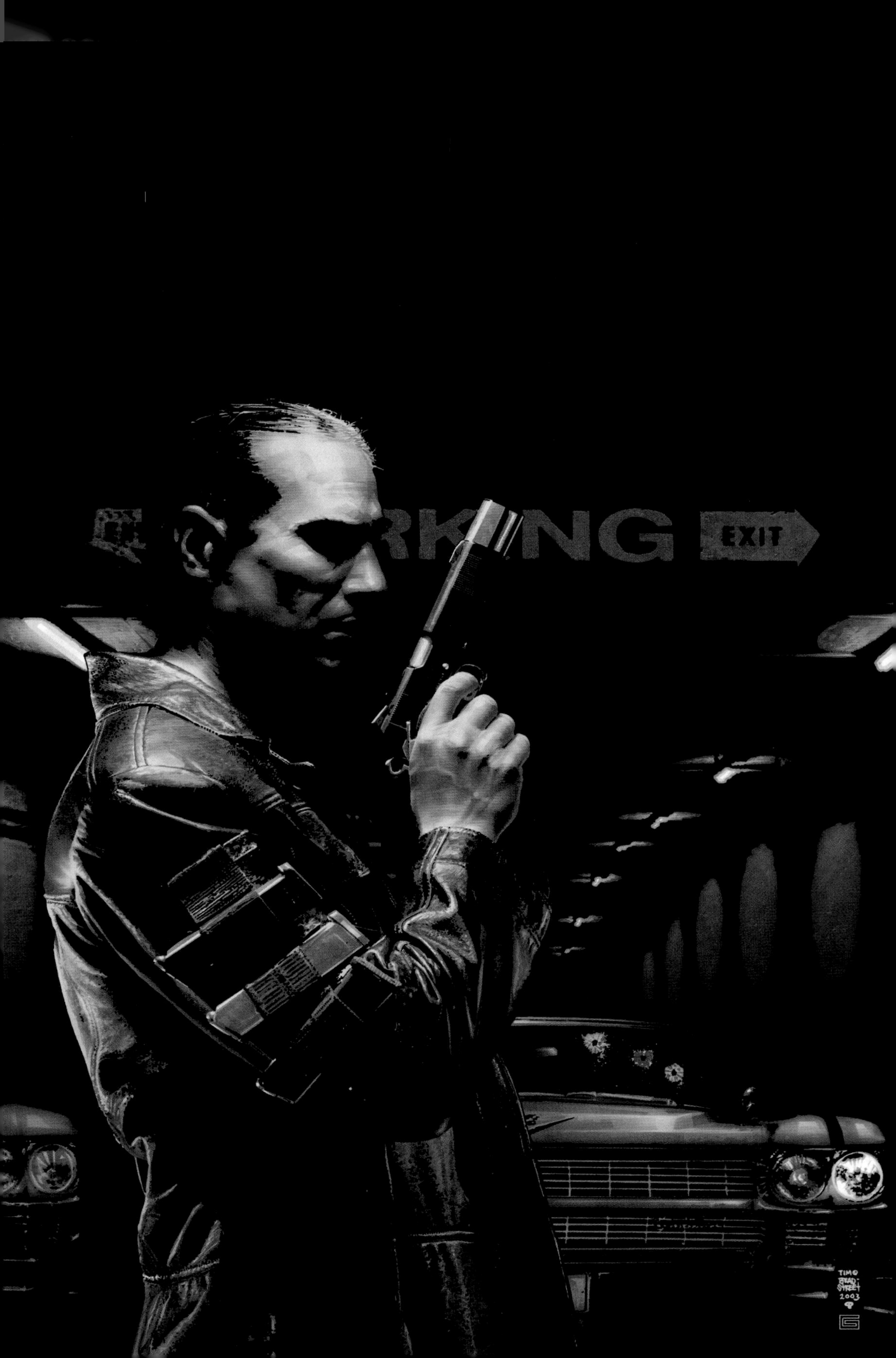
EXIT

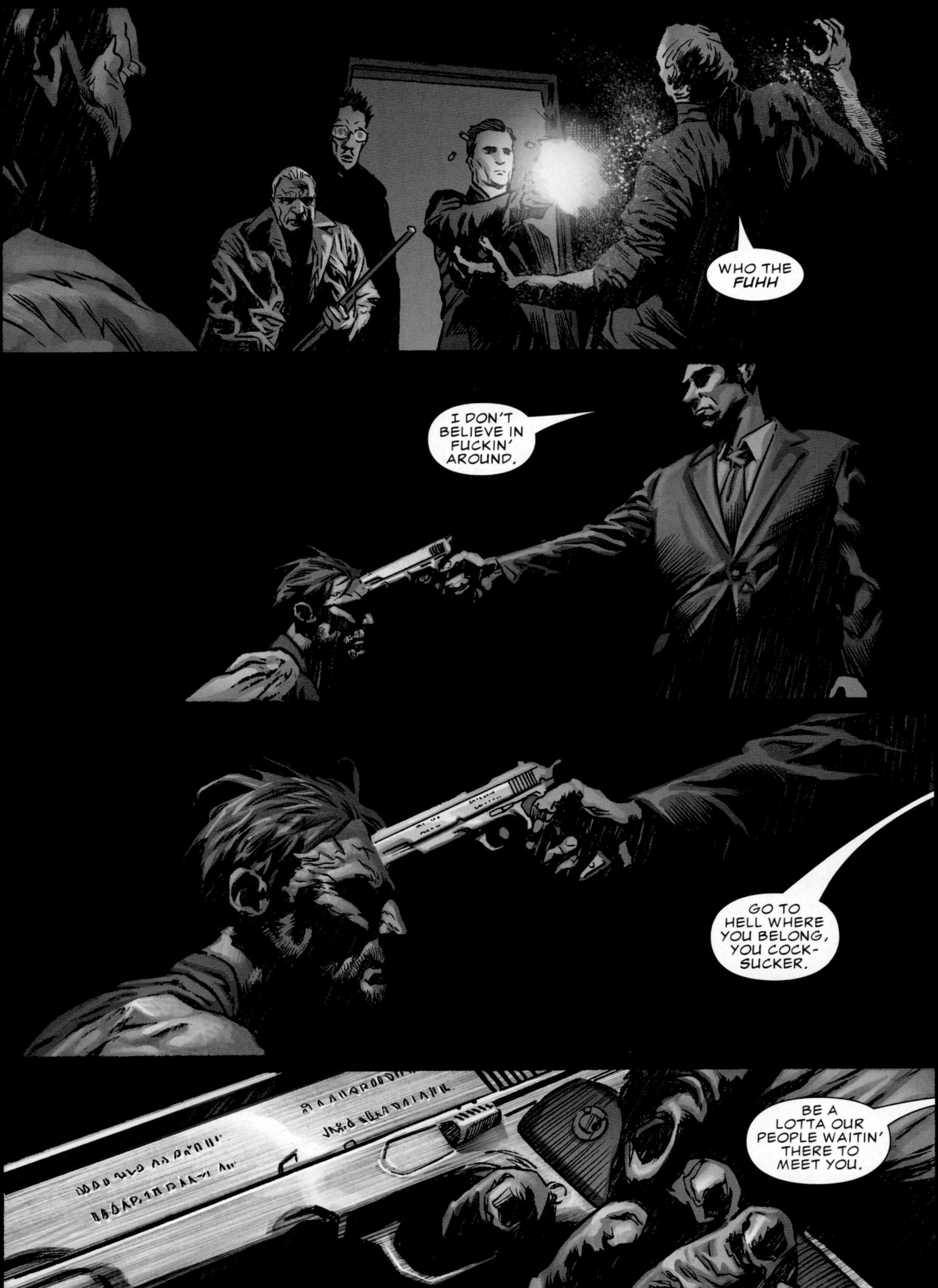
WHO THE *FUHH*
I DON'T BELIEVE IN FUCKIN' AROUND.
GO TO HELL WHERE YOU BELONG, YOU COCK-SUCKER.
BE A LOTTA OUR PEOPLE WAITIN' THERE TO MEET YOU.

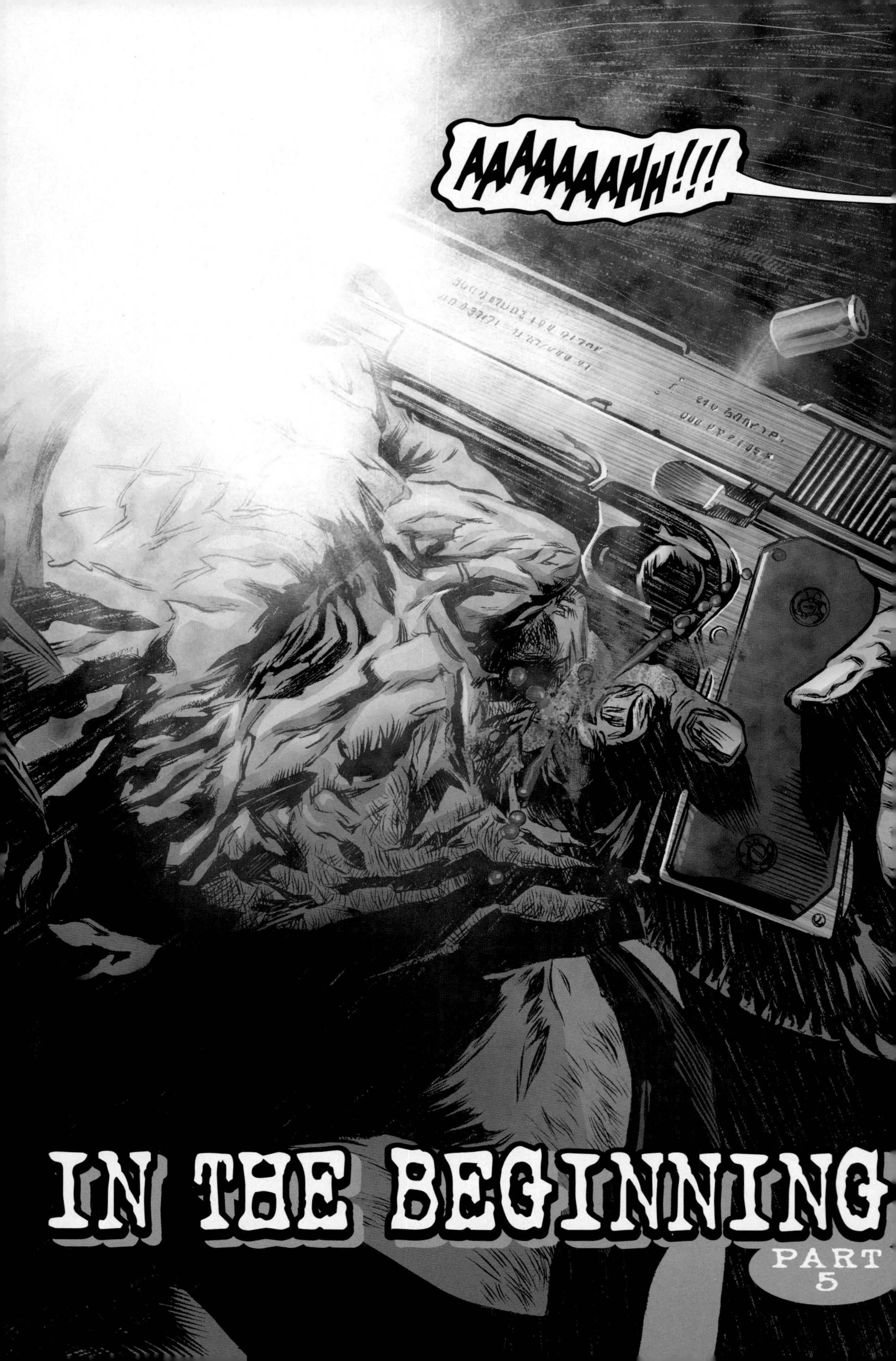
AAAAAAAHH!!!
IN THE BEGINNING
PART 5

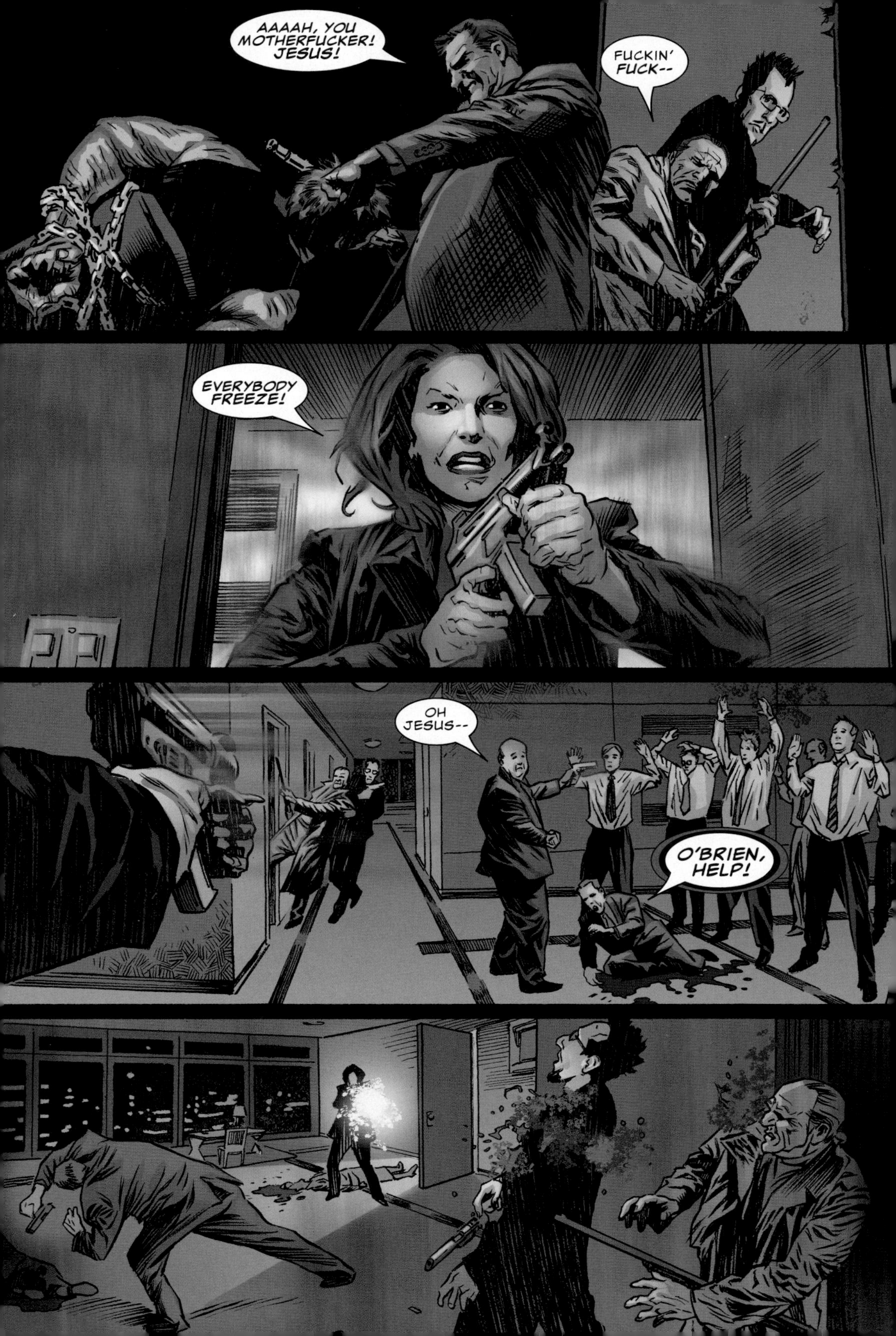
AAAAH, YOU MOTHERFUCKER! JESUS!
FUCKIN' FUCK--
EVERYBODY FREEZE!
OH JESUS--
O'BRIEN, HELP!

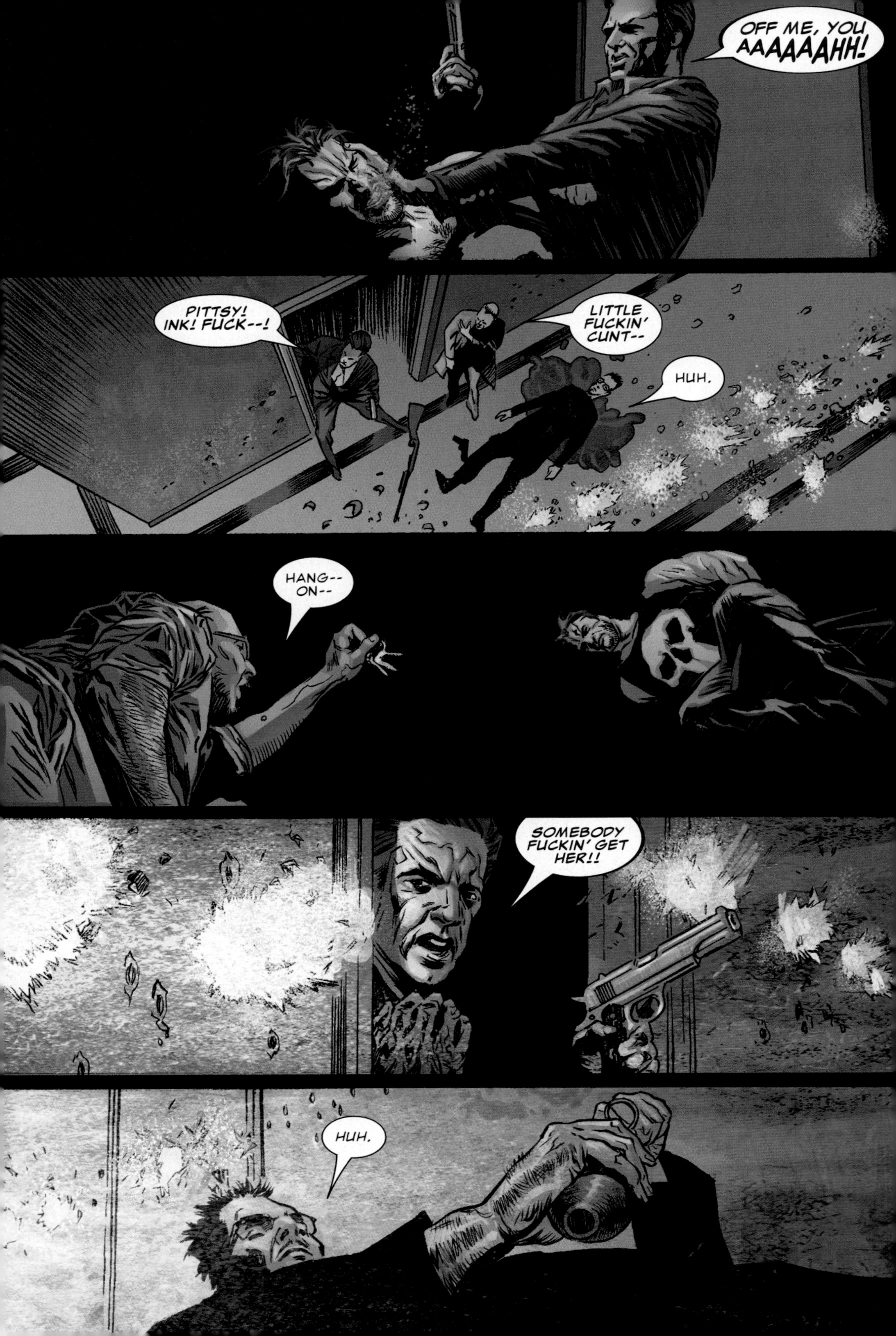
OFF ME, YOU AAAAAAHH!
PITTSY! INK! FUCK--!
LITTLE FUCKIN' CUNT--
HUH.
HANG-- ON--
SOMEBODY FUCKIN' GET HER!!
HUH.

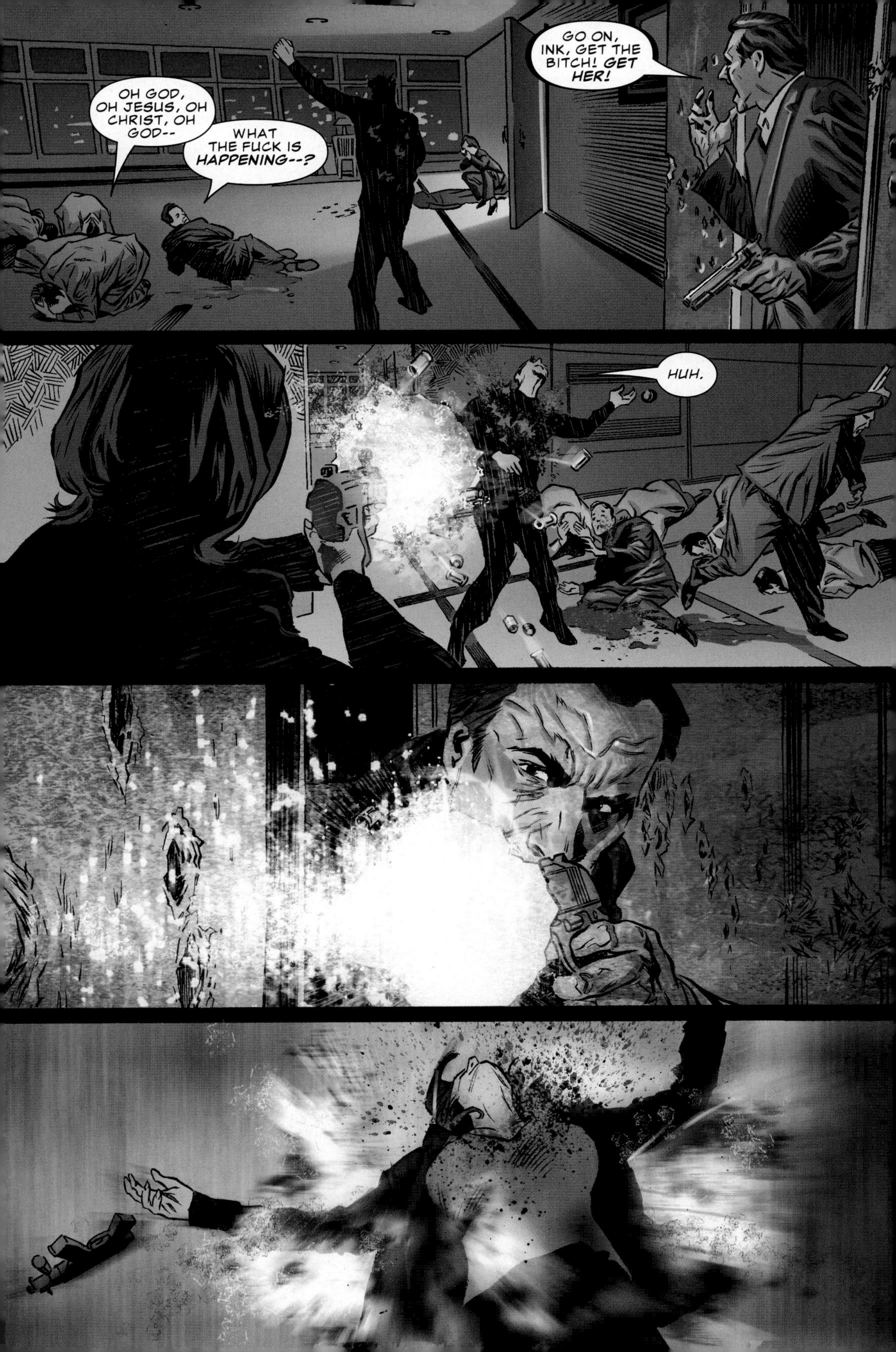
OH GOD, OH JESUS, OH CHRIST, OH GOD--
WHAT THE FUCK IS HAPPENING--?
GO ON, INK, GET THE BITCH! GET HER!
HUH.

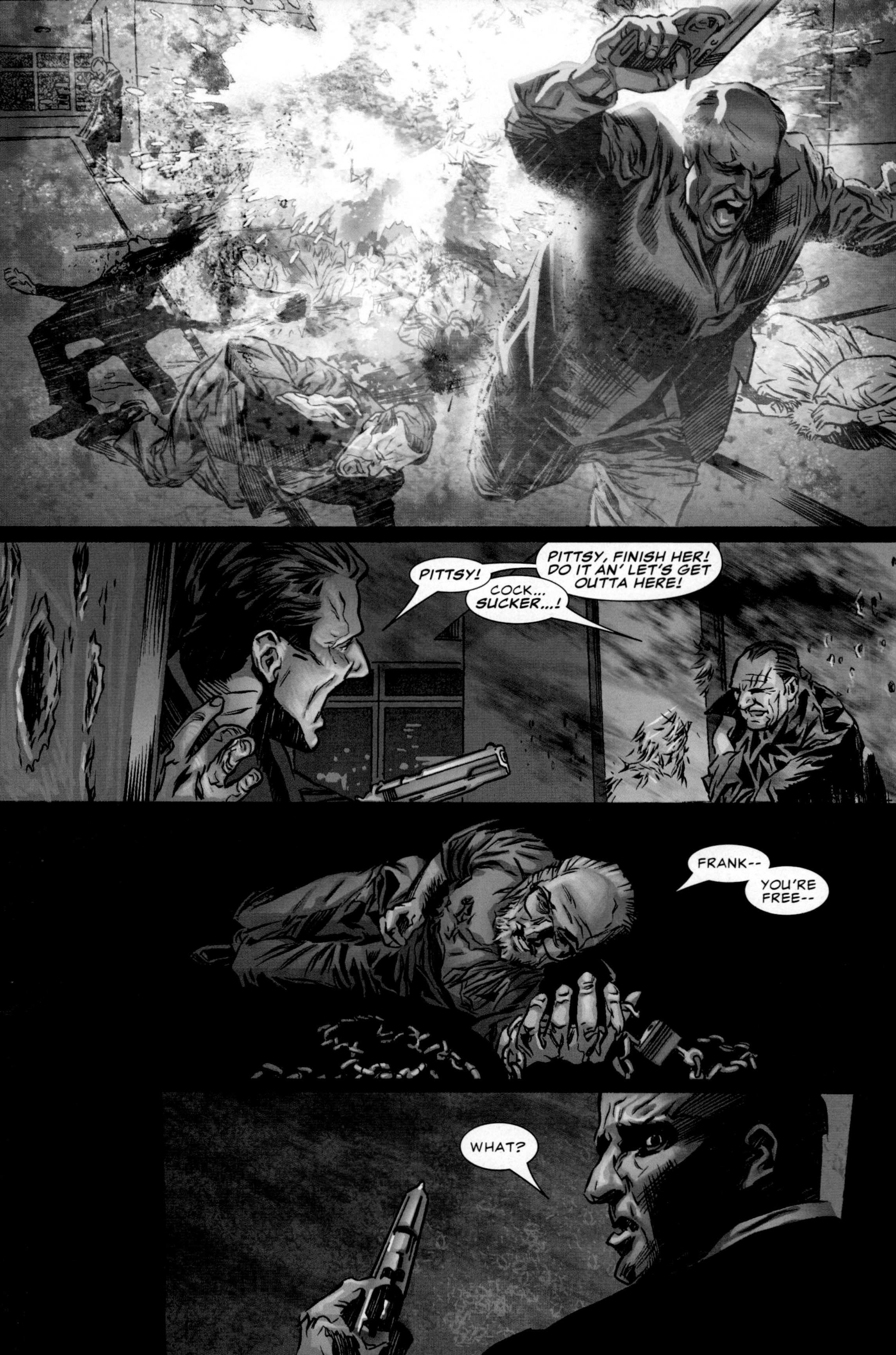
PITTSY!
PITTSY, FINISH HER! DO IT AN' LET'S GET OUTTA HERE!
COCK... SUCKER...!
FRANK--
YOU'RE FREE--
WHAT?

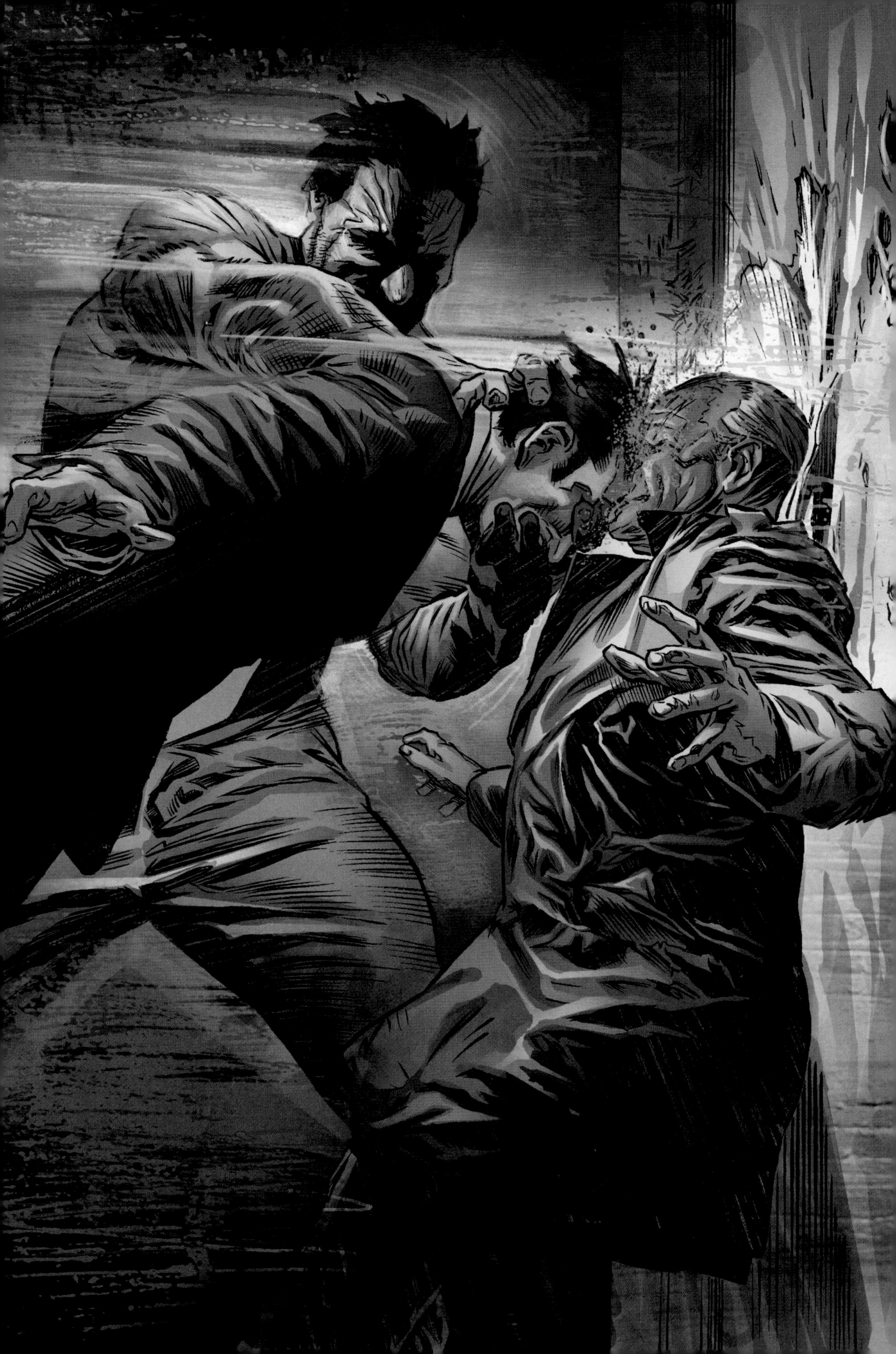

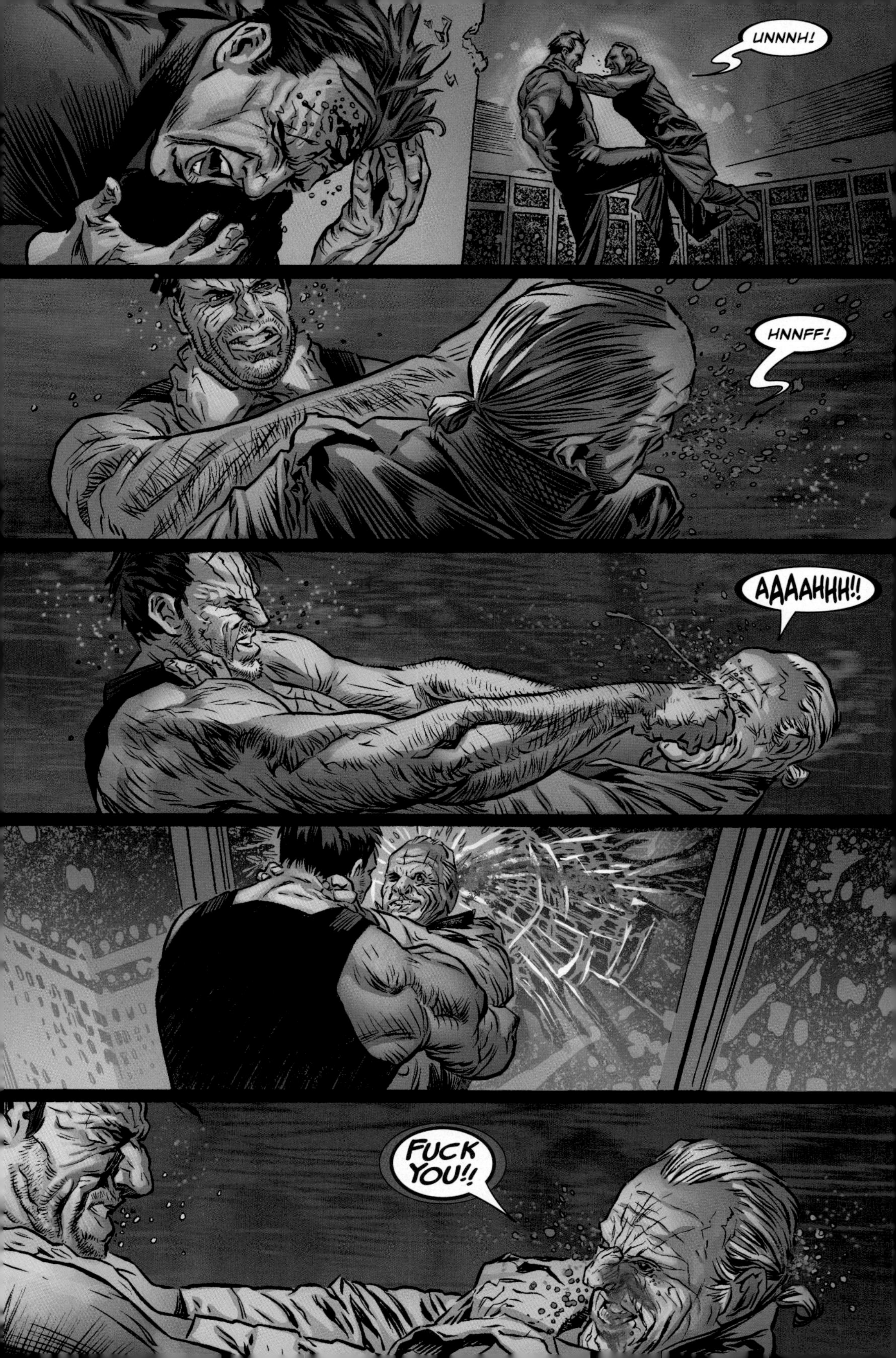
UNNNH!
HNNFF!
AAAAHHH!!
FUCK YOU!!

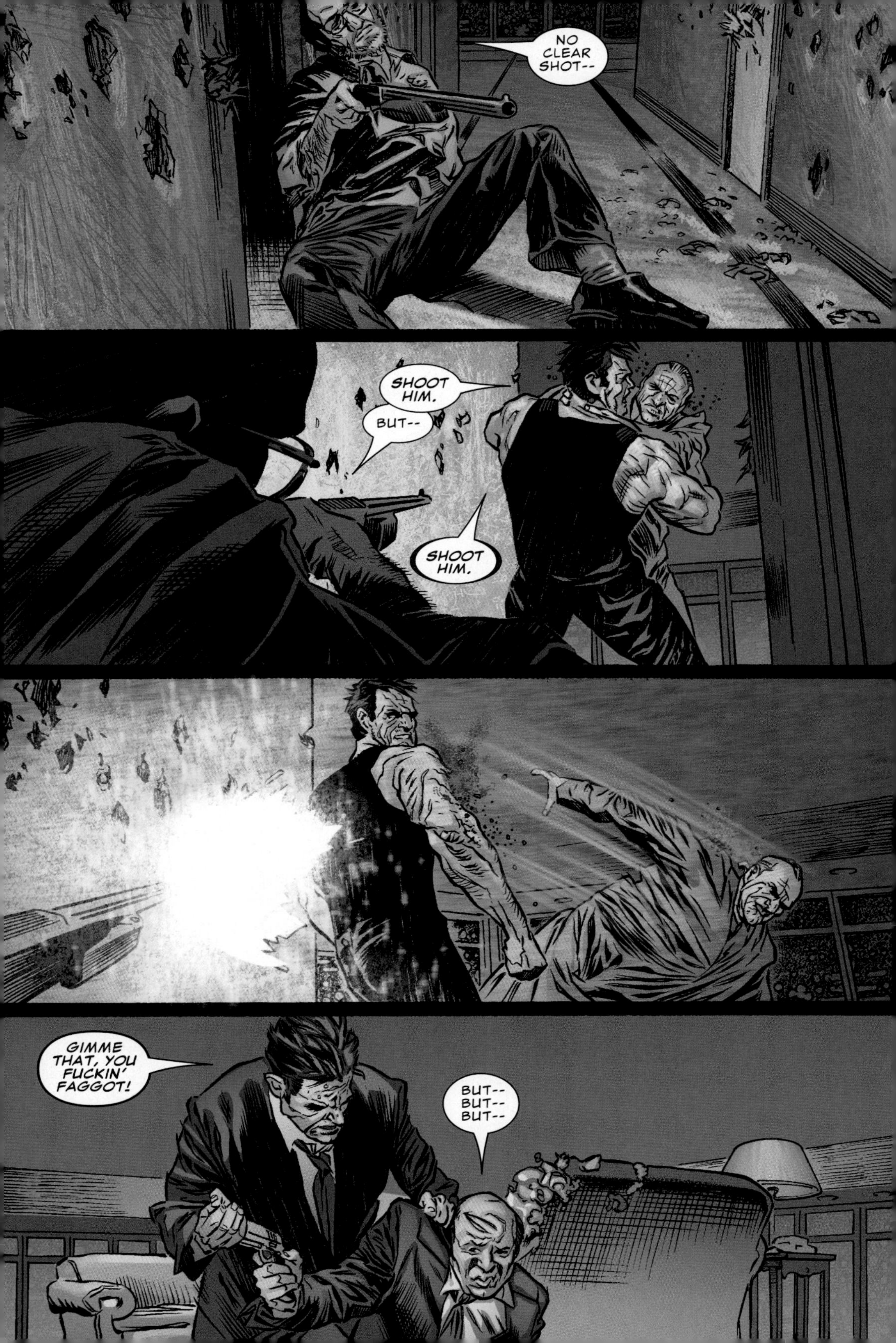
NO CLEAR SHOT--
SHOOT HIM.
BUT--
SHOOT HIM.
GIMME THAT, YOU FUCKIN' FAGGOT!
BUT-- BUT-- BUT--

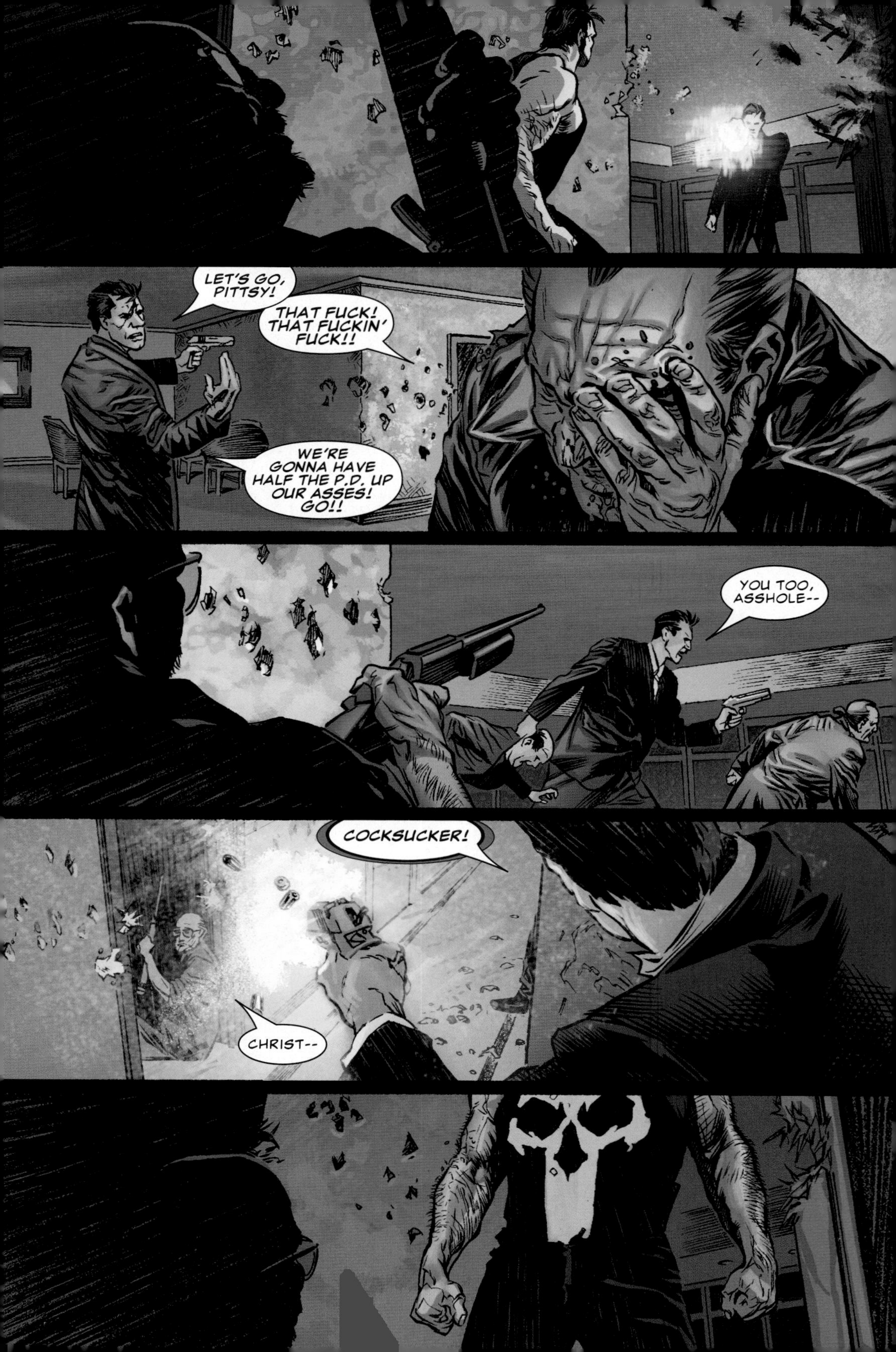
LET'S GO, PITTSY!
THAT FUCK! THAT FUCKIN' FUCK!!
WE'RE GONNA HAVE HALF THE P.D. UP OUR ASSES! GO!!
YOU TOO, ASSHOLE--
COCKSUCKER!
CHRIST--

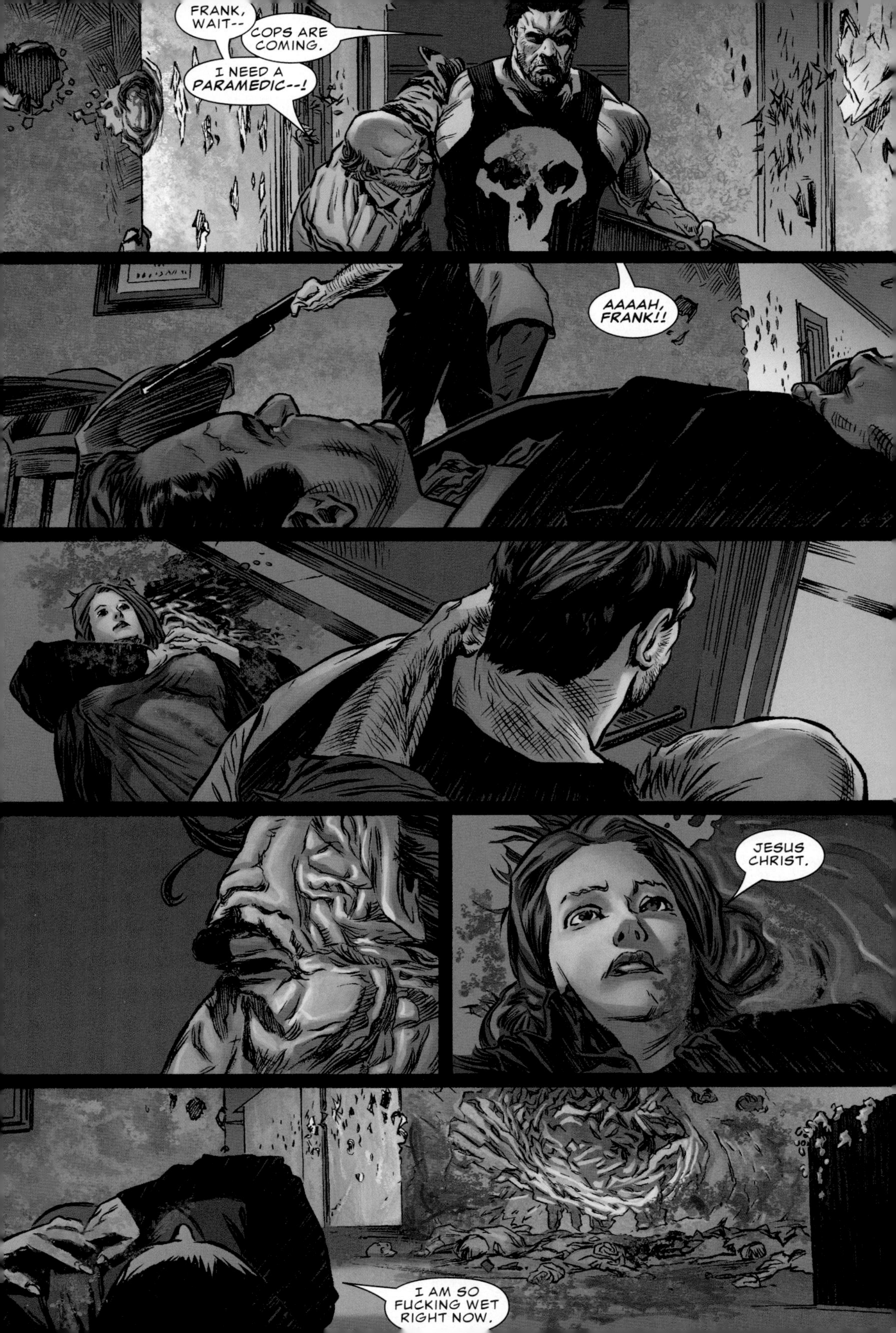
FRANK, WAIT--
COPS ARE COMING.
I NEED A PARAMEDIC--!
AAAAH, FRANK!!
JESUS CHRIST.
I AM SO FUCKING WET RIGHT NOW.

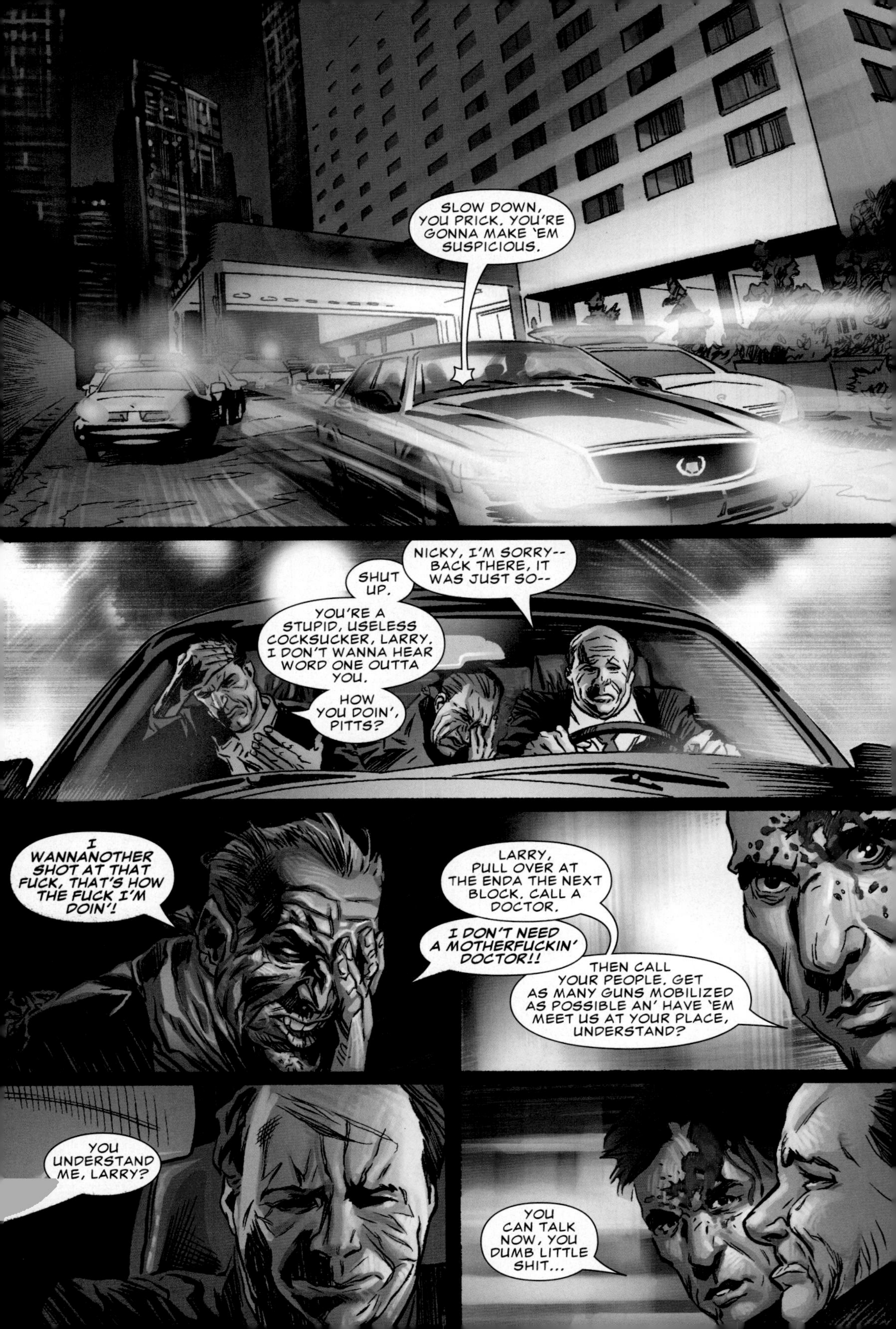
SLOW DOWN, YOU PRICK. YOU'RE GONNA MAKE 'EM SUSPICIOUS.
NICKY, I'M SORRY-- BACK THERE, IT WAS JUST SO--
SHUT UP.
YOU'RE A STUPID, USELESS COCKSUCKER, LARRY. I DON'T WANNA HEAR WORD ONE OUTTA YOU.
HOW YOU DOIN', PITTS?
I WANNANOTHER SHOT AT THAT FUCK, THAT'S HOW THE FUCK I'M DOIN'!
LARRY, PULL OVER AT THE ENDA THE NEXT BLOCK. CALL A DOCTOR.
I DON'T NEED A MOTHERFUCKIN' DOCTOR!!
THEN CALL YOUR PEOPLE. GET AS MANY GUNS MOBILIZED AS POSSIBLE AN' HAVE 'EM MEET US AT YOUR PLACE, UNDERSTAND?
YOU UNDERSTAND ME, LARRY?
YOU CAN TALK NOW, YOU DUMB LITTLE SHIT...

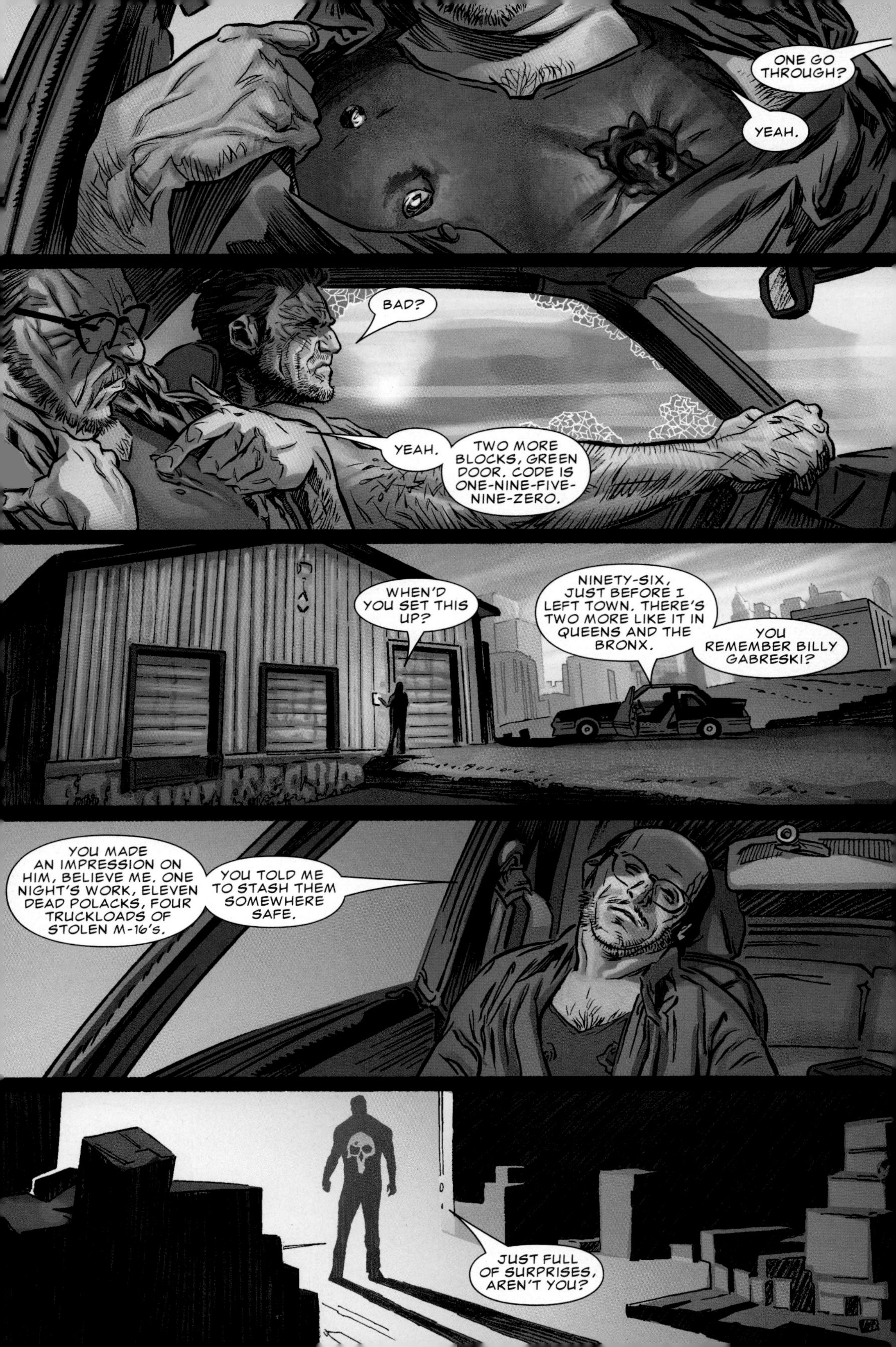
ONE GO THROUGH?
YEAH.
BAD?
YEAH.
TWO MORE BLOCKS, GREEN DOOR. CODE IS ONE-NINE-FIVE-NINE-ZERO.
WHEN'D YOU SET THIS UP?
NINETY-SIX, JUST BEFORE I LEFT TOWN. THERE'S TWO MORE LIKE IT IN QUEENS AND THE BRONX.
YOU REMEMBER BILLY GABRESKI?
YOU MADE AN IMPRESSION ON HIM, BELIEVE ME. ONE NIGHT'S WORK, ELEVEN DEAD POLACKS, FOUR TRUCKLOADS OF STOLEN M-16'S.
YOU TOLD ME TO STASH THEM SOMEWHERE SAFE.
JUST FULL OF SURPRISES, AREN'T YOU?

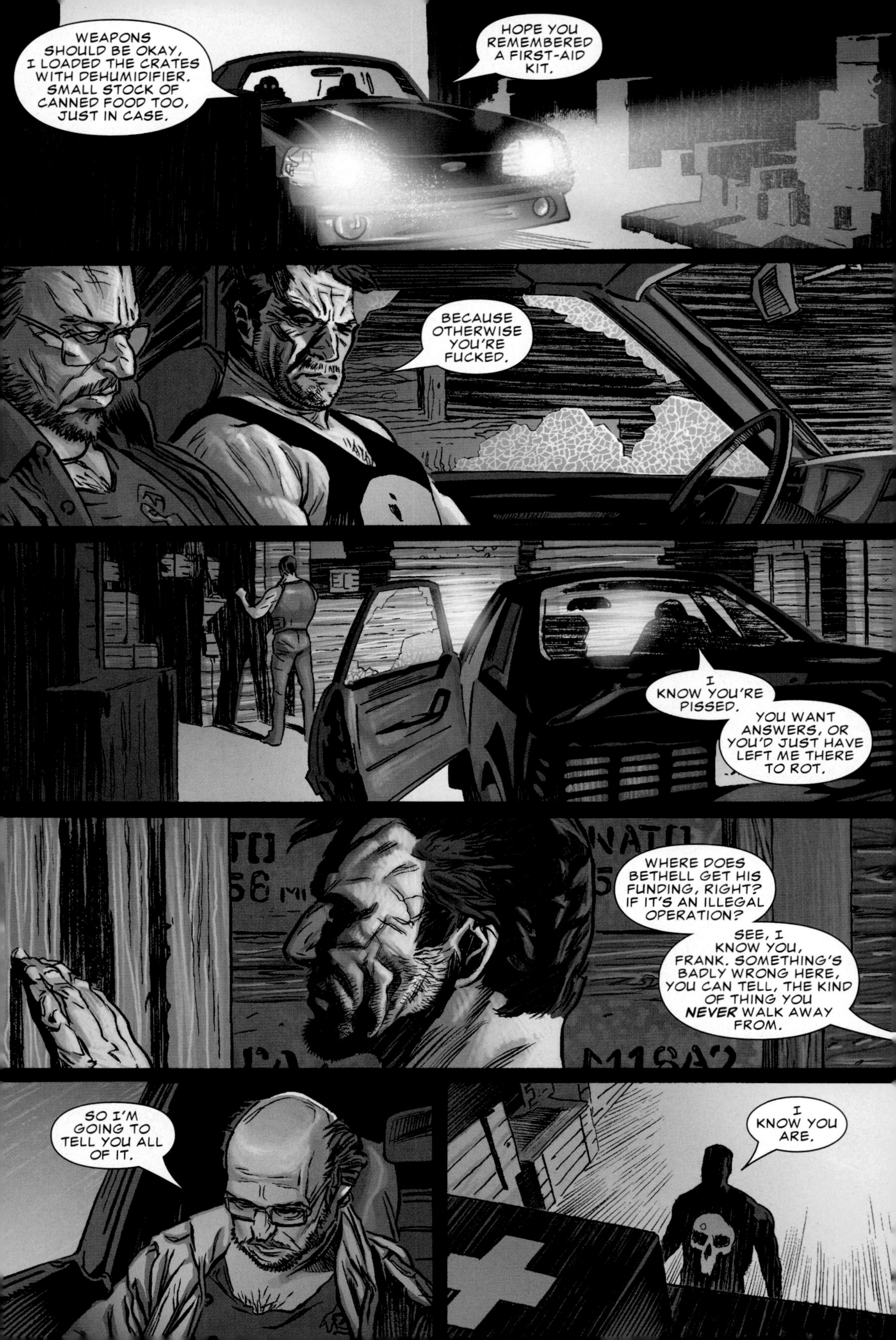
WEAPONS SHOULD BE OKAY, I LOADED THE CRATES WITH DEHUMIDIFIER. SMALL STOCK OF CANNED FOOD TOO, JUST IN CASE.
HOPE YOU REMEMBERED A FIRST-AID KIT.
BECAUSE OTHERWISE YOU'RE FUCKED.
I KNOW YOU'RE PISSED.
YOU WANT ANSWERS, OR YOU'D JUST HAVE LEFT ME THERE TO ROT.
WHERE DOES BETHELL GET HIS FUNDING, RIGHT? IF IT'S AN ILLEGAL OPERATION?
SEE, I KNOW YOU, FRANK. SOMETHING'S BADLY WRONG HERE, YOU CAN TELL, THE KIND OF THING YOU **NEVER** WALK AWAY FROM.
SO I'M GOING TO TELL YOU ALL OF IT.
I KNOW YOU ARE.

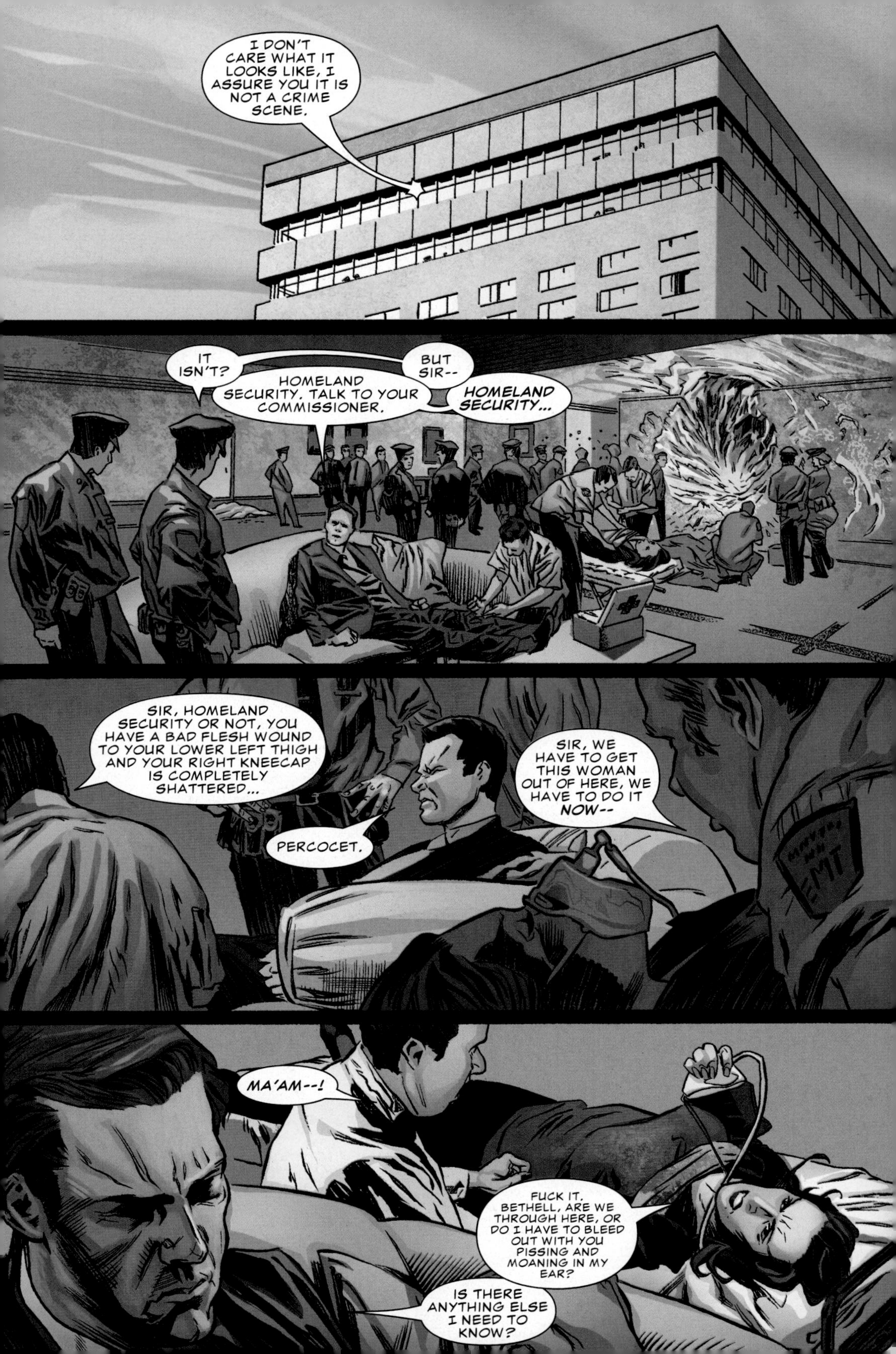
I DON'T CARE WHAT IT LOOKS LIKE, I ASSURE YOU IT IS NOT A CRIME SCENE.
IT ISN'T?
BUT SIR--
HOMELAND SECURITY. TALK TO YOUR COMMISSIONER.
HOMELAND SECURITY...
SIR, HOMELAND SECURITY OR NOT, YOU HAVE A BAD FLESH WOUND TO YOUR LOWER LEFT THIGH AND YOUR RIGHT KNEECAP IS COMPLETELY SHATTERED...
PERCOCET.
SIR, WE HAVE TO GET THIS WOMAN OUT OF HERE, WE HAVE TO DO IT NOW--
MA'AM--!
FUCK IT. BETHELL, ARE WE THROUGH HERE, OR DO I HAVE TO BLEED OUT WITH YOU PISSING AND MOANING IN MY EAR?
IS THERE ANYTHING ELSE I NEED TO KNOW?

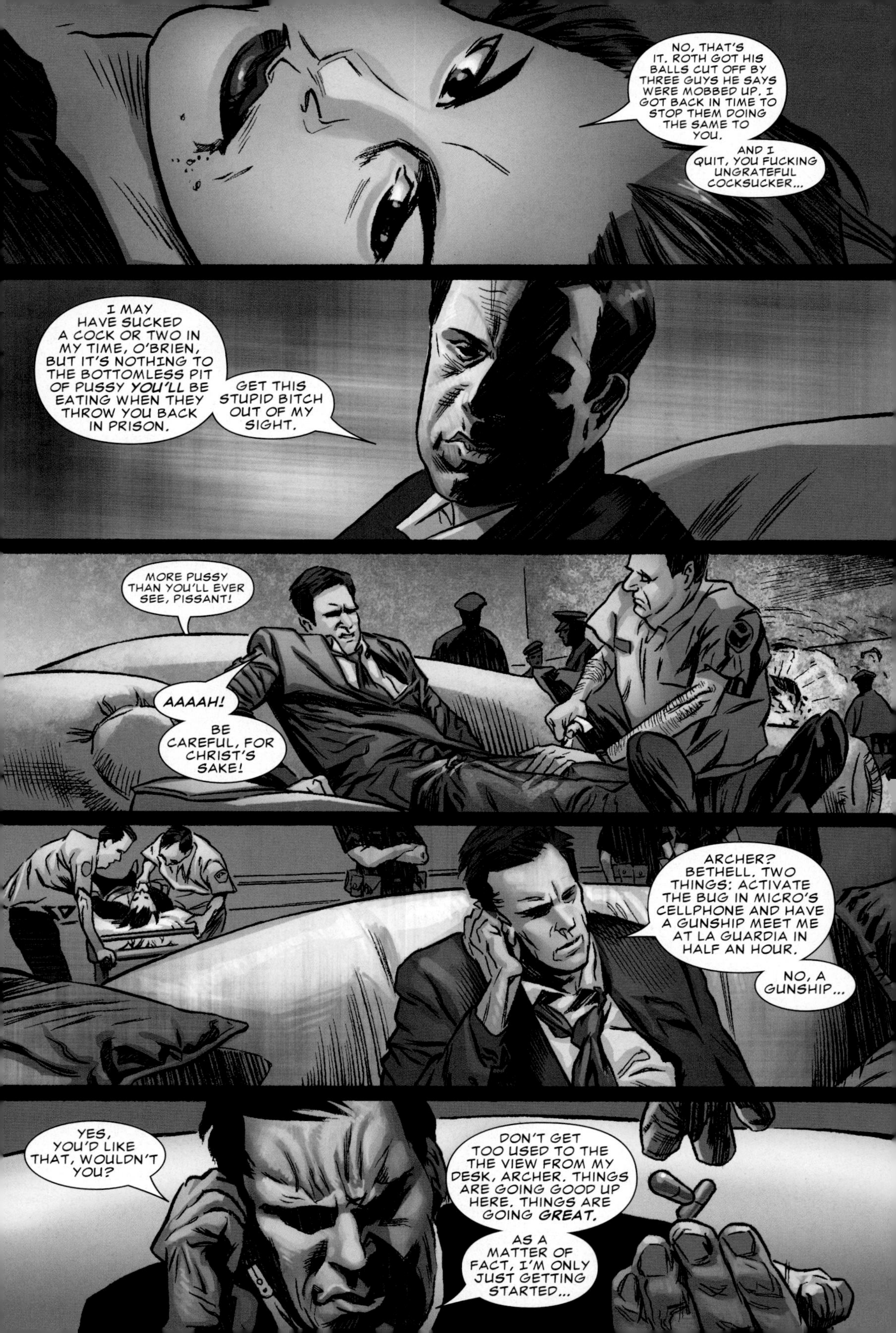
NO, THAT'S IT. ROTH GOT HIS BALLS CUT OFF BY THREE GUYS HE SAYS WERE MOBBED UP. I GOT BACK IN TIME TO STOP THEM DOING THE SAME TO YOU.
AND I QUIT, YOU FUCKING UNGRATEFUL COCKSUCKER...
I MAY HAVE SUCKED A COCK OR TWO IN MY TIME, O'BRIEN, BUT IT'S NOTHING TO THE BOTTOMLESS PIT OF PUSSY YOU'LL BE EATING WHEN THEY THROW YOU BACK IN PRISON.
GET THIS STUPID BITCH OUT OF MY SIGHT.
MORE PUSSY THAN YOU'LL EVER SEE, PISSANT!
AAAAH!
BE CAREFUL, FOR CHRIST'S SAKE!
ARCHER? BETHELL. TWO THINGS: ACTIVATE THE BUG IN MICRO'S CELLPHONE AND HAVE A GUNSHIP MEET ME AT LA GUARDIA IN HALF AN HOUR.
NO, A GUNSHIP...
YES, YOU'D LIKE THAT, WOULDN'T YOU?
DON'T GET TOO USED TO THE THE VIEW FROM MY DESK, ARCHER. THINGS ARE GOING GOOD UP HERE. THINGS ARE GOING GREAT.
AS A MATTER OF FACT, I'M ONLY JUST GETTING STARTED...

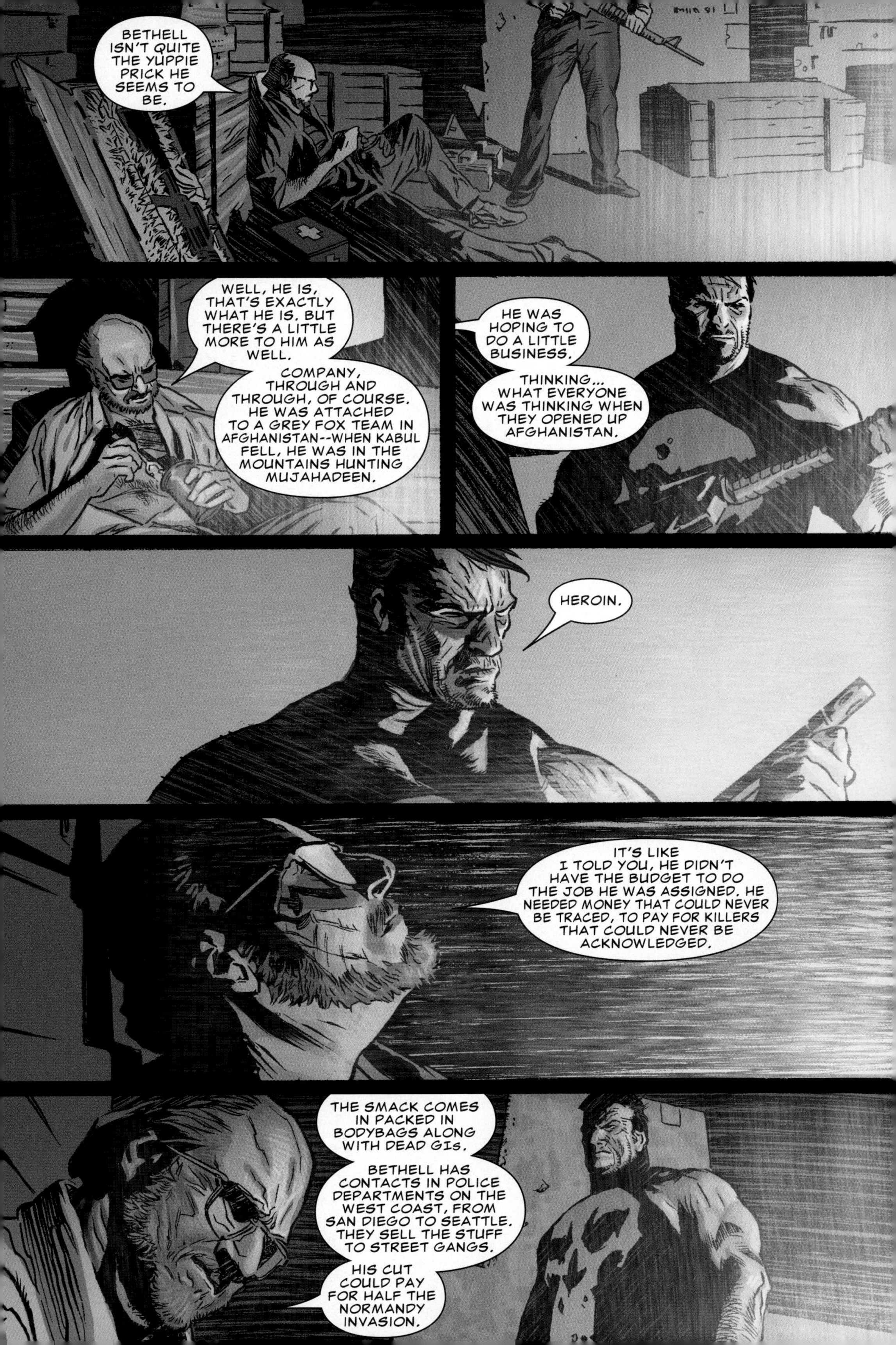
BETHELL ISN'T QUITE THE YUPPIE PRICK HE SEEMS TO BE.
WELL, HE IS, THAT'S EXACTLY WHAT HE IS. BUT THERE'S A LITTLE MORE TO HIM AS WELL.
COMPANY, THROUGH AND THROUGH, OF COURSE. HE WAS ATTACHED TO A GREY FOX TEAM IN AFGHANISTAN--WHEN KABUL FELL, HE WAS IN THE MOUNTAINS HUNTING MUJAHADEEN.
HE WAS HOPING TO DO A LITTLE BUSINESS.
THINKING... WHAT EVERYONE WAS THINKING WHEN THEY OPENED UP AFGHANISTAN.
HEROIN.
IT'S LIKE I TOLD YOU, HE DIDN'T HAVE THE BUDGET TO DO THE JOB HE WAS ASSIGNED. HE NEEDED MONEY THAT COULD NEVER BE TRACED, TO PAY FOR KILLERS THAT COULD NEVER BE ACKNOWLEDGED.
THE SMACK COMES IN PACKED IN BODYBAGS ALONG WITH DEAD GIs.
BETHELL HAS CONTACTS IN POLICE DEPARTMENTS ON THE WEST COAST, FROM SAN DIEGO TO SEATTLE. THEY SELL THE STUFF TO STREET GANGS.
HIS CUT COULD PAY FOR HALF THE NORMANDY INVASION.

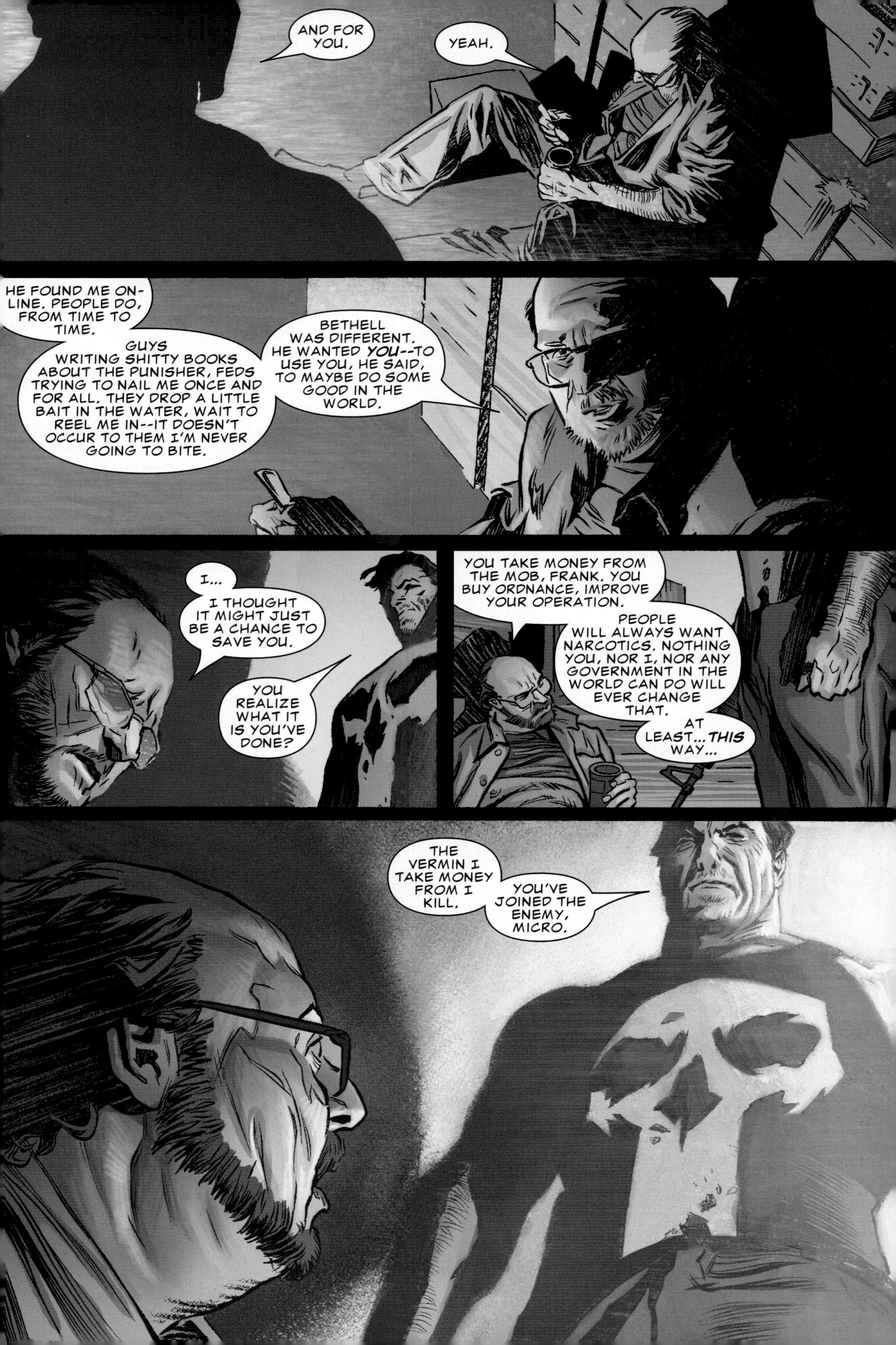
AND FOR YOU.
YEAH.
HE FOUND ME ON-LINE. PEOPLE DO, FROM TIME TO TIME.
GUYS WRITING SHITTY BOOKS ABOUT THE PUNISHER, FEDS TRYING TO NAIL ME ONCE AND FOR ALL. THEY DROP A LITTLE BAIT IN THE WATER, WAIT TO REEL ME IN--IT DOESN'T OCCUR TO THEM I'M NEVER GOING TO BITE.
BETHELL WAS DIFFERENT. HE WANTED *YOU*--TO USE YOU, HE SAID, TO MAYBE DO SOME GOOD IN THE WORLD.
I...
I THOUGHT IT MIGHT JUST BE A CHANCE TO SAVE YOU.
YOU REALIZE WHAT IT IS YOU'VE DONE?
YOU TAKE MONEY FROM THE MOB, FRANK. YOU BUY ORDNANCE, IMPROVE YOUR OPERATION.
PEOPLE WILL ALWAYS WANT NARCOTICS. NOTHING YOU, NOR I, NOR ANY GOVERNMENT IN THE WORLD CAN DO WILL EVER CHANGE THAT.
AT LEAST... **THIS** WAY...
THE VERMIN I TAKE MONEY FROM I KILL.
YOU'VE JOINED THE ENEMY, MICRO.

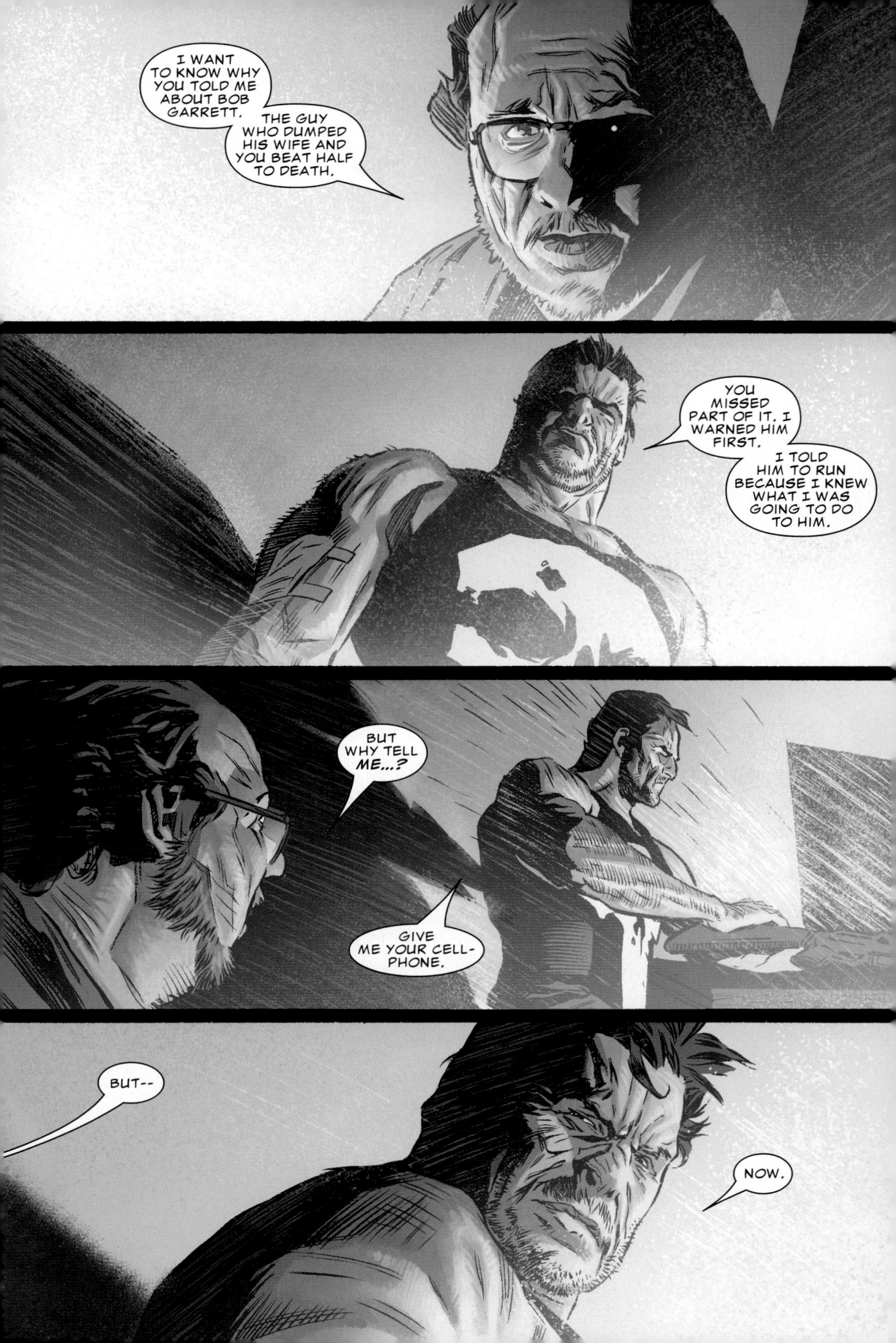
I WANT TO KNOW WHY YOU TOLD ME ABOUT BOB GARRETT.
THE GUY WHO DUMPED HIS WIFE AND YOU BEAT HALF TO DEATH.
YOU MISSED PART OF IT. I WARNED HIM FIRST.
I TOLD HIM TO RUN BECAUSE I KNEW WHAT I WAS GOING TO DO TO HIM.
BUT WHY TELL *ME*...?
GIVE ME YOUR CELL-PHONE.
BUT--
NOW.

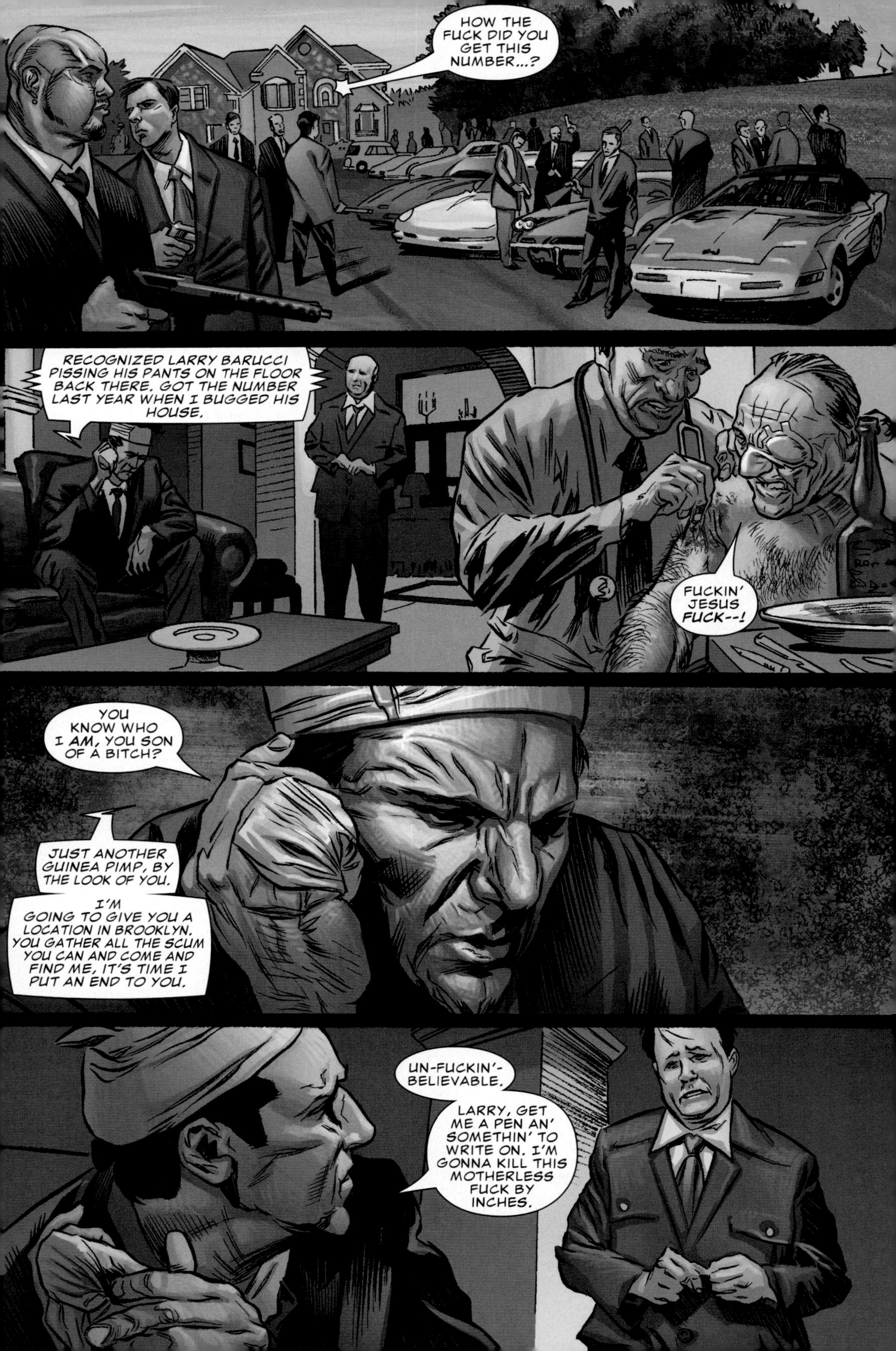

HOW THE FUCK DID YOU GET THIS NUMBER...?
RECOGNIZED LARRY BARUCCI PISSING HIS PANTS ON THE FLOOR BACK THERE. GOT THE NUMBER LAST YEAR WHEN I BUGGED HIS HOUSE.
FUCKIN' JESUS FUCK--!
YOU KNOW WHO I AM, YOU SON OF A BITCH?
JUST ANOTHER GUINEA PIMP, BY THE LOOK OF YOU.
I'M GOING TO GIVE YOU A LOCATION IN BROOKLYN. YOU GATHER ALL THE SCUM YOU CAN AND COME AND FIND ME, IT'S TIME I PUT AN END TO YOU.
UN-FUCKIN'-BELIEVABLE.
LARRY, GET ME A PEN AN' SOMETHIN' TO WRITE ON. I'M GONNA KILL THIS MOTHERLESS FUCK BY INCHES.

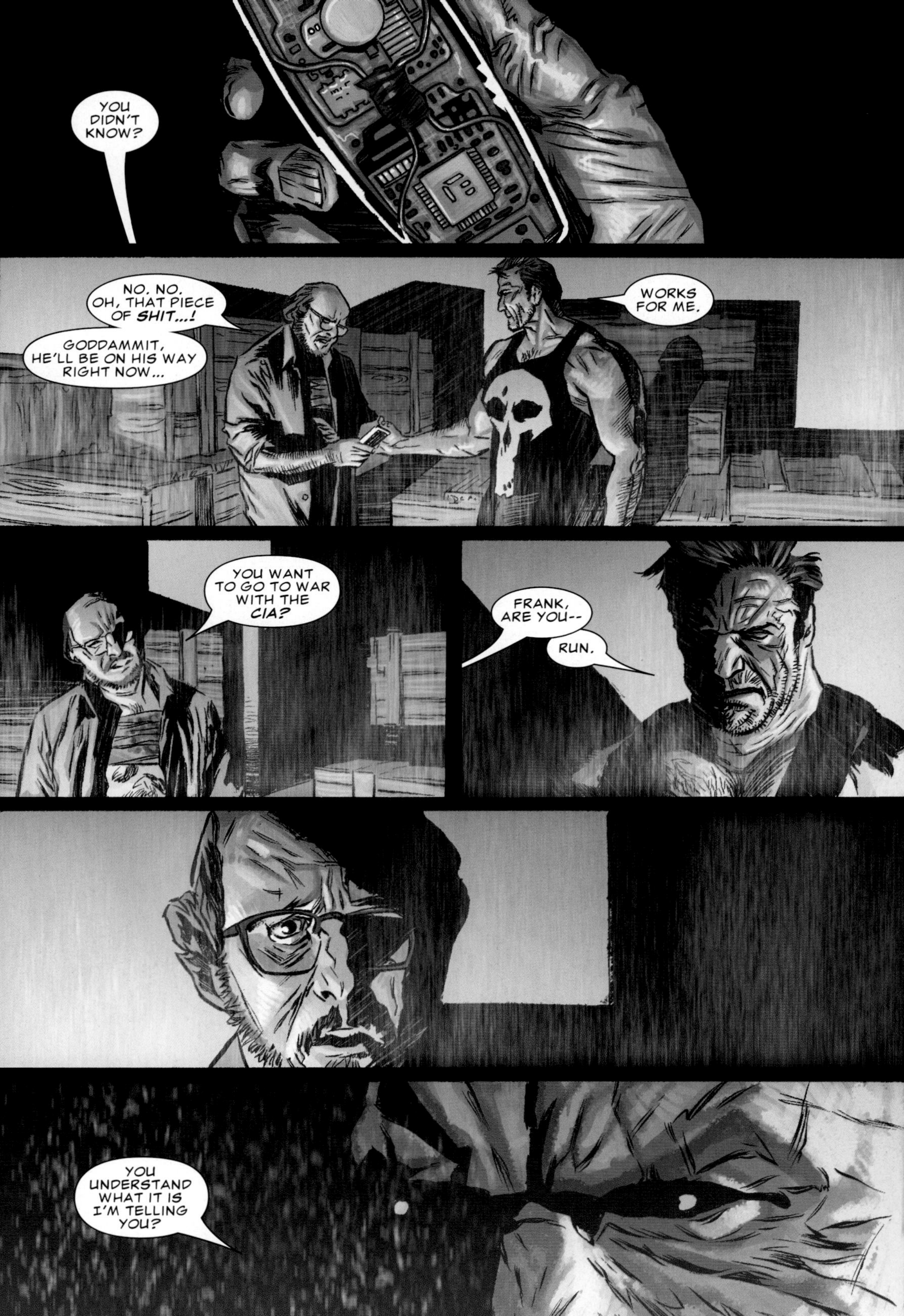
YOU DIDN'T KNOW?
NO. NO. OH, THAT PIECE OF SHIT...!
GODDAMMIT, HE'LL BE ON HIS WAY RIGHT NOW...
WORKS FOR ME.
YOU WANT TO GO TO WAR WITH THE CIA?
FRANK, ARE YOU--
RUN.
YOU UNDERSTAND WHAT IT IS I'M TELLING YOU?

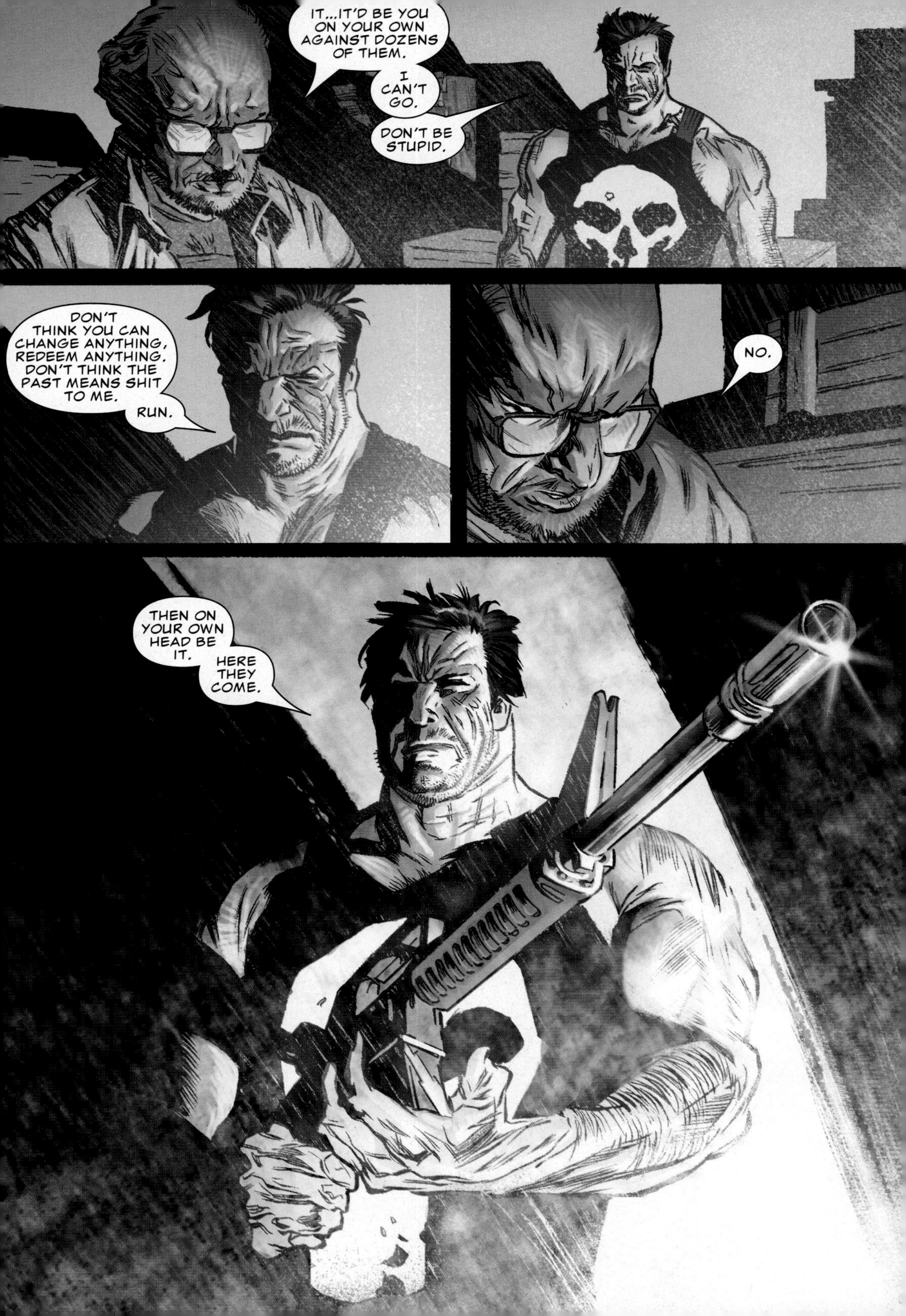
IT...IT'D BE YOU ON YOUR OWN AGAINST DOZENS OF THEM.
I CAN'T GO.
DON'T BE STUPID.
DON'T THINK YOU CAN CHANGE ANYTHING, REDEEM ANYTHING. DON'T THINK THE PAST MEANS SHIT TO ME.
RUN.
NO.
THEN ON YOUR OWN HEAD BE IT.
HERE THEY COME.

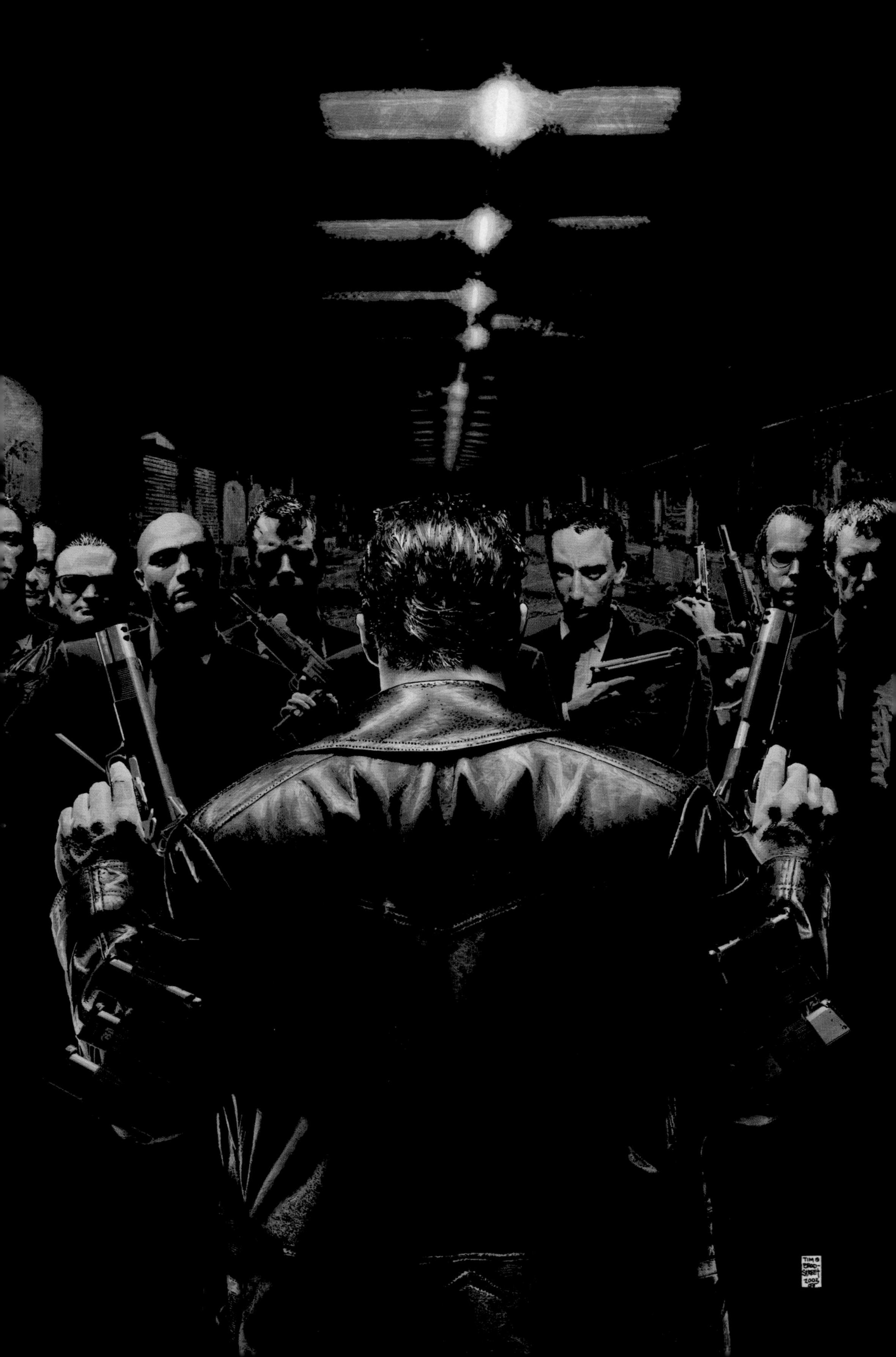
TIM
BRAD-
STREET

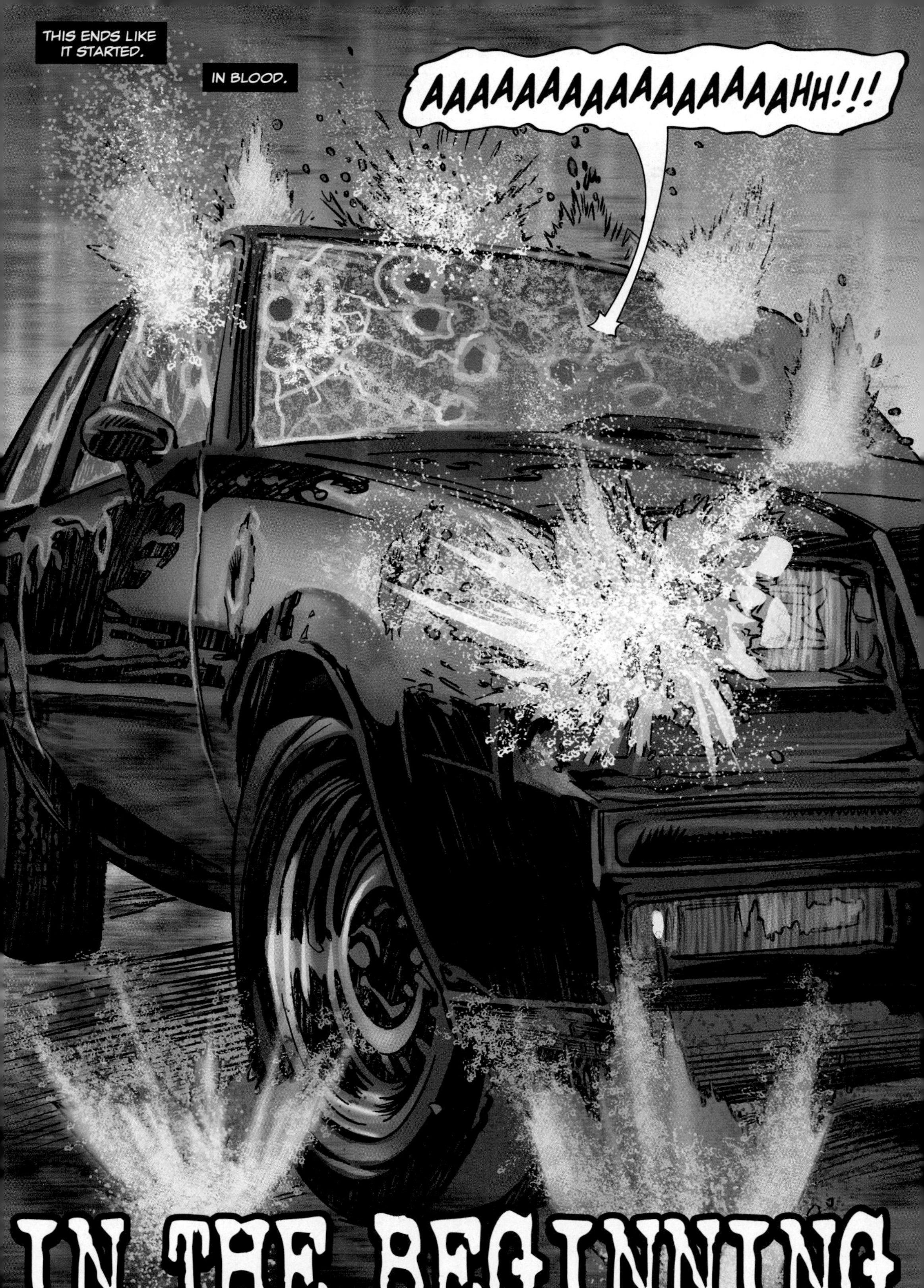
THIS ENDS LIKE IT STARTED.
IN BLOOD.
AAAAAAAAAAAAAAAAAHH!!!

IN THE BEGINNING
CONCLUSION

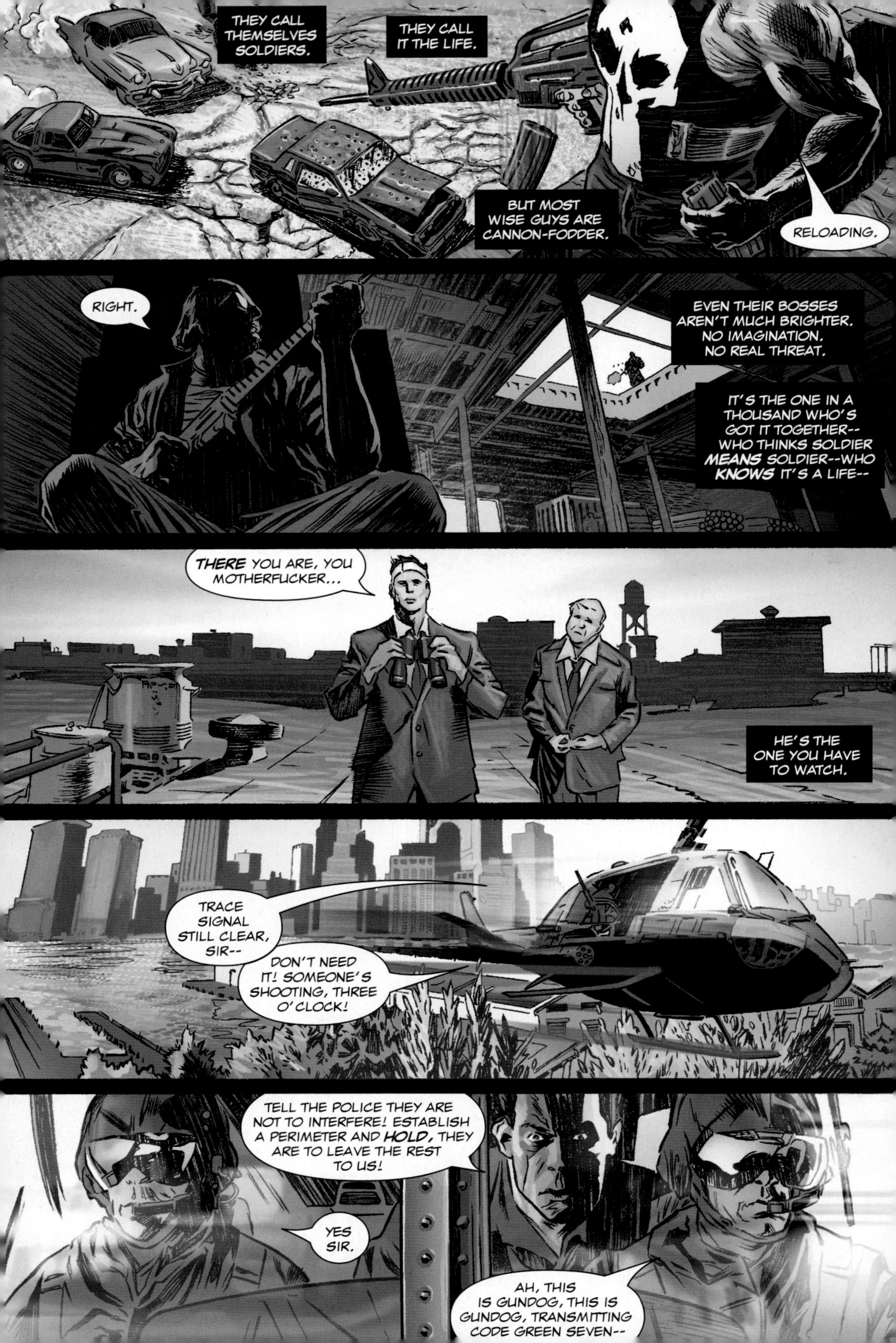
THEY CALL THEMSELVES SOLDIERS.
THEY CALL IT THE LIFE.
BUT MOST WISE GUYS ARE CANNON-FODDER.
RELOADING.
RIGHT.
EVEN THEIR BOSSES AREN'T MUCH BRIGHTER. NO IMAGINATION. NO REAL THREAT.
IT'S THE ONE IN A THOUSAND WHO'S GOT IT TOGETHER-- WHO THINKS SOLDIER MEANS SOLDIER--WHO KNOWS IT'S A LIFE--
THERE YOU ARE, YOU MOTHERFUCKER...
HE'S THE ONE YOU HAVE TO WATCH.
TRACE SIGNAL STILL CLEAR, SIR--
DON'T NEED IT! SOMEONE'S SHOOTING, THREE O'CLOCK!
TELL THE POLICE THEY ARE NOT TO INTERFERE! ESTABLISH A PERIMETER AND HOLD, THEY ARE TO LEAVE THE REST TO US!
YES SIR.
AH, THIS IS GUNDOG, THIS IS GUNDOG, TRANSMITTING CODE GREEN SEVEN--

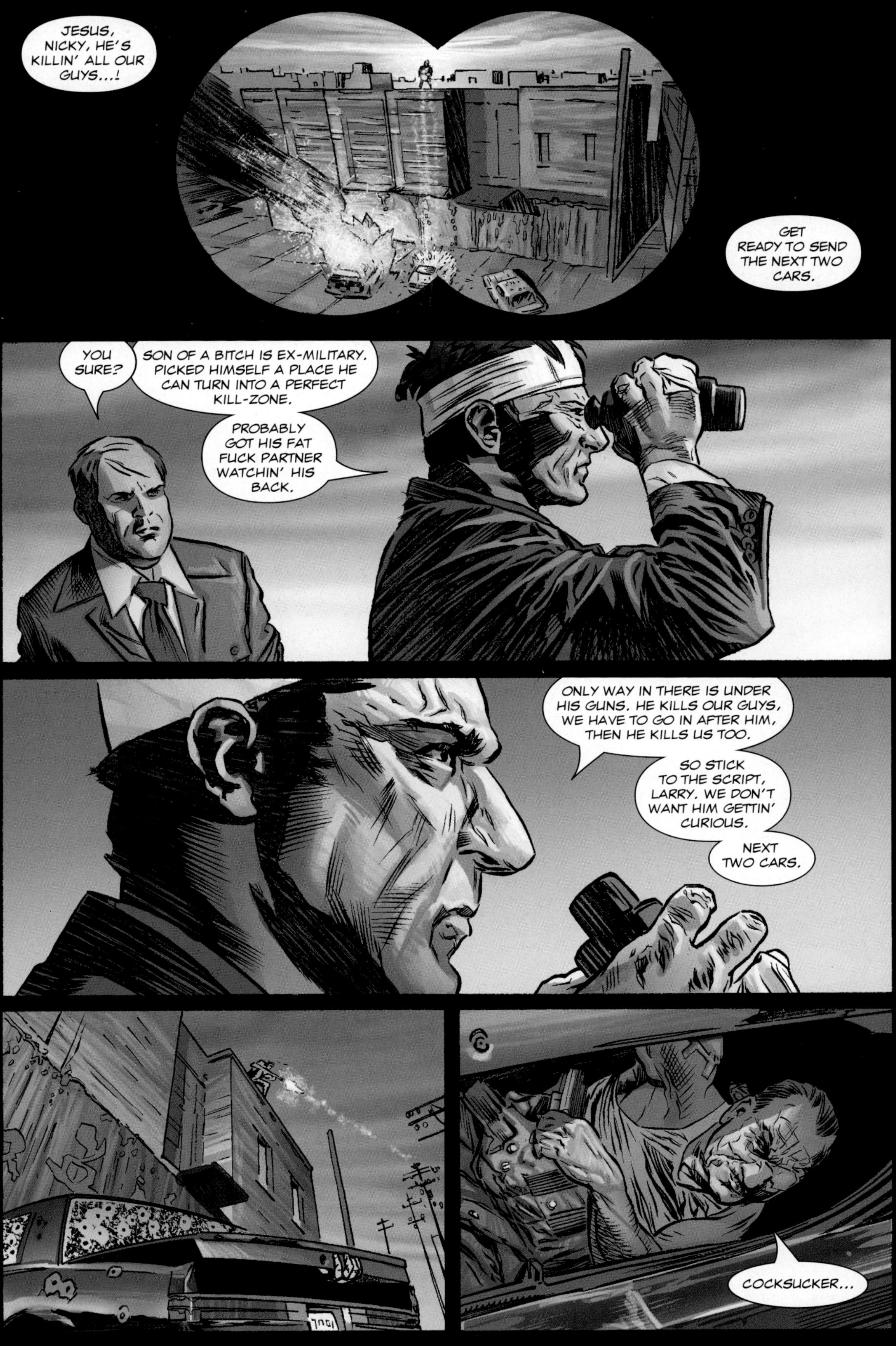
JESUS, NICKY, HE'S KILLIN' ALL OUR GUYS...!
GET READY TO SEND THE NEXT TWO CARS.
YOU SURE?
SON OF A BITCH IS EX-MILITARY. PICKED HIMSELF A PLACE HE CAN TURN INTO A PERFECT KILL-ZONE.
PROBABLY GOT HIS FAT FUCK PARTNER WATCHIN' HIS BACK.
ONLY WAY IN THERE IS UNDER HIS GUNS. HE KILLS OUR GUYS, WE HAVE TO GO IN AFTER HIM, THEN HE KILLS US TOO.
SO STICK TO THE SCRIPT, LARRY. WE DON'T WANT HIM GETTIN' CURIOUS.
NEXT TWO CARS.
COCKSUCKER...

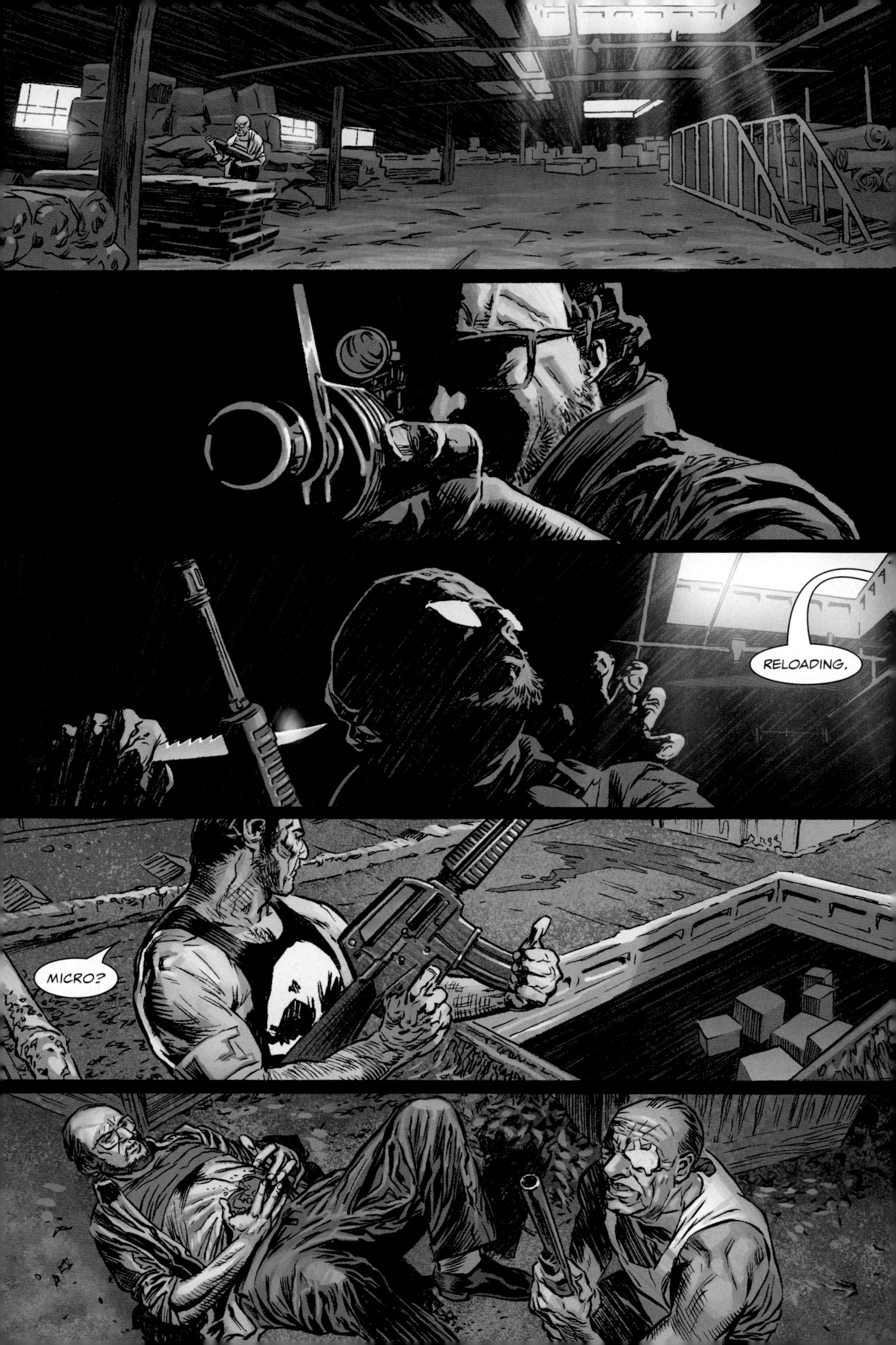
RELOADING.
MICRO?

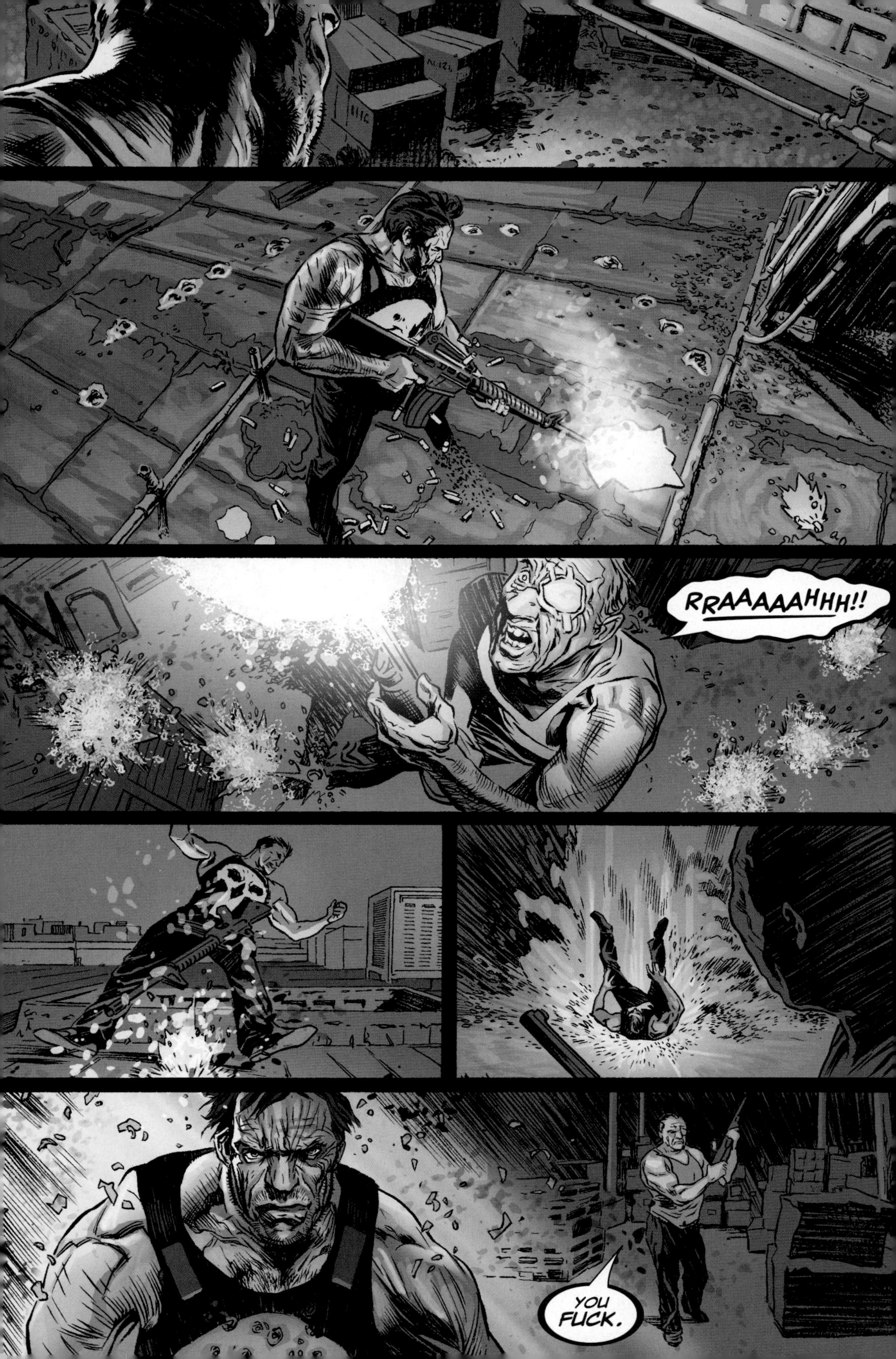
RRAAAAAHHH!!
YOU FUCK.

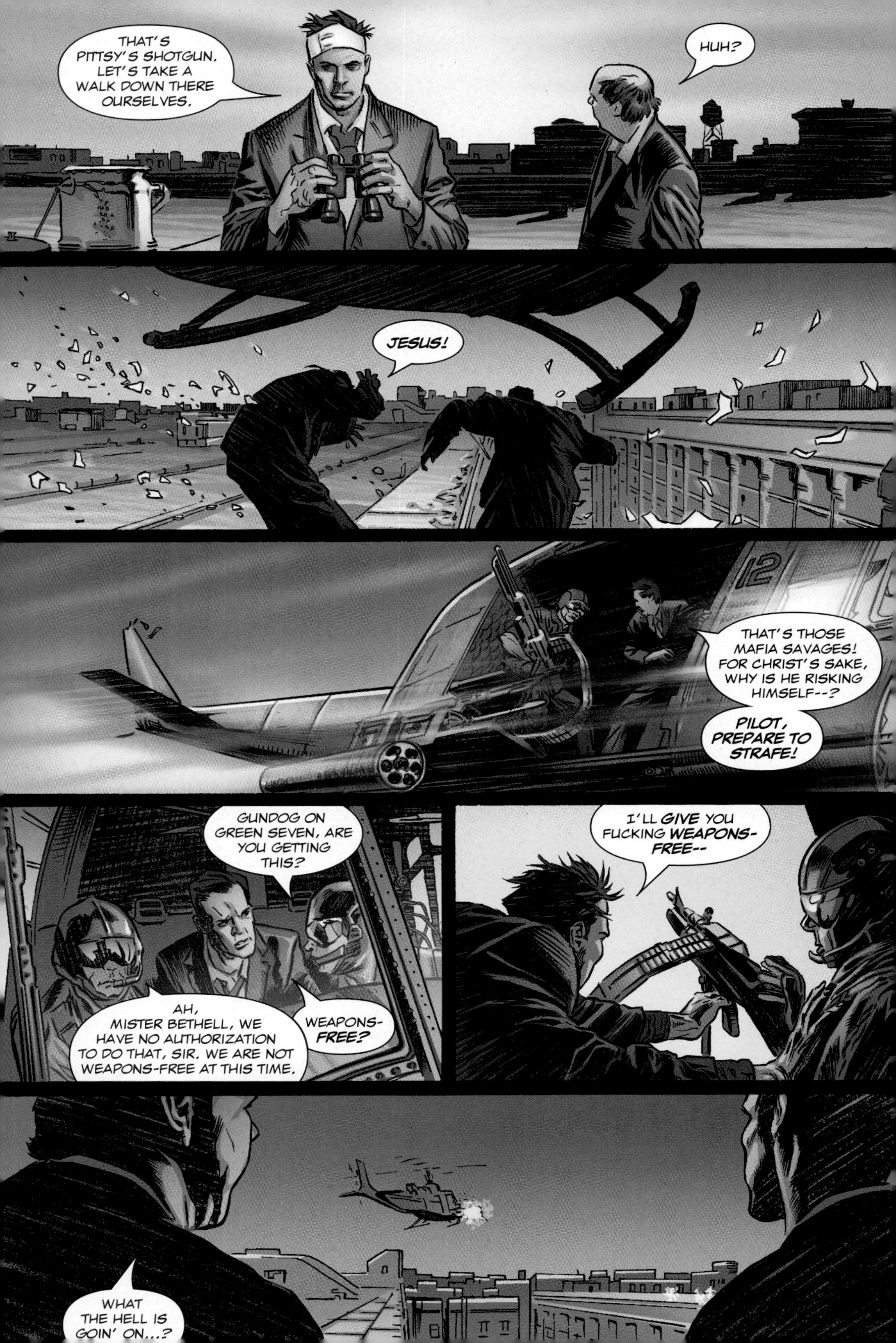
THAT'S PITTSY'S SHOTGUN. LET'S TAKE A WALK DOWN THERE OURSELVES.
HUH?
JESUS!
12
THAT'S THOSE MAFIA SAVAGES! FOR CHRIST'S SAKE, WHY IS HE RISKING HIMSELF--?
PILOT, PREPARE TO STRAFE!
GUNDOG ON GREEN SEVEN, ARE YOU GETTING THIS?
AH, MISTER BETHELL, WE HAVE NO AUTHORIZATION TO DO THAT, SIR. WE ARE NOT WEAPONS-FREE AT THIS TIME.
WEAPONS-FREE?
I'LL GIVE YOU FUCKING WEAPONS-FREE--
WHAT THE HELL IS GOIN' ON...?

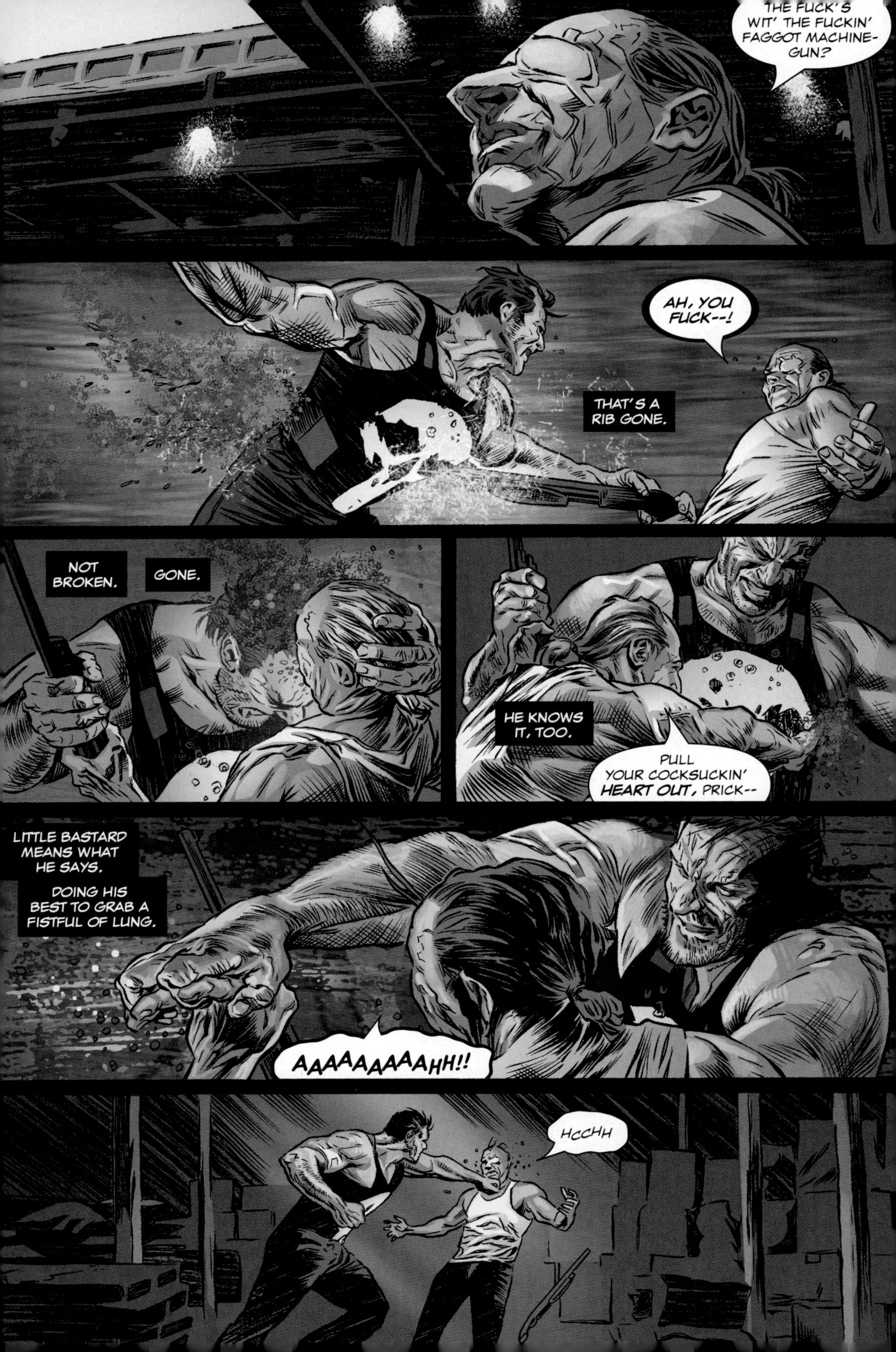
THE FUCK'S WIT' THE FUCKIN' FAGGOT MACHINE-GUN?
AH, YOU FUCK--!
THAT'S A RIB GONE.
NOT BROKEN.
GONE.
HE KNOWS IT, TOO.
PULL YOUR COCKSUCKIN' HEART OUT, PRICK--
LITTLE BASTARD MEANS WHAT HE SAYS.
DOING HIS BEST TO GRAB A FISTFUL OF LUNG.
AAAAAAAAAHH!!
HCCHH

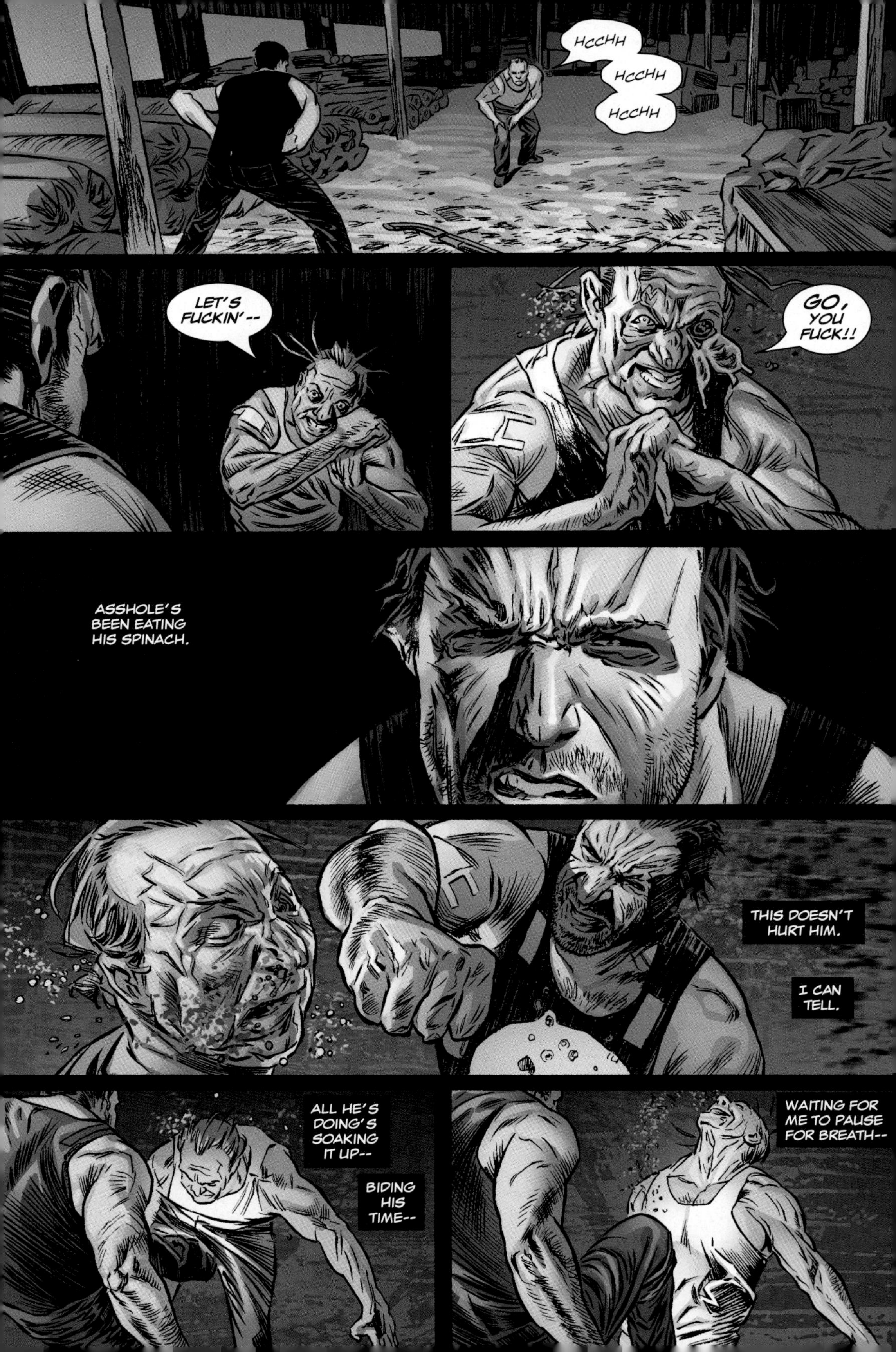
HCCHH
HCCHH
HCCHH
LET'S FUCKIN'--
GO, YOU FUCK!!
ASSHOLE'S BEEN EATING HIS SPINACH.
THIS DOESN'T HURT HIM.
I CAN TELL.
ALL HE'S DOING'S SOAKING IT UP--
BIDING HIS TIME--
WAITING FOR ME TO PAUSE FOR BREATH--

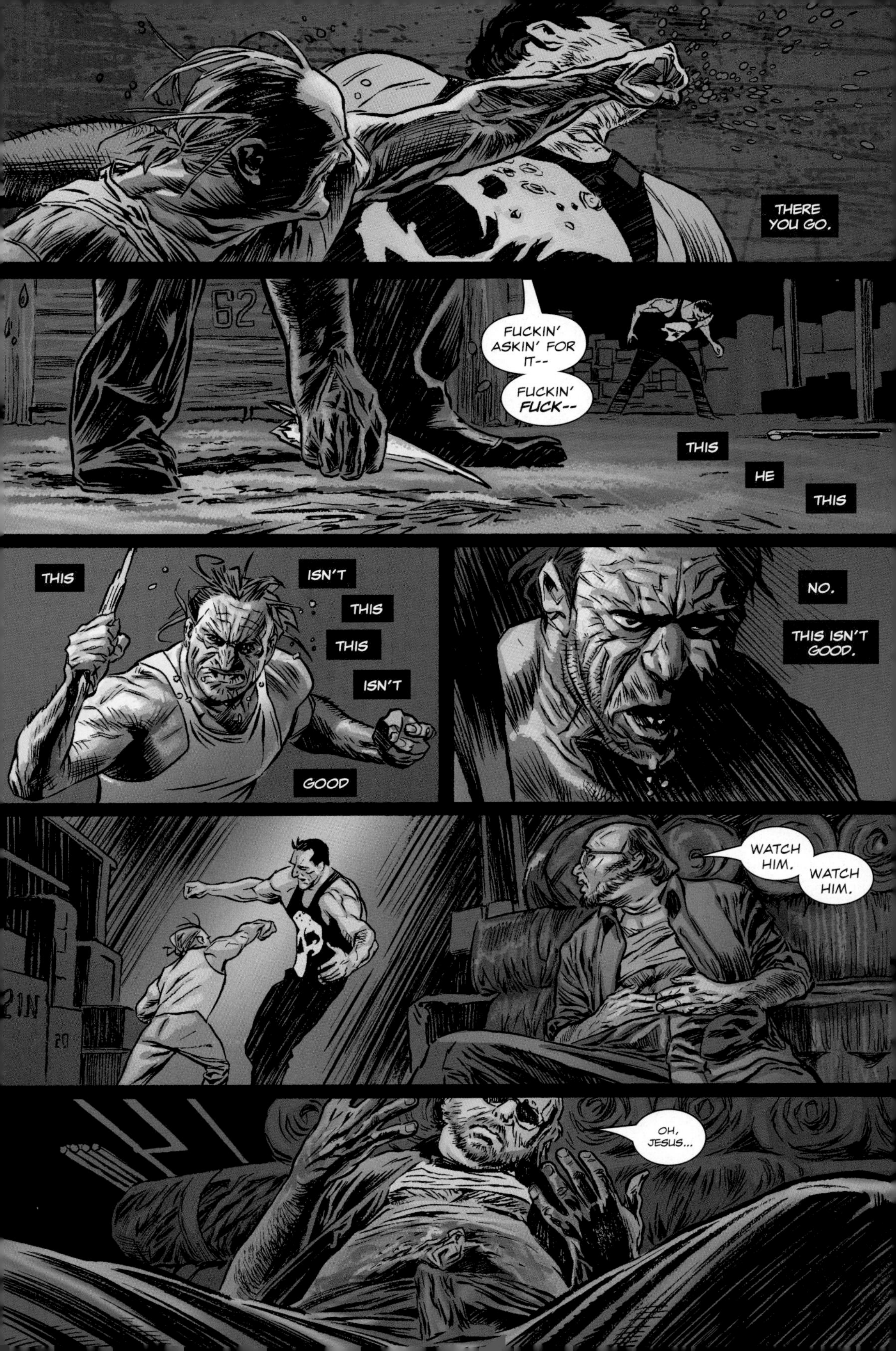
THERE YOU GO.
FUCKIN' ASKIN' FOR IT--
FUCKIN' FUCK--
THIS
HE
THIS
THIS
ISN'T
THIS
THIS
ISN'T
GOOD
NO.
THIS ISN'T GOOD.
WATCH HIM.
WATCH HIM.
OH, JESUS...

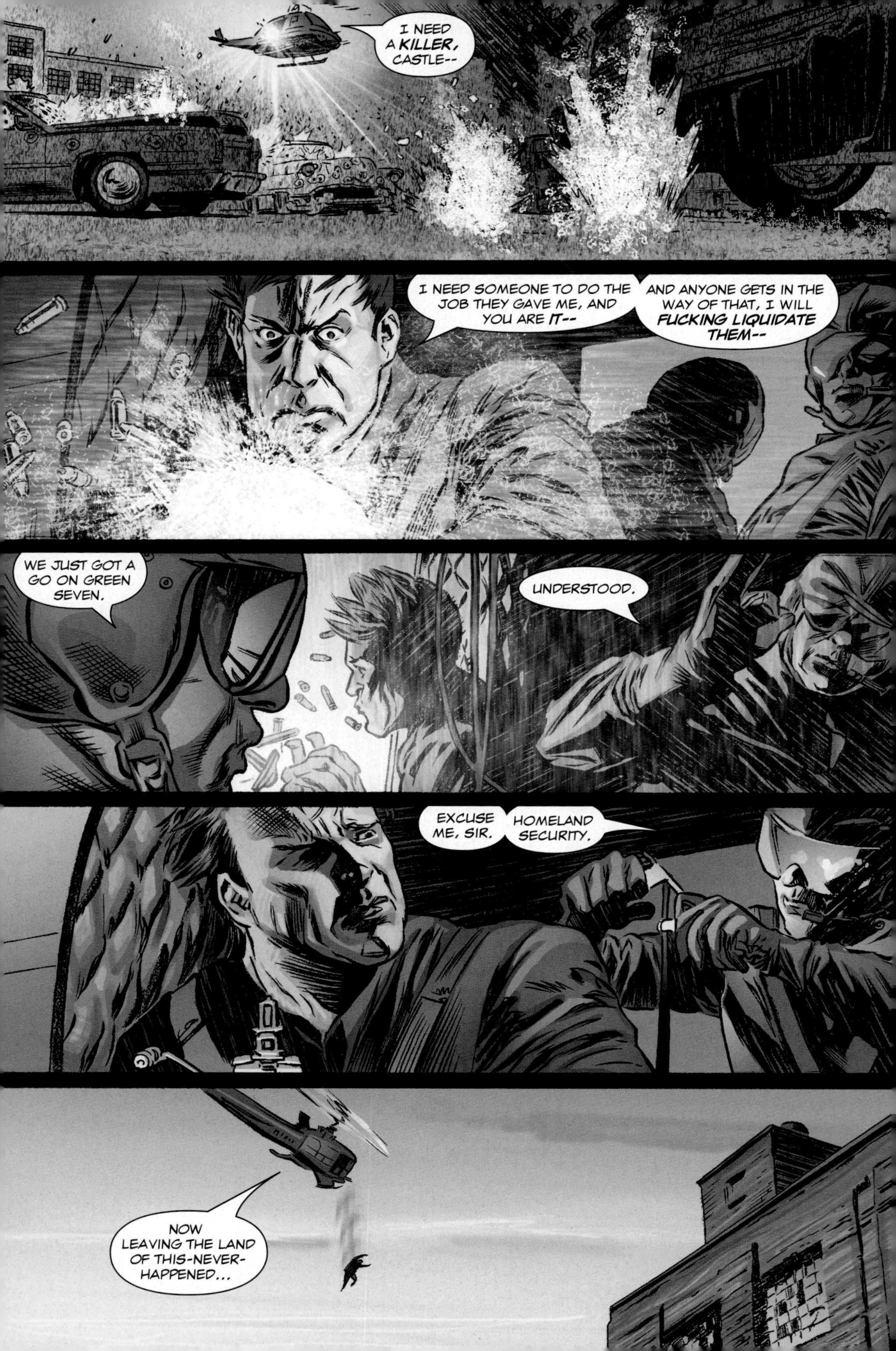
I NEED A **KILLER,** CASTLE--
I NEED SOMEONE TO DO THE JOB THEY GAVE ME, AND YOU ARE *IT--*
AND ANYONE GETS IN THE WAY OF THAT, I WILL ***FUCKING LIQUIDATE THEM--***
WE JUST GOT A GO ON GREEN SEVEN.
UNDERSTOOD.
EXCUSE ME, SIR.
HOMELAND SECURITY.
NOW LEAVING THE LAND OF THIS-NEVER-HAPPENED...

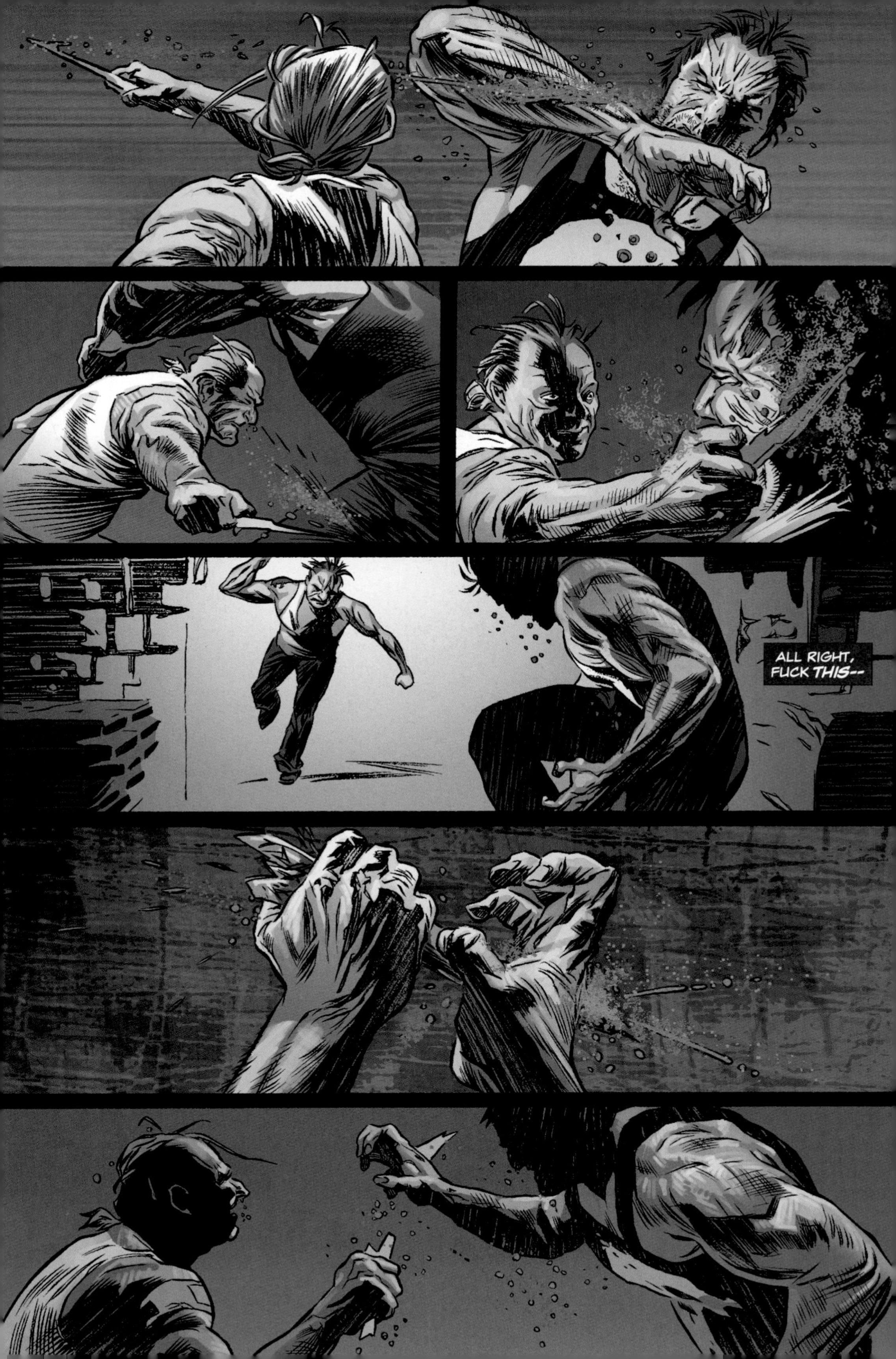
ALL RIGHT, FUCK THIS--

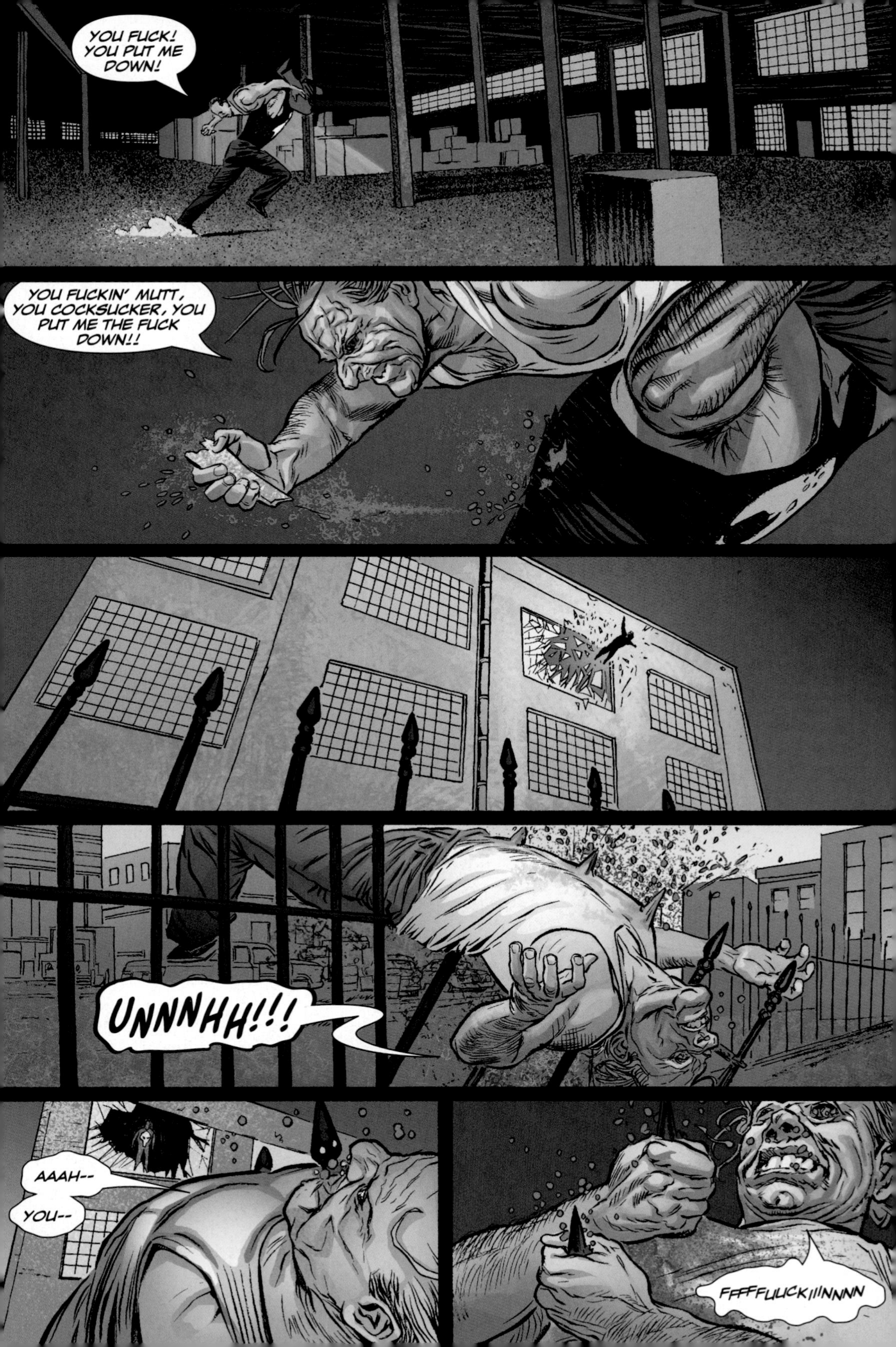
YOU FUCK! YOU PUT ME DOWN!
YOU FUCKIN' MUTT, YOU COCKSUCKER, YOU PUT ME THE FUCK DOWN!!
UNNNHH!!!
AAAH--
YOU--
FFFFFUUCKIIINNNN

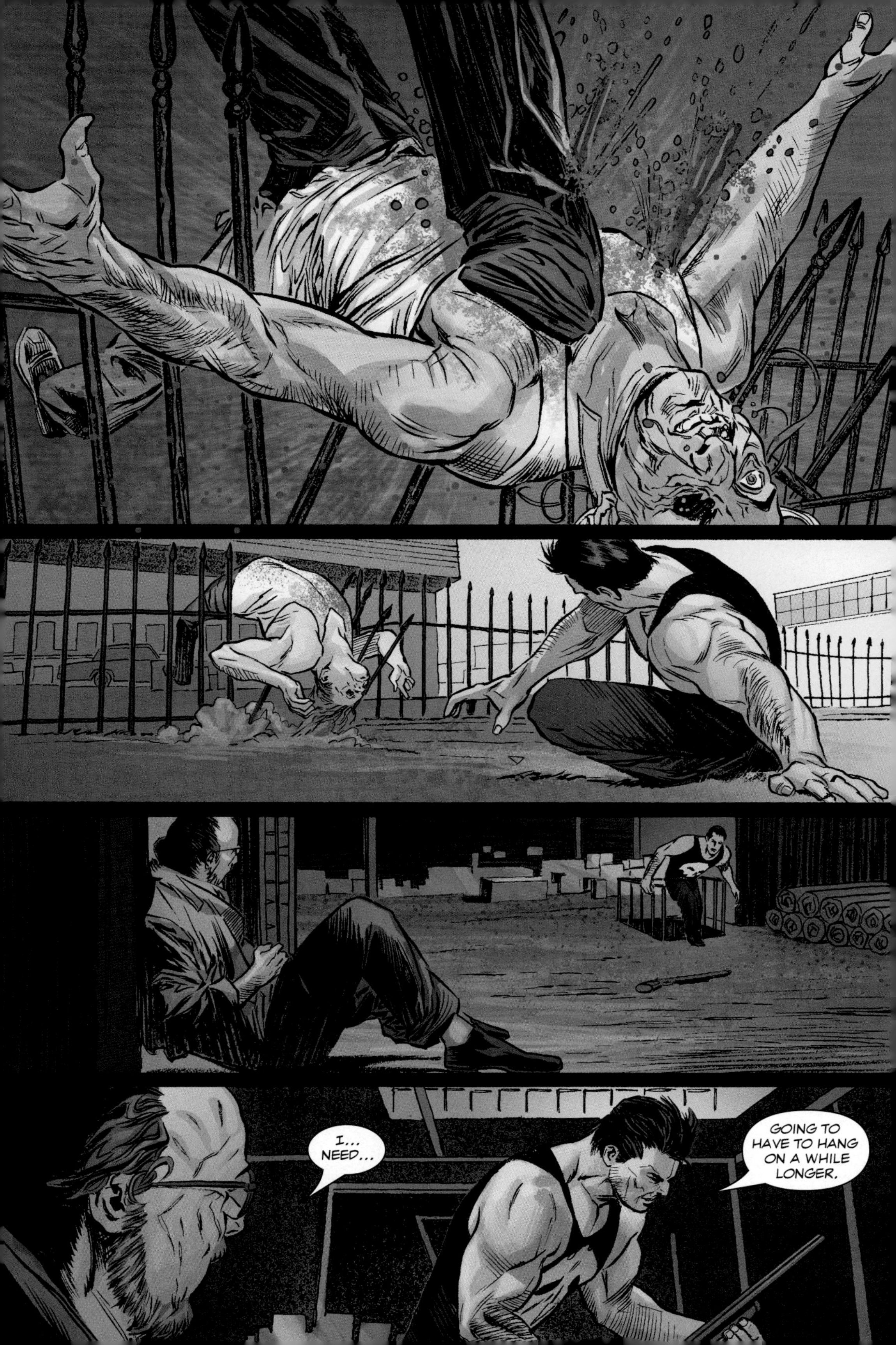
I... NEED...
GOING TO HAVE TO HANG ON A WHILE LONGER.

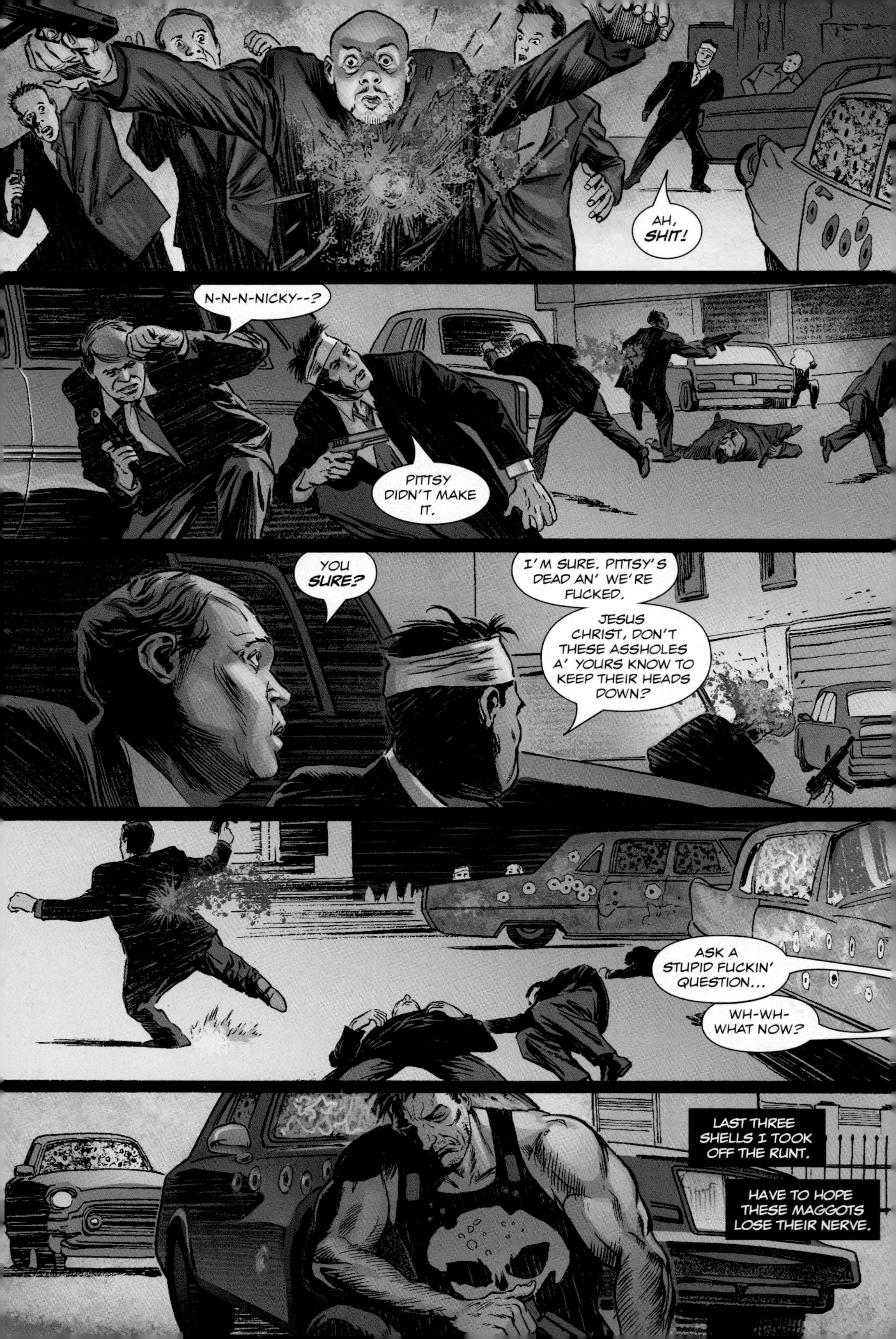
AH, SHIT!
N-N-N-NICKY--?
PITTSY DIDN'T MAKE IT.
YOU SURE?
I'M SURE. PITTSY'S DEAD AN' WE'RE FUCKED.
JESUS CHRIST, DON'T THESE ASSHOLES A' YOURS KNOW TO KEEP THEIR HEADS DOWN?
ASK A STUPID FUCKIN' QUESTION...
WH-WH-WHAT NOW?
LAST THREE SHELLS I TOOK OFF THE RUNT.
HAVE TO HOPE THESE MAGGOTS LOSE THEIR NERVE.

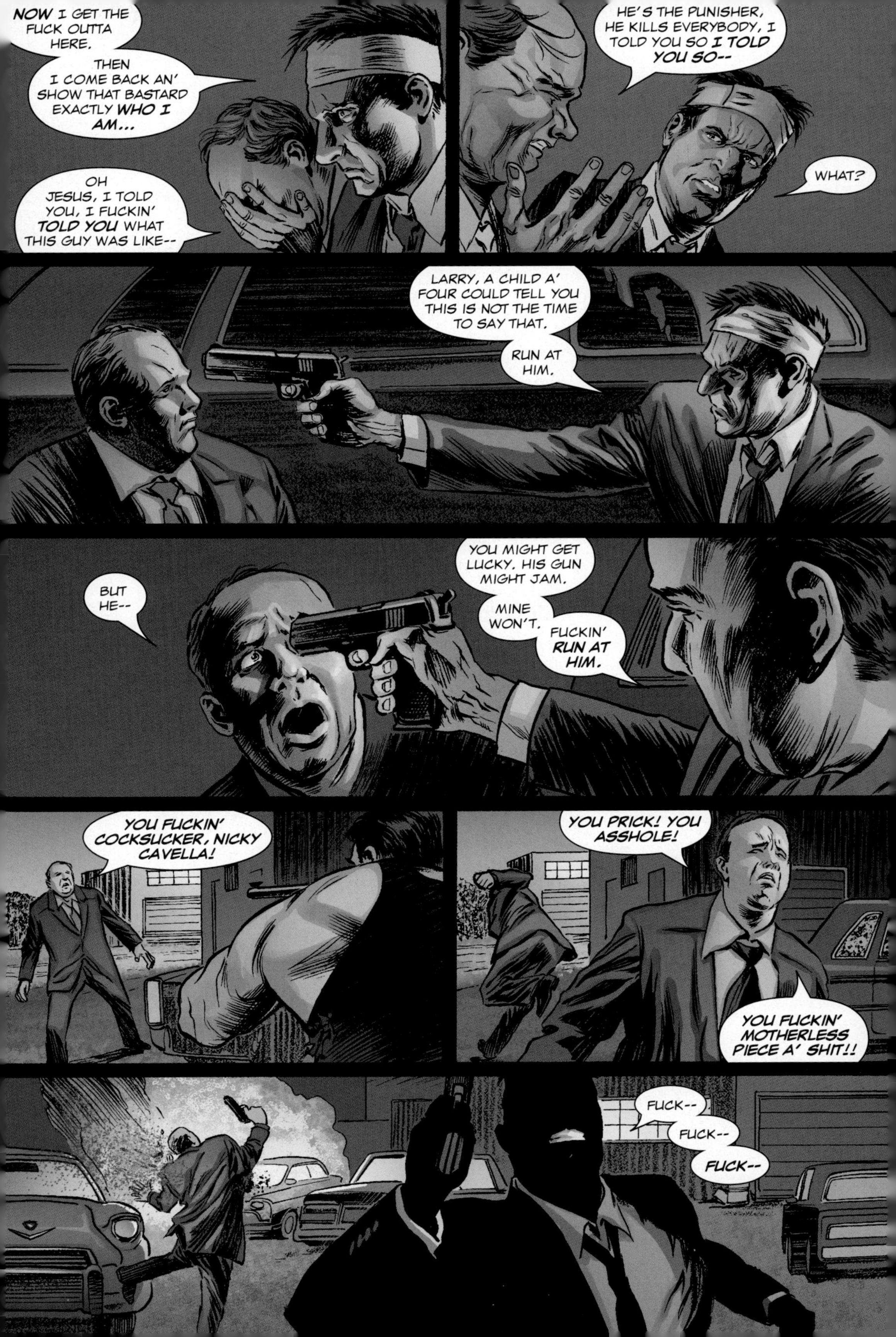
NOW I GET THE FUCK OUTTA HERE.
THEN I COME BACK AN' SHOW THAT BASTARD EXACTLY WHO I AM...
OH JESUS, I TOLD YOU, I FUCKIN' TOLD YOU WHAT THIS GUY WAS LIKE--
HE'S THE PUNISHER, HE KILLS EVERYBODY, I TOLD YOU SO I TOLD YOU SO--
WHAT?
LARRY, A CHILD A' FOUR COULD TELL YOU THIS IS NOT THE TIME TO SAY THAT.
RUN AT HIM.
BUT HE--
YOU MIGHT GET LUCKY. HIS GUN MIGHT JAM.
MINE WON'T.
FUCKIN' RUN AT HIM.
YOU FUCKIN' COCKSUCKER, NICKY CAVELLA!
YOU PRICK! YOU ASSHOLE!
YOU FUCKIN' MOTHERLESS PIECE A' SHIT!!
FUCK--
FUCK--
FUCK--

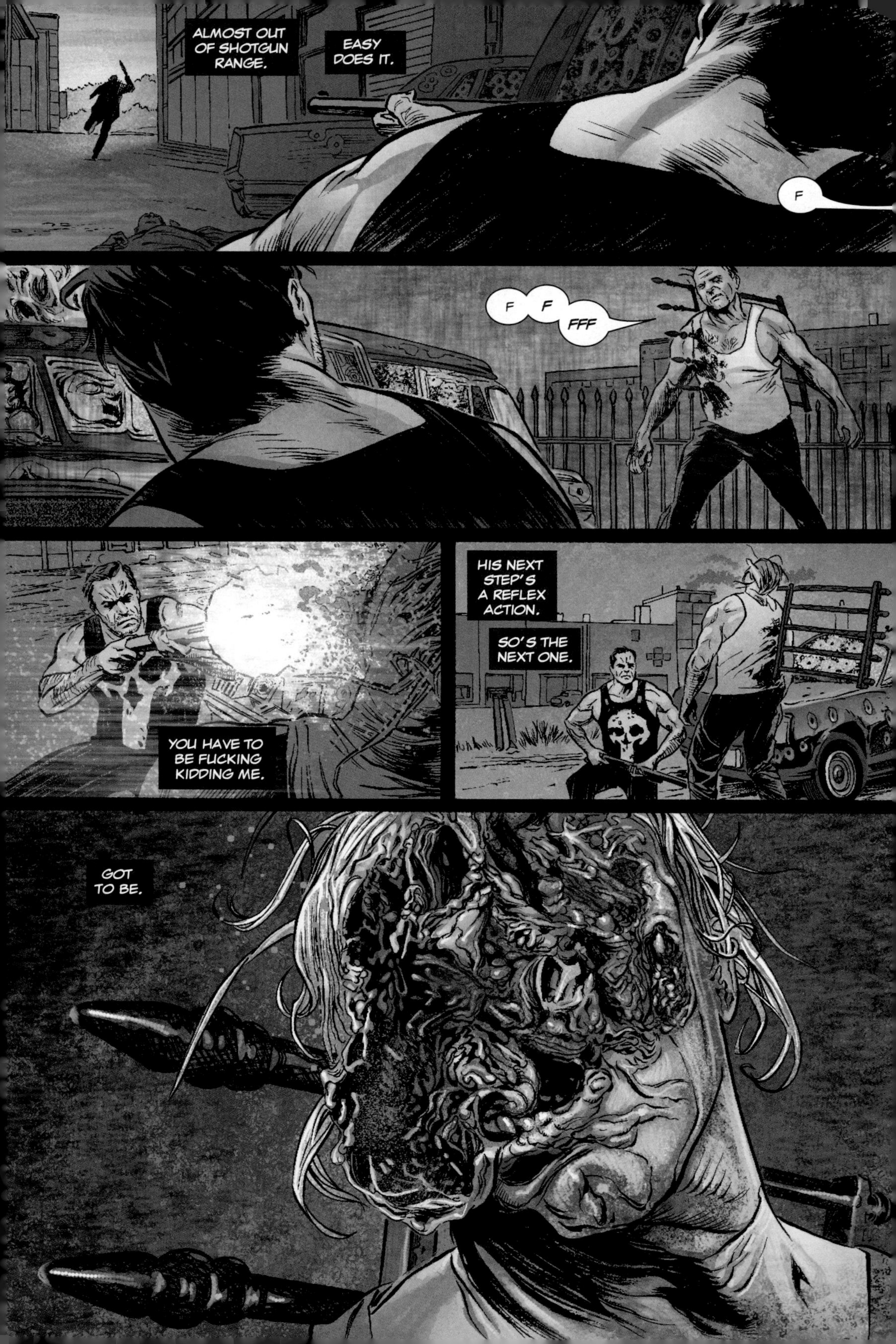
ALMOST OUT OF SHOTGUN RANGE.
EASY DOES IT.
F
F F FFF
YOU HAVE TO BE FUCKING KIDDING ME.
HIS NEXT STEP'S A REFLEX ACTION.
SO'S THE NEXT ONE.
GOT TO BE.

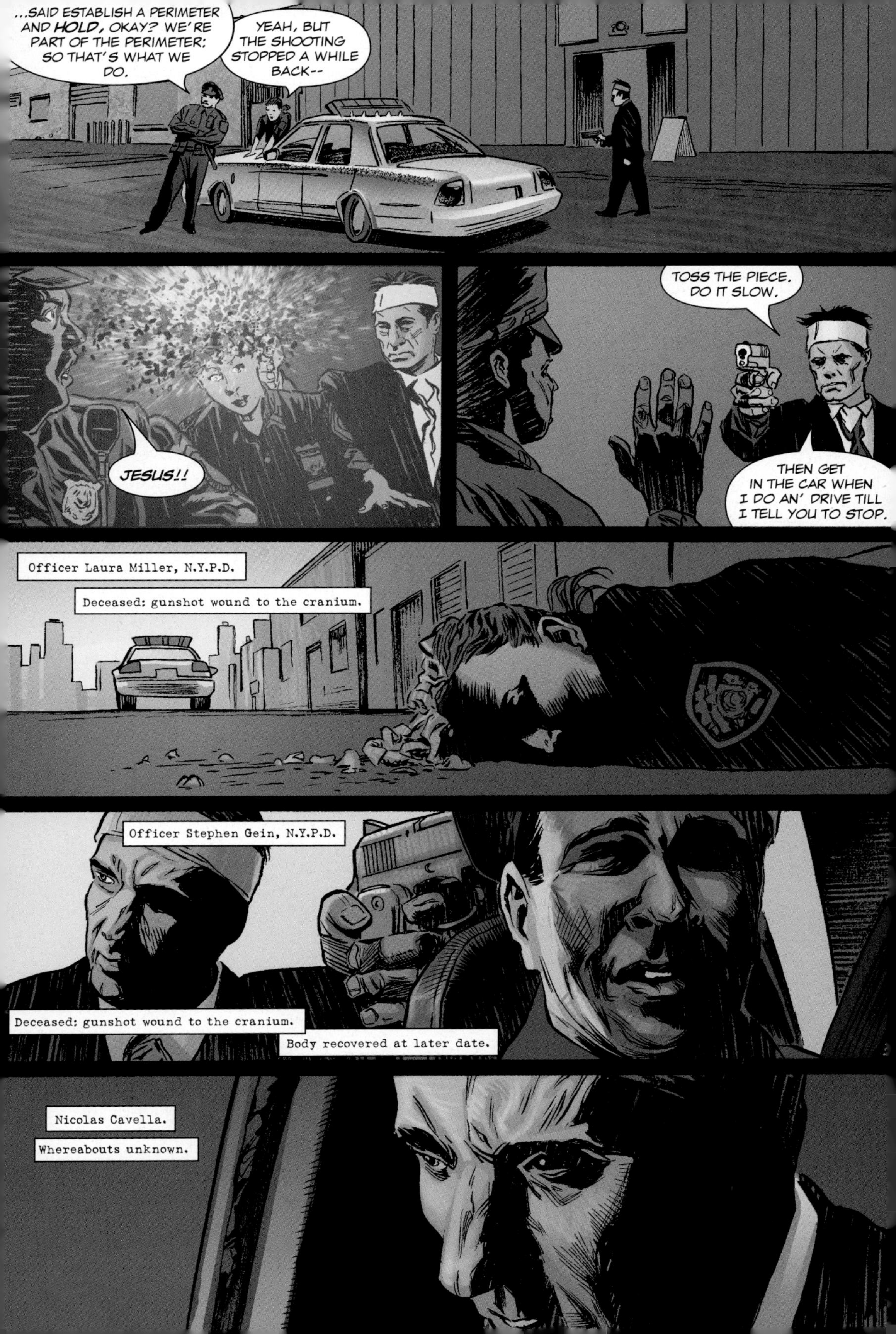
...SAID ESTABLISH A PERIMETER AND HOLD, OKAY? WE'RE PART OF THE PERIMETER: SO THAT'S WHAT WE DO.
YEAH, BUT THE SHOOTING STOPPED A WHILE BACK--
JESUS!!
TOSS THE PIECE. DO IT SLOW.
THEN GET IN THE CAR WHEN I DO AN' DRIVE TILL I TELL YOU TO STOP.
Officer Laura Miller, N.Y.P.D.
Deceased: gunshot wound to the cranium.
Officer Stephen Gein, N.Y.P.D.
Deceased: gunshot wound to the cranium.
Body recovered at later date.
Nicolas Cavella.
Whereabouts unknown.

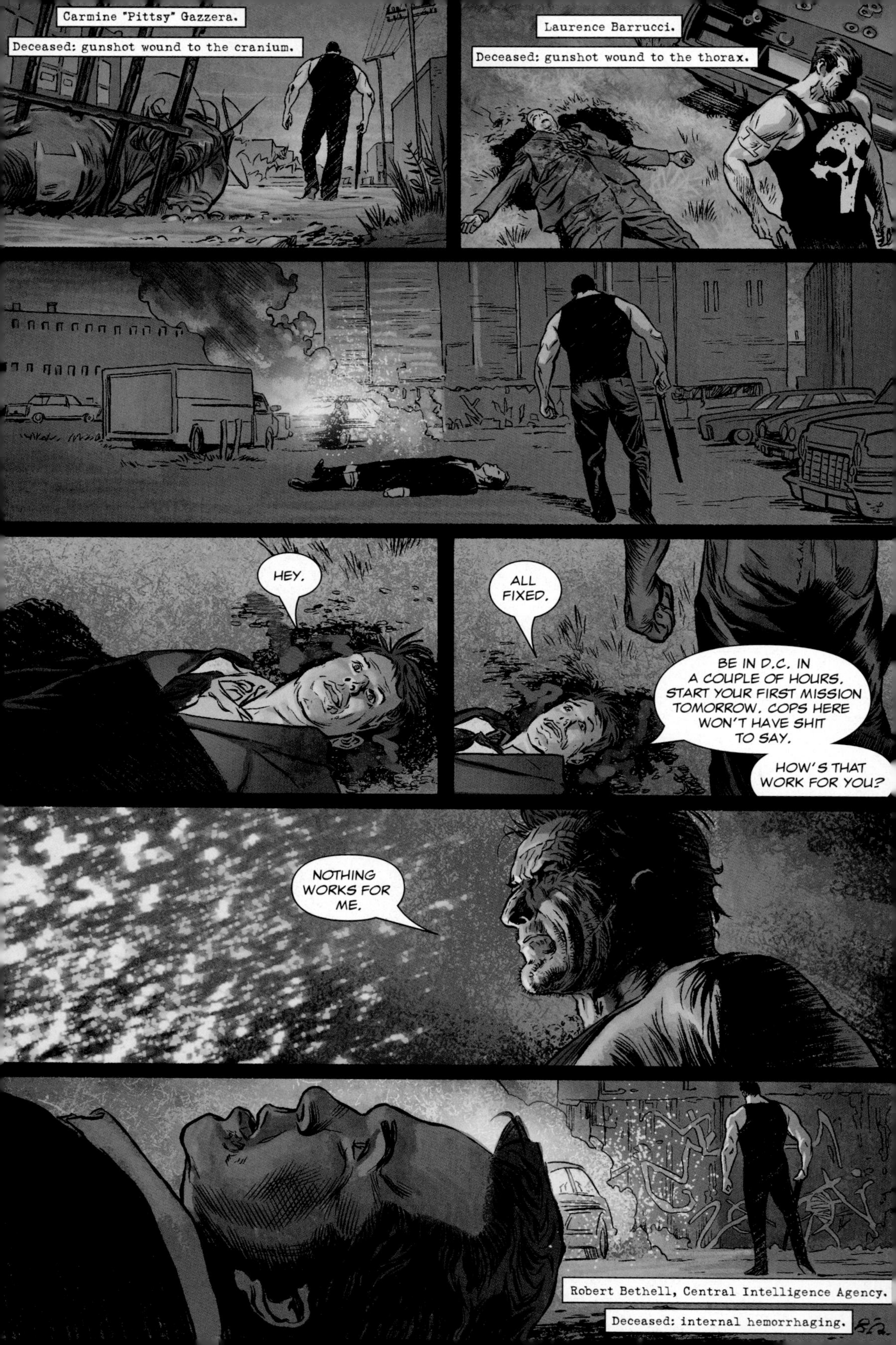
Carmine "Pittsy" Gazzera.
Deceased: gunshot wound to the cranium.
Laurence Barrucci.
Deceased: gunshot wound to the thorax.
HEY.
ALL FIXED.
BE IN D.C. IN A COUPLE OF HOURS. START YOUR FIRST MISSION TOMORROW. COPS HERE WON'T HAVE SHIT TO SAY.
HOW'S THAT WORK FOR YOU?
NOTHING WORKS FOR ME.
Robert Bethell, Central Intelligence Agency.
Deceased: internal hemorrhaging.

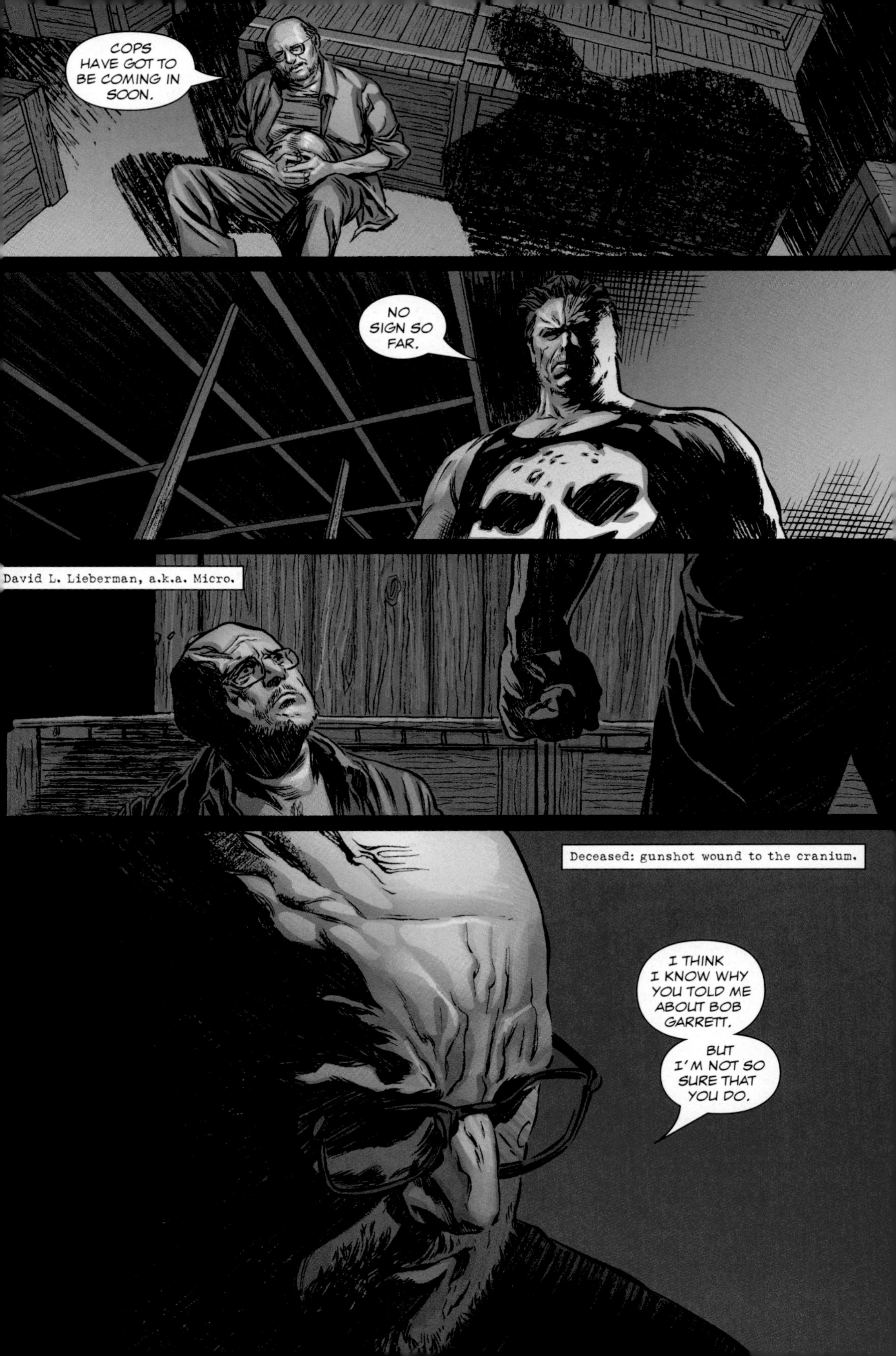
COPS HAVE GOT TO BE COMING IN SOON.
NO SIGN SO FAR.
David L. Lieberman, a.k.a. Micro.
Deceased: gunshot wound to the cranium.
I THINK I KNOW WHY YOU TOLD ME ABOUT BOB GARRETT.
BUT I'M NOT SO SURE THAT YOU DO.

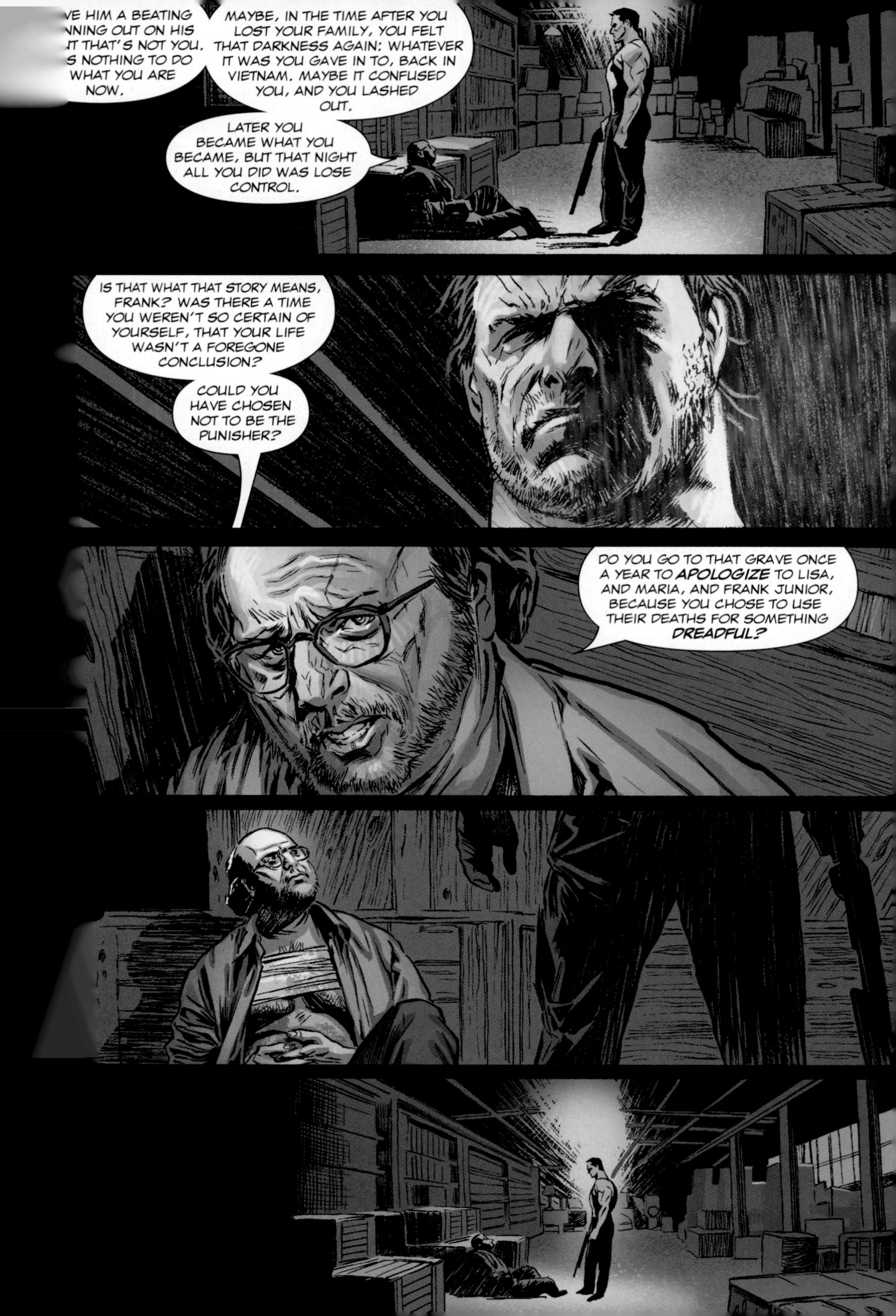
VE HIM A BEATING NNING OUT ON HIS T THAT'S NOT YOU. S NOTHING TO DO WHAT YOU ARE NOW.
MAYBE, IN THE TIME AFTER YOU LOST YOUR FAMILY, YOU FELT THAT DARKNESS AGAIN: WHATEVER IT WAS YOU GAVE IN TO, BACK IN VIETNAM. MAYBE IT CONFUSED YOU, AND YOU LASHED OUT.
LATER YOU BECAME WHAT YOU BECAME, BUT THAT NIGHT ALL YOU DID WAS LOSE CONTROL.
IS THAT WHAT THAT STORY MEANS, FRANK? WAS THERE A TIME YOU WEREN'T SO CERTAIN OF YOURSELF, THAT YOUR LIFE WASN'T A FOREGONE CONCLUSION?
COULD YOU HAVE CHOSEN NOT TO BE THE PUNISHER?
DO YOU GO TO THAT GRAVE ONCE A YEAR TO APOLOGIZE TO LISA, AND MARIA, AND FRANK JUNIOR, BECAUSE YOU CHOSE TO USE THEIR DEATHS FOR SOMETHING DREADFUL?

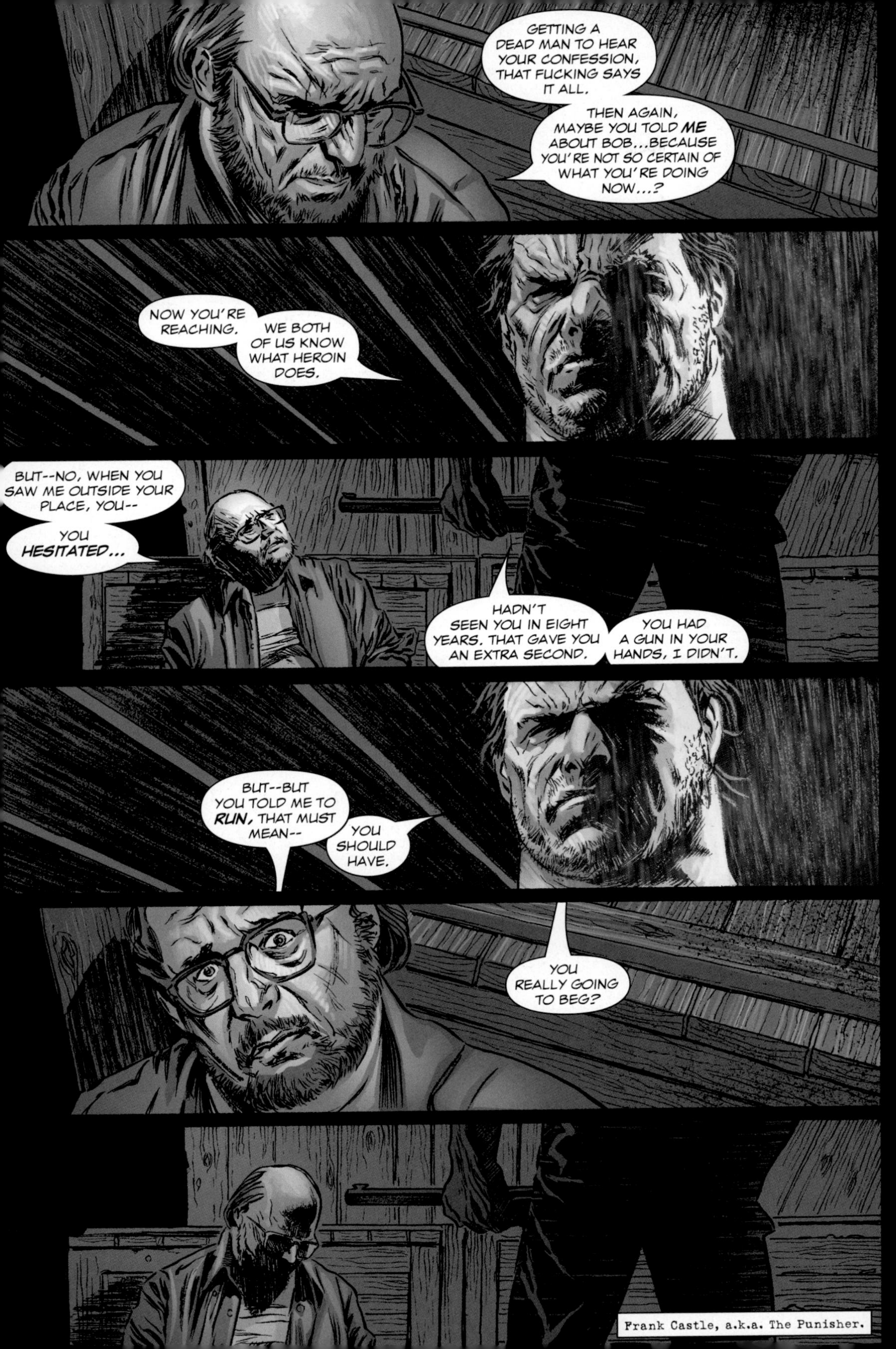
GETTING A DEAD MAN TO HEAR YOUR CONFESSION, THAT FUCKING SAYS IT ALL.
THEN AGAIN, MAYBE YOU TOLD ME ABOUT BOB...BECAUSE YOU'RE NOT SO CERTAIN OF WHAT YOU'RE DOING NOW...?
NOW YOU'RE REACHING.
WE BOTH OF US KNOW WHAT HEROIN DOES.
BUT--NO, WHEN YOU SAW ME OUTSIDE YOUR PLACE, YOU--
YOU HESITATED...
HADN'T SEEN YOU IN EIGHT YEARS. THAT GAVE YOU AN EXTRA SECOND.
YOU HAD A GUN IN YOUR HANDS, I DIDN'T.
BUT--BUT YOU TOLD ME TO RUN, THAT MUST MEAN--
YOU SHOULD HAVE.
YOU REALLY GOING TO BEG?
Frank Castle, a.k.a. The Punisher.

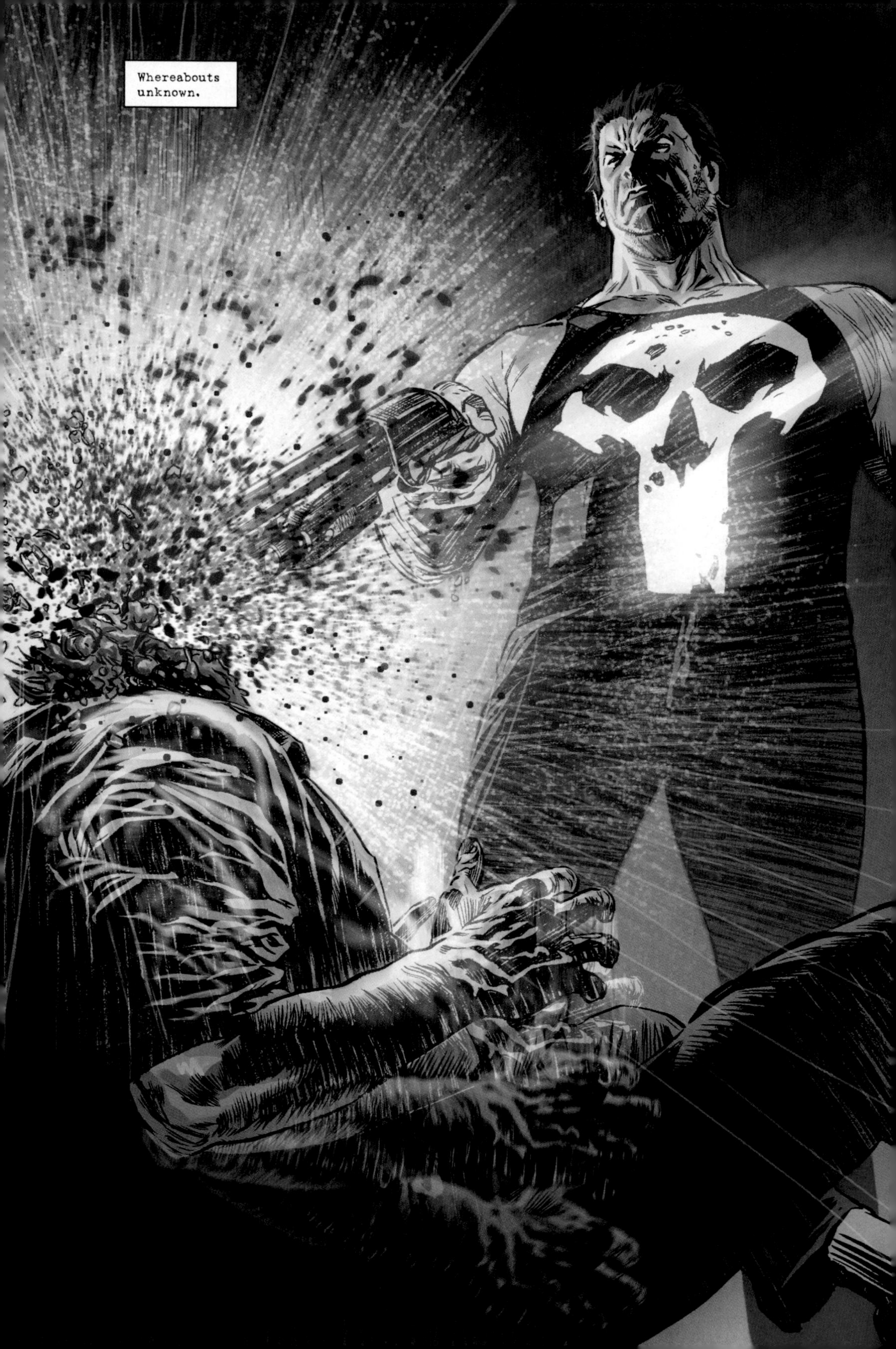
Whereabouts
unknown.

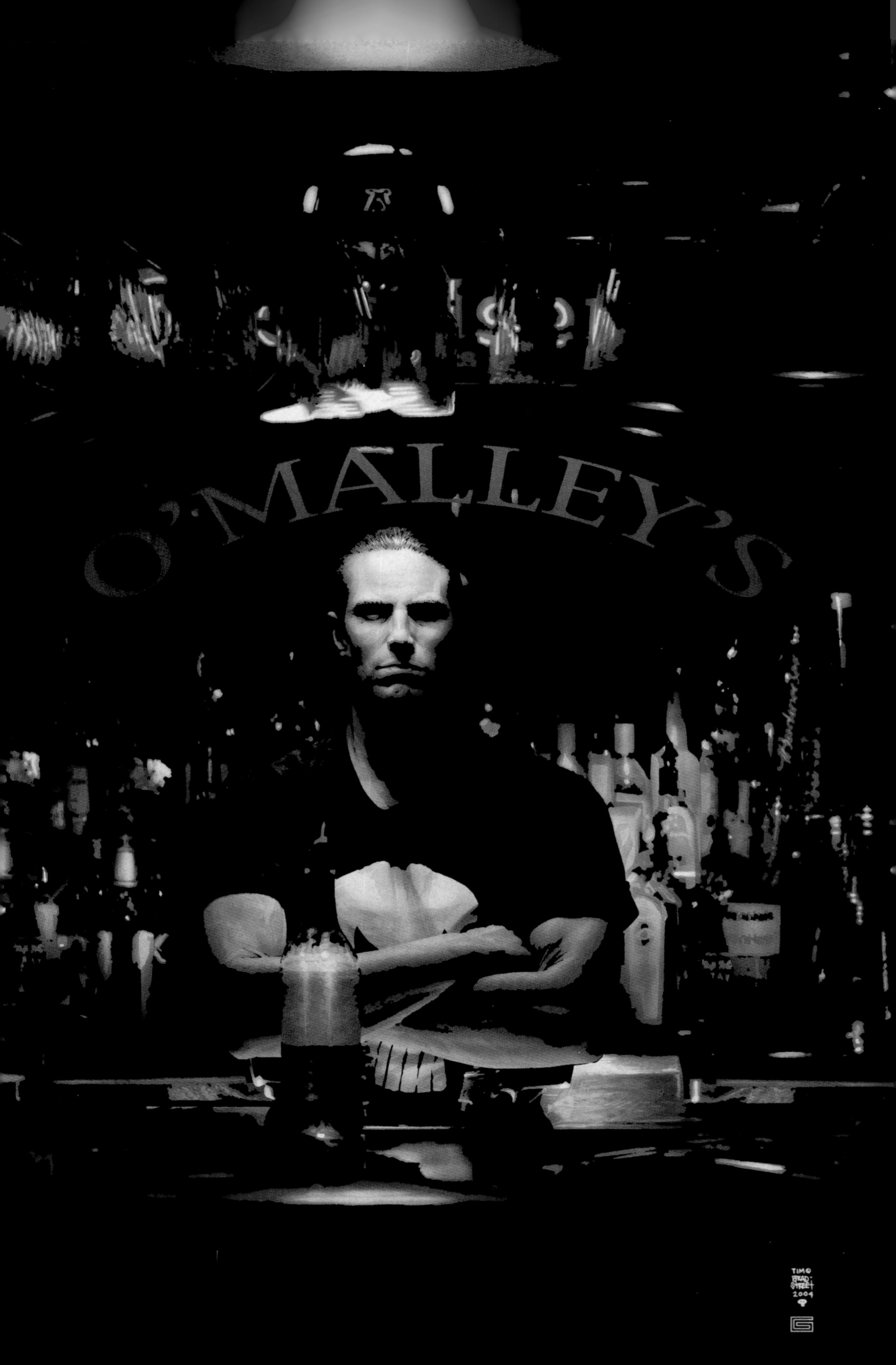
O'MALLEY'S

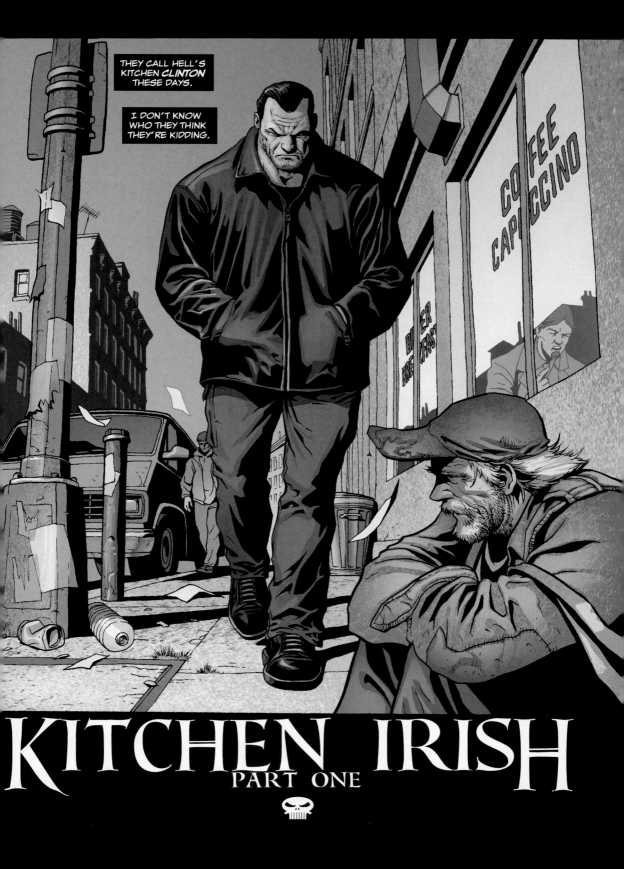

THEY CALL HELL'S KITCHEN *CLINTON* THESE DAYS.

I DON'T KNOW WHO THEY THINK THEY'RE KIDDING.

KITCHEN IRISH
PART ONE

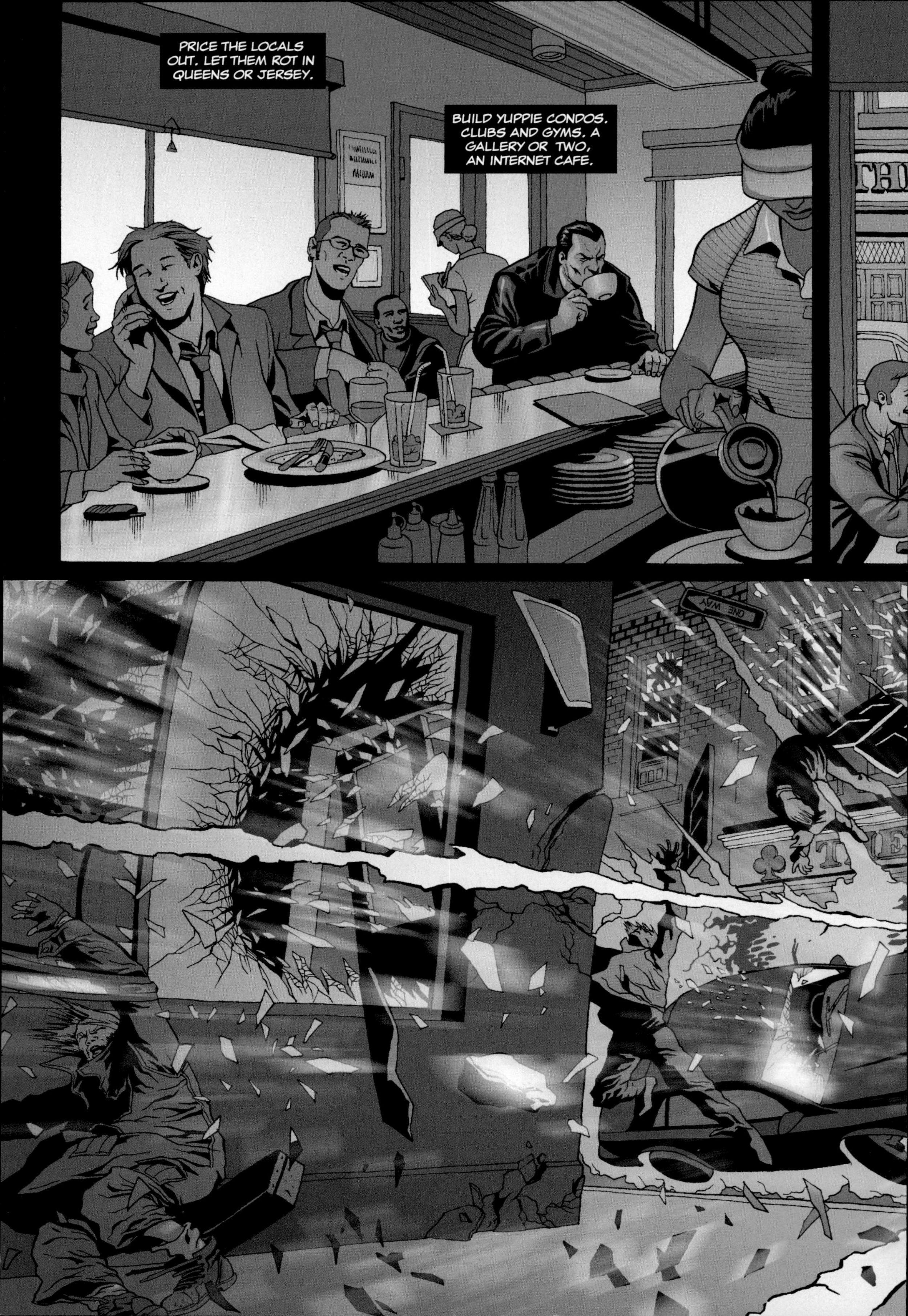
PRICE THE LOCALS OUT. LET THEM ROT IN QUEENS OR JERSEY.
BUILD YUPPIE CONDOS. CLUBS AND GYMS. A GALLERY OR TWO, AN INTERNET CAFE.
ONE WAY

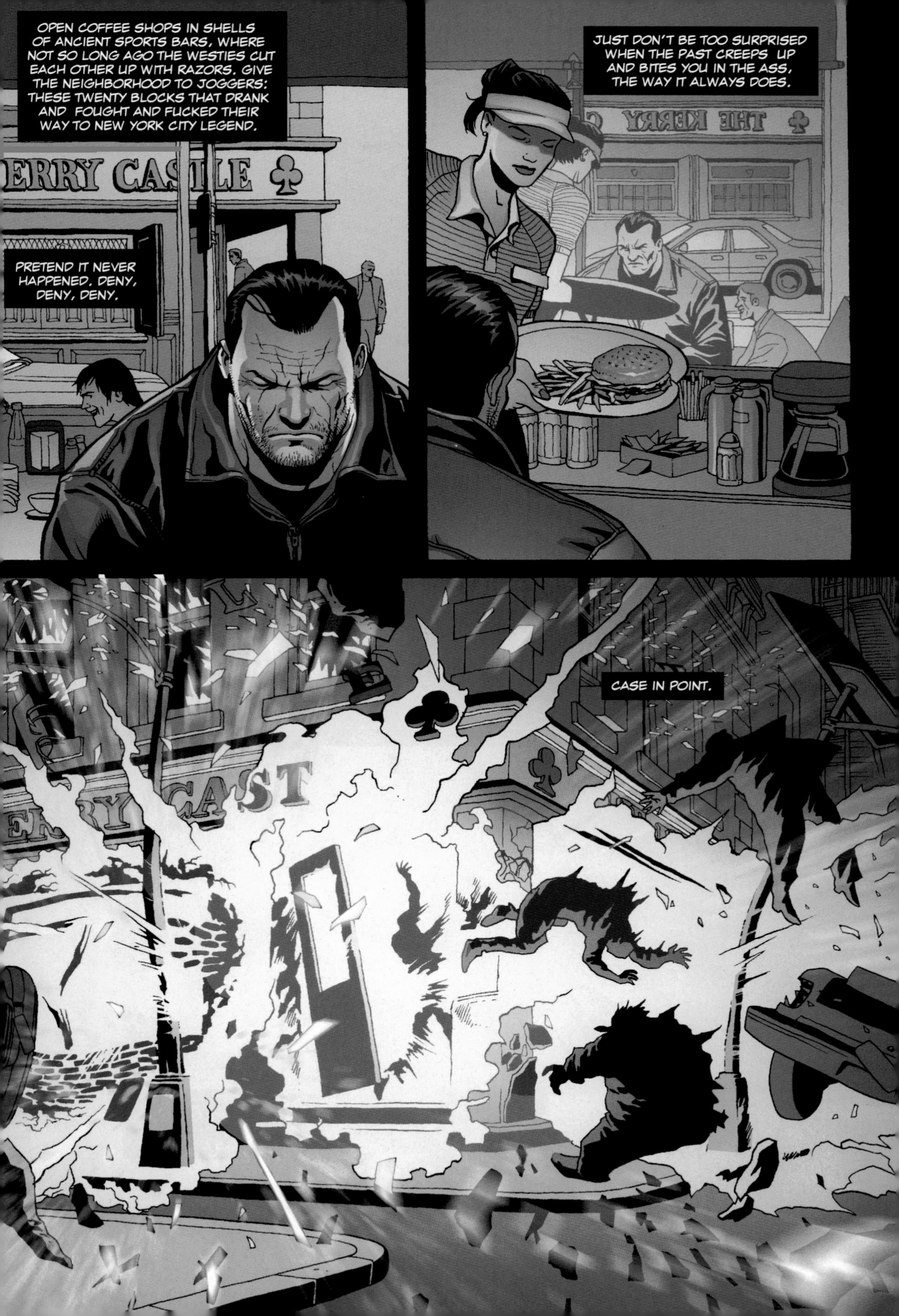
OPEN COFFEE SHOPS IN SHELLS OF ANCIENT SPORTS BARS, WHERE NOT SO LONG AGO THE WESTIES CUT EACH OTHER UP WITH RAZORS. GIVE THE NEIGHBORHOOD TO JOGGERS: THESE TWENTY BLOCKS THAT DRANK AND FOUGHT AND FUCKED THEIR WAY TO NEW YORK CITY LEGEND.
PRETEND IT NEVER HAPPENED. DENY, DENY, DENY.
JUST DON'T BE TOO SURPRISED WHEN THE PAST CREEPS UP AND BITES YOU IN THE ASS, THE WAY IT ALWAYS DOES.
CASE IN POINT.

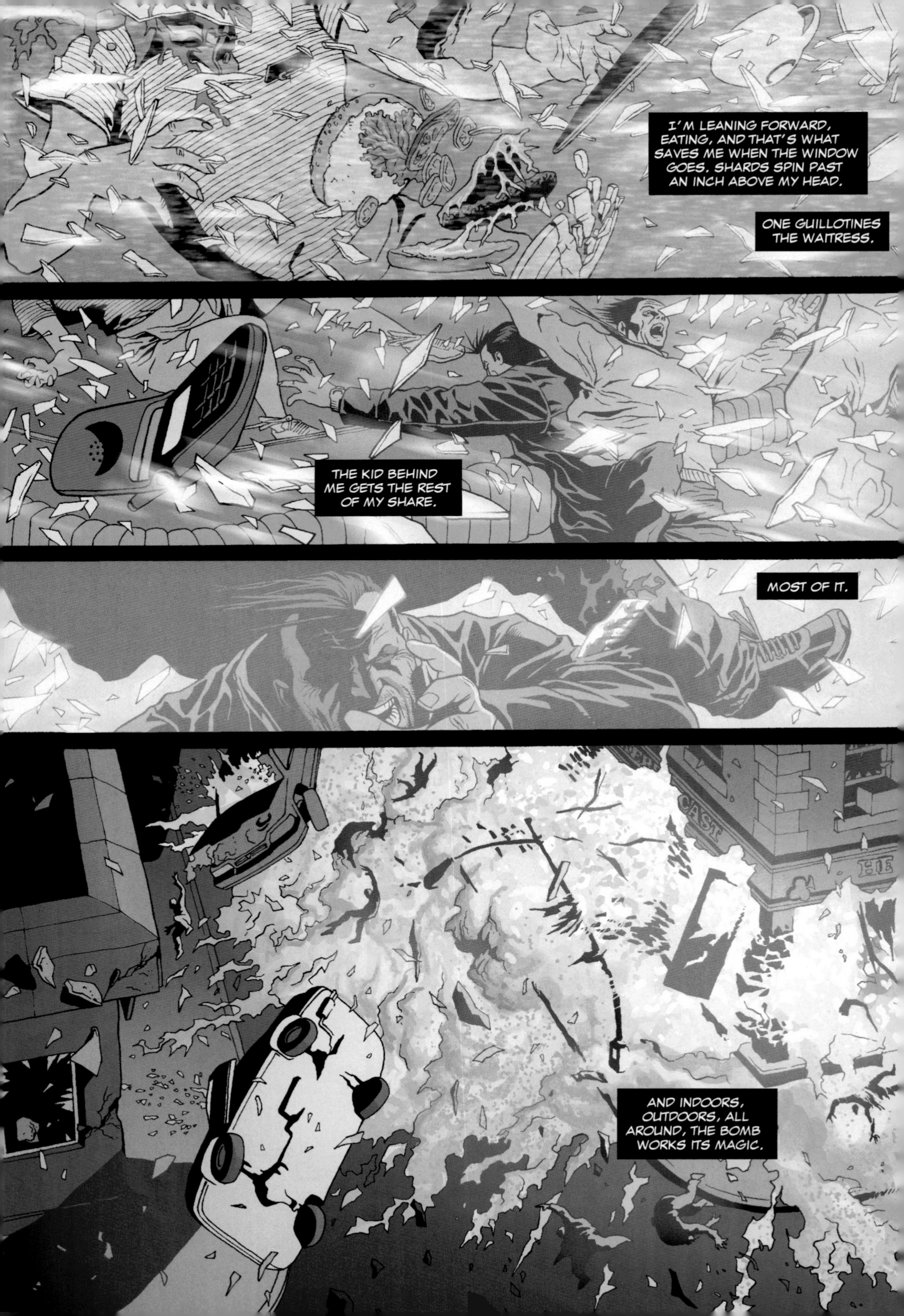
I'M LEANING FORWARD, EATING, AND THAT'S WHAT SAVES ME WHEN THE WINDOW GOES. SHARDS SPIN PAST AN INCH ABOVE MY HEAD.
ONE GUILLOTINES THE WAITRESS.
THE KID BEHIND ME GETS THE REST OF MY SHARE.
MOST OF IT.
CAST
HE
AND INDOORS, OUTDOORS, ALL AROUND, THE BOMB WORKS ITS MAGIC.

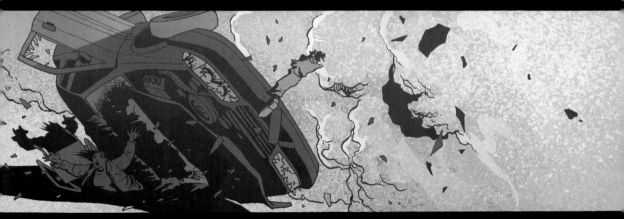

WHEN I WAKE I'M
HALFWAY INTO SHOCK,
WHICH TAKES A MOMENT
TO SUPPRESS.

THERE'S A NOISE
LIKE SOMEONE'S
CHOKING.

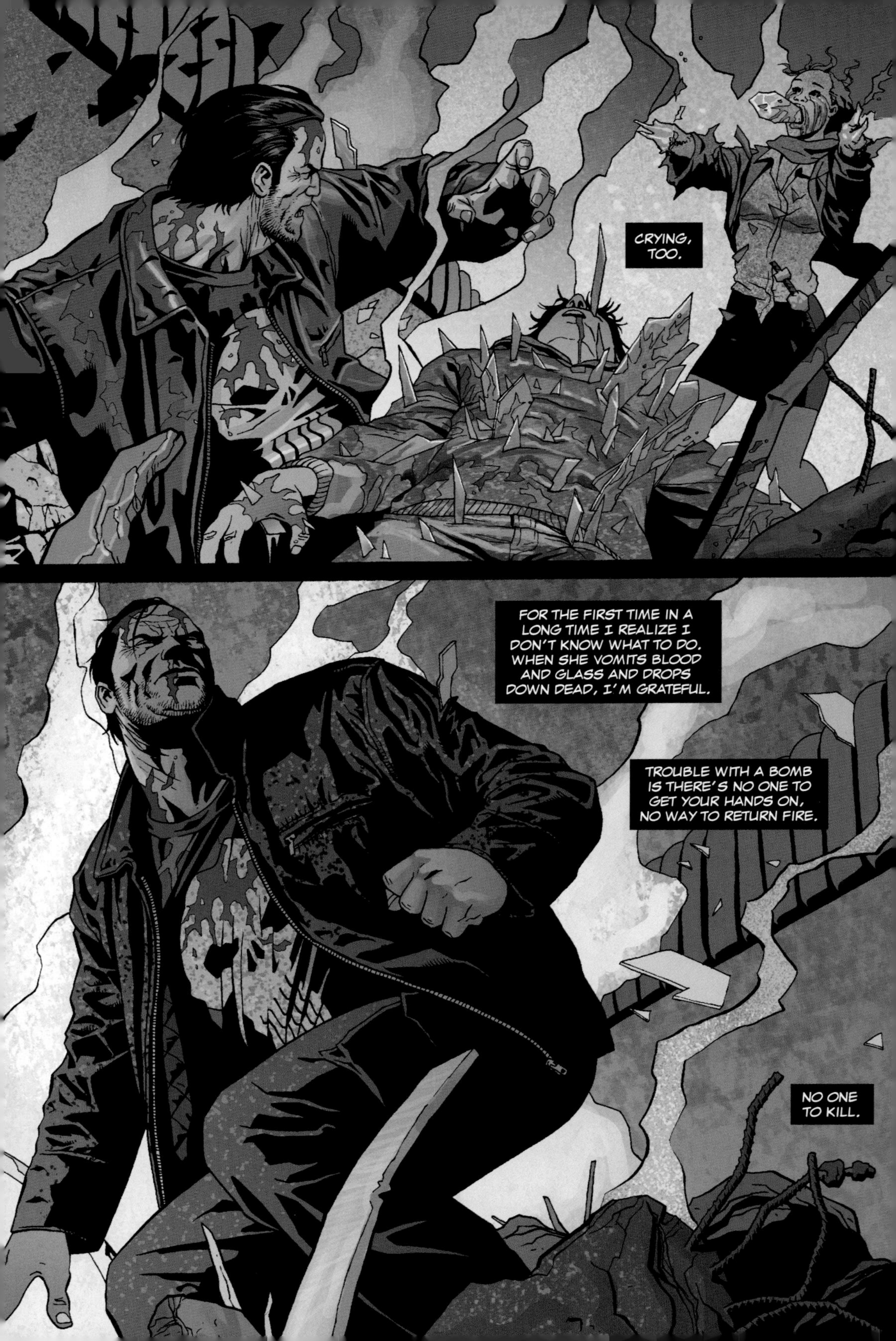
CRYING, TOO.
FOR THE FIRST TIME IN A LONG TIME I REALIZE I DON'T KNOW WHAT TO DO. WHEN SHE VOMITS BLOOD AND GLASS AND DROPS DOWN DEAD, I'M GRATEFUL.
TROUBLE WITH A BOMB IS THERE'S NO ONE TO GET YOUR HANDS ON, NO WAY TO RETURN FIRE.
NO ONE TO KILL.

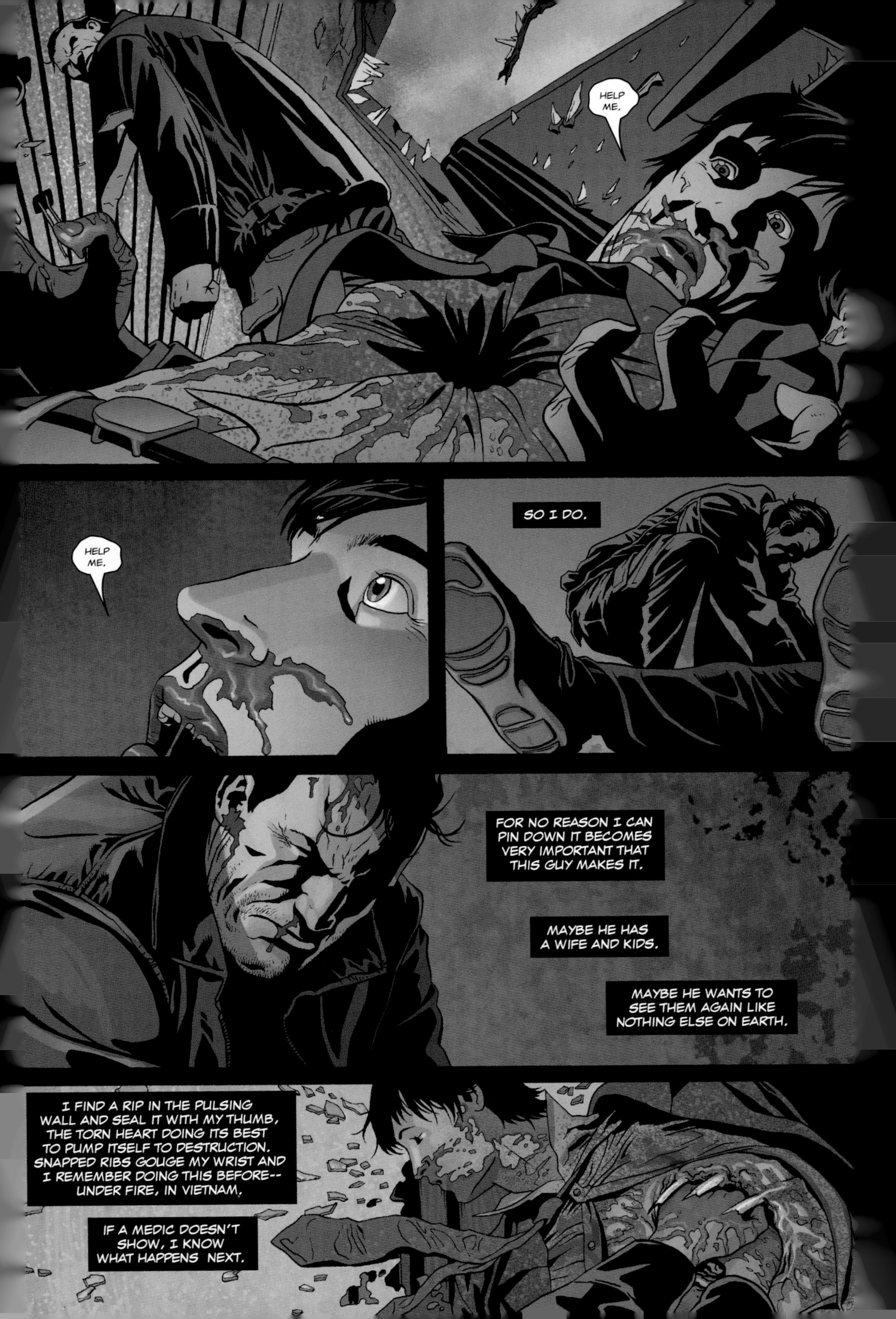
HELP ME.
HELP ME.
SO I DO.
FOR NO REASON I CAN PIN DOWN IT BECOMES VERY IMPORTANT THAT THIS GUY MAKES IT.
MAYBE HE HAS A WIFE AND KIDS.
MAYBE HE WANTS TO SEE THEM AGAIN LIKE NOTHING ELSE ON EARTH.
I FIND A RIP IN THE PULSING WALL AND SEAL IT WITH MY THUMB, THE TORN HEART DOING ITS BEST TO PUMP ITSELF TO DESTRUCTION. SNAPPED RIBS GOUGE MY WRIST AND I REMEMBER DOING THIS BEFORE-- UNDER FIRE, IN VIETNAM.
IF A MEDIC DOESN'T SHOW, I KNOW WHAT HAPPENS NEXT.

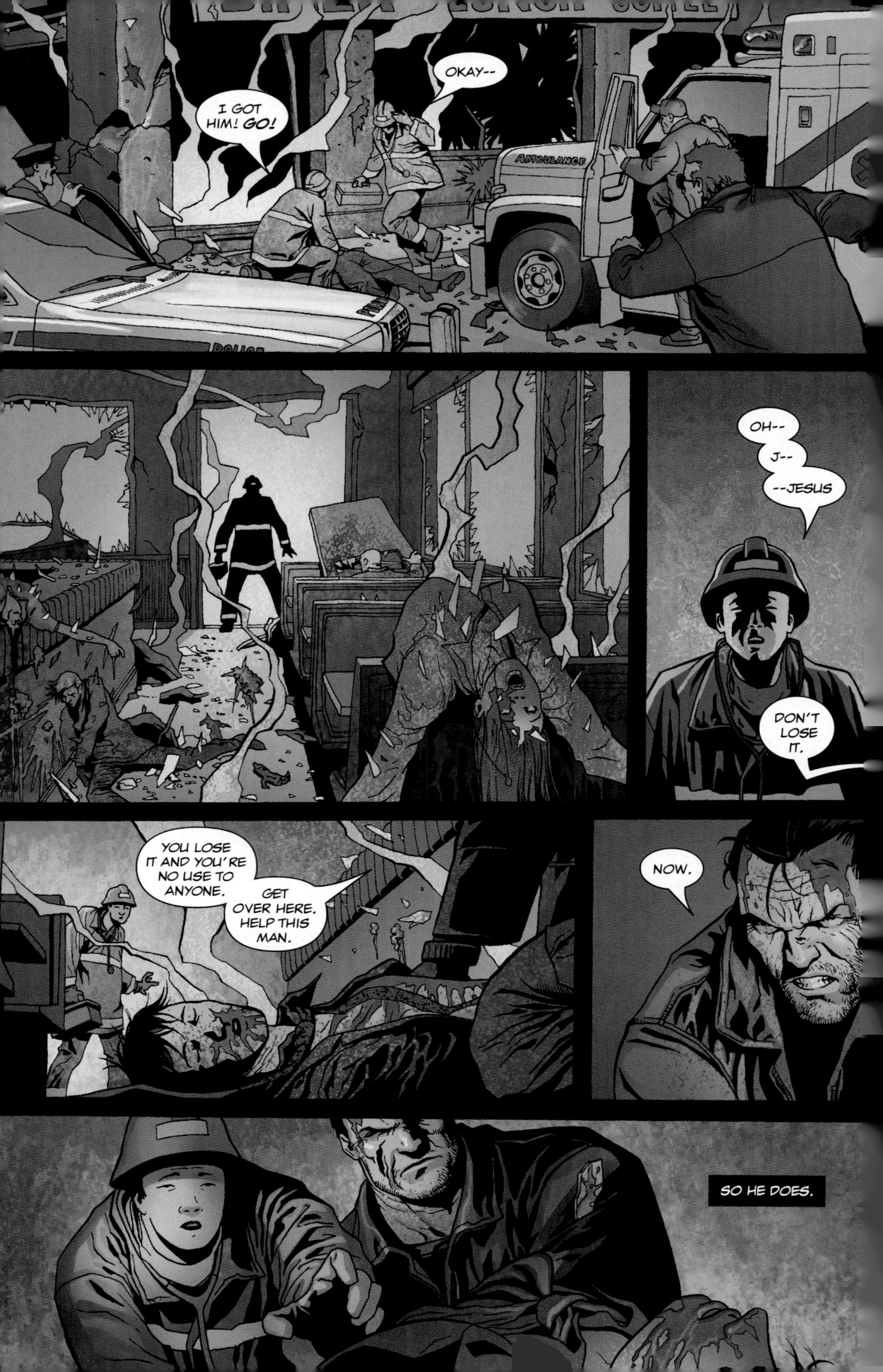
OKAY--
I GOT HIM! GO!
OH--
J--
--JESUS
DON'T LOSE IT.
YOU LOSE IT AND YOU'RE NO USE TO ANYONE.
GET OVER HERE. HELP THIS MAN.
NOW.
SO HE DOES.

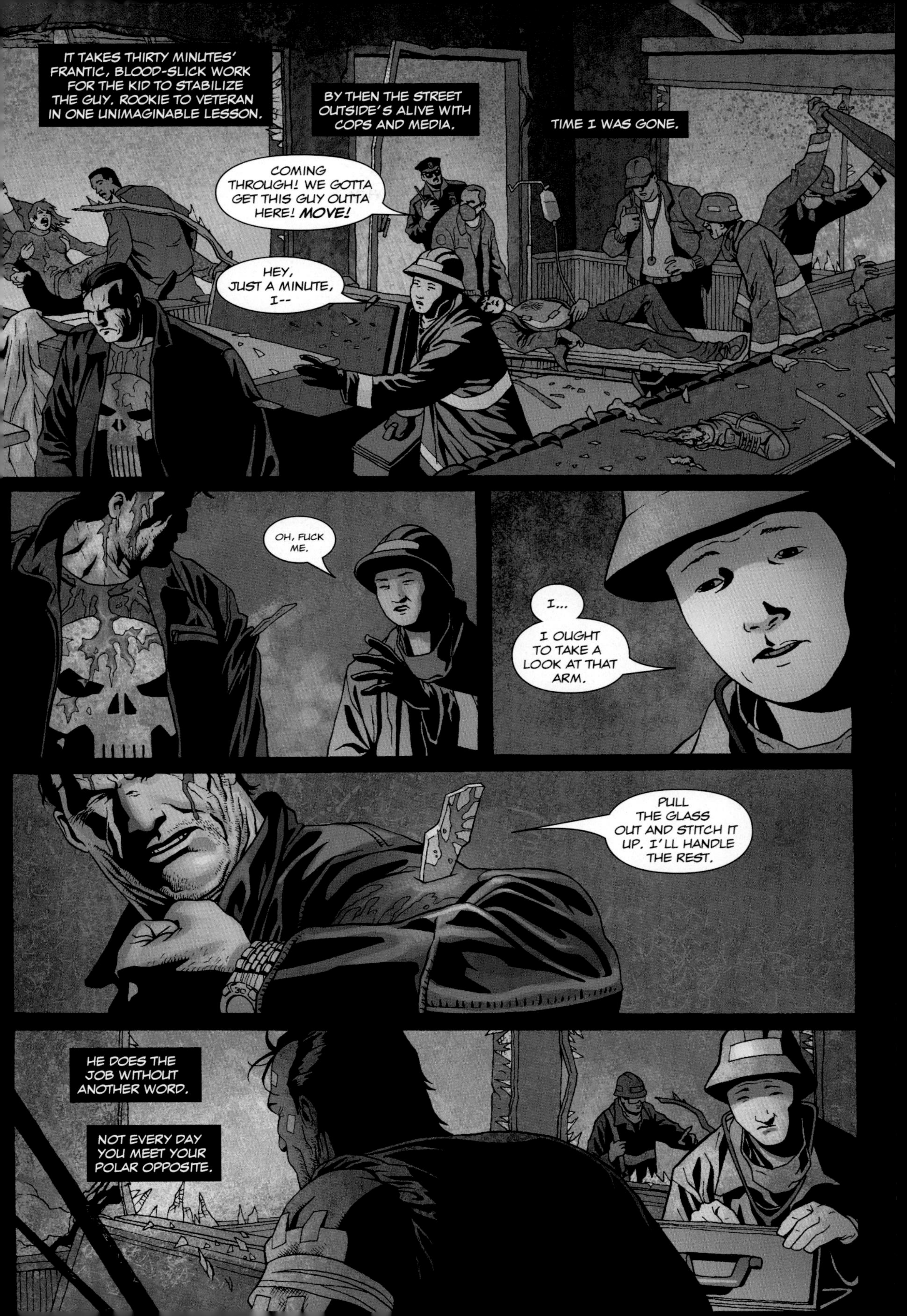
IT TAKES THIRTY MINUTES' FRANTIC, BLOOD-SLICK WORK FOR THE KID TO STABILIZE THE GUY. ROOKIE TO VETERAN IN ONE UNIMAGINABLE LESSON.
BY THEN THE STREET OUTSIDE'S ALIVE WITH COPS AND MEDIA.
TIME I WAS GONE.
COMING THROUGH! WE GOTTA GET THIS GUY OUTTA HERE! MOVE!
HEY, JUST A MINUTE, I--
OH, FUCK ME.
I...
I OUGHT TO TAKE A LOOK AT THAT ARM.
PULL THE GLASS OUT AND STITCH IT UP. I'LL HANDLE THE REST.
HE DOES THE JOB WITHOUT ANOTHER WORD.
NOT EVERY DAY YOU MEET YOUR POLAR OPPOSITE.

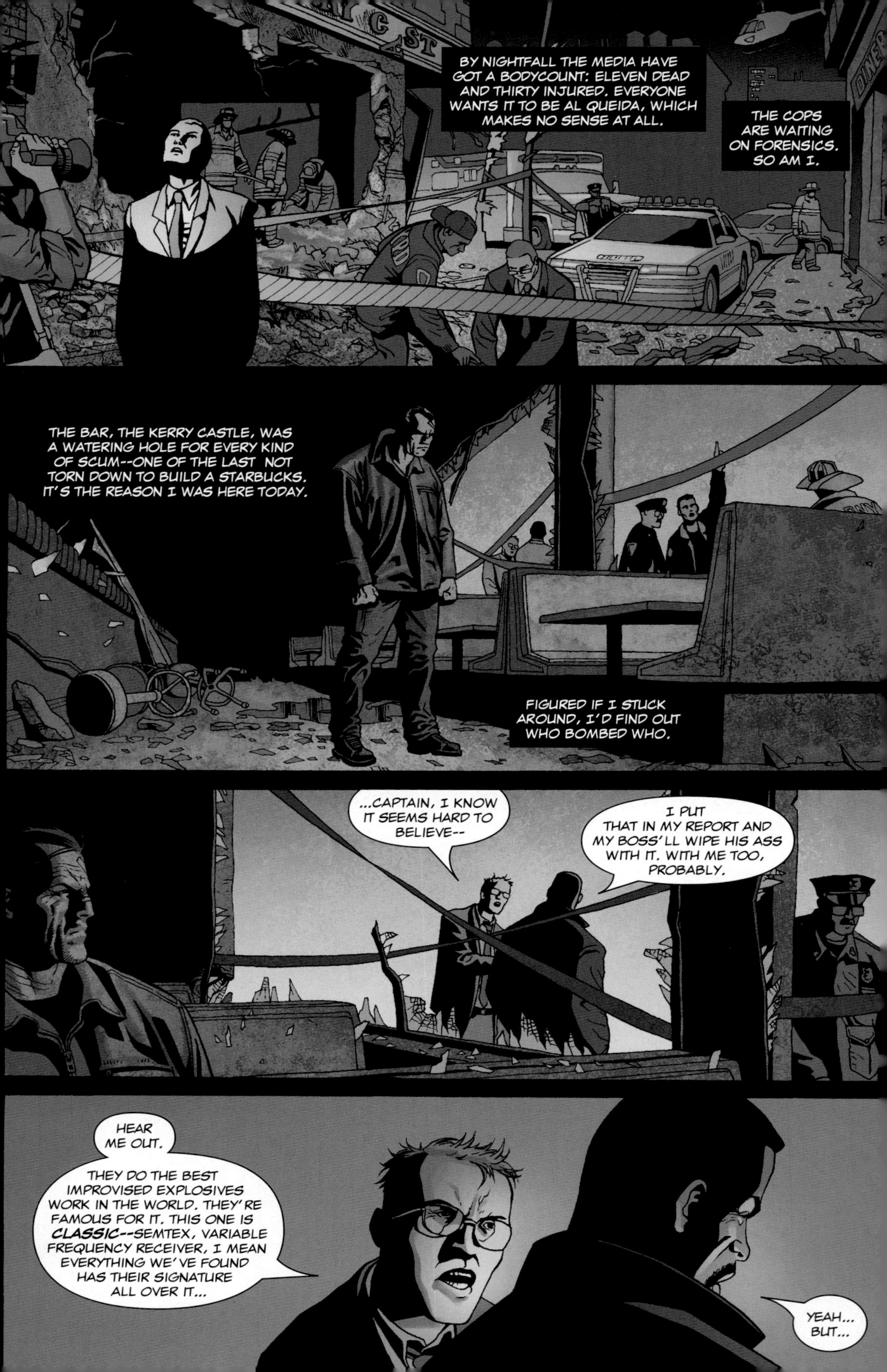

BY NIGHTFALL THE MEDIA HAVE GOT A BODYCOUNT: ELEVEN DEAD AND THIRTY INJURED. EVERYONE WANTS IT TO BE AL QUEIDA, WHICH MAKES NO SENSE AT ALL.
THE COPS ARE WAITING ON FORENSICS. SO AM I.
THE BAR, THE KERRY CASTLE, WAS A WATERING HOLE FOR EVERY KIND OF SCUM--ONE OF THE LAST NOT TORN DOWN TO BUILD A STARBUCKS. IT'S THE REASON I WAS HERE TODAY.
FIGURED IF I STUCK AROUND, I'D FIND OUT WHO BOMBED WHO.
...CAPTAIN, I KNOW IT SEEMS HARD TO BELIEVE--
I PUT THAT IN MY REPORT AND MY BOSS'LL WIPE HIS ASS WITH IT. WITH ME TOO, PROBABLY.
HEAR ME OUT.
THEY DO THE BEST IMPROVISED EXPLOSIVES WORK IN THE WORLD. THEY'RE FAMOUS FOR IT. THIS ONE IS ***CLASSIC***--SEMTEX, VARIABLE FREQUENCY RECEIVER, I MEAN EVERYTHING WE'VE FOUND HAS THEIR SIGNATURE ALL OVER IT...
YEAH... BUT...

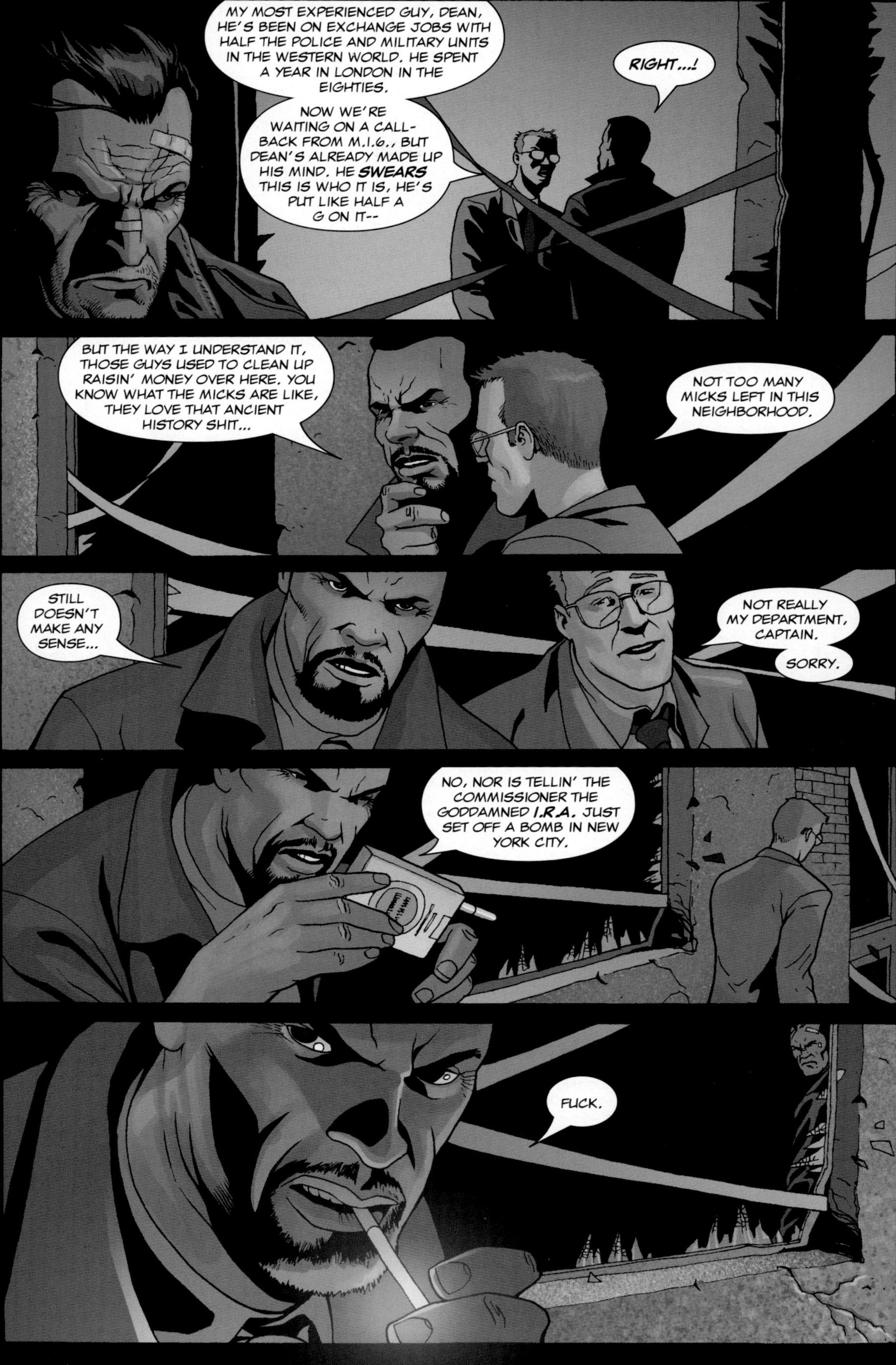
MY MOST EXPERIENCED GUY, DEAN, HE'S BEEN ON EXCHANGE JOBS WITH HALF THE POLICE AND MILITARY UNITS IN THE WESTERN WORLD. HE SPENT A YEAR IN LONDON IN THE EIGHTIES.
NOW WE'RE WAITING ON A CALL-BACK FROM M.I.6., BUT DEAN'S ALREADY MADE UP HIS MIND. HE SWEARS THIS IS WHO IT IS, HE'S PUT LIKE HALF A G ON IT--
RIGHT...!
BUT THE WAY I UNDERSTAND IT, THOSE GUYS USED TO CLEAN UP RAISIN' MONEY OVER HERE. YOU KNOW WHAT THE MICKS ARE LIKE, THEY LOVE THAT ANCIENT HISTORY SHIT...
NOT TOO MANY MICKS LEFT IN THIS NEIGHBORHOOD.
STILL DOESN'T MAKE ANY SENSE...
NOT REALLY MY DEPARTMENT, CAPTAIN.
SORRY.
NO, NOR IS TELLIN' THE COMMISSIONER THE GODDAMNED I.R.A. JUST SET OFF A BOMB IN NEW YORK CITY.
FUCK.

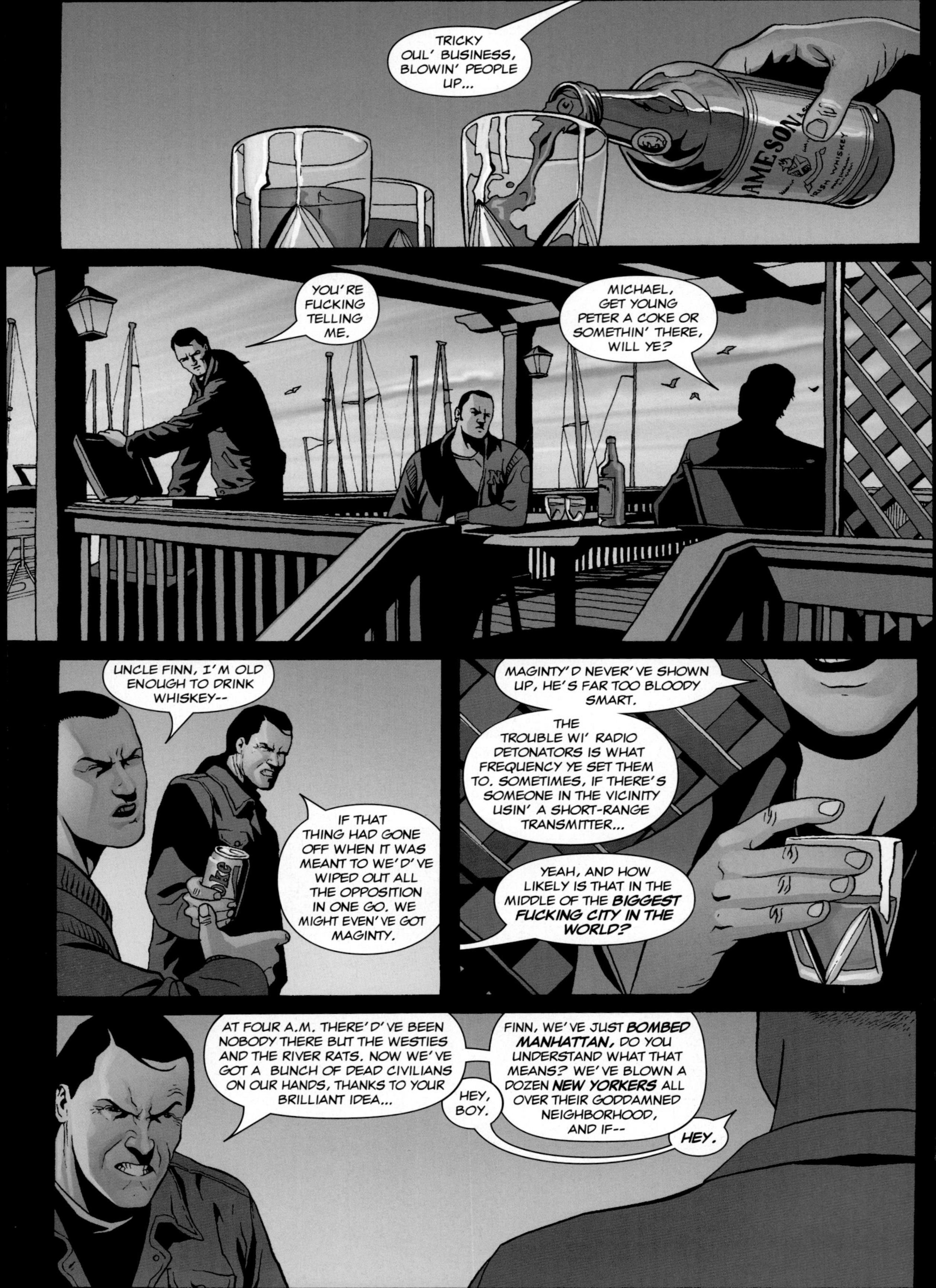
TRICKY OUL' BUSINESS, BLOWIN' PEOPLE UP...
YOU'RE FUCKING TELLING ME.
MICHAEL, GET YOUNG PETER A COKE OR SOMETHIN' THERE, WILL YE?
UNCLE FINN, I'M OLD ENOUGH TO DRINK WHISKEY--
IF THAT THING HAD GONE OFF WHEN IT WAS MEANT TO WE'D'VE WIPED OUT ALL THE OPPOSITION IN ONE GO. WE MIGHT EVEN'VE GOT MAGINTY.
MAGINTY'D NEVER'VE SHOWN UP, HE'S FAR TOO BLOODY SMART.
THE TROUBLE WI' RADIO DETONATORS IS WHAT FREQUENCY YE SET THEM TO. SOMETIMES, IF THERE'S SOMEONE IN THE VICINITY USIN' A SHORT-RANGE TRANSMITTER...
YEAH, AND HOW LIKELY IS THAT IN THE MIDDLE OF THE **BIGGEST FUCKING CITY IN THE WORLD?**
AT FOUR A.M. THERE'D'VE BEEN NOBODY THERE BUT THE WESTIES AND THE RIVER RATS. NOW WE'VE GOT A BUNCH OF DEAD CIVILIANS ON OUR HANDS, THANKS TO YOUR BRILLIANT IDEA...
FINN, WE'VE JUST **BOMBED MANHATTAN,** DO YOU UNDERSTAND WHAT THAT MEANS? WE'VE BLOWN A DOZEN **NEW YORKERS** ALL OVER THEIR GODDAMNED NEIGHBORHOOD, AND IF--
HEY, BOY.
HEY.

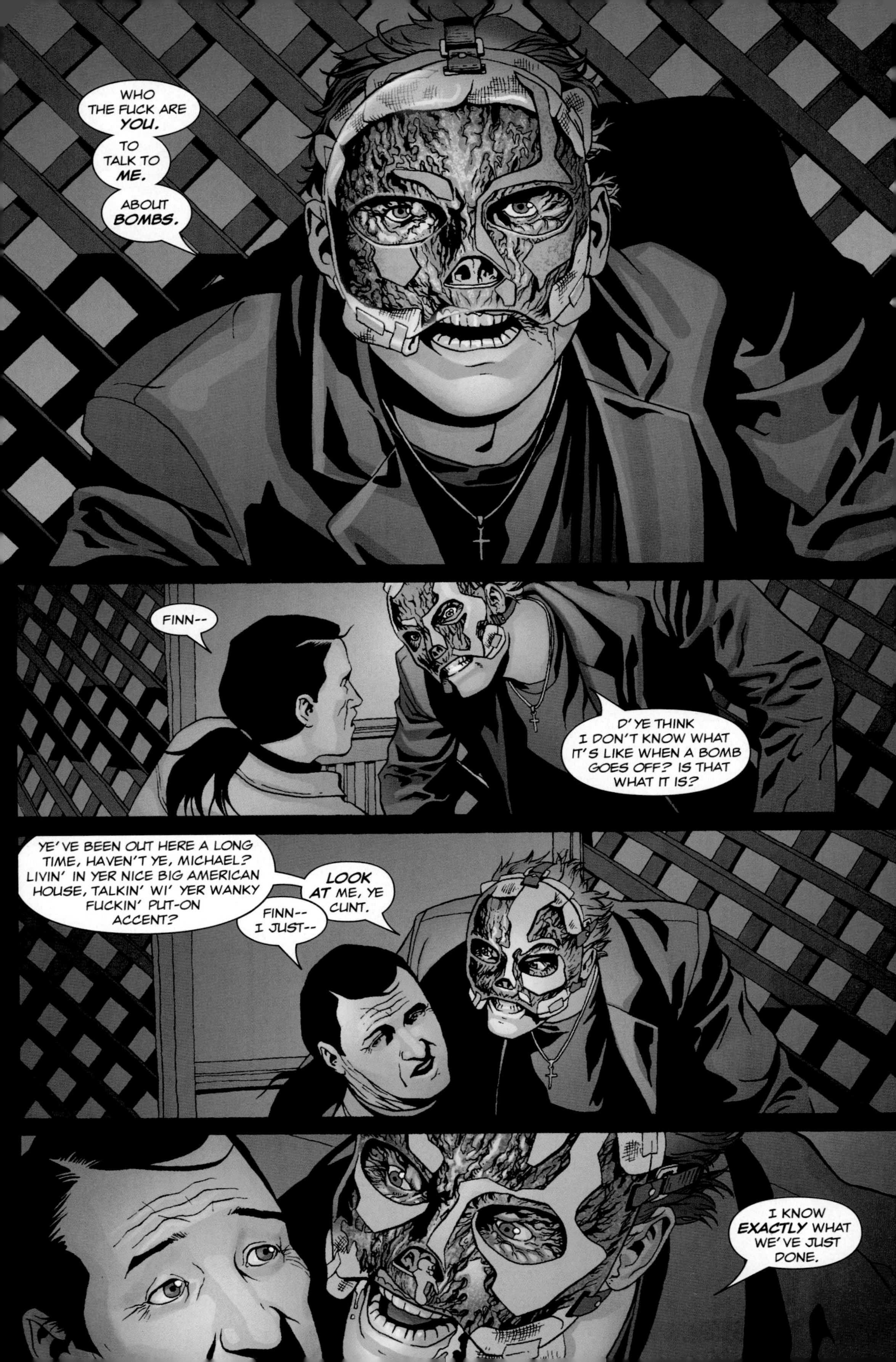
WHO THE FUCK ARE YOU.
TO TALK TO ME.
ABOUT BOMBS.
FINN--
D'YE THINK I DON'T KNOW WHAT IT'S LIKE WHEN A BOMB GOES OFF? IS THAT WHAT IT IS?
YE'VE BEEN OUT HERE A LONG TIME, HAVEN'T YE, MICHAEL? LIVIN' IN YER NICE BIG AMERICAN HOUSE, TALKIN' WI' YER WANKY FUCKIN' PUT-ON ACCENT?
FINN-- I JUST--
LOOK AT ME, YE CUNT.
I KNOW EXACTLY WHAT WE'VE JUST DONE.

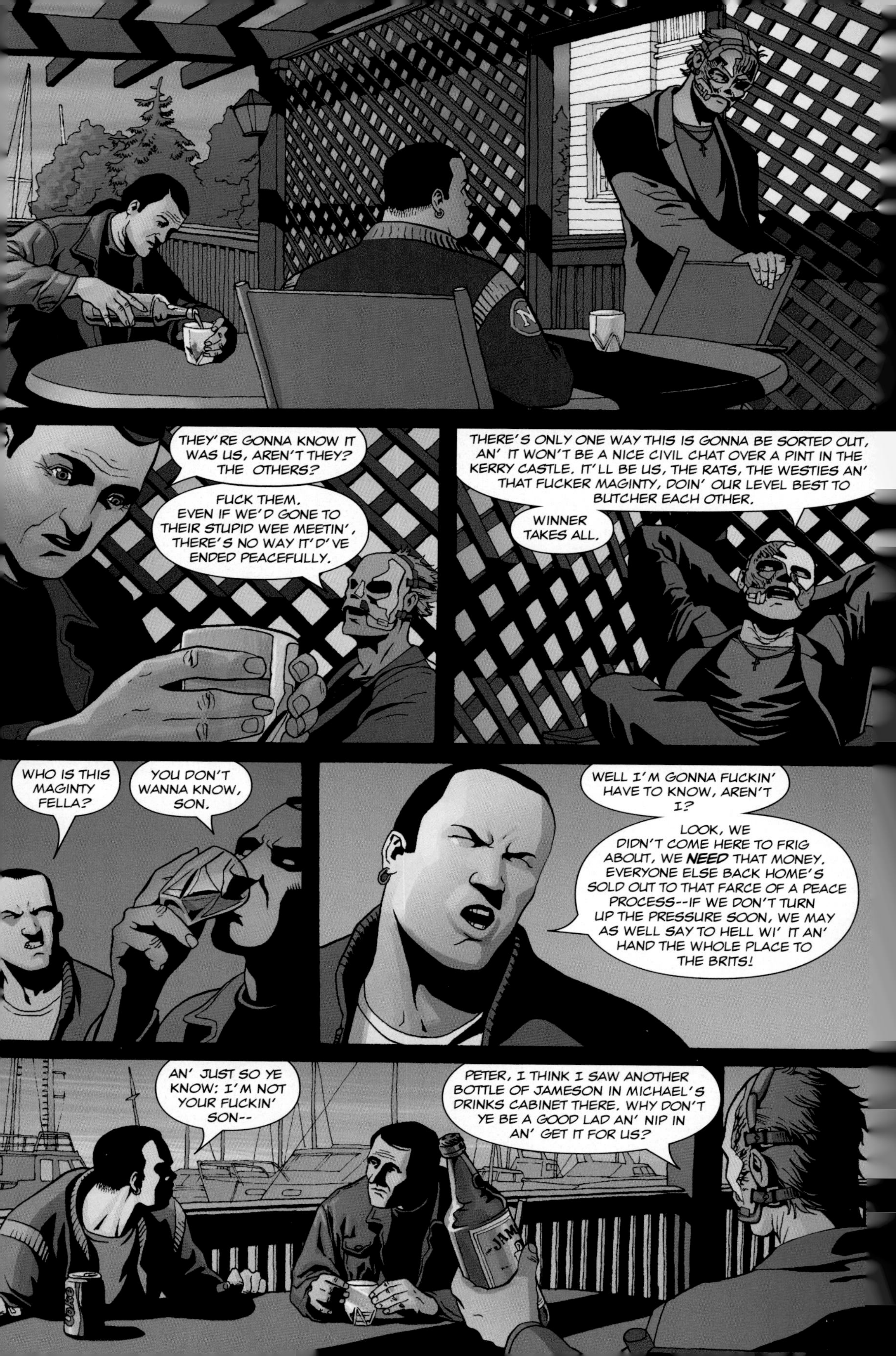
THEY'RE GONNA KNOW IT WAS US, AREN'T THEY? THE OTHERS?
FUCK THEM. EVEN IF WE'D GONE TO THEIR STUPID WEE MEETIN', THERE'S NO WAY IT'D'VE ENDED PEACEFULLY.
THERE'S ONLY ONE WAY THIS IS GONNA BE SORTED OUT, AN' IT WON'T BE A NICE CIVIL CHAT OVER A PINT IN THE KERRY CASTLE. IT'LL BE US, THE RATS, THE WESTIES AN' THAT FUCKER MAGINTY, DOIN' OUR LEVEL BEST TO BUTCHER EACH OTHER.
WINNER TAKES ALL.
WHO IS THIS MAGINTY FELLA?
YOU DON'T WANNA KNOW, SON.
WELL I'M GONNA FUCKIN' HAVE TO KNOW, AREN'T I?
LOOK, WE DIDN'T COME HERE TO FRIG ABOUT, WE NEED THAT MONEY. EVERYONE ELSE BACK HOME'S SOLD OUT TO THAT FARCE OF A PEACE PROCESS--IF WE DON'T TURN UP THE PRESSURE SOON, WE MAY AS WELL SAY TO HELL WI' IT AN' HAND THE WHOLE PLACE TO THE BRITS!
AN' JUST SO YE KNOW: I'M NOT YOUR FUCKIN' SON--
PETER, I THINK I SAW ANOTHER BOTTLE OF JAMESON IN MICHAEL'S DRINKS CABINET THERE. WHY DON'T YE BE A GOOD LAD AN' NIP IN AN' GET IT FOR US?

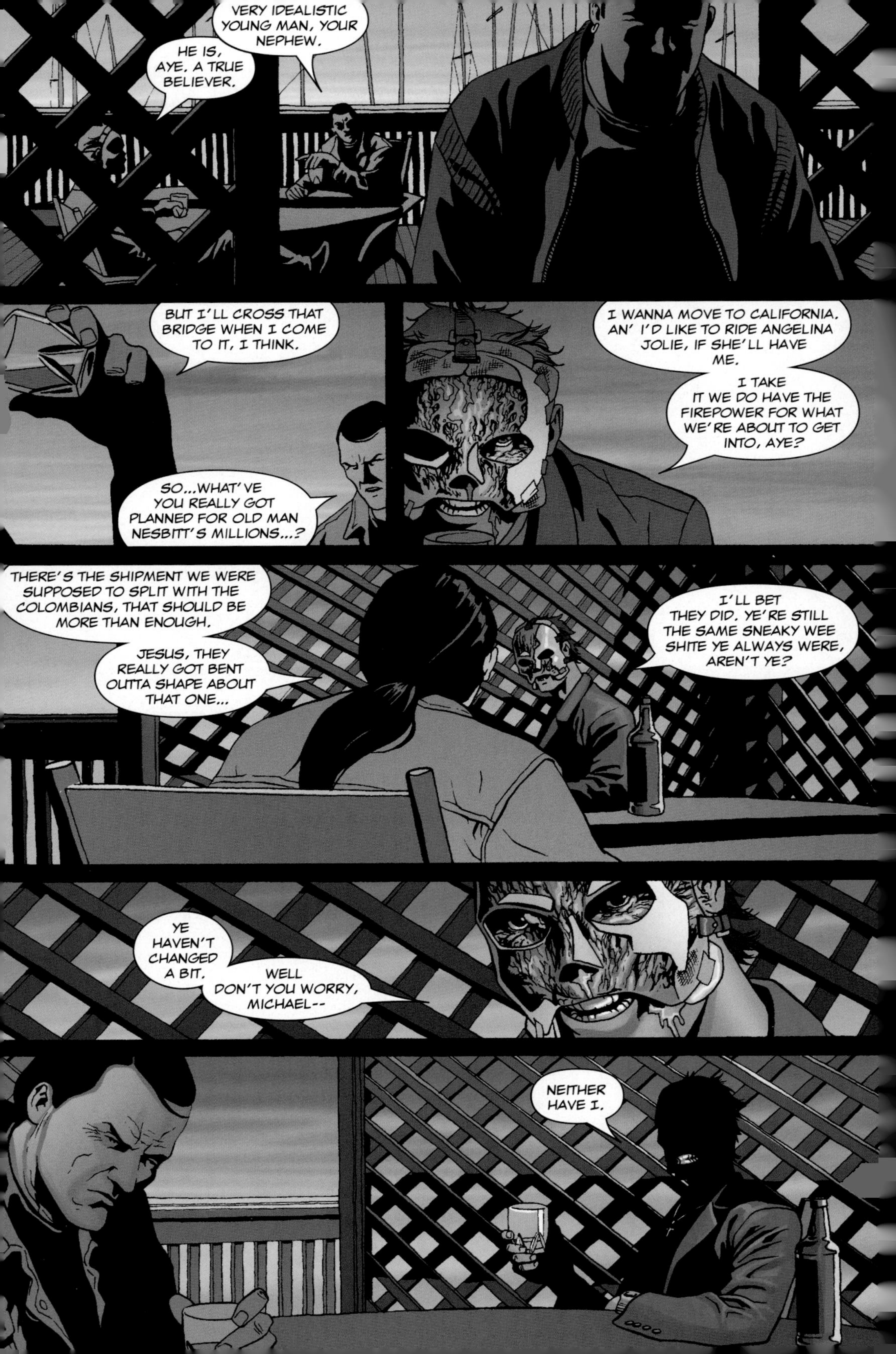
VERY IDEALISTIC YOUNG MAN, YOUR NEPHEW.
HE IS, AYE. A TRUE BELIEVER.
BUT I'LL CROSS THAT BRIDGE WHEN I COME TO IT, I THINK.
SO...WHAT'VE YOU REALLY GOT PLANNED FOR OLD MAN NESBITT'S MILLIONS...?
I WANNA MOVE TO CALIFORNIA. AN' I'D LIKE TO RIDE ANGELINA JOLIE, IF SHE'LL HAVE ME.
I TAKE IT WE DO HAVE THE FIREPOWER FOR WHAT WE'RE ABOUT TO GET INTO, AYE?
THERE'S THE SHIPMENT WE WERE SUPPOSED TO SPLIT WITH THE COLOMBIANS, THAT SHOULD BE MORE THAN ENOUGH.
JESUS, THEY REALLY GOT BENT OUTTA SHAPE ABOUT THAT ONE...
I'LL BET THEY DID. YE'RE STILL THE SAME SNEAKY WEE SHITE YE ALWAYS WERE, AREN'T YE?
YE HAVEN'T CHANGED A BIT.
WELL DON'T YOU WORRY, MICHAEL--
NEITHER HAVE I.

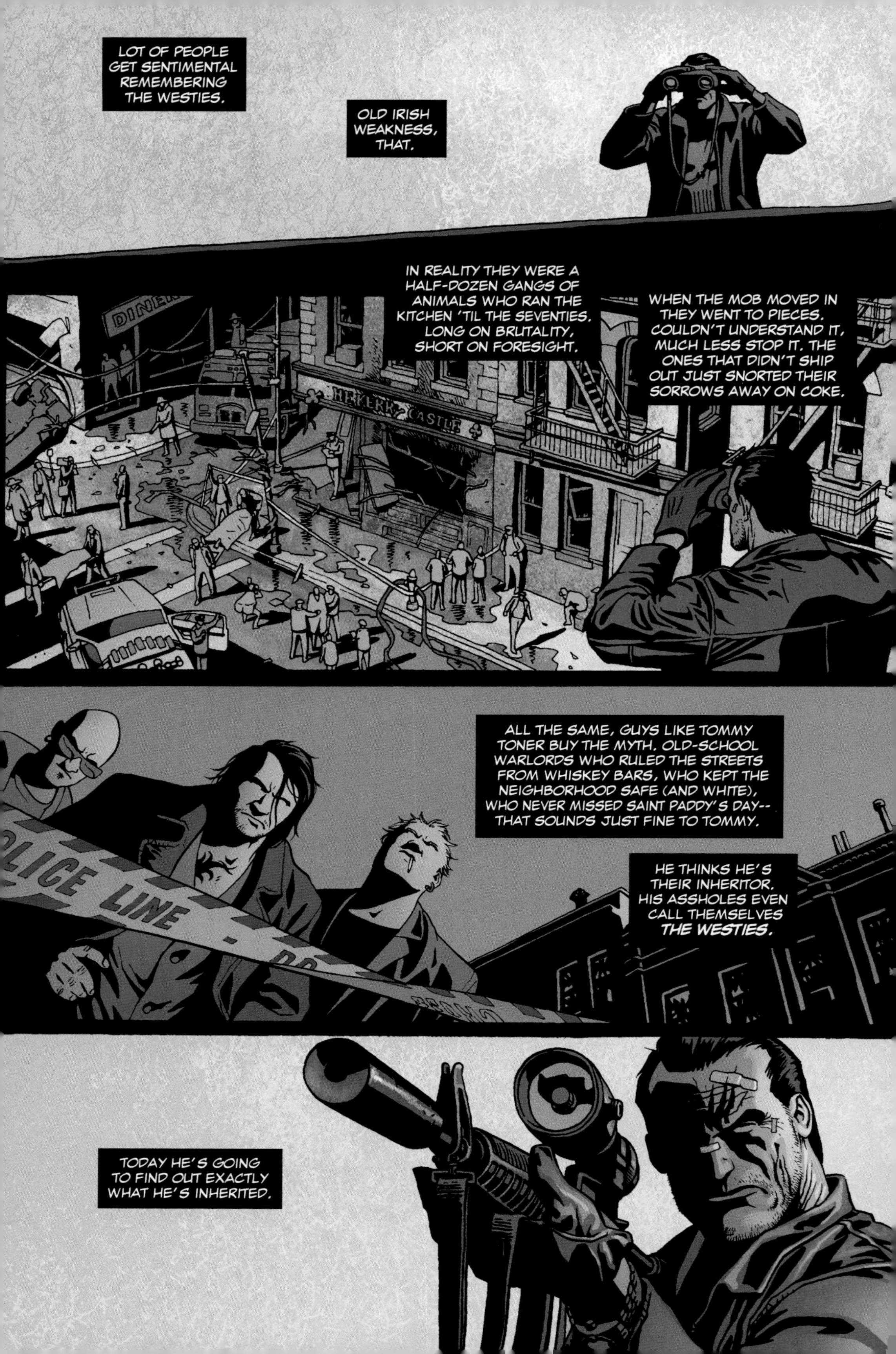
LOT OF PEOPLE GET SENTIMENTAL REMEMBERING THE WESTIES.
OLD IRISH WEAKNESS, THAT.
IN REALITY THEY WERE A HALF-DOZEN GANGS OF ANIMALS WHO RAN THE KITCHEN 'TIL THE SEVENTIES. LONG ON BRUTALITY, SHORT ON FORESIGHT.
WHEN THE MOB MOVED IN THEY WENT TO PIECES. COULDN'T UNDERSTAND IT, MUCH LESS STOP IT. THE ONES THAT DIDN'T SHIP OUT JUST SNORTED THEIR SORROWS AWAY ON COKE.
DINER
ALL THE SAME, GUYS LIKE TOMMY TONER BUY THE MYTH. OLD-SCHOOL WARLORDS WHO RULED THE STREETS FROM WHISKEY BARS, WHO KEPT THE NEIGHBORHOOD SAFE (AND WHITE), WHO NEVER MISSED SAINT PADDY'S DAY-- THAT SOUNDS JUST FINE TO TOMMY.
HE THINKS HE'S THEIR INHERITOR. HIS ASSHOLES EVEN CALL THEMSELVES THE WESTIES.
LICE LINE
TODAY HE'S GOING TO FIND OUT EXACTLY WHAT HE'S INHERITED.

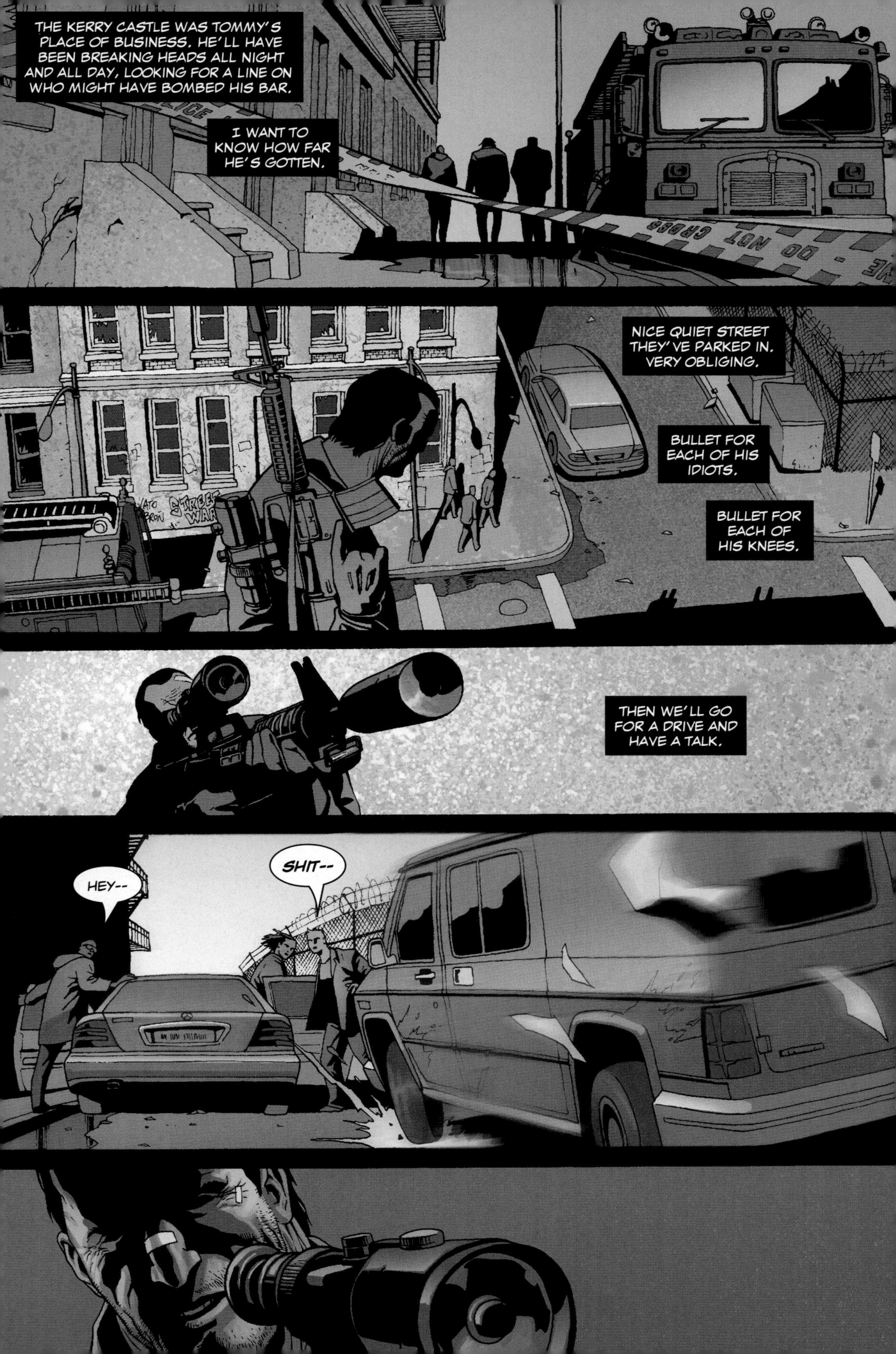
THE KERRY CASTLE WAS TOMMY'S PLACE OF BUSINESS. HE'LL HAVE BEEN BREAKING HEADS ALL NIGHT AND ALL DAY, LOOKING FOR A LINE ON WHO MIGHT HAVE BOMBED HIS BAR.
I WANT TO KNOW HOW FAR HE'S GOTTEN.
DO NOT CROSS
NICE QUIET STREET THEY'VE PARKED IN. VERY OBLIGING.
BULLET FOR EACH OF HIS IDIOTS.
BULLET FOR EACH OF HIS KNEES.
THEN WE'LL GO FOR A DRIVE AND HAVE A TALK.
HEY--
SHIT--

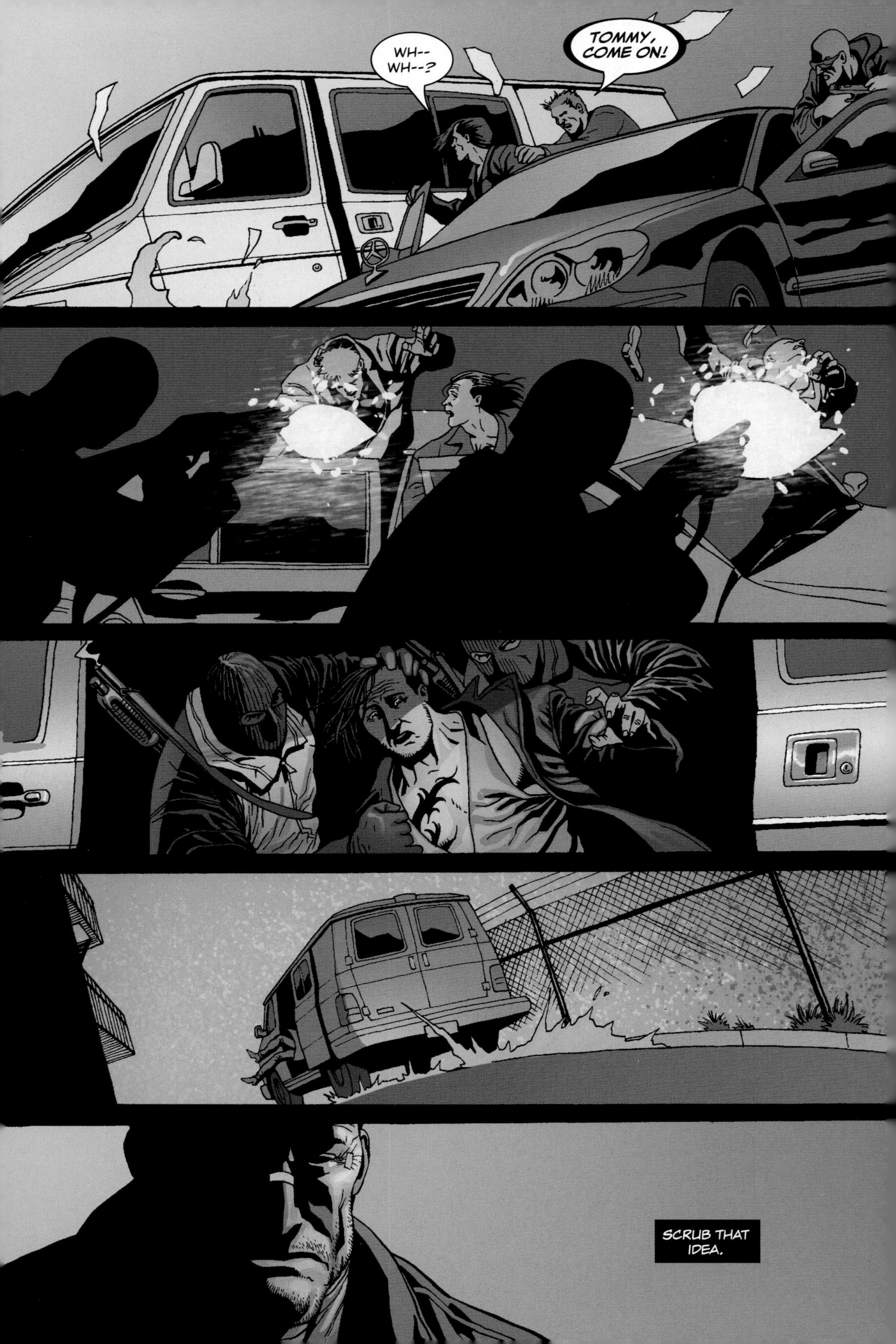
WH-- WH--?
TOMMY, COME ON!
SCRUB THAT IDEA.

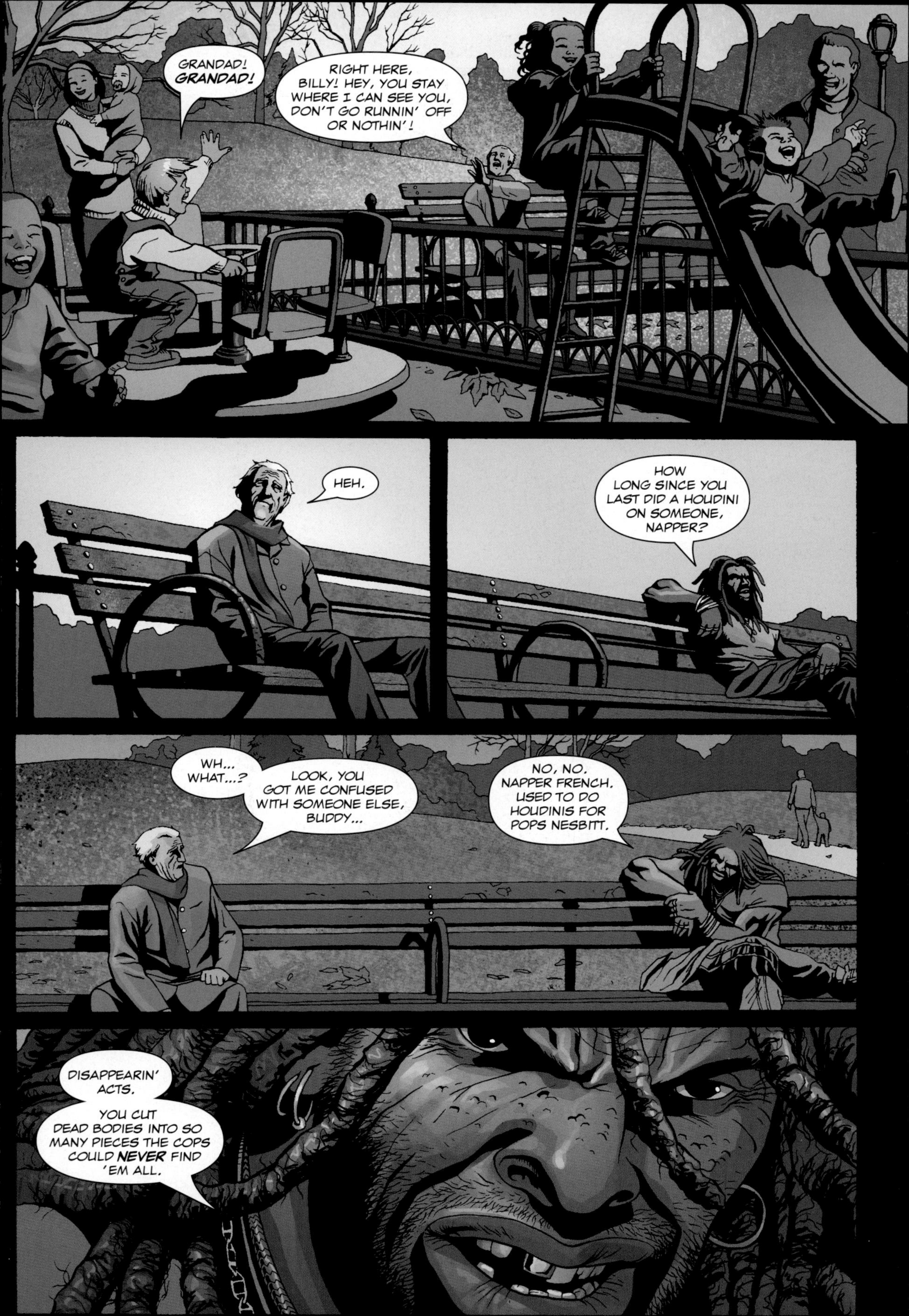
GRANDAD! **GRANDAD!**
RIGHT HERE, BILLY! HEY, YOU STAY WHERE I CAN SEE YOU, DON'T GO RUNNIN' OFF OR NOTHIN'!
HEH.
HOW LONG SINCE YOU LAST DID A HOUDINI ON SOMEONE, NAPPER?
WH... WHAT...?
LOOK, YOU GOT ME CONFUSED WITH SOMEONE ELSE, BUDDY...
NO, NO. NAPPER FRENCH. USED TO DO HOUDINIS FOR POPS NESBITT.
DISAPPEARIN' ACTS.
YOU CUT DEAD BODIES INTO SO MANY PIECES THE COPS COULD **NEVER** FIND 'EM ALL.

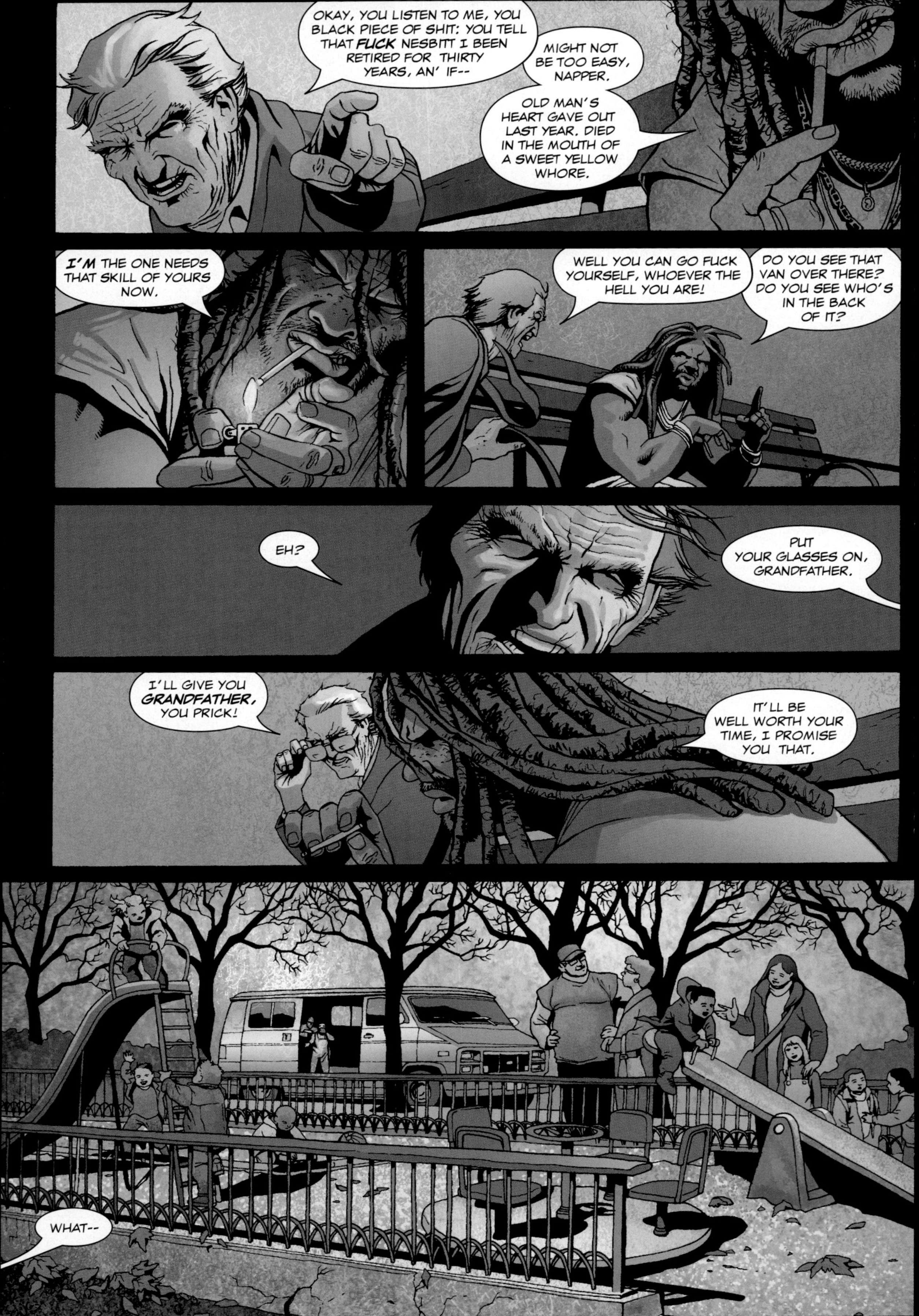
OKAY, YOU LISTEN TO ME, YOU BLACK PIECE OF SHIT: YOU TELL THAT FUCK NESBITT I BEEN RETIRED FOR THIRTY YEARS, AN' IF--
MIGHT NOT BE TOO EASY, NAPPER.
OLD MAN'S HEART GAVE OUT LAST YEAR. DIED IN THE MOUTH OF A SWEET YELLOW WHORE.
I'M THE ONE NEEDS THAT SKILL OF YOURS NOW.
WELL YOU CAN GO FUCK YOURSELF, WHOEVER THE HELL YOU ARE!
DO YOU SEE THAT VAN OVER THERE? DO YOU SEE WHO'S IN THE BACK OF IT?
EH?
PUT YOUR GLASSES ON, GRANDFATHER.
I'LL GIVE YOU GRANDFATHER, YOU PRICK!
IT'LL BE WELL WORTH YOUR TIME, I PROMISE YOU THAT.
WHAT--

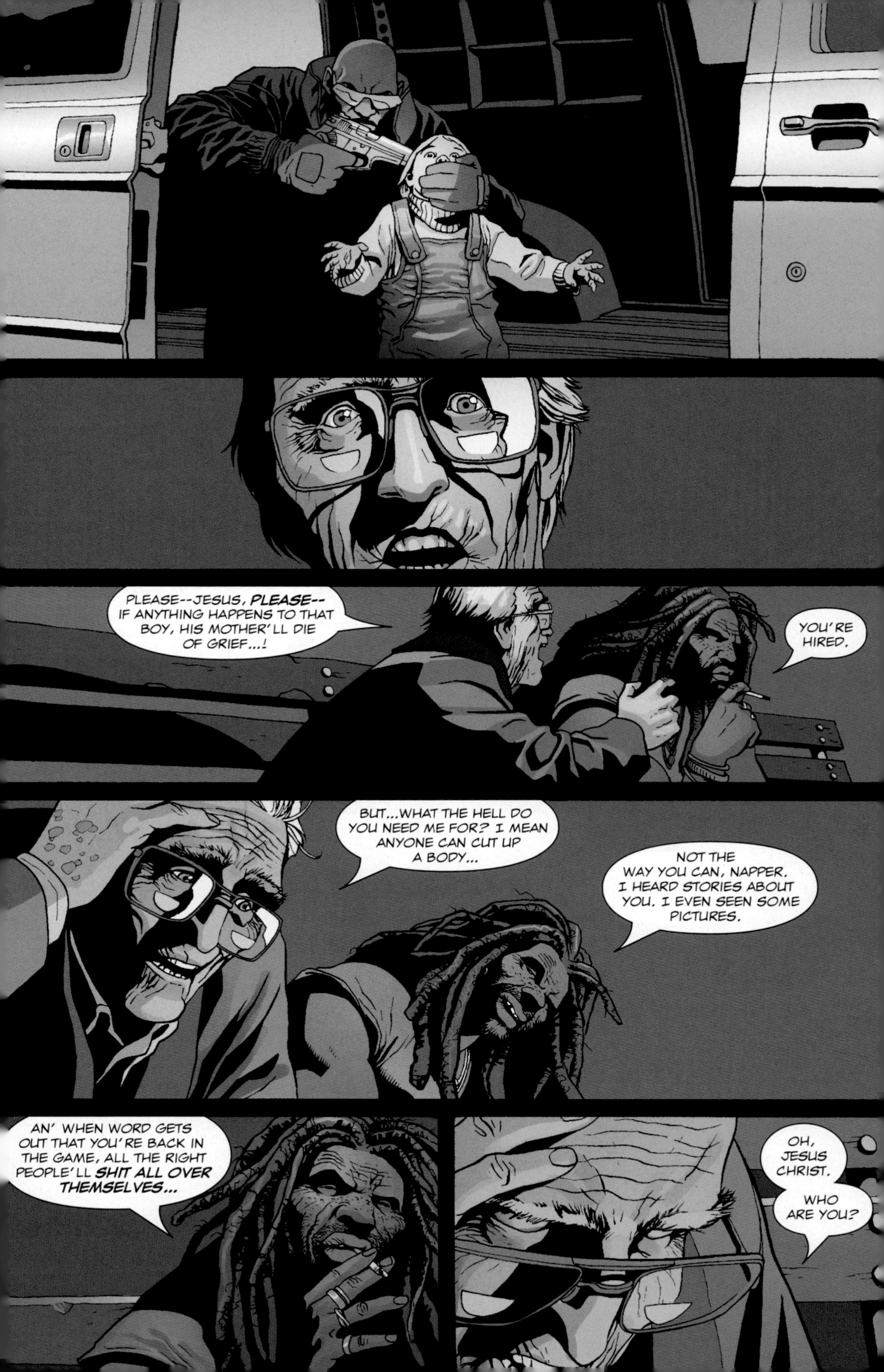
PLEASE--JESUS, PLEASE-- IF ANYTHING HAPPENS TO THAT BOY, HIS MOTHER'LL DIE OF GRIEF...!
YOU'RE HIRED.
BUT...WHAT THE HELL DO YOU NEED ME FOR? I MEAN ANYONE CAN CUT UP A BODY...
NOT THE WAY YOU CAN, NAPPER. I HEARD STORIES ABOUT YOU. I EVEN SEEN SOME PICTURES.
AN' WHEN WORD GETS OUT THAT YOU'RE BACK IN THE GAME, ALL THE RIGHT PEOPLE'LL SHIT ALL OVER THEMSELVES...
OH, JESUS CHRIST.
WHO ARE YOU?

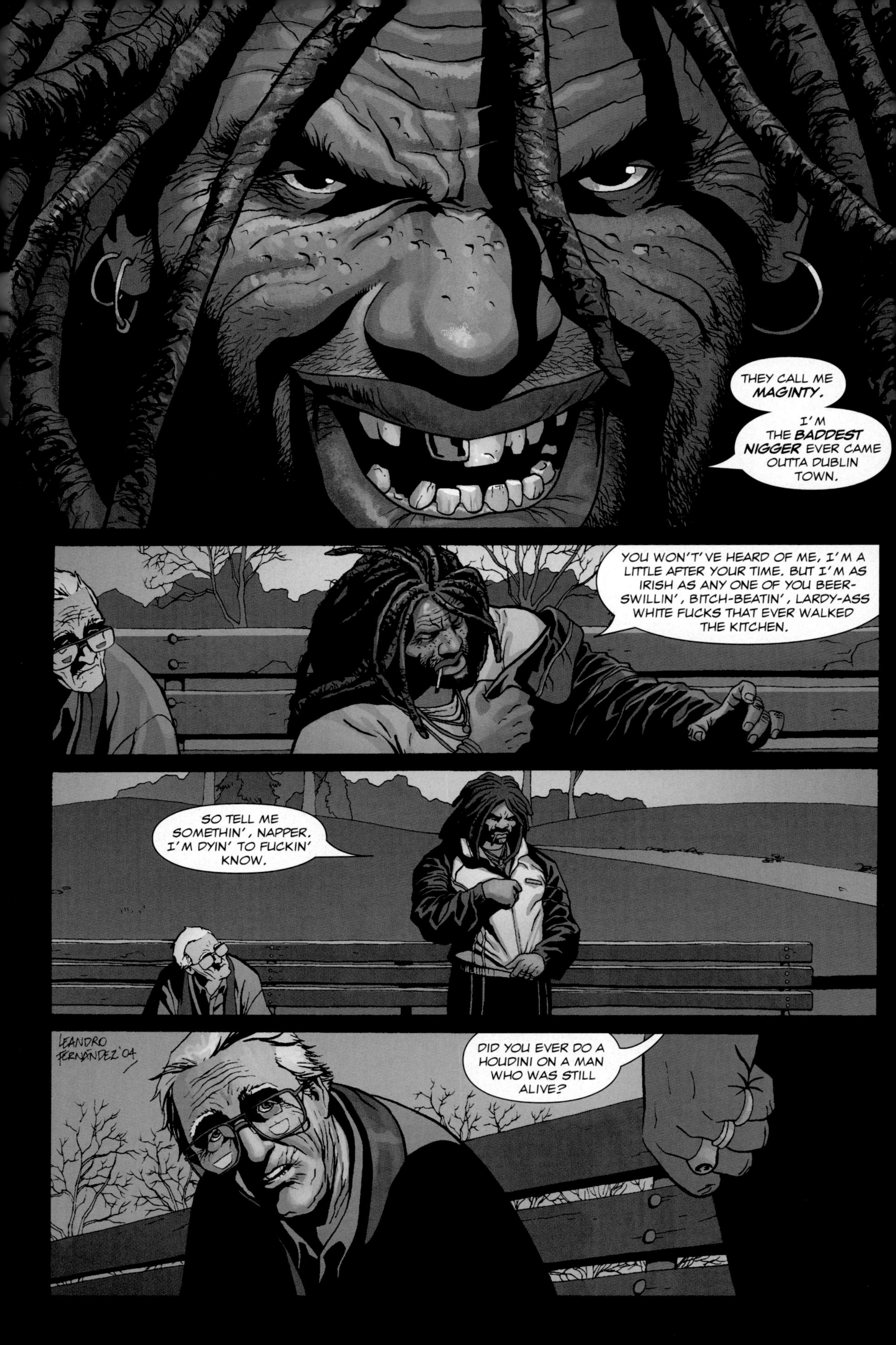
THEY CALL ME MAGINTY.
I'M THE BADDEST NIGGER EVER CAME OUTTA DUBLIN TOWN.
YOU WON'T'VE HEARD OF ME, I'M A LITTLE AFTER YOUR TIME. BUT I'M AS IRISH AS ANY ONE OF YOU BEER-SWILLIN', BITCH-BEATIN', LARDY-ASS WHITE FUCKS THAT EVER WALKED THE KITCHEN.
SO TELL ME SOMETHIN', NAPPER. I'M DYIN' TO FUCKIN' KNOW.
LEANDRO FERNÁNDEZ '04
DID YOU EVER DO A HOUDINI ON A MAN WHO WAS STILL ALIVE?

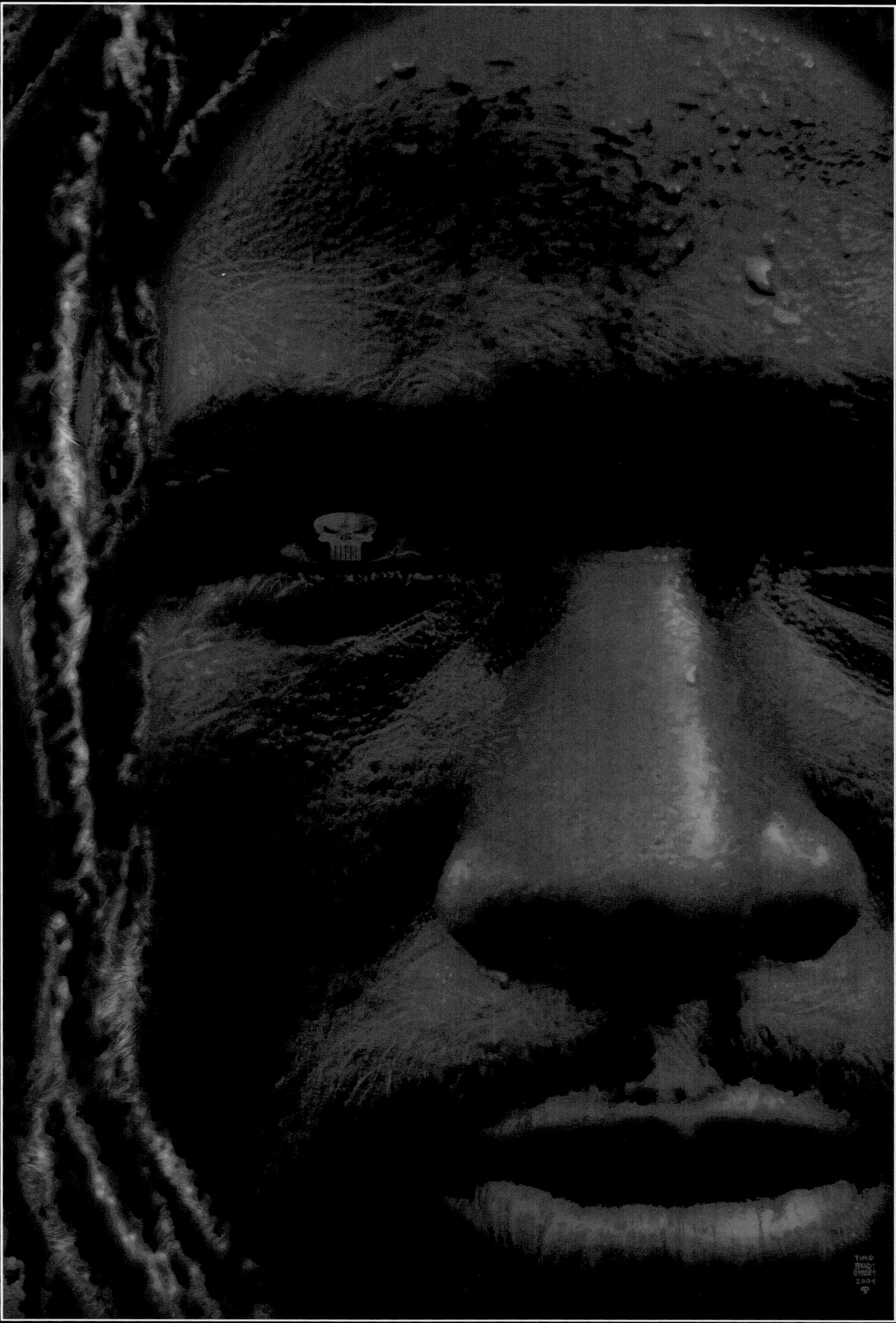

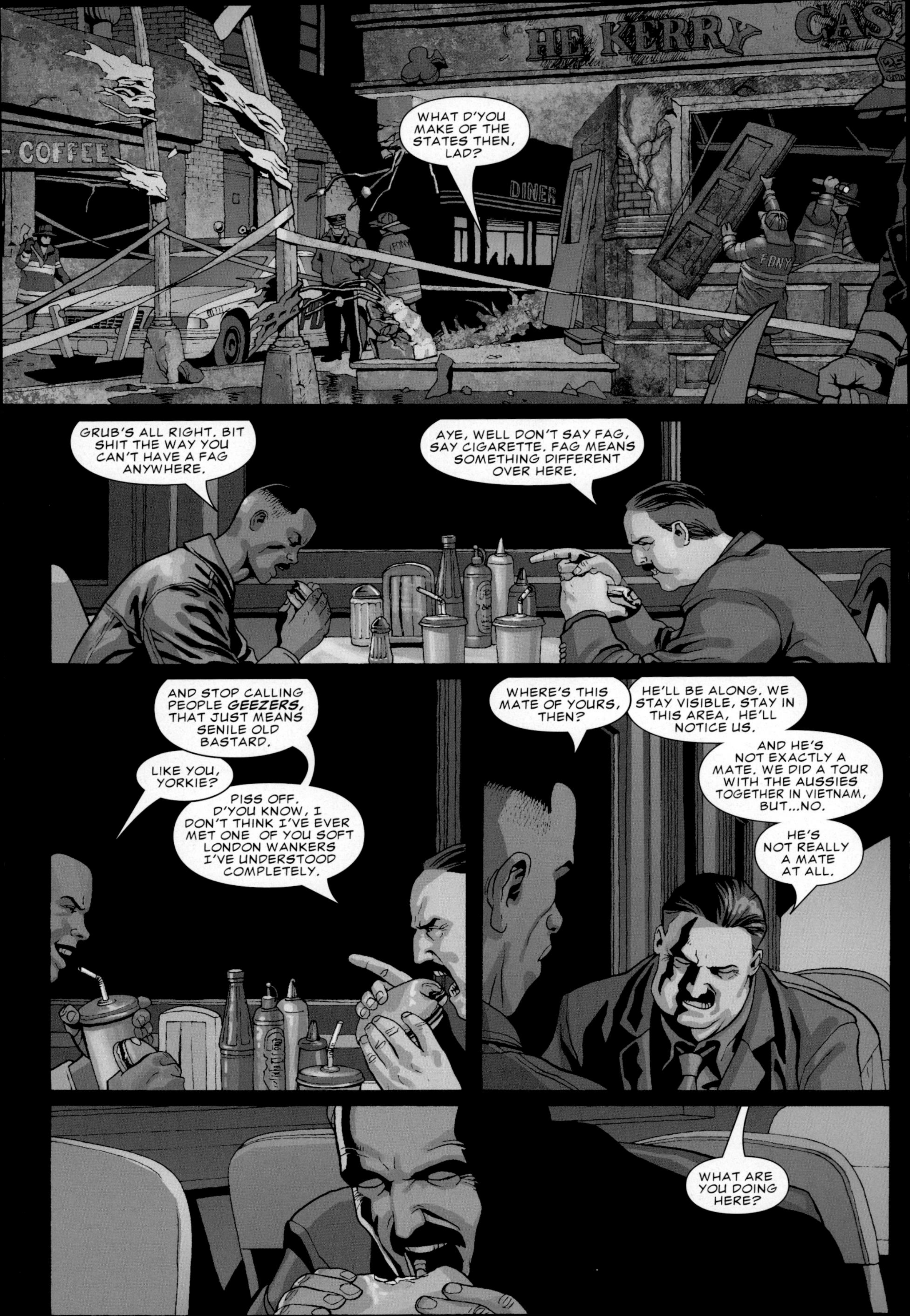
HE KERRY CAS
COFFEE
DINER
FDNY
WHAT D'YOU MAKE OF THE STATES THEN, LAD?
GRUB'S ALL RIGHT. BIT SHIT THE WAY YOU CAN'T HAVE A FAG ANYWHERE.
AYE, WELL DON'T SAY FAG, SAY CIGARETTE. FAG MEANS SOMETHING DIFFERENT OVER HERE.
AND STOP CALLING PEOPLE *GEEZERS,* THAT JUST MEANS SENILE OLD BASTARD.
LIKE YOU, YORKIE?
PISS OFF. D'YOU KNOW, I DON'T THINK I'VE EVER MET ONE OF YOU SOFT LONDON WANKERS I'VE UNDERSTOOD COMPLETELY.
WHERE'S THIS MATE OF YOURS, THEN?
HE'LL BE ALONG. WE STAY VISIBLE, STAY IN THIS AREA, HE'LL NOTICE US.
AND HE'S NOT EXACTLY A MATE. WE DID A TOUR WITH THE AUSSIES TOGETHER IN VIETNAM, BUT...NO.
HE'S NOT REALLY A MATE AT ALL.
WHAT ARE YOU DOING HERE?

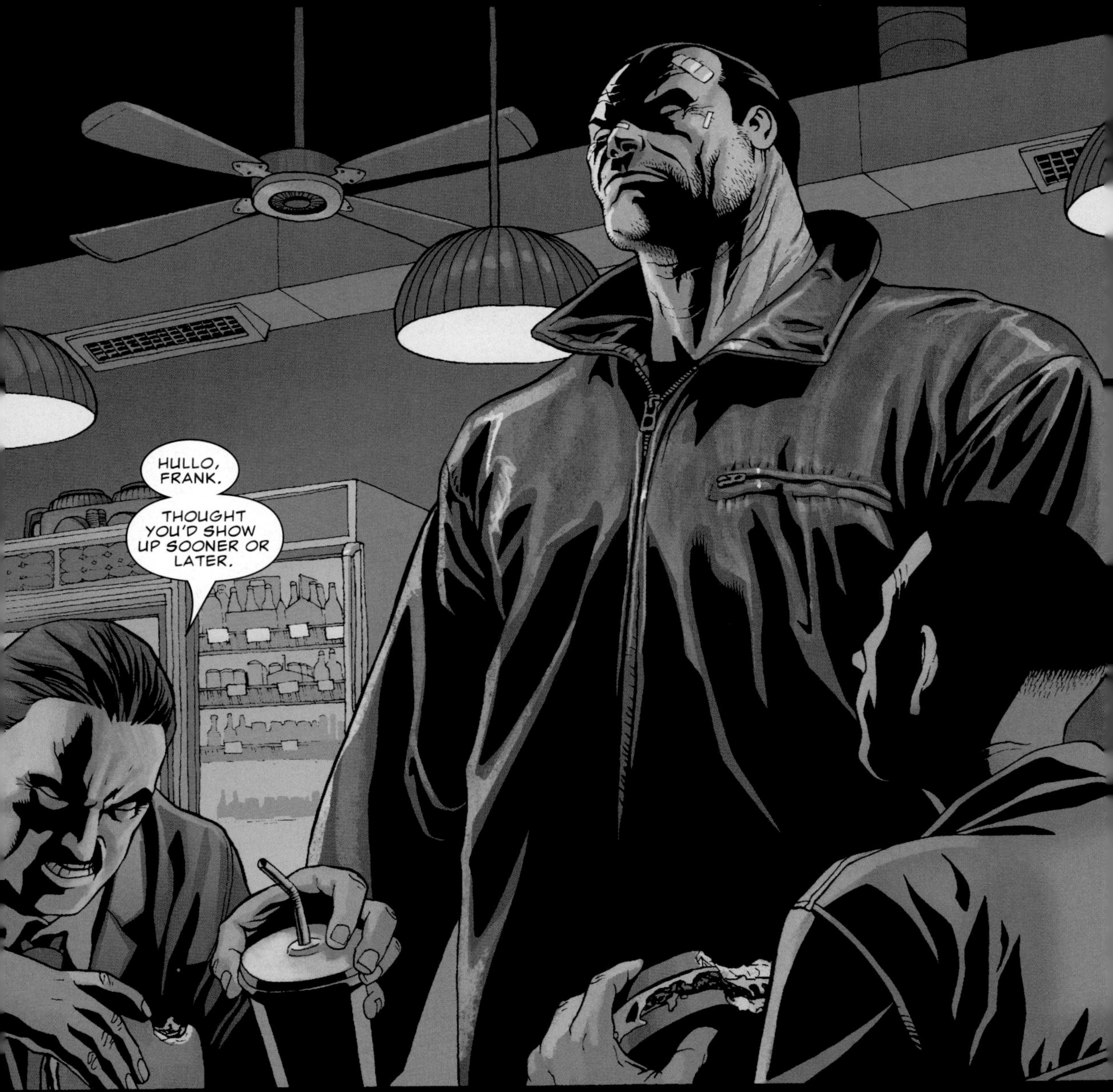
HULLO, FRANK.
THOUGHT YOU'D SHOW UP SOONER OR LATER.

KITCHEN IRISH

PART TWO

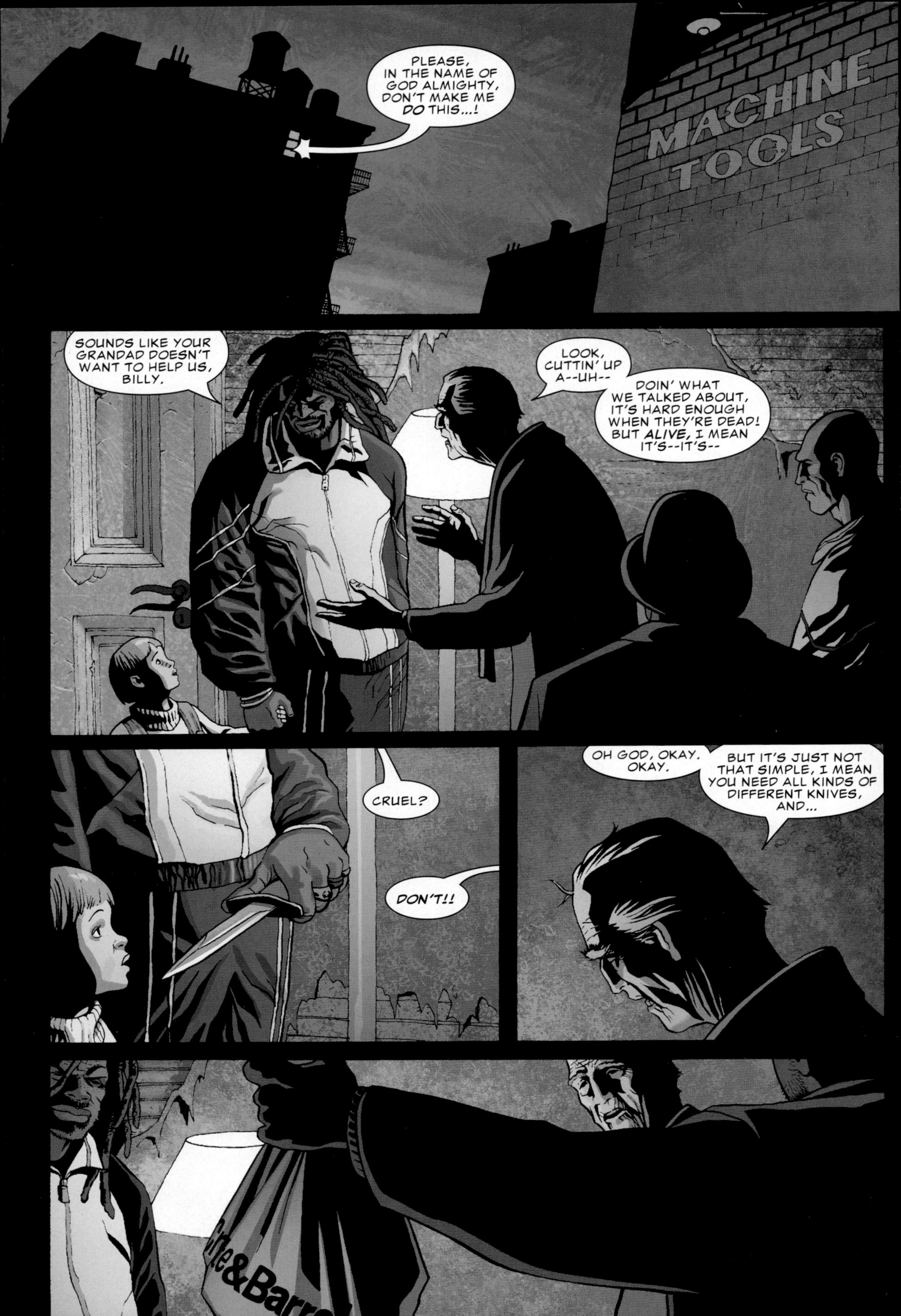
PLEASE, IN THE NAME OF GOD ALMIGHTY, DON'T MAKE ME *DO* THIS...!
MACHINE TOOLS
SOUNDS LIKE YOUR GRANDAD DOESN'T WANT TO HELP US, BILLY.
LOOK, CUTTIN' UP A--UH--
DOIN' WHAT WE TALKED ABOUT, IT'S HARD ENOUGH WHEN THEY'RE DEAD! BUT *ALIVE*, I MEAN IT'S--IT'S--
CRUEL?
DON'T!!
OH GOD, OKAY. OKAY.
BUT IT'S JUST NOT THAT SIMPLE, I MEAN YOU NEED ALL KINDS OF DIFFERENT KNIVES, AND...

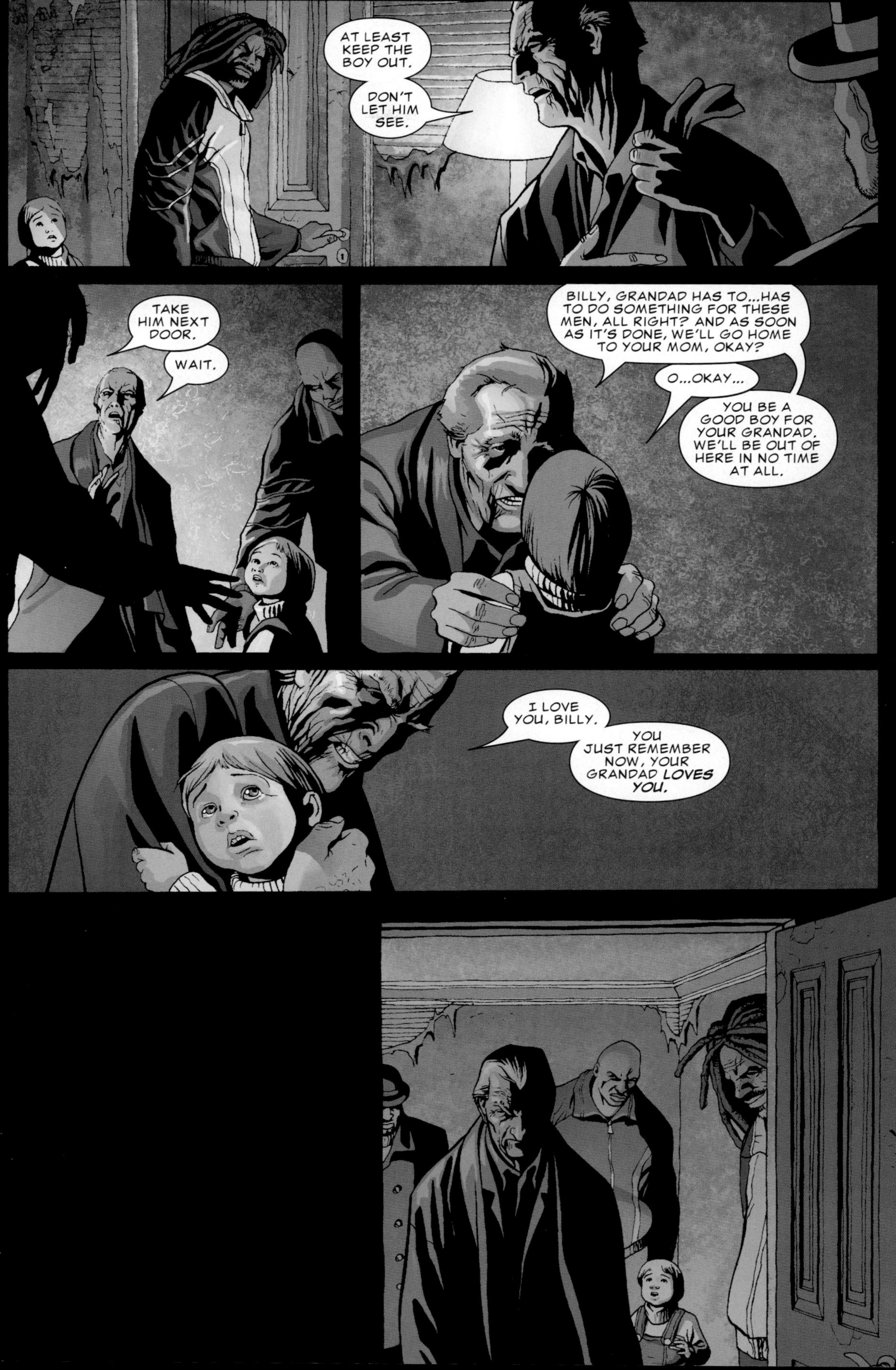
AT LEAST KEEP THE BOY OUT.
DON'T LET HIM SEE.
TAKE HIM NEXT DOOR.
WAIT.
BILLY, GRANDAD HAS TO...HAS TO DO SOMETHING FOR THESE MEN, ALL RIGHT? AND AS SOON AS IT'S DONE, WE'LL GO HOME TO YOUR MOM, OKAY?
O...OKAY...
YOU BE A GOOD BOY FOR YOUR GRANDAD. WE'LL BE OUT OF HERE IN NO TIME AT ALL.
I LOVE YOU, BILLY.
YOU JUST REMEMBER NOW, YOUR GRANDAD LOVES YOU.

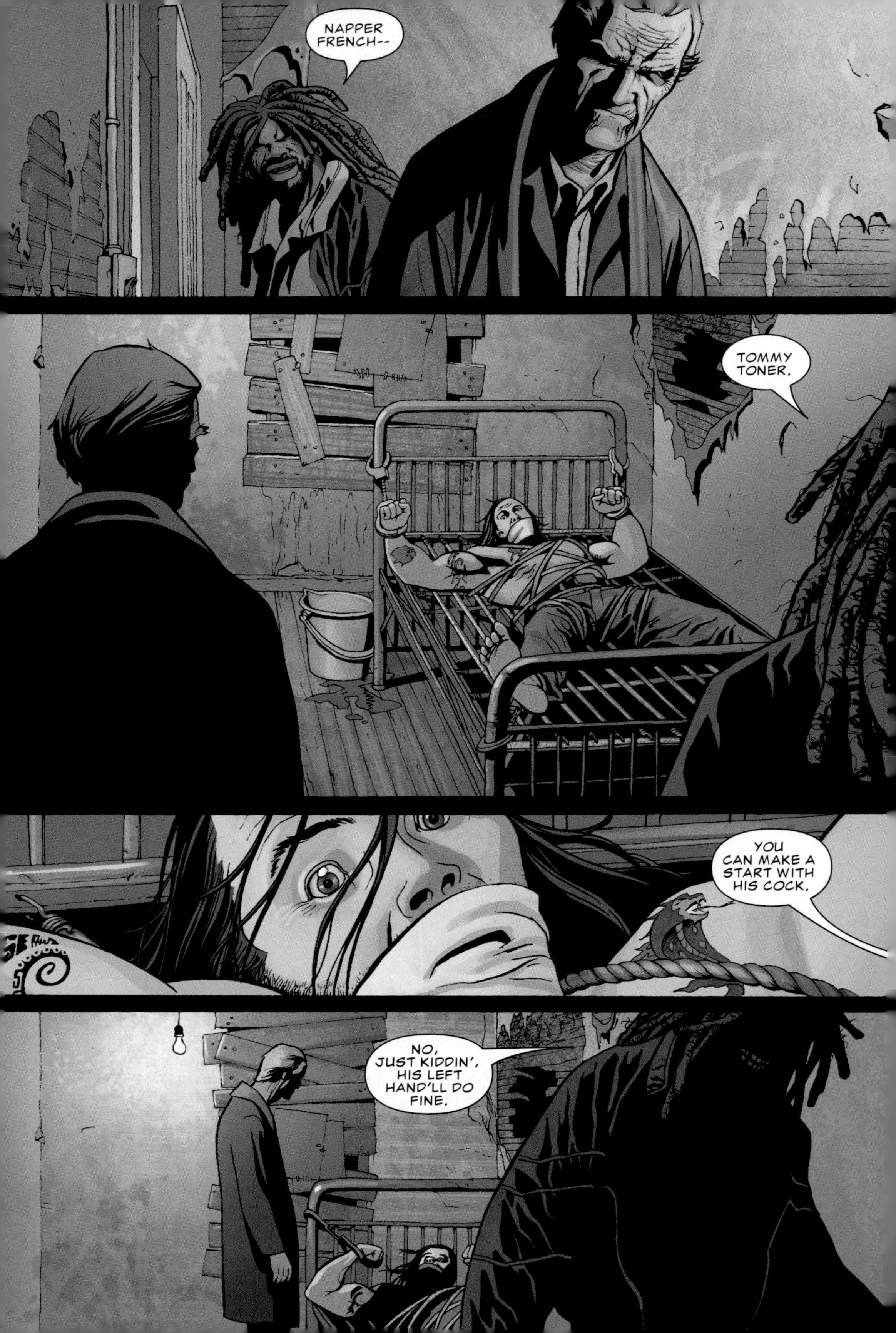
NAPPER FRENCH--
TOMMY TONER.
YOU CAN MAKE A START WITH HIS COCK.
NO, JUST KIDDIN', HIS LEFT HAND'LL DO FINE.

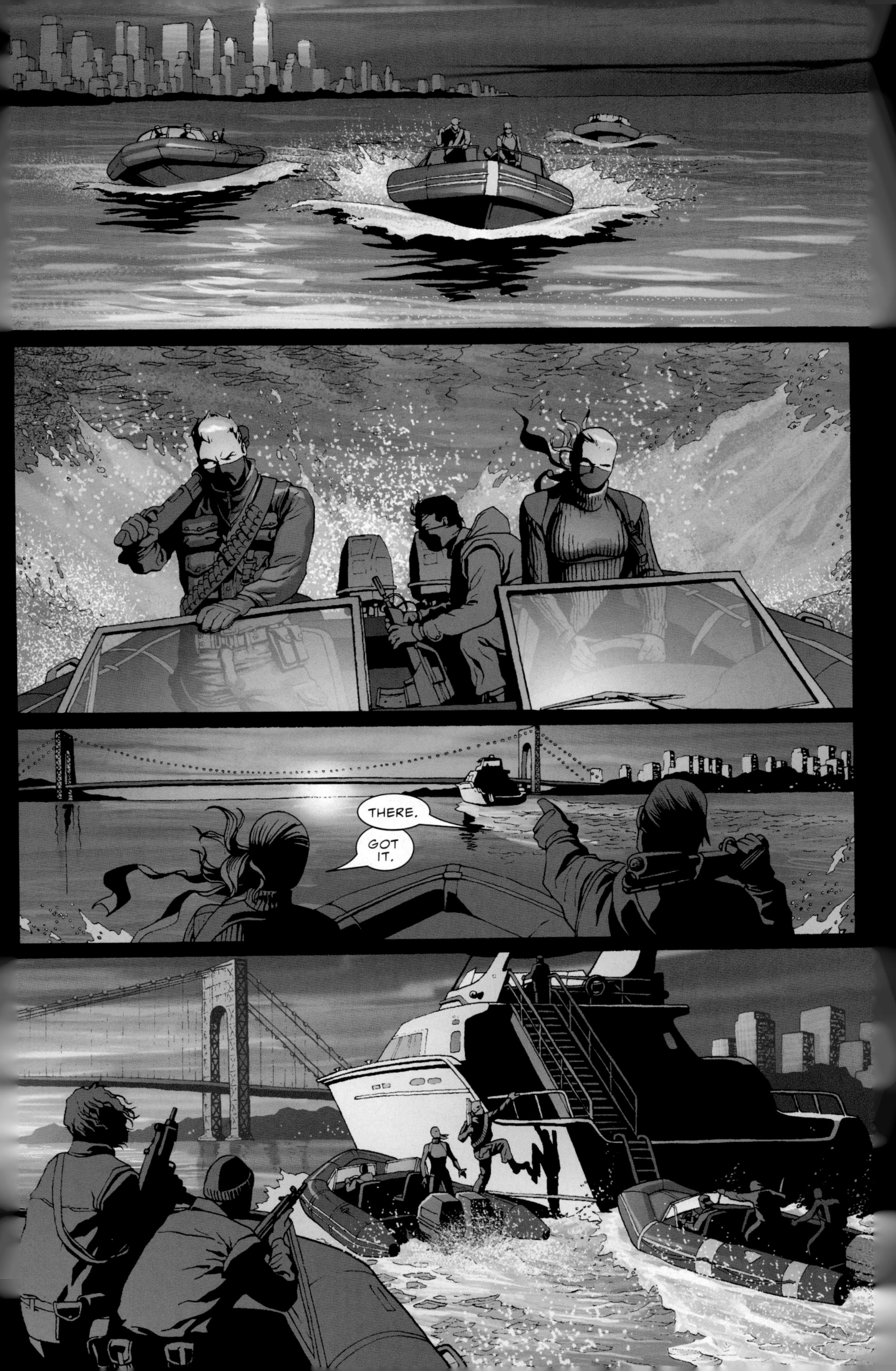
THERE.
GOT IT.

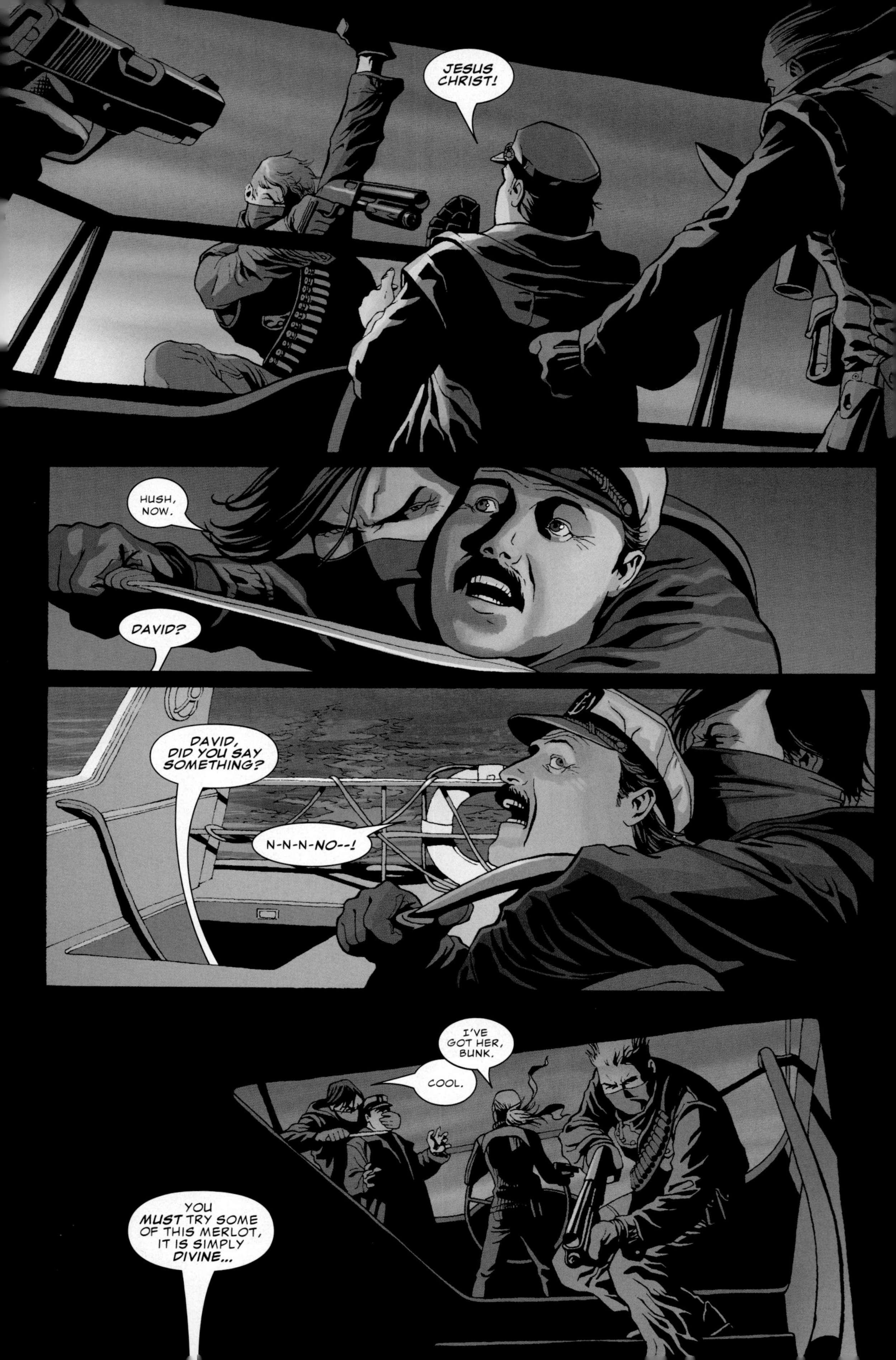
JESUS CHRIST!
HUSH, NOW.
DAVID?
DAVID, DID YOU SAY SOMETHING?
N-N-N-NO--!
I'VE GOT HER, BUNK.
COOL.
YOU MUST TRY SOME OF THIS MERLOT, IT IS SIMPLY DIVINE...

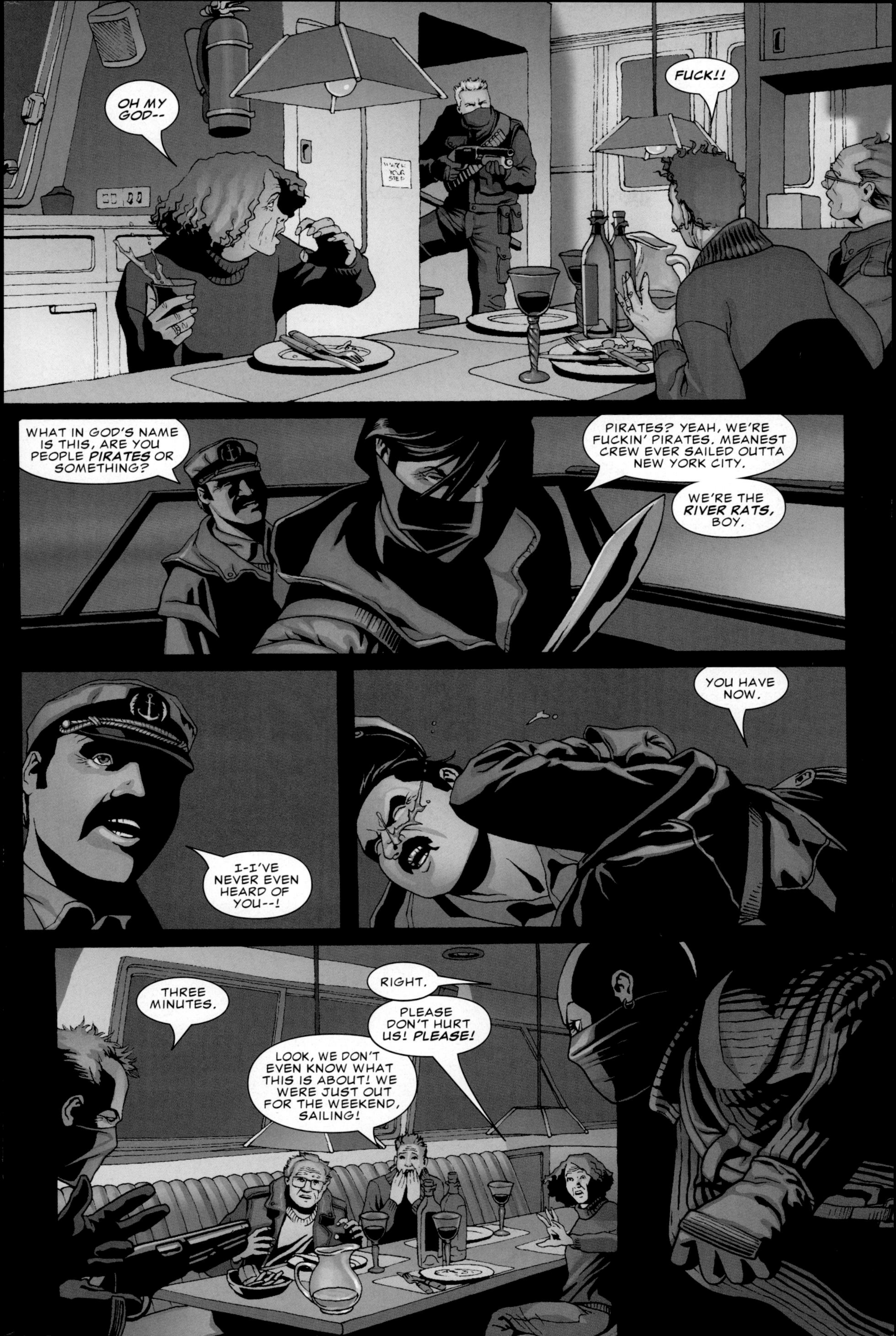
OH MY GOD--
WATCH YOUR STEP
FUCK!!
WHAT IN GOD'S NAME IS THIS, ARE YOU PEOPLE **PIRATES** OR SOMETHING?
PIRATES? YEAH, WE'RE FUCKIN' PIRATES. MEANEST CREW EVER SAILED OUTTA NEW YORK CITY.
WE'RE THE **RIVER RATS,** BOY.
I-I'VE NEVER EVEN HEARD OF YOU--!
YOU HAVE NOW.
THREE MINUTES.
RIGHT.
PLEASE DON'T HURT US! **PLEASE!**
LOOK, WE DON'T EVEN KNOW WHAT THIS IS ABOUT! WE WERE JUST OUT FOR THE WEEKEND, SAILING!

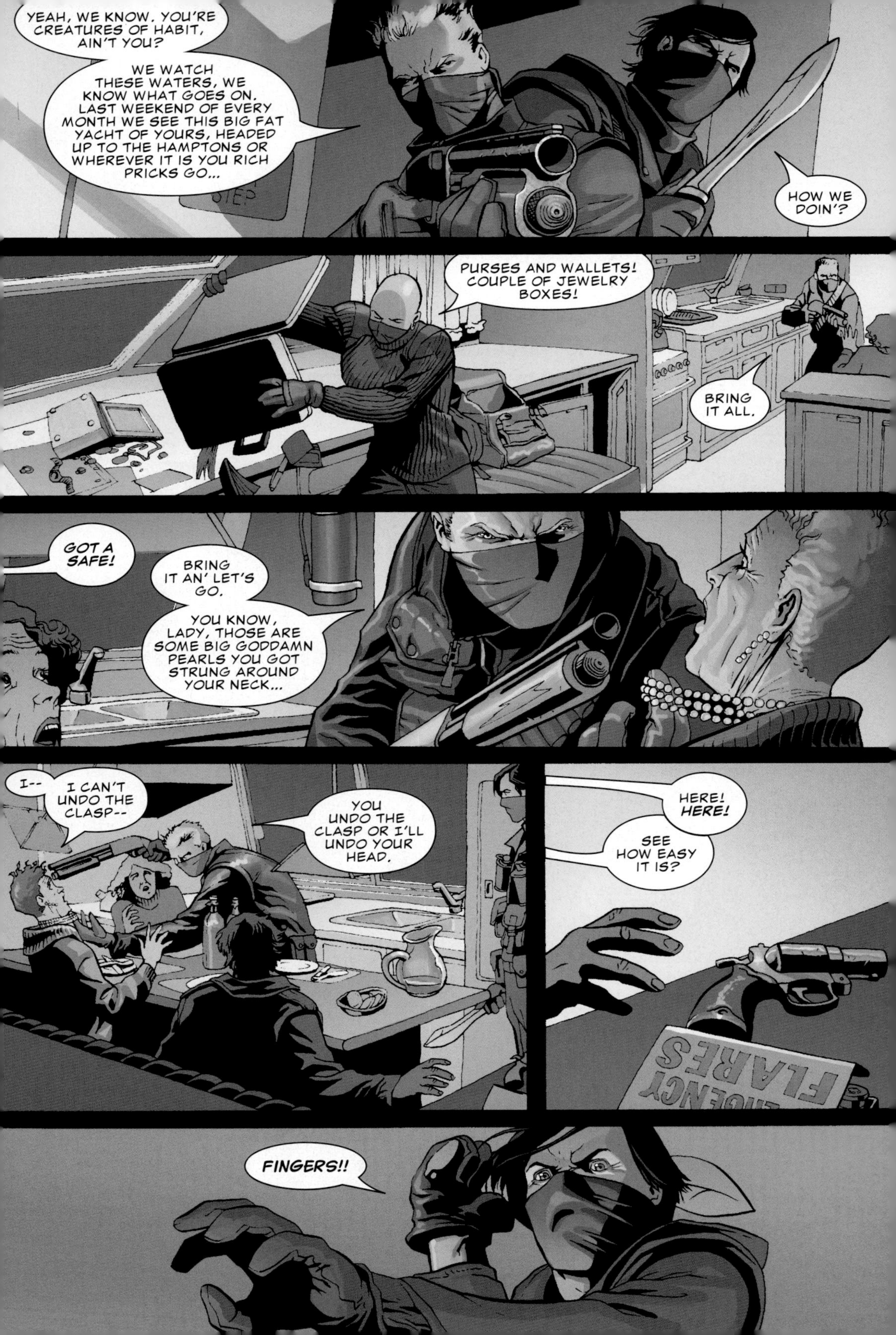
YEAH, WE KNOW. YOU'RE CREATURES OF HABIT, AIN'T YOU?
WE WATCH THESE WATERS, WE KNOW WHAT GOES ON. LAST WEEKEND OF EVERY MONTH WE SEE THIS BIG FAT YACHT OF YOURS, HEADED UP TO THE HAMPTONS OR WHEREVER IT IS YOU RICH PRICKS GO...
HOW WE DOIN'?
PURSES AND WALLETS! COUPLE OF JEWELRY BOXES!
BRING IT ALL.
GOT A SAFE!
BRING IT AN' LET'S GO.
YOU KNOW, LADY, THOSE ARE SOME BIG GODDAMN PEARLS YOU GOT STRUNG AROUND YOUR NECK...
I--
I CAN'T UNDO THE CLASP--
YOU UNDO THE CLASP OR I'LL UNDO YOUR HEAD.
HERE! HERE!
SEE HOW EASY IT IS?
FLARES
FINGERS!!

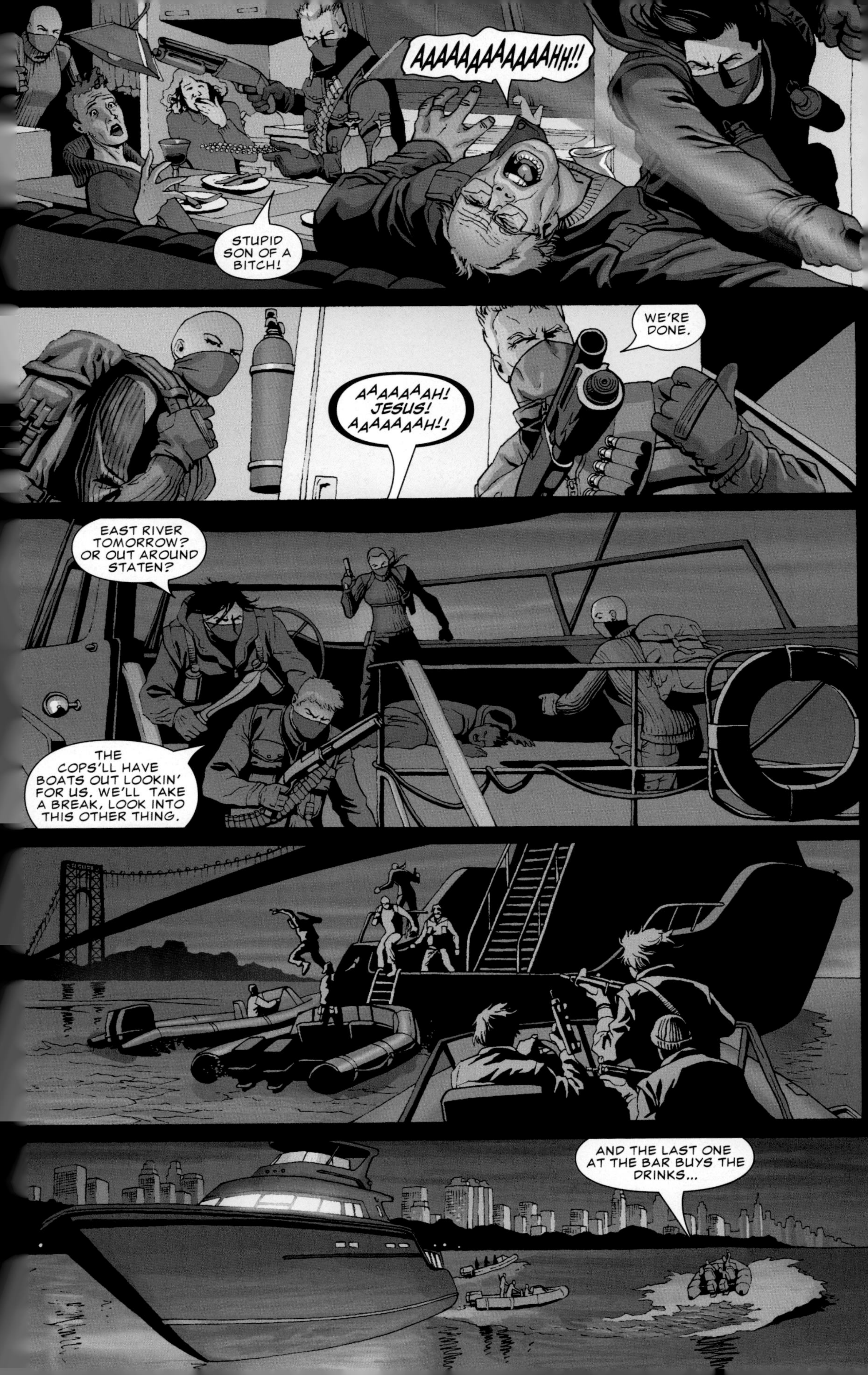
AAAAAAAAAAAAHH!!
STUPID SON OF A BITCH!
WE'RE DONE.
AAAAAAAH! JESUS! AAAAAAAH!!
EAST RIVER TOMORROW? OR OUT AROUND STATEN?
THE COPS'LL HAVE BOATS OUT LOOKIN' FOR US. WE'LL TAKE A BREAK, LOOK INTO THIS OTHER THING.
AND THE LAST ONE AT THE BAR BUYS THE DRINKS...

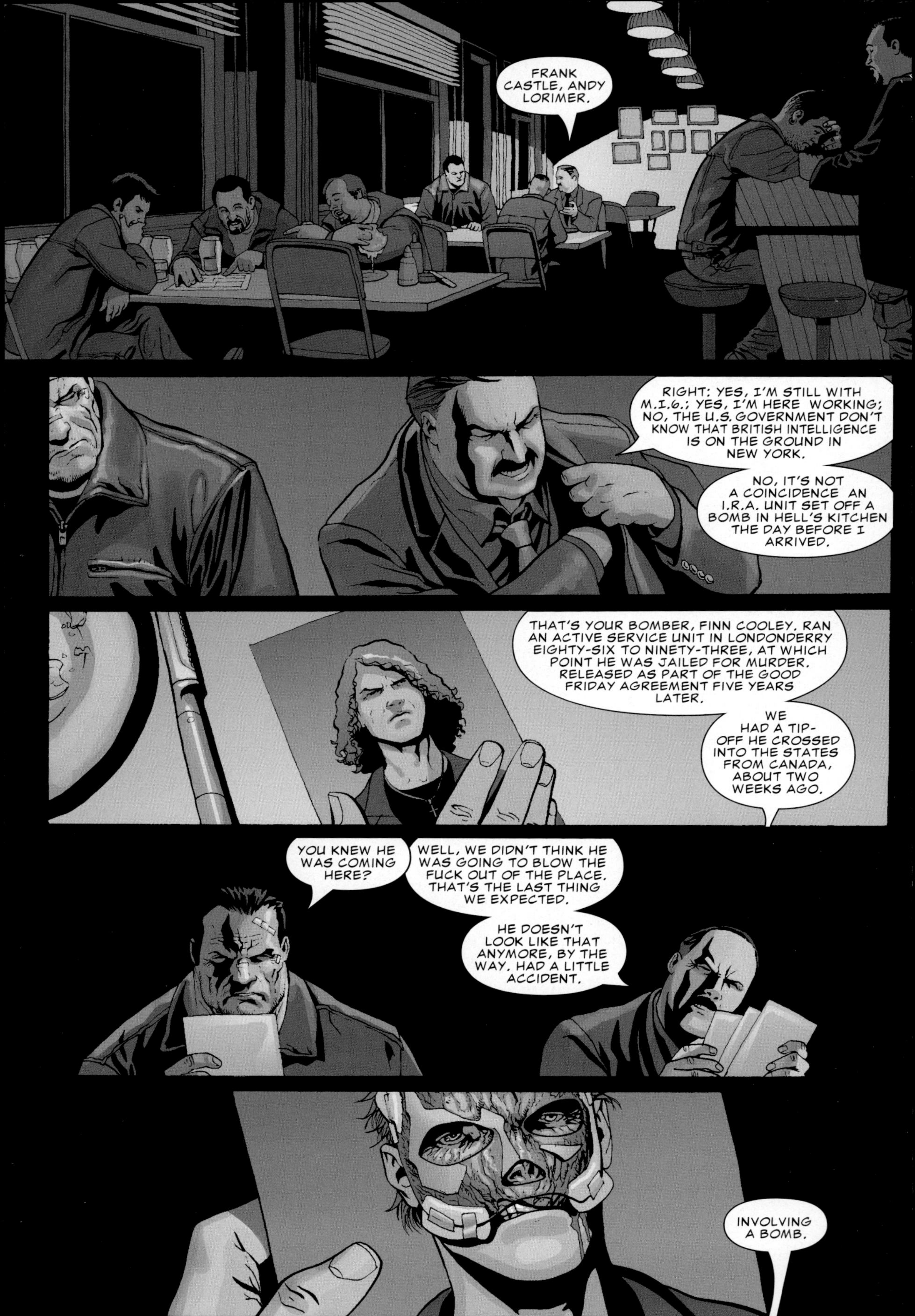
FRANK CASTLE, ANDY LORIMER.
RIGHT: YES, I'M STILL WITH M.I.6.; YES, I'M HERE WORKING; NO, THE U.S. GOVERNMENT DON'T KNOW THAT BRITISH INTELLIGENCE IS ON THE GROUND IN NEW YORK.
NO, IT'S NOT A COINCIDENCE AN I.R.A. UNIT SET OFF A BOMB IN HELL'S KITCHEN THE DAY BEFORE I ARRIVED.
THAT'S YOUR BOMBER, FINN COOLEY. RAN AN ACTIVE SERVICE UNIT IN LONDONDERRY EIGHTY-SIX TO NINETY-THREE, AT WHICH POINT HE WAS JAILED FOR MURDER. RELEASED AS PART OF THE GOOD FRIDAY AGREEMENT FIVE YEARS LATER.
WE HAD A TIP-OFF HE CROSSED INTO THE STATES FROM CANADA, ABOUT TWO WEEKS AGO.
YOU KNEW HE WAS COMING HERE?
WELL, WE DIDN'T THINK HE WAS GOING TO BLOW THE FUCK OUT OF THE PLACE. THAT'S THE LAST THING WE EXPECTED.
HE DOESN'T LOOK LIKE THAT ANYMORE, BY THE WAY. HAD A LITTLE ACCIDENT.
INVOLVING A BOMB.

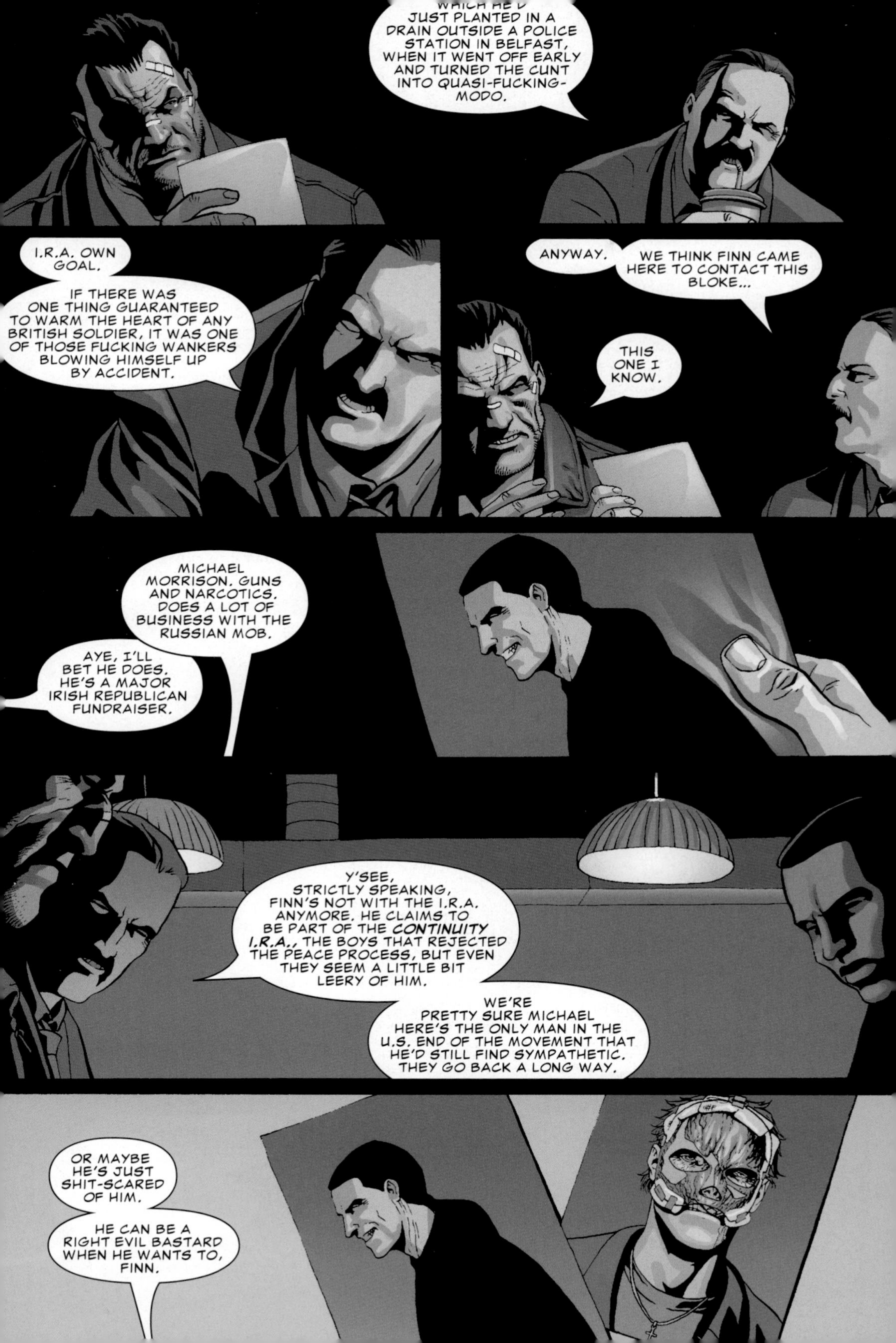
WHICH HE'D JUST PLANTED IN A DRAIN OUTSIDE A POLICE STATION IN BELFAST, WHEN IT WENT OFF EARLY AND TURNED THE CUNT INTO QUASI-FUCKING-MODO.
I.R.A. OWN GOAL.
IF THERE WAS ONE THING GUARANTEED TO WARM THE HEART OF ANY BRITISH SOLDIER, IT WAS ONE OF THOSE FUCKING WANKERS BLOWING HIMSELF UP BY ACCIDENT.
ANYWAY.
WE THINK FINN CAME HERE TO CONTACT THIS BLOKE...
THIS ONE I KNOW.
MICHAEL MORRISON. GUNS AND NARCOTICS. DOES A LOT OF BUSINESS WITH THE RUSSIAN MOB.
AYE, I'LL BET HE DOES. HE'S A MAJOR IRISH REPUBLICAN FUNDRAISER.
Y'SEE, STRICTLY SPEAKING, FINN'S NOT WITH THE I.R.A. ANYMORE. HE CLAIMS TO BE PART OF THE *CONTINUITY I.R.A.*, THE BOYS THAT REJECTED THE PEACE PROCESS, BUT EVEN THEY SEEM A LITTLE BIT LEERY OF HIM.
WE'RE PRETTY SURE MICHAEL HERE'S THE ONLY MAN IN THE U.S. END OF THE MOVEMENT THAT HE'D STILL FIND SYMPATHETIC. THEY GO BACK A LONG WAY.
OR MAYBE HE'S JUST SHIT-SCARED OF HIM.
HE CAN BE A RIGHT EVIL BASTARD WHEN HE WANTS TO, FINN.

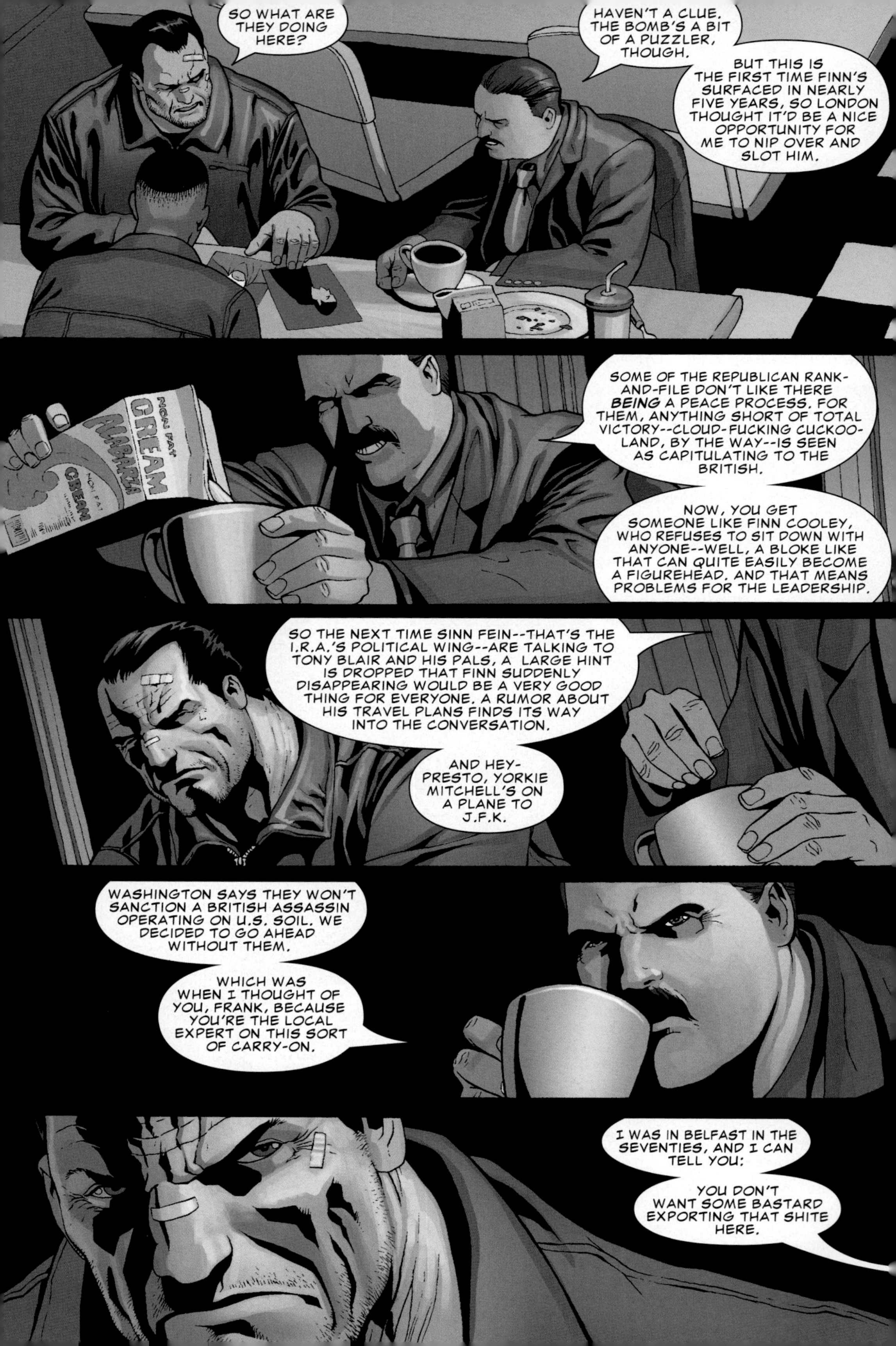

SO WHAT ARE THEY DOING HERE?
HAVEN'T A CLUE. THE BOMB'S A BIT OF A PUZZLER, THOUGH.
BUT THIS IS THE FIRST TIME FINN'S SURFACED IN NEARLY FIVE YEARS, SO LONDON THOUGHT IT'D BE A NICE OPPORTUNITY FOR ME TO NIP OVER AND SLOT HIM.
NON FAT CREAM
SOME OF THE REPUBLICAN RANK-AND-FILE DON'T LIKE THERE *BEING* A PEACE PROCESS. FOR THEM, ANYTHING SHORT OF TOTAL VICTORY--CLOUD-FUCKING CUCKOO-LAND, BY THE WAY--IS SEEN AS CAPITULATING TO THE BRITISH.
NOW, YOU GET SOMEONE LIKE FINN COOLEY, WHO REFUSES TO SIT DOWN WITH ANYONE--WELL, A BLOKE LIKE THAT CAN QUITE EASILY BECOME A FIGUREHEAD. AND THAT MEANS PROBLEMS FOR THE LEADERSHIP.
SO THE NEXT TIME SINN FEIN--THAT'S THE I.R.A.'S POLITICAL WING--ARE TALKING TO TONY BLAIR AND HIS PALS, A LARGE HINT IS DROPPED THAT FINN SUDDENLY DISAPPEARING WOULD BE A VERY GOOD THING FOR EVERYONE. A RUMOR ABOUT HIS TRAVEL PLANS FINDS ITS WAY INTO THE CONVERSATION.
AND HEY-PRESTO, YORKIE MITCHELL'S ON A PLANE TO J.F.K.
WASHINGTON SAYS THEY WON'T SANCTION A BRITISH ASSASSIN OPERATING ON U.S. SOIL. WE DECIDED TO GO AHEAD WITHOUT THEM.
WHICH WAS WHEN I THOUGHT OF YOU, FRANK, BECAUSE YOU'RE THE LOCAL EXPERT ON THIS SORT OF CARRY-ON.
I WAS IN BELFAST IN THE SEVENTIES, AND I CAN TELL YOU:
YOU DON'T WANT SOME BASTARD EXPORTING THAT SHITE HERE.

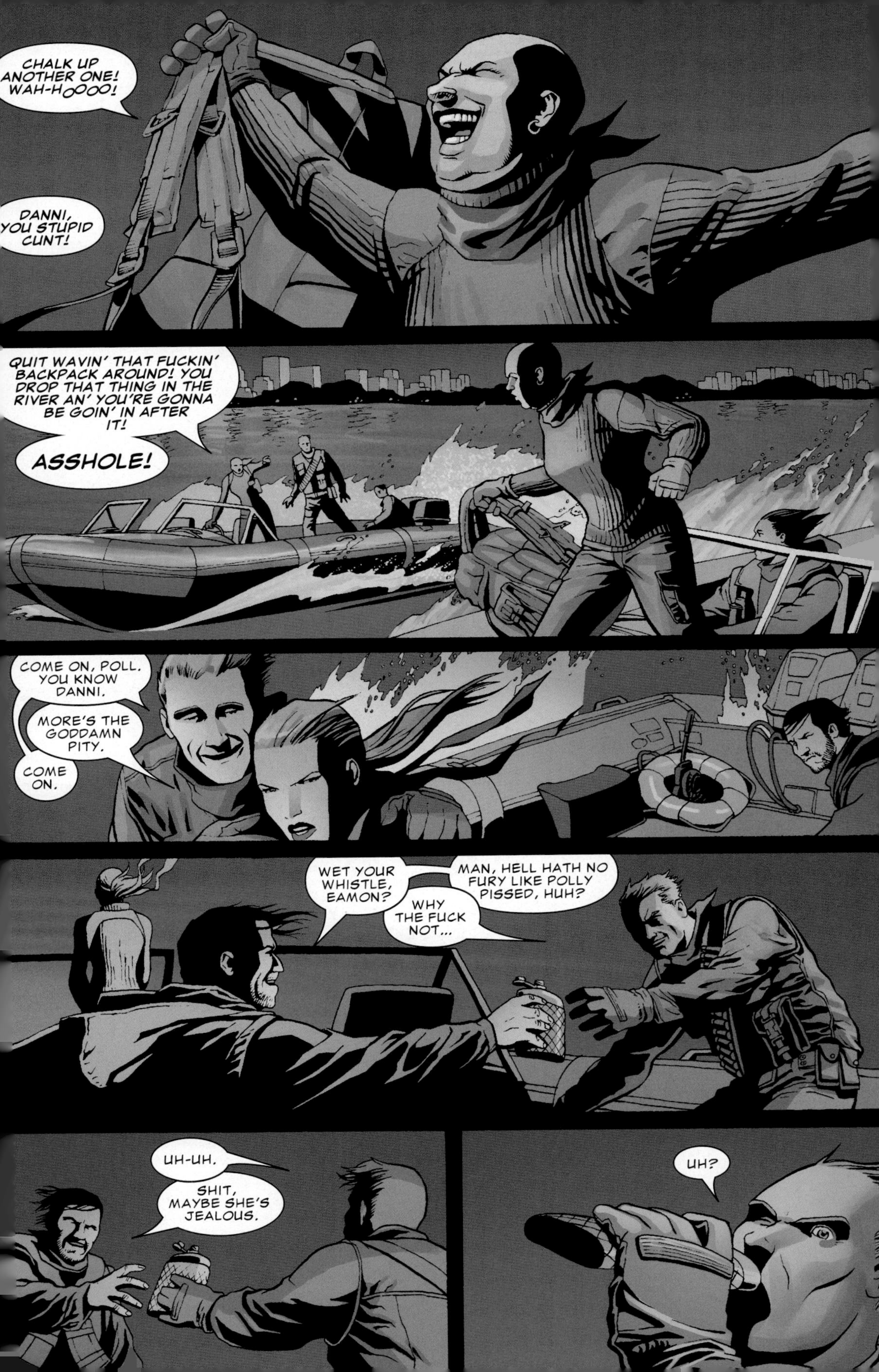
CHALK UP ANOTHER ONE! WAH-HOOOO!
DANNI, YOU STUPID CUNT!
QUIT WAVIN' THAT FUCKIN' BACKPACK AROUND! YOU DROP THAT THING IN THE RIVER AN' YOU'RE GONNA BE GOIN' IN AFTER IT!
ASSHOLE!
COME ON, POLL. YOU KNOW DANNI.
MORE'S THE GODDAMN PITY.
COME ON.
WET YOUR WHISTLE, EAMON?
WHY THE FUCK NOT...
MAN, HELL HATH NO FURY LIKE POLLY PISSED, HUH?
UH-UH.
SHIT, MAYBE SHE'S JEALOUS.
UH?

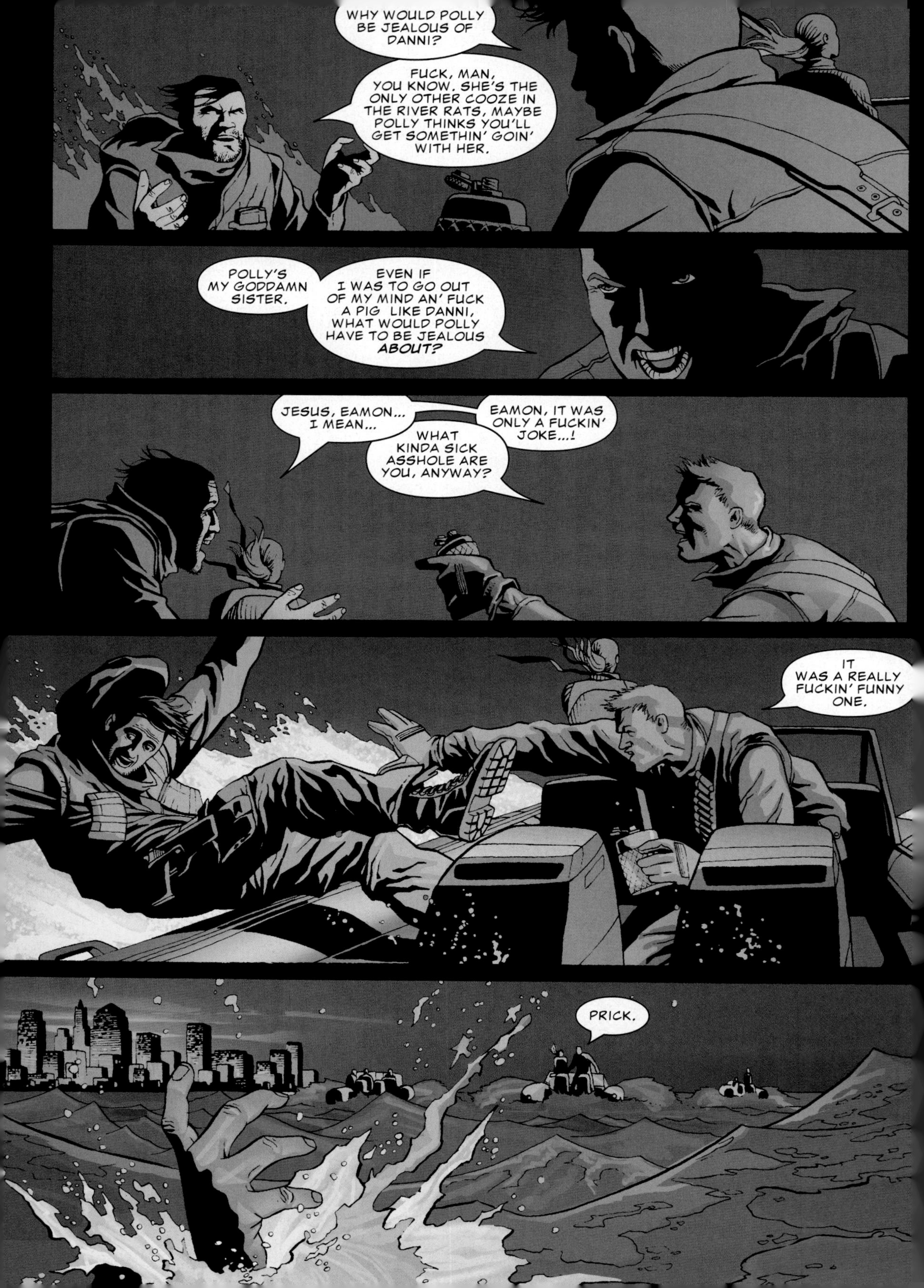
WHY WOULD POLLY BE JEALOUS OF DANNI?
FUCK, MAN, YOU KNOW. SHE'S THE ONLY OTHER COOZE IN THE RIVER RATS, MAYBE POLLY THINKS YOU'LL GET SOMETHIN' GOIN' WITH HER.
POLLY'S MY GODDAMN SISTER.
EVEN IF I WAS TO GO OUT OF MY MIND AN' FUCK A PIG LIKE DANNI, WHAT WOULD POLLY HAVE TO BE JEALOUS *ABOUT?*
JESUS, EAMON... I MEAN...
WHAT KINDA SICK ASSHOLE ARE YOU, ANYWAY?
EAMON, IT WAS ONLY A FUCKIN' JOKE...!
IT WAS A REALLY FUCKIN' FUNNY ONE.
PRICK.

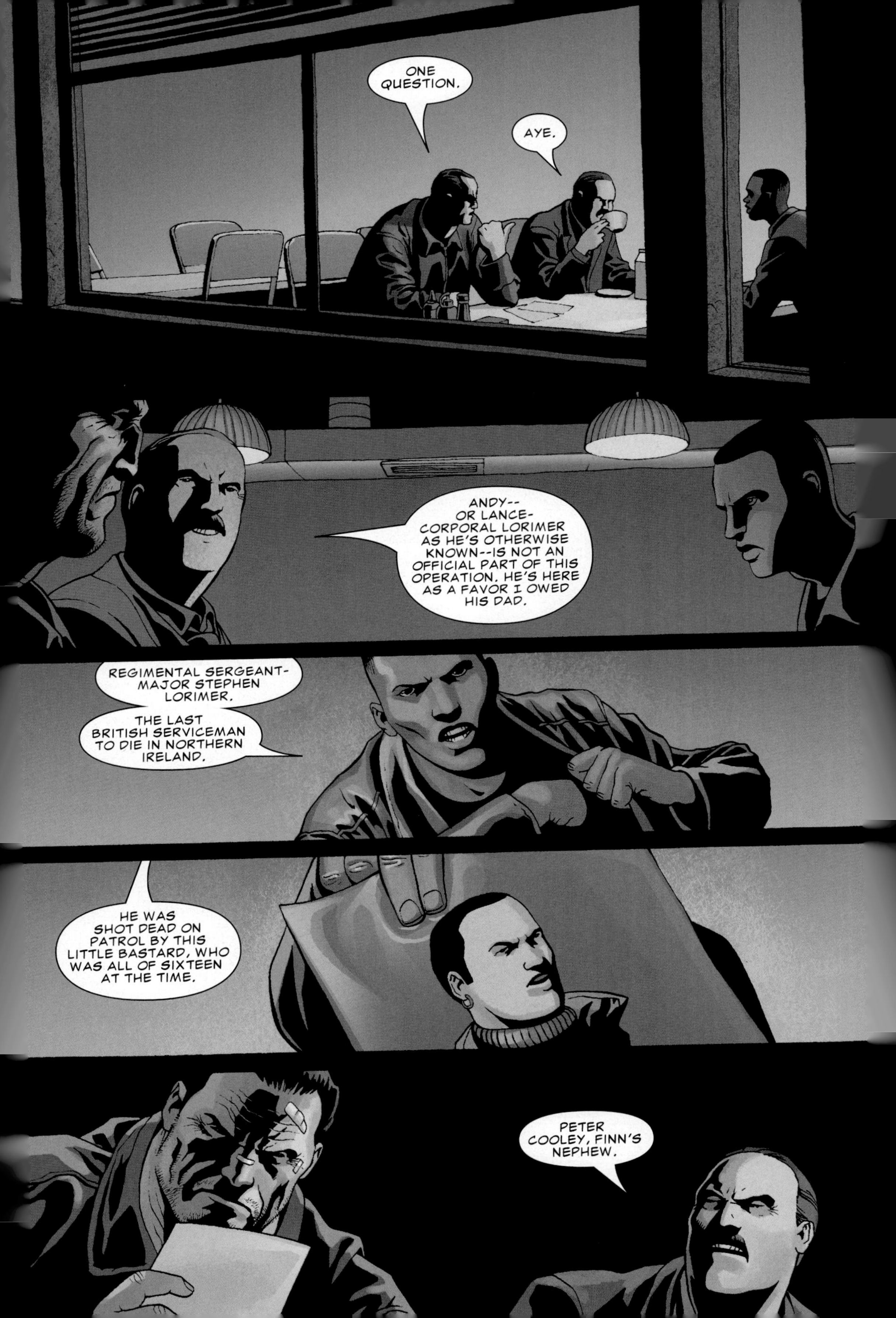
ONE QUESTION.
AYE.
ANDY-- OR LANCE-CORPORAL LORIMER AS HE'S OTHERWISE KNOWN--IS NOT AN OFFICIAL PART OF THIS OPERATION. HE'S HERE AS A FAVOR I OWED HIS DAD.
REGIMENTAL SERGEANT-MAJOR STEPHEN LORIMER.
THE LAST BRITISH SERVICEMAN TO DIE IN NORTHERN IRELAND.
HE WAS SHOT DEAD ON PATROL BY THIS LITTLE BASTARD, WHO WAS ALL OF SIXTEEN AT THE TIME.
PETER COOLEY, FINN'S NEPHEW.

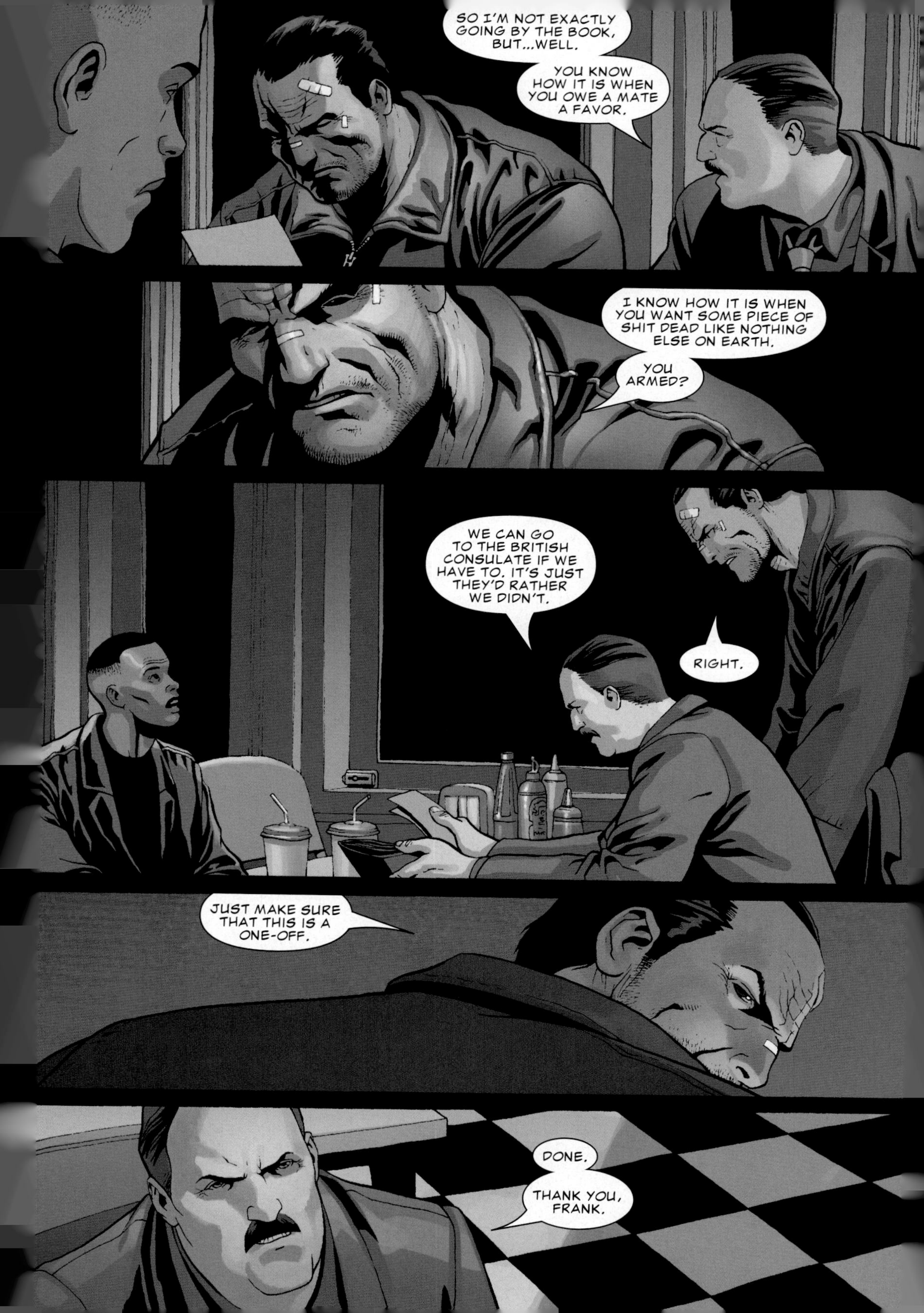
SO I'M NOT EXACTLY GOING BY THE BOOK, BUT...WELL.
YOU KNOW HOW IT IS WHEN YOU OWE A MATE A FAVOR.
I KNOW HOW IT IS WHEN YOU WANT SOME PIECE OF SHIT DEAD LIKE NOTHING ELSE ON EARTH.
YOU ARMED?
WE CAN GO TO THE BRITISH CONSULATE IF WE HAVE TO. IT'S JUST THEY'D RATHER WE DIDN'T.
RIGHT.
JUST MAKE SURE THAT THIS IS A ONE-OFF.
DONE.
THANK YOU, FRANK.

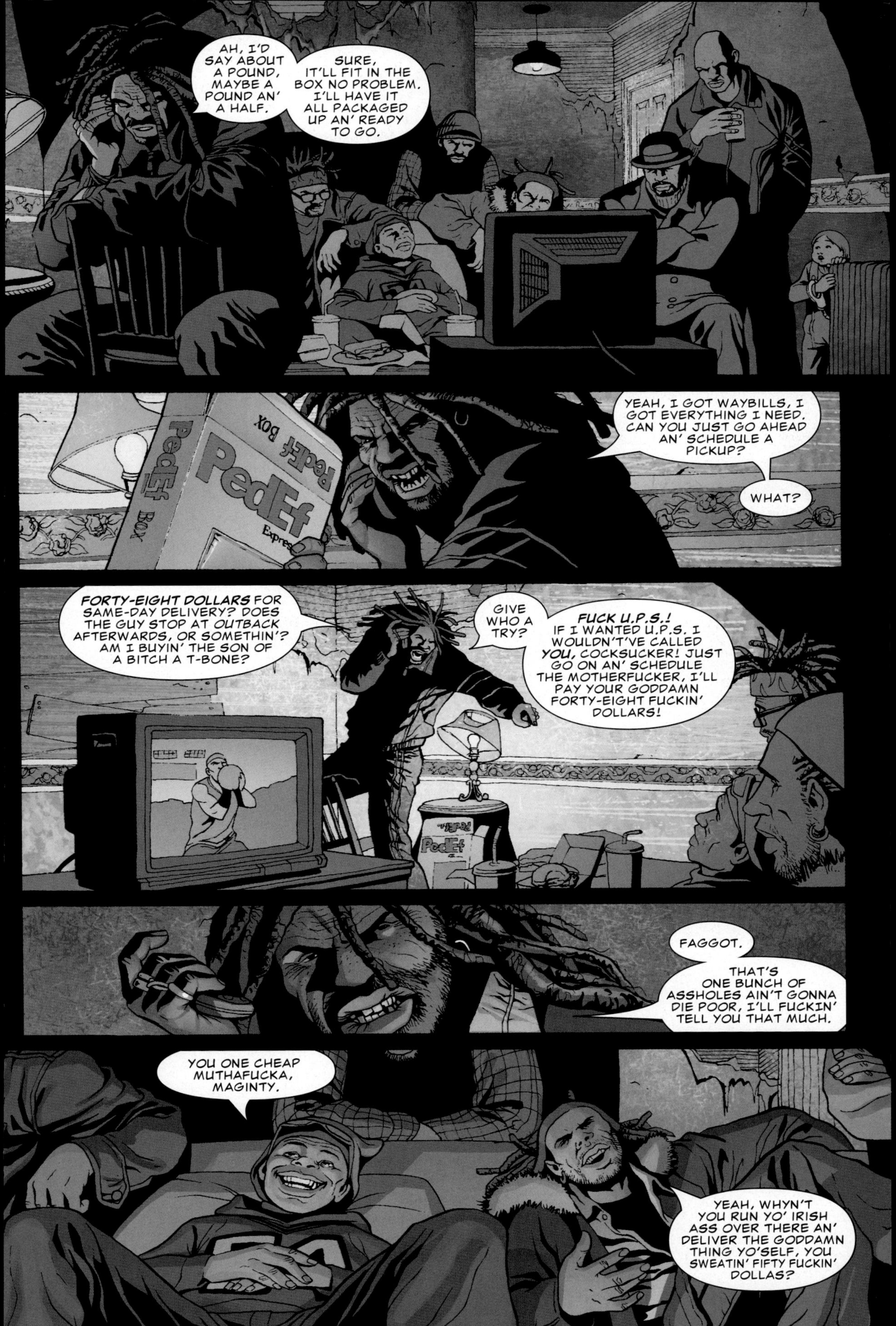
AH, I'D SAY ABOUT A POUND, MAYBE A POUND AN' A HALF.
SURE, IT'LL FIT IN THE BOX NO PROBLEM. I'LL HAVE IT ALL PACKAGED UP AN' READY TO GO.
PedEf BOX
PedEf
YEAH, I GOT WAYBILLS, I GOT EVERYTHING I NEED. CAN YOU JUST GO AHEAD AN' SCHEDULE A PICKUP?
WHAT?
FORTY-EIGHT DOLLARS FOR SAME-DAY DELIVERY? DOES THE GUY STOP AT OUTBACK AFTERWARDS, OR SOMETHIN'? AM I BUYIN' THE SON OF A BITCH A T-BONE?
GIVE WHO A TRY?
FUCK U.P.S.! IF I WANTED U.P.S. I WOULDN'T'VE CALLED YOU, COCKSUCKER! JUST GO ON AN' SCHEDULE THE MOTHERFUCKER, I'LL PAY YOUR GODDAMN FORTY-EIGHT FUCKIN' DOLLARS!
FAGGOT.
THAT'S ONE BUNCH OF ASSHOLES AIN'T GONNA DIE POOR, I'LL FUCKIN' TELL YOU THAT MUCH.
YOU ONE CHEAP MUTHAFUCKA, MAGINTY.
YEAH, WHYN'T YOU RUN YO' IRISH ASS OVER THERE AN' DELIVER THE GODDAMN THING YO'SELF, YOU SWEATIN' FIFTY FUCKIN' DOLLAS?

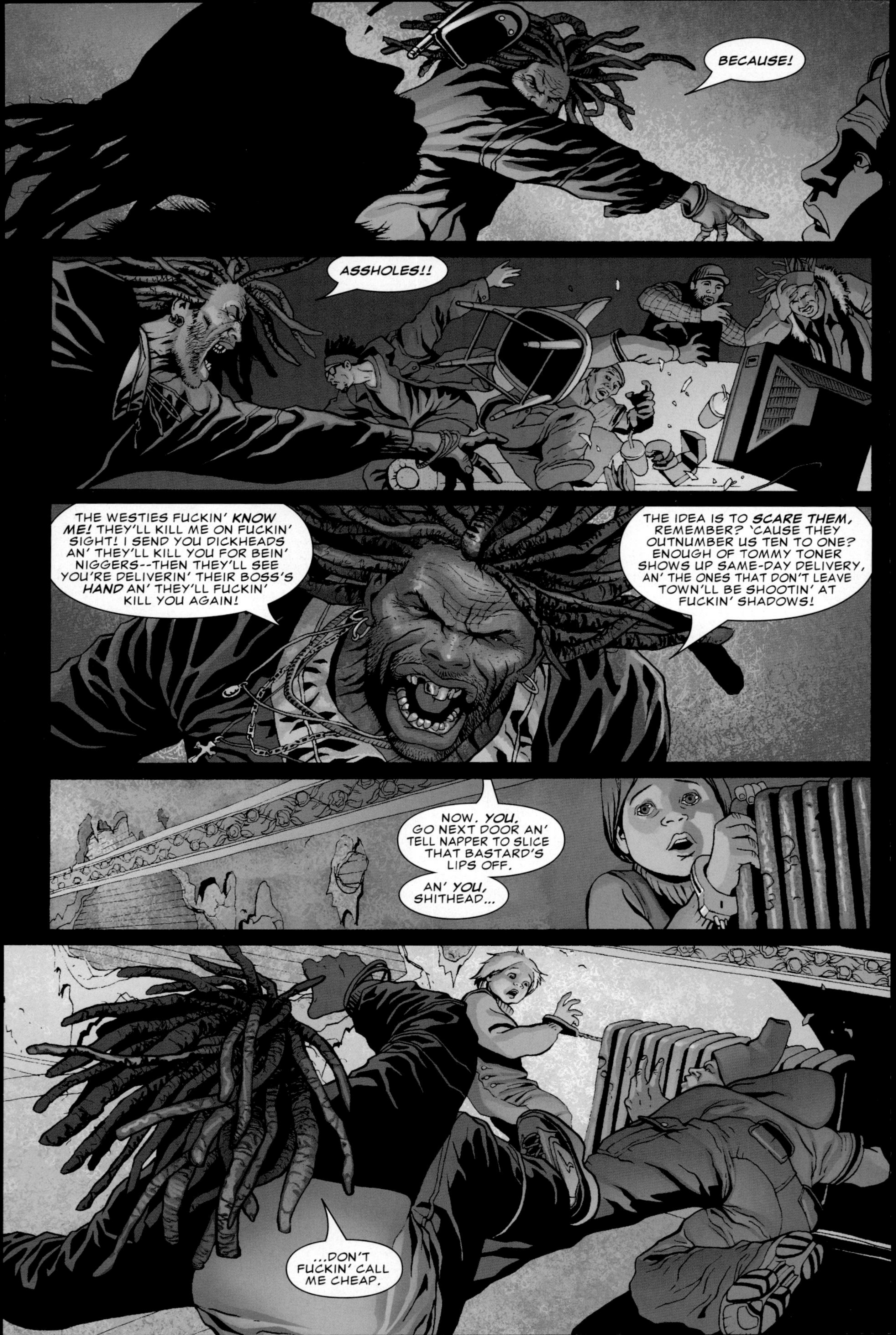
BECAUSE!
ASSHOLES!!
THE WESTIES FUCKIN' KNOW ME! THEY'LL KILL ME ON FUCKIN' SIGHT! I SEND YOU DICKHEADS AN' THEY'LL KILL YOU FOR BEIN' NIGGERS--THEN THEY'LL SEE YOU'RE DELIVERIN' THEIR BOSS'S HAND AN' THEY'LL FUCKIN' KILL YOU AGAIN!
THE IDEA IS TO SCARE THEM, REMEMBER? 'CAUSE THEY OUTNUMBER US TEN TO ONE? ENOUGH OF TOMMY TONER SHOWS UP SAME-DAY DELIVERY, AN' THE ONES THAT DON'T LEAVE TOWN'LL BE SHOOTIN' AT FUCKIN' SHADOWS!
NOW. YOU. GO NEXT DOOR AN' TELL NAPPER TO SLICE THAT BASTARD'S LIPS OFF.
AN' YOU, SHITHEAD...
...DON'T FUCKIN' CALL ME CHEAP.

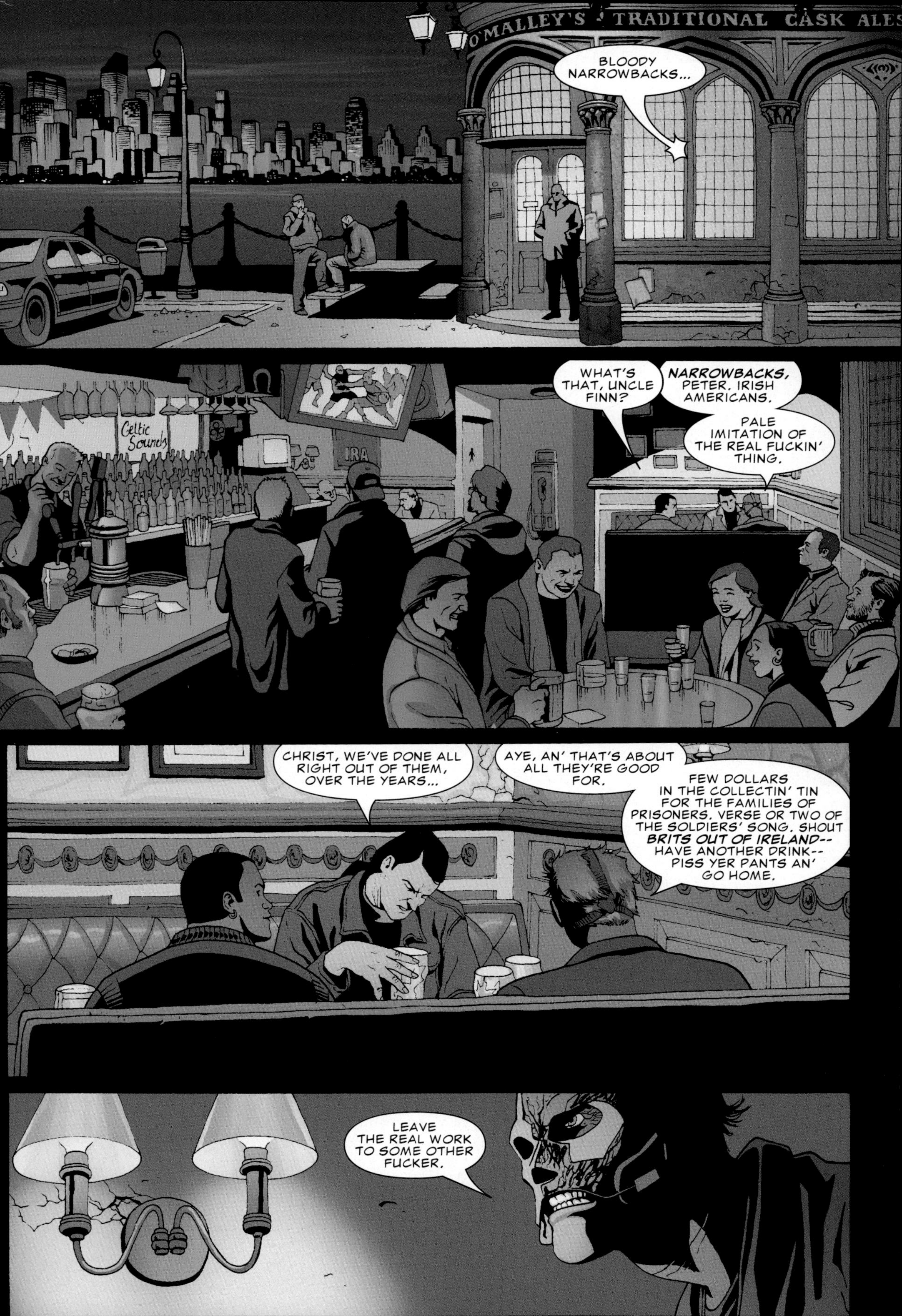
O'MALLEY'S TRADITIONAL CASK ALES
BLOODY NARROWBACKS...
WHAT'S THAT, UNCLE FINN?
NARROWBACKS, PETER. IRISH AMERICANS.
PALE IMITATION OF THE REAL FUCKIN' THING.
Celtic Sounds
IRA
CHRIST, WE'VE DONE ALL RIGHT OUT OF THEM, OVER THE YEARS...
AYE, AN' THAT'S ABOUT ALL THEY'RE GOOD FOR.
FEW DOLLARS IN THE COLLECTIN' TIN FOR THE FAMILIES OF PRISONERS. VERSE OR TWO OF THE SOLDIERS' SONG. SHOUT BRITS OUT OF IRELAND-- HAVE ANOTHER DRINK-- PISS YER PANTS AN' GO HOME.
LEAVE THE REAL WORK TO SOME OTHER FUCKER.

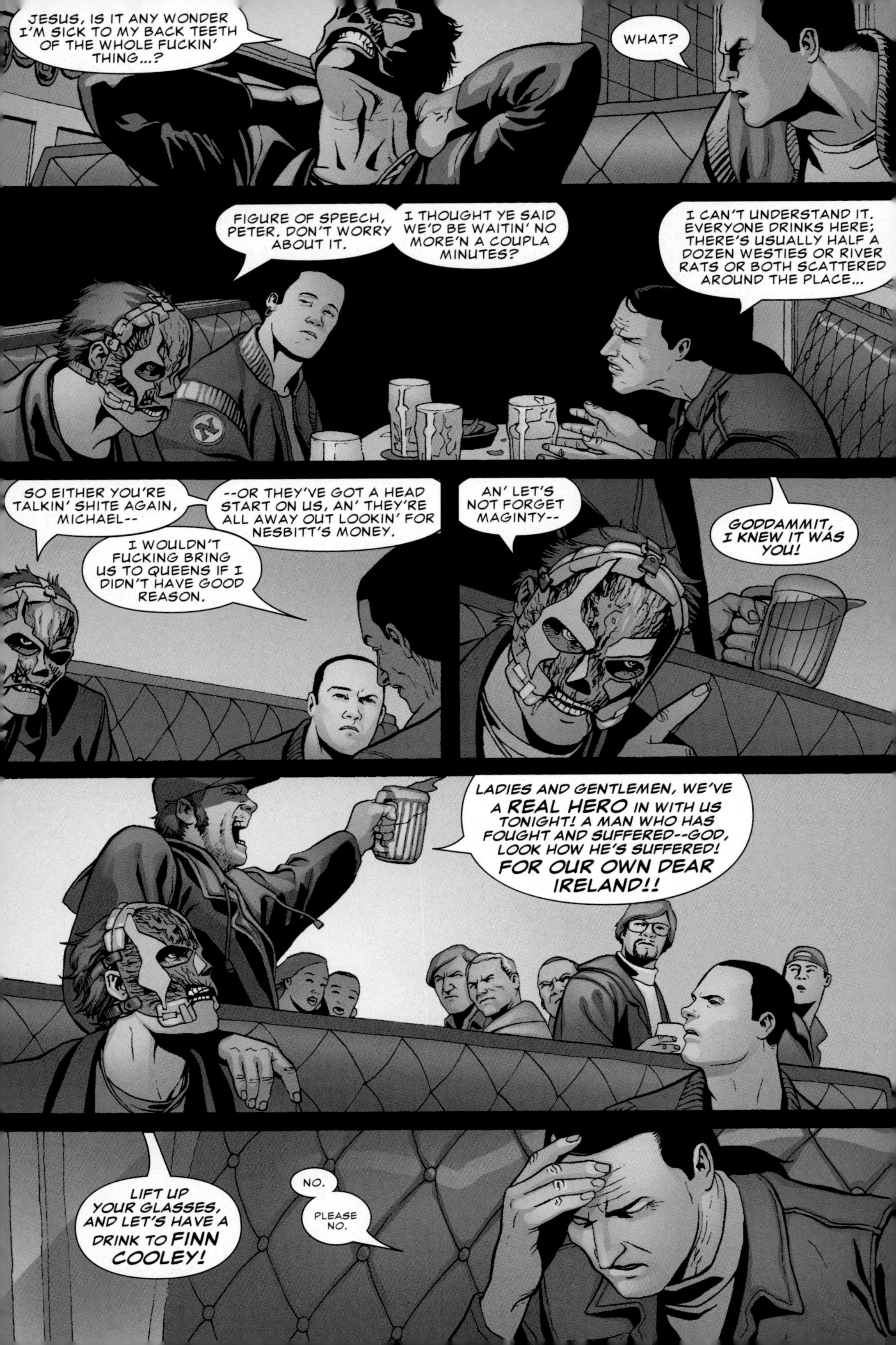
JESUS, IS IT ANY WONDER I'M SICK TO MY BACK TEETH OF THE WHOLE FUCKIN' THING...?
WHAT?
FIGURE OF SPEECH, PETER. DON'T WORRY ABOUT IT.
I THOUGHT YE SAID WE'D BE WAITIN' NO MORE'N A COUPLA MINUTES?
I CAN'T UNDERSTAND IT. EVERYONE DRINKS HERE; THERE'S USUALLY HALF A DOZEN WESTIES OR RIVER RATS OR BOTH SCATTERED AROUND THE PLACE...
SO EITHER YOU'RE TALKIN' SHITE AGAIN, MICHAEL--
--OR THEY'VE GOT A HEAD START ON US, AN' THEY'RE ALL AWAY OUT LOOKIN' FOR NESBITT'S MONEY.
I WOULDN'T FUCKING BRING US TO QUEENS IF I DIDN'T HAVE GOOD REASON.
AN' LET'S NOT FORGET MAGINTY--
GODDAMMIT, I KNEW IT WAS YOU!
LADIES AND GENTLEMEN, WE'VE A REAL HERO IN WITH US TONIGHT! A MAN WHO HAS FOUGHT AND SUFFERED--GOD, LOOK HOW HE'S SUFFERED! FOR OUR OWN DEAR IRELAND!!
LIFT UP YOUR GLASSES, AND LET'S HAVE A DRINK TO FINN COOLEY!
NO.
PLEASE NO.

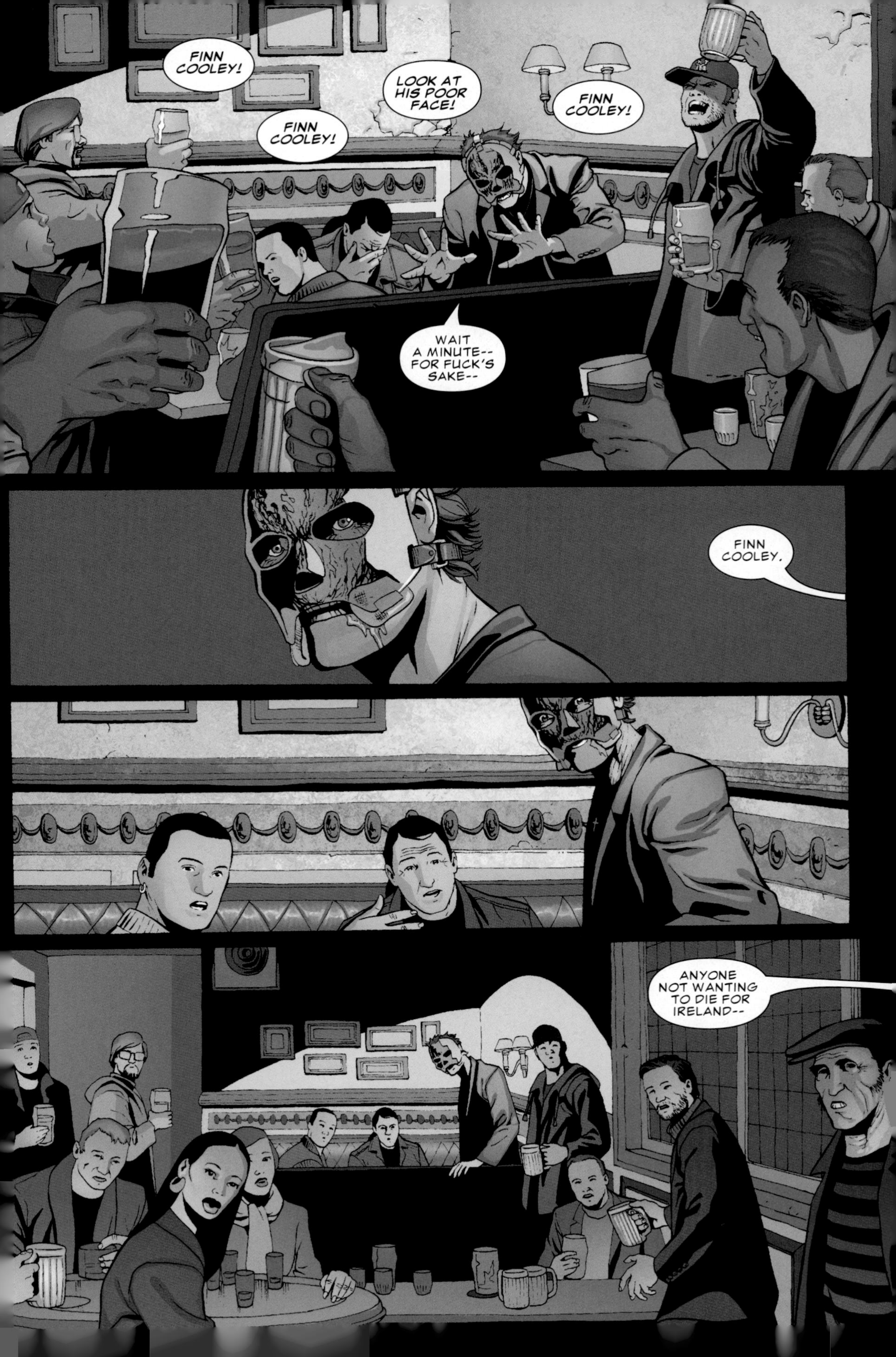
FINN COOLEY!
FINN COOLEY!
LOOK AT HIS POOR FACE!
FINN COOLEY!
WAIT A MINUTE-- FOR FUCK'S SAKE--
FINN COOLEY.
ANYONE NOT WANTING TO DIE FOR IRELAND--

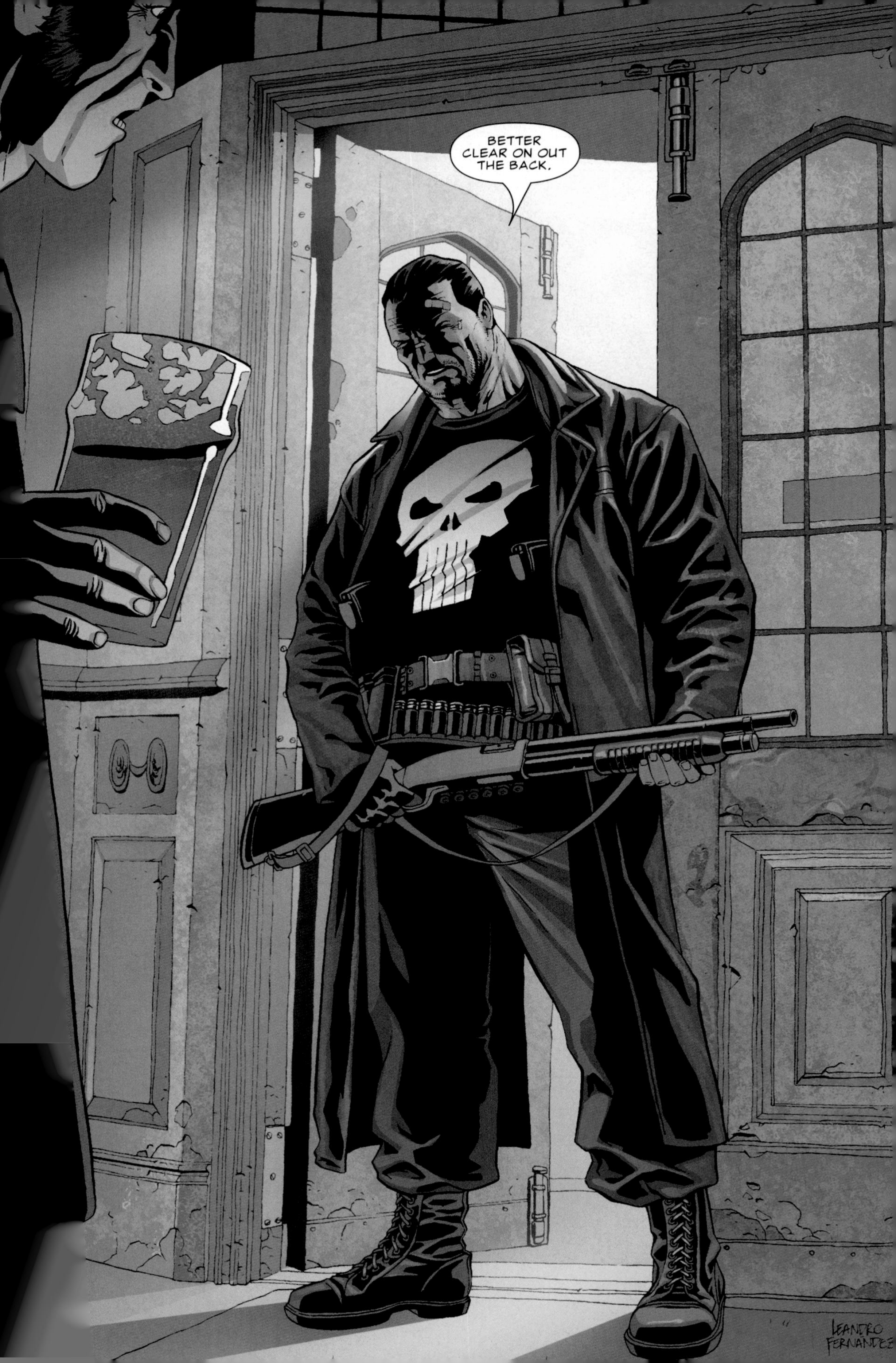
BETTER CLEAR ON OUT THE BACK.
LEANDRO FERNANDES

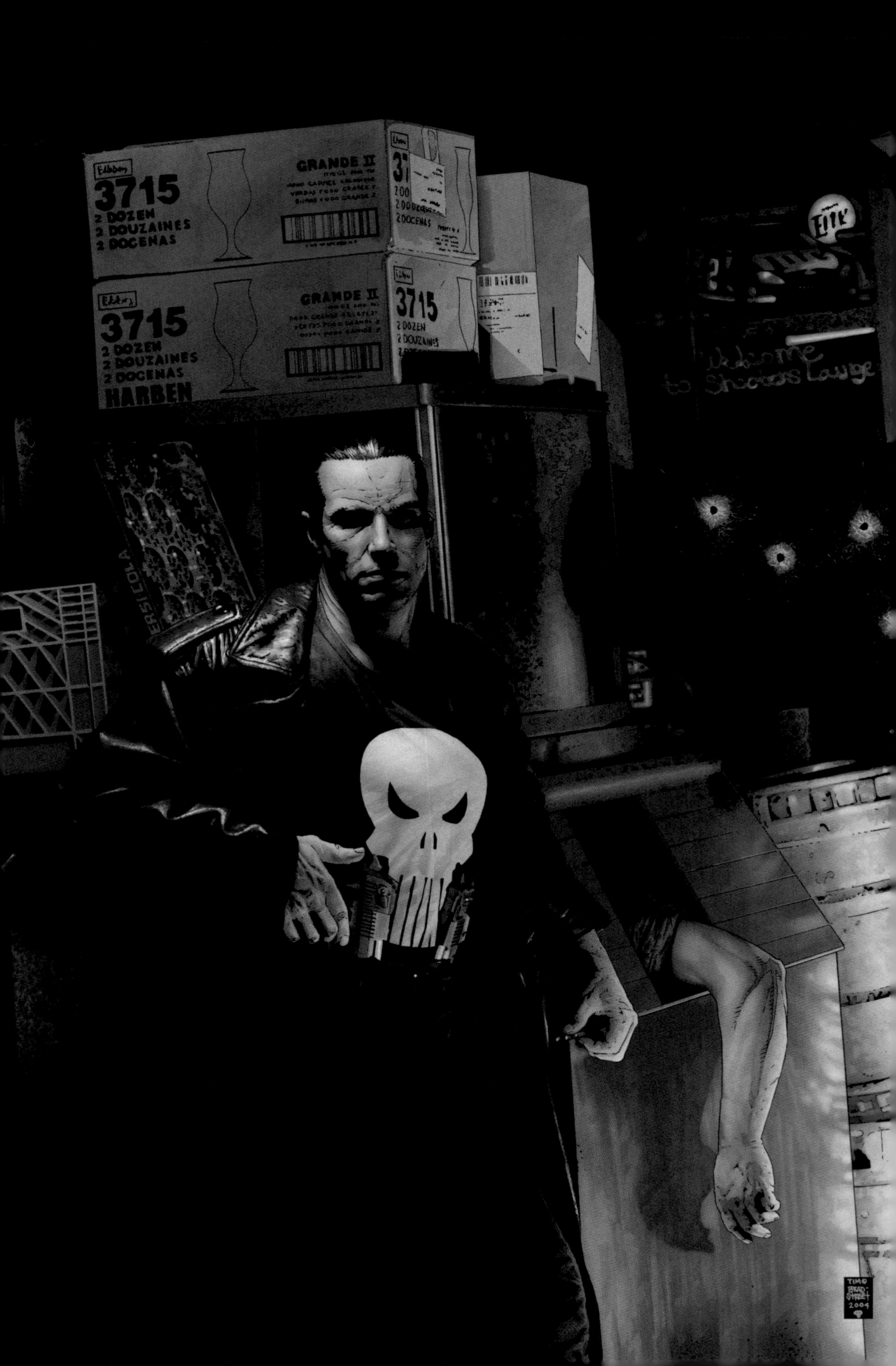
3715
2 DOZEN
2 DOUZAINES
2 DOCENAS
GRANDE II
3715
2 DOZEN
2 DOUZAINES
2 DOCENAS
HARBEN
GRANDE II
3715
2 DOZEN
TIMO
BRAD-
STREET
2004

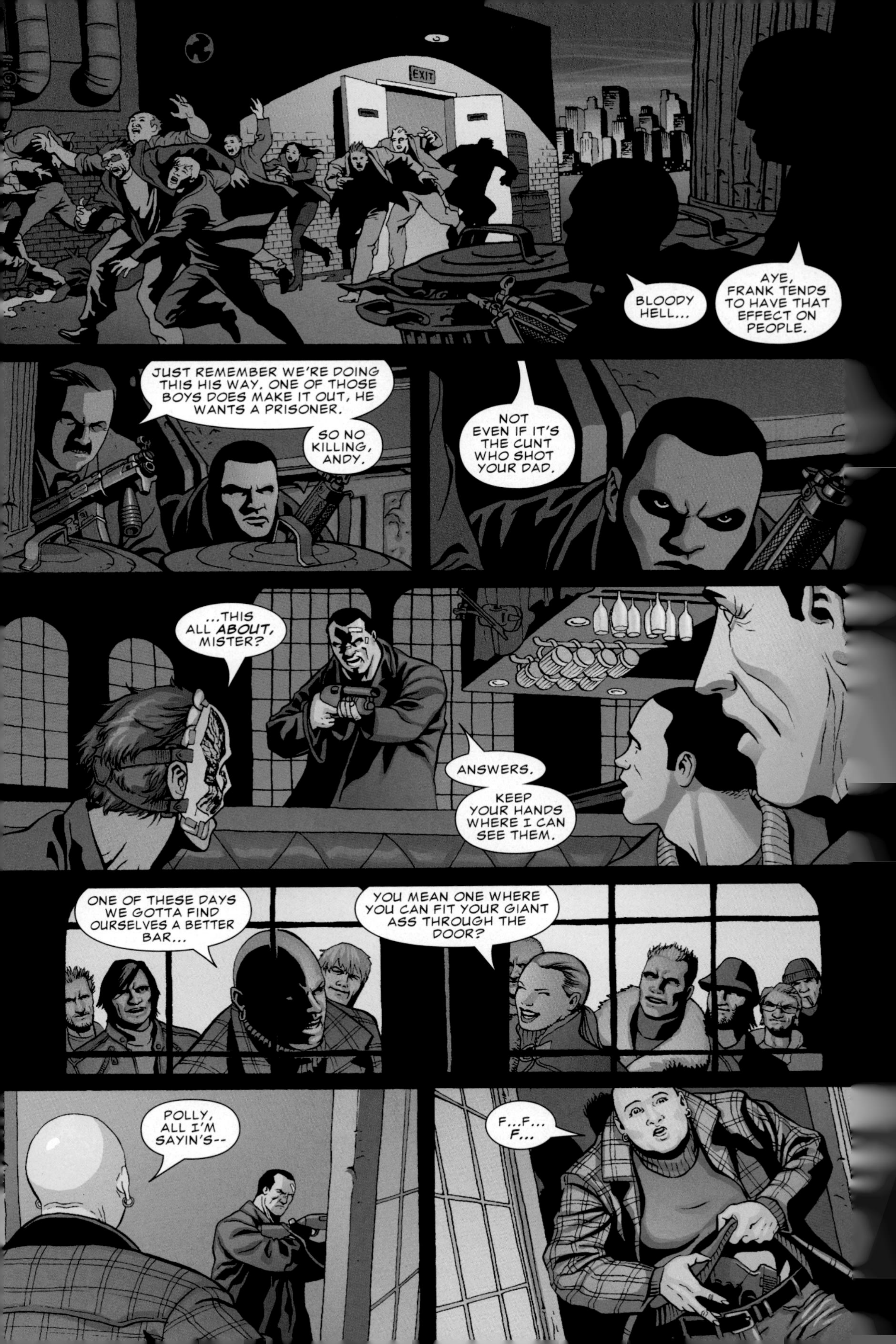
EXIT
BLOODY HELL...
AYE, FRANK TENDS TO HAVE THAT EFFECT ON PEOPLE.
JUST REMEMBER WE'RE DOING THIS HIS WAY. ONE OF THOSE BOYS DOES MAKE IT OUT, HE WANTS A PRISONER.
SO NO KILLING, ANDY.
NOT EVEN IF IT'S THE CUNT WHO SHOT YOUR DAD.
...THIS ALL ABOUT, MISTER?
ANSWERS.
KEEP YOUR HANDS WHERE I CAN SEE THEM.
ONE OF THESE DAYS WE GOTTA FIND OURSELVES A BETTER BAR...
YOU MEAN ONE WHERE YOU CAN FIT YOUR GIANT ASS THROUGH THE DOOR?
POLLY, ALL I'M SAYIN'S--
F...F... F...

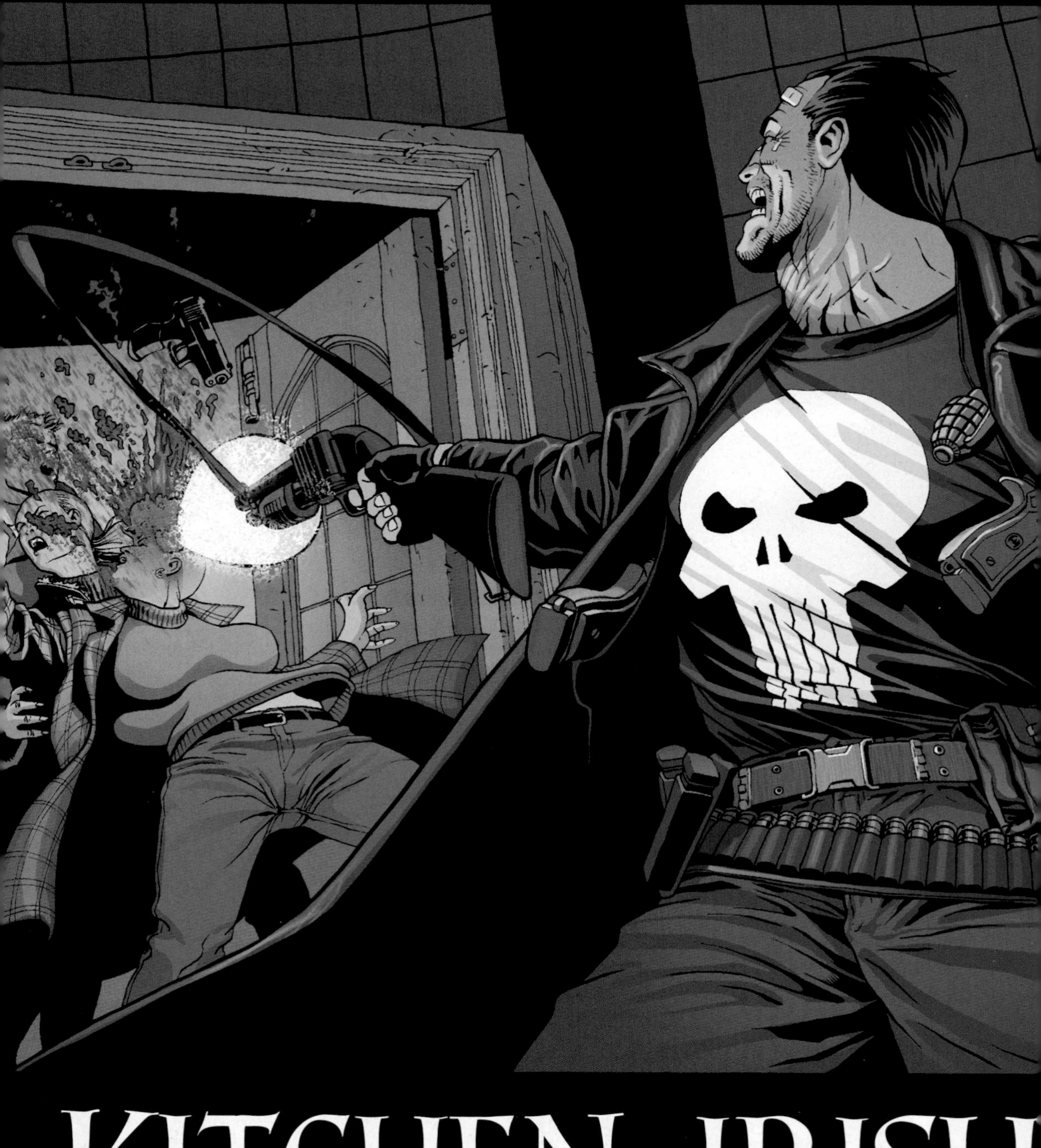

KITCHEN IRISH

PART THREE

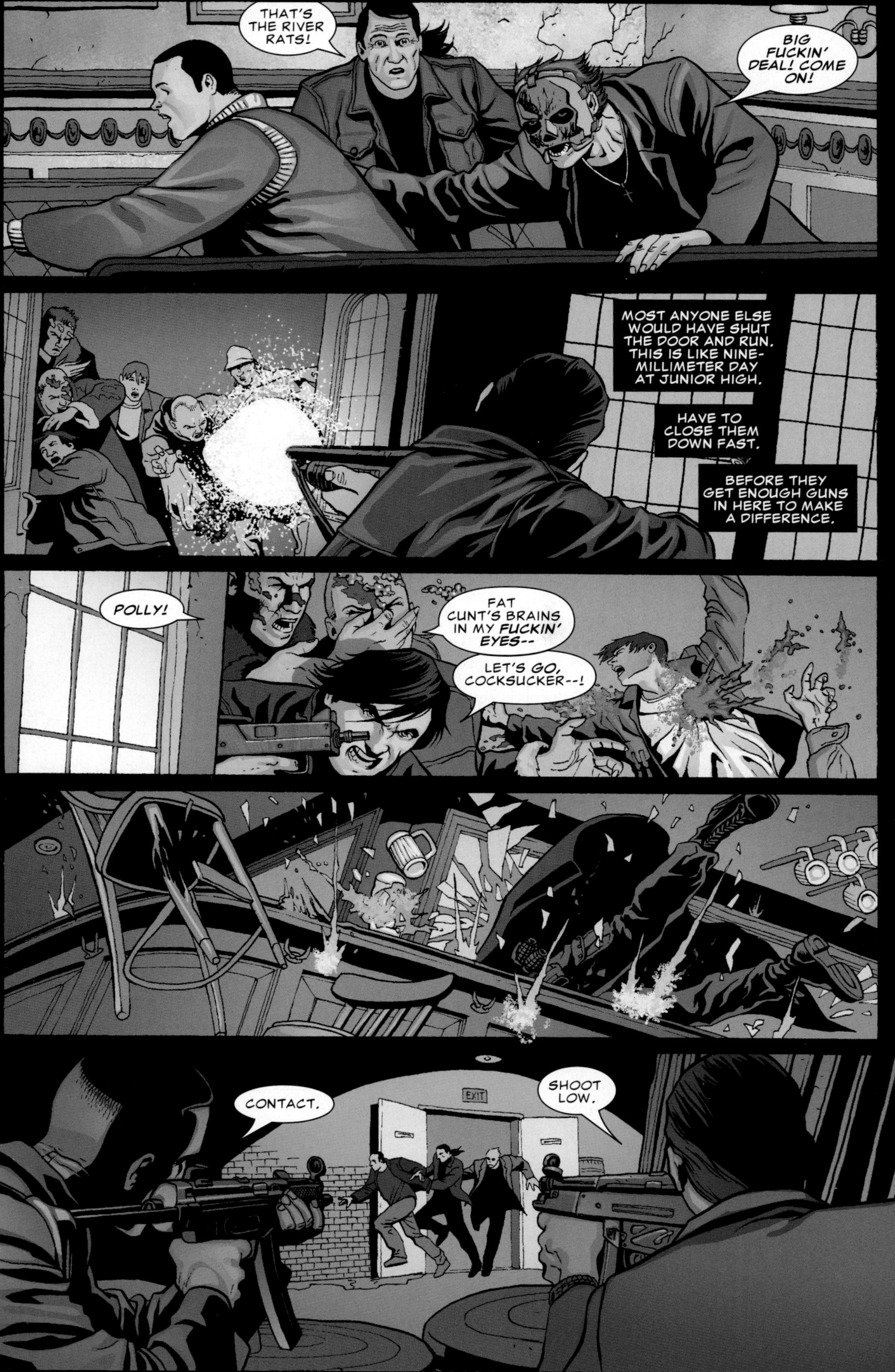

THAT'S THE RIVER RATS!
BIG FUCKIN' DEAL! COME ON!
MOST ANYONE ELSE WOULD HAVE SHUT THE DOOR AND RUN. THIS IS LIKE NINE-MILLIMETER DAY AT JUNIOR HIGH.
HAVE TO CLOSE THEM DOWN FAST.
BEFORE THEY GET ENOUGH GUNS IN HERE TO MAKE A DIFFERENCE.
POLLY!
FAT CUNT'S BRAINS IN MY FUCKIN' EYES--
LET'S GO, COCKSUCKER--!
EXIT
CONTACT.
SHOOT LOW.

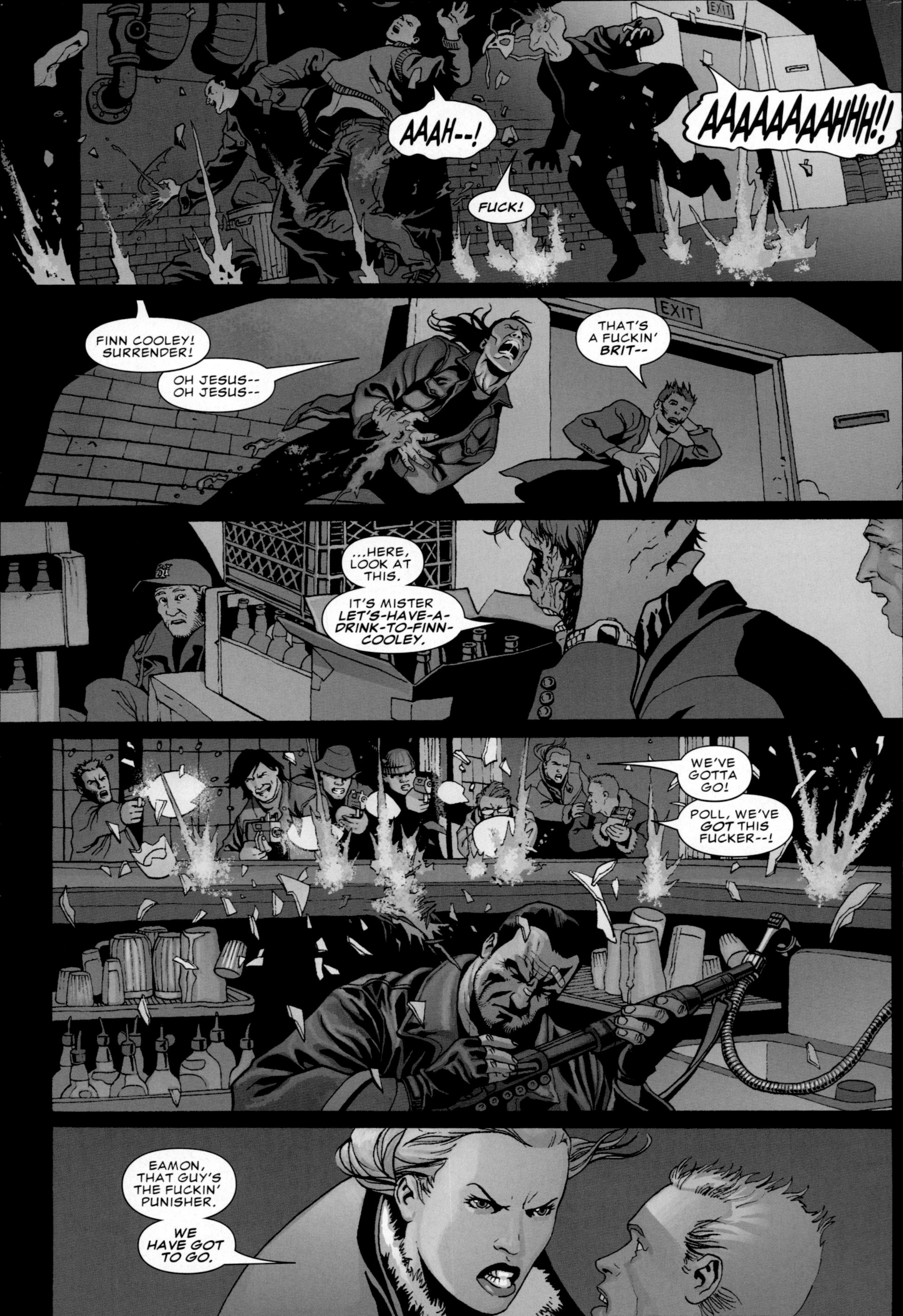
EXIT
AAAH--!
AAAAAAAAHHH!!
FUCK!
FINN COOLEY! SURRENDER!
OH JESUS-- OH JESUS--
EXIT
THAT'S A FUCKIN' BRIT--
...HERE, LOOK AT THIS.
IT'S MISTER LET'S-HAVE-A-DRINK-TO-FINN-COOLEY.
WE'VE GOTTA GO!
POLL, WE'VE GOT THIS FUCKER--!
EAMON, THAT GUY'S THE FUCKIN' PUNISHER.
WE HAVE GOT TO GO.

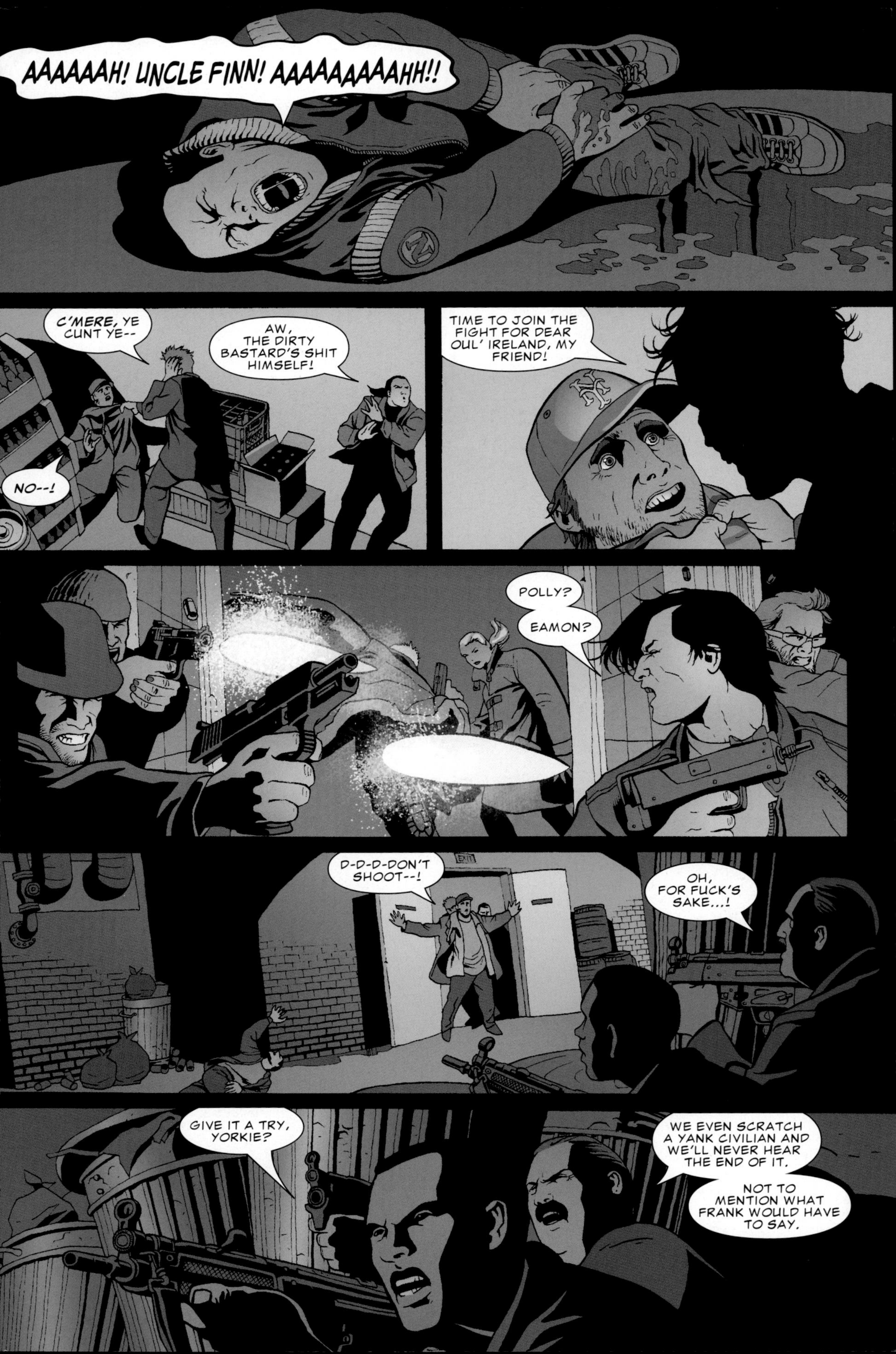
AAAAAAH! UNCLE FINN! AAAAAAAAAHH!!
C'MERE, YE CUNT YE--
AW, THE DIRTY BASTARD'S SHIT HIMSELF!
NO--!
TIME TO JOIN THE FIGHT FOR DEAR OUL' IRELAND, MY FRIEND!
POLLY?
EAMON?
D-D-D-DON'T SHOOT--!
OH, FOR FUCK'S SAKE...!
GIVE IT A TRY, YORKIE?
WE EVEN SCRATCH A YANK CIVILIAN AND WE'LL NEVER HEAR THE END OF IT.
NOT TO MENTION WHAT FRANK WOULD HAVE TO SAY.

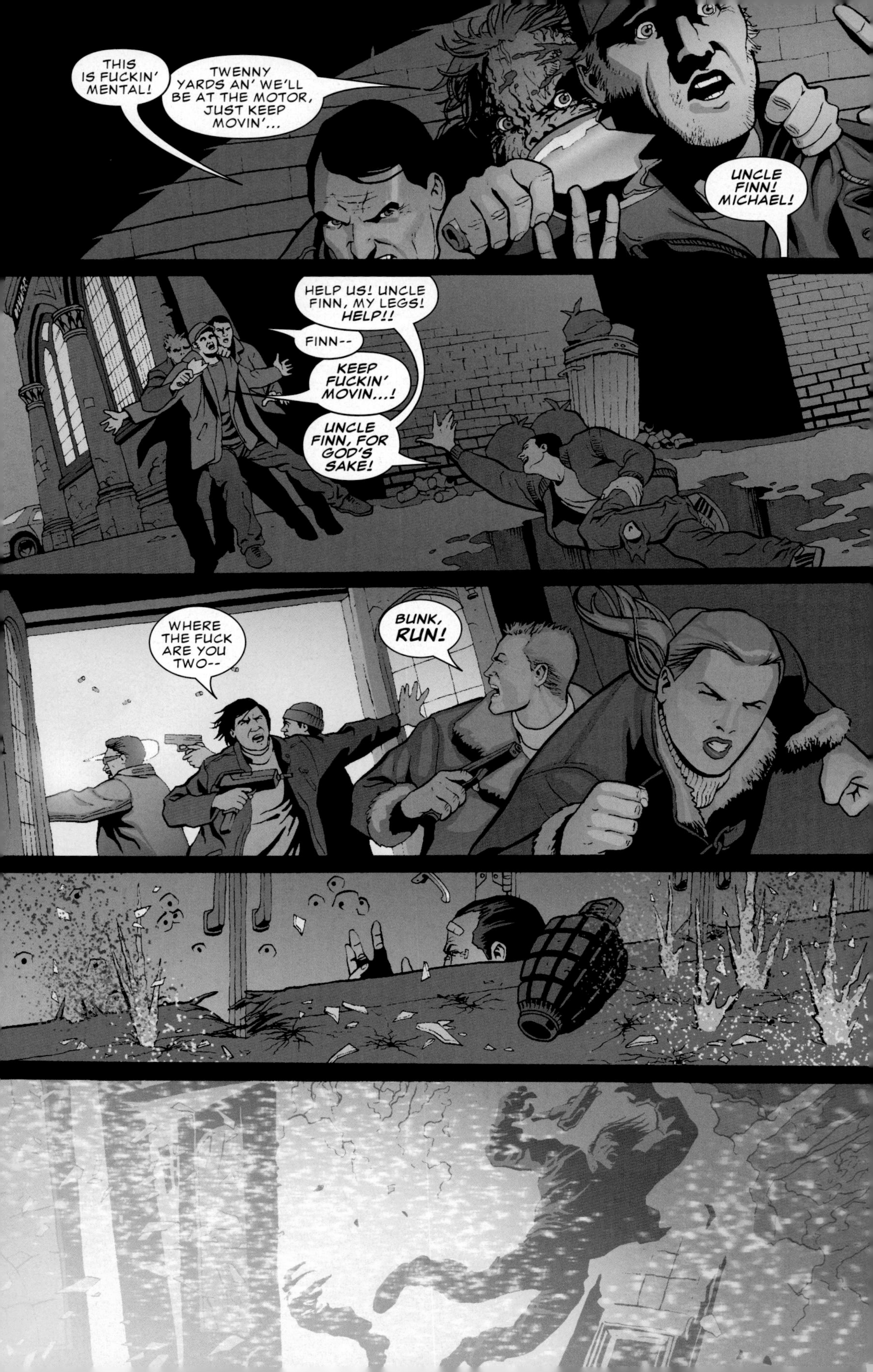
THIS IS FUCKIN' MENTAL!
TWENNY YARDS AN' WE'LL BE AT THE MOTOR, JUST KEEP MOVIN'...
UNCLE FINN! MICHAEL!
HELP US! UNCLE FINN, MY LEGS! HELP!!
FINN--
KEEP FUCKIN' MOVIN...!
UNCLE FINN, FOR GOD'S SAKE!
WHERE THE FUCK ARE YOU TWO--
BUNK, RUN!

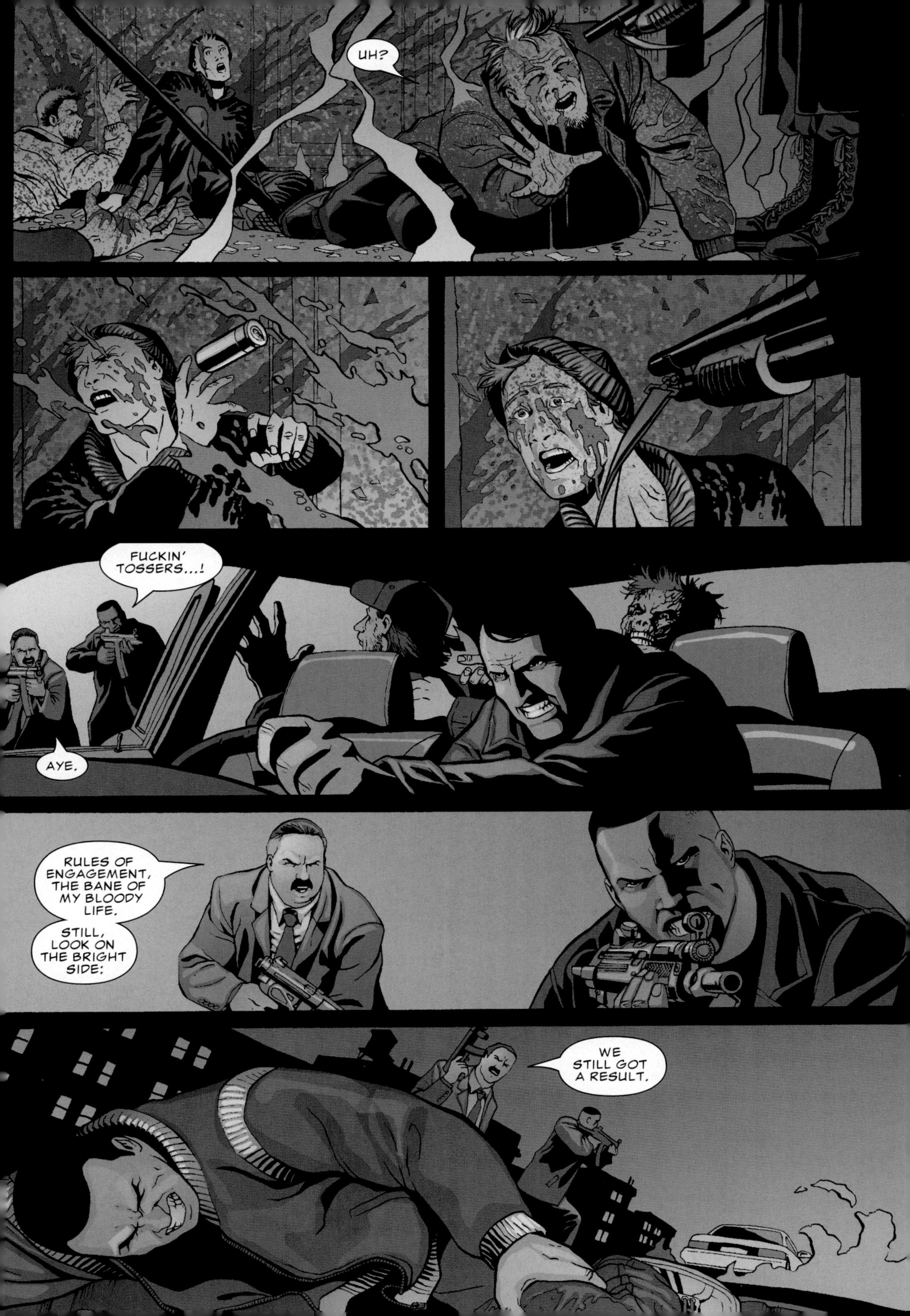
UH?
FUCKIN' TOSSERS...!
AYE.
RULES OF ENGAGEMENT, THE BANE OF MY BLOODY LIFE.
STILL, LOOK ON THE BRIGHT SIDE:
WE STILL GOT A RESULT.

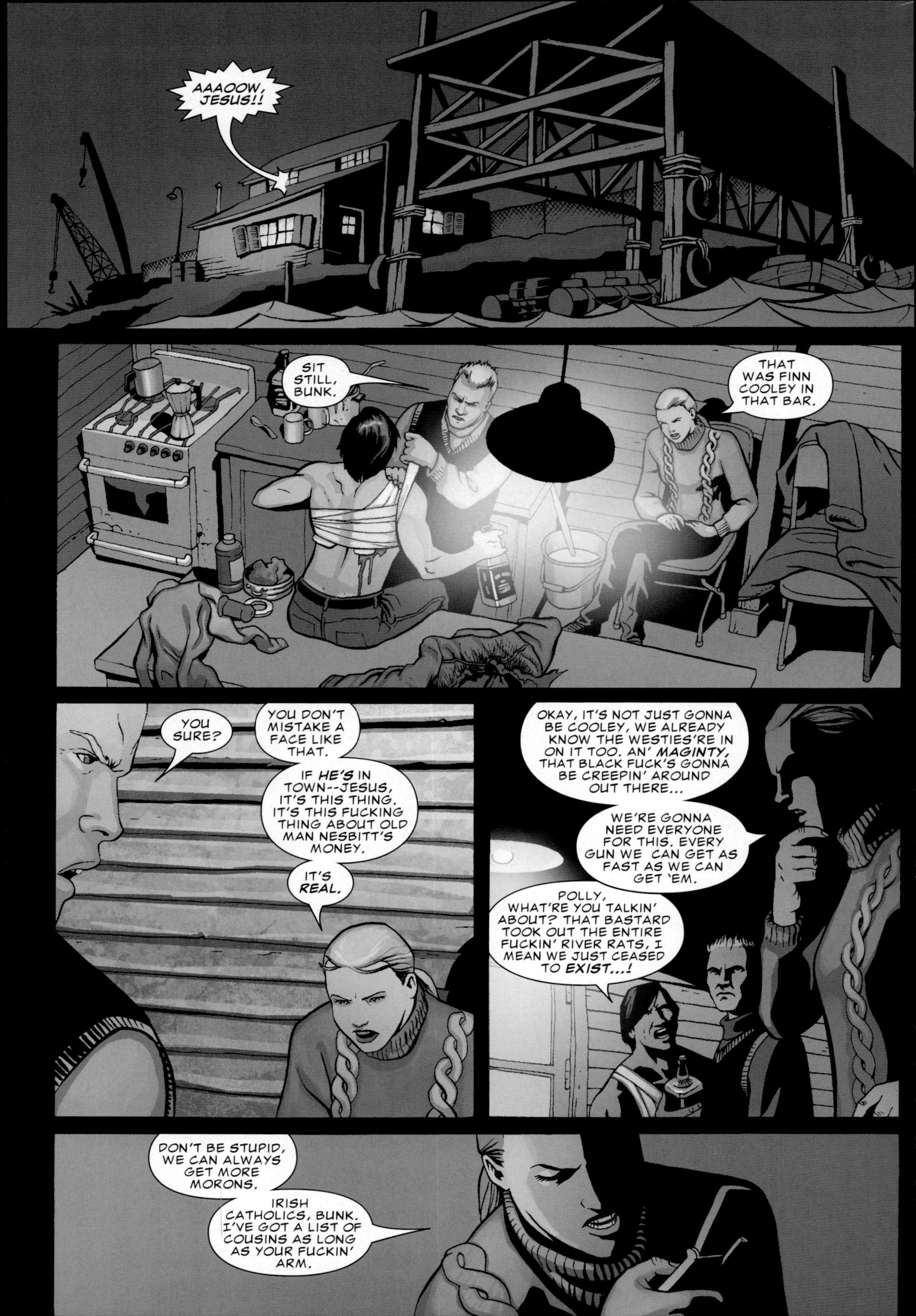

AAAOOW, JESUS!!
SIT STILL, BUNK.
THAT WAS FINN COOLEY IN THAT BAR.
YOU SURE?
YOU DON'T MISTAKE A FACE LIKE THAT.
IF HE'S IN TOWN--JESUS, IT'S THIS THING. IT'S THIS FUCKING THING ABOUT OLD MAN NESBITT'S MONEY.
IT'S REAL.
OKAY, IT'S NOT JUST GONNA BE COOLEY, WE ALREADY KNOW THE WESTIES'RE IN ON IT TOO. AN' MAGINTY, THAT BLACK FUCK'S GONNA BE CREEPIN' AROUND OUT THERE...
WE'RE GONNA NEED EVERYONE FOR THIS. EVERY GUN WE CAN GET AS FAST AS WE CAN GET 'EM.
POLLY, WHAT'RE YOU TALKIN' ABOUT? THAT BASTARD TOOK OUT THE ENTIRE FUCKIN' RIVER RATS, I MEAN WE JUST CEASED TO EXIST...!
DON'T BE STUPID, WE CAN ALWAYS GET MORE MORONS.
IRISH CATHOLICS, BUNK. I'VE GOT A LIST OF COUSINS AS LONG AS YOUR FUCKIN' ARM.

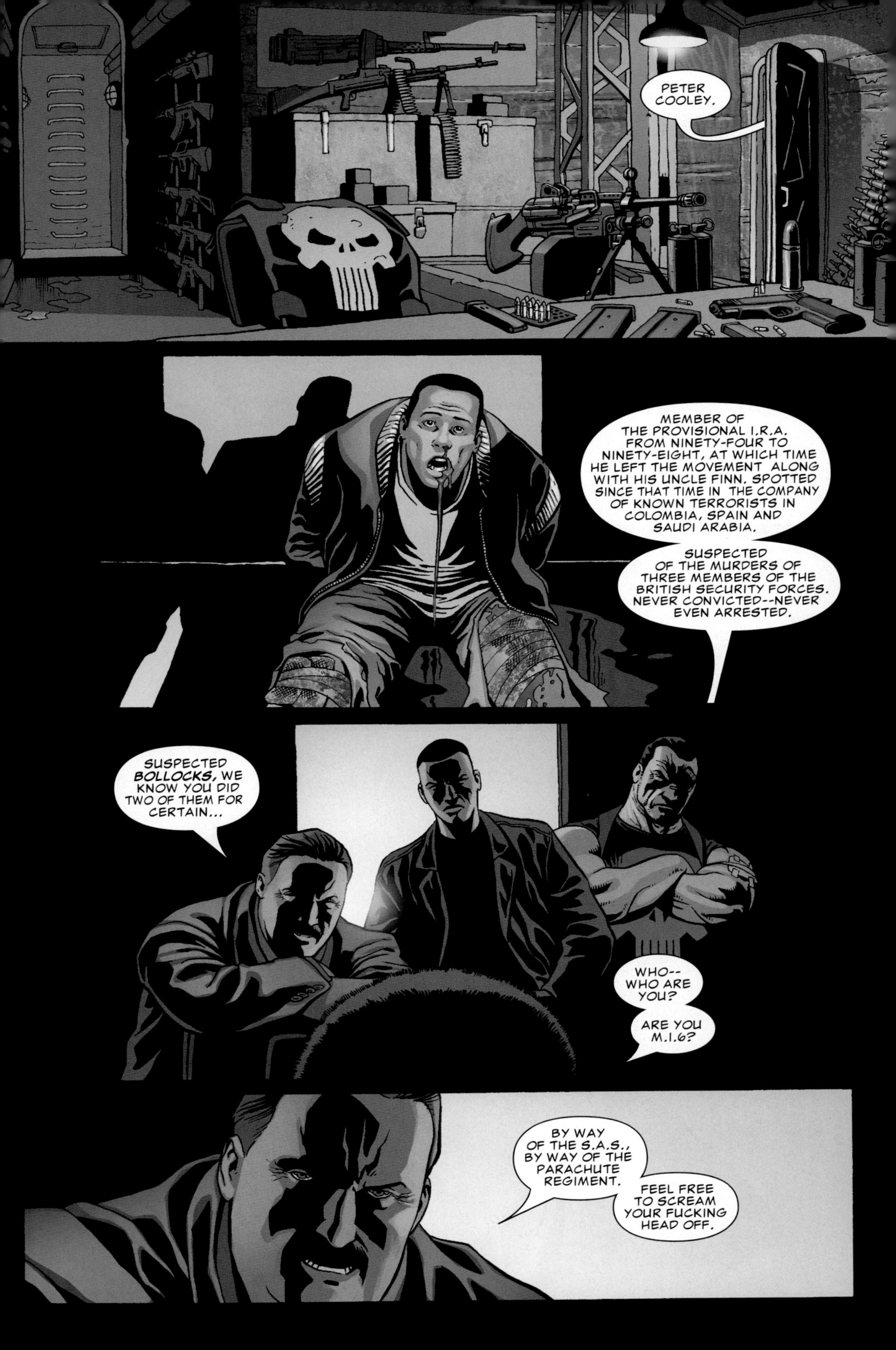
PETER COOLEY.
MEMBER OF THE PROVISIONAL I.R.A. FROM NINETY-FOUR TO NINETY-EIGHT, AT WHICH TIME HE LEFT THE MOVEMENT ALONG WITH HIS UNCLE FINN. SPOTTED SINCE THAT TIME IN THE COMPANY OF KNOWN TERRORISTS IN COLOMBIA, SPAIN AND SAUDI ARABIA.
SUSPECTED OF THE MURDERS OF THREE MEMBERS OF THE BRITISH SECURITY FORCES. NEVER CONVICTED--NEVER EVEN ARRESTED.
SUSPECTED BOLLOCKS, WE KNOW YOU DID TWO OF THEM FOR CERTAIN...
WHO--WHO ARE YOU?
ARE YOU M.I.6?
BY WAY OF THE S.A.S., BY WAY OF THE PARACHUTE REGIMENT.
FEEL FREE TO SCREAM YOUR FUCKING HEAD OFF.

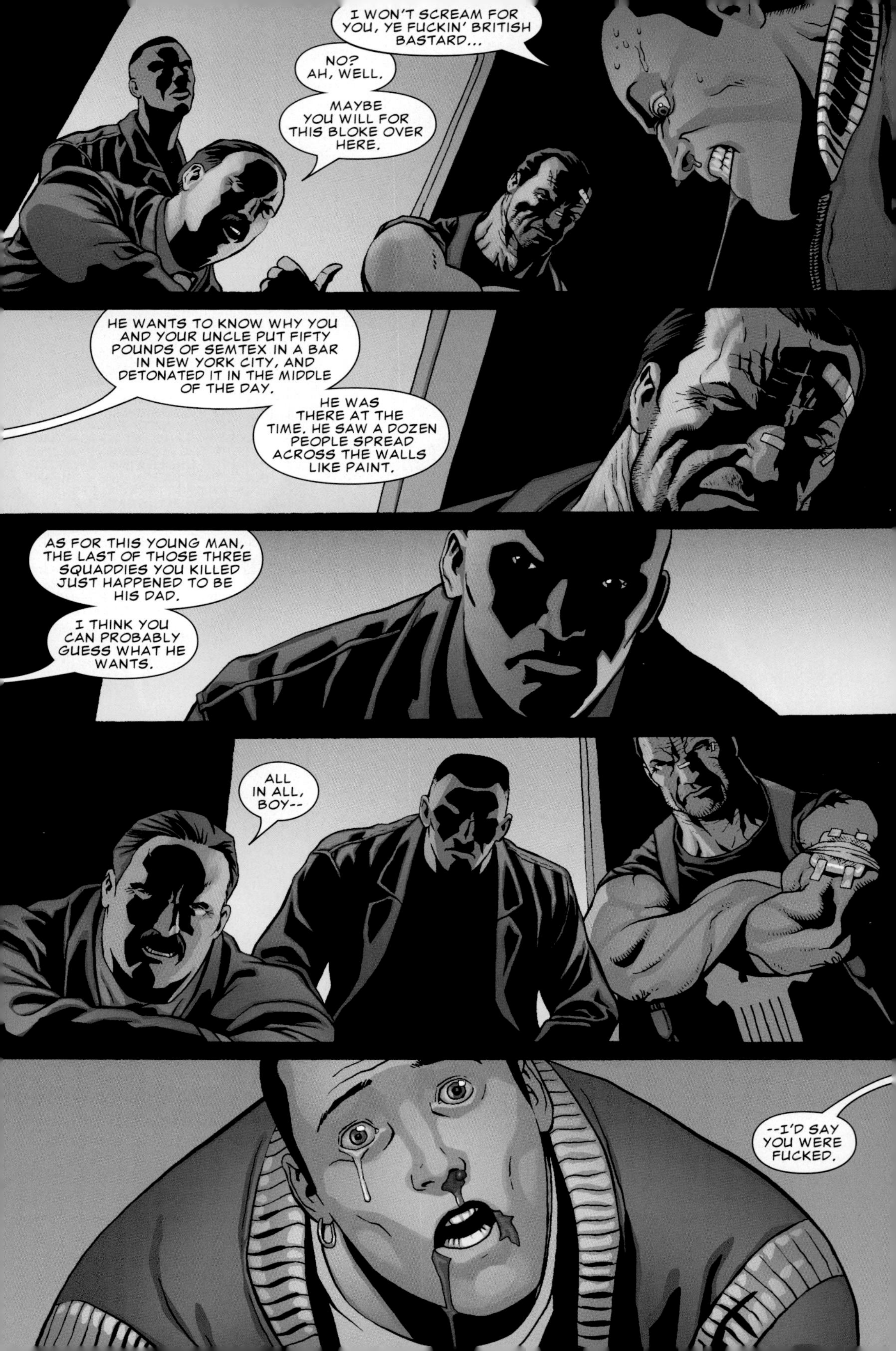
I WON'T SCREAM FOR YOU, YE FUCKIN' BRITISH BASTARD...
NO? AH, WELL.
MAYBE YOU WILL FOR THIS BLOKE OVER HERE.
HE WANTS TO KNOW WHY YOU AND YOUR UNCLE PUT FIFTY POUNDS OF SEMTEX IN A BAR IN NEW YORK CITY, AND DETONATED IT IN THE MIDDLE OF THE DAY.
HE WAS THERE AT THE TIME. HE SAW A DOZEN PEOPLE SPREAD ACROSS THE WALLS LIKE PAINT.
AS FOR THIS YOUNG MAN, THE LAST OF THOSE THREE SQUADDIES YOU KILLED JUST HAPPENED TO BE HIS DAD.
I THINK YOU CAN PROBABLY GUESS WHAT HE WANTS.
ALL IN ALL, BOY--
--I'D SAY YOU WERE FUCKED.

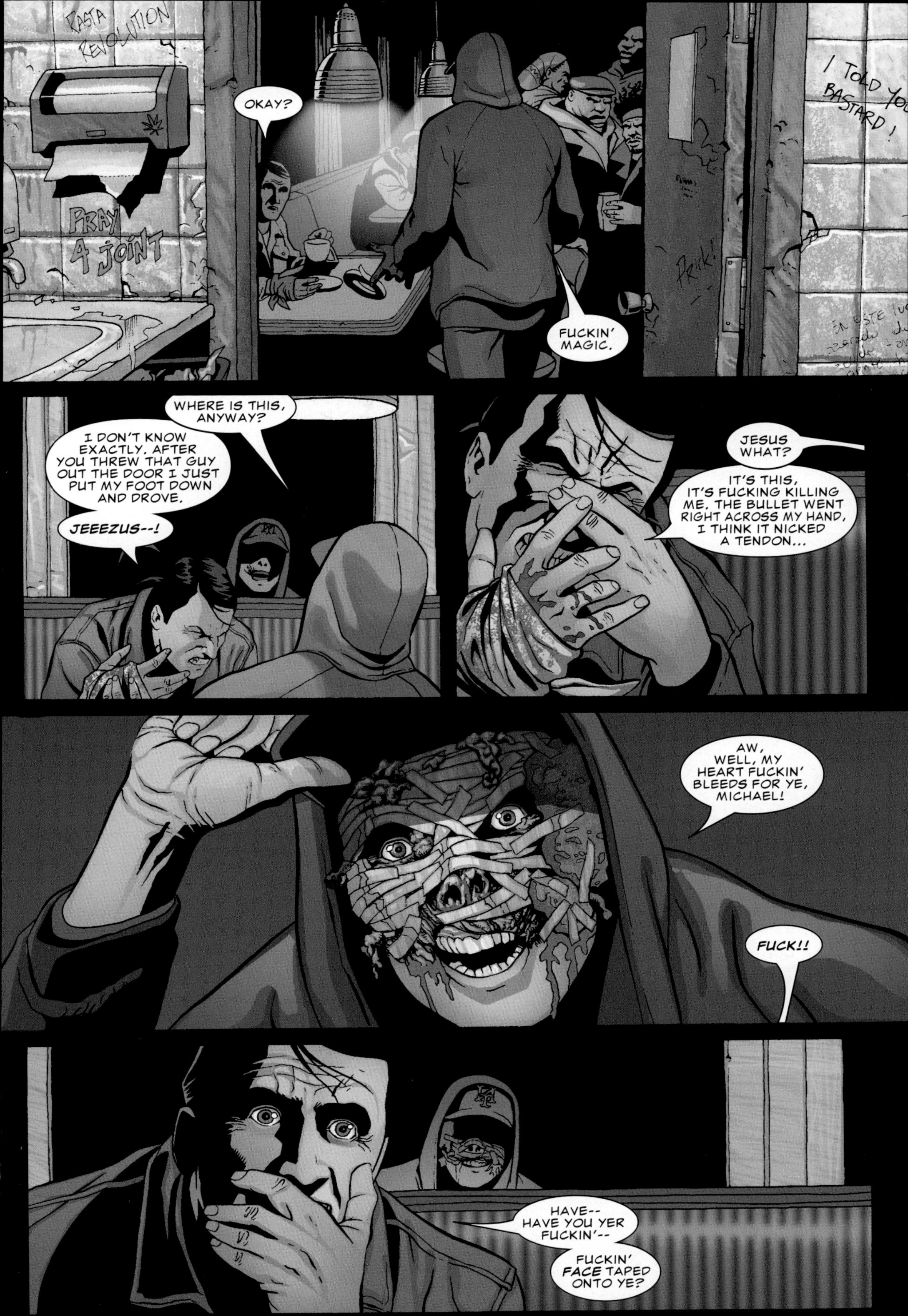
RASTA REVOLUTION
PRAY 4 JOINT
OKAY?
FUCKIN' MAGIC.
WHERE IS THIS, ANYWAY?
I DON'T KNOW EXACTLY. AFTER YOU THREW THAT GUY OUT THE DOOR I JUST PUT MY FOOT DOWN AND DROVE.
JEEEZUS--!
JESUS WHAT?
IT'S THIS, IT'S FUCKING KILLING ME. THE BULLET WENT RIGHT ACROSS MY HAND, I THINK IT NICKED A TENDON...
AW, WELL, MY HEART FUCKIN' BLEEDS FOR YE, MICHAEL!
FUCK!!
HAVE-- HAVE YOU YER FUCKIN'--
FUCKIN' FACE TAPED ONTO YE?

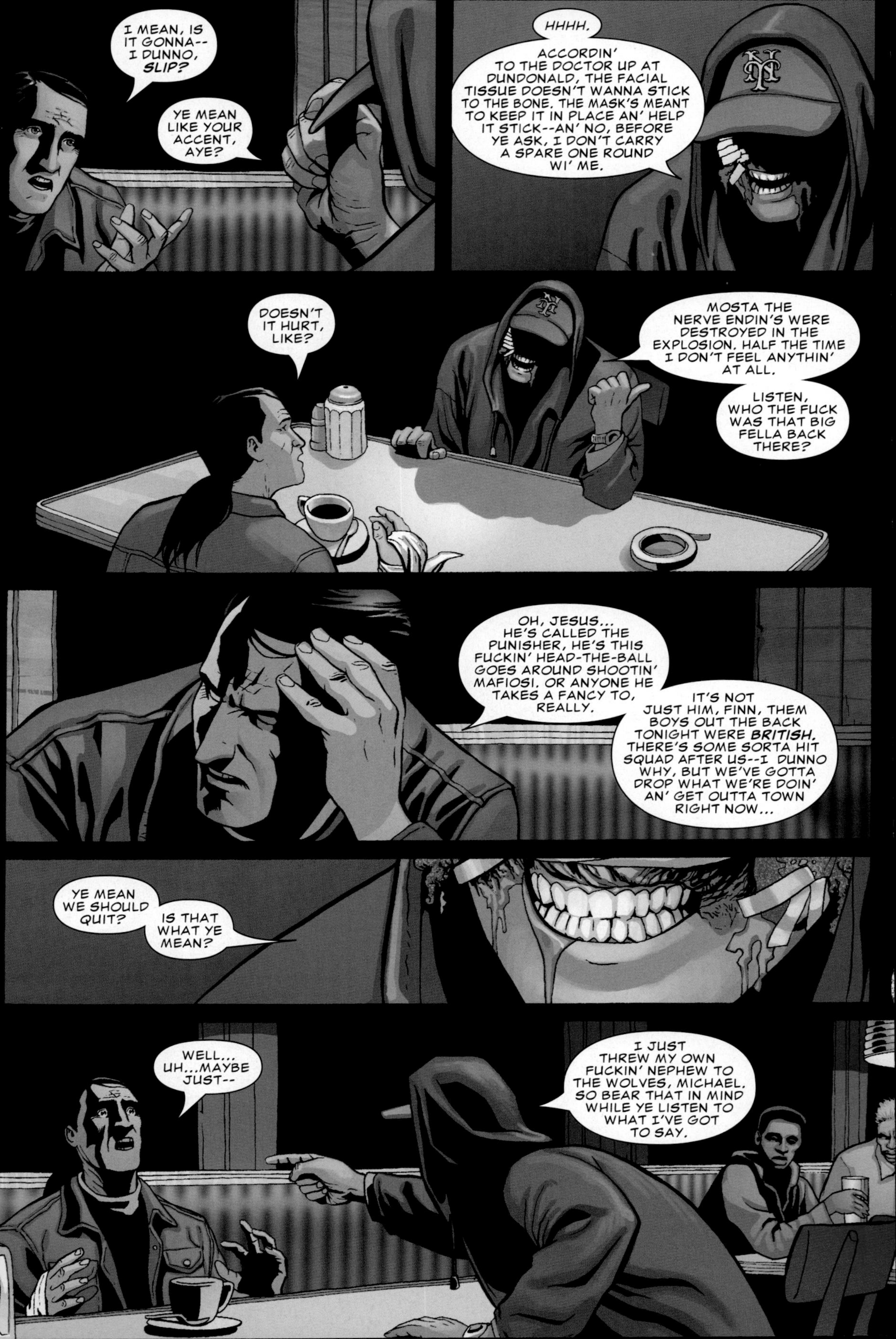

I MEAN, IS IT GONNA-- I DUNNO, *SLIP?*
YE MEAN LIKE YOUR ACCENT, AYE?
HHHH.
ACCORDIN' TO THE DOCTOR UP AT DUNDONALD, THE FACIAL TISSUE DOESN'T WANNA STICK TO THE BONE. THE MASK'S MEANT TO KEEP IT IN PLACE AN' HELP IT STICK--AN' NO, BEFORE YE ASK, I DON'T CARRY A SPARE ONE ROUND WI' ME.
DOESN'T IT HURT, LIKE?
MOSTA THE NERVE ENDIN'S WERE DESTROYED IN THE EXPLOSION. HALF THE TIME I DON'T FEEL ANYTHIN' AT ALL.
LISTEN, WHO THE FUCK WAS THAT BIG FELLA BACK THERE?
OH, JESUS... HE'S CALLED THE PUNISHER, HE'S THIS FUCKIN' HEAD-THE-BALL GOES AROUND SHOOTIN' MAFIOSI, OR ANYONE HE TAKES A FANCY TO, REALLY.
IT'S NOT JUST HIM, FINN, THEM BOYS OUT THE BACK TONIGHT WERE *BRITISH.* THERE'S SOME SORTA HIT SQUAD AFTER US--I DUNNO WHY, BUT WE'VE GOTTA DROP WHAT WE'RE DOIN' AN' GET OUTTA TOWN RIGHT NOW...
YE MEAN WE SHOULD QUIT?
IS THAT WHAT YE MEAN?
WELL... UH...MAYBE JUST--
I JUST THREW MY OWN FUCKIN' NEPHEW TO THE WOLVES, MICHAEL, SO BEAR THAT IN MIND WHILE YE LISTEN TO WHAT I'VE GOT TO SAY.

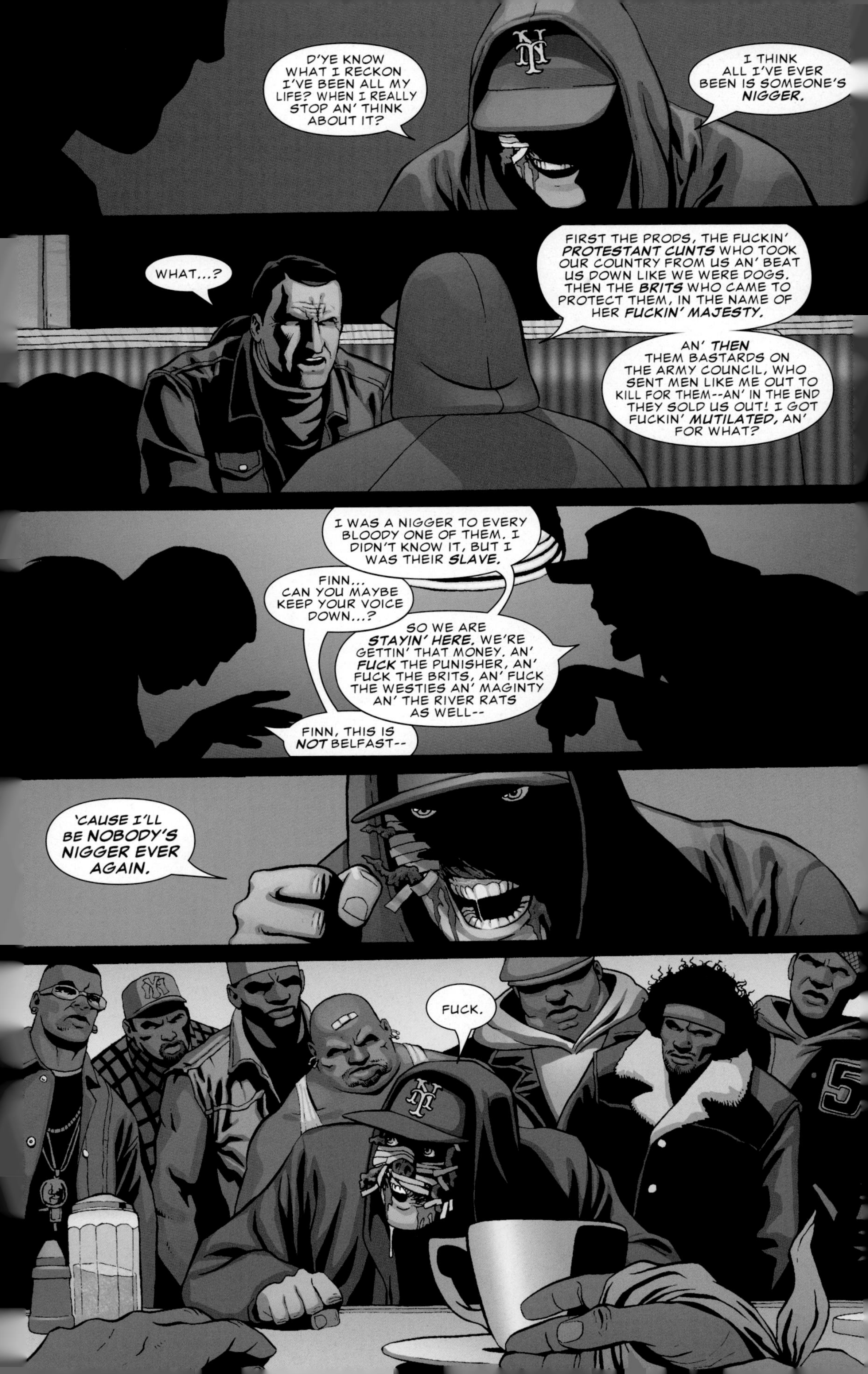
D'YE KNOW WHAT I RECKON I'VE BEEN ALL MY LIFE? WHEN I REALLY STOP AN' THINK ABOUT IT?
I THINK ALL I'VE EVER BEEN IS SOMEONE'S NIGGER.
WHAT...?
FIRST THE PRODS, THE FUCKIN' PROTESTANT CUNTS WHO TOOK OUR COUNTRY FROM US AN' BEAT US DOWN LIKE WE WERE DOGS. THEN THE BRITS WHO CAME TO PROTECT THEM, IN THE NAME OF HER FUCKIN' MAJESTY.
AN' THEN THEM BASTARDS ON THE ARMY COUNCIL, WHO SENT MEN LIKE ME OUT TO KILL FOR THEM--AN' IN THE END THEY SOLD US OUT! I GOT FUCKIN' MUTILATED, AN' FOR WHAT?
I WAS A NIGGER TO EVERY BLOODY ONE OF THEM. I DIDN'T KNOW IT, BUT I WAS THEIR SLAVE.
FINN... CAN YOU MAYBE KEEP YOUR VOICE DOWN...?
SO WE ARE STAYIN' HERE. WE'RE GETTIN' THAT MONEY, AN' FUCK THE PUNISHER, AN' FUCK THE BRITS, AN' FUCK THE WESTIES AN' MAGINTY AN' THE RIVER RATS AS WELL--
FINN, THIS IS NOT BELFAST--
'CAUSE I'LL BE NOBODY'S NIGGER EVER AGAIN.
FUCK.

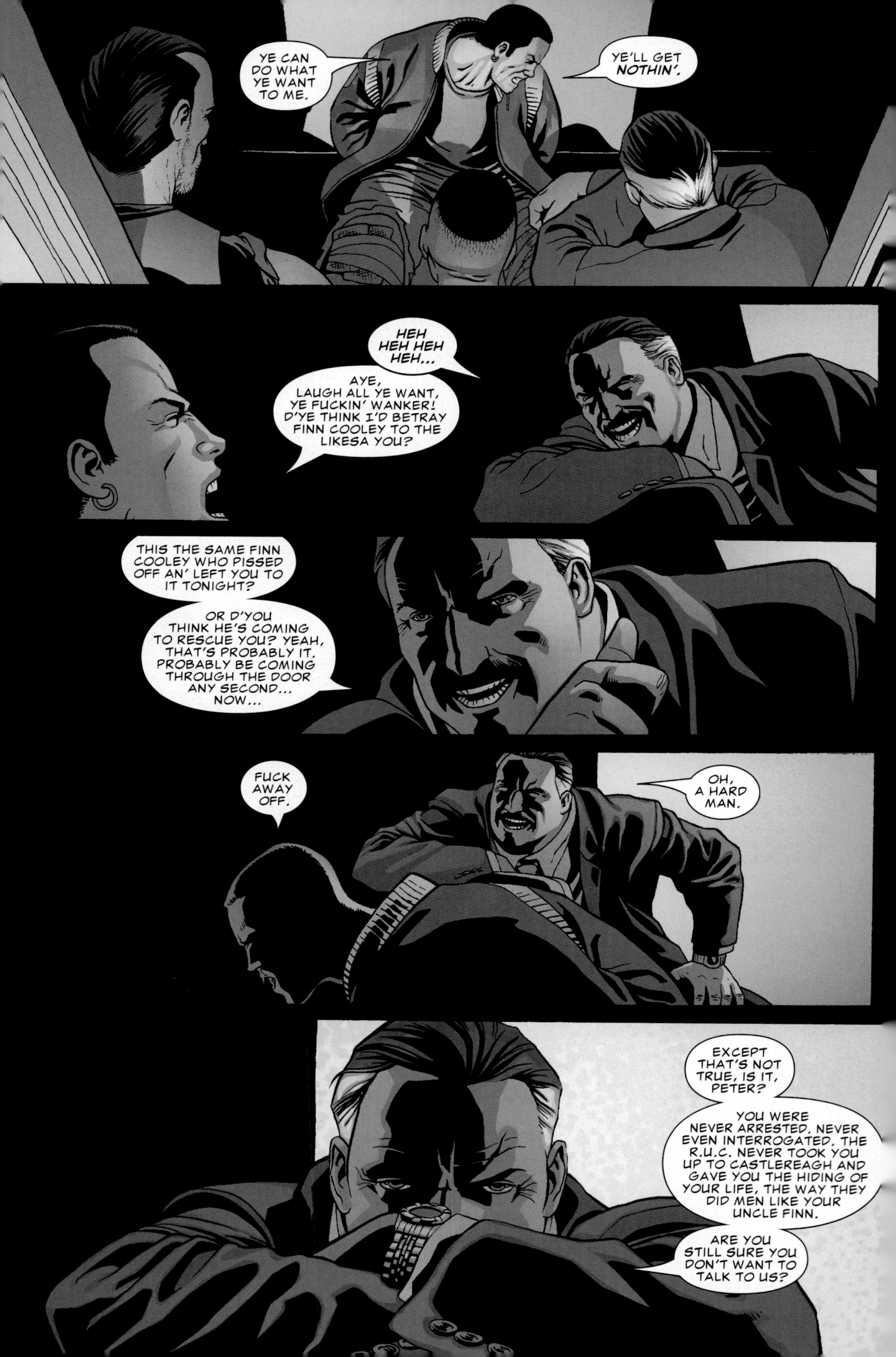
YE CAN DO WHAT YE WANT TO ME.
YE'LL GET NOTHIN'.
HEH HEH HEH HEH...
AYE, LAUGH ALL YE WANT, YE FUCKIN' WANKER! D'YE THINK I'D BETRAY FINN COOLEY TO THE LIKESA YOU?
THIS THE SAME FINN COOLEY WHO PISSED OFF AN' LEFT YOU TO IT TONIGHT?
OR D'YOU THINK HE'S COMING TO RESCUE YOU? YEAH, THAT'S PROBABLY IT. PROBABLY BE COMING THROUGH THE DOOR ANY SECOND... NOW...
FUCK AWAY OFF.
OH, A HARD MAN.
EXCEPT THAT'S NOT TRUE, IS IT, PETER?
YOU WERE NEVER ARRESTED. NEVER EVEN INTERROGATED. THE R.U.C. NEVER TOOK YOU UP TO CASTLEREAGH AND GAVE YOU THE HIDING OF YOUR LIFE, THE WAY THEY DID MEN LIKE YOUR UNCLE FINN.
ARE YOU STILL SURE YOU DON'T WANT TO TALK TO US?

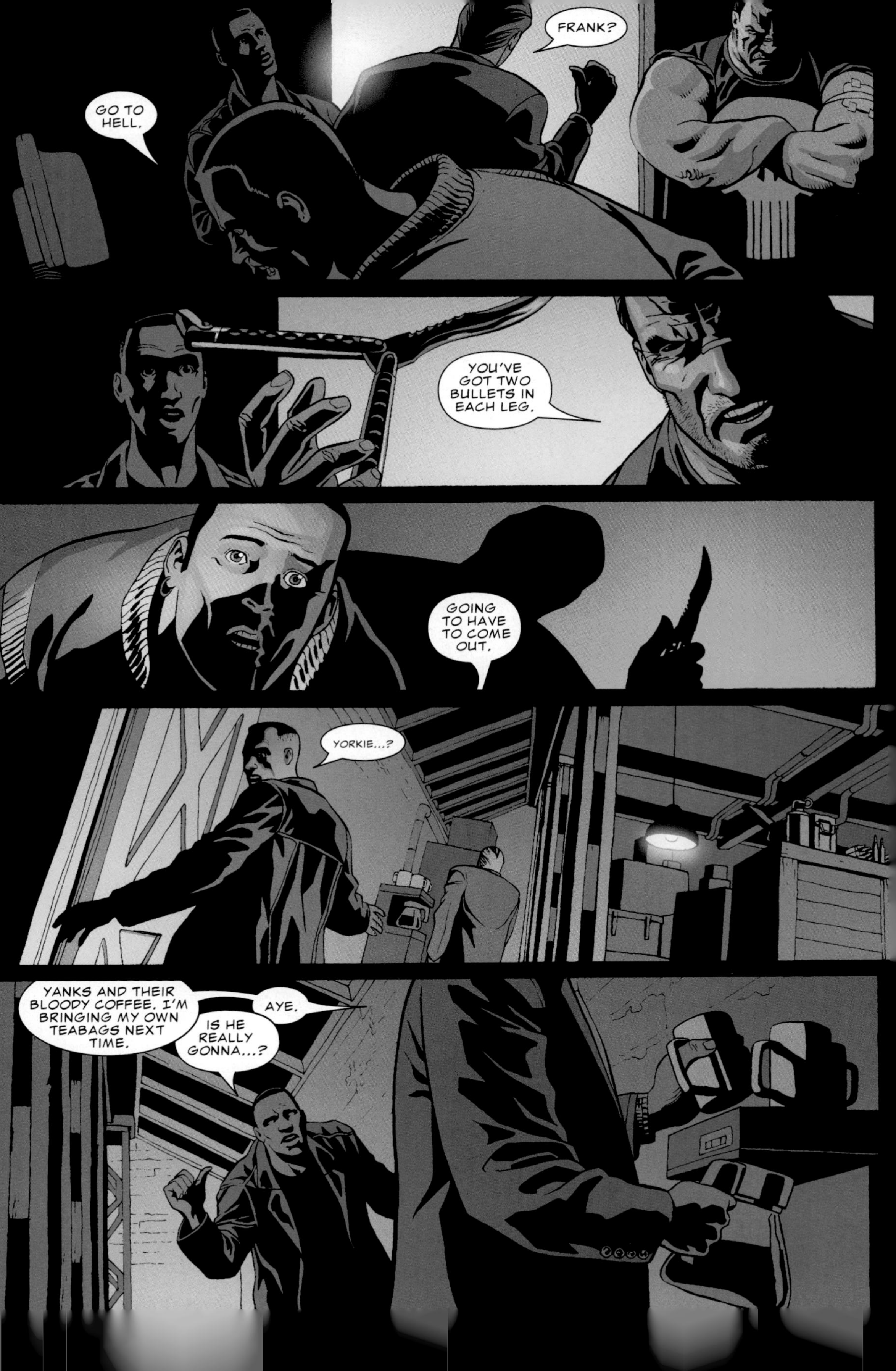
FRANK?
GO TO HELL.
YOU'VE GOT TWO BULLETS IN EACH LEG.
GOING TO HAVE TO COME OUT.
YORKIE...?
YANKS AND THEIR BLOODY COFFEE. I'M BRINGING MY OWN TEABAGS NEXT TIME.
AYE.
IS HE REALLY GONNA...?

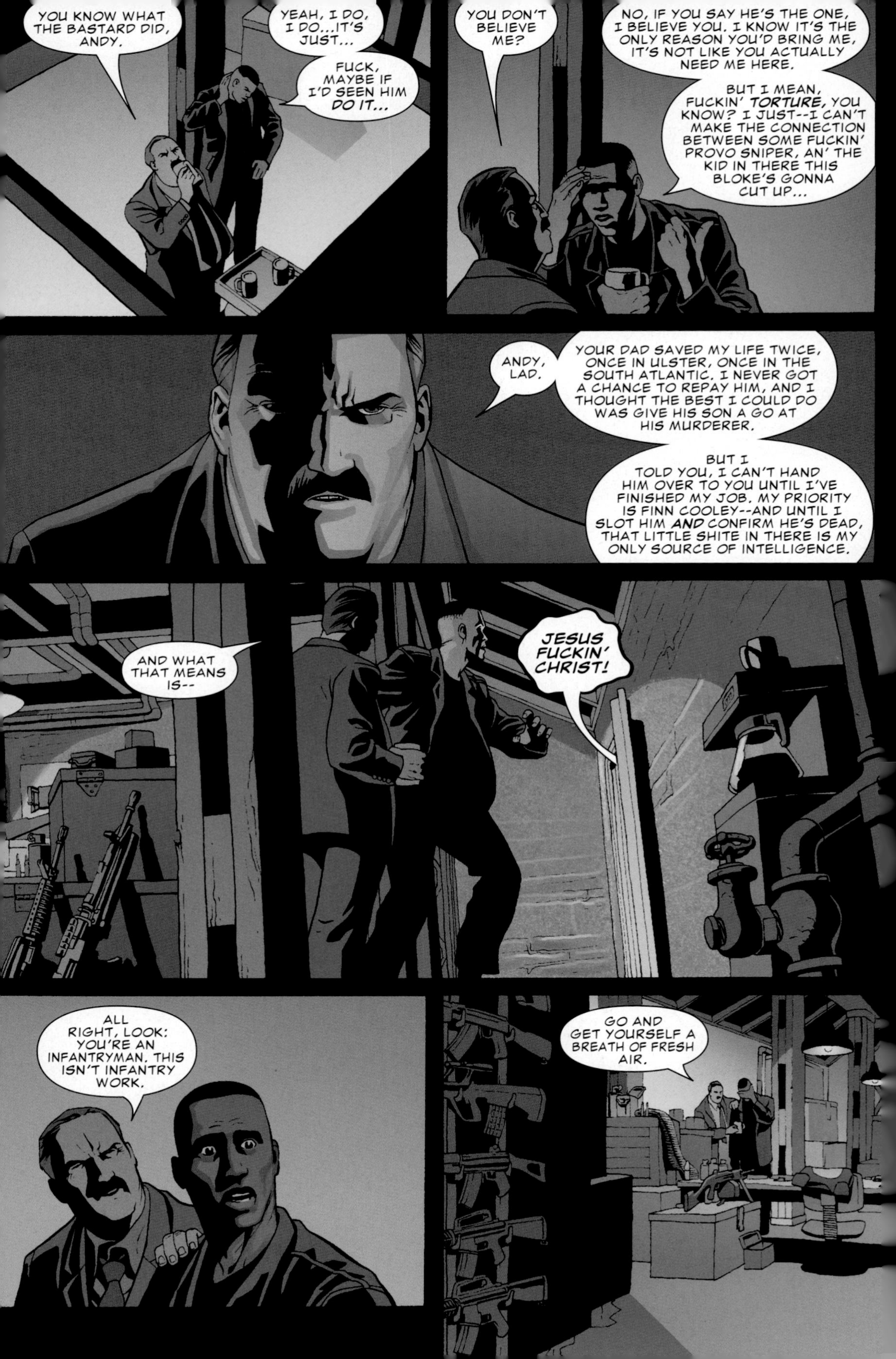

YOU KNOW WHAT THE BASTARD DID, ANDY.
YEAH, I DO, I DO...IT'S JUST...
FUCK, MAYBE IF I'D SEEN HIM *DO IT...*
YOU DON'T BELIEVE ME?
NO, IF YOU SAY HE'S THE ONE, I BELIEVE YOU. I KNOW IT'S THE ONLY REASON YOU'D BRING ME, IT'S NOT LIKE YOU ACTUALLY NEED ME HERE.
BUT I MEAN, FUCKIN' ***TORTURE,*** YOU KNOW? I JUST--I CAN'T MAKE THE CONNECTION BETWEEN SOME FUCKIN' PROVO SNIPER, AN' THE KID IN THERE THIS BLOKE'S GONNA CUT UP...
ANDY, LAD.
YOUR DAD SAVED MY LIFE TWICE, ONCE IN ULSTER, ONCE IN THE SOUTH ATLANTIC. I NEVER GOT A CHANCE TO REPAY HIM, AND I THOUGHT THE BEST I COULD DO WAS GIVE HIS SON A GO AT HIS MURDERER.
BUT I TOLD YOU, I CAN'T HAND HIM OVER TO YOU UNTIL I'VE FINISHED MY JOB. MY PRIORITY IS FINN COOLEY--AND UNTIL I SLOT HIM ***AND*** CONFIRM HE'S DEAD, THAT LITTLE SHITE IN THERE IS MY ONLY SOURCE OF INTELLIGENCE.
AND WHAT THAT MEANS IS--
JESUS FUCKIN' CHRIST!
ALL RIGHT, LOOK: YOU'RE AN INFANTRYMAN. THIS ISN'T INFANTRY WORK.
GO AND GET YOURSELF A BREATH OF FRESH AIR.

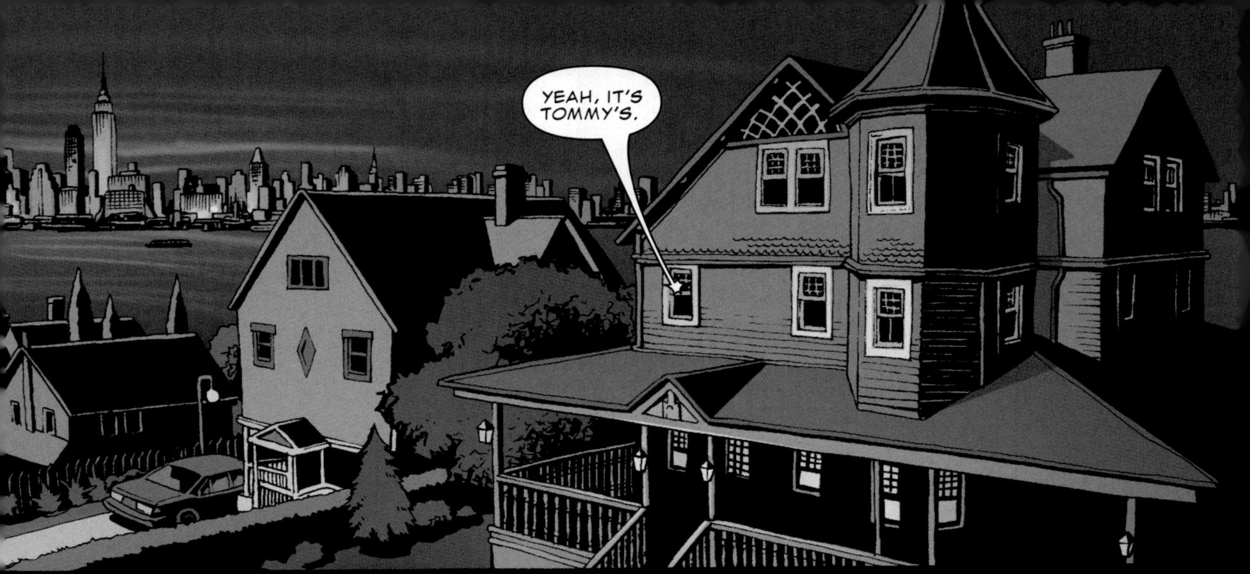
YEAH, IT'S TOMMY'S.

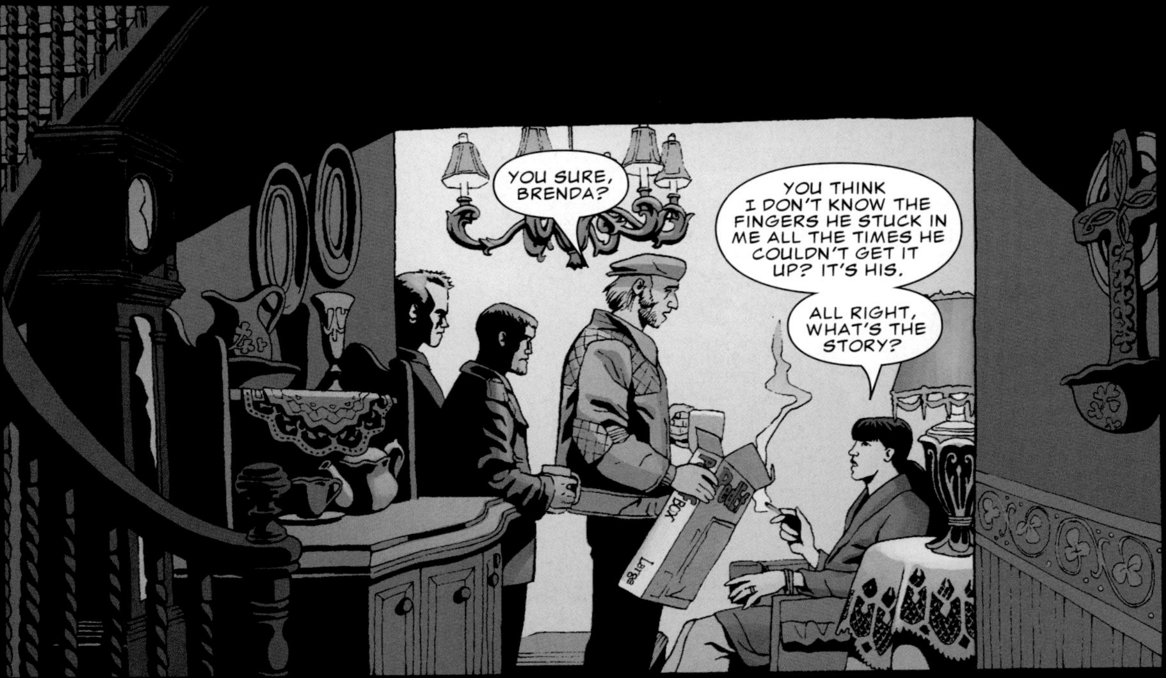
YOU SURE, BRENDA?
YOU THINK I DON'T KNOW THE FINGERS HE STUCK IN ME ALL THE TIMES HE COULDN'T GET IT UP? IT'S HIS.
ALL RIGHT, WHAT'S THE STORY?

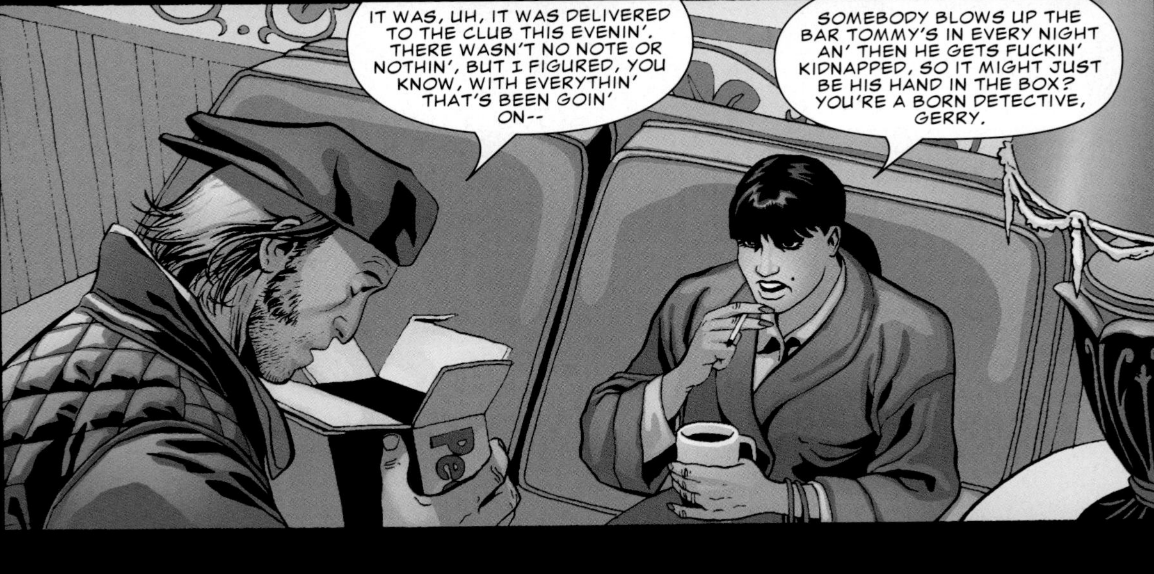
IT WAS, UH, IT WAS DELIVERED TO THE CLUB THIS EVENIN'. THERE WASN'T NO NOTE OR NOTHIN', BUT I FIGURED, YOU KNOW, WITH EVERYTHIN' THAT'S BEEN GOIN' ON--
SOMEBODY BLOWS UP THE BAR TOMMY'S IN EVERY NIGHT AN' THEN HE GETS FUCKIN' KIDNAPPED, SO IT MIGHT JUST BE HIS HAND IN THE BOX? YOU'RE A BORN DETECTIVE, GERRY.

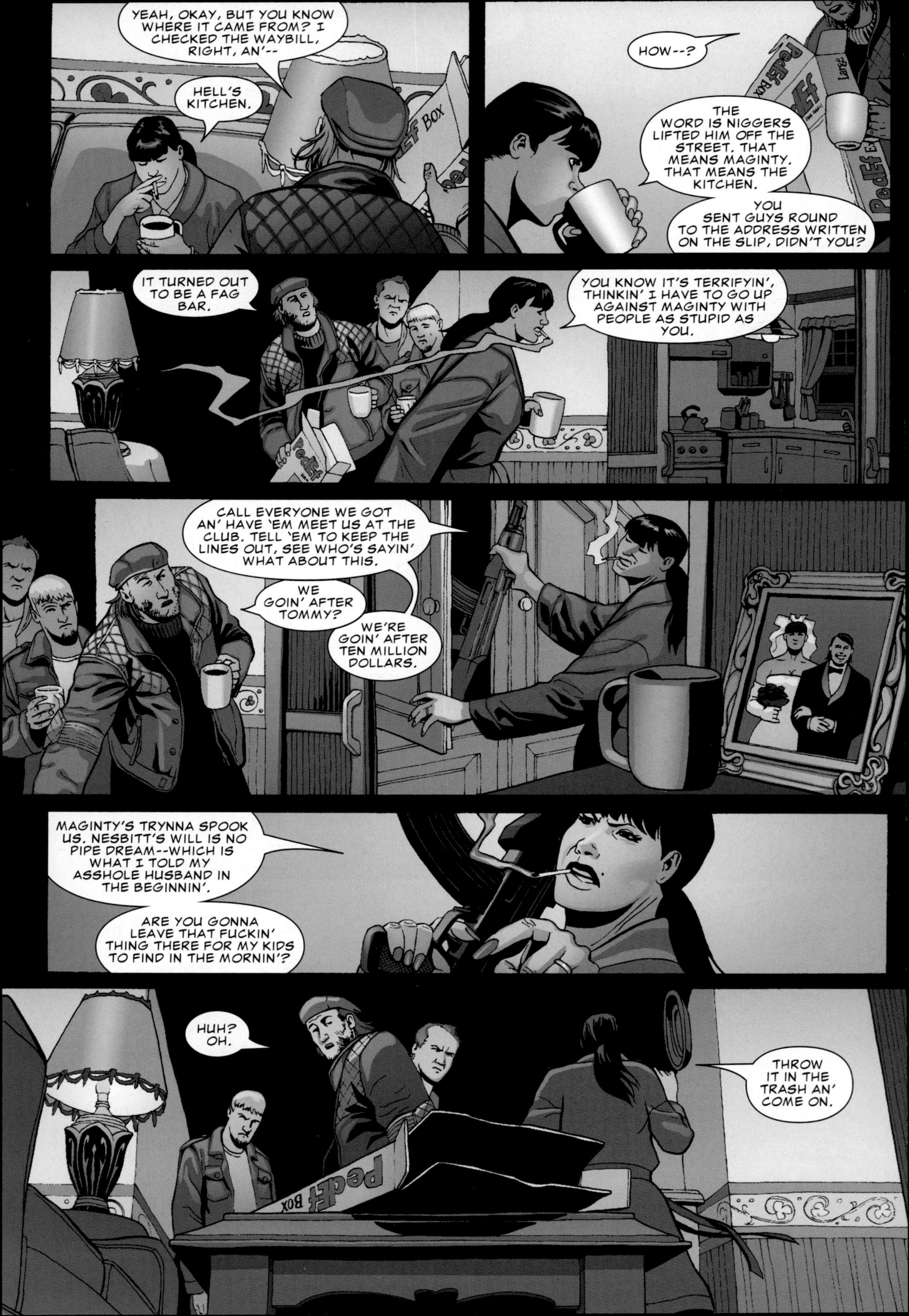
YEAH, OKAY, BUT YOU KNOW WHERE IT CAME FROM? I CHECKED THE WAYBILL, RIGHT, AN'--
HELL'S KITCHEN.
HOW--?
THE WORD IS NIGGERS LIFTED HIM OFF THE STREET. THAT MEANS MAGINTY. THAT MEANS THE KITCHEN.
YOU SENT GUYS ROUND TO THE ADDRESS WRITTEN ON THE SLIP, DIDN'T YOU?
IT TURNED OUT TO BE A FAG BAR.
YOU KNOW IT'S TERRIFYIN', THINKIN' I HAVE TO GO UP AGAINST MAGINTY WITH PEOPLE AS STUPID AS YOU.
CALL EVERYONE WE GOT AN' HAVE 'EM MEET US AT THE CLUB. TELL 'EM TO KEEP THE LINES OUT, SEE WHO'S SAYIN' WHAT ABOUT THIS.
WE GOIN' AFTER TOMMY?
WE'RE GOIN' AFTER TEN MILLION DOLLARS.
MAGINTY'S TRYNNA SPOOK US. NESBITT'S WILL IS NO PIPE DREAM--WHICH IS WHAT I TOLD MY ASSHOLE HUSBAND IN THE BEGINNIN'.
ARE YOU GONNA LEAVE THAT FUCKIN' THING THERE FOR MY KIDS TO FIND IN THE MORNIN'?
HUH? OH.
THROW IT IN THE TRASH AN' COME ON.

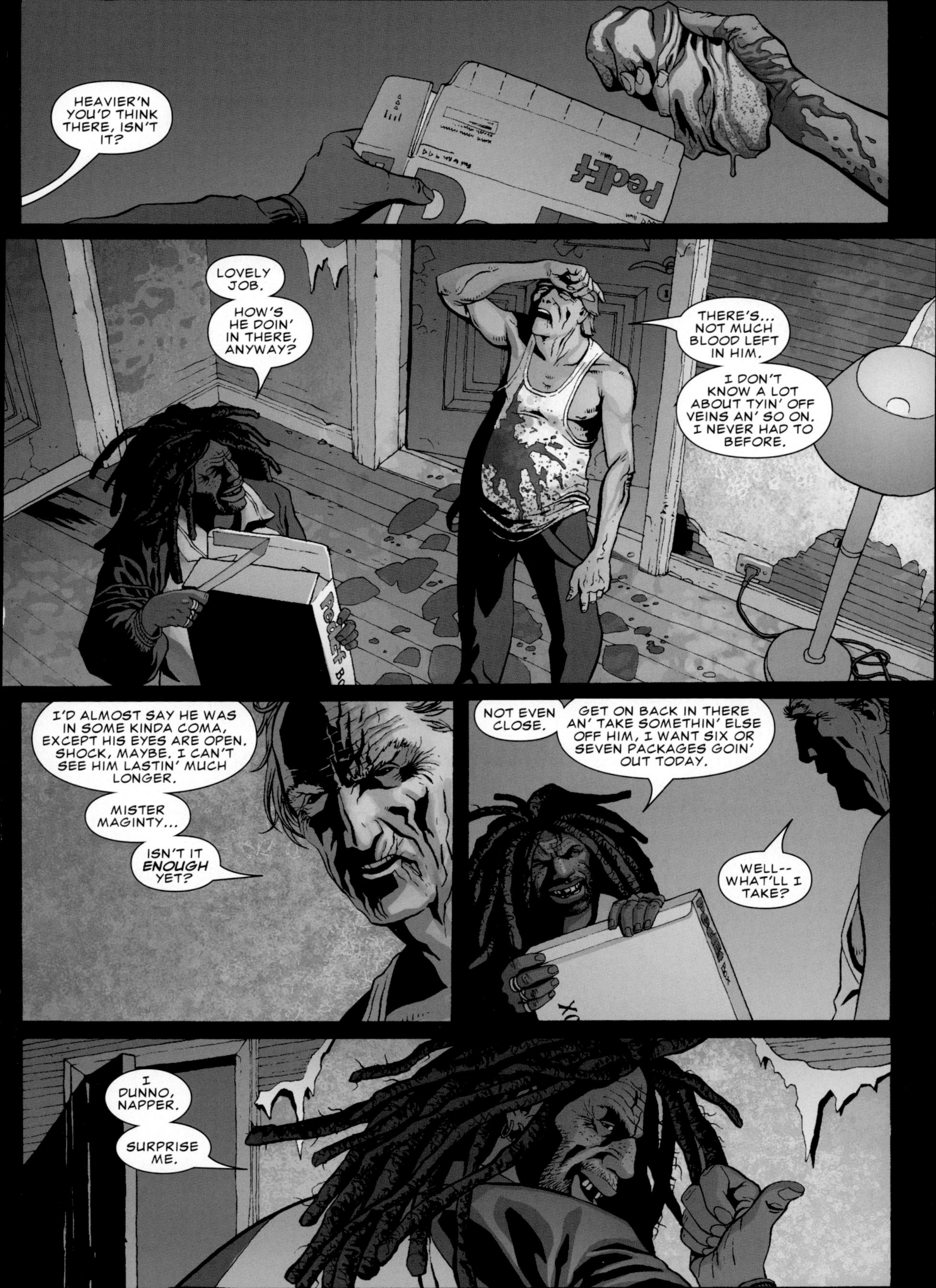
HEAVIER'N YOU'D THINK THERE, ISN'T IT?
LOVELY JOB.
HOW'S HE DOIN' IN THERE, ANYWAY?
THERE'S... NOT MUCH BLOOD LEFT IN HIM.
I DON'T KNOW A LOT ABOUT TYIN' OFF VEINS AN' SO ON. I NEVER HAD TO BEFORE.
I'D ALMOST SAY HE WAS IN SOME KINDA COMA, EXCEPT HIS EYES ARE OPEN. SHOCK, MAYBE. I CAN'T SEE HIM LASTIN' MUCH LONGER.
MISTER MAGINTY...
ISN'T IT *ENOUGH* YET?
NOT EVEN CLOSE.
GET ON BACK IN THERE AN' TAKE SOMETHIN' ELSE OFF HIM, I WANT SIX OR SEVEN PACKAGES GOIN' OUT TODAY.
WELL-- WHAT'LL I TAKE?
I DUNNO, NAPPER.
SURPRISE ME.

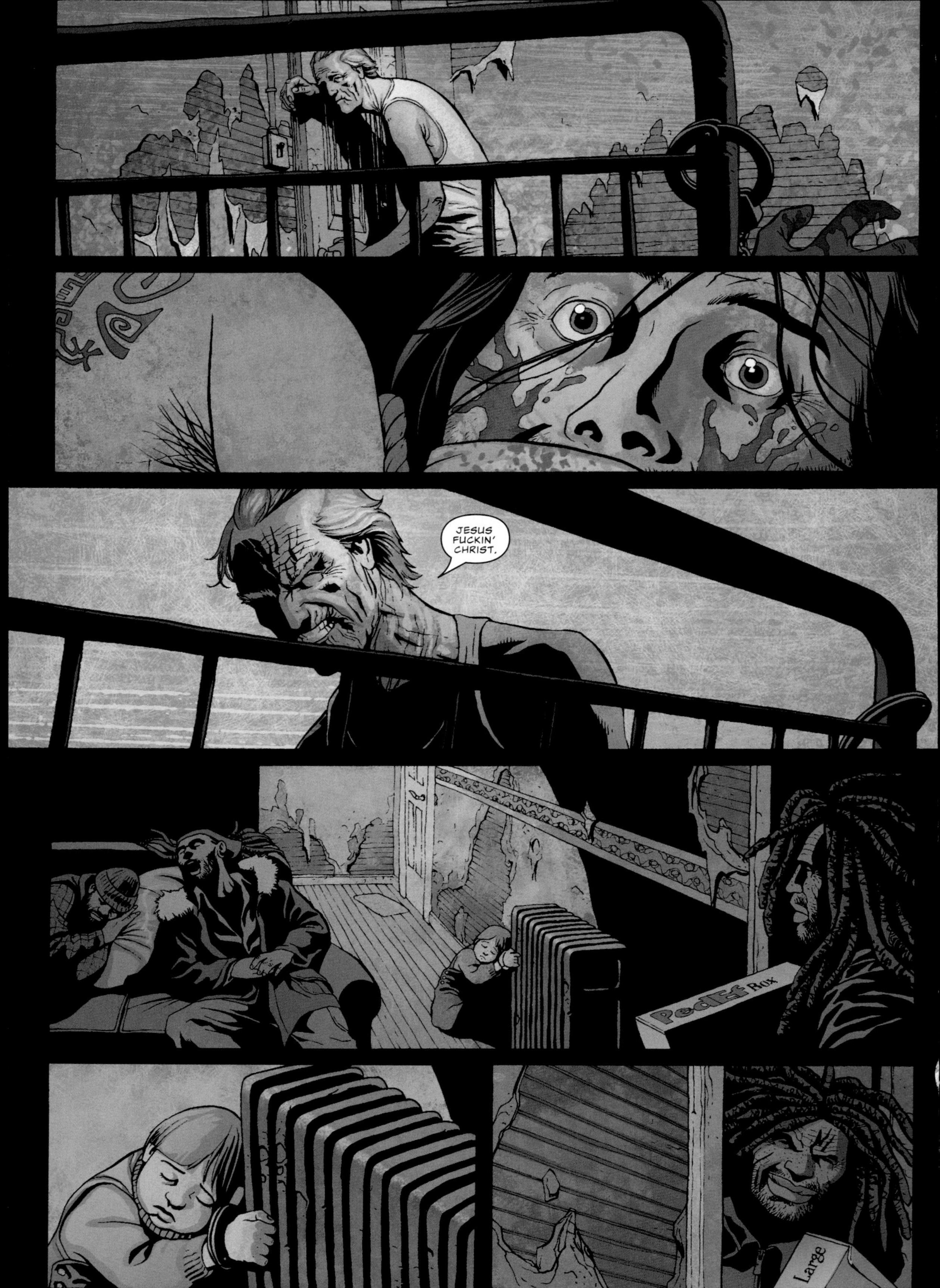
JESUS FUCKIN' CHRIST.
PedEf Box
Large

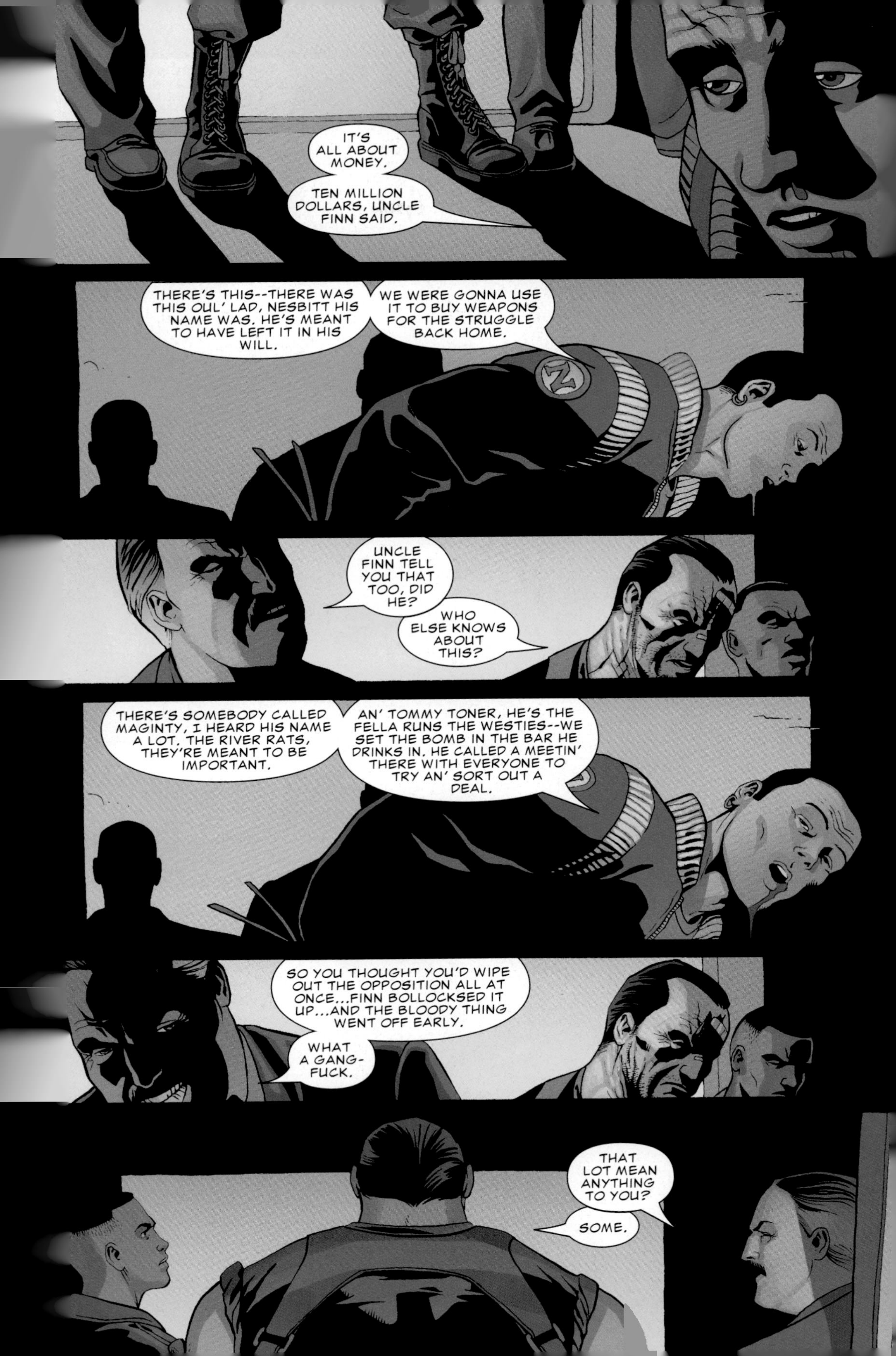

IT'S ALL ABOUT MONEY.
TEN MILLION DOLLARS, UNCLE FINN SAID.
THERE'S THIS--THERE WAS THIS OUL' LAD, NESBITT HIS NAME WAS. HE'S MEANT TO HAVE LEFT IT IN HIS WILL.
WE WERE GONNA USE IT TO BUY WEAPONS FOR THE STRUGGLE BACK HOME.
UNCLE FINN TELL YOU THAT TOO, DID HE?
WHO ELSE KNOWS ABOUT THIS?
THERE'S SOMEBODY CALLED MAGINTY, I HEARD HIS NAME A LOT. THE RIVER RATS, THEY'RE MEANT TO BE IMPORTANT.
AN' TOMMY TONER, HE'S THE FELLA RUNS THE WESTIES--WE SET THE BOMB IN THE BAR HE DRINKS IN. HE CALLED A MEETIN' THERE WITH EVERYONE TO TRY AN' SORT OUT A DEAL.
SO YOU THOUGHT YOU'D WIPE OUT THE OPPOSITION ALL AT ONCE...FINN BOLLOCKSED IT UP...AND THE BLOODY THING WENT OFF EARLY.
WHAT A GANG-FUCK.
THAT LOT MEAN ANYTHING TO YOU?
SOME.

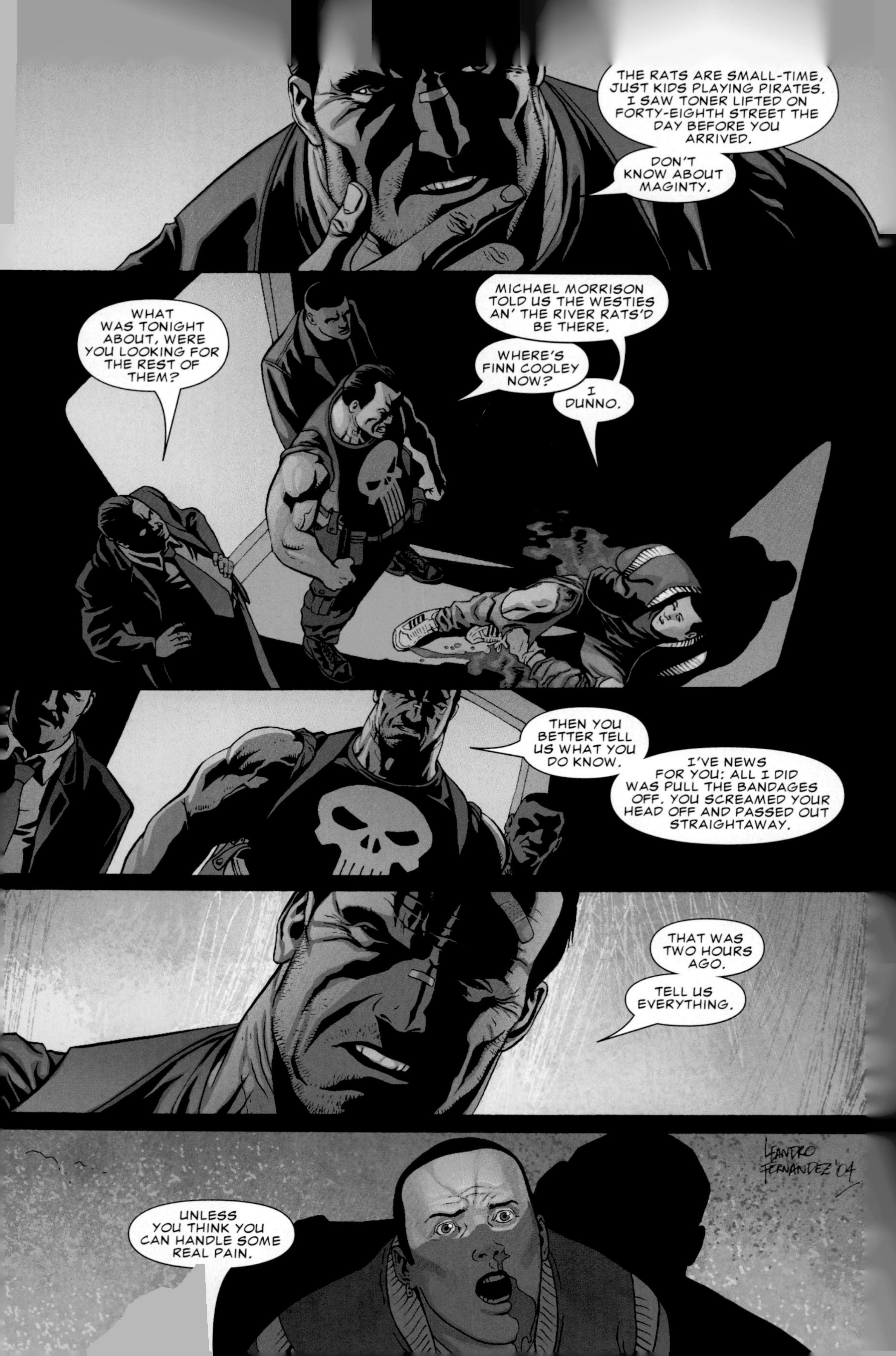
THE RATS ARE SMALL-TIME, JUST KIDS PLAYING PIRATES. I SAW TONER LIFTED ON FORTY-EIGHTH STREET THE DAY BEFORE YOU ARRIVED.
DON'T KNOW ABOUT MAGINTY.
WHAT WAS TONIGHT ABOUT, WERE YOU LOOKING FOR THE REST OF THEM?
MICHAEL MORRISON TOLD US THE WESTIES AN' THE RIVER RATS'D BE THERE.
WHERE'S FINN COOLEY NOW?
I DUNNO.
THEN YOU BETTER TELL US WHAT YOU DO KNOW.
I'VE NEWS FOR YOU: ALL I DID WAS PULL THE BANDAGES OFF. YOU SCREAMED YOUR HEAD OFF AND PASSED OUT STRAIGHTAWAY.
THAT WAS TWO HOURS AGO.
TELL US EVERYTHING.
LEANDRO FERNANDEZ '04
UNLESS YOU THINK YOU CAN HANDLE SOME REAL PAIN.

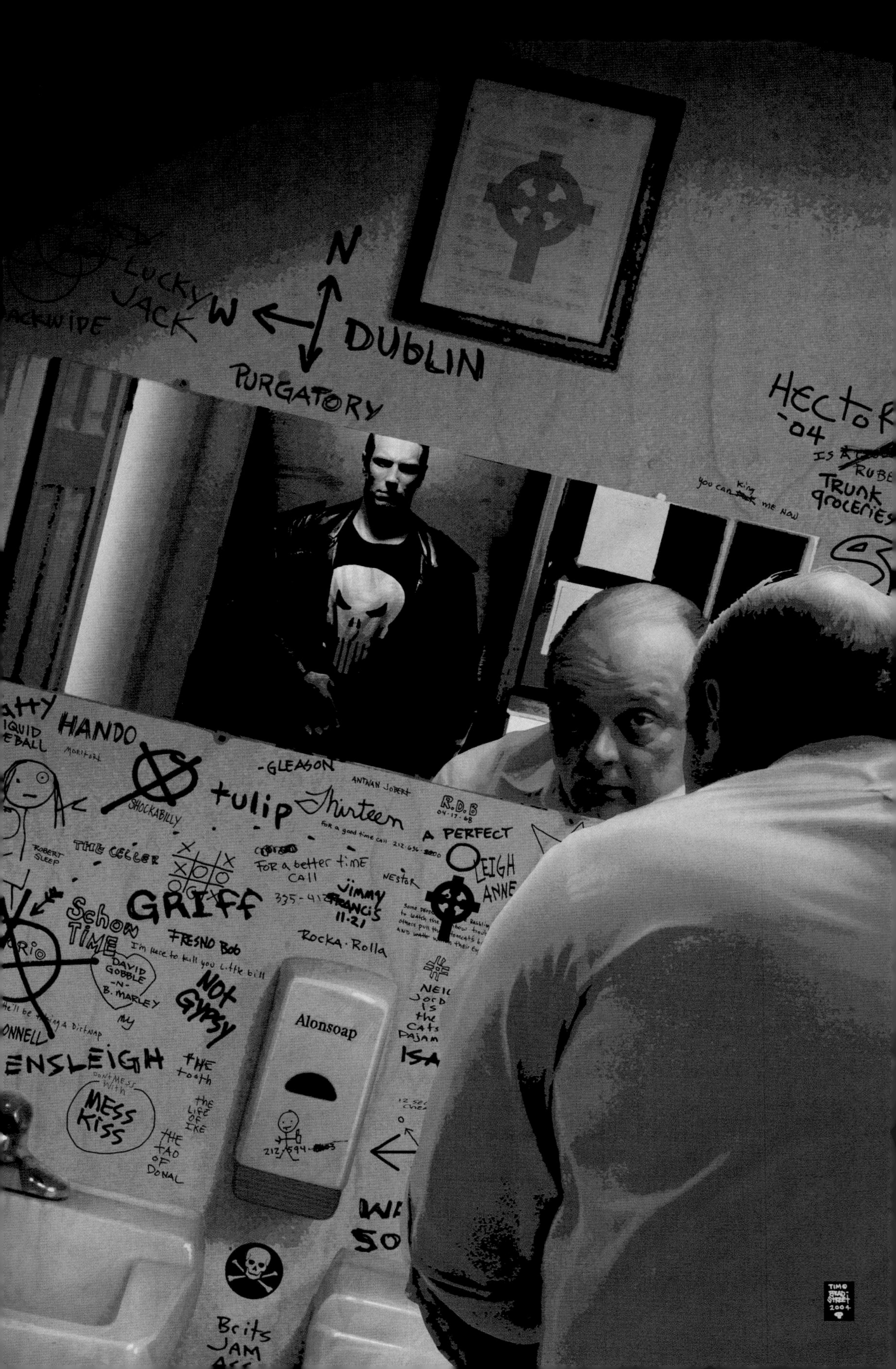
N
LUCKY JACK
W
DUBLIN
PURGATORY
HECTOR
-04
TRUNK
groceries
HANDO
-GLEASON
SHOCKABILLY
tulip
ANTWAN JOBERT
Thirteen
R.D.B
04-17-68
A PERFECT
LEIGH
ANNE
ROBERT SLEEP
THE CELLER
For a better time
Call
NESTOR
Jimmy
Francis
11.21
GRIFF
Schow
TIME
FRESNO Bob
I'm here to kill you little bill
Rocka-Rolla
DAVID
GOBBLE
-N-
B. MARLEY
NOT
GYPSY
Alonsoap
MESS
KISS
THE
tooth
the
LIFE
OF
IKE
THE
TAO
OF
DONAL
TIMO
BRAD-
STREET
2004

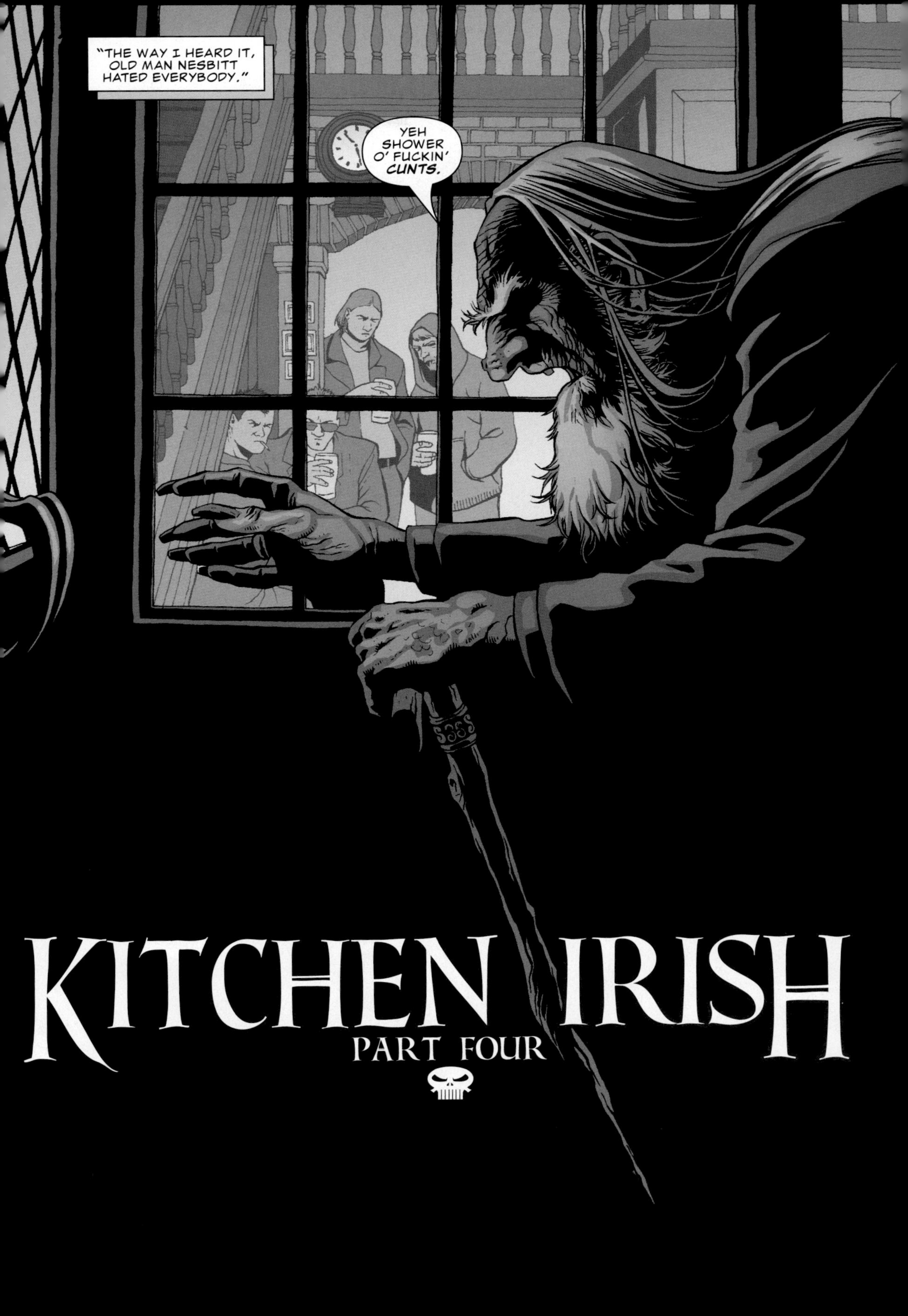
"THE WAY I HEARD IT, OLD MAN NESBITT HATED EVERYBODY."
YEH SHOWER O' FUCKIN' CUNTS.
KITCHEN IRISH
PART FOUR

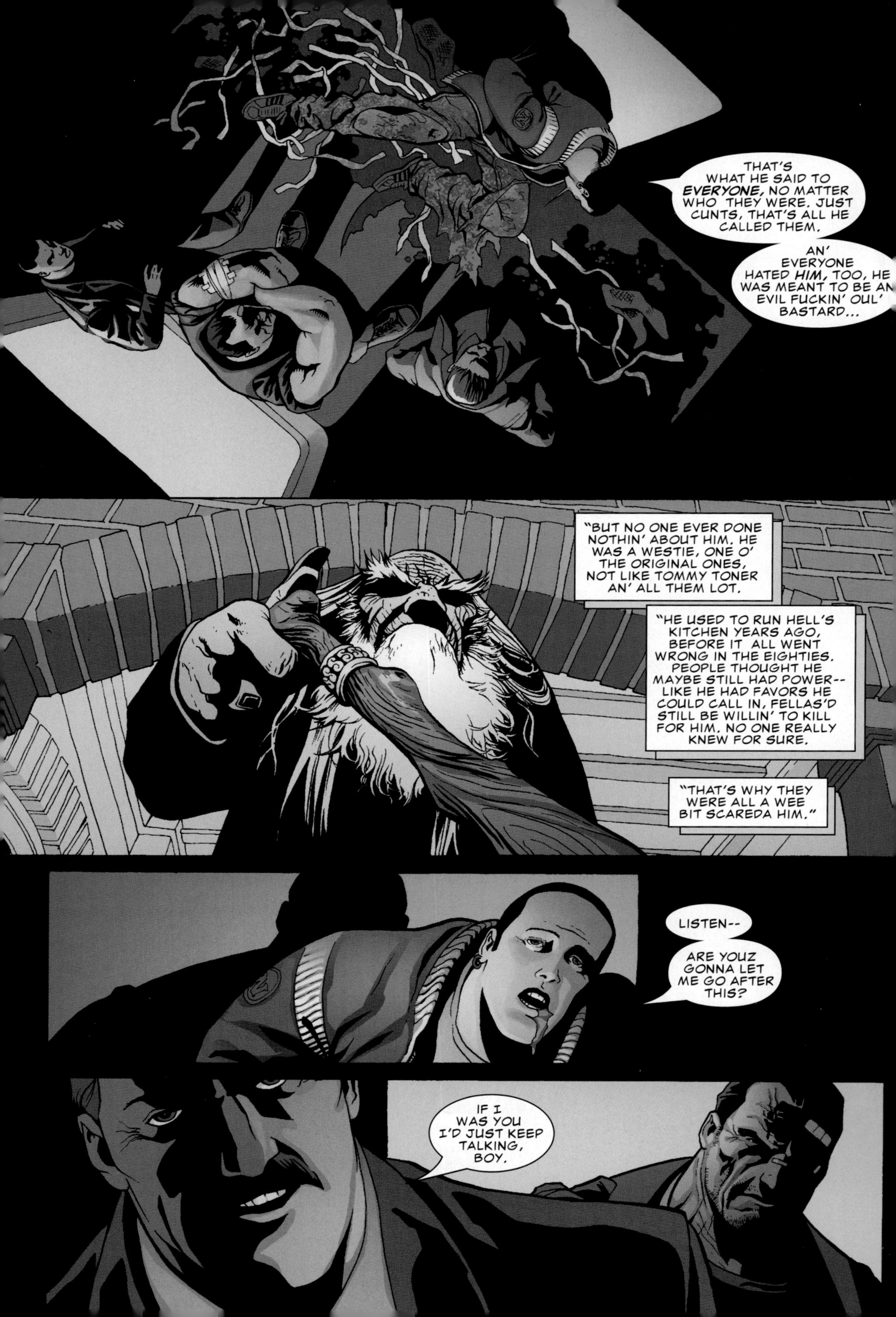
THAT'S WHAT HE SAID TO EVERYONE, NO MATTER WHO THEY WERE. JUST CUNTS, THAT'S ALL HE CALLED THEM.
AN' EVERYONE HATED HIM, TOO, HE WAS MEANT TO BE AN EVIL FUCKIN' OUL' BASTARD...
"BUT NO ONE EVER DONE NOTHIN' ABOUT HIM. HE WAS A WESTIE, ONE O' THE ORIGINAL ONES, NOT LIKE TOMMY TONER AN' ALL THEM LOT.
"HE USED TO RUN HELL'S KITCHEN YEARS AGO, BEFORE IT ALL WENT WRONG IN THE EIGHTIES. PEOPLE THOUGHT HE MAYBE STILL HAD POWER-- LIKE HE HAD FAVORS HE COULD CALL IN, FELLAS'D STILL BE WILLIN' TO KILL FOR HIM. NO ONE REALLY KNEW FOR SURE.
"THAT'S WHY THEY WERE ALL A WEE BIT SCAREDA HIM."
LISTEN--
ARE YOUZ GONNA LET ME GO AFTER THIS?
IF I WAS YOU I'D JUST KEEP TALKING, BOY.

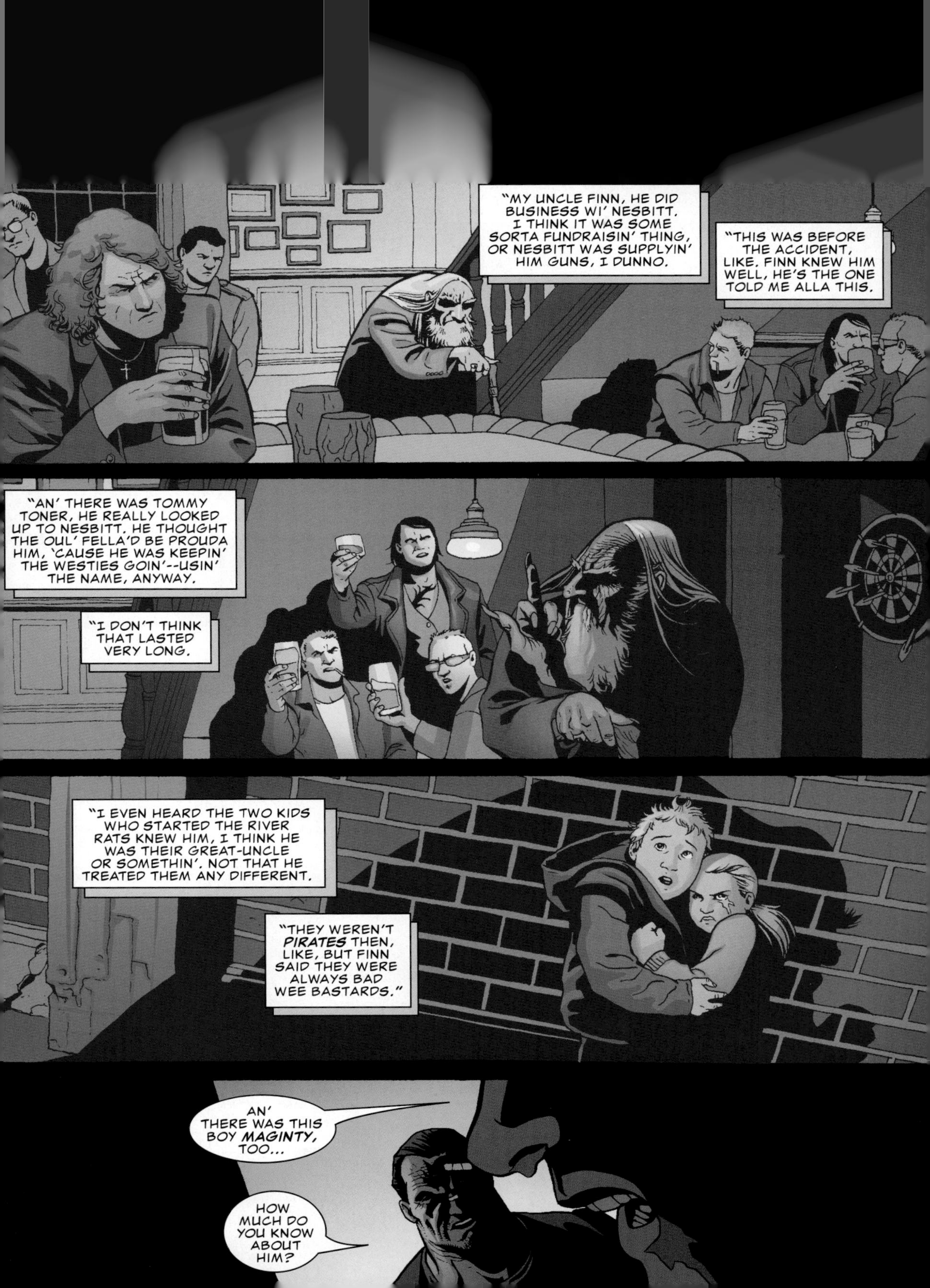
"MY UNCLE FINN, HE DID BUSINESS WI' NESBITT. I THINK IT WAS SOME SORTA FUNDRAISIN' THING, OR NESBITT WAS SUPPLYIN' HIM GUNS, I DUNNO.
"THIS WAS BEFORE THE ACCIDENT, LIKE. FINN KNEW HIM WELL, HE'S THE ONE TOLD ME ALLA THIS.
"AN' THERE WAS TOMMY TONER, HE REALLY LOOKED UP TO NESBITT. HE THOUGHT THE OUL' FELLA'D BE PROUDA HIM, 'CAUSE HE WAS KEEPIN' THE WESTIES GOIN'--USIN' THE NAME, ANYWAY.
"I DON'T THINK THAT LASTED VERY LONG.
"I EVEN HEARD THE TWO KIDS WHO STARTED THE RIVER RATS KNEW HIM, I THINK HE WAS THEIR GREAT-UNCLE OR SOMETHIN', NOT THAT HE TREATED THEM ANY DIFFERENT.
"THEY WEREN'T PIRATES THEN, LIKE, BUT FINN SAID THEY WERE ALWAYS BAD WEE BASTARDS."
AN' THERE WAS THIS BOY MAGINTY, TOO...
HOW MUCH DO YOU KNOW ABOUT HIM?

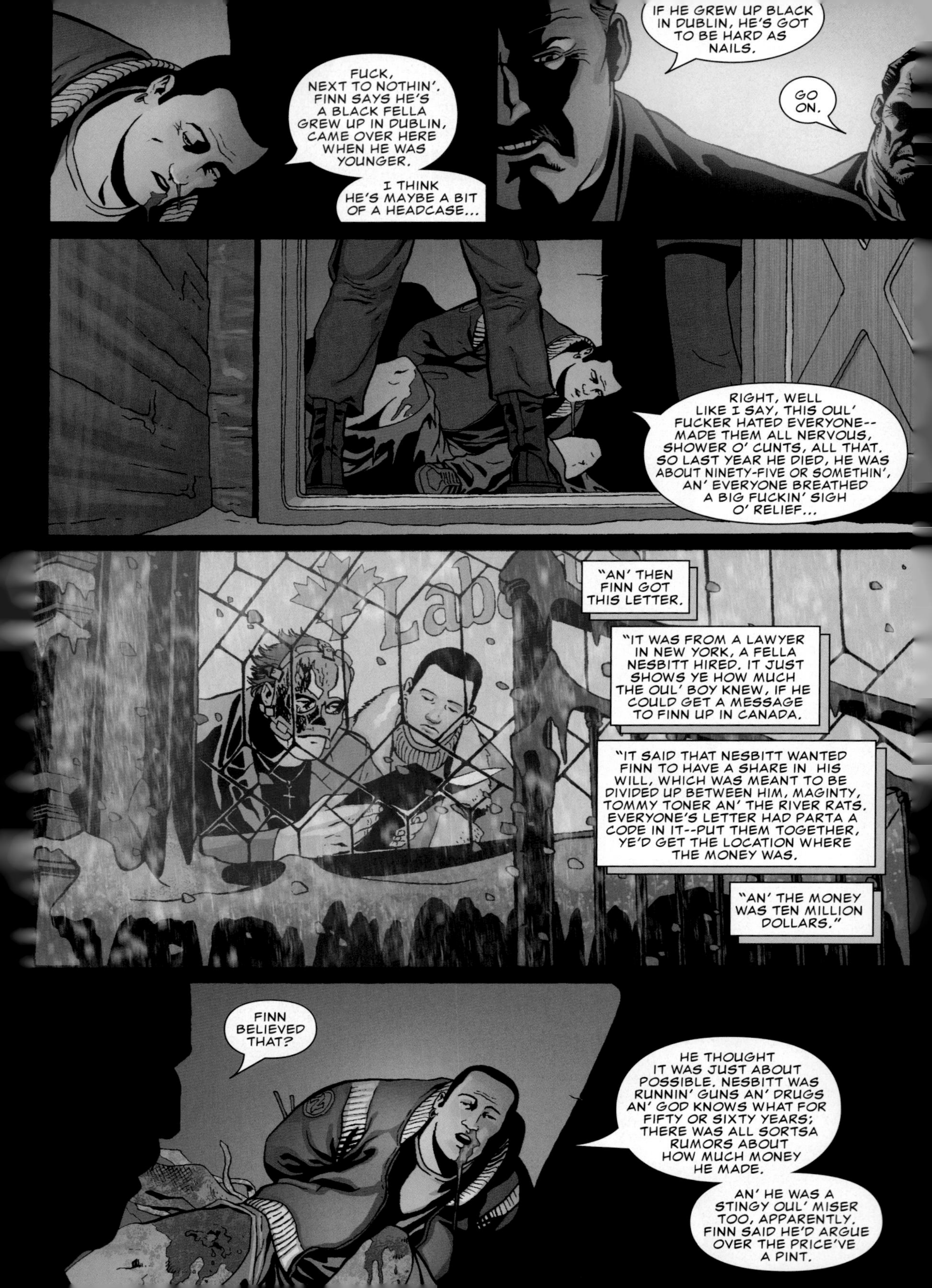
FUCK, NEXT TO NOTHIN'. FINN SAYS HE'S A BLACK FELLA GREW UP IN DUBLIN, CAME OVER HERE WHEN HE WAS YOUNGER.
I THINK HE'S MAYBE A BIT OF A HEADCASE...
IF HE GREW UP BLACK IN DUBLIN, HE'S GOT TO BE HARD AS NAILS.
GO ON.
RIGHT, WELL LIKE I SAY, THIS OUL' FUCKER HATED EVERYONE-- MADE THEM ALL NERVOUS, SHOWER O' CUNTS, ALL THAT. SO LAST YEAR HE DIED, HE WAS ABOUT NINETY-FIVE OR SOMETHIN', AN' EVERYONE BREATHED A BIG FUCKIN' SIGH O' RELIEF...
"AN' THEN FINN GOT THIS LETTER.
"IT WAS FROM A LAWYER IN NEW YORK, A FELLA NESBITT HIRED. IT JUST SHOWS YE HOW MUCH THE OUL' BOY KNEW, IF HE COULD GET A MESSAGE TO FINN UP IN CANADA.
"IT SAID THAT NESBITT WANTED FINN TO HAVE A SHARE IN HIS WILL, WHICH WAS MEANT TO BE DIVIDED UP BETWEEN HIM, MAGINTY, TOMMY TONER AN' THE RIVER RATS. EVERYONE'S LETTER HAD PARTA A CODE IN IT--PUT THEM TOGETHER, YE'D GET THE LOCATION WHERE THE MONEY WAS.
"AN' THE MONEY WAS TEN MILLION DOLLARS."
FINN BELIEVED THAT?
HE THOUGHT IT WAS JUST ABOUT POSSIBLE. NESBITT WAS RUNNIN' GUNS AN' DRUGS AN' GOD KNOWS WHAT FOR FIFTY OR SIXTY YEARS; THERE WAS ALL SORTSA RUMORS ABOUT HOW MUCH MONEY HE MADE.
AN' HE WAS A STINGY OUL' MISER TOO, APPARENTLY. FINN SAID HE'D ARGUE OVER THE PRICE'VE A PINT.

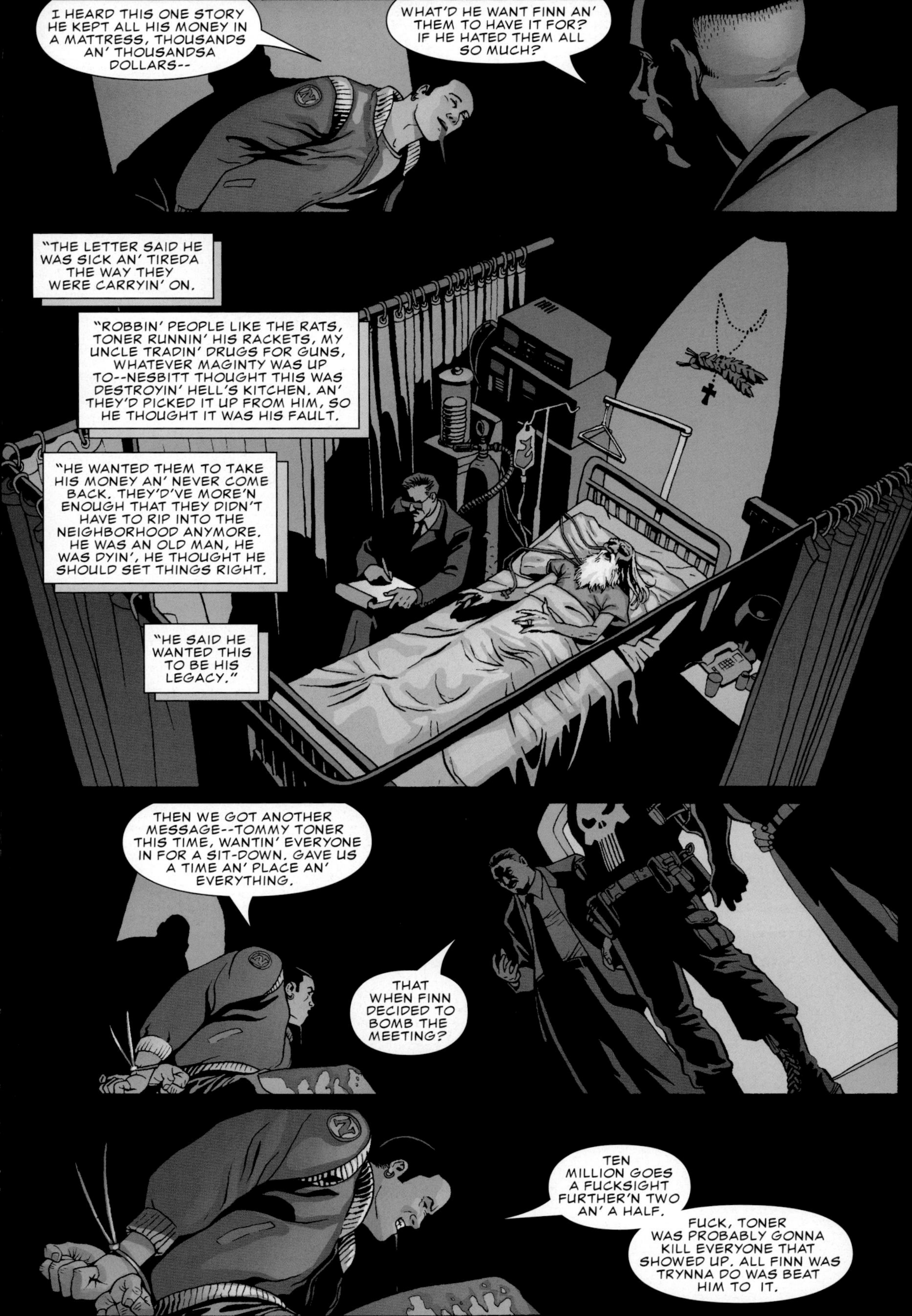
I HEARD THIS ONE STORY HE KEPT ALL HIS MONEY IN A MATTRESS, THOUSANDS AN' THOUSANDSA DOLLARS--
WHAT'D HE WANT FINN AN' THEM TO HAVE IT FOR? IF HE HATED THEM ALL SO MUCH?
"THE LETTER SAID HE WAS SICK AN' TIREDA THE WAY THEY WERE CARRYIN' ON.
"ROBBIN' PEOPLE LIKE THE RATS, TONER RUNNIN' HIS RACKETS, MY UNCLE TRADIN' DRUGS FOR GUNS, WHATEVER MAGINTY WAS UP TO--NESBITT THOUGHT THIS WAS DESTROYIN' HELL'S KITCHEN. AN' THEY'D PICKED IT UP FROM HIM, SO HE THOUGHT IT WAS HIS FAULT.
"HE WANTED THEM TO TAKE HIS MONEY AN' NEVER COME BACK. THEY'D'VE MORE'N ENOUGH THAT THEY DIDN'T HAVE TO RIP INTO THE NEIGHBORHOOD ANYMORE. HE WAS AN OLD MAN, HE WAS DYIN', HE THOUGHT HE SHOULD SET THINGS RIGHT.
"HE SAID HE WANTED THIS TO BE HIS LEGACY."
THEN WE GOT ANOTHER MESSAGE--TOMMY TONER THIS TIME, WANTIN' EVERYONE IN FOR A SIT-DOWN. GAVE US A TIME AN' PLACE AN' EVERYTHING.
THAT WHEN FINN DECIDED TO BOMB THE MEETING?
TEN MILLION GOES A FUCKSIGHT FURTHER'N TWO AN' A HALF.
FUCK, TONER WAS PROBABLY GONNA KILL EVERYONE THAT SHOWED UP. ALL FINN WAS TRYNNA DO WAS BEAT HIM TO IT.

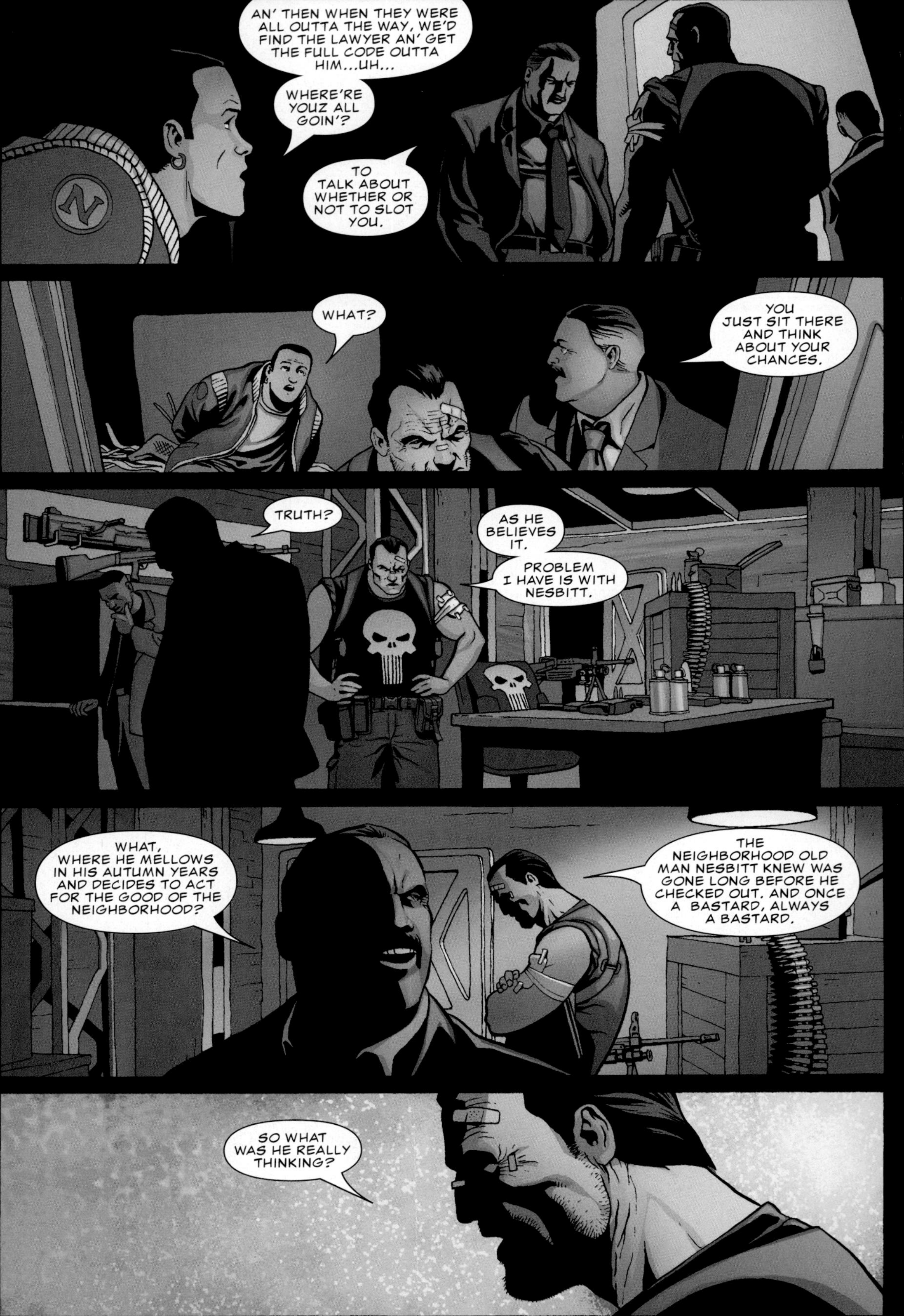
AN' THEN WHEN THEY WERE ALL OUTTA THE WAY, WE'D FIND THE LAWYER AN' GET THE FULL CODE OUTTA HIM...UH...
WHERE'RE YOUZ ALL GOIN'?
TO TALK ABOUT WHETHER OR NOT TO SLOT YOU.
WHAT?
YOU JUST SIT THERE AND THINK ABOUT YOUR CHANCES.
TRUTH?
AS HE BELIEVES IT.
PROBLEM I HAVE IS WITH NESBITT.
WHAT, WHERE HE MELLOWS IN HIS AUTUMN YEARS AND DECIDES TO ACT FOR THE GOOD OF THE NEIGHBORHOOD?
THE NEIGHBORHOOD OLD MAN NESBITT KNEW WAS GONE LONG BEFORE HE CHECKED OUT. AND ONCE A BASTARD, ALWAYS A BASTARD.
SO WHAT WAS HE REALLY THINKING?

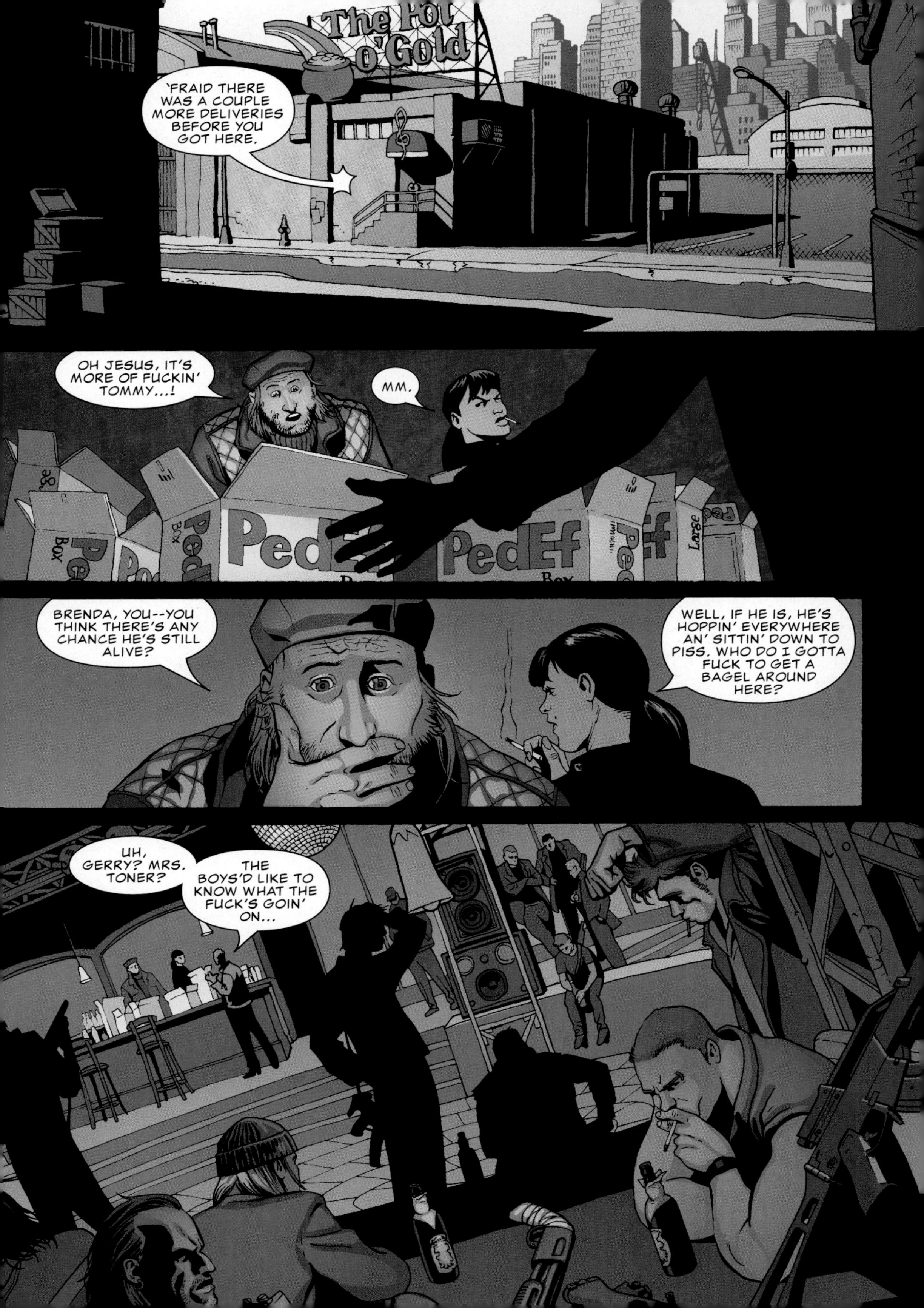
The Pot o'Gold
'FRAID THERE WAS A COUPLE MORE DELIVERIES BEFORE YOU GOT HERE.
OH JESUS, IT'S MORE OF FUCKIN' TOMMY...!
MM.
PedEf
BRENDA, YOU--YOU THINK THERE'S ANY CHANCE HE'S STILL ALIVE?
WELL, IF HE IS, HE'S HOPPIN' EVERYWHERE AN' SITTIN' DOWN TO PISS. WHO DO I GOTTA FUCK TO GET A BAGEL AROUND HERE?
UH, GERRY? MRS. TONER?
THE BOYS'D LIKE TO KNOW WHAT THE FUCK'S GOIN' ON...

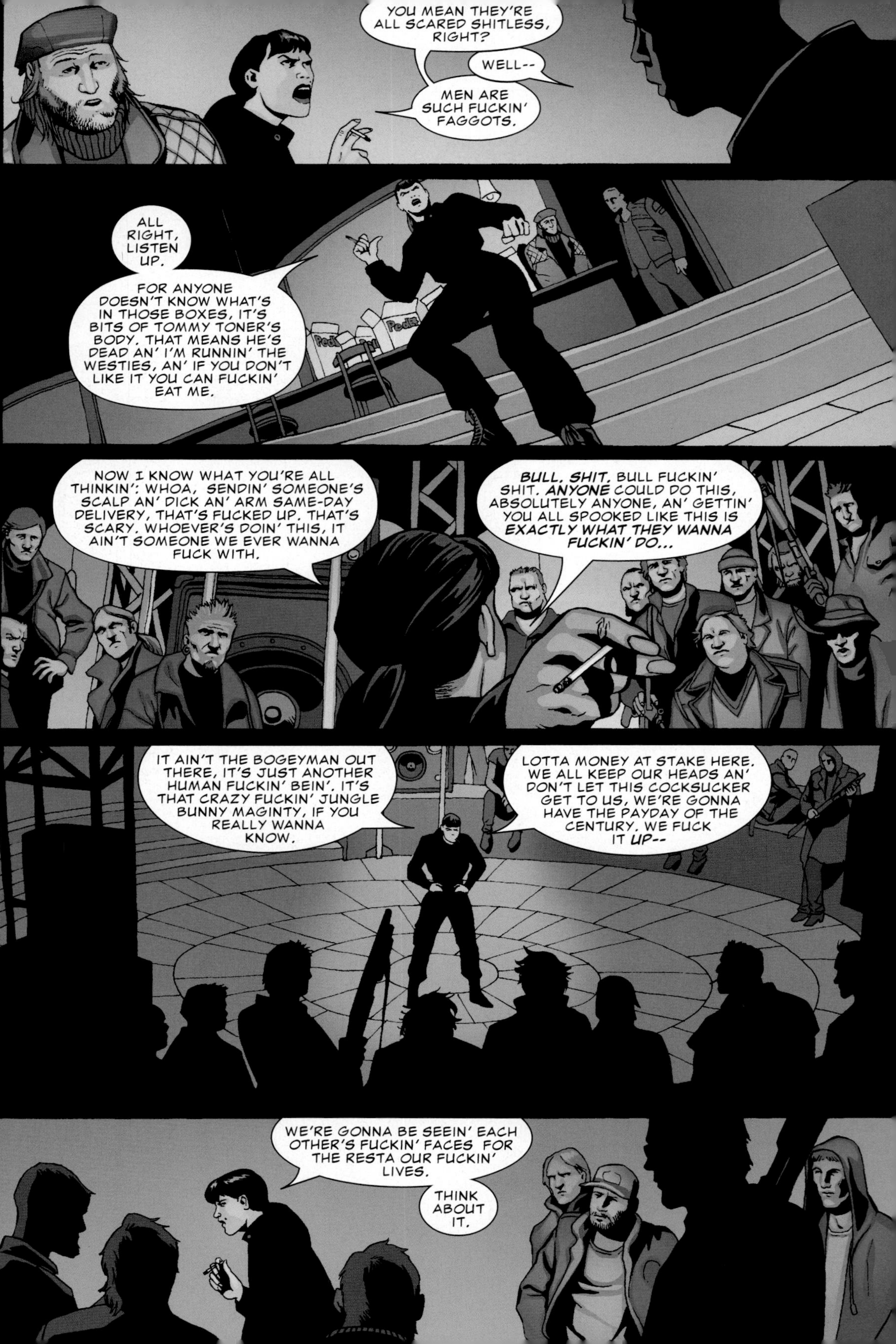
YOU MEAN THEY'RE ALL SCARED SHITLESS, RIGHT?
WELL--
MEN ARE SUCH FUCKIN' FAGGOTS.
ALL RIGHT, LISTEN UP.
FOR ANYONE DOESN'T KNOW WHAT'S IN THOSE BOXES, IT'S BITS OF TOMMY TONER'S BODY. THAT MEANS HE'S DEAD AN' I'M RUNNIN' THE WESTIES, AN' IF YOU DON'T LIKE IT YOU CAN FUCKIN' EAT ME.
NOW I KNOW WHAT YOU'RE ALL THINKIN': WHOA, SENDIN' SOMEONE'S SCALP AN' DICK AN' ARM SAME-DAY DELIVERY, THAT'S FUCKED UP. THAT'S SCARY. WHOEVER'S DOIN' THIS, IT AIN'T SOMEONE WE EVER WANNA FUCK WITH.
BULL. SHIT. BULL FUCKIN' SHIT. *ANYONE* COULD DO THIS, ABSOLUTELY ANYONE, AN' GETTIN' YOU ALL SPOOKED LIKE THIS IS *EXACTLY WHAT THEY WANNA FUCKIN' DO...*
IT AIN'T THE BOGEYMAN OUT THERE, IT'S JUST ANOTHER HUMAN FUCKIN' BEIN'. IT'S THAT CRAZY FUCKIN' JUNGLE BUNNY MAGINTY, IF YOU REALLY WANNA KNOW.
LOTTA MONEY AT STAKE HERE. WE ALL KEEP OUR HEADS AN' DON'T LET THIS COCKSUCKER GET TO US, WE'RE GONNA HAVE THE PAYDAY OF THE CENTURY. WE FUCK IT *UP*--
WE'RE GONNA BE SEEIN' EACH OTHER'S FUCKIN' FACES FOR THE RESTA OUR FUCKIN' LIVES.
THINK ABOUT IT.

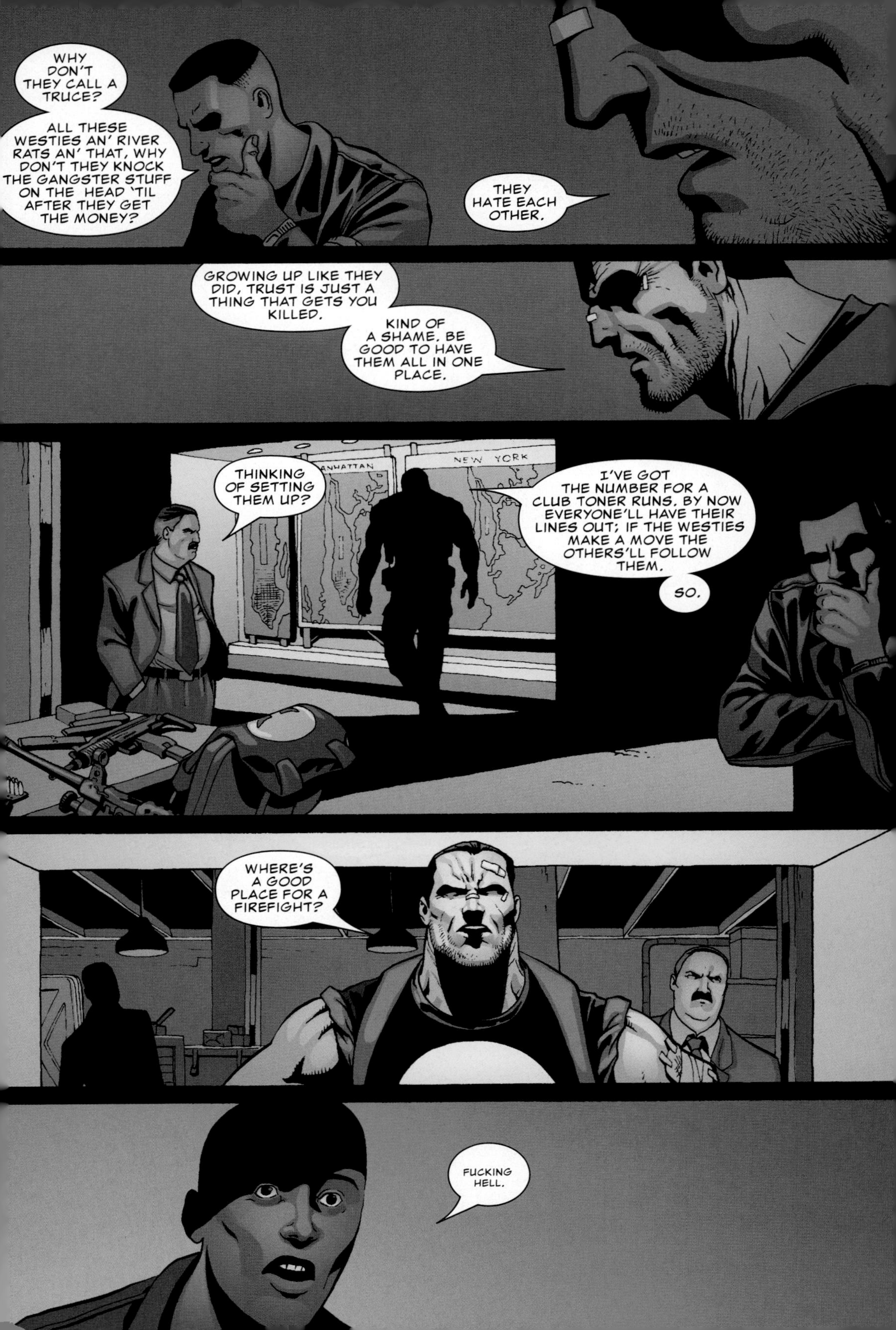
WHY DON'T THEY CALL A TRUCE?
ALL THESE WESTIES AN' RIVER RATS AN' THAT, WHY DON'T THEY KNOCK THE GANGSTER STUFF ON THE HEAD 'TIL AFTER THEY GET THE MONEY?
THEY HATE EACH OTHER.
GROWING UP LIKE THEY DID, TRUST IS JUST A THING THAT GETS YOU KILLED.
KIND OF A SHAME. BE GOOD TO HAVE THEM ALL IN ONE PLACE.
THINKING OF SETTING THEM UP?
NEW YORK
I'VE GOT THE NUMBER FOR A CLUB TONER RUNS. BY NOW EVERYONE'LL HAVE THEIR LINES OUT; IF THE WESTIES MAKE A MOVE THE OTHERS'LL FOLLOW THEM.
SO.
WHERE'S A GOOD PLACE FOR A FIREFIGHT?
FUCKING HELL.

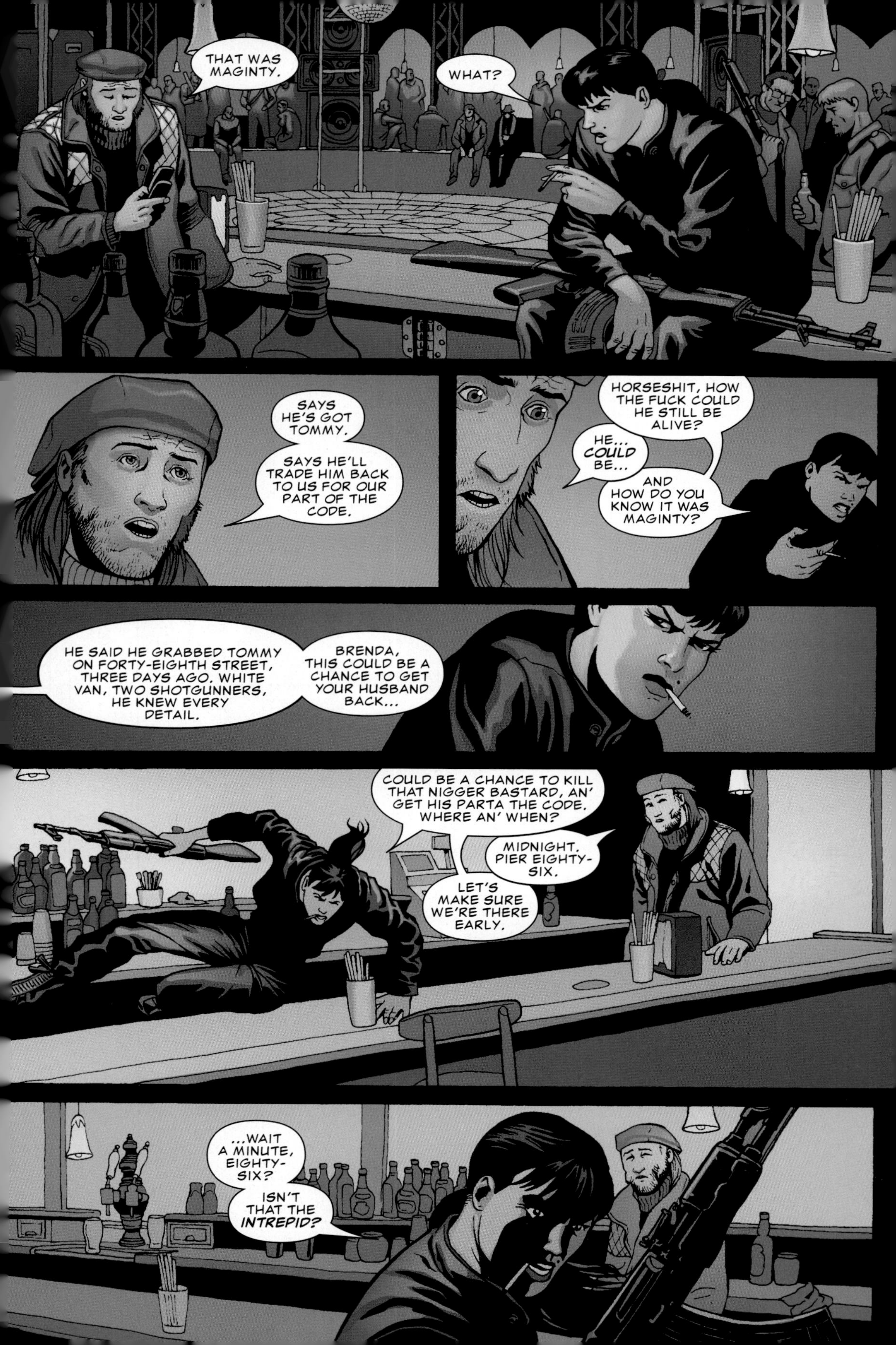
THAT WAS MAGINTY.
WHAT?
SAYS HE'S GOT TOMMY.
SAYS HE'LL TRADE HIM BACK TO US FOR OUR PART OF THE CODE.
HORSESHIT, HOW THE FUCK COULD HE STILL BE ALIVE?
HE... *COULD* BE...
AND HOW DO YOU KNOW IT WAS MAGINTY?
HE SAID HE GRABBED TOMMY ON FORTY-EIGHTH STREET, THREE DAYS AGO. WHITE VAN, TWO SHOTGUNNERS, HE KNEW EVERY DETAIL.
BRENDA, THIS COULD BE A CHANCE TO GET YOUR HUSBAND BACK...
COULD BE A CHANCE TO KILL THAT NIGGER BASTARD, AN' GET HIS PARTA THE CODE. WHERE AN' WHEN?
MIDNIGHT. PIER EIGHTY-SIX.
LET'S MAKE SURE WE'RE THERE EARLY.
...WAIT A MINUTE, EIGHTY-SIX?
ISN'T THAT THE *INTREPID?*

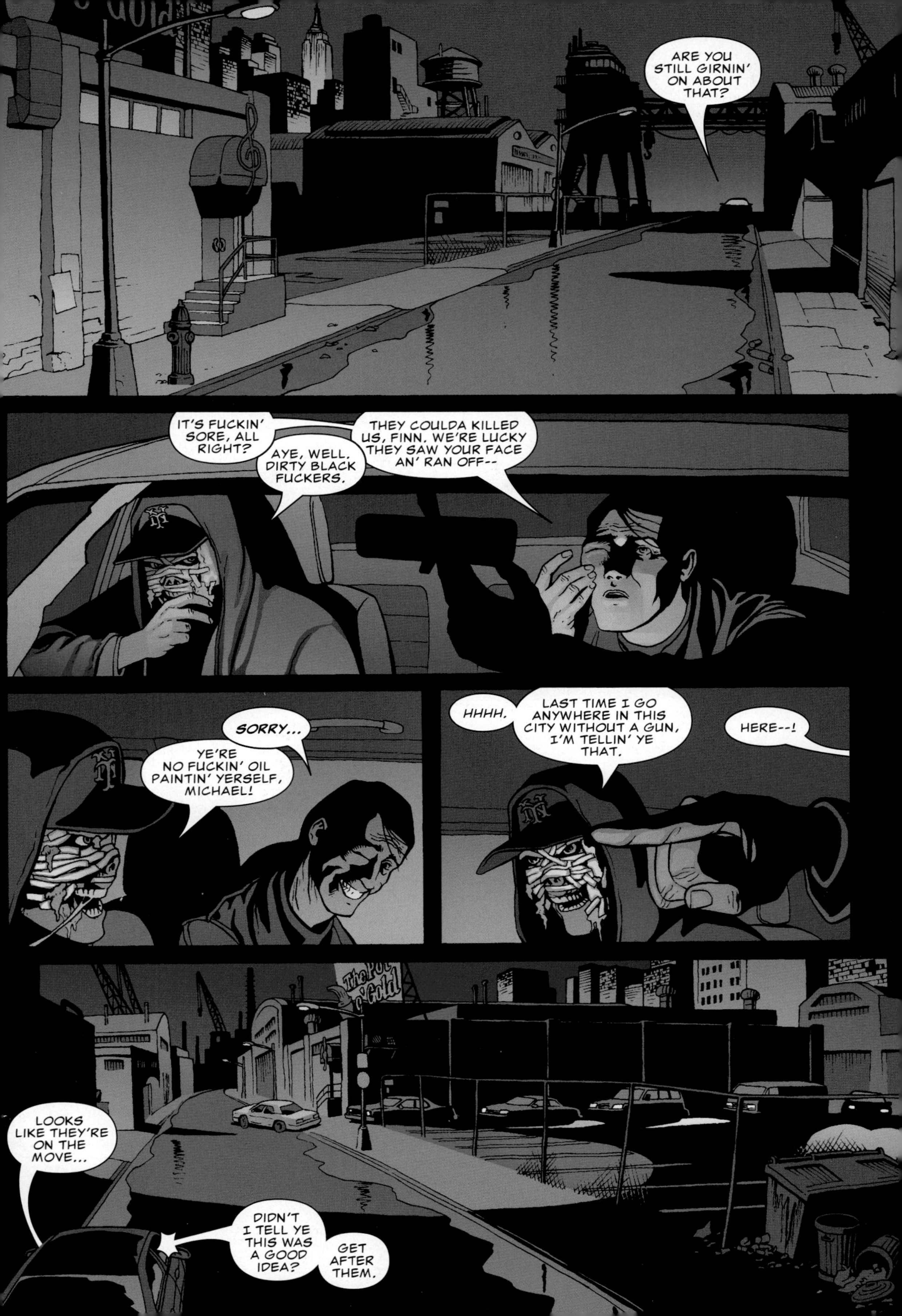
ARE YOU STILL GIRNIN' ON ABOUT THAT?
IT'S FUCKIN' SORE, ALL RIGHT?
AYE, WELL. DIRTY BLACK FUCKERS.
THEY COULDA KILLED US, FINN. WE'RE LUCKY THEY SAW YOUR FACE AN' RAN OFF--
SORRY...
YE'RE NO FUCKIN' OIL PAINTIN' YERSELF, MICHAEL!
HHHH.
LAST TIME I GO ANYWHERE IN THIS CITY WITHOUT A GUN, I'M TELLIN' YE THAT.
HERE--!
LOOKS LIKE THEY'RE ON THE MOVE...
DIDN'T I TELL YE THIS WAS A GOOD IDEA?
GET AFTER THEM.

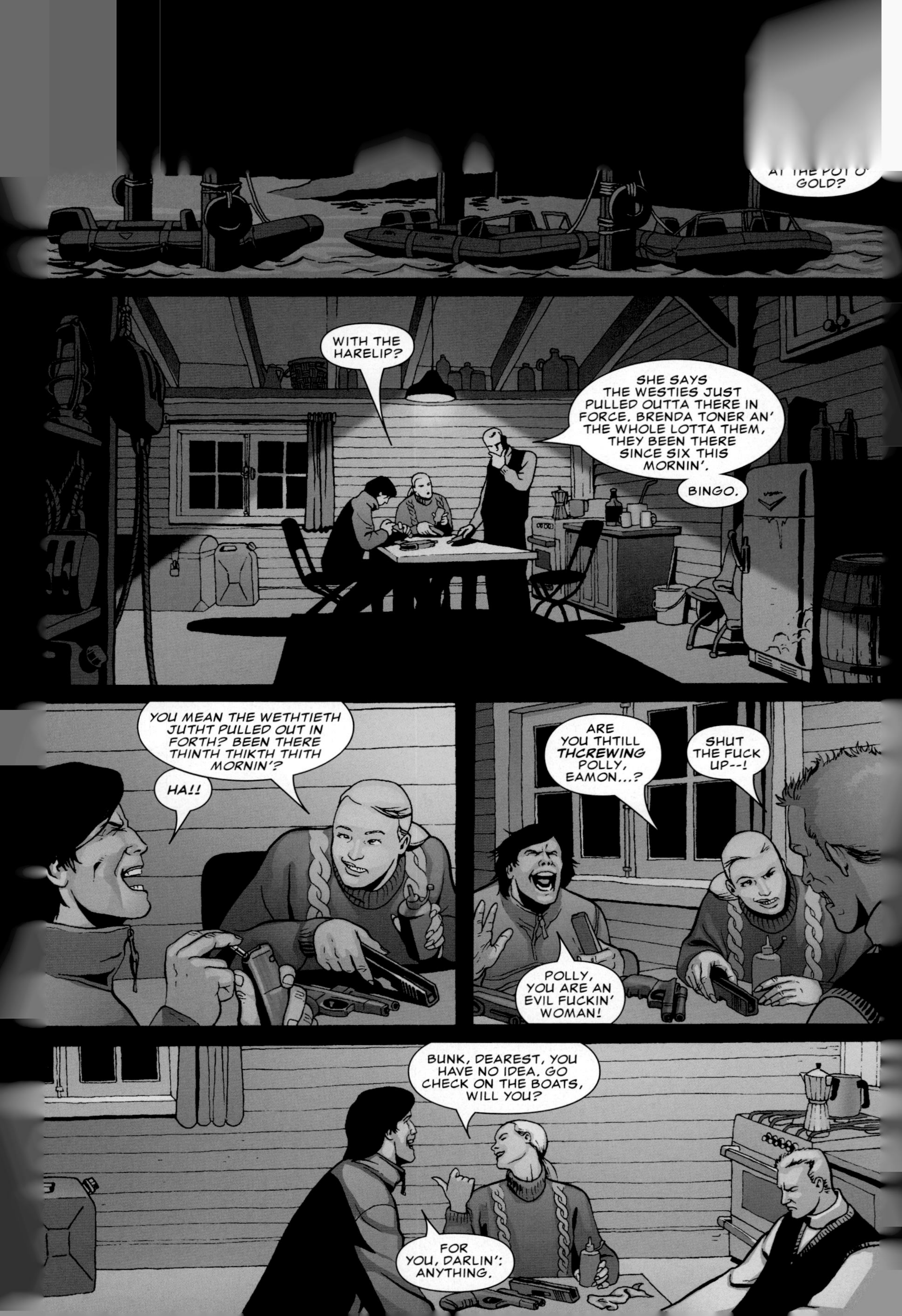

AT THE POT O' GOLD?
WITH THE HARELIP?
SHE SAYS THE WESTIES JUST PULLED OUTTA THERE IN FORCE. BRENDA TONER AN' THE WHOLE LOTTA THEM, THEY BEEN THERE SINCE SIX THIS MORNIN'.
BINGO.
YOU MEAN THE WETHTIETH JUTHT PULLED OUT IN FORTH? BEEN THERE THINTH THIKTH THITH MORNIN'?
HA!!
ARE YOU THTILL **THCREWING** POLLY, EAMON...?
SHUT THE FUCK UP--!
POLLY, YOU ARE AN EVIL FUCKIN' WOMAN!
BUNK, DEAREST, YOU HAVE NO IDEA. GO CHECK ON THE BOATS, WILL YOU?
FOR YOU, DARLIN': ANYTHING.

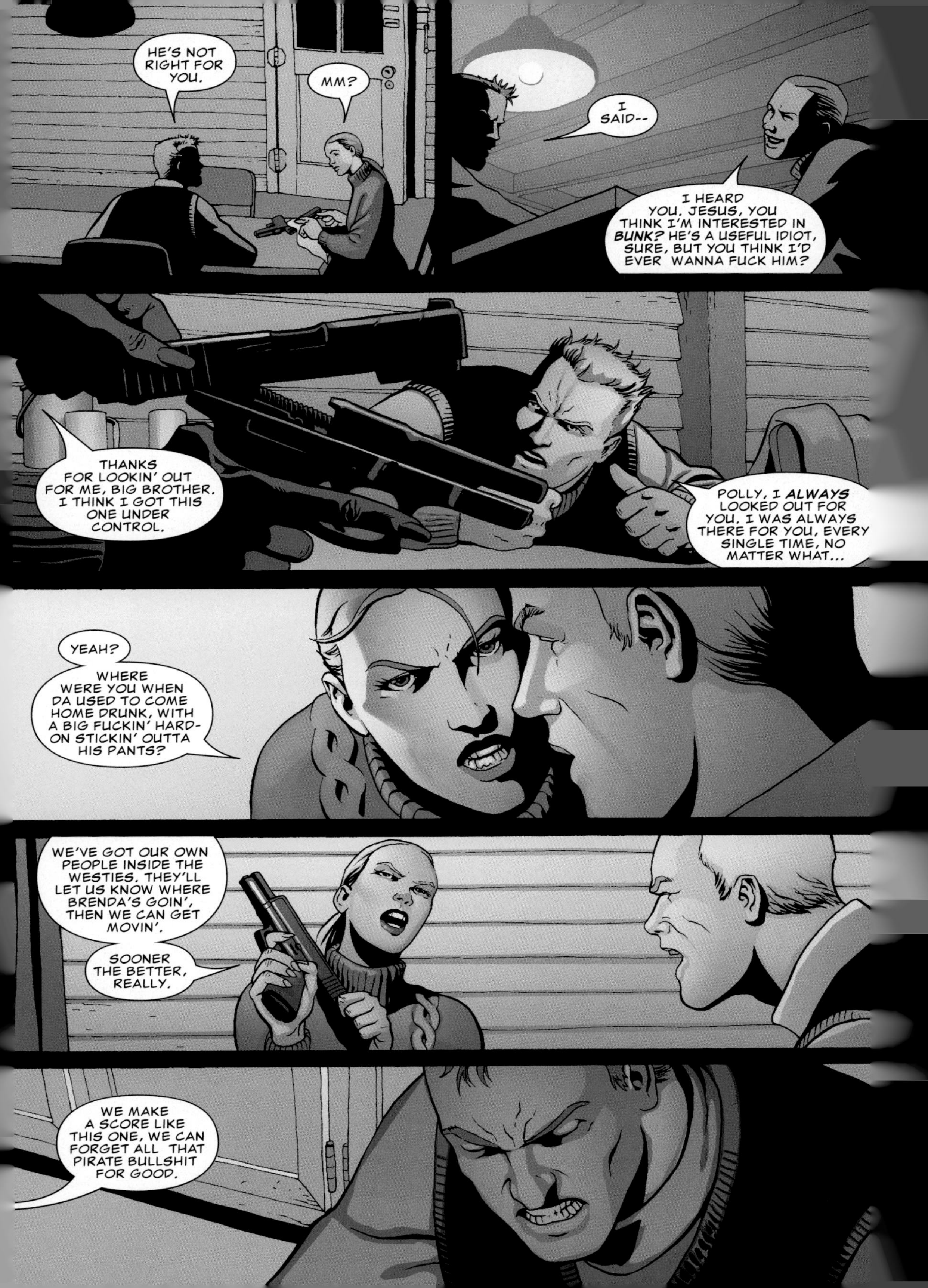

HE'S NOT RIGHT FOR YOU.
MM?
I SAID--
I HEARD YOU. JESUS, YOU THINK I'M INTERESTED IN BUNK? HE'S A USEFUL IDIOT, SURE, BUT YOU THINK I'D EVER WANNA FUCK HIM?
THANKS FOR LOOKIN' OUT FOR ME, BIG BROTHER. I THINK I GOT THIS ONE UNDER CONTROL.
POLLY, I ALWAYS LOOKED OUT FOR YOU. I WAS ALWAYS THERE FOR YOU, EVERY SINGLE TIME, NO MATTER WHAT...
YEAH?
WHERE WERE YOU WHEN DA USED TO COME HOME DRUNK, WITH A BIG FUCKIN' HARD-ON STICKIN' OUTTA HIS PANTS?
WE'VE GOT OUR OWN PEOPLE INSIDE THE WESTIES. THEY'LL LET US KNOW WHERE BRENDA'S GOIN', THEN WE CAN GET MOVIN'.
SOONER THE BETTER, REALLY.
WE MAKE A SCORE LIKE THIS ONE, WE CAN FORGET ALL THAT PIRATE BULLSHIT FOR GOOD.

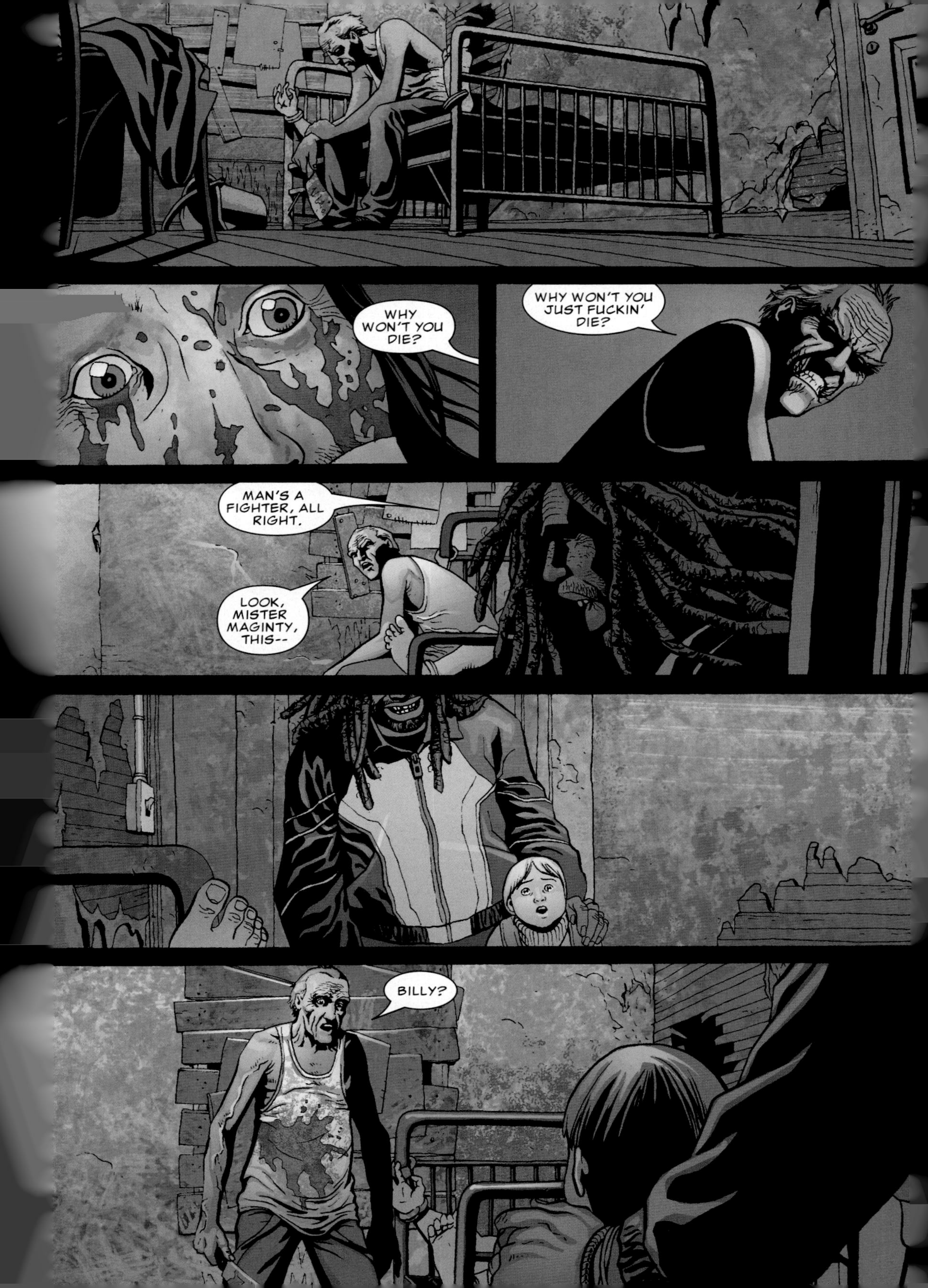
WHY WON'T YOU DIE?
WHY WON'T YOU JUST FUCKIN' DIE?
MAN'S A FIGHTER, ALL RIGHT.
LOOK, MISTER MAGINTY, THIS--
BILLY?

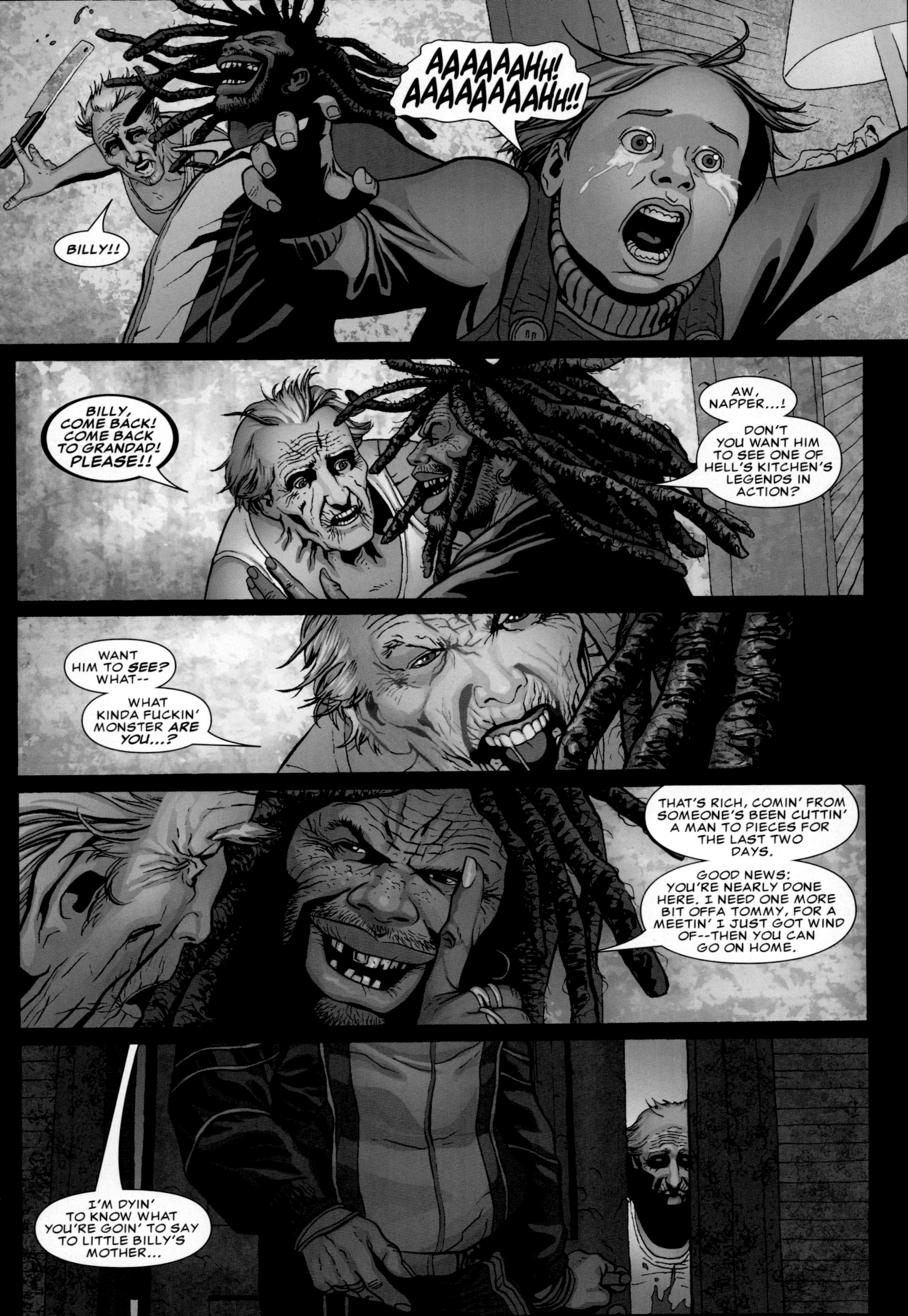
AAAAAAHH! AAAAAAAAHH!!
BILLY!!
BILLY, COME BACK! COME BACK TO GRANDAD! PLEASE!!
AW, NAPPER...!
DON'T YOU WANT HIM TO SEE ONE OF HELL'S KITCHEN'S LEGENDS IN ACTION?
WANT HIM TO SEE? WHAT--
WHAT KINDA FUCKIN' MONSTER ARE YOU...?
THAT'S RICH, COMIN' FROM SOMEONE'S BEEN CUTTIN' A MAN TO PIECES FOR THE LAST TWO DAYS.
GOOD NEWS: YOU'RE NEARLY DONE HERE. I NEED ONE MORE BIT OFFA TOMMY, FOR A MEETIN' I JUST GOT WIND OF--THEN YOU CAN GO ON HOME.
I'M DYIN' TO KNOW WHAT YOU'RE GOIN' TO SAY TO LITTLE BILLY'S MOTHER...

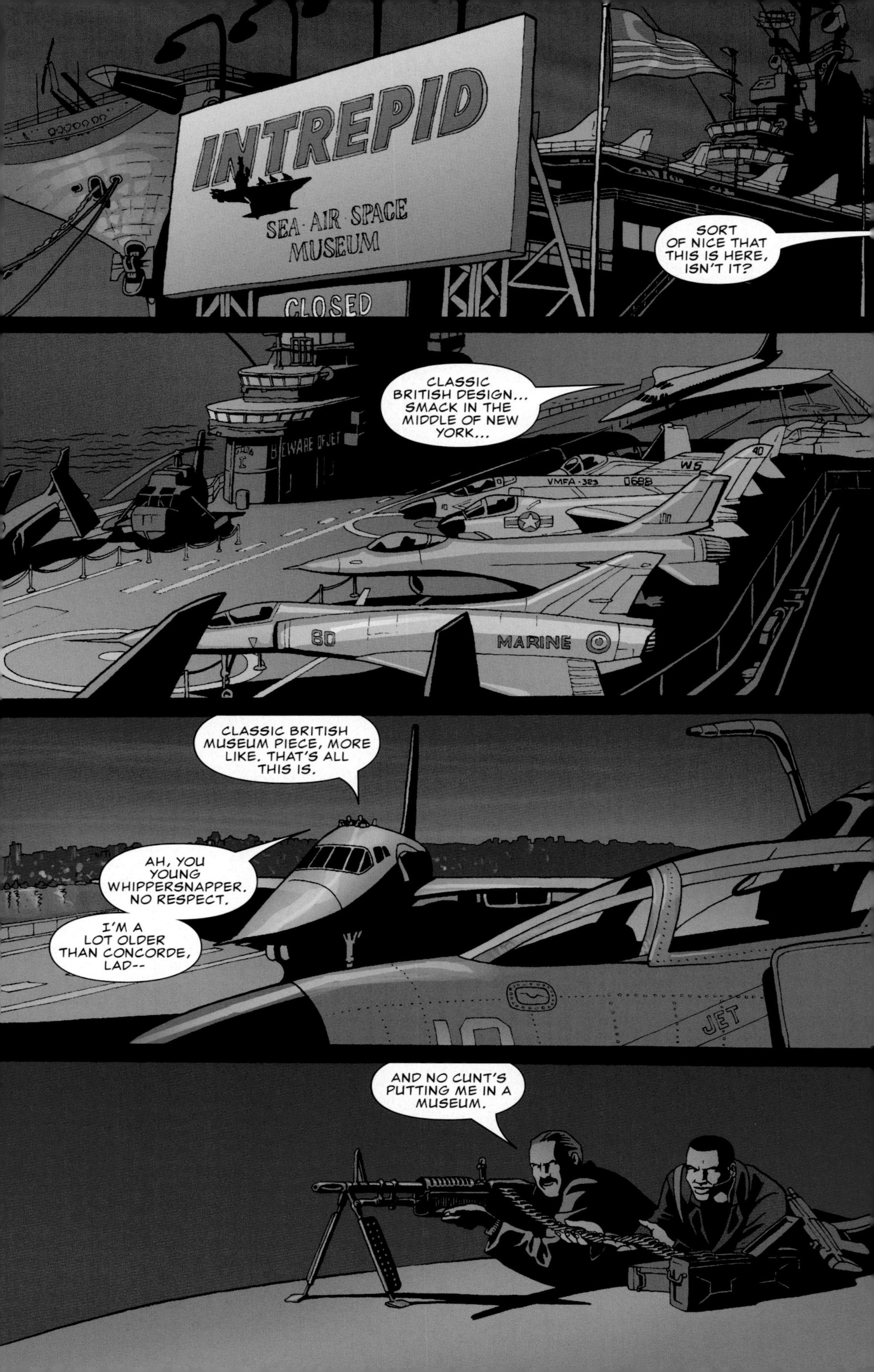
INTREPID
SEA·AIR·SPACE MUSEUM
CLOSED
SORT OF NICE THAT THIS IS HERE, ISN'T IT?
CLASSIC BRITISH DESIGN... SMACK IN THE MIDDLE OF NEW YORK...
BEWARE OF JET
VMFA-323
MARINE
CLASSIC BRITISH MUSEUM PIECE, MORE LIKE. THAT'S ALL THIS IS.
AH, YOU YOUNG WHIPPERSNAPPER. NO RESPECT.
I'M A LOT OLDER THAN CONCORDE, LAD--
JET
AND NO CUNT'S PUTTING ME IN A MUSEUM.

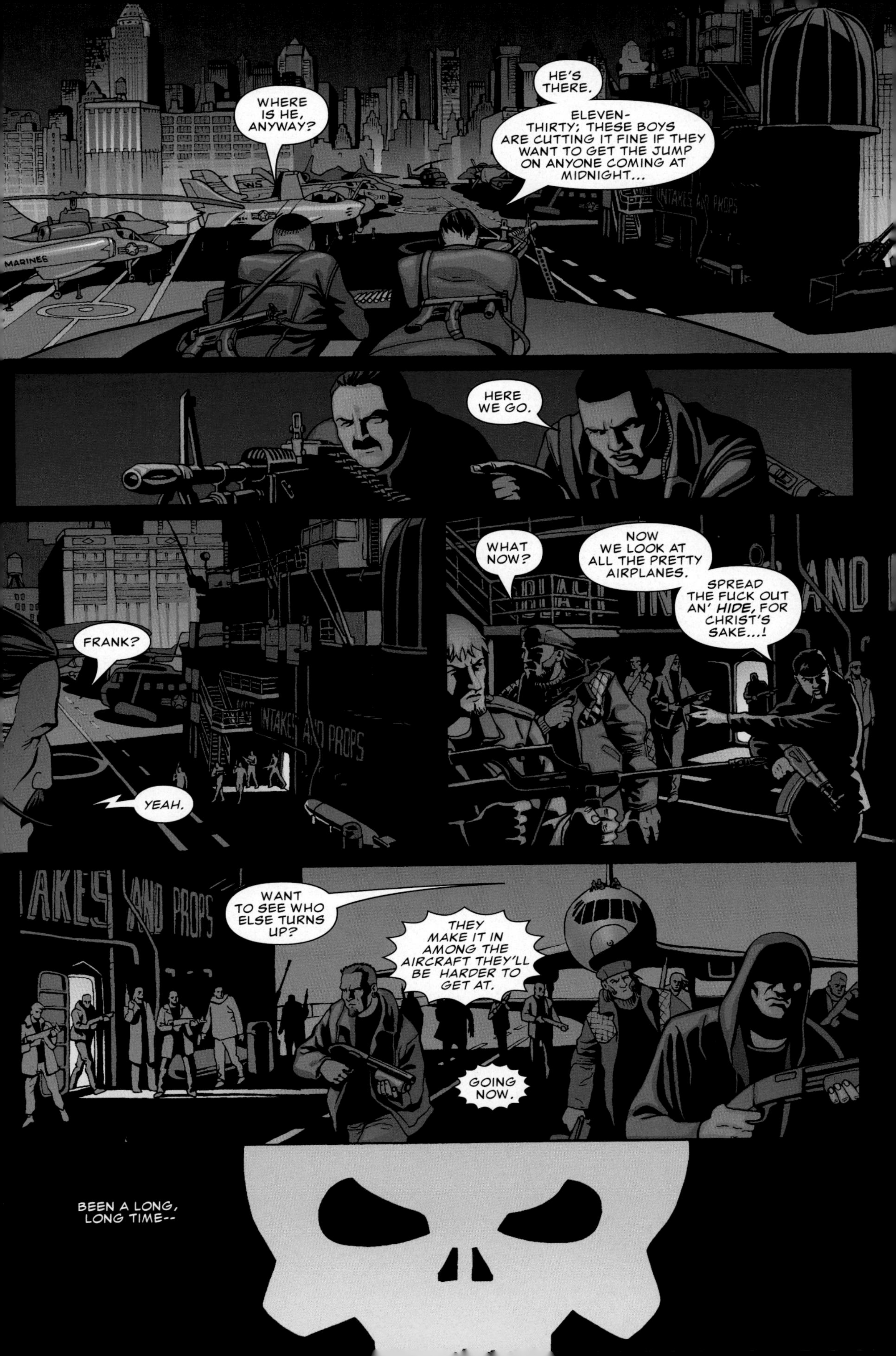
WHERE IS HE, ANYWAY?
HE'S THERE.
ELEVEN-THIRTY; THESE BOYS ARE CUTTING IT FINE IF THEY WANT TO GET THE JUMP ON ANYONE COMING AT MIDNIGHT...
MARINES
INTAKES AND PROPS
HERE WE GO.
FRANK?
YEAH.
WHAT NOW?
NOW WE LOOK AT ALL THE PRETTY AIRPLANES.
SPREAD THE FUCK OUT AN' *HIDE*, FOR CHRIST'S SAKE...!
WANT TO SEE WHO ELSE TURNS UP?
THEY MAKE IT IN AMONG THE AIRCRAFT THEY'LL BE HARDER TO GET AT.
GOING NOW.
BEEN A LONG, LONG TIME--

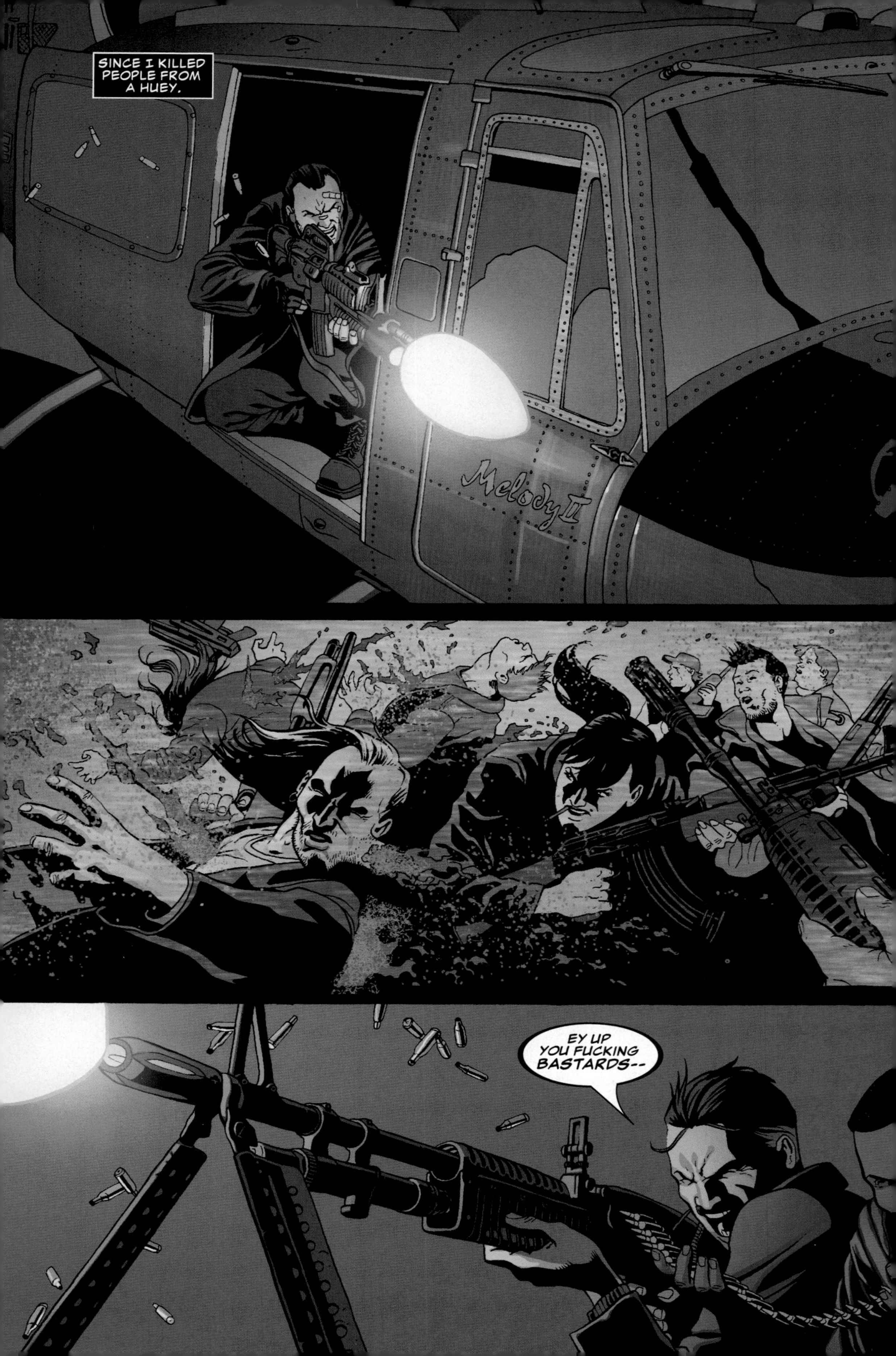
SINCE I KILLED PEOPLE FROM A HUEY.
Melody II
EY UP YOU FUCKING BASTARDS--

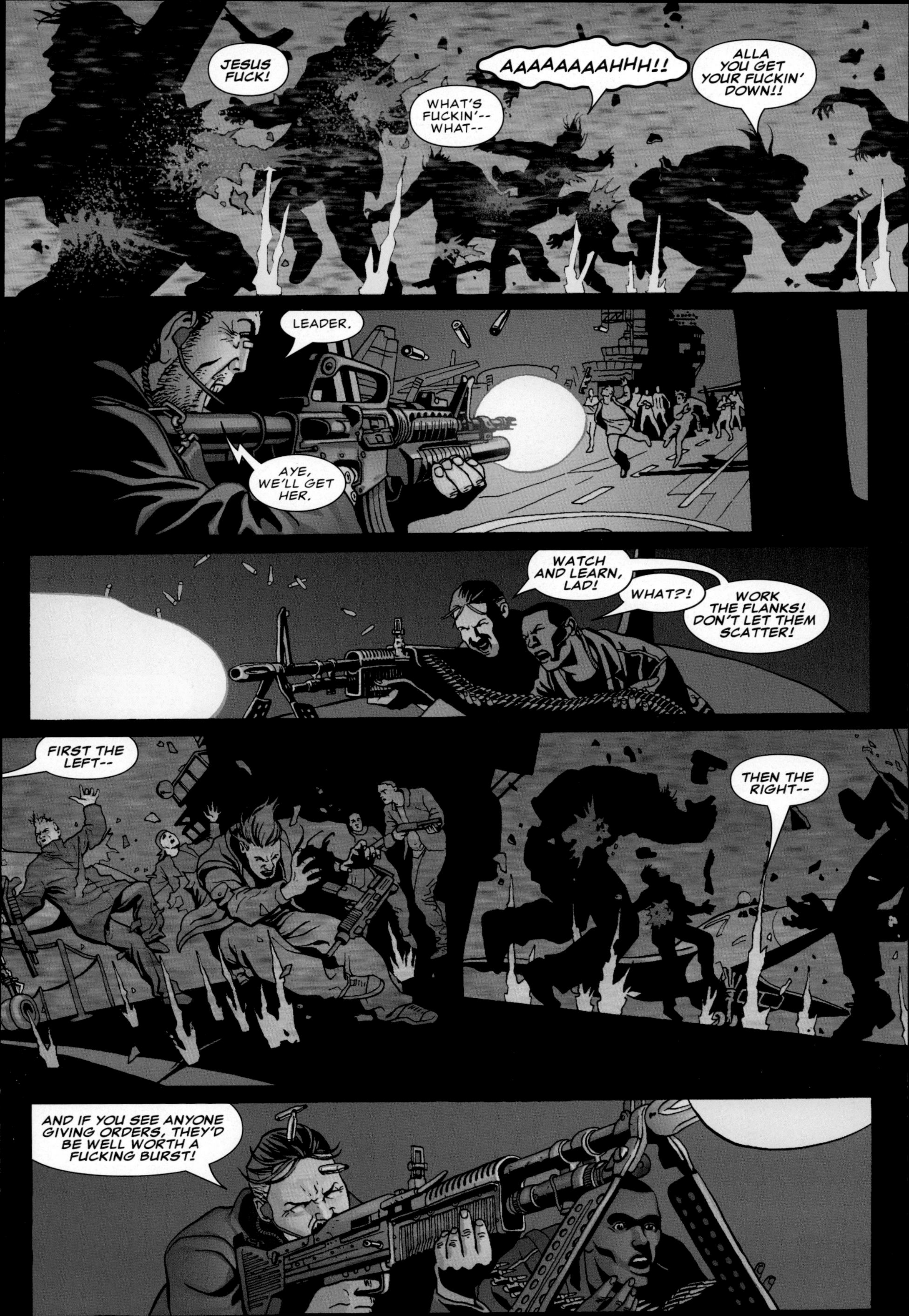
JESUS FUCK!
WHAT'S FUCKIN'-- WHAT--
AAAAAAAAHHH!!
ALLA YOU GET YOUR FUCKIN' DOWN!!
LEADER.
AYE, WE'LL GET HER.
WATCH AND LEARN, LAD!
WHAT?!
WORK THE FLANKS! DON'T LET THEM SCATTER!
FIRST THE LEFT--
THEN THE RIGHT--
AND IF YOU SEE ANYONE GIVING ORDERS, THEY'D BE WELL WORTH A FUCKING BURST!

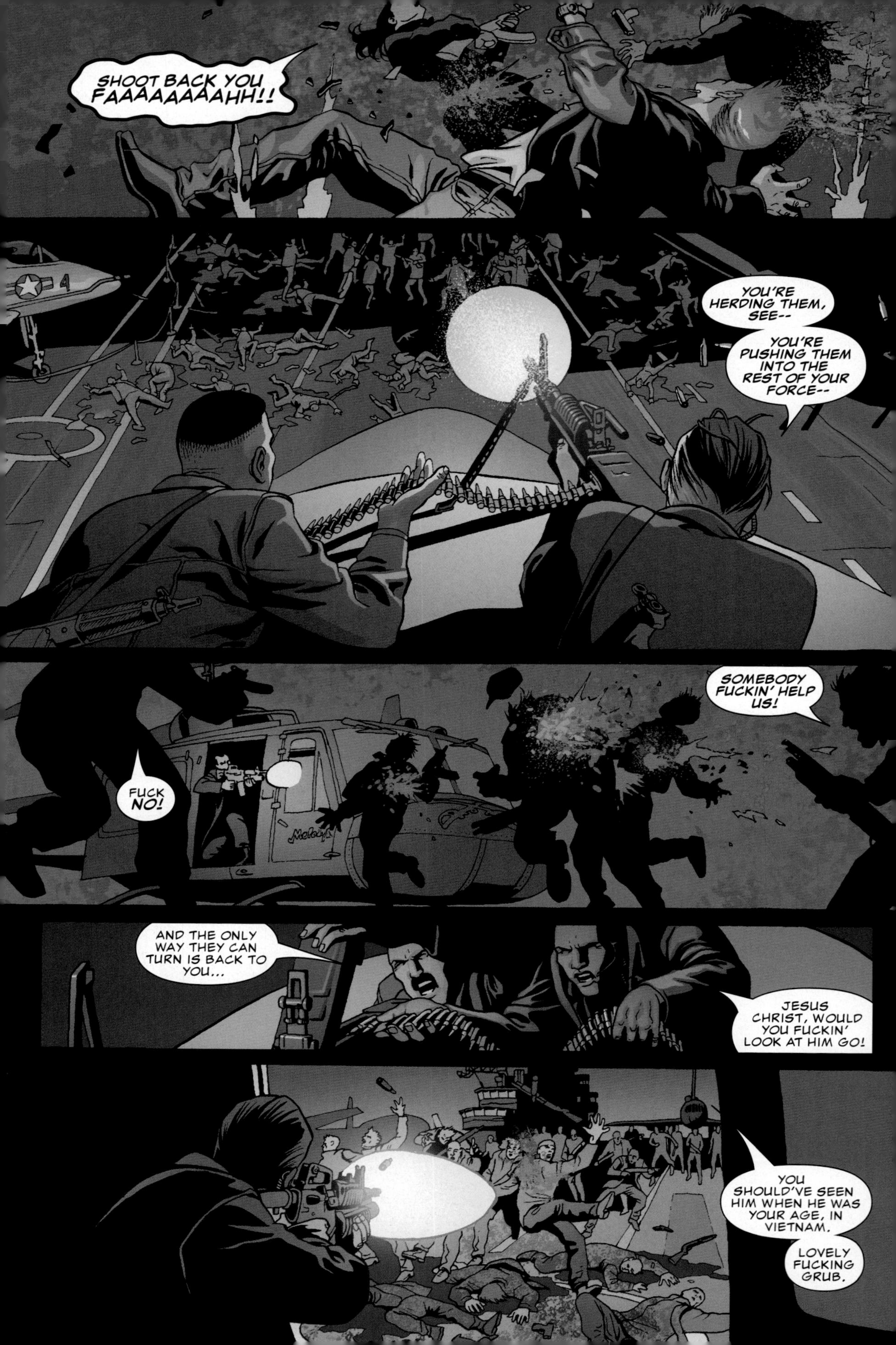

SHOOT BACK YOU FAAAAAAAAHH!!
YOU'RE HERDING THEM, SEE--
YOU'RE PUSHING THEM INTO THE REST OF YOUR FORCE--
SOMEBODY FUCKIN' HELP US!
FUCK NO!
AND THE ONLY WAY THEY CAN TURN IS BACK TO YOU...
JESUS CHRIST, WOULD YOU FUCKIN' LOOK AT HIM GO!
YOU SHOULD'VE SEEN HIM WHEN HE WAS YOUR AGE, IN VIETNAM.
LOVELY FUCKING GRUB.

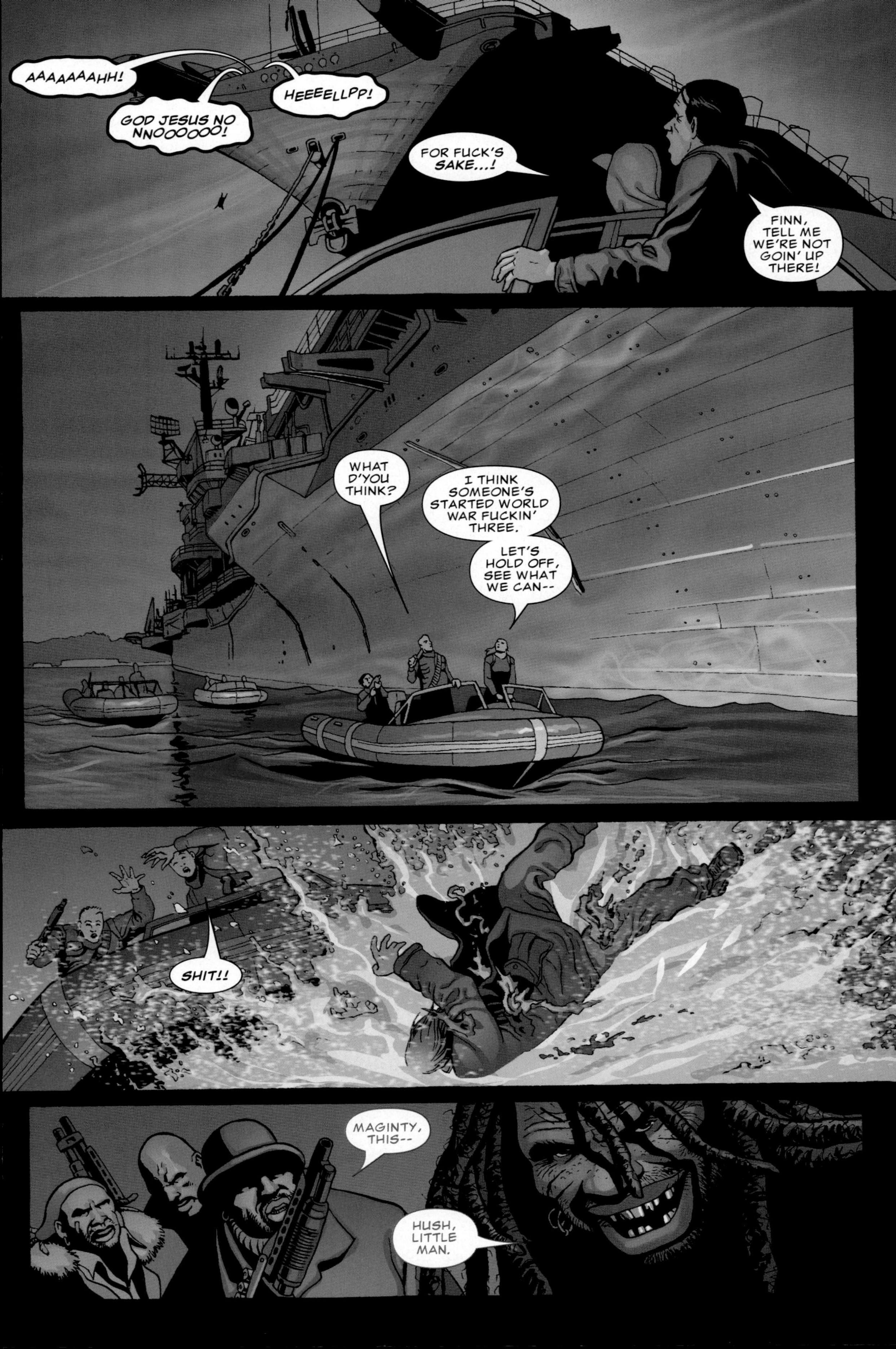
AAAAAAAHH!
GOD JESUS NO NNOOOOOO!
HEEEELLPP!
FOR FUCK'S SAKE...!
FINN, TELL ME WE'RE NOT GOIN' UP THERE!
WHAT D'YOU THINK?
I THINK SOMEONE'S STARTED WORLD WAR FUCKIN' THREE.
LET'S HOLD OFF, SEE WHAT WE CAN--
SHIT!!
MAGINTY, THIS--
HUSH, LITTLE MAN.

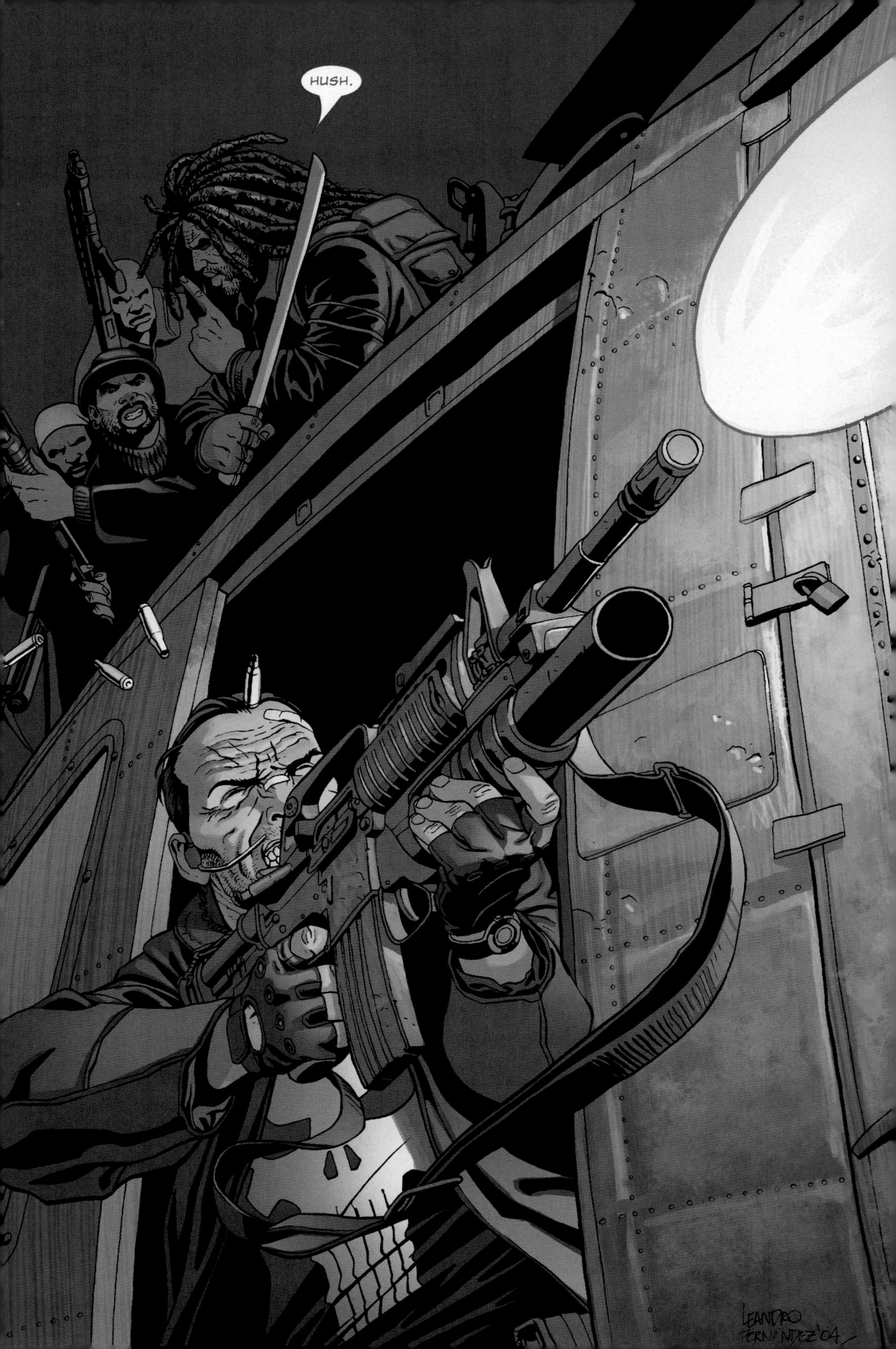
HUSH.
LEANDRO FERNANDEZ '04

PUNISHER #11

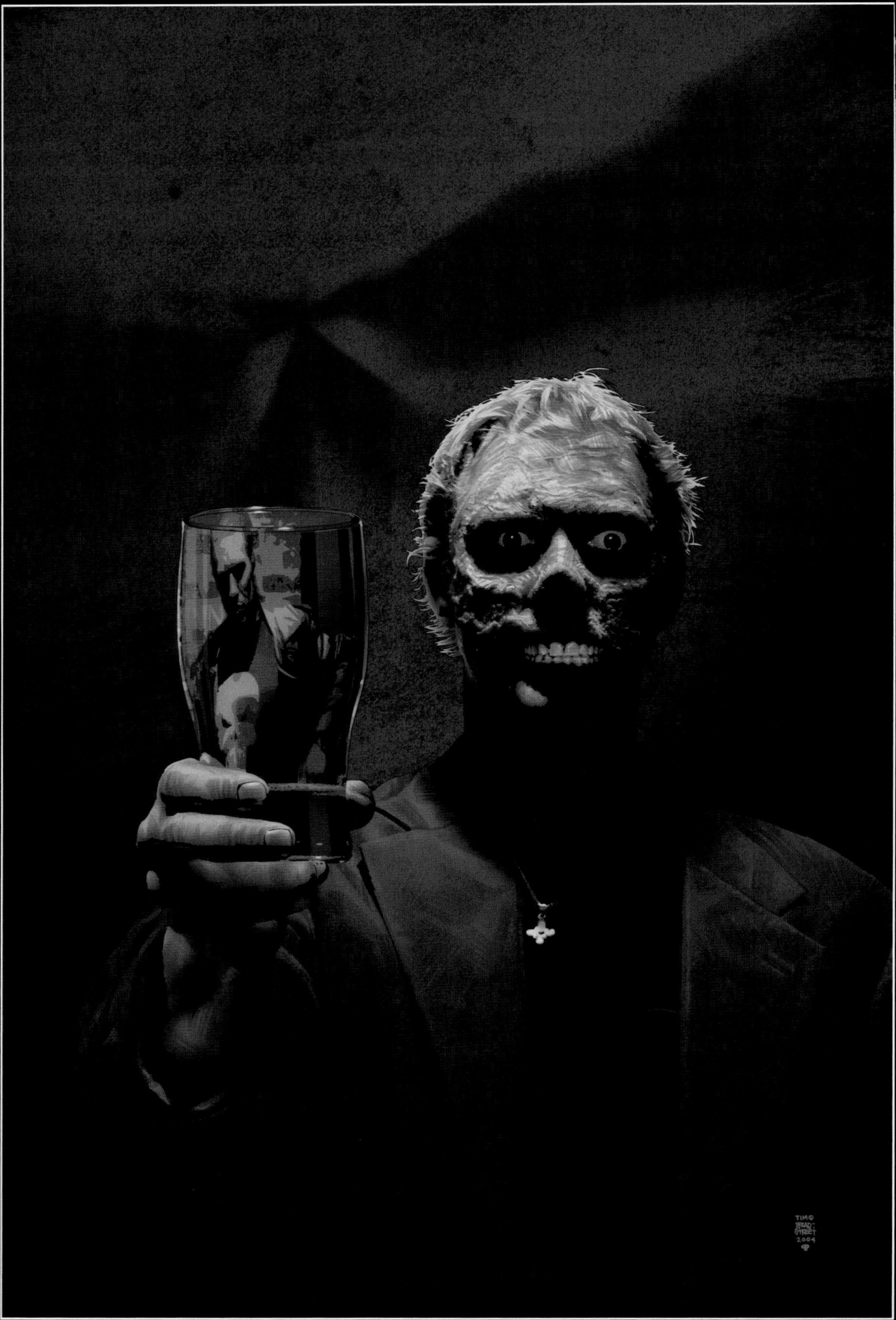
TIM
BRAD-
STREET
2004

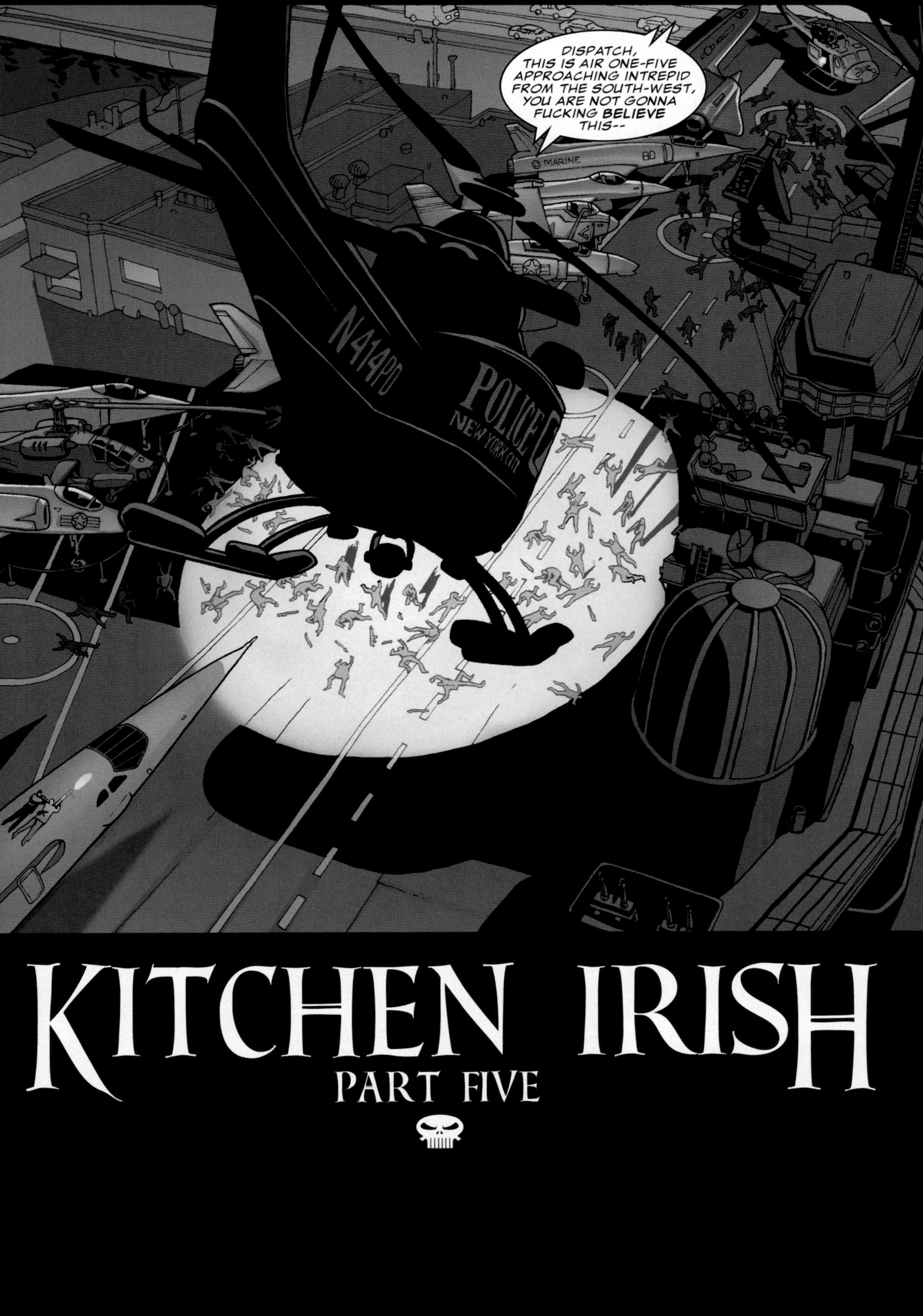
DISPATCH, THIS IS AIR ONE-FIVE APPROACHING INTREPID FROM THE SOUTH-WEST, YOU ARE NOT GONNA FUCKING BELIEVE THIS--
N414PD
POLICE
NEW YORK CITY
MARINE

KITCHEN IRISH

PART FIVE

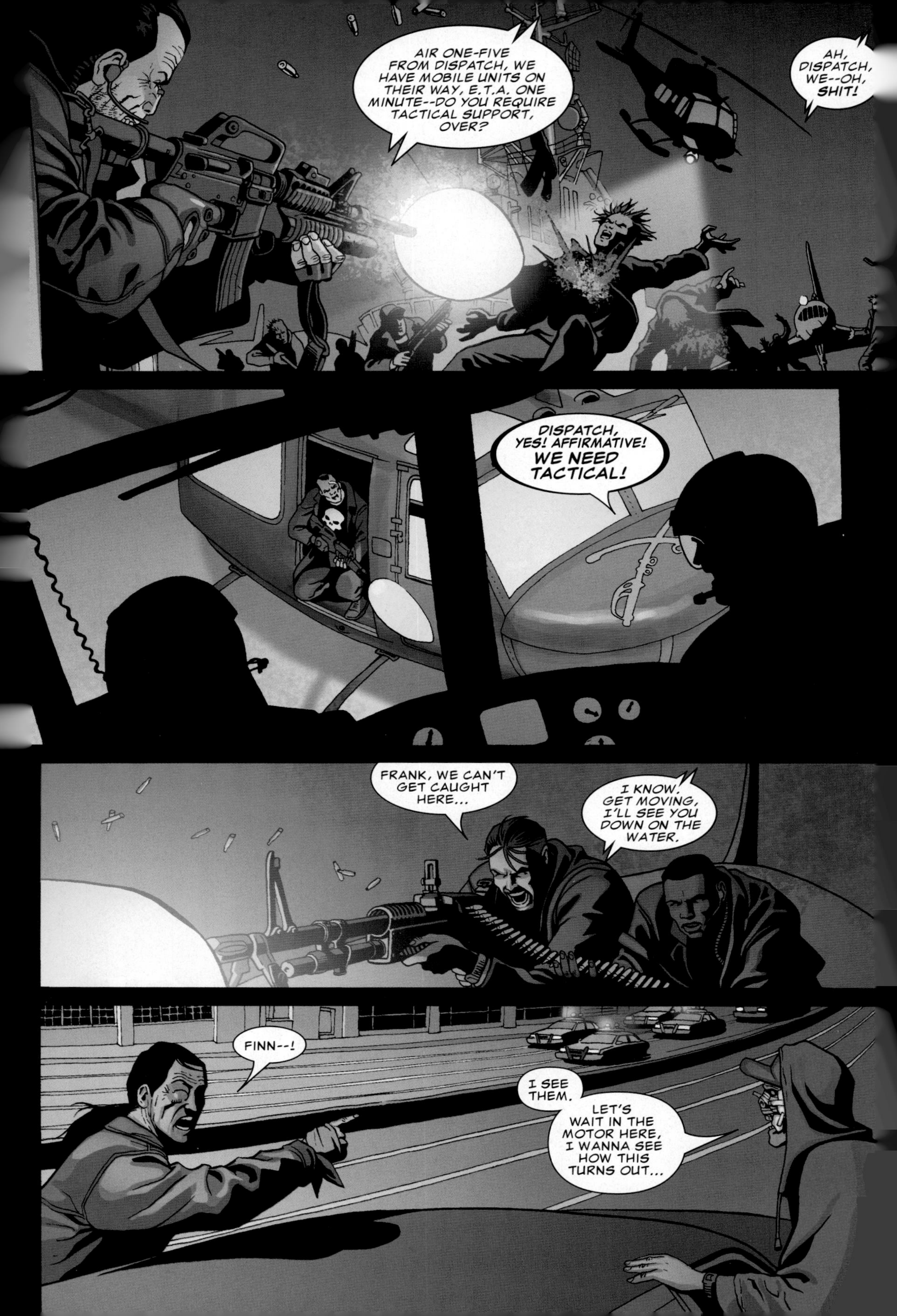
AIR ONE-FIVE FROM DISPATCH, WE HAVE MOBILE UNITS ON THEIR WAY, E.T.A. ONE MINUTE--DO YOU REQUIRE TACTICAL SUPPORT, OVER?
AH, DISPATCH, WE--OH, SHIT!
DISPATCH, YES! AFFIRMATIVE! WE NEED TACTICAL!
FRANK, WE CAN'T GET CAUGHT HERE...
I KNOW. GET MOVING, I'LL SEE YOU DOWN ON THE WATER.
FINN--!
I SEE THEM.
LET'S WAIT IN THE MOTOR HERE, I WANNA SEE HOW THIS TURNS OUT...

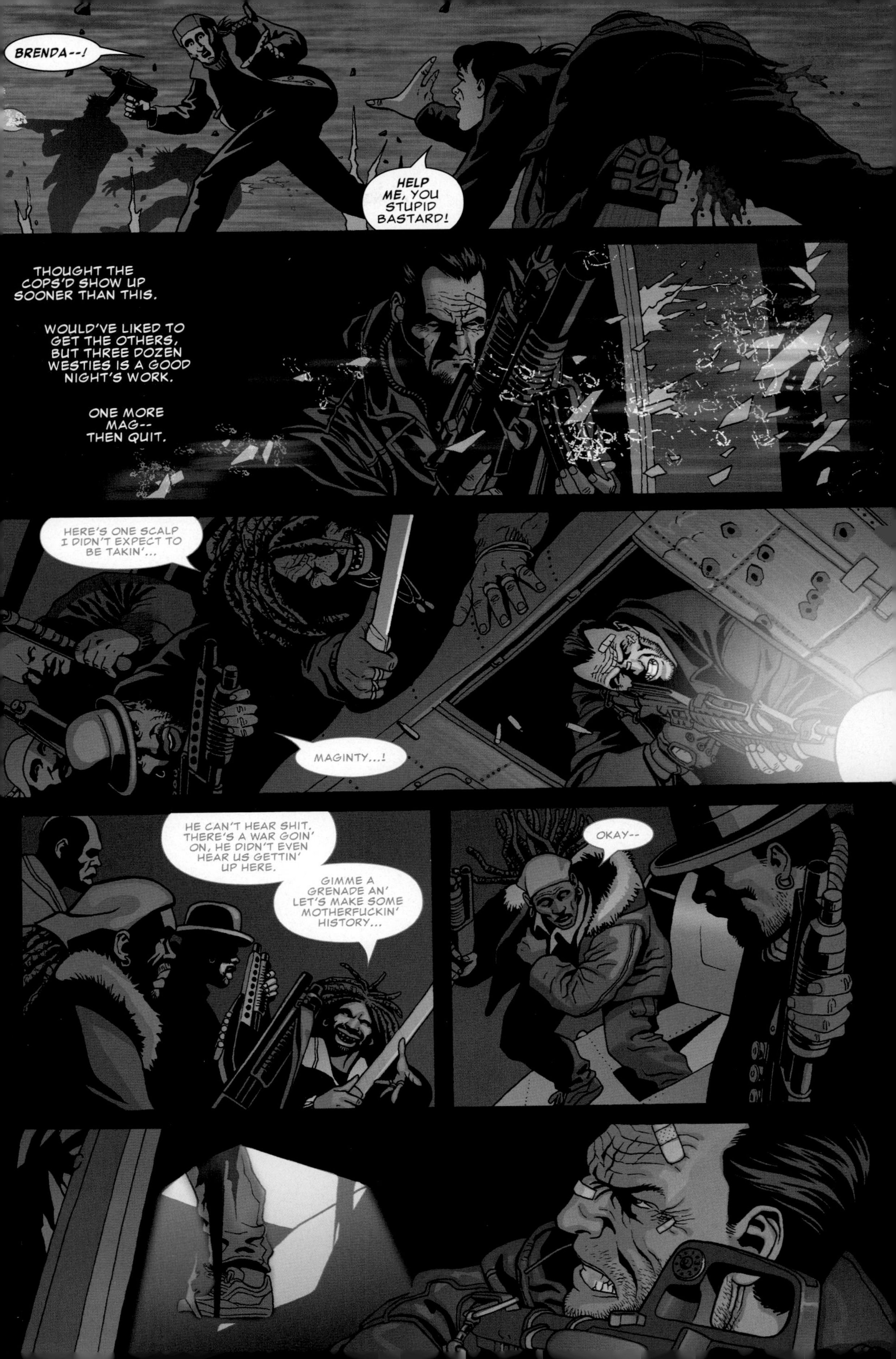

BRENDA--!
HELP ME, YOU STUPID BASTARD!
THOUGHT THE COPS'D SHOW UP SOONER THAN THIS.
WOULD'VE LIKED TO GET THE OTHERS, BUT THREE DOZEN WESTIES IS A GOOD NIGHT'S WORK.
ONE MORE MAG-- THEN QUIT.
HERE'S ONE SCALP I DIDN'T EXPECT TO BE TAKIN'...
MAGINTY...!
HE CAN'T HEAR SHIT. THERE'S A WAR GOIN' ON, HE DIDN'T EVEN HEAR US GETTIN' UP HERE.
GIMME A GRENADE AN' LET'S MAKE SOME MOTHERFUCKIN' HISTORY...
OKAY--

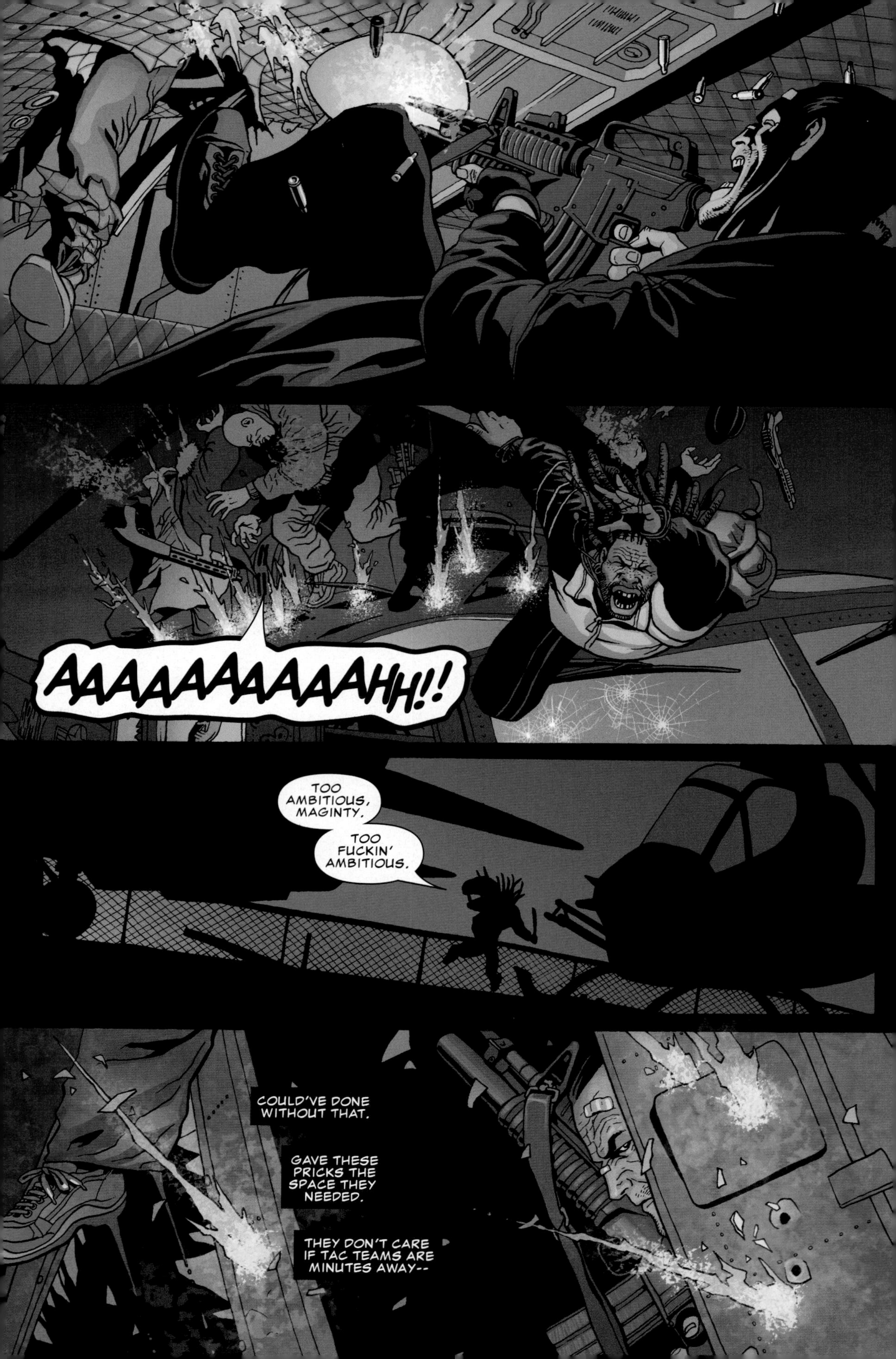
AAAAAAAAAAAHH!!
TOO AMBITIOUS, MAGINTY.
TOO FUCKIN' AMBITIOUS.
COULD'VE DONE WITHOUT THAT.
GAVE THESE PRICKS THE SPACE THEY NEEDED.
THEY DON'T CARE IF TAC TEAMS ARE MINUTES AWAY--

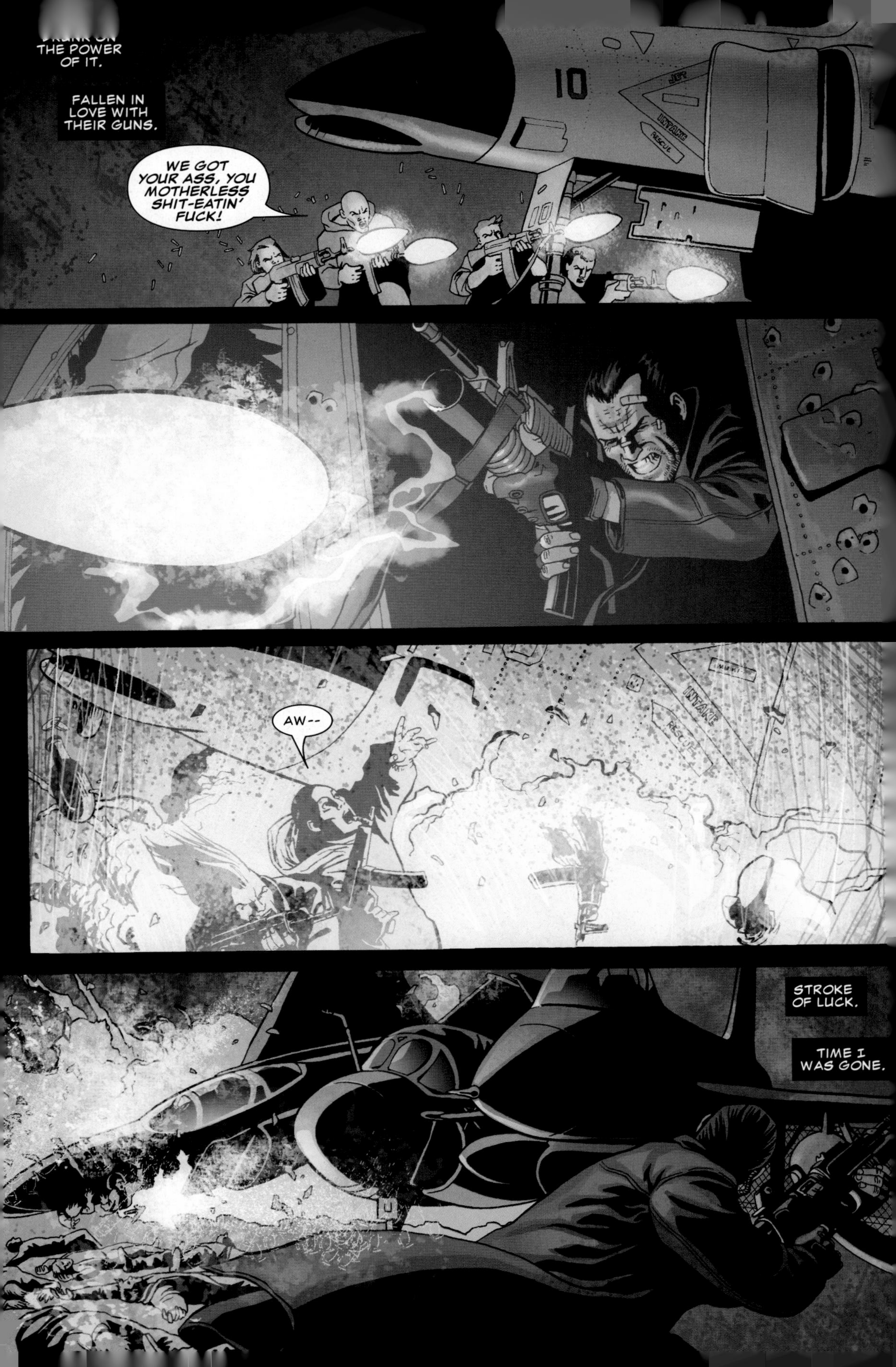
THE POWER OF IT.
FALLEN IN LOVE WITH THEIR GUNS.
WE GOT YOUR ASS, YOU MOTHERLESS SHIT-EATIN' FUCK!
AW--
STROKE OF LUCK.
TIME I WAS GONE.

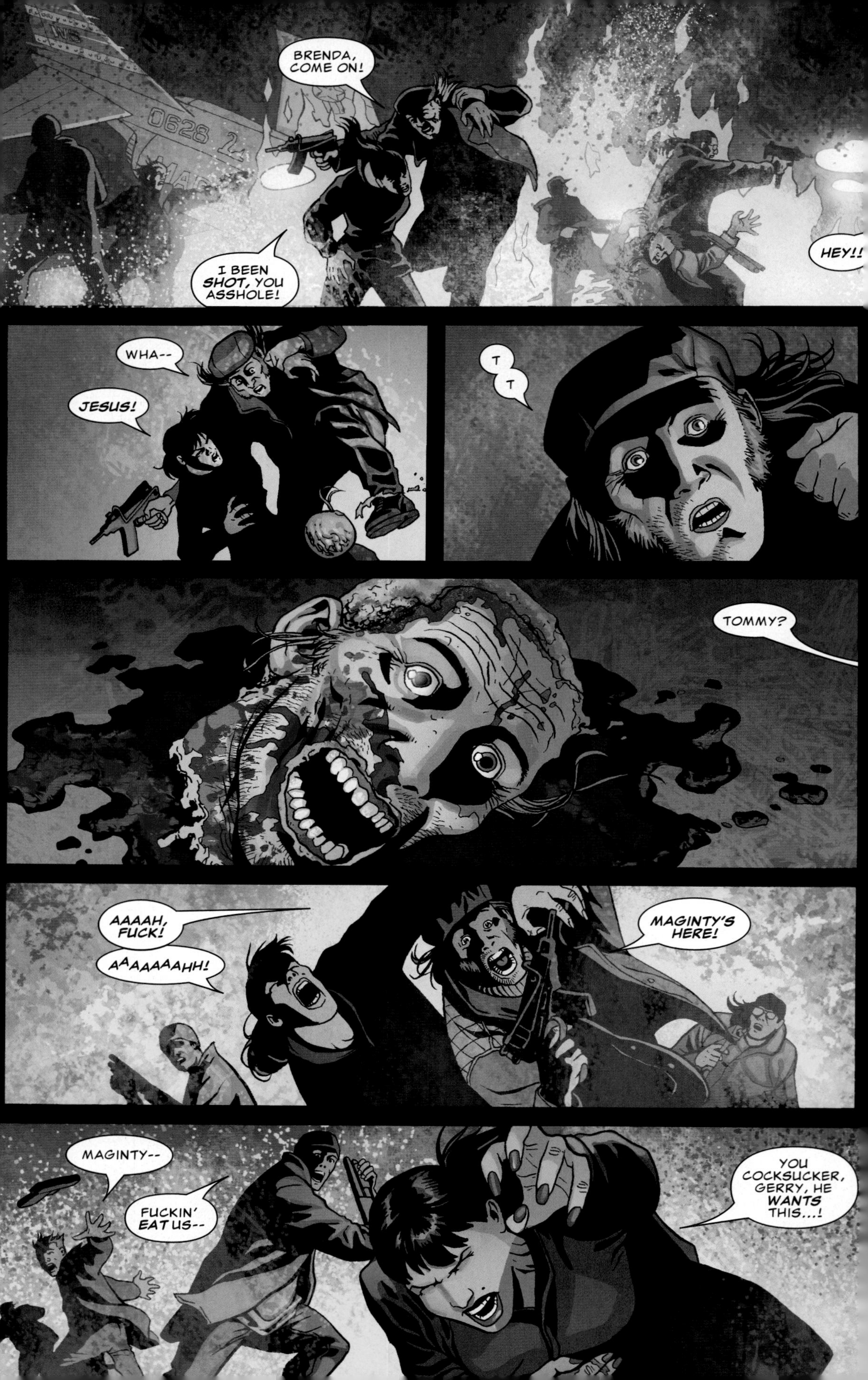
BRENDA, COME ON!
I BEEN SHOT, YOU ASSHOLE!
HEY!!
WHA--
JESUS!
T
T
TOMMY?
AAAAH, FUCK!
AAAAAAAHH!
MAGINTY'S HERE!
MAGINTY--
FUCKIN' EAT US--
YOU COCKSUCKER, GERRY, HE WANTS THIS...!

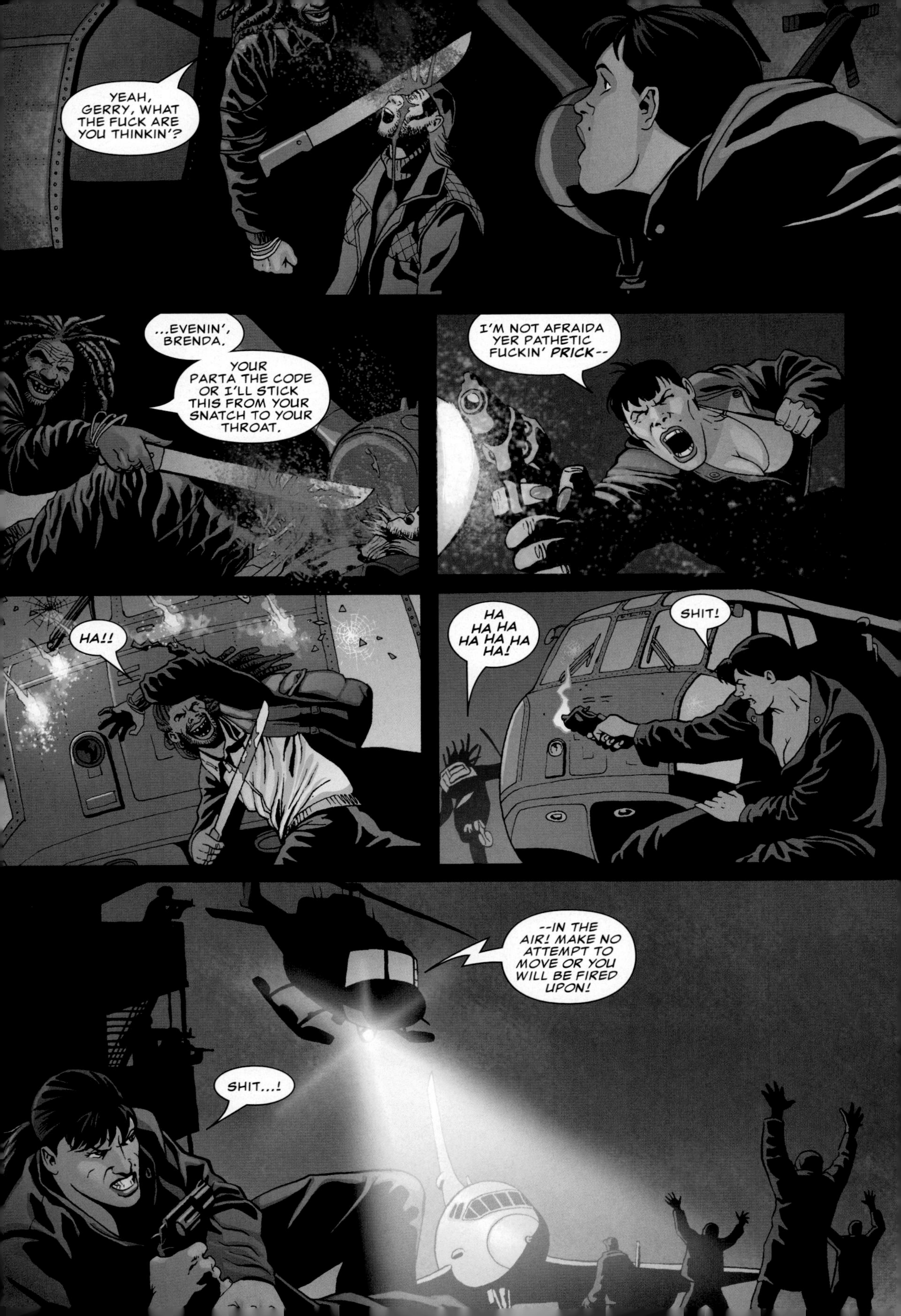
YEAH, GERRY, WHAT THE FUCK ARE YOU THINKIN'?
...EVENIN', BRENDA.
YOUR PARTA THE CODE OR I'LL STICK THIS FROM YOUR SNATCH TO YOUR THROAT.
I'M NOT AFRAIDA YER PATHETIC FUCKIN' PRICK--
HA!!
HA HA HA HA HA HA HA!
SHIT!
--IN THE AIR! MAKE NO ATTEMPT TO MOVE OR YOU WILL BE FIRED UPON!
SHIT...!

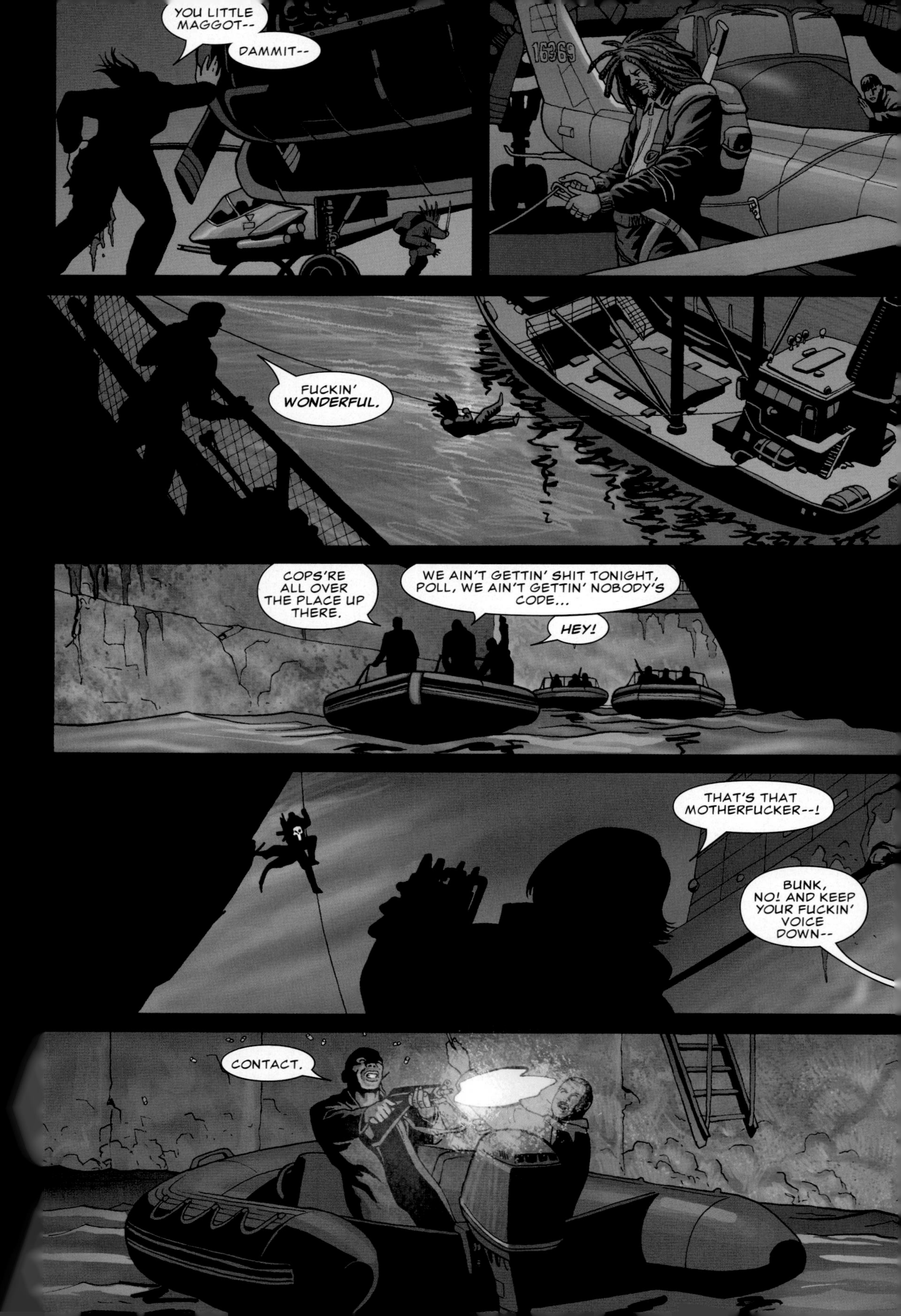
YOU LITTLE MAGGOT--
DAMMIT--
FUCKIN' *WONDERFUL.*
COPS'RE ALL OVER THE PLACE UP THERE.
WE AIN'T GETTIN' SHIT TONIGHT, POLL, WE AIN'T GETTIN' NOBODY'S CODE...
HEY!
THAT'S THAT MOTHERFUCKER--!
BUNK, NO! AND KEEP YOUR FUCKIN' VOICE DOWN--
CONTACT.

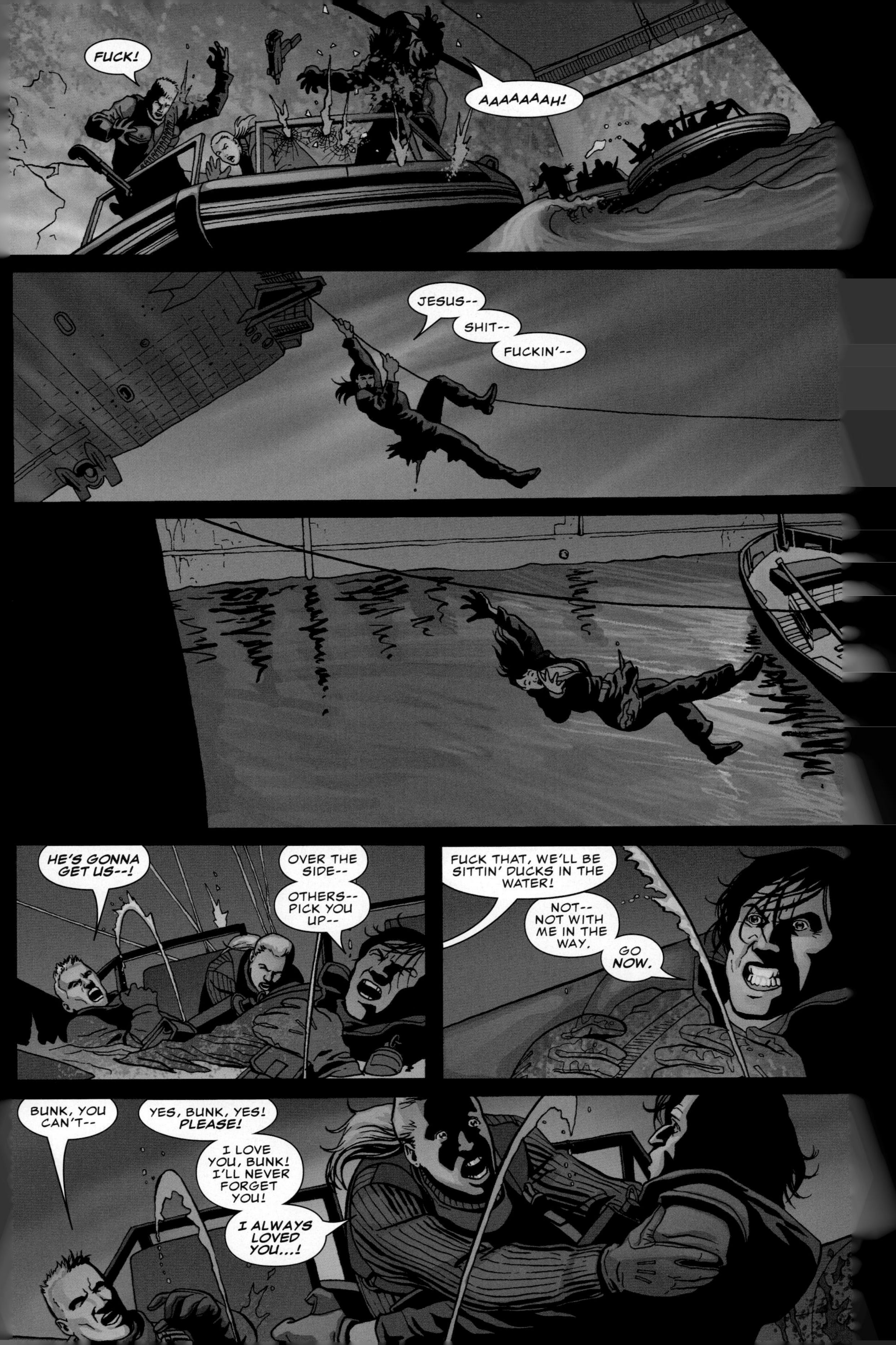
FUCK!
AAAAAAAH!
JESUS--
SHIT--
FUCKIN'--
HE'S GONNA GET US--!
OVER THE SIDE--
OTHERS-- PICK YOU UP--
FUCK THAT, WE'LL BE SITTIN' DUCKS IN THE WATER!
NOT-- NOT WITH ME IN THE WAY.
GO NOW.
BUNK, YOU CAN'T--
YES, BUNK, YES! PLEASE!
I LOVE YOU, BUNK! I'LL NEVER FORGET YOU!
I ALWAYS LOVED YOU...!

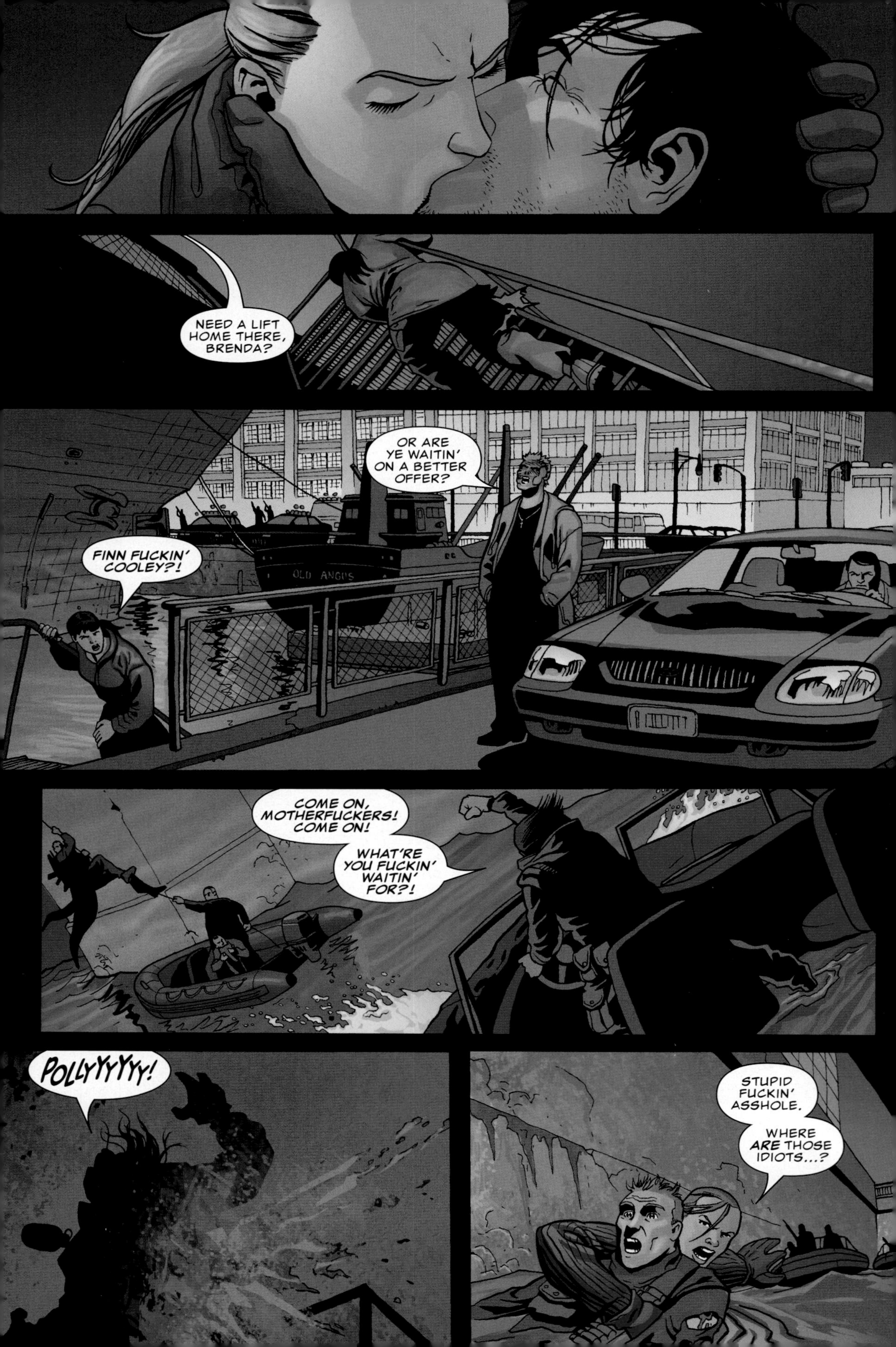
NEED A LIFT HOME THERE, BRENDA?
OR ARE YE WAITIN' ON A BETTER OFFER?
FINN FUCKIN' COOLEY?!
COME ON, MOTHERFUCKERS! COME ON!
WHAT'RE YOU FUCKIN' WAITIN' FOR?!
POLLYYYYYY!
STUPID FUCKIN' ASSHOLE.
WHERE ARE THOSE IDIOTS...?

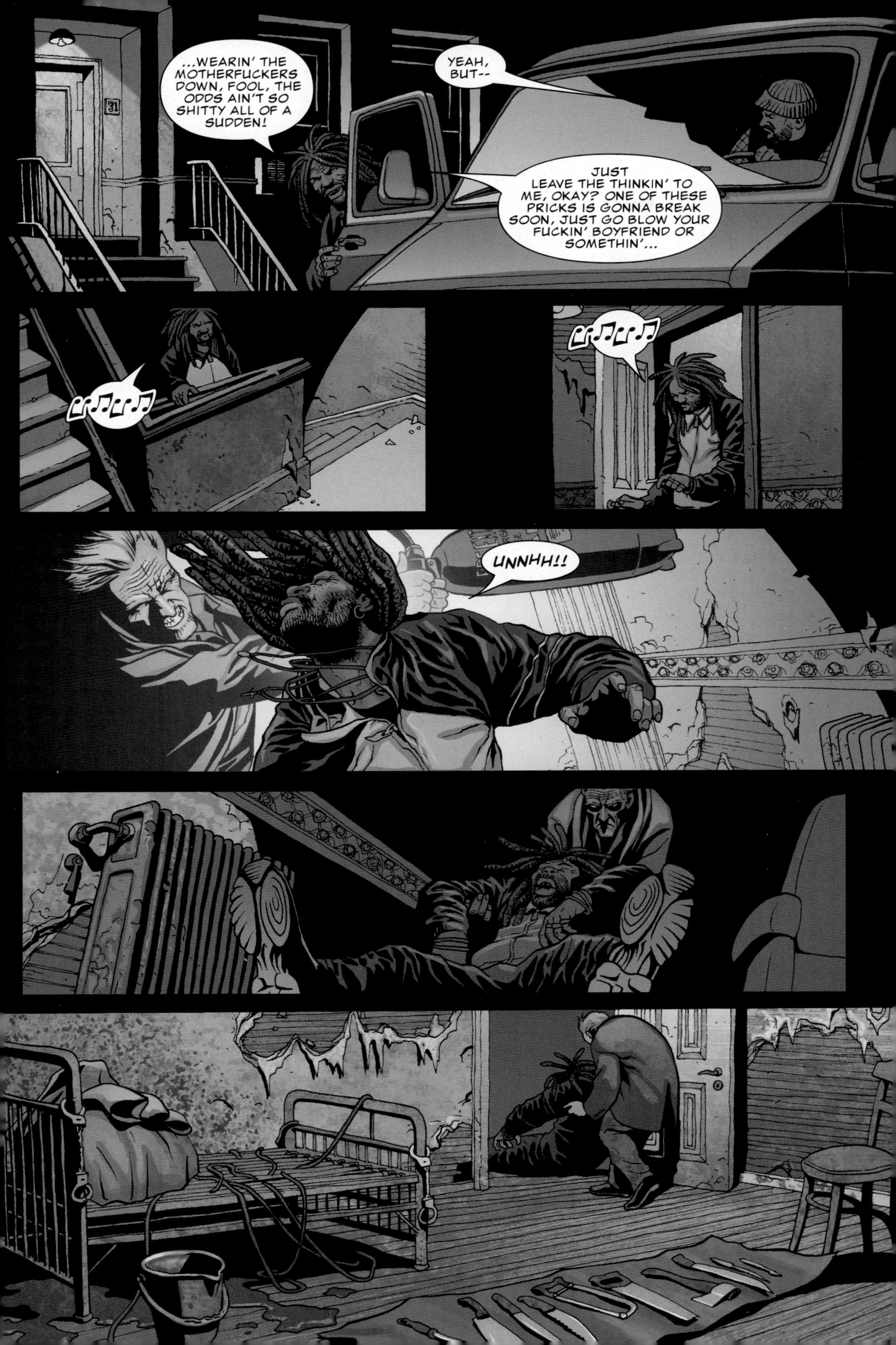
...WEARIN' THE MOTHERFUCKERS DOWN, FOOL, THE ODDS AIN'T SO SHITTY ALL OF A SUDDEN!
YEAH, BUT--
JUST LEAVE THE THINKIN' TO ME, OKAY? ONE OF THESE PRICKS IS GONNA BREAK SOON, JUST GO BLOW YOUR FUCKIN' BOYFRIEND OR SOMETHIN'...
31
UNNHH!!

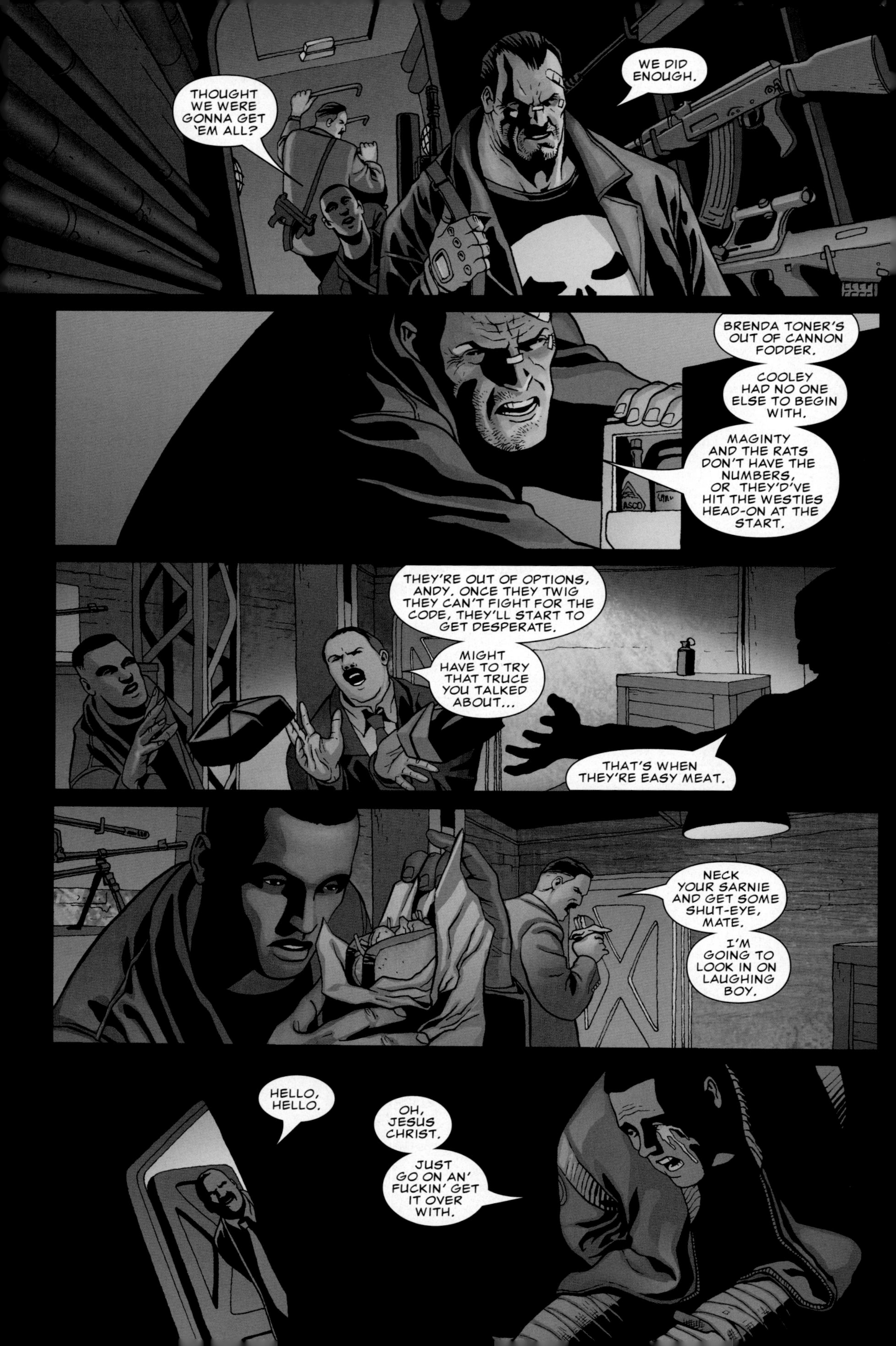
THOUGHT WE WERE GONNA GET 'EM ALL?
WE DID ENOUGH.
BRENDA TONER'S OUT OF CANNON FODDER.
COOLEY HAD NO ONE ELSE TO BEGIN WITH.
MAGINTY AND THE RATS DON'T HAVE THE NUMBERS, OR THEY'D'VE HIT THE WESTIES HEAD-ON AT THE START.
THEY'RE OUT OF OPTIONS, ANDY. ONCE THEY TWIG THEY CAN'T FIGHT FOR THE CODE, THEY'LL START TO GET DESPERATE.
MIGHT HAVE TO TRY THAT TRUCE YOU TALKED ABOUT...
THAT'S WHEN THEY'RE EASY MEAT.
NECK YOUR SARNIE AND GET SOME SHUT-EYE, MATE.
I'M GOING TO LOOK IN ON LAUGHING BOY.
HELLO, HELLO.
OH, JESUS CHRIST.
JUST GO ON AN' FUCKIN' GET IT OVER WITH.

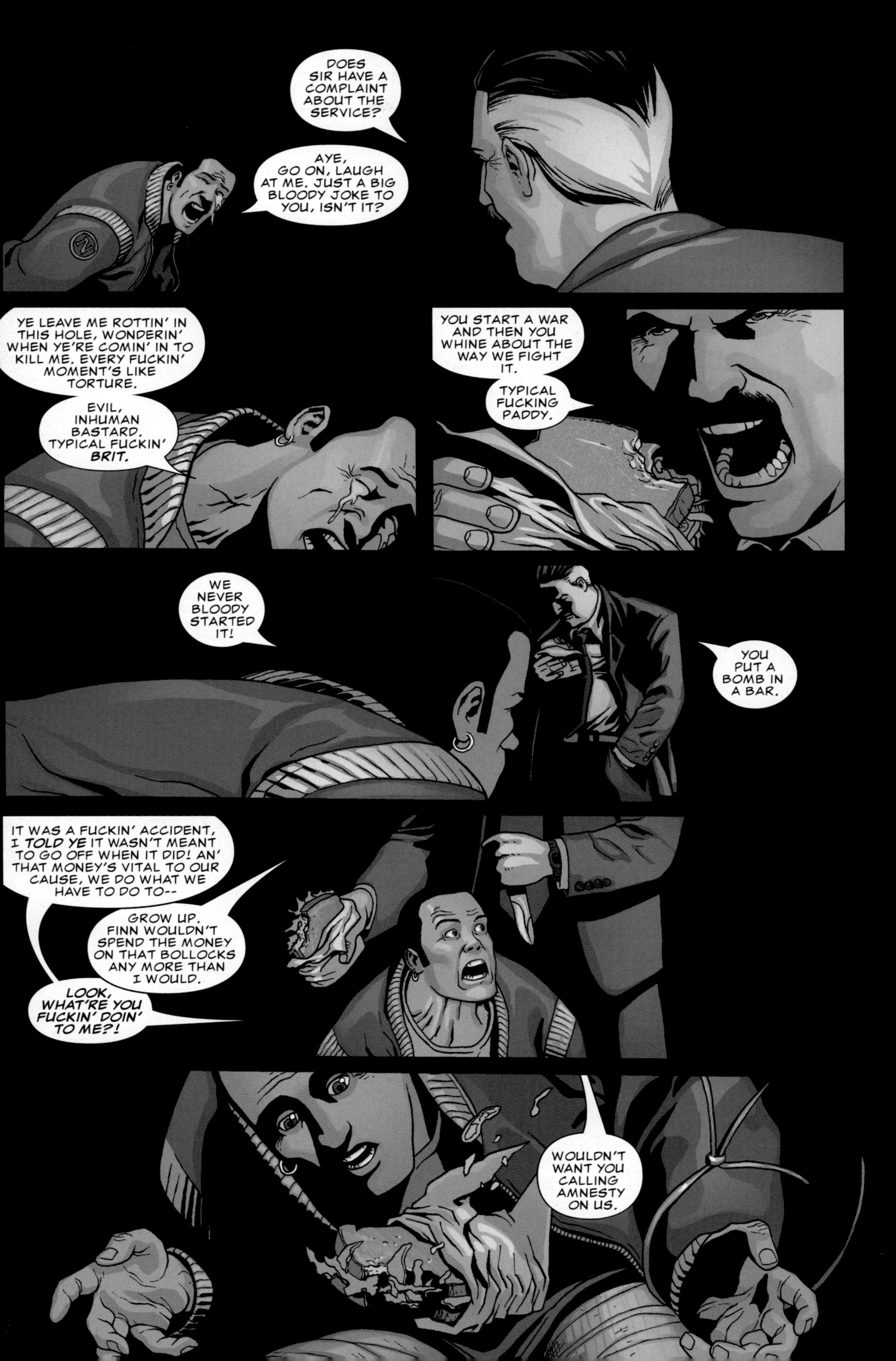
DOES SIR HAVE A COMPLAINT ABOUT THE SERVICE?
AYE, GO ON, LAUGH AT ME. JUST A BIG BLOODY JOKE TO YOU, ISN'T IT?
YE LEAVE ME ROTTIN' IN THIS HOLE, WONDERIN' WHEN YE'RE COMIN' IN TO KILL ME. EVERY FUCKIN' MOMENT'S LIKE TORTURE.
EVIL, INHUMAN BASTARD. TYPICAL FUCKIN' *BRIT.*
YOU START A WAR AND THEN YOU WHINE ABOUT THE WAY WE FIGHT IT.
TYPICAL FUCKING PADDY.
WE NEVER BLOODY STARTED IT!
YOU PUT A BOMB IN A BAR.
IT WAS A FUCKIN' ACCIDENT, I *TOLD YE* IT WASN'T MEANT TO GO OFF WHEN IT DID! AN' THAT MONEY'S VITAL TO OUR CAUSE, WE DO WHAT WE HAVE TO DO TO--
GROW UP. FINN WOULDN'T SPEND THE MONEY ON THAT BOLLOCKS ANY MORE THAN I WOULD.
LOOK, WHAT'RE YOU FUCKIN' DOIN' TO ME?!
WOULDN'T WANT YOU CALLING AMNESTY ON US.

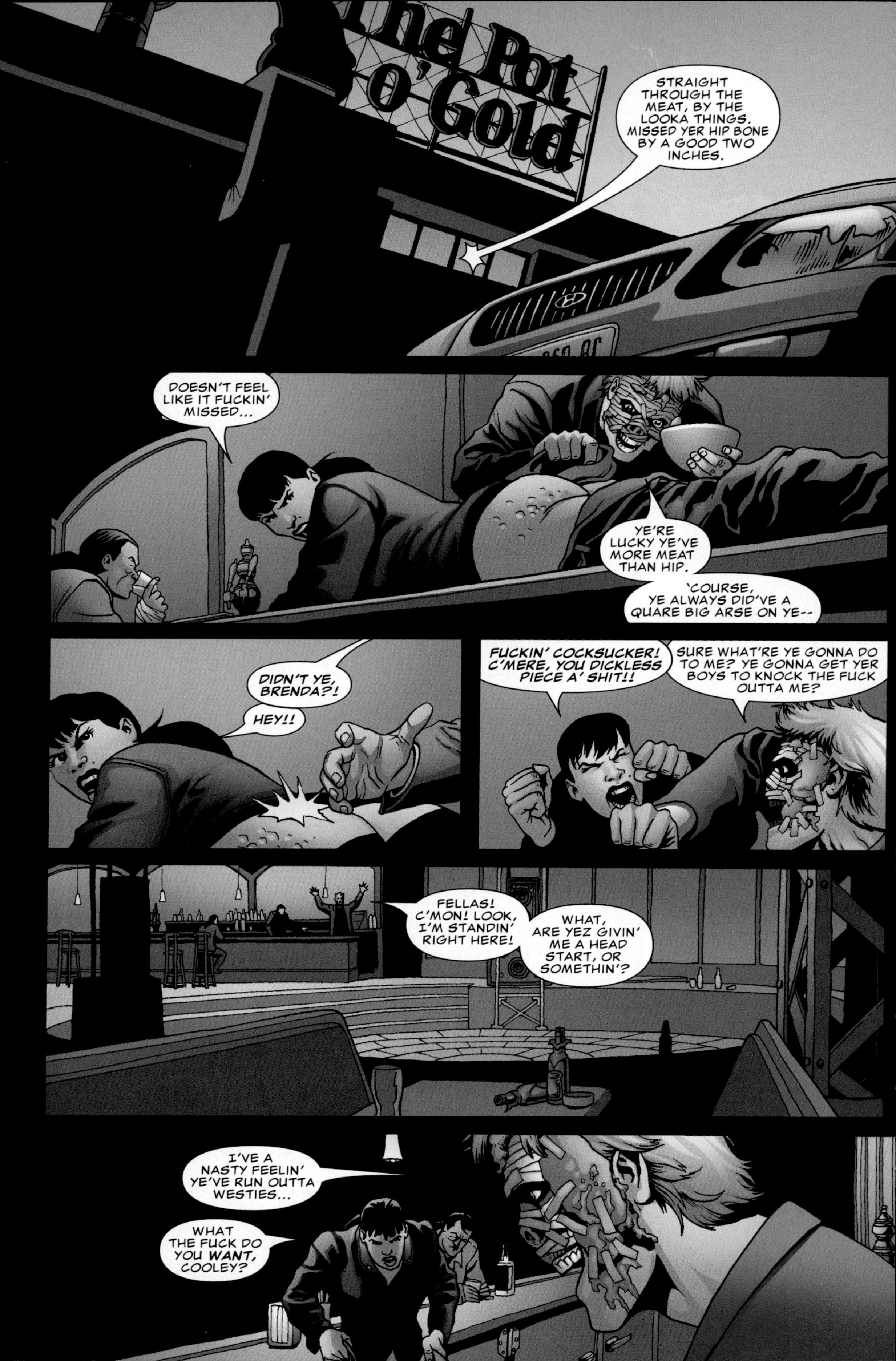
The Pot o' Gold
STRAIGHT THROUGH THE MEAT, BY THE LOOKA THINGS. MISSED YER HIP BONE BY A GOOD TWO INCHES.
DOESN'T FEEL LIKE IT FUCKIN' MISSED...
YE'RE LUCKY YE'VE MORE MEAT THAN HIP.
'COURSE, YE ALWAYS DID'VE A QUARE BIG ARSE ON YE--
DIDN'T YE, BRENDA?!
HEY!!
FUCKIN' COCKSUCKER! C'MERE, YOU DICKLESS PIECE A' SHIT!!
SURE WHAT'RE YE GONNA DO TO ME? YE GONNA GET YER BOYS TO KNOCK THE FUCK OUTTA ME?
FELLAS! C'MON! LOOK, I'M STANDIN' RIGHT HERE!
WHAT, ARE YEZ GIVIN' ME A HEAD START, OR SOMETHIN'?
I'VE A NASTY FEELIN' YE'VE RUN OUTTA WESTIES...
WHAT THE FUCK DO YOU WANT, COOLEY?

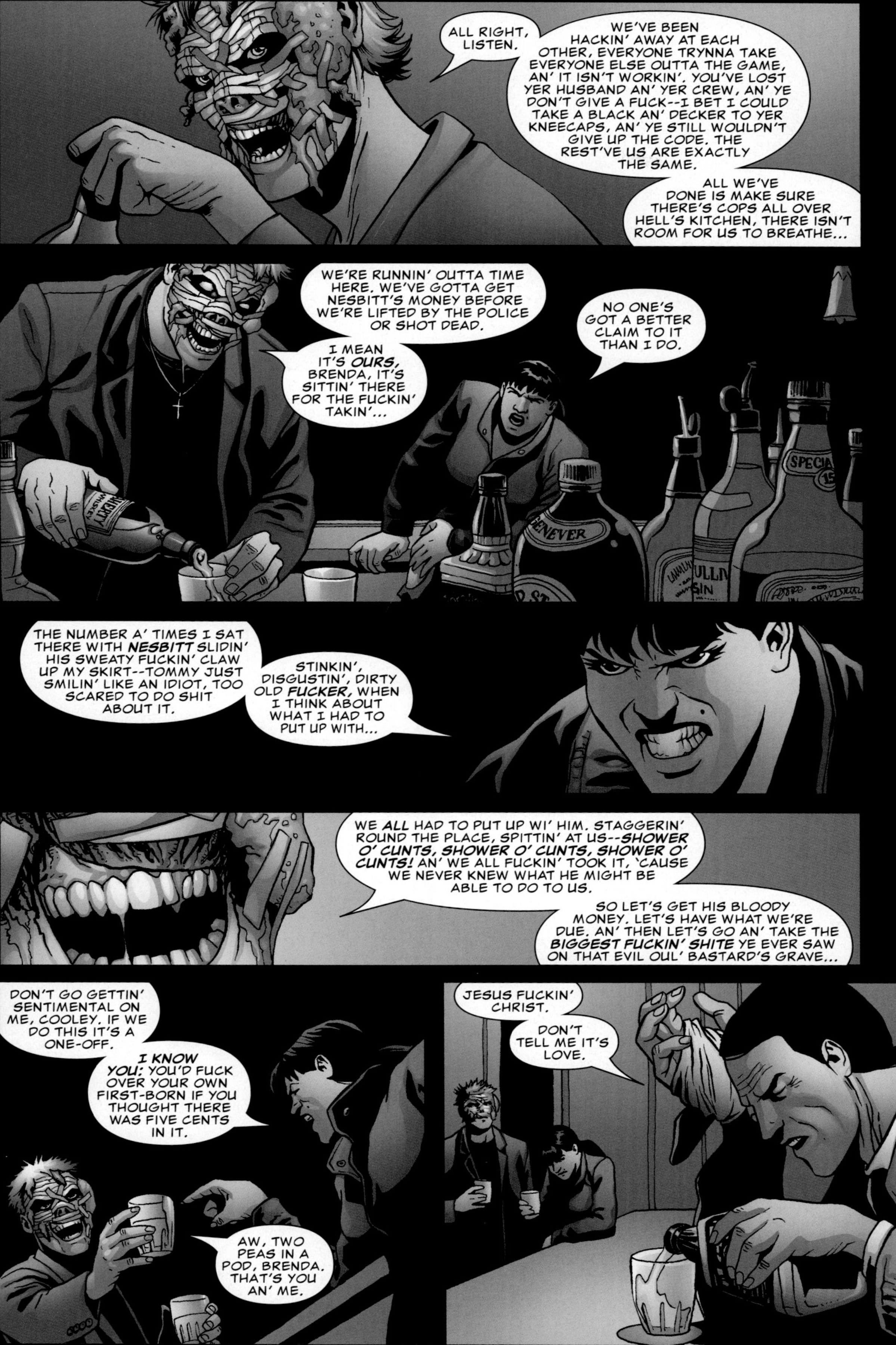

ALL RIGHT, LISTEN.
WE'VE BEEN HACKIN' AWAY AT EACH OTHER, EVERYONE TRYNNA TAKE EVERYONE ELSE OUTTA THE GAME, AN' IT ISN'T WORKIN'. YOU'VE LOST YER HUSBAND AN' YER CREW, AN' YE DON'T GIVE A FUCK--I BET I COULD TAKE A BLACK AN' DECKER TO YER KNEECAPS, AN' YE STILL WOULDN'T GIVE UP THE CODE. THE REST'VE US ARE EXACTLY THE SAME.
ALL WE'VE DONE IS MAKE SURE THERE'S COPS ALL OVER HELL'S KITCHEN, THERE ISN'T ROOM FOR US TO BREATHE...
WE'RE RUNNIN' OUTTA TIME HERE. WE'VE GOTTA GET NESBITT'S MONEY BEFORE WE'RE LIFTED BY THE POLICE OR SHOT DEAD.
I MEAN IT'S OURS, BRENDA, IT'S SITTIN' THERE FOR THE FUCKIN' TAKIN'...
NO ONE'S GOT A BETTER CLAIM TO IT THAN I DO.
GENEVER
SPECIA
THE NUMBER A' TIMES I SAT THERE WITH NESBITT SLIDIN' HIS SWEATY FUCKIN' CLAW UP MY SKIRT--TOMMY JUST SMILIN' LIKE AN IDIOT, TOO SCARED TO DO SHIT ABOUT IT.
STINKIN', DISGUSTIN', DIRTY OLD FUCKER, WHEN I THINK ABOUT WHAT I HAD TO PUT UP WITH...
WE ALL HAD TO PUT UP WI' HIM. STAGGERIN' ROUND THE PLACE, SPITTIN' AT US--SHOWER O' CUNTS, SHOWER O' CUNTS, SHOWER O' CUNTS! AN' WE ALL FUCKIN' TOOK IT, 'CAUSE WE NEVER KNEW WHAT HE MIGHT BE ABLE TO DO TO US.
SO LET'S GET HIS BLOODY MONEY. LET'S HAVE WHAT WE'RE DUE. AN' THEN LET'S GO AN' TAKE THE BIGGEST FUCKIN' SHITE YE EVER SAW ON THAT EVIL OUL' BASTARD'S GRAVE...
DON'T GO GETTIN' SENTIMENTAL ON ME, COOLEY. IF WE DO THIS IT'S A ONE-OFF.
I KNOW YOU: YOU'D FUCK OVER YOUR OWN FIRST-BORN IF YOU THOUGHT THERE WAS FIVE CENTS IN IT.
AW, TWO PEAS IN A POD, BRENDA. THAT'S YOU AN' ME.
JESUS FUCKIN' CHRIST.
DON'T TELL ME IT'S LOVE.

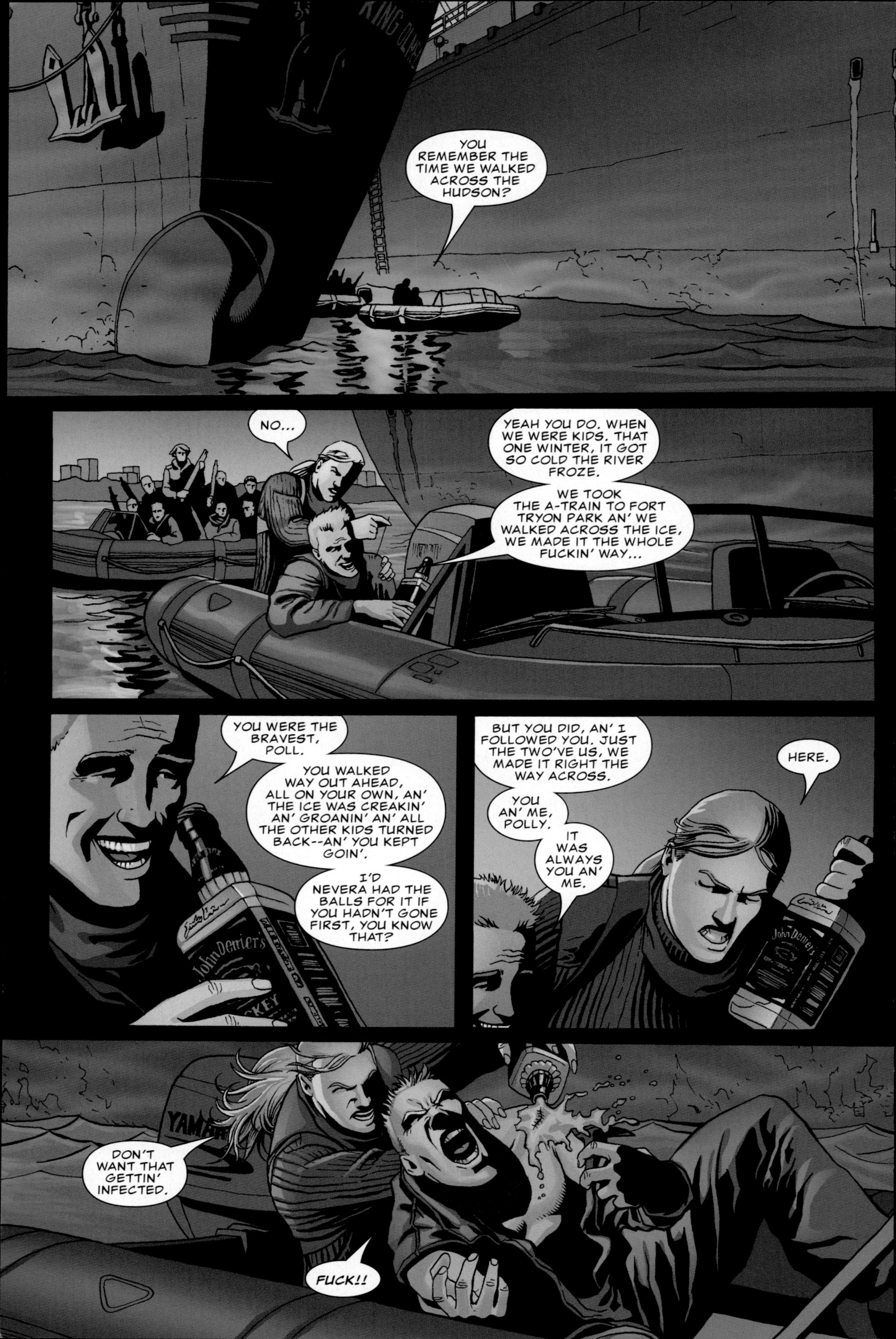
YOU REMEMBER THE TIME WE WALKED ACROSS THE HUDSON?
NO...
YEAH YOU DO. WHEN WE WERE KIDS. THAT ONE WINTER, IT GOT SO COLD THE RIVER FROZE.
WE TOOK THE A-TRAIN TO FORT TRYON PARK AN' WE WALKED ACROSS THE ICE, WE MADE IT THE WHOLE FUCKIN' WAY...
YOU WERE THE BRAVEST, POLL.
YOU WALKED WAY OUT AHEAD, ALL ON YOUR OWN, AN' THE ICE WAS CREAKIN' AN' GROANIN' AN' ALL THE OTHER KIDS TURNED BACK--AN' YOU KEPT GOIN'.
I'D NEVERA HAD THE BALLS FOR IT IF YOU HADN'T GONE FIRST, YOU KNOW THAT?
BUT YOU DID, AN' I FOLLOWED YOU. JUST THE TWO'VE US, WE MADE IT RIGHT THE WAY ACROSS.
YOU AN' ME, POLLY.
IT WAS ALWAYS YOU AN' ME.
HERE.
DON'T WANT THAT GETTIN' INFECTED.
FUCK!!

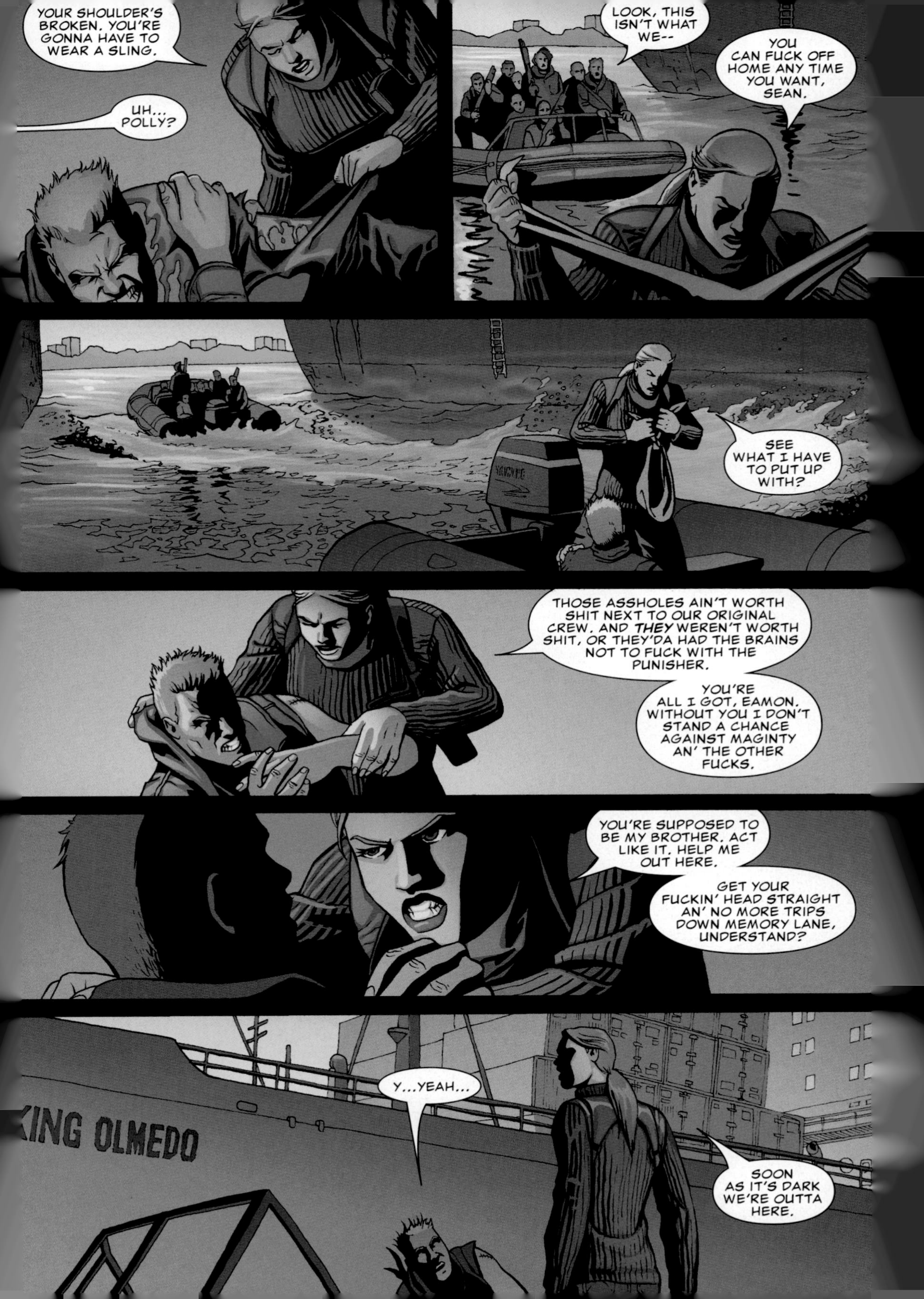
YOUR SHOULDER'S BROKEN. YOU'RE GONNA HAVE TO WEAR A SLING.
UH... POLLY?
LOOK, THIS ISN'T WHAT WE--
YOU CAN FUCK OFF HOME ANY TIME YOU WANT, SEAN.
SEE WHAT I HAVE TO PUT UP WITH?
THOSE ASSHOLES AIN'T WORTH SHIT NEXT TO OUR ORIGINAL CREW. AND THEY WEREN'T WORTH SHIT, OR THEY'DA HAD THE BRAINS NOT TO FUCK WITH THE PUNISHER.
YOU'RE ALL I GOT, EAMON. WITHOUT YOU I DON'T STAND A CHANCE AGAINST MAGINTY AN' THE OTHER FUCKS.
YOU'RE SUPPOSED TO BE MY BROTHER. ACT LIKE IT. HELP ME OUT HERE.
GET YOUR FUCKIN' HEAD STRAIGHT AN' NO MORE TRIPS DOWN MEMORY LANE, UNDERSTAND?
Y...YEAH...
SOON AS IT'S DARK WE'RE OUTTA HERE.
KING OLMEDO

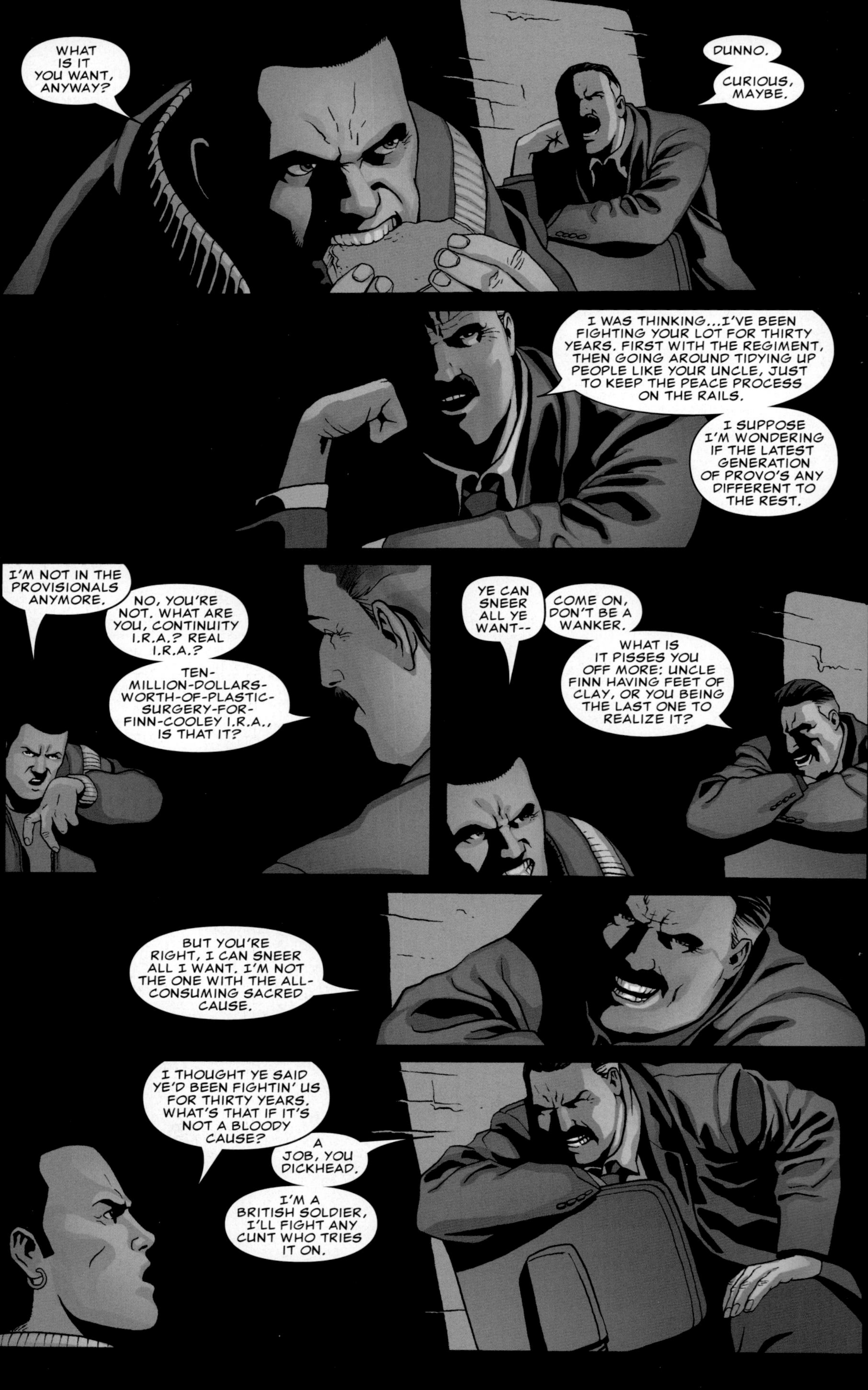
WHAT IS IT YOU WANT, ANYWAY?
DUNNO.
CURIOUS, MAYBE.
I WAS THINKING...I'VE BEEN FIGHTING YOUR LOT FOR THIRTY YEARS. FIRST WITH THE REGIMENT, THEN GOING AROUND TIDYING UP PEOPLE LIKE YOUR UNCLE, JUST TO KEEP THE PEACE PROCESS ON THE RAILS.
I SUPPOSE I'M WONDERING IF THE LATEST GENERATION OF PROVO'S ANY DIFFERENT TO THE REST.
I'M NOT IN THE PROVISIONALS ANYMORE.
NO, YOU'RE NOT. WHAT ARE YOU, CONTINUITY I.R.A.? REAL I.R.A.?
TEN-MILLION-DOLLARS-WORTH-OF-PLASTIC-SURGERY-FOR-FINN-COOLEY I.R.A., IS THAT IT?
YE CAN SNEER ALL YE WANT--
COME ON, DON'T BE A WANKER.
WHAT IS IT PISSES YOU OFF MORE: UNCLE FINN HAVING FEET OF CLAY, OR YOU BEING THE LAST ONE TO REALIZE IT?
BUT YOU'RE RIGHT, I CAN SNEER ALL I WANT. I'M NOT THE ONE WITH THE ALL-CONSUMING SACRED CAUSE.
I THOUGHT YE SAID YE'D BEEN FIGHTIN' US FOR THIRTY YEARS. WHAT'S THAT IF IT'S NOT A BLOODY CAUSE?
A JOB, YOU DICKHEAD.
I'M A BRITISH SOLDIER, I'LL FIGHT ANY CUNT WHO TRIES IT ON.

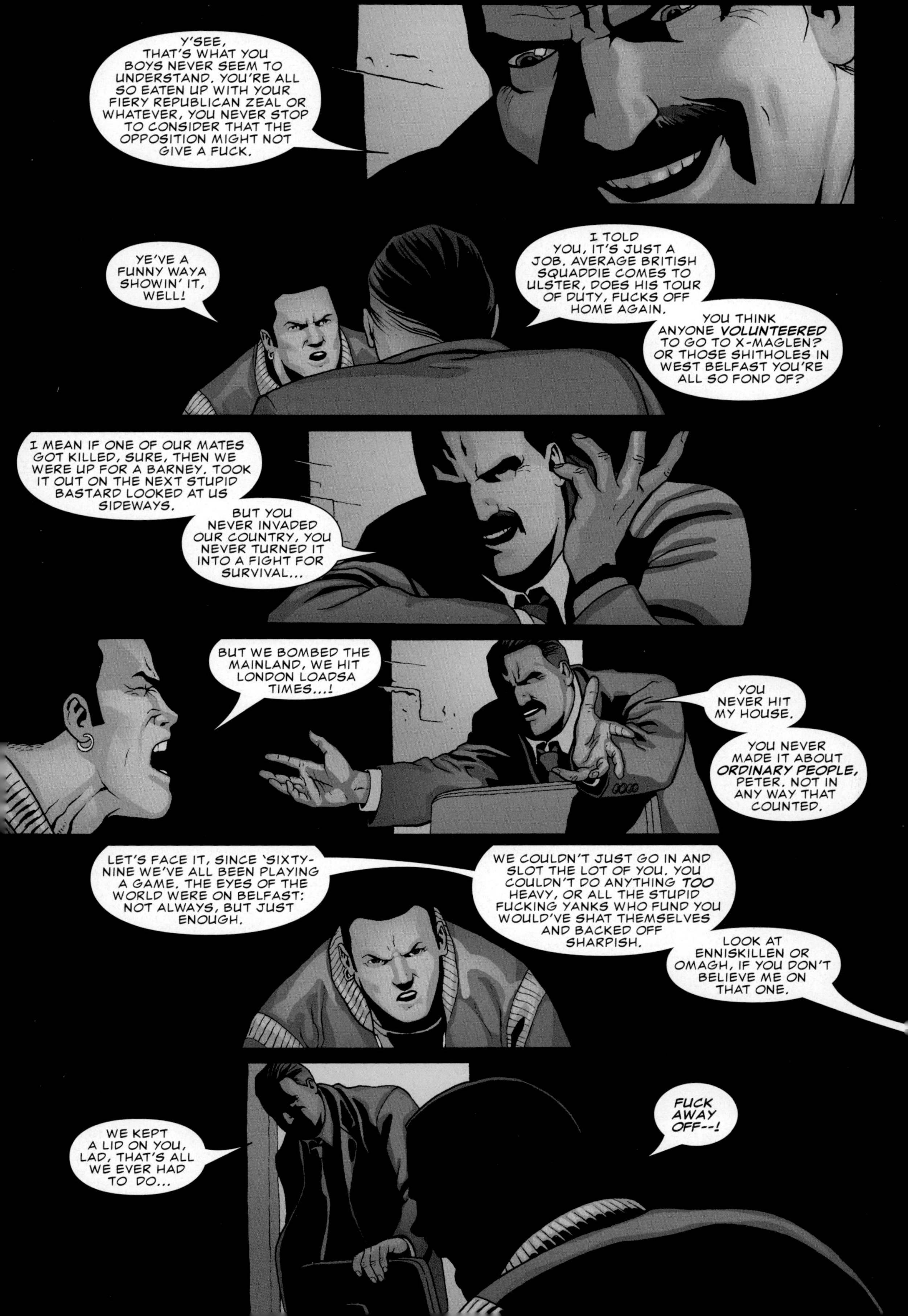
Y'SEE, THAT'S WHAT YOU BOYS NEVER SEEM TO UNDERSTAND. YOU'RE ALL SO EATEN UP WITH YOUR FIERY REPUBLICAN ZEAL OR WHATEVER, YOU NEVER STOP TO CONSIDER THAT THE OPPOSITION MIGHT NOT GIVE A FUCK.
YE'VE A FUNNY WAYA SHOWIN' IT, WELL!
I TOLD YOU, IT'S JUST A JOB. AVERAGE BRITISH SQUADDIE COMES TO ULSTER, DOES HIS TOUR OF DUTY, FUCKS OFF HOME AGAIN.
YOU THINK ANYONE VOLUNTEERED TO GO TO X-MAGLEN? OR THOSE SHITHOLES IN WEST BELFAST YOU'RE ALL SO FOND OF?
I MEAN IF ONE OF OUR MATES GOT KILLED, SURE, THEN WE WERE UP FOR A BARNEY. TOOK IT OUT ON THE NEXT STUPID BASTARD LOOKED AT US SIDEWAYS.
BUT YOU NEVER INVADED OUR COUNTRY, YOU NEVER TURNED IT INTO A FIGHT FOR SURVIVAL...
BUT WE BOMBED THE MAINLAND, WE HIT LONDON LOADSA TIMES...!
YOU NEVER HIT MY HOUSE.
YOU NEVER MADE IT ABOUT ORDINARY PEOPLE, PETER. NOT IN ANY WAY THAT COUNTED.
LET'S FACE IT, SINCE 'SIXTY-NINE WE'VE ALL BEEN PLAYING A GAME. THE EYES OF THE WORLD WERE ON BELFAST: NOT ALWAYS, BUT JUST ENOUGH.
WE COULDN'T JUST GO IN AND SLOT THE LOT OF YOU. YOU COULDN'T DO ANYTHING TOO HEAVY, OR ALL THE STUPID FUCKING YANKS WHO FUND YOU WOULD'VE SHAT THEMSELVES AND BACKED OFF SHARPISH.
LOOK AT ENNISKILLEN OR OMAGH, IF YOU DON'T BELIEVE ME ON THAT ONE.
WE KEPT A LID ON YOU, LAD, THAT'S ALL WE EVER HAD TO DO...
FUCK AWAY OFF--!

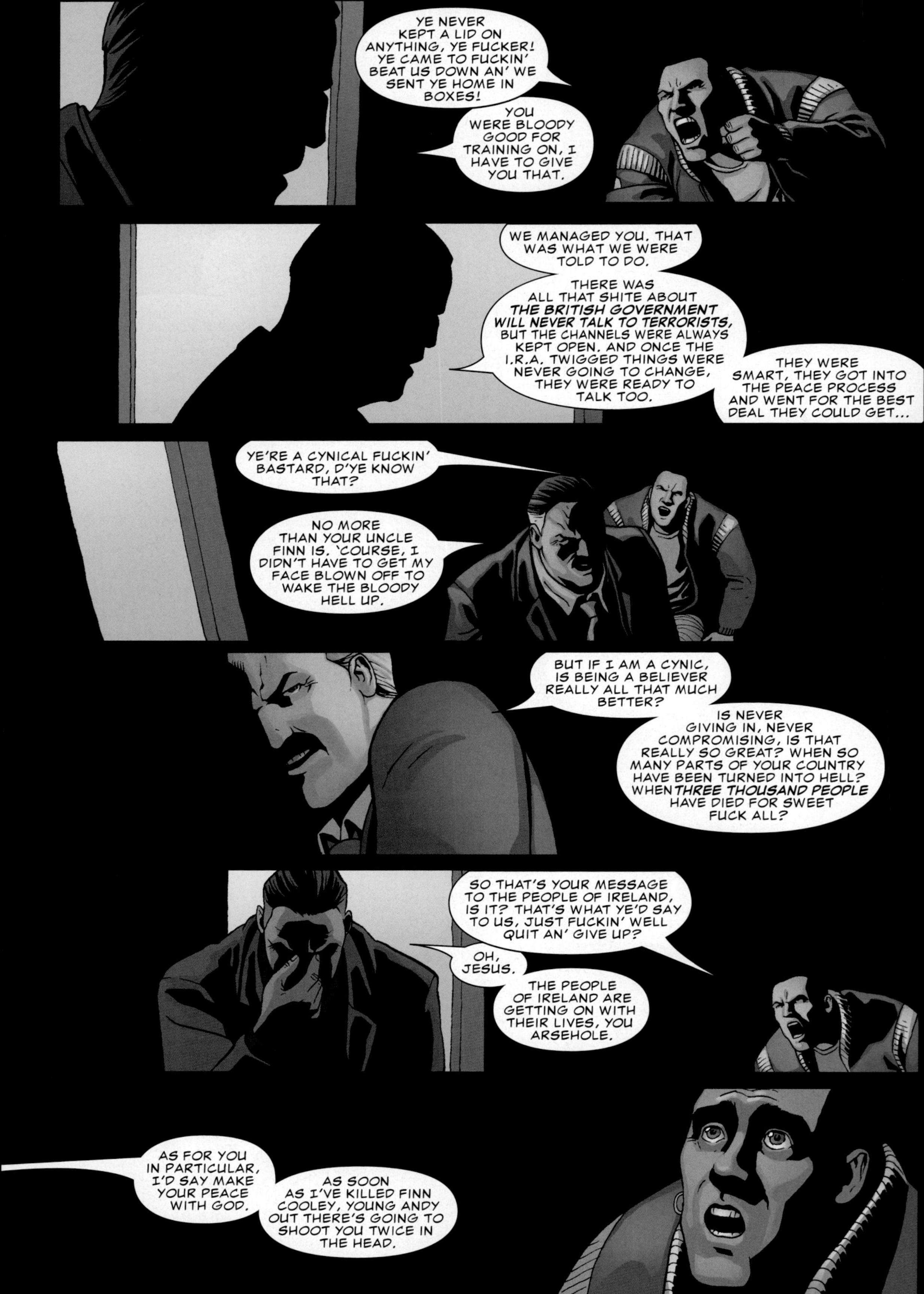
YE NEVER KEPT A LID ON ANYTHING, YE FUCKER! YE CAME TO FUCKIN' BEAT US DOWN AN' WE SENT YE HOME IN BOXES!
YOU WERE BLOODY GOOD FOR TRAINING ON, I HAVE TO GIVE YOU THAT.
WE MANAGED YOU. THAT WAS WHAT WE WERE TOLD TO DO.
THERE WAS ALL THAT SHITE ABOUT *THE BRITISH GOVERNMENT WILL NEVER TALK TO TERRORISTS,* BUT THE CHANNELS WERE ALWAYS KEPT OPEN. AND ONCE THE I.R.A. TWIGGED THINGS WERE NEVER GOING TO CHANGE, THEY WERE READY TO TALK TOO.
THEY WERE SMART, THEY GOT INTO THE PEACE PROCESS AND WENT FOR THE BEST DEAL THEY COULD GET...
YE'RE A CYNICAL FUCKIN' BASTARD, D'YE KNOW THAT?
NO MORE THAN YOUR UNCLE FINN IS. 'COURSE, I DIDN'T HAVE TO GET MY FACE BLOWN OFF TO WAKE THE BLOODY HELL UP.
BUT IF I AM A CYNIC, IS BEING A BELIEVER REALLY ALL THAT MUCH BETTER?
IS NEVER GIVING IN, NEVER COMPROMISING, IS THAT REALLY SO GREAT? WHEN SO MANY PARTS OF YOUR COUNTRY HAVE BEEN TURNED INTO HELL? WHEN *THREE THOUSAND PEOPLE* HAVE DIED FOR SWEET FUCK ALL?
SO THAT'S YOUR MESSAGE TO THE PEOPLE OF IRELAND, IS IT? THAT'S WHAT YE'D SAY TO US, JUST FUCKIN' WELL QUIT AN' GIVE UP?
OH, JESUS.
THE PEOPLE OF IRELAND ARE GETTING ON WITH THEIR LIVES, YOU ARSEHOLE.
AS FOR YOU IN PARTICULAR, I'D SAY MAKE YOUR PEACE WITH GOD.
AS SOON AS I'VE KILLED FINN COOLEY, YOUNG ANDY OUT THERE'S GOING TO SHOOT YOU TWICE IN THE HEAD.

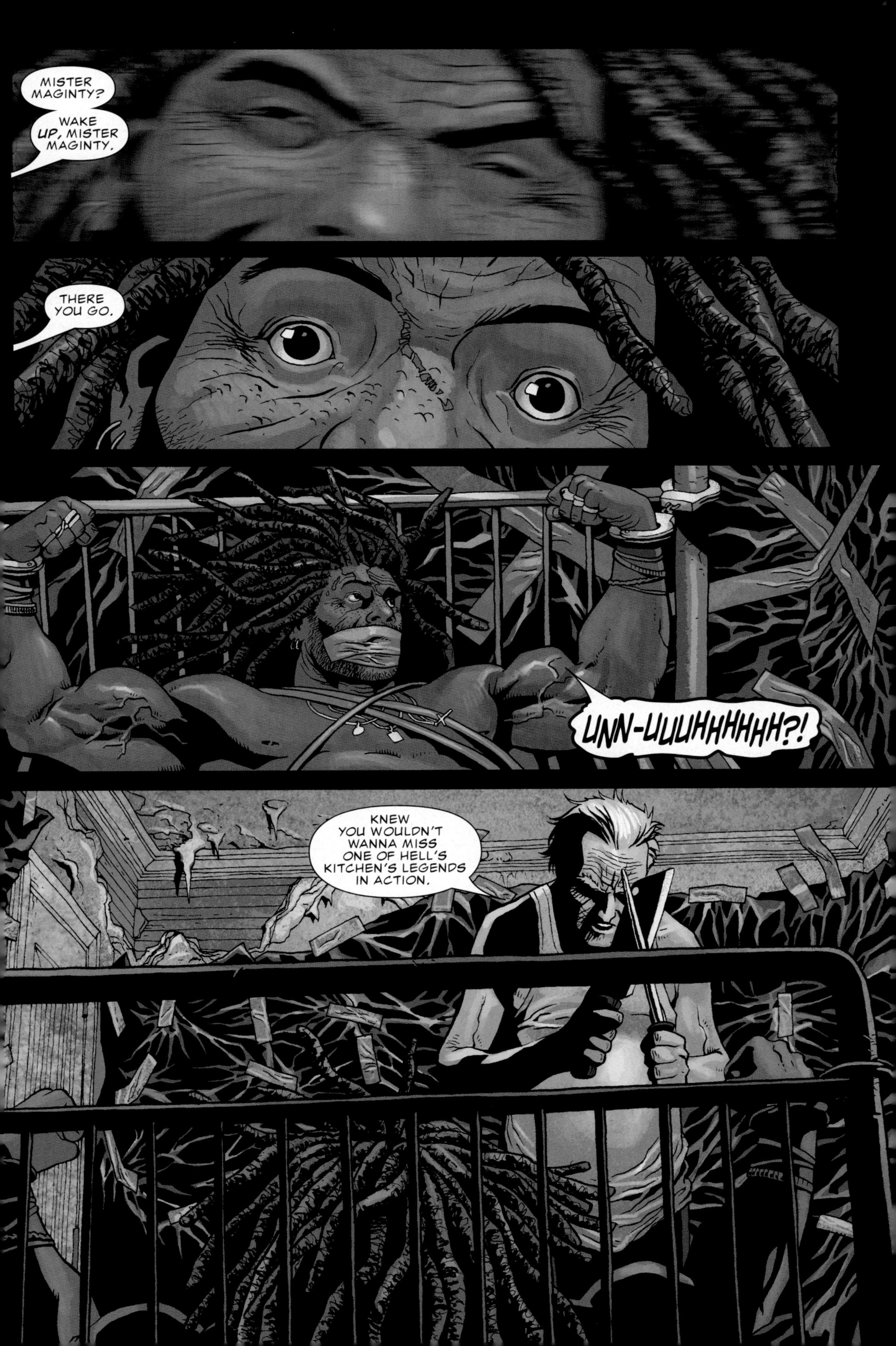
MISTER MAGINTY?
WAKE UP, MISTER MAGINTY.
THERE YOU GO.
UNN-UUUHHHHHH?!
KNEW YOU WOULDN'T WANNA MISS ONE OF HELL'S KITCHEN'S LEGENDS IN ACTION.

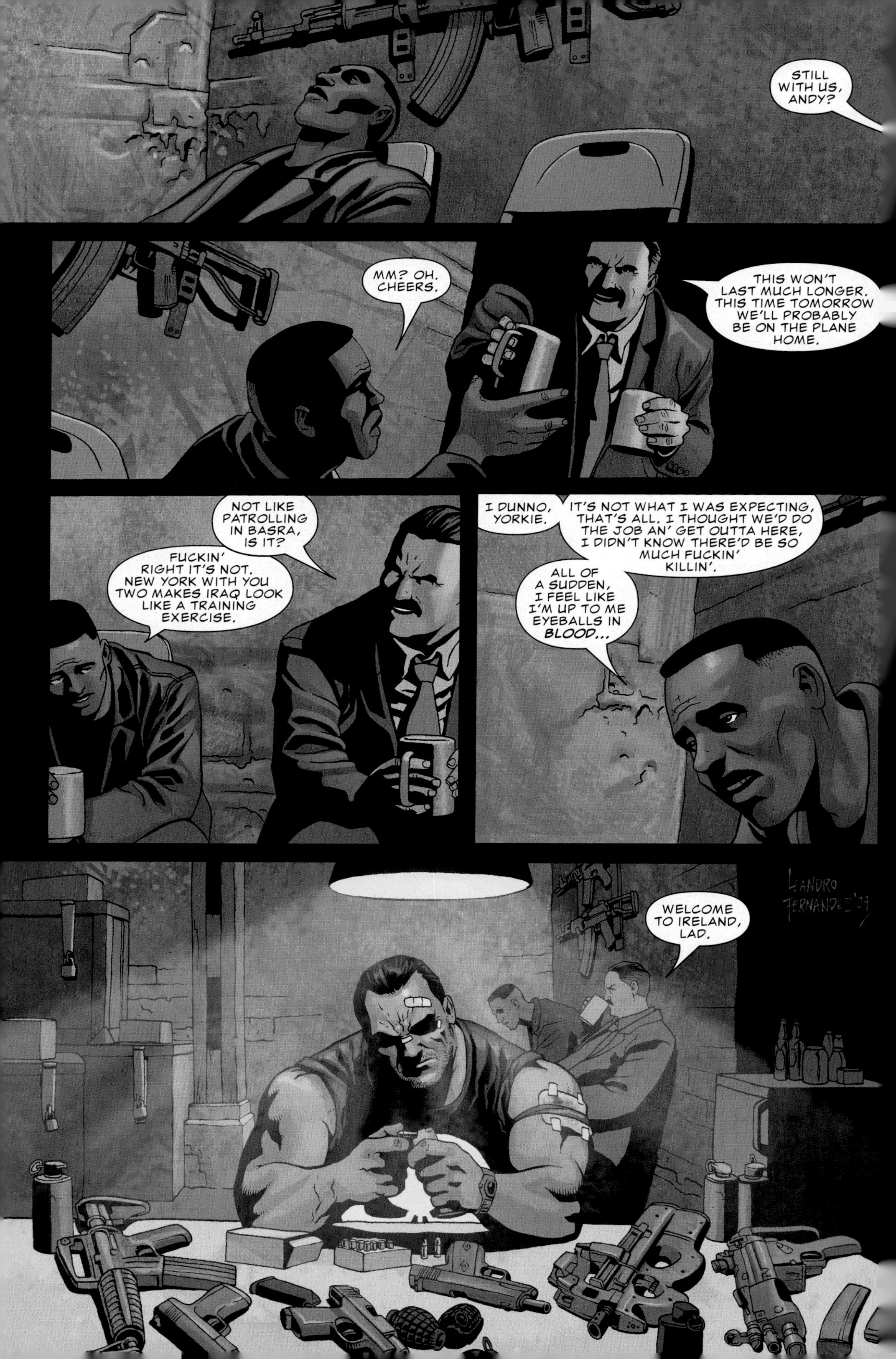
STILL WITH US, ANDY?
MM? OH. CHEERS.
THIS WON'T LAST MUCH LONGER. THIS TIME TOMORROW WE'LL PROBABLY BE ON THE PLANE HOME.
NOT LIKE PATROLLING IN BASRA, IS IT?
FUCKIN' RIGHT IT'S NOT. NEW YORK WITH YOU TWO MAKES IRAQ LOOK LIKE A TRAINING EXERCISE.
I DUNNO, YORKIE.
IT'S NOT WHAT I WAS EXPECTING, THAT'S ALL. I THOUGHT WE'D DO THE JOB AN' GET OUTTA HERE, I DIDN'T KNOW THERE'D BE SO MUCH FUCKIN' KILLIN'.
ALL OF A SUDDEN, I FEEL LIKE I'M UP TO ME EYEBALLS IN *BLOOD...*
LEANDRO FERNANDEZ '09
WELCOME TO IRELAND, LAD.

PUNISHER #12

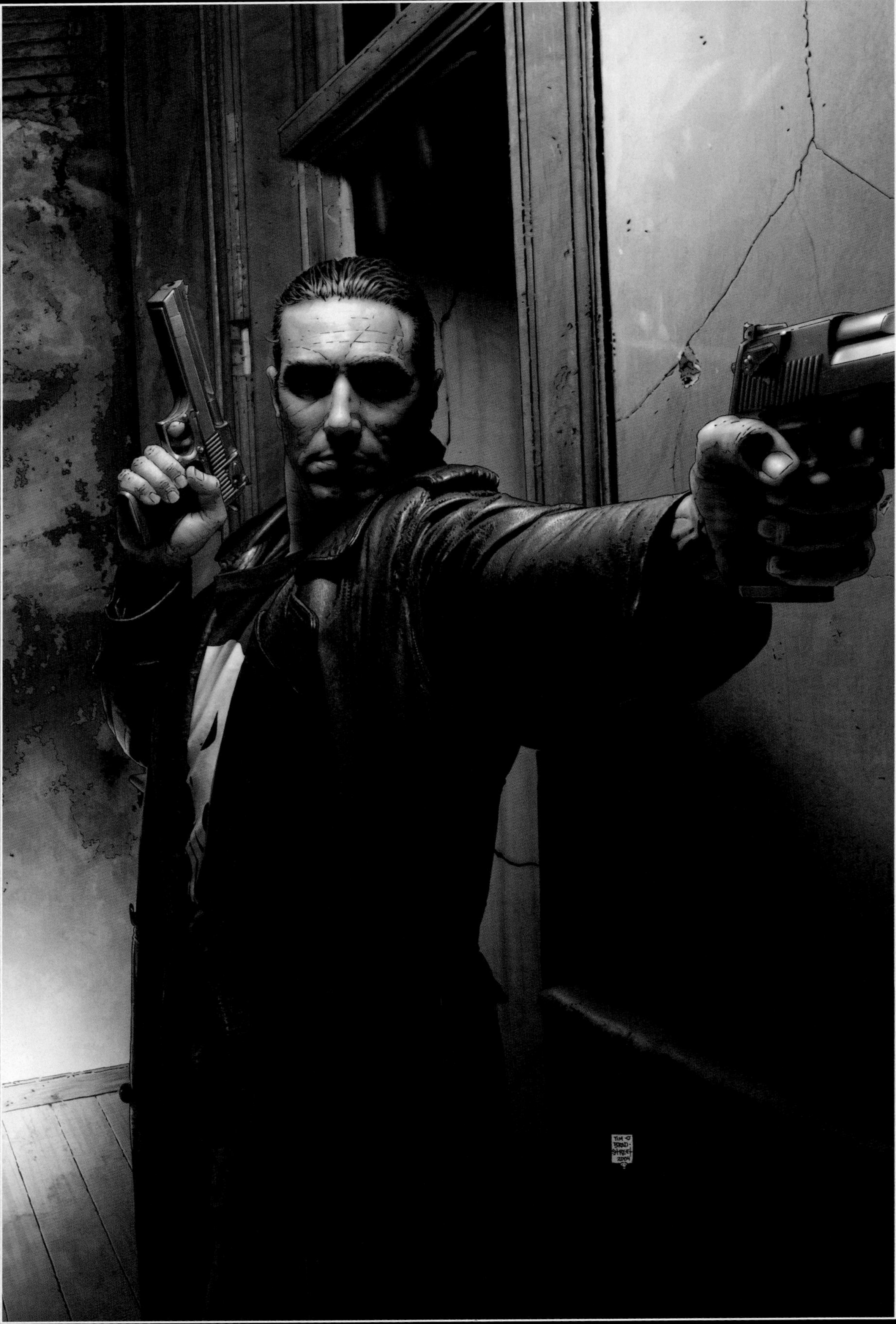

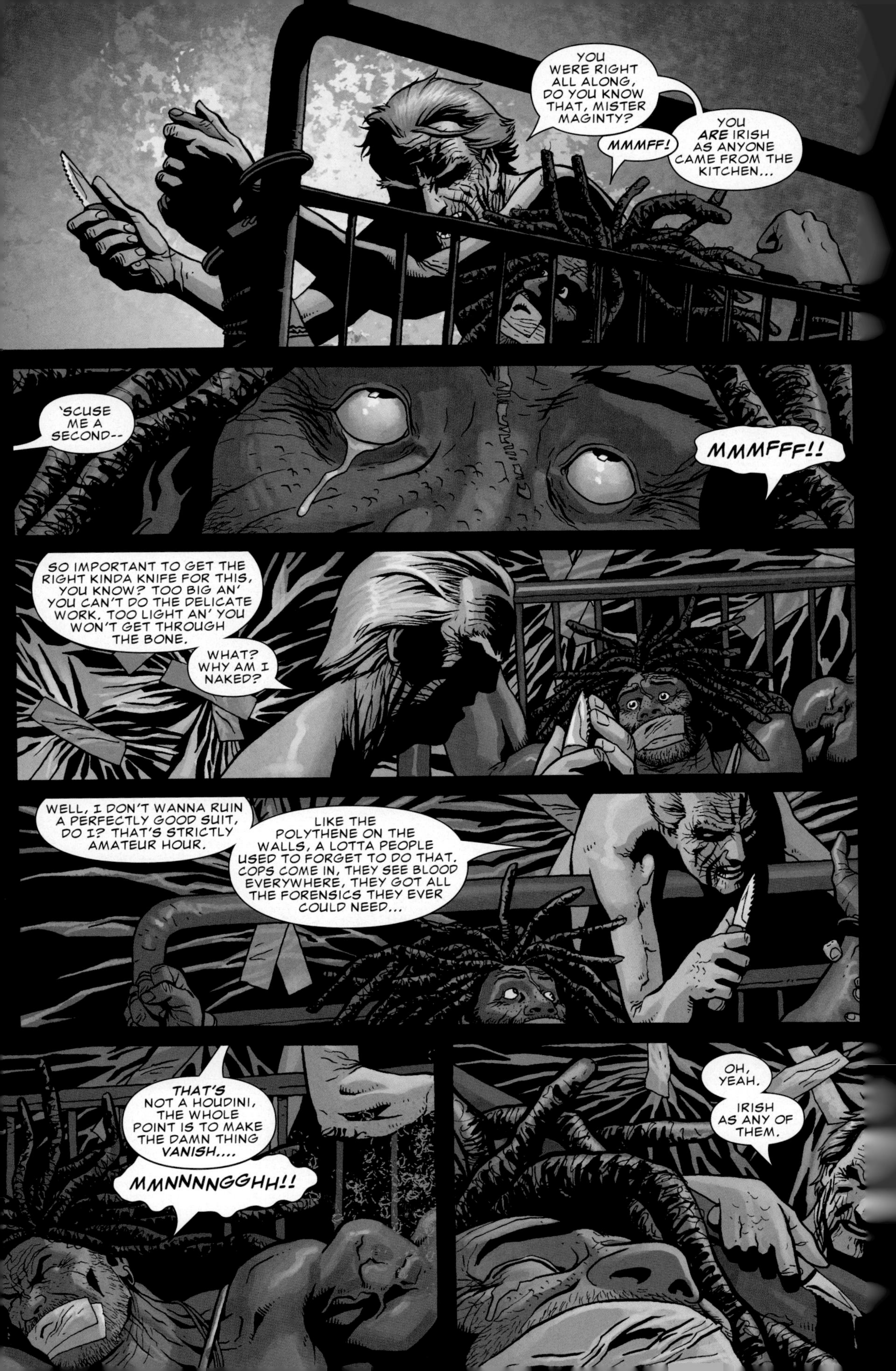
YOU WERE RIGHT ALL ALONG, DO YOU KNOW THAT, MISTER MAGINTY?
MMMFF!
YOU ARE IRISH AS ANYONE CAME FROM THE KITCHEN...
'SCUSE ME A SECOND--
MMMFFF!!
SO IMPORTANT TO GET THE RIGHT KINDA KNIFE FOR THIS, YOU KNOW? TOO BIG AN' YOU CAN'T DO THE DELICATE WORK. TOO LIGHT AN' YOU WON'T GET THROUGH THE BONE.
WHAT? WHY AM I NAKED?
WELL, I DON'T WANNA RUIN A PERFECTLY GOOD SUIT, DO I? THAT'S STRICTLY AMATEUR HOUR.
LIKE THE POLYTHENE ON THE WALLS, A LOTTA PEOPLE USED TO FORGET TO DO THAT. COPS COME IN, THEY SEE BLOOD EVERYWHERE, THEY GOT ALL THE FORENSICS THEY EVER COULD NEED...
THAT'S NOT A HOUDINI, THE WHOLE POINT IS TO MAKE THE DAMN THING VANISH....
MMNNNNGGHH!!
OH, YEAH.
IRISH AS ANY OF THEM.

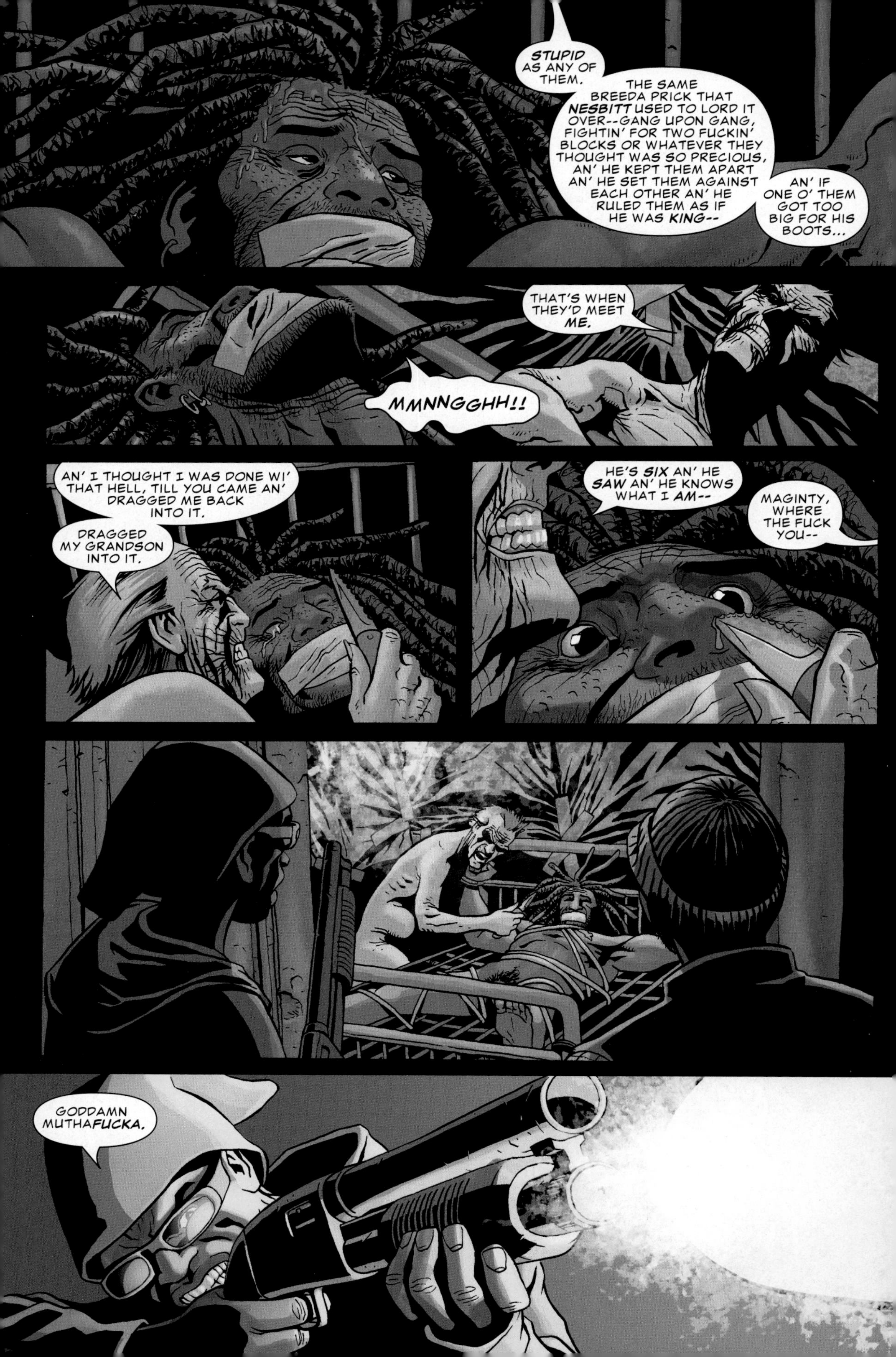
STUPID AS ANY OF THEM.
THE SAME BREEDA PRICK THAT NESBITT USED TO LORD IT OVER--GANG UPON GANG, FIGHTIN' FOR TWO FUCKIN' BLOCKS OR WHATEVER THEY THOUGHT WAS SO PRECIOUS, AN' HE KEPT THEM APART AN' HE SET THEM AGAINST EACH OTHER AN' HE RULED THEM AS IF HE WAS KING--
AN' IF ONE O' THEM GOT TOO BIG FOR HIS BOOTS...
THAT'S WHEN THEY'D MEET ME.
MMNNGGHH!!
AN' I THOUGHT I WAS DONE WI' THAT HELL, TILL YOU CAME AN' DRAGGED ME BACK INTO IT.
DRAGGED MY GRANDSON INTO IT.
HE'S SIX AN' HE SAW AN' HE KNOWS WHAT I AM--
MAGINTY, WHERE THE FUCK YOU--
GODDAMN MUTHAFUCKA.

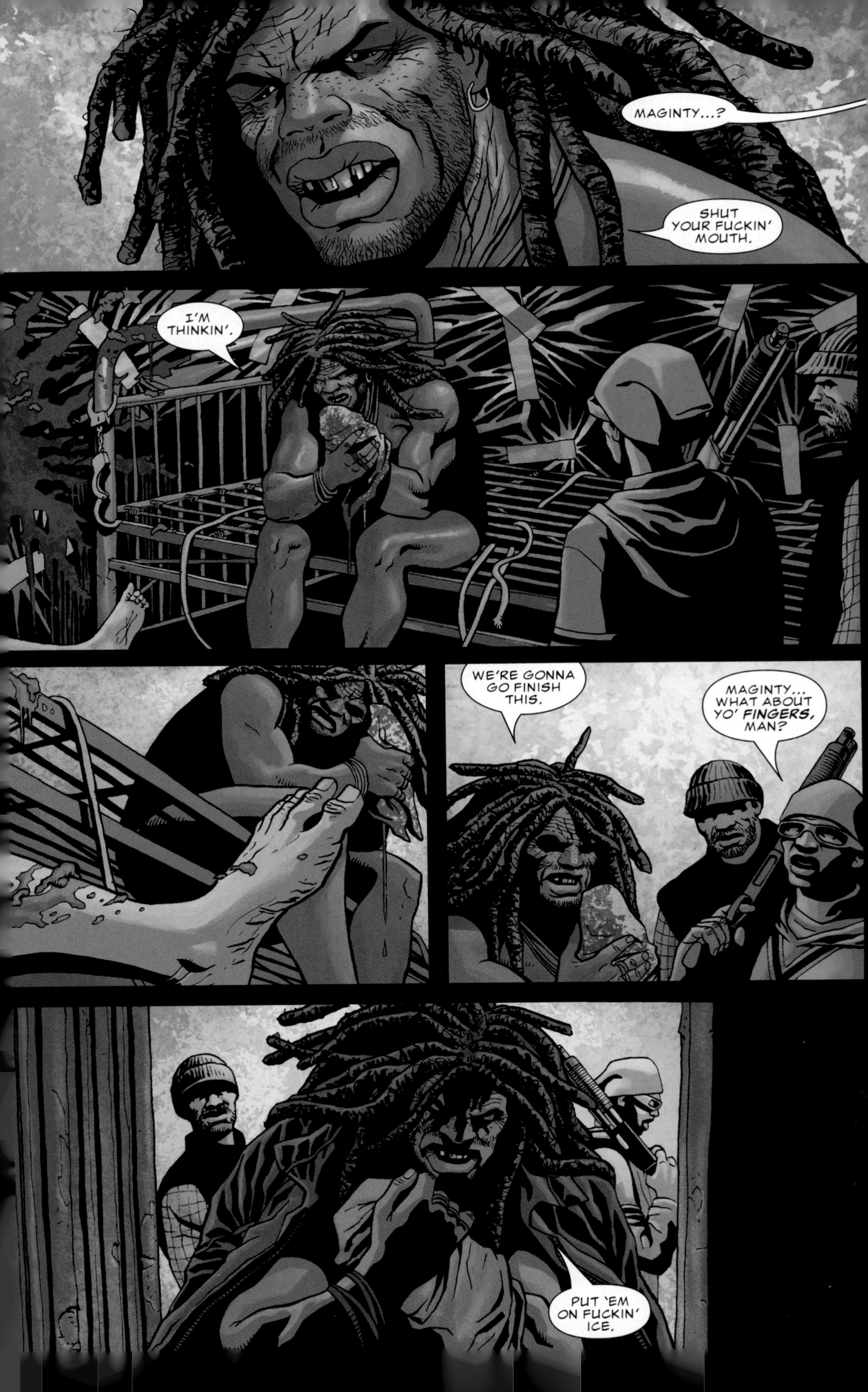
MAGINTY...?
SHUT YOUR FUCKIN' MOUTH.
I'M THINKIN'.
WE'RE GONNA GO FINISH THIS.
MAGINTY... WHAT ABOUT YO' **FINGERS,** MAN?
PUT 'EM ON FUCKIN' ICE.

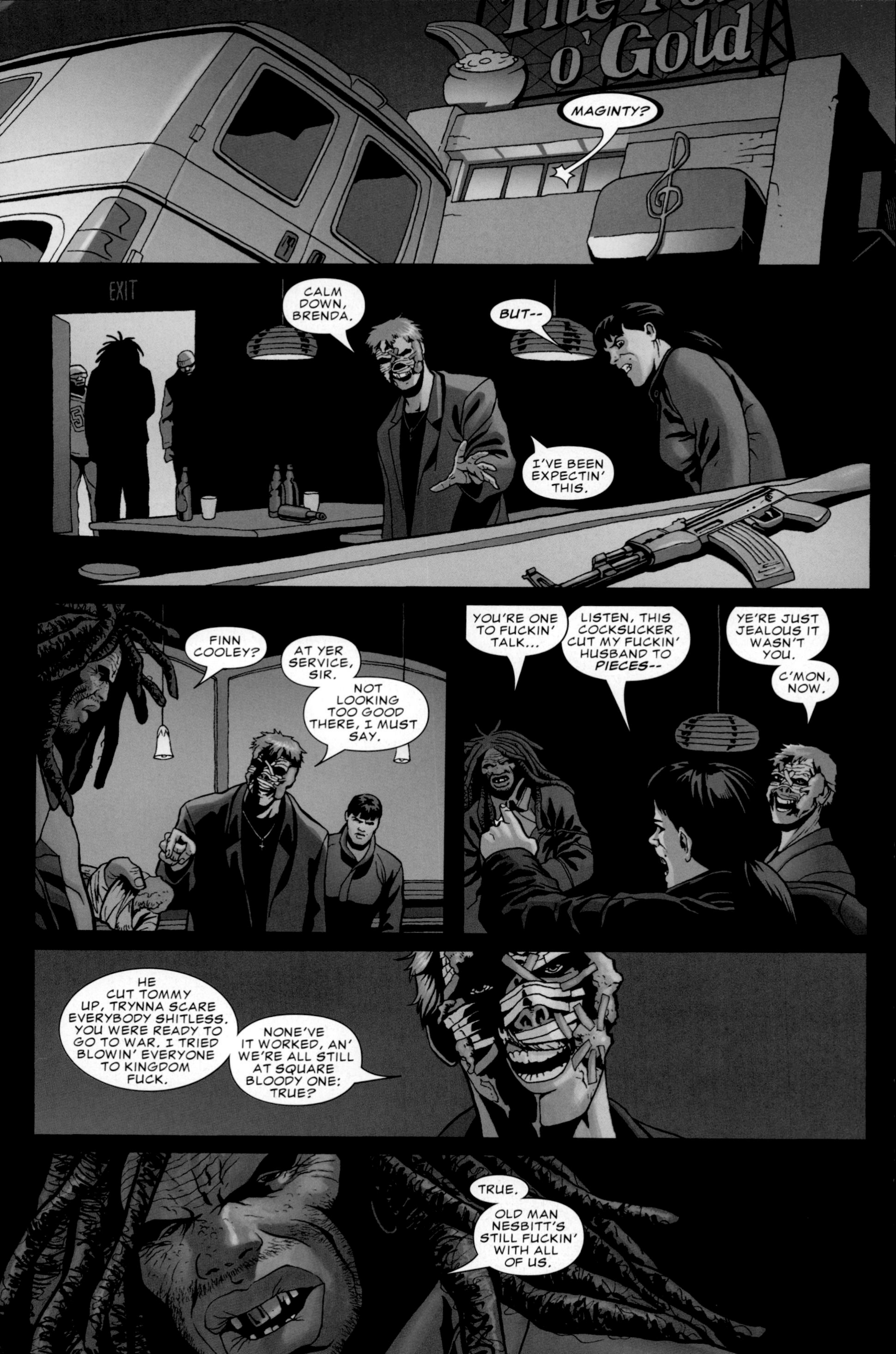
o'Gold
MAGINTY?
EXIT
CALM DOWN, BRENDA.
BUT--
I'VE BEEN EXPECTIN' THIS.
FINN COOLEY?
AT YER SERVICE, SIR.
NOT LOOKING TOO GOOD THERE, I MUST SAY.
YOU'RE ONE TO FUCKIN' TALK...
LISTEN, THIS COCKSUCKER CUT MY FUCKIN' HUSBAND TO *PIECES*--
YE'RE JUST JEALOUS IT WASN'T YOU.
C'MON, NOW.
HE CUT TOMMY UP, TRYNNA SCARE EVERYBODY SHITLESS. YOU WERE READY TO GO TO WAR. I TRIED BLOWIN' EVERYONE TO KINGDOM FUCK.
NONE'VE IT WORKED, AN' WE'RE ALL STILL AT SQUARE BLOODY ONE: TRUE?
TRUE.
OLD MAN NESBITT'S STILL FUCKIN' WITH ALL OF US.

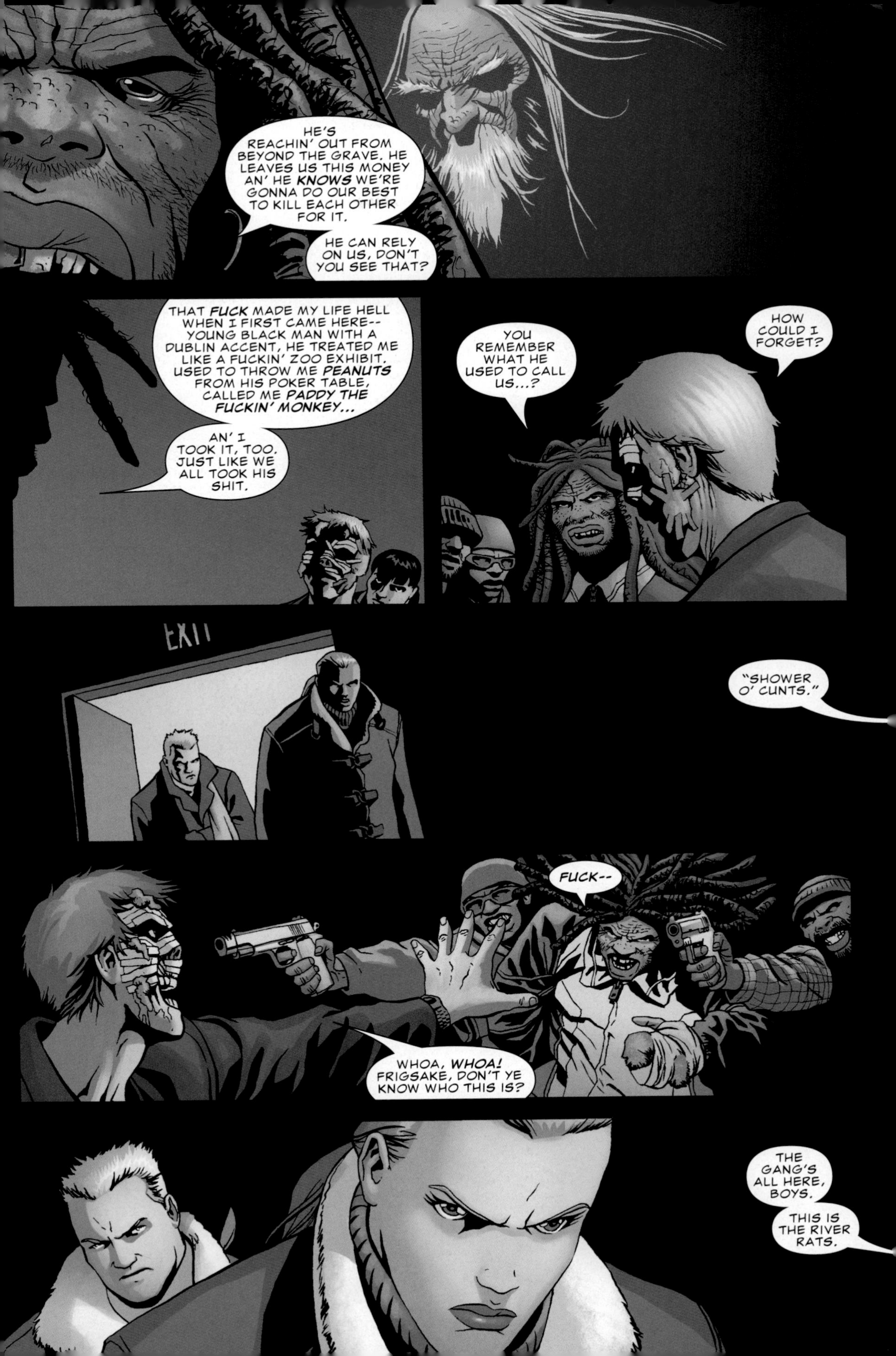
HE'S REACHIN' OUT FROM BEYOND THE GRAVE. HE LEAVES US THIS MONEY AN' HE KNOWS WE'RE GONNA DO OUR BEST TO KILL EACH OTHER FOR IT.
HE CAN RELY ON US, DON'T YOU SEE THAT?
THAT FUCK MADE MY LIFE HELL WHEN I FIRST CAME HERE-- YOUNG BLACK MAN WITH A DUBLIN ACCENT, HE TREATED ME LIKE A FUCKIN' ZOO EXHIBIT. USED TO THROW ME PEANUTS FROM HIS POKER TABLE, CALLED ME PADDY THE FUCKIN' MONKEY...
AN' I TOOK IT, TOO. JUST LIKE WE ALL TOOK HIS SHIT.
YOU REMEMBER WHAT HE USED TO CALL US...?
HOW COULD I FORGET?
EXIT
"SHOWER O' CUNTS."
FUCK--
WHOA, WHOA! FRIGSAKE, DON'T YE KNOW WHO THIS IS?
THE GANG'S ALL HERE, BOYS.
THIS IS THE RIVER RATS.

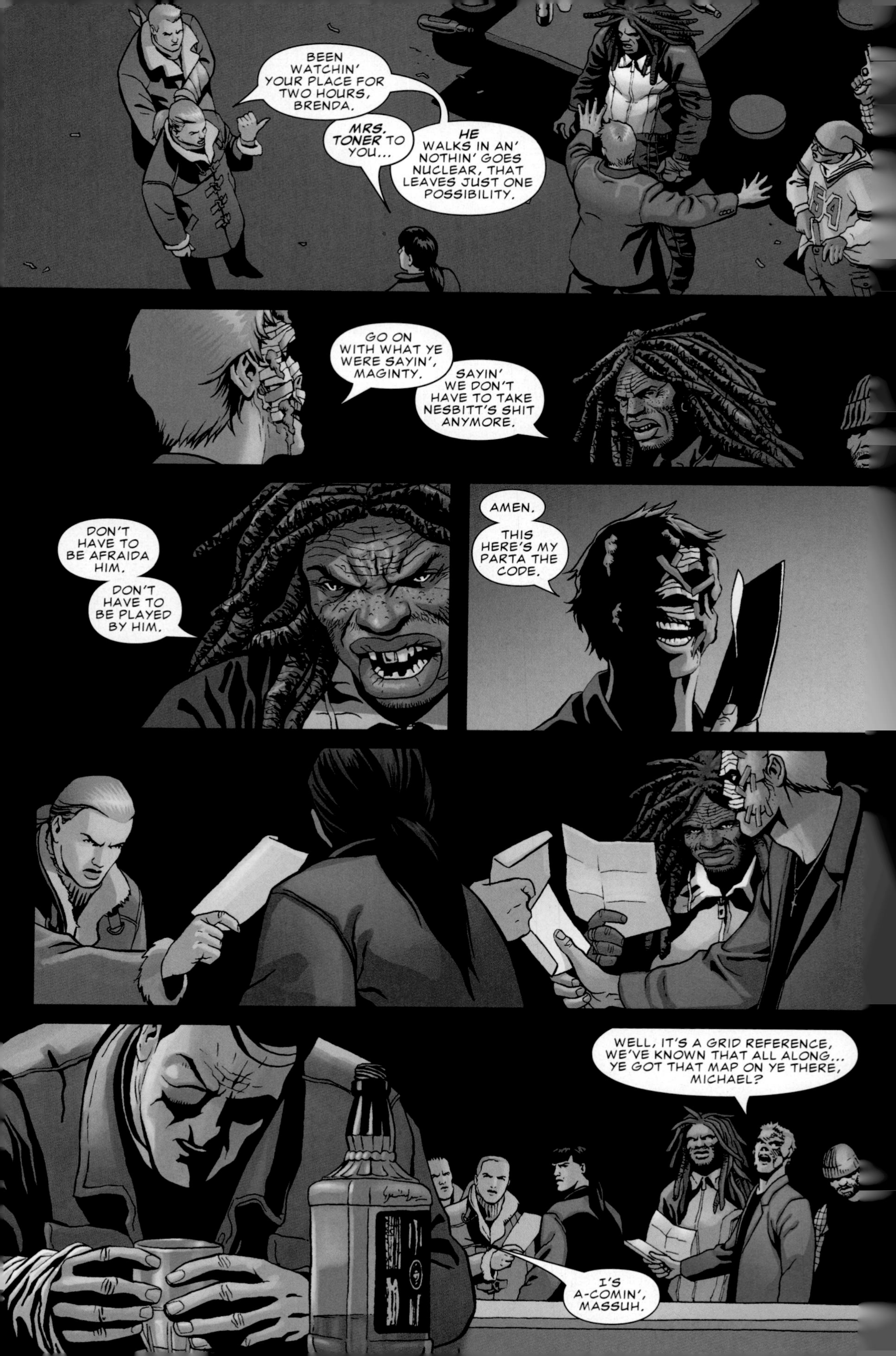
BEEN WATCHIN' YOUR PLACE FOR TWO HOURS, BRENDA.
MRS. TONER TO YOU...
HE WALKS IN AN' NOTHIN' GOES NUCLEAR, THAT LEAVES JUST ONE POSSIBILITY.
GO ON WITH WHAT YE WERE SAYIN', MAGINTY.
SAYIN' WE DON'T HAVE TO TAKE NESBITT'S SHIT ANYMORE.
DON'T HAVE TO BE AFRAIDA HIM.
DON'T HAVE TO BE PLAYED BY HIM.
AMEN.
THIS HERE'S MY PARTA THE CODE.
WELL, IT'S A GRID REFERENCE, WE'VE KNOWN THAT ALL ALONG... YE GOT THAT MAP ON YE THERE, MICHAEL?
I'S A-COMIN', MASSUH.

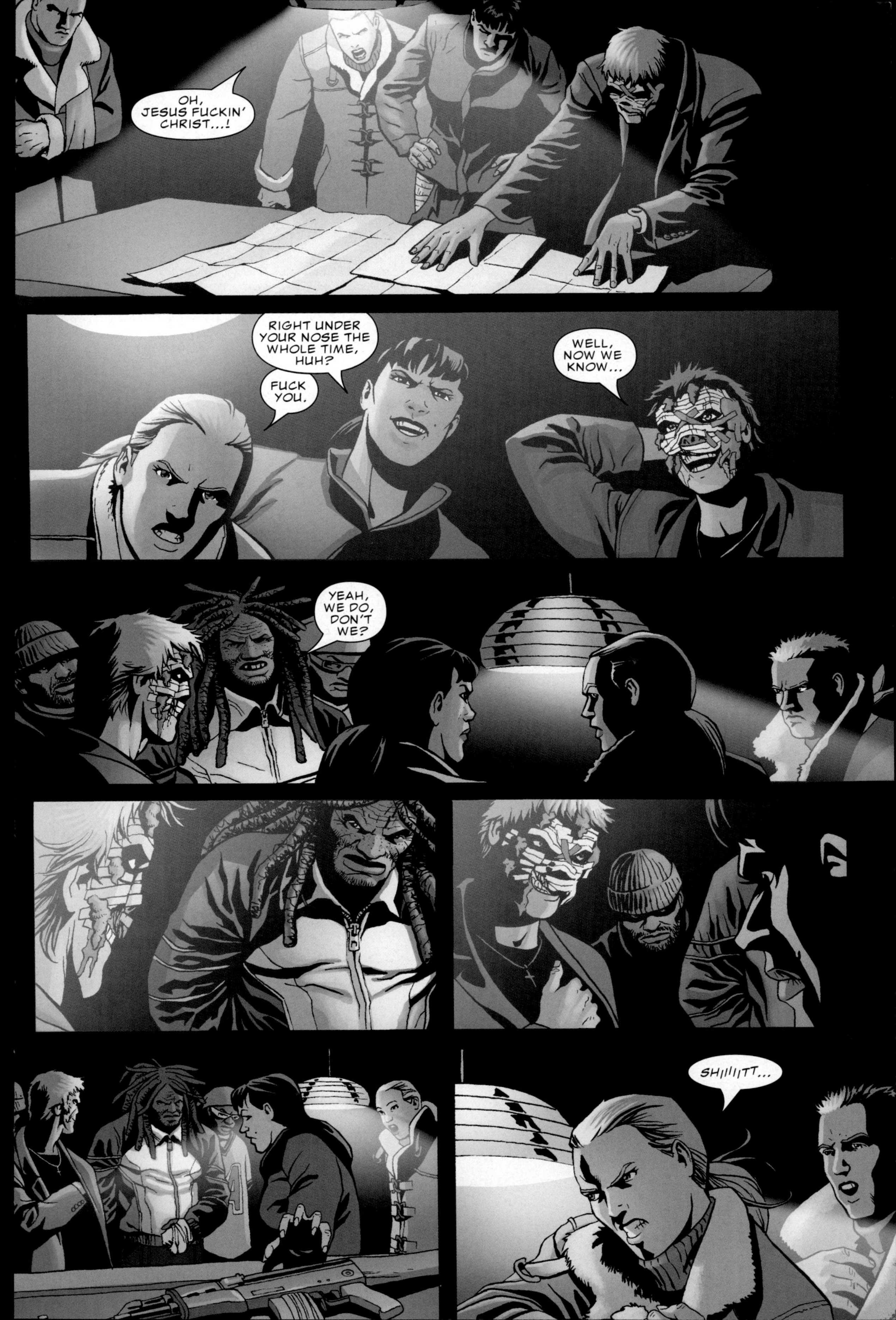
OH, JESUS FUCKIN' CHRIST...!
RIGHT UNDER YOUR NOSE THE WHOLE TIME, HUH?
FUCK YOU.
WELL, NOW WE KNOW...
YEAH, WE DO, DON'T WE?
SHIIIIITT...

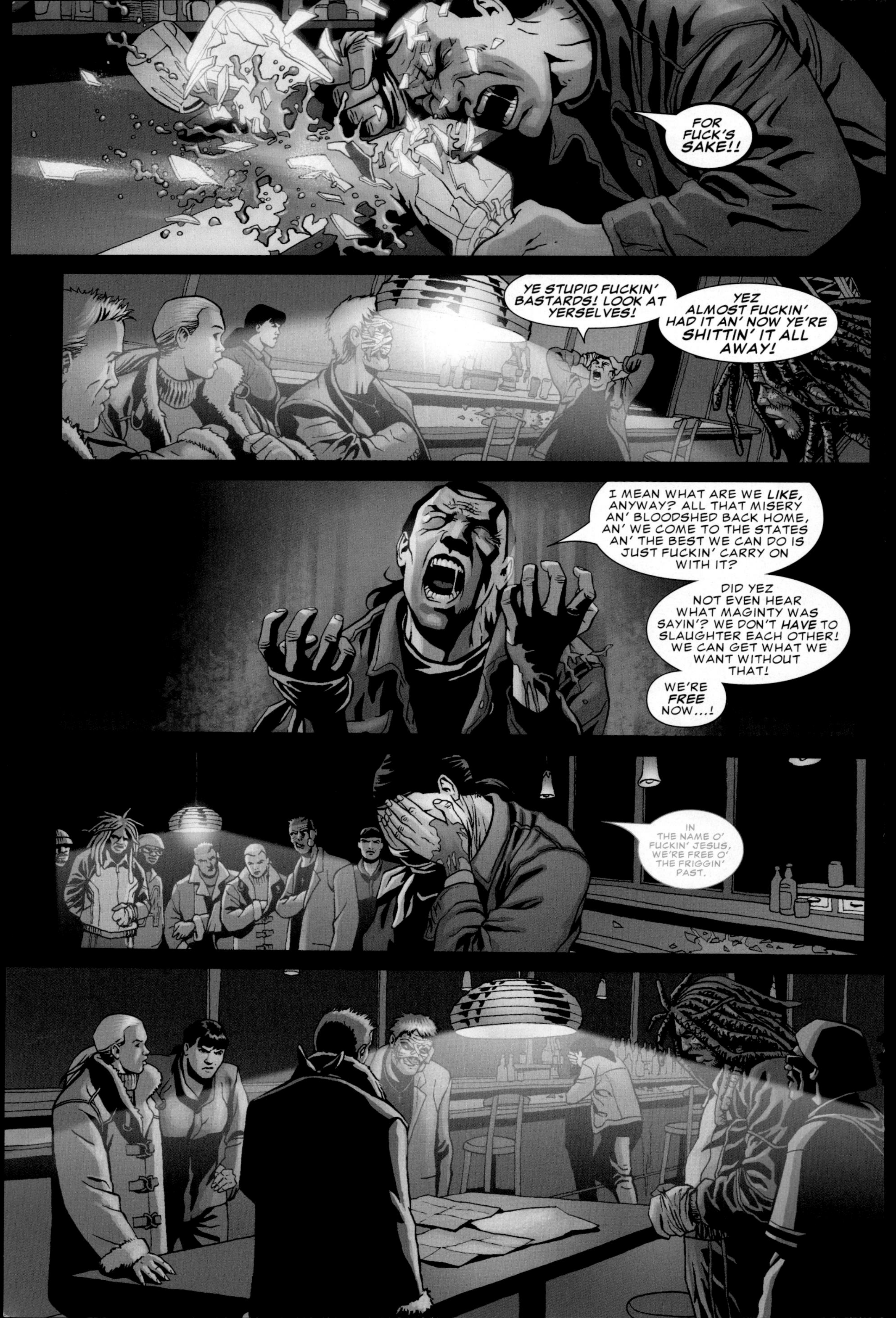
FOR FUCK'S SAKE!!
YE STUPID FUCKIN' BASTARDS! LOOK AT YERSELVES!
YEZ ALMOST FUCKIN' HAD IT AN' NOW YE'RE SHITTIN' IT ALL AWAY!
I MEAN WHAT ARE WE LIKE, ANYWAY? ALL THAT MISERY AN' BLOODSHED BACK HOME, AN' WE COME TO THE STATES AN' THE BEST WE CAN DO IS JUST FUCKIN' CARRY ON WITH IT?
DID YEZ NOT EVEN HEAR WHAT MAGINTY WAS SAYIN'? WE DON'T HAVE TO SLAUGHTER EACH OTHER! WE CAN GET WHAT WE WANT WITHOUT THAT!
WE'RE FREE NOW...!
IN THE NAME O' FUCKIN' JESUS, WE'RE FREE O' THE FRIGGIN' PAST.

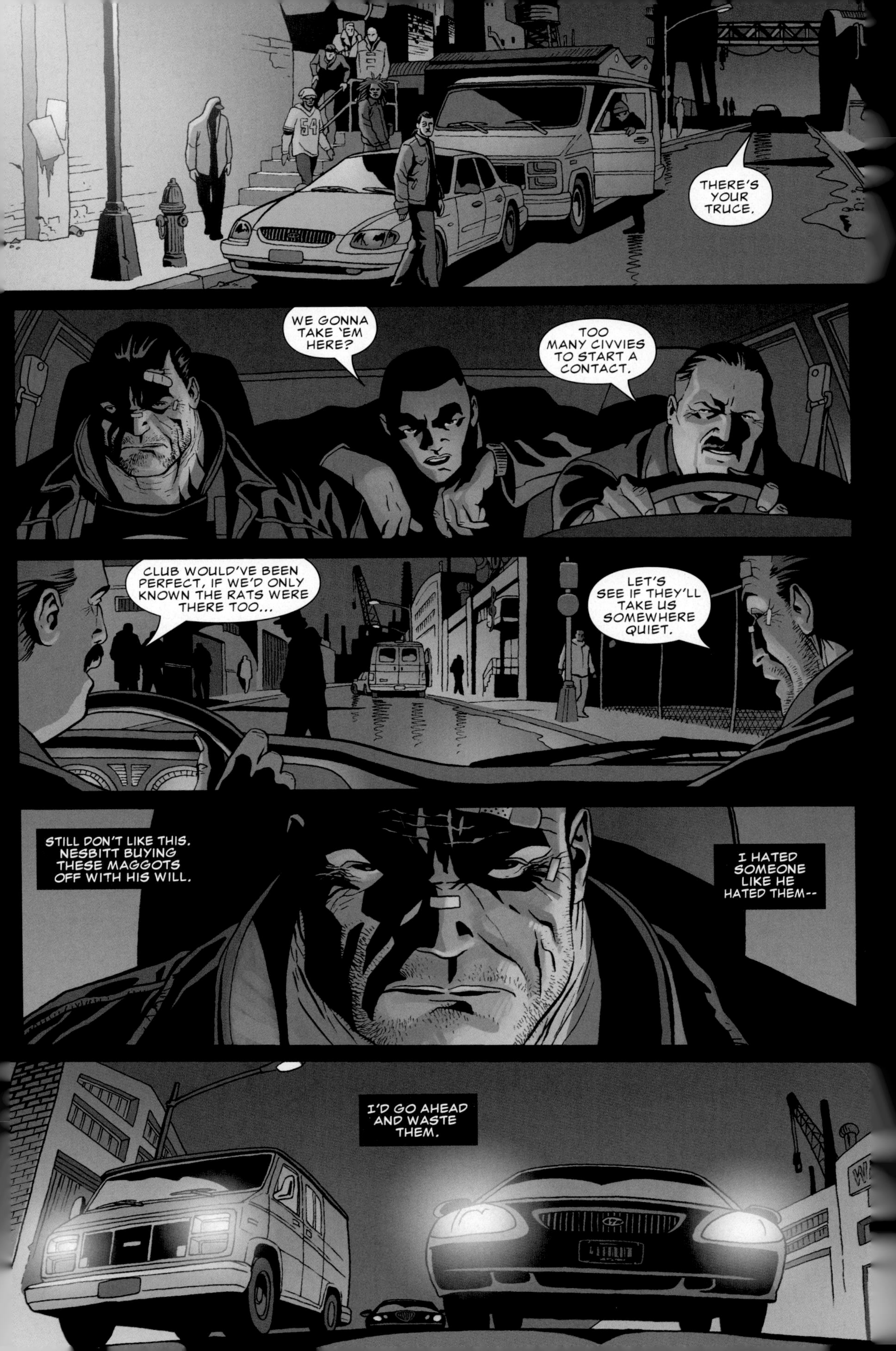
THERE'S YOUR TRUCE.
WE GONNA TAKE 'EM HERE?
TOO MANY CIVVIES TO START A CONTACT.
CLUB WOULD'VE BEEN PERFECT, IF WE'D ONLY KNOWN THE RATS WERE THERE TOO...
LET'S SEE IF THEY'LL TAKE US SOMEWHERE QUIET.
STILL DON'T LIKE THIS. NESBITT BUYING THESE MAGGOTS OFF WITH HIS WILL.
I HATED SOMEONE LIKE HE HATED THEM--
I'D GO AHEAD AND WASTE THEM.

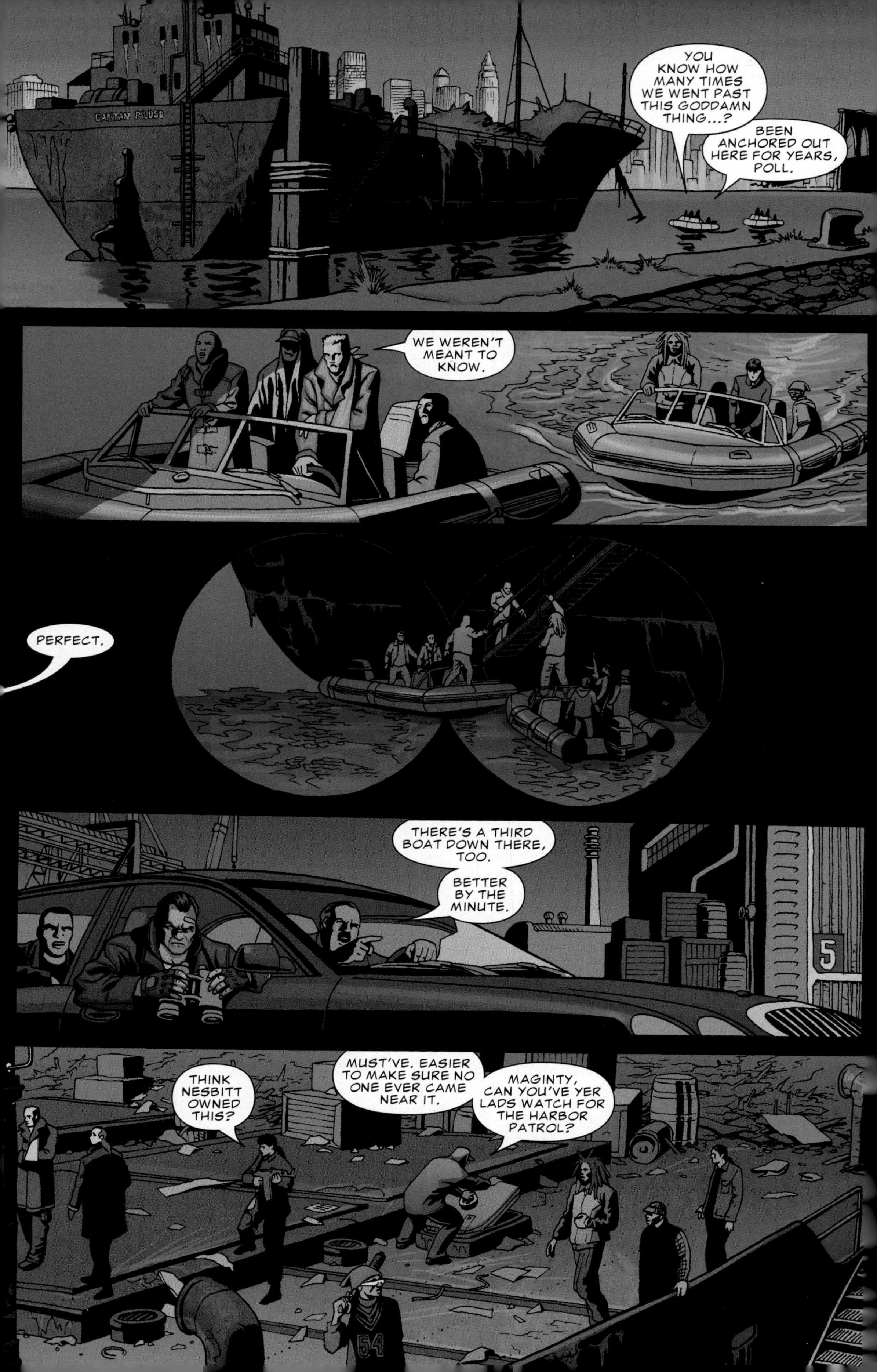
CAPITAN PILUSO
YOU KNOW HOW MANY TIMES WE WENT PAST THIS GODDAMN THING...?
BEEN ANCHORED OUT HERE FOR YEARS, POLL.
WE WEREN'T MEANT TO KNOW.
PERFECT.
THERE'S A THIRD BOAT DOWN THERE, TOO.
BETTER BY THE MINUTE.
5
THINK NESBITT OWNED THIS?
MUST'VE. EASIER TO MAKE SURE NO ONE EVER CAME NEAR IT.
MAGINTY, CAN YOU'VE YER LADS WATCH FOR THE HARBOR PATROL?
54

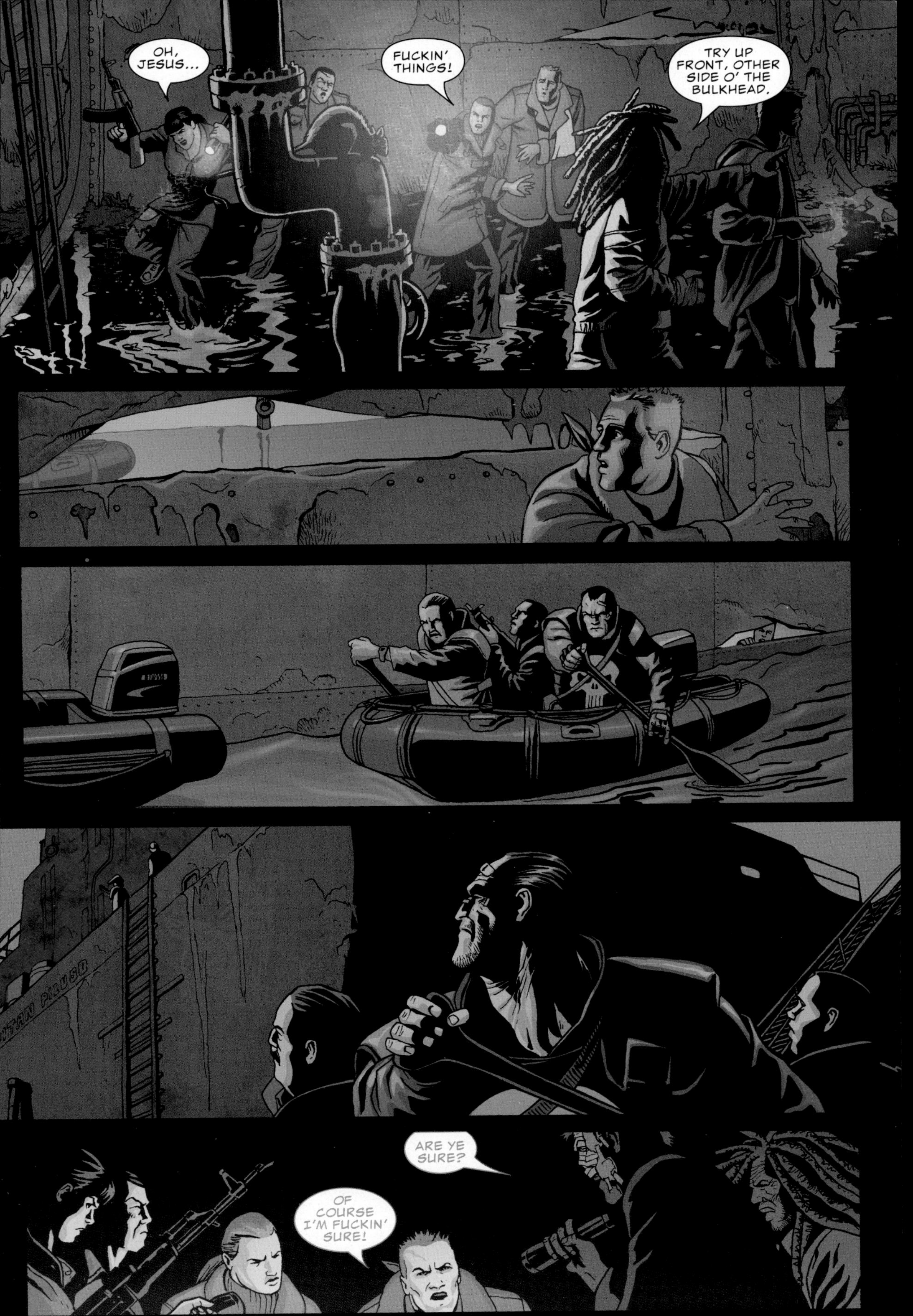
OH, JESUS...
FUCKIN' THINGS!
TRY UP FRONT, OTHER SIDE O' THE BULKHEAD.
ARE YE SURE?
OF COURSE I'M FUCKIN' SURE!

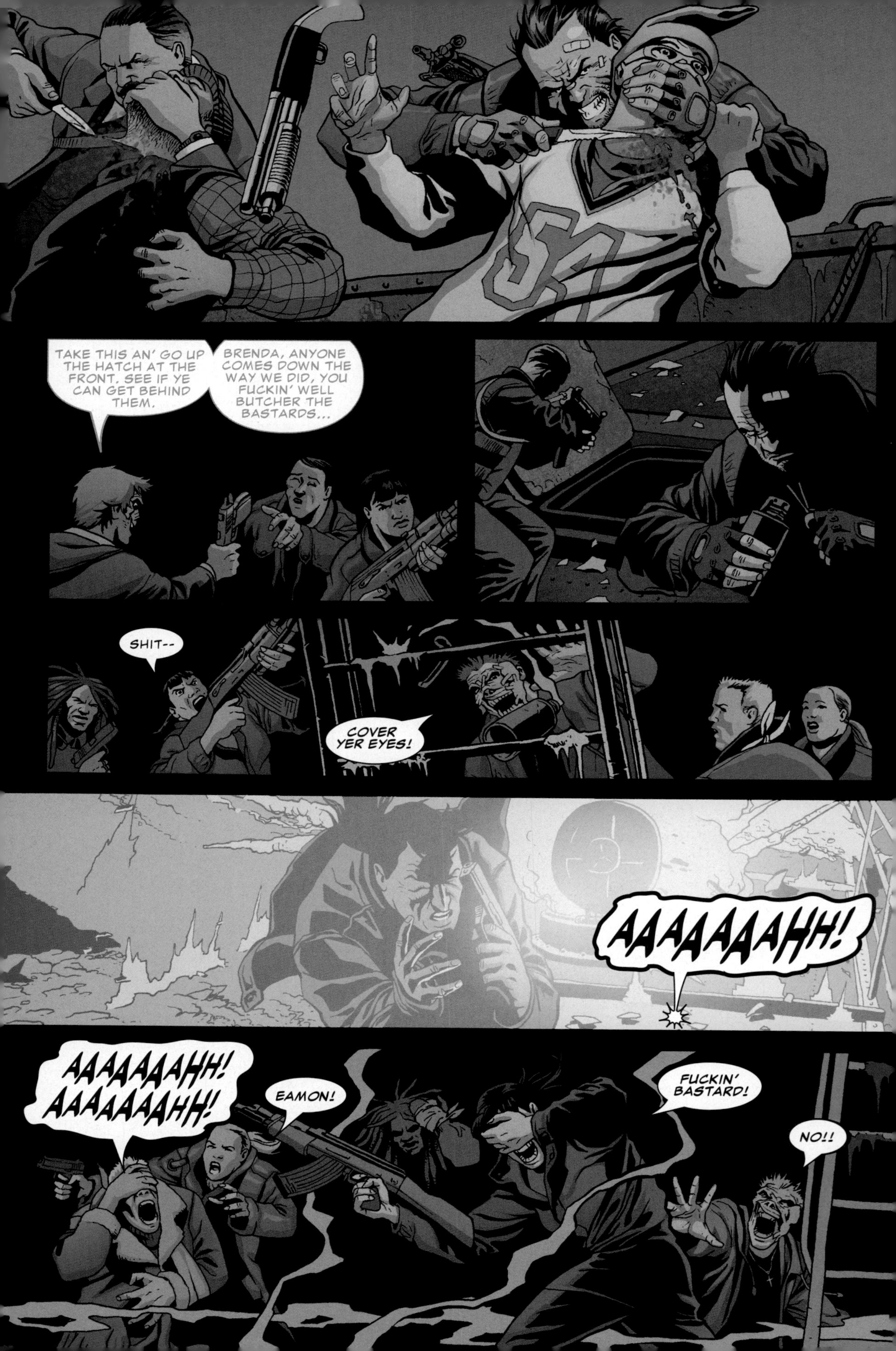
TAKE THIS AN' GO UP THE HATCH AT THE FRONT. SEE IF YE CAN GET BEHIND THEM.
BRENDA, ANYONE COMES DOWN THE WAY WE DID, YOU FUCKIN' WELL BUTCHER THE BASTARDS...
SHIT--
COVER YER EYES!
AAAAAAAHH!
AAAAAAAHH! AAAAAAAHH!
EAMON!
FUCKIN' BASTARD!
NO!!

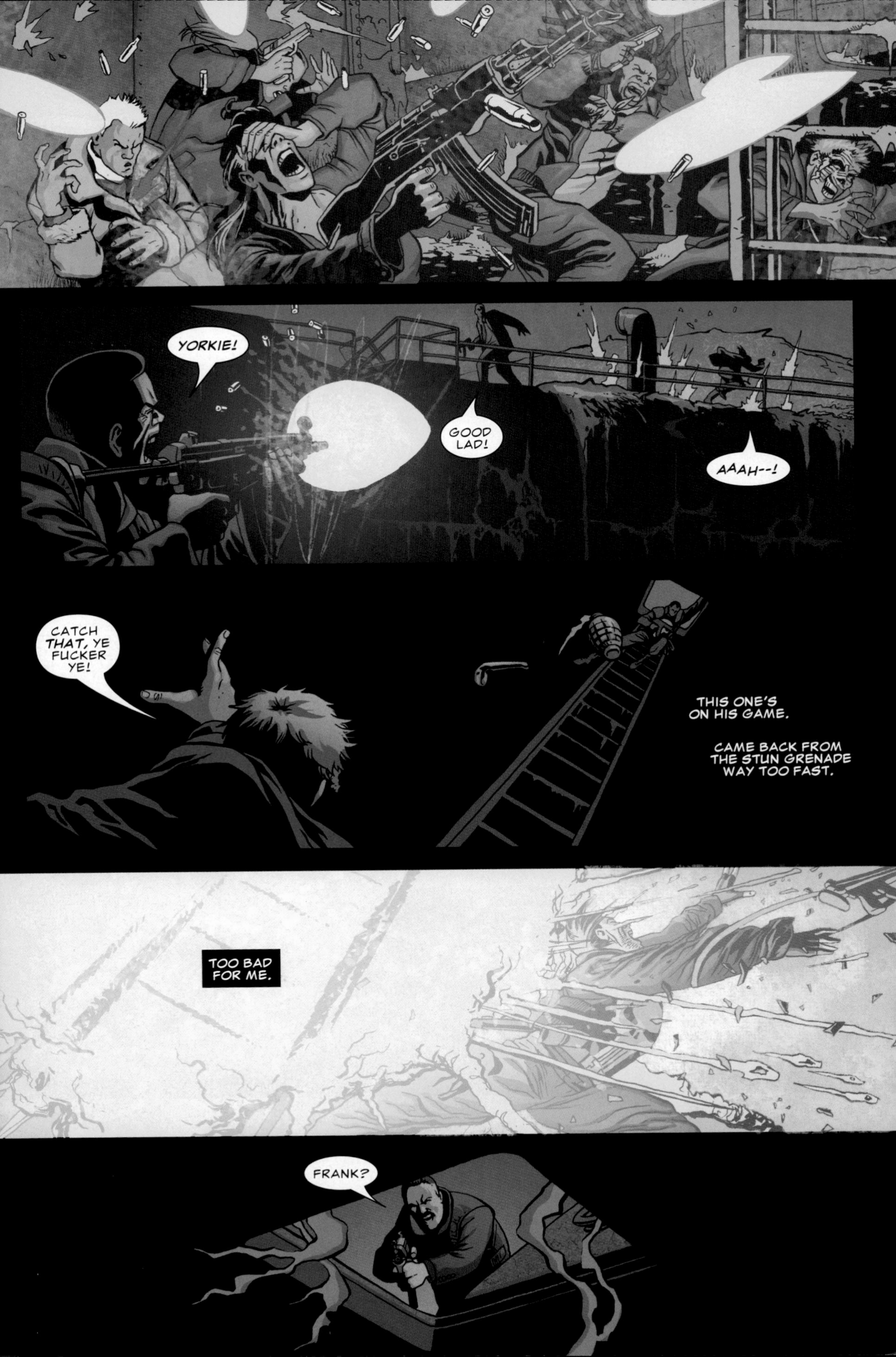
YORKIE!
GOOD LAD!
AAAH--!
CATCH THAT, YE FUCKER YE!
THIS ONE'S ON HIS GAME.
CAME BACK FROM THE STUN GRENADE WAY TOO FAST.
TOO BAD FOR ME.
FRANK?

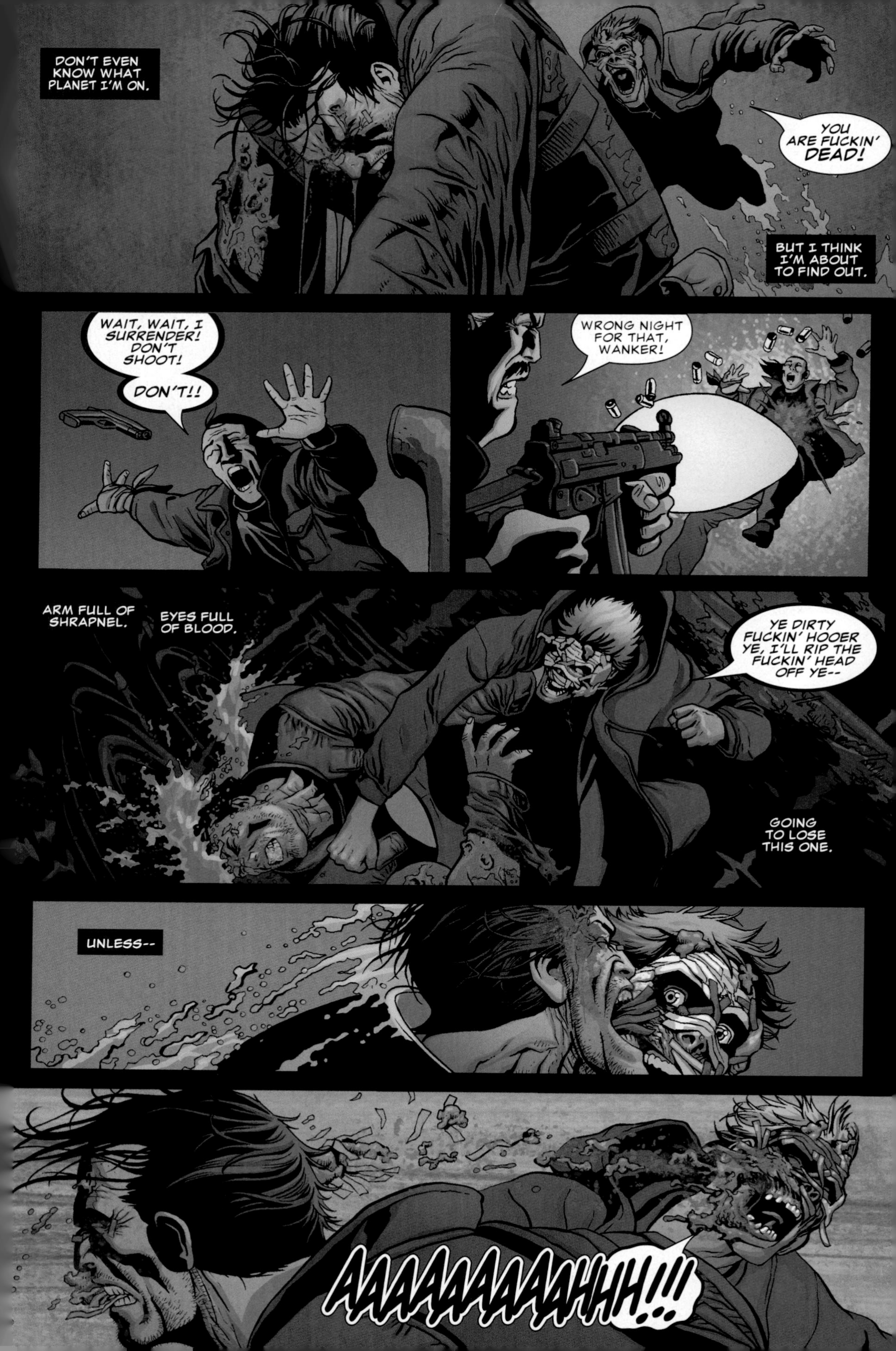
DON'T EVEN KNOW WHAT PLANET I'M ON.
YOU ARE FUCKIN' DEAD!
BUT I THINK I'M ABOUT TO FIND OUT.
WAIT, WAIT, I SURRENDER! DON'T SHOOT!
DON'T!!
WRONG NIGHT FOR THAT, WANKER!
ARM FULL OF SHRAPNEL.
EYES FULL OF BLOOD.
YE DIRTY FUCKIN' HOOER YE, I'LL RIP THE FUCKIN' HEAD OFF YE--
GOING TO LOSE THIS ONE.
UNLESS--
AAAAAAAAAHHH!!!

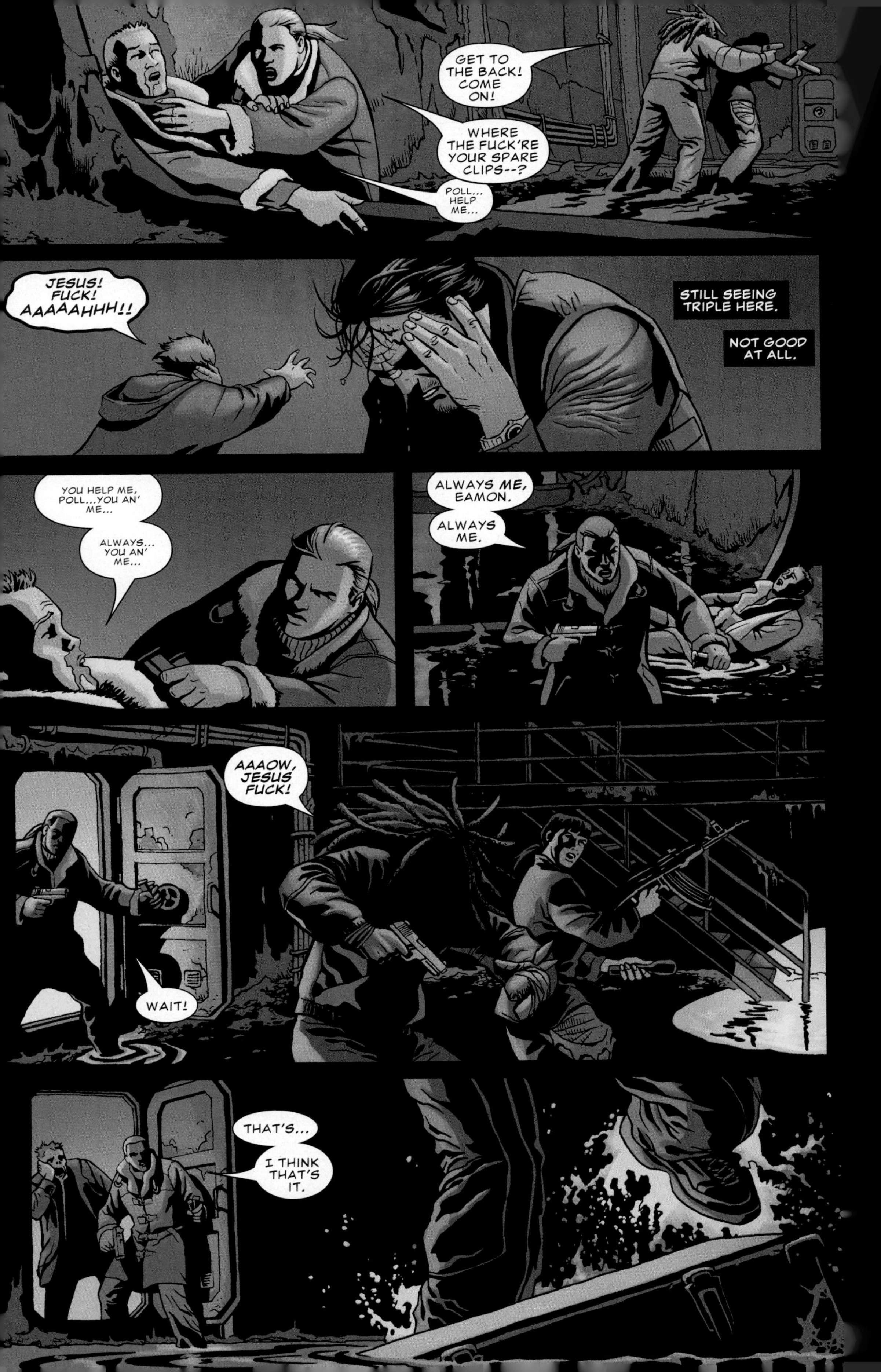
GET TO THE BACK! COME ON!
WHERE THE FUCK'RE YOUR SPARE CLIPS--?
POLL... HELP ME...
JESUS! FUCK! AAAAAHHH!!
STILL SEEING TRIPLE HERE.
NOT GOOD AT ALL.
YOU HELP ME, POLL...YOU AN' ME...
ALWAYS... YOU AN' ME...
ALWAYS ME, EAMON.
ALWAYS ME.
AAAOW, JESUS FUCK!
WAIT!
THAT'S...
I THINK THAT'S IT.

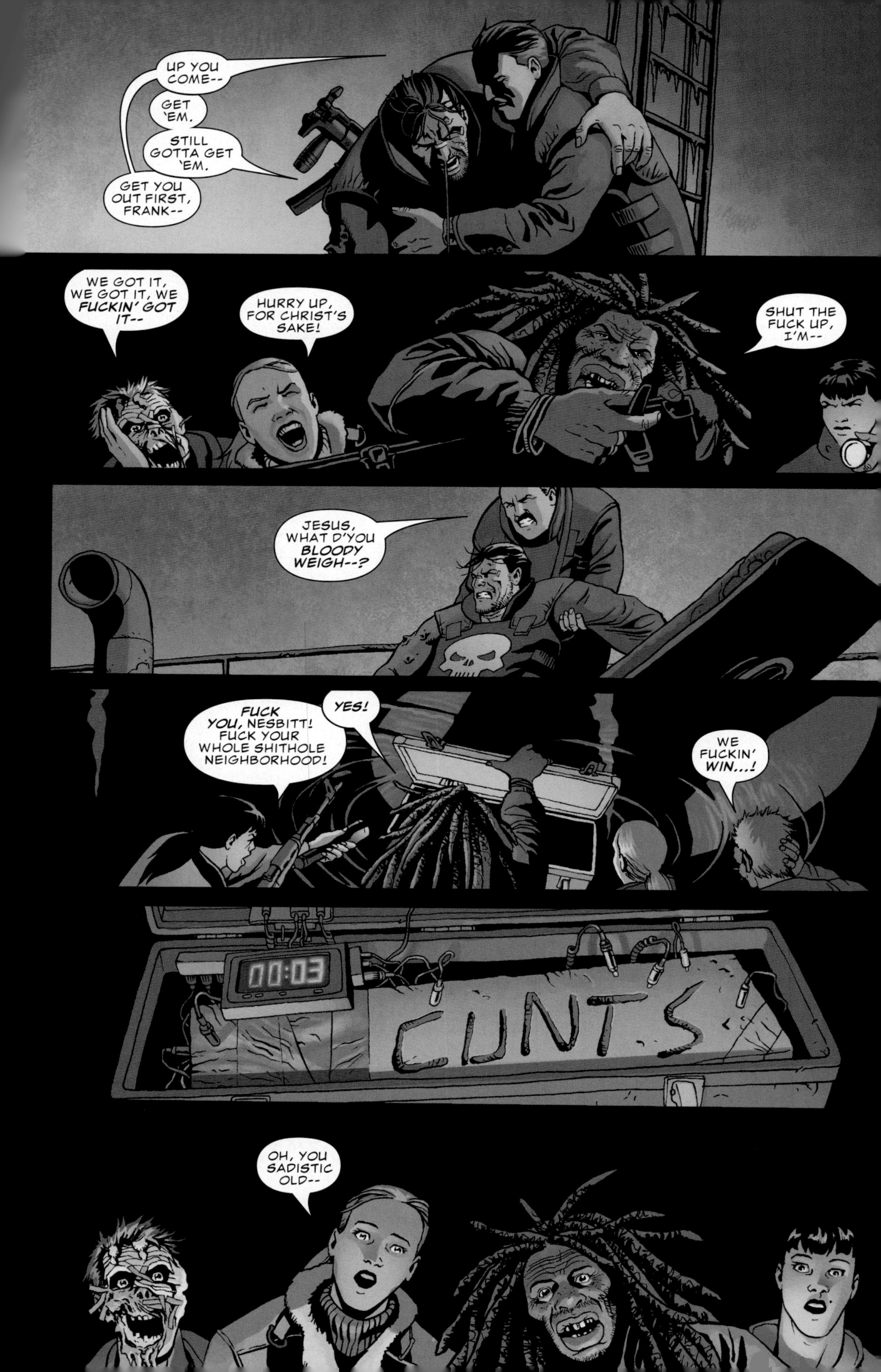
UP YOU COME--
GET 'EM.
STILL GOTTA GET 'EM.
GET YOU OUT FIRST, FRANK--
WE GOT IT, WE GOT IT, WE *FUCKIN' GOT IT*--
HURRY UP, FOR CHRIST'S SAKE!
SHUT THE FUCK UP, I'M--
JESUS, WHAT D'YOU *BLOODY WEIGH*--?
FUCK YOU, NESBITT! FUCK YOUR WHOLE SHITHOLE NEIGHBORHOOD!
YES!
WE FUCKIN' *WIN...!*
00:03
CUNTS
OH, YOU SADISTIC OLD--

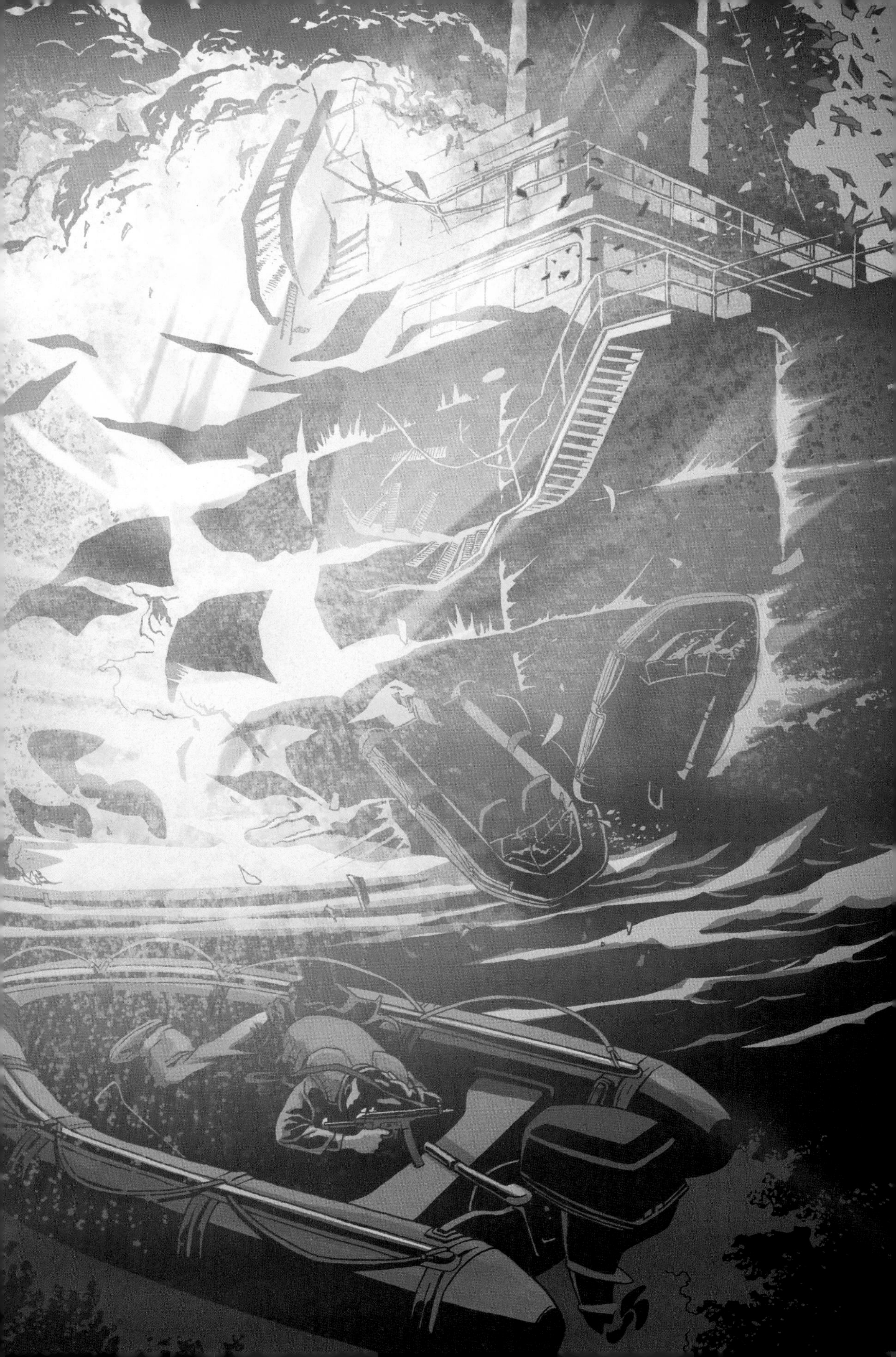

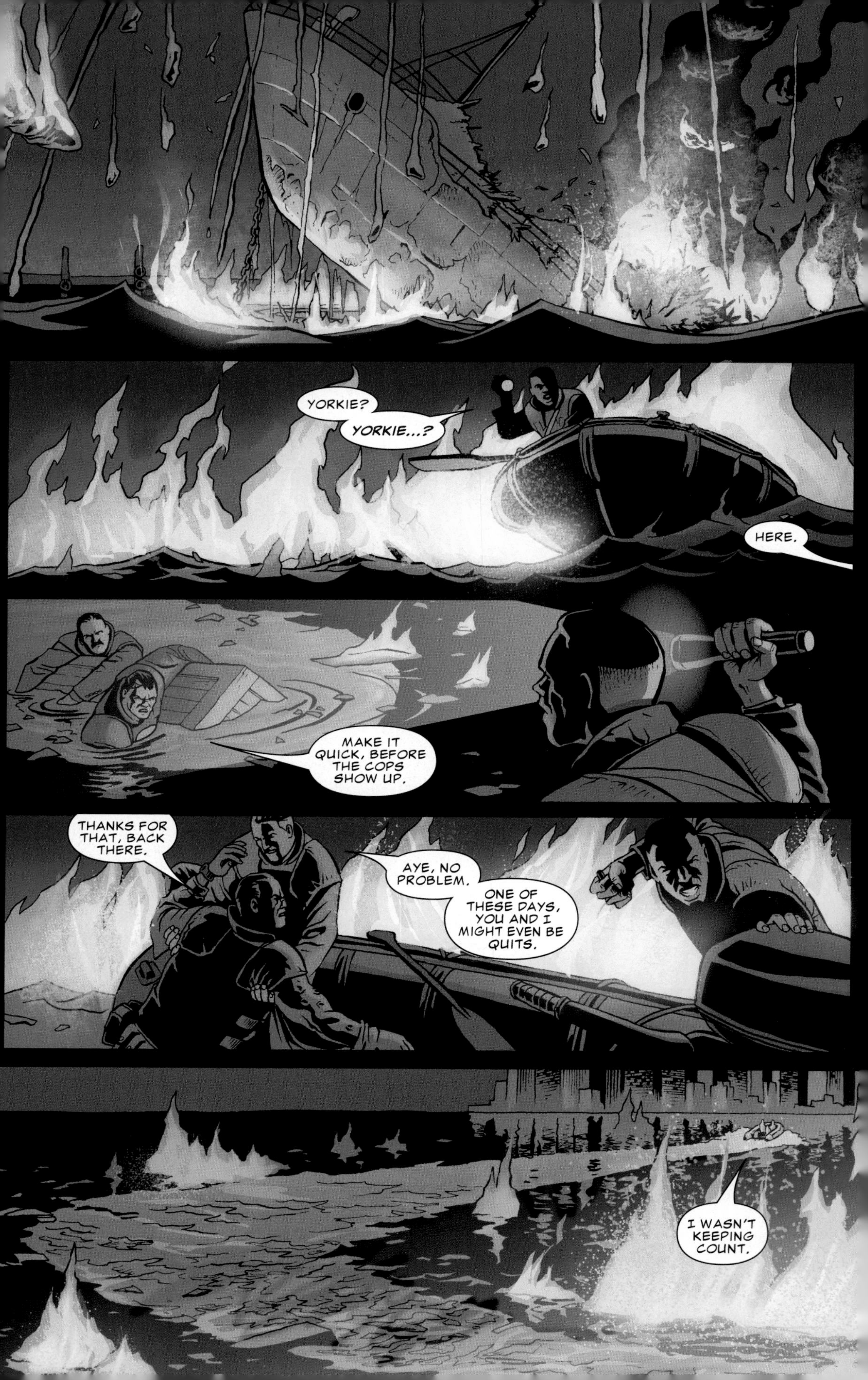
YORKIE?
YORKIE...?
HERE.
MAKE IT QUICK, BEFORE THE COPS SHOW UP.
THANKS FOR THAT, BACK THERE.
AYE, NO PROBLEM.
ONE OF THESE DAYS, YOU AND I MIGHT EVEN BE QUITS.
I WASN'T KEEPING COUNT.

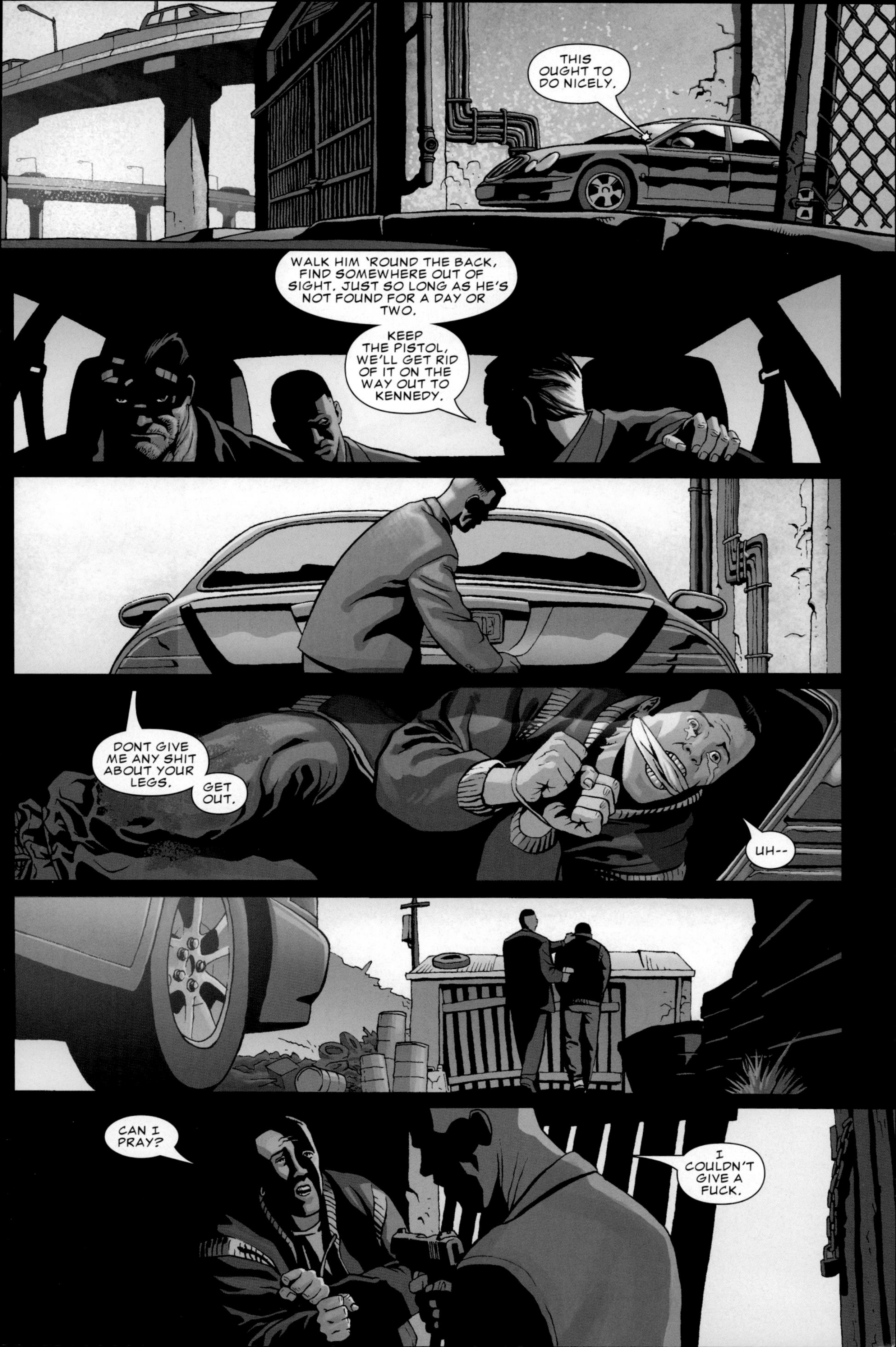

THIS OUGHT TO DO NICELY.
WALK HIM 'ROUND THE BACK, FIND SOMEWHERE OUT OF SIGHT. JUST SO LONG AS HE'S NOT FOUND FOR A DAY OR TWO.
KEEP THE PISTOL, WE'LL GET RID OF IT ON THE WAY OUT TO KENNEDY.
DONT GIVE ME ANY SHIT ABOUT YOUR LEGS.
GET OUT.
UH--
CAN I PRAY?
I COULDN'T GIVE A FUCK.

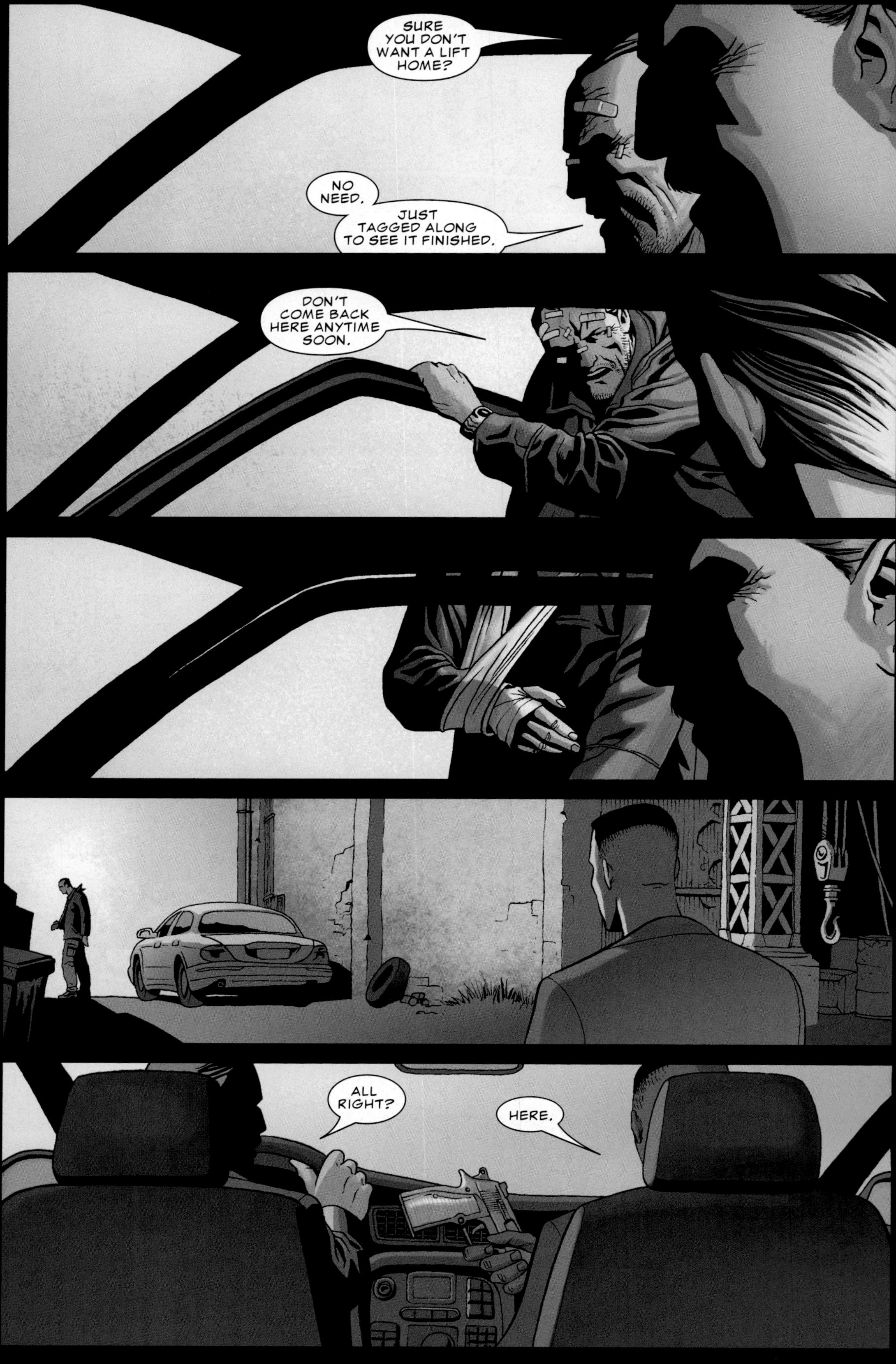
SURE YOU DON'T WANT A LIFT HOME?
NO NEED.
JUST TAGGED ALONG TO SEE IT FINISHED.
DON'T COME BACK HERE ANYTIME SOON.
ALL RIGHT?
HERE.

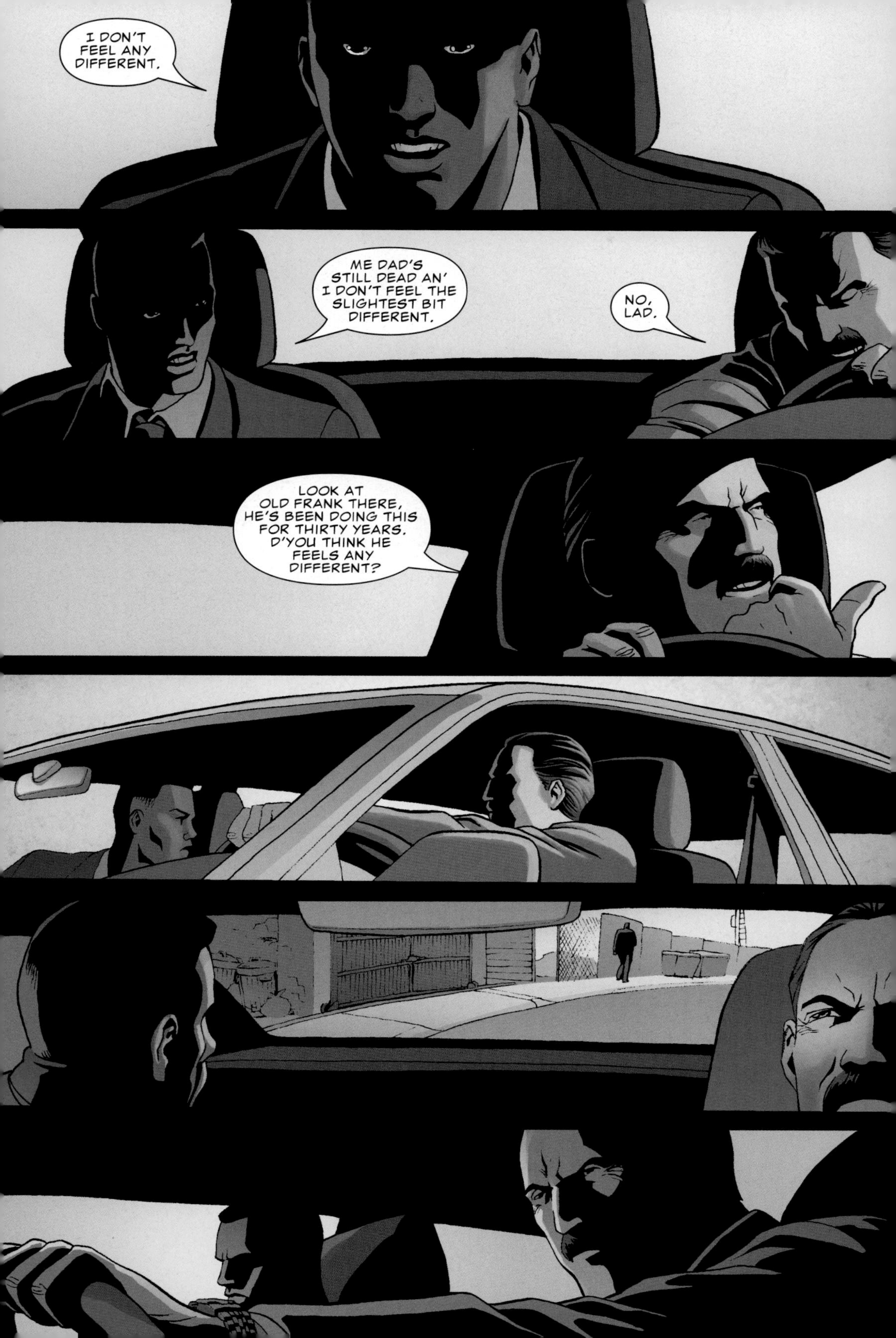

I DON'T FEEL ANY DIFFERENT.
ME DAD'S STILL DEAD AN' I DON'T FEEL THE SLIGHTEST BIT DIFFERENT.
NO, LAD.
LOOK AT OLD FRANK THERE, HE'S BEEN DOING THIS FOR THIRTY YEARS. D'YOU THINK HE FEELS ANY DIFFERENT?

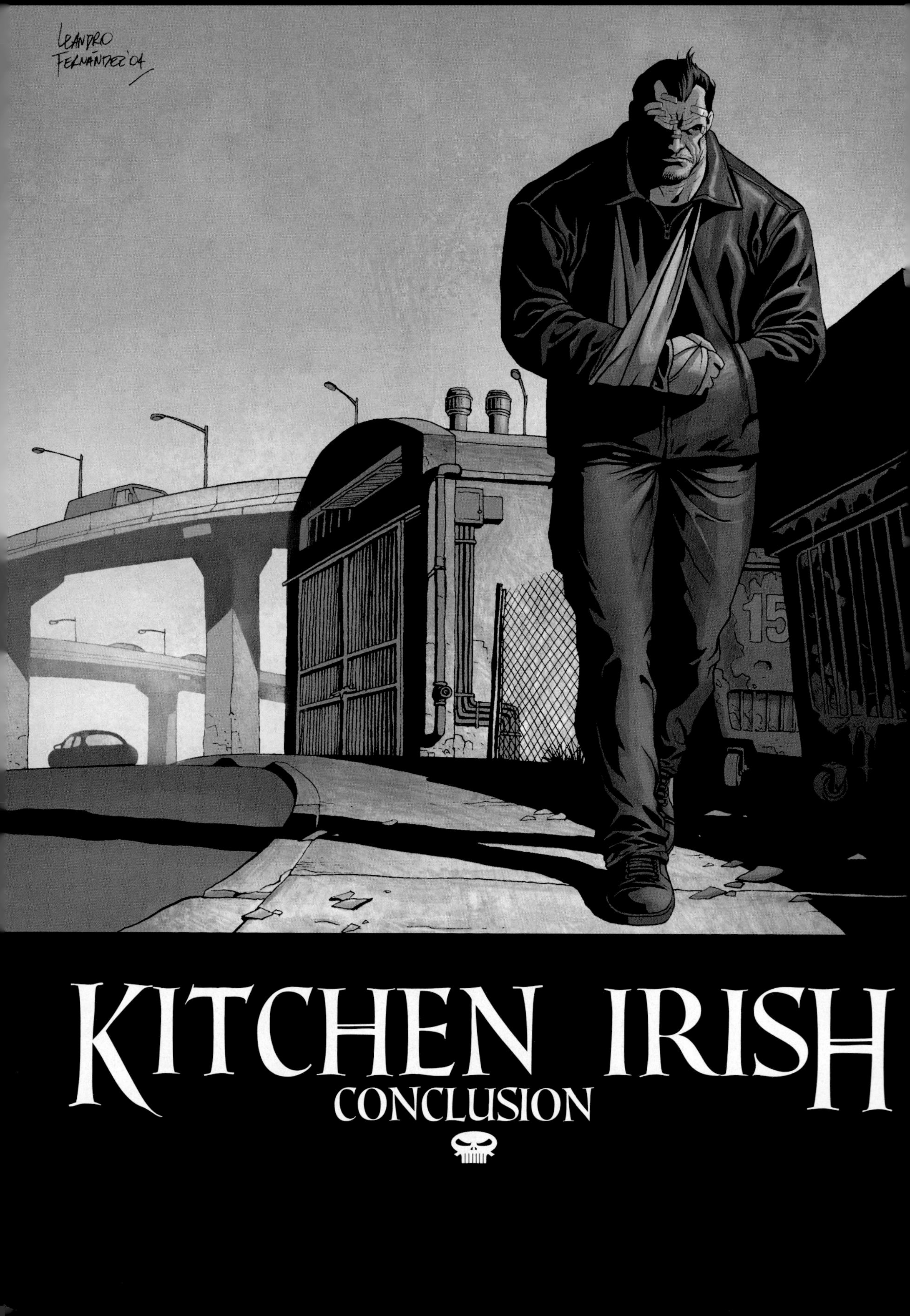
LEANDRO FERNANDEZ '04
15

KITCHEN IRISH
CONCLUSION

BORN COVER SKETCHES

By Wieslaw Walkuski

#1

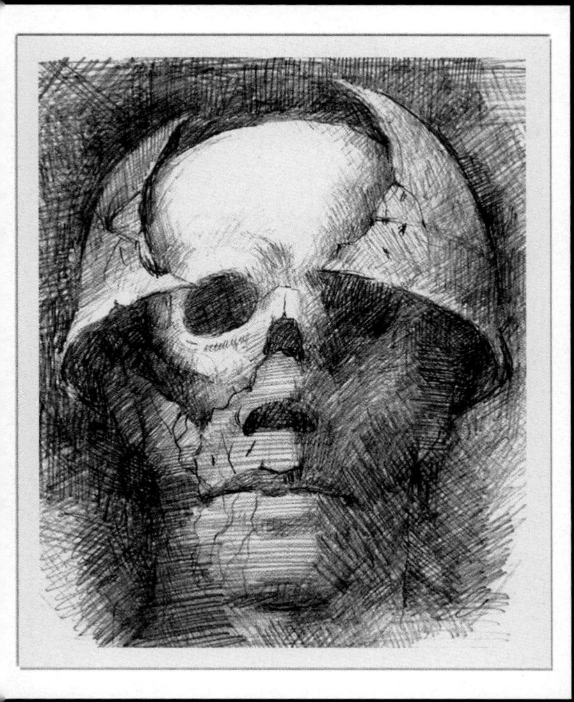

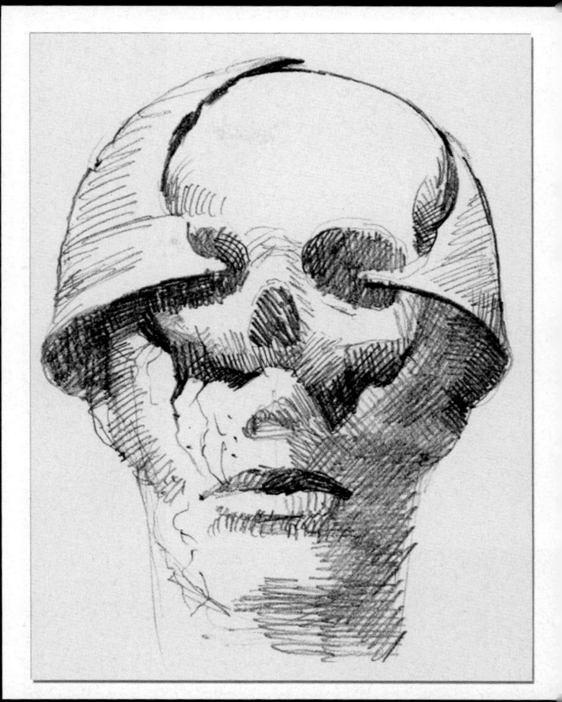

#2

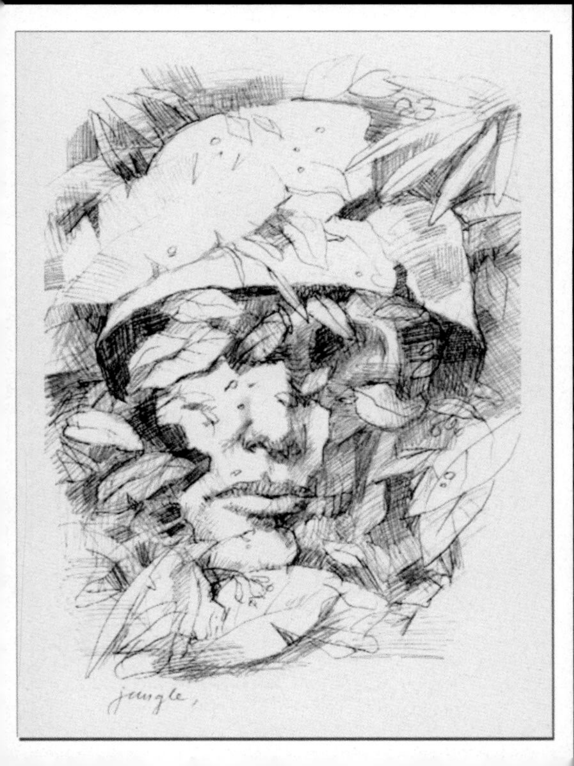
jungle,

#4

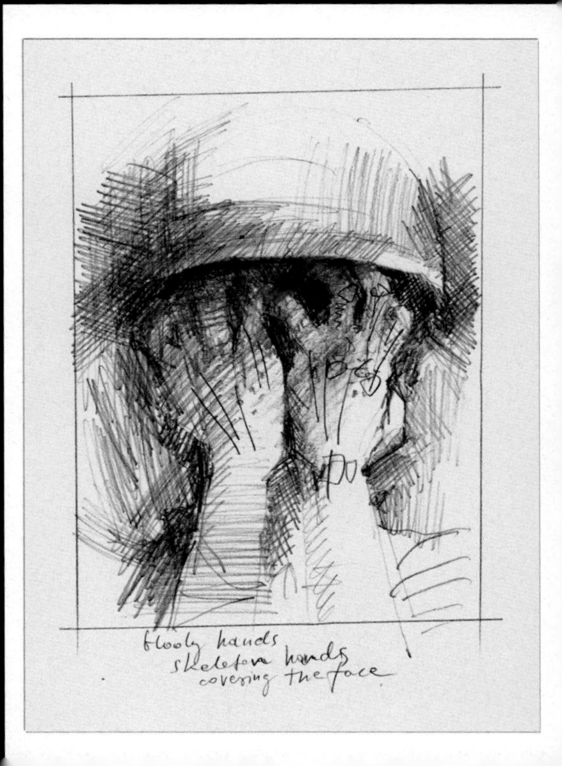
bloody hands
skeleton hands
covering the face

#3

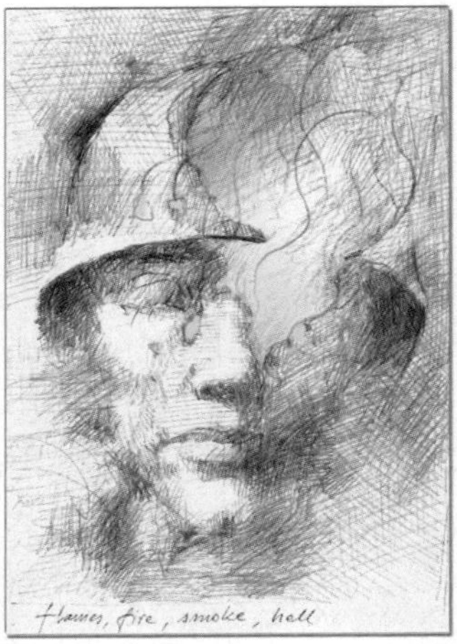
flames, fire, smoke, hell

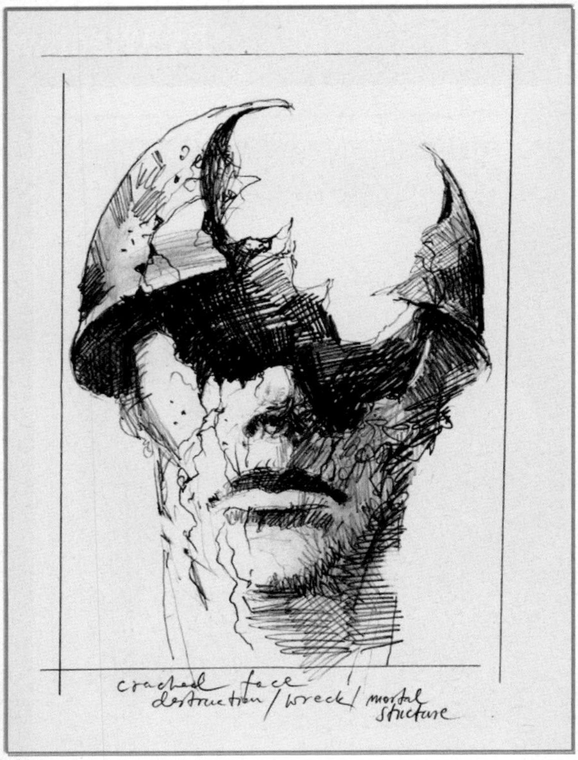
cracked face
destruction / wreck / mortal
structure

UNUSED

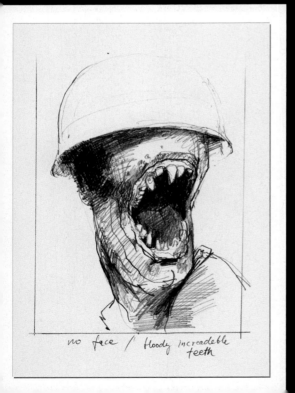

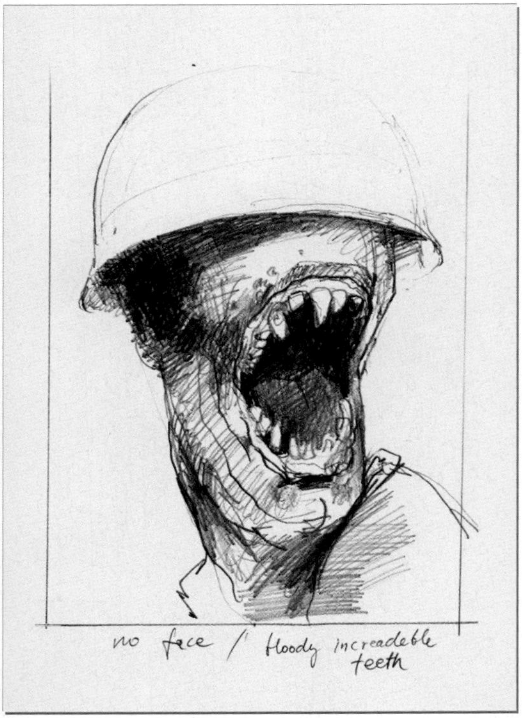
no face / bloody increadeble
teeth

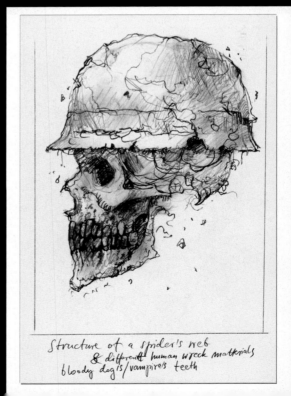

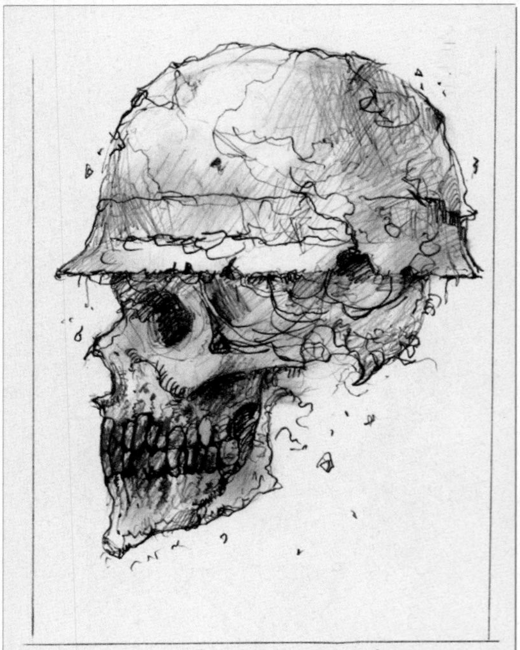
Structure of a spider's web
& different human wreck matterials
bloody dog's/vampire's teeth

THOUGHTS ABOUT BORN
by Darick Robertson

My own father, Ira D. Robertson, and my uncle both fought in World War II. As a result I grew up with a lot of respect for people in the military, despite my own liberal political views. I have a deep respect for the people that put themselves in harm's way and the bravery involved to fight for an ideal or even for a sense of duty. When I began gathering research for this project, I bought hardcover books collecting *Life* magazine pictures by renowned photojournalists like Larry Burrows (who died in Vietnam, and took some incredible pictures). I watched documentaries to get a better understanding of the politics involved and found many web sites put up by veterans sharing their experiences. I started to experience the war in another way entirely, the way only truth captured on film can affect you.

When assistant editor Nick Lowe (whose assistance was INVALUABLE to this project) offered his father David Lowe's personal photo album from Vietnam, it was such an incredible opportunity that I immediately promised I would take the best of care of the book.

Looking through the album was a profound experience. Many simple things people wouldn't think to photograph get captured when someone is just taking snapshots of the people they're with and the things that they're doing throughout the course of the day. I really wanted to capture those details. It felt important to me, because while the Punisher is fictional, the Vietnam War was not, and like Nick's father, David, there are many veterans still alive today to whom the Vietnam war is very much a reality to them, not the stuff of fiction. This is a story of what that war did to this character, but I wanted to show my respect for the people who really went through it. I felt it was important to capture those details as a way of showing respect for the experience. By immersing my imagination in the reality of that environment, I felt I could bring more to the characters and their performances. I did all I could to capture the details of the place and equipment they were wearing and using.

Nick told me that his father was really impressed with *Born*. David Lowe went so far as to even send copies of "Born" along to his veteran buddies.

That means more to me than any other compliment I received for my work on this series.

Fire Support Basecamp Hampton,
February 1969

Photo courtesy of David Lowe

VIETNAM PHOTO REFERENCE

Courtesy of David Lowe

Cu Chi, August 1969

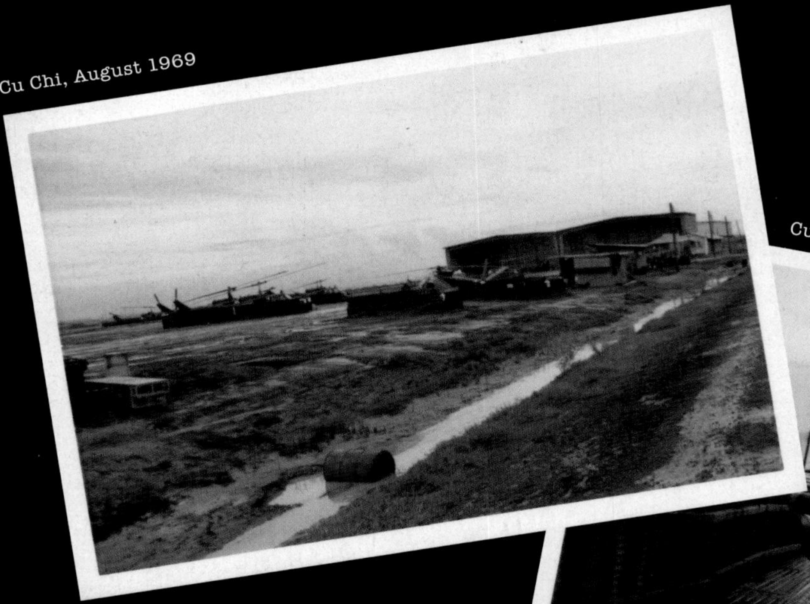

Cu Chi, August 1969

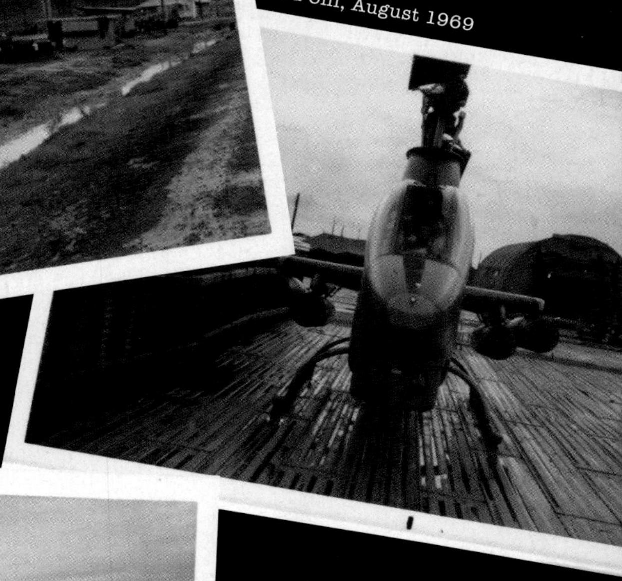

V

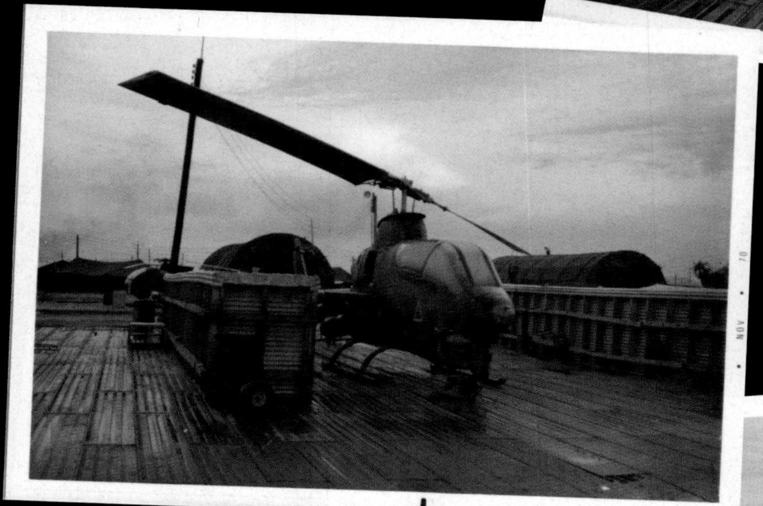

Cu Chi, August 1969

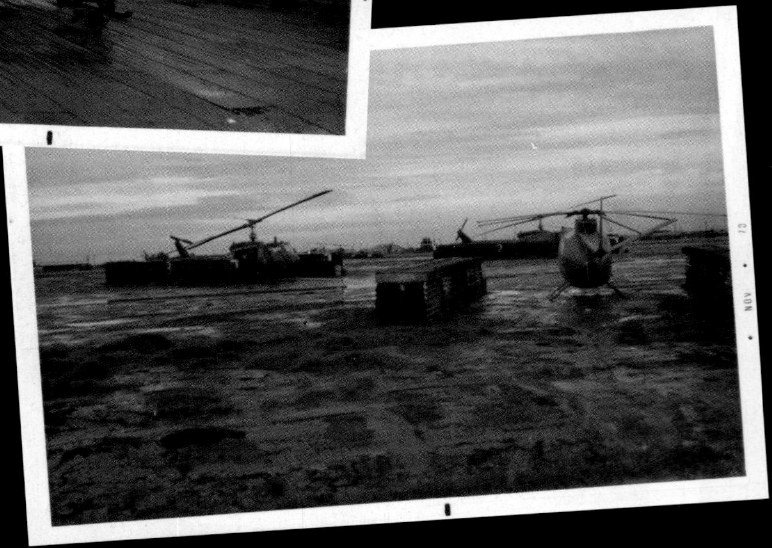

Fire Support Basecamp Hampton, February 1969

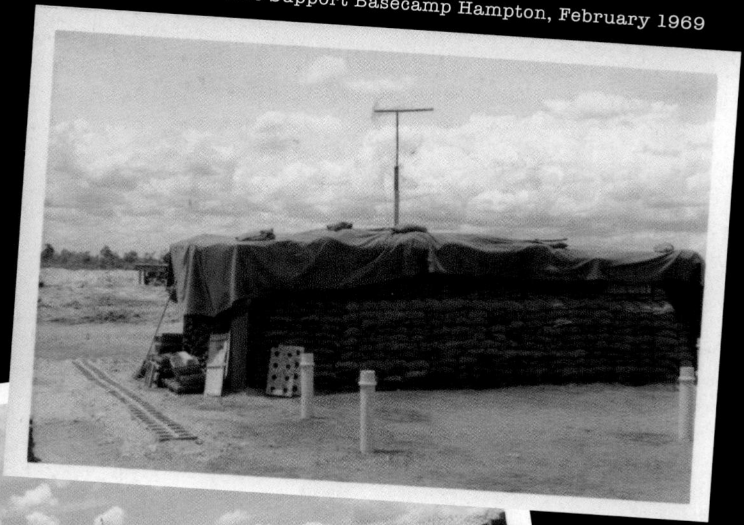

Fire Support Basecamp Hampton, February 1969

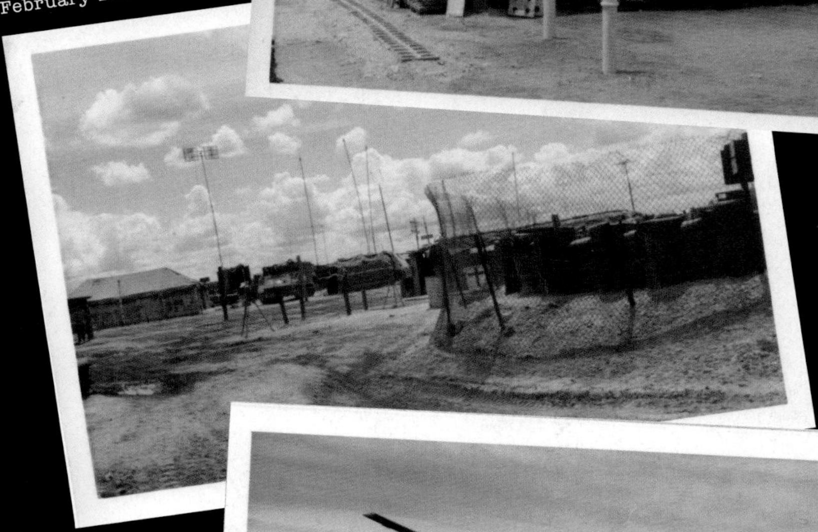

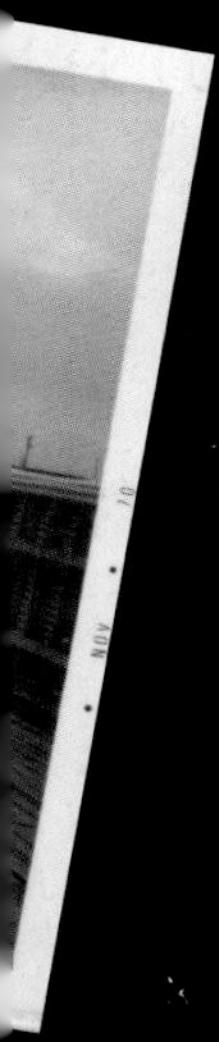

Cu Chi, August 1969

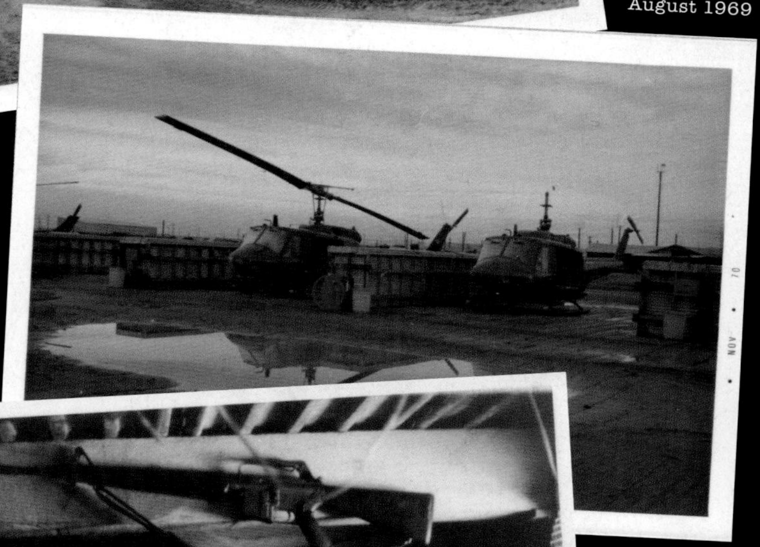

Fire Support Basecamp Hampton, February 1969

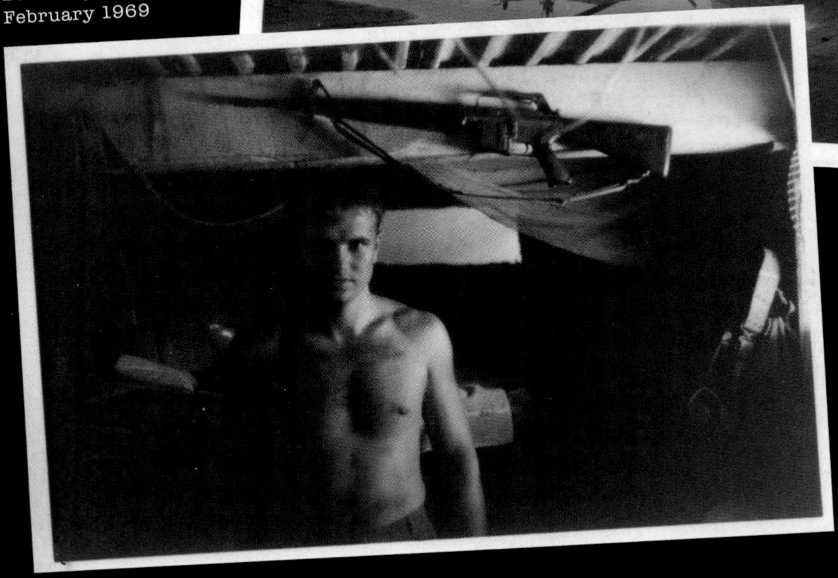

CHARACTER DESIGNS
by Darick Robertson

When I first spoke to Garth about what he wanted Frank to look like, Garth emphasized to me that he's young, but had seen too much to look young. I thought about that and laughed at myself because the first designs I did for Frank in Nam were comparable to his present-day look. I sort of smacked my forehead and thought "Duh; of course he's young."

So I did these sketches while reading the script on a plane to Germany. I liked the bald one, but thought it was a little too extreme. This was a story of a man about to go to extremes, not about one who already had. The other version is a Mohawk haircut, similar to those worn by the Screaming Eagles in WWII. The fact that I was emulating the wrong war steered me away from that design.

The final sketch captured something that I didn't expect to find in Frank: innocence. I ultimately felt the right way to go was to show the young man as much as possible, so he would contrast by the end, the way that Charlie Sheen transforms in *Platoon*. So I wrote the name "Castle" under it, as my chosen concept. Garth liked that one too.

The thumbnail for the splash stayed pretty much intact from the layout to the finished page and was the first page I worked on when beginning the series.

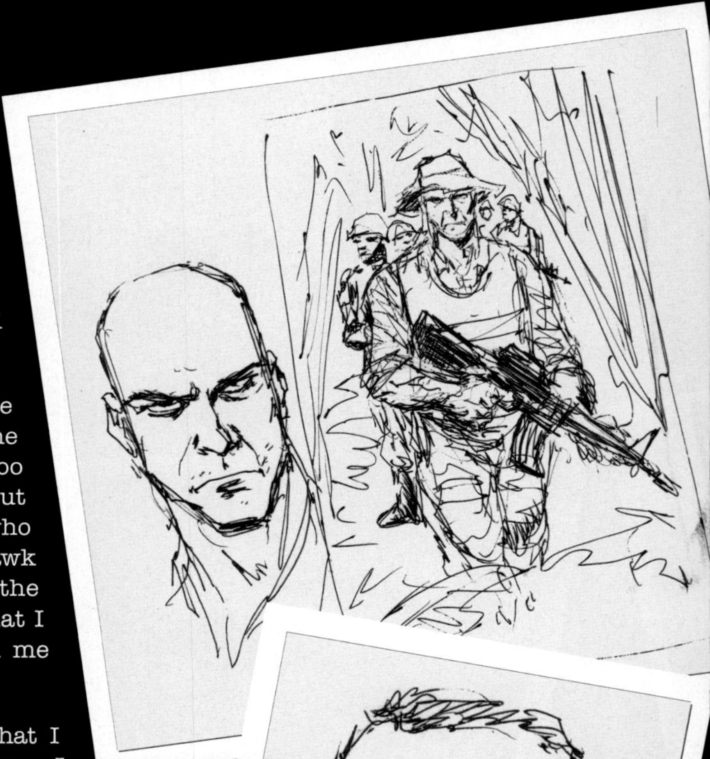

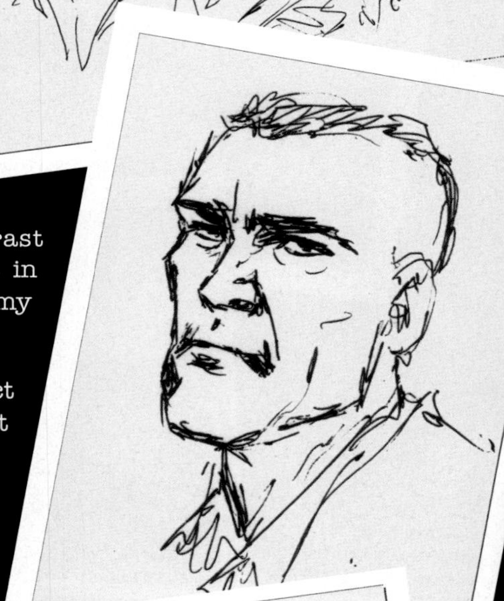

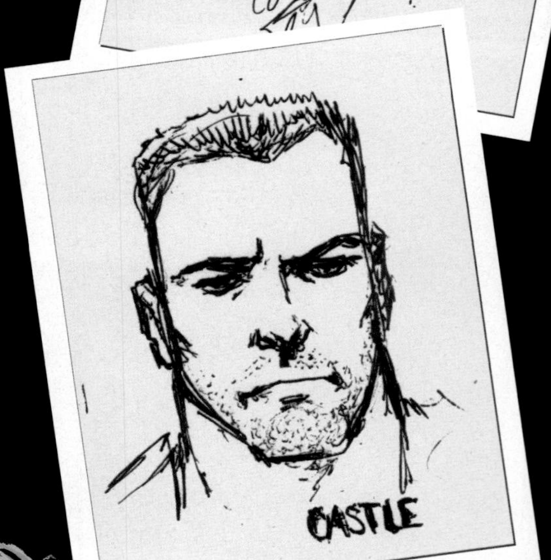
CASTLE

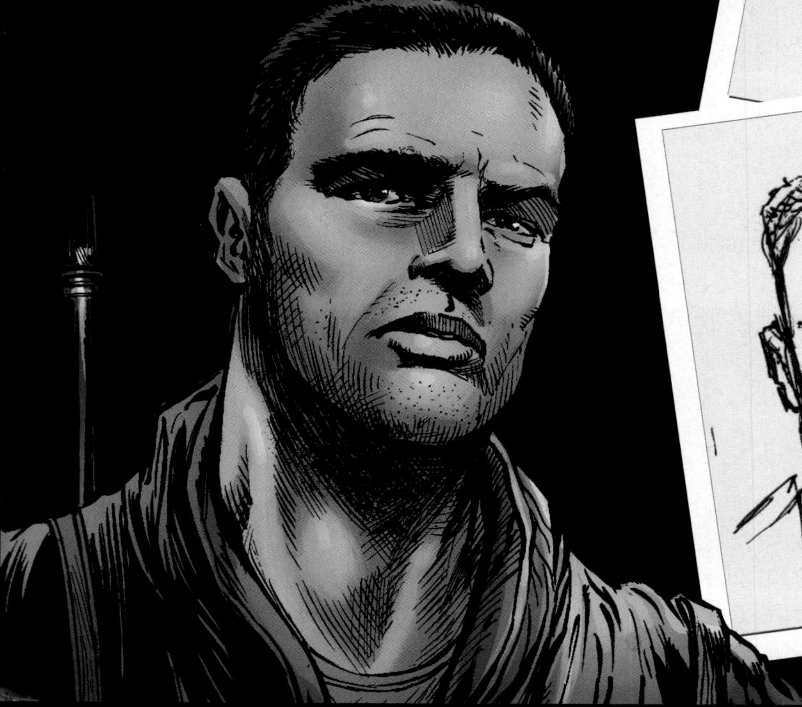

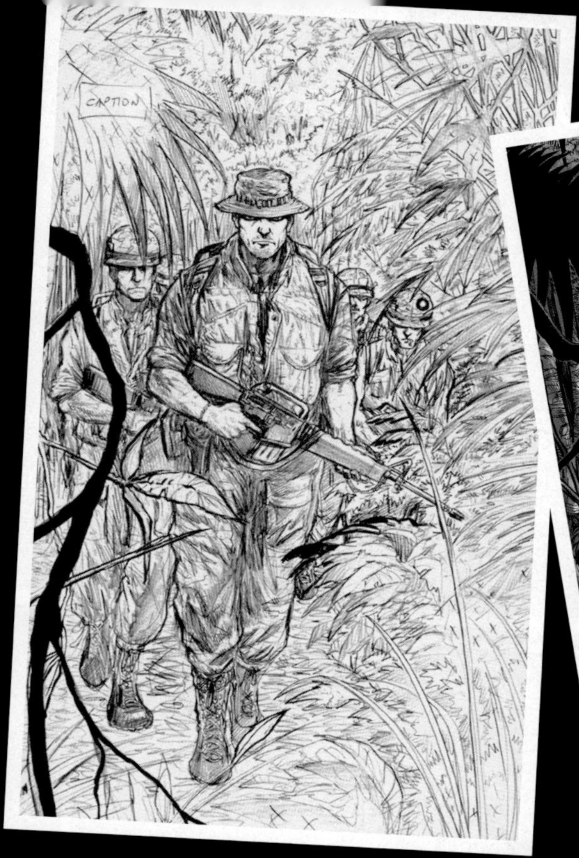
CAPTION

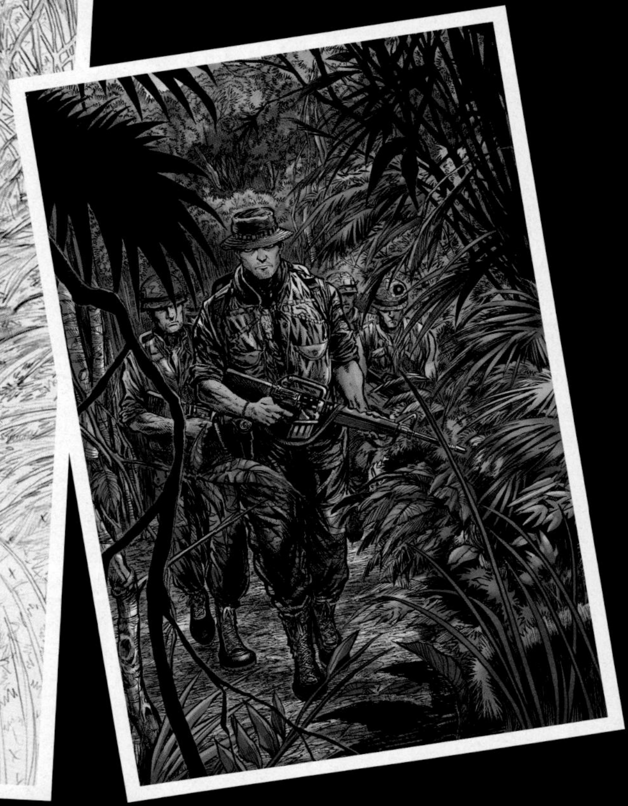

I have a bad habit of working my character designs out right there on the page, which means I rarely have any really juicy sketchbook stuff for these sections. I have to see the character performing the script in front of my eyes before I can determine if the design is working. So these designs for Angel and Stevie are really just batted out based on what I was reading about them in the script. (You can see I needed practice drawing Vietnam-era Marine combat helmets, as Stevie's is way too small.) I sometimes like to ask Garth what actors he pictures when scripting. He didn't have a lot of suggestions for Stevie and Angel, but described their personalities well. I knew he wanted strength of character and innocence in Stevie; the second page that I drew to show Garth was page 5 from issue one, and he broke into a wide grin when he saw it, so I figured I nailed it.

With Angel, I just wanted him to look lost and angry.

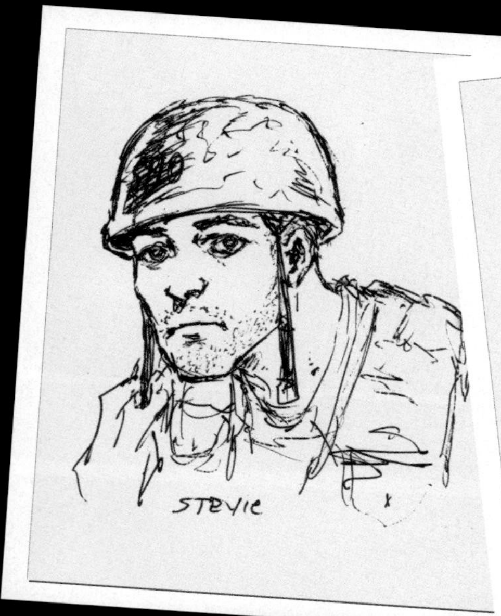
STEVIE

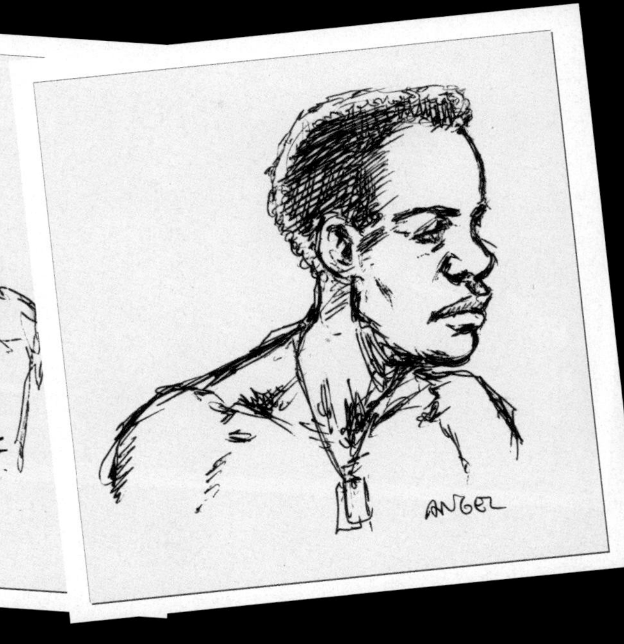
ANGEL

LAYOUTS FOR BORN #2 PAGE 15
by Darick Robertson

This was an important moment in the story and I drew it out badly a couple of times before going to my sketchbook to get the angle right. I didn't want to glorify the woman's death, and even though the book was a MAX title, sometimes it's better to leave the violence to the imagination.

What was important in this scene was the distance the soldiers give Frank and their lack of action to intervene. In my sketch I drew their reactions, but when I was laying it out on the page, I felt that logically they would back off when seeing the gun and by focusing solely on Frank and his action, you couldn't be distracted by anything else but that which was happening in the moment — Frank's mercy kill, and the evidence of his growing into a sociopath.

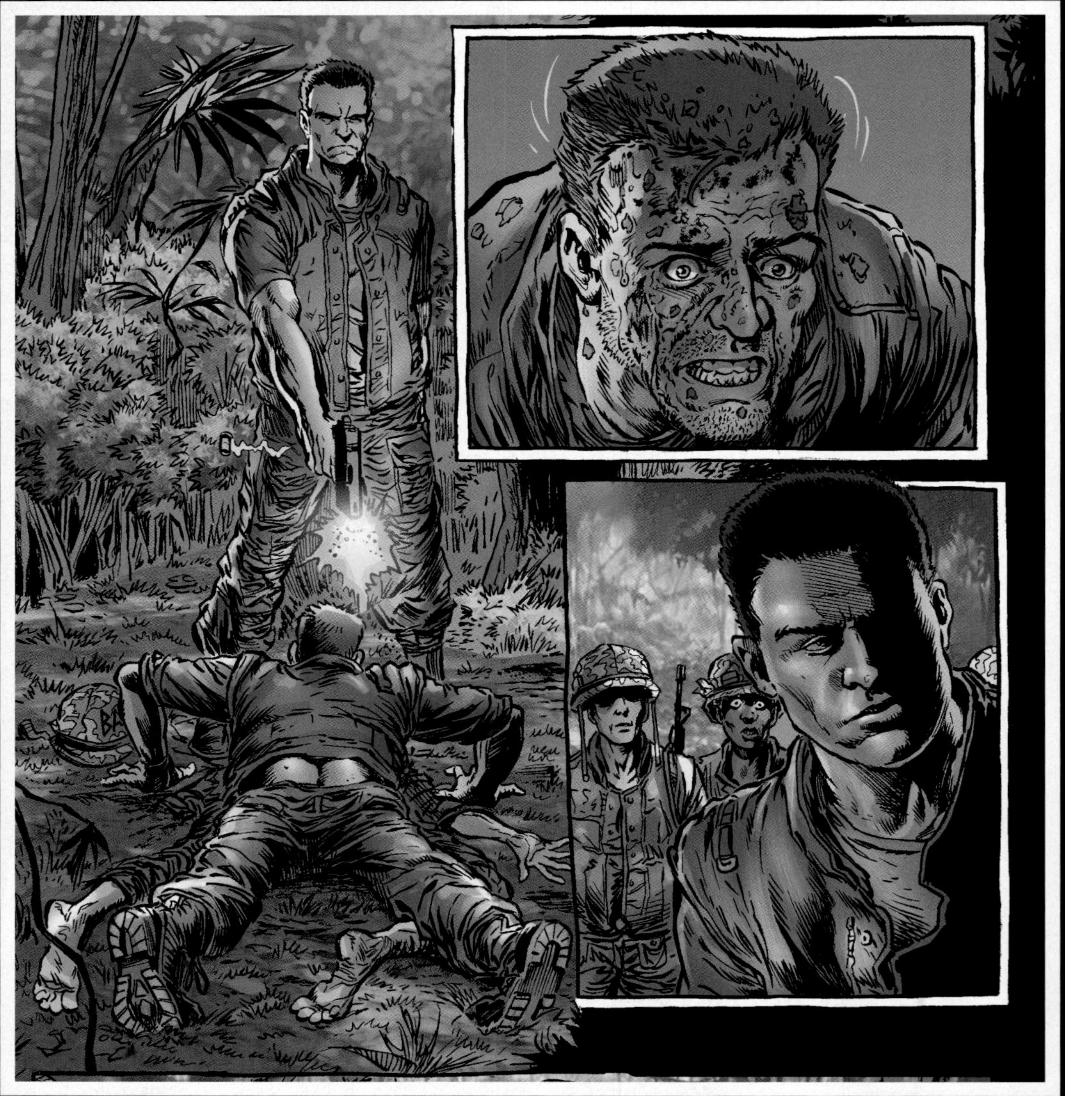

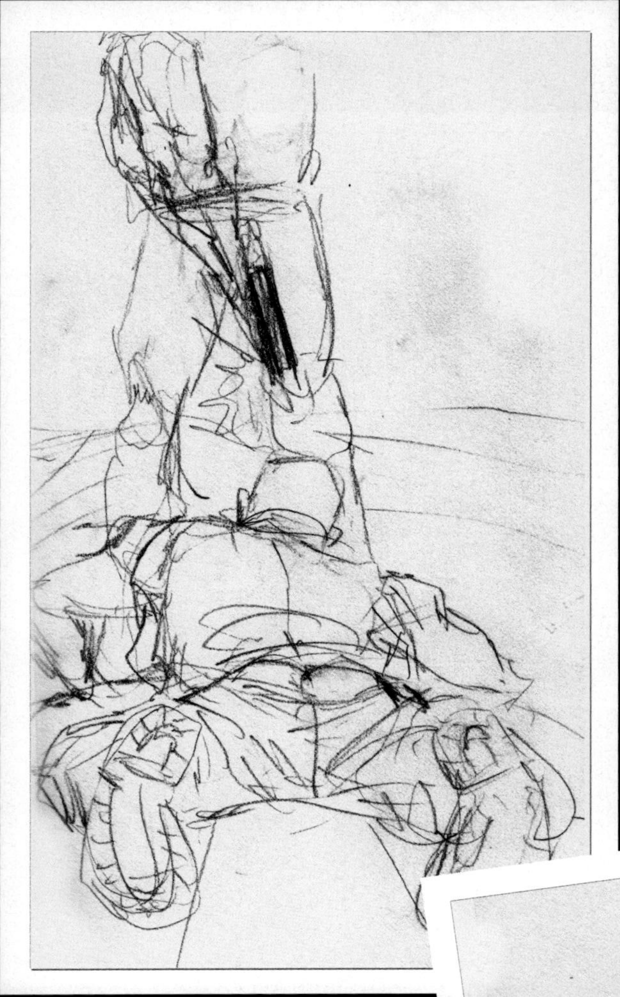

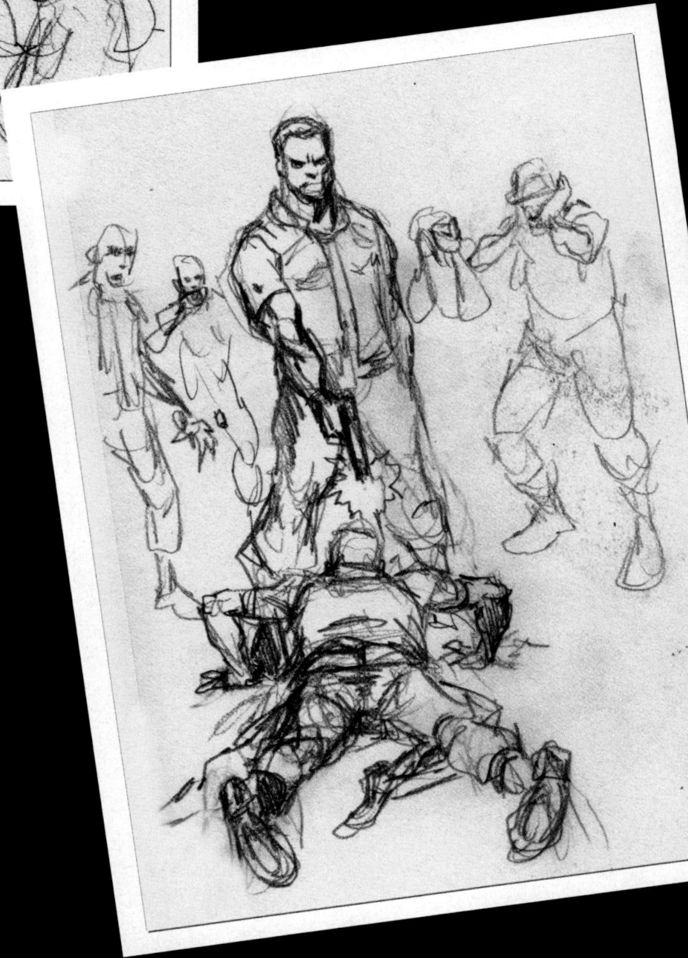

LAYOUTS FOR BORN #1 PAGE 2
by Darick Robertson

This was the most challenging part of issue one for me. I really wanted to give the scene room and atmosphere, but still had to tell the sequence in pages with five panels. This was one of those sequences that if I'd had all the time and room that I needed, I would have drawn each panel as double-page spreads to really give the size of that C-4 plane and the crash its due.

So I did this layout while reading the script, coincidentally on a plane flying over the Atlantic. I was so excited about this series that I was eager to lay it out as I read it.

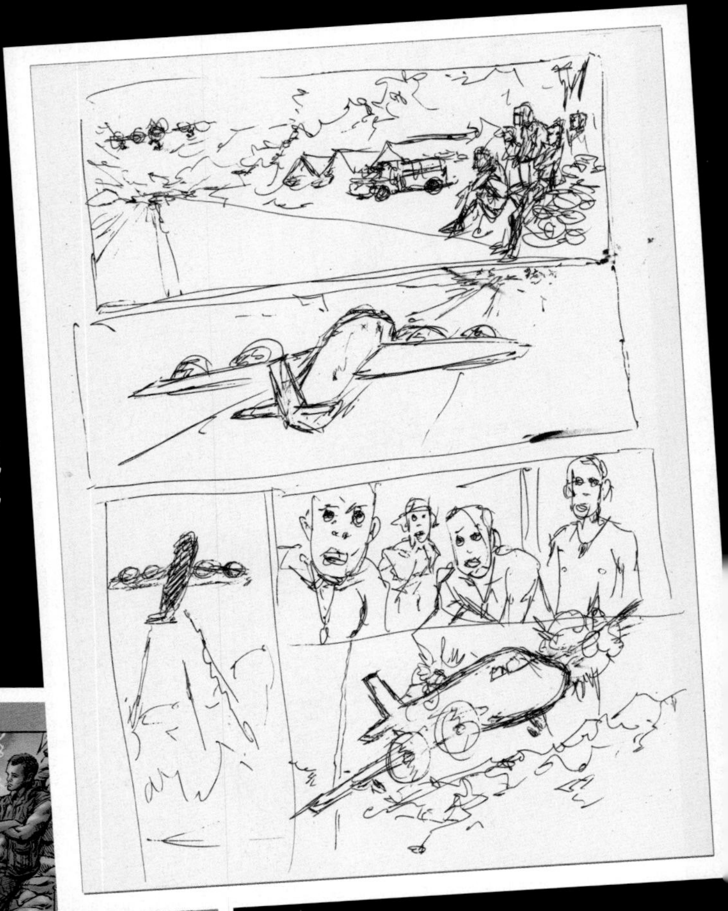

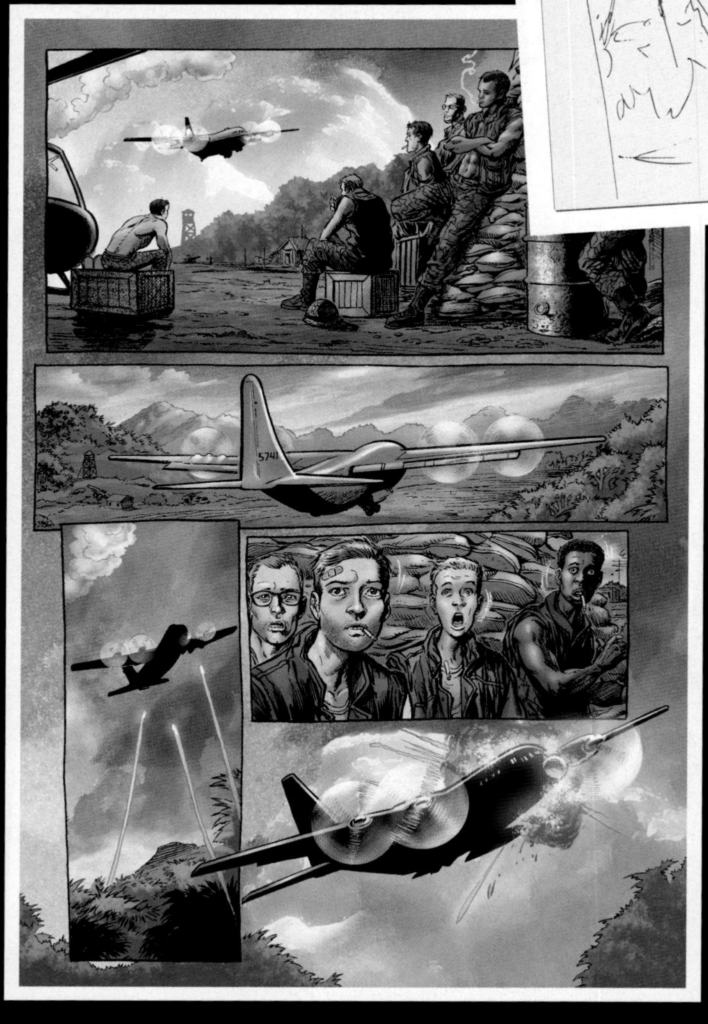
5741

PUNISHER DESIGN BY LEWIS LAROSA

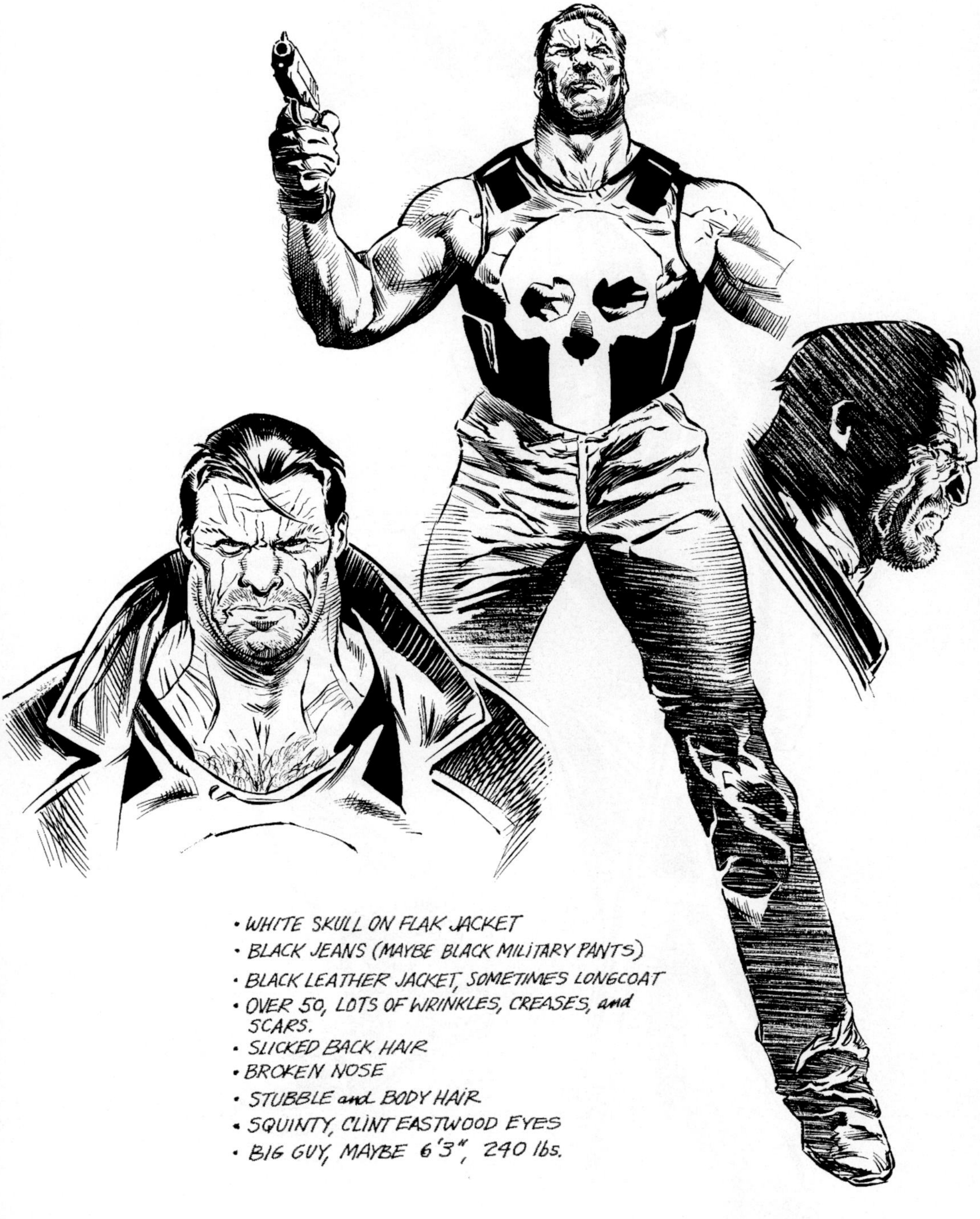

• WHITE SKULL ON FLAK JACKET
• BLACK JEANS (MAYBE BLACK MILITARY PANTS)
• BLACK LEATHER JACKET, SOMETIMES LONGCOAT
• OVER 50, LOTS OF WRINKLES, CREASES, and SCARS.
• SLICKED BACK HAIR
• BROKEN NOSE
• STUBBLE and BODY HAIR
• SQUINTY, CLINT EASTWOOD EYES
• BIG GUY, MAYBE 6'3", 240 lbs.

PUNISHER DESIGN BY LEANDRO FERNANDEZ

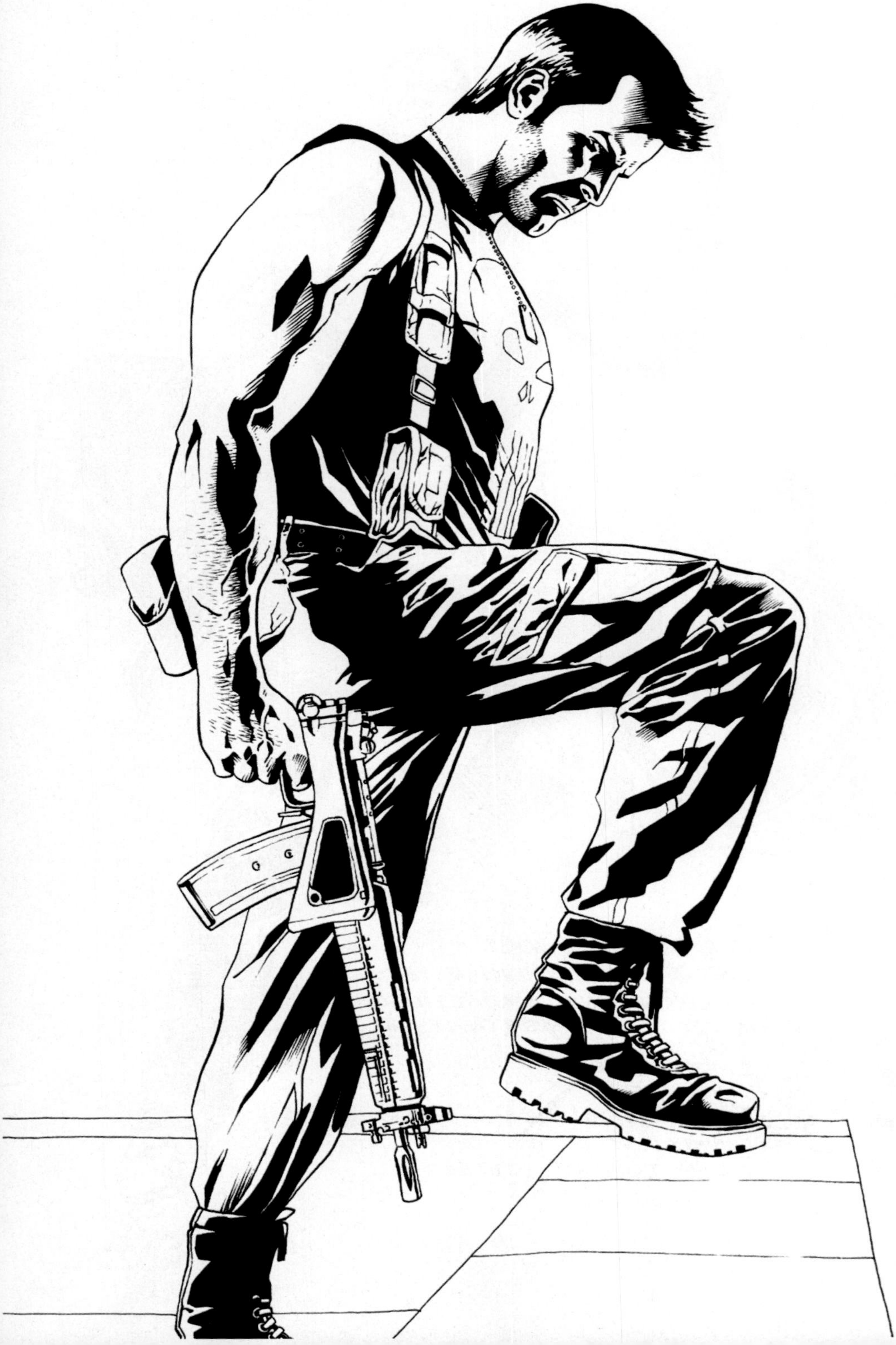

PUNISHER #7

From layouts to finished colors.
Pencils/inks by Leandro Fernandez. Colors by Dean White.

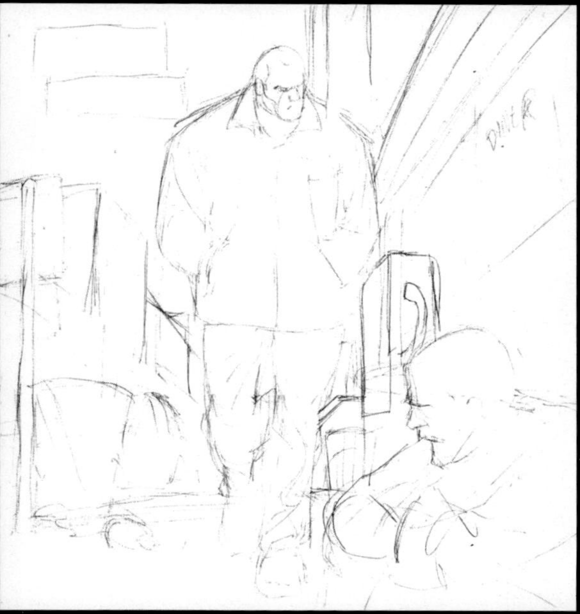

Page 1 Layout

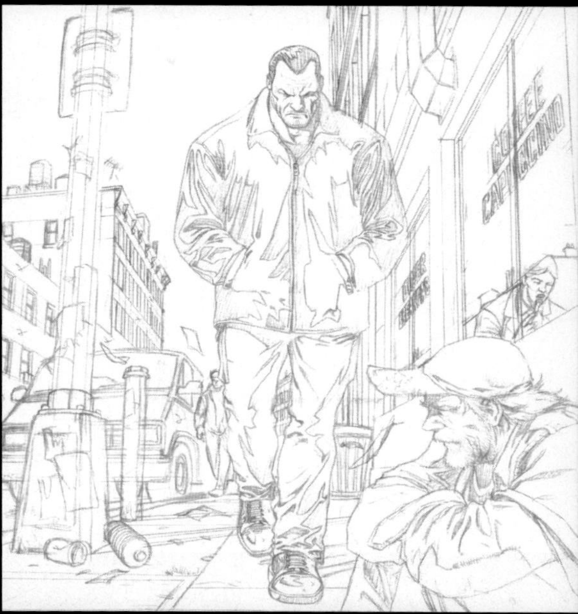

Page 1 Pencils

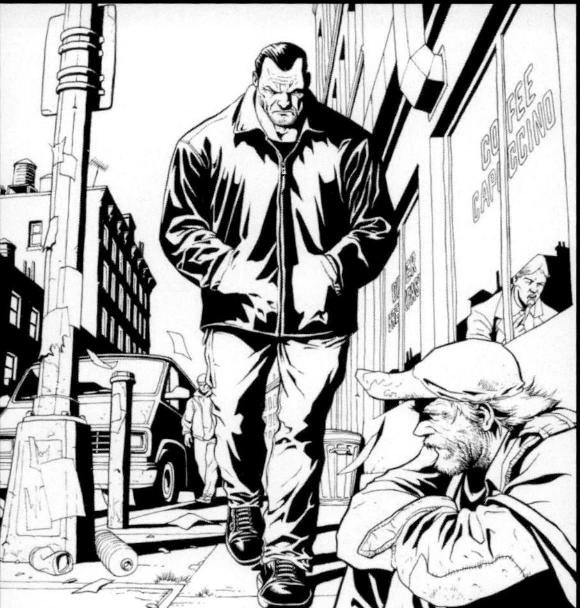

Page 1 Inks

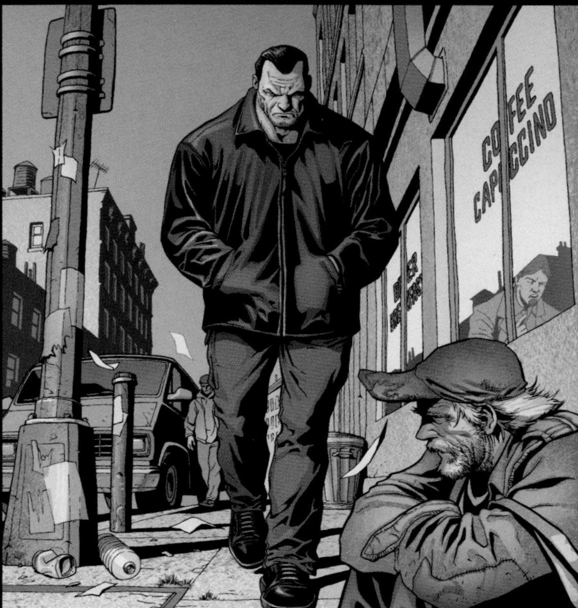

Page 1 Colors

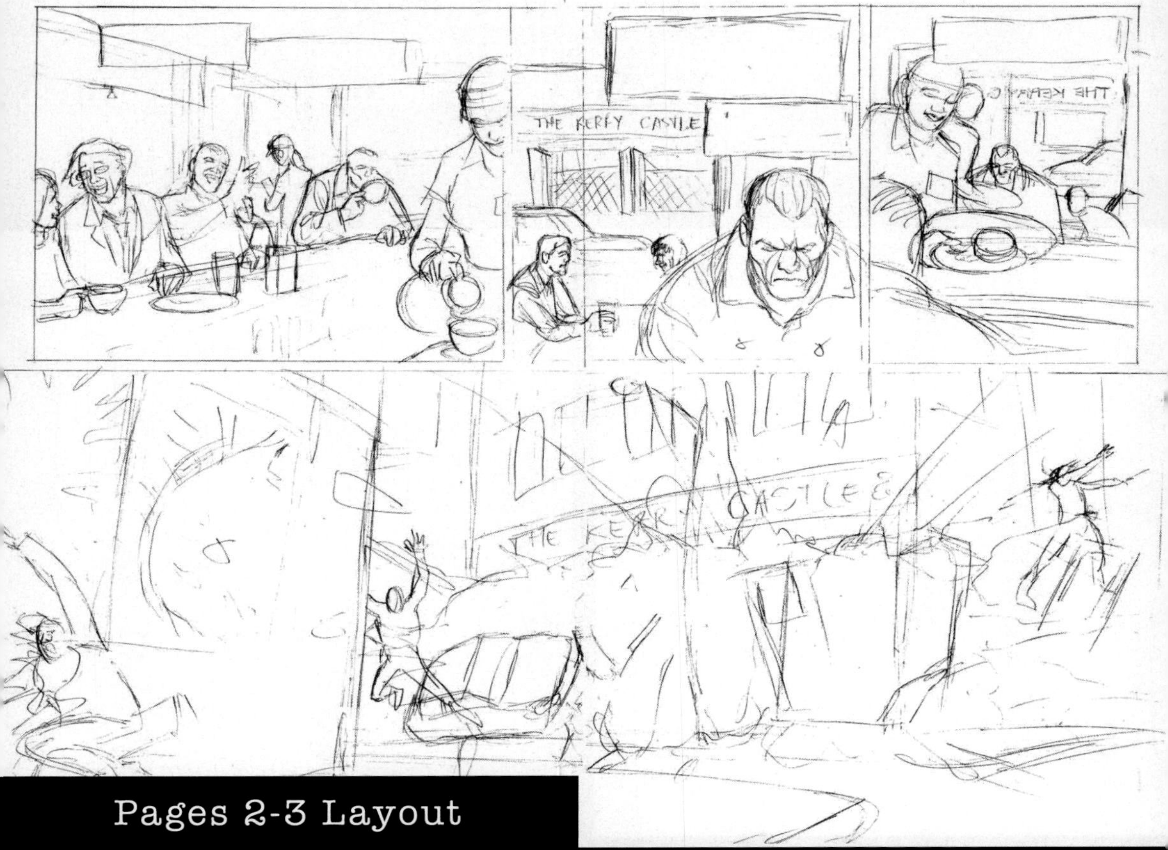
THE KERRY CASTLE

Pages 2-3 Layout

Pages 2-3 Pencils

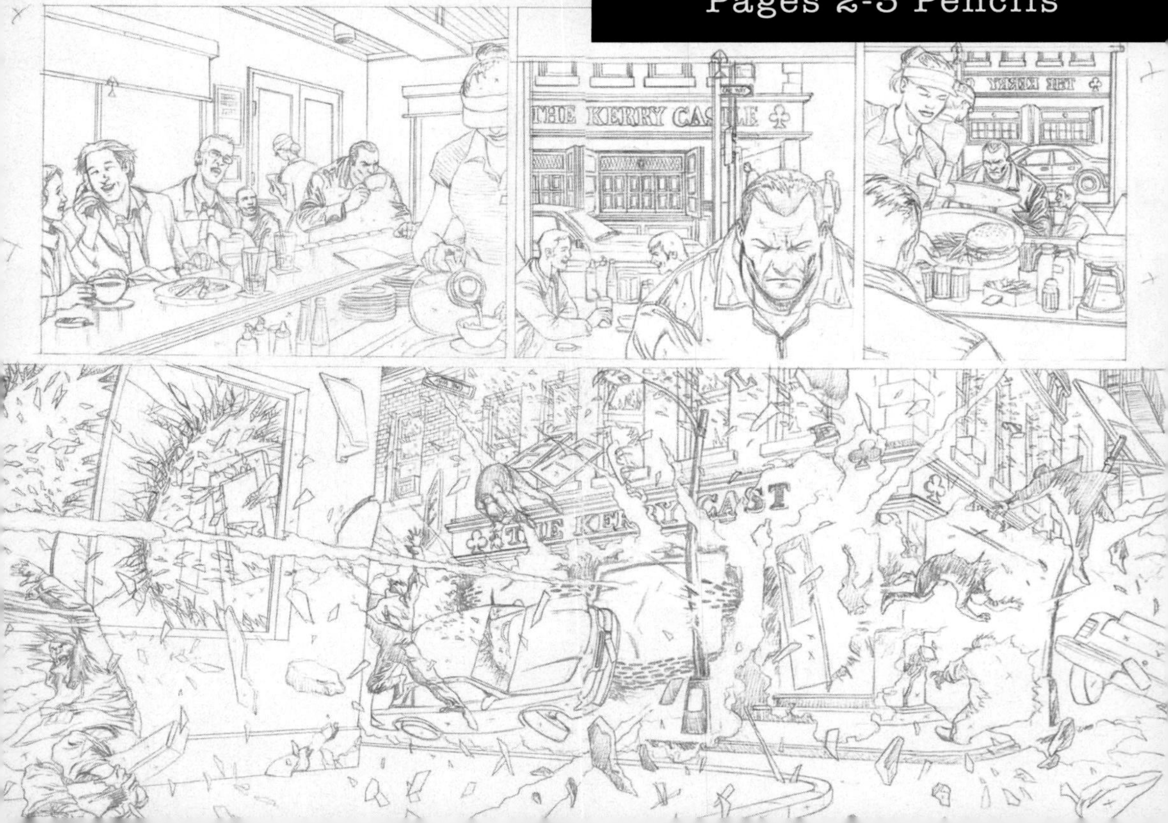
THE KERRY CASTLE
THE KERRY CAST

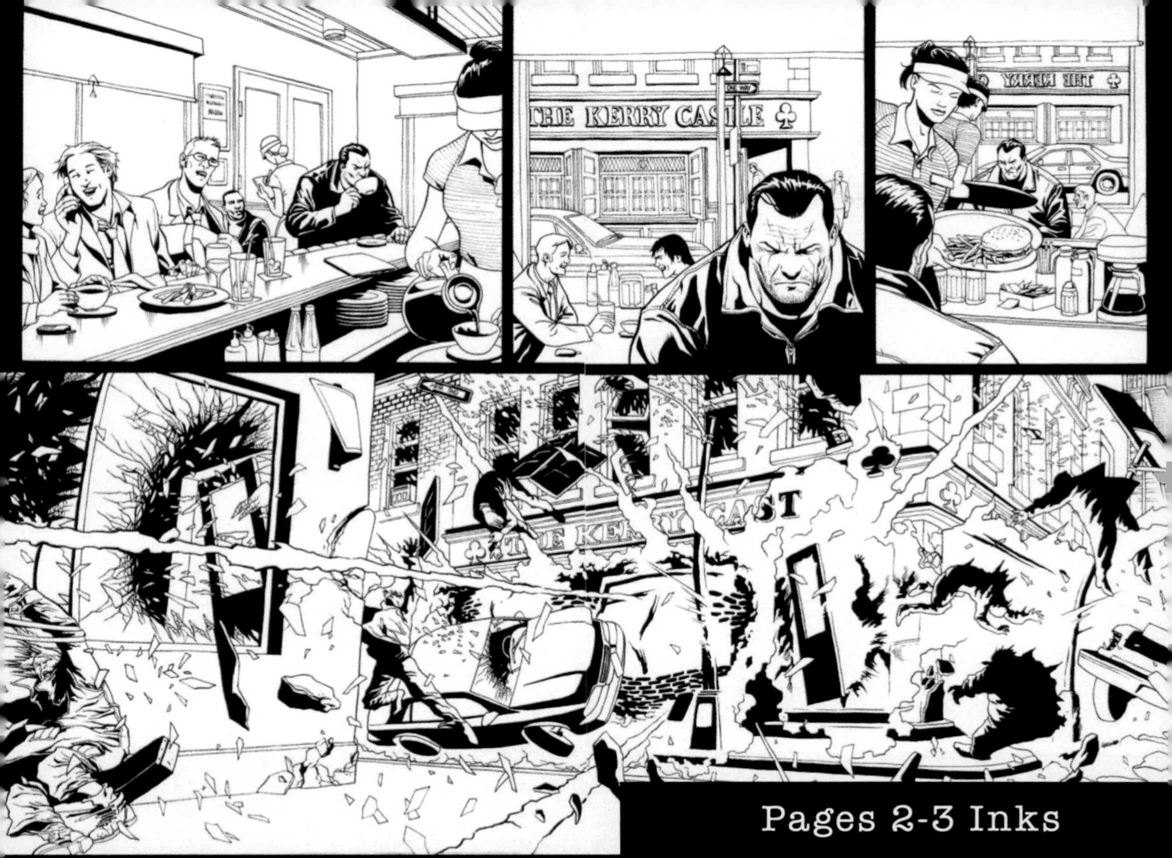
THE KERRY CASTLE

Pages 2-3 Inks

Pages 2-3 Colors

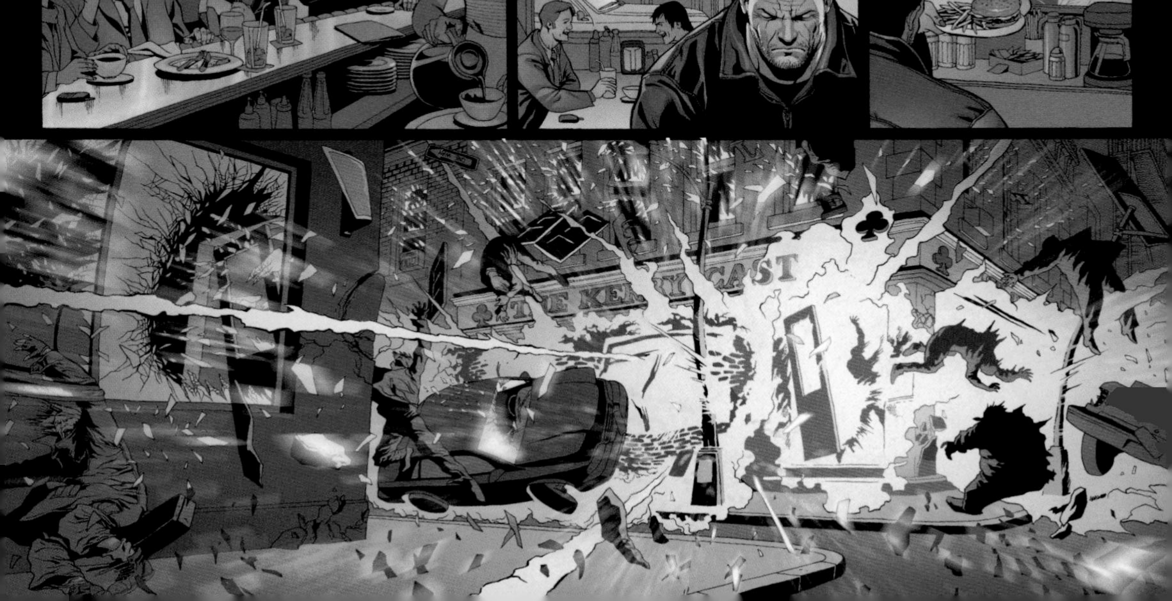
THE KERRY CASTLE

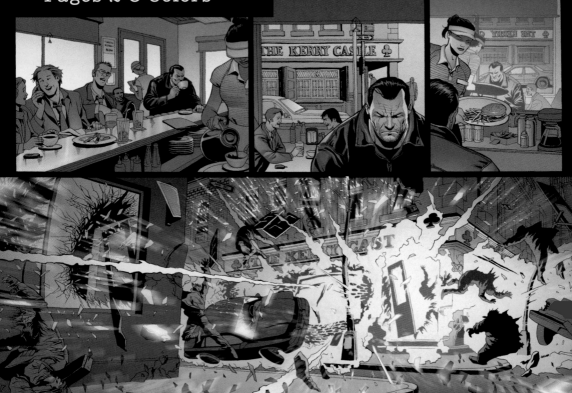

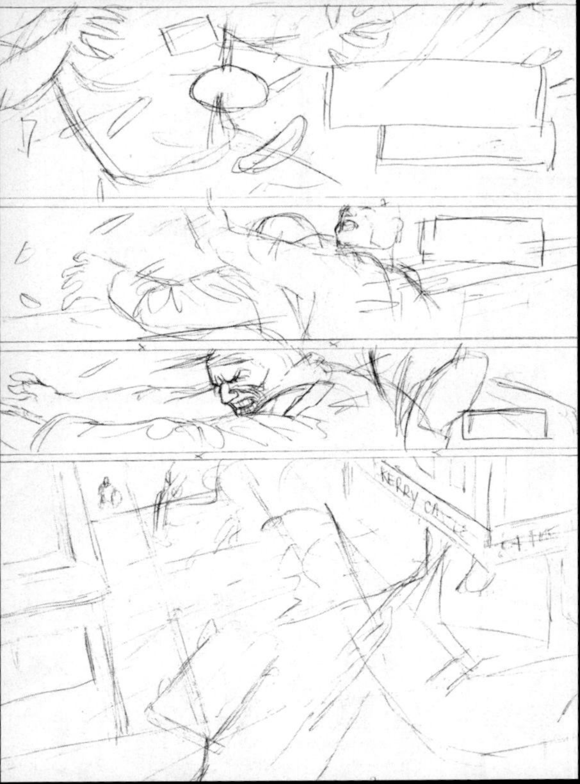

Page 4 Layout

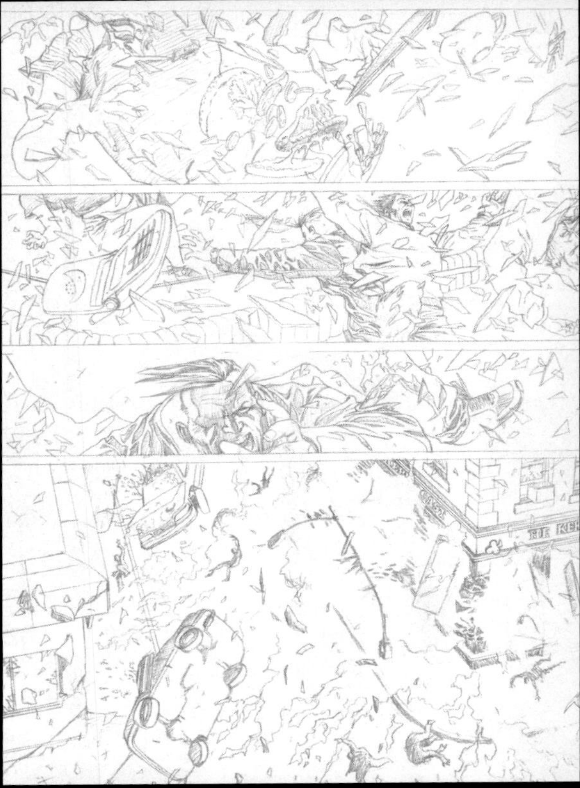

Page 4 Pencils

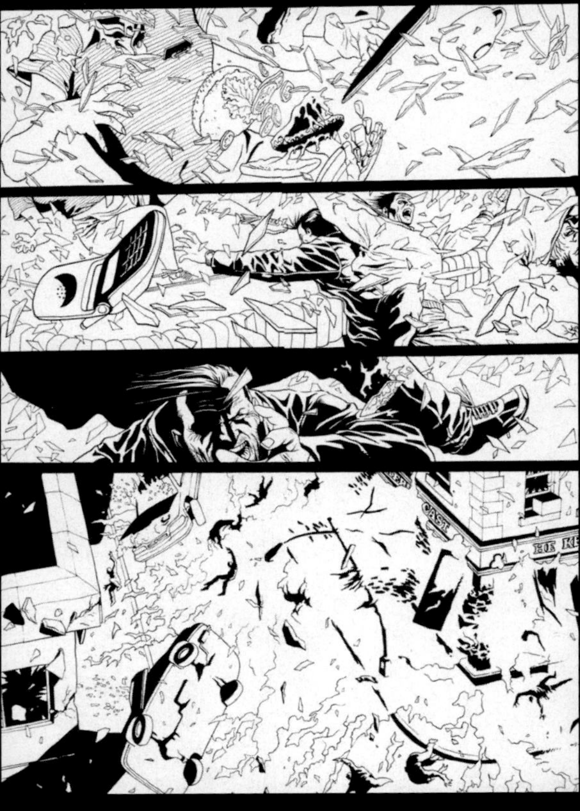

Page 4 Inks

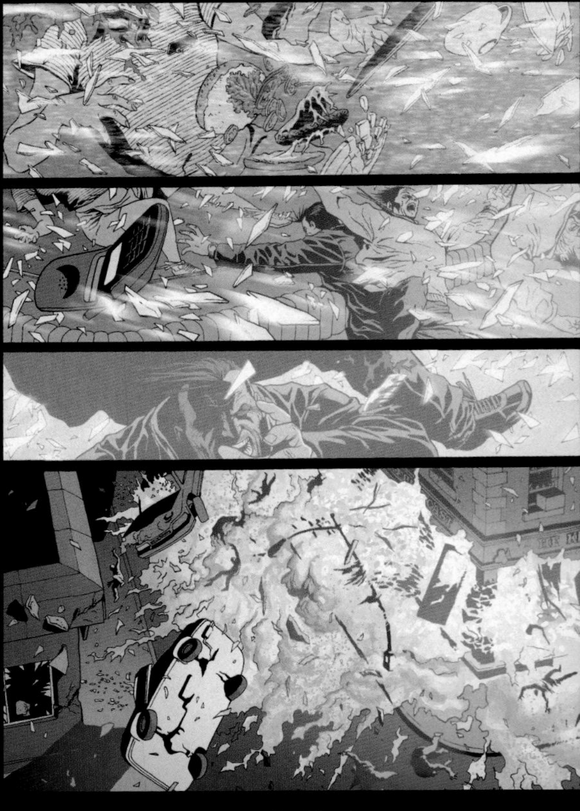

Page 4 Colors

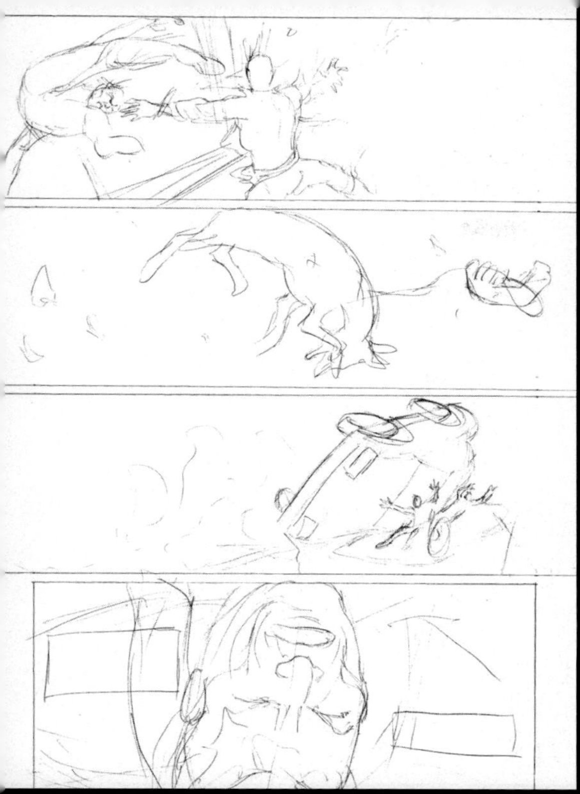

Page 5 Layout

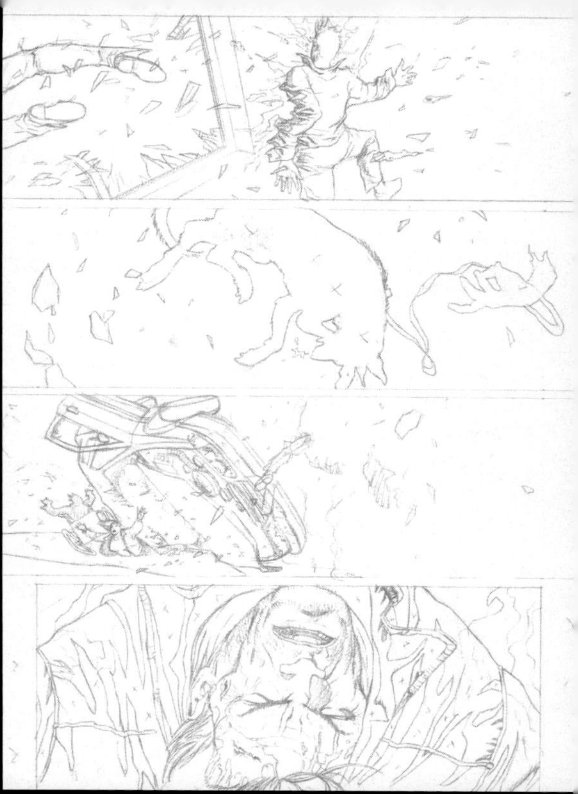

Page 5 Pencils

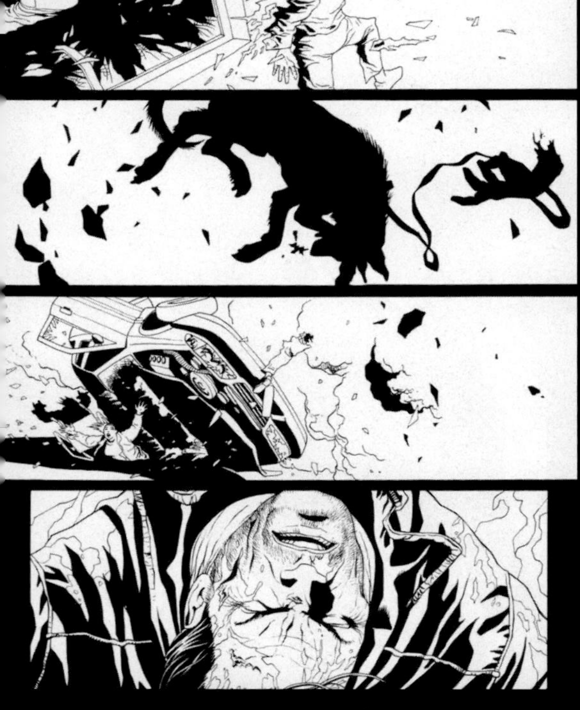

Page 5 Inks

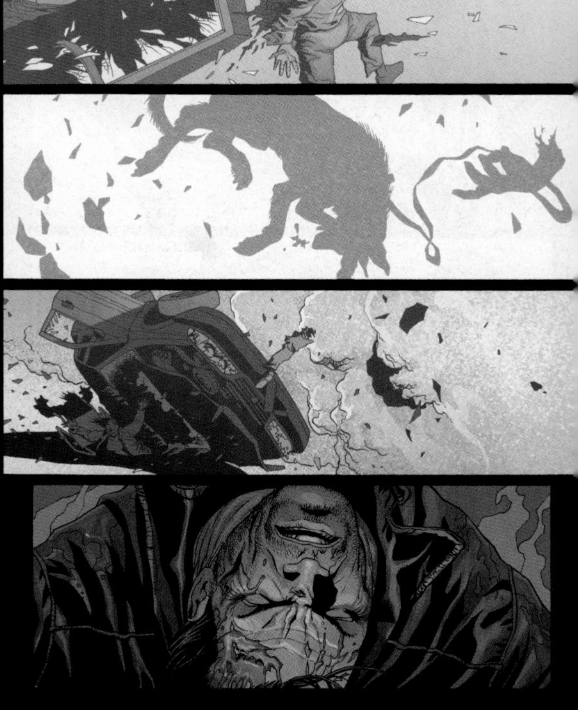

Page 5 Colors

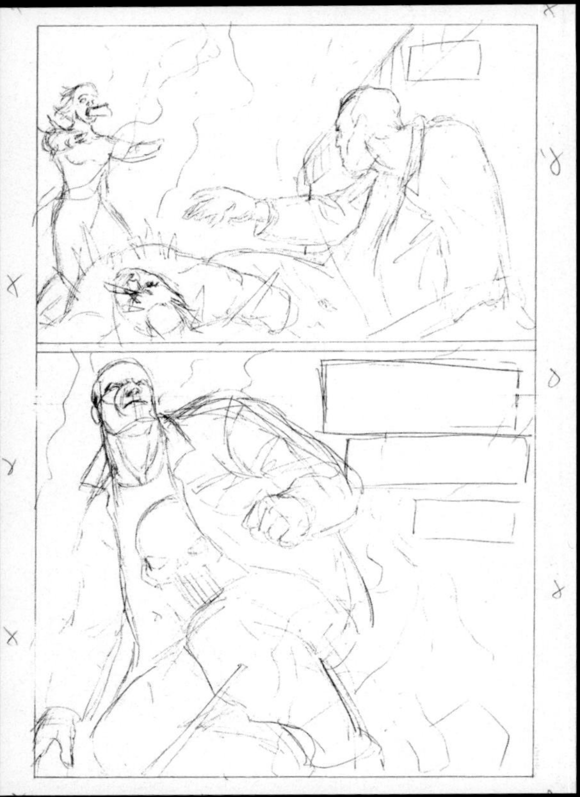

Page 6 Layout

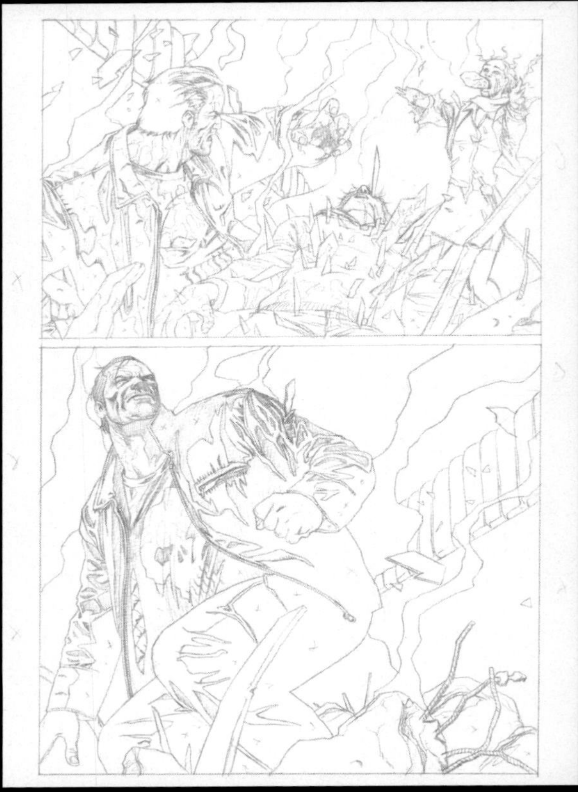

Page 6 Pencils

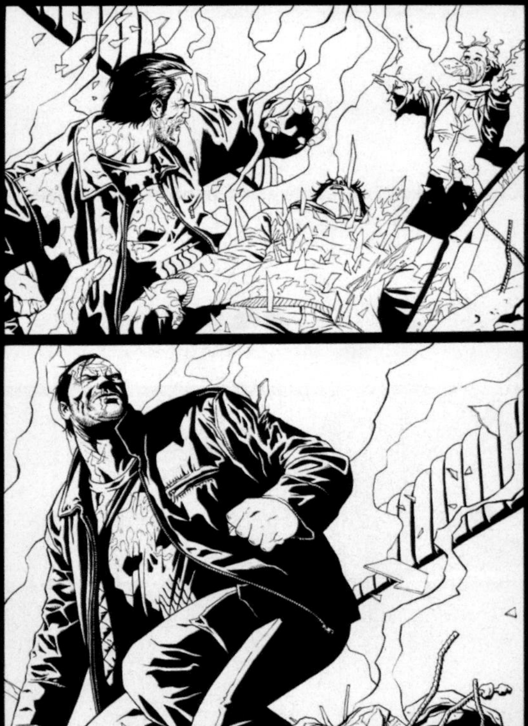

Page 6 Inks

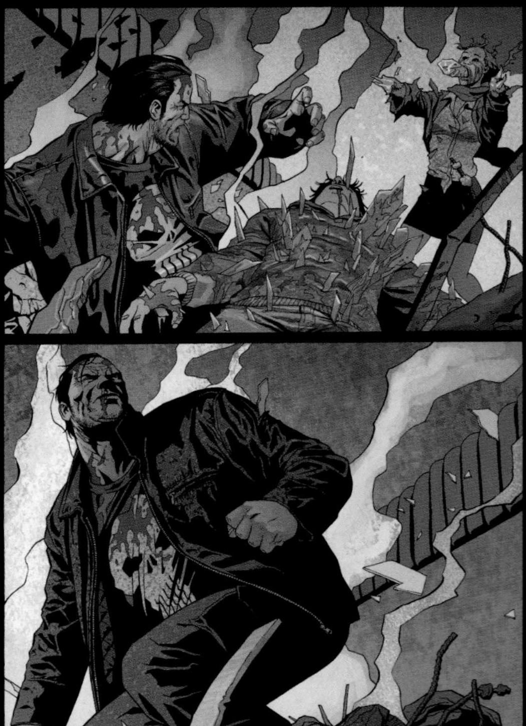

Page 6 Colors

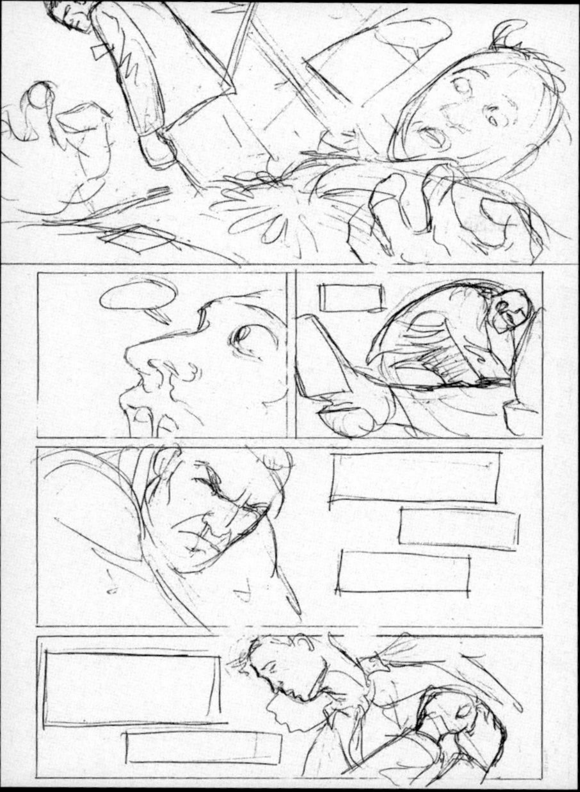

Page 7 Layout

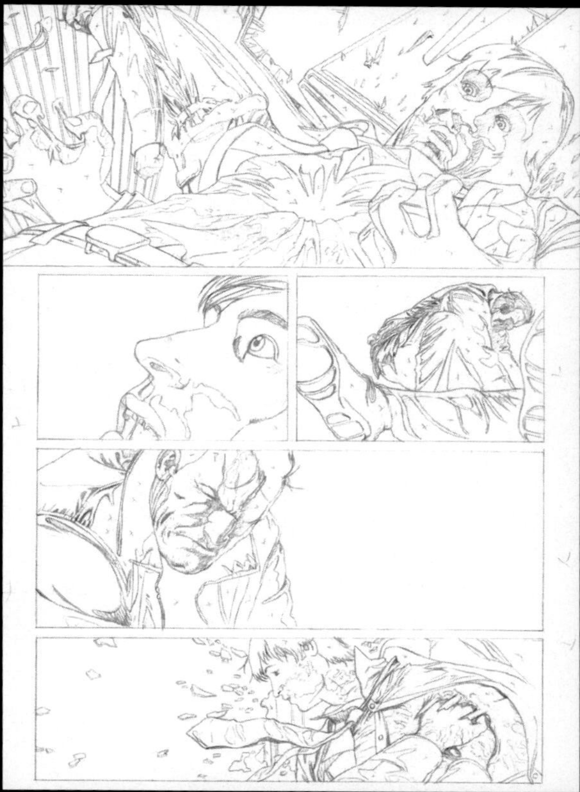

Page 7 Pencils

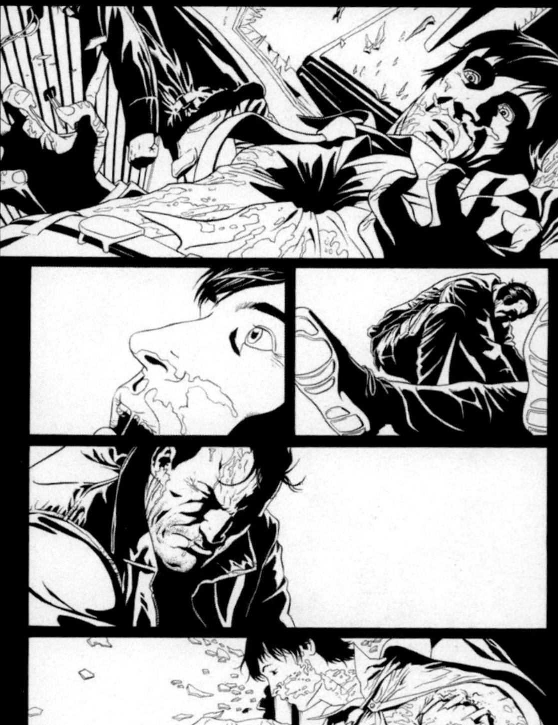

Page 7 Inks

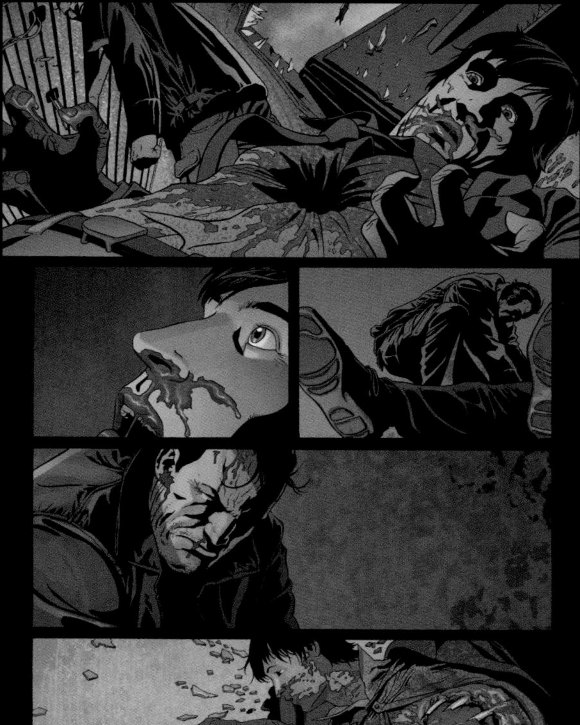

Page 7 Colors

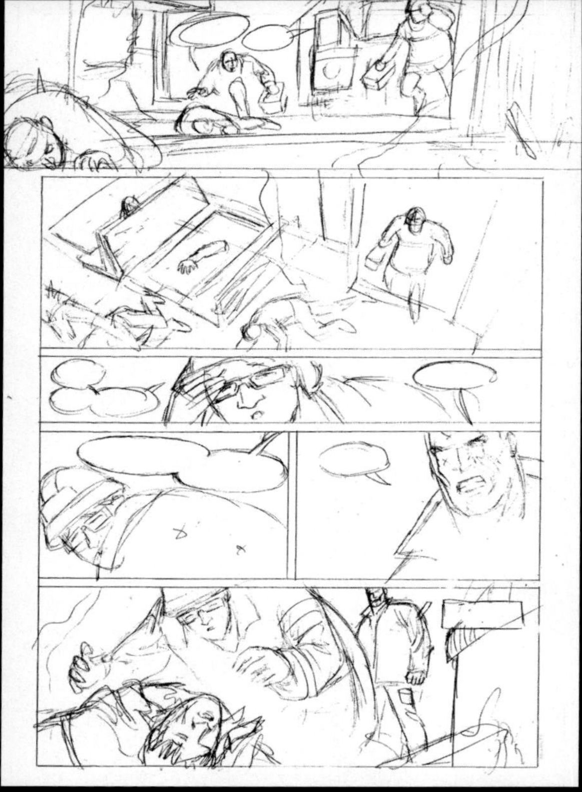

Page 8 Layout

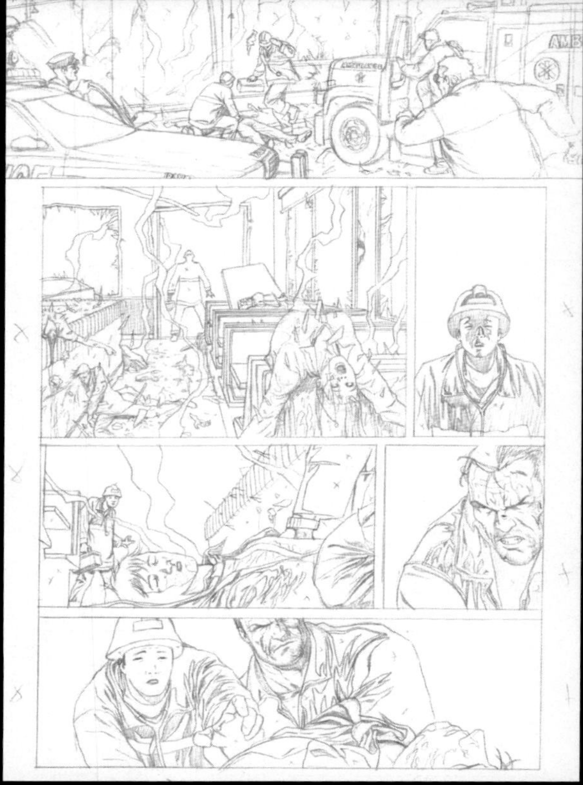

Page 8 Pencils

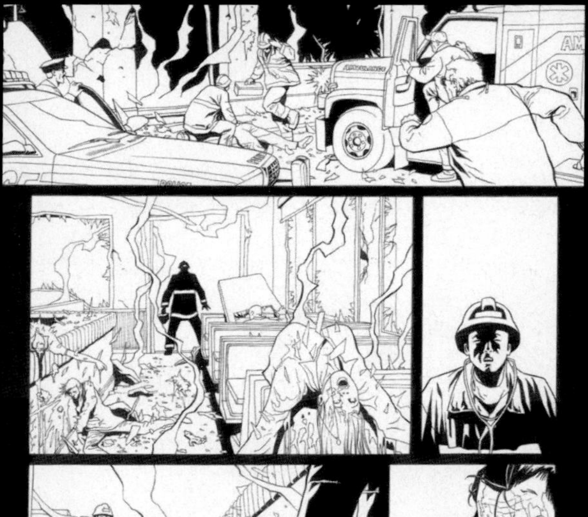

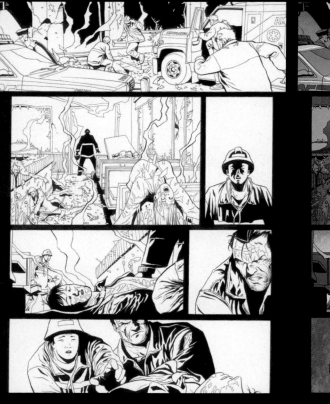

Page 8 Inks

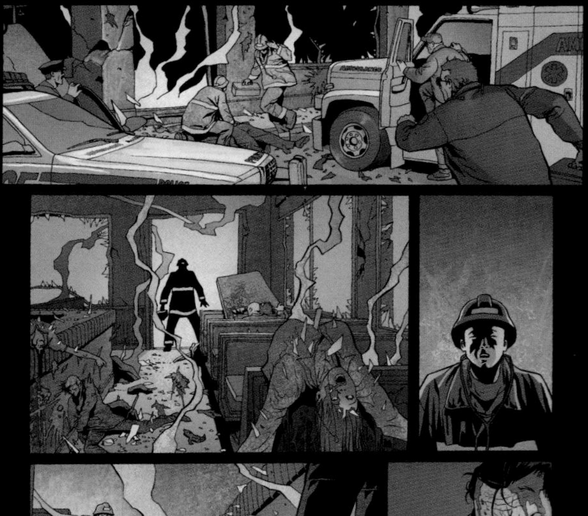

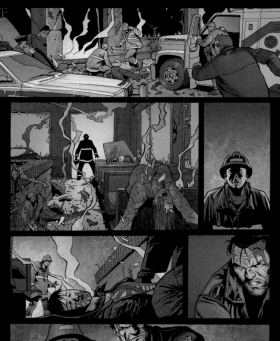

Page 8 Colors

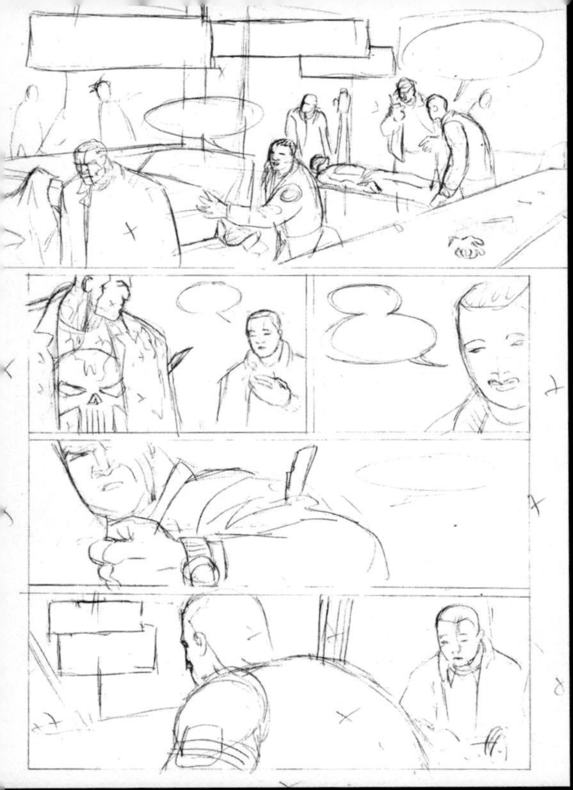

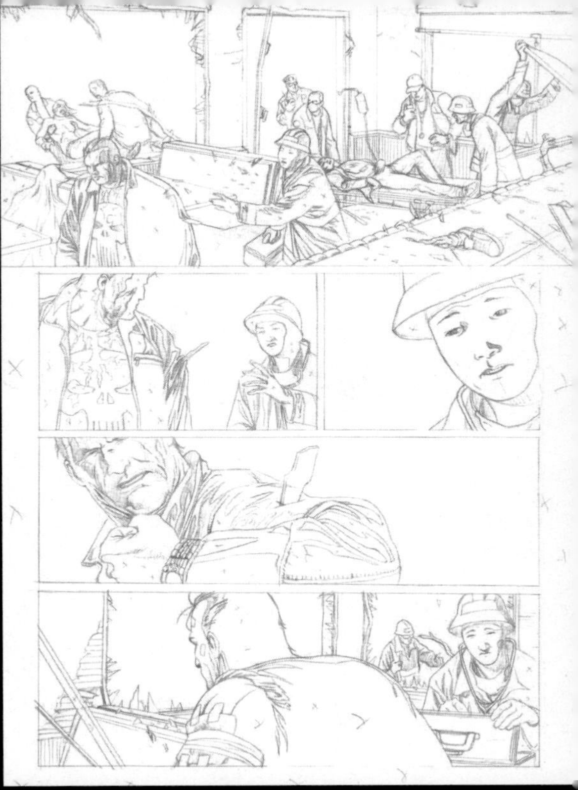

Page 9 Layout

Page 9 Pencils

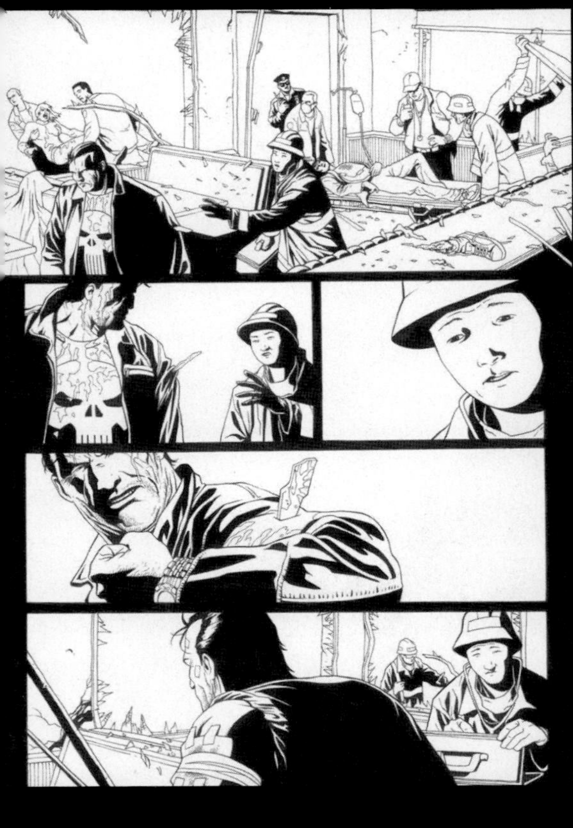

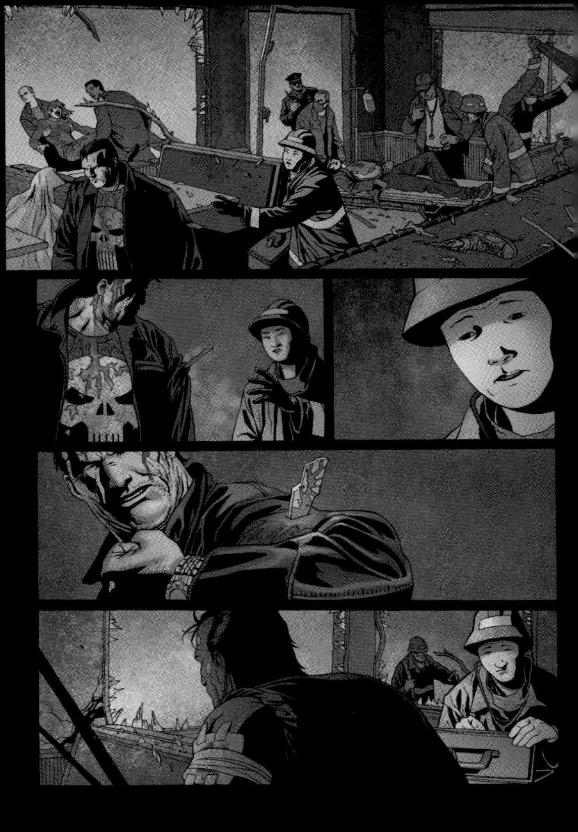

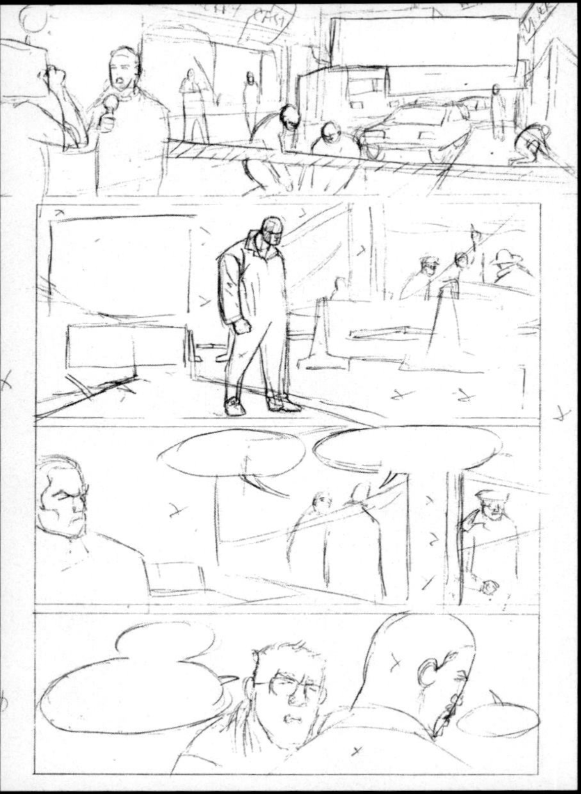

Page 10 Layout

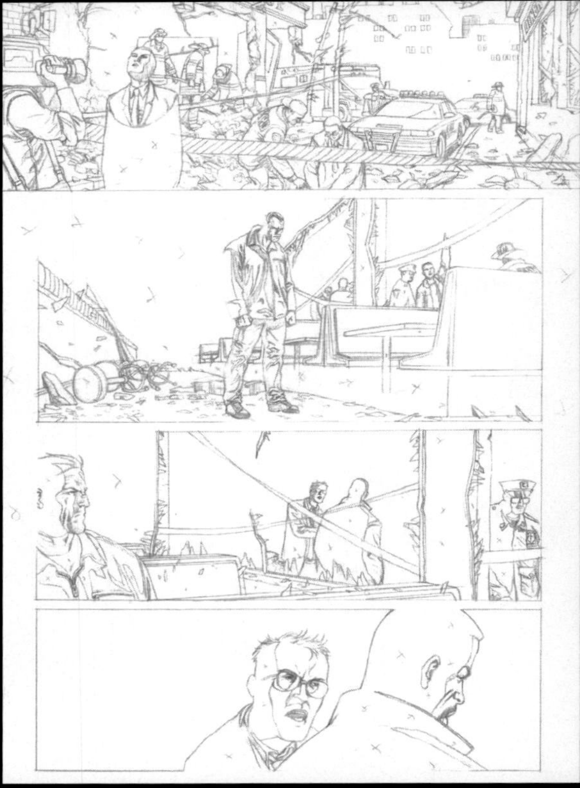

Page 10 Pencils

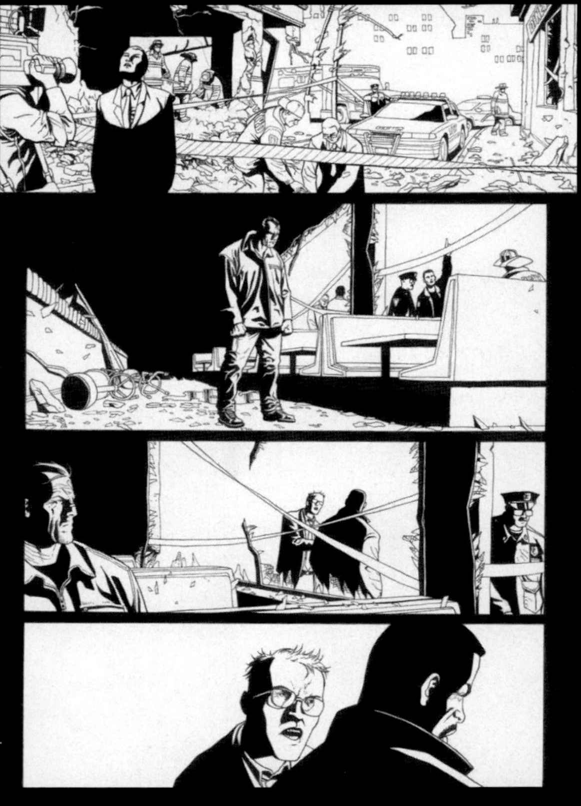

Page 10 Inks

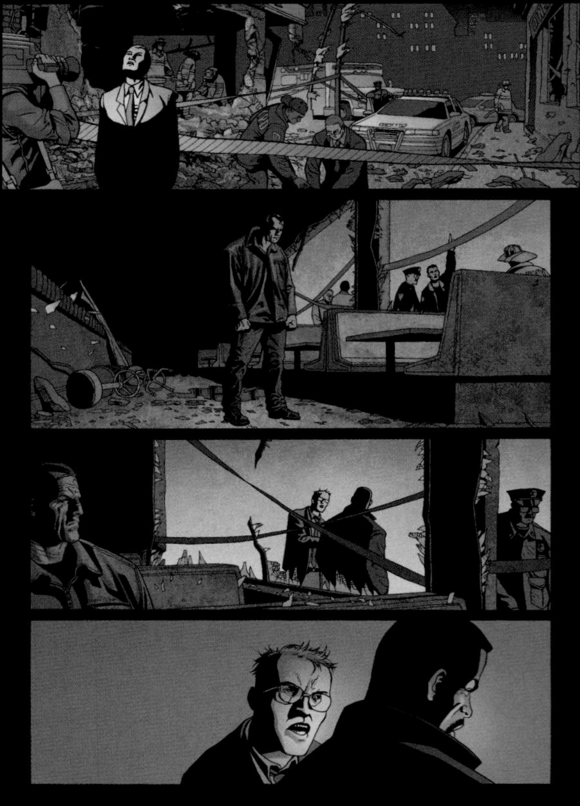

Page 10 Colors

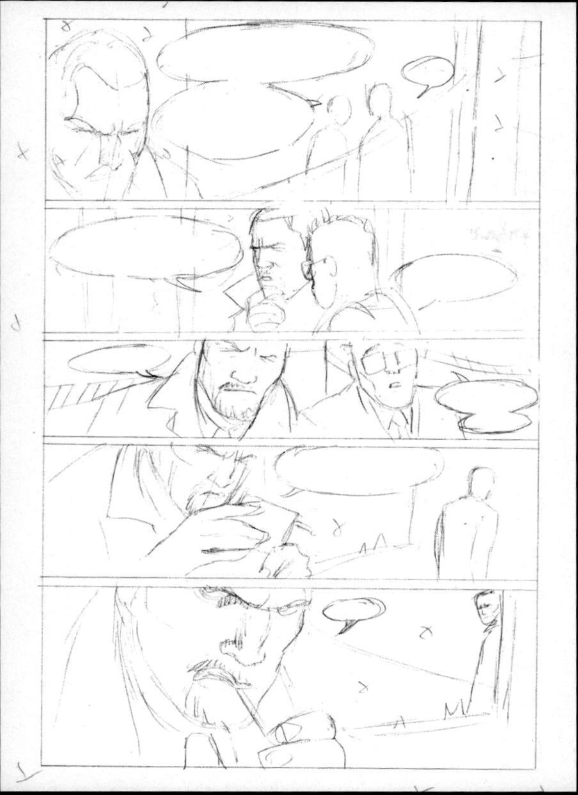

Page 11 Layout

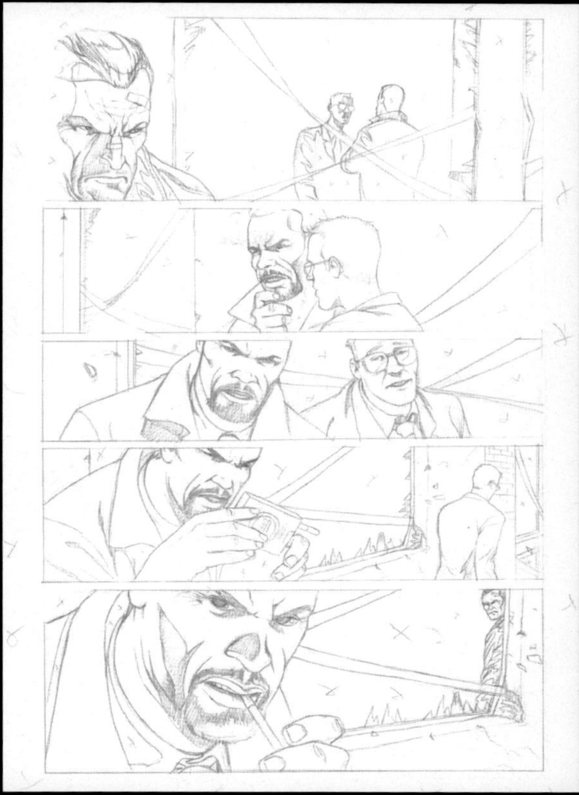

Page 11 Pencils

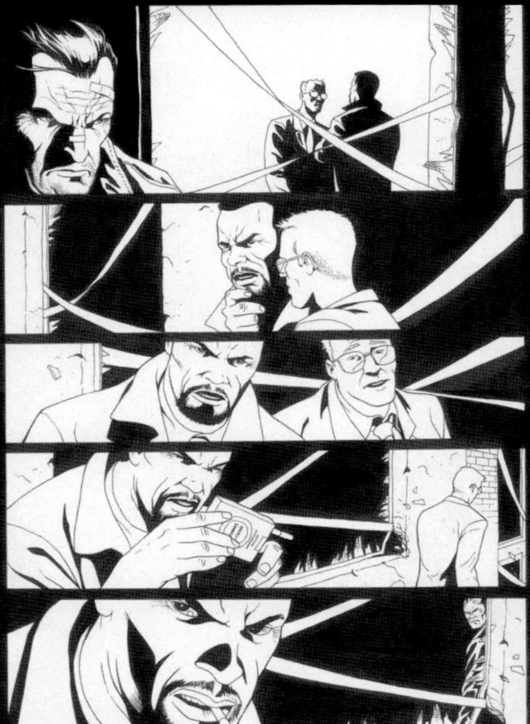

Page 11 Inks

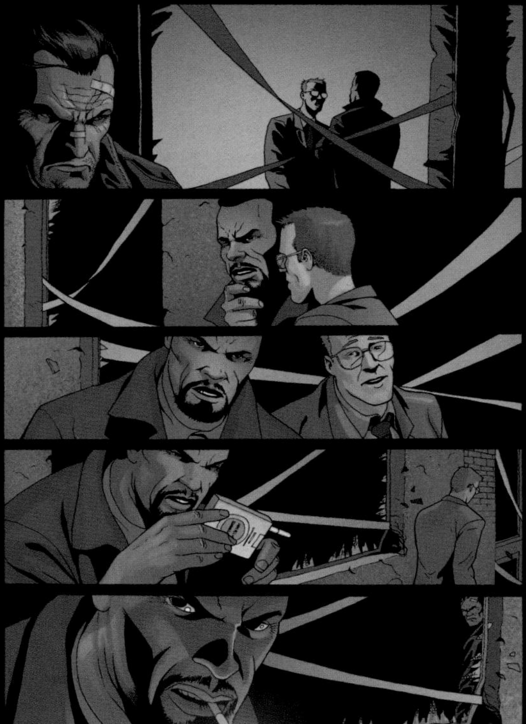

Page 11 Colors

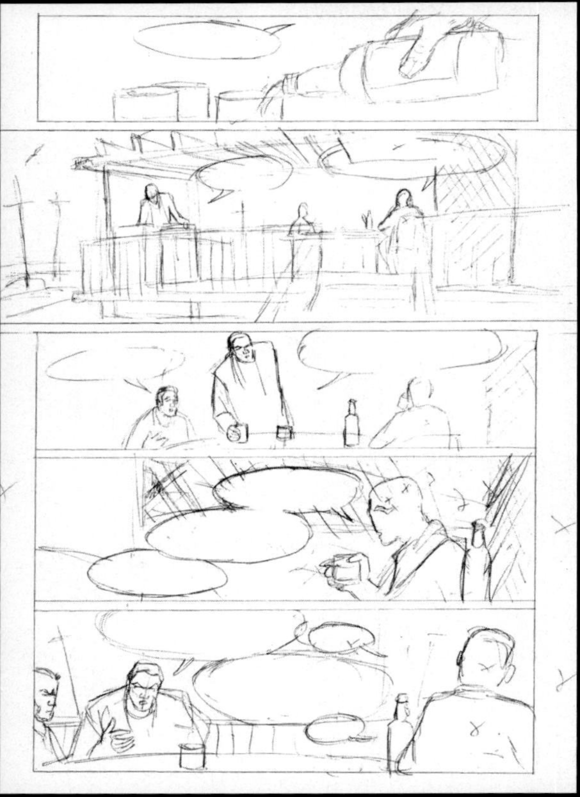

Page 12 Layout

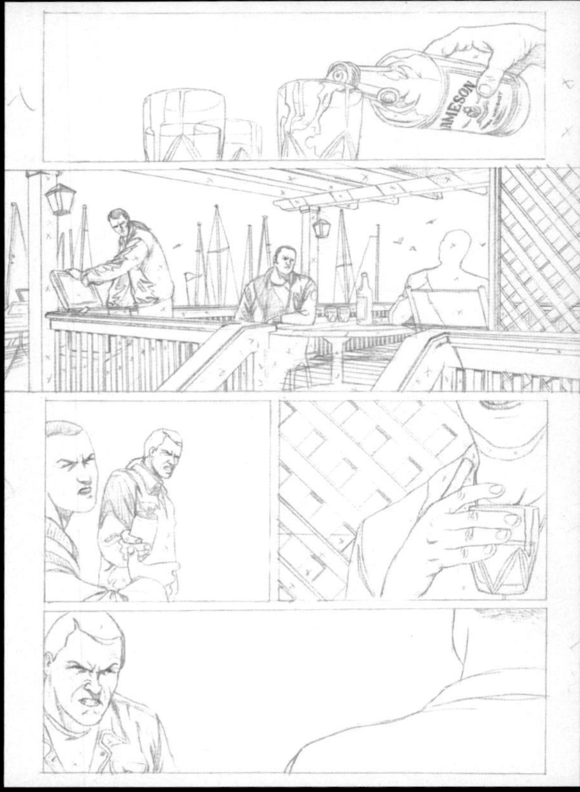

Page 12 Pencils

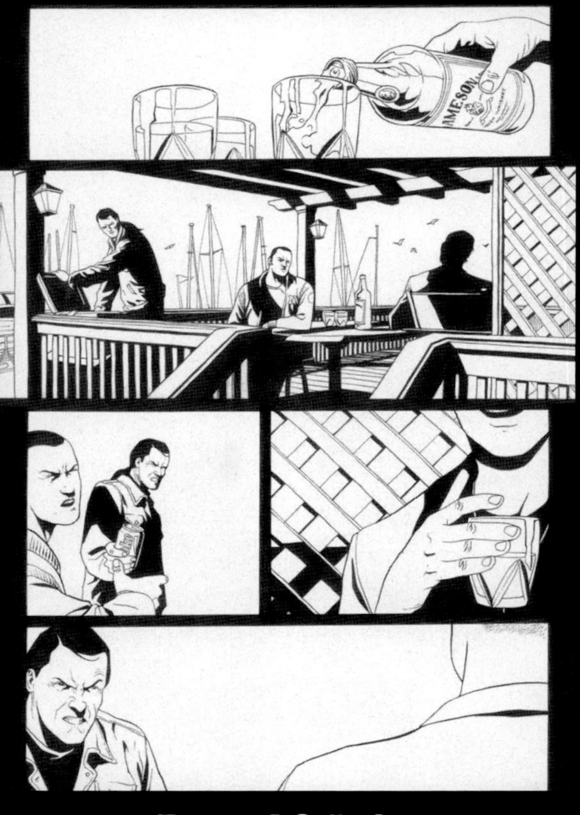

Page 12 Inks

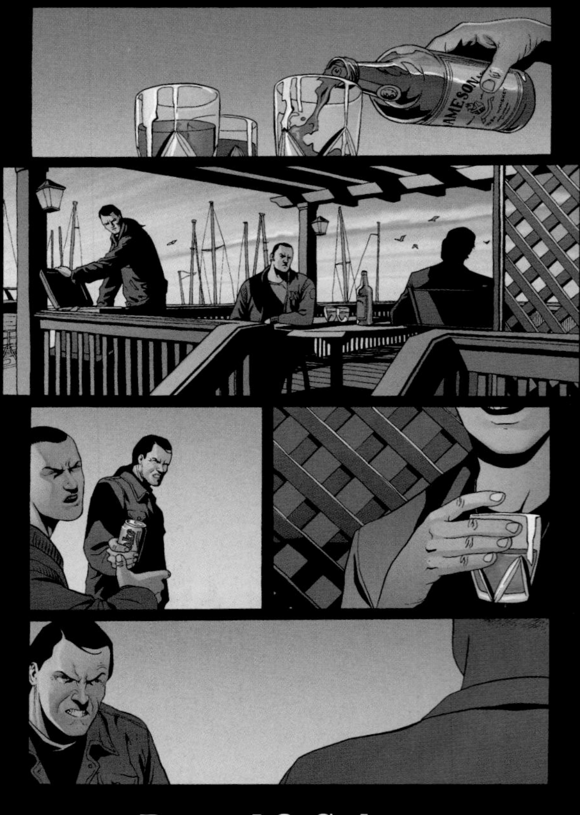

Page 12 Colors

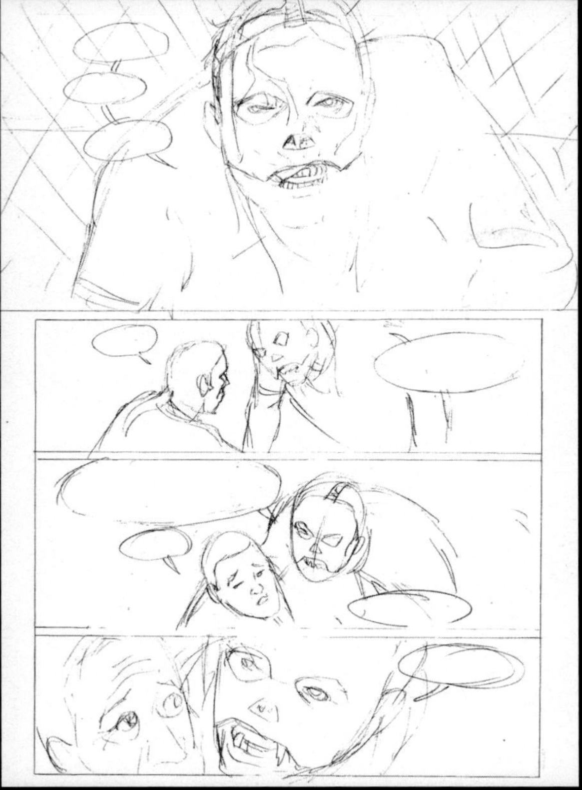

Page 13 Layout

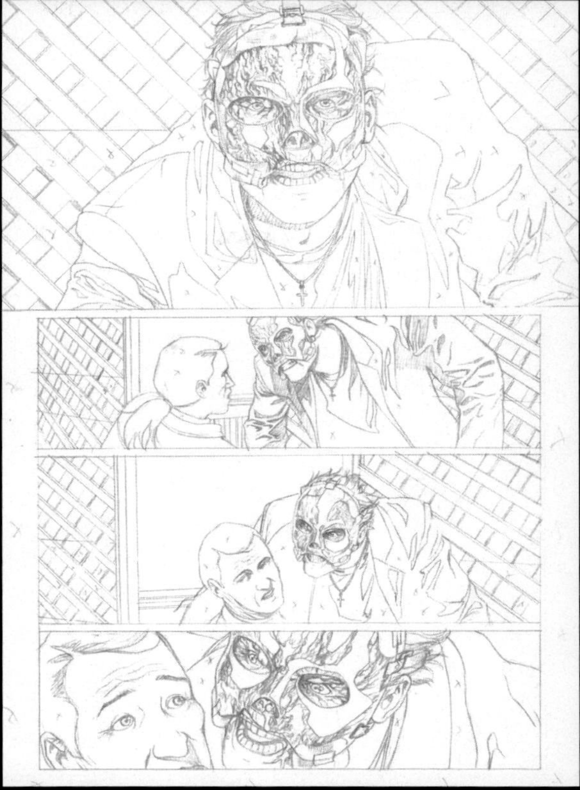

Page 13 Pencils

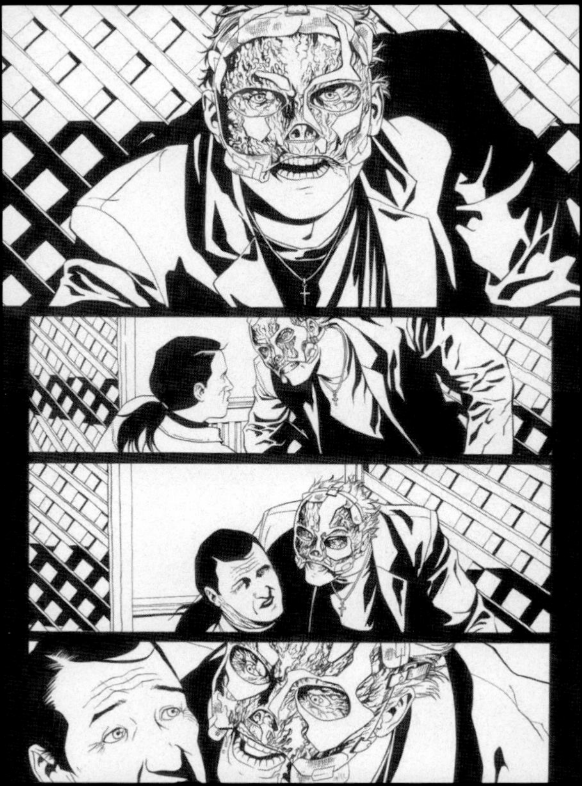

Page 13 Inks

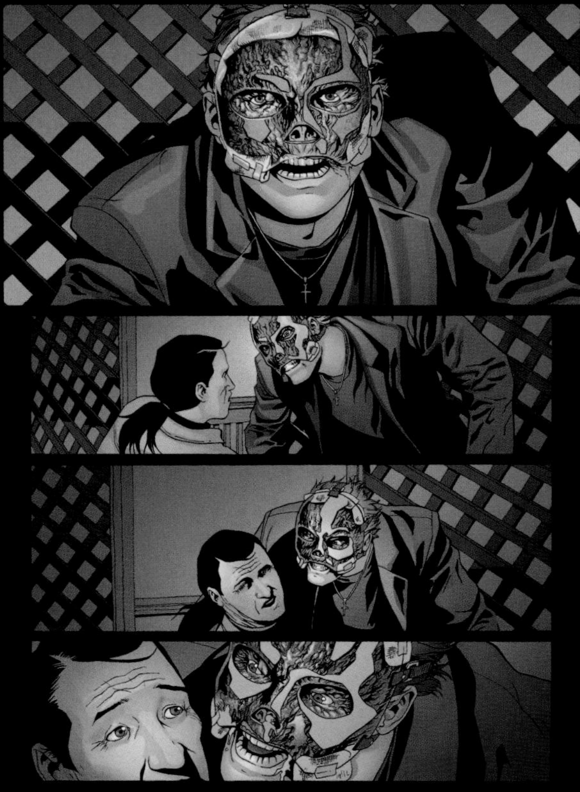

Page 13 Colors

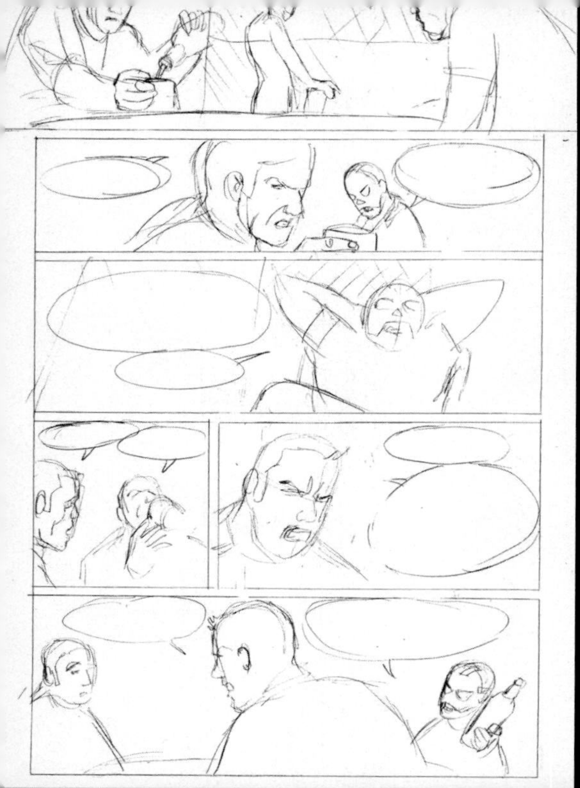

Page 14 Layout

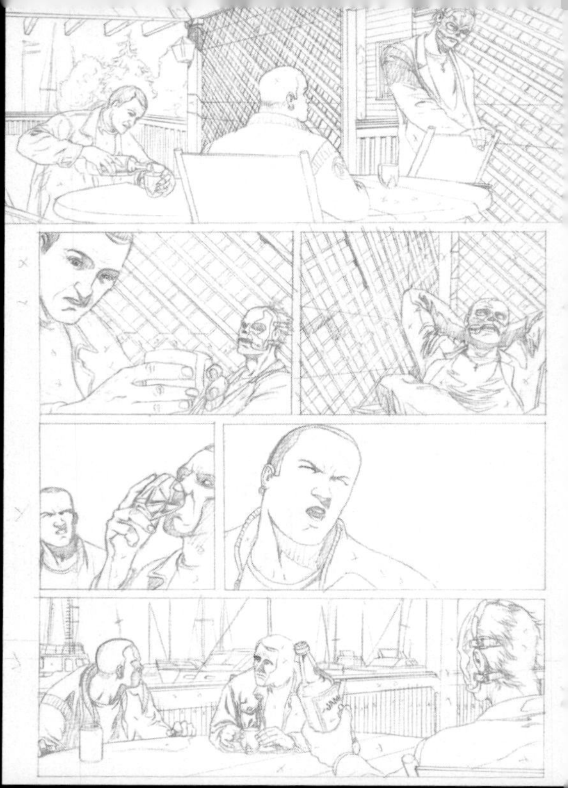

Page 14 Pencils

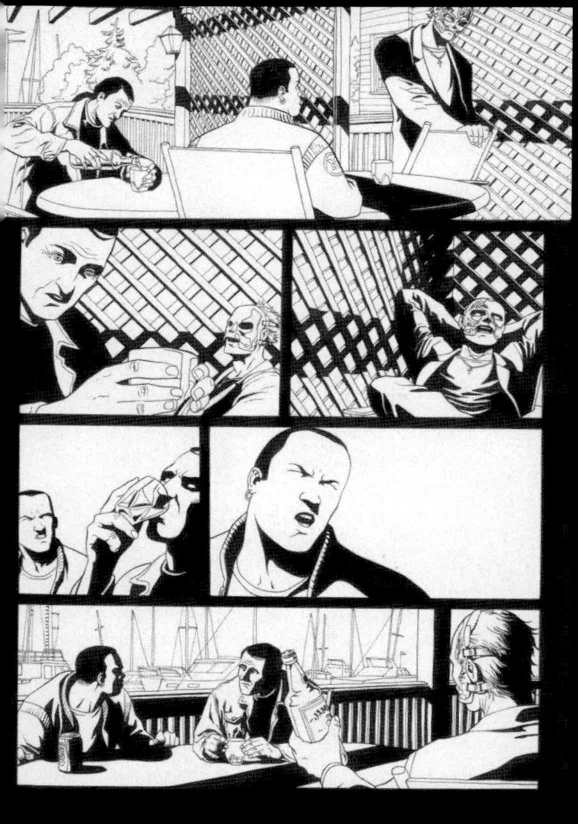

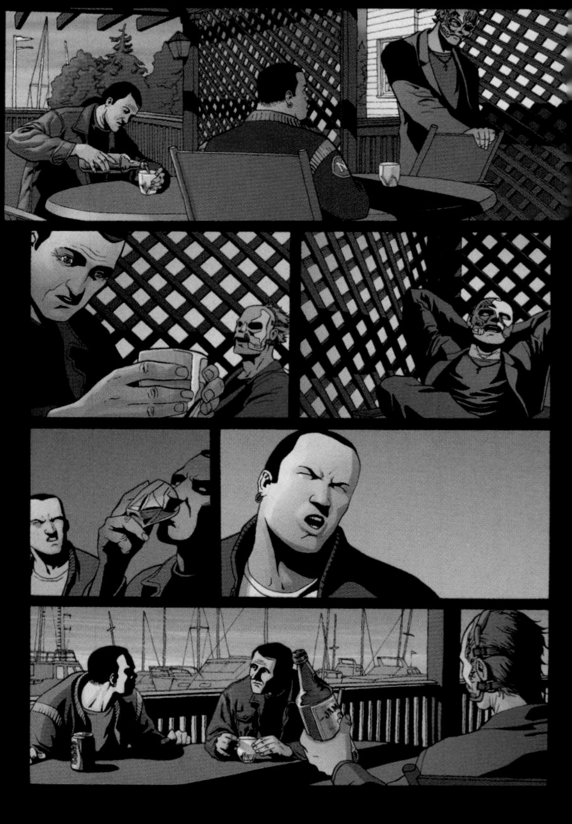

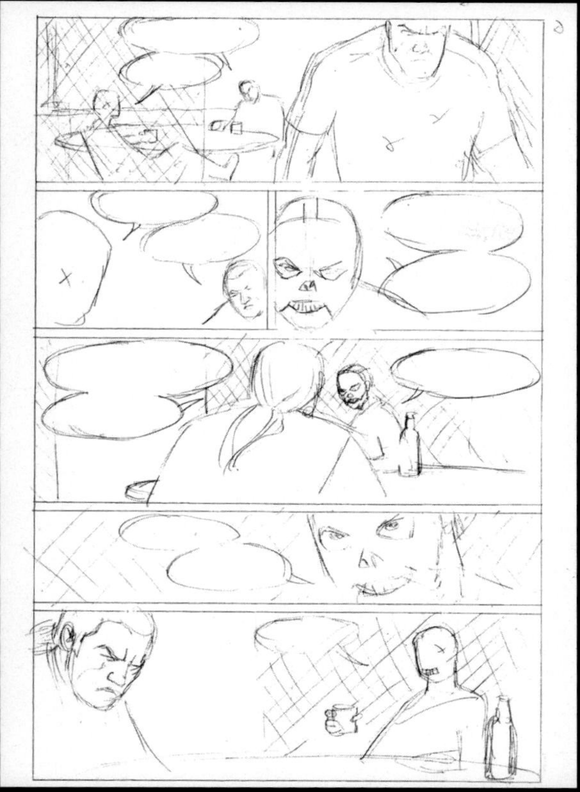

Page 15 Layout

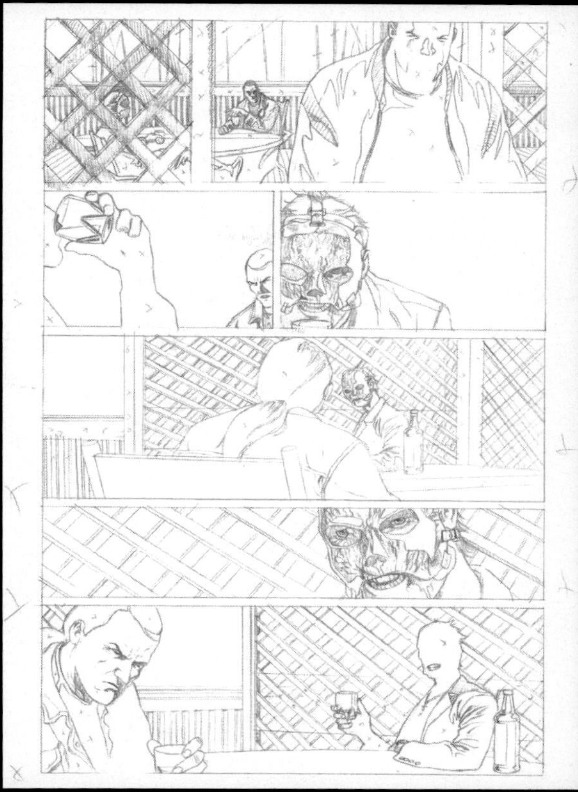

Page 15 Pencils

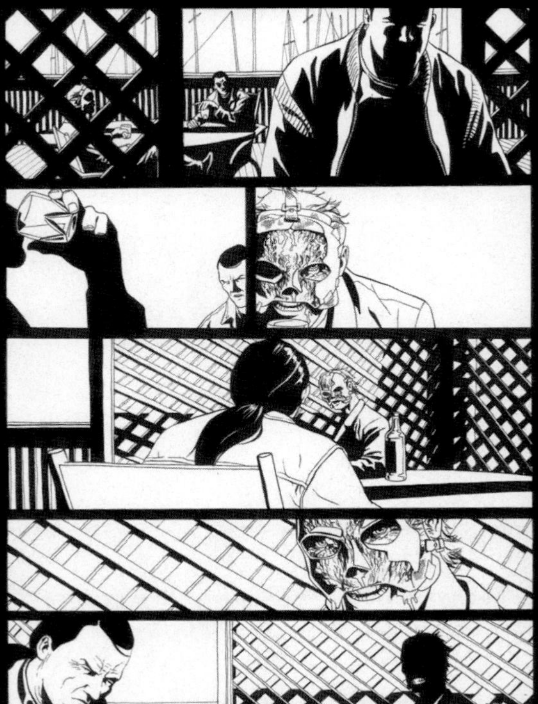

Page 15 Inks

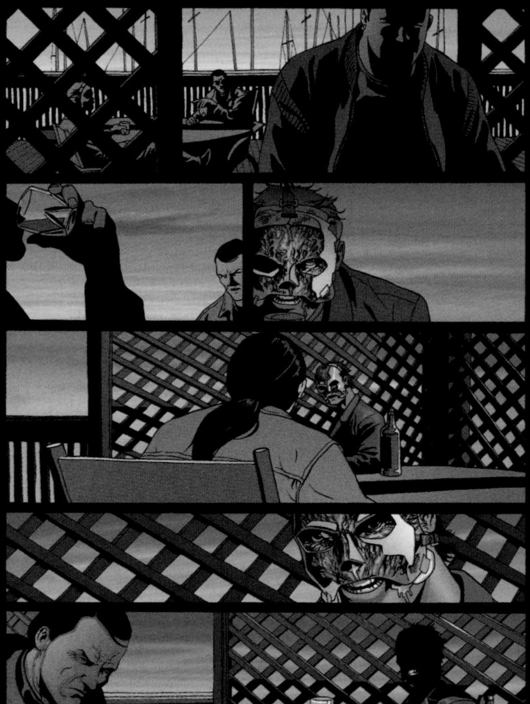

Page 15 Colors

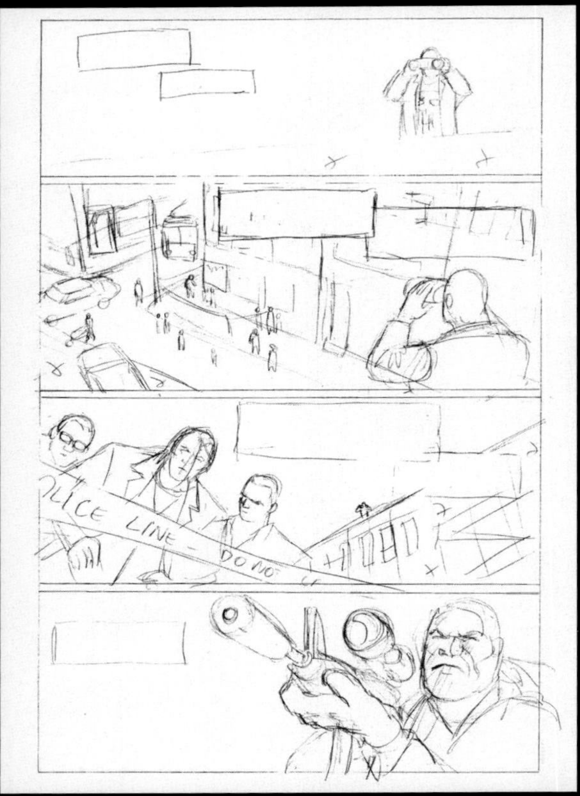

Page 16 Layout

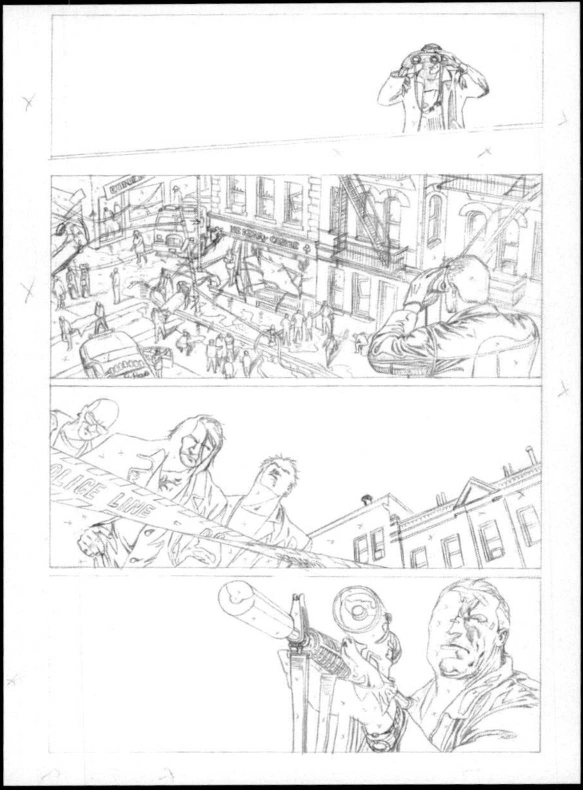

Page 16 Pencils

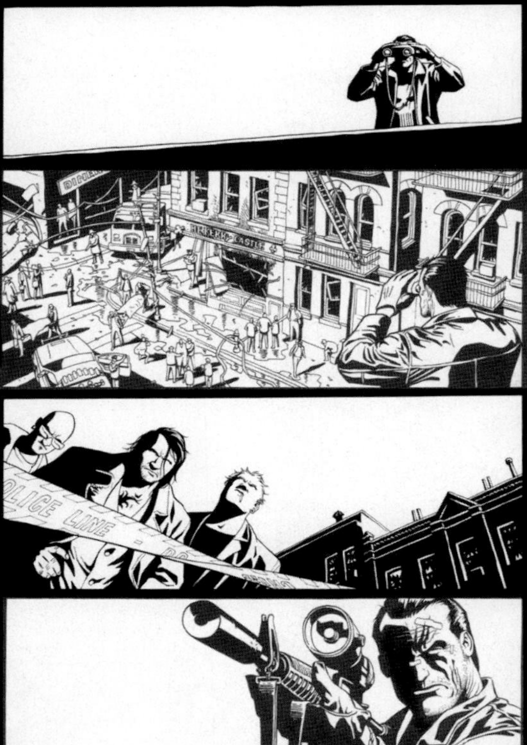

Page 16 Inks

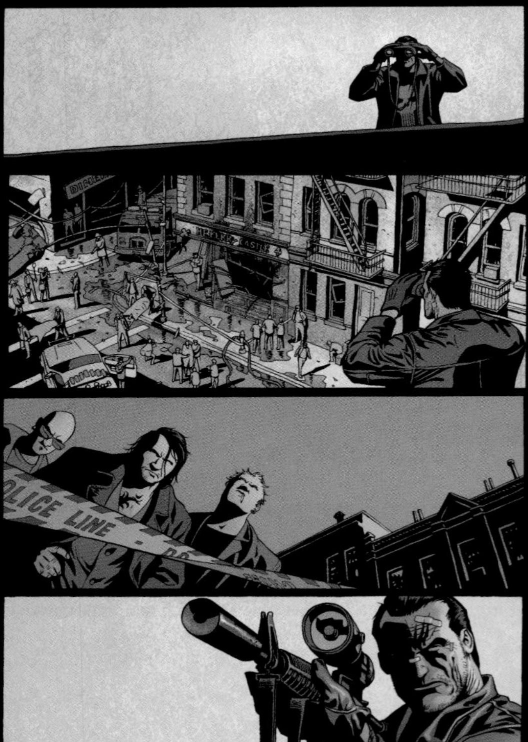

Page 16 Colors

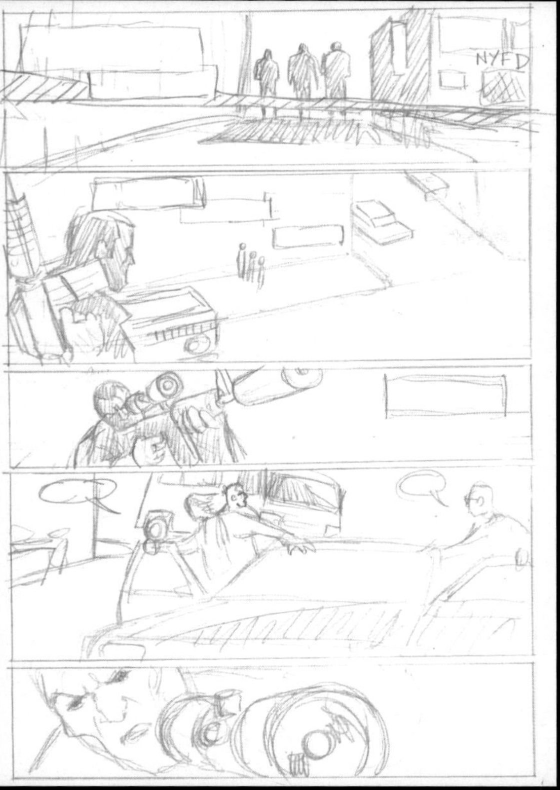
NYFD

Page 17 Layout

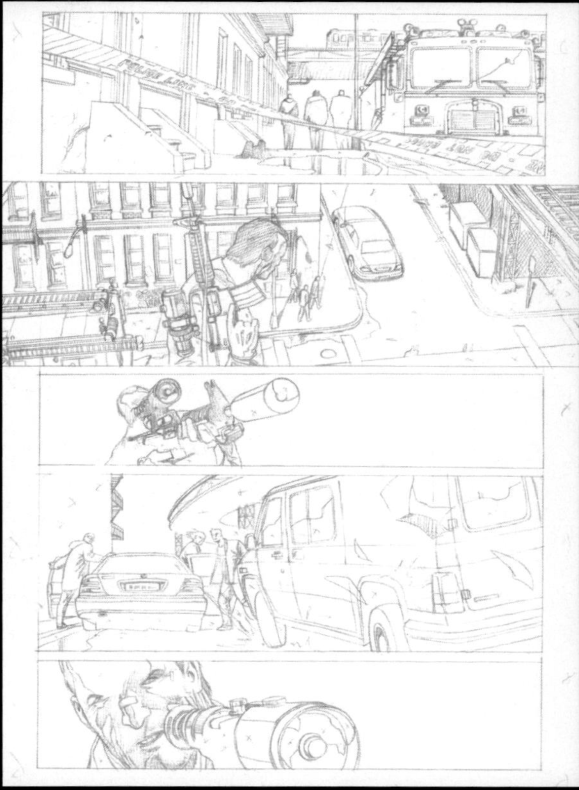

Page 17 Pencils

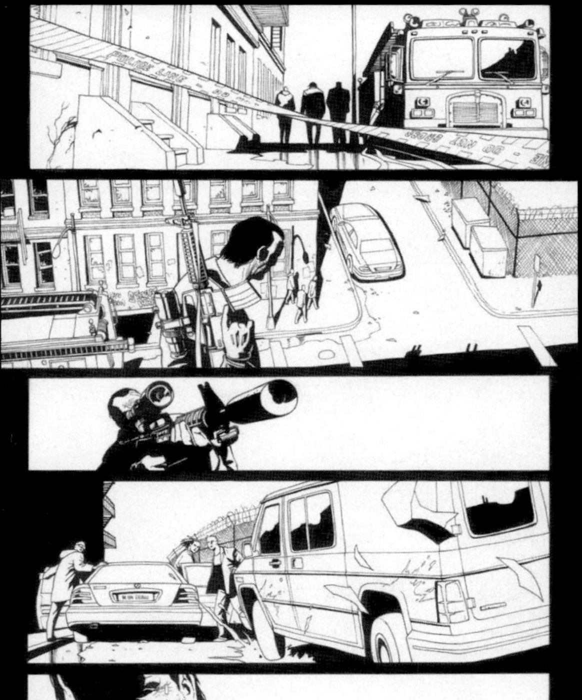

Page 17 Inks

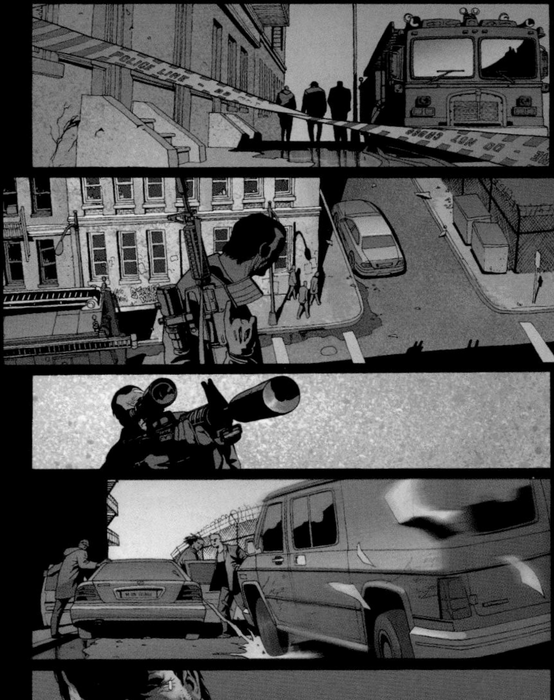

Page 17 Colors

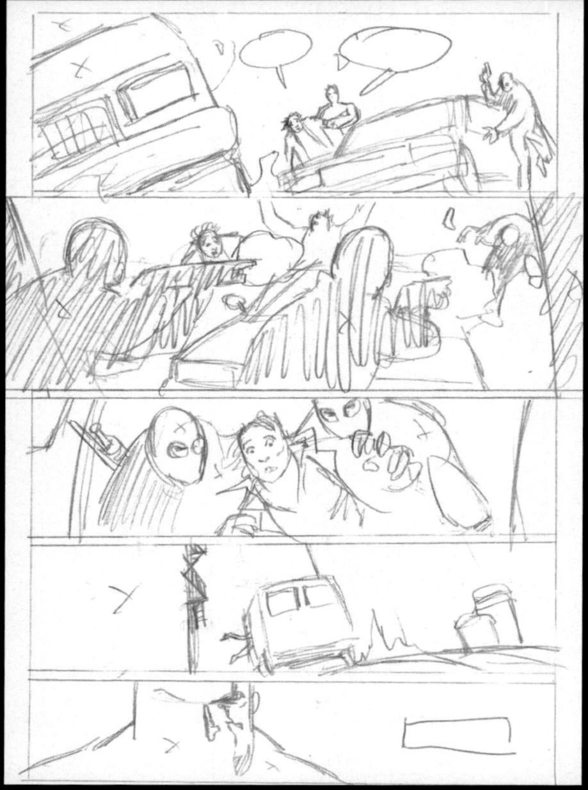

Page 18 Layout

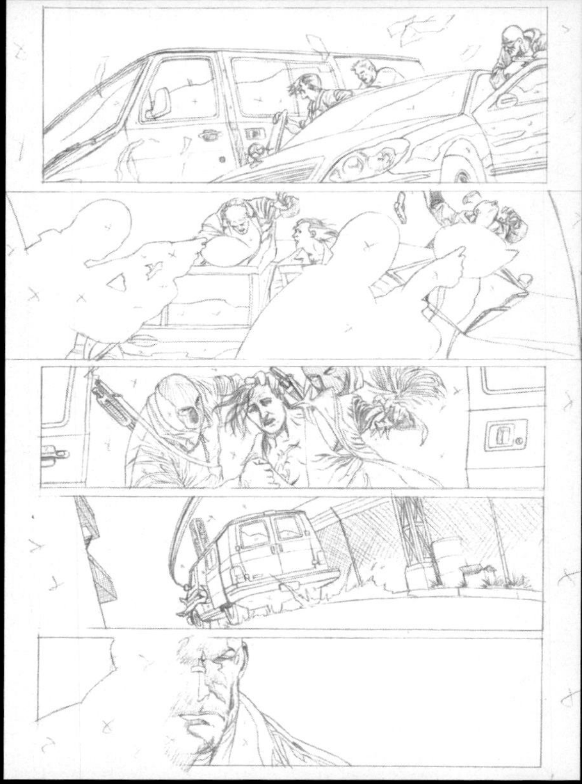

Page 18 Pencils

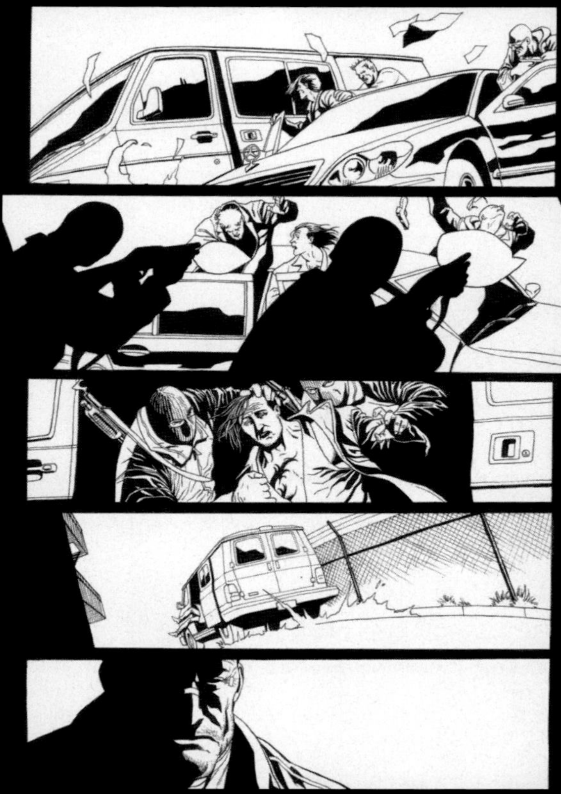

Page 18 Inks

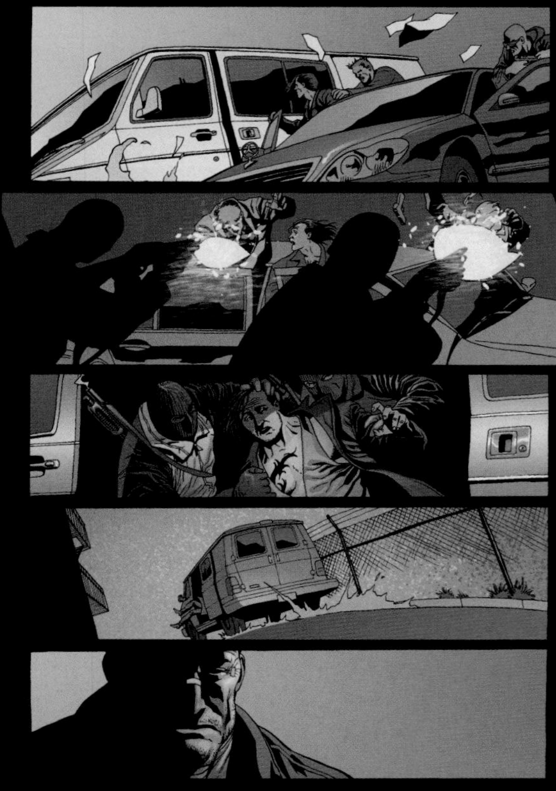

Page 18 Colors

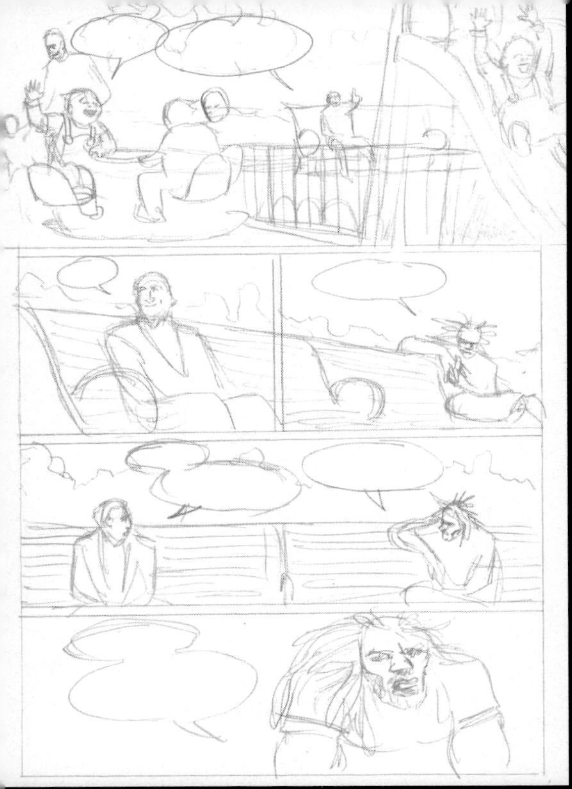
Page 19 Layout

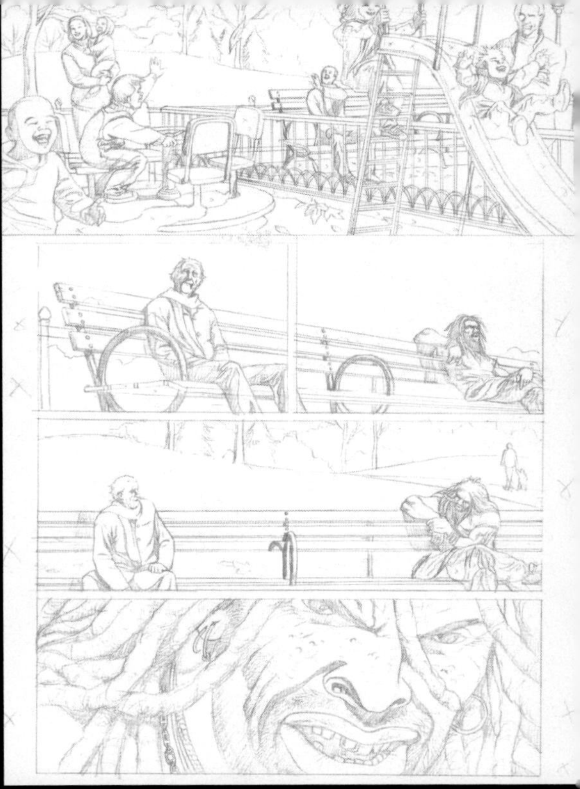
Page 19 Pencils

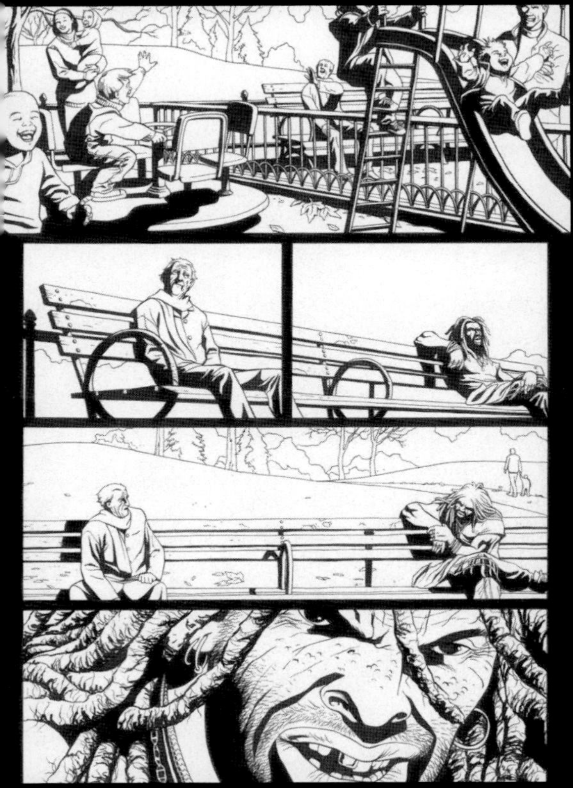
Page 19 Inks

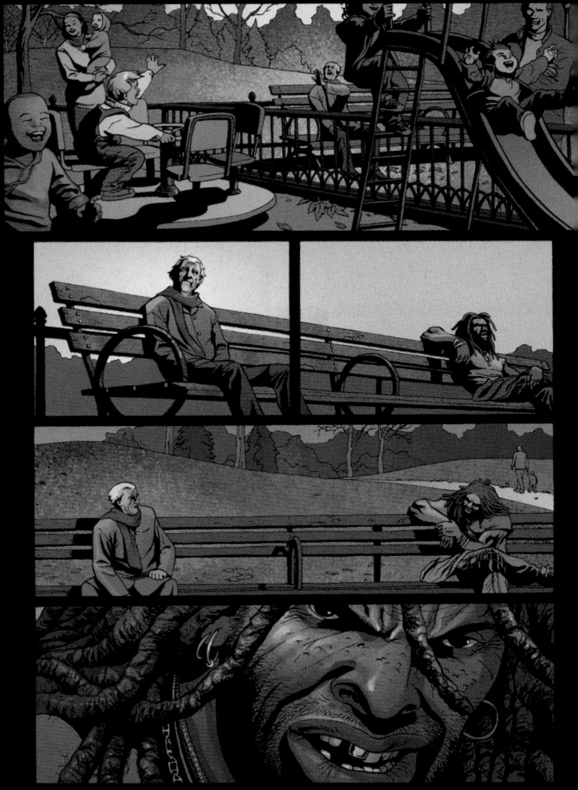
Page 19 Colors

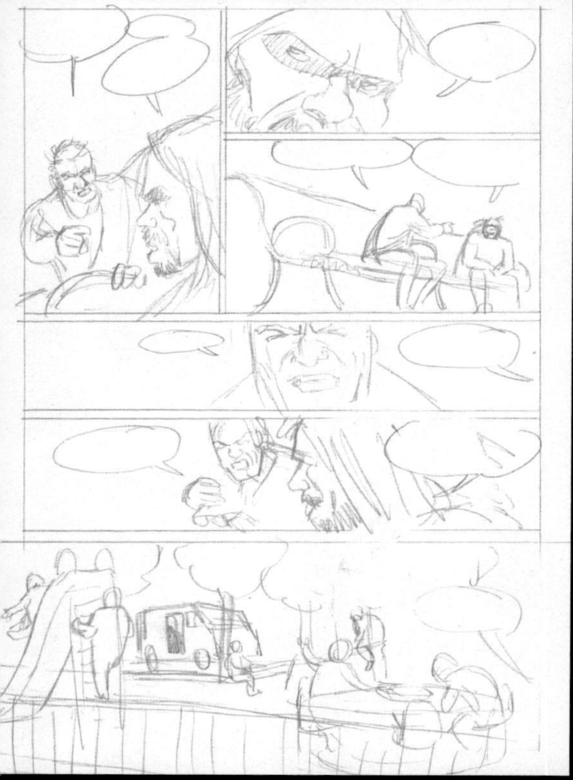

Page 20 Layout

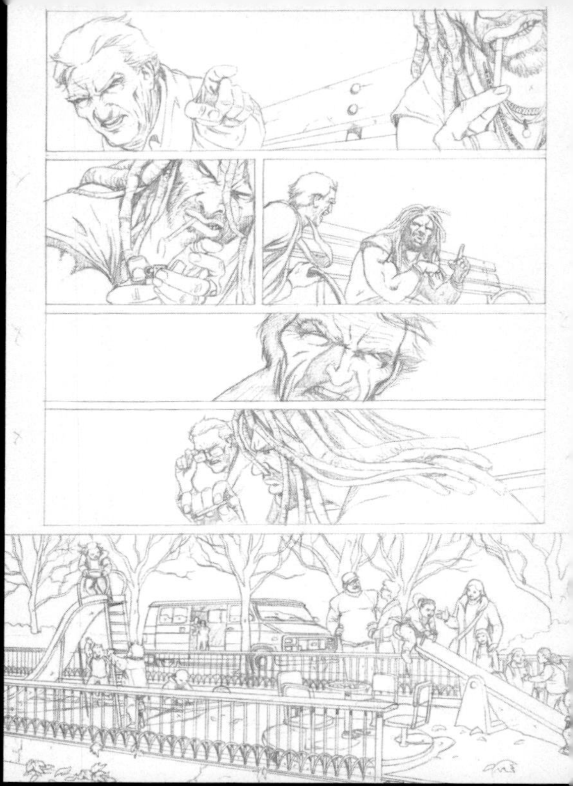

Page 20 Pencils

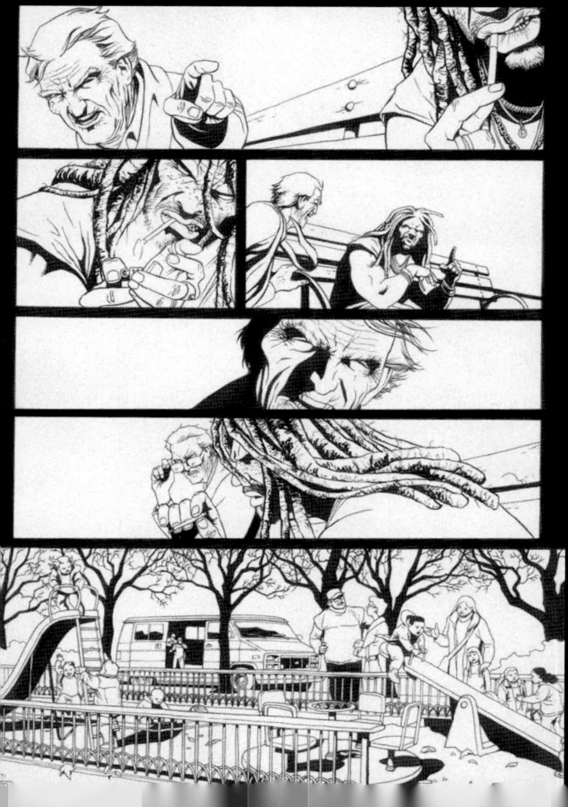

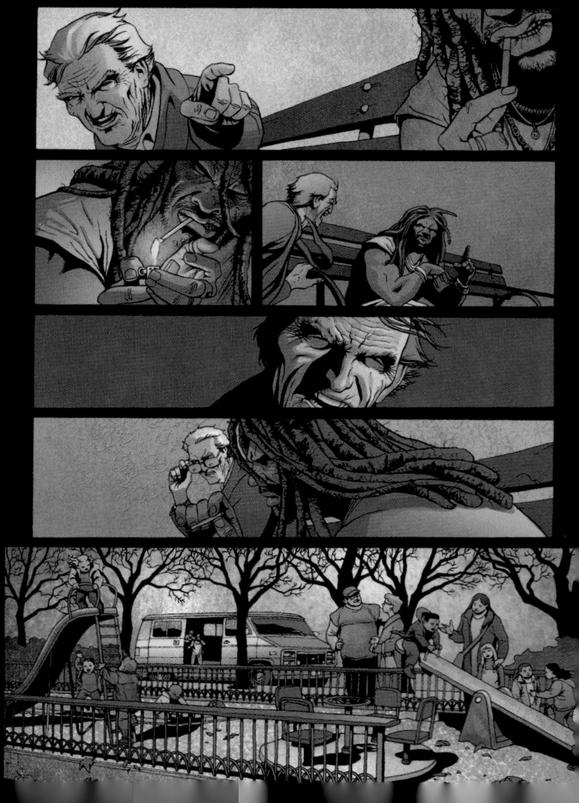

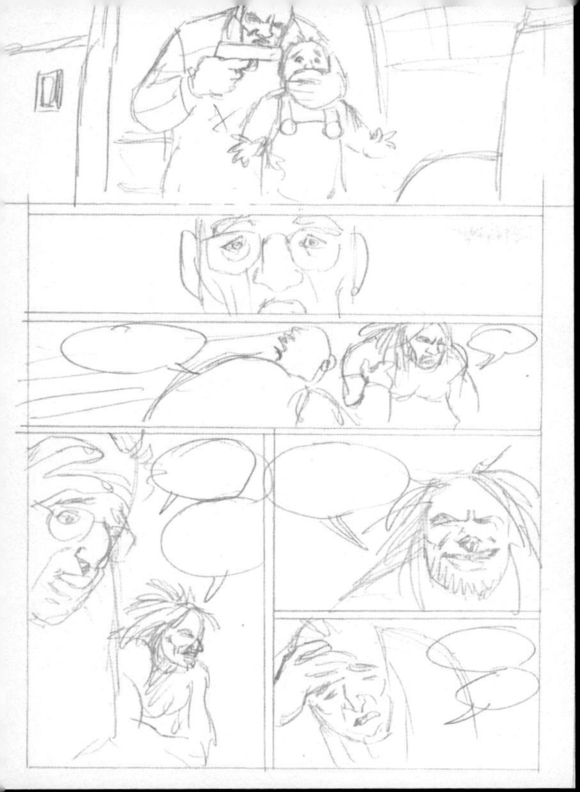

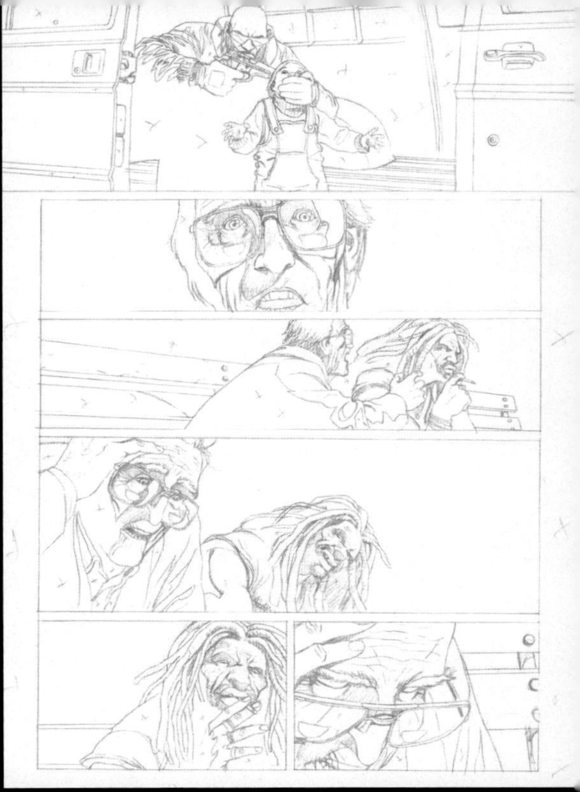

Page 21 Layout

Page 21 Pencils

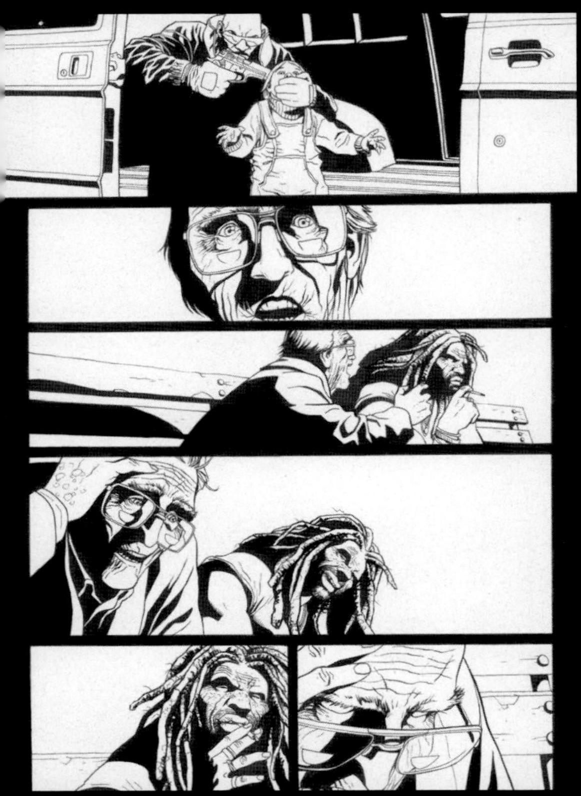

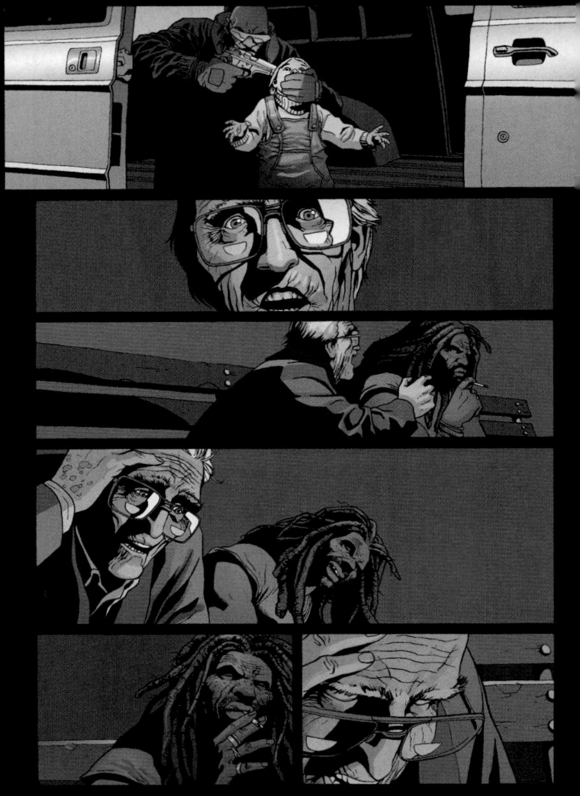

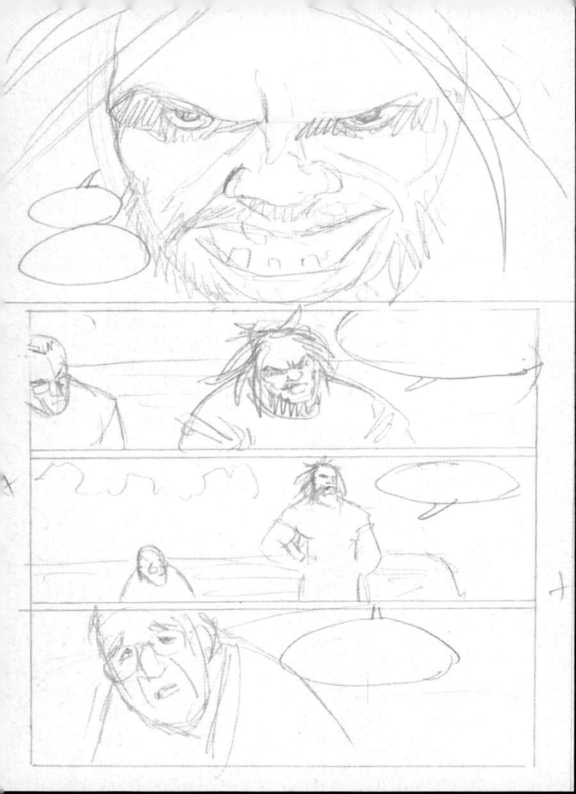

Page 22 Layout

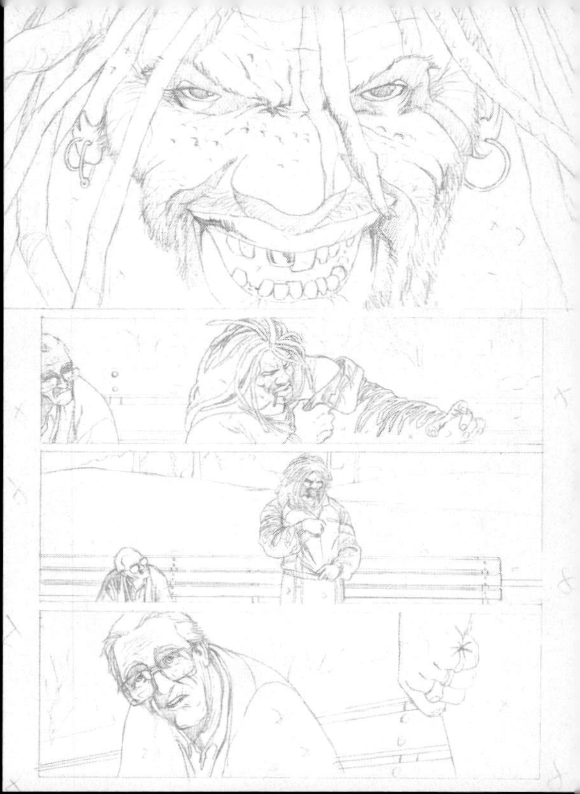

Page 22 Pencils

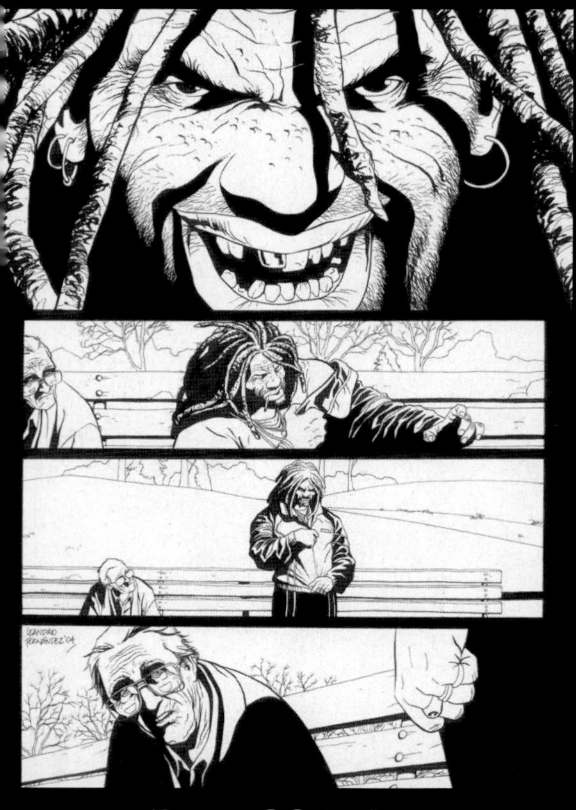

Page 22 Inks

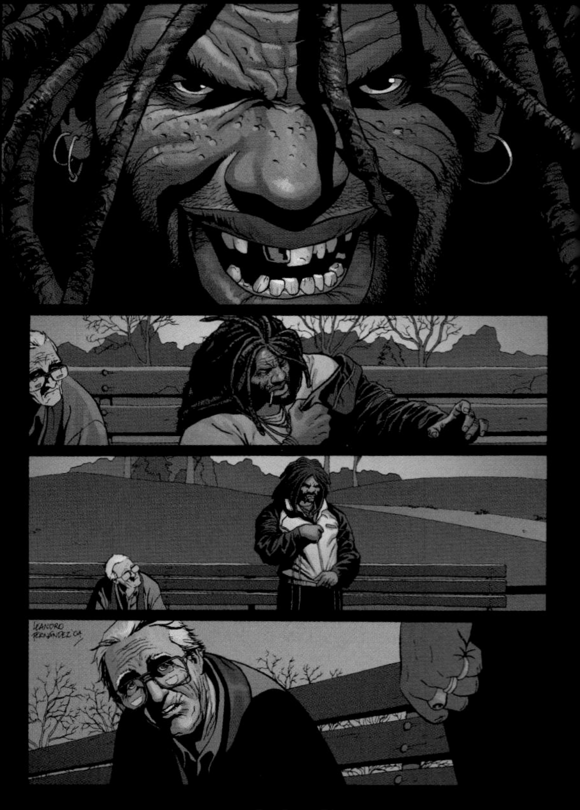

Page 22 Colors